Praise for *The Creation of the M*

"Typically brilliant, exuberant. . . . A remarkably rich book that carries its length and impressive learning with great style." —*Financial Times*

"[A] sumptuous and spicy volume. . . . Porter possesses a deft style."
—*Washington Post Book World*

"Porter has amassed a wealth of evidence to make his case. . . . [His] viewpoint is refreshing." —*Wall Street Journal*

"A provocative and illuminating survey, looking back from the age of the web to the vibrant, interlocking networks of the first recognisably 'modern'—if not wholly enlightened—century." —*Sunday Times* (London)

"Is a term like 'British Enlightenment' an oxymoron? . . . Part of the power of Roy Porter's new book is that you stop asking questions like that in the first chapter. . . . Porter doesn't so much argue as hammer home his brilliantly selected evidence."
—*The Guardian* (London)

"Roy Porter is on a mission to rescue the Enlightenment from what he sees as its Frenchification, and to give Britain due credit instead. . . . [H]e succeeds admirably. . . . A delight, with sensible organization, a lucid and engaging style, a good balance between generalization and example, and a strong grasp of nuance."
—*Fort Worth* (Texas) *Morning Star Telegram*

"Splendid . . . Porter puts his case vigorously and he has a genius for apt quotations which bring his narrative to life." —*Sunday Telegraph* (London)

"A superb guide to the intellectual life of the period, which . . . conveys an enormous amount of learned information lightly. . . . This is a book which has understood the age, which sees it clearly and, a surprisingly rare virtue, loves and sympathises with its dashing, dazzling spirit. . . . Brilliant, lucid and admirable." —*Observer* (London)

"Intellectual history at its best." —*Richmond* (Virginia) *Times Dispatch*

"The culmination of an astonishingly prolific and impressive career."
—*The Scotsman*

THE CREATION OF THE MODERN WORLD

The Untold Story of the British Enlightenment

ROY PORTER

W. W. Norton & Company
New York • London

To Natsu, the love of my life

Copyright © 2000 by Roy Porter
First American edition 2000
First published as a Norton paperback 2001

Originally published in England under the title *Enlightenment:
Britain and the Creation of the Modern World*

The text of this book is composed in Monotype Baskerville with the display set in Monotype Baskerville
Manufacturing by Quebecor Fairfield

ISBN 0-393-04872-1
ISBN 0-393-32268-8 pbk.

W. W. Norton & Company, Inc., 500 Fifth Avenue, New York, N.Y. 10110
www.wwnorton.com

W. W. Norton & Company Ltd., Castle House, 75/76 Wells Street, London W1T 3QT

1 2 3 4 5 6 7 8 9 0

CONTENTS

CONTENTS

LIST OF ILLUSTRATIONS

(Photographic acknowledgements in brackets, where applicable)

ACKNOWLEDGEMENTS

My interest in the Enlightenment stems from the time when, as a member of the proverbial class of '68, I had the great good fortune to be taught by Jack Plumb and Quentin Skinner at Christ's College, Cambridge. Jack showed me that the eighteenth century, far from being the stylized high political comedy of manners so commonly presented, was rather a time of turbulence, indeed a great watershed; Quentin for his part whetted my appetite for the challenges of intellectual history. How these marvellous teachers opened my mind would have warmed the hearts of the protagonists of this book.

Typed by candlelight in 1974 during the miners' strike power cuts, my first ever lectures given to the Cambridge history faculty were on the English Enlightenment – then, for sure (and still now, I suspect) a topic which raised quizzical eyebrows. During the intervening quarter century, my passion for the subject has never flagged, and I have always meant to put my views down on paper.

Over the years, many scholars have challenged me and helped clarify my thinking. I should particularly like to thank Mikuláš Teich, whose proposal in the late 1970s that we should stage a seminar series on 'The Enlightenment in National Context' made my thinking less pitifully parochial. Special thanks also to Sylvana Tomaselli, who has long been a devoted reader of everything I have written on and around this subject and a critic blessed with that candour so dear to enlightened radicals.

I owe much to the writings of many other scholars who, explicitly or obliquely, have been addressing this topic. John Pocock, Margaret Jacob, J. C. D. Clark and, for Scotland, Nicholas Phillipson must be singled out. In their contrasting ways and with their very disparate opinions, each has insisted there is a problem to be addressed.

Over the twelve months it took to write, chapters and drafts of this book have been read by Hannah Augstein, Bill Bynum, Luke Davidson, Brian Dolan, Alex Goldbloom, Fiona MacDonald, Michael Neve, Clare Spark, Christine Stevenson, Jane Walsh and Andrew Wear. To them I am deeply grateful for a welter of invaluable comments, criticisms, stimuli and friendly support.

I spent many happy years at the Wellcome Institute for the History of Medicine in London, recently disbanded by the Wellcome Trust. I am delighted to acknowledge the enormous support given to me by individual members of the staff, notably my secretary Frieda Houser, research assistant Caroline Overy and at the Xerox machine Andy Foley and Stuart Fricker. Additional exemplary research assistance has been provided by Sally Scovell and Sharon Messenger, and retyping of the seemingly endless drafts has been done by the tireless Sheila Lawler, Jan Pinkerton and Tracey Wickham, with help from Gill Doyle and Joanna Kafouris. Jed Lawler has helped a computer illiterate. At Penguin, I am very grateful to Sally Holloway, Cecilia Mackay and Janet Dudley for their expert copy-editing, picture-researching and indexing respectively. I am profoundly grateful to the British Academy for awarding me a fellowship under their research leave scheme for the academic year 1998–9, during which this book, so long stalled, has been completed.

Thanks to my publisher, Simon Winder, whose faith in this book has taken the practical form of a flow of helpful comments. I should finally like to pay tribute to Gill Coleridge, my literary agent. Over the last decade she has brought method to the mess of my literary life, in a manner that has simply made all the difference. What more can I say?

'It is a history-book, Sir, (which may possibly recommend it to the world) of what passes in a man's own mind.'
LAURENCE STERNE, *The Life and Opinions of Tristram Shandy*
(1759–67)

'I am a true Englishman, formed to discover nothing but to improve anything.'
WILLIAM GODWIN, cited in Don Locke,
A Fantasy of Reason (1980)

'So convenient a thing is it to be a *reasonable creature*, since it enables one to find or make a reason for everything one has a mind to do.'
BENJAMIN FRANKLIN, *Autobiography* (1793)

'Within limits, the Enlightenment was what one thinks it was.'
NORMAN HAMPSON, *The Enlightenment* (1968)

'Distrust is a necessary qualification of a student in history.'
SAMUEL JOHNSON, 'Review of the Account of the Conduct of the Duchess of Marlborough' (1742)

'Many of the books which now croud the world, may be justly suspected to be written for the sake of some invisible order of beings, for surely they are of no use to any of the corporeal inhabitants of the world.'
SAMUEL JOHNSON, 'A Review of Soame Jenyns' (1757)

'I'm sick of Portraits and wish very much to take up my Viol da Gamba and walk off to some sweet Village where I can paint Landskips and enjoy the fag End of Life in quietness and ease.'

THOMAS GAINSBOROUGH, letter to William Jackson (*c.* 1760)

'The Husbandman puts his seed in the Ground & the Goodness, Power, & Wisdom of God have pledged themselves, that he shall have Bread, and Health, & Quietness in return for Industry, & Simplicity of Wants, & Innocence. The AUTHOR scatters his seed – with aching head, and wasted Health, & all the heart-leapings of Anxiety – & the Folly, the Vices, the Fickleness of Man promise him Printers' Bills & the Debtors Side of Newgate, as full & sufficient Payment.'

SAMUEL TAYLOR COLERIDGE, letter to Thomas Poole
(Tuesday, 13 December 1796)

'I am now trying an Experiment very frequent among Modern Authors; which is, to write upon Nothing.'

JONATHAN SWIFT, *A Tale of a Tub, and Other Satires* (1704)

'I wonder, however, that so many people have written, who might well have left it alone.'

SAMUEL JOHNSON, *A Journey to the Western Islands of Scotland*
(1775)

'No expectation is more fallacious than that which authors form of the reception which their labours will find among mankind. Scarcely any man publishes a book, whatever it be, without believing that he has caught the moment when the publick attention is vacant to his call, and the world is disposed in a particular manner to learn the art which he undertakes to teach.'

SAMUEL JOHNSON, Preface to Richard Rolt,
Dictionary of Trade and Commerce (1756)

'A man may write at any time, if he will set himself doggedly to it.'

SAMUEL JOHNSON in James Boswell,
The Life of Samuel Johnson (1791)

INTRODUCTION

[T]he historiography of enlightenment in England remains that
of a black hole.

J. G. A. POCOCK[1]

A few preliminaries will make this book more approach-
able. For starters, terms of art, which are as inescapable as they are
unsatisfactory. In John Pocock's opinion, the phrase '"the" (or "an")
"English Enlightenment" does not ring quite true'.[2] Maybe; but,
following his own example, I shall be using it all the same. It is
admittedly an anachronistic term, but it captures, I believe, the
thinking and temper of a movement, one of whose leading lights
could declare, 'our first concern, as lovers of our country, must be to
enlighten it'.[3] I have, however, avoided the term 'pre-Enlightenment',
since that confuses rather than clarifies (is it supposed to denote a
status quo ante or something more akin to a prelude?).[4] I shall, however,
refer to the 'early' or the 'first' Enlightenment, alluding roughly to
pre-1750 developments or, approximately, to what is mainly covered
in the first eleven chapters of my book. I also write of the 'late' or
'second' Enlightenment, indicating in broad terms what happened
after the middle of the century, or what may be found in the latter
part of the book, that is, the enlightened critique of Enlightenment.
'The long eighteenth century' sometimes serves as a shorthand for
the entire span from Restoration to Regency, and other chronological
markers, like 'Georgian' and 'Hanoverian', are used equally elas-
tically.

Over the years Pocock and others have been urging that, to
avoid making progressive voices sound too much like a caucus or a

conspiracy, we should drop the definite article and maybe also the capital letter, and speak not of 'The Enlightenment' but rather of 'enlightenment', or better still 'enlightenments'. I fully endorse this typically shrewd suggestion, which is particularly germane to Britain where there never emerged, as some think there did in France, *un petit troupeau des philosophes* – a little flock, a party of humanity. The British avant-garde was not a network of persecuted rebels or underground samizdat authors, destined to hand down the torch of liberal democracy to Kennedy's America or Blair's Britain. They are better likened to the mixed clientele talking, talking, talking in a hot, smoky and crowded coffee house; men sharing broad convictions and sympathies but differing, and agreeing to differ, on matters dear to their hearts.

Mention of 'men' leads to the vexed issue of gendered language. Like those coffee house politicians, the great majority of the thinkers discussed below are male. The idiom they used – 'man of letters', 'man of mode', 'the common man', etc. – was gendered through and through, as were their assumptions: when thinkers like John Locke spoke of 'man', there doubtless lurked a generic if tacit notion of 'mankind' in general, but the people they actually envisaged as doing the teaching and preaching, writing and enlightening, were male. They did not think much of women in such public contexts, and when they did, they singled them out specifically. This silently gendered language reflected a man's world as defined by dominant male élites; and, to catch the tones of the times, I largely follow their practice here.[5]

One further note on terms. The Act of Union (1707) united the parliaments of England and Scotland, creating Great Britain. Scotland thereby accepted the Act of Settlement, enacted by Westminster in 1701, which designated the Hanoverians as Queen Anne's successors. A second Act of Union of 1801 incorporated Ireland into the 'United Kingdom'. My usage of national terms in the following pages will be less technically constitutionalist. I often employ 'English' as a shorthand for 'English language', and the terms 'English' and 'British' somewhat interchangeably when referring to ideas and developments broadly shared by élites living in the British Isles, since practically all enlightened thinking was then actually coming out of English heads, especially during the first third of the eighteenth century. By contrast to this 'lumping' habit, 'English' and 'Scottish' will be distinguished when I am specifically addressing regional traditions and themes, and I shall devote much of chapter 10 to developments characteristic of the Scottish Enlightenment.[6] Numerous thinkers of Irish and Welsh extraction – John Toland and Richard Price, for example – also achieved eminence, but, except fleetingly in chapters 10 and 20, I do not focus on controversies taking place *within* and *about* Ireland and Wales. Usage will be clarified by context; if this laxity sometimes seems confusing or is galling to modern nationalist sensibilities, it reflects the realities of a time when 'English' was commonly applied to people born anywhere in 'our Isles'.[7]

In this book far too many themes receive short measure. I do not give much space to political debate, literature and the arts, to tides of taste, the commercialization of culture or the forging of nationalism. Apart from space constraints, the reasons are plain: splendid books have appeared recently in all these areas and, rather than redigging sound foundations, I have instead tried to build on the spade work of my fellow historians.[8] Likewise, few extended exegeses of major philosophies are offered here. Once again, in many instances, fine studies already exist,[9] and in any case my chief concern lies less with the intricacies of, say, Hobbes, Hume, Hutton or Hazlitt than with the interplay of activists, ideas and society.

Historians of the Scottish Enlightenment may feel particularly aggrieved: does not the north British contribution deserve greater attention? Don't the literati of Aberdeen, St Andrews and Glasgow, not to mention the 'Athens of the North' itself, New Town and all, warrant chapters all to themselves? I would not scant the brilliance of the Caledonian contribution but, once again, notable studies already exist upon which I shall draw; and since my interest is more with meanings and impacts than with origins, I have, perhaps cavalierly, chosen to splice Scottish thinkers into the British story as a whole.[10]

I greatly regret that more is not said here about Continental influences upon Britain, and the reciprocal uptake of British thinking overseas. Insular history has no virtues, and any claims staked below about the Englishness of the English Enlightenment, or about 'English exceptionalism',[11] must rest on firmer foundations than 'fog over the Channel' obliviousness to developments elsewhere. I can only plead that adequate discussion of such issues would have made a long book lengthier still, and that it would require research into the literati of Milan, Mainz and Madrid far beyond my competence.[12]

Numerous other issues cry out for greater attention – the controversies which raged over mind and body, Heaven and Hell, the afterlife, the soul and the *je ne sais quoi* of the self, to name just a few. I have an excuse for some of these omissions: I plan to address such topics in my next book, which will examine the triangle of the moral, the material and the medical in the anglophone Enlightenment.

Next, a word on where I stand. Enlightenment historiography has been distorted by hindsight, and remains unashamedly *parti pris*. Progressives have long praised the *philosophes* for being the begetters of the Rights of Man, or have traced a lineage from them to the American Republic – indeed, the distinguished American historian Henry Commager once claimed that Europe dreamed the Enlightenment and America made that dream come true.[13] For their part, right-wing scholars, echoing Burke and the Abbé Barruel, have blamed the Enlightenment for handing the Terror its ideological ammunition, while Rousseau's doctrine of the general will supposedly begat 'totalitarian democracy', lethally sanctioning fascism, Nazism and Stalinism.[14] In some quarters it has become almost *de rigueur* to paint the Enlightenment black. After the Second World War, 'totalitarian' became the epithet for an Enlightenment whose managerial rationality was alleged to have imposed an 'administered life' which inexorably reduced society to 'a universal concentration camp'.[15] Echoing such readings, Michel Foucault held that, despite its rhetoric, the true logic of the Enlightenment was to control and dominate rather than to emancipate.[16] Certain modern literary critical circles take a no less jaundiced view. 'The "new" eighteenth century to be found in postmodernist scholarship,' Terry Castle drily observes, 'is not so much an age of reason, but one of paranoia, repression, and incipient madness.'[17] 'These days,' remarked Eric Hobsbawm in 1997, in a similar vein, 'the Enlightenment can be dismissed as anything from superficial and intellectually naive to a conspiracy of dead white men in periwigs to provide the intellectual foundation for Western imperialism'.[18] Voltaire likened history to a box of tricks we play on the dead, and none would gainsay that objectivity is a mirage; yet I believe these Foucauldian and postmodernist readings are wilfully lopsided, and I shall show how and why below.

I find enlightened minds congenial: I savour their pithy prose, and feel more in tune with those warm, witty, clubbable men than with, say, the aggrieved Puritans who enthral yet appal Christopher Hill or with Peter Gay's earnestly erotic Victorians. I trust, however, that this book will be read as a work of analysis rather than one of advocacy or apology. The Enlightenment is not a good thing or a bad thing, to be cheered or jeered. Apart from anything else, heroes-and-villains judgementalism would be absurd, because, as I shall insist *ad nauseam*, there never was a monolithic 'Enlightenment project'. Enlightened thinkers were broad-minded, they espoused pluralism, their register was ironic rather than dogmatic. 'The Enlightenment was not a crusade,' observes Mark Goldie, 'but a tone of voice, a sensibility.'[19] Tolerance was central, and protagonists could shake hands on some matters while shaking fists on others. For much of his career, Joseph Priestley, that unflagging religio-political liberal, looked upon Edmund Burke as a sympathizer, though their amity ended abruptly with the French Revolution. Then again, while Priestley took issue with the infidel Edward Gibbon's account of its rise, they shared, in large measure, criticisms of the corruptions of Christianity. Priestley even made a point of publishing his polemical exchanges with his co-Nonconformist Dr Richard Price, in the candid if quaint conviction that dissent should be seen as the spur to truth.[20] Little was fixed, debate came before doctrine, and culture wars went on among the enlightened as well as against their foes.

In short, we must be sensitive to chiaroscuro so as to descry the Enlightenment's contours, attending to its limits no less than its liberations, in recognition (as ever) that what permitted some truths to be interrogated was that others remained self-evident. We must resist being seduced by its slogans, and neither hypostatize the Enlightenment as the manifest destiny of humanity nor, conversely, diabolize it as a plot of dead white males: rather it should be seen as a cluster of overlapping and interacting élites who shared a mission to modernize. Our social vantage on enlightened ideologues must be nuanced, taking in the view 'from below' as well as 'from above', from the provinces as well as the metropolis, embracing female no less than male responses.[21] It must be capacious enough to disclose how particular preferences led some (Jeremy Bentham, for instance) to proceed in the name of cost-efficient rationality, while others, like John Wilkes, played the liberty trump. To some (David Hume, for example) enlightenment was primarily a matter of emancipation from religious bigotry within the political *status quo*; for others, like Dr Richard Price, it meant a pathway to political liberty picked out by Providence.[22]

Avoiding taking sides, this book strives to make sense of what moved progressive intellectuals by laying bare their thinking, in the light of Locke's dictum that we must understand a thinker's terms, 'in the sense he uses them, and not as they are appropriated, by each man's particular philosophy, to conceptions that never entered the mind' of that author.[23] This is a particularly important undertaking because the world they were making is the one we have inherited, that secular value system to which most of us subscribe today which upholds the unity of mankind and basic personal freedoms, and the worth of tolerance, knowledge, education and opportunity. As the Enlightenment's children, we should try to fathom our parents.

As ever, that is not straightforward. While in the eighteenth century progressive intellectuals backed many causes now typically approved, they also espoused others which today we find abhorrent. John Locke championed the natural freedom of mankind, yet 'The Fundamental Constitutions of Carolina', framed by him in 1669, granted free men in the new colony absolute jurisdiction over their slaves.[24] Bentham deplored the criminalization of homosexuality, yet proposed castrating rapists and tattooing convicts – all on the basis of the greatest happiness principle.[25] Mary Wollstonecraft vindicated the rights of women, but out-misogynized most women-haters. 'The age of enlightenment,' Ronald Knox once noted, 'was also an age of fanaticisms.'[26] Complexities, convolutions and contradictions leap out from my pages.

'Reason, with most people, means their own opinion': thus wrote the saturnine William Hazlitt.[27] Without succumbing wholly to that Hazlittian mulishness born of defeat, we must beware presentism and recognize that every age, especially perhaps the age of reason, rationalizes in its own way and has its own meaning codes, spoken and implicit. To utilitarians, rationality did not only spell personal freedom; it was also disciplinary, a tool in the forging of that efficient regime in which the rational would regulate the rest. The fact that Benthamism thus spelt social control is, however, no argument for abandoning 'Enlightenment' as a historical category: it is merely a caveat against simplistic 'all is for the best in the best of all possible enlightenments' readings.[28] Nothing could be sillier than to tightlace the dead into today's conceptual corsets. The most we can hope to do is to understand them – all the hectoring in the world will not change them! Far from judging saints and sinners, this book problematizes the progressives in the battle for the mind.

While cheerfully acknowledging my massive debts to fellow historians, I also draw gratefully upon the work of literary scholars. Even the best historians have rarely done justice to the remarkable insights afforded by literary investigations into Grub Street and the republic of letters, into authorship and readership, into genres, canons and registers, and into fictionalizations of self and society. In what follows I highlight the part played by poets, critics and novelists in debates over identity, individuality and subjectivity, and the role of the imagination in the politics of the gendered self, in the belief that the eighteenth century was truly, as Johnson thought, an 'age of authors'.[29]

Enlightened avant-gardes condemned the fossilized, prized novelty (while also mistrusting it) and thrived upon controversy, self-criticism and self-celebration. Through the medium of print, public opinion was materializing in a manner uncannily prefiguring the late twentieth-century data revolution and those contemporary expressions of the electric information explosion, the Internet and the World Wide Web. The progress of print was a development upon which those two mighty adversaries Samuel Johnson and David Hume for once found themselves of a mind. 'The mass of every people must be barbarous where there is no printing and consequently knowledge is not generally diffused,' ruled Johnson;[30] there had been, sensed Hume, 'a sudden and sensible change in the opinions of men within these last fifty years, by the progress of learning and liberty'.[31] The print revolution and the rise of the reading public brought new cadres of knowledge-mongers into being, serving as society's eyes, ears, brains and mouthpieces.[32] How curious that this budding British intelligentsia has been ignored. This book aims to make a modest contribution to changing that, rethinking Albion's Enlightenment and shedding light on the 'black hole'.

(Note: I have tried to give full citations to the quotations I have used. I have not, however, been scrupulously consistent in following original punctuation and capitalization.)

I

A BLIND SPOT?

The eighteenth century sailed forward into an era of unparalleled stability . . . No ferment of ideas or memories remained.

PERRY ANDERSON[1]

The year 1783 brought the launching not just of the American Republic but also, more modestly, of the Berliner Mittwochgesellschaft (Wednesday Club), a debating society typical of those then sprouting in German cities. In a local periodical, one of its members broached the question: 'What is enlightenment?' Strenuous debate followed. Three hundred and sixty miles to the east, in Königsberg, a professor of philosophy offered his contribution. In his 'Answer to the Question: What is Enlightenment?' (1784), the great Immanuel Kant deemed that 'if it is now asked whether we live at present in an enlightened age, the answer is: No', although he did add, 'we do live in an age of enlightenment': Europe was in the throes of *becoming* enlightened.[2] How?

To secure 'man's release from his self-incurred immaturity', Kant judged, people must think for themselves under the watchword *sapere aude* – 'dare to know' – a tag from the Roman poet Horace.[3] Yet it was not so simple. The thinker must indeed 'dare to know'; nevertheless, in his capacity as clergyman or civil servant, his primary duty lies in serving his church and obeying his prince – in Kant's case, Frederick the Great, king of Prussia, an enlightened monarch, no doubt, and a fan of Voltaire, but a man Machiavellian, militaristic and autocratic. Subjects, Kant concluded, were duty-bound to swallow dissent and uphold the royal will so as to preclude disorder.

Kant's denial that his age was enlightened is often endorsed by historians.[4] Yet, taken for historical fact, it is utterly misleading. It may well apply to his own university city, the modern Kaliningrad, on Russia's Baltic coast, east of Poland, where he had been born in 1724 and would die eighty years later – in his entire life the philosopher, while boldly voyaging in the mind, never ventured his gouty toes outside East Prussia. His daily constitutional was almost as far as he ever went – and such a regular was he that the locals were said to set their watches by the professorial tread.[5]

Not all that many Königsbergers, one suspects, had *sapere aude* hung over their beds. And Kant's denial arguably applies more broadly to Prussia at large, a feudal kingdom manned by hereditary serfs whose forced labour sustained a haughty landed nobility, a cadre of tame officials and a fearsome military machine. Despite Frederick's own advanced postures and policies, Prussia qualifies for the epithet 'enlightened' only in a somewhat Pickwickian sense. 'A government, supported by an army of 180,000 men,' tersely commented the English traveller John Moore, 'may safely disregard the criticisms of a few speculative politicians, and the pen of the satirist.'[6]

A faithful state functionary, Professor Kant's ideal of freedom was as timid as the man himself. Elsewhere in Europe, the question of enlightenment had been raised and, many were sure, resolved, decades before Berlin's Wednesday talking shop was even dreamed up. However sublime a philosopher, as a culture-watcher Kant was fated to be a man on the margins, hardly *au fait* with political realities to the west, where phrases like 'this enlightened age' had long been ten-a-penny.[7] In England, Ambrose Philips's magazine the *Free-Thinker* had adopted Horace's '*sapere aude*' as its masthead as early as 1718, launching an assault on superstition; and in a nation in which formal censorship had ceased back in 1695, such an assertion of free-thinking raised few eyebrows – the Mittwochgesellschaft, by contrast, positively gave its imprimatur to press censorship.[8]

Already, by Phillips's time, Englishmen prided themselves upon living in the light. A full three-quarters of a century before Kant,

Anthony Ashley Cooper, the 3rd Earl of Shaftesbury, had addressed a comrade in the Netherlands in far more spirited terms:

There is a mighty Light which spreads its self over the world especially in those two free Nations of England and Holland; on whom the Affairs of Europe now turn; and if Heaven sends us soon a peace suitable to the great Successes we have had, it is impossible but Letters and Knowledge must advance in greater Proportion than ever . . . I am far from thinking that the Cause of Theisme will lose anything by fair Dispute. I can never . . . wish better for it than when I wish the Establishment of an intire Philosophicall Liberty.[9]

As this book will stress, the Whig peer's elation at enjoying 'intire Philosophicall Liberty' in a free and progressive country was shared by many of his contemporaries. How peculiar, then, that historians have had so little to say about the role of English thinkers in the European Enlightenment as a whole!

Complex revisionisms mark our times. For long the 'age of reason' was slighted by Anglo-American scholars as an arid or pretentious interlude, personified by know-alls such as Voltaire and oddballs such as Rousseau. More recently, however, the Enlightenment has been achieving recognition – sometimes notoriety – as a movement decisive in the making of modernity.[10] The American historian Peter Gay reinstated the *philosophes* as dauntless critics, wrestling with problems of modern life which still tax us today.[11] And since then, our understanding of the *Aufklärung* has been further enriched. We can now see it as stretching far beyond the 'little flock of *philosophes*' celebrated by Gay: today's cultural historians point to the ferment of new thinking amongst the reading public at large, stimulated *via* newspapers, novels, prints and even pornography – the Enlightenment should be viewed not as a canon of classics but as a living language, a revolution in mood, a blaze of slogans, delivering the shock of the new. It decreed new ways of seeing, advanced by a range of protagonists, male and female, of various nationalities and discrete status, professional and interest groups.[12]

This image of an *engagé* Enlightenment, criticizing, cajoling and calling for practical improvement on a broad front, represents a major advance upon the dated image of periwigged poseurs prattling on in Parisian salons. In this welcome revisionism, however, the role of Britain remains oddly neglected. That is nothing new. In his establishing of the Enlightenment pantheon, Ernst Cassirer's magisterial and profoundly influential *The Philosophy of the Enlightenment*, translated from the German in 1951, had not so much as mentioned Bolingbroke and Bentham, Priestley, Price and Paine or Godwin and Wollstonecraft (the Enlightenment's premier husband-and-wife team), or that astonishing polymath Erasmus Darwin, let alone Anglo-Scottish political economy – no Adam Smith! – or lay preachers like Addison and Steele. From his philosophical eyrie, Cassirer patronized those few English thinkers he did deign to discuss: 'among the leaders of this movement', he concluded of the Deists, 'there is no thinker of real depth and of truly original stamp'.[13]

Cassirer's erudition proved justifiably influential, and his neglect of England characterized his successors. Leonard Marsak's anthology *The Enlightenment* presented no readings at all from English writers, while Lester Crocker's equivalent barely did better, with a token four out of fifty.[14] The pattern thus set a generation ago continues: James Schmidt's recent *What Is Enlightenment?* contains thirty-four essays, not one of which focuses on England.[15] A survey of religion and philosophy in Georgian Britain got by without using the term 'Enlightenment' at all; Christopher Hill likewise, deprecating the mystifying rationality of 'Yahoo society'; and literary historians have often opted for the label 'Augustan', partly because 'age of reason' has been thought to suggest a 'winter of the imagination'.[16] And when not thus ignored, English achievements have been denied. Henry Steele Commager rated England 'a bit outside the Enlightenment', while a fellow American pronounced as recently as 1976, 'the term "English Enlightenment" would be jarring and incongruous if it were ever heard'.[17] This book will, I trust, be a jarring experience.

Such scholarly disdain has deep roots. Unlike the self-styled *lumières* or *illuminati* across the Channel, Georgian gentlemen did not in so many words term themselves 'enlighteners', nor did the phrase 'the Enlightenment' enter English usage until the mid-Victorian era, even then being used to curl a lip at Voltaire and the other facile scoffers of that 'age of reason' which the Romantics and Victorians so abhorred.[18] The term continues to carry pejorative airs: the 1973 edition of *The Shorter Oxford English Dictionary* glosses it as denoting 'shallow and pretentious intellectualism, unreasonable contempt for authority and tradition, etc., applied *esp.* to the spirit and aims of the French philosophers of the 18th c.' – a definition proud to perpetuate not just English philistinism but Oxonian deference to 'authority and tradition'.[19]

It does not come as a surprise, therefore, that no book exists called 'The English Enlightenment' or 'The British Enlightenment'; the nearest is John Redwood's *Reason, Ridicule and Religion* (1976), which is at least subtitled 'The Age of Enlightenment in England, 1660–1750'. Written by a fellow of All Souls, Oxford, who, hardly by chance, went on to become a far right Conservative Party politician and outspoken Eurosceptic, it advances a decidedly rum case: incapable of mounting a truly rational critique of Throne and Altar, rationalist enemies of the Establishment had instead, rather caddishly, stooped to raillery and ridicule.[20] Subsequent neo-conservative historians like J. C. D. Clark, who also did time at All Souls, have in effect denied by silence an Anglo-Enlightenment, holding that Hanoverian England remained a 'confessional state' with Church and King beliefs supreme. For all its scholarship and intelligence, Clark's reading is highly idiosyncratic: eyes glued on the political superstructure, he overlooks the zest for change bubbling up in society at large. Yet his stress on the durability of hidebound High Church and Tory convictions is valuable in its own way, since it highlights the intensity of ideological conflict, and so reminds us that enlightened attitudes formed not some bland background music to events but a partisan voice, expressive of sectional interests and divided élites.[21]

There are, of course, distinguished exceptions to this academic blind spot – J. G. A. Pocock and Margaret Jacob, in particular, have made a point of utilizing the term, and what follows will draw greatly and gratefully upon their pioneering scholarship. Nevertheless, there has been no study of the 'British Enlightenment' as such, nor any debate on 'English Enlightenment' comparable to those over the scientific and industrial revolutions.[22]

What makes all this so very odd is that the *philosophes* themselves looked to England as the birthplace of the modern. Anglophiles in France, Italy and the Holy Roman Empire celebrated Britain's constitutional monarchy and freedom under the law, its open society, its prosperity and religious toleration. 'The English are the only people upon earth,' declared Voltaire in his significantly titled *Lettres philosophiques ou Lettres anglaises* (1733), the first grenade lobbed at the *ancien régime*,

who have been able to prescribe limits to the power of Kings by resisting them; and who, by a series of struggles, have at last established that wise Government, where the Prince is all powerful to do good, and at the same time is restrain'd from committing evil; where the Nobles are great without insolence, tho' there are no Vassals; and where the People share in the government without confusion.[23]

However idealized, Voltaire's homage was at least based upon first-hand experience. After a spat with the Chevalier de Rohan, the young writer had been roughed up by the nobleman's bully boys and thrown into the Bastille, and was released only on condition that he went into exile. Resident in England for three years from 1726, he enjoyed the companionship of poets and politicians and plunged into the works of English scientists, philosophers and religious free-thinkers.[24]

The *Lettres* saluted England as a 'nation of philosophers' and the cradle of liberty, tolerance and sense, using it, like Montesquieu later, as a stick to beat his own *patrie*. Francis Bacon was the prophet of modern science, Isaac Newton had revealed the laws of the universe, and John Locke had demolished Descartes and rebuilt philosophy on the bedrock of experience.[25] Together, their teachings beat a path between dogmatism and scepticism, opening up new views of nature, morals and society.

A *philosophe* of a younger generation, Denis Diderot felt no less ardent. Reflecting on the 'two countries in Europe in which philosophy is cultivated', he drew a telling distinction: 'In England, philosophers are honoured, respected; they rise to public offices, they are buried with the kings . . . In France warrants are issued against them, they are persecuted, pelted with pastoral letters . . . Do we see that England is any the worse for it?'[26]

France 'owes to England', the *Journal encyclopédique* was to acknowledge, 'the great revolution which has taken place in everything which can contribute to render peoples more happy and States more flourishing'.[27] Progressives in Paris formed an informal English fanclub, while a popular comedy of the 1760s guyed the Anglomaniac who had 'Hogard' and 'Hindel' on his lips, drank only tea, read nothing but Shakespeare and Pope and declared: 'The teachers of mankind have been born in London, and it is from them we must take lessons.'[28] There was even a touch of truth in that caricature, as Edward Gibbon – hardly a vulgar chauvinist – found when visiting Paris just after the inglorious Bourbon defeat in the Seven Years War: 'Our opinions, our fashions, even our games, were adopted in France; a ray of national glory illuminated each individual, and every Englishman was supposed to be born a patriot and a philosopher.'[29]

Continentals lapped up English ideas. Take another Anglophile, the Piedmontese nobleman Alberto Radicati di Passerano. 'He absorbed the more violent and polemical elements from English deism,' the great Italian historian Franco Venturi once observed:

He dreamed of a world without property or authority, and, at the same time, showed enthusiasm for the mixed government of the British Isles, which he experienced during his difficult and troubled exile. He combined the most diverse elements from the commonwealthmen in a curious and original way . . . Every aspect of this example, both the ideological and the political, reveals particularly well the penetration on the continent of the ideas formed in England at the turn of the century.[30]

Continental savants were galvanized by English innovations in politics and ethics, epistemology, aesthetics and even *belles lettres* – so much so that Diderot was led to exclaim that 'without the English, reason and philosophy would still be in the most despicable infancy in France'.[31] Religious critiques infiltrated France through the works of Toland, Tindal, Collins, Wollaston, Woolston and those Deistical aristocrats Shaftesbury and Bolingbroke, spreading even farther afield, *via* Leibniz and the Electress Sophia to the German states, and into Italy through Giannone.[32]

English moral benevolism also rippled to the Continent. Diderot's passion for *vertue* was kindled by his translating Shaftesbury;[33] other *philosophes* applauded Pope's *An Essay on Man* (1733–4), while Rousseau found balm in Addison and Steele, confessing, '*The Spectator* particularly pleased me, and improved my mind.'[34] Later on, British utilitarianism spurred legal reformers, a Spaniard declaring 'the grand Baintham' to have been 'the most universal genius which the world ever produced – a Solon, a Plato, and a Lope de Vega'.[35] Nor was exporting less brisk in the natural sciences – with Newtonian gravitation finally weaning the French off their beloved Cartesian 'vortices'[36] – and also in the practical arts: 'France owes to England the great revolution which has taken place in her literature,' gushed the *Journal encyclopédique* in 1758:

How many excellent works . . . have appeared in recent years upon the useful arts – upon agriculture . . . upon commerce, finance, manufactures, navigation and the colonies, in short upon everything which can contribute to render peoples more happy and States more flourishing.[37]

The peerless *Encyclopédie* itself, launched in 1751 by Diderot and d'Alembert and completed in twenty-eight volumes, originated in a scheme to translate Ephraim Chambers's *Cyclopaedia*, which had appeared back in 1728.[38]

Even British fiction became fashionable. *Robinson Crusoe* (1726) took Germany by storm – by 1760 over forty sequels had appeared; so did the verse of Ossian, the 'Scottish Homer', at a later date; while sentimental drama and novels ravished Continental hearts: 'O

Richardson, Richardson, man unique in my eyes,' sang Diderot of the author of *Pamela*, 'thou shalt be my reading at all times!'[39] In short, so a French critic confessed in 1768, once English letters had been tasted, 'a revolution quickly took place in our own: the Frenchman . . . no longer welcomed or valued anything that had not something of an English flavour about it'.[40]

Contemporary comment thus suggests it was an English sun which lit up many of the Continental children of light. How, in that case, do we explain modern verdicts like R. R. Palmer's?

At a banal level – that of historical tastes – the paradox is easily accounted for: 'The Enlightenment is ordinarily thought of as a French affair.'[41] By custom, the movement is assumed to be Francophone, albeit perhaps finding its metaphysical apotheosis among German philosophers. 'There were many philosophes,' ruled Gay, 'but there was only one Enlightenment' – and that was France-centred, headed by that Voltairian party of humanity which championed the modern trinity of atheism, republicanism and materialism.[42] Leonard Marsak dubbed the Enlightenment 'primarily a French phenomenon'; it was 'pre-eminently and focally French', agreed Lester Crocker, while Robert Darnton has recently restated that it was 'in Paris in the early eighteenth century' that enlightenment took off.[43]

Such readings owe much to the assumption current ever since Edmund Burke and the Abbé Barruel that the Enlightenment's climax – or nadir – lay in what Palmer styled 'democratic revolution', enshrined first in the American and then in the French Revolutions.[44] The fact that there was no English revolt to match, indeed that John Bull proved the bulwark of counter-revolution, seems to lend support to the idea that there can have been no English Enlightenment worthy of the name.

Indeed, small surprise that historians should belittle British developments if the Enlightenment's defining features are taken to be the atheism, republicanism and materialism supposedly fired by the *philosophes*' big guns and sparking the French Revolution. Hailed thus as the authorized prophets of the modern,[45] must not the avant-garde have been 'radical' to the very marrow? Gay freely bestows bouquets like 'revolutionaries', 'skeptics', 'democrats' and 'atheists'; and if the Enlightenment is primarily to be read, following him, as the 'rise of modern paganism', it must make sense to put into the foreground Voltaire's *écrasez l'infâme*, along with d'Holbach's atheistic material-ism.[46] Hence, finding in England few pagans or insurrectionists panting to throttle the last king with the guts of the last priest, how easy it is to conclude that the 'English Enlightenment' must be a misnomer or an oxymoron.[47]

Yet in sober truth few French *philosophes*, and virtually none of their German, Italian or Dutch *confrères*, were devoted democrats, materialists or atheists.[48] The shrill rhetoric of some *philosophes*, and the loathing many truly felt for cardinals and even kings, should not be mistaken for practical plans to turn society itself upside-down. Dazzling sloganizing made the French Enlightenment central to later radical mythologies and reactionary demonologies alike, but the links between the High Enlightenment and revolutionary activity were anything but clear cut.[49] Many *philosophes*, as revolutionaries them-selves complained, had feathered nests for themselves under the *ancien régime* – d'Alembert, after all, held four more sinecures than Dr Johnson.[50] To what extent, and until when, would Voltaire or Diderot, had they lived to see the Revolution, have applauded its actual course – one which beheaded the chemist Lavoisier and drove Condorcet to suicide, and was criticized by latter-day *philosophes* like Raynal and Marmontel? Looking at the Enlightenment retrospec-tively through modern political lenses creates a fatally distorting teleology.

Anglophone developments have also been skipped over thanks to the intellectualist fallacy dear to academics who, echoing Cassirer's verdict on the Deists, prize 'profundity' above all and rate dead thinkers on an abstrusity scale. Given this scholarly snobbery, such seminal figures as the idiosyncratic Shaftesbury, the ironist Toland, the suave Steele or the populist Paine get low marks. Even the decision to call his book the *philosophy* of the Enlightenment perhaps involved Cassirer in a distortion, a betrayal even, of its spirit, especially insofar as he imagined the *philosophes* stumblingly trying, *avant la lettre*, to write *The Critique of Pure Reason*. After all, scholasticism was the last thing activists were trying to advance.

Anyone embracing Cassirer's criteria would certainly find English discourse pretty low grade, though they might award more points to Scottish academics like Thomas Reid and Dugald Stewart for their methodical manuals of methodology.[51] Undoubtedly England produced no Kant, but that is not the point: there is no earthly reason why systematic metaphysics should be taken as the acme of enlightenment.[52] Thinkers like Locke abhorred *l'esprit de système* and swept aside the old scholastic cobwebs; the most ingenious way of becoming foolish was to be a system-monger, quipped Shaftesbury, who made ridicule the test of truth. England's modernizers had no stomach for indigestible scholastic husks; they were not ivory-towered academics but men (and women) of letters who made their pitch in the metropolitan market place and courted the public, hoping, with Joseph Addison, who supported Cicero's praise of Socrates for bringing philosophy down from the heavens, to make it 'dwell in Clubs and Assemblies, at Tea-Tables and in Coffee Houses'.[53] Selling philosophy to urbanites, and uniting the man of letters to the man of the world, English thinkers made it their business to be palatable, practical and pleasing.

If academics have misled themselves with monolithic and anachronistic models of what 'true enlightenment' must have been, things are changing. Recent scholarship has been in a disaggregating mood, replacing the old essentialist assumptions of a pure and unitary (for which, read French) movement with a pluralism, appreciative of a variety of blooms, from Dublin to Lublin, from York to New York, each with its own seeds and soil, problems, priorities and programmes. In place of the old emphasis on superstars, wider enlightened circles are now being investigated from perspectives which accommodate E. P. Thompson's 'peculiarities of the English' – alongside, of course, those of the Prussians, the Poles and the Portuguese.[54] Today it seems arbitrary and anachronistic to rule that only crusaders for atheism, republicanism and materialism deserve the adjective 'enlightened'; the time is ripe, as Thompson himself might surely have said, to rescue the English Enlightenment from the 'enormous condescension of posterity'.[55]

To trace the part played by British thinkers in the making of modernity, better mappings are needed of the contacts and circuits of literati and their listeners. The loops between London, Edinburgh and Dublin, between the metropolis and the provinces, between cultures high and low, religious and secular, male and female, must all be traced. Appealing against guilty verdicts on the treason of the intellectuals – Perry Anderson's withering 'no ferment of ideas or memories' – Thompson points to the formation of 'scores of intellectual enclaves, dispersed over England, Wales and Scotland, which made up for what they lost in cohesion by the multiplicity of initiatives afforded by these many bases'.[56] J. H. Plumb likewise has guided the bedazzled eye away from the 'peaks of culture': 'too much attention, it seems to me,' he wrote, 'is paid to the monopoly of ideas amongst the intellectual giants, too little to their social acceptance. Ideas acquire dynamism when they become social attitudes and this was happening in England.'[57] These are some of the challenges this book takes up. I shall now turn to the core problems of the British Enlightenment, and signpost the key themes covered in the chapters to follow.

Britain experienced profound transformations during the long eighteenth century: the overthrow of absolutism, accelerating population growth, urbanization, a commercial revolution marked by rising disposable income, the origins of industrialization. Shifts in consciousness helped to bring these changes about, to make sense of and level criticism at them, and to direct public attention to modernity, its delights and its discontents.[58]

Striking changes were afoot in 'high culture'. Protestant scripturalism – the belief that every word of the Bible had been dictated by the Holy Ghost – was refined into a new rational faith, attended by more optimistic models of man's lot under the Supreme Being (see chapter 5). Basking in Newton's glory, the new science was acclaimed and extended to pastures new, natural and social alike. Scientific methods, political arithmetic, probabilistic thinking, systematic observation, experiment and quantification and appeals to the yardstick of Nature all gained prestige and applicability (see chapter 6).

Partly as a consequence of these new beliefs, vast intellectual capital was vested in creating sciences of man and society. Hobbes, Locke and their successors anatomized the mind and emotions, and recognizable precursors of today's social and human sciences – psychology, economics, anthropology, sociology and so forth – took shape (see chapters 3, 7, 17). Divine Right and other prescriptive dogmas which had buttressed a static, hierarchical social order were assailed by critical thinking on power, leading to the felicific calculus, to utilitarian reformism and to the Rights of Man (see chapters 8 and 18).

I shall be scrutinizing these and many other innovations in scientific, theological, psychological, social and political discourse, by focusing on such key figures as Newton, Locke, Bernard de Mandeville, David Hartley, Erasmus Darwin, Priestley, Paine, Bentham, Godwin and Wollstonecraft, and examining the publicizing of their ideas by Addison and Steele, Defoe, Pope and Sterne and a host of other poets, preachers and popularizers. Much work has been done on such past masters, but it remains fragmentary; the pieces have yet to be put together and the full jigsaw revealed.

Big ideas must be contextualized in terms of broader transformations in casts of mind, habits of thinking and shades of sensibility, and their diffusion among the reading public must be addressed, so that the practical consequences of enlightened ideologies can be grasped. Only then will the fundamental revisions wrought in public outlooks become clear: biblicism and providentialism were being challenged by naturalism; custom was elbowed aside by an itch for change and faith in the new. In many fields – in moral quandaries, self-identity, artistic taste, reading habits, leisure pursuits – deference to tradition was spurned as antiquated, backward or plebeian by boosters conjuring up brighter futures there for the taking. Central to enlightened modernizing were the glittering prospects of progress conveyed through print.

In Britain, at least, the Enlightenment was thus not just a matter of pure epistemological breakthroughs; it was primarily the expression of new mental and moral values, new canons of taste, styles of sociability and views of human nature. And these typically assumed practical embodiment: urban renewal; the establishment of hospitals, schools, factories and prisons; the acceleration of communications; the spread of newspapers, commercial outlets and consumer behaviour; the marketing of new merchandise and cultural services. All such developments repatterned the loom of life, with inevitable repercussions for social prospects and agendas of personal fulfilment.

England's avant-garde enjoyed different prospects from those to be expected elsewhere. Activists were not thwarted at every twist and turn by monarchical *fiat*, *lettres de cachet* or an ossified *status quo* in State, Church and society. Quite the reverse. After the Glorious Revolution of 1688, the very statute book incorporated much of the enlightened wish list: freedom of the person under habeas corpus, the rule of law, Parliament, religious toleration, and so forth. Furthermore, unlike elsewhere, neither censorship, police spies nor petrified ecclesiastical protocols stopped the articulate and ambitious from pursuing their goals, be they experiments in free-thinking and -living, self-enrichment or the pursuit of pleasure. Promoters of enlightened rationality did not need to storm barricades, for doors swung open within the system, giving some plausibility to Bacon's oft-quoted maxim: *faber suae quisque fortunae* ('each man [is] the maker of his own fortune'). Not until late in the eighteenth century did the Enlightenment's new men feel radically alienated from the English Establishment.

Hardly surprisingly, therefore, one trait of enlightened England was a buoyant pragmatism, underpinned by a Baconian philosophy of action. The proof of 'pudding time' lay in the uses of freedom, the enjoyment of well-being. Foreign visitors marvelled at England's thriving hive. 'The English are great in practical mechanics,' declared the Swiss-American Louis Simond,[59] while Pastor Moritz from

Prussia drooled over English improvements, right down to the knack of 'roasting slices of buttered bread before the fire ... called "toast"'.[60] Predictably, English piety was also esteemed for its emphasis on works not words: 'religion in England, in towns, and even in the smallest villages,' envied the Abbé Prévost, 'finds its expression in hospitals for the sick, homes of refuge for the poor and aged of both sexes, schools for the education of the children'.[61]

Conversely, when on Grand Tour, the enlightened British were not slow to bridle at Continental benightedness, and were shocked by the misery they met. Finding the peasantry of the Palatinate 'poor and wretched', Elizabeth Montagu drew the hackneyed contrast between starving yokels and 'princes so magnificent'.[62] 'I cannot help thinking they groan under oppression,' commented Tobias Smollett, lamenting the 'poverty, misery, and dirt, among the commonalty of France'.[63]

British pragmatism was more than mere worldliness: it embodied a *philosophy* of expediency, a dedication to the art, science and duty of living well in the here and now. Lord Chesterfield's commendation to his son of hedonism and *savoir vivre* finessed Locke's dictum that 'Our Business here is not to know all things, but those which concern our Conduct' – Pope's view that 'the proper study of mankind is man'.[64] Would it be fanciful to suggest that Prime Minister Walpole's preferred self-presentation as 'no saint, no Spartan, no reformer' had an enlightened tint? The displacement of Calvinism by a confidence in cosmic benevolism blessed the pursuit of happiness, and to this end Britons set about exploiting a commercial society pregnant with opportunities, and the practical skills needed to drive it.[65]

Modernizers faced pressing predicaments. Above all, in the 'great scramble' of a market society,[66] how could a stable order be achieved which would facilitate the pursuit of happiness? Enlightened crusaders waved the liberty banner, legitimizing such claims through Lockean liberalism and the moral and psychological formulae known as benevolism, sensationalism, associationism and utilitarianism. Did not each man best know how best to pursue pleasure? 'Virtue is the conformity to a rule of life,' explained the Revd John Gay, 'directing the actions of all rational creatures with respect to each other's happiness.'[67] Glossing a famous phrase from Pope's *An Essay on Man*, another respected Anglican divine, the Revd William Paley, deemed that 'whatever is expedient is right' – a breathtaking maxim to come from the pen of a Cambridge tutor and member of the Church of England.[68] Sanctifying self-interest and private judgement, Joseph Priestley urged: 'it is most advisable to leave every man at perfect liberty to serve himself'.[69] Even the sober Joseph Butler, later a bishop, doubted we were justified in pursuing virtue, 'till we are convinced that it will be for our happiness, or, at least, not contrary to it'.[70] And egoism in practice had a pretty free run amidst the trappings of what admittedly remained a confusing and cluttered hierarchy. The endorsement from Locke to Smith of the inviolability of private property, and the assurance that 'the inconveniences which have arisen to a nation from leaving trade quite open are few',[71] found expression in economic liberalism and *laissez-faire* (see chapters 11 and 17).

It has furthermore been argued that it was enlightened England which brought, at least amongst genteel and professional people, the first flowering of 'affective individualism' within the conjugal family: greater exercise of choice as regards marriage partner, some degree of female emancipation from stern patriarchy, and for children from the parental rod (see chapters 12 and 15). Over from France, Madame du Boccage found that the daughters of the gentry 'live in much less constraint than young ladies amongst us'.[72] Writers and artists similarly basked in unwonted opportunities. 'How sweet this bit of freedom really is!' exclaimed Haydn in 1791, on one of his money-spinning London concert tours. 'I had a kind prince, but sometimes was I obliged to be dependent on base souls. I often sighed for release, and now I have it in some measure.'[73]

This emancipation of the ego from hidebound tradition and the stern judgementalism of elders, family and peers, this rejection or attenuation of the ancestral 'moral economy',[74] was widely thought worth the risk as a feelgood factor became programmed into enlightened expectations. Conviction grew that the time was ripe to cast off from the old world and set sail for a cape of Good Hope; Moderns could and should outdo Ancients. The auguries were auspicious: human nature was not flawed by the Fall; desire was desirable, society improvable, knowledge progressive and good would emerge from what Priestley dubbed man's 'endless cravings'.[75]

All this chimed with a new faith in Nature at large: Newton's universe, like society itself, was doubtless composed of myriad atoms, yet its ensemble comprised a harmonious and resplendent natural order, which man had a right to explore and master through natural science and the practical arts (see chapter 6). And confidence also grew about the Divine Order. God's benevolence resolved the theodicy problem: Satan was but a metaphor, evil at bottom mere error. Providence – Smith's 'invisible hand' – had bid self-love and social be the same in a programme of amelioration;[76] 'private vices' were, fortunately, 'public benefits'; and self-interest could also be enlightened. In Shaftesbury's sunny phrase: 'The Wisdom of what rules, and is First and Chief in nature, had made it to be according to the private Interest and Good of everyone, to work towards the general Good'[77] – or, in the less lofty sentiments of Frederick Eden, 'the desire of bettering our condition . . . animates the world [and] gives birth to every social virtue'.[78]

Thus heartened, Albion's polite and commercial people seized their chance to express themselves, to escape the iron cages of Calvinism, custom and kinship – and even to indulge their 'whims'.[79] Acquisitiveness, pleasure-seeking, emotional and erotic self-discovery, social climbing and the joys of fashion slipped the moral and religious straitjackets of guilt, sin and retribution (see chapter 12). Harshness towards children was relaxed, while philanthropy kindled sympathy towards lunatics and dumb animals, the deaf and disabled (see chapters 15 and 16).[80] Yet, enlightened élites still had to prove that self-emancipation and pleasure-seeking could actually be ventured without precipitating the moral ruin and social chaos widely feared. Sodom and Gomorrah, Babylon and Rome – all had collapsed; the pious bloodshed of the Civil War and Interregnum had left deep scars; and the libertinism of the Cavalier Court was a salutary reminder of how hedonism not only destroyed itself through the bottle, pox or pistol, but also meant sinister alliances with Popish tyranny. Hobbes had hurled down a challenge: since man was incurably selfish, could not Leviathan alone curb his excesses? No more than Divine Right kingship or the theocracy of saints was Hobbism an option admissible to enlightened minds.

Hence the problem lay in ensuring that private fulfilment did not subvert public orderliness. And any proposed solution had to take into account certain singular features of English society. For one thing, having bid absolutism good riddance at the Glorious Revolution, enlightened élites were confronted with a truculent populace.[81] Rowdy street politics, mused the Prussian Johann Wilhelm von Archenholz, was the price the nation paid for freedom: 'The idea of liberty,' he wrote, 'and the consciousness of protection from the laws, are the reasons why the people in general testify but little respect for their superiors.'[82] Subjects who could not be hammered had to be humoured. Madame du Boccage did not mince her words: 'In France we cringe to the great, in England the great cringe to the people.'[83]

Furthermore, England's free market economy, itself fanned by enlightened individualism, depended on consumerism permeating down through the social strata. With the renaissance of provincial towns, the growth of communications and service industries and the commercialization of news, information and leisure, an expanding public hankered to participate in pleasures traditionally exclusive to the élite (see chapter 11). 'It is evident,' observed Madame Roland about England, 'that man, whatever he may be, is here reckoned something, and that a handful of rich does not constitute the nation.'[84]

It was under these circumstances, with plaudits to freedom pealing out from Parliament, press and pulpit, that opinion-makers spelt out their strategies for accommodating egoism within a stable social fabric. One choice lay in embracing inclusiveness. Whilst propagandists spoke for propertied and privileged élites, theirs was an ideology which espoused universalism: potentially, at least, reason was an attribute enjoyed by the whole nation, including women and the plebs. The best bid for accommodation and harmony would thus lie in assimilating the 'people' within the 'public' – all, that is, who qualified themselves for entry by their industry, civility, affluence or manifest loyalty. Impossible to impose by the sword, order might thereby be achieved through what Hume styled 'opinion', equality under the law, meritocratic social mobility, the reduction of civil and religious disabilities and the manipulation of allegiance and rising expectations.[85] The corollary of this was, of course, that those who could not or would not play the conformity game were to be stigmatized: religious fanatics, obdurate lawbreakers and the idle and undeserving poor would be subjected to increasingly severe measures of disapproval and discipline.[86] But in a society dismissive of predestination and doubtful about ancestral pedigree *per se*, few aspirant males were automatically debarred by birth or blood.

Enlightened opinion tried out various strategies for achieving inclusiveness. One involved philanthropy and 'paternalism'.[87] The needy and the 'unfortunate' could be bought off by a humanitarianism realized in schools, hospitals, dispensaries, asylums, reformatories and other charitable outlets. The beauty of such enlightened largesse lay in fostering amongst the *bien pensants* the glow of a superior sensibility (see chapter 16).[88]

Another assimilation strategy lay in displays of social openness. Foreigners were astonished to see how the 'Quality' consented to mingle with, rather than seclude themselves from, the nation at large. The hustings, sporting events, spas, pleasure gardens and urban parades – all encouraged social concourse. It startled the Prussian Carl Philip Moritz to find that in England 'officers do not go in uniform but dress as civilians'. Having puzzled over what made St James's Park so special, he concluded: 'It is the astonishing medley of people.' The French traveller P. J. Grosley reacted similarly to London's resorts: 'The pleasures of Vauxhall and Ranelagh unite both sexes, and all ranks and conditions.' And what was it about cricket? 'Everyone plays it,' César de Saussure concluded, 'the common people and also men of rank.' And the English stagecoach? Why, responded Louis Simond, it contained 'passengers of all sexes, ages, and conditions'. Likewise the coffee house: '[W]hat a lesson,' remarked the Abbé Prévost, 'to see a lord, or two, a baronet, a shoemaker, a tailor, a wine-merchant, and a few others of the same stamp poring over the same newspapers. Truly the coffee houses . . . are the seats of English liberty.'[89]

While historians point to a widening gulf between élite and popular culture,[90] in England counter-currents were also at work. No doubt outrageous hamming went on in the public theatricals of the grandees, flouncing around at Vauxhall or at the hustings, but much of the population expected to participate in the modern partiality for amusement, display, fashion and preening. Enlightened fables sold social success to hopefuls like William Hogarth's 'industrious apprentice', while improving books for children courted those

> Who from a State of Rags and Care,
> And having Shoes but half a Pair;
> Their Fortune and their Fame would fix,
> And gallop in a Coach and Six.[91]

Carrots lured those bent on embourgeoisement: the Lord Mayor's coach, Archdeacon Paley noted, was not for *his* benefit, but for society's – to fire the prentice boy's ambition.[92] Money offered an *entrée* into a modern commercial dream world which led all to entertain hopes and allowed quite a few to realize them.

In what seemed, especially to foreigners, a society perilously short of legal and regal subordination, integrative gestures also marked other enlightened strategies. As will become clear, reconciliatory strands were woven into enlightened discourse - confidence in the compatibility of individual *and* society, money *and* gentility, self-love *and* conscience, science *and* religion, even men *and* women. The tragic mind set of Stoicism and the otherworldly fixations of Christianity yielded to a faith in man's temporal capacity to remould himself and, in the course of time, surmount dichotomies. Whereas Christian humanism gloried in arduous choice - witness *Samson Agonistes* or *Rasselas* – the enlightened always wanted, nay, *expected* to have their cake and eat it.

Addressing nagging fears that individualism would dig its own grave, it has here been suggested that one bid for harmony was to vest faith in the equilibrium expected to emerge from social roles and market forces. Another lay in putting confidence in a validating framework of natural order and religio-ethical teachings. Critical darts were doubtless hurled at the so-called metaphysical mumbo-jumbo which legitimized oppression – be it Platonism or predestination – but there were very few utter cynics or sceptics determined to deny cosmic truth altogether.[93] There was a desire to destabilize and dismantle, yet we must never scant the enlightened desire to replace exploded systems with a superior orderliness, the urge not just to probe and puncture but to prove, preach and prescribe. Obsolete teachings were rejected, partly for being untrue, but chiefly because, whilst promising godly order, they had patently – witness the Wars of Religion – failed to deliver.

To enlightened minds, the past was a nightmare of barbarism and bigotry: fanaticism had precipitated bloody civil war and the axing of Charles Stuart, that man of blood, in 1649. Enlightened opinion repudiated old militancy for modern civility. But how could people adjust to each other? Sectarianism, that sword of the saints which had divided brother from brother, must cease; rudeness had to yield to refinement. Voltaire saw this happening before his very eyes in England's 'free and peaceful assemblies':

Take a view of the *Royal Exchange* in *London*, a place more venerable than many courts of justice, where the representatives of all nations meet for the benefit of mankind. There the Jew, the Mahometan, and the Christian transact together as tho' they all profess'd the same religion, and give the name of Infidel to none but bankrupts. There the Presbyterian confides in the Anabaptist, and the Churchman depends on the Quaker's word. And all are satisfied.[94]

This passage squares with the enlightened belief that commerce would unite those whom creeds set asunder. Moreover, by depicting men content, and content to be content – differing, but agreeing to differ – the *philosophe* pointed towards a rethinking of the *summum bonum,* a shift from God-fearingness to a selfhood more psychologic-ally oriented. The Enlightenment thus translated the ultimate ques-tion 'How can I be saved?' into the pragmatic 'How can I be happy?' – thereby heralding a new praxis of personal and social adjustment.

This accent on refinement was no footling obsession with petty punctilio; it was a desperate remedy meant to heal the chronic social conflict and personal traumas stemming from civil and domestic tyranny and topsy-turvy social values. Politeness could be taught by education – Locke and his successors stressed 'learning in the uses of the world' – and perfected by practice. 'The great art,' preached James Boswell, 'of living easy and happy in society is to study proper behaviour, and even with our most intimate friends, to observe politeness.'[95] (That raucous drunk never learned.)

Above all, the refinement of the self was to be a function of energetic sociability. Solitude – 'one of the greatest obstacles to pleasure and improvement'[96] – bred hypochondria: cooped up in his study, the costive scholar succumbed to spleen. '[N]othing,' deplored David Hartley, 'can easily exceed the Vain-glory, Self-conceit, Arro-gance, Emulation, and Envy, that are found in the eminent Professors of the Sciences.'[97] To be enlightened, a gentleman had to be sociable, or, in Johnson's coinage, 'clubbable' (and the Great Cham's own Literary Club boasted the top minds of the day). Clubs like Mr Spectator's, masonic lodges, taverns, coffee houses and friendly societies – miniature free republics of rational society – sprang up to promote fellowship and good feeling.[98] And the enlightened set about devising the arts and crafts of pleasing. Human nature was malleable; people must cheerfully accommodate each other; good breeding, conversation and discreet charm were the lubricants which would overcome social friction, contributing 'as much as possible to the Ease and Happiness of Mankind'.[99] 'We polish one another,' reflected Shaftesbury, 'and rub off our corners and rough sides by a sort of amicable collision.'[100] The rational arts of ease, good humour, sympathy, restraint and moderation, based upon acceptance of human nature – all marked the new felicific formulae.[101] This book will stress these distinctively British enlightening strategies: the drive not to subvert the system, but to secure it so as to achieve individual satisfaction and collective stability, within the post-1688 framework.

Regardless of the fortunes of this or that ideology, a deeper transformation was afoot: the rise and triumph of lay and secular public opinion, the fourth estate, the information society, involving the birth, infancy and troubled adolescence of the modern intelligentsia.[102] Many features mark Britain's men of letters (notably a paradoxical anti-intellectualism), which make sense only when seen in terms of the unique circumstances of the Enlightenment's birth pangs. Enlightened opinion-makers gazed upon their navels, pondering their self-identity and their strategies for the seduction of society by the printed word – as did such satirists as Swift, who pricked their pretensions. The pen is mightier than the sword, Bulwer Lytton was soon to proclaim; that *aperçu* would have sounded more curious still without the enlightenment experience.[103]

2

THE BIRTH OF
AN IDEOLOGY

'Tis well an Old Age is out,
And time to begin a New.

JOHN DRYDEN[1]

I am here in a country which hardly resembles the rest of
Europe. This nation is passionately fond of liberty ... every
individual is independent.

MONTESQUIEU[2]

The half-century after 1660 brought decisive transformations to British power politics and its clashing ideologies. Years of
civil strife led to the beheading of the Lord's anointed, Charles I, on
30 January 1649, the establishment of a republic, the abolition of the
House of Lords and the Bench of Bishops, and to the rule of the
Major Generals and Cromwell's doomed Protectorate – events which
drove the young John Locke to despair of 'this great Bedlam England'.[3] During the Interregnum, England's traditional governors had
been bruised and battered, as God's own nation was redeemed or
ravaged by New Model Army pikemen, chiliastic preachers and
antinomian agitators advancing 'New Jerusalem' schemes which
ranged from the communism of the Diggers to Ranter free love.
Hence the audible relief at the Restoration. 'Never so joyfull a day,'
John Evelyn recorded in his diary the day Charles II rode into
London: 'I stood in the Strand and beheld it and blessed God.'[4] It
was not only the King who hoped never again to have to go on his
travels; the old political nation was bent on stabilization, and for
many in the Cavalier Parliament this meant vengeance against and

repression of those who had turned the world upside-down and, as the 1662 Fifth Monarchist Rising showed, had every intention of doing so again.[5]

Measures were passed to ram the lid back on. The Anglican Church was restored, with its bishops, courts and most of its privileges. Censorship was reimposed. The so-called Clarendon Code – the Corporation Act (1661), the Act of Uniformity (1662), the Conventicle Act (1662), the Five Mile Act (1665) and the Test Acts (1661, 1673) – harassed non-Anglicans, curbing their rights to preach, teach and hold office. The Act of Uniformity, for example, required all clergy and schoolmasters to subscribe to a declaration of conformity to the Anglican liturgy and to forswear disloyal oaths.[6] The next decades saw the apogee of Divine Right preaching and of royal thaumaturgical healing. Thomas Hobbes might be the Devil incarnate, but he was hardly alone in looking to a mighty sovereign to end feuding and fanaticism.[7]

In some ways, the Restoration worked. Building on Cromwell's recent conquests overseas, trade prospered. The Court exuded a louche brilliance and the 'Merrie Monarch' a winning charm, at least for those who had loathed the Puritan Zeal-of-the-land-busies. Culturally and artistically, a dazzling half-century followed, with the work of Wren, Gibbons, Lely, Kneller, Purcell, and the dramas of Dryden, Aphra Behn, Etheridge, Wycherley, Congreve, Vanbrugh and Farquhar,[8] while the Royal Society, chartered in 1662, promised to best the world in science.[9]

Restoring order, however, proved easier said than done. Interregnum England had grown fatally factionalized, and everyone had scores to settle. No realist could expect that the entire kingdom would now flock back into the Anglican fold; the Court dallied with Catholicism, while many of the middling sort had put down sturdy sectarian roots – an identity given permanence once the repressive Clarendon Code alienated even mainstream Protestant dissent. Politicians locked horns over law and liberty, the religious settlement, Crown–Parliament relations and foreign alignments. As commercial policy began to count for more to what was becoming a 'trading nation', and Louis XIV's militarism grew more threatening, discord deepened and parties formed.[10]

Meanwhile, Charles was playing with fire. His Declaration of Indulgence (1672) opportunistically suspended statutes against Nonconformists and Catholics – a measure he was soon forced to rescind, but which inevitably deepened debates over the accommodation ('comprehension') or the muzzling of dissent.[11] A little before, he had acted treacherously, in the secret clauses of the Treaty of Dover (1670), by providing for England's conversion to Catholicism in return for the Sun King's gold, in a move meant to secure Crown independence from Parliament. Smelling a rat, the more extreme Whigs, led by the Earl of Shaftesbury, fell to conspiracies, desperate at all costs to stave off re-Catholicization. This clove the political nation: the succession of Charles II's Papist brother, James, was feared since it posed palpable threats to Protestantism, and hysteria was whipped up by the fabricated 'Popish Plot'. Radical Whigs resorted to desperate measures in the Exclusion Crisis, backing the succession of the Duke of Monmouth, Charles's illegitimate, but at least Protestant, son.[12] Spying was met by counter-espionage, accusation by counter-charge. Outmanoeuvred, Shaftesbury fled, and his secretary, John Locke, joined him in exile. Radicals who, like them, found refuge in the Dutch republic, that hotbed of dissidence, conspired with *émigrés* from France, especially after Louis' Revocation of the Edict of Nantes (1685) created a Huguenot diaspora which fed pan-Protestant paranoia.

Contained in the twilight years of Charles's reign, crisis erupted after James II's accession in 1685. Monmouth's revolt ended ingloriously at Sedgemoor but, in the wake of that débâcle, the arbitrariness of royal repression alienated top politicians and bishops, mighty aristocrats, urban corporations and the universities. Natural conservatives temporarily found themselves bedfellows with hotheads in repudiating a regime contemptuous of legality and rights, one increasingly ruling through prerogative and smelling of Popery. When James's consort, Mary of Modena, belatedly gave birth to an heir (spurious, according to the 'warming-pan legend'), events were triggered which led to an invitation to William of Orange, the Dutch stadtholder, to invade and eject James Stuart.[13]

Yet James's 'abdication' in the bloodless 'Glorious Revolution' of November 1688 sparked as many problems as it solved. The Bill of Rights, imposed upon William in the Revolutionary Settlement as a condition for his accession to the throne, guaranteed regular (triennial) parliaments, security of person and property, broad toleration for Protestants and other freedoms. In effect, contrary to its own basic instincts, the political nation had been driven, in the name of safeguarding rights and religion, to pass measures which, at the Restoration, would certainly have been regarded as dangerously unsettling. Stuart folly, parliamentary factionalism and the fickleness of fate had brought about what proved an irreversible liberalization of the constitution – one which most of the élite wanted to be final.[14]

Yet, the genie was out of the bottle once again, as during the Interregnum; the demons raised by James could not be silenced. Quite the reverse. The post-1688 political machinery was untried, office was up for grabs, allegiances were volatile and the principles and policies of William and Mary's regime became matters of raging controversy. Radical arguments repudiating Divine Right and patriarchalism[15] had been enunciated to rationalize first resistance to, and then the expulsion of, James. But by what title did William himself reign and rule? Had such a right been conferred upon him by the nation? If so, did that amount to popular sovereignty? If a 'Protestant wind' had blown him to Torbay in 1688, did Providence bless each and every victorious usurper? Could prelates who had broken their sacred oaths of allegiance to James then in conscience swear fealty to William?

Moreover, 1688 could nowise be a final solution.[16] Jacobite counter-coups long remained threatening. Orangism dragged England into the 'world war' against France, that finale of the Wars of Religion. William's strategic rapprochement with Protestant Dissenters put the Church of England under ever greater strain, and religious tensions intensified with the arrival of some 80,000 Huguenot refugees, fanning anti-Catholic panic. The 'pacification' of

Ireland, the cost of William's 'grand alliance' wars and the expansion of the executive and standing army (serving, many averred, Dutch rather than British interests) further deepened divisions.[17]

If things cooled somewhat with the less controversial reign of Queen Anne, her own failure to produce a surviving heir reopened the succession sore. Questions of principle – who *was* the legitimate successor, and on whose say-so? – became inseparable from the jockeyings of Whigs and Tories to gain and retain the ever fatter spoils of office.[18] The post-1688 years hence brought the 'rage of party' in a 'divided nation' split over the fundamentals of Church and State, King and Parliament, Whig and Tory, High and Low Church, subject and citizen – satirized by Swift in terms of Big and Little Enders. And all these controversies were occurring amid momentous institutional and economic change at home, with the foundation of the Bank of England (1694), the new money markets and the Stock Exchange, and the mushrooming of the 'fiscal military state'[19] – all against a backdrop of a ravaged, war-torn Europe in which the Protestant cause sometimes seemed close to ruin at the hands of the dreaded Sun King.

These times of crisis brought pamphlets, prints and other propaganda galore, from all sides and slants, penned by brilliant polemicists. It was this crescendo of religio-political controversy from the 1680s that formed the catalyst of enlightenment, unleashing volleys of polemics damning tyranny and priestcraft in the names of freedom, property, autonomy and reason,[20] advanced especially by those militant Whigs who formed the 'Country' faction.[21] To appreciate the momentous intellectual consequences of these developments, it will be helpful first to examine the radicalization of John Locke.[22]

The Restoration found Locke holding a 'studentship' (in effect, a fellowship) at Christ Church, Oxford. Somerset-born in 1632, he had been ten years old when his father had taken up arms against Charles I and twenty-one when he thus saluted Oliver Cromwell: 'You, Sir, from Heav'n a finish'd hero fell.'[23] Though of Puritan stock, he hated the Interregnum turmoil, and his early thinking took a conservative turn, prizing order above all, as is evident from his 'Two Tracts on Government' (written in 1660–61 but not published), which championed passive obedience and upheld the magistrate's right to impose religious uniformity.[24]

Declining to take holy orders, Locke became physician and secretary to Lord Ashley (later Shaftesbury), serving on the Council of Trade during his master's chancellorship of the Exchequer in 1672. Inescapably entangled in exclusionist politics, he may have helped Shaftesbury cook up the 'Popish Plot'. Under surveillance after the Rye House Plot (1682), he burned or buried his papers and fled to the United Provinces, his studentship being withdrawn on royal command. In Rotterdam he fell in with conspiring Whig refugees and the Remonstrants, those liberal Dutch Nonconformists who upheld a minimal religious creed; moving to Utrecht, he was again at the thick of intrigues, probably advising Viscount Mordaunt on the Monmouth Rebellion, and being ordered out of town in 1686 when James II sought his extradition along with other suspects.

Returning to England after the Glorious Revolution, Locke played a central role in its vindication, publishing anonymously the *Two Treatises of Government* (1690), a radical work written at the time of the Exclusion Crisis in order to legitimize rebellion in terms of a contractual theory of government (see chapter 8).[25] He exerted considerable sway as adviser to the Junto Whigs, Somers, Halifax and Mordaunt. As an Excise commissioner, he became active in the growing fiscal bureaucracy; serving on the Board of Trade, he was energetic in commercial policy; he was also an original subscriber to the Bank of England, while, together with Halifax and Isaac Newton, he presided over the 'great recoinage' of 1694–6. Enlightened thinkers liked to view philosophers as piloting the ship of state: Locke provided the perfect prototype.

Over the course of forty years, the habitually watchful philosopher had undergone a profound radicalization, one indicative of how bold minds were driven by darkening times into enlightened convictions. Back in the early 1660s, fearing religious turmoil, Locke had been a champion of order and obedience in Church and State. Responding to circumstances, he turned into the leading theorist of toleration: Locke unfolded anti-innatist arguments in the *Essay concerning Human Understanding* (1690) (see the discussion in chapter 3); his *Two Treatises on Government* spelt out theories of government accountability and the right of resistance; and his religious orthodoxy crumbled as he became, almost certainly, a closet Unitarian (see chapter 5). In short, the Restoration conservative turned into a philosophical radical. 'I think that both Locke and my Lord Shaftesbury were as arrant atheists as Spinoza,' an informant told Dr Charlett, master of University College, Oxford, in 1706, while Locke was also damned as a man of 'very bad principles' by the Oxford Tory Thomas Hearne.[26]

Appraising these decisive decades, the distinguished American historian Margaret Jacob has claimed that enlightened thinking first found voice in the contexts of these domestic politico-religious broils and of the Sun King's imperial ambitions. Naming 1689 as its nativity, she has declared that 'the Enlightenment at large, in both its moderate and radical forms, began in England' with the Glorious Revolution, following hard on the heels of Isaac Newton's *Principia* (1687).[27] While finessing her formulations over the years,[28] Jacob has consistently situated the movement's onset in that conjunction of political crisis and intellectual revolution, buoyed up by the stimulating social atmosphere provided by swarms of refugees, pamphlet wars, coffee houses and clubs, and the international web of the republic of letters.

Luck and logic meant that with George I's succession in 1714, the subsequent botched Jacobite invasion and the resulting entrenchment of the Hanoverian dynasty, progressive ideologies triumphed. Constitutional and politico-religious liberties were vindicated, and the personal powers of the Crown and the pretensions of High-flying bishops were curbed in what proved an unshakeable commitment to the quadruple alliance of freedom, Protestantism, patriotism and prosperity.[29] This chain of events produced strange kinks, however: progressive thinkers, hitherto automatically oppositional, now found themselves brokers of power under the new dynasty.[30] No longer did they have to fear constant harassment, for most opinions could be published with impunity once the lapse of the Licensing Act (1695) put an end to pre-publication censorship. Though laws against blasphemy, obscenity and seditious libel remained on the statute book, and offensive publications could still be presented before the courts, the situation was light years away from that obtaining in France, Spain or almost anywhere else in *ancien régime* Europe – or that faced by Locke in exile.[31] This exceptional freedom of expression sparked print wars which gave the battles for minds their enduring energies, and which led enlightened activists ultimately to devour their own parents.

In these circumstances, enlightened ideologies were to assume a unique inflection in England: one less concerned to lambast the *status quo* than to vindicate it against adversaries left and right, high and low. Poachers were turning gamekeepers; implacable critics of princes now became something more like apologists for them; those who had held that power corrupted now found themselves, with the advent of political stabilization, praising the Whig regime as the bulwark of Protestant liberties. These are paradoxes which have been brilliantly teased out by the historian John Pocock.

In a series of distinguished writings, Pocock has analysed the advanced discourses which vindicated the post-1688 and post-1714 settlements against the motley mix of Jacobites, High-flyers, Dissenting enthusiasts and 'Good Old Cause' republicans seemingly threatening to drag Britain back into civil strife and wars of faith. Sights trained on the school of Peter Gay, he challenges 'the paradigm of Enlightenment as radical liberation which has made it so hard to speak of an English Enlightenment at all'.[32] The English, in his view, were uniquely able to enjoy an enlightenment without *philosophes* precisely because, at least after 1714, there was no longer any *infâme* to be crushed.[33] Since a broadly liberalized regime was already in power, what was chiefly required was its defence against diehards and the ghosts of Laud, Strafford ('Black Tom Tyrant') and Cromwell. Hostility to religion as such would have been misplaced because, after the Act of Toleration (1689), faith functioned within the framework of what Locke memorably dubbed 'the reasonableness of Christianity'.

There was no further need to contemplate regicide because Great Britain was already a mixed monarchy, with inbuilt constitutional checks on the royal will; nor would radicals howl to string up the nobility, since they had abandoned feudalism for finance. What Pocock tentatively calls the 'conservative enlightenment' was thus a holding operation, rationalizing the post-1688 settlement, pathologizing its enemies and dangling seductive prospects of future security and prosperity. The Enlightenment became established and the established became enlightened.[34]

A seemingly paradoxical instance of an intellectual vanguard vindicating the *status quo*, the English Enlightenment derived its identity, Pocock holds, from the reaction to the traumatic experiences of the Stuart century; it was the ideology of a post-Puritan ruling order which made England both the most modern and (eventually) the most counter-revolutionary state in Europe.[35] Or, more provocatively, being 'too modern to need an Enlightenment', England 'was already engaged upon the quarrel with modernity itself.'[36] Especially after 1714, enlightened ideologues thus enlisted in defence of the new Whig order, one perpetuating certain features of the *ancien régime*,[37] but notably unlike the other great monarchies.

Supplementing such views, Margaret Jacob has further shown how the Newtonian universe was recruited to bolster the new constitutional order against its foes.[38] Repudiating alike the scandalous materialism of Hobbes and Spinoza and also the outmoded occultism of the sectaries, Newtonian cosmology afforded the perfect paradigm for a modern, stable, harmonious Christian polity ruled by law, not caprice.[39] God and the Georges were the constitutional monarchs respectively of the universe and the nation. A garden laid out at Richmond by George II's consort, Queen Caroline, rooted these new teachings in busts of Newton, Samuel Clarke and Locke, planted there because 'they were the Glory of their Country, and stamp'd a Dignity on Human Nature'; they would serve as expressions of faith in the trinity of experimental science, rational religion and Revolution principles.[40]

This realignment of enlightened propaganda so as to validate the

Georgian order naturally sparked fierce divisions among advanced thinkers.[41] Dissenting voices came from 'country' or 'true' Whigs, 'Good Old Cause' radicals alarmed and outraged at the pestiferous growth of patronage, placemen and politicking, adamant that 1688 and 1714 had not gone far enough in muzzling throne and altar. Ideological affinities ironically emerged between such agitators and the Tories, who had been so deftly outflanked after 1714. Cornered by Walpole into long-term opposition, Tory wits sported a libertarianism of their own: Jonathan Swift, otherwise the great scourge of the trendy literati, could carve as his political epitaph: 'Fair liberty was all his cry'.[42] Such a pilfering of liberal clothes does not, of course, turn the Tories into Enlightenment men, it merely reveals the quick-change masquerading of an age when enlightened propagandists providentially found themselves, for once, calling the shots.

Rancorous in the extreme, late Stuart and early Hanoverian ideological enmities did not then just peter out: there was no 'end of ideology' slumber. Throughout the century, self-styled progressives continued to wage war – sometimes phoney – on darkness and despotism; indeed, there continued to be droves of dyed-in-the-wool Non-Jurors, Jacobites, Tories, anti-Newtonians and anti-Lockeans, while Oxford remained a den of disaffection (its classic lost causes were not all born losers).[43] Moreover, enlightened publicists inevitably made new enemies – not just peppery wits, congenital naysayers and doomsters, but Methodists and Evangelicals convinced that rational religion in a mechanical universe was the slippery slope towards unbelief and anarchy. Meanwhile, enlightened critics continued down the decades to target the citadels of power, as with Jeremy Bentham's exposures of the arcana of the law. For some, the logic of rational religion did indeed inexorably lead to rejection of Christianity, while the radical distrust of power authorized by Locke and others might teach that government itself was an unnecessary evil. Later chapters will explore how the sleuths of enlightenment continued to track new monsters.

*

As the new century dawned and the Act of Union was signed (1707), the Moderns could thus pride themselves upon living in the light, because Great Britain's constitutional and ecclesiastical framework seemed to guarantee fundamental freedoms. There were other grounds, too, for self-congratulation. The times seemed pregnant not just with change but with improvement, and halcyon days beckoned: would not trade, industry, enterprise and the new science spell a sparkling contrast to all that was *passé*, vulgar or rustic?

The civilizations of Greece and Rome were still, of course, revered; nearer home, however, lay the conspicuous success story of the Golden Age Dutch republic, acclaimed by such respected figures as Sir William Temple;[44] and, though progress was far from uniform, many declared that England, too – if not yet Scotland – was enjoying rapid and remarkable commercial changes and bourgeois self-enrichment, developments driven by and especially visible in London, headquarters of print, pleasure and politeness.

London dominated Britain as no other European capital: 'This city is now what ancient Rome once was,' boasted the *London Guide*; 'the seat of Liberty, the encourager of arts, and the admiration of the whole world.'[45] And not only was enlightenment overwhelmingly a metropolitan bloom but, within the city itself, the axis of culture was itself shifting.

The arts had always been watered by ecclesiastical, royal and noble patronage; the pre-Reformation Church had commissioned artworks, and courtly culture had found expression in lavish ceremonial, in exquisite art collections and in splendid edifices like Inigo Jones's Whitehall Banqueting House.[46] From the late seventeenth century, however, the cultural centre of gravity was conspicuously migrating away from Court into metropolitan spaces at large – into coffee houses, taverns, learned societies, salons, assembly rooms, debating clubs, theatres, galleries and concert rooms; formerly the minions of monarchy, the arts and letters were to become the consorts of commerce and the citizenry.[47]

Between the Restoration and George III's coronation a hundred years later, culture became one of the capital's key growth sectors.

Swarms of promoters, publishers, journalists and middlemen looked for openings, employment and profit not only, and certainly no longer primarily, to the King and his courtiers – the first three Georges were either boorish or stingy – but to chocolate house, club and society clienteles. This shift from Court to Town helped make London the metropolis *à la mode*. Visitors marvelled at the ceaseless throb of activity, the flutter of news, personalities, fashion, talk and diversion to be found from Cheapside to Chelsea. They were astonished by the bustle of the rebuilt post-Fire City to the east, and by the sumptuous display of the developing West End, by the brilliant shops around the Strand and Piccadilly, by theatres and exhibitions, exchanges and markets, the river teeming with shipping and royal parks shimmering with promenaders. The capital became a non-stop parade, bursting with sites for culture-watchers, a festival of the senses offering convivial, culinary and sexual pleasures in its taverns, pleasure gardens and bagnios, places where fame and fortune could be made – and lost.[48] London became a lead character in its own right in Georgian art and thought, if often cast in the villain's role:

> Here malice, rapine, accident, conspire,
> And now a rabble rages, now a fire;
> Their ambush here relentless ruffians lay,
> And here the fell attorney prowls for prey;
> Here falling houses thunder on your head,
> And here a female atheist talks you dead.[49]

As an addictive imaginary space, London was endlessly praised or pilloried by essayists like Addison, Steele and Defoe, by Pope, Swift, Gay, Fielding and other poets and novelists, and by artists like Hogarth: Londoners evidently could not get enough.[50]

Seminal for news, novelty and gossip were the coffee houses. That Restoration innovation spread rapidly, a 1739 survey finding a staggering tally of 551 – ten times more than in Vienna! – to say nothing of the 447 taverns and 207 inns also in the capital. Initially they sprang up around the Royal Exchange and the Custom House in the City, serving as clearing houses for news, foreign and domestic.

Clients of the East India Company and other booming financial institutions (including, from 1694, the Bank of England) clinched their deals amid the smoke. Lloyd's coffee house moved to Lombard Street in 1691 to become the focus of marine insurance, while the tragicomedy of the South Sea Bubble was played out in and around Jonathan's and Garraway's in Exchange Alley.[51]

If business provided the initial rationale, the coffee house soon became crucial to cultural networking. Dryden held court at Will's in Covent Garden, where Pope was later an *habitué*; Addison patronized nearby Button's, and the Tory wits went to the Smyrna in Pall Mall. The Bedford was popular with thespians; Old Slaughter's in St Martin's Lane became the artists' haunt; and, when in London, Edinburgh cronies gathered at the British coffee house, by Charing Cross.[52] Newspapers and pamphlets were laid on – the Chapter coffee house even had its own library – while critics held forth and debates raged on the latest opera, political squib, Court scandal or heretical sermon. Taverns, too, functioned as news centres. 'Ask any landlord why he takes the newspapers,' pronounced the young William Cobbett, later in the century, 'he'll tell you that it attracts people to his house.'[53] All such institutions thus worked to put their clienteles in the know: 'We are become a Nation of Statesmen,' declared *The Craftsman* magazine; 'our Coffee-houses and Taverns are full of them.'[54] The happy conjunction of culture-seekers and a commercial outlet tailor-made for them was plain to foreigners. 'What attracts enormously in these coffee-houses are the gazettes and other public papers,' wrote the Swiss visitor César de Saussure; 'all Englishmen are great newsmongers. Workmen habitually begin the day by going to coffee-rooms in order to read the latest news.'[55] The Irish clergyman Dr Thomas Campbell noted at the Chapter 'a specimen of English freedom', when 'a whitesmith in his apron & some of his saws under his arm, came in, sat down and called for his glass of punch and the paper, both of which he used with as much ease as a Lord'.[56]

The coffee house served as the prototype of the club, many of which were modelled on the fictional specimen immortalized in the

Spectator. Of the 2,000 clubs and other societies said to exist in early Georgian London, some were social (like the Sublime Society of Beefsteaks at the Bedford), some debating (like the Robin Hood Society), and others artistic (like the Society of Dilettanti).[57] The Kit-Cat became the rendezvous for Whig grandees and men of letters, while pride of place later went to Dr Johnson's Literary Club, whose gatherings at the Turk's Head in Gerrard Street, Soho, included the politician Edmund Burke, the painter Joshua Reynolds, the playwright Oliver Goldsmith, the naturalist Sir Joseph Banks, the musicologist Charles Burney, the theatre men David Garrick, Richard Brinsley Sheridan and George Colman, the historian Edward Gibbon, the orientalist Sir William Jones and the economist Adam Smith. Where else could such a galaxy of talent be habitually found?[58]

Clubs came in all guises: the Spitalfields Mathematical Society was a self-improvement club for tradesmen; the 'Society for the Encouragement of Learning', established in 1731 'to institute a republic of letters for promoting the Arts and Sciences', was probably a masonic lodge.[59] Convivial and political clubs abounded, like the Sons of Freedom, or the Antigallicans, who campaigned on behalf of John Wilkes. Self-styled custodians of culture, clubs fulfilled certain of the functions of the Paris salon or the university the capital then lacked: they established circuits of conversation.[60]

Private in format like the club but public in its façade was that British innovation freemasonry. Modelled as a microcosm of the Commonwealth, with its members divided into the three estates of apprentices, journeymen and masters, the lodge promoted enlightened conduct: brotherhood, benevolence, conviviality, liberty, civilization. The 'Royal Art', proclaimed the movement's *Constitutions*, had been practised by the 'free born . . . from the beginning of the world, in the polite nations'.[61]

Freemasonry achieved phenomenal success. In 1717 the London lodges affiliated to form the Grand Lodge of England, with its own Grand Master. Within eight years, there were fifty-two lodges in Great Britain alone, while by 1768 nearly 300 British lodges had been founded, including eighty-seven in the metropolis. The lodge created a social milieu rejoicing in British constitutionalism and prosperity, and dedicated to virtue and humanity under the Great Architect;[62] yet masonry was also riddled with typically British ideological tensions, combining deference to hierarchy with a measure of egalitarianism, acceptance of distinction with social exclusivity and commitment to rationality with a taste for mysteries and ritual.[63]

Overall, the proliferation of clubs, societies and lodges joined with the expansion of the press and Grub Street to boost culture as a flourishing print-based communications enterprise serving a varied public at large (see chapter 4).

London supported numerous other public platforms for staging modern ideas and values, flaunting political and artistic allegiances and promoting the new. The most prominent of these pulpits of modernity was the theatre. Condemned as threats to godly order, playhouses had been closed down by the Puritans. Re-established in 1660, the theatre initially took its cue from royal and noble patronage, but in time began to pitch for wider audiences and tastes, as auditoria grew ever larger – late eighteenth-century Drury Lane seated a staggering 3,611, and even Norwich's theatre held over a thousand.

Mingling sensation and instruction rather like television today, and regaling audiences with costume drama, great lives, history, satire and moral mazes, theatre broadened outlooks and tastes while also serving as a sounding board for opinion and politics. Taken as a burlesque on Sir Robert Walpole, John Gay's *Beggar's Opera* (1728) thus proved phenomenally popular, being performed sixty-two times and enjoyed by up to 40,000 people in its first season alone. When in 1763 the aristocratic libertine the Earl of Sandwich welshed on his drinking companion John Wilkes, he quickly became dubbed 'Jemmy Twitcher', the thief who betrayed Gay's hero, Macheath, and it proved a sobriquet that stuck.[64]

Complementing the theatre as fare for the fancy were London's new art galleries. There was the Shakespeare Gallery in Pall Mall, where the art dealer John Boydell specialized in paintings of scenes from the Bard; and the Poets' Gallery in Fleet Street, which featured works inspired by famous lines of British verse. Founded in 1769, the Royal Academy held annual exhibitions whose appeal was enormous: an amazing 1,680 visitors jammed into Somerset House one Friday in 1769 for the RA show![65]

Museums, too, were novelties. Founded by an act of parliament in 1753, the British Museum was the first public museum in Europe intended 'not only for the inspection and entertainment of the learned and the curious, but for the general use and benefit of the public'.[66] Numerous private-venture museums sprang up, too. 'The birds of paradise, and the humming birds, were I think among the most beautiful,' wrote Susan Burney, Fanny's sister, returning from a visit to Sir Ashton Lever's museum (or 'Holophusikon', in his hifalutin phrase) in Leicester Square. 'There are several pelicans – flamingoes – peacocks (one quite white) – a penguin. Among the beasts a hippopotamus (sea-horse) of an immense size, an elephant, a tyger from the Tower – a Greenland bear and its cub – a wolf – two or three leopards.'[67] Other commercial operations, like 'eidophysicons' or magic lanterns, cashed in on novelty and sensation, bringing the wonders of the world to the curious. In 1773 a listing of the sights of London declared, if with a touch of exaggeration, that there were 'Lions, Tygers, Elephants, &c. in every Street in Town'. Cherokee chiefs taking tea, midgets and giants, stone-eaters and other freaks, 'philosophical fireworks', chess-playing automata, lectures on health, sexual rejuvenation or mesmerism – all these, and scores more besides, titivated the fancy, sparked controversy and became part of the cultural baggage of anyone wanting to pass as a somebody.[68]

Such developments owed much to a new breed of entrepreneur. John Rich, the theatrical manager, decked playhouses out with sophisticated stage machinery and lavish scenery; the opera impresario J. J. Heidegger staged *risqué* masquerades; Jonathan Tyers, proprietor of Vauxhall Pleasure Gardens, patronized artists and composers.[69] The swelling metropolitan public could thus share, at modest cost, in a new and refined world of art, letters and performance, becoming better informed, exercising taste and basking in contemporary refinement: 'there is nothing like a playhouse for fine prospects', one playgoer reputedly exclaimed, '. . . without fatigue, and trouble, one can see all Europe, *well lighted for a shilling*'.[70]

Not to be outdone, provincial cities for their part developed their own sites for news, events and culture. While mirroring the metropolis – 'we . . . imitate your fashions, good and evil', proclaimed a Newcastle writer[71] – they also forged distinctive regional identities. In York, Exeter, Bristol, Norwich and elsewhere, political and cultural activity generated venues for recitals, plays and concerts, notably the elegant all-purpose assembly rooms (still highly visible), where local élites gathered for balls, charity fundraisers, music-making and performances. Comfortable coaching inns, shopping parades, parks and stylish squares tempted the gentry to linger in town beyond the calls of business, in a show of urbanity. Meanwhile, Bath and other spas boomed, seductively if implausibly claiming to combine the recovery of health with the pursuit of pleasure.[72]

The enjoyments quickened and quenched by these new public amenities fed off economic growth at large. England was now a premier 'trading nation', ran the cliché, whose natives could take pride in being 'a polite and commercial people'.[73] Colonization, British domination of the slave trade and rapid overseas expansion fed rising consumption at home.[74] London, proclaimed Addison, had become 'a kind of Emporium for the whole Earth', a view extended to the nation at large by Daniel Defoe's *Tour Thro' the Whole Island of Great Britain* (1724–7), that national anthem to progress, agricultural, commercial and industrial.[75] The Revd Alexander Catcott, his parish in the Atlantic boom port of Bristol, gloried in Britain's mercantile ascendancy: 'Our island has put on quite a different face, since the increase of commerce among us.'[76] In defiance of traditional snobberies, trade was held up as a source not just of profit but of civilization:

> Commerce gives Arts, as well as *Gain*;
> By Commerce wafted o'er the Main . . .[77]

And not only civilization: trade, so the boosters claimed, promoted confidence, harmony and unity, fostering contacts and gathering the ends of the nation into a single circuit. Better post roads, turnpikes and coaching services dramatically abridged time and distance. In 1754 the Newcastle to London trip had taken six days; within thirty years that had been halved. The four and a half days needed to get from Manchester to London at mid-century had been slashed to twenty-eight hours by 1788. Improved roads boosted traffic, serving as socio-economic multipliers; the pace of life quickened and remote areas were sucked into the national economy of consumption, news and fashion. As of 1740, only one stagecoach a day had rattled its way from Birmingham to London; by 1763 there were thirty. Arthur Young – like Defoe, a non-stop proselytizer – gushed at the idea of the nation on the move:

The general impetus given to circulation; new people – new ideas – new exertions – fresh activity to every branch of industry; people residing among good roads, who were never seen with bad ones, and all the animation . . . and industry, which flow with a full tide . . . between the capital and the provinces.[78]

However, not all were of that mind. 'I am just old enough,' groused John Byng in 1790, 'to remember Turnpike roads few, and those bad . . . But I am of the very few, perhaps alone, who regret the times . . . now, every abuse, and trickery of London are ready to be play'd off upon you.'[79] How impertinent the provinces had grown!

Better roads spelt better post. Traditionally the mail simply followed the axial post roads out of London, but thanks to the development of 'cross-posts', a veritable lattice of routes emerged. By 1756 there were daily services – Sundays excepted – from London west to Plymouth and to Bristol, Swansea and Pembroke; the Holyhead post road had a weekday service, with services on to Ireland, while the Great North Road also carried the mail daily. By contrast, most provincial cities in France were receiving the Paris mail only twice a week.[80]

Such improvements found their most extreme form in the hothouse of London. 'The new Penny Post Office,' beamed *The Times* in 1794, is likely to prove such a very great accommodation to the public . . . there will be six deliveries each day in all parts of the town . . . Persons putting in letters by nine in the morning . . . may receive answers from London the same afternoon.[81]

The impact must have been like the coming of e-mail.

Such developments brought a revolution in consciousness. Time was, mused George Colman, when travel had been 'like the caravan over the deserts of Arabia'; but all that had become a thing of the past thanks to 'the amendment of the roads . . . the manners, fashions, amusements, vices, and follies of the metropolis, now make their way to the remotest corners of the land'.[82] The result was a 'global village' effect, netting within the national culture provincials who 'scarce half a century ago . . . were regarded as a species, almost as different from those of the metropolis, as the natives of the Cape of Good Hope'.[83] Now, exclaimed the Swiss-American visitor Louis Simond fifty years later, 'nobody is provincial in this country'.[84] And in all this, London remained the prime mover in a nation much taken by its own energies. 'I look upon your city as the best place of *improvement*,' remarked Dr South in the 1690s; 'from the school we go to the university, but from the universities to London.'[85]

Small wonder, then, that the British talked themselves up as a singularly free and fortunate race – indeed, one uniquely enlightened. This 'enveloping haze of patriotic self-congratulation'[86] was, of course, fostered by propaganda. 'We enjoy at this Hour,' declared the *Daily Courant* on 13 June 1734,

an uninterrupted Peace, while all the rest of Europe is either actually engaged in War, or is on the very Brink of it. Our Trade is at a greater Heighth than ever, while other Countries have scarce any, thro' their own Incapacity, or the Nature of their Government. We are free from Religious Disturbances, which distract almost every other Nation. Our liberties and our Properties are perfectly secure.[87]

Set to verse, such sentiments became the bombast of the Scot James Thomson:

> The nations, not so blest as thee,
>   Must in their turn to tyrants fall;
> While thou shalt flourish great and free,
>   The dread and envy of them all.
>   'Rule, Britannia, rule the waves;
>   Britons never will be slaves.'[88]

At the drop of a hat, it seems, natives launched into self-congratulation. 'Hail Britain, happiest of countries! Happy in thy climate, fertility, situation, and commerce; but still happier in the peculiar nature of thy laws and government,' sang the Irish-born Oliver Goldsmith.[89] Charles Churchill hit upon another 'Hail':

> Hail, LIBERTY! A glorious word,
> In other countries scarcely heard . . .[90]

Rarely had Britons felt so truculently triumphalist, or puffed themselves up so chauvinistically – witness the engravings of Hogarth, who signed himself ironically 'Britophil'. Touring Italy in 1729, Lord Hervey – Pope's 'Sporus' – came out in couplets:

> Throughout all Italy beside,
> What does one find, but Want and pride?
> Farces of Superstitious folly,
> Decay, Distress, and Melancholy:
> The Havock of Despotick Power,
> A Country rich, its owners poor . . .[91]

It had not been so very long previously, it is worth remembering, that Italy had been the very cynosure of the English (if also considered the sink of depravity). A trip to Lisbon in 1775 similarly made Thomas Pelham bubble: 'with what joy and gratitude must every Englishman reflect on the happiness of his own nation in comparison of any other'.[92]

The bullish chorus, brilliantly satirized by the 'Britophil' Hogarth, did not escape foreigners. The people will tell you, observed the Swiss visitor de Saussure, 'that there is no country in the world where such perfect freedom may be enjoyed as in England'.[93] Doubtless, in their cups, Squire Booby and his drinking companions cursed mercenary placemen and those damn'd dogs the Excise men but, travelling abroad, they pilloried or pitied the natives (while enjoying the paintings and the painted ladies) and plumed themselves upon living in a land 'great and free'. Enlightenment and patriotism made a heady brew.

Enlightenment was more than talk, however; there was quite literally more light around. 'Most of the streets are wonderfully well lighted,' remarked de Saussure, new to London, 'for in front of each house hangs a lantern or a large globe of glass, inside of which is placed a lamp which burns all night.'[94] Some time later, the Prussian Archenholz marvelled: 'In Oxford-street alone there are more lamps than in all Paris.'[95] Pastor Moritz, too, was 'astonished at the unusually good lighting of the streets, compared with which Berlin makes a pretty poor show'.[96] A German princeling, the story ran, thought all the bright lights had been got up specially to honour him.[97]

Taste and technology each played its part. Leaded casements were replaced by big sash windows;[98] interior design *à la* Adam went in for pale and creamy tints; and, from the 1780s, the new Argand oil lamp made all the difference indoors after dark. Its tubular wick and glass chimney produced a continuous bright and almost smoke- and smell-free light far superior to candles. Birmingham's Lunar Society had been at work on the idea in the 1770s, and when the Swiss Louis Argand patented his version, Matthew Boulton of Birmingham won the exclusive manufacturing rights.[99]

Nor was gas far behind. Boulton's friend, the engineer William Murdoch, gas-lit his own house in 1792; and ten years later he illuminated Boulton and Watt's factory to celebrate the Peace of Amiens – a 'luminous spectacle . . . as novel as it was astounding', spouted an enthusiast.[100]

Light has always been a potent symbol. Its creation was God's first

act (*fiat lux*: 'Let there be light'), while the miracle of the final day of
Creation was the light of human reason (*lumen animae*). Isaiah tells us
that 'the men who walked in darkness' had seen 'a great light', while,
in the New Testament, St John speaks neo-Platonically of 'the true
Light which lighteth every man that cometh into the world'. Sinners
saw 'as through a glass, darkly', but Jesus would be the 'light of the
world'.[101] The Vulgate for its part calls the Lord 'my illumination' –
Dominus illuminatio mea (the Oxford University Press's motto); while
Cambridge Platonists, following Psalm 20, spoke of reason as the
'candle of the Lord', an illumination divinely implanted in the soul.[102]

Light bore secular meanings, too. If the metaphor was one to
which the Sun King laid claim, Albion later made it her own, because
of the conceit that it was an Englishman who had, scientifically
speaking, actually *discovered* light – that is, eludicated its principles: as
the peerless Newton explained in his *Opticks* (1704), light propagates
itself through particles and white light comprises a spectrum of the
colours and obeys the laws of reflection and refraction.[103]

> Even *Light itself*, which every thing displays,
> Shone undiscover'd, till his brighter mind
> Untwisted all the shining robe of day . . .[104]

– though James Thomson's lines were plonking by contrast to Pope's
sublime:

> Nature, and Nature's Laws lay hid in Night:
> God said, *Let Newton be! and All was Light.*[105]

It is, of course, no accident that, after Newton, the chief light-struck
natural philosopher was that enlightened polymath Joseph Priestley,
author of *The History and Present State of Discoveries Relating to Vision,
Light, and Colours* (1772).[106]

Light and enlightenment pervaded public consciousness. The
'Light of Knowledge', claimed William Young in 1722, was 'now
universally breaking on the world';[107] sixty years on, Gilbert Stuart
spoke of 'this enlightened age of philosophy and reflexion';[108] Abraham Tucker popularized Locke in his *The Light of Nature Pursued* (1768);

Gibbon celebrated his 'free and enlightened country'; the Lunar Society, that gathering of Midlands intellectual aristocracy, met monthly at full moon (to make their journey home easier); Thomas Spence praised the 'Sun of Liberty'; and Mary Wollstonecraft was jubilant over – while Burke jeered at – 'this enlightened age'.[109] As Tom Paine so succinctly put it, 'What we have to do is as clear as light.'[110]

As a marker of how light's secular, practical connotations had come to the fore, Samuel Johnson defined 'to enlighten' as 'to illuminate, to supply with light, to instruct, to furnish with increase of knowledge, to cheer, to exhilarate, to gladden, to supply with sight, to quicken in the faculty of vision'.[111] Assuredly, light was thus integral to the natural order; but it could also be a manmade searchlight, piercing the gloom, dispelling darkness. Light's spell is evident in the intense interest taken in the science of sight. 'Were there no example in the world, of contrivance except that of the *eye*,' declared the Cambridge divine William Paley, 'it would be alone sufficient to support the conclusion which we draw from it, as to the necessity of an intelligent Creator.'[112] Above all, light was crucial to the newly dominant epistemology, as empiricism turned the problem of knowing into a matter of seeing: to know was henceforth to see. John Locke's *Essay concerning Human Understanding* (1690) was paradigmatic for a host of later texts which explained cognition through visual metaphors, the mind as a *camera obscura*.[113] No accident, perhaps, that Lemuel Gulliver was English literature's first bespectacled hero.[114]

With light so supercharged, enlightenment became a rallying cry. 'Why are the nations of the world so patient under despotism?' demanded the Revd Richard Price. 'Is it not because they are kept in darkness, and want knowledge? Enlighten them and you will elevate them.'[115] Almost inevitably, Tom Paine – not just a political radical but a designer of smokeless candles – also milked that image in his *The Rights of Man* (1792), claiming the transparency of truth: 'the sun needs no inscription to distinguish him from darkness'.[116] Light, he held, was God's gift, a natural asset – no wonder William

Pitt's notorious window tax was so bitterly resented, a radical squib branding the Prime Minister 'Mr Billy Taxlight'.[117]

All this resplendence made light intoxicating, and there arose an excited sense of involvement in change among a people for whom *sapere aude* came to mean *facere aude* – not just to know but to act as well. Grumble though he might that all was 'running mad after innovation', Samuel Johnson could compliment 'his own age' for 'its superiority' over the Ancients – 'in every respect', that was, 'except in its reverence for government'.[118] Indeed, Boswell records that great cant hater protesting that 'I am always angry when I hear ancient times praised at the expence of modern times.'[119] 'The age we live in is a busy age in which knowledge is rapidly advancing towards perfection,' enthused the young Jeremy Bentham, launching a 60-year career dedicated to reforming the house of the Hanoverians according to the yardstick of utility. 'In the natural world, in particular, every thing teems with discovery and with improvement.'[120]

There were many Englands, but one was the stage of thrusting achievers, sold on science, dedicated to the diffusion of rational knowledge and eager for innovation – be it practical, artistic or intellectual. They were men devoted to the promotion of a new material well-being and leisure; aspiring provincials, Dissenters, sceptics and political realists resentful at the traditional authority imbued in Church and State. Such Moderns it was who were the fomenters of the Enlightenment.[121]

3

CLEARING AWAY
THE RUBBISH

Reason is the glory of human nature.

ISAAC WATTS[1]

More like a communing of clubbable men than a clique or a conspiracy, the Enlightenment derived its coherence in Britain largely from a shared currency of images and idioms – it was as much a language as a programme. Powerful among these, as we have seen, was light: 'this enlightened age'. Another keyword was emancipation: Moderns dramatized deliverance and studied escapology.[2] Some societies crave the transcendence of the otherworldly; others revere custom, or, as with Renaissance Italy, hanker after a previous golden age.[3] The enlightened, by contrast, aimed to break the chains and forge a new future.

Emancipation might be portrayed in terms of a natural maturing or coming of age, a growing out of swaddling bands. What was generally envisaged, however, was something more violent and traumatic: snatching off a blindfold or bursting free from a straitjacket. Bogged down in semantic quicksands, fettered in 'mind-forg'd manacles',[4] or hoodwinked by sinister foes, enlightened spirits craved escape from the murk of time or the mental maze. Narratives of emancipation were not, of course, without precedent – folklore abounds in tales of captors and captives, romances are travelogues of the search, and the Christian master narrative is itself a 'doomed and redeemed' tale of Paradise lost and regained.[5] But what distinguishes the Enlightenment is the secularity of its model of mankind questing freedom through the Socratic 'know yourself' and its modern corollary, 'do it yourself'.

Escape scenarios gained their immediacy from two experiences, one negative, the other positive. Firstly there was the threat of malignant forces which had wreaked destruction in the past and were still darkening the present. In Britain, as elsewhere, Protestantism had never felt secure against a Catholicism cast not merely as erroneous and corrupt, but as evil incarnate, the Whore of Babylon, the Beast of the Apocalypse. Partly thanks to the Council of Trent (1545–63), Rome had had at its disposal the Index of Prohibited Books, the Inquisition, the Society of Jesus and other battalions of the Church Militant, which had then gone about their work with fire and faggot, leaving a gory toll of carnage and martyrs. The Protestant alliance had been mauled in the Thirty Years War; now Louis XIV was renewing the assault. What gave Britons such fitful sense of common cause and shared identity as they did possess was anti-Catholicism, a visceral loathing of 'the insupportable Yoke of the most Pompous and Tyrannical *Policy* that ever enslav'd Mankind under the name or shew of *Religion*'.[6] Such fears were readily fanned so long as Jacobitism was waiting in the wings.

As chapter 5 will detail, enlightened minds inherited Protestant anti-Catholicism and then rationalized it. Rome was demonized as the inveterate foe. The perverse apotheosis of self-abasement and slavish submission to tyranny, Popery sanctified theological dogmatism, ritualized idolatry, drilled windows into men's souls and denied the post-Gutenberg duty of all believers to read God's Book by the candle of Reason.[7]

Enlightened anti-Catholicism furthermore presumed guilt by association. Basing their creed on the Bible alone, Protestants denounced the dependency of Romish dogma upon Eastern gnosticism, Hellenistic Platonism, neo-Aristotelianism and other non-Christian sources: key tenets of Catholicism such as transubstantiation and purgatory had been shown to possess no scriptural basis whatever, being fabricated entirely on scholastic metaphysics, Church tradition and Vatican decrees. As the 'new science' assailed Platonism and Thomism with Cartesian systematic doubt or Baconian empiricism, it was inevitable that the citadel of scholastic theology would also be sapped, so dubious were its metaphysical foundations. Welding Protestantism to enlightened thinking, Locke was to assert in his *The Reasonableness of Christianity* (1695) that all that was required of a Christian was to profess that the Bible was the word of God and Jesus the Messiah. Such professions aside, theology (that is, the knowledge of God) was essentially beyond man's needs, powers and business.[8]

The academic heritage was trashed over and again by enlightened propagandists as a tragicomedy of errors – gazing up at the heavens, pedants had stumbled into a ditch. Thus Plato, proceeding – according to Viscount Bolingbroke – 'like a bombast poet and a mad theologian', had 'diverted men from the pursuit of truth'.[9] Gibbon likewise lamented misguided learning. 'Several of these masters,' he jeered at the neo-Platonists of late Antiquity, 'were men of profound thought and intense application; but, by mistaking the true object of philosophy, their labours contributed much less to improve than to corrupt the human understanding.' In the medieval period, further-more, so prone to 'credulity and submission', monkish casuists had contracted 'the vices of a slave', and for fifteen hundred years meta-physics had perpetuated a sterile obscurantism.[10]

Once hitched to the papal propaganda machine, otherwise innocu-ous sophistries had turned positively dangerous. Rome commanded a fiendish indoctrination department in which iniquity trapped inno-cence, be it through devious dogma or gaudy images. The Antichrist's evil empire was endlessly portrayed as a lethal threat to the freeborn Englishman's enjoyment of his God-given faculties.[11]

It was not just from Popery that post-Restoration élites were seeking deliverance, however: collective memories had also been scarred by the Civil War. The Calvinist dogma of predestination had bred 'enthusiasm', that awesome, irresistible and unfalsifiable conviction of personal infallibility (see chapter 5). Presbyterians, anti-nomian 'mechanic preachers' spewing up prophecies as the spirit moved them, and other self-elected saints had loosed torrents of chiliastic bloodshed. Those experiences came back as nightmares: still in the 1780s the unflappable Edward Gibbon could descry in the Gordon rioters rampaging through the capital the ghosts of Roundhead fanatics – bogeymen soon recycled in Burke's *Reflections* (1790).[12] If Popery was the epitome of despotism, imposed from above, Puritanism was anarchy incarnate, breaking out from below. Who could say which was the more pernicious?[13]

Luckily, light was dawning, hinting that this long reign of delusion, devastation and death might nearly be over. Holy war was going out of fashion: Europe-wide, princes and even prelates were becoming more wary about heretic- and witch-burning, while the mental tide was turning, as is evident from the popularity of burlesques of the bigots:

> Such as do build their faith upon
> The holy text of pike and gun
> Decide all controversies by
> Infallible artillery . . .
> As if religion were intended
> For nothing else but to be mended.[14]

In particular – this is the positive development – natural science was making headway as a solid platform for knowledge. Telescopes and microscopes were revealing new worlds, infinitely distant, infinitely large or small; anatomy was laying bodily structures bare, and England's own William Harvey had discovered the circulation of the blood. Observation and experiment were revealing Nature's laws, while inventions like the airpump and, a bit later, Newcomen's steam engine were contributing to that 'effecting of all things possible' trumpeted by Bacon; and meantime, brave new worlds were being discovered by circumnavigators. So if the Civil War left an acrid stench, there were also harbingers of hope.

This intellectual watershed was signposted in the 'battle of the books'.[15] The Renaissance had venerated classical achievements in philosophy, science, letters and the arts; Hippocrates and Galen remained the medical bibles; and humanists continued to uphold the geocentric (earth-centred) and homocentric (man-centred) cosmos espoused by Greek science, with man at the hub and as the measure of the divinely created system. Xenophon, Cicero, Livy, Virgil and other classical poets, philosophers, moralists, historians and statesmen chaired the school of virtue in which students of culture should enrol. Renaissance 'anticomania' was consoling: wisdom was already set in stone, the custodian of civilization.

To enlightened eyes, however, the humanist tenet that what had come first was best had been overtaken by time: after all, as Bacon and Hobbes pointed out, it was the Modern Age which was truly old. Historical scholarship produced a new optic on the past, challenging the Renaissance identification with the Ancients and accentuating the radical differences between the old world of Antiquity and the new one marked by guns and printing. Authentic new worlds had been discovered, above all America, disclosing scenes of exotic life unknown to Aristotle or Ptolemy. The seventeenth century moreover proved intellectually revolutionary. The dazzling 'new sciences' of astronomy, cosmology and physics pioneered by Kepler and Galileo challenged the cosy commonplaces of both Greek philosophy and the Bible. Heliocentric astronomy decentred the earth, reducing it to a tiny, minor planet nowhere in particular in that dauntingly infinite universe newly glimpsed through the telescope, whose immense spaces frightened not only Pascal. And this 'new astronomy' was complemented by a new 'mechanical philosophy', which stripped Nature of its purposive vitality, reducing it to a machine made up of material particles governed by universal laws, whose motions could be given mathematical expression. If daunting and dangerous, science was also full of promise.

Empirical discoveries fostered a new spirit, eager to question authorities, even the Bible, a sceptical turn robustly expressed in the *Dictionnaire* (1697) of that unbiddable Huguenot Pierre Bayle.[16] Many of Europe's greatest minds of Bayle's generation concluded that, in the search for truth, neither implicit faith in the Bible nor automatic reliance on the Ancients would any longer suffice. If, as late as 1690, William Temple's *Essay upon the Ancient and Modern Learning* upheld the superiority of the Ancients, William Wotton's *Reflections upon Ancient and Modern Learning* (1694) countered that, in the sciences at least, they had been wholly eclipsed by the Moderns. It remained hotly disputed, however, whether Antiquity's achievements in poetry, drama and the fine arts had been, or could be, excelled: would the contemporary Homer please step forward? But Moderns like Alexander Pope had their own solution to that problem: the classics could be translated, simplified and modernized to meet the needs of modern audiences.[17]

Such confusions, crises and controversies frame the key enlightenment escape strategy, the demand for a clear-out and clean-up of the lumber house of the mind, condemned as dark, dilapidated and dangerous, unfit for habitation: metaphysics was dismissed as moonshine and traditional teachings were ridiculed as fictions, frauds, fantasies, fables or fallacies.[18] Bigotry, dogmatism and overweening system-building were damned by Moderns equally eager to deride 'old wives' tales' and other hand-me-down folk wisdom: obsolete orthodoxies in all shapes and sizes had to be swept away. Magic, mysticism, scholasticism and all other houses of cards or castles of error must be demolished, and knowledge rebuilt on firm foundations. Enlightened publicists thus set about cleansing, scouring, sifting, sieving, winnowing the mental grain from the chaff, echoing the injunctions of the Helmontian chemist and doctor George Thomson back in the 1660s: 'Works, not Words; Things, not Thinking . . . Operation, not meerly Speculation.'[19] Emancipation would not come easily: 'the Bulk of Mankind in all Ages, and in all Countries, are violently attached to the Opinions, Customs, and even Habits, which they have been used to', averred the free-thinker John Trenchard, adopting the patronizing air favoured by enlightened authors when putting down 'folly'. 'Sounds, Shews, Prejudices, vain and idle Terrors, Phantoms, Delusions . . . operate more upon them than true and strong Reasons.'[20]

It became *de rigueur* to denounce the bad old ways of the bad old days. George Berkeley, philosopher, mathematician and later bishop, prompted himself: 'Mem.: to be eternally banishing Metaphisics etc. and recalling Men to Common Sense.'[21] Locke's pupil, the 3rd

Earl of Shaftesbury, similarly condemned 'all that Dinn & Noise of Metaphysicks, all that pretended studdy'.[22] Where then lay true inquiry? 'To philosophize, in a just Signification, is but To carry Good-Breeding a step higher'[23] – thinking could be rescued from the academic eunuchs if undertaken by gentlemen in a liberal spirit.

Crucial to these truth strategies – impatience with obscurity and a prizing of clarification and transparency – was distrust of what the Royal Society's apologist Thomas Sprat dubbed 'the cheat of words'. Taking their cue from the 'new science', enlightened thinkers set *res* over *verba*; words must not be reified, reality must replace rhetoric. Sprat called for language to 'return back to primitive purity, and shortness, when men deliver'd so many things, almost in an equal number of words'.[24] He was not so 'lost in lexicography', mused Samuel Johnson, 'as to forget that words are the daughters of the earth, and that things are the sons of heaven'.[25] Since 'words are so apt to impose on the understanding,' despaired Berkeley, 'I am resolved in my inquiries to make as little use of them as possibly I can.'[26]

Setting reality above verbality, the coming English empiricism also looked favourably on quantification. Were not numbers, at least, unambiguous and trustworthy? 'Instead of using only comparative and superlative Words and intellectual Arguments,' explained Sir William Petty, a founder fellow of the Royal Society, 'I have taken the course . . . to express myself in Terms of *Number*, *Weight*, or *Measure*.'[27]

Eternal intellectual vigilance was essential, however, because inanity was endemic and error infectious. Their feared triumph in a cacophonous babel formed the nightmare vision of Alexander Pope's *Dunciad* (1728), the climax of which depicted the final eclipse of reason at the hands of the Queen of Dulness:

> Lo! thy dread Empire, CHAOS! is restor'd;
> Light dies before thy uncreating word:
> Thy hand, great Anarch! lets the curtain fall;
> And Universal Darkness buries All.[28]

Pope's abhorrence of quack versification reflected the suspicion of fabling and fiction, as expressed in the notorious put-down of poetry itself attributed to the Cambridge professor Isaac Barrow: 'a kind of ingenious nonsense'. Though hardly one of its front-men, Pope shared the Enlightenment's hatred of *a priori* scholiasts, logic-choppers, pedants, know-alls and other dunces: in its warnings to man to heed his limits, his *Essay on Man* reads like Locke in heroic couplets.[29]

Like natural science, philosophy had to be built anew on rock solid foundations. It would have to be transparent, stripped of verbiage, dead wood and ancestor-worship. It must be self-critical, grounded in Nature and squaring with common sense and experience. Only clear thinking, plain words, candour and modesty would end the reign of error. Hopelessly clipped, counterfeited and compromised, the debased intellectual coinage had to be replaced by a sound currency.[30]

In the framing of such convictions, the printing press played a key, if double-edged, role. The printed word was praised as the guarantor of plain, stable fact – by contrast, for instance, to the imprecisions, instabilities and exaggerations inherent in handed-down word-of-mouth teachings. In that sense, it complemented the Baconian science of hard, solid facts. But the printed book was readily fetishized, and authors ossified into authorities. The 'battle of the books' largely hinged upon the ambiguities of books as the repositories of truth.[31]

The emancipatory bid central to the identity of enlightening élites was symbolically presided over by three intrepid intellectuals of earlier generations.[32] One was Descartes, who in his *Discourse on Method* (1637) coolly announced his Copernican revolution in thinking, notably the commitment to universal doubt and to clear and distinct reasoning derived from first principles: 'I think, therefore I am.' Though the senses were irreparably deceptive, reason was capable of establishing truth, and, almost to justify his confidence, his *Geometry* (1637) trail-blazed co-ordinate geometry and algebra, and his *Principles of Philosophy* (1644) set out a mechanical philosophy in which God directed a mechanical universe sustained by 'cause and effect' contact action and propelled through a swirl of vortices (*tour-billons*).

With its promise of a renovation of thinking on a rationalist footing – *cogito ergo sum* – Descartes' philosophy enjoyed a vogue in England around the Restoration, being taken up by, among others, Cambridge Platonists like Henry More. By validating the immaterial soul, Descartes particularly appealed to anti-Calvinists keen to reinstate the dignity of *homo rationalis*. But its *a priorism* never convinced.[33] The Frenchman's clockwork universe could easily be dismissed as crypto-atheistic;[34] moreover, his denial of consciousness to any creatures except humans struck many English writers as both implausible (did not animals have sense organs?) and heartless, flying in the face of Divine Benevolence. And the physiological basis of Cartesian dualism – body and soul fundamentally distinct and joined only *via* the obscure isthmus of the pineal gland deep in the brain – seemed makeshift. Gland jokes ran and ran.[35]

Not least, advances in natural philosophy subverted Descartes' physics, especially his vortices and plenum, and the mechanics of billiard-ball contact action. Since English scientists led the field in discrediting these views – notably *via* Newton's void space gravitational astrophysics and Boyle's airpump demonstrations of the vacuum – Descartes' star waned rapidly in Britain: a Frenchman would leave the world full on quitting Paris, quipped Voltaire, but find it a vacuum on arriving in London.[36]

Happily Descartes' reputation could be played off against that of native English thinkers, in particular Francis Bacon, apotheosized in the Enlightenment.[37] The philosophical Lord Chancellor's programme for the reform and revitalization of natural philosophy was first outlined in his *Advancement of Learning* (1605), where, to hold at bay churchmen hostile to prying into God's secrets, science was diplomatically demarcated from theology, thereby validating unfettered investigation.

Bacon opened his reformation of knowledge by rejecting blind worship of authorities like Aristotle: bad science buried itself in musty books instead of first-hand observation of the Book of Nature.

Repudiating syllogisms, which toyed with terms while ignoring physical reality, he unfolded a new logic. Inquiry should start with faithful records of natural phenomena, proceeding to derive from them 'aphorisms' (system-free inferences); it would then gather these up into generalizations, and use 'negative instances' to falsify faulty ones.

While science had to start with the senses, Bacon warned of the distortions, both individual and social, inherent in perception, defining the four 'idols' (or illusions) which warped sense experience: those of the cave, herd, theatre and market place. (Philosophical anti-idolatry of this kind clearly mirrored its Protestant twin.) These hazards could be overcome through a controlled ascent from fact to theory, then moving on to the acid test of practice, in the generation of discoveries and inventions beneficial to mankind. Science should be a collective enterprise, best organized in research groups ('Solomon's Temple'), and its cumulative findings would pilot progress, mental and material alike.

Synthesized in the *Instauratio Magna* (1620), Bacon's thinking was to prove immensely influential. His reformist blueprints were taken up first in the Civil War era and then by the Royal Society in the 1660s, which acknowledged the 'father of experimental philosophy' as its inspiration. Voltaire eulogized the man d'Alembert was to hail as 'the greatest, the most universal, and the most eloquent of philosophers', underwriting as he did so much of the enlightened agenda: the assault on bibliolatry; the iconoclastic rejection of tradition, speculation and *a priori* systems; the grounding of inquiry in observation; and experiment and the conviction that science must serve mankind. Indeed, the Baconian mapping of knowledge via the three fundamental faculties of the mind – memory, reason and imagination – was embraced in the 'Preliminary Discourse' to the *Encyclopédie*. With his adoption as the Royal Society's mascot, enlightened Britain gained a big-name philosopher of her own – and one who was Lord Chancellor to boot.

The third modern philosopher definitive of enlightened self-understanding was the most problematic – yet also propitious. It is not surprising that Thomas Hobbes was bent on politico-philosophical cleansing, since he had been driven into exile in the Civil War, whose horrors pervaded his mature thinking.[38] In *Leviathan* (1650) and other writings, root and branch reform of language and logic were deemed indispensable to future peace and order, and he himself proposed a severe philosophical purge through a radical nominalism and materialism targeted against spurious scholastic terms: 'For *True* and *False* are attributes of Speech, not of *Things*.'[39] Woolly thinking and false dogmatism spelt chaos: 'For words are wise mens counters, they do but reckon by them; but they are the mony of fooles.'[40] Words must never be allowed to take on a life of their own; entities must not unnecessarily be multiplied and all fictions must be banished – directives whose drastic implications included Hobbes's denial of the immaterial as utter nonsense: 'The *universe* . . . is corporeall, that is to say, body . . . and that which is not Body, is no part of the Universe.'[41] And that was that. The implications were momentous: no spirit, no lords spiritual.

It was with this nominalist, materialist and monist pencil that Hobbes redrew human nature. Man was a machine, mere matter in motion; thoughts and feelings were stirrings in the sense organs induced by external pressures and producing in turn those brain waves called ideas; imagination was the consciousness of ideas which persisted in the mind after the original stimuli had died away, and memory was their recollection. All such activities went on independently of speech and hence (*pace* Descartes) were common to animals as well as humans.

Men and beasts were also of a piece in possessing 'passions', disturbances in the internal organs matching images in the brain, incessantly reactivated by external stimuli. What counted emotionally was not only the satisfaction of present desires but the assurance that future needs would also be gratified. Hence felicity could have no *finis ultimus*, being rather 'a continuall progresse of the desire, from one object to another'.[42] It did, however, have an absolute negation, and that was death. Hedges against violent death, including ruthless self-defence, were therefore essential. No man being an island, a 'perpetual contention for honour, riches, and authority' resulted, entailing the notorious nightmare of a state of Nature in which the life of man was 'solitary, poore, nasty, brutish and short'.[43] While the Hobbesian view of life as 'a perpetuall and restlesse desire of power after power, that ceaseth onely in Death' was thus dismal – a kind of secular Calvinism – his philosophical determinism was offered as providing the first principles for a salutary politics of absolutism and obedience, and hence a recipe for order.[44]

For Restoration wits, Hobbism might also rationalize a black comedy of egoistic power play – the 'Malmesbury monster', or English Machiavelli, could serve as an alluring mentor for rakes like Rochester who endorsed his kneejerk anti-clericalism. Critics, however, were appalled by his corrosive denial of normative natural law and the Christian Deity as traditionally understood.[45] Effectively dethroning, or at least defaming, God, Hobbes's mordant material-ism seemed aimed not only at 'vain philosophy, and fabulous tra-ditions' – like angels, demons and other 'abstract essences' bred by fevered imaginations – but against Christianity as such.[46] Hobbists became targets: in 1668, one Daniel Scargill, a fellow of Corpus Christi College, Cambridge, was expelled from the university for having 'asserted several Impious and Atheistical Tenets to the great dishonour of God', while in 1683 Oxford consigned *Leviathan* to the flames, together with his *De Cive* (1642).[47]

For all his own disclaimers, Hobbes thus became execrated as tantamount to an atheist. That is what made him so useful to enlightened philosophers. So long as they piously disowned him, they could also quietly incorporate many aspects of his conceptual rubbish-cleansing: tactical Hobbes-bashing allowed them to pass as more correct than they actually were.

This enlightened cleansing of 'the Rubbish of the Schools', was brought to a rousing climax by David Hume:

When we run over libraries, persuaded of these principles, what havoc must we make? If we take in our hand any volume of divinity or school metaphysics, for instance, let us ask, *Does it contain any abstract reasoning concerning quantity or number?* No. *Does it contain any experimental reasoning concerning matters of fact and existence?* No. Commit it then to the flames; for it can contain nothing but sophistry and illusion.[48]

The way forward lay not in 'school metaphysics' but intellectual humility: debunking infallible oracles, laying sound foundations in facts and figures and creating a culture of criticism. If there were strict limits to human knowledge, no matter, since God had surely given men powers sufficient to discharge their earthly offices. Herein lay the enormous appeal of Locke's image of the philosopher as 'an Under-Labourer in clearing Ground a little, and removing some of the Rubbish, that lies in the way to Knowledge', so as to beat a path for the true 'master-builders' – that is, such scientists as Robert Boyle, Thomas Sydenham and Isaac Newton, who were actually raising the temple of truth.[49]

Far and away the key philosopher in this modern mould, however, was John Locke. From the 1670s, as we have seen, he became politically radicalized, thereafter playing a decisive part in political debate, economic policy, currency reform, and in promoting religious toleration. His *Essay concerning Human Understanding* (1690) was his masterwork, presenting a persuasive vision of the new man for the new times, grounded upon an analysis of the workings of the mind in the making of true knowledge.[50]

In stark contrast to Descartes, Hobbes and the other rationalists, Locke's truth claims were models of modesty. To the Galileo-idolizing Hobbes, reason could range omnipotent; for Locke, any straying from the empirical straight and narrow led into mental minefields. While Hobbes proposed proofs *modo geometrico*, Locke saw no scope for Euclidian certainty. Man was a limited being, and reason just sufficient for human purposes.[51] His anti-*a priorism* and his distrust of pure reason were backed by the relativistic anthropological evidence adduced in his *Essay*, which documented the stunning diversity of beliefs and customs worldwide, from the atheists of Soldania Bay in southern Africa to the Mingrelians, a people professing Christianity who nevertheless buried their children alive, and others who devoured their own infants.[52] Such confirmation of the boundless variety of human beliefs and customs underpinned Locke's extreme mistrust of alleged innate cognitive and ethical truths, and the systems of certainty built on them. Yet full-blown scepticism was not in order: knowledge was achievable as a construct out of the interplay of mind and nature.

Language itself was a mare's nest. 'All the Art of Rhetorick,' Locke growled, 'is for nothing else but to insinuate wrong Ideas, move the Passions, and thereby mislead the Judgement.'[53] Harping on man's capacity for deception and delusion, he highlighted 'the several *wilful* faults and neglects which men are guilty of in this way of communication'.[54] Linguistic abuse took many forms: new words were coined unanchored to clear ideas, old ones got garbled, Humpty-Dumpty fashion. Philosophers actually basked in obscurity, 'by either applying old words to new and unusual significations, or introducing new and ambiguous terms without defining either; or else putting them so together as may confound their ordinary meaning' – this last, Locke drily observed, passed under the 'esteemed names of *subtlety* and *acuteness*'.[55] 'Names without ideas' were but 'empty sounds', while 'he that applies his names to ideas different from their common use . . . speaks gibberish'.[56] Lockeans prided themselves on plain speaking.

Just as ideas were not innate, words themselves were not God-given: no more than absolute *political* power had indefeasible *verbal* authority been bestowed upon Adam, wrote the refuter of Sir Robert Filmer's patriarchalist political theorizings (see chapter 8). Speech, rather, was consensual, and the relations between signified and signifier were essentially conventional. Language was at bottom pragmatic and functional, best when tailored for 'ease and dispatch'.[57] It needed to be properly policed.

The intellectual garden was thus choked with weeds. To root them out, Locke laid down certain fundamental ground rules for tackling such basic questions as: what do I know? – and how do I know it? To begin with, it was essential to distinguish 'assent' from 'knowledge'. Assent (or 'faith') was owed to the testimony of whoever revealed God's word. Before assent could be given, however, there must be certainty that it really was revelation; this required not blind trust but judgement.[58] 'How a rational Man,' Locke assured a supporter, 'that should enquire and know for himself, can content himself with a Faith or Religion taken upon trust . . . is to me astonishing.'[59]

Locke had no truck with the fideist line that reason and faith were at odds, for the latter was properly 'nothing but a firm assent of the mind: which . . . cannot be accorded to anything but upon good reason'. Gullibility was not piety. To accept a book, for instance, as revelation without checking out the author was gross superstition – how could it honour God to suppose that faith overrode reason, for was not reason no less God-given?[60]

In a typically enlightened move, Locke restricted the kinds of truths which God might reveal: revelation could not be admitted contrary to reason, and 'faith can never convince us of anything that contradicts our knowledge'. Yet there remained matters on which hard facts were unobtainable, as, for instance, Heaven or the resurrection of the dead: 'being beyond the discovery of reason', such issues were 'purely matters for faith'.[61]

In short, Locke raised no objections to revealed truth as such, but whether something 'be a divine revelation or no, reason must judge' – it was the constant court of appeal. The *credo, quia impossibile est* of the early Church fathers might seem the acme of devotion, but it 'would prove a very ill rule for men to choose their opinions or religion by'. Unless false prophets were strenuously avoided, the mind would fall prey to 'enthusiasm', that eruption of the 'ungrounded fancies of a man's own brain'. Doubtless, God *might* speak directly to holy men, but Locke feared the exploitation of popular credulity, and urged extreme caution.[62]

These directives of Locke on faith and reason, set out in his *Essay* (1690) and then in *The Reasonableness of Christianity* (1695), proved enormously influential in staking out an enlightened epistemology which made reason a citadel against superstition and enthusiasm. His distinctive Christian beliefs will be examined further in chapter 5.

By contrast to the 'assent' of faith, natural 'knowledge' was derived from the senses – though these, Locke always warned, 'reach but a very little way'.[63] Whereas revelation gave grounds for certainty, 'knowledge' garnered from sense experience stopped at probability. Here Locke shared Bacon's impatience with scholastic syllogisms, which chopped logic 'without making any addition to it'.[64] Empirical knowledge, by contrast, traded in honest matters of fact and, though limited, could be cumulative and progressive.

Knowledge – as distinct from faith and sham syllogizing – was of two kinds. One was intuitive. This, the more certain but restricted in scope, consisted of truths requiring no proof: for instance, a semicircle is less than a whole circle.[65] The other type ('demonstration') arose from the acquisition and assimilation of sense data, and would generate 'probable' knowledge. While inevitably lacking the certitude of revelation or intuition, this formed the main stock of truth available to mortals. Locke agreed with Sydenham, Boyle, Newton and their peers in stressing the limits of man's powers, but that was no insuperable problem: 'our business here is not to know all things, but those which concern our conduct'.[66]

Turning to the actual operations of the understanding, Locke denied Descartes' innate ideas.[67] The mind of a newborn infant was like an 'empty cabinet', a *tabula rasa*, or a piece of 'white Paper',[68] and knowledge was acquired only by experience, that is to say, through the five senses:

Methinks the *Understanding* is not much unlike a Closet wholly shut from light, with only some little openings left, to let in external visible Resemblances, or *Ideas* of things without: would the pictures coming into a dark room but stay there, and lie so orderly as to be found upon occasion, it would very much resemble the understanding of a man.[69]

'Ideas' arose from an external material thing (e.g. snow) provoking first a sensation and then a reflection which involved an 'idea': thus the sensation of snow would lead to the idea of 'white',[70] an 'idea' thus being the 'object of the understanding'. Locke's usage was original: 'ideas' are in our minds, not only when we think but also when we see or respond to any sense inputs. The objects of perception were thus not *things* but *ideas*, which stemmed from objects in the external world but which also depended upon the mind for their existence.

Deriving thus from sensations, ideas were at first 'simple', but later, thanks to 'reflection', they could be combined so as to become 'complex'. For instance, from the repetition of similar sensations, the ideas of time and space were in due course built up, while from movement there arose the idea of agency and power. To be authentic, an idea had to originate from something external and, in ascertaining the knowability of the outside world, it was vital to discriminate between 'primary' and 'secondary' qualities, that is, those truly inherent in the actual world as distinct from those which merely clocked up some response in the observer. A statement about volume (a 'primary' quality) was very different from one about smell: the latter (a 'secondary' quality) said nothing essential about the substance in question, only about the nose of the sniffer. That was a distinction strategic to Locke, partly because it enabled him, while denying innate ideas, to stave off charges of scepticism; in the event, however, it proved unsustainable.[71]

Plotting epistemological pathways, Locke proceeded from sensation and reflection to perception, that is, thinking itself. This involved contemplation, the retention of past experiences and the ability to recall them. Memory was thus integral to the understanding, as were wit and judgement.[72] Wit implied the facile juxtaposition of ideas, if perhaps fancifully and without fixed order; judgement demonstrated a precise discrimination between them. Largely taken from Hobbes, Locke's distinction was to prove highly influential in aesthetics and literary criticism.[73]

Through exercise of judgement and habitual association of ideas, complex ideas could be built up, such as those of order, beauty or liberty.[74] The idea of freedom thus arose from the fact that a person felt able to act or desist from acting when he chose. Here lay one of Locke's many rebuttals of Hobbes. For the latter, liberty was a matter of power: a person was free to do whatever he had the power to do. The political liberal in Locke rejected this, for an act could be voluntary, in the sense of being an act of will, but none the less not truly 'free', if it were the product of external coercion (e.g. a gun to the head). But though Locke rebutted Hobbes's authoritarian politics, they shared much common ground in their approaches to genuine knowledge and the workings of the mind. Hobbes had reduced thought to the mechanics of motion; Locke too embarked upon a comparable simplification:

> our original ideas . . . all might be reduced to these very few primary and original ones, viz. extension, solidity, mobility, or the power of being moved; which by our senses we receive from body; perceptivity or the power of perception, or thinking; motivity, or the power of moving; which by reflection we receive from our minds.[75]

Far more than Hobbes, Locke was impressed by the Baconian philosophy of the Royal Society (of which he was elected a fellow in 1668); its commitment to observation and experiment provided the grounding for his philosophy of science. He was enthralled, for instance, by the microscope, which hinted at yet further unseen worlds, awaiting investigation: 'that which is now the yellow colour of gold would then disappear and instead of it we should see an admirable texture of parts, of a certain size and figure. This microscopes plainly discover to us.'[76] Patient observation and experiment would certainly prove fruitful; but, Locke warned, conclusions must not outrun the evidence. Forever limited to the perceivable and measurable, science could say nothing about inner reality.[77] In his corrective to scholastic and Cartesian arrogance, Locke thus proposed promoting knowledge by respecting its boundaries. Though 'demonstrable' knowledge, the harvest of experience, could never be more than probable, it was nevertheless useful and progressive.[78]

Alongside his defences of toleration and political liberty, Locke thus set the enlightened agenda with his endorsement of the mind's progressive capacities. In dismissing Platonic and Cartesian *a priorism*, in asserting that knowledge was the art of the probable and in holding that the way forward lay in empirical inquiry, he replaced rationalism with reasonableness in a manner which became programmatic for the Enlightenment in Britain.

While Locke was radical, he demolished to rebuild, and anatomized to root out pathological terms and tenets. To some he seemed alarmingly sceptical, because he judged received truths and innate ideas false or misleading. Yet, playing down the Fall, he resolutely insisted on the capabilities of the human understanding: the existence of God could be known, as could Nature and Nature's laws. He sought not to deny truth but to set it on a sound basis. His philosophy proved a great watershed, and he became the presiding spirit of the English Enlightenment.

Locke's legacy proved controversial.[79] Many of his views – his insistence upon reason as the judge of revelation, his denial of innate ideas and moral absolutes, his hints as to thinking matter, his radical suggestions on identity and consciousness and his audible silence on the Trinity (see chapters 5 and 7) – laid him open to attack; even Isaac Newton, normally an ally, once accused him of being a 'Hobbist'.[80] He was, as noted, denounced in his alma mater, while Bishop Stillingfleet sniffed atheism in his religion.[81] His conviction that all knowledge derived from experience was unsettling, and his 'way of ideas' got up noses. Against Matthew Tindal's Lockean view that the 'idea' of government must be analysed, Jonathan Swift thus railed:

Now, it is to be understood, that this refined Way of Speaking was introduced by Mr *Locke* . . . All the former Philosophers in the World, from the Age of *Socrates* to ours, would have ignorantly put the Question, *Quid est Imperium*? But now it seemeth we must vary our Phrase; and since our modern Improvement of Human Understanding, instead of desiring a Philosopher to describe or define a Mouse-trap, or tell me what it is; I must gravely ask, what is contained in the Idea of a Mouse-trap?[82]

Nevertheless, Locke's empiricism took root. John Harris's influential encyclopaedia *Lexicon Technicum* (1704) followed him in defining ideas as 'whatsoever the Mind perceives in itself', and the second edition (1710) declared innatism conclusively refuted. 'It is much to be suspected,' opined William Wollaston in 1722, 'there are no such *innate* maxims as they pretend', while Chambers' *Cyclopaedia* (1728) averred that 'our great Mr *Locke* seems to have put this Matter out of dispute'.[83]

Lockean empiricism pointed the way to advances in scientific investigation. The Irish gentleman William Molyneux broached the exciting, if unsettling, implications that followed from the denial of innate ideas. For instance, would someone born blind, but subsequently given sight by surgery, be immediately able to distinguish a cube from a sphere? – was there, in other words, an innate idea of shape? Molyneux thought not: no one given sight for the first time could possibly judge. Locke agreed, acknowledging the point in the second edition of his *Essay* – a further blow to innatism.[84] The rationalist Leibniz, for his part, demurred: a blind man, newly given sight, should be able to identify shapes and their differences. Berkeley, by contrast, supported Locke–Molyneux. Drawing on a case history published by the surgeon William Cheselden in the Royal Society's *Philosophical Transactions*, he maintained in his *Essay Towards a New Theory of Vision* (1709) that a newly sighted blind boy could not immediately 'see' a thing – that is, could not match visual appearances with distances as perceived by touch.[85] Cheselden had been well aware that Lockean experientialism had made such an individual a key test case, and his account was in turn cited by, among others, Voltaire, Diderot, Condillac, Buffon and Kant.[86] Relating the eye to the I, Locke's epistemology thus stimulated studies in what would later be called experimental psychology.

'Locke is universal,' declared William Warburton.[87] By 1760, the *Essay* had raced through nine English editions, as well as four in his collected works, and Latin versions came out in London and on the Continent. Sales in France were predictably sluggish. Though a French translation was issued in 1700, twenty-five years later copies were still lying around unsold. From the 1730s, however, owing to Voltaire's *Lettres anglaises* (1733), French interest quickened. Meanwhile, in Britain, attacks were parried by supporters such as

Catharine Cockburn, whose *Defence of Mr Locke's Essay on the Human Understanding* was published anonymously in 1702, while a host of writers publicized his views. Bolingbroke, for instance, proclaimed the potential, yet also the limits, of human knowledge – notions versified in Pope's *Essay on Man*.[88]

Locke was also boiled down for students, notably in Isaac Watts's *Logic* (1724), which reached a twentieth edition by 1779.[89] A devoted follower, that diligent Nonconformist expressed his admiration in a poem and an ode upon Locke's death: the *Essay*, he claimed, 'has diffused fairer Light through the World in numerous Affairs of Science and of Human Life', and he went on to declare that many chapters were 'worthy of Letters of Gold'.[90] Locke's hold over British philosophy increased as Watts's and later textbooks became standard; and, if somewhat unevenly, his thinking permeated higher education. Even Oxford showed a flicker of interest. A move had been made there in 1703 to suppress the *Essay*, but in 1744 the student reading lists mentioned Locke's 'Metaphysics', that is his *Essay*. Eleven years later, however, his alma mater repented of its rashness and Locke again disappeared.[91]

By contrast with this predictable fate in Tory Oxford, Locke's philosophy rapidly entered the arts curriculum in Whig Cambridge. In 1739, the *Advice to a Young Student*, written for undergraduate use by Daniel Waterland, master of Magdalene College, praised the *Essay* for actually explaining the reasoning process, rather than, as with earlier logics, merely defining terms of art. Waterland's book shows that scholasticism was fast vanishing from enlightened Cambridge, having been supplanted by Hobbes, Descartes, Leibniz, Butler, Berkeley, but especially by Locke.[92] He was also taken up in the Scottish universities, initially in the classes of John Stevenson, professor of logic at Edinburgh from 1730, although there it was Bacon who became the prince of the Moderns.[93]

Meanwhile, the implications of Locke's empiricism were teased out, sketched in, challenged and contested, and it became the first base for the sensationalism of Hume (with his 'impressions') and for Hartley's elaboration of the association of ideas. Abraham Tucker's

Light of Nature Pursued (1768) reads as a fulsome if prolix gloss on the thinker who had succeeded in 'clearing away that incumbrance of innate ideas, real essences and such like rubbish'.[94] Bent upon exploding fictions and the lies of language, Jeremy Bentham also paid heartfelt tribute: 'Without Locke I could have known nothing.'[95]

It was the *Spectator*, however, which introduced Locke to the reading public at large. The finest publicity agent any philosopher ever had, Joseph Addison popularized his ideas on wit, judgement, personal identity, the labyrinths of language and, above all, aesthetics in an astonishing sequence of essays on the 'Pleasures of the Imagination'.[96] Not least, addressing the problem of understanding Nature, he dramatized Lockean views on primary and secondary qualities with his habitual light touch:

our Souls are at present delightfully lost and bewildered in a pleasing Delusion, and we walk about like the Enchanted Hero of a Romance, who sees beautiful Castles, Woods, and Meadows . . . but upon the finishing of some secret Spell, the fantastick Scene breaks up, and the disconsolate Knight finds himself on a barren Heath, or in a solitary Desart.[97]

The comic possibilities of that rather disorienting distinction were seized upon in the *Guardian*'s account of Jack Lizard's return home from college, where his student mind had clearly been turned: 'for the first Week he dealt wholly in Paradoxes . . . When the Girls were sorting a Set of Knots, he would demonstrate to them that all the Ribbands were of the same Colour; or rather, says *Jack*, of no Colour at all.'[98]

Maintaining that Locke's *Essay* was the book which, the Bible aside, dominated the Georgian century, Kenneth MacLean has documented its uptake from the intellectually serious – key quotations in Samuel Johnson's *Dictionary* – right across the spectrum to jokey allusions and knowing name-dropping.[99] An advertisement in the *Covent Garden Journal* for 14 April 1752 thus puffed a caution against crime written by Henry Fielding as particularly suitable for the young, since 'those Ideas which they then join together, as Mr Locke judiciously observes, they are never after capable of separating'.[100] Evidently, Locke's name sold books.

Laurence Sterne likewise took it for granted that readers of *Tristram Shandy* would know, or would wish to be thought to know, 'the sagacious *Locke*'. Near the beginning, our hero observes that his father's custom of winding up the clock on the first Sunday night of every month

was attended with but one misfortune, which, in a great measure, fell upon myself, and the effects of which I fear I shall carry with me to my grave; namely, that from an unhappy association of ideas, which have no connection in nature, it so fell out at length, that my poor mother could never hear the said clock wound up, – but the thought of some other things unavoidably popped into her head – and *vice versa*: – Which strange combination of ideas, the sagacious Locke, who certainly understood the nature of these things better than most men, affirms to have produced more wry actions than all other sources of prejudice whatsoever.[101]

The *tabula rasa* also formed a talking point elsewhere in that novel and in many other books besides. In Mary Hays's *Memoirs of Emma Courtney* (1796) we are told quite explicitly that the mind begins as a blank sheet of paper.[102] Samuel Richardson's heroine Pamela acquired her grasp of the infant mind from Locke's *Some Thoughts concerning Education* (1693), obligingly presented to her by her husband-to-be;[103] and some years later Lord Chesterfield sent his son a copy of the same book, with the key passages marked, to teach him what 'a very wise, philosophical, and retired man, thinks'.[104] Those who wanted to be in the know evidently had to be up with Locke.

Crucial to the repertoire of the British Enlightenment was the Lockean model of the mind maturing through experience from ignorance to knowledge, and the paradigm it suggested for the progress of mankind at large. The individual could gain practical knowledge through the senses, could reason through words, and could find out his duties to God and his fellows. Being error-prone, man was imperfect; being educable, he was improvable. Mistakes could be expunged and advance would come by trial and error.[105] What made Locke the great teacher of the Enlightenment, it has been said, was his offering 'a plausible account of the new science as valid knowledge, intertwined with a theory of rational control of the self', while bringing the two together under the ideal of rational self-responsibility.[106]

4

PRINT CULTURE

Books and the Man I sing.

ALEXANDER POPE[1]

The chief glory of every people arises from its authors.

SAMUEL JOHNSON[2]

The present age, if we consider chiefly the state of our own country, may be stiled with great propriety *The Age of Authors*.

SAMUEL JOHNSON[3]

Society is held together by communication and information.

SAMUEL JOHNSON[4]

Crucial to the Enlightenment were the battles of the pen – against sword, censor, and rival pen. In paper wars, wit, erudition and criticism targeted darkness, dullness and despotism. Most dramatically in France, *philosophes* wielded the quill against Church and State, which retaliated by overseeing and harassing writers and publishers *via* the Index of Prohibited Books and the censor's office, police cells, the courts and even the Bastille. Both Voltaire and Diderot were locked up, and they and other *philosophes* spent time in exile. On the eve of the Revolution more than 160 censors were on Louis XVI's thought-police's payroll; to evade their attentions, elaborate networks had been devised to smuggle contraband publications across the borders from the Netherlands and Switzerland.[5]

They did these things differently in England. Censorship had been reinstated at the Restoration after the publishing free-for-all of the

Civil War and Interregnum, but the Glorious Revolution of 1688 put paid to that.[6] In 1695 the Licensing Act was allowed to lapse – partly out of resentment at the Stationers' Company's monopoly – and the old system of pre-publication censorship never returned. Hitherto restricted to London, York and Oxbridge, printing became a free market, and nothing stood in the way of any bold writer or bookseller willing to run the risk of post-publication prosecution, and perhaps prison or the pillory – and that, as Daniel Defoe found after conviction for his *Short Way with Dissenters* (1702), could prove a passport to popularity. Among the vaunted post-1688 shibboleths was freedom of the press, that liberty which 'protects all the rest', as the *London Evening Post* self-servingly proclaimed in 1754.[7]

Printed materials mushroomed. About 6,000 titles had appeared in England during the 1620s; that number climbed to almost 21,000 during the 1710s, and to over 56,000 by the 1790s.[8] Some individual sales were impressive. Samuel Richardson's *Pamela* (1740) went through five editions in twelve months, Defoe's *Robinson Crusoe* (1719) and Tobias Smollett's *Roderick Random* (1748) had print runs of 5,000 in their first year, while Henry Fielding's *Amelia* (1751) sold as many in just a week.[9]

Pamphlets went like hot cakes. Defoe's *True-Born Englishman* (1701), a political verse satire, enjoyed nine regular editions in four years and suffered a dozen pirated editions, totalling some 80,000 copies.[10] A few years later three tracts associated with the Sacheverell controversy sold over 50,000 apiece; and in 1776 Richard Price's *Observations on the Nature of Civil Liberty* did as well.[11] Between 1660 and 1800 over 300,000 separate book and pamphlet titles were published in England, amounting perhaps to 200 million copies all told.[12] As will be clear even from these crude numbers, unlike many of their Continental cousins, English men of letters hardly constituted a 'literary underground', forced to wage guerrilla wars against the powers that be. Rather they formed part of an emergent culture industry, staking out self-identities as critics, knowledge-mongers and opinion-makers, addressing a growing public, and used as well as abused by the authorities.

*

The arrival of print was represented as a great watershed. While the invention of writing was the most wonderful of all human discoveries, declared William Worthington, making us 'Masters of other Men's labours and studies, as well as of our own', printing itself, the progressive Anglican Edmund Law was sure, had 'contributed infinitely to the perfection and progress of the sciences'.[13] Literacy too was prized, with the Scots in particular proud of their parochial schools, springboards to college for the 'lad o' pairts'.[14] In England, between the cracks of the broad but decaying grammar school heritage, thousands of commercial ventures and Nonconformist academies sprang up, as did charity schools early in the century and Sunday schools later.[15]

Of course, sights might be set low: parish schools often taught reading but not writing, and assigned pupils only the Bible and other pious texts distributed by the Society for the Promotion of Christian Knowledge. But the reading eye can never be blinkered – that is why many voices were raised, from that of the arch-cynic Bernard de Mandeville to the rabid *Anti-Jacobin Review*, against the folly of teaching the plebs to read at all and so giving them ideas above their station: ignorance, thought Soame Jenyns, was the best 'opiate' of the poor.[16]

Readers rejoiced: Edward Gibbon gloried in his 'early and invincible love of reading, which I would not exchange for the treasures of India',[17] while ordinary working men wrote of lives revolutionized through the habit. Sent to market by his grazier father, the young John Cannon would slip away to a local gardener's to read the 'large history of that learned and warlike Jew, Josephus Ben Gurion', which was the 'first foundation of my steady and unwearied adherence to English history'. Becoming a revenue officer and schoolteacher and serving as the local scribe, Cannon later loaned out books in the spirit of his horticultural mentor.[18] Tramping to find work, the 14-year-old autodidact William Cobbett spied Swift's *A Tale of a Tub* in a bookseller's window. He forked out his entire capital – threepence – found a haystack and began to read. *Eureka!* – 'the book', he recalled, 'was so different . . . it delighted me beyond description; and it produced what I have always considered a sort of birth of intellect'. Cobbett rose to become the people's tribune, the self-styled 'great enlightener of the people of England'.[19] Something similar happened to the Lancashire weaver's son Samuel Bamford, another who would pay tribute to the 'blessed habit of reading'. His earliest love was a perennial favourite: 'The first book which attracted my particular notice was "The Pilgrim's Progress", with rude wood-cuts.'[20] Bunyan led to Milton, to Pope, and on then to the rest of English literature, fortifying that sense of independence which turned Bamford into a radical. His contemporary John Clare, born into a near-illiterate peasant family in the Northamptonshire fens, learned his letters, stole time out from his work and, hiding behind hedges to read, grew familiar with that supreme self-help fable *Robinson Crusoe*, then turned into an angry poet, protesting against exploitation and enclosures.[21] Crucial to plebeian self-respect was the empowerment offered by books.[22]

The reading habit changed cultural allegiances. 'The poorer sort of farmers, and even the poor country people in general,' commented James Lackington in the 1790s, 'shorten the winter nights by hearing their sons and daughters read tales, romances, etc. and on entering their houses, you may see *Tom Jones*, *Roderick Random*, and other entertaining books, stuck up on their bacon-racks.'[23] 'Prodigious numbers in inferior or *reduced* situations of life', he gloried, had thus been 'benefited', rescued as they now were from wasting their time on 'less rational purposes'.[24] Lackington's account of reading as enlightenment was patently self-serving, coming as it did from one who not only made his living as a bookseller but who prided himself upon selling knowledge cheap. A self-made man, he turned his 'Temple of the Muses' in Finsbury Square into one of London's landmarks, its sign boasting: 'CHEAPEST BOOKSELLERS IN THE WORLD'. By 1792 he was claiming a staggering turnover of 'more than one hundred thousand volumes annually', boosted by his giant catalogues and his brainwave of cheap remaindering.[25]

Lackington was not alone in sensing the power of print. 'General literature now pervades the nation through all its ranks,' Samuel Johnson had earlier stated, every house now being 'supplied with a closet of knowledge'.[26] Referring back to the 1760s, when he had been lent *Gulliver's Travels* and the *Spectator* by a fellow apprentice, Thomas Holcroft similarly pointed to the difference: back in his childhood, an ale house might have a few old English ballads, but 'books were not then, as they fortunately are now . . . to be found in almost every house'.[27]

These print-led shifts in consciousness hinged partly on high literacy rates – although, already impressive by European standards by 1700, British literacy levels did not rise very sharply in the next century.[28] What mattered, rather, was not the sum total of readers but the fact that reading became second nature to a major swathe of the nation, and that the glass screen dividing those within the print club from the rest came to count for more: illiterates were mercilessly taunted, while reading proffered an admission ticket into the cultural magic circle, even for those of no great wealth or status. Indeed, the key polarity in Georgian England, it has been suggested, was not that between patrician and plebeian, or rich and poor, but that between those swimming in the metropolitan culture pool created by print and those excluded, those whose culture was still essentially oral – perhaps what Sir James Mackintosh had in mind when he said that the spread of 'the art of Printing had . . . provided a channel by which the opinions of the learned' passed 'to the shop and the hamlet'.[29]

Autodidacts like Cobbett were particularly inspired by their early encounters with modern writings – with Defoe, Swift and Smollett, with newspapers and magazines. This reflected a shift from 'intensive' to 'extensive' reading.[30] Traditionally, a 'common reader' would treasure a shelf of hallowed texts, perusing them time and again – precisely the picture Holcroft painted. 'My master's whole library,' Lackington remarked of his cobbler employer, 'consisted of a school-size Bible, Watts's Psalms and Hymns, Foot's Tract on Baptism, Culpeper's Herbal, the History of the Gentle Craft, and an imperfect volume of Receipts in Physic, Surgery etc. and the Ready Reckoner.' The Bible, some religious texts and a few 'how-to' books – such had been an artisan's treasury of wisdom.[31]

The new breed of 'extensive' readers, by contrast, had access to a far greater range of materials, largely up to date, which they might run through, before returning them to the circulating library, handing them on or turning them into bumf. The individual item became less sacred, and the reader more desultory, accustomed, commented the bluestocking Frances Boscawen, 'not to read strictly, but *feuiller*'.[32] It was a shift which was widely condemned: 'Reading is now sunk at best into a Morning's Amusement,' growled that arch-grumbler the Revd John Brown.[33] That the new habits were not all trivialization, however, is shown by the diary of the mid-century Sussex grocer Thomas Turner. Rather impressively, that godly but gadabout fellow owned more than seventy books and periodicals, including works by such flagship enlighteners as Locke, Addison, Tillotson, Steele, Sterne and Edward Young, as well as Shakespeare and Milton; his diary mentions a further fifty books read in the decade after 1754, along with periodicals and newspapers. Of an evening, if he was not getting drunk, Turner might intone Tillotson's sermons to his chums,[34] and, when trade was slack, he would sit in his shop poring over such weighty works as Locke's *Some Thoughts concerning Education*. Since Turner doubled as village schoolteacher, he may well have spread enlightened outlooks to his pupils, perhaps even following Locke's educational hints.[35]

As Turner's diary confirms, prominent in the print explosion were newspapers, magazines and other ephemera. The newspaper itself was still news. The new century inherited the *Post Boy*, *Post-Man* and *Flying-Post*; the first successful daily, the *Daily Courant*, began under Queen Anne; more followed – the *Evening Post*, the *St James's Evening Post*, the *Whitehall Evening-Post*, the *London Journal*, the *Daily Post*, the *London Evening-Post*, the *Daily Advertiser* and so forth – while the *London Gazette* served as the nation's official organ. Up to 1700, all were printed in London – by 1712 the capital had about a score of single-sheet papers, selling some 25,000 copies a week – but a provincial press soon emerged, beginning with the *Norwich Post* in 1701. By 1760, 200,000 copies were being sold a week of the thirty-five provincial papers, and sales had doubled by 1800. Every big town had its own paper before the century was out.[36]

The annual total sale of newspapers in 1713 was around the 2.5 million mark. By the 1770s, when there were nine London dailies and fifty provincial weeklies, the figure was over 12 million; by 1801, when London alone was served by thirteen daily and ten tri-weekly newspapers, it had leapt to 16 million. 'Their cheapness brings them into universal use,' commented Johnson on the medium's take-off; 'their variety adapts them to everyone's taste.'[37] New worlds flashed before people's eyes – and novelty, as George Crabbe noted in 1785, was the big draw:

> I sing of NEWS, and all those vapid sheets
> The rattling hawker vends through gaping streets.[38]

'There is no Humour in my Countrymen,' declared Mr Spectator, 'which I am more inclined to wonder at than their general Thirst after News.'[39]

Provincial papers served as beacons to the region in which they were distributed, teaching a widening public not just of kings and battles but of the fads, sensations and excitements of the moment – indeed they *created* that public in the first place. Founded in 1736, by the end of the century the *Salisbury Journal* was selling over 4,000 copies an issue (more than most Paris newspapers) and it made its self-made proprietor Benjamin Collins rich – he died worth a staggering £100,000. Alongside news local and national, it dished up a minestrone of events, announcements, books, features and odds and ends. In all, around 200 teachers in seventy-eight Wessex towns inserted ads in the *Journal* in its first thirty-four years, a good pro-portion of which were for brand new schools,[40] showing that the press and education worked hand in hand to galvanize minds, and bearing out Johnson's dictum that 'knowledge is diffused among our people by the news-papers'.[41]

Newspapers changed assumptions and made things happen. 'A lady will offer five guineas reward for a little lost dog worth fivepence,' wrote the Swiss de Saussure in 1725:

A husband will warn the public not to lend or sell his wife anything on credit . . . A quack will advertise that he will cure all ailments. A person who has been robbed promises a reward to whoever will help him to recover his stolen property. Entertainments and spectacles are advertised; also offers of houses, domains, furniture, carriages, horses for sale or on hire, books, pamphlets, etc., and by reading these papers you know of all the gossip and of everything that has been said and done in this big town.[42]

Small wonder the invention was hailed as a dynamo of change. 'One of the improvements of life in which the present age has excelled all that have gone before', it was noted in 1753, 'is the quick circulation of intelligence, by the multitudes of newspapers'[43] – while the nostalgic for their part knew what to blame. In 1768 the crusty Alexander Catcott – he was, among other things, a passionate anti-Newtonian – snarled that 'every man in this Enlightened age (having been fully instructed by those genteel and easy conveyances of knowledge, newspapers and magazines)' presumed to have 'the liberty of making a philosophy (and I might add indeed a religion) for himself'.[44] If extreme, the Bristol clergyman's diatribe contained a core of truth, as did Josiah Tucker's telling retort in 1774 that 'this country is as much news-mad and news-ridden as ever it was popery-mad and priest-ridden'.[45]

A parallel agent of cultural change was the periodical, popularized by Daniel Defoe's *Review* (1704–13). Through the persona of Isaac Bickerstaff, Richard Steele then edited and largely wrote the *Tatler*, which appeared thrice-weekly from 1709. The first *Spectator* followed on 1 March 1711, with another of those tags from Horace beloved of the Georgians: *ex fumo dare lucem* ('to turn the darkness light').[46] Posing as the musings of 'Mr Spectator', this collaboration between Steele and Joseph Addison appeared daily, Sundays excepted, until December 1712 (nos. 1–555), priced at just one penny. With other collaborators, Addison then put out a second series which ran three times a week from June to December 1714 – all told, a staggering 635 numbers.

As will be explored in chapter 7, the *Tatler* and the *Spectator* brought enlightened views and values to the public at large, polishing manners, popularizing the new philosophy and refining tastes.[47] By splicing dramatized scenes with moral chats and readers' correspondence, genuine and fictitious, a collusive sense of shared superiority was forged through the medium of the daily essay, often read out at home or in that 'place of general Resort', the coffee house.[48] The novelty of it all was not lost on Samuel Johnson. Before the *Tatler* and *Spectator*, he observed, 'England had no masters of the common life. No writers had yet undertaken to reform either the savageness of neglect, or the impertinence of civility.'[49]

Fired by their success, scores more periodicals followed. Prominent were the *Examiner* (1710–14), partly written by Swift; Steele's own *Guardian* (1713); Ambrose Philips' bi-weekly *Free-Thinker* (1718–21), with its '*sapere aude*' masthead – popular enough to warrant a three-volume reprint; and Aaron Hill's *Plain Dealer* (1724–5). The very titles tell all. Henry Fielding's *Covent-Garden Journal* mixed essays with news, as did his *Grub-street Journal* (1730–37). A signal innovation was the *Female Spectator*, which appeared in 1744.[50] Edited by the dramatist and novelist Eliza Haywood (though ostensibly the work of an all-women 'club'), it was the first magazine written by, for and about women, being filled with items on love, marriage and the family, female education, etiquette and health (including warnings against the hysteria induced by excessive tea-drinking).[51]

After the *Tatler* and *Spectator*, the prime periodical, however, was the evergreen and significantly titled *Gentleman's Magazine: or, Monthly Intelligencer*, a general interest offering, founded in 1731 by Edward Cave, a Midlander like Johnson, who astutely passed himself off as 'Sylvanus Urban, Gent.' The *Gentleman's* boasted it contained 'more in Quantity, and greater Variety, than any Book of the Kind and Price' (just sixpence). To prove its range, after a lengthy 'View of the Weekly Disputes and Essays in this Month', the first issue devoted four pages to poems and six to a 'Monthly Intelligencer', and included sections on marriages and deaths, promotions, accidents and 'lost and stolen', stock prices, bills of mortality, foreign news, books and bankrupts, together with an essay on credulity (witchcraft in

Pennsylvania), gardening hints and abridgements of the news and comment papers. It built a circulation of over 10,000 copies and, of course, a far larger readership.[52]

More followed, including Johnson's *Rambler* (twice-weekly, 1750– 52, running to over 200 issues). His 'Idler' column appeared in the weekly *Universal Chronicle* (1758–60) and Goldsmith's 'Chinese Letters' in the *Public Ledger* (1760–61). In time, specialized titles arrived, given over to topics like fashion. Book review magazines came in too. First there were the *Monthly* (1749) and the *Critical* (1756); then in 1783 John Murray started up the *English Review*, in 1788 Joseph Johnson launched the *Analytical Review*, in 1793 came Rivington's *British Critic*, and three years later the *Monthly Magazine* – between them, they founded the meta-genre of works about new books.[53] By 1800, a staggering 250 periodicals had been launched in England, creating a spirited cultural sounding-board and exchange: 'a periodical paper of instruction and entertainment', reflected Boswell, himself a columnist, 'may be reckoned one of the happiest inventions of modern times'.[54]

Real and fabricated alike, audience participation was a key attraction, persuading readers at large, as with phone-ins today, to regard themselves as on the inside of the sets that mattered. Reader input was the very *raison d'être* of the *Athenian Gazette, or Casuistical Mercury, Resolving All the Most Nice and Curious Questions Proposed by the Ingenious* (1691), whose format lay in answering readers' questions – on points of fact, morals and conduct. Later renamed the *Athenian Mercury*, this 'all your questions answered' scrapbook was the brainchild of the eccentric John Dunton. Despite the Fall, he remarked in his garrulous autobiography, 'the desire for Knowledge is undestroyed'; and it was to afford the curious 'some glimmering apparition of Truth' that he launched his weekly miscellany, printing in its 580 numbers the answers to close on 6,000 questions, their subjects ranging from female education to the immortality of the soul. You could, for instance, find out 'How shall a man know when a Lady loves him?' or 'Whether 'tis Lawful for a Man to beat his Wife'.[55] It was later put out in bound volumes, twenty in all, plus various supplements like the *Young Students' Library*, which provided among other scientific items an abstract of Locke's *Essay on Human Understanding*, another of Thomas Sprat's *History of the Royal Society* (1667), and some 'Observations on Mr Boyle's Specifick Remedies', the chemist's foray into popular health.[56] Dunton's *Athenian Mercury* provides a benchmark of cultural change, signalling the point when 'Mr Public'[57] was beginning to look to journalists for guidance in life, perhaps in the process sidelining parents, parsons and other venerable authorities.

All such publications, of course, entailed wider innovations within the print business. The relentless demands of newspapers and magazines for copy turned authorship into a trade. Only from around 1700 did the 'author by profession' make his mark on the literary landscape. Writing, remarked Daniel Defoe in 1725, 'is becoming a very considerable Branch of the English Commerce . . . The Booksellers are the Master Manufacturers or Employers. The several Writers, Authors, Copyers, Sub-Writers and all other operators with Pen and Ink are the workmen.'[58] The plight of such 'hirelings with Pen and Ink' was caught by Henry Fielding in *The Author's Farce* (1730), in the lament of the arch-hack Blotpage:

> How unhappy's the fate
> To live by one's pate
> And be forced to write hackney for bread!
> An author's a joke
> To all manner of folk
> Wherever he pops up his head, his head,
> Wherever he pops up his head.[59]

Blotpage was new to the literary scene. In 1763, supping with Johnson and Goldsmith, Boswell noted how odd it was to be 'sitting with London authors by profession': Sawney McHackit had not yet appeared in Old Reekie.[60]

The scribblers' headquarters was Grub Street, an actual location (by the Barbican) as well as an image.[61] Defined by Johnson as 'a street near Moorfields, much inhabited by writers of small histories, dictionaries, and temporary poems', it was a wry joke to its own denizens, who self-mockingly referred to the 'University of Grub-street', that 'fruitful Nursery of tow'ring Genius's!'[62] Meanwhile, they were despised by princes of the pen like Alexander Pope, fearful of being dragged down into the gutter by the drudges scratching away for the 'buzzing tribe' of Paternoster Row booksellers, those 'pimps of literature'.[63]

Life was not easy for one of that new breed, the 'author by trade', who, as poignantly evoked in Johnson's *Life of Mr Richard Savage* (1744), strained for bread and fame – how Johnson knew, being a poor bookseller's son himself![64] Their status was rising, however, if slowly – and only for some. This owed a little to a series of copyright acts, which extended the Lockean sanctity of an Englishman's estate to literary property. 'Nothing [is] more a Man's own than his Thoughts and Inventions,' avowed the critic John Dennis; 'wit', agreed Lord Chesterfield, 'is a sort of property'.[65]

Complex new copyright laws confirmed publishers' rights while also holding out some entitlements to authors. London's 'booksellers' (publishers) had traditionally enjoyed a national monopoly (aside from the university presses) under the protective canopy of the Stationers' Company. The lapse of the Licensing Act spurred the hundred or so metropolitan booksellers to combine to defend their corner, setting up congers, or associations, which monopolized shares in copyright.[66] Subsequent to the 1710 Act, however, it was no longer clear that they controlled exclusive copyrights, and certainly not for any more than twenty-one years (from the date of the Act) over the works of the dead – Shakespeare, for instance. Books already in print would be protected for fourteen years, renewable for a further fourteen if the author or owner was still alive.

In this unsettled situation, publishers found it paid to strike deals with favoured authors, who proved able to negotiate more handsome rewards. Oliver Goldsmith secured 800 guineas for his *History of Animated Nature* (1774), while the Scottish historian William Robertson received a huge £4,500 for his *History of Charles V* (1772).[67] Successful authors and publishers thus thrived alike in what had become a booming industry. 'I respect Millar, Sir,' declared

Johnson of a top bookseller, 'for he has raised the price of literature.'[68]

No doubt there is truth in Hogarth's portrayal of the hapless 'distrest poet'; Adam Smith was to deride 'that unprosperous race of men commonly called men of letters', and one protested that 'there is no Difference between the Writer in his Garret, and the Slave in the Mines'.[69] Yet professional authors were winning their place in the sun. Little of any value was written in either the garret or the palace, remarked Gibbon, perhaps correctly.[70] Certainly a growing number of writers, himself included, escaped these stultifying extremes, gaining pecuniary success and public cachet alike. 'My book was on every table, and almost on every toilette,' the historian gloated, recalling the appearance of his *The History of the Decline and Fall of the Roman Empire* (1776–81); 3,500 copies sold in just over a year.[71] Before 1700 those authors who were not independent gentlemen had typically sought patronage, and some – Gay and Prior, for instance – continued to be so favoured.[72] But patronage could feel like prostitution and it irked many, not just Johnson. In any case, by the 1730s the golden age of royal and noble literary sponsorship marked by Lords Somers, Montagu, Halifax, Harley and the Kit-Cat Club was waning. Writers, however, found that, instead of drowning, they were actually buoyed up by the market, which provided them with a measure of independence. Johnson, for one, never rued the new situation in which the author looked to the public, and the pen was independent of the pension. Visiting Glasgow, he was given the old rigmarole as to how trade and learning did not mix, but, as ever, he had no truck with cant:

JOHNSON: . . . Now learning itself is a trade. A man goes to a bookseller, and gets what he can. We have done with patronage.

Enter the biographer with his usual asinine interjection:

BOSWELL: It is a shame that authors are not now better patronized.
JOHNSON: No, Sir. If learning cannot support a man, if he must sit with his hands across till somebody feeds him, it is as to him a bad thing, and it is better as it is. With patronage, what flattery! What falsehood!

BOSWELL: But is it not the case now, that instead of flattering one person, we flatter the age?
JOHNSON: No, Sir! The World always lets a man tell what he thinks, his own way.[73]

While Johnson cursed Lord Chesterfield for letting him down as protector to his *Dictionary*, his complaint was not about the noble lord's failure to bankroll it – finance to the tune of about £5,000, after all, came from the booksellers. What piqued the lexicographer was Chesterfield's failure to provide 'one Act of assistance, one word of encouragement, or one smile of favour'. Hence the barbed put-down:

The shepherd in Virgil grew at last acquainted with Love, and found him a native of the rocks. Is not a Patron, my Lord, one who looks with unconcern on a Man struggling for Life in the water, and when he has reached ground encumbers him with help.[74]

– and the significant substitution when Johnson revised *The Vanity of Human Wishes* in 1749:

> There mark what ills the scholar's life assail,
> Toil, envy, want, the *Patron*, and the jail.

(The line had originally indicted not the patron but 'the garret'.)[75]

While Tory wits mourned the demise of courtly patronage in Walpole's 'degenerate' age, Johnson was not alone in viewing it as a blessing in disguise for authors by profession – an escape from being patronized. The poets of England, opined Goldsmith, 'no longer depend on the great for subsistence; they have now no other patrons but the public, and the public, collectively considered, is a good and generous master'.[76]

Literature became a commodity circulating in all shapes and sizes. John Wesley turned out fourpenny pocket-sized abridgements of classics like *Paradise Lost* – Milton for the masses – as well as a dictionary and a nine-page English grammar.[77] New packages were also pioneered, for instance publishing by parts. The first edition of

Johnson's *Dictionary* (1755), of which 2,000 copies were printed, cost £4 10s.; hard on its heels came a second, brought out in 165 weekly sections at sixpence each. Smollett's *Complete History of England* (1757–8) sold 10,000 copies in sixpenny weekly numbers.[78]

In addition, enterprising publishers began to market cheap sets of the standard English poets and playwrights at the knock-down price of a shilling or so – in effect, paperbacks. This was made possible by a 1774 copyright ruling which established that after the expiry of the protected period (a maximum of twenty-eight years), a text entered the public domain. The old cartels could now be smashed. John Bell launched his *Poets of Great Britain Complete from Chaucer to Churchill* series, which came out between 1776 and 1792 in 109 volumes, at 1s. 6d. each – or just 6d. on tatty paper.[79] Soon John Cooke was competing, with his editions of the British poets, prose writers and dramatists, in sixpenny weekly numbers.[80] Young William Hazlitt gobbled up English literature through Cooke's books which regularly arrived by mail order at his parental home ('a perpetual gala-day'). Another 1770s innovation was William Lane's Minerva Press and Library, notorious for its salacious and sentimental novels.[81]

Thus, more made its way into print, more cheaply. Books also became easier of access, particularly as provincial publishing brought a bookshops boom. Under the Licensing Acts printing had been a London monopoly and provincials had had to make do without printed broadsides and handbills, advertisements, theatre programmes, tickets, receipts or other trade items. In 1700 Birmingham had no bookseller, while as late as the 1720s Lincoln had a towncrier but no newspaper or printer. All that changed fast. By 1740, there were about 400 printing outlets in nearly 200 towns, and, by the 1790s, this had risen to nearly 1,000 in more than 300 centres. In 1800, Newcastle-upon-Tyne could boast not only twenty printers but twelve booksellers and three engravers as well. 'There are now as many Booksellers as there are Butchers,' observed the Londoner William Blake.[82]

Nor was it even necessary to buy, as hosts of book clubs and libraries – circulating, proprietary and subscription – came into being. By 1800 there were about a hundred in the metropolis and a thousand in the provinces.[83] Some were huge: in 1793 Bell's London circulating library claimed to hold 150,000 volumes – including the kinds of *belles lettres* and Minerva Press fiction which drove Sir Anthony Absolute to apoplexy.[84] Though most libraries kept large stocks of history, travel and the like, it was the novels, play texts and light reading which were seized off the shelves.

The print boom bred new varieties of men of letters. 'In opulent or commercial society,' observed Adam Smith, theorist of the division of labour, 'to think or reason comes to be, like every other employment, a particular business, which is carried on by a very few people.'[85] Among the emergent breeds was the critic, that self-appointed judge, censor and reformer of the republic of letters – and object of vilification:

> So, Nat'ralists observe, a Flea
> Hath smaller Fleas that on him prey,
> And these have smaller yet to bite 'em,
> And so proceed *ad infinitum* . . .[86]

Thus wrote Swift, while Cobbett for his part called 'those who carry on the trade of critic . . . a base and hireling crew'.[87] Even so, the critic was enlightened man incarnate, the caustic Restoration wit purified into the more civilized character required in the age of politeness, standing for freedom of speech and rational argument against dogmatism and absolutism.[88]

Mr Critic overlapped somewhat with the satirist for, especially in the early Enlightenment, the burlesque, the spoof and the parody formed ideal vehicles for free-thinking, opposition and subversion. And his younger brother was Mr Reviewer. Johnson might slight the business as an 'epidemical conspiracy for the destruction of paper',[89] but reviewing, like criticism, filled the sails of the ship of print. It told readers what to think and say, while nurturing a much-desired (if despised) cultural narcissism in circles eager to hear themselves talked about and liking the sound of their own voices.[90]

The crony of them all was Mr Spectator, arbiter of standards and ubiquitous commentator. Hinting that there was no coffee house which he did not frequent, that Addisonian persona assumed a universal status, transcending the particular identities of the individual members of his club – the cleric, man of fashion, merchant, country gentleman and soldier – to become the cosmopolite, the very epitome of sweet reason, composure and tolerant pluralism.[91]

These literary identities were part and parcel of the key Enlightenment reinvention of the persona of the thinker, signalled by Adam Smith's remark about the trade of thinking. Proposing to bring 'Philosophy out of Closets and Libraries, Schools and Colleges, to dwell in Clubs and Assemblies, at Tea-Tables and in Coffee Houses', Joseph Addison, the first great media man, sought to turn the philosopher into a man of letters and thus a man of the world.[92] Thinking was not for academics alone and must be rescued from the 'monkish' seminaries which bred arcane pomposity; what was needed was discussion not disputation, conversation not controversy, politeness not pedantry. 'If Philosophy be, as we take it, the Study of Happiness,' remarked the 3rd Earl of Shaftesbury, 'must not everyone, in some manner or other, either skilfully or unskilfully philosophize?'[93] It was not thus a matter of metaphysics but of *savoir vivre*: 'The Taste of Beauty, and the Relish of what is decent, just, and amiable, perfects the Character of the Gentleman and the Philosopher.'[94]

David Hume concurred in urging a reincarnation for the philosopher: 'The separation of the learned from the conversable world', he maintained, had been 'the great defect of the last age'; learning had 'been as great a loser by being shut up in colleges and cells', while philosophy had gone to ruin 'by this moping recluse method of study, and became as chimerical in her conclusions, as she was unintelligible in her style and manner of delivery'. Where lay the fault? Thinking had been monopolized by self-absorbed academics 'who never consulted experience in any of their reasonings, or who never searched for that experience, where alone it is to be found, in common life and conversation'. Things, however, were on the mend. 'It is with great pleasure I observe', he noted, that men of letters in this age have lost in a great measure that shyness and bashfulness of temper, which kept them at a distance from mankind; and, at the same time, that men of the world are proud of borrowing from books their most agreeable topics of conversation.[95]

Hume's life itself played out the impasse of the thinker – and its Enlightenment resolution. In his twenties, the Scotsman slithered into a career crisis. He abandoned his legal studies and launched himself on to the troubled waters of philosophy. He wrestled with his daring experimental science of the self, abandoning the philosophy of first principles and *a priori* reason for the unremitting examination of every scratch of sensation upon the consciousness, under a ruthless and sceptical honesty – studies that were to lead to his *Treatise of Human Nature* (1739).

For a while, he studied at fever pitch, but then succumbed to fatigue and ennui: 'I could no longer raise my Mind to that pitch, which formerly gave me such excessive Pleasure.' He tried to work, but by the spring of 1730 he was experiencing severe physical and mental pains. Not least, those doughty 'Reflections against Death, & Poverty, & Shame & Pain' which he had read in the works of the Stoics had the clean contrary effect on him, for they merely accentuated the fact that he was sick.

Hume grew mentally disordered, but he was unwilling to believe his condition was purely in the head, for that would have implied a disturbing loss of self-control. His doctor was not deceived: 'he laughed at me, & told me . . . I had fairly got the Disease of the Learned'. He was prescribed 'a Course of Bitters, & Anti-hysteric Pills', claret and riding. His nerves and spirits needed reinvigorating. During the next eighteen months, Hume's health went up and down. Still he wished to believe it was no mental or personality disorder, for that would have implied either madness or malingering. Yet he could not disguise that his condition had some psychic tinge. The best parallel to his condition, Hume noted, lay in the strange sicknesses of religious *dévots*. Painting a self-deprecating portrait of the philosopher as a young religious enthusiast, he can hardly have felt flattered by his fate.

Arguably this acutely self-monitored mental breakdown was critical in shaping Hume's philosophical temper and credo. For it was
living proof of the frailty of pure, isolated, abstract reason. Thinking
could not divorce itself from sensation, and sensation was rooted in
the body. Nervous collapse surely convinced Hume that his own
special philosophical project – to delve into sensations to resolve the
problem of identity – entailed the kind of morbid introspection that
was making him sick. Philosophy was autobiography.

From his sickness Hume emerged a new breed of philosopher, in
ways notably paralleled nearly a century later in the outcome of John
Stuart Mill's nervous breakdown, which transformed a scientific
utilitarian into a libertarian individualist. Those who wallowed in
morbid introspection remained religious enthusiasts; understanding
and overcoming the condition led to Humean philosophy. What
pulled him out of his depression was not some religious illumination
but 'Nature herself'. By rejoining the world and regaining his sociability, he restored his mental equilibrium: 'I dine, I play a game of
back-gammon, I converse, and am merry with my friends; and when
. . . I wou'd return to these speculations, they appear so cold, and
strain'd, and ridiculous, that I cannot find in my heart to enter into
them any farther.'[96] 'Be a philosopher,' he concluded; 'but amidst all
your philosophy be still a man.'[97]

Once his *Treatise* had fallen 'deadborn from the press',[98] Hume took
to writing Spectatorial essays and history, not as an abandonment of
philosophy but as its superior, modern expression. Reckoning that
'Addison, perhaps, will be read with pleasure, when Locke shall be
entirely forgotten',[99] he set about burnishing his style and switched
careers. After applying unsuccessfully in 1744 for the chair of moral
philosophy at Edinburgh, he settled in that city seven years later,
where, with his new identity as a man of letters, he gained a reputation
in literary circles for essays and for his *History of Great Britain* (1754–
62). Appointed secretary to the British embassy in Paris in 1763, he
turned into a prominent salon figure, befriending such *philosophes*
as Diderot and d'Holbach, and he later served in London as an
undersecretary of state before finally retiring to Edinburgh. The

philosopher had successfully metamorphosed into a man of letters and man of affairs.[100]

In his vastly influential *Lectures on Rhetoric and Belles Lettres* (1783), Hugh Blair approached the question of the thinker and his public from a further angle. What did readers of serious books want? Doubtless they hoped 'for instruction, not for entertainment', but readability must be a plus: 'The same truths, and reasonings, delivered in a dry and cold manner, or with a proper measure of elegance and beauty, will make very different impressions on the minds of men.' Indeed, Blair extolled 'good Writing'. Particularly valuable were illustrations from history and the affairs of great men, 'for they take Philosophy out of the abstract, and give weight to Speculation, by shewing its connection with real life, and the actions of mankind'.[101]

Moreover, it was now insisted, unlike its monkish ancestor, enlightened philosophy should and would be useful. Assuredly it was the 'trade' of the philosopher, noted Adam Smith, 'not to do any thing, but to observe every thing'. However, even this art of observation must be use-oriented;[102] the true philosopher was no armchair daydreamer – James Watt of steam-engine fame, for example, amply deserved the accolade.[103] In the notion broached by Smith and others that Mr Spectator, alias the universal observer, was the model thinker, philosophy itself was redirected and revitalized: no metaphysical mystery exclusive to cloistered bookworms, it was to be that rational understanding of the real world which would drive the Enlightenment.[104]

Bearing out the Baconian dictum that knowledge is power, print proved the great engine for the spread of enlightened views and values (see chapter 15).[105] Alongside chapbooks, prayer books, jest books and what have you, the presses spewed forth improving teach-yourself guides, educational treatises and advice manuals by the score, from gardening to gymnastics, carpentry to cookery – Hannah Glasse's *The Art of Cookery Made Plain and Easy* (1747) even tailored recipes to servants, to save 'the Ladies a great deal of Trouble'.[106]

The children's book was also born,[107] and prints and picture books blossomed.[108]

Monumental reference works appeared, including Johnson's *Dictionary of the English Language* (1755). John Harris's *Lexicon Technicum* (1704) was the first modern English encyclopaedia, weighted on the scientific and technical side.[109] Inspired by Harris, Ephraim Chambers compiled a more comprehensive work, entitled *Cyclopaedia: or, An Universal Dictionary of Arts and Sciences*, published in 1728 in two folio volumes, with plates, at four guineas. Chambers was to be honoured by election to the Royal Society of London and burial in Westminster Abbey.[110] In 1778 the Dissenting minister Abraham Rees re-edited Chambers in four volumes – it appeared in 418 weekly numbers – and he later cranked out a further edition, before planning his *Cyclopaedia, Or an Universal Dictionary of Arts and Sciences . . . Biography, Geography and History*, a vast undertaking completed in 1819 in thirty-nine quarto volumes.[111]

Meanwhile, the *Encyclopaedia Britannica* had appeared, also in parts (the first appearing in 1768), at a cost of 6d. each on plain paper, with over a hundred parts in all. Its 2,670 quarto pages with 160 copperplate engravings cost just £12.[112] Ten thousand copies were printed of the third edition (1787–97) – France, with three times the population of Britain, had a mere 4,500 subscribers for its *Encyclopédie*. All human knowledge was thus made readily available, for the first time, in English and within reach of middle-class pockets.[113]

Though far from every title flew under the 'enlightened' ensign – mountains of devotional literature were published – print became indelibly linked in the public mind with progress. And, through the printed word, a specifically national culture was crystallizing, aided by works that taught what every educated Briton should know, particularly about home-bred achievements. Horace Walpole's *Anecdotes of Painting in England*, published from 1762, was the first history of English art; Thomas Warton's *History of English Poetry* (1774–81) complemented Dr Johnson's *Lives of the Poets* (1779–81); Sir Joshua Reynolds's *Discourses*, on matters of taste, came out between 1769 and 1791, while in music Sir John Hawkins's *A General History of the Science and Practice of Music* (1776) was counterpointed in the same year by Charles Burney's polished *A General History of Music*.[114]

Early in the century, Shaftesbury had protested that 'the British Muses' were 'yet in their mere infant-state'.[115] But critical and popular editions of British writers and biographical dictionaries of native worthies, like the *Biographia Britannica* (1747–66), allayed cultural anxieties and boosted national pride. Bardolatry boomed, especially after David Garrick's Shakespeare jubilee staged in 1769 at Stratford-upon-Avon. Anthologized in works of the 'beauties of Shakespeare' genre, the Bard became the national saint – chips of his chair were on sale as relics: 'Shakespear,' mused the playwright-scholar Arthur Murphy, 'is a kind of establish'd Religion in Poetry.'[116] Poets' Corner in Westminster Abbey became a tourist must; the trade cards of London booksellers fêted heroes like Shakespeare, Addison and Pope, alongside such philosophers and divines as Locke, Newton, Boyle, Clarke and Archbishop Tillotson; while a temple of British worthies, designed by the Viscount Cobham on his country estate at Stowe, sported busts of Shakespeare, Bacon, Milton, Newton, Locke and Inigo Jones, amid the regulation generals and royals. Voltaire was impressed: 'The English have so great a Veneration for exalted Talents, that a Man of Merit in their Country is always sure of making his Fortune. Mr Addison was rais'd to the Post of Secretary of State in England. Sir Isaac Newton was made Warden of the Royal Mint. Mr Congreve had a considerable Employment.'[117] Writers and thinkers had become national assets.

'Meantime, the pamphlets and half-sheets grow so upon our hands,' groaned Swift in 1710, 'it will very well employ a man every day from morning till night to read them.' His solution? Never to open any![118] The doctor Thomas Beddoes was another who grumbled about the welter of print – all those endless pamphlets and periodicals befuddling the brain. 'Did you see the papers today? Have you read the new play – the new poem – the new pamphlet – the last novel?' – that was all you heard. 'You cannot creditably frequent intelligent company, without being prepared to answer these questions, and the progeny that springs from them.' The consequence? 'You must needs hang your heavy head, and roll your bloodshot eyes over thousands of pages weekly. Of their contents at the week's end, you will know about as much as of a district, through which you have been whirled night and day in the mail-coach.'[119] Yet that didn't sap his ardour for enlightenment, or still his quill.

Be they reactionaries like Swift or radicals like Beddoes, many feared truth was being buried in the avalanche of textual production. 'It comes to pass, that Weekly Essays, amatory Plays and Novels, political Pamphlets, and books that revile Religion; together with a general *Hash* of these, served up in some *Monthly Mess* of *Dulness*,' bewailed the Revd John Brown, 'are the Meagre *literary Diet* of Town and Country.'[120] Old fogeys feared what Johnson memorably and approvingly called 'a nation of readers' – for his part, however, the lexicographer never doubted the benefits of literacy, even if he also muttered that 'this teeming of the press in modern times . . . obliges us to read so much of what is of inferior value, in order to be in the fashion'.[121]

What made critical reactions to the diffusion of knowledge, and the culture industry sustaining it, so caustic was that this cornucopia of secular information, instant opinion and urbane values, purveyed by the *Monthly Mess*, was new and unprecedented. People seemed to be picking up beliefs from their reading like apples from a barrel. Moreover, amid the welter of essays, *belles lettres* and novels, life and letters seemingly mirrored each other in a looking-glass world – no accident, surely, that the prime Scottish periodical was actually titled the *Mirror*.[122]

It was a turning point. The print boom was bringing into being an intelligentsia, separate from (though overlapping with) the clergy, a 'commonwealth of polite letters' linked to the public at large *via* the publishing industry.[123] Print technologies and surplus wealth were supporting cultural performers who became established as self-appointed tribunes of the people, sustained by infrastructures created by impresarios, critics and capitalists. The writer's status became irrevocably bound up with his relations to the public –

indeed, his public relations – as he projected himself as the nation's eyes, ears and voice, a figure commanding public presence, notoriety even. The business of writing and the reading public were two sides of the coin of print capitalism.

Writers were, of course, confronted by the problem of how to train these raw cultural audiences, how to forge taste while affecting to follow it. Some did not hide their contempt: 'the Vulgar', alias 'bipedal reptiles', spat one, now expected respectful treatment as 'the Public'.[124] But if satirists disdained its supposed boorish ignorance, later authors tended to be more accepting of the public, recognizing that their fame depended on its applause. 'The public is seldom wrong,' declared Gibbon;[125] 'I rejoice to concur with the common reader,' Johnson tellingly commented, *à propos* Thomas Gray's *Elegy Written in a Country Church-Yard* (1751).[126] If such tributes involved a dollop of flattery, they also reflected the familiar, if fragile, relations in the Enlightenment between thinkers and the public.

5

RATIONALIZING RELIGION

The universal Disposition of this Age is bent upon a rational religion.

THOMAS SPRAT[1]

... before Christianity was entirely reasoned out of these kingdoms ...

EDWARD MOORE[2]

What did God require of mankind, who could know His will, and by what means? These questions lay at the very heart of enlightened thinking.[3] This must be kept in mind, if two errors are to be avoided. One is the assumption that it was an age of downright religious apathy, when 'cassock'd huntsmen and fiddling priests' kept fine cellars and mistresses, congregations slumbered, the wits blasphemed, the Quality flouted the Commandments, and even grave Quakers turned gay. Hogarth's engravings, the diary of Parson Woodforde – a man devoted more to beef than to the Bible – Gibbon's damnation of the 'fat slumbers of the Church' and other familiar vignettes lend some credence to this caricature.[4] An early *Spectator* paper insinuated that the value of Sunday church-going was essentially temporal, it being 'the best method that could have been thought of for the polishing and civilizing of mankind'[5] – and even this may not have worked, since congregations were dwindling.[6] 'The Church in Danger' was the cry not only of *iure divino* High-flyers, and many bewailed the tide of 'unbelief': 'no age, since the founding and forming the Christian Church,' lamented Daniel Defoe in 1722, 'was ever like, in open avowed atheism, blasphemies, and heresies, to the

96

age we now live in'.[7] No one in England believed any longer, quipped Montesquieu around the same time.[8]

Indifference and unbelief, however, if present, were far from the norm. Many, notably Nonconformists, staunchly upheld the austerities of their grandfathers. Weekly in church or chapel, the Protestant nation heard Bible religion preached from the pulpit, and indeed sang it, in what proved to be the golden age of English hymnody.[9] Rigorism survived – high-profile divines still damned even the theatre: 'a Player cannot be a living member of Christ,' thundered William Law.[10] Amongst prominent laymen, Samuel Johnson upheld eternal hellfire and believed the 'quiver of Omnipotence' was 'stored with arrows',[11] while Jonas Hanway, rescuer of unfortunates and popularizer of the umbrella, insisted that 'to learn how to die . . . is the great business of living'.[12] If we imagine mass indifference, the polemics of Deists and the raillery of sceptics make no sense.[13] Religion was still a burning issue, if now only in a metaphorical sense.

And what of the other *canard*, the view – the converse of the former – that the scoffers' attacks were but the paper darts of crankish nobodies? 'Who, born within the last forty years,' demanded Edmund Burke in 1790, 'has read one word of Collins, and Toland, and Tindal, and Chubb, and Morgan, and that whole race who called themselves Free Thinkers? Who now reads Bolingbroke? Who ever read him through?'[14] The Deist challenge associated with such figures, Burke blustered, had not just been seen off; it had been impotent in the first place. The English, in other words, did not even come near to producing that *écrasez l'infâme* warcry which typified their Continental cousins, and Christianity remained snug until the Victorian honest doubters and the *Origin of Species*.[15]

But that is also a simplistic view. Mary Wollstonecraft certainly did not share Burke's confidence. 'It is the fashion now for young men to be deists,' his feminist foe tut-tutted, 'and many a one [have] improper books sent adrift in a sea of doubts.'[16] In this, the pious Anglican, wary of 'wandering reason', was echoing churchmen's fears regarding the inroads made by free-thinking. 'It is come, I know not how, to be taken for granted, by many persons,' agonized Joseph Butler, later bishop of Durham, 'that Christianity is . . . now at length discovered to be fictitious.'[17]

For all Burke's put-downs, the English Deists were novel, incisive and influential – Voltaire and other *philosophes* were deeply in their debt.[18] And it was for quite other reasons that Bolingbroke and co. were less widely perused in Burke's day: by then their writings had done their work. Samuel Johnson once remarked of the Renaissance courtesy books that 'if they are now less read', it was 'only because they have effected that reformation which their authors intended';[19] the same holds for Augustan Deism. Threats to a gentleman's privilege of being religious on his own terms – threats from High Churchmen, Non-jurors, Puritans and later from Methodists and other enthusiasts – had been resisted, had withered away or were becoming marginalized to a 'lunatic fringe'.[20] Legislation won toleration for Protestants; prorogued in 1717, Convocation did not thereafter meet for over a century, depriving the Church of its 'parliament'; and the Church courts lost their bite. By 1800 courtly prelates of the lustre of a Laud were extinct, and no longer were there menacing clerical conspirators like Bishop Atterbury, dazzling demagogues like Henry Sacheverell or pulpit polemicists like Dean Swift.[21] In important respects England had grown 'laicized',[22] and the world the Deists and Mr Spectator had wanted, one secure against Popish and Puritan theocracy, had largely been realized.[23]

Indeed, ecclesiastics had been busily secularizing themselves, pursuing lives barely different from those of their neighbours: 'A foreigner is surprised,' observed the Swiss traveller de Saussure, 'to find the clergy in public places, in taverns, and eating-houses, where they smoke and drink just like laymen; but, as they scandalize no one, you quickly get accustomed to this sight.'[24] What made the name of many a leading Anglican divine was not divinity or devoutness but achievements in other spheres: William Derham and Gilbert White in science and natural history, Richard Bentley, William Warburton and Richard Hurd in scholarship, George Berkeley in philosophy,

Thomas Percy and Lawrence Sterne in literature, Edward Young and George Crabbe in poetry, William Gilpin in aesthetics, Horne Tooke in philology and Thomas Robert Malthus in political economy, to say nothing of the hundreds of country parsons who dabbled in verse and antiquities or prosecuted poachers.[25] Masquerading as a travelling Spaniard, Robert Southey contrasted religion Iberian and Anglican-style:

With us, every thing is calculated to remind us of religion. We cannot go abroad without seeing some representation of Purgatory, some cross which marks a station, an image of Mary the most pure, or a crucifix . . . There is nothing of all this in England. The clergy here are as little distinguished from the laity in their dress as in their lives. Here are no vespers to unite a whole kingdom at one time in one feeling of devotion; if the bells are heard, it is because bell-ringing is the popular music.[26]

Enlightened minds ceased to equate religion with a body of commandments, graven in stone, dispensed through Scripture, accepted on faith and policed by the Church. Belief was becoming a matter of private judgement, for individual reason to adjudicate within the multi-religionism sanctioned by statutory toleration. The Anglican Church, meanwhile, lost its monopolies over education and the enforcement of morals. As religion became subjected to reason, Christianity ceased to be a 'given' and became a matter of analysis and choice. And, for some, that meant scepticism or rejection.

As the seventeenth century drew to its close, one call was heard ever louder: religion and reason were one and must pull together. 'There is nothing so intrinsically rational as religion is,' Benjamin Whichcote had urged – and Locke concurred with that respected Cambridge Platonist.[27] History showed why that alliance mattered, as it looked back in anger upon the wars of religion, be it Papists or Puritans who had commanded the 'infallible artillery'.[28] What the political nation sought was a rational religion, involving the destruction of idolatry and priestly power. Enlightenment in Britain took place within, rather than against, Protestantism.

Religion, held the enlightened, must be rational, as befitted the mind of God and the nature of man. Rejecting the bogeyman of a vengeful Jehovah blasting wicked sinners,[29] enlightened divines instated a more optimistic (pelagian) theology, proclaiming the benevolence of the Supreme Being and man's capacity to fulfil his duties through his God-given faculties, the chief of these being reason, that candle of the Lord. The Creator should be seen less as Jahweh, the Lord of Hosts, than as a constitutional head of state. 'God is a monarch,' opined Viscount Bolingbroke, 'yet not an arbitrary but a limited monarch': His power was limited by His reason.[30]

As we have seen, Locke's epistemology had a place for revealed truth, which commanded 'assent' or faith.[31] Reason for its part could validate the existence of the Father of Light, verify the Bible as revelation and back the basics: Christ was the Messiah, the sole tenet upon which the disciples had insisted – not for them any Thirty-nine Articles, Westminster Confession or even Athanasian Creed. Beyond that, how could man fathom omniscience?[32]

Here lay the prospect of a creed, adapted to 'labouring and illiterate men', and free of those sophistries with which 'wranglers in religion have filled it', as though the stairway to heaven wound through the 'academy'. Scripture, Locke held, was simple, 'to be understood in the plain, direct meaning of the words and phrases'.[33] Revealed in Scripture and Nature, God's will must be divined through use of the understanding, for

Reason is natural revelation, whereby the eternal Father of light, and Fountain of all knowledge, communicates to mankind that portion of truth which he has laid within the reach of their natural faculties.[34]

And His requirements were not beyond human capacities but could be met by sober conduct:

the business of men is to be happy in this world by the enjoyment of the things of nature subservient to life, health, ease, and pleasure, and by the comfortable hopes of another life when this is ended.[35]

Precisely what Locke thought cardinal to Christianity was set out in his *The Reasonableness of Christianity, as Delivered in the Scriptures* (1695), published five years after the *Essay concerning Human Understanding*. Brushing off the scholastic encrustations, he restored the Gospel to its pristine purity. The key truth – that Jesus was the Messiah, proclaiming the coming of the Kingdom – admittedly needed clarification. The Jews had thought of a messiah as a prophet, priest and king; but 'though these three offices,' commented the anti-clerical philosopher,

be in holy writ attributed to our Saviour, yet I do not remember that he anywhere assumes to himself the title of a priest, or mentions anything relating to his priesthood ... but the Gospel, or the good news of the kingdom of the Messiah, is what he preaches everywhere, and makes it his great business to publish to the world.[36]

Another problem: Christ had declared that none would be admitted to his Kingdom who did not accept him.[37] What, then, of that hoary quandary, the fate of the millions who had not heard the Word? Locke's consoling answer – one showing the centrality of natural law to his thinking – referred to the parable of the talents: the Lord would not expect ten talents from him to whom He had given but one. Independently of revelation, man was governed by the law of reason, and he should make use of 'this candle of the Lord, so far as to find what was his duty'.[38] Even without Christ, reason pointed to the just life under natural law.

What, then, was the point of Christ's coming? Since Locke did not believe the Messiah had been sent to bear the sins of the world, again his answer hinged on natural law. Reason had indeed revealed the Deity, but the truth had grown clouded, and the people had been fooled by crafty clerics peddling false gods: 'vice and superstition held the world,' he explained, 'the priests everywhere, to secure their empire, having excluded reason from having any thing to do in religion'.[39] Through such cheats, sight had been lost of the 'Wise Architect'. While the discerning built on the rock of reason, that alone failed to persuade the herd. The Greeks had had their Socrates, but such philosophers made no impact on the rabble, and when St Paul had visited Athens, he had found its denizens sunk in superstition as if the sage had never existed, wallowing in ceremonies and sacrifices to the neglect of reason's 'clear and convincing light'.[40] 'In this state of darkness and error . . . our Saviour found the world. But the clear revelation he brought with him dissipated this darkness', and made the 'one invisible true God' known.[41] Christ thus came not to reveal new truths but to 'republish' those obscured by evil and error.

In Locke's plain man's guide to Christianity, no one accepting the Messiah need flounder in theological niceties. 'Religious creeds I leave to others,' he shrugged; 'I only set down the Christian religion as I find our Saviour and his apostles preached it.'[42] Like other enlightened thinkers, what concerned Locke was Christ's moral mission – faith was futile without works, religion was a school of virtue.

Locke was a cautious radical. By casting Christ as a moral guide, and especially by his silence on the Trinity, he seemed to be slipping towards Arianism, the denial of Jesus's divinity. Yet, unlike later Deists, he had no qualms about Scripture: revelation and reason were not antagonists but allies. Even so, he had come far from his Calvinist youth and Oxford orthodoxy; dogmas had given way to the duty of inquiry. In all this he was not alone.[43]

Small surprise, perhaps, that a philosophical physician like Locke held that the horrors of the age owed much to an over-mighty clergy, insisted that articles of faith submit to reason and urged toleration. It is more remarkable that a churchman who acceded to the see of Canterbury in 1689 should espouse comparable views: that is what Voltaire and others found so extraordinary about John Tillotson. 'All the duties of Christian religion which respect God,' he stressed, assuming a thoroughly Lockean air, 'are no other but what natural light prompts men to, excepting the two sacraments, and praying to God in the name and by the mediation of Christ.'[44] Like his friend Locke, Tillotson taught that Christianity was simple and squared with man's nature:

Two things make any course of life easy; present pleasure, and the assurance of a future reward. Religion gives part of its reward in hand, the present comfort and satisfaction of having done our duty; and, for the rest, it offers us the best security that Heaven can give.[45]

What made religion easy was that it was rational – the prelate might have pipped Locke to the catch phrase 'the reasonableness of Christianity'. In Tillotson's appeal to common sense, the mysteries of faith, so attractive to earlier pious men like Sir Thomas Browne, were superseded. 'The laws of God are reasonable, that is, suitable to our nature and advantageous to our interest,' the Latitudinarian glossed the reassuring text, 'His Commandments are not Grievous', in what proved the most popular sermon of the century to come.[46]

Tillotson thus fused Pelagianism and benevolence in a creed which, he trusted, all Englishmen would feel able to endorse. After all, was not Jesus a consummate gentleman? 'The Virtues of his Life are pure, without any Mixture of Infirmity and Imperfection testimonial of good character', began his character reference for the Messiah.

He had Humility without Meanness of Spirit; Innocency without Weakness; Wisdom without Cunning; and Constancy and Resolution in that which was good, without Stiffness or Conceit, and Peremptoriness of Humour: In a word, his Virtues were shining without Vanity, Heroical without anything of Transport, and very extraordinary without being in the least extravagant.[47]

Warning his flock not to be 'righteous overmuch' – far too dangerously 'enthusiastic'! – Tillotson gallantly rescued Jesus from any aspersions of fanaticism.

The Archbishop's middle-of-the-roadism struck a chord with enlightened élites in a controversy-weary age. But his rationalist distaste for Catholicism unwittingly gave a hostage to fortune, since his arguments against Papism could easily be used against Anglicanism itself. Tillotson rejected transubstantiation on the grounds that it contravened the testimony of the senses; half a century later David

Hume effortlessly extended this very appeal to the senses to miracles at large.[48]

While many enlisted reason in the cause of Christianity, the turn of the century divine who strove hardest to prove that Christianity was not merely reasonable but demonstrable by reasoning was Samuel Clarke. Cambridge-educated, he first attracted attention by defending the proposition that 'no article of the Christian faith is opposed to reason'.[49] Later, in his Boyle Lectures of 1704 (see chapter 6) Clarke sought to prove the existence, omnipresence, omnipotence, omniscience, infinite wisdom and beneficence of the Creator, precisely as in a proof in Euclidian geometry. It was a contradiction in terms, for example, to suppose that there could have been an infinite succession of dependent beings going back through all eternity. There must, therefore, be an eternal Being, whose non-existence would constitute a nonsense. *Pace* Spinoza, the universe could not be this necessary Being, for matter could be destroyed without contradiction.

Man's duties were clear, Clarke insisted, thanks to the universality and immutability of the laws of nature. Like mathematics, moral laws were founded upon 'the eternal and necessary differences of things'. To deny the compelling nature of such laws was as absurd as to say that 'a square is not double to a triangle of equal base and height'.[50] Proving God against atheists by such philosophical subtleties left him open, however, to Anthony Collins's gibe that no one doubted His existence until Clarke tried to prove it.[51]

Furthermore, verifying Christianity by logic alone failed to resolve doctrinal disputes. Having sifted no fewer than 1,251 New Testament texts, Clarke was forced to concede in his *Scripture-doctrine of the Trinity* (1712) that the Bible supported neither the Athanasian (Trinitarian) nor the Arian (Unitarian) position. The conclusion that the Trinity was a subject upon which a Christian might incline either way may have contented Clarke, but it raised suspicions of heterodoxy – and allegedly cost this doyen of learning a bishopric.[52]

Clarke's confidence that Christianity was confirmed by cosmic order as revealed by the new philosophy became standard to the new natural theology dear to Latitudinarian hearts. In his *Physico-Theology* (1713), the Revd William Derham, himself a fellow of the Royal Society, thus concluded his survey of Creation: 'the works of God are so visible to all the world . . . that they plainly argue the vileness and perverseness of the atheist'.[53] He gloried in a designer universe presided over by a humane Creator, rather as in Joseph Addison's rhyming of Psalm XIX:

> The unwearied Sun from day to day
> Does his Creator's power display;
> And publishes to every land
> The work of an Almighty hand.[54]

The terraqueous globe was made for man who, guided by the laws of God and Nature, was to lead a virtuous, industrious and happy life. Whereas dons and divines had previously sought out demons, ghosts and wonders as ammunition against atheism, Latitudinarians saluted universal order, explained by Newtonian laws, as the surer proof of the Almighty hand; Satan's evil empire and all such talk was reduced to a bugaboo. Rational religion discredited – indeed, voiced positive disgust for – the Calvinist Lord of Vengeance, baroque demonology and all its attendant theological wranglings (just how many of the damned would the bottomless pit house?). It began to dismiss fire and brimstone eschatology as the prattle of deluded Dissenters or mad Methodists, even if the zealots' fixation with portents and prophesyings might serve as a salutary reminder of the grotesque pandemonium of the Interregnum.

'Religious toleration is the greatest of all evils,' judged Thomas Edwards in 1646; 'it will bring in first scepticism in doctrine and looseness of life, then atheism.'[55] Once so orthodox, such views seemed increasingly insupportable. The new temper carried a key implication. If religion was rational and basic truths plain, what justification could there be for compulsion?[56] Pragmatic consider-ations were in any case pointing the other way. Persecution had actually bred heresy, and did not the multiplication of sects and the divisions of the Christians palpably discredit any confession's claim to be God's chosen?

Locke became the high priest of toleration, his thinking feeding off his anti-innatist epistemology. In an essay of 1667, which spelt out the key principles expressed in his later *Letters on Toleration*, Locke denied the prince's right to enforce religious orthodoxy, reasoning that the 'trust, power and authority' of the civil magistrate were vested in him solely to secure 'the good, preservation and peace of men in that society'. Hence princely powers extended solely to externals, not to faith, which was a matter of conscience. Any state intervention in faith was 'meddling'.[57]

To elucidate the limits of those civil powers, Locke divided religious opinions and actions into three. First, there were speculative views and modes of divine worship. These had 'an absolute and universal right to toleration', since they did not affect society, being either private or God's business alone. Second, there were those – beliefs about marriage and divorce, for instance – which impinged upon others and hence were of public concern. These 'have a title also to toleration, but only so far as they do not tend to the disturbance of the State'. The magistrate might thus prohibit publication of such convictions if they would disturb the public good, but no one ought to be forced to forswear his opinion, for coercion bred hypocrisy. Third, there were actions good or bad in themselves. Respecting these, Locke held that civil rulers should have 'nothing to do with the good of men's soul or their concernments in another life' – it was for God to reward virtue and punish vice, and the magistrate's job simply to keep the peace. Applying such principles to contemporary realities, Locke advocated toleration, but with limits: Papists should not be tolerated, because their beliefs were 'absolutely destructive of all governments except the Pope's'; nor should atheists, since any oaths they took would be in bad faith.

As a radical Whig in political exile in the Dutch republic, Locke wrote the first *Letter on Toleration*, which was published, initially in Latin, in 1689. Echoing the 1667 arguments, this denied that Christianity could be furthered by force. Christ was the Prince of

Peace; his gospel was love, his means persuasion; persecution could not save souls. Civil and ecclesiastical government had contrary ends; the magistrate's business lay in securing life, liberty and possessions, whereas faith was about the salvation of souls. A church should be a voluntary society, like a 'club for claret'; it should be shorn of all sacerdotal pretensions. While Locke's views were contested – Bishop Stillingfleet, for example, deemed them a 'Trojan Horse'[58] – they nevertheless won favour in an age inclined, or resigned, to freedom of thought and expression in general.

Like Locke, the so-called Toleration Act of 1689 had an eye first and foremost to practical politics, and did not grant full toleration. Officially an 'Act for Exempting their Majesties' Protestant Subjects, Dissenting from the Church of England, from the Penalties of Certain Laws', it stated that Trinitarian Protestant Nonconformists who swore the oaths of Supremacy and Allegiance and accepted thirty-six of the Thirty-nine Articles could obtain licences as ministers or teachers.[59] Catholics and non-Christians did not enjoy rights of public worship under the Act – and non-Trinitarians were left subject to the old penal laws. Unitarians, indeed, were further singled out by the Blasphemy Act of 1697, which made it an offence to 'deny any one of the persons in the holy Trinity to be God'. There was no official Toleration Act for them until 1813, and in Scotland the death penalty could still be imposed – as it was in 1697 – for denying the Trinity.[60]

Scope for prosecution remained. Ecclesiastical courts still had the power of imprisoning for atheism, blasphemy and heresy (maximum term: six months). Occasional indictments continued under the common law, and Parliament could order books to be burned. Even so, patriots justly proclaimed that England was, alongside the United Provinces, the first nation to have embraced religious toleration – a fact that became a matter of national pride. 'My island was now peopled, and I thought myself very rich in subjects; and it was a merry reflection which I frequently made, how like a king I looked,' remarked Defoe's castaway hero, Robinson Crusoe; 'we had but three subjects, and they were of different religions. My man Friday was a pagan and a cannibal, and the Spaniard was a Papist: however, I allowed liberty of conscience throughout my dominions.'[61]

Two developments made toleration a *fait accompli*: the lapse of the Licensing Act in 1695, and the fact that England had already been sliced up into sects. It was, quipped Voltaire, a nation of many faiths but only one sauce, a recipe for confessional tranquillity if culinary tedium: 'If there were only one religion in England, there would be danger of despotism, if there were only two they would cut each other's throats; but there are thirty, and they live in peace.'[62] No longer could faith be expected to unify the kingdom. 'The heretical sects in this country are so numerous,' commented Robert Southey, ventriloquizing his visiting Spaniard,

that an explanatory dictionary of their names has been published. They form a curious list! Arminians, Socinians, Baxterians, Presbyterians, New Americans, Sabellians, Lutherans, Moravians, Swedenborgians, Athanasians, Episcopalians, Arians, Sublapsarians, Supralapsarians, Antinomians, Hutchinsonians, Sandemanians, Muggletonians, Baptists, Anabaptists, Paedobaptists, Methodists, Papists, Universalists, Calvinists, Materialists, Destructionists, Brownists, Independants, Protestants, Huguenots, Nonjurors, Seceders, Hernhutters, Dunkers, Jumpers, Shakers, and Quakers, &c. &c. &c. A precious nomenclature![63]

Heterogeneity fostered a climate in which religion was up for questioning – a fact recognized with evident exasperation by one author writing in 1731: 'I shall examine no further than is absolutely necessary whether God is Spirit or Matter, or Both, or Neither, or Whether the World is eternal or not.'[64]

Among the many burning debates, a major one concerned the nature and destiny of the soul. For Locke, the reality of the spiritual was, *pace* Hobbes, plain: 'For, whilst I know by seeing, or hearing, etc., that there is some corporeal being without me, the object of that sensation, I can more certainly know that there is some spiritual being within me that sees and hears.'[65] Though its 'substance' was unknown, it was no harder to accept spirit than matter, for 'the motion of body [itself] is cumbered with some difficulties, very hard and perhaps impossible to be explained or understood by us'.[66] Locke thus validated the soul and reassured critics that 'the resurrection of the dead' was for him 'an article of the Christian Faith'.[67] The crux of his polemic on this matter with Edward Stillingfleet, bishop of Worcester, lay rather in his denial that what was requisite for a heavenly transition was the resurrection of the *same* body. Did not the flesh change over time?

your lordship will easily see, that the body he had, when an embryo in the womb, when a child playing in coats, when a man marrying a wife, and when bed-rid, dying of a consumption, and at last, which he shall have after his resurrection; are each of them his body, though neither of them be the same body, the one with the other.[68]

The important point, held Locke, was that, when the dead arose at the last trump, the *person* would be judged. While necessary in this mortal life, the body was incidental. For enlightened thinkers like Locke, the quintessence of the person was the mind; for a prelate, by contrast, concerned with the meting out of eternal rewards and punishments, the flesh could not be omitted from the equation. Stillingfleet spied in Locke's elevation of 'ideas' over 'substance' the slippery slope to scepticism; he was not alone.

Likewise, while Locke endorsed the resurrection of the dead, he did not hold that personal immortality hinged upon the soul's *immateriality*. It had been an orthodox Christian–Platonist belief, lately bolstered by Cartesianism, that consciousness entailed immateriality. For Locke, however, it was not for man to dogmatize: Why might not the Maker endow suitably complex matter with the property of thinking? He reassured those fearful that linking thought to matter was tantamount to denying the soul that immortality itself would not thereby be imperilled: whether the soul be immaterial or not did not affect the likelihood of resurrection.[69]

Another controversy which embroiled Locke, and later grew more intense, centred on Arianism, that is, denial of Christ's divinity. Perhaps because he studiously held his tongue on the Trinity, Locke was accused of supporting heresy, for instance by John Edwards in

Socinianism Unmasked (1696),[70] and thereafter it proved easy for Arians, insistent that neither reason nor the Bible gave any support to Trinitarianism, to imply that they had the great philosopher's endorsement[71] – indeed, some historians hold that Locke's deepest impact on enlightened thought lay in the encouragement his silence tacitly gave to Socinianism.[72] It certainly became a common accusation against Latitudinarians that they were crypto-Arians, or worse – Tillotson being thus accused of a Hobbism which reduced 'God to matter and religion to nature': 'His politics are Leviathan, and his religion is latitudinarian . . . He is owned by the atheistical wits of all England as their true primate and apostle.'[73] The free inquiry which toleration permitted – that is, allowing people to differ – inexorably spelt the spread of heterodoxy.

Toleration thus finally drew the persecutor's fangs. Locke had taught that the only safe church was a voluntary society denied the power of the sword; for the enlightened, this disarming of the priesthood was a decisive step towards exposing religion, like everything else, to the rays of reason and the salutary power of criticism.

Conflicts over toleration and points of doctrine were inflamed and sustained by an anti-clericalism bent upon clipping the wings of sacerdotalism. From the 1660s, Locke himself was chiding the 'crafty men' who had fuelled the Civil War with 'coals from the altar', and the 'sharp-sighted' Popish mystagogues sworn to ruling consciences.[74] 'Priestcraft' was a term coined at the time of the Exclusion Crisis:

> In pious times, e'r priestcraft did begin,
> Before polygamy was made a sin.[75]

opened John Dryden's *Absolom and Achitophel* (1681). John Toland then made that slight his trademark, seeing priestcraft as a plot in which 'the bulk of mankind, are retain'd in their Mistakes by their Priests', and greeting the new century with a pointed epigram:

> Religion's safe, with priestcraft is the war,
> All friends to priestcraft, foes of mankind are.[76]

Anti-clericalism was also the stalking horse of such 'True Whigs' as Anthony Collins, Robert Molesworth, Walter Moyle, Henry Neville, James Tyrrell and other members of the 'Grecian Tavern set', committed to crushing 'monkish' tyranny.[77] Further whipped up by John Trenchard's and Thomas Gordon's *The Independent Whig* (1720–21) (see chapter 8), clergy-bashing culminated in Richard Baron's compilation *The Pillars of Priestcraft and Orthodoxy Shaken* (1768). Quoting the *philosophes* alongside the English Deists and dictating 'everlasting reasons for opposing all priests', Baron pledged to 'emancipate the minds of men, and to free them from those chains in which they have been long held to the great disgrace both of reason and Christianity'.[78] Such calumnies made the bellicose Bishop Warburton apoplectic: how dare scurrilous free-thinkers picture the clergy as 'debauched, avaricious, proud, vindictive, ambitious, deceitful, irreligious and incorrigible'?[79]

While the anti-clerical tempest eventually abated, partly because ecclesiastics actually became less visible and vocal as pillars of power, clergy-baiting remained a trump card in enlightened rhetoric. Tom Paine lambasted priestcraft, alias persecution; 'Mr Malthus,' remarked the inveterate Jeremy Bentham, 'belongs to that profession to which acknowledgement of error is rendered impossible',[80] while his disciples, Francis Place and James Mill, proved feisty priest-haters.[81] 'Tyranny & cruelty,' the peasant poet John Clare confided to his journal in 1824, 'appear to be the inseparable companions of Religious Power & the aphorism is not far from truth that says: "All priests are the same."'[82] Religion was evidently too important to entrust to the clergy.

Shielded by state toleration and with anti-clerical animosity rife, controversy raged as to what sort of religion modern man should espouse. Precisely which beliefs actually commanded sober assent? For Locke, as we have seen, Christianity, rightly understood, was rational. Others, self-styled or so-called Deists, granted that reason lighted the way to a knowledge of a Supreme Being and of man's duties – atheism was as blind as superstition – but further held that Christianity either added nothing at all to 'natural religion' or contained foolish and false elements, and hence must be purged, reinterpreted or rejected.

Deists came in many colours. A *soi-disant* 'Christian Deist' and supporter of Locke's anti-innatism was the All Souls fellow William Wollaston, whose *Religion of Nature Delineated* (1724) sold an impressive 10,000 copies.[83] Rather like Samuel Clarke, Wollaston held that religious truths were as plain as Euclid, clear to all who contemplated Creation. So why was there Revelation at all? It was all a 'belt and braces' operation, obligingly provided by the Deity for the unthinking vulgar, who were no better at religion than at geometry. 'Double Truth' theories of this kind were the Deists' stock in trade.

A fellow All Souls champion of civil theology was Matthew Tindal, who opened his career by taking potshots at High-flyers.[84] His later *Christianity as Old as the Creation, or the Gospel a Republication of the Religion of Nature* (1730) – it became the 'Deists' Bible' – asserted that 'God, at all times, has given mankind sufficient means of knowing whatever he requires of them'. Those 'means' lay in rationality.[85] Whereas reason was timeless and ubiquitous, the Bible had been but a late and local edition of truth – no one, surely, could think God would first have revealed His laws in that way?[86]

Can it be supposed an infinitely good and gracious Being, which gives men notice, by their senses, what does good or hurt to their bodies, has had less regard for their immortal parts, and has not given them at all times, by the light of their understanding, sufficient means to discover what makes for the good of their souls?[87]

To deny salvation to those denied the Bible would make God odious. Tindal instead commended a creed based exclusively on the Creation, that is, on universal reason; for 'God's will is so clearly and fully manifested in the Book of Nature, that he who runs may read it'.[88]

Like most Deists, Tindal assumed an original monotheism, a belief in the one true God, a pure and pristine natural religion revealed by the light of reason.[89] How, then, had this clear and simple truth been perverted? It was all the clergy's fault:

the pride, ambition, and covetousness of the priests . . . has been the cause
. . . of the great corruption of religion.[90]

Nor was the damage produced by the priestly lickspittles of civil
despots confined to Catholics:

Nay, have not the Protestant clergy been every jot as much, if not more
zealous and industrious than the Popish, to enslave the people, and promote
arbitrary power.[91]

Denounced by his own college chaplain as 'Spinoza revived',[92]
Tindal plied other Deist lines. He mocked those who unthinkingly
or disingenuously took Scripture as the truth merely because the
Bible said so – a circular argument. 'It's an odd jumble,' he bantered,
'to prove the truth of a book by the truth of the doctrines it contains,
and at the same time conclude those doctrines to be true because
contained in that book.'[93] He also picked at Scripture's loose threads.
The only way to uphold its supposed infallibility, he declared, was,
upon stumbling across contradictions, to twist and torture the meaning; for instance, confronted by glaring inconsistencies, apologists
had often contended that God must have been talking down to the
ignorant Jews. Tindal, however, would have none of these evasions,
venturing instead some biblical criticism of his own.

There were, of course, entrenched canons of scriptural interpretation, deriving from Renaissance philology: the erudition of Scaliger,
Heinsius, Grotius, Casaubon and many other scholars was justly
acclaimed,[94] and giant strides were being made in textual criticism
by the French Catholic Richard Simon. Stimulated in part by Pierre
Bayle, however, heterodox views now issued from the English Deists,
determined to expose those 'absurdities' planted by crafty priests.

Read with candour, Tindal claimed, many theological doctrines
and biblical stories were silly, and cast the Creator in bad odour.
The doctrine of exclusive salvation was monstrous: how could Jesus
be the saviour of mankind, if virtuous pagans predeceasing him
would find Heaven's gate bolted? And what of the contradictions
between the universal goodness of the Divine Essence as revealed by

the light of Nature, and Jehovah's often contemptible behaviour as recorded in the Scriptures, where, for example, natural order was violated to punish men for crimes they had not committed, as when Elijah caused three and a half years of drought? If God had in bygone days breached the laws of Nature to scourge the innocent, who could be sure He would not stoop so low again? Old Testament justice was bizarre indeed. How weird to find Elisha calling down the wrath of the Lord upon children for calling him bald! Exposed thus to the glare of reason, the Scriptures, especially the Old Testament, began to seem like a patchwork of problems.

One solution was urged by Thomas Woolston, a fellow of Sidney Sussex College, Cambridge, whose thinking owed much to Anthony Collins.[95] His *Six Discourses* (1727–30) observed that, taken literally, much of the Bible defied plain common sense or was quite unedifying – the lewd and cruel acts of King David, the impostures of that renegade Pharisee Paul, and the absurd tale of Balaam's ass. In cursing somebody's fig tree just to make a point, Jesus had violated the sanctity of private property (that is, had behaved as badly as a Stuart). How could evil spirits have been driven into the Gadarene swine? – everyone knew the Jews did not keep pigs. Nor could Jesus really have seen – at least, not without a miraculous telescope – all the kingdoms of the world from any conceivable mountain. Such narratives were plainly inane or impious.

Healing miracles also posed a problem. Since it was unclear exactly which diseases Jesus had healed, how could it be affirmed that his cures were supernatural? 'Faith and imagination' were probably involved. In some – such as curing blindness with spittle – there was clearly no miracle: 'our *Surgeons*, with their Ointments and Washings' could achieve as much. Other, more dramatic, miracles Woolston simply denied: the raising of Lazarus was all 'Fable and Forgery'. In his final discourse, he tackled the Resurrection, recycling the old argument that Christ's body had disappeared because zealots had absconded with it.[96]

None of that mattered, however, because, following Origen, Woolston ruled that the biblical narratives were intended to be read not literally but rather spiritually: thus, the ass on which Christ had ridden into Jerusalem actually meant the Church. It is hard to tell whether he was sincere in such allegorizing (or rationalizing) or simply sending up the earnest scriptural literalism of an age which set inordinate store by 'matter of fact', 'evidences', 'testimonies' and 'eye witness'.[97] Opprobrium and legal penalties were heaped on Woolston's head, but what impressed Voltaire, at least, most were the huge sales his works enjoyed.

Criticism was thus being levelled against religious hokum among others by respectable men of the cloth salaried by venerable institutions. Deism's support was wider, however: lawyers, country gentlemen and doctors aplenty cracked anti-clerical jokes, snickered at superstition and engaged in raillery and even sacrilege, as with Francis Dashwood's Hellfire Club with its satanic rites. Deism even had its petty bourgeois pundits in the provinces. A candlemaker by trade – how apt! – Thomas Chubb of Salisbury made it his business, in the name of purification, to pit true religion against the 'corrupt doctrines' of Christianity: the immaculate conception, the Trinity, the atonement and the plenary inspiration of Scripture.[98] Junking such theological trash, Chubb defended rationality, praised benevolence as 'a part of the human constitution',[99] 'vindicated' human nature and backed Locke on the eternal validity of natural law. While taking the philosopher to task on points of detail – the fiction of the state of nature was a feeble footing for man's rights to 'life, liberty, and estate' – he nevertheless fully endorsed Locke's championing of liberty of thought, that essential human attribute. 'It hath pleased God to make man a free, accountable creature,' he declared, 'by planting in him an understanding . . . in the use of which he is capable of . . . judging . . . of the truth or falseness of things.'[100] Prizing freedom, Chubb dismissed original sin, predestination and special providence as equally pernicious, since all taught a cruel fatality in which men's 'actions are not . . . their own free choice'. While religion was ennobling, ritual was demeaning, and reason alone would dispel the dross and teach a virtuous life under God.

*

In their different ways, figures like Wollaston and Chubb candidly meant to rescue religion from graceless zealots. Other critics of sacerdotal rigmaroles – Woolston was one – seem more devious. And if his game is hard to guess, what are we to make of that most corrosive critic of the churches, John Toland?[101]

Born in Ireland in 1671 of Catholic parents – his father, it seems, was a priest – Toland converted to Protestantism in his youth. Sent to school by some 'eminent dissenters', he attended the university of Leiden, where he became familiar with Locke. He then went on to lead a bohemian life as a scholar, being protected at various times by Whigs and Deists like the 3rd Earl of Shaftesbury – but also by the Tory Lord Harley. A wily controversialist, Toland loved stealing the clothes off the backs of such respectable figures as Tillotson and Locke, playing authority off against authority and covering his tracks with tongue-in-cheek disavowals. He seems to have stated his fundamental tenet, however, in his early masterpiece, *Christianity Not Mysterious* (1696) : 'reason is the only foundation of all certitude . . . there is nothing in the Gospel contrary to reason nor above it.'[102] As he outlined his approach, he sowed, as ever, doubts in the process: 'I prove first, that the true religion must necessarily be reasonable and intelligible. Next I show that these requisite conditions are found in Christianity.'[103] In Christianity indeed, but not as the churches had ever interpreted it!

Toland held, probably disingenuously, that true Christianity's superiority lay in making plain what was mysterious in other faiths. A return was needed to primitive simplicity, discarding the Trinity and other such mumbo-jumbo. Holding that 'the Doctrines of the Gospel are not contrary to *Reason*', he deemed that the belief that religion contains mysteries

is the undoubted Source of all the *Absurdities* that ever were seriously vented among *Christians*. Without the Pretence of it, we should never hear of the *Transubstantiation*, and other ridiculous Fables of the Church of *Rome*; nor of any of the *Eastern Ordures*, almost all receiv'd into this *Western Sink*.[104]

From such assertions the reader may infer that received faith was mostly bad faith.

Christianity Not Mysterious created a great furore, being presented by the Grand Jury of Middlesex and ordered to be burnt by the Irish Parliament. Though Locke was not mentioned by name, contemporaries anxiously sensed in Toland's work Locke's teachings being drawn out to their logical conclusions. Prizing reason as the foundation of all certitude, like Locke, Toland held that reason alone could determine what was revealed, for in His wisdom God had made everything, Revelation included, answerable to it.[105] But there agreement ended. Whereas Locke believed Christianity passed the reason test, Toland demanded that anything mysterious about Christianity must be discarded. While seemingly endorsing Locke's philosophy of truth, *Christianity Not Mysterious* thus proposed a significantly different tie between reason and revelation. Locke had maintained that whatever was delivered in an authenticated revelation must be accepted; Toland, by contrast, held that each particular of Scripture must be judged according to its conformity to 'common Notions': nothing that was 'above reason' passed muster. His requirement that religion be mystery-free thus threatened the status of the Bible as revealed truth.

In all this, Toland was also trading in typical Deist fashion on distinctions between the credulous herd and 'the rational and thinking part', who could discover for themselves plain truths about God. To the wise, the 'marvels' of Scripture were all susceptible to down-to-earth explanations – the pillar of cloud and fire, for instance, was no miracle at all, but simply a signal contained in an iron pot hoisted on top of a pole.[106] 'We shall be in Safety,' advised his *Pantheisticon* (1720), 'if we separate ourselves from the Multitude; for the Multitude is a Proof of what is worst'[107] – at best children to be humoured, at worst credulous fools, colluding with those sinister mystery-mongers who, from cradle to grave, had reduced life itself to lies:

We no sooner see the Light, but the grand Cheat begins to delude us from every Quarter. The very Midwife hands us into the World with superstitious Ceremonys, and the good women assisting at the Labour have a thousand

Spells to avert the Misfortune, or to produce the Happiness of the Infant; making several ridiculous Observations, to discover the Omen of his future State of Life. Nor is the Priest in some places behindhand with these Gossips, to initiate him betimes into his Service, by pronouncing certain Forms of Words as so many powerful Charms.[108]

Reason alone could deliver man from his spellbound condition and restore the true, simple, natural religion of the 'antient Egyptians, Persians, and Romans' who had 'no sacred Images or Statues, no peculiar Places or costly Fashions of Worship', but simply worshipped God and pursued virtue.[109]

If Toland was the most insidious of the Deists, the one packing the most powerful punch was Anthony Collins.[110] His line was simplicity itself: 'As it is every Man's natural right and duty to think, and judge for himself in matters of opinion; so he should be allow'd freely to profess his opinions.' There was one proviso made by this Cambridge-educated gentleman lawyer, living on his Essex estate: that 'those opinions do not tend to the disturbance of society'.[111]

Collins was a personal friend of Locke's.[112] In a long letter to the elderly philosopher he attacked John Norris's *An Essay towards the Theory of the Ideal or Intelligible World* (1701–4) for its Platonism, derided syllogistic logic, denied Descartes' belief that animals lacked consciousness and defended the possibility of thinking matter. Unsurprisingly, Locke was delighted by this swingeing attack on his critics and endorsement of his *Essay*.[113]

Like Toland, Collins loved pitting orthodoxy against orthodoxy and mischievously recruited Tillotson to his cause, taking up arms against Samuel Clarke in defence of Locke on the soul.[114] His *Priestcraft in Perfection* (1709) denied the Church's right to dictate ceremonies, and anti-clericalism crackles in his writings – the 'laity are the calves and sheep of the priests'.[115] Collins's clergy-baiting continued with his notorious *Discourse of Free-thinking* (1713),[116] a devastating exposition of the 'vile arts' and feuds among the divines, coupled with a defence of reason against authority which deified Socrates as a 'very great freethinker'.[117]

A pointer for later Deism lay in Collins's attack on the credit of Scripture. Drawing on Le Clerc, Simon and other modern Bible scholars, his *Discourse of the Grounds and Reasons of the Christian Religion* (1724) exposed the shakiness of the old proof of divine inspiration from the fulfilment of prophecy, demonstrating that it all hung – or rather fell – on forced readings. In his attempt to prove the literal realization of prophecies, the Cambridge theologian William Whiston had had to top and tail them in a quite arbitrary and ludicrous manner![118] Soon prophecy would prove rational Christianity's Achilles' heel.

Deists professed to be purifying the faith. The more radical among them, however, did not merely challenge the abuses of the churches and the theologians' fibs; they developed historical, psychological and political critiques of received religion as such, if often masking their attacks through assaults on pagan absurdities, Catholic frauds or Anglican errors. Religion *per se* was pure, honouring God and teaching virtue; why then had it always gone bad?

In England this radical critique, initiated by Hobbes (see chapter 3),[119] was extended by Charles Blount, an enigmatic figure whose prose proceeded by disclaimer and denial. His *Great is Diana of the Ephesians*, subtitled *On the Original of Idolatry* (1680), was typical of the Deist 'parallel theology' strategy: exposure of the absurdities of heathen fables invited the *cognoscenti* to read the nonsense of Christianity between the lines. How, for example, could the story of the Fall, with its talking snake, etc., be taken literally?[120] Blount provoked fierce responses, notably Charles Leslie's *Short and Easy Method with the Deists* (1698), which vindicated the Bible as pure matter of fact.[121]

By the 1710s, a more devastating critique was gaining ground, a critique of historical religion itself, seen through the lenses of power politics and psychopathology. Natural religion, the argument ran, had originally embraced monotheism, though that had to be encoded in secret hieroglyphic and symbolic languages so as to protect it from the vulgar.[122] That original purity had been squandered, however, and religion had become polarized in every society, with a pure version for the élite and a debased one for *hoi polloi*. How so? In framing their explanations, the English Deists drew on an armoury of resources: Bayle's *exposés* of priestly imposture; Dutchman Balthasar Bekker's *De Betoverde Weereld* (1691–3), translated into English in 1695 as *The World Bewitch'd* (a book which in effect denied the reality of the Devil); Bernard Fontenelle's exposure of oracles; and assorted medical pathologies of demoniacs.[123]

Religion came in two sorts, held John Trenchard in his *Natural History of Superstition* (1709): true and false. Belief in a benevolent Creator and in the gospel of love was the marrow of truth. All other manifestations were false, and it was upon these that his investigation of the blight of superstition focused, surveying cults and creeds worldwide and through time. Long before Hume and the *philosophes*, Trenchard posed the key questions of religious psychology. Why were people so superstitious? Why did they cook up bizarre cults and perform unnatural acts in God's name? How could they be duped by priestly machinations? What led *soi-disant* prophets to credit their own hallucinations and others to believe them?

Seeking the 'causes of our Passions and Infirmities', Trenchard located in human nature the reasons why the mind, for all its glories, had been betrayed into superstition.[124] There was 'something innate in our Constitutions' – a psycho-physiological analogue of original sin – which bred susceptibility to delusions. Man sought to avoid pain. Obsessed with death and hence with fears of pain and punishment in a hereafter, he felt driven to identify potential persecutors.[125] But the causes of things were hidden and, in his anxieties, he embraced either flights of fancy or the tales of seers in inventing pagan gods and all the accompanying baggage of divination, catalogued by Trenchard in a passage adapted from Bekker:

To these Weaknesses and our own, and Frauds of others, we owe the Heathen Gods and Goddesses, Oracles and Prophets, Nimphs and Satyrs, Fawns and Tritons, Furies and Demons, most of the Stories of Conjurers and Witches, Spirits and Apparitions, Fairies and Hobgoblins, the Doctrine

of Prognosticks, the numerous ways of Divination, viz. Oniromancy, Sidero-
mancy, Tephranomancy, Botonomancy, Crommyomancy, Cleromancy,
Aeromancy, Onomatomancy, Arithomancy, Geomancy, Alectryomancy,
Cephalomancy, Axinomancy, Coscinomancy, Hydromancy, Onycho-
mancy, Dactylomancy, Christallomancy, Cataptromancy, Gastromancy,
Lecanomancy, Alphitomancy, Chiromancy, Orneomancy, and Necro-
mancy, Horoscopy, Astrology and Augury, Metoposcopy and Palmistry,
the fear of Eclipses, Comets, Meteors, Earthquakes, Inundations, and any
uncommon Appearances and so forth.[126]

Abandoning themselves to exalted rituals, primitive people 'saw'
visions and experienced the supernatural. Lifting from Bayle a
hypothesis to explain such 'tripping', Trenchard posited that
bodily stimuli produced phantom images which then failed to be
falsified by facts 'when the Organs of Sense . . . are shut and locked
up' – which might occur during sleep, in delirium, madness, sickness
or shock, cases when the internal phantoms 'reign without any
Rival'.[127]

This appropriation of Locke's empiricist epistemology explained
how 'inner light' visionaries became cut off from the outward senses,
the only true 'conduits of knowledge'. Hallucinations thereby became
confused with reality, as the victims transmogrified their 'Clouds and
Foggs' into 'Deities', some seeing 'beatifick visions', others 'Divels
with instruments of Fear and Horrour' – a victim might think he was
a bottle, a corpse, a god, or who knows what. 'Many instances of this
kind', glossed Trenchard, are 'to be seen in Bedlam'.[128]

Drawing thus on the literature of lunacy, Trenchard reduced
religious visions to psycho-physiological stimuli. Fasting or flagella-
tion induced delirious psychic states, while those famed for abnormal
piety were invariably melancholic hermits, their revelations mere
symptoms of disease.[129] Initially spewed forth by a lone fanatic,
such phantasms might then spread rapidly in a religious epidemic
explained by the mechanical philosophy: 'Everything in Nature is in
constant Motion, and perpetually emitting Effluviums and minute
Particles of its Substance, which operate upon, and strike other

Bodies.'[130] Not witchcraft but medical science would thus account for children falling into fits in the presence of old hags and other supposed manifestations of the black art.

The 3rd Earl of Shaftesbury advanced similar views, extolling, in his *Soliloquy* (1710), 'study of Human Affection' (we would call it psychology) as the demarcator of true from false faith: 'By this Science Religion itself is judged, Spirits are search'd, Prophecys prov'd, Miracles distinguish'd.'[131] Sickened by the slavish religio-politics of High-flyers and Non-jurors, the Whig aristocrat proceeded to psychologize religious transports in his influential *Letter concerning Enthusiasm* (1711). Having watched the antics of the Pentecostal 'French prophets' speaking in tongues in London, Shaftesbury, like Trenchard, ridiculed enthusiasts of all stripes – Catholics, Jews, Puritans, Huguenots, persecutors and inquisitors.[132] Men had projected their bile on to their gods: 'For then it is we see wrath, and fury, and revenge, and terrors in the Deity: when we are full of disturbances and fears within.'[133] His accounts of sacred contagion matched Trenchard's: 'The fury flies from face to face; and the disease is no sooner seen than caught. And thus is Religion also Pannick.'[134] But while the splenetic fantasized savage and jealous deities, the great-souled man would never attribute vengefulness to his Maker. And so Deists like Shaftesbury, for whom Christianity was properly a religion of humanity, looked to psychopathology to explain the grotesque eruptions of apocalyptic mayhem, hellfire and damnation which had disgraced the faith.

Deism thus cross-examined religion naturalistically, socially and psychologically. Unlike the noble creed of the wise, what had prevailed in the churches were the wild-eyed terrors of the stupid, stoked and exploited by cynical priests. It fell to David Hume to complete the enlightened psychopathologization of religion.

Espousing the Royal Society's Baconian motto *'nullius in verba'*, enlightened minds put their money on matters of fact, rules of evidence and scientific method. Rational Protestants like Locke reasoned that Christianity deserved credence precisely because the

Bible narratives constituted authenticated historical truth, while scriptural scholars amassed testimonies of miracles and evidence for the fulfilment of prophecy. Biblical authority thus hinged not on blind faith but hard evidence, substantiated, like verified history at large, by dependable eyewitness accounts.

Collins's *Discourse of the Grounds and Reasons of the Christian Religion* and similar works started chipping away at the credibility of prophecies and miracles. The sceptic's task was made easier, since Protestant polemics had already tactically narrowed the pool of miracles: those performed by Christ and the Apostles were valid, whereas subsequent ones were scorned as mere Popish impostures or popular marvels for which the data were faked or flimsy. The 'age of miracles' had long since ceased: once the Gospel had been preached, why should God need further recourse to marvellous means?

The disputability of the distinction between miracles for which the evidence was copper-bottomed and those for which it was flimsy begged questions from principled critics and opportunist scoffers alike – and all the more so as 'miracles' were still happening in front of people's very eyes, even in urbane Cartesian Paris.

On 1 May 1727, François de Paris, a revered Jansenist deacon, had died and was buried in the parish cemetery of Saint-Médard. Mourners flocked to his grave and 'miraculous' healings of apparently incurable diseases – tumours, blindness, deafness – were posthumously wrought by this holy man. Was it not odd – unscientific, impious, even – for Protestants to deny so peremptorily 'miracles' like these, for which there seemed abundant contemporary testimony, while upholding those alleged to have occurred thousands of years earlier among the primitive Jews of Palestine?[135]

A major challenge to the convenient Protestant 'end of the age of miracles' formula came from Conyers Middleton, a fellow of Trinity College, Cambridge. A divine and classical scholar of sceptical temper, Middleton enjoyed likening Catholic ceremonies and superstitions to heathen polytheism: all that incense recalled Virgil's description of the temple of Venus, and worshippers still knelt before images in converted pagan temples whose demigods had been replaced by saints. Paganism, implied his *Letter from Rome* (1729), was thus a dress rehearsal for Catholicism.

Middleton then moved on to miracles. His *Free Enquiry into the Miraculous Powers Which are Supposed to Have Subsisted in the Christian Church from the Earliest Ages* (1749) was ostensibly intended to demonstrate biblical miracles and query post-biblical miracle claims, but its sly insinuation was that the selfsame criticisms could be levelled at the New Testament events themselves. It was, in effect, all or nothing: Protestants could not have their cake and eat it.[136]

Contemporaneously, David Hume – who felt scooped by Middleton on miracles[137] – was developing a radical critique of religion in all its manifestations. His early 'On Miracles' (1748) took Tillotson's anti-transubstantiation argument to its logical, though unintended, conclusion. Alleged miracles contradicted all sense experience of the uniformity of nature. The irresistible conclusion must be that witnesses to such 'miracles' were deceived – or deceivers – rather than that cosmic order had been breached.[138] 'There is not to be found, in all history,' he insisted,

any miracle attested by a sufficient number of men, of such unquestioned goodness, education and learning, as to secure us against all delusion in themselves; of such undoubted integrity as to place them beyond all suspicion of any design to deceive others; of such credit and reputation in the eyes of mankind as to have a great deal to lose in case of their being detected in any falsehood, and at the same time attesting facts, performed in such a public manner and in so celebrated a part of the world as to render the detection unavoidable. All which circumstances are requisite to give us a full assurance of the testimony of men![139]

Conclusive stuff; but the reader was then backhandedly invited to take this sceptical finale for a vindication of piety. Since 'our most holy religion is founded on Faith', and since no other made such a play of it, Christianity was evidently the cream of the crop: 'we may conclude that the Christian Religion not only was at first attended with miracles, but even at this day cannot be believed by any reasonable person without one'.[140]

In his 'Natural History of Religion' (1757), Hume trained his scepticism against the self-satisfied platitudes of the Deists, reasoning that their much-vaunted pristine monotheism or natural religion was but wish fulfilment. In reality, all religion had its origins in fear and ignorance, and the first faiths had been crude and polytheistic. Savages, after all, still were polytheistic, as were the masses (and, by implication, Roman Catholics, with their saint cults, and Trinitarians) in civilized nations. Polytheism, the first expression of the religious impulse, bred superstition, that opium of the people, and superstition spawned priests. Credited with supernatural powers, the magic man could placate the angry gods by sacrifices, incantations and rituals.[141]

In time, the progress of the mind drew monotheism out of polytheism, clarity out of confusion. Monotheism, however, in its turn bred enthusiasm, defined in Johnson's *Dictionary* as 'a vain belief of private revelation, a vain confidence of divine favour or communication'. In his exalted, self-deifying state, the enthusiast experienced transcendent raptures and soaring highs, credited to the presence of his god. 'Every whimsy is consecrated,' Hume stated, 'human reason, and even morality are rejected as fallacious guides: And the fanatic madman delivers himself over, blindly, and without reserve, to . . . inspiration from above.'[142] The zealot had little need for clerics, his was a priesthood of all believers – that was why enthusiasm was so politically explosive. As with the first Quakers, the enthusiast, under divine direction, became a social anarchist, a menace to law and order. The Puritans' success in the Civil War was due to enthusiasm: convinced theirs was a holy war, the saints never hesitated to attack Throne and Altar. Superstition, however, brought political perils of its own, for priests formed sinister interest groups, insinuating themselves into power or setting up as rival states within the state. Hume's strategic distinction between enthusiasm – fanatically intolerant but driving men to assert their liberties – and the superstition which made men law-abiding through cowed objection – was to prove highly influential, notably in Gibbon's *Decline and Fall*.[143]

Thus Hume sabotaged Christianity by advancing a naturalistic account of the religious impulse, while equally discrediting the Deist myth of prehistoric monotheism. So what was left of religion? 'The whole is a riddle, an enigma, an inexplicable mystery. Doubt, uncertainty, suspense of judgement, appear the only result of our most accurate scrutiny concerning this subject.'[144] Was, then, the nature of things utterly inscrutable? That was the question which underlay his *Dialogues concerning Natural Religion*, written around 1751 but published only after his death, in 1779. In that work, modelled on Cicero, philosophical inquiry further challenged the religious truth claims both of Christianity and of rationalism: there was no natural religion. Hume's unresolved three-way colloquy between the orthodox Demea, the rationalist believer Cleanthes and the sceptic Philo pointed to the conclusion that no religious hypothesis explained the order of Nature or the existence of evil. Attempts to deduce a just God or a meaning of life from the riddles of the universe were just a rope of sand:

While we argue from the course of nature and infer a particular intelligent cause which first bestowed and still preserves order in the universe, we embrace a principle which is still uncertain and useless. It is uncertain because the subject lies entirely beyond the reach of human experience. It is useless because . . . we can never on that basis establish any principles of conduct and behaviour.[145]

There was no convincing theodicy: the Deist or 'rational Christian' just God was at best a 'mere *possibility* and hypothesis'.

Hume's critique of the claim that a knowledge of God and His attributes could be derived from the facts hinged on the critique of causality in his *Treatise of Human Nature* and *Enquiry concerning Human Understanding* (see chapter 7 below). The concept of causation was doubtless the basis of all knowledge, but causality was not itself a demonstrable fact. Experience showed the succession of events, but did not reveal any necessity in that succession – it was habit which created the expectation that one event would invariably follow on from another. Custom was not knowledge, however, and did not strictly justify projections from the past to the future, from the known to the unknown. Causality was thus not a principle definitively derived from the order of things but a mental postulate. Belief in a rational order of Nature was only a premise, albeit one that was useful, even essential.[146]

Pitting believers against rationalists, the *Dialogues* found the case for religion, be it Christian or Deist, unproven – and atheism likewise: doubt was the only honest and honourable option. However, that did not mean that religion had no use at all. Hume perhaps sympathized with his character Cleanthes when he stated: 'The proper office of religion is to regulate the heart of men, humanize their conduct, infuse the spirit of temperance, order and obedience.'[147] To that, enlightened Christians and Deists alike could happily say amen.

In his dying days, Hume informed James Boswell that he had 'never entertained any belief in Religion since he began to read Locke and Clarke'.[148] Some years previously he had called religiosity nothing but 'sick men's dreams'.[149] And as early as 1742, he had detected a 'sudden and sensible change in the opinions of men within these last fifty years', thanks to the progress of learning and liberty:

Most people, in this island, have divested themselves of all superstitious reverence to names and authority: The clergy have much lost their credit: Their pretensions and doctrines have been ridiculed; and even religion can scarcely support itself in the world. The mere name of *king* commands little respect; and to talk of a king as God's vice-regent on earth, or to give him any of those magnificent titles, which formerly dazzled mankind, would be to excite laughter in every one.[150]

Le bon David was, of course, trailing his coat with a majestic flourish, but he was surely right to link a decline in faith to the enlightened assault on authority at large, a process to which he contributed handsomely.

Whilst Hume remained a sceptic – on a visit to Paris he claimed never to have been in the company of atheists – others, however, were to come out as open atheists, including the one-time Dissenting minister William Godwin, followed by his future son-in-law, Percy Bysshe Shelley, author of *The Necessity of Atheism* (1811).[151] Historically, this was a remarkable development. 'Atheist' had long been a term bandied about as an insult, but it was not until the eighteenth century that atheism was taken up as a principled rejection of religion as such, for being both incredible and immoral.

On the whole, however, English free-thinkers tended not to take their quarrel with orthodoxy to such extremes – perhaps because they were hardly made to suffer for their heterodoxy, or driven to court martyrdom. On failing to win a professorship, Hume could denounce 'the cabals of the Principal, the bigotry of the clergy, and the credulity of the mob',[153] and Gibbon for his part might bridle at British benightedness,[154] but infidelity did not stop the former from becoming librarian to the Edinburgh Faculty of Advocates or from holding diplomatic posts, just as the latter's impieties did not prevent him from becoming the age's most fêted historian.[155] Enlightened thinkers and a nation jealous to uphold freedoms and suspicious of clericalism generally rubbed along easily enough with each other in a climate in which religion was valued amongst the élite principally for teaching virtue and the rule of law.

Amid suspicions that Locke himself had been a closet Arian, Unitarianism in time proved a Trojan horse and the spur to radical politics and religion (see chapter 18).[156] Above all, the 'potent magic of religion' came under scrutiny[157] as mainstream observance became divested of supernatural and spiritual elements – hence the violent antipathy among rational Christians and Deists alike to John Wesley, who upheld the reality of witchcraft and Satan's power in the world: Methodism was 'wild and pernicious Enthusiasm', according to the bishop of Exeter.[158] Enlightened thought approved religion so long as its basis was rational rather than numinal. 'I hope no reader imagines me so weak to stand up in the defence of real Christianity, such as used, in primitive times (if we may believe the writers of those ages) to have an influence upon men's belief and actions,' ironized Swift on the obsolescence of old-time religion:

to offer at the restoring of that, would indeed be a wild project; it would be to dig up foundations: to destroy at one blow all the wit, and half the learning of the kingdom: to break the entire frame and constitution of things: to ruin trade, extinguish arts and sciences, with the professors of them; in short, to turn our courts, exchanges, and shops, into deserts.[159]

At century's end, William Blake indignantly concurred: 'Spirits are Lawful, but not Ghosts; especially Royal Gin is Lawful Spirit.'[160] The Enlightenment had little quarrel with true religion (designed to make men good) but feared the magic of the sacred in the hands of the priests.

6

THE CULTURE
OF SCIENCE

And new philosophy calls all in doubt

JOHN DONNE[1]

Deep into the seventeenth century, the new science remained highly enigmatic. Copernicus, Kepler, Galileo and all the other investigators now enshrined in the 'scientific revolution' pantheon met incomprehension and resistance, and not just from the Vatican;[2] their theories were found fanciful, false or frightening. Late in life, the learned Milton had still by no means given whole-hearted assent even to heliocentric astronomy – or perhaps he could not see why planetary orbits mattered much by contrast to the sacred tragedy of the Fall:

> Think onely what concernes thee and thy being;
> Dream not of other Worlds.[3]

For moralists and wits, the new science spelt confusion rather than clarification and closure. Theorists were accused of the vanity of dogmatizing or of sowing scepticism, and the proliferation of systems – Aristotelianism, Paracelsianism, Helmontianism, Epicureanism, Cartesianism, Gassendism, Democritism and a host of other '-isms' besides – seemed as scandalous in natural philosophy as in faith. Hypotheses mushroomed, as in the cosmogonical war following the publication of Thomas Burnet's *Sacred Theory of the Earth* (1681): a dozen or so geological speculators made, unmade and remade the globe, and stalemate ensued. System rancorously contradicted system, riding roughshod over received readings of the Bible, to the extent that it could be said that Burnet, himself an Anglican divine, held that

All the books of Moses
Were nothing but supposes . . .
That as for Father Adam
And Mrs Eve his Madam,
And what the devil spoke, Sir,
'Twas nothing but a joke, Sir,
And well invented flam.[4]

For their part, curiosity-mongers were mocked for petty-mindedness: why ever collect all those fleas and fossils?

O! would the Sons of Men once think their Eyes
And Reason giv'n them but to study *Flies*![5]

Thomas Shadwell's *The Virtuoso* (1676) paraded Sir Nicholas Gim-crack as a hobby-horsical blockhead, blithely indifferent to matters of genuine utility – he loved only the 'speculative' side of swimming – while in *Gulliver's Travels* (1726), Swift satirized the learned of Lagado, bent on extracting sunbeams from cucumbers and reducing life to geometry. The foibles of *savants* were manna to satirists.[6]

Though the Royal Society, chartered in 1662, potentially possessed intellectual prestige, it too laid itself open to derision.[7] Meanwhile, hardliners warned that the new science compromised Scripture and pre-empted Providence. Cartesian matter in motion mechanism debarred God from the clockwork universe and deemed Creation lifeless, soulless and without conscious purpose, while other brands of the new philosophy for their part reeked of Aristotelian eternalism, Democritan chance or Lucretian determinism; the Cambridge Platonist Ralph Cudworth's vast *True Intellectual System of the Universe* (1678) excoriated all such stepping stones to atheism.[8]

Despite such conflicts and confusions, the new science, or 'natural philosophy' as it was known,[9] was after all recruited remarkably swiftly and successfully into enlightened discourse, and thereafter the two constituted a formidable alliance. This was partly a result of the good fortune for patriots in already having the Baconian programme to draw upon, trumpeting in *The New Atlantis* (1627) the 'effecting of all things possible'. 'The Human Understanding is unquiet,' Bacon had stressed; 'it cannot stop or rest, and still presses onward.'[10] His ringing aphorisms – *Antiquitas saeculi juventus mundi* ('Antiquity was the youth of the world'), 'Knowledge is power', and so forth – were morale-boosters to the Moderns in the battle of the books.[11] Systematized in the *Novum Organum* (1620), Baconianism became a key enlightenment resource. With dogmatic scholasticism and magicians' fantasies both being replaced by inductive method and experimental investigation, natural philosophy would match and extend the achievements of those 'useful arts' which the Lord Chancellor so extolled. In his *The History of the Royal Society of London* (1667), Bishop Sprat hitched Bacon to the Royal Society, stressing both the role of practical men in furthering science and its part in material progress.[12]

The post-Restoration assimilation of the new science into progressive ideologies was speeded up by another extraordinary stroke of luck, a constellation of phenomenal 'natural philosophers', who not only won international glory for their discoveries but were also anxious to allay fears and promote what we would now call the public understanding of science. Courting public approval – their denunciations of Descartes, Spinoza and Hobbes helped in this – they wove the new science into a progressive philosophy.

Incomparably important to the marriage of science and enlightenment were the career, achievements and image of Sir Isaac Newton.[13] A childhood genius born in 1642, Newton went up to Cambridge University in 1661, becoming a fellow of Trinity College in 1667 and just two years later Lucasian professor of mathematics. By then he had already made giant strides in two branches of that subject, differentiation and integration. As early as October 1666 he wrote a dazzling tract setting out the basics of the calculus – the fact that he did not publish it at the time was to precipitate, forty years later, a violent dispute with the German philosopher Gottfried Leibniz over who got there first. Newton also undertook early experimental investigations into light, showing that sunlight was heterogeneous, and that colours arose from the separation of white light into its component rays.

Around 1670 he became engrossed in two other fields of inquiry, alchemy and theology. He read widely in alchemy, experimenting in his personal laboratory and composing treatises. Though he never published any of these – the art was losing respectability – they probably influenced his scientific thinking at large.[14] Theologically, Newton convinced himself earlier than Locke, and far more radically, that the doctrine of the Trinity was false; he became a closet Arian. He also devoted himself to Scripture, reading the Apocalypse and the Book of Daniel as prognosticating the rise of the Trinitarian heresy. His theological searches foreshadowed many prominent enlightened positions, although, as with his alchemy, he confined his Arian views to a trusted circle.[15]

In 1684, a visit from fellow physicist Edmond Halley recalled Newton to his earlier interests. Two and a half years of intense application led to his masterpiece, the *Philosophiae Naturalis Principia Mathematica*, published in 1687.[16] The *Mathematical Principles of Natural Philosophy* laid out a new science of dynamics which linked Kepler's laws of the heavenly orbits to Galileo's kinematics of terrestrial motion. Not only did Newton offer a comprehensive account of the forces holding the solar system together, but he also deduced an astonishing generalization, that of universal gravitation: every particle of matter in the universe is attracted to every other with a force varying directly as the product of their masses and inversely as the square of their distance. The clarity and power of that law, the coping stone of the new conception of Nature, ensured that the *Principia* dominated enlightened thinking about Nature.

In 1704 Newton published his second great book, the *Opticks*, which expounded his findings about light reached over thirty years earlier and concluded with sixteen 'Queries', speculations destined to shape experimental science. Finally, he returned to theology. His posthumously published *Chronology of Ancient Kingdoms Amended* (1728) and *Observations on the Prophecies* (1733) set about rectifying biblical chronology – falsified by Popery and priestcraft – in the light of astronomical data.[17]

Newton had left Cambridge in 1696 to become warden (and later master) of the Royal Mint, and in 1703 the Royal Society elected him president, an office he held until his death in 1727. He was knighted in 1705, the first scion of science to be so recognized. Meanwhile he was gathering about him a circle of protégés. David Gregory, John Keill, Roger Cotes, William Whiston and Colin Maclaurin gained university chairs through Newton's patronage, while Francis Hauksbee and J. T. Desaguliers found Royal Society employment with his help. These acolytes pursued the priority dispute with Leibniz over the calculus, with Keill and John Freind acting as Newton's champions and the divine Samuel Clarke waging the campaign on a more philosophical plane.[18] Through having such followers, Newton became Newtonianism.[19]

Newton's authority was, of course, founded upon his *Principia*, but, being mathematically incredibly demanding, it was more revered than read. Popularization was needed. Initially this was the work of disciples such as Henry Pemberton, author of *A View of Sir Isaac Newton's Philosophy* (1728), but in time a wider group became involved, including authors overseas, such as the Italian Francesco Algarotti, whose *Newtonianismo per le dame* (1737) was translated into English as *Sir Isaac Newton's Philosophy Explain'd for the Use of the Ladies* (1739).[20]

Newtonian mathematical cosmology was quickly assimilated into the educational curriculum at his *alma mater*. Among the enthusiasts was Richard Bentley, the brilliant classicist and master of Trinity, who delivered the first of the Boyle Lectures (see below). Bentley in turn patronized Roger Cotes, the first Plumian professor of astronomy and editor of the second edition of the *Principia* (1709), and William Whiston, Newton's protégé and successor as Lucasian professor.[21]

Newton's fame spread beyond Britain, especially in the Dutch republic through the experimenters Pieter van Musschenbroek and W. J. 'sGravesande, while Herman Boerhaave gave medicine a Newtonian slant. French acceptance was slower, on account of the entrenched Cartesian plenism. While Voltaire grappled manfully with the technicalities, his *Lettres philosophiques* (1734) mainly promoted

Newton as an intellectual hero,[22] and nor was it until the 1730s that such Newtonian sympathizers as Clairaut and Maupertuis became prominent in the Académie Royale des Sciences.[23]

Newton's work proved crucial in various ways.[24] The *Principia* endorsed a mathematical approach, which was to be applied to rational mechanics. The *Opticks*, on the other hand, opened up experimental inquiries into heat, light, magnetism and electricity, partly through the new theory of matter offered in the concluding 'Queries', further amplified in the 1706 and 1717 editions, where the Newtonian notion of force was extended from planetary gravitation to the microscopic intercorpuscular interactions, with a view to resolving problems like chemical affinity. Newton also introduced in the 1717 'Queries' the idea of the aether, a super-fine fluid composed of mutually repulsive particles. This proved a flexible theoretical resource, giving rise in later thinking to other hypothetical subtle fluids, designed to explain electricity, heat, etc.

Newton was the god who put English science on the map, an intellectual colossus, flanked by Bacon and Locke.

> Let Newton, Pure Intelligence, whom God
> To mortals lent to trace His boundless works
> From laws sublimely simple, speak thy fame
> In all philosophy.[25]

sang James Thomson in his 'Ode on the Death of Sir Isaac Newton' (1727). Wordsworth was later more Romantic:

> Newton with his prism and silent face,
> . . . a mind for ever,
> Voyaging through strange seas of thought alone.[26]

'Newton' the icon proved crucial to the British Enlightenment, universally praised except by a few obdurate outsiders, notably William Blake, who detested him and all his works.[27]

What was crucial about Newton – apart from the fact that, so far as his supporters were concerned, he was a Briton blessed with omniscience – was that he put forward a vision of Nature which, whilst revolutionary, reinforced latitudinarian Christianity. For all but a few diehards,[28] Newtonianism was an invincible weapon against atheism, upholding no mere First Cause but an actively intervening personal Creator who continually sustained Nature and, once in a while, applied a rectifying touch.[29] Like Locke, furthermore, the public Newton radiated intellectual humility. Repudiating the *a priori* speculations of Descartes and later rationalists, he preferred empiricism: he would 'frame no hypotheses' (*hypotheses non fingo*),[30] and neither would he pry into God's secrets. Thus, while he had elucidated the law of gravity, he did not pretend to divine its causes. Not least, in best enlightened fashion, Newtonian science set plain facts above mystifying metaphysics. In Newtonianism, British scientific culture found its enduring rhetoric: humble, empirical, co-operative, pious, useful.[31] 'I don't know what I may seem to the world, but, as to myself,' he recalled, in his supreme soundbite,

I seem to have been only like a boy playing on the sea shore, and diverting myself in now and then finding a smoother pebble or a prettier shell than ordinary, whilst the great ocean of truth lay all undiscovered before me.[32]

In all respects, Newton chimed with the approved public image of the Royal Society, and with other leading lights of Restoration natural philosophy, in particular the Hon. Robert Boyle. Conspicuous for his philosophical modesty while well-born to boot, that pioneer chemist also pursued his researches from the stance of altruistic piety, insistent that investigation of Nature was the road to God.[33]

It was providential that Newton's *Principia* was published in 1687, on the eve of the Glorious Revolution. Himself the MP for his university and a staunch Whig, Newton, like Locke, was soon rewarded under William and Mary with high office, and his science was enlisted to back the new moral and political order, chiefly *via* the Boyle Lectures, a sermon series endowed by Boyle's will to be read annually from London pulpits 'for proving the Christian Religion against notorious infidels'. Delivering the first series in 1692 (published as the *Confutation of Atheism*), Newton's protégé Richard Bentley used the *Principia* to demonstrate God's providential design for the universe. Samuel Clarke, in 1704–5, and other early lecturers also drew on Newton to bolster Latitudinarian Anglicanism, and to hammer home the value of empirical inquiry, intellectual freedom and rational religion. These lectures not only boosted the Christian faith, however; they helped reinforce the position of the new political regime.[34]

The affinities between the Newtonian cosmos and the post-1688 polity were played up. In the year after the master's death, his disciple J. T. Desaguliers produced an explicit application of physics to politics in *The Newtonian System of the World: The Best Model of Government, an Allegorical Poem* (1728), where the British monarchy was celebrated as the guarantor of liberty and rights: 'attraction is now as universal in the political, as the philosophical world'.

> What made the Planets in such Order move,
> He said, was Harmony and mutual Love.[35]

God himself was commended as a kind of constitutional monarch:

> His Pow'r, coerc'd by Laws, still leaves them free,
> Directs but not Destroys their Liberty.[36]

The *Principia* thus provided an atomic explanatory model not just for Nature but for society too (freely moving individuals governed by law). For Desaguliers, no praise was sufficient for the genius who had finally revealed the ways of God to man:

> Newton the unparallel'd, whose Name
> No Time will wear out of the Book of Fame,
> Coelestiall Science has promoted more,
> Than all the Sages that have shone before.[37]

It was particularly fortunate that Newton had apostles assiduous in guarding his image. For, as is now known from scrutiny of his private papers, he was in reality far from the flawless figure cosmeticized for public consumption. He had plunged deeply into esoterica, his idiosyncratic Arianism was profoundly heretical and he was jealous and browbeating to boot. Public exposure of such traits would have blown his cover as an enlightened idol. Newton himself, however, kept his speculations private, and he left it to loyal juniors like Whiston to try out in public his more chancy speculations, such as anti-Trinitarianism – sometimes to their cost (Whiston was dismissed from his Cambridge chair).[38]

After his death, Newton's findings – indeed the new science in general – were occasionally deployed to dispute or erode Christian teachings, as by the Deist geologist James Hutton, or the unabashed pantheist who touted the eternity of the Earth, George Hoggart Toulmin.[39] In Britain, however, thanks to the Newtonian synthesis, natural philosophy remained remarkably in tune with the rational Christianity of the moderate Enlightenment – a holy alliance embodied in a lively tradition of natural theology, culminating in William Paley's influential *Natural Theology* (1802). A strategic example opened that work: from a watch we infer a watchmaker;[40] from natural contrivances, such as the human body, we could, by the same logic, infer a Divine Clockmaker, reasoning 'thro' Nature up to Nature's God':

The pivot upon which the head turns, the ligament within the socket of the hip joint, the pulley or trochlear muscles of the eye; the epiglottis, the bandages which tie down the tendons of the wrist and instep, the slit or perforated muscles at the hands and feet, the knitting of the intestines to the mesentery.[41]

Could all this be the work of blind chance?[42]

The Enlightenment secured the triumph of a radical new rendering of the very constitution of Nature.[43] After 1660, the Aristotelian metaphysics of elements, humours, substances, qualities and final causes, so long dominant in the universities, as well as rival Renaissance neo-Platonic and hermetic visions of a spiritual universe, were finally superseded by models of Nature viewed as matter in motion, governed by laws capable of mathematical expression. This enthronement of the mechanical philosophy, the key paradigm switch of the 'scientific revolution', in turn sanctioned the new assertions of man's rights over Nature so salient to enlightened thought.[44]

Pioneered in France by Pierre Gassendi, Marin Mersenne and especially by Descartes, and in England by Hobbes, the mechanical philosophy's key feature lay in its ontology of microscopic corpuscles interacting by contact. These possessed only the 'primary qualities' of size, shape and motion: all other ('secondary') properties – like smell, colour or taste – were deemed the subjective products of interaction with human sense organs. For Cartesianism, the universe was a plenum, matter was inert and passive and motion depended on billiard-ball contact – all other supposed modes of action were ridiculed as vulgar or mystical, relics of discredited magic. Challenging Descartes in his revised version of the mechanical philosophy, Newton affirmed action at a distance in a matter theory in which force assumed a central role, being associated with gravity and applicable to many other phenomena.

In its diverse and contested forms, the mechanical philosophy achieved towering prestige in the early Enlightenment, and not just in the physical sciences. 'Clockwork' thinking, for example, invaded physiology and medicine; 'iatromechanism', advanced among others by the Scottish physicians Archibald Pitcairne and George Cheyne, cast the human body as a system of pulleys, springs and levers, pipes and vessels, its fluids being governed by the laws of hydraulics. Life itself was potentially explicable within the new mechanical paradigm.

By the middle of the eighteenth century, however, strict mechanism was being judged incapable of accounting for the full complexities of living phenomena, especially properties like growth and reproduction. The Scottish surgeon John Hunter, the 'father' of British physiology, substituted a vitalism, which held that organized matter had an inherent vital force which distinguished it from the inorganic. Seemingly paradoxically, vitalism was thereby recruited to bolster materialism: having banished belief in the natural qualities and manifestations of the soul and other spiritual powers ('anima'), enlightened thinkers such as Erasmus Darwin then found the mechanical philosophy inadequate to explain those special features of living matter (such as generation) which the 'animists' had high-lighted; hence they extended the power of self-organization to all matter, by analogy with such phenomena as crystal growth.[45]

In Britain, enlightened theorizings of matter and inquiries into chemistry and branches of experimental physics like the study of heat were dominated by Newtonianism. It diverged sharply from the Cartesian brand of mechanism, for not only did Newtonianism embrace the vacuum – as proved by airpump experiments – but it held that the quantity of matter (strictly defined) in the universe was tiny; in Joseph Priestley's graphic image, 'all the solid matter in the solar system might be contained within a nut-shell'.[46] 'Solid' bodies, in other words, were largely void space, which resisted disintegration or penetration thanks to the intensity of the forces acting between their component particles. The prime example of these inter-particular forces was gravitation, but in the speculative 'Queries' to the *Opticks*, Newton also floated the idea of analogous microscopic forces, introducing, as we have seen, the 'aether' to explain electrical phenomena and even gravity itself.

The Newtonian matter model underwent challenge and change. In the 1720s and 1730s, Robert Greene and John Rowning held that attractive and repulsive forces acted antagonistically so as to sustain activity in Nature.[47] This assertion marks an important juncture in enlightened matter theory: while for Newton force had been an expression of divine intervention, later theorists increasingly assumed that matter was inherently active and that Nature was sustained independently of God's immediate will.

This move was made possible by the uptake and modification of aether theories. From the 1740s, they were popularized by works such as Bryan Robinson's *Dissertation on the Aether of Sir Isaac Newton* (1743), and similar sorts of 'subtle fluids' were proposed in domains such as electricity, magnetism and physiology. The Scot James Hutton applied them to heat, and then to geology in his *Theory of the Earth* (1795). A friend of David Hume and Adam Smith, Hutton ventured a true secularization of Nature: light, heat and electricity were modifications of a single aetherial substance, which acted as a principle of repulsion to counter attraction; interacting with gravitational matter, the circulation of aetherial (repulsive) matter through the universe maintained movement independently of what the Deist Hutton scorned as the vulgar notion of divine supervention.[48] Partly on these grounds, he could present the Earth as indefinitely old – it showed 'no vestige of a beginning – no prospect of an end'.[49] 'Nature's God' was thus in retreat.

This secularization of matter theory is also visible in thinking about force, as Newtonian 'forces' were assimilated into the 'powers' which Locke had ascribed to matter, notably the power to affect the senses. In his *Disquisitions Relating to Matter and Spirit* (1777), Joseph Priestley boldly proposed that matter was, in reality, reducible to such Lockean 'powers': 'particles' were actually nothing more than spheres of attractive and repulsive forces circling a nucleus. Since these forces comprised the Lockean powers making us aware of matter's existence, the core of each particle was quite unknowable. Thus, concluded Priestley, we had no grounds for concluding that there was really anything there at all: the existence of a material substrate independent of its powers was one of those redundant hypotheses a true Newtonian would not wish to 'feign'; Newton's 'solid', inert matter was thus an illusion.

The beauty of this argument for Priestley, *qua* enlightened materialist, was that it collapsed the problematic Cartesian distinction between matter and spirit. All matter became in effect spiritualized, or vice versa, and the mysteries of mind/body dualism dissolved.[50] His adversaries, however, condemned such views as smacking of that strand of French materialism which held that matter was alive, thus raising the bogey of Locke's 'thinking matter'. The development of matter theory thus brought together a clutch of concerns – epistemology, mind–body relations and God's government of the physical world – which made it central to enlightened attempts to formulate a science of natural order.

It was not only, of course, the physical sciences which developed, even if, thanks to Newton, they seemed the most spectacular. By the middle of the eighteenth century, knowledge of all aspects of Nature was advancing on a broad front. Carolus Linnaeus arrived at a system for classifying the kingdoms which natural historians studied, while works like Oliver Goldsmith's 8-volume *History of the Earth and Animated Nature* (1774) popularized the living world for the new reading public, and opened up new aesthetic prospects, as will be shown in chapter 13.[51]

Newton's principate proved momentous for enlightened thinking. It bolstered confidence that Nature had finally been fathomed, and created a model of a material reality, amenable to observation and experiment, which squared perfectly with Locke's empiricism. No longer alive or occult but rather composed of largely inert matter, Nature could be weighed, measured – and mastered. The mechanical philosophy fostered belief that man was permitted, indeed dutybound, to apply himself to Nature for (in Bacon's words) the 'glory of God and the relief of man's estate'. Since Nature was not, after all, sacred or 'ensouled', there could be nothing impious about utilizing and dominating it. The progressiveness of science thus became pivotal to enlightened propaganda. The way was now well-lit, as bright as light itself.[52]

Science was energetically promoted amongst the public. Initially in London's coffee houses, lecturers began to offer demonstrations with globes, orreries and other instruments displaying the marvels of the clockwork universe, while performing chemical, magnetic, electrical and airpump experiments besides.[53] In the spring of 1713, for instance, Newton's protégé William Whiston was holding forth on mathematics and science at both Douglas's coffee house in St Martin's Lane and at the Marine coffee house near the Royal Exchange – typical Whig haunts. The most illustrious popularizer, however, was the Royal Society's official experimenter, Desaguliers. In that same year he offered a course on Newtonian science in twenty-one lectures, providing to 'such as are altogether unskilled in Mathematics' experimental proof of the reality of the vacuum, while also catering for interest in 'mechanical engines in general'. Mechanical principles would be applied to the operations of levers, weights and pulleys, and to ballistics – warfare offered major opportunities for applied science.[54]

Such lecturing might also launch a fashionable career, as demonstrated by that of Adam Walker. Befriended by Priestley, the inventor and astronomy lecturer performed at the Haymarket Theatre in 1778, while in glamorous George Street, off Hanover Square, he put on a lecture series each winter, which brought him to the notice of London's intelligentsia – even if Fanny Burney found him 'vulgar in conversation'. About 1781 Walker built a magnificent 20-foot orrery consisting of luminous globes of various sizes to represent the planets and displaying the workings of the solar system in a darkened auditorium, which he named the Eidouranion. He also doubled as a visiting science lecturer at Westminster, Winchester and other public schools. At Eton, one member of his audience, Percy Bysshe Shelley, was 'completely captivated' by his discourses on astronomy, electricity, chemistry, magnetism and hydrostatics – as is plain to see from Shelley's philosophical poetry.[55] Medicine too had its popularizers – the Scot James Graham, for instance, gave demonstrations of medical electricity and sexual rejuvenation in his Temple of Health off the Strand in London, where he displayed his 'Celestial Bed'.[56]

Science popularization spread to the provinces, Desaguliers himself lecturing to the very first provincial scientific and literary society, the Spalding Gentlemen's Society in Lincolnshire. As early as 1712, the *Newcastle Courant* publicized the proposals of Dr James Jurin, physician and master of the Royal Free Grammar School, 'for carrying on by subscription a compleat Course of Mechanicks, by which Gentlemen unacquainted with any part of the Mathematicks in the Space of 12 or 18 Months by meeting 3 Times a Week for an Hour at a Time may be enabled to compute the Effect of any Machine whatsoever'. Jurin was yet another Newtonian, who, under a different enlightenment hat, was also a pioneer of smallpox inoculation.[57]

Whiston lectured in Bristol in 1724; James Ferguson – one of a host of Scots who took the high road south – performed in Bath and Bristol in the 1760s and 1770s; James Arden, Henry Moyes, John

Warltire, Benjamin Martin and others brought science to the West Country. Early in his career Martin lectured in Gloucester, Salisbury, Newbury, Oxford, Chichester, Bath, Reading, York, Scarborough and Ipswich, and in 1747 he set up his pitch in Birmingham for the first time.[58] By the end of the century few towns of any significance had not been milked by itinerant lecturers offering courses of a dozen or twenty lectures over a few weeks, supplementing their income meanwhile by selling their books, apparatus and medical nostrums, by performing land surveys or by giving private tuition. In short, 'knowledge', as Benjamin Martin reflected, 'is now become a fashionable thing, and philosophy is the science à la mode; hence, to cultivate this study is only to be in taste, and politeness is the inseparable consequence'.[59]

Science entered and shaped the world of the educated in many ways. An instrument trade flourished – an erudite gentleman or lady of means might be expected to own a microscope or a telescope, alongside a cabinet of beetles or stuffed birds.[60] Popular science books appeared, some for children, and encyclopaedias played a major role in its dissemination.[61] But while science thus staked its place in polite culture, it was also promoted as utilitarian, an engine of national progress. 'None has more improved the Mechanic Arts,' noted the Frenchman Guy Miège, enthusing over the English alliance of science, technology and industry. 'Here are made the best Clocks, Watches, Barometers, Thermometers, Air Pumps, and all Sorts of *Mathematical Instruments* . . . For Merchandize and Navigation, except the *Hollanders*, none come near them.'[62] The *Collection for Improvement of Husbandry and Trade* (1692), put out by apothecary, entrepreneur and fellow of the Royal Society John Houghton, was one of scores of works which proclaimed the economic benefits expected from the link-up of science and know-how.[63] Such claims grew louder. 'The study of the useful arts and sciences and of modern languages,' declared the *New and Old Principles of Trade Compared* (1788), 'are [*sic*] superior to the study of the languages and the works of taste of decayed nations.'[64] 'Read the history of mankind,' barked another booster;

consider the gradual steps of civilization from barbarism to refinement, and you will not fail to discover that the progress of society from its lowest and worst to its highest and most perfect state has been uniformly accompanied and chiefly promoted by the happy exertions of man in the character of a mechanic or engineer. Let all machines be destroyed, and we are reduced in a moment to the condition of savages.[65]

It was just such thinking which underlay the aims of the Society for the Encouragement of Arts, Commerce and Manufactures (1754), located just off the Strand, which offered premiums to reward innovators in various aspects of the practical and decorative arts. Bandying around buzz words like 'experiments', its founder, William Shipley, floated projects designed to turn technical expertise to economic advantage, including, rather enterprisingly, shoes waterproofed with tin foil (cost: 1d. a pair), while others dreamed – ominously! – of making 'coffee of English materials'.[66] In the 1770s James Barry produced a suite of paintings to decorate the Society's great hall. The train of philosophers, scientists and others painted by the artist began with the Ancients and culminated with contemporary British adepts, like Newton, portrayed as the new Olympians.[67]

A prime promoter of the enlightened alliance of science, utility and philanthropy under the banner of improvement was the Quaker John Coakley Lettsom.[68] Born in 1744 in the West Indies, where his father was a plantation owner, Lettsom was sent to England for his education, studying medicine in London and Edinburgh. On his father's death in 1767, he returned to the Caribbean as heir to the family estates. There he performed a deed both pious and enlightened: 'The moment I came of age,' he later recalled, 'I found my chief property was in slaves, and without considering of future support, I gave them freedom, and began the world without fortune, without a friend.'[69]

Setting up in medical practice in London, Lettsom proved highly successful. In 1782, he noted that 'sometimes for the space of a week, I cannot command twenty minutes' leisure in my own house'.[70]

Acquiring many prominent patients, including Lord Shelburne, patron of Priestley and Bentham, his busy practice made him wealthy – by 1800, his earnings amounted to a princely £12,000 annually. Prosperity underwrote philanthropy – 'who will thank us for dying rich!'[71] Indefatigably charitable, Lettsom was a founder of several forward-looking institutions. In 1770, he launched the General Dispensary in Aldersgate Street, the first of its kind, and became one of its physicians. This provided free outpatient treatment to the poor through a resident apothecary, and inaugurated domiciliary visiting. In 1774 he assisted in founding the (Royal) Humane Society, to pioneer techniques and publicize the practice of resuscitating the drowned; he was the driving force behind the Royal Sea Bathing Infirmary at Margate (1791), a convalescent home for the tubercular; and he also helped found the Medical Society of London (1773), whose very Addisonian aim was to unite improvement and conviviality.

Building a house in suburban Camberwell, Lettsom there laid out a fortune on a museum, library and botanical garden. Like other enlightened Quakers, he valued sociability and the exchange of knowledge, keeping up a correspondence with (among others) George Washington, Benjamin Rush, Benjamin Franklin, Erasmus Darwin and Albrecht von Haller. Despite his Quaker pacifism, Lettsom became physician to the Camberwell Volunteer Infantry in 1803, declaring, 'May I fall by the sword rather than live to see this free country the domain of a Corsican murderer and usurper!'[72]

Lettsom enthused over useful knowledge, scientific experimentation, medical advance and moral improvement; a tireless writer, he produced pamphlets against drunkenness, while his *The Natural History of the Tea Tree with Observations on its Medical Qualities, and Effects of Tea-Drinking* (1772) exposed the evils of that pernicious habit. Among a plethora of projects, he was an advocate of soup kitchens for the poor, and his passion for education led him to write on the management of boarding schools, giving advice as to games, diet, attire and cleanliness. This busy bee also fittingly directed attention to beehives, 'as appendages both of ornament and utility to the gardens about the metropolis': within twenty miles of London, up to

50,000 hives might be maintained, enriching the nation by a guinea *per* hive *per annum*.

In 1801 Lettsom collected his improving ideas into the 3-volume *Hints Designed to Promote Beneficence, Temperance, and Medical Science*, which gave instruction on such varied subjects as poverty, discharged prisoners, prostitution, infectious fevers, a Samaritan society, crimes and punishments, wills and testaments, lying-in charities, the deaf and dumb, village societies, the blind, a society for promoting useful literature, religious persecution, Sunday schools, the Philanthropic Society, dispensaries, hydrophobia, sea-bathing infirmaries, and 'A Substitute for Wheat Bread' – Indian corn made a thrifty porridge. It all amounted to a veritable enlightenment *omnium gatherum*.

If piqued at his exclusion, as a Quaker, from the fellowship of the Royal College of Physicians, Lettsom was a passionate champion of science and his own profession. He waged newspaper wars against quacks, became an early advocate of smallpox vaccination and also championed John Howard, the hospital and prison reformer.

As well as botany, fossils, medicine and natural history, Lettsom was an enthusiast for scientific agriculture, playing a part in the introduction into Britain of the mangelwurzel. All such scientific and philanthropic activities were the more remarkable, because, like his physician contemporary Erasmus Darwin, his works tended to be written in his carriage while scurrying about to see his patients. Like others featured in later chapters – Darwin himself, Richard Lovell Edgeworth and Joseph Priestley, for instance – Lettsom exemplifies the ardent promotion of practical, science-based improvement by enlightened Englishmen.

A contemporary of Lettsom who, in a crammed career, united science, improvement and utility on a more elevated plane within the Establishment was Sir Joseph Banks.[73] Born to wealth, young Banks drifted from Eton to Oxford without apparent intellectual passions, but there he became fascinated by botany and, finding that the professor did not lecture, he imported a substitute from Cambridge, out of his own pocket.

Inheriting broad Lincolnshire acres, Banks built himself a mansion in Soho Square which he turned into a salon, club, library and natural history museum – his curator, Dr Daniel Solander, one of Linnaeus's protégés, presided over a great and growing collection of botanical specimens. A mutual interest in agriculture won Banks the friendship of George III, who made him Keeper of the Royal Gardens at Kew. Every inch an Englishman – stout country squire, farmer, fisherman, sheriff of Lincolnshire and gout-sufferer – Banks was no less an enlightened cosmopolite. During the forty-two years he presided, ever more autocratically, over the Royal Society, disbursing hospitality and patronage, he combined internationalism with an ardent patriotism. Anticipating Jenner's dictum that 'the sciences are never at war', he conferred upon Benjamin Franklin the Royal Society's gold medal for his zeal in protecting Captain Cook during the American War of Independence; and in the French wars he intervened to save beleaguered *savants*, rescuing the geologist Dolomieu from a Naples dungeon.

Banks's long career throbbed with activity on behalf of science, which he valued as progressive knowledge and a national asset. While still a young man he explored Newfoundland and Labrador and botanized in Iceland; he visited Fingal's Cave in the Hebrides, reciting Ossian before recording its dimensions; and he sailed with Cook in 1769 to the South Seas, on one of the first great international scientific enterprises, to observe the transit of Venus, and brought home 17,000 new plants to stock his bulging Soho Square cabinet.

Banks promoted Botany Bay – named after his own passion – as an ideal site for a convict colony, and thereafter proved a booster and benefactor to New South Wales. He experimented with Spanish merino sheep to improve the breeds sent to Australia, got Captain Bligh to export the breadfruit tree from Polynesia to the Caribbean and imported mangoes from Bengal. As patron of the African Society, he helped send John Ledyard up the Nile, and Mungo Park up the Niger. High-minded if self-important, adventurous yet autocratic, a man with a deep sense of social responsibility but scarcely a trace of Christian piety, for half a century Banks devoted his wealth to advancing science, learning and wealth creation – an awfully English *philosophe*.

Science's growing prestige broadened horizons and bred hope: all was open to inquiry, measurement and analysis. Apparatus would do its bit: telescopes, microscopes, barometers, thermometers, hydrometers, theodolites, pumps and prisms – such technical devices were the auxiliaries of a new science which was not about vain and vaporous lucubrations but the busy, hands-on probing of Nature. Every month the *Gentleman's Magazine* reported daily barometric pressure, temperature and the bills of mortality for the City of London, all neatly tabulated, just like stocks and shares. Science had 'too long made only a work of the Brain and the Fancy', Robert Hooke had conceded in his *Micrographia* (1665); 'it is now high time that it should return to the plainness and soundness of Observations on material and obvious things'.[74] True scientific method was to 'begin with the Hands and Eyes, and to proceed on through the Memory, to be continued by the Reason; nor is it to stop there, but to come about to the Hands and Eyes again, and so, by a continual passage round from one Faculty to another'.[75] Adopt this method, and what indeed could bind Prometheus?

Probabilistic thinking to some extent replaced Providence,[76] while the conviction grew that social no less than natural events were fundamentally governed by natural law – and hence were in principle amenable to scientific enumeration, explanation and control. 'No Laws can set Prices in Trade,' declared Sir Dudley North in his *Discourses Upon Trade* (1691), 'the rates of which, must and will make themselves': commerce was subject to underlying regularities, and prices, like water, would find their own level.[77]

The psychological and aesthetic dynamics of fathoming Nature were pondered by Adam Smith in a long meditation on the history of astronomy. Addressing Plato's point that philosophy begins in wonder, he proposed that it was the mind's uneasiness with the strange which provided the driving force for attempts to eliminate perplexity through theories, models and formulae. He accentuated the psychological side of science – it began with unease at the unexpected, and would, it was hoped, be followed by relief upon assimilating irregularities into the familiar. A scientific theory gave satisfaction when it overcame disquiet at anomalies.

That was not, however, the only reason for the intellectual dissatisfaction which propelled scientific theorizing: a good explanation must be clear, coherent and easy to grasp. When, in a valiant attempt to accommodate all the observed phenomena, a theory (Smith instanced Ptolemaic astronomy) grew over-intricate and unwieldy, disaffection would set in, and a new and simpler model would be needed (in this case, Copernican heliocentrism). 'Philosophy is the science of the connecting principles of nature,' he summarized, in a formulation reminiscent of Hume.

Nature, after the largest experience that common observation can acquire, seems to abound with events which appear solitary and incoherent with all that go before them, which therefore disturb the easy movement of the imagination; which makes its ideas succeed each other, if one may say so, by irregular starts and sallies; and which thus tend, in some measure to introduce . . . confusions and distractions . . . Philosophy, by representing the invisible chains which bind together all those disjointed objects, endeavours to introduce order into this chaos of jarring and discordant appearances.[78]

The savage mind thus encountered disorder everywhere, and the progress of science was the quest for regularity. Uniformity and order were the desiderata of the striving, restless progressive mind, at least as much as they were present in Nature. Smith thus wove the rise of science into that wider evolutionary history of the human mind advanced in the conjectural histories of civilization discussed below in chapter 10. A confidant of Hume and, like him, no Christian, Smith acclaimed science as 'the great antidote to the poison of enthusiasm and superstition'.[79]

As well as thus discrediting 'superstition', Newtonianism served enlightened goals by demarcating 'true' sciences from the 'pseudo' – those which were 'occult', 'magical' and 'vulgar'. This happened conspicuously in the discrediting of astrology.[80] Throughout the Renaissance, that ancient art had remained integral to a shared, indeed dominant culture, acceptable to courtiers, clergy and country folk alike, which peaked in England around 1650 with the work of the adepts William Lilly and his great rival, the royalist John Gadbury, both of whom enjoyed national followings.[81] After the Restoration, however, educated sympathies cooled decisively. The triumph of the new science contributed much to this rejection. Ptolemaic geocentric cosmology had posited correspondences between macrocosm and the microcosm, the celestial spheres and mankind. But if, as the new astronomy revealed, the heavens were neither perfect nor unchanging, the Earth was but a paltry planet in an infinite universe and the cosmos was governed by mechanical second causes, then astrology had many questions to answer.

The disavowal of astrology was also, however, a socio-cultural reaction. The art had been indelibly tainted during the Civil War by plebeian radicalism and wild republican prophesyings, leaving it vulnerable to attack as treacherous and vulgar. By 1700 such fellows of the Royal Society who had been sympathetic to astrology – John Aubrey, for instance – were all dead, and no top-flight metropolitans stepped into their shoes.

Though its appeal waned amongst the enlightened, however, the art retained a popular following. Provincial adepts continued to practise, albeit on the margins. Like other manifestations of the occult – palmistry or physiognomy, for instance – astrology was not killed off by science; rather, it found new niches in a modulating cultural environment.[82] Almanac sales held up, but their profile changed. Many became more 'rational', some early eighteenth-century productions shedding prophecies altogether; other compilers repudiated judicial astrology, one, Richard Saunders, feeding the reader with 'A Discourse on the Invalidity of Astrology'. Openly hostile, his almanac derided astrology's want of scientific foundations, mocking Lilly, Gadbury and the 'frightful stuff' put out by the self-promoting Whig zealot John Partridge.[83]

As Shaftesbury would have been pleased to find, ridicule worked.

Pierre Bayle's *Dictionnaire* (1697) mocked astrology as puerile – he did not even trouble readers with formal disproofs! Such dismissiveness was infectious. In his 'Predictions for the Year 1708', Jonathan Swift, writing under the pseudonym of Isaac Bickerstaff, lampooned the political predictions of the old astrologers, his chief target being again John Partridge. 'Bickerstaff' foretold that Partridge would die of a fever at 11 p.m. on 29 March 1708 – followed by Louis XIV on 29 July, and the Pope six weeks later. A solemn account duly appeared of Partridge's predestined demise. The hapless astrologer tried to prove his continued existence, but his posthumous protestations proved futile. Among the élite, astrology had been reduced to a joke.[84]

Earnest popular educators, for their part, were of the view that it was not ridicule but the march of the mind which would finally see off the footling art. Over a century after Swift's lampoon, *The British Almanac* for 1828, published by the Society for the Diffusion of Useful Knowledge, while providing a wealth of terrestrial and celestial data, was quite astrology-free. 'From that hour,' it was piously declared, 'the empire of astrology was at an end.' Like Partridge's, this obituary also proved wildly premature.[85]

Other practices underwent similar revamping. From the late seventeenth century, fortune-telling, dowsing, palmistry, metopos-copy, physiognomy and similar arcana lost credence among the élite, while continuing to be practised up and down the country by amateurs. Top people likewise distanced themselves from old magical medicine, including the botanical lore of emblems and correspond-ences; after Queen Anne, British monarchs stopped touching for the King's Evil (in France the Bourbons touched on until 1830).[86] Ancient wisdom lost its legitimacy as a scientific posture muscled in. 'I could write a better book of cookery than has ever yet been written,' boasted Samuel Johnson; 'it should be a book upon philosophical principles.'[87]

Science's key contribution to enlightened thinking lay in its underwriting belief in intellectual advance and its staking a claim to be the gold standard of positive knowledge. There were innumerable progress stories along these lines. Thus Chambers' *Cyclopaedia* (1738) traced the birth of the healing arts with Hippocrates and their corruption by the medievals:

At length, however, they [Galen's errors] were purged out and exploded by two different means; principally indeed by the restoration of the pure discipline of Hippocrates in France; and then also by the experiments and discoveries of alchymists and anatomists; till at length the immortal Harvey overturning, by his demonstrations, the whole theory of the antients, laid a new and certain basis of the science. Since his time, Medicine is become free from the tyranny of any sect, and is improved by sure discoveries in anatomy, chymistry, physics, botany, mechanics &c.[88]

Sketch after sketch of medicine's progress elaborated such conclusions. Looking back over the previous two thousand years in his *Strictures on the Gout* (1775), the medical writer Samuel Wood chided the 'unenlightened state of the ancient Practitioners', with whom 'all was mere conjecture'. 'There could be no Physiology at all,' he insisted, 'before our immortal Hervey's Discovery of the Circulation of the Blood'; but 'since these lights have shone in upon us, all the ancient conjectures, reasonings, and systems, must vanish like morning clouds before the sun'.[89] All told, Wood insisted, it is 'evident we have greatly the advantage of our ancestors', and theoretical advances had borne practical fruit: 'we now see many diseases cured with facility, with which the afflicted of those days bore, and closed a wretched existence'. In a recital of enlightened platitudes, he looked forward with confidence to the conquest of diseases long held incurable, including his personal speciality, gout.

Expectations of brilliant breakthroughs also coloured the more grandiose medical dreams of Thomas Beddoes, chemist, physician, researcher, educator, poet, pamphleteer – indeed, 'Mr Late Enlightenment' incarnate. An ardent experimentalist, Beddoes saluted the French revolution in chemistry no less than in politics.[90] Looking to science to produce transformations in health, he read history as a tale of progress: while equivocal about the Ancients – he criticized

Plato's 'mystic passages' – and dismissive of the Dark Ages as a fog of priestly superstition, he hailed the achievements of the sixteenth and seventeenth centuries as beyond praise.[91]

Touting the applicability of the new gas chemistry to respiratory disorders, Beddoes predicted in 1793 that 'from chemistry, which is daily unfolding the profoundest secrets of nature', hopes could be entertained for 'a safe and efficacious remedy for one of the most frequent painful and hopeless of diseases', that is, consumption (tuberculosis). Inspired by late Enlightenment perfectibilism, he foresaw that 'however remote medicine may at present be from such perfection', there was no reason to doubt that 'the same power will be acquired over living, as is at present exercised over some inanimate bodies, and that not only the cure and prevention of diseases, but the art of protracting the fairest season of life and rendering health more vigorous will one day half realize half the dream of Alchemy'.[92] Chemistry thus portended a medical millennium. 'In a future letter,' he informed his Lunar Society friend Erasmus Darwin,

I hope to present you with a catalogue of diseases in which I have effected a cure ... Many circumstances indeed seem to indicate that a great revolution in this art is at hand ... And if you do not, as I am almost sure you do not, think it absurd to suppose the organization of man equally susceptible of improvement from culture with that of various animals and vegetables, you will agree with me in entertaining hopes not only of a beneficial change in the practice of medicine, but in the constitution of human nature itself.[93]

Beddoes's Promethean expectations of how science would revolutionize life were undergirded by his enlightened vision of *Homo sapiens* as a creature of infinite possibility: the mind was not cursed by original sin or trammelled by innate ideas. Beddoes the empiricist set no bounds to improvement: Nature's truths lay open to the senses, and education itself was, in the widest sense, experimental.[94]

Science seemed the master key to progress. 'Not to insist on the great advancements in arts and science which have originated from *natural philosophy*,' maintained the Dissenting doctor John Aikin, 'what man of enlarged ideas will deny, that the *philosophy of the human mind*, of *law*, of *commerce*, of *government*, of *morals*, and I will add, of *religion*, have greatly contributed to any superiority this age may claim over former periods?'[95] In short, what could shackle the mind? Joseph Priestley pictured intelligence endlessly triumphing under divine guidance: 'knowledge . . . will . . . be increased; nature including both its materials and its laws, will be more at our command'.[96] Science thereby figured as the basis of a brighter future in all realms. 'The English hierarchy (if there be anything unsound in its constitution),' he maintained, 'has reason to tremble even at an air pump or an electrical machine.'[97]

The reason of science did not, however, seem so reasonable to everyone, all the time. It was, after all, Priestley who spent his last days, Newton-like, poring over the prophecies of the Book of Daniel, while the astronomer William Herschel was confident about finding inhabitants on the moon. Was science's title as the guardian of reason assured? Was it not susceptible to some enlightened criteria of humility?[98]

7

ANATOMIZING
HUMAN NATURE

Know then thyself, presume not God to scan;
The proper study of Mankind is Man.

ALEXANDER POPE[1]

Upon the whole, I desire to take my Catalogue of Virtues from
Cicero's Offices, not from the Whole Duty of Man.

DAVID HUME[2]

And who are you? said he.
– Don't puzzle me; said I.

LAURENCE STERNE, *Tristram Shandy*[3]

With the displacement of scripturalism that was brought
about by rational religion, the need to resolve the human condition
moved centre stage in Enlightenment thinking. ' 'Tis evident, that all
the sciences have a relation, greater or less, to human nature,'
declared David Hume in his thematically titled *A Treatise of Human
Nature* (1739–40): not only were epistemology, ethics, aesthetics and
politics all anchored in human nature, but even mathematics and
the natural sciences were 'in some measure dependent on the science
of Man'.[4] Evidently Pope had got it right: the proper study of mankind
indeed was man.

The recoil from Protestant bibliolatry demanded a wholesale
refiguring of man's character and destiny. Reformation theology had
preached woeful truths: man was fallen, his passions were base,
sinners could not achieve salvation by their own efforts, while
Calvinists held that implacable Divine Will had predestined all but

the saints to eternal perdition. Through the Fall, Paradise had been lost, and such progress as there might be towards redemption would have to be a pilgrim's. For Bunyan, the *via dolorosa* to the Celestial City wound through Vanity Fair, where Christian and his companion Faithful were pelted by the mob, set in irons and hurled into a cage as a public spectacle. Faithful was sentenced to be burnt at the stake while for Christian, although he escaped and 'came to a delicate plain, called Ease', this was more the beginning of his trials than the end: 'at the farthest side of that plain was a little hill called Lucre', beyond which lay Doubting Castle.[5]

This saga of fallen man expelled into a vale of tears is captured by an event in the childhood of the Dissenter Isaac Watts. One day, the pious story runs, his mother came across some of the young lad's verses. Doubting his authorship on account of their merit, she quizzed him about them. To prove that they were his the boy composed for her an acrostic:

> **I** am a vile polluted lump of earth,
> **S**o I've continued ever since my birth,
> **A**lthough Jehovah grace does daily give me,
> **A**s sure this monster Satan will deceive me,
> **C**ome therefore, Lord, from Satan's claws relieve me.
>
> **W**ash me in Thy blood, O Christ,
> **A**nd grace divine impart,
> **T**hen search and try the corners of my heart,
> **T**hat I in all things may be fit to do
> **S**ervice to thee, and sing thy praises too.[6]

Young Watts was in a bind: to prove his talents – something verging on the sin of pride – required him to attest his depravity. Enlightened thinking was to discount such doctrines as demeaning to God and man alike: 'there is nothing which I contemplate with greater Pleasure', avowed Richard Steele, 'than the Dignity of Human Nature'.[7]

This is not to say, however, that Augustinian gloom was immediately and universally replaced by enlightened glee. Throughout the century, many moralists, variously disposed towards the enlightened agenda, continued to propound sober moral precepts couched in that Christian humanist idiom in which Hamlet had imagined man 'crawling between heaven and earth'.[8] Widespread in appeal was a dignified Stoicism derived from Cicero and Seneca, which warned against the vanity of human wishes and the snares of the senses – there was more in life to be endured than enjoyed, ruled Samuel Johnson. Christian Stoicism highlighted the polar forces of good and evil battling in the human breast – angel against animal, spirit against flesh, reason against appetite.[9] In this model of man, the human condition was defined by its antinomies, and by the unavoidability of taxing choices. Set on a stage in which fantasy and falsehood had to be combated, 'man's chief merit', deemed Johnson, 'consists in resisting the impulses of his nature'.[10]

No more in this Ciceronian than in the Calvinist scenario was there a sunny hedonism, a primrose path to pleasure. 'Something is always wanting to happiness,' explained Johnson's *Rambler*, for, as he remarked elsewhere, 'in all sublunary things there is something to be wished which we must wish in vain' – man, in short, 'is not born for happiness'.[11] What was crucial for such grave philosophies was not diversion but dignity and integrity: the disavowal of false gods and fatuous expectations. Six years before the storming of the Bastille, Johnson warned that 'the age is running mad after innovation'.[12] Debunking the inane and conceited cult of the new was, of course, also central to Burke's *Reflections* (1790).[13]

Such traditionalists poured scorn on naive optimism about the human condition. The Augustan satirists particularly ridiculed the facile follies of puffed-up sciolists. In his *A Tale of a Tub* (1704) and elsewhere, Swift conjured up a motley crew of modern philosophers, poets, professors and pedagogues, all suffering from obsessive solipsism. 'I am now trying an Experiment very frequent among Modern Authors,' the *Tale*'s asinine narrator blurts out, 'which is, to write upon Nothing.'[14] Such blether epitomized the modern infatuation with singularity, one blithely eager, in the name of the new science, to reduce human beings to machines or puppets. Humanists like

Johnson and Burke abhorred any apparent relinquishing of the lofty, if daunting, human obligation to exercise free will and moral choice. Swift's notorious 'modest proposers' and all the other panacea pedlars pilloried in Augustan satire were traitors to man's higher duties. Pope for his part presented rogues' galleries of his own, notably with his portrayal of the hacks in *The Dunciad* (1728), bloated with their own genius. Time and again, conservative moralists levelled their wrath or wit against modern man, that wretch who, duped by a frivolous faith in progress, had abandoned his humanity and given himself over to facile optimism and glib apologetics.[15] Moral probity required recognition that, in Pope's words, man was 'born but to die, and reas'ning but to err'. Indeed, the most eloquent warning against all such self-exculpatory hubris came from Pope:

> Plac'd on this isthmus of a middle state,
> A being darkly wise, and rudely great:
> With too much knowledge for the Sceptic side,
> With too much weakness for the Stoic's pride,
> He hangs between; in doubt to act, or rest,
> In doubt to deem himself a God, or Beast;
> In doubt his Mind or Body to prefer;
> Born but to die, and reas'ning but to err;
> Alike in ignorance, his reason such,
> Whether he thinks too little, or too much;
> Chaos of Thought and Passion, all confus'd;
> Still by himself abus'd, or disabus'd;
> Created half to rise, and half to fall;
> Great lord of all things, yet a prey to all;
> Sole judge of Truth, in endless Error hurl'd
> The glory, jest, and riddle of the world![16]

In his exposure of human pretensions, Pope held a fine line. While humbling pride, he was nevertheless more sanguine than Milton or Bunyan in urging man's capacity to know, and thus perhaps redeem, himself – indeed, in some moods he seems to be striking up enlightened melodies. After all, though a Catholic, Pope had drunk in

Bolingbroke's natural religion and Shaftesbury's benevolism, and his confidence in the passions prefigured Hume:

> The surest Virtues thus from Passions shoot,
> Wild Nature's vigor working at the root.[17]

While sympathetic towards such classical values, modern thinkers for their part did not dwell on the tragic or on puncturing pretensions: theirs was an ardent desire to promote positive views of human potential.[18] Every age, of course, has its admixture of optimists and pessimists, and such categories are themselves deeply problematic; yet it would be odd to deny that enlightened minds felt hopeful about the human condition.

Conspicuous among the new optimists was the 3rd Earl of Shaftesbury.[19] Tutored by Locke, though assuredly no clone, Shaftesbury derided Hobbes's grim teachings: in dwelling on the dismal master passions of fear and that lust for power which ended only in death, had not the author of *Leviathan* 'forgot to mention Kindness, Friendship, Sociableness, Love of Company and Converse, Natural affection, or anything of this kind'?[20] Hobbes, however, was not Shaftesbury's sole bugbear; hellfire preachers had equally traduced mankind with their deluded dogma that good nature and religion were at odds. Rejecting all such misanthropy, be it secular or Christian, and venerating the Cambridge Platonists, Shaftesbury exalted man as a naturally sociable being and commended a disinterested love of virtue: 'If Eating and Drinking be natural, Herding is so too. If any Appetite or Sense be natural, the Sense of Fellowship is the same.'[21]

Shaftesbury also talked up man's capacities: reason and ridicule, criticism and conversation would dispel error and further the cause of truth. 'Good humour', he held, 'is not only the best security against enthusiasm, but the best foundation of piety and true religion', while a 'Freedom of Raillery' was 'a Liberty in decent Language to question every thing, and an Allowance of unravelling or refuting any Argument, without offence'.[22] His *Characteristicks* (1711) shared similar goals to those of the *Spectator*, which began in the same year: to cajole readers out of bad habits and to coax them into better ones. And exactly like that magazine, his writing – conversational and dialogic in form – proved highly popular, with *Characteristicks* going through at least ten editions by the 1790s; evidently it struck a chord with a reading public keen to be sweet-talked into feeling good about itself.[23]

The new hopefulness was often predicated upon claims to lay bare the springs of human nature, so as to gain at long last a true grasp of what would later be called individual psychology: once understood, the human animal or machine could be fine-tuned to play its optimal social role. Both post-Vesalian anatomy and the new mechanical philosophy sanctioned the project of probing beneath the skin or the skull: in order for the workings of the human motor to be mastered, first it had to be stripped down. The classic early expression of this view was *Leviathan*.[24] But what Hobbes purported to find – *homo lupus homini* – was no less repugnant to the enlightened than to the divines, wounding human dignity as much as it supposedly implied atheism. Nevertheless, the Hobbesian invitation to take man to pieces retained its appeal.

The quest had many champions and took various forms. Newton predictably proved crucial, seemingly indicating the road ahead in the final pages of the *Opticks*: 'And if natural Philosophy in all its Parts, by pursuing this Method, shall at length be perfected,' stated its Query 31, 'the Bounds of Moral Philosophy will be also enlarged.'[25] Sir Isaac thus held out the prospect of a true science of human nature grounded upon natural science – one, as we shall see, which tempted David Hume.[26]

A popular approach to the subject lay in specifying man's place within the order of Nature. A long-established tradition, associated with jurists like Grotius and Pufendorf, had elucidated man's duties under natural law.[27] Implicit, and often explicit, in such accounts lay suppositions about the uniformity of man. Echoing the classical *quod semper, quod ubique, quod ab omnibus* ('always, everywhere and by everyone'), it was held that, in order to be scientific, accounts of rights and duties must transcend local and temporal variations so as to home in upon the quintessence. Only when shown to possess a universality comparable to the laws of motion would a rendition of human nature carry proven explanatory power and the ring of authenticity. If, as Hume held, mankind was presumed 'much the same' at all times and in all places, it was realistic to aspire 'to discover the constant and universal principles of human nature'.[28]

Natural law theories were commonly hitched to a conjectural anthropology which sometimes questioned and sometimes confirmed the accepted order of the here and now by invoking a *status quo ante*.[29] The thought experiment of positing man in an original state of Nature, divested of all but essential needs, wants and faculties, proved popular, influentially so in Locke's *Two Treatises of Government* (1690).[30] How far existing society was 'natural' or 'unnatural' could be tested by reconstructing the transition from square one. Indeed, it was even possible to retrace the inquiry one stage further: at what (chrono)logical point had man transcended the merely *animal* and become distinctively human? – the issue behind Lord Monboddo's evolutionary speculations (see chapter 10).[31]

The tracing of such a passage from 'Nature' to 'society' was not, however, in the main meant to be taken literally and temporally, but more by way of a just-so story, and the Scottish professor Adam Ferguson insisted that inquiry into the human essence must not be confused with authentic historical narrations. Asked 'where the state of nature is to be found',

We may answer, It is here; and it matters not whether we are understood to speak in the island of Great Britain, at the Cape of Good Hope, or the Straits of Magellan . . . If the palace be unnatural, the cottage is so no less; and the highest refinements of political and moral apprehension, are not more artificial in their kind, than the first operations of sentiment and reason.[32]

If elucidation of human nature could thus entail anthropological reconstruction of mankind's station in space and time, be it grounded in the archives or the imagination, a journey into the interior could equally be conducted. We must 'search accurately into the constitution of our nature', observed Francis Hutcheson, professor of moral philosophy at Glasgow University, in 1747, 'to see what sort of creatures we are';[33] 'it must be by an anatomy of the mind', pronounced Thomas Reid, a Scottish philosopher of the next generation, 'that we can discover its powers and principles'.[34] Central to the enlightened programme was analysis of the understanding. To such philosophers it no longer seemed profitable, in Milton's way, to inscribe the human actor in scenarios of sin and Satan, faith and the Fall; likewise the gladiatorial struggle within the breast between good and evil, spirit and flesh, as conjured up by Johnsonian humanism, could now appear more sermon than science.[35] Away with such rhetoric! What was needed was a dispassionate, objective study of human faculties, motives and behaviour.

For thinkers espousing Lockean empiricism, the key to the mechanisms of the mind and emotions lay in a sensationalist analysis of the production of consciousness and character *via* environmental stimuli. That carried a further implication: the understanding of selfhood in general and of the individual self in particular meant prioritizing interiority. What had once been taken as objective, external commands and eternal fitnesses needed to be recast as the products of trains of associations, as functions of inner powers, outgrowths of circumstances and experience: truths graven upon tablets of stone became psychologized. Heretofore profoundly suspect, subjectivity was now being tentatively validated.

One domain in which this new accent on subjectivity was explored and esteemed early on was the aesthetic. It was, after all, more plausible and less threatening to personalize taste than to do the same to morality itself – indeed, the notion that love of beauty required the exercise of superior individual aesthetic judgement had an evident appeal. As noted in chapter 3, the *Spectator* popularized Locke's empiricist aesthetics, but the internalization of the appreciation of beauty owed most to Shaftesbury, who sought at the same time to dignify 'taste' by associating it with the transcendent.[36] Loveliness, he claimed, was objectively real, it was the splendour of the divine Nature about which he rhapsodized; but appreciation of such loveliness was not something which any Tom, Dick or Harry instinctively experienced or had the right to pronounce upon; while seeded in the human heart, it needed cultivation. Taste involved not only an exquisite, intuitive discrimination beyond mechanical calculation, but also a relish verging on enthusiasm: aesthetic transports implied a participation in the grander cosmic whole, transcending gross self-gratification.

Shaftesbury's aesthetic creed – that beauty followed universal standards, but only the great-souled man, who had nurtured his taste, would recognize and cherish it – agreed with his teachings on morality. Creation was inherently good, he said, hence virtue did not consist in slavish Calvinist or Hobbesian obedience to external decrees. And man's end lay in a disinterested pursuit of virtue which would lead to self-perfection. Virtue stemmed from a benign disposition, which was of a piece with good breeding. Exercise of taste and virtue were thus comparable activities.[37]

Shaftesbury's view that beauty, though not lying in the eye of the beholder, at least required a generous spirit to perceive it, was extended by his follower and systematizer Francis Hutcheson,[38] whose *Inquiry concerning Beauty, Order, Harmony, Design* (1725) drew on Locke's 'way of ideas': 'the word beauty is taken for the idea raised in us, and a sense of beauty for our power of receiving this idea'.[39] Hutcheson held that pulchritude did not simply dwell in and radiate from the object but was inseparable from acts of perception. His psychologizing style of thinking was predictably taken further along the relativistic road by David Hume: 'Beauty,' Hume concluded in 1757, 'is no quality in things themselves: it exists merely in the mind . . . Each mind perceives a different beauty.'[40] It was central also to the young Burke, whose *Philosophical Enquiry into the Sublime and the Beautiful*, of the same year, presented a reading of sublimity which was essentially sensationalist: aesthetic categories were primarily defined by imaginative experiences, involving emotions like terror (see chapters 9 and 13). 'When any object, either of sublimity or beauty is presented to the mind,' explained the Scot Archibald Alison later, in 1790, in his development of similar themes, 'I believe every man is conscious of a train of thought being immediately awakened in his imagination, analogous to the character or expression of the original object.'[41] Lockean associationism – Alison's 'constant connection between the sign and the thing signified' – thus came to govern enlightened analyses of aesthetic experience. Subjectivity did not, however, preclude science in such matters, for aesthetic associations were regarded by Hume and others as being no less definite – and hence no less determinable – than gravity itself.[42] Beauty had been assimilated into the mechanisms of the mind.

As issues like beauty, traditionally regarded as decreed by the order of Nature and mandated by the canons of classical criticism, were reconfigured as psychological, elucidation of the workings of that psyche obviously became more pressing. What precisely was the 'self' within? Was it, as taught by Christian dualism, the immortal and immaterial soul – or some annexe or inflexion of it? Or was it something altogether more mundane, to do simply with the senses, and with powers like judgement and memory? How was this *je ne sais quoi* to be known? By introspection – or by an anatomy of the brain or nerves? These were the big issues confronting enlightened moralists.

In this context, the pressing question became that of self-identity: what did it mean to be an 'I'? 'The word Person,' Hobbes had commented,

is Latin [and] signifies the *disguise,* or *outward appearance* of a man, counter-feited on the State; and sometimes more particularly that part of it, which disguiseth the face, as a Mask or visard . . . So that a *Person* is the same that an *Actor* is, both on the Stage and in common Conversations; and to *Personate,* is to Act, or Represent himself, or an other.[43]

Hobbes, as ever, points in two directions; on the one hand his was a subversive materialism which reduced the psyche to cerebral matter in motion; on the other, his quest for a philosophy of cast-iron order led him to focus on the outward manifestations of a man.

The connection of personhood to inner consciousness was broached in the second edition of the *Essay concerning Human Understanding* (1694), where Locke declared that 'self is not determined by Identity or Diversity of Substance, which it cannot be sure of, but only by identity of consciousness':

Person, as I take it, is the name for this *self*. Where-ever a Man finds, what he calls *himself*, there I think another may say is the same *Person* . . . This personality extends it *self* beyond present Existence to what is past, only by consciousness.[44]

The person was thus fundamentally not fixed in the flesh but in the understanding, held Locke, using 'consciousness' in the sense of the 'totality of the impressions, thoughts, and feelings, which make up a person's conscious being'.[45] By thus making the self-presence of the soul hinge on such fleeting occurrences as impressions and sensations, he seemed to his critics to come perilously close to dissolving it completely. This gave him no cause for unease, however: as he saw it, his reading, far from opening the floodgates to scepticism and unbelief, afforded a nobler vision of the mind, detached thereby from the dross of corporeality. He certainly entertained no doubts as to the real presence of the self. 'For if I know I feel pain,' he wrote,

it is evident I have as certain perception of my own existence, as of the existence of the pain I feel: or if I know I doubt, I have as certain perception of the existence of the thing doubting, as of that thought which I *call doubt*. Experience then convinces us, that we have an *intuitive knowledge* of our own existence.[46]

Such teachings nevertheless potentially destabilized beliefs about the permanent integrity of the self. Locke's pupil Shaftesbury relished such ruminations, his turn of thinking taking an introspective, not to say narcissistic, direction. For the earl, the theoretical question 'What is a person?' bled into the personal 'Who am *I*?' While staunchly upholding a patrician endorsement of rank and status, he grew absorbed in the enigmas of selfhood, reflecting on the riddle of identity that 'I [may] indeed be said to be lost, or have lost My Self' – a conclusion with infinitely regressive Shandyesque possibilities.[47]

The subversive repercussions of such speculations as to the unity, permanency and identity of the self were explored in controversies over duty, accountability and determinism. Many arose out of the necessitarian teachings of Joseph Priestley and William Godwin,[48] but such conflicts had first crystallized in exchanges between Samuel Clarke and Anthony Collins. For the Christian rationalist, continuity was of the essence of the conscious mind; its omnipresence confirmed the immortal soul, which was in turn a validation of the Supreme Intellect. Challenging these orthodoxies, Collins teased out the implications of Locke's suggestion that consciousness, while assuredly the seat of the understanding, was nevertheless intermittent and fragmented: thinking, Collins stressed, did not go on all the time – for instance, during sleep – while trances, forgetfulness and delirium proved that perception was discontinuous and divisible.[49] Such instances provided golden opportunities for this free-thinking lawyer. 'Let us consider to what Ideas we apply the Term Self,' he proposed, giving such unsettling speculations a provocative spin:

If a Man charges me with a Murder done by some body last Night, of which I am not conscious; I deny that I did the Action, and cannot possibly attribute it to my *Self*, because I am not conscious that I did it. Again, suppose me to be seized with a short Frenzy of an Hour, and during that time to kill a Man, and then to return to my *Self* without the least Consciousness of what I have done; I can no more attribute that Action to my *Self*, than I could the former, which I supposed done by another. The mad Man and the sober Man are really two as distinct Persons as any two Other Men in the World.[50]

Collins's tantalizing forensic speculations not only problematized notions of personal responsibility in the moral and legal spheres but also challenged doctrines of sacred responsibility and punishment. Such debates over identity were destined to run and run, especially once rekindled by Hume (see below).

Perhaps in order to obviate the risk entailed in post-Lockean speculations that the *cogito*, that backbone of public man, would disintegrate if theological or Stoic absolutes were discarded, certain moral philosophers set about making an inventory of the divine anatomy of the mind. Notable here was the school of 'faculty psychology', which shone especially in the Scottish universities, as a 'middle way' seeking to forge a moral philosophy which was credibly modern yet would reassure both the Kirk and civic patrons that moral philosophy was basically about teaching man his God-given duties.

Along these lines, Francis Hutcheson at Glasgow – 'I am called New Light here,' he quipped – developed an elaborate classification, derived from introspection, of the mental faculties with which man had been endowed, designed to demonstrate the reality of the 'moral sense' (regarded as an inner power rather like gravity) and so rebut scepticism and Bernard de Mandeville's cynical egoism.[51] Daringly, in the light of Presbyterian politics, Hutcheson's blueprint for the internal chambers of the mind was framed within a naturalistic ethic – 'the action is best,' he declared, sidestepping discussion of sin, 'which procures the greatest happiness for the greatest numbers'.[52] His pioneering utilitarianism – the test of morality lay not in conscience but in consequences – was given respectability by his insistence that it was God Himself who had implanted in the machinery of the mind the disposition to virtue, a moral sense naturally tending to goodness.[53] Such sentiments bring out Hutcheson's multiple commitments: his espousal of the natural (that is, God-given) goodness of mankind; of adaptation and final causes; and of happiness as a criterion and moral goal. Equally evident is his determination to replace the *a priori* with the empirical, since it was to 'our structure and frame' – rather than the Commandments or Clarkean eternal fitnesses – that he looked for 'clear evidences showing the proper business of mankind'.[54]

Analysis of the make-up of human nature, proposed Hutcheson in his *A Short Introduction to Moral Philosophy* (1747), must take into account both body and soul. Of these, the soul was the 'nobler' part, endowed with two classes of powers, the understanding and the will. The former 'contains all the powers which aim at knowledge', while the latter has 'all our desires pursuing happiness and eschewing misery'.[55]

What Hutcheson meant by the understanding was the sum of all the powers designed to yield knowledge. These included the senses – those powers of the soul by which (Lockean) ideas were raised when encountering certain objects. Some senses (like sight) were external, depending on bodily organs stimulating feelings or notions in the soul when an impression was made on the body; others were internal – otherwise known as consciousness or reflection. There were also reflex or subsequent senses, among which he listed aesthetic appreciation (already discussed); the enjoyment derived from the discovery of truth; sympathy or fellow feeling; the desire for action; and conscience or the 'moral sense'

by which we discern what is graceful, becoming, beautiful and honourable in the affections of the soul, in our conduct of life, our words and actions . . . What is approved by this sense, we count right and beautiful, and call it virtue; what is condemned, we count base and deformed and vicious.[56]

This sense of good and evil was universal, being divinely implanted at all times and places. There was also the sense of honour and shame, founded upon the moral sense yet distinct from it and operating in the light of consciousness of the approval of our fellows; and lastly the Shaftesburian sense of ridicule, vital for correcting human frailties.

Complementing the understanding was the will, which orchestrated the pursuit of happiness. Such wishes came in two sorts, selfish and disinterested. Among the former were stable passions – the desire for good for one's self, an aversion to evil, joy when good was attained or sorrow when evil ensued – and also turbulent, blind and impetuous impulses, including the itch for power, renown or gold. The disinterested passions included calm desires (such as benevolence or good will), aversion, joy (which might take such forms as pride, arrogance and ostentation) and sorrow (including shame, remorse and dejection). Then there were passionate desires – 'nor have we names settled to distinguish always the calm from the passionate', added Hutcheson, apparently defeated at last by the daunting taxonomic task he had taken on.

In the organization of the psyche there were finally also 'dispositions relating equally to understanding and will'. These were four. First was the (Lockean) disposition to associate ideas or affections, 'however disparate or unlike, which at once have made strong impressions on our mind' – in Hutcheson's view, it was to this leaning that we owed 'our power of memory, or recalling of past events, and even the faculty of speech'. Second, there were habits, for 'such is the nature both of the soul and body, that all our powers are increased and perfected by exercise'. Then there was the desire to obtain whatever appeared a means to a desirable end, such as wealth and power. Last, there were the powers of eloquence.[57]

Hutcheson thus internalized morality – virtuous behaviour stemmed from inner impulses – while skirting scepticism by stressing how these feelings were divinely implanted as part of a structured consciousness. Rather as with Linnaeus's contemporaneous botany, inventories of the mind such as Hutcheson's might be self-confessedly artificial, being drawn up largely for heuristic and pedagogic purposes, but they were also meant, in a rather literal way, as natural-historical taxonomies of the powers with which the Divine Artificer had endowed man, that *animal rationalis* brought into this world to practise virtue and achieve happiness. Such schemes became the bedrock of academic moral philosophy in the Common Sense philosophy which shored up the syllabuses of Scottish (and North American) universities, partly in order to serve as a sandbag against the floodtides of Mandevillian cynicism and Humean scepticism.[58]

Philosophies like Hutcheson's were tacitly part of what was beginning to be known as 'psychology'.[59] In traditional charts of knowledge, the study of the mind or soul had fallen under the heading of 'pneumatology', that is, the philosophy of 'incorporeal' substances (God, angels, etc.), a pursuit located in turn within the domain of divinity. Enlightened discourse, by contrast, began to map out a field of natural knowledge pertaining to the mind which was distinct from the theological study of the immortal soul. Thus Chambers' *Cyclopaedia* (1727) defined psychology as 'a Discourse Concerning the Soul' which constituted a part not of theology but rather of anthropology, that is, the natural study of man at large.[60] The *Cyclopaedia* glossed soul and mind in Lockean terms. By associating the soul with physiology and logic, and by shifting the study of the mind from pneumatology to psychology, Chambers' text established the latter as part of the new philosophy.[61] David Hartley, discussed below, similarly spoke in 1749 of 'psychology, or theory of the human mind', setting it within 'natural philosophy'.[62] With the soul thus becoming psychologized, as by Locke, and even materialized, as by Hartley and his editor, Priestley, enlightened thought withdrew the study of man from the theological. A new and essentially naturalistic or secular understanding of the psyche was thereby being framed.

Embracing fresh approaches to the mind, enlightened thinking thus ensured that ethics, while continuing to draw upon Plato, Aristotle, Xenophon, Cicero, the Bible, Renaissance humanists like Erasmus and Montaigne and many other revered authorities, should square with, indeed must be derived from, empirical and introspective investigation of the faculties and dispositions comprising man's natural endowment. Any such claim would previously have counted for less, in view of the doctrine of the Fall. But with a Pelagian theology resurgent, it was now deemed to be man's business not, as Johnson put it, to 'resist the impulses of his nature', but to train those affections. That in turn depended upon resolving the conundrum of human nature itself.

So what was man's make-up? There was, needless to say, no single enlightened view, but rather difference, debate and dialogue. Battle lines were drawn, however, at the beginning of the century by Bernard de Mandeville, a Rotterdam-born physician who had settled in London. Cartesian by education and an admirer of the pungent moral satires of La Bruyère and La Rochefoucauld, Mandeville delighted in anatomizing man, or taking readers behind the scenes of this comedy of manners.[63] According to him, the removal of the masks revealed Hobbesian egoism, an itch for power and a pride in reputation. 'Disinterested' behaviour turned out to be self-seeking, and 'virtue' concealed selfishness and an insatiable hunger for gratification and aggrandizement.[64]

Like Freud later, Mandeville was fascinated by the obsessive denial of the desires of the flesh dictated by moralists and divines, and was particularly intrigued by obsessional sexual 'Thou shalt nots'. Males and females alike, explained his *The Virgin Unmask'd* (1709), were perennially on heat; both sexes craved the satisfaction of carnal hunger. Yet *mores* spelt out elaborate rules for deferring or rationing erotic gratification. Ladies in particular were expected to remain chaste, or at least cultivate a reputation for 'virtue'.[65] Mandeville did not positively object to such devices in the economy of erotic regulation – they negotiated discordant desires and made the system work – but he loved daring hypocrites to come clean.

While Mandeville never strayed far from matters sexual, at the heart of his non-medical writings was another dialectic of desire and denial: the appetite for gain and fame. Time and again, he addressed what he identified as the central paradox of his age. Individuals were manifestly availing themselves of every opportunity to acquire wealth and esteem; money, possessions, display and conspicuous consumption – all conferred power and prestige. Yet acquisitiveness was conducted in the face of official fusillades against greed; what everyone actually did was denounced as luxury and vice. Why so? These were the issues addressed in his notorious *The Grumbling Hive: or, Knaves Turn'd Honest* (1705), a 433-line moral tale in doggerel hexameters, later festooned with lengthy prose commentaries and reissued as *The Fable of the Bees: or Private Vices, Public Benefits* (1714), a work which swelled with every infamous edition.[66]

Mandeville imagined a successful 'hive'. All the bees were ambitious egoists, buzzing to get on by all possible means – to turn an honest penny by labour, trade and other ways, but also through shadier enterprises, such as swindles, frauds and theft:

> All trades and Places knew some Cheat,
> No Calling was without Deceit.[67]

In macrocosm, collective conduct replicated the individual: the national hive at large was, in other words, proud, aggressive and warlike. Being thus active and assertive, individuals and community flourished alike:

> Thus every Part was full of Vice,
> Yet the whole Mass a Paradise;
> Flatter'd in Peace, and fear'd in Wars,
> They were th'Esteem of Foreigners,
> And lavish of their Wealth and Lives,
> The Ballance of all other Hives.
> Such were the Blessings of that State;
> Their Crimes conspired to make 'em Great.[68]

What was the secret, the grand arcanum, of the thriving hive? Mandeville's answer was provocative: what made the world go round was vice – or, translated from Christian censure into plain English, self-interest.

> Thus Vice nurs'd Ingenuity,
> Which join'd with Time and Industry
> Had carry'd Life's Conveniences
> It's real Pleasures, Comforts, Ease,
> To such a Height, the very Poor
> Liv'd better than the Rich Before,
> And Nothing could be added more.[69]

Or rather nothing, that is, until moral rigorism had its say. Corruption was rife, thundered the godly; the system fostered vanity and greed and it created artificial desires which outran needs; it was wanton and wasteful; it excited the appetites of the flesh instead of quelling them; it begat the itch for luxury and debauchery. All this, they insisted, must end.

What happened, then, when, in virtue's name, a regime of self-denial was inaugurated? Frugality became king, double-dealing was outlawed – and the consequence was abject decline. Rectitude and austerity had no need for a bustling market economy; demand disappeared and idleness and poverty set in. If righteousness was to rule, he concluded, you had to forsake the gratifications of civilization and take to munching acorns.

So, for the cynical Mandeville – ironically, no less than for his

Stoic adversaries – choice was of the essence. It was possible to have wealth, employment and pleasure, refinement, sophistication and politeness – in a word, the Addisonian trappings – by pursuit of what the morality-mongers dubbed vice. Or you could be, in the well-worn phrase, poor but honest. What irked or amused him was the myopic folly or flagrant hypocrisy of those who blithely berated profligacy, deaf to the implications of their own oratory.

Why did 'morality' precipitate untoward consequences? It was because of false consciousness, induced by clergy and others, about the nature and purposes of morality itself. That was why Mandeville appended to the 1723 edition of the *Fable* a 'Search into the Nature of Society'. Properly understood, true morality should be a matter not of the *denial* of desires but of their regulation.[70] Human nature was nakedly selfish. In the state of nature, Mandevillian man was essentially Hobbesian, driven by basic wants (food, survival, sex, and so on) and seeking to satisfy them in the crudest ways. Such bare-faced egoism inevitably bred conflict, and conflict-management had to be undertaken by a wise legislator decreeing conventional codes so as to civilize egoism. Possessive instincts were to be governed by property laws, and lust tamed by matrimony. The envy which initially led to filching other people's belongings became normalized into labour, exchange and the love of lucre. Thus, properly understood, society was a cunningly contrived mill for refining naked egoism into more peaceful and profitable means for the fulfilment of wants, at the cost of some deferral of gratification and much moral posturing. And why not? After all, even respectability has its pleasures.

Moral codes and conduct were identity cards to be carried to ensure observation of the niceties. Honour and shame provided the spur. Those abiding by the rules of the game, no matter how cynically, would be esteemed, while others would be showered in obloquy. Given human vanity, the distribution of acclaim and disgrace pro-vided powerful inducements to ensure that the merry-go-round of life kept turning.

Ultimately, what made the system tick was 'that strong Habit of Hypocrisy, by the Help of which, we have learned from our Cradle to hide even from ourselves the vast Extent of Self-Love, and all its different Branches';[71] and what preachers dubbed baseness was, when suitably masked, a vital social energy. 'Vices are inseparable from great and potent Societies,' taunted Mandeville, 'and it is impossible their Wealth and Grandeur should subsist without.'[72] And the ultimate moral of it all?

> Then leave complaints; Fools only strive
> To make a great an honest hive . . .
> Fraud, luxury and pride must live
> While we the benefits receive.[73]

Mandeville, in other words, would deny his contemporaries the easy moral self-congratulation they craved:

> T'enjoy the world's conveniences,
> Be famed in war, yet live in ease,
> Without great vices, is a vain
> Eutopia seated in the brain.[74]

Inevitably, he was reviled by Christian moralists (as the 'man devil') for having had the temerity to stand up for depravity. 'Vice and luxury have found a Champion and a Defender,' carped the critic John Dennis, 'which they never did before.'[75]

Relentlessly reminding readers that human nature was depraved, that greed and envy were vicious, and love of money the root of all evil, Mandeville was, so to speak, confirming what rigorists had been preaching all along. But the message of *The Virgin Unmask'd* and *The Fable of the Bees* was not repentance: quite the reverse. Man was indeed self-interested, but was that not *desirable*? Greed, lust, vanity and ambition were beneficial, if pursued in socially sanctioned ways. Properly directed on the world's stage, selfishness produced social harmony. Long before Hume or Smith, Mandeville was thus suggesting that 'private vices' would beget 'public benefits' – Mandeville looked to a legislator to effect them, Smith for his part to an 'invisible hand'.

Such transvaluations were far from unique. Did not Pope propose in his *An Essay on Man* that, rightly managed, 'self love and social' would prove the same?[76] Mandeville, however, took unique delight in playing the *enfant terrible*, twitting Shaftesbury's lofty idealism.[77] In return, as we have seen, Shaftesbury's acolyte Hutcheson retaliated, upholding human decency under a benevolent God;[78] and numerous other moralists developed philosophies, examined in chapter 11, which unequivocally repudiated vice and aligned virtue with enlightened self-interest.

The great advocate of exploring man scientifically was David Hume, whose *A Treatise of Human Nature*, appearing in 1739–40, was, as specified in its subtitle, 'An Attempt to Introduce the Experimental Method of Reasoning into Moral Subjects'.[79] Partly perhaps for personal reasons – he had had a nervous breakdown in his twenties – Hume made it clear that the 'science of man' was necessarily sceptical in tendency: it was essential to ask 'Where am I, or what? From what causes do I derive my existence, and to what condition shall I return?'[80] From this standpoint he explored the grounding of belief – received 'truth' was largely wishful thinking, betraying a readiness to be deceived – and he famously criticized sloppy metaphysicians and theologians for illegitimate thought leaps from 'is' to 'ought'. Aspiring to become the 'Newton of the moral sciences', Hume sought to establish a rigorous account of the mind derived from 'careful and exact experiments', the 'only solid foundation' being grounded in 'experience and observation'.[81] *A priorism* was out: 'any hypothesis, that pretends to discover the ultimate original qualities of human nature, ought at first to be rejected as presumptuous and chimerical'.[82]

Hume, indeed, drove Locke's empiricism further, dissolving the latter's category of knowledge ('demonstration') into 'belief'. It was not that Hume was bent upon showing that it was a random or unintelligible universe, only that man's mental equipment for understanding it was imperfect: 'When I reflect on the natural fallibility of my judgment, I have less confidence in my opinions than when I only consider the objects concerning which I reason.'[83] He was, however, prepared to fall back on the general experience of uniformity: 'Would you know,' he famously asked, 'the sentiments, inclinations, and course of life of the Greeks and Romans? Study well the temper and actions of the French and English . . . Mankind are so much the same, in all times and places.' And on that basis, he was confident of the feasibility of a science meant to 'discover the constant and universal principles of human nature'.[84]

The first book of the *Treatise* addressed key topics relating to the mental faculties, knowledge and belief. Claiming to eliminate all concepts not derived from experience and observation, Hume held that our knowledge of the self and of the world was limited to perceptions (impressions) derived from observation and introspection. All legitimate ideas or thoughts were to be traced back to sense impressions or to internal impressions or feelings, and to associations derived therefrom. The old scholastic doctrine of substance was empty verbiage, and neither could causal powers be discovered – one must submit to 'constant conjunctions' which stopped short at belief in the uniformity of nature.[85]

For these reasons, no fixed self was knowable (or, by implication, there at all). Taking up Locke's discussion of identity (see above), Hume drove it to sceptical conclusions: since experience was made up of 'impressions', and these – for Hume, as for Collins – were discrete, there was, in truth, no such demonstrably constant unity as a 'person', merely atomized impressions of continuity. Personal identity was thus highly contingent and wreathed in doubt. Truths still self-evident to the theist Locke could not survive the sceptical Hume's scrutiny. Peering into himself he discovered, he reported, no coherent, sovereign self, only a flux of perceptions. During sleep, existence in effect ceased. Given the inability to meld disparate perceptions, identity was thus 'merely a quality which we attribute to them, because of the union of their ideas in the imagination when we reflect on them . . . Our notions of personal identity proceed entirely from the smooth and uninterrupted progress of the thought along a train of connected ideas.'[86]

If the first book of the *Treatise* was thus shockingly sceptical in its thrust, the second and third, on the passions and morals respectively, struck more positive notes. Analysis of such desires as pride and humility, love and hate, uncovered an internal feeling or sentiment called the 'moral sense'.[87] In delineating the workings of propensities integral to human existence, Hume noted that Christian theologians and Platonists alike had condemned the appetites, the former deploring them as sinful, the latter demanding their mastery by reason. For Hume, by contrast, feelings were the true springs of such vital social traits as the love of family, attachment to property and the desire for reputation. Pilloried passions like pride were the very cement of society. Dubbing its denigrators 'monkish', Hume defended pride when well regulated; indeed, magnanimity, that quality attributed to all the greatest heroes, was 'either nothing but a steady and well-establish'd pride and self-esteem, or partakes largely of that passion'. Besides, 'hearty pride' was essential to society, whose hierarchy of ranks, fixed by 'our birth, fortune, employments, talents or reputation', had to be maintained if it were to function smoothly. A person needed pride to acquit himself well in his station – indiscriminate humility would reduce social life to chaos. Much that had traditionally been reproved as egoistically immoral he reinstated as beneficial.[88]

Hume drew attention to the logical chasm between the real world and the duties commanded by sacred books, commended by authorities, or rationally deduced, as by Clarke or Wollaston, from the fitnesses of things. Telling man that he 'ought' to struggle against his nature was about as useful as urging planets to resist gravity. Unlike the cynical Mandeville, the complacent and socially conservative Hume wanted not to outrage readers but to reconcile them to the actualities of human emotions, beliefs and conduct, and to guide them to social usefulness.[89]

What mattered in that respect was that desirable social conduct arose not from reason but out of feelings. Hence, in a celebrated paradox, Hume maintained that reason was and ought to be 'the slave of the passions' – since the emotions, like gravity, constituted motives and hence controlled what people were actually moved to do.[90] Reason *per se* could not initiate action, for it was not of itself a motive. ''Tis not contrary to reason,' he reflected outrageously, 'to prefer the destruction of the whole world to the scratching of my finger.' Strictly speaking, there was no such thing as the civil war between reason and the passions, as imagined by Plato – that question had been badly posed: reason 'can never pretend to any other office than to serve and obey' the passions.[91]

Hence mankind should cultivate rather than curb natural leanings. Immense harm could result, as in the English Civil War, when normal inclinations were abandoned and men became the pawns of wild imaginings which invariably proved disorienting and destructive. Since there were no transcendental truths, innate ideas or *a priori* precepts, it paid to follow custom, that 'great guide of human life'. The Enlightenment's most uncompromising investigator of human nature thus ironically reached conclusions whose implications were highly conservative, for as a moralist Hume was a down-to-earth pragmatist, basing his prescriptions on utility and the need for social reassurance.

Conduct was thus programmatically naturalized. Society had developed so as to meet certain basic needs – for security, self-esteem, and so forth. The science of human nature confirmed that these pragmatic actions were grounded in psychological realities, and hence were not to be disavowed lightly in the name of any specious transcendental value system, abstract metaphysics or utopian vision. What Mandeville showed in satire, Hume demonstrated through science.

The two Davids – Hume and Hartley – were very different individuals but their philosophies are surprisingly convergent. Like Hume, Hartley's thinking involved an inquiry into human nature that was conceptually radical, upending conventional ideas of the make-up of the mind; and, as with Hume, the implications of his analysis were in practice rather conservative. Indeed, Hartley's was even more conventional, since, by contrast to the unbeliever Hume, he upheld the essentials of Christianity, albeit occasionally giving them a rather eccentric twist.[92]

The son of a poor Anglican clergyman, Hartley studied at Cambridge at precisely the time when Newtonian mathematics and Lockean philosophy were coalescing to form the core curriculum. He went on to hold a fellowship at Jesus College until he was forced to relinquish it, as was normal practice, upon his marriage in 1730.[93] While sincere as a Christian, Hartley had doubts about the Thirty-nine Articles. These precluded him, like many others, from taking holy orders, and so he studied medicine instead. Elected a fellow of the Royal Society, Hartley moved in superior intellectual circles, his friends including the Society's president, Sir Hans Sloane, the Revd Stephen Hales (famous for his physiological experiments) and Joseph Butler, the leading Anglican theologian.

Observations on Man, His Frame, His Duty, and His Expectations, published in 1749, presented a comprehensive philosophy of man considered in respect both of his earthly existence and a future state. Convinced that all knowledge was derived from experience, Hartley drew heavily upon Locke's associationist empiricism, but whereas the wary Locke had avoided entangling himself with the material basis of thought,[94] the younger man plunged in boldly, persuaded that the mysteries of the mind could be resolved by modern physical science.

Hartley also digested the innovative associationist utilitarianism of the Revd John Gay's *Preliminary Dissertation Concerning the Fundamental Principle of Virtue or Morality* (1731), which proposed a pleasure and pain psychology as the key to a philosophy of action. Following Locke and Gay,[95] Hartley dismissed innatist theories of cognition and morality, holding that complex ideas were concatenated from simple ones by repeated inputs of the 'sensations of the soul': anything else was mystery-mongering. Through the principle of association, primary sensations were capable of being compounded *via* complex combinations into pleasures and pains, which came in six different classes – imagination, ambition, self-interest (divided into gross and refined), sympathy, theopathy and the moral sense – each of which was factitious.

Man was thus a machine programmed for happiness, and

Christianity's transcendental teleology of human improvement was validated by experience itself. 'Some Degree of Spirituality,' declared Hartley 'is the necessary Consequence of passing through Life. The sensible Pleasures and Pains must be transferred by Association more and more every day, upon things that afford neither sensible Pleasure nor sensible Pain in themselves, and so beget the intellectual Pleasures and Pains.'[96] This was beyond dispute, since on balance pleasures outnumbered pains, so that 'Association . . . has a Tendency to reduce the State of those who have eaten of the Tree of the Knowledge of Good and Evil, back again to a paradisiacal one'.[97] The mind had been divinely designed in such a way that experience and association invariably led to higher truths. A child, for instance, came to associate its parents with the pleasures derived from them, and would in due course, forgetting the original motive, learn to love them. Conversely, the miser, initially associating money with the pleasure derived from what it would buy, would equally forget the original association and in the end experience pure greed.[98] Feelings and values were thus constructs arising out of mental activity, and educational and environmental influences should optimally be organized so as to secure the association of pleasure with socially desirable objects. Man might never rise to altruism in the strictest sense, but he was certainly capable of benevolence. And benevolence, held Hartley,

has also a high Degree of Honour and Esteem annexed to it, procures us many Advantages, and Returns of Kindness, both from the Person obliged and others; and is most closely connected with the Hope of Reward in a future State, and with the Pleasures of Religion, and of Self-approbation, or the Moral Sense . . . It is easy therefore to see, how such Associations may be formed in us, as to engage us to forego great Pleasure, or endure great Pain, for the sake of others.[99]

Drawing on associationism as an explanatory principle, Hartley went beyond Locke and set it upon physical foundations, that is, the anatomy of the nervous system and the physiology of 'motions excited in the brain'. For his scientific axioms he turned to Newton. In the

'Queries' to the *Opticks*, Newton had shown how light vibrated in a medium. Such vibrations impacted upon the retina, Hartley explained; having impinged upon the eye, these corpuscular motions then set off further undulating waves which passed along the nerves to the brain. The association of ideas was thus materialized in terms of reiterated vibrations in the white medullary matter of the brain and spinal cord, resulting in lasting traces which formed the physical substrate of complex ideas, memory and dispositions.

Unlike La Mettrie and other French *philosophes*, Hartley framed his materialist psycho-physiology in terms of an overarching Christian theology: materialism could nowise be the road to atheism, precisely because it had been God who, in His wisdom, had endowed matter with all its powers. Furthermore, the necessitarianism entailed by such materialism was, to Hartley, the surest guarantee of the unbroken operation of cause and effect, of the uniformity of Nature, and hence of God's boundless empire. Determinism predicated a strict chain of causes both physical and moral, which led inexorably back to the First Great Cause. Indeed, the second volume of the *Observations* extended the system to account for man's prospects beyond the grave.

Hartley's thinking proved critical to the late Enlightenment science of man. It gave learning theory and the moral sense firm naturalistic moorings, and, though he was himself devout, his unification of sensation, motion, association and volition within a mechanistic theory of consciousness and action pointed to the secularization of the concept of utility. His was a model which came to be prized as the fountainhead of psychological, biological and social truths, providing the stimulus for the associationist tradition in psychology and pedagogics. Hartley's conjectural physiology of the nervous system also offered prototypes for the sensory motor theories later influential in neurophysiology, comprising distant ancestors of Pavlovian notions of conditioned reflexes.

Hartley's influence was widespread – an early enthusiasm for his work led Coleridge to name his first-born Hartley. In his 1775 edition of the *Observations*, retitled the *Theory of the Human Mind*, Joseph Priestley, though omitting the neurology, valued Hartleyan determinism since it put associationism at the service of a Unitarian philosophy of nature. Erasmus Darwin, by contrast, made Hartley's neurological mechanisms the basis for the scheme of medical classification advanced in his *Zoonomia* (1794) and for the evolutionism of his *Temple of Nature* (1803), and William Godwin's arguments in his *Enquiry concerning Political Justice* (1793) for inevitable progress drew on Hartley's moral meliorism. Hartley, indeed, proved more influential than Hume in the late Enlightenment, since his vision of human perfectibility – a predetermined tendency to happiness, scientifically intelligible, under a benevolent Deity – was precisely the doctrine of human nature needed by progressives, marrying as it did science and piety and discounting the abhorrent selfishness of Hobbes or Mandeville. Its Achilles heel lay in its unsettling and, to many, offensive materialism. As so often, enlightened solutions proved jarring to tender sensibilities, and so provided perennial provocations of controversy.

Sidestepping pulpit pontifications and formal metaphysics, enlightened thinkers thus put the study of human nature on a footing which was naturalistic, empirical and analytical. Of course, any natural science of man was open to the charge that it reduced the Christian pilgrim, created in God's image, to a beast, puppet or machine, driven by the gross laws of matter in motion: hence the sting of Swiftian satire. But the new scientific approach to human nature caught on, notably in the rooting and shooting of the human and social sciences.[100] 'In our universities, what a change has been gradually accomplished since the beginning of the eighteenth century!' exclaimed Dugald Stewart at its close:

The Studies of Ontology, of Pneumatology, and of Dialectics, have been supplanted by that of the Human Mind, conducted with more or less success, on the plan of Locke's *Essay*; and in a few seats of learning, by the studies of Bacon's *Method of Inquiry* of the Principles of Philosophical criticism, and of the Elements of Political Economy.[101]

Beyond those seminaries, the transformation from Pilgrim to the man of sense was even greater.

8

THE SCIENCE
OF POLITICS

freedom is the first blessing of our nature

By the time David Hume proposed in an essay of 1741 that politics should be reduced to a science, the idea was a cliché – indeed, it had been the subject of a sardonic joke in *Gulliver's Travels* (1726), where the hero chided the Brobdingnagians for their 'ignorance' in 'not having hitherto reduced *Politicks* into a *Science*, as the more acute Wits of Europe have done'.[2] And, as we have seen, in 1728 Desaguliers had produced his *The Newtonian System of the World: The Best Model of Government*, which vindicated the social order through science and proclaimed that he had 'considered Government as a phenomenon . . . most perfect' when it 'does most nearly resemble the natural government of our system, according to the laws settled by the all-wise and almighty architect of the universe'.[3]

But if the State was thus construed as being open to scientific analysis, in practice politics itself remained a cockpit of rival rhetorics, and the central plank in enlightened platforms was freedom:

Freedom from absolutism (the constitutional monarchy); freedom from arbitrary arrest, trial by jury, equality before the law, the freedom of the home from arbitrary entrance and search, some limited liberty of thought, of speech, and of conscience, the vicarious participation in liberty (or in its semblance) afforded by the right of parliamentary opposition and by elections and election tumults . . . as well as freedom to travel, trade, and sell one's own labour.[4]

Small wonder freedom roused such passions, for, in the eyes of Whiggish modernizers, the Stuarts had been bent upon extinguishing it. Charles I had dispensed with Parliament; Charles II had played fast and loose with both that institution and the Anglican Church, while his stops of the Exchequer had undermined security of property and financial confidence; and then James II had subverted the sanctity of the law by arbitrary arrests and by tampering with urban corporations, university tenures and other forms of property. Moreover, both Charles and James, admiring Catholic absolutism overseas, had used the royal prerogative and dispensing powers recklessly. Sir Robert Filmer's *Patriarcha* (1680) had deemed monarchy divine, and Jacobitism would long retain its furtive following.[5]

The most signal repudiation of such thinking came from John Locke, whose *Two Treatises of Government*, written during the Exclusion Crisis, was published in 1690.[6] In the First Treatise, Locke rebutted passive obedience and discounted Filmer's notion of the Divine Right monarchs handed down from God *via* Adam: such patriarchalism forged 'Chains for all Mankind'.[7] He also repudiated the view that 'all Government in the World is the product only of Force and Violence, and that Men live together by no other Rules but that of Beasts, where the strongest carries it' – although Hobbes went unmentioned as the author of 'might is right'.[8] Defining political power as 'a *Right* of making Laws . . . for the Publick Good', Locke denied that its source lay either in Adam or in arms: political legitimacy could spring only from consent, as was explained in a just-so story of the transition from a state of nature.[9]

Locke conjured up an original pre-government condition in which men went about their business bound by all the basic rights and duties of civil society (such as abstaining from theft and violence), precisely because 'the state of nature has a law of nature to govern it, which obliges everyone: and Reason, which is that law, teaches all mankind, who will but consult it, that being all equal and independent, no one ought to harm another in his life, health, liberty, or possessions'. This law of Nature was binding because it was God's edict and men were His 'property'.[10]

Political society was then set up by the voluntary agreement of 'all', to protect those God-given rights and properties recognized by reason in the state of Nature: 'the great and chief end of men's uniting into commonwealths, and putting themselves under government, is the preservation of their property'.[11] Government was dutybound to uphold the contract agreed by the people, who retained an indefeasible residual authority over their rulers. In the state of Nature, in other words, the individual was autonomous, though bound by the law of Nature; in civil society action became subject to public judgement – private persons became public persons, and private acts were replaced by public ones, in a transformation designed to strengthen the protection of life, liberty and property.[12] An ultimate right was retained to resist a government in breach of its contract – a right not to be activated individually but exercised by the 'people' (a notion left studiously vague): 'the Community may be said in this respect to be always the Supreme Power'.[13] So long as government functioned justly, this residual popular power was not to be used. But if the prince were to seek to 'enslave, or destroy them', the people were entitled to '*appeal to Heaven*' – though precisely how, the judicious Locke left unstated. Moreover, he was quick to reassure nervous readers that this right did not 'lay a perpetual foundation for disorder', since it would not be used until 'the Inconvenience is so great, that the Majority feel it, and are weary of it'. The nation would thus be slow to rebel:[14] even 'Great mistakes in the ruling part . . . will be born by the People without muting or murmur', and recourse would be had to resistance only after 'a long train of Abuses, Prevarications, and Artifices'.[15] Locke was walking his perennial tightrope: anarchy was no answer to tyranny.

Locke's defence of liberty rested on his theory of property. Confronting Filmer's claim that 'God gave the World to Adam and his Posterity',[16] he cited the Scripture text stating that God had 'given the Earth to the Children of Men, given it to Mankind in common'.[17] In the state of Nature, a man lawfully made his own the land upon which he laboured:

Though the Earth, and all inferior Creatures be common to all Men, yet every Man has a *Property* in his own Person. This no Body has any Right to but himself. The *Labour* of his Body, and the *Work* of his Hands, we may say, are properly his. Whatsoever then he removes out of the State that Nature hath provided, and left it in, he hath mixed his *Labour* with, and joyned to it something that is his own, and thereby makes it his *Property*.[18]

Work thereby debarred others from the products of one's labour.[19] The basic 'value added' principle – by adding something to the land over and above 'Nature', labour created an inviolable title – solved for Locke the problem of how 'the Property of labour should be able to over-ballance the Community of Land' – a solution doubtless attractive to propertied readers enjoying the highly unequal fruits of agrarian capitalism at a time when enclosure was gathering momentum.[20] Since property thus preceded government, it could not be meddled with by the prince.

A further and crucial modification of the state of Nature arose from the consensual 'Invention of Money',[21] which led to lawful consent to 'larger Possessions, and a Right to them', and thereby sanctioned all the changes industry brought. 'The desire to having more than Men needed altered the intrinsick value of things',[22] and added what would later be called exchange value to use value.

Needs, explained Locke, had initially been met through barter. By the exchange of 'Plumbs that would have rotted in a Week, for Nuts that would last good for his eating a whole Year' no injury was done by natural man to the conservation of Creation, for 'he wasted not the common Stock'.[23] Barter thus squared with the law of Nature, since no 'waste' resulted: what would contravene it was not the 'largeness of his Possession', but rather the 'perishing of any thing uselessly in it'.[24] Next followed the invention of money, drawing on 'some lasting thing that Men might keep without spoiling', such as gold.[25] Some (Locke presumed) being more industrious than others, the advent of a money economy inevitably brought a 'disproportionate and unequal Possession of the Earth',[26] thereby sanctioning differential wealth and encouraging accumulation and saving.

Crudely put, capitalism enjoyed the blessing of God's laws, while absolutism did not.

Though Locke sought to allay fears – the right of rebellion was a last resort – the radical potential of his politics could hardly be gainsaid. Indeed, looking back from the 1780s, the pragmatic Josiah Tucker bemoaned the unsettling tendencies of Lockean theory as hijacked by the contemporary 'new-light' men, that is, Dissenters like Richard Price. With its postulates of a state of Nature and an original compact, contractarianism was rooted, Tucker growled, not in realities but in precisely those metaphysical will-o'-the-wisps the enlightened scorned. That was what made it so serviceable in the 1770s to the American rebels and then in the 1790s to Painites back home.[27]

In his own lifetime, however, Locke's political formulations proved somewhat beside the point. The *Two Treatises* had initially been penned to justify the 1st Earl of Shaftesbury's exclusionist policies.[28] Published, however, in 1690 in the afterglow of the Glorious Revolution, his oppositional theory of an original contract was virtually redundant – indeed, even a potential irritation for triumphant Whigs by then seeking not to legitimize resistance to tyranny but to vindicate the new Williamite order. After 1688, it has been observed, the key question was not whether 'a ruler might be resisted for misconduct, but whether a regime founded on patronage, public debt, and professionalization of the armed forces did not corrupt both governors and governed'.[29]

Not surprisingly, then, alternative discourses of freedom moved centre stage. Prominent among them was one which drew upon the analysis of the rise and fall of states developed by Machiavelli in his *Discourses* on Livy's history of Rome, and which had been trimmed to British circumstances by James Harrington's *Oceana* (1656).[30] Followers of Harrington explained the flourishing (or failure) of liberty in political societies in terms of their socio-political health (or pathology). Initially developed by anti-Stuart Whigs, the theory was subsequently levelled by dissident ('Country' or 'True') Whigs against post-1688 administrations ('Court Whigs') before, thanks to the twists of politics, being exploited by opposition Tories, notably Viscount Bolingbroke, for their own ends. Posing as a public-spirited, non-party censor of political morality, Bolingbroke's paper, *The Craftsman*, sermonized on maladministration and corruption, targeting in particular the great oligarch Robert Walpole – a classic case of stealing one's enemy's ideological clothes.[31]

This 'civic tradition', a body of ideas owing much to Polybius and other Graeco-Roman thinkers, addressed the historical and institutional realities of the body politic.[32] The essentials of a sound state lay in a regular constitution which involved elected assemblies and a division of powers amongst the various legislative, executive and judicial functions; and in a military force recruiting the citizenry in public defence. The polity's make-up was broadly speaking republican, and political liberty hinged on participation both in arms and in senates. The converse of the virtuous and free body politic was despotism – an irregular, unconstitutional state which depended for its defence on standing armies and mercenaries, and consigned the populace to political slavery.[33]

A constitution and a citizen army were not, however, sufficient to guarantee permanent freedom. The people themselves had to possess true public spirit (*virtù*) and moral fibre: only thereby could political liberty be sustained. Such *esprit* in turn depended on the right foundations: economically, a citizen had to be 'independent' – that is, free from needing to engage directly in productive or commercial activity. In Aristotelian terms, a clear demarcation was to be drawn between property-owners on the one hand and on the other those whose lot it was to sustain them – tradesmen, artisans, women and the plebs.

If, however, citizens ended up sordidly setting private interests above public virtue, then, according to this civic tradition, the community would sink in sleaze, a malignancy threatening the very soul of the commonwealth. Greed and apathy would speed the decay of institutions and the consequent loss of political *virtù* and liberty.

Pamphleteers and coffee house pundits voiced fears of the ruin allegedly being wrought by commercial society, in particular by the *nouveaux riches*, by their paper money, stocks, shares and banks, the National Debt and other new and shady forms of financial dealing, all suspected to be spawning deception, double-dealing and dependence. The gentry and freeholders, England's backbone, were supposedly growing enfeebled, while the new City plutocrats lorded it in conspicuous luxury.

A prominent instance of this neo-Roman discourse of political freedom was John Trenchard and Thomas Gordon's *Cato's Letters* (1720–23). A Whig MP, Trenchard had co-written with Walter Moyle the definitive 'Commonwealth' attack on William III's standing army. Although he had initially penned pamphlets for Walpole, he grew disillusioned, and, with Lord Molesworth, led the parliamentary attack in 1720 on the minister's handling of the South Sea Bubble.[34] Collaborating with Gordon, he then produced 'Cato's' letters in the anti-Walpole weekly the *London Journal*. For three years, 'Cato' slammed the 'Robinocracy' (Walpole's regime) and the moneymongering to blame for the Bubble, vilifying mere 'money' in the name of landed independence and exposing the 'Murtherers of our Credit' who had imperilled the sacred 'Security of Property'.[35]

Trenchard and Gordon, however, also grafted their neo-Harringtonian ideas on to Lockean contractarianism. The doctrine of inalienable rights enunciated by 'Cato' clearly echoed the *Second Treatise*. 'All Men are born free,' he proclaimed:

No Man has Power over his own Life, or to dispose of his own Religion; and cannot consequently transfer the Power of either to any body else. Much less can he give away the Lives and Liberties, Religion or acquired Property of his Posterity, who will be born as free as he himself was born, and can never be bound by his wicked and ridiculous Bargain.[36]

Liberty, that 'unalienable Right of all Mankind', was likewise defined in Lockean terms as 'the Power which every Man has over his own Actions, and his Right to enjoy the Fruit of his Labour, Art, and Industry'.[37] Not only were such rights defended but 'men are naturally equal', 'Cato' further boldly asserted, and 'no Man was ever born above all the rest, nor below them all'.[38] Far from being authorized *à la* Filmer by 'the immediate Revelation of God', governments were the creations of peoples, set up to safeguard their rights; hence force could 'give no Title'.[39] It had been precisely this 'Principle of People's judging for themselves, and resisting lawless Force' which had sanctioned the 'late happy *Revolution*'. And lest readers feared resistance might go too far, 'Cato' stressed, echoing Locke, that subjects were so wary of disturbing the peace that they would not resort to protest until grievances grew intolerable – indeed, the true danger was that they would tarry too long, for 'tyranny has engrossed almost the whole Earth, and . . . makes the World a Slaughter-house'.[40] Eternal vigilance was imperative.

The early Enlightenment liberty platform thus had many planks: Lockean natural liberty was dovetailed into civic humanist political anatomy and other traditions besides – the Anglo-Saxon self-government ideal and its corresponding 'Norman yoke' theory, and the ubiquitous celebration of Common Law and the constitution:[41]

> Then was the full and perfect plan disclos'd
> Of BRITAIN's matchless *Constitution*, mixt
> Of mutual checking and supporting Powers,
> KINGS, LORDS, and COMMONS.[42]

was celebrated by James Thomson's 'Goddess of Liberty' in his poem *Liberty* (1735).

Post-1688 England was thus the land of the free, destined to teach the world a lesson: 'The sentiment of liberty, and the ever-active protection of the laws,' groused the Prussian visitor von Archenholz, 'are the cause why the common people testify but little consideration for persons of quality, and even for persons in office.'[43] Indeed, such swagger had some basis in political realities. Flaunting the freedom of the press, journalists boasted of their role as guardians of British independence. 'Those who declaim against the Liberties taken by News Papers . . . know not what they say,' declared the *London Evening Post* in 1754; 'it is this Liberty, that . . . protects all the rest.'[44] Provincial papers echoed the chorus. 'Every Englishman must be sensible that by encouraging a News Paper,' affirmed the *Reading Mercury*, 'he contributes to the support of the Liberty of the Press.'[45] According to arguments recited in Thomas Hayter's *Essay on the Liberty of the Press* (1755), William Bollan's *The Freedom of Speech and Writing upon Public Affairs Considered* (1766) and similar works, freedom of speech was the cornerstone of all the others. It was 'the great palladium of British freedom', pronounced the jurist William Blackstone, while the pamphleteer 'Junius' styled it 'the palladium of all the civil, political, and religious rights of an Englishmen'.[46] This turned into a veritable Whig mantra: 'Against despotism of any kind or in any shape,' declared Richard Sheridan, 'let me but array a free Press, and the liberties of England will stand unshaken.'[47] The rationale behind free speech was spelt out by the bookseller John Almon. Man was, by nature, a communicative creature. As society expanded, it had become necessary to supplement the spoken word with the written, to ensure communication across great distances. Since liberty of *speech* was a fundamental right, liberty of the *press*, Almon concluded, must follow.[48]

Characteristically pragmatic arguments were further adduced by David Hume: press freedom was, paradoxically, a stabilizing factor, posing no danger to public order. The public was neither as gullible nor as menacing as the scaremongers alleged, and private reading actually lowered the political temperature:

A man reads a book or pamphlet alone and cooly. There is none present from whom he can catch the passion by contagion . . . The liberty of the press, therefore, however abused, can scarce ever excite popular tumults . . .

It has also been found, as the experience of mankind increases, that the *people* are no such dangerous monster as they have been represented, and that it is in every respect better to guide them, like rational creatures, than to lead or drive them, like brute beasts. Before the United Provinces set the example, toleration was deemed incompatible with good government; and it was thought impossible, that a number of religious sects could live together in harmony and peace . . . ENGLAND has set a like example of civil liberty; and though this liberty seems to occasion some small ferment at present, it has not as yet produced any pernicious effects.[49]

In short, champions of freedom exulted in English traditions and the 'sacred' constitution – Horace Walpole slept with a copy of Magna Carta on one side of his bed and Charles I's death warrant on the other.[50] The Glorious Revolution was freedom's meridian. The period prior to 1688 had been characterized by intellectual 'mysteries' and by Popery, John Taylor reflected, before

LIBERTY at the Revolution, O bright, auspicious Day! reared up her heavenly Form, and smiled upon our happy Land. Delivered from the fears of Tyranny and Persecution, Men began freely to use their Understandings.[51]

And these Whig myths assumed an enlightened hue: freedom was not just a political blessing but also the cradle of culture. 'Where Absolute Power is,' insisted the 3rd Earl of Shaftesbury, 'there is no Publick.'[52] Freedom, by contrast, spelt civilization: 'All Politeness is owing to Liberty. We polish one another, and rub off our Corners and rough Sides by a sort of amicable Collision.'[53]

Civic humanism saw freedom as guaranteed by independent freehold property: only the landed truly had a stake in the country, unlike the moneybags benefiting from paper money and the public debt arising out of the founding of the Bank of England in 1694. Neo-Harringtonians feared the subversion of the ancient constitution by unscrupulous dealers whose hands were soiled by filthy lucre and place-hunting. 'Landed men,' held Bolingbroke, 'are the true owners of our political vessel; the moneyed men, as such, are but passengers in it.'[54]

How was this danger to be forestalled? England, some insisted, should heed the examples of ancient Greece or the Roman republic, as depicted by Cato or Plutarch. 'The Grecian commonwealths, while they maintained their liberty, were the most heroic confederacy that ever existed,' held James Harris, 'they were the politest, the bravest, and the wisest of men.'[55] Yet were not such visions hopelessly at odds with reality? Hanoverian Britain was growing richer, more self-assured and centralized, and who could credibly deny that England's new greatness on the world's stage derived from trade, conquest and a powerful executive? All these, however, according to civic humanist dogma, were dire threats to liberty.[56] So did the Whig ascendancy in reality subvert that very freedom it was purporting to defend? And if so, was British liberty just a shadow or even a sham?[57] Many, of course, cried yes, wrung their hands and continued to intone the rhetoric of 'corruption' – notably the Revd John Brown, whose doom-laden *Estimate of the Manners and Principles of the Times* (1757) diagnosed national decay caused by the cancer of commerce.[58] Yet these Jeremiads were being challenged by new enlightened discourses, anxious to vindicate commercial society.

Enlightened thinking, as we have seen, shunned the scholastic: it wanted not just to understand the world but to influence it. In this drive, none were more influential than Joseph Addison and Richard Steele, whose *Tatler, Spectator* and *Guardian* promoted key enlightened positions.[59] Ideas were meant to be spread, and to that end they looked forward to the day 'when Knowledge, instead of being bound up in Books, and kept in Libraries and retirement, is thus obtruded upon the Publick; when it is canvassed in every Assembly, and exposed upon every Table'.[60]

Adopting the persona of 'Isaac Bickerstaff', Richard Steele edited the thrice-weekly *Tatler* (1709), dedicated to the reformation of manners and morals: 'The general Purpose of this Paper, is to expose the false Arts of Life, to pull off the Disguises of Cunning, Vanity, and Affectation, and to recommend a general Simplicity in our Dress, our Discourse, and our Behaviour.'[61] While it also included news coverage and a miscellany of essays, letters and information, social improvement was central from the start.

Two months after the final *Tatler* was published, with sales approaching 4,000, the first *Spectator* appeared, on 1 March 1711. It was an immediate hit. '*The Spectator*,' enthused John Gay, 'is in everyone's hands, and a constant topic for our morning conversation at the tables and coffee houses.'[62] By the tenth issue Addison was boasting, 'there are already three thousand of them distributed every day' – and on his guess of 'twenty readers to every paper' that meant 'about three-score thousand disciples in London and Westminster'.[63] Gentleman's clubs met to discuss the magazine and it was read from Scotland to Surinam. And although the real public reached by those pioneering media men was sizeable, even more significant perhaps was their conquest of the public imagination: they were the talk of the town. While cleverly sustaining an air of elitist intimacy, Mr Spectator, the man about town, was the first media man.

Devoted to uniting 'merriment with decency' while instructing in taste and morality, the *Spectator*'s 'morning lectures' were to be varied, light and crisp, so that 'the busy may find time, and the idle may find patience' to scan them. Ignorance, dogmatism, violence, boorishness, inanity, divisiveness – whatever militated against politeness was targeted. Promoting propriety, good manners and style, its lay sermons declared war on false values, foppery and folly – and low taste, like puns.

In the absence of political or religious unanimity, good taste was made the new social adhesive which would cement propertied élites together. Civilized role-playing and the poised presentation of self by the *honnête homme* flourishing among 'the Fraternity of Spectators'[64] became paramount on an urban stage in which all doubled as actors and audience. Piously doffing his hat, Addison noted that, whilst St Augustine had called life 'a Pilgrimage', Epictetus for his part had deemed the world 'a Theatre, where everyone has a Part allotted to him' and would be judged accordingly. Of the two, it was the classical moralist whom Addison chiefly commended – although, along with Steele, he was arguably the most influential Christian of his age.[65]

'There cannot a greater judgment befall a country than such a dreadful spirit of division that rends a government into two distinct people . . . A furious Party spirit, when it rages in its full Violence, exerts it self in civil war and bloodshed.'[66] Such wounds must be healed. 'My paper has not in it a single word of news, a reflection on politicks, nor a stroke of party,' boasted the irenic Addison; he would advance 'no fashionable touches of infidelity, no obscene ideas, no satyres upon priesthood, marriage, and the like popular topicks of ridicule'.[67] Politics and scandal might sell, but he aimed to draw 'men's minds off from the bitterness of party' and forge consensus.[68] Yet, of course, the *Spectator*'s anti-politics were utterly political, preaching moderation and acceptance of modernity, rather like that sworn foe of 'Men of Heat', Daniel Defoe, and later David Hume. New political extremism was as ruinous as old enthusiasm; the divided society had to be knitted together and political passions needed to be managed.[69] Beguiling with their style and mocking the manners of the vulgar, the out of date and fashionable affectations alike, the *Tatler* and the *Spectator* sold the young idea of lifestyle politics, offered alluring glimpses of social success and peddled hope: 'Half the misery of human life,' Addison wrote, 'might be extinguished, would men alleviate the general curse they lie under, by mutual offices of compassion, benevolence, and humanity.'[70] Yet the price of improvement was regulation and 'Mr Spectator', writing from his coffee house nook, fantasized himself as the universal eye, meting out correction by naming and shaming. 'Inspectors' would be sent to check abuses, rather as with the Society for the Reformation of Manners, except that while that body policed the poor, the *Spectator* was to examine the élite.[71] Appearances counted, after all: all aspects of the individual, readers were reminded – demeanour and decorum, attire and attitudes – were social signs making character and status legible, and hence demanded attention if self and society were to rub along.

Appearing day in, day out, the *Spectator* and its lookalikes became the oracles of modern élites conversing with themselves – and liking what they heard. In the first instance their appeal, in their conversational essays featuring familiar characters – the original soap opera heroes? – was to smart urbanites but, in due course, they captured the reading nation at large, as they were reprinted and imitated over and again. In the 1760s, Edinburgh's high priest of taste, the Revd Hugh Blair, could comment that it was 'in the hands of everyone'; 'there is scarcely an individual', concurred Vicesimus Knox, cleric, schoolmaster and man of letters, 'who has not digested the Spectators'.[72] Many testified to its impact: Voltaire used it to improve his English, it taught Benjamin Franklin style, while another American, James Madison, recalled that it inculcated 'just sentiments, an appetite for knowledge, and a taste for the improvement of the mind and manners'.[73] Spectatorial periodicals were thus bibles of enlightened behaviour.

Addison and Steele were writing for political animals who had grown up seeing the city through jaundiced eyes – as Babylon, Rome or Vanity Fair – indeed, they themselves could portray it as a den of dissimulation, where ideals were subservient to interest and taste to tawdriness.[74] Displacing this Augustinian or neo-Harringtonian bogey, they invoked an alternative image of a flourishing public realm founded upon benevolence. Spurred by altruism rather than advantage, true friendship would blossom in the relaxed, face to face environment of the tavern, coffee house or exchange, in the company of companions drawn from different walks of life – gentry, clergy, soldiers, merchants. Man's natural capacity for virtue would thereby be released and good living thrive. The modern city was capable of cradling, no less than corrupting, virtue. Once virtue shook hands with commerce, the asceticism of the Puritans and the anxieties of the humanists could be thankfully consigned to the past.

Thanks in large measure to Addison and Steele, a new politics began to displace those traditional rhetorics, especially as the post-1714 regime truly did seem to deliver the promised peace and prosperity. 'Public liberty, with internal peace and order, has flourished almost without interruption,' sang David Hume of the startling transformations so perceptible in his own lifetime:

Trade and manufactures, and agriculture, have increased: The arts, and sciences, and philosophy, have been cultivated. Even religious parties have been necessitated to lay aside their mutual rancour; and the glory of the nation has spread itself all over Europe; derived equally from our progress in the arts of peace, and from valour and success in war.[75]

Promoting practical morality was central to Hume's project, perhaps explaining his decision, after completing his *Treatise of Human Nature* in 1740, to abandon systematic philosophy for polite essay-writing *à la* Addison. As a vehicle for moralizing on human conduct, the essay suited his genius and his aims. Addison and Steele had addressed the aspirations of propertied urbanites, teaching them how to negotiate their private happiness in a complex society; Hume recognized that this emergent commercial order still needed defending, not least against noisy moralists.

Challenging civic humanism's sacred cows, Hume held that market society went hand in glove with liberty. 'If we trace commerce in its progress, through Tyre, Athens, Syracuse, Carthage, Venice, Florence, Genoa, Antwerp, Holland, England, etc.,' he submitted, 'we shall always find it to have fixed its seat in free governments.'[76] Far from causing corruption, economic development was integral to social improvement. Supplanting the evils of scarcity and privation, the abundance of material goods produced by the market promised 'the chief advantage of society', and this could be secured by gathering larger populations together to improve security and capitalize on economies of scale and the division of labour.[77]

Greed detonated disorder, the civic humanists had claimed, and it was to this stumbling block that Hume turned his attention in the *Treatise*. The 'insatiable, perpetual, universal' passion for acquisition was, he admitted, 'directly destructive of society', but not if 'curbed so as to ensure security of possession'. Such essential stability was provided by justice, which established the rules of property and its transfer, and the duty of contract-keeping. Justice was not, however, some innate idea or eternal fitness discerned by *a priori* reason; government itself arose only gradually, when peoples had to provide for external security by defending themselves against aggressors. Unlike in Locke's thinking, justice was thus consequential – a virtue which, Hume insisted, in a much-misread distinction, was 'artificial' without being at all 'arbitrary'. Derivative rather than primary, justice was the product of conventions, just as government was an outgrowth of necessity not reason.[78]

Hume disparaged Locke's state of nature as a futile fiction. Justice and morality had come about pragmatically, over time, by trial and error, in line with human wants:

After men have found by experience, that their selfishness and confin'd generosity, acting at their liberty, totally incapacitate them for society; and at the same time have observ'd, that society is necessary to the satisfaction of those very passions, they are naturally induc'd to lay themselves under the restraint of such rules, as may render their commerce more safe and commodious ... *Thus self-interest is the original motive to the* establishment *of justice: but a* sympathy *with public interest is the source of the* moral approbation, *which attends that virtue.*[79]

War had first inured men to leaders. They, in time, would tend to assume responsibility for justice once possessions accrued. Recognition would follow that it was in everybody's true interests to set the administration of justice, along with defence, in the hands of office-holders whose repute would lie in the competent performance of those functions. Government was thus not, as for Locke, a necessary evil but rather the source and sign of social progress. Out of the need for, and utility of, government stemmed the duty of allegiance to it.[80]

Hume then proceeded to address the implications of economic improvement. The neo-Harringtonians had got it wrong: luxury was a good thing, ensuring motives for obedience to government and creating a desirable environment for social life. Flying in the face of ancient wisdom, Hume held that Rome's decline had not stemmed from the import of 'Asiatic' luxury: excessive conquests and the ineptitude of imperial government had been to blame.[81] The truth was that progress in the arts was favourable to liberty, for it fostered a stable social order. In 'rude unpolished nations', landowners and their underlings were hopelessly at odds, provoking social strife. Under the early tyrannies the populace were slaves, who did not 'enjoy the necessaries of life in plenty or security':[82] neither learning nor trade could have developed in such conditions. It was only with the rooting of law in 'free governments' that improvement could begin. Aspiring to liberty, the citizens of early republics sought to curb power by instituting the rule of law. This in turn fostered and channelled productive energies, and so such republics became seedbeds for the encouragement of knowledge, skills and arts. The foreign contacts of the early Greeks, with all their 'neighbouring and independent states, inconnected together by commerce and policy', also boosted the rise of civilization. The rivalries of small eastern Mediterranean polities prevented the stifling uniformity characteristic of monolithic empires. Thus, Hume concluded, laws and institutions, stability and order – the preconditions of commerce and culture alike – were originally 'the sole growth of republics'.[83]

Hume's trump card, however, was his claim that modern monarchies were closer, in essentials, to republics than to their nominal forebears: 'It may now be affirm'd of civiliz'd Monarchies, what was formerly said in Praise of Republics alone, *that they are a Government of Laws, not of men.*'[84] Slavery had been the ruin of ancient despotisms – since slaves were not allowed family life, slave populations had had to be restocked by war. Early city states had not proved more viable, however, headed as they were by citizen élites holding women, foreigners and slaves in subjection. The open assemblies typical of early democracies were unwieldy, and rotation of office had foundered on the reefs of faction and feuds. Political chaos ensued and ancient polities had been torn apart by *coups d'état*, ostracism and vendettas, creating turmoil and driving cities into interminable wars for booty and honour. Consequent depopulation hindered economic development, while the glamour of politics and warfare meant that productive labour was despised. The slave labour and incessant warfare of early regimes, in short, did not favour economic growth. Nevertheless, despite all the turmoil, at least the seeds of civilization had been sown. Cultivation of the arts, manual and liberal, stimulated the mind and softened cruel passions:

The more those refined arts advance, the more sociable men become; nor is it possible, that, when enriched with science, and possessed of a fund of conversation, [men] should be contented to remain in solitude, or live with their fellow-citizens in that distant manner, which is peculiar to ignorant and barbarous nations . . . Thus industry, knowledge, and humanity are linked together by an indissoluble chain, and are found . . . to be peculiar to the more polished, and . . . the more luxurious ages.[85]

Enlightened optimism blazons here in Hume's confidence in the civilizing power of the passions. Government and freedom were not at odds: no authority, no liberty.

Thus, in Hume's vision, the advance of civilization required neither saints nor heroes; impersonal forces drove men to accomplish collectively what none had individually willed: 'The spirit of the age affects all the arts; and the minds of men, being roused from their lethargy, and put into a fermentation, turn themselves on all sides, and carry improvement into every art and science.'[86] It was in this context that his Addisonian entreaties were entered against the reckless political partisanship tearing England apart.

So how were virtue and happiness to be realized in Hume's modern commercial world, despite its courtiers, fops and speculators? He took up Addison's answer: the good life was to be practised, not in the great world of affairs – on the battlefield or the Senate House floor – but amongst family and friends, in a sociable setting where the buffetings of fortune could be avoided and self-esteem secured. It was a private milieu which had to be constructed and cherished – people had to learn to cultivate the art, as Adam Smith was shortly to explain, of seeing themselves as others saw them. The past had belonged to might; civilization must now look to mind, as swords were beaten into teaspoons. Private spaces had to be carved out in which people felt relaxed enough to tolerate each other's opinions and value respect above righteousness. Confidence, conciliation and conversation would abrade idiosyncrasy, affectation and prejudice. The Spectatorial values adopted by Hume held that beliefs and actions should be tempered by self-criticism, detachment and a desire to cultivate domestic affection and friendship: only thus could social approval be secured. Here, finally, lies the contribution of Adam Smith.

Addison and Steele were no academics, and Hume never got a chair. Yet in a fascinating turnabout, their teachings were to acquire a more formal expression, when the Glasgow professor Adam Smith became the philosopher of Mr Spectator.[87] Based on a course of lectures delivered to his students, Smith's *Theory of Moral Sentiments* (1759) spelt out the principles of morals and social living appropriate for self-improving middling sorts immersed in a modern, commercial society, a few rungs down the social scale from the *habitués* of Mr Spectator's club. Lecturing to young Scots, Smith elevated the ego of commercial man above the civic virtues of the classical republican, dwelling particularly on the wealth, freedom and political wisdom needed to sustain a commercial polity.

While anxious, like other Scottish philosophers, to introduce the methods of the natural into the moral sciences, Smith had ethical aims which were primarily practical: to instruct his students in their roles as citizens (as is clear from his discussion of the significantly titled 'impartial spectator').[88] Addressing the psychological fact that 'we desire both to be respectable and to be respected', he proposed that 'happiness arises from the consciousness of being beloved'. Virtue, as Locke had taught, was a learnt behaviour; the desire to be praiseworthy was acquired, not innate;[89] and the 'impartial spectator' was the device Smith proposed to help people cope and achieve respect in complex social situations posing conflicting choices.

The 'impartial spectator' was many things for Smith. It could be the identity of a real person ('the attentive spectator') in concrete situations, whose approval was valued. On a higher plane, the 'impartial spectator' lay more within the imagination than in the world – he was the 'supposed spectator of our conduct'. At the most sophisticated level, the figure was thoroughly internalized as 'the abstract and ideal spectator', or, in other words, conscience. This internal tribunal – 'the demi-god within the breast' – was thus a monitor, an *alter ego*, conjured up to negotiate social intricacies. 'When I endeavour to examine my own conduct,' Smith meditated:

when I endeavour to pass sentence upon it, and either to approve or condemn it, it is evident that, in all such cases, I divide myself, as it were, into two persons; and that I, the examiner and judge, represent in a different character from that other I, the person whose conduct is examined into and judged of.[90]

Overall, the impartial spectator was a 'looking-glass by which we can in some measure, with the eyes of other people, scrutinize the propriety of our own conduct'.[91]

Smith's theory of interpersonal adjustment deriving from sympathy – putting ourselves in others' shoes – should be read in the context of the practical morality already advanced by Addison and Steele and Hume, with their recognition that society was complex and required subtle skills in taxing social situations to help people lead useful, happy and virtuous lives and avail themselves of expanding opportunities. It was absurd for moderns to imagine escaping from the swirl of prejudice, fashion and fantasy by retreating into Catonic severity: contemporaries could live virtuously only by cultivating social sites such as the home, the coffee house, tavern and salon, where those from different walks of life would converse as friends and peers and learn tolerance, moderation and mutual respect.[92]

Prizing relationships between independently minded individuals, Smith aimed to show how they could acquire a sense of justice, public responsibilities and personal identity. Distrusting monolithic politico-economic institutions, he valued face to face relationships and voluntary groupings – reflecting Hume's *aperçu* that the club might serve as a model for the moral history of society itself.[93] By considering how others would appear to us, and by looking into society's mirror, noted Smith, we 'suppose ourselves the spectators of our own behaviour'.[94] As the inimitable Robert Burns put it,

> O wad some Pow'r the giftie gie us
> Tae see oursels as ithers see us![95]

In some ways, Smith's philosophy reflected Mandeville's egoism, but whereas the *Fable*'s author believed that people conformed because they were bent on praise, Smith deemed they also wanted to be praiseworthy: his was an internalized view of moral motives, appropriate to a dawning age of sentiment.[96]

Enlightened political discourse vindicated commercial society by planting it in the soil of British liberties. Addison and Steele undertook the popularizing mission, Hume and Smith provided the theory. Ploughing his own furrow, and challenging, if more urbanely than Mandeville, the self-images of the age, Hume set the agenda for later twists in enlightened political discourse, ones concerned to vindicate commercial society and establish its conduciveness – indeed, indispensability – to peace, prosperity and sociability. How far economic development would square with liberal politics will be further examined in chapter 17.

Initially at least, Hume's scientific analysis of politics and apology for the *status quo* had little cause to clash with Whig defences of freedom. Even Joseph Priestley, eventually a firebrand, could sound rather Humean early in his career, demoting 'civil liberty' below 'personal freedom'. 'Happiness is in truth the only object of legislation of intrinsic value,' he maintained, 'and what is called political liberty is only one of the means of obtaining this end. With the advantage of good laws, a people though not possessed of political power may yet enjoy a great degree of happiness.'[97] In due course, however, this early accommodation would become problematic.

9

SECULARIZING

The Augustan journalists and critics were the first intellectuals
on record to express an entirely secular awareness of social and
economic changes going on in their society.

J. G. A. POCOCK[1]

The long eighteenth century brought an inexorable, albeit
uneven, quickening of secularization, as the all-pervasive religiosity
typical of pre-Reformation Catholicism gave way to an order in
which the sacred was purified and demarcated over and against a
temporal realm dominating everyday life. In towns at least, churches
were ceasing to be the main assemblies and clerics the chief authorities, and the daily round and the ritual year were becoming detached
from the liturgy and the Christian calendar. Already characteristic
of Protestant and commercial society, such changes were furthered
by enlightened imperatives.[2]

In the new climate of criticism and with the tempo of life accelerating, old ways were challenged, and no longer did hallowed custom
or 'God's will' automatically provide answers to life's questions. With
material culture burgeoning, 'business' (in both senses of the term)
counting and the national pulse quickening, practical calculations
meant more. Time – the transient and temporal rather than the eternal
– became money, indeed became property: Samuel Pepys was
pleased as Punch to acquire his first timepiece. 'There are now a
great many large Clocks in London,' commented the French traveller
Henri Misson fifty years later; 'almost every Body has a Watch.'[3]

With time growing precious to a commercial people, the English
became noted as a nation on the move. They 'walk very fast',

recorded the French traveller Grosley, 'their thoughts being entirely engrossed by business, they are very punctual to their appointments'.[4] Ever strapped for time, Londoners even came to rely on the fast-food takeaway. 'I happened to go into a pastrycook's shop one morning,' wrote Robert Southey, donning his Spanish persona:

and inquired of the mistress why she kept her window open during this severe weather – which I observed most of the trade did. She told me, that were she to close it, her receipts would be lessened forty or fifty shillings a day – so many were the persons who took up buns or biscuits as they passed by and threw their pence in, not allowing themselves time to enter. Was there ever so indefatigable a people![5]

Time discipline was stressed as task orientation yielded to time orientation. Factory hours even became punctuated by clocking-on, with John Whitehurst designing special timepieces for use in his friend Josiah Wedgwood's Etruria works.[6] 'Above all things,' advised Sir John Barnard, 'learn to put a due value on Time.'[7] Even aristocrats got the message. 'There is nothing which I more wish that you should know and which fewer people do know than the true use and value of Time,' Lord Chesterfield cautioned his son:

I knew a gentleman, who was so good a manager of his time, that he would not even lose that small portion of it which the calls of nature obliged him to pass in the necessary house, but gradually went through all the Latin poets in those moments. He bought, for example, a common edition of Horace, of which he tore off gradually a couple of pages, carried them with him to that necessary place, read them first and then sent them down as a sacrifice to Cloacina; that was so much time fairly gained, and I recommend you to follow his example . . . it will make any book which you shall read in that manner very present in your mind.[8]

Prayers and pieties continued, but in the ubiquitous worldly atmosphere devout habits of trusting to Providence were challenged by a new eagerness to practise self-help and take charge where possible – indeed, to be 'provident'. In respect of illness, for instance, there was a tide of hospital foundations. Medieval hospitals had been 'hospices', holy places of 'hospitality' for the needy, setting the good death and salvation above surgery; and most of those had been destroyed by the Reformation. The new foundations were, however, centres of care and treatment for the sick poor (the rich were still nursed at home). Five great new London hospitals were founded through bequests and private philanthropy: the Westminster (1720), Guy's (1724), St George's (1733), the London (1740) and the Middlesex (1745). Provincial and Scottish infirmaries followed and specialist institutions, such as the Foundling Hospital in Bloomsbury for abandoned babies, lying-in hospitals, 'lock' hospitals for venereal diseases and 'Magdalene' institutions for prostitutes, were also set up, while new dispensaries provided drugs for outpatients.[9] The evocatively named Humane Society, founded in London in 1774, publicized rescue techniques, especially for cases of drowning. Based on a Dutch precursor, it supplied equipment, awarded prizes and distributed pamphlets which instructed in mouth-to-mouth resuscitation, tobacco enemas and electrical stimulation. Promoted by eminent physicians like John Coakley Lettsom and supported by the Quality, it publicized its views in periodicals such as the *Gentleman's Magazine*, while newspapers explained first aid techniques.[10] Human intervention was now meant to snatch victims from their fate.

Various occurrences hitherto explained supernaturally, such as madness and suicide, were also secularized as part of this 'disenchantment of the world'.[11] Infanticide ceased to be viewed as the product of bewitchment, being reinterpreted in the civil context of child murder.[12] In due course the Revd Thomas Robert Malthus, despite – or perhaps because of – being an Anglican clergyman, could claim to demonstrate in his *Essay on the Principle of Population* (1798) that incontestable 'acts of God' like war and famine had, after all, nothing to do with the Devil or the Horsemen of the Apocalypse but followed automatically from the numerical imbalance of man's appetites for food and sex.[13]

Tabulation of statistics, publicly in bills of mortality, helped turn accidents into regularities in a growing culture of quantification.[14] Falling sick had traditionally flagged the arbitrariness of existence, or rather had pointed to the essentially providential meaning of things. When mortal affliction had struck, heads had turned upwards. But now physicians strove to extend their control by plotting biomedical regularities. The physiological operations of the body were weighed, measured and numbered, and there followed actuarial computations such as differential life expectations, essential for insurance, annuities and so on – it is no accident that those late Enlightenment luminaries Richard Price and William Frend were both prominent actuaries. Mortality crises became objects of investigation by army, navy and civilian doctors, especially after 1750, in expectation that once periodicities in smallpox and other epidemics were established, such infections might be predicted, and thence controlled.[15] It is significant that it was the ardent Newtonian, secretary of the Royal Society and prominent physician James Jurin who clinched the statistical case for smallpox inoculation.[16]

Many domains underwent what, from a twentieth-century viewpoint, has been called the 'taming of chance', though it might less anachronistically be deemed the denial or distancing of the transcendental.[17] That was exemplified in the rise of social scientific frames of thinking – the belief that social happenings should be explicable in terms of impersonal, universal law, expressed within the categories of such emergent disciplines as political economy, anthropology, sociology, psychology and demography.[18] All this went with myriad slight, but cumulatively significant, day-to-day indications that polite and propertied society, afflicted by adversity or the unknown, was growing less disposed to look to the Hand of God, and certainly not to the wiles of Satan. Whilst the environment remained hazardous, unsafe and disease-ravaged, risk might now be managed through superior information – about epidemics, prices, crises, wars or weather trends – purveyed by the press, and also through practical agencies like banks, annuities, firepumps, smallpox inoculation and casualty admission in hospitals.[19] Life and fire insurance expanded: John Byng noted in the 1790s that even waggons could be seen emblazoned with the Phoenix Insurance emblem, 'which is a novel safeguard, many having taken fire'.[20] Faced with a household rat problem, the Restoration astrologer Elias Ashmole had tried talismans to ward them off; by the next century professional ratcatchers were advertising their services in the papers. The staging of public lotteries – their philosophy of luck seemingly at odds with Providentialism – symbolizes this more secular bent.[21] Meanwhile, much else that was time-hallowed was now being questioned as superstitious, irrational or primitive, as for instance duelling and the aristocratic honour code at large.[22]

Enlightened thinking challenged attitudes to body and health, confronting custom with reason and the spiritual with the secular. Addressing childbirth, progressive doctors urged that the episcopally licensed 'ignorant' midwives be abandoned in favour of medically trained male obstetricians, who, expert in anatomy, would for the most part leave parturition to wise and gentle Nature or in emergencies use the newly invented forceps.[23] Once safely delivered, babies should no longer be subjected to swaddling – another symbolical mode of confinement! – but be allowed to romp freely and, as Nature intended, be breast- not artificially fed, and suckled not by wetnurses but by their own mothers.[24] Toddlers should not be mollycoddled but encouraged to exercise freely in fresh air, so as to harden and grow up strong. Reason, nature and health were thus said to go hand in hand, and superstition would wither under science's sunlight. This new 'childbirth package' gained credence because it chimed with polite and progressive opinion: the appeal to modern science, to reason, to the blandishments of the 'natural', to familial affection. The switch from 'peasant' midwife to graduate *accoucheur*, from 'custom' (wetnursing) to 'Nature' (the maternal breast), from 'superstition' (swaddling as a support for weak bones) to 'science' (activity promotes sturdiness) – all harmonized with the dream of escape from ignorance into information, from the prejudiced past into the brave new future. Indeed, the switch from the dim, closed birthing-room into birth by daylight aptly captures the essence of 'enlightenment'.[25]

Given due attention to bodily health, why, speculated Dr Erasmus Darwin and others, should lifespans not be prolonged? And if death must finally supervene, advanced thinkers wanted it shorn of the traditional horrors of hellfire. Christianity had traditionally portrayed death as the threshold to futurity. To the Catholic the final dispensing of grace was paramount: a good man who died without the sacraments (for example, by not confessing his sins) might be consigned to Hell, the sinner who received them, saved. The Protestant with his non-sacerdotal strategy was instructed to meet his Maker with conscious fortitude. Regarded primarily as a religious event, the Christian deathbed had thus staged high drama, and the *ars moriendi* (art of dying) scripted the conquest of Death, to prove it held no terrors. Of course, it did; and abundant records attest the intractable fears entertained by Christians such as Samuel Johnson and James Boswell of what the Beyond might hold, be it oblivion or the abyss (Johnson, for one, feared eternal damnation).

Combating such morbidity, the enlightened sought to demystify death by promoting frankness towards physical annihilation.[26] Central to this, for rational Christians, Deists, sceptics and atheists alike, was an onslaught upon the theology of eternal punishment, that perverted fiction of priestcraft designed to terrorize the credulous and so maximize ecclesiastical power and profit. The enlightened also commended dignity at the end, tempting Christians to haunt the deathbeds of pagans, in hopes of last-minute conversion or signs of chinks in their stoical composure. Imposing himself on the dying Hume, the anxious James Boswell was scandalized by the unbeliever's departing 'easy'.[27] There was, broadly speaking, a move away from the pious 'good death' scripted by the old *ars moriendi*, in which the dying person called upon God and denounced the Devil, towards the ideal of a peaceful passing, aided, if need be, by the opiates newly at the doctor's disposal.[28]

Some accepted oblivion ('After Death, nothing is,' opined Rochester),[29] and notions of the afterlife itself were also changing.[30] In his Lockean *The Light of Nature Pursued* (1768), Abraham Tucker accepted that the melancholy appearance of a lifeless body was shocking; but 'it is to the imagination only, not the understanding; for whoever consults this faculty will see at first glance, that there is nothing dismal in all these circumstances'. To learn how to die peacefully, it was necessary, he reasoned, to conquer the nightmarish phantasms associated with funerary rituals, and the attendant palaver of Hell, damnation and demons.[31]

Secularization also infiltrated the social rituals surrounding death. Testamentary references to God were being pared down to formal preambles; the typical English will came to serve almost exclusively as an instrument for transmitting property within the family; and the elaborate funeral sermon was giving way to the obituary notice in the press.[32]

And what about the lower orders? Was their living and dying to remain a matter of prayer, popular nostrums and Providence? Education in popular health became a crusade waged by progressive doctors. First published in 1769, and often reprinted, William Buchan's *Domestic Medicine* expounded to the common reader an enlightened philosophy of health to be pursued through reason, temperance, hygiene and heeding Nature's laws. The sick no longer needed to abandon themselves to their fate: knowledge and skill would save lives.[33] Committed to 'rendering medicine more extensively beneficial to mankind', the Edinburgh-trained Buchan embraced a democratic, late Enlightenment medical populism. If the people were ignorant about illness, it was because 'physic is still engrossed by the faculty'. For far too long physicians had made medicine a mystery, a closed shop using a dead tongue and serving the sordid greed of those who would 'make a trade of it'. Popery had spawned priestcraft; seeking likewise to 'disguise and conceal the art', physicians had set up doctorcraft.[34]

'While men are kept in the dark, and told that they are not to use their own understanding in matters that concern their health,' explained Buchan, drawing on familiar, telltale metaphors, 'they will be the dupes of designing knaves.' Monopoly perpetuated ignorance. Quoting Benjamin Rush, the top American physician and one of the signatories to the Declaration of Independence, Buchan later waxed indignant that doctors had for so long exercised a 'monopoly over many artificial remedies'. But 'a new order of things is rising in medicine too, as well as in government'. The modern age thus demanded the democratization of medicine, and that meant freedom of information. 'It is no more necessary,' he explained, 'that a patient should be ignorant of the medicine he takes to be cured by it, than that the business of government should be conducted with secrecy in order to insure obedience to just laws.'[35]

So what future did he envision? Most disorders and accidents, Buchan insisted, could be self-treated: from diarrhoea to dislocated necks, few bedside problems lay beyond a sensible layman or woman – one simply needed to avoid silly folk saws and professional mystifications. Buchan thus scolded the

horrid custom immediately to consign over to death every person who has the misfortune by a fall, or the like, to be deprived of the appearance of life. The unhappy person, instead of being carried into a warm house, and laid by the fire, or put in a warm bed, is generally hurried away to a church, or barn, or some other cold damp house, where, after a fruitless attempt has been made to bleed him . . . he is given over for dead, and no further notice taken of him.

Such fatal folly was the result of 'ignorance', 'supported by an ancient superstitious notion, which forbids the body of any person supposed to be killed by an accident to be laid in an house that is inhabited' – views 'contrary to all the principles of reason, humanity and common sense'.[36]

Buchan's book fanfared the ideal of medicine for the people, by the people.[37] Yet with health, as with everything else, enlightened thinking was not of a piece. Even doctors wedded to Buchan's impeccably liberal politics did not necessarily share his faith in a people's medicine; for, like a pilotless ship, self-medication could be perilous.

One radical physician confronting this dilemma was Thomas Beddoes, already mentioned in chapter 6. A Midlands tanner's son, Beddoes was so ardent in his support for the French Revolution that in 1793 he was effectively drummed out of his position as reader in chemistry at Oxford University. Retiring to private practice in the

Bristol suburb of Clifton, where he opened his Pneumatic Institution in 1799, Beddoes hoped to cure tuberculosis by means of the newly discovered oxygen and nitrous oxide (laughing gas). While also writing anti-Pitt diatribes and health care manuals for the well-to-do, Beddoes produced medical tracts targeted at the lower orders, whose vulgar errors irked him. Education was the answer – people had to 'unlearn' their mistakes, and not meddle. Lay physic was bad physic and therapeutics should be left to the trained.[38]

In touting this medical variant of enlightened absolutism, Beddoes was departing from Buchan's dictum that medicine could be a plain art open to all. Popular ignorance must indeed end, but what the people must know was not medicine but healthy living, based on good diet, exercise and moderation. Above all, he wished to apply 'physiological knowledge to domestic use'. In line with the sense-based pedagogics championed by Locke, Rousseau and Beddoes's own father-in-law, Richard Lovell Edgeworth, a start should be made by 'teaching children accurately to distinguish the parts of the body'.[39]

Buchan, Beddoes and other progressive physicians criticized the *status quo* in society and medicine alike, bludgeoning vested interests for conniving in ignorance and holding that injustice and oppression undermined the people's health. Beddoes accused Pitt's high-tax, inflationary and warmongering policies of impoverishing labourers, and denounced medicine as a 'sick trade' perverted by fortunes and fashion. Medicine thus affords a clear-cut case, one among many, of the practical application of enlightened thinking, confirming that it was not mere vacuous coffee house chatter but an action philosophy.[40]

Health management finds parallels in attempts to regulate other domains: irregularity was Jeremy Bentham's *bête noire* and the rationalization of the legal and administrative systems his *raison d'être*. The 'lottery of the law' made crime and punishment scandalously arbitrary, the pillory being a mere 'game of chance'.[41] Reformers particularly aimed to end that absurd confusion of ferocity and leniency displayed by the Bench which negated all hopes of deterrence.[42] In a similar vein, Bentham also protested against the absurdities of the Poor Law, where 'in a cluster of small pauper establishments, straggling over England, dispersed and unconnected . . . all is opacity and obscurity'. Likewise, addressing local administration, he groaned that 'every thing is insulated, every thing is particular; every thing is out of reach, every thing is out of knowledge: and while every thing is growing worse and worse, every thing is out of the reach of cure'. Muddle must yield to method.[43]

Other anomalies and abuses became targets for streamlining and rationalization. Calendar reform was introduced when England (finally) went over to the Gregorian system in 1753;[44] English replaced Norman French as the language of the law;[45] and cricket received its rules in 1744, while the next year saw the appearance of Edmund Hoyle's immortal *The Polite Gamester, Containing Short Treatises on the Games of Whist, Quadrille, Backgammon and Chess.*

Language reform had its advocates. Amid xenophobic braying against the invasions of Gallic neologisms, proposals were published for academies to standardize and monitor English,[46] the *Gentleman's Magazine* urging that 'a proper person or committee be appointed, to ascertain all such words as are wanting in our language, to convey clearly and precisely such ideas as naturally arise in the mind of every man'.[47] In the preface to his *Dictionary* (1754), Samuel Johnson urged that regularity should finally be brought to the English tongue – that language 'copious without order, energetick without rules' – although, like Ephraim Chambers, he rejected French-style academies as dictatorial.[48] Often reprinted, Joseph Priestley's *The Rudiments of English Grammar* (1761) simplified grammar – and chastised David Hume for his Frenchified style; while John Walker's *Pronouncing Dictionary of English* (1774) provided 'rules to be observed by the natives of Scotland, Ireland, and London, for avoiding their respective peculiarities' – the corrective agenda being as ever politically loaded.[49] Describing English as the third and superior 'classical' language, the Irish Thomas Sheridan argued in his *British Education: or the Source of the Disorders of Great Britain* (1756) for making Britain's literary heritage the basis for modern polite instruction:

as models of style, Milton in the poetic, and Shakespeare in the dramatic, Swift, Addison, Dryden, and Sir William Temple . . . in prose, may be considered as truly classical, as the Virgil, Caesar, Tully, and Sallust of the Romans; nor is there any reason that they should not be handed down as such equally to the end of time.[50]

Nor did the applied arts escape the systematizers. In 1728 Batty Langley published *New Principles of Gardening* (1728), followed in 1747 by his, at first blush, paradoxical *Gothic Architecture, Improved by Rules and Proportions* (Georgian gothic was regularly irregular). Even William Hogarth, that bulldog champion of English liberties against foreign tyranny, expected his *The Analysis of Beauty* (1753) to fix 'the fluctuating ideas of Taste'.[51] Such projects for ordering and regularizing typically, however, met with scant success, as Bentham's chequered career makes so clear. Quite apart from those intent upon leaving well alone, enlightened counterarguments championed English 'freedom' over Continental centralization – a prejudice which stalled proposals to conduct a national census and which was to run and run under the Podsnapian Victorians.[52]

In certain domains the eighteenth century brought remarkable secularization in perceptions and practice alike. Take madness. Before the Restoration, insanity was commonly read as a spiritual condition, be it demonic possession or divine genius. In medical writings after 1660, however, the idea that lunacy could be an affliction of the soul, and thus genuinely endanger salvation, ceased to be admissible – that was too close to the demonologists' dogmas for comfort. Physicians instead assigned lunacy to some or other somatic ailment: 'Every change of the Mind', maintained Dr Nicholas Robinson (not coincidentally, an ardent Newtonian), 'therefore, indicates a Change in the Bodily Organs' – the presumption being that, if an organic pathology were diagnosed, the immortal soul automatically escaped aspersions of impairment, while the authenticity of the malady was also reassuringly confirmed. It was no mere matter of 'imaginary Whims and Fancies' – that too would have been stigmatizing – precisely because, as Robinson insisted, it arose from 'the real, mechanical Affections of Matter and Motion'.[53]

Partly because madness had been regarded as integral to man's lapsarian condition, hardly any specialist institutions for the insane had been endowed. In almost the only exception, London's Bethlem Hospital (Bedlam), inmates had often been chained and neglected, and hidebound therapeutics of blood-lettings and emetics long remained the staple treatments. Its doors open to gawping sightseers, Bethlem was a satirist's delight.[54]

All this changed. With enlightened physicians discarding demono-logical in favour of disease models, lunatics were declared sick, not possessed, and therefore amenable to treatment and cure. For this the right environment was needed – that is, asylums, preferably in rural surroundings, far from the madding crowd. Private and charitable madhouses sprang up, while Bethlem ended public visiting around 1770. From about then, recourse to sedation or mechanical restraint was, in its turn, challenged by new techniques of interper-sonal management. Authentically psychological illnesses became conceivable for, with the secularization of psychology (see chapter 7), it became possible to speak of a 'disordered understanding' without the insinuation of diabolical possession of the immortal soul. By 1798, the specialist mad-doctor Alexander Crichton could evoke the heritage of 'our British Psychologists', that is, Locke, Hartley, Reid, Stewart, Priestley and Kames.[55] Neo-Lockean theories professed to show how insanity could be read as the outcome of personal tragedy – for instance, loss, grief or unrequited love. Educated in Lockean Cambridge, Dr William Battie regarded all madness as 'deluded imagination',[56] a notion which flowed, of course, from Locke's doc-trine of the (mis)association of ideas. For Thomas Arnold, Lockean psychiatrist and Leicester madhouse-keeper, 'the imagination is too active when it is for ever busily employed'.[57]

And once madness was no longer attributed to supernatural powers, unbelievers like Dr Erasmus Darwin could switch the blame for mass hysteria and religious melancholy to fanatics and Methodists, and cast enthusiasm as itself a symptom of mental derangement. No longer did the Devil drive you insane: now believing in the Devil or in hellfire was, for physicians like him, a mark of madness.[58]

In these circumstances, 'moral therapy' became the magic word: the mad, like everyone else, were to be treated with reason, calmness and good example. Visiting the prestigious York Retreat, opened in 1796, Louis Simond found it 'admirably' managed, 'almost entirely by *reason* and kindness: it was instituted by Quakers. Most of the patients move about at liberty, without noise and disorder.'[59] In the case of insanity, enlightened thinkers thus plumed themselves that benighted religious explanations, and the neglect and cruelty supposedly accompanying them, were being supplanted by reason and humanity. It is noteworthy that the York Retreat, though run by Quakers for Quakers, employed exclusively secular therapies.

Changing responses to suicide afford marked parallels.[60] In Christendom 'self-murder' had been both a sin and a crime, an offence against God and King, the business of courts ecclesiastical and civil. Since Tudor times juries had routinely returned verdicts of *felo de se* (wilful self-murder), imposing severe posthumous punishments: the suicide was denied Christian burial, the corpse being interred at a crossroads, a stake through the heart; and the felon's property was forfeited to the Crown. This cruel treatment expressed Protestant theological rigorism – suicide as a wilful mutiny against God – while also marking the tenacious assertion of royal rights under the new monarchy. Puritanism redoubled the punitiveness.

As in so many other walks of life, the Restoration brought a transformation. It soon become standard for coroners' courts to reach a *non compos mentis* verdict, whether or not there was any real history or independent sign of mental instability in the victim: was not suicide itself sufficient proof of derangement? This 'medicalization' or 'psychologization' of self-destruction sanctioned a churchyard burial and put a stop to the escheat of the victim's possessions – a notable assertion of community will against the Crown at the very moment when Locke was affirming against Filmer the natural right to property.

Shifting philosophies of the self, in any case, led the élite to commend 'Antique Roman' apologies for suicide as noble-minded. On 4 May 1737, having filled his pockets with rocks, Eustace Budgell, a one-time contributor to the *Spectator*, drowned himself in the Thames. Found on his desk was a suicide note: 'What Cato did, and Addison approved, cannot be wrong.'[61] David Hume and others offered enlightened defences of suicide.[62] While fashionable society condoned the deed, holding that death was preferable to dishonour, enlightened opinion, eager to outflank bigotry, abandoned punitiveness for pity. The poet Thomas Chatterton, who poisoned himself in 1770 at the age of seventeen, provided the role model for the Romantic suicide cult.[63]

These changes – which made Britain notorious as the suicide capital of the world – in many ways bear out historian Keith Thomas's account first of the intensification of Christian Providentialism in the Reformation century, and then its later withering under a Weberian *Entzauberung*, prompted by the laser beams of science and rationalism.[64] But they offer no support to another popular reading of early Modern cultural history, the one which posits a growing post-Restoration chasm between élite and popular culture. High and low alike, the various post-1660 suicide scenarios followed parallel courses. Public responses to patrician rakes who blew their brains out were not dissimilar to those towards big-bellied milkmaids who disappeared in duckponds (the two events might not be unrelated): formerly vilified, the suicide now often attracted sympathy. The Anglican Parson Woodforde had nothing but sympathy for the suicides he knew.[65] 'Is it?' asked Pope –

> Is it, in heav'n a crime to love too well?
> To bear too tender, or too firm a heart,
> To act a Lover's or a *Roman's* part?
> Is there no bright reversion in the sky,
> For those who greatly think, or bravely die?[66]

Crucial to this reconceptualization of suicide was the rise of print culture. The role heretofore played by the Church in fixing its meaning – overwhelmingly punitive – was usurped by the media, whose line was humanitarian through and through. Newspapers and magazines turned suicides into 'human interest' stories, indeed sensations, and encouraged vicarious, often morbid, public involvement, with the printing of suicide notes, last letters and tales of blighted love. Here, as elsewhere, the media gave voice to new secular meanings, expressive of enlightened 'humanitarian narratives'.[67] Like life itself, suicide was secularized.

This shift in status from pariah, malefactor or sinner to object of pity, evident in the cases of lunatics and suicides (themselves often assimilated to the insane), was mirrored in many other walks of life, where what had heretofore attracted religious or moral blame might now find ambivalent exculpation. The quandaries of how to balance individual responsibility over and against moral judgementalism and the sociological gaze were to loom large in a spectrum of debates over vice and poverty, in controversies over free will and determinism, and in the consequentialist philosophy of utilitarianism (see chapter 16).

Perhaps the most telling instance of the rejection of traditional Christian dogmas in favour of new secular models is the discrediting of witchcraft, a shift which occurred against a backdrop of controversy regarding the reality and agency of spirits in general.[68] As is highlighted by the critiques levelled by materialists like Hobbes, historic Christianity – élite and popular alike – was spirit-drenched. During his Yorkshire childhood in the 1730s, recalled Joseph Priestley, 'it was my misfortune to have the idea of darkness, and the ideas of malignant spirits and apparitions, very closely connected'. Rendered 'too full of terror' by his strict Calvinist upbringing, he remembered 'reading the account of the "man in an iron cage" in the *Pilgrim's Progress* with the greatest perturbation'. Recollection of that 'state of ignorance and darkness', he affirmed, 'gives me a peculiar sense of the value of rational principles of religion'.[69] Jeremy Bentham had a similarly horrifying memory of his own youth, some twenty years later: 'This subject of ghosts has been among the torments of my life, the devil was everywhere in it and in me too.' Commenting, like Priestley, on his early reading of Bunyan, he exclaimed: 'how much less unhappy I should have been, could I have acknowledged my superstitious fears!'[70] As mature intellectuals, both totally repudiated the spirits which had brought them to youthful fears and tears.

The prime example of the public disavowal of spirits is witchcraft. Belief in the terrestrial intervention of Satan and his satellites had long been upheld, not just by the churches, in line with the Bible ('Thou shalt not suffer a witch to live,' the Lord told his people through Moses (Exodus XXII: 18)), but by such leading intellectuals as Robert Burton.[71] That consensus crumbled after 1650.[72] To a degree this was due to rationalist philosophers like Hobbes, whose materialism ruled out by definition the real presence of evil spirits. 'The opinion that rude people have of fairies, ghosts and goblins and the power of witches' was blamed in his *Leviathan* on the incapacity to distinguish 'dreams' from 'sense'. 'As for witches,' he held, 'I think not that their witchcraft is any reall power' – though he approved of the punishment of such impostors for the 'false beliefe they have, that they can do such mischiefe'.[73]

What is most evident in post-Restoration England, however, is not the triumph of *a priori* denials but a widespread *de facto* waning of belief on grounds of experience and humanity. 'I believe in general,' held Addison in the *Spectator*, 'that there is, and has been such a thing as witchcraft' – a feint that established his *bona fides*; yet he could 'give no credit to any particular instance of it'. That deft formula established, he went on to explain how those mistaken for witches were pitiable old women victimized by the 'ignorant and credulous'. Great danger was in store once some old crone – call her Moll White – had got the 'Reputation of a Witch'.

If she made any Mistake at Church, and cryed *Amen* in a wrong place, they never failed to conclude that she was saying her Prayers backwards . . . If the Dairy Maid does not make her Butter come so soon as she would have it, *Moll White* is at the bottom of the Churn. If a Horse sweats in the Stable, *Moll White* has been upon his Back.[74]

And thus he concluded with a call for an end to persecution:

I hear there is scarce a village in *England* that has not a *Moll White* in it. When an old Woman begins to doat, and grow chargeable to a Parish, she is generally turned into a Witch, and fills the whole Country with extravagant Fancies, imaginary Distempers, and terrifying Dreams.[75]

Addison's views squared with those set out in the Revd Francis Hutchinson's influential *An Historical Essay Concerning Witchcraft* (1718), a work lacking the theoretical barbs of Balthazar Bekker's Cartesian *De Betoverde Weereld* (*The Bewitched World*) (1691–3) but perhaps for that reason all the more effective.

A Whig who rose to become a bishop, Hutchinson, like Locke and Addison, upheld spirits, declaring that 'sober belief' in 'good and bad spirits [was] part of every good Christian's faith', while at the same time insisting that such convictions were totally different from 'the fantastick doctrines that support the vulgar opinion of witchcraft'.[76] 'The credulous multitude,' he little doubted, 'will ever be ready to try their tricks, and swim the old women, and wonder at and magnify every unaccountable symptom and odd accident.'[77] But education would in time erode error. 'Witchcraft' was explicable by natural causes; scriptural references to it had been mistranslated; popular ghost lore was fiddle-faddle;[78] the confessions of 'old Women' were 'not to be regarded', and the conceit of compacts with the Devil he dismissed with a Lockean hand wave as 'meer Imagination'.[79]

While rehearsing the scepticism of Johannes Weyer, Reginald Scot, John Webster and Balthasar Bekker, Hutchinson probed the psychology of the witch craze as social panic. Though never denying witchcraft in principle, and shrewdly appending two sermons against Sadduceeism – one affirming Christ's miracles, the other the reality of angels – he noted that witchcraft was rife mainly in backward Catholic kingdoms, and submitted that what triggered panics were rabble-rousing books and meddlesome witch-finders.

Hutchinson was the epitome of the moderate, progressive humanitarian Whig thinker so prominent in enlightened England. While Hobbes the ultra reduced 'superstition' to rank fraud, the Anglican divine judiciously made allowance for self-deception, hysteria, social pressure and labelling. It was all too easy for people to be talked into believing they were witches – 'old women are apt to take such fancies of themselves'. 'Imagine a poor old creature,' he appealed to his readers' sympathies,

under all the weakness and infirmities of old age, set like a fool in the middle of a room, with a rabble of the town round about her house: then her legs tied cross, that all the weight of her body might rest upon her seat. Then she must continue her pain four and twenty hours, without any sleep or meat . . . what wonder was it, if when they were weary of their lives, they confessed any tales that would please.[80]

A case like that of Jane Wenham, the last English 'witch' to be condemned (in 1714), showed 'how impossible it is for the most innocent Persons to defend themselves'. A meek crone living in a 'barbarous parish', she it was, in Hutchinson's view, who was the real victim of *maleficium,* and so the one who truly merited pity.[81] Beliefs like those of Addison and Hutchinson took root amongst educated élites, capitalizing upon snobberies against the benighted and rancour towards priestcraft. In his essay 'Of Witchcraft' (1724), Thomas Gordon thus accused priests of whipping up fears about witchcraft because it was they who enjoyed the official monopoly in countering it. In this they had been aided by mob credulity, but England was now mending: 'an old Woman may be miserable now, and not be hanged for it'. The Deist Whig piqued himself upon his liberal sentiments – he was 'so much a heretick as to believe, that God Almighty, and not the Devil, governs the World'; like all enlightened spokesmen, he had no desire to dwell in a devil-infested world.[82]

Such humanitarian views, oozing condescension, rang out from press and pulpit alike as the idiom of the *bien pensants.* In a sermon preached in 1736 after a suspected witch was 'swum', a Leicestershire parson, Joseph Juxon, called witchcraft into doubt with an appeal to compassion. Suspects were typically 'such as are destitute of friends, bow'd down with years, laden with infirmities; so far from annoying others, as not to have it in their power to take care of themselves'. Yet so prevalent were alarms and superstition that 'there is always a party formed . . . against these poor, ignorant and helpless creatures'. Accusations had to be nipped in the bud, not least because, though 'persons of ill fame be accused first . . . yet the suspicion may fall at last upon those of unblemished character and reputation', precipitating 'havock'. The élite certainly did not want to run the risk of being incriminated themselves![83]

Witchcraft, magic and the supernatural continued to be debated long after the repeal of the witchcraft statutes in 1736. Many seized the Addisonian moral high ground, picking on sitting targets and deploring hidebound views – 'the world has perhaps been imposed upon' by no one more than pretenders to occult powers, declared the anonymous *A System of Magick* in 1727.[84] Brought out in 1736 to coincide with repeal, *A Discourse on Witchcraft*, also anonymous, complimented Englishmen for living in an enlightened land at a happy time when the 'impostures' of priests and the folly of the 'vulgar' were finally being laid to rest.[85]

Colluding in a cosy superiority with its sophisticated readers, the press took pleasure in exposing sensational manifestations of witchcraft practices or bizarre superstitions. 'The ridiculous notion of witches and witchcraft still prevails amongst the lower sort of people,' declared one such paper in 1773, before reciting a cruel ducking meted out in Wiltshire to an alleged witch.[86] In another Wessex village, 'one Sarah Jellicoat escaped undergoing the whole discipline usually inflicted by the . . . unthinking vulgar on witches', thanks, in true enlightened manner, to the timely inter- vention of 'some humane gentlemen and the vigilance of a discreet magistrate'.[87]

In that age of conspicuous humanity, the witch, like the prostitute, could even become the *heroine* of a narrative, typecast as sad, lonely and bigot-beset. Such sentimental strains were already present in Hutchinson – when Jane Wenham 'was denied a few Turnips' by vicious parishioners, readers were told, 'she laid them down very submissively'.[88] Christopher Smart's *The Genuine History of the Good*

Devil of Woodstock (1802) invited similar identification: the villagers were brutish to poor Jane Gilbert, called her witch and did her injury; but, sustained in part by compassionate social superiors, she bore it like a good Christian; finally she came into a legacy and behaved with exemplary benevolence to her erstwhile persecutors.[89]

With witches and ghosts discredited, the demonic and magical did not so much disappear from polite culture as change their face and place. The supernatural was sanitized and culturally revamped in the flourishing domains of entertainment and print culture. There was, of course, nothing wholly new in this. The supernatural had always been a staple of the arts – *viz.* the ghost in *Hamlet* or the witches in *Macbeth*.[90] Yet the witch was to undergo a role change on the English stage. Shakespeare's witches had been sinister and supernatural; those, by contrast, in Thomas Shadwell's *The Lancashire-Witches* (1681) and *Tegue o Divelly the Irish Priest* (1682) provided crude comic relief in pot-boiling anti-Papist pro-Whig burlesque; they were made to fly across the boards, courtesy of stage machinery, in an aptly dramatic exposure of the absurdity of it all. The popularity of his portrayal shows how the witch had become a political football, exploited by enlightened Whigs to lampoon sinister Tories and the wild Irish in the Popish Plot panic. A few years later, Allan Ramsay's pastoral drama *The Gentle Shepherd* (1715) introduced a new figure: a harmless 'witch' invested, however, with supernatural powers by fearful, credulous rustics: Ramsay was, of course, the Scottish Addison.[91]

Fantasy devils also loom large in the kitsch supernatural stage props of Augustan satire, notably Pope's *The Rape of the Lock* (1712). His *Dunciad* evoked a demonic universe in which infernal goddesses – 'Dulness' and 'Cloacina' – possessed mortals and required pro-pitiation in a mock-classical extravaganza with bit parts for Gorgons, dragons, fiends and wizards. Satire also explains the supernatural apparatus in William Hogarth's engraving *Credulity, Superstition and Fanaticism* (1762). Originally titled *Enthusiasm Delineated*, this conjured up the (by then thankfully) ludicrous confederation of Satan, witches and spirits, so as to mock the Methodists. A hysterical congregation appears in the throes of frenzy, while a thermometer, propped up on Joseph Glanvill's once esteemed pro-spirit *Sadducismus Triumphatus* (1681) and on John Wesley's sermons, takes the temperature of the Methodists' intellects on a scale rising from 'despair' up to 'raving madness'. The source of all this mental mania? An enthusiast ranting in the pulpit astride a broomstick and topped by a steeple hat, clutching in one hand a puppet of Satan and in the other a witch doll.[92] The Augustans could thus still stage the supernatural, but chiefly by camping it up. 'A poet who should now make the whole action of his tragedy depend upon enchantment and produce the chief events by the assistance of supernatural agents,' pondered Samuel Johnson, his finger as ever on the cultural pulse, 'would be censured as transgressing the bounds of probability, be banished from the theatre to the nursery, and condemned to write fairy tales instead of tragedies.'[93]

Witch personae thus flourished as comic grotesques at the very time when real ones were fast fading from the consciousness, if not the nightmares, of the educated. In due course witchiness would find further incarnations: while the Devil perhaps metamorphosed into the Negro, provocatively blending blackness with virility,[94] the village hag would be superseded by the *femme fatale* and the vamp – although the shawl-clad crone, with her cottage, cat and cauldron, was to enjoy an afterlife in Romantic fairy tales, children's fiction and the movies.[95]

In such artistic migrations, the supernatural assumed a new symbolic reality, with the *psychological* truth of witch lore and the supernatural coming into the open, marking the late Enlightenment plunge into interiority. A century after John Locke had warned against exposing children to tales of '*Sprights*', the Romantic Charles Lamb imaginatively savoured the ambivalences of being spooked by ghosts and goblins. Assuming the persona of a little girl who believed her aunt was a witch, 'I shrunk back terrified and bewildered to my bed', he wrote, 'where I lay in broken sleeps and miserable fancies, till the morning'.[96] Here Lamb psychologized and sexualized the witch figure in a manner perennially fascinating to late Enlightenment fantasists.

This refiguring of the supernatural from the transcendental to the psychological flags wider developments in poetics. The dark, devilish and disturbing elements then being laundered from religion by reason were returning, sanitized, in new artistic genres. In particular, the cult of the sublime aestheticized the supernatural. In his *Philosophical Enquiry into the Origin of Our Ideas of the Sublime and the Beautiful* (1757), Edmund Burke provided the classic psychological explanation of the allure of the 'terrible': the sublime was terror enjoyed in security. Dread of ghosts, demons, the unknown and the uncanny could now be enjoyed from the comfort and safety of one's theatre box or parlour sofa.[97]

The new aesthetics had implications which went far beyond admiration for mountains and spectres: it recuperated religion by psychologizing it.[98] For some it could even reinvest the very notion of the holy, seemingly discredited by the withering Enlightenment critique of irrationalist mystification. Seminal in this respect were Robert Lowth's lectures on Hebrew poetry. Professor of poetry in Oxford, Lowth delivered (in Latin) lectures in which the sacred poetry of the Hebrews was praised as 'the only specimens of the primeval and genuine poetry'.[99] In treating the religious as artistic, he was part of a trend. In a discussion of the New Testament demons and miracles, Anthony Blackwall replaced rationalist fixation on the evidences of Christianity by a psychology of faith. The man in the Bible possessed with Legion, he suggested, was brilliantly dramatized:

Who is not shocked with horror and trembling at the first appearance of the raging Demoniac . . . Then with what religious awe, reverence and tenderness of devotion do we view the mild Saviour of the human race commanding the infernal Legion to quit their possession to the miserable sufferer![100]

Here Scripture was theatricalized, its spiritual authority seen as depending on the suspension of disbelief.[101] Turning to the raising of Lazarus, Blackwall likewise underscored the dramatic qualities of suspense and amazement, almost as though the truth of the biblical miracles was vested primarily in their appeal to lofty Shaftesburian sensibilities.[102]

Nor was he alone in casting the Bible as what Edgar Allan Poe would style a work of mystery and imagination. In James Usher's *Clio or, Discourse on Taste* (1769) enthusiasm was applauded for its power to excite terror, curiosity and pious exultation: 'In the sublime we feel ourselves alarmed, our motions are suspended, and we remain for some time until the emotion wears off, wrapped in silence and inquisitive horror.' Following Burke, Usher observed that the obscurity, irregularity and awe constituting the sublime were primarily associated with the 'idea of invisible and immense power' – in a word, God, who thus became a psychological entity. Moderns might deride such emotions as superstitious, but terror and awe were integral to human experience.[103]

The role of the sublime in psychologizing, aestheticizing, and thereby revalidating the supernatural stands out in the cult of the Gothic, a genre heralded by Horace Walpole's *The Castle of Otranto* (1765) and continued in the novels of Mrs Radcliffe (with her rationalized 'explained supernatural'), Matthew Lewis, author of *Ambrosio, or the Monk*, and, in a more complex fashion, in Mary Shelley's *Frankenstein* (1818).[104] Supernaturalizing the everyday, such works traded in stock elements: the mist-shrouded castle, the villain vowed to Satan, demons, phantoms, sorcerers and shrews, a flirtation with the weird, the uncanny and the bizarre – and, underpinning all, a Burkean obsession with terror and the infinite unknown. Elements like ghosts triggered new sexual frissons in a return of the repressed as the old demonological themes of possession, while incubi and succubi were internalized and eroticized by that quintessential late Enlightenment artist Henry Fuseli.[105] Romanticism played a key part in the conversion of the supernatural from Scripture to studio, study, stage – and, later, screen: in the nineteenth century it would be writers and artists who would explore those issues of innocence and evil, the terrestrial and the eternal, which had so long been the prerogative of divines – before being overtaken, in their turn, by psychoanalysts, a tendency acknowledged in T. E. Hulme's adage that 'Romanticism . . . is spilt religion'. For Romantics, artistic creativity redefined the holy: 'Imagination', held Blake, 'is the Divine Body of the Lord Jesus, blessed for ever.'[106]

In such matters as spirit possession, madness, suicide and witchcraft, changing attitudes and practices attest a signal development: a waning of the hold over the élite enjoyed by the literal word of the Bible and its theocentric vision.[107] Challenges to Scripturalism materialized in other fields as well, including interpretations of the history of mankind itself, to be examined below.

Enlightened thinkers sought to rationalize life in terms of a model of natural order which replaced an active God with an active man. The hubris of such arrogations of omniscience and omnipotence afforded golden opportunities to satirists bent upon deflating rationalist monsters: apostles of modernity, Swift never tired of showing, were possessed by the demons of reason.[108] 'The world is persuaded, not without some colour of reason,' confessed Jeremy Bentham in the 1770s, with the cheery self-mockery of youth, 'that all reformers and system-mongers are mad . . . I dreamt t'other night that I was a founder of a sect; of course, a personage of great sanctity and importance: it was called the sect of the Utilitarians.'[109] Parodying himself as enthusiast rather tickled him: 'There came out to me a good man named Ld. S.' – that is, Lord Shelburne – 'and he said unto me, what shall I do to be saved? I yearn to save the nation. I said unto him – take up my book and follow me.'[110]

Despite this disconcerting tendency of reason to turn crazy, the Enlightenment brought a fundamental value shift, landmarked for instance by the repeal of the witchcraft statutes, the passing of Divine Right theories of government and the end of touching for the King's Evil.[111] The magic also went out of medicine: viper flesh, pike jaw and unicorn horn vanished from the pharmacopoeia. The Medieval Christian endorsement of 'wonder', with its horror of 'forbidden knowledge', gave way to the enlightened underwriting and validation of 'curiosity' and scorn for 'marvels'.[112]

The programmatic shift from Christian Providentialism to more secular, scientific world views must, however, be kept in perspective. After all, everyone still craved glimpses of the extraordinary. Daniel Defoe's *Essay on the History and Reality of Apparitions* (1727) dramatized the traditional spirit world of pneumatology while also anticipating modern parapsychology.[113] The London earthquakes of February 1750 provoked panic, with the hellfire preacher William Romaine and his episcopal counterpart Thomas Sherlock both urging their flocks to repent before the threat of divine punishment. 'In after ages it will hardly be believed', recorded Tobias Smollett,

that on the evening of the eighth day of April, the open fields, that skirt the metropolis, were filled with incredible numbers of people . . . who waited in the most fearful suspense until morning, and the return of day disproved the truth of the dreadful prophecy.[114]

Spectacular episodes like the Cock Lane ghost affair in the 1760s, a metropolitan media hype, involving the alleged appearance of a ghost at a city of London lodging house, are reminders of the enduring power of supernaturalism, just as sensations like the Mary Toft affair – the Surrey woman who in 1726 convinced many people, including the Royal Surgeon and Anatomist, that she had given birth to rabbits – demonstrate popular credulity.[115]

Integral to a profound transformation of mentalities, secularization and naturalization also had their social dimension, demarcating the enlightened from the rest. The devaluing of marvels was no triumph of abstract rationality but a shift in the identity of intellectuals, for whom wonder and wonders became dismissed as vulgar, the very antithesis of what it meant to be in the stadium of light.[116] In any case, such changes lay no less in rhetoric than in realities; nor must they simply be deemed as 'progress', for one man's rationality is another's credulity. 'Superstition is said to be driven out of the World,' commented Hester Thrale in 1790; 'no such Thing, it is only driven out of Books and Talk'.[117]

IO

MODERNIZING

We must consider how very little history there is: I mean real
authentick history.

SAMUEL JOHNSON[1]

The Georgian century brought rapid and profound socio-
economic transformation, opened, closed and punctuated by political
revolutions. Small wonder that enlightened thinkers felt driven to
address the dynamics of change, and to formulate theories which
linked past, present and future, ultimately in terms of overarching
visions of progress.[2]

History-writing itself was changing. Renaissance philologists had
pioneered the recovery, editing and scholarly study of documents,
while in the seventeenth century headway had been made in the use
of inscriptions, coins and archaeological evidence. These traditions
continued, but the preoccupations of such mere 'antiquarians' were
challenged in the Enlightenment by a new breed of philosophic
historians, erudite yet eager to create an intelligible, instructive and,
not least, entertaining past, presented in polished prose. 'The advantages found in history seem to be of three kinds,' wrote Hume: 'as it
amuses the fancy, as it improves the understanding, and as it streng-
thens virtue.'[3]

Innovative features distinguished the outlooks of this new history.
Sir Walter Raleigh's *History of the World* (1614), William Howell's
History of the World (1680–85), Cardinal Bossuet's synoptic *Histoire
universelle* (1681) and other standard texts, were 'God's eye' narratives,
beginning at the Creation and tracing the providential handing down
of civilization by God to His chosen people. Between 1669 and 1678

Theophilus Gale published four parts of a massive work, *The Court of the Gentiles*, demonstrating that all arts and sciences arose from the Jewish people – from Adam, Moses (skilled historian and philosopher), Seth and Enoch (astronomy), Noah (navigation), Solomon (architecture) and Job (a great philosopher).[4] Such Bible-centred readings were on the way out.

Indeed, historians like Hume and Gibbon now approached the rise of Christianity itself from a naturalistic standpoint, adopting a detached and often ironic stance. Hume's *History of England* (1754–62) was unremittingly hostile to the manifestations of religion: monks and ascetics were power-mad hypocrites; the Church conducted itself through deceit and superstition; the Crusades had been fired by fanaticism and greed; doctrinal bickerings were fatuous.[5] Here lay the overture to Gibbon's lordly irony. Chapters 15 and 16 of his *Decline and Fall of the Roman Empire* exposed Christianity's human, rather than Providential, sources, its growth being explained not by Providence but by secondary causes: the inflexible and intolerant zeal of the Christians, inherited from the Jews; the doctrine of a future life; the miraculous powers claimed by the primitive Church; the austerity of Christian morals; and the organization of the 'Christian republic'.[6] Conjectural history, discussed below, replaced scriptural accounts of origins with sweeping narratives of social evolution.

Scorning dry-as-dust antiquarianism,[7] enlightened historians targeted their works at wider audiences. Patriotic histories were popular, Gilbert Burnet's *History of the Reformation* (1679–1715) being but the foremost in a long line of Protestant-Whig histories celebrating the march of national freedom *via* the Reformation and the Glorious Revolution.[8] Even the very superior Gibbon ('an Englishman, a philosopher, and a Whig') was not above a touch of chauvinism. 'We contemplate the gradual progress of society from the lowest ebb of primitive barbarism, to the full tide of modern civilization,' he swelled:

We contrast the naked Briton who might have mistaken the sphere of Archimedes for a rational creature, and the contemporary of Newton, in whose school Archimedes himself would have been a humble disciple. And we compare the boats of osier and hides that floated along our coasts with the formidable navies which visit and command the remotest shores of the ocean. Without indulging the fond prejudices of patriotic vanity, we may assume a conspicuous place among the inhabitants of the earth.[9]

Yet that cosmopolite also typically wrote sympathetically about Islam, and pondered how the history of Europe would seem to a future New Zealander.

Hume defined the historian's task as being 'to remark the rise, progress, declension, and final extinction of the most flourishing empires: the virtues, which contributed to their greatness, and the vices which drew on their ruin'.[10] Applied to English history, this meant putting the accent on socio-cultural phenomena: 'The rise, progress, and decline of art and science,' he reflected, 'are curious objects of contemplation, and intimately connected with a narration of civil transactions.'[11] Looking back to what he typically called 'the dark ages', he dismissed many of the chronicles as mere fable and, good *philosophe* as he was, contrasted the boringness of barbarians with those 'convulsions of a civilized state' which generally 'compose the most instructive . . . part of its history'.[12]

In the light of the uniformitarian conviction that human nature was ever and everywhere the same, enlightened historians posited that the past was intelligible in terms of the hidden springs of action; and, motives being constant, that made it relevant to the present.[13] Later 'historicists' would upbraid such thinking as anachronistic, since it failed to probe into the minds of the dead. That charge would not, however, have fazed enlightened historians, who prized their own 'philosophical' stance – history was philosophy teaching by example. And, as Bolingbroke's dictum makes clear,[14] enlightened history was positively intended to be didactic, providing lessons for statesmen while also broadening outlooks: 'history', he claimed, 'serves to purge the mind of those national partialities and prejudices, that we are apt to contract in our education'.[15] The greatest of its morals was that human affairs – with few exceptions, notably

[1]

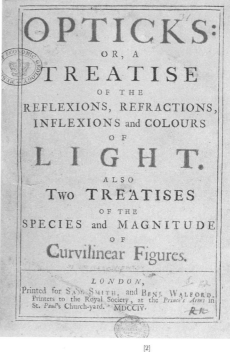

[2]

Light

The Enlightened English believed they had a special corner on light, since it was Newton who in his Opticks (1704) had first revealed the true scientific nature of that mysterious entity [2]. With tremendous patriotic pomp, a host of celebratory images deified the incomparable Sir Isaac [1]. Advances in light technology resulted, amongst other things, in improved light-houses [3], alongside domestic lighting and street illumination; while the diffusion of useful and entertaining knowledge was aided by the invention of the magic lantern [4].

[3]

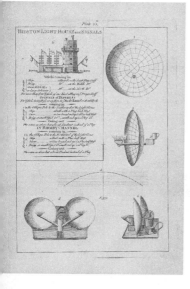

[4]

[5]

[6]

[7]

[8]

[9]

Words

Edward Gibbon gloried in his 'early and invincible love of reading, which I would not exchange for the treasures of India', and many would have agreed. But different sorts of readers and reading met with more or less approval. The gentleman with his feet up on the sofa reading Horace's Odes was obviously a good thing [5], but the bookworm in his Cambridge study gave off the odour of the past [6], the cottager at his door might have caused raised eyebrows, had he not been reading the Bible [7], and the ecstatic female philosopher was an object lesson in the dangers of a little learning [9]. Alexander Pope himself insisted that the proper study of mankind was man, yet books could help in that: the tomes in front of the tomb include Locke and Newton as well as Pope [8].

[12]

The Family

The nuclear family was prized by the enlightenment as a natural institution, particularly in its progressive form, with stiff patriarchal authoritarianism being replaced by close and friendly links between husband and wife, and parents and children [10]. Indoors and out, polite society liked to be painted in informal groups, playing with children and pets [11, 13]. John Bacon's drawing room is significantly emblazoned with the icons of the age: a telescope, an air-pump, and cameos of Milton, Bacon and Newton [12].

[13]

[14]

Reform

'I am a true Englishman', declared William Godwin, 'formed to discover nothing but to improve anything', and in that he reflected the spirit of an age which itched to change the old ways, and make everything better, faster, more efficient, or cheaper. In the countryside, the English took pride in their rational farming methods [**14**], while communications between towns were sped by turnpike roads and timetabled stagecoach services ('very commodious and warm') [**15**]. The Foundling Hospital showed humanitarian care to abandoned babies [**16**], and, contrariwise, Tyburn showed the terrible fate awaiting the idle and incorrigible [**17**]. In 1783, Tyburn itself became the victim of improvements.

[15]

BRISTOL, 1758.

WILLIAM JAMES's
LONDON and *BRISTOL*
CONSTANT
STAGE-WAGGONS:
(Late Mr. SAMUEL SARTAIN'S)

Load at St. *Peter's*-Pump, BRISTOL, | Set out from his House in the *Old-Market*,

Every { Saturday / Monday / Wednesday } Afternoon. | Every { Monday / Tuesday / Thursday } Morning.

Arrives at the THREE CUPS, in *Bread-*Street, LONDON, | Set out from the THREE CUPS, in *Bread-*Street, LONDON,

Every { Friday / Saturday / Tuesday } At Noon. | Every { Saturday / Monday / Wednesday } Morning.

And Returns to BRISTOL,
Every *Thursday, Friday,* and *Monday* Noon.

For the greater Convenience, GOODS and PASSENGERS are put down and taken up at the *Black* and *White Bears,* and *White Horse Cellar* in *Piccadilly.*

₊ These are the most EXPEDITIOUS WAGGONS that go from BRISTOL to LONDON, being only four Nights on the Road. They are likewise made very commodious and warm for PASSENGERS, who will meet with the best of USAGE.

All GENTLEMEN, MERCHANTS, and OTHERS, may depend upon the utmost Care being taken of all GOODS, &c. that may be intrusted with me, and their FAVOURS thankfully acknowledged,

By their most obedient and obliged humble Servant,
WILLIAM JAMES.

For further Particulars enquire of WM. JAMES, at his House in the *Old-Market,* or of THO. COX, or JOHN GULLICK, at the Warehouse in St. *Peter-street, Bristol* ; or RICHARD EDWARDS, at the *Three Cups* in *Bread-street, London.*

Design'd & Engrav'd by W.ᵐ Hogarth

The IDLE 'PRENTICE Executed at Tyburn.

Proverbs Chap: I. Verf: 27,28.
When fear cometh as desolation, and their
destruction cometh as a Whirlwind; when
distress cometh upon them, then they shall
call upon God, but he will not answer.

Plate 11

Publish'd according to Act of Parliam.t Sep. 30. 174

[18]   [19]

Leisure

The Moderns aimed to get the mix right between business and pleasure. The English liked to think of themselves as not wasting time – hence the habit (not just amongst poor chimney-sweep boys) of buying take-away meals from street-sellers [18]. But that was meant to give them more time for leisure. Those seeking cheap elegance could find it for a few shilling at Ranelagh Gardens with its magnificent rotunda (the Georgian 'Dome'!) [19]; somewhat more rough-and-tumble was a free-for-all wintry skate on the Serpentine, captured here by Rowlandson [20].

[20]

Graeco-Roman Antiquity – had been a nightmare of crime and folly, from which humanity must awake and escape.[16]

Enlightened histories claimed to be replacing error with truth, but they were in reality trading new myths for old – their own mentalities were mythopoeic too. Yet, however blind to their own myth-making, the enlightened were energetic anatomists of myth, going beyond accounts of individual fables to shape grand anthropologies – or pathologies – of the myth-making imagination itself.

The museum of mythology – and that principally meant Graeco-Roman legends – was approached from various vantage points, which, for simplicity, might be called the Christian, the Deist, and the rationalist.[17] According to Christian thinking, myth – that is, paganism – was intrinsically false, though heathen fables might be instructively read as corruptions of biblical truths. Samuel Shuckford's *The Sacred and Profane History of the World Connected* (1728), a typical instance, confidently assimilated all non-biblical traditions to Scripture by taking biblical chronology, characters and events as the gold standard. In his 'euhemerist' reading of myth as coded history, the ancient gods were actually Noah and his sons, disguised under other names and dressed up in the garb of paganism.[18] For the foremost late-century Christian mythographer Jacob Bryant, Noah had variously been styled Prometheus, Deucalion, Atlas, Theuth, Zuth, Xuthus, Inachus, Osiris, Helius, Zeus, Dios, Dionysos, Bacchus, Naus and Nous, in local myths derived from adulterated versions of true Judaeo-Christianity.[19] The same Christian-privileging habit is conspicuous in William Warburton. His *The Divine Legation of Moses* (1737–41) defended Christian orthodoxy by paradoxically embracing the free-thinkers' claim that the doctrine of Heaven and Hell was a purely human device, contrived for political reasons. Such being the case, the Bishop deduced that Hebrew theocracy must have been *divinely* directed, since the Old Testament made no mention of future rewards and punishments.[20]

For its part, the Deist approach premised, as already seen, primitive monotheism. From that it followed that both pagan polytheism and Christian doctrines (with their quasi-polytheistic Trinity and saints) were degenerate versions of the primal cult of the Supreme Being. Exploring 'The Origin of Idolatry and Reasons of Heathenism' in his *Letters to Serena* (1704), John Toland thus contrasted foolish pagan fables with pure monotheism:

The most ancient Egyptians, Persians, and Romans, the first Patriarchs of the Hebrews . . . had no sacred Images or Statues, no peculiar Places or costly Fashions of Worship; the plain Easiness of their Religion being most agreeable to the Simplicity of the Divine Nature.[21]

Myth had become the chosen vehicle for imparting religious or moral doctrines, explained Toland, because fables were so beguiling. The trouble was that, in due course, the legends of the Greeks, Egyptians and Hebrews had provided monkish writers with models for the 'art of lying': 'The bare, naked, or simple way of Instructing by Precept, being found jejune and nauseous, a mixture of *Fable* was therefore thought necessary to sweeten and allure the minds of men, naturally Superstitious and Credulous.'[22] The gilding of religious doctrines with myth proved the teachings themselves mendacious, and priestcraft peddled parables to conceal its repellent and ridiculous doctrines. Fables were acceptable, however, to Toland if they were open inducements to virtue, Aesop for his part being an author who tended 'to the discrediting of Vice [and] the encouraging of Vertue'.[23]

The rationalist view diagnosed myth as symptomatic of the infantile folly of fearful beings trapped in ignorance, that mother of superstition. Its fountainheads were Pierre Bayle, Bernard de Fontenelle, author of *De l'origine des fables* (1724), and David Hume, all of whom exposed myth as a symptom of primitive mentality. The savage mind involved a frenzied imagination compulsively fabulizing the world. And if at first glance it was just a pile of nonsense, mythology could actually be read as a coded record of primitive man's attempts to get to grips with the world – the primitive mentality was like a child's. In his *Dictionnaire historique et critique* (1697), Bayle also pointedly derided the absurd and immoral tales of Greek and Roman mythology, so as to juxtapose them against parallel biblical episodes: Jupiter was an adulterer and – lo and behold! – so was King

David. From Charles Blount onwards, such outlooks also proved influential in Britain.[24]

The evaluation of myths grew less hostile. 'It is absurd,' insisted Adam Ferguson, in standard fashion, 'to quote the fable of the Iliad or the Odyssey, the legends of Hercules, Theseus, or Oedipus, as authorities in matter of fact relating to the history of mankind.' Yet that was not the whole story, for, he continued,

> they may, with great justice, be cited to ascertain what were the conceptions and sentiments of the age in which they were composed, or to characterize the genius of that people, with whose imaginations they were blended, and by whom they were fondly rehearsed and admired.[25]

Ferguson's view, that where historical data were wanting myths afforded windows on to bygone mentalities, achieved wide acceptance, not least with Herder in Germany. Distinguishing between nations which had developed their own myths and those which had borrowed others', Ferguson expressed his respect for Greek mythology: 'the passions of the poet pervaded the minds of the people, and the conceptions of men of genius being communicated to the vulgar, became the incentives of a national spirit'.[26] Like Vico, he recommended the comparative study of myths for the illumination it might afford into the mindsets of aboriginal and less sophisticated peoples.[27] Others, however, were unimpressed. 'The machinery of the Pagan is uninteresting to us,' dogmatized the no-nonsense Samuel Johnson: 'when a Goddess appears in Homer or Virgil, we grow weary.'[28]

The desire to forge a natural, rather than a sacred, history also shows in contemporary investigations into language. That was a hot topic: Descartes signally ruled that it was speech which differentiated animals and humans;[29] questions of the purity and pathology of language were, as already shown in chapter 3, crucial to enlightened understandings of the fortunes of truth; while the progress of language became widely accepted as an index of the rise (or fall) of civilization.[30] Above all, the origin of speech became a field in which the authority of the Bible itself was necessarily at stake. Was language truly, as Genesis stated, God's gift? If so, how could it have become corrupted? And why were there so many different tongues? Once the Adamic origin of language had been challenged, however, would not the Old Testament version of human history itself, indeed the very truth status of Scripture, be threatened? No wonder debate flared.[31]

Renaissance philology had built on the Bible. Speech, according to Genesis, went back to the garden of Eden, when God had mandated Adam to name all things. And key features of the scriptural account had become enshrined in philological orthodoxy: the first words were names. At God's instigation Adam had labelled the animals; his names indexed sounds to sights. In turn, the confusion of tongues, according to Genesis, stemmed from the Tower of Babel and man's sacrilegious attempt to ascend into Heaven. In short, sacred theories held that all mankind had originally spoken the same tongue, while later differentiation was thereafter divinely ordained, at Babel, to thwart man's pride.

Herein lay a scheme granting words maximum significance. Since the Bible made Adam's namings prelapsarian, it was widely held by humanists that such pristine labels must have been 'essential'; hence, to decipher the original language of mankind, as recorded in Hebrew, would, it was hoped, reveal long-occluded sacred truths about Creation, and etymology would illuminate the secrets of mind, both divine and human. Popular amongst grammarians, this view of language as originally transparent, definitive and true gave hope for the restoration of that purity, and thus bolstered the dreams of the likes of John Wilkins, bishop of Chester and fellow of the Royal Society, for a universal language which would reverse Babel and reunify speech. The possibility of a new and 'perfected' tongue later intrigued religious writers like William Worthington and John Gordon, who saw the globalization of a single language as a step towards the consummation of godly knowledge. A universal language, insisted Priestley, would be 'one of the last and greatest achievements of human genius'.[32]

Enlightened theorists dissented from some or all of the old philological tenets. While few British writers contradicted the Adamic theory head on – Mandeville was one – critics elaborated alternative naturalistic explanations of glottogenesis, treating language as a human invention or a natural acquisition, much like the other arts. In a Hobbist, nominalist manner, Locke stressed that the signification of words was 'perfectly arbitrary'.[33]

Once the question of the divine donation had been raised it became: How could speech actually have been developed? Some held that language had arisen from 'natural' correspondences between particular utterances and the properties of the objects designated, which had supposedly triggered particular sound sequences in the mind. Advocates made much of natural onomatopoeia ('bang', 'hiss', etc.) and man's instinctive eloquence. There were, after all, other 'natural' communications, such as gestures, which did not even need to be voiced. 'In the first ages of the world,' observed William Warburton, 'mutual converse was upheld by a mixed discourse of words and actions . . . this practice subsisted long after the necessity was over; especially amongst the eastern people' (naturally given to wild gesticulations).[34] Man had thus a natural gift for bodily expression, but crucial were the gestures produced with the voice, the '*cris naturels*' or interjections, venting some inward passion – desire, want, hunger, fear. Repetition would lead to memorization and for the reproduction of sounds for mutual information. Use of simple vocal signs extended the scope of mental operations, which in turn improved the signs, increased their number and made them more familiar.[35] Language, it was thus commonly argued, had arisen from necessity, and then gone hand in glove with mental and social progress.

In his *Of the Origin and Progress of Language* (1773–92), Lord Monboddo accepted Locke's view that etymology clarified epistemology, for 'the origin of language' could not be grasped 'without inquiring into the origin of ideas'.[36] Hence, he argued, 'from the study of language, if it be properly conducted, the history of the human mind is best learned', especially, he thought, 'in the first steps of its progress, of which it is impossible there can be any other record than what is preserved in language'.[37]

The Scottish judge proposed a wholly naturalistic and evolutionary theory of glottogenesis all his own.[38] On anatomical and other grounds, he had convinced himself that the orang-utan was an as-yet speechless variety of the human species.[39] Meaningful articulation was so demanding that only man had managed to acquire it. Speech was not innate, for 'not only solitary savages, but a whole nation' – that is, the great apes – 'have been found without the use of speech':

They are exactly of the human form; walking erect, not upon all-four, like the savages that have been found in Europe; they use sticks for weapons; they live in society; they make huts of branches of trees, and they carry off negroe girls, of whom they make slaves.[40]

Cartesians had claimed, noted Monboddo, that 'language is natural to man; and that therefore whatever animal does not speak; is not a man'.[41] But that begged the question, since the orang-utan's want of speech was purely fortuitous, thus scotching the assumption that language radically distinguished man from the animals. Rather than man being unique, Nature here, as everywhere else, showed continuity: orang-utans were humans who until now lacked speech. The history of language was thus a chapter in the wider bio-social evolution of *homo sapiens*.[42]

In mythology, philology and other fields such as racial origins and diversification, or the physical development of the Earth itself, scriptural narratives were being refuted, rationalized or metaphorized by naturalistic accounts highlighting development over time.[43] While few thinkers in Britain dismissed the historicity of the Bible root and branch, many sidelined or ignored it, substituting natural for divine causes, gradual developments for miraculous interventions and, explicitly or not, a longer timescale than the Pentateuch allowed.[44]

The histories of human society and culture had, moreover, traditionally been read as sagas of corruption, a declension from Eden or the Golden Age.[45] In the 'Ancients versus Moderns' debate and elsewhere, such pessimistic readings were being challenged, however, by a growing belief in improvement. Nowhere was this more evident than where change was most wanted, needed and dramatic: on the periphery.[46]

The eighteenth century brought conflicts of allegiances for intellectuals, torn between cosmopolitan leanings and local loyalties. Being a 'citizen of the world' was attractive for those steeped in Graeco-Roman values and disgusted by sectarian and chauvinistic bigotry. Yet there was a growing clamour, too, for national identity: enlightened libertarianism, after all, demanded independence from oppressors, while a new fascination with roots and race, with the vernacular, customs and history was fostering feelings of nationhood which transcended dynastic fealties.[47]

The myths singling out and occasionally cementing the English have been central to this book, above all pride in Anglo-Saxon political liberties, and the *entente cordiale* between liberal Protestantism, rational religion, commercial success and the civilizing process. Notionally at least, it was not only the English who were included within such enlightened formulae – 'Britons never never never shall be slaves,' sang the Scot Thomson in a masque called *Alfred*.[48] But sentiments among the non-English were not always so clear cut: the Scots, Welsh and Irish – to say nothing of Britons overseas, as in the Thirteen Colonies – were liable to feel split. Doubtless it would be wrong to antedate or exaggerate 'Celtic nationalisms' among the intellectuals, and non-English Britons had little compunction about calling themselves 'English' when it suited[49] – a mark, surely, of the fact that so many prominent 'Celtic' luminaries had gladly quit their native heath to seek fame and fortune in the Great Wen. The traffic of Scots along the high road south was notorious;[50] and those Welsh- and Irish-born who might be fielded in any Enlightenment first team – for instance, Richard Price, Sir William Jones and Robert Owen, Richard Steele, John Toland, Sir Hans Sloane, the Sheridans, Laurence Sterne, Oliver Goldsmith and Edmund Burke – chose not to pass their adult lives in their mother country. Those who stayed at home and passed as patriots might sound none too enamoured. 'I reckon no man is thoroughly miserable,' commented Jonathan Swift, dean of St Patrick's cathedral in Dublin, 'unless he be condemned to live in Ireland', alias 'this isle of slaves'. His solution to the Hibernian problem was proffered, of course, in *A Modest Proposal* (1729), which suggested that Irish babies would make delicious eating, 'whether Stewed, Roasted, Baked, or Boiled; and I make no doubt, that it will equally serve in a Fricasie, or a Ragoust'.[51]

Georgian Wales remained rural and sparsely populated; it boasted no polite city or university, and some bishops never even saw their see. The Welsh gentry had no reputation for learning – and well into the nineteenth century Thomas Peacock expected to wring a laugh, in his novel *Headlong Hall* (1816), out of the idea of a Welsh squire, his Harry Headlong, actually owning some books.[52]

There were some lights, however. Edward Morgan, who hailed from the Vale of Glamorgan and passed as Iolo Morganyg, was a Unitarian and a devotee of Voltaire and other *philosophes*, sharing their hatred of priestcraft. He launched the cult of Madoc, the medieval Welshman who, so it was told, had sailed west and discovered America, planting his compatriots amid the Great Plains. With Welsh emigration to the New World rising, the itch to unearth that long-lost intrepid tribe naturally grew – an interest fed by Dr John Williams, a learned divine resident in Sydenham, south of London, with his *An Enquiry into the Truth of the Tradition Concerning the Discovery of America by Prince Madog ab Owen Gwynedd about AD 1170* (1791).[53] Especially with the revolt of the Thirteen Colonies, the Madocians could be hailed as frontiersmen of liberty, the very first people to fling off the English yoke. His nationalist libertarian rhetoric was later reinforced by Jacobinism.[54]

Morganyg was also fascinated by philology (he deduced affinities between Welsh and pristine Hebrew), and by Druidic myth, literature and history (the Druids were presented as prototype Jacobins).[55] Aiming to revive bardic traditions, he fancied the Eisteddfod as a kind of national cultural academy: back in the days of Aneirin and

Taliesin, Arthur and his knights had been Welsh poetry's sponsors. Familiarizing himself with the *Gorsedd*, an ancient open-air bardic gathering, Morganyg conjured up its reincarnation, complete with robes, ranks and rituals. The first revived *Gorsedd* was staged by the London Welsh on Primrose Hill in 1792, contributing to the 'invention of tradition'. Cambro-Briton revivalism was, at this time, largely metropolitan, backed by the *Gwyneddigon*, the energetic London Welsh society.

Ireland was different: a cauldron of conflict, with rival populations sundered by language, land, ethnicity, faith, wealth and the savage anti-Catholic penal code; and the Protestant ascendancy was bitterly resented. In Dublin, Cork and a few other cities, Ireland also boasted seats of civilization – in Dublin's case, a parliament, an ancient university and a fringe of professional corporations.

Georgian Ireland spawned institutions dedicated to modernizing, in particular the Dublin Society. Founded in 1731 for 'the improvement of Husbandry, Manufactures and other useful Arts', its members were primarily Protestant gentlemen of the landowning classes, with a sprinkling of bishops, judges, barristers, doctors and the military. It was practical in its orientation: agricultural treatises were circulated, new implements tried, experiments performed and premiums offered to those producing the top crops. Visiting in 1770, Arthur Young, while none too impressed overall by Irish agronomy, met many an improving landlord. Dublin also boasted theatres and assembly rooms for polite culture – Handel visited in 1741 to conduct *The Messiah* – while the Irish Parliament and courts upheld proud traditions of oratory; Trinity College, where Berkeley taught early in his career, sported famous debating societies; and to stir up science, the Royal Irish Academy was founded in 1785.[56]

From Swift through to Burke's denunciations of the Test Acts, controversies raged over Irish rights. It was not, however, until the 1790s that grievances were voiced in an idiom directly coloured by enlightened (by then, also revolutionary) claims.[57]

*

Scotland was different again.[58] Unlike Wales, it was a populous country with big cities; unlike Ireland, it was overwhelmingly Protestant and not quasi-colonial. Cultivating distinguished traditions of humanist learning and, thanks to its Calvinism, a deep commitment to schooling, Scotland retained its own Kirk, legal and educational system, enduring sources of cultural prestige even after it lost its parliament upon the Act of Union (1707). The university cities of Edinburgh, Glasgow and, to a lesser degree, Aberdeen and St Andrews possessed high concentrations of divines, lawyers, doctors and leisured gentlemen, many doubling as men of letters. There were thus deep-seated cultural practices, rooted in the professions, landowning classes and the universities.[59]

If the nation was also in turmoil – riven, beyond the mid-century, by the conflicts of loyalty, interest and ideology centred on Jacobitism – opportunities were beckoning for the rapid economic and social development of a people who, before the Union, had been desperately backward and impoverished. For some, the surrender of political sovereignty in 1707 was a national humiliation; for others, the tangible cultural, intellectual and social advances – the progress of 'civil society' – made that loss mainly a matter for the nostalgic.[60] What is significant, however, is that no Scottish thinker could avoid an acute awareness of change, actual and anticipated; many hence felt obliged to theorize the transformations the nation was, or should be, undergoing.

How far the Scottish Enlightenment was homegrown remains highly contested.[61] Many believed the torch came from outside, specifically from metropolitan polite culture. 'The appearance of *Tatlers*, *Spectators*, and *Guardians* in the reign of Queen Anne', thought Ramsay of Ochtertyre, had anglicized the philistine Scot into 'a polite scholar'.[62] 'The constant flux of information and of liberality from abroad,' agreed Dugald Stewart, 'may help to account for the sudden burst of genius, which to a foreigner must seem to have sprung up in this country by a sort of enchantment, soon after the Rebellion of 1745.'[63]

London, for its part, certainly lured the literati. 'Scotland is but a

narrow place,' lamented the architect Robert Adam in 1755, explaining his need for 'a greater, a more extensive, and more honourable
scene, I mean an English Life', and bantering to his sister in Edinburgh that it was a 'pity' that 'such a genius' as himself 'should be
thrown away upon Scotland'.[64] Meanwhile, David Hume, bent on
deleting his Scotticisms, styled London 'the Capital of my own
Country' and declared to his crony Adam Smith: 'Scotland is too
narrow a place for me.'[65] Hume was no rabid patriot: pre-Union
Scotland had lagged; the Scots had not then even amounted to a civil
society, having been 'the rudest, perhaps, of all European Nations; the
most necessitous, the most turbulent, and the most unsettled';[66] while
her kings had never managed to uphold order. Yet he could equally
growl about the 'Barbarians who inhabit the Banks of the Thames',[67]
deny that significant intellectual work was coming out of England and
crow over Caledonia's triumphs. 'Is it not strange,' he propositioned
Gilbert Elliot in 1757,

that, at a time when we have lost our Princes, our Parliaments, our
independent Government, even the Presence of our chief Nobility, are
unhappy in our accent and Pronunciation, speak a very corrupt Dialect of
the Tongue which we make use of; is it not strange, I say, that, in these
Circumstances, we shou'd really be the People most distinguish'd for Literature in Europe?[68]

However, to draw rigid distinctions between the English and
Scottish enlightened traditions is anachronistic, largely because such
a delineation merely reflects later nationalisms. In philosophy, moral
and natural science, the common ground between those north and
south of the Tweed outweighs the contrasts. English and Scottish
thinkers were in constant dialogue, be it Francis Hutcheson absorbing
Shaftesbury so as to rebut Mandeville, or the long-running materialism dispute between Joseph Priestley and Thomas Reid, James Beattie and the other 'Common Sense' philosophers.[69] Given a shared
tongue and shared readerships, it is hardly surprising that the traditions fed off each other. A swelling tide of English students attended
Edinburgh University after 1750, while many leading Scots, like

Hume, Smith and Smollett, passed a part of their careers in England, or even further afield. Being cosmopolitan counted for much with the enlightened Scot.

Whatever its ingredients, the catalyst of the Scottish Enlightenment is clear. In 1707, the nation's élite traded in political independence for a Union with England which promised better economic times,[70] and then went on to reject the Jacobite calls to arms. By the time of the battle of Culloden (16 April 1746), the Union was visibly bearing socio-economic fruit,[71] which left Samuel Johnson astonished when visiting the Highlands (that 'Nation just rising from barbarity') in the 1770s:

There was perhaps never any change of national manners so quick, so great, and so general . . . We came thither too late to see what we expected . . . a system of antiquated life. The clans retain little now of their original character, their ferocity of temper is softened, their military ardour is extinguished, their dignity of independence is depressed, their contempt of government subdued, and the reverence for their chiefs abated.[72]

Remarkable developments attended the post-Union decades. Early on, power struggles erupted in an embattled Kirk dominated since 1688 by Calvinist doctrinaires in the Covenanting mould. In 1696 an Edinburgh teenager, Thomas Aikenhead, was convicted of blasphemy and put to death, and witches were still being executed.[73] From 1714 John Simpson, professor of theology at Glasgow, was harassed for heresy; Archibald Campbell, professor of church history at St Andrews, was also charged with heresy, in 1736, for his *A Discourse Proving that the Apostles were No Enthusiasts* (1730); and so were Francis Hutcheson in 1738, William Leechman, professor of divinity at Glasgow, in 1744, and David Hume in 1756. Lord Kames was subjected to attacks from zealots for the deterministic philosophy expressed in his *Essays on the Principles of Morality and Natural Religion* (1751),[74] while the Revd John Home came under attack for writing a stage play.

The Kirk's hardline leadership was, however, in the course of time successfully challenged by the 'Moderates', eager to temper faith with reason and modern learning.[75] In the end the Moderate cause predominated, as is evident in the illustrious careers of its leading lights, the Revd Hugh Blair and the Revd William Robertson. The Edinburgh-educated Blair showed his colours by publishing a favourable review of Hutcheson's *System of Moral Philosophy* in the first *Edinburgh Review*, which praised his treatment of morality, if taking issue with his excessively aesthetic view of benevolence. Between 1776 and 1788, Blair occupied the newly created position of professor of rhetoric and *belles-lettres* at Edinburgh, bringing out his influential *Lectures* (1783), which praised the *Spectator* and even endorsed the novel as a literary form. If Blair won greatest public acclaim at the time for his defence of Ossian, he was lastingly remembered for his Latitudinarian sermons, which also made him rich – he was the first Edinburgh cleric to own a carriage.[76] Robertson for his part became, with Hume and Gibbon, one of the great triumvirate of British Enlightenment historians, publishing his *History of Scotland* in 1759, his *History of the Emperor Charles V* in 1769 and his *History of America* in 1777.[77] Becoming principal of Edinburgh University and then leader of the Moderates in the Church of Scotland, he was appointed moderator of the General Assembly in 1763 – evidence of how far the Church of Scotland had by then liberalized itself.

After the Union, culture advanced on a broad front. Newspapers emerged, such as the *Edinburgh Evening Courant*, Ruddiman's *Weekly Mercury*, the *Scots Magazine* and the *Caledonian Mercury* (which boasted a circulation of 1,400 by 1739).[78] Clubs and improvement societies also sprang up. The Easy Club met from 1712 under the poet Allan Ramsay, significantly to read the *Spectator*. The Mirror Club did much the same, while the Select Society (1754–64), of which Adam Smith was a founder member, was a debating club for men of rank.[79] The Honourable Society for the Improvement in the Knowledge of Agriculture (1723–45) also catered for the élite. 'The more these refined arts advance, the more sociable men become,' commented Hume on the role of such voluntary associations:

They flock into cities; love to receive and communicate knowledge; to show their wit or breeding . . . Particular clubs and societies are every where formed: Both sexes meet in an easy and sociable manner; and the tempers of men, as well as their behaviour, refine apace . . . Thus *industry*, *knowledge*, and *humanity*, are linked together, by an indissoluble chain.[80]

The success of such clubs in bringing gentlemen together was especially crucial as, unlike England, Scotland had never had a corps of professional writers. As late as the 1730s, noted Dugald Stewart, the trade of authorship was unknown in Scotland – there was no Edinburgh Grub Street – and it was gentlemen, lawyers, divines, academics and doctors who did the writing in the 'Athens of the North'.[81]

Meanwhile, the universities themselves were modernizing. In particular, at Edinburgh and Glasgow the old regenting system (in which the professor was forced to act like a schoolmaster, teaching everything) gave way to specialized professorships.[82] Despite nepotistic tendencies, the universities housed a galaxy of talent, philosophical, scientific and medical, and many eminent works followed from within and without the academy.

In 1754, the original *Edinburgh Review* was founded by a band of literati including Blair and Smith. Though it survived for only two numbers – evidently it was precocious to the point of prematurity – it provided a pointer to the future. 'This country which is just beginning to attempt figuring in the learned world,' remarked Smith in the second and final number, 'produces as yet so few works of reputation, that it is scarce possible a paper which criticizes upon them chiefly, should interest the public for any considerable time.' The priority lay in absorbing Continental works and, in order to set an example, Smith embarked on an account of the *Encyclopédie*, no less.[83] Regarding it as its mission to regularize Scottish writing, the *Review* censured 'vulgarity' of language; the uphill 'progress in knowledge' in north Britain, explained the preface to the first number, arose from the 'difficulty of a proper expression' in a country lacking a refined standard of writing.[84]

With polarities thus staring them in the face – between lively England and languishing Scotland, but also between the advancing Lowlands and the backward Highlands – Scottish thinkers could hardly avoid producing theoretical models highlighting social contrast and change. Perhaps the most ambitious emerged from one of the rare Highlander protagonists, Adam Ferguson, a man whose careers propitiously spanned those of soldier, clergyman and professor. His *An Essay on the History of Civil Society* (1767) analysed the moral and material headway of nations towards commercial society, notably in two historical discussions of social development – 'Of the History of Rude Nations' and 'Of the History of Policy and Arts'. The last three parts – 'Of Consequences that Result from the Advancement of Civil and Commercial Arts', 'Of the Decline of Nations' and 'Of Corruption and Political Slavery' – presented, as the titles make clear, historico-moral cost–benefit analyses of the transition to modernity.[85] Offering a conspectus on developments 'from rudeness to civilization', his diagnosis of the problems of advanced commercial society voiced civic humanist disquiet regarding Scottish attempts to pursue economic development while remaining virtuous. Born on the borderline of primitive and advanced societies in a nation seeking a new kind of commercial and constitutional liberty, Ferguson was deeply engaged with Scottish problems, even if his *Essay* discussed backward economies without ever naming the Highlands, commercialization without dwelling on England and the State without alluding to the Union. The big issue was the place – or replaceability – of traditional civic virtue in the modern state. Would not modernization sap vital traditions of martial and civic spirit and in the end undermine liberty? Surely the price of affluence would be too high?[86]

The *Essay* engaged in tacit dialogue with David Hume, who demurred from Ferguson while, like him, silently mapping Scotland old and new on to a broader historical canvas. Hume conducted his own comparison of polities ancient and modern, by addressing the contrast between Sparta (for which read medieval Scotland) and modern commercial society.[87] As the exemplar of a free society, Sparta had long been celebrated by Scottish 'Commonwealthmen' from Andrew Fletcher of Saltoun[88] to Ferguson, but Hume torpedoed the anti-luxury case for Spartan virtue: trade, he held, spelt not corruption but civility, peace and progress.[89] Countering the old glorification of Spartan valour, recently boosted by Rousseau's *Discours* on the arts and sciences (1750), he subverted the civic human-ist tradition which prized the landed warrior as the cornerstone of a free society. Essaying a 'science of man' derived from 'cautious observation of human life',[90] Hume held that warrior states like Sparta were both undesirable and obsolete, whereas the 'ages of refinement' brought by modern commerce were 'both the happiest and most virtuous'.[91]

Hume set the 'arts of luxury' in historical context. His initial phase – soon to reappear as Adam Smith's first state of society – was the 'savage state', a subsistence economy devoted to hunting and fishing. Thereafter societies went on to pursue agriculture, which in time could support 'superfluous hands', free to apply themselves to the arts. With many acquiring the 'opportunity of receiving enjoyments with which they would otherwise have been unacquainted', well-being spread.[92]

Sparta stood out as the stark exception to such developments – indeed, as the perfect model of 'classical' virtue, it had been held up as a moral reproach to lesser nations. What had happened in Sparta was that its extra hands had been devoted not to economic but to military activity. A tension evidently existed between the 'greatness of the state' (its military machine) and the 'happiness of the subject'.[93]

Ages of luxury were happier, their happiness consisting in three ingredients: 'indolence', 'action' and 'pleasure' – this last being clearly linked with action, for action invigorated the mind, thereby satisfying natural appetites and inhibiting unnatural ones.[94] In praising action Hume was, however, celebrating not Cicero's preoccupation with the *res publica* – involvement in affairs of state – but the private pursuit of 'industry'. People were roused to activity or industry by the desire for a more 'splendid way of life' and for the 'pleasures of luxury'.[95] These had been despised by classical moralists and Christians alike because they pandered to the gratification of bodily desires, but Hume dissociated himself from such reproaches and praised 'inno-cent' luxury; only monks and others 'disordered by the frenzies of enthusiasm' could denounce innocuous things like good food or clothing. Indeed Hume counterargued that the refinement of pleasure which luxury brought actually spelt a *reduction* in coarse indulgence – it was the barbarian hordes who were the gluttons, not the courtiers of Versailles with their 'refinements of cookery'. Moralistic attacks on 'excess' in modern commercial society were thus off-beam.[96]

Whereas savage nations like Sparta remained lacking in social graces and humanity, the advent of industry unleashed progressive forces. 'Every art and science' was improved, 'profound ignorance' was banished and the 'pleasures of the mind as well as those of body' cultivated.[97] Hume rebutted the trite moralistic castigation of urban corruption, that supposed sink of debauchery which lured innocent peasants off the land. Underpinning that hackneyed antipathy to the urban was the Harringtonian model, upheld by Ferguson, of the virtuous citizen with plough and sword. For Hume the consummate Modern, by contrast, civilization, civility and the civic life were of a piece;[98] sociability and humanity encouraged 'laws, order, police, discipline'; and it was in 'polished' ages that 'industry, knowledge and humanity were interlinked by an indissoluble chain'.[99]

Sparta's kings put warfare before welfare. For Hume, however, 'humanity' itself demanded that tempers and manners be 'softened',[100] echoing 'the doctrine of the *doux commerce*' spelt out by Montesquieu's *De l'esprit des lois* (1748).[101] One sign of that desirable softening of manners was that modern wars had become less 'brutal', while, over time, courage – that virtue supreme in uncultivated nations – had also been played down. Such a softening, soothed Hume, did not mean a collapse into effeminacy – the might of contemporary France and England clearly proved that 'luxury' did not lead to military decrepitude![102]

Hume paraded his positive alternative to the Spartan ideal of the 'strict moralists', the 'modern' notion of liberty, a view soon to be more fully elucidated by his friend Adam Smith. Spartan society had been stymied by its rigid polarization, divided between helots and 'the soldiers or gentlemen'.[103] One desirable consequence of the growth of luxury lay in the ending of such crude divisions. Slavery was 'disadvantageous' to happiness, whereas in a commercial society the population at large would be happy, as all its members would 'reap the benefit of these commodities'.[104]

Hume clinched his case with an appeal to the science of man. Sparta was exceptional, 'violent and contrary to the more natural and usual course of things' – impossible, had it not actually existed![105] Modern states should not – indeed *could* not – return to that way of being: Sparta was a world we had luckily lost. The notion of a modern city as a 'fortified camp' with its inhabitants fired with a 'passion for the public good'[106] hardly rang true, for 'our strongest attention is confin'd to ourselves'.[107] Governments must manage subjects by those feelings that truly moved them – they must 'animate them with a spirit of avarice and industry, art and luxury'.[108]

For Hume, avarice, that *bête noire* of the 'severe moralists', was, paradoxically, the 'spur' to 'civil Liberty'[109] and to that 'exercise and employment' for which 'there is no craving or demand of the human mind more constant and insatiable'.[110] Avarice operated 'at all times, in all places and upon all persons'[111] – a universality significant for the Humean science of man which looked to 'principles as universal as possible'.[112] Hence understanding of politics must not be based upon freaks like Sparta, rated 'a prodigy' by everyone 'who has considered human nature'.[113]

It would require, suggested Hume, in a telltale choice of words, 'a miraculous transformation' to rid mankind of vice.[114] Magistrates must handle men as they are, and play off one vice against others less prejudicial to society. Government could not impose the 'good life' by *fiat*. Rather, since human nature was fixed, a ruler had to channel the passions constructively, to promote well-being. Sparta had got it wrong: 'industry and arts and trade', properly understood, would increase 'the power of the sovereign'; but such an increase should not, as in the case of Spartan militarism, be bought at the cost of 'the happiness of the subjects'.[115]

Whereas a commercial nation was potent, observed the enlightened philosopher, the non-trading society was going nowhere:

soldiers were at bottom ignorant, insolent and idle. A civilized nation, *because* of its other attributes, would constitute an effective military power, not least because, in a rich nation, an army could be raised through taxes.[116]

Above all, commercial society was progressive, argued Hume, alluding to 'the great advantage of *England* above any nation at present in the world'. This success consisted not simply in possessing a 'multitude of mechanical arts' but in the 'great number of persons to whose share the productions of these arts fall', for 'every person if possible ought to enjoy the fruits of his labour'. The equitable spreading of benefits harmonized with human nature.[117] All in all, the enlightened science of man taught a clear lesson: Scotland should anglicize herself as swiftly as possible.

Hume thus blew the trumpet for the modern: Scotland should not copy Sparta, nostalgia was wasted on that imagined community. Time had moved on, partly because of the human impulse for improvement. Unlike Ferguson, and even to some degree Adam Smith, for whom modernization brought harm as well as gain, Hume was fully optimistic about the direction of social change.

Such assumptions became inscribed in the model of an unfolding plan of history, driven by a spring. It became a characteristic of post-1750 thinking, particularly in Scotland, to hold that societies almost necessarily passed through a series of stages, with all elements of their development – economic, moral, legal, cultural and political – symbiotically interacting. One for whom such a model became second nature was Hume's kinsman Henry Home, Lord Kames.[118] After producing his early *Essay on the Principles of Morality and Natural Religion* (1751) – a work ruled dangerous by the Kirk – that judge and inexhaustible speculator on the human condition turned, in his *Historical Law-Tracts* (1758), to a history of the origin and development of law, concluding in 1774 with the expansive *Sketches of the History of Man*, a 4-volume anthropology of morals which traces the historical development of all manner of social institutions.[119]

Addressing the law, Kames boldly held that legal rationality itself was not timeless but had to be historicized: 'The law of a country is in perfection when it corresponds to the manners of the people, their circumstances, their government. And as these are seldom stationary, the law ought to accompany them in their changes.'[120] Analysing man's 'remarkable propensity for appropriation', the law lord deemed that 'without private property there would be no industry, and without industry, men would remain savages forever'. At 'the dawn of society', he explained, individuals defended their belongings and sought personal revenge. In due course, third parties were called in to adjudicate when property disputes arose. Such judges steadily acquired powers of intervention in disputes, and civil jurisdiction made headway. Criminal jurisdiction progressed more slowly, however, for 'revenge, the darling privilege of undisciplined nature, is never tamely given up'.[121] All the same, vendettas proved so disruptive that governments eventually assumed the mantle of proceeding against blood feuds.[122]

From the history of law, Kames was led to adumbrate a wider philosophy of social change: 'Hunting and fishing, in order for sustenance, were the original occupations of man. The shepherd life succeeded; and the next stage was that of agriculture.'[123] Such 'progressive changes' could be found 'universally', but it was only at the agrarian stage that there emerged 'the true spirit of society, which consists in mutual benefits, and in making the industry of individuals profitable to others as well as to themselves'.[124]

Others mapped out similar patterns in establishing, in Sir John Dalrymple's words, 'how men arrived from the most rude to the most polished state of society'. In his *History of Edinburgh, from the Earliest Accounts to the Present Time* (1787) Alexander Kincaid paints 'a general picture of the manners of the time throughout all Scotland' which paid special attention to 'barbarity' conceived as a cultural rather than a strictly economic phase.[125] Such ideas, however, found their fullest expression in the four-stage theory spelt out by Adam Smith and later by his follower John Millar in their attempts to historicize Montesquieu's map of manners into a natural history of mankind.[126] 'The four stages of society are hunting, pasturage, farming, and commerce,' explained Smith, in a thought experiment which sounds more like Crusoe than Rousseau:

If a number of persons were shipwrecked on a desert island their first sustenance would be from the fruits which the soil naturally produced, and the wild beasts which they could kill. As these could not at all times be sufficient, they came at last to tame some of the wild beasts that they might always have them at hand. In process of time even these would not be sufficient; and as they saw the earth naturally produce considerable quantities of vegetables of its own accords, they would think of cultivating it so that it might produce more of them. Hence agriculture, which requires a good deal of refinement before it could become the prevailing employment of a country ... The age of commerce naturally succeeds that of agriculture.[127]

The dynamic tensions arising in each successive stage would spark the transition to the next. Herds thus led to the 'inequality of fortune' which 'first gave rise to regular government. Till there be property there can be no government', since its very point was to 'defend the rich from the poor'.[128]

It was John Millar who elaborated these views. Like all progressive Scots, this professor of law at Glasgow praised the colossal benefits accruing from the Glorious Revolution and the Act of Union: 'From this happy period, therefore, commerce and manufacturers assumed a new aspect, and continuing to advance with rapidity, produced innumerable changes in the state of society, and in the character and manners of the people.'[129] His quasi-materialist version stressed the economic logic of the four stages. The first object of mankind was, it went without saying, 'to procure subsistence, to obtain the necessaries, comforts and conveniences of life'. Thereafter, their aim was 'to defend their persons and their acquisitions against the attacks of one another'. At first, because property itself was simple, political arrangements were as well, but greater wealth required that 'its government ought to be the more complicated'. For that reason, by 'tracing the progress of wealth we may thus expect to discover the progress of government'.[130]

Millar itemized the four successive states. First there were savages, 'people who live by hunting and fishing and by gathering the spontaneous fruits of the earth'; then came the age of the shepherds; then husbandmen; and lastly commercial peoples.[131] Overall, he told a tale of progress comprehensive and unalloyed:

their prospects are gradually enlarged, their appetites and desires are more and more awakened and called forth in pursuit of the several conveniences of life; and the various branches of manufacture, together with commerce, its inseparable attendant, and with science and literature, the natural offspring of ease and affluence, are introduced, and brought to maturity.[132]

The environment played a certain part in such developments, explaining why some societies progressed more than others, but, like Smith, Millar essentially ascribed progress to man's nature itself, 'a disposition and capacity for improving his condition', which 'has every where produced a remarkable uniformity in the several steps of his progression'.[133]

In the philosophies of Hume, Smith and Millar, improvement was virtually guaranteed and the path of progress everywhere became legible. Assessing Smith's contributions, Dugald Stewart thus praised his *Dissertation on the Origin of Language* (1761) as 'a specimen of a particular sort of enquiry' typical of the times, the attempt to explain the 'marked difference between the institutions, ideas, manners and arts of the past and those of the present'. In examining 'by what gradual steps the transition has been made from the first simple efforts of uncultivated nature, to a state of things so wonderfully artificial and complicated', hard facts were, admittedly, few and far between, and so the answers had to be sought in another source, conjecture: 'our conclusions *a priori*, may tend to confirm the credibility of facts, which, on a superficial view, appeared to be doubtful or incredible'. Such speculative accounts, Stewart insisted, did not merely serve to gratify curiosity: they had their scientific value, showing how change 'may have been produced by natural causes'. The procedure was worthy of a name: 'I shall take the liberty of giving the title of Theoretical or Conjectural History.'[134] Progress had thus become so important a theoretical weapon in the enlightened armoury that when data were lacking to support it, conjecture would serve in their place.

With the querying of the sufficiency of the Bible to explain the human condition, attempts to make sense of the great canvas of history took on a new urgency, while rapid material and social change inspired attempts to position the present in terms of ongoing processes. Theories of transition from rudeness to refinement took hold, particularly in Scotland, in view of the nation's rapid development – from the savage to the Scotsman, from Eden to Edinburgh. Modernization did not only bring prosperity, it was a comprehensive force spreading civility to all departments of life: 'the improvements in the state of society, which are the effects of opulence and refinement', trumpeted Millar, will 'dispose the father to behave with greater mildness and moderation in the exercise of his authority. As he lives in greater affluence and security, he is more at leisure to exert the social affections, and to cultivate those arts which tend to soften and humanize the temper.'[135] Progress was humanizing.

The Scots felt mighty pleased to be enlightened – and affluent – at last.[136] And, proud of their sturdy academic and philosophical traditions, they rationalized that confidence through elevated theories of the human mind and its ameliorating powers. No mere theorist of social change, Adam Ferguson also produced, for example, his *Institutes of Moral Philosophy* (1796). After chapters on 'The History of the Species', which sketched in the anthropological background, Ferguson then went on to tackle 'The History of the Individual', which looked at consciousness, sense and perception, observation, memory, imagination, abstraction, reasoning, foresight, propensity, sentiment, desire and volition. Man's intellectual potential itself knew no bounds.[137]

As a historian of mental progress Ferguson was followed by Dugald Stewart, another typically polymathic professor from a typically Scottish academic dynasty. In 1772 Stewart junior took over the mathematical classes at Edinburgh of his failing father. Six years later he also undertook to lecture for Ferguson and, on the latter's resignation in 1785, he transferred to the chair of moral philosophy, proving a huge success. All his key books – the *Elements of the Philosophy of the Human Mind* (1792), the *Philosophical Essays* (1810) and *The Philosophy of the Active and Moral Powers of Man* (1828) – disclose a common programme: a Baconian philosophy of mental development.

Natural philosophy had acquired the status of science, Stewart held, when inquiry, freed from metaphysical speculation, was directed towards discovering, by observation and experiment, the laws governing the connection of physical phenomena. Natural science had progressed by bringing these uniformities under laws of greater generality capable of comprehending disparate phenomena: the philosophy of mind must advance by similar means.

For Stewart the great desideratum was a *unitary* human science, though one which would be two-pronged, embracing a science of society (including economics and politics) and a science of consciousness. The phenomenon of consciousness, he stressed, had to be addressed unbiased by speculation, and the laws of their relations validated inductively. The science of mind would seek a knowledge of the 'general laws of our constitution', paralleling Newtonian principles in physics, and, like them, promote the deductive explanation of a galaxy of facts.

Though the science of mind presupposed 'the principles of common sense', that favourite term of Thomas Reid was erroneous, for it made his appeal to 'common sense' against scepticism sound like an appeal to the vulgar against the educated. Stewart instead chose to speak of 'the fundamental laws of human belief'.

Stewart derived from earlier Scottish thinkers an idea which became his leitmotiv, almost an *idée fixe*: the unity of the 'philosophical sciences' – logic, moral and political philosophy, political economy and aesthetics, all dependent on the philosophy of mind. For this, the study of human nature 'considered as one great whole' was required, grounded upon psychology in its widest sense. He was also concerned to integrate his natural philosophical views within rational religion. The soul was not something of which we were introspectively conscious; our knowledge of it, rather, was entirely 'relative', derived from the phenomenon of consciousness. The immateriality of the mind created expectations of life after death, and tendencies deep-seated in human nature needed a future life for their realization – for instance, the irreducible notions of right and wrong required and suggested divine government. Stewart represented the culmination of Scottish academic attempts to discover in history the progressive manifestation of mind.

Central to enlightened hopes was the goal of extending scientific thinking to man and society. Living in a rapidly changing society with a strong university tradition, it is little surprise that the Scots were so prominent in that movement, contributing particularly clear and coherent philosophies of progress.

II

HAPPINESS

The present is the Age of Pastime, the Golden Reign of Pleasure

SAMUEL FAWCONER[1]

Oh Happiness! our being's end and aim!
Good, Pleasure, Ease, Content! Whate'er thy name

ALEXANDER POPE[2]

What is the pulse of this so busy world?
The love of pleasure . . .

EDWARD YOUNG[3]

I will tell you in what consists the *summum bonum* of human life:
it consists in reading *Tristram Shandy*, in blowing with a pair of
bellows into your shoes in hot weather, and roasting potatoes
under the grate in cold.

ARCHDEACON PALEY[4]

The Enlightenment's great historical watershed lay in the
validation of pleasure. This chapter, rounding off the first half of this
book, will explore the increasing embracement, however uneven and
qualified, of the pursuit of temporal happiness as the *summum bonum*.

It would be absurd to imply that before the Enlightenment there
were no profligates, no cakes and ale, or that the pleasures of the
senses and imagination were utterly frowned upon. In Antiquity,
Epicurus and his followers had advocated a hedonism which priorit-
ized, if not the gratification of desire at least the avoidance of pain.[5]
Pagan bacchanalia were well known to the Renaissance,[6] while

pastoral painting and poetry blazoned bucolic golden age idylls in which bounteous Nature freely yielded up her fruits.[7] The Christian calendar had its feasts no less than its fasts – the Twelve Days of Christmas, Plough Sunday and Monday, Shrove Tuesday, All Fools' Day and any number of saints' days – while trades had their particular festive days: for example, St Crispin's for shoemakers, St Paul's for tinners. Familiar themes – the revels of Bacchus and Venus, the cornucopia and the flowing bowl – show that, both in reality and in the artistic imagination, there had always been times and places of holiday, abandonment and enjoyment.

Yet sensualism had been decisively rejected. Plato had pictured the appetites as a mutinous crew – only Captain Reason would prevent shipwreck – while the Stoics for their part dismissed hedonism as a bubble: the wise must disdain fleeting pleasures and find truth in the immaterial and eternal. Stoicism thus somewhat anticipated the Christian rejection of carnality, true blessedness coming only through abstinence and asceticism.[8] Concupiscence was the consequence of Original Sin; through omnipresent images of the Expulsion, the *danse macabre* and the *memento mori*, Christians had been taught that this was a vale of tears in which labour was a cursed reminder of the Fall, egoism was evil and pride had to be cast out of the heart: according to Sir Thomas Browne, 'there is no happiness within the circle of flesh'. Signalling the Church's anxieties about the seductive pleasures of objects, the deadly sins singled out for censure were envy and avarice, lust and even, somewhat bathetically, gluttony. In this valley of the shadow of death, the mortification of the flesh was the release of the spirit.[9]

Many such God-fearing Christians remained – Gibbon smirked at how such killjoys divested the God they adored of 'every amiable attribute'.[10] Samuel Johnson, whose *Rasselas* (1759) showed that the Happy Valley was not happy at all, offered what might be called an infelicific calculus: 'Infelicity is involved in corporeal nature, and interwoven with our being; all attempts therefore to decline it wholly are useless and vain.'[11]

*

While there were some sunny intervals, hedonism in itself was wholly deprecated within traditional Christianity. The Enlightenment's novelty lay in the legitimacy it accorded to pleasure, not as occasional binges, mystical transports or blue-blooded privilege, but as the routine entitlement of people at large to pursue the senses (not just purify the soul) and to seek fulfilment in this world (and not only in the next).

This transformation, as seen, came about partly *within* Christianity, for Latitudinarianism presented a benevolent God as author of a harmonious universe in which earthly joys presaged heavenly rewards. 'To do good is the most pleasant enjoyment in the world,' explained Archbishop Tillotson, 'it is natural, and whatever is so, is delightful.'[12] 'There should not always be Storms or Thunder,' ruled the Marquis of Halifax; 'a clear Sky would sometimes make the Church look more like Heaven.'[13]

More importantly, hedonism also emerged beyond the Church, thanks to the reinstatement of classical ideas and to enlightened philosophies of human nature. The new science promoted mechanical models of man essentially as a machine motivated to pursue pleasure and avoid pain. In *Leviathan* (1651), Hobbes advanced a negative hedonism, oriented primarily towards avoiding pain and death, while for his part Mandeville touted a cynical egoism: all actually pursue selfish pleasure, if hypocritically denying it.[14] For their challenges to traditional precepts, humanistic and Christian, Hobbes and Mandeville were pilloried, but their essential message won gradual if guarded acceptance: self-fulfilment rather than denial should be embraced, because it is inherent in human nature and beneficial to society. Later thinkers glossed these otherwise shocking conclusions. Taking distinct guises in different fields of discourse, they are worth reviewing briefly.

One, as mentioned, lay within divinity itself. By 1700, natural theology was achieving high prominence, picturing God as the benign Architect of a perfect universe. Following in Sir Isaac's footsteps, the Boyle lecturers presented the Earth as a law-governed habitat meant for mankind's use.[15] Man could garner the fruits of the soil, tame the animals and quarry the crust.[16] Cosmic optimism of course begged endless questions, being satirized by Voltaire's *Candide* and Samuel Johnson's *Rasselas* – that meeting of ideological opposites, both published in 1759 after the Lisbon earthquake killed 30,000 people.[17] The natural theology of design remained extremely influential, however, culminating in the Christian utilitarianism of the Revd William Paley, who cooed: 'it is a happy world after all'.[18]

The union of earthly and divine happiness was expressed in similarly blunt utilitarian terms by Abraham Tucker, who compared Heaven to a 'universal bank, where accounts are regularly kept and every man debited or credited for the least farthing he takes out or brings in'. The divine depository had many advantages over the Bank of England; not only was the security perfect, but the rate of interest was enormous; whenever the Christian was in need, said Tucker, 'the runner angel' would 'privately slip the proper sum into my hand at a time when I least expect it'. He calculated that our entire suffering might be equivalent to a minute of pain once in every twenty-two years.[19]

Paralleling this new Christian eudemonism ran traditions of moral philosophy and aesthetics espoused by Lord Shaftesbury and his admirer Francis Hutcheson. Scorning gravity and the grave, Shaftesbury's rhapsodies to the pleasures of virtue pointed the way for those who would champion the virtues of pleasure.[20] And while Hutcheson despised the work of Mandeville, his formulations (in particular his precocious expression of the 'greatest happiness' principle) nudged morality in the same psychological direction.[21]

Early Enlightenment philosophers endowed ethics with a new, and hopefully sounder basis in psychology. Morality had traditionally been cast as an objective system of divine laws or cosmic fitnesses: absolute right and wrong, duty and justice. Increasingly, virtue was refigured as a matter of heeding inner promptings – goodness lay not in obeying commandments but in harnessing motives. It was newly emphasized that, contrary to Augustinian rigorism, human nature was not hopelessly depraved; rather, passions were naturally benign – and in any case pleasure was to be derived from sympathy. Virtue was, in short, part and parcel of a true psychology of pleasure – indeed, its own reward.[22] Good taste and good morals fused in an aesthetic of virtue.

Such shifts in divinity and ethics matched changes in social perception. Pilgrim had traditionally been a character in a divine drama whose denouement had come right at the beginning of Act One in the original sinner expelled from Paradise. Enlightened thinkers, however, looked through rosier lenses: civilization was making rapid and wholesale changes to both the natural and the built environment as science and technology were asserting man's powers over Nature. People were changing, too – and, in any case, were seen to vary radically the world over, in physique and appearance, outlooks, prospects and expectations. Viewed thus, *homo rationalis* was not, after all, some transcendental soul occupying a preordained place in the Great Chain of Being, but the plastic product of multiple external influences and stimuli; man was not just *homo faber* but *homo hominis faber*, maker of his own destiny; mankind was born not in Filmerian chains, but, as Locke argued, naturally free.[23]

Like Nature at large, man comprised a machine made up of parts, open to scientific study through the techniques of a 'moral anatomy' which would unveil psychological no less than physical laws of motion.[24] Building on such naturalistic postulates, thinkers championed individualism, the right to self-improvement – and to *happiness*. *Robinson Crusoe* (1719) fantasized man in the state of nature in terms of the dilemma of the shipwreck having to (re)invent civilization (almost) single-handedly and forge his own destiny. In fact, it became common, as in Mandeville, to represent society as a hive made up of individuals, each pulsating with needs, desires and drives, either colluding or colliding. 'The wants of the mind are infinite,' asserted the property developer and physician Nicholas Barbon,[25] expressing views which pointed towards Adam Smith's celebration of 'the uniform, constant and uninterrupted effort of every man to better his condition'.[26]

The natural right to pursue one's own interests became an Enlightenment commonplace. The paradox that self-interest was preferable to shows of public virtue, mooted by Mandeville, was maintained, less scandalously but more persuasively, by Hume and Smith. 'Self Love,' asserted Josiah Tucker, 'is the great Mover in human Nature'; and since the 'principle of self-interest', according to Sir James Steuart, was 'the universal spring of human actions', it followed that

the best way to govern a society, and to engage everyone to conduct himself according to a plan, is for the statesman to form a system of administration, the most consistent possible with the interest of every individual, and never to flatter himself that his people will be brought to act . . . from any other principle than private interest.[27]

This atomization of the public good into disparate interests amounted to a privatization of virtue.

Questions of good and evil, right and wrong, virtue and vice, were thus recast in the early Enlightenment from dogma about duties into matters of fact about human nature. How do we know? Are we mere machines, or do we have free will? Or, perhaps, as in Lord Kames's suggestion (see chapter 10), do we merely *think* we have free will? Should we follow our impulses? Can we help doing so? For posing such questions, enlightened thinkers have often been credited as the first modern analysts of social man, the first sociologists and anthropologists, social psychologists, penologists and so forth.[28]

By postulating the mind as a *tabula rasa* and thus viewing man as radically pliable, capable of indeterminate change, Locke proved immensely influential. Denying not just the Cartesian *cogito* but also stark doctrines of human depravity, *An Essay concerning Human Understanding* (1690) and *Some Thoughts concerning Education* (1693) presented man's make-up as entirely a product of learning from experience, through the association of ideas.[29] A child of circumstances, man in turn possessed the capacity to transform his milieu; ever challenged by that environment he was continually changing.[30] Above all, reason, that candle of the Lord, guided him in the rational pursuit of happiness. 'I will faithfully pursue that happiness I propose to myself,' stated Locke, 'all innocent diversions and delights, as far as they will contribute to my health, and consist with my improvement, condition, and my other more solid pleasures of knowledge and reputation, I will enjoy.'[31] While in David Hartley's philosophy, rational hedonism found the soil in which to put down materialist roots[32] the Unitarian Joseph Priestley, as will be explored in chapter 18, set the pursuit of happiness within a determinist yet Providential theory of progress.

These epistemologies of learning were incorporated by enlightened thinkers into psychological models which portrayed action as essentially driven by hedonic impulses. Reversing traditional priorities, David Hume cast reason as the slave of the passions: confidence in the emotions would contribute to social cohesion and benefit. Properly channelled and polished, 'self love and social' would prove 'the same'.[33]

Projecting man as an ensemble of stimuli and responses, activated by sense inputs, sensationalist psychology sanctioned a new practical hedonism. 'Pleasure is now the principal remaining part of your education,' Lord Chesterfield instructed his son. The well-tempered pursuit of happiness in the here and now – indeed, the *right* to happiness – became the talk of *belles lettrists*.[34] 'Man is generally represented as an animal formed for, and delighted in, society,' stressed Henry Fielding:

in this state alone, it is said, his various talents can be exerted, his numberless necessities relieved, the dangers he is exposed to can be avoided, and many of the pleasures he eagerly affects enjoyed. In short, by good-breeding . . . I mean the art of pleasing, or contributing as much as possible to the ease and happiness of those with whom you converse.[35]

Among the polite, the teachings of *Pilgrim's Progress* thus began to sound quaintly *passé*. 'Happiness is the only thing of real value in existence,' asserted Soame Jenyns: 'neither riches, nor power, nor wisdom, nor learning, nor strength, nor beauty, nor virtue, nor religion, nor even life itself, being of any importance but as they contribute to its production.'[36] The codification of such views was utilitarianism, and Bentham's greatest happiness principle would chime with the new political economy systematized by Adam Smith: egoism pursued in accordance with free market competition would result, courtesy of the 'Invisible Hand', in the common good (see chapter 17).[37]

Enlightened thinking thus advanced new models of man and rationales for happiness. The plasticity of human nature meant people could be educated or conditioned, so as to be continually making and remaking themselves. Not least, confidence grew that the natural order would deliver not just pleasure but harmonious progress. And that was partly because 'new hedonist' was not 'old rake' in another guise, but the man or woman of sensibility who could pursue satisfaction through sociable behaviour, and whose good nature would tender pleasure as well as take it. We thus finally revert to the crucially important Addison and Steele.

The *Spectator* ridiculed various human failings, especially Puritan scrupulosity and Cavalier libertinism: the sanctimonious devalued Divine Benevolence, while rakes ruined themselves with drunken debauchery. A third way was proposed, that of the *honnête homme*, whose moderate pursuit of rational pleasures in social settings would produce lasting enjoyment. Stressing urbanity, politeness, rationality and moderation, Addisonianism authorized smart pursuits – light reading, tea-table conversation, the pleasures of the town – adjudged personally gratifying while socially harmonious. Enlightened thought thus gave its blessing to the pursuit of pleasure, precisely because it redefined the pleasures it was desirable to pursue. Overall, the English ideology, voiced through Lockean psychology, the Spectatorial stylistics of the self, utilitarianism and political economy, promoted refined hedonism and enlightened self-interest within consumer capitalism.[38]

Only the most cocksure quantitative historian would assert that some societies achieve more pleasure than others, or are more pleasure-loving. Bentham's felicific calculus notwithstanding, pleasure is hard to measure.[39] It can be said, however, that desire assumes different forms from era to era. It would therefore be worthwhile examining the shifting sites of and outlets for the enlightened pleasure quest – responses to growing affluence within a commercial economy which left more people with more money spare to spend or squander.[40]

Pleasure-taking was transformed by changes in material culture – the built environment, the availability of urban pleasure sites, resorts indoor and outdoor and the 'pleasure machines' through which discriminating consumers might find pastime and amusement.[41] An effervescent 'feel-good' factor buoyed people up – indeed, it was a society in which, by the 1780s, one could actually soar up into the air for the first time in human history, thanks to the hot-air balloon – or, failing that, buy a souvenir balloon hat;[42] while, from 1808, in a 'steam circus' enclosure in Euston Square, you could even be driven on rails round and round by the *Catch-me-who-can*, the first ever passenger steam locomotive, designed by the Cornish engineer Richard Trevithick. But *who* took *which* pleasures? With affluence spreading, enjoyments once for the few were opened, often to the many and occasionally to the masses: enlightened pleasures were meant, within reason, to be for the greatest number.

Traditionally, exclusiveness had been what gave the spice. Only the leisured classes had had the time and the money to devote themselves to conspicuous pleasure – and so it fell to them to define what pleasure and leisure were. But, because of these grandee associations, such values might also be disdained as symptoms of privileged profligacy. The lower orders were 'debauched' by idleness, thundered preachers, the great 'corrupted' by leisure.

Grandees experienced their relaxations through a value system framed by their classical education. Free time was the prized privilege of noble birth, lack of leisure the penalty of poverty, or a mark of the mercenariness of the miserly tradesman, proverbially obsessed with filthy lucre. The burden of perpetual toil bespoke dependency; leisure, by contrast, permitted cultivation of mind and body and promoted that greatness of soul eulogized by Aristotle and echoed by Shaftesbury.[43]

Landed society by no means despised *negotium* (business) : it consti-tuted, after all, an immensely ambitious, wealth-accumulating élite, cultivating economic interests as energetic agrarian capitalists and exercising sway as politicians, magistrates and military leaders. But grandees particularly prized *otium* (ease); they subscribed to Horace's ideals of the good life (*integer vitae, sceleris purus*); not least, being receptive to enlightened values, they recognized that their enduring authority must depend upon not might but magic, a conspicuous show of enviable lifestyles. They thus formed a 'leisure class', devoted to conspicuous cultural consumption.[44] For the ruling class, business and pleasure traditionally went hand in glove. The eagerness of the affluent middle classes to buy themselves into landed leisure, even at the risk of ruin, bespeaks its awesome appeal. Yet enjoyments were also emerging which were quintessentially urban and bourgeois: in a new twist, pleasure and leisure were becoming commercialized.[45]

Pre-industrial Britain had sustained highly traditional modes of leisure, organized around the rhythms of agrarian life, Christian festivals and the political calendar, with their bells, bonfires and beanfeasts.[46] 'Old Leisure' had worn a bucolic air. The propertied classes disported themselves on their estates, symbolically through hunting and shooting, rites and rights devoutly upheld by ever more bloody game laws. Holkham, Houghton, Blenheim and the other great houses cemented the association of the country estate with aristocratic enjoyments like art, book-collecting and antiquarianism. With the exception of the Grand Tour, that youthful rite of passage, patrician pleasures clustered around the familial acres, although it was also found necessary to have an urban headquarters, ideally in the fashionable West End.[47]

The lower orders for their part traditionally gained sporadic release through village sports, merrymaking, fairs and the drinking festivals associated with trades (apprenticeship rituals) and the rural calendar (harvest home, etc.). These, however, were to meet increasing opposition as preachers and magistrates denounced idleness and the disorder of saturnalian bouts of drunken dissipation, accompanied by riot and later telltale bastard births. Rural leisure was to grow more exclusively class-specific, and so it was essentially in the urban public sphere that pleasure catered to the many.[48]

The rights and wrongs of leisure and pleasure were hotly debated, but social change and commercial opportunism left the moralists behind. Evangelicals like William Law might still denounce the stage, but new modes of pleasure came into vogue willy-nilly, and the public voted with its feet, flocking to the theatre, to cricket matches, prize fights, spectacles and spas. An entertainment industry arose, controlled by professional actors, theatre managers, painters, sportsmen, art dealers, journalists, critics and back-up teams of cultural brokers. For the first time, the market supported a permanent pool of pleasure professionals.[49] All this, of course, had its critics. But new lobbies of enlightened economists and progressive social commentators began to argue that market culture, sport, print and leisure were economically productive entities, forces for civilization and social cohesion, and indices of improvement.

The leisure and pleasure industries could expand, thanks, of course, to commercial energies and the 'consumer revolution'.[50] In curtains and carpets, plate and prints, households were acquiring new consumer durables. Homes grew more comfortable as domestic goods which hitherto had been the preserve of the rich became more common: upholstered chairs, tablecloths, glass- and china-ware, tea services, looking-glasses, clocks, bookcases, engravings and bric-à-brac to put on the wall or the mantelshelf. For children, shop-bought toys, games and jigsaw puzzles made their appearance. Alongside old favourites like the Bible and *Foxe's Book of Martyrs* (1554), magazines, novels, play texts, sermons, political pamphlets, almanacs and other ephemera tickled a taste for news and novelty, expanded horizons, made people more aware of how the other half lived, and so fed rising material and imaginative expectations.[51]

The urban space itself was restyled. The Georgian city served increasingly as a sociocultural centre, designed for spending time and money on enjoyments.[52] Shops became more attractive, bright and airy, luring in customers with the latest fashions.[53] The traditional shop had been a workshop; now it became a retail outlet displaying ready-made goods.[54] Foreigners were bowled over: 'Every article is made more attractive to the eye than in Paris or in any other town,' commented the German novelist Sophie von La Roche: 'behind great glass windows absolutely everything one can think of is neatly, attractively displayed, and in such abundance of choice as almost to make one greedy.'[55] Browsing was such fun: 'What an immense stock, containing heaps and heaps of articles!' she exclaimed, visiting Boydell's, the capital's biggest print dealer. Shopping became an eye-opening pastime.[56]

What better epitome of the Georgian love of pleasure than the pleasure garden? Up to two hundred or so such resorts sprouted among London's suburban villages, with their fishponds and fireworks, musicians and masquerades, ideal for trysts.[57] Laid out with walks, statues and tableaux, Vauxhall became London's first great fashionable resort. Bands played, there was dancing, or one could sup in gaily decorated alcoves amid the groves. Right by Chelsea Hospital, Ranelagh Gardens opened in 1742. Vying with Vauxhall, its chief attraction was a rotunda, 150 feet in diameter, with an orchestra in the centre and tiers of boxes. Open to all with a few shillings to spare, pleasure gardens and resorts crowned the Georgian pleasure revolution.[58]

Various forms of entertainment, like the theatre, were also now targeted at middle-brow audiences.[59] Traditionally, sports had been community rituals, integrated into the agricultural and religious year – village football, for instance, on Shrove Tuesday.[60] Now paid sportsmen emerged, as did the paying spectator. Pugilism got big, and such star professional prize fighters emerged as Daniel Mendoza, Tom Cribb and 'Gentleman' John Jackson, drawing crowds of thousands to their barefist bouts.[61] Cricket too became a spectator sport; as with horseracing, much of its appeal lay in the gambling.[62] Sports journalism whipped up the interest.

Like sport, other activities hitherto largely homemade or exclusive to courtly and noble patrons became organized, commercialized, professionalized, nationalized and discussed in literate culture. Georgian England supported a wide range of concerts and other musical events; Handel's *Water Music* (1717) and *Music for the Royal Fireworks* (1749) were first performed at Vauxhall, while piety and pleasure met in his sacred oratorios. Top continental musicians chose to do concert tours in London and some, Handel above all, settled because career opportunities were more inviting than those offered as a courtly kapellmeister.[63]

Shows and spectacles abounded. The great swathe of streets from Fleet Street and the Strand, up through Charing Cross and into Leicester Square, Soho and Piccadilly, hosted halls, booths and displays mixing sensationalism, news and wonder. Roll up for the 'Ethiopian Savage'! 'This astonishing Animal,' reported the *Daily Advertiser* on 4 June 1778, 'is of a different species from any ever seen in Europe, and seems to be a link between the Rational and Brute Creation . . . and is allowed to be the greatest Curiosity ever exhibited in England.' The next year Robert Barker set up his Panorama, a display of huge paintings, in Leicester Place, and in nearby Lisle Street James Loutherbourg opened his Eidophusikon (magic lantern) – to say nothing of the menageries at the Tower and Exeter Change in the Strand and the raree-shows drawing the crowds to Bartholomew Fair at Smithfield every September.[64]

In such developments it was market forces that mattered.[65] The drive for museums and galleries in Georgian England typically came from leisure and educational entrepreneurs bent upon bringing their wares to the people and seeking to profit out of novelties, curiosities and commercial openings, and the public hunger for experience.[66] This commercialization of leisure did not put a stop to traditional folk pleasures – indeed, in some ways it positively fostered amateur and community activities. For example, with the publication of sheet music, spurred by the enterprising John Walsh, it was easy for home musicmakers to be playing Boyce or Arne on their viols or flutes soon after such music had been composed.[67] From Pepys onwards, letters and diaries give ample evidence of a joyous, if also uneasy, indulgence of pleasure. It was a time, for example, when conspicuous delight was taken in food, helped by low prices and the introduction of exotica like pineapples. And the pleasures of the table were washed down by those of the bottle. Drinking, judged Samuel Johnson, was life's second greatest pleasure.[68]

Moderns might argue, of course, that the true barometer of a civilization's proclivities lies in its erotic culture. Samuel Johnson's number one pleasure, however, leaves relatively few records, and is unusually subject to sensationalist distortion. Nevertheless, it is clear that sex was publicly flaunted in eighteenth-century England in a manner historically atypical – one perhaps bearing comparison with our own times.[69] The most visible index was, of course, prostitution. There were said to be up to 30,000 streetwalkers in London alone – James Boswell's journals suggest it was impossible (for that young man about town, at least) to saunter down the Strand or in St James's Park without being defeated by the attentions of hordes of harlots.[70] Escaping a Presbyterian upbringing, Boswell had an itch for pleasure at large – 'I felt a completion of happiness,' he wrote in 1772, *à propos* being in Johnson's company: 'I just sat and hugged myself in my own mind.'[71] As *l'homme moyen sensuel* he judged there was no 'higher felicity on earth enjoyed by man than the participation of genuine reciprocal amorous affection with an amiable woman'.[72] And he practised with gusto what he preached, performing many sexual feats while a young man about town in 1763, among others taking a whore (wearing a condom, for safe sex) on the recently opened Westminster Bridge.[73]

The post-censorship age brought an explosion in the production of erotica.[74] A significantly titled best-seller was John Cleland's *Memoirs of a Woman of Pleasure* (1749), popularly known as *Fanny Hill*. Whilst the very notion of a 'woman of pleasure' evidently betrays macho prejudices – the female as sex object – it conveys a confidence in erotic enjoyment. In that book, Mrs Cole, the bawd, 'considered pleasure of one sort or other as the universal port of destination, and every wind that blew thither a good one, provided it blew nobody any harm'.[75] Cleland turned that 'harlot's progress' which had been a tragedy for Hogarth into a triumph: Fanny enjoyed and profited from her profession, while also falling in love with her very first client, whom she finally married – thus combining pleasure, gain and romance all in one implausible enlightened fantasy.[76]

Prostitution aside, moderns devoted themselves to erotic pleasures. Rather than condemning sexuality as lust, as in Augustinian theology, or regarding it primarily in procreative terms, Georgian sex advice literature maintained that sex constituted a pleasure in its own right and a contribution to conjugality.[77] The leading physician Dr Erasmus Darwin, who sired fourteen children, twelve of them legitimate, panegyrized love as 'the purest source of human felicity, the cordial drop in the otherwise vapid cup of life'.[78]

The most flagrant male sexual icon in the Restoration era had been the rake, its paragon (or evil genius) being John Wilmot, Earl of Rochester. 'The restraining a man from the Use of Women,' Bishop Burnet wrote of that libertine, 'he thought unreasonable impositions on the freedom of Mankind.' The philosophy behind Rochester's self-image as a 'fucking machine' was Hobbesian.[79] Mandeville later rationalized anti-Puritan libidinal release; his *A Modest Defence of the Public Stews; or An Essay Upon Whoring* (1724) spoke not of curbing, but of channelling the discharge of sexual impulses.[80] If the rake Lovelace was the villain of Samuel Richardson's sentimental *Clarissa* (1748), John Wilkes's *Essay on Woman* (1763) showed how free love could be assimilated into an enlightened pursuit of freedom in general:

> Since Life can little more supply
> Than just a few good fucks, and then we die.[81]

Addisonian politeness was, however, undermining Rochester's roistering, as the favoured image of sexual gratification became that of the *honnête homme*, or 'man of sense'. Lord Chesterfield famously informed his son that liaisons were part of a young man's education, and desirable, so long as they were conducted with decorum.[82]

Eroticism and enlightenment further converged with the production of full-blown erotic philosophies upon the discovery (or invention) of paganism, a neo-classical taste for a civilization simple, elegant and natural. A key figure in this was the outright materialist and hedonist Erasmus Darwin, whose *The Botanic Garden* (1791), popularizing the Linnean sexual system of plant classification, implied polygamy amongst the plants:

> Sweet blooms GENISTA in the myrtle shade,
> And *ten* fond brothers wood the haughty maid.
> *Two* knights before thy fragrant altar bend,
> Adored MELISSA! and *two* squires attend.[83]

Hailing 'the Deities of Sexual Love', Darwin wedded his scientific botany to ancient mythology, conjuring up a cast of nymphs and sylphs in classical and oriental tales offered as mythologizations of natural processes.[84] The Greek myths he viewed as anthropomorphic representations of natural truths: pagan mythology was preoccupied by love precisely because natural man – before the inauspicious triumph of Christian asceticism – perceived that Nature was driven by sex.[85]

Darwin's acquaintance with fertility cults and rites stemmed from accounts of the recently excavated Herculaneum and Pompeii. England's ambassador to Naples, Sir William Hamilton, was a collector of *objets d'art*, a critic of Catholicism, the advocate of an unbiblical geological timescale and a proponent of paganism.[86] His 'Account of the Remains of the Worship of Priapus', a demonstration that pagan phallic ceremonies survived veiled in modern Catholicism, was put out privately in 1786 by Richard Payne Knight, a wealthy connoisseur, together with his own 'Discourse' on the same subject. Payne Knight for his part held that the vestiges of phallic worship (such as maypoles) present in all faiths, not least Christianity, proved that the phallus was 'a very rational symbol of a very natural and philosophical system or religion' – that is, enlightened Nature-worship. Ancient Greece constituted the Golden Age, the only period when 'the advantages of savage joined to those of civilized life'. Enthusiastic about the Greeks' festive celebration of the generative principle, he predictably censured Judaeo-Christianity: 'the Jews . . . being governed by a Hierarchy, endeavoured to make it aweful and venerable to the people, by an appearance of rigour and austerity'.

Organized religion had always been inimical to personal happiness and a tool of political oppression to boot, and Payne Knight damned 'two of the greatest curses that ever afflicted the human race, dogmatical theology, and its consequent, religious persecution'.[87] Attacking the indissolubility of marriage, he held that there were 'many causes which ought to justify divorce, as well as that of adultery on the part of the woman'. Together with Godwin and Darwin, he became a butt of reactionary abuse, censured in the 1790s in the anti-Jacobin *The Pursuits of Literature* for undermining the morals of the nation.[88]

Jeremy Bentham, too, was a sexual liberal, deploring bigotry and asceticism, and terming copulation a 'cup of physical sweets'. He wrote in favour of matrimonial visits for convicts locked up in his panopticon while, seeking legalization of 'irregularities of all sorts in the venereal appetite', he called for the future toleration of 'vice' (that is, homosexuality), for irregular desire was simply a matter of 'tastes', just like a love of oysters. In any case, homosexuality was a victimless crime, 'free from worry to third persons'. No more than religious dissent should 'sexual nonconformity' be penalized.[89]

This is not the place to survey eighteenth-century sexual orientations – it would be folly to reduce them all to inflections of enlightened sentiments – but it is worth insisting that during this period old sexual taboos were being widely attacked as benighted prejudices, and the legitimacy of erotic pleasure championed. Evidence of this is to be found in the manuscripts of the Scot Robert Wallace, author of an extraordinary essay which was not only enthusiastic about sexual pleasure but also in some measure egalitarian.[90] His 'Of Venery, or of the Commerce of the two Sexes' held that 'love & lust are very nearly allied', and that 'the most bashful virgin or chastest matron has often more lust or inclination to Venery than the greatest prostitute'.[91] Idealized or Platonic love was – like all things Platonic – an illusion:

Seldom I believe can a man admire the good qualities of a fine woman's mind and conduct without a secret wish to be familiar with her person. Virtue, honour, prudence, may restrain him from any indecency, but his regard is allwayes mixed with something sensuall. If his health & the temperament of his body be vigorous he would gladly rush into her embraces: What women feel I know not but perhaps the most bashful virgin or chastest matron may not be without the same sort of passionate Desires.[92]

While conceding that 'fornication should be Discouraged', Wallace believed that it should be 'only gently punished': he insisted that want of chastity should not 'be accounted a very great blot even upon a woman's character'. After all, who denied that a widow might remarry? The public fixation upon female chastity showed how the moral majority had 'gone into foolish, whimsicall, unnaturall, absurd, ill founded conceits on this head'. Desire was natural, and there was 'no foundation in nature for placing so much happiness in the sole enjoyment of a woman'. Hence, he would 'encourage a much more free commerce of the sexes than is allowed by our customs & permitt women to make proposals as well as men'.[93] What is astonishing is that Wallace was a Presbyterian minister and moderator of the General Assembly of the Church of Scotland.

It is hard to take the hedonic pulse of the past. Help is afforded, however, by visual evidence. The prints of Hogarth and others provide plentiful evidence that the English did not merely indulge in pleasures, but wanted to be *recorded* enjoying themselves. Alongside images of plebeian Beer Street and Southwark Fair, with a good time being had by all, Hogarth also depicted respectable bourgeois families, not, as their grandparents might have been shown, overshadowed by the *memento mori* of a skull or, like their Victorian grandchildren, engaged in solemnly improving activities, but rather amusing themselves, taking tea, playing with their children or pets, having a stroll, fishing, visiting pleasure gardens – doing all the Addisonian things, often with happy expressions on their faces.[94] It is no accident that the Victorians, who prided themselves on the importance of being earnest and whose Queen was not amused, looked back with stern disapproval upon their pleasure-loving, enlightened forebears.[95]

12

FROM GOOD SENSE
TO SENSIBILITY

Oh! the number of miserables that novels have sent to perdition!

ARTHUR YOUNG[1]

It was public men holding forth on public matters who dominated early Enlightenment debate. The state had to be set upon a legitimate basis of law and freedom, religion made rational and tolerant, philosophy purged, reason rectified, the new science promoted and urban living elevated on to a superior plane of polite sociability. Matching the Classicism and Palladianism shaping the visual arts, the prestigious genres in literature were noble and civic – tragedy and the epic, as befitted those wearing the senatorial purple whose education had beaten into them a love of Antiquity; while, in a different register, Augustan satire purported to correct public manners and morals.

For their part, the pacesetters of the early Enlightenment formed a coherent and powerful élite which included a fair sprinkling of noblemen (for instance, Shaftesbury and Bolingbroke), MPs (such as Addison and Steele, Trenchard and Gordon), upper clergy (notably Archbishop Tillotson), academics (like Newton and Locke), lawyers (like Anthony Collins), and all their ilk. Uniting top people political and literary, the high-profile Whig Kit-Cat Club was headed by the titled – the dukes of Newcastle, Somerset, Devonshire, Manchester, Dorset and Montagu, the earls of Lincoln, Bath, Wilmington, Carbery, Carlisle, Berkeley and Halifax. Only Tonson the publisher and Vanbrugh the playwright-architect did not hail from landed or wealthy backgrounds. The same applies to the wider constituency. The *Tatler*, for instance, boasted an impressive proportion of aristocratic and genteel subscribers. Of the 752 names on its subscription list, one in ten was an English peer; there were furthermore thirty-five Scottish or Irish lords, twenty-six peers' sons and as many ladies from aristocratic families. Include the eight bishops, and the list contains 166 aristocratic names, or 22 per cent of the total.[2]

That situation changed, socially, intellectually and culturally, during the course of the century. The focus of intellectual inquiry shifted to enlightenment *within* – the personal became the political.[3] To some degree this entailed a distancing or disengagement from ideals formerly promoted, critiques of the old critiques. Censure was levelled, for example, at the 'insincere' mask of Addisonian decorum, especially when it assumed such an eminently parodiable form as Lord Chesterfield's letters to his son – the Earl, in Dr Johnson's classic double-barrelled put-down, displayed the morals of a whore and the manners of a dancing master.[4]

Such shifts reflected an ongoing internal logic. With domestic peace and prosperity succouring consumption and print capitalism, more people had the time and leisure to participate in the openings afforded by polite culture and revalue themselves and their place in the world. Whether in the guise of activist or audience, the pool of cultural players encompassed ever larger numbers of women and provincials, and more middle- and even lower-class figures. Parties from beyond the old charmed clique of the great and the good achieved entry into this widening circle – a development encouraged and legitimized by enlightened *vox populi* universalism – if nevertheless retaining some sense of identity as 'excluded'.[5] The swelling band of these marginal people, simultaneously insiders and outsiders, inevitably bred tensions, and it is they who will be addressed in this chapter, which traces the dialectic of 'inner enlightenment' mainly after 1750 and examines new discursive modes of figuring the self and its dilemmas.

It was enlightened philosophy which forged modern renderings of the individual psyche and of 'psychology' (see chapter 7). A synergism emerged between Lockean philosophies of mind and the models of subjectivity touted in such less rigid genres as novels, *belles lettres*, portraits, diaries and letters. This dialectic had key implications for emergent individualism, self-consciousness, self-definition and self-improvement: it is no accident that the word 'autobiography' first appeared at this time – or indeed that, in writing about the soul, the traditional Puritan genre of spiritual self-examination was supplemented by more secular modes of confession.[6] There were also rethinkings of sex and gender as, in enlightened self-fashionings, the voice of women became more influential, from early romance writers like Delariviere Manley, through the sentimental novelists, up to Mary Wollstonecraft and her sister Jacobins. (For the voice of women, see also chapter 14.)

The new selves – marked by the fictional Tristram Shandy – blazoning themselves forth in first-person epistles and fictions were often defiantly unconventional, decentred from canonical structures, self-absorbed and drunk on their own singularity. In a forsaking of classical precepts, the doubtful became prized over the definite, the incomplete over the finished, the rough over the suave, the capricious over the constant: flux, striving and mutability all acquired a new frisson. With growing regard being expressed for authenticity, experience, feeling and 'truth within the breast', a mutiny was in the air against tradition, convention, patriarchy and their totemic authority symbols.[7]

This rebelliousness ironically idolized one monumental male icon: Jean-Jacques Rousseau. In confessional mode, Rousseau gloried in a selfhood which was infinitely fascinating: his ringing 'If I am not better, at least I am different' became the unofficial late Enlightenment credo before it was adopted by Romanticism.[8] One's duty, in Addison's eyes, had been to sparkle as a convivial conformist; in the gospel of the *Confessions*, it was in the unbiddable rough diamond that true value lay; the spirit of nonconformity became *de rigueur* and self-preoccupation prized. The new privileging of inner experience subverted hard and fast classical distinctions between the inner and the outer, fact and fantasy, and taught individuals to remake themselves as originals, following inner promptings: 'I know my own heart,' Anne Lister told her diary, echoing Rousseau.[9]

One signature of such changes was the reopening of the creativity debate. Locke's *tabula rasa* had seemingly settled the matter: all were born much of a muchness, innate genius no more existed than innate ideas, and differentials in mind and character were the products of experience. 'Dr Johnson denied that any child was better than another, but by difference of instruction,' recorded Boswell in 1773.[10] By a nice irony, such anti-innatist views were also upheld by Lord Chesterfield, who taught his son the impeccably egalitarian sentiment that men – though hardly women – started intellectually on a level: 'A drayman is probably born with as good organs as Milton, Locke, or Newton.'[11] Priestley too denied that there was anything special about Newton's mind; Adam Smith concurred: 'The difference of natural talents in different men is, in reality, much less than we are aware of';[12] and so did Godwin: 'Genius . . . is not born with us, but generated subsequent to birth.'[13]

Such Lockean views squared with classical teachings about literary production. For pundits like Pope, artistry was neither a gift nor supernaturally inspired; it was, he said, in his *Essay on Criticism* (1711) at bottom a matter of craftsmanship:

> True wit is nature to advantage dressed;
> What oft' was thought, but ne'er so well expressed.[14]

Joshua Reynolds judged likewise: his aesthetics had no truck with fancy conceptions of divine illumination or spontaneous creativity. He found not merely pretentious but 'pernicious' all talk of 'waiting the call and inspiration of Genius' or 'attending to times and seasons when the imagination shoots with the greatest vigour'. Neither a 'divine gift' nor a 'mechanical trade', painting was a skill, demanding training, knowledge and practice, and novelty counted for less than the 'ne'er so well expressed'.[15] Imagination was, of course, prized – Addison celebrated the 'pleasures of the imagination', a phrase incorporated into Mark Akenside's 1744 poem of that title. But it had to be tempered with learning, wit and judgement, so as to nip in the bud that 'dangerous prevalence of imagination' which could lead to madness.[16]

All this was challenged by new thinking emerging around the middle of the century, which refigured genius into a celebration of uniqueness. Mechanistic models of mental operations, notably the association of ideas, became supplanted by organic images of creative processes modelled on vegetative growth.[17] In his *Conjectures on Original Composition* (1759), the Anglican clergyman-poet Edward Young paid tribute to originality and creativity – Nature 'brings us into the world all *originals*. No two faces, no two minds, are just alike.'[18] 'The common judgment of humanity' and all the other critical nostrums vaunted by the Addisonians were now denounced as insipidly jejune: individuality must be given its head. Deriding slavish imitation, Young sent poets back for inspiration to Nature, where 'genius may wander wild'. Instead of the consensus the Augustans courted, singularity was to be valued: 'Born Originals, how comes it to pass that we die Copies?' bemoaned Young: 'That meddling Ape Imitation, as soon as we come to years of Indiscretion (so let me speak), snatches the Pen, and blots out nature's mark of Separation, cancels her kind intention, destroys all mental Individuality.'[19] Shakespeare was fortunate to have read in two books only, the book of Nature and the book of man; and 'if Milton had spared some of his learning, his muse would have gained more glory'. The greatest geniuses were those who went to Nature's school, and knew no other teacher, and the artist's first rule must be to have none: 'Thyself so reverence as to prefer the native growth of thy own mind to the richest import from abroad.'[20]

Taking a similar tack, William Sharpe's *A Dissertation upon Genius* (1755) and Alexander Gerard's *An Essay upon Genius* (1774)[21] put originality first, seeing literary creation, by analogy with natural growth, as the outpouring of the original healthy psyche. The 'vegetative' genius capable of true 'soul' was defended from imputations of irrationality: 'A perfect judgement is seldom bestowed by Nature,' held Gerard, 'even on her most favoured sons; but a very considerable degree of it always belongs to real genius.'[22]

The rethinking of genius brought the rehabilitation of enthusiasm. Mercilessly reviled by early Enlightenment religious critics, enthusiasm was reinvented as the fervent sensibility – one which, for that reason, thankfully lacked any public threat. Thus sanitized and privatized, it made its comeback first of all in the aesthetic sphere, with Joseph Warton's *The Enthusiast: or Lover of Nature* (1744) extolling gothic wildness and prizing Nature over art.[23] Divested of its former apocalyptic garb, enthusiasm blossomed into a florid aesthetics, as private reading kindled the imagination and provided food for feelings.[24] Denying Reynolds's neo-classical dictum that 'enthusiastick admiration seldom promotes knowledge', William Blake replied that it was 'the first Principle of Knowledge & its Last'. 'Mere enthusiasm,' conceded Reynolds, 'will carry you a little way' – 'Meer Enthusiasm,' retorted Blake, 'is the All in All!'[25]

The key late Enlightenment concept which validated the inner self was sensibility.[26] It drew, of course, upon earlier sources. The *Spectator* had appealed to superior males to repudiate traditional machismo: draw-can-sir rakes and Sir Tunbelly Clumseys alike were absurd and inadmissible relics of a barbaric past; while ladies, for their part, were taught no longer to sit in silent submission but to feel. And in the fashioning of the sensitive soul, other vital ingredients were to hand. Material culture, print media and prosperity gave a growing slice of society opportunities for self-cultivation, as 'longing as a permanent mode' became the 'key to the understanding of modern consumerism'.[27] Mediated through mirrors and magazines,[28] a heightened emotional investment was made in hearth, home and private affection. If, in twentieth-century narratives, notably the psychoanalytic, the family has routinely been depicted as thwarting self-realization,[29] the new Enlightenment domesticity liberated individuality.

In examining and intensifying the sense of self, enlightened thinkers drew on new psycho-physiological models. Challenging the divinely delivered Christian soul or Cartesian *cogito*, post-Lockean thinking presented consciousness as infinite potentiality, a sum of shifting sensations, reliant on an indeterminate and trembling network of nerves and fibres discharging signals between the outside world and the inner *je ne sais quoi*.[30] Neurology had just acquired its name, and popular doctrines of the nerves presented the human animal as neither a Platonic *homo rationalis* nor a Christian original sinner, but as an embodied self, wafted by the breezes of experience, vibrating with impressions, emotions and sympathy conducted via the nervous system. Symptomatic here is the coining by the Newtonian physician George Cheyne of the label 'the English malady'.[31] A malaise of introspection and depression, this new bittersweet complaint bore a formal resemblance to traditional Burtonian melancholia, but with subtle and significant differences. The melancholic had been a solitary or outsider, like Jacques in *As You Like It*. The sufferer from the English malady, by contrast, was, according to Cheyne, a creature of politeness: it was the pressures and pleasures of a mobile, open, affluent society which precipitated this quintessential Enlightenment disorder, which arose, he insisted, from the assaults on the nervous system produced by modern lifestyles, with their social emulation, copious eating and drinking, lounging, tight lacing, late hours and heady, competitive talk. Cheyne emphasized its rank-specific aetiology: the malady was unknown in simpler, primitive societies or among rustics, all of whom were too neurologically impoverished to be capable of falling victim. The Enlightenment thus formulated not just progress but its verso: the idea of diseases of civilization, afflicting meritocrats of feeling.[32]

It is also telling that, two generations later, in his *A View of the Nervous Temperament* (1807), Thomas Trotter argued that the nervous crises identified by his predecessor had not merely proliferated but, like enlightenment in general, were percolating down the social scale, to afflict the middle classes – and women too.[33] A mobile, pressure-cooker society, Trotter argued, made its citizens live on their nerves. They took to stimulants – the banes of tea and tobacco, alcohol and narcotics. Powerful habit-forming stimulants were increasingly consumed, but the law of diminishing returns applied. The result? Pain, insomnia, hypochondria and other injurious consequences, which in turn demanded medicaments, some of which – opium above all – produced devastating side effects, and were themselves habit-forming. Driven by morbid cravings for stimulants, modern society, with its 'fast lane' living, was becoming, Trotter argued, an addicted society.[34] Nervousness bred narcissism, which itself triggered hypochondria and hysteria. Diseases of civilization and of the imagination came to afflict the self-conscious in a dramatic medicalization of the promise and pitfalls of modernity.[35]

The man and woman of feeling, too good for a bad world, thus became *à la mode*,[36] and fascination grew with those 'fine folks' blessed, or cursed, with superfine feelings, electrically exquisite, elegantly refined. Among the smart set, and in the *belles lettres* which refracted and ratified modish opinion and images, morality itself might, following Shaftesbury, take on an aesthetic, subjective air, embracing personal leanings and longings (see chapter 7). No longer was duty graven on Mosaic tablets, deduced from Euclidian cosmic fitnesses or dictated by social convention; rather, for the man or woman of sensibility the good was what felt right, the impulsive outpourings of the honest and virtuous heart touched by desire or distress. Truth was internalized and privatized, as Descartes' clean-cut *cogito* dissolved into Hume's bundles of impressions, wishes and desires.[37]

With relationships between personalities and print becoming an ever more intense force field, fiction emerged as the choice medium for 'rethinking the self'. Novels were precisely that: novel – constituting one of the literary genres born since the invention of printing.[38] In the forging of fiction's imaginative empire, especially after 1750, it was the novel which took pride of place, associated from its inception with individualism and a certain political liberalism. Defoe's influential narratives invited identification with the protagonist as outsider or loner – Robinson Crusoe, Moll Flanders[39] – and these were followed by novels of sensibility. Sarah Fielding's *The Adventures of David Simple* (1744), Henry Brooke's *The Fool of Quality* (1765–70), Oliver Goldsmith's *The Vicar of Wakefield* (1764), Laurence Sterne's *Tristram Shandy* (1759–67) and *A Sentimental Journey* (1767), and Henry Mackenzie's *The Man of*

Feeling (1771) were just the most pioneering or popular of scores of tear-jerkers which grabbed readers' sympathies and fed vicarious emotional identification. Mackenzie has his hero, the orphan Harley, go to London, where he is taken in by sharks and swindlers, but also meets virtue in the guise of a penitent prostitute, Miss Atkins, whom he befriends. Returning home, he encounters a broken-down soldier who turns out to be his childhood mentor, Edwards, whose doleful tale of misfortune and sacrifice wrings yet more tears from Harley. Arriving home, they find that Edwards's son is dead, leaving two orphan children. Harley catches a fever while nursing his old tutor; this, together with unrequited love, brings about first sickness and then a welcome death. The formula ran and ran.[40]

'My dear girl, take the pen,' exclaims the hero of Richardson's *Sir Charles Grandison* (1753–4), 'I am too sentimental.' Popularized by Sterne, that very term sentimental – roughly, 'emotion-full' – was dismissed by John Wesley as absurd. 'I casually took a volume of what is called *A Sentimental Journey Through France and Italy*. Sentimental!' he exploded: 'What is that? It is not English; he might as well say Continental. It is not sense. It conveys no determinate idea.'[41] Sentimentality was further popularized in periodicals like the *Lady's Magazine* (1770–1832). That successful monthly's diet of fiction specialized in cliché-packed tales: first love, then parental objection or some other hitch to courtship; next, some twist of plot, and finally a resolution thanks to the authorial invisible hand. Such a formula proved the magazine's fictional mainstay for half a century.[42]

Sentimental novelists often, however, drew on personal experience. Left by her husband with a gaggle of young children, Charlotte Smith projected herself as a shabby-genteel heroine in a hateful world. In novel after novel – *Emmeline* (1788), *Ethelinde* (1789), *Celestina* (1791), *Desmond* (1792), *The Old Manor House* (1793), *The Wanderings of Warwick* (1794), *The Banished Man* (1794), *Montalbert* (1795), *Marchmont* (1796), and *The Young Philosopher* (1798) – her heroines suffered at the hands of legal chicanery and male power, be it that of despotic fathers, ghastly husbands, duplicitous lawyers, conniving parsons and all manner of other blackguards and bullies. She kept herself afloat

– financially and emotionally – by churning out one or two such formulaic novels a year.[43]

While ringing the changes in their melodramatizations of sensibility and suffering, the moral centre of gravity in sentimental novels always lay in the man or woman of feeling hurt by a heartless world.[44] They dramatized virtue in distress in a more intimate and private register than the etiquette manual or sermon. Moral struggle might well be painted in black and white – integrity pitted against infamy, loyalty against lucre – but in the novel such quandaries were portrayed not as the cosmic allegory of a pilgrim's progress or the stoic grandeur of a Brutus, Cato or Lucretia, but individuated within common-or-garden bourgeois settings. Modern dilemmas were questions of divided loyalties to mercenary parents, or heart against head, in plots which dealt not with Miltonic sin and salvation but the troubled heart and the panting breast. In sentimental narratives the generous man or woman of sensibility would confront the crimes and cruelties of the world – would, above all, *feel* such evils – and respond with oceans of tears. Treading a *via dolorosa* and armed only with humanity, the hero or heroine would find malice or misfortune lurking everywhere, which thus accentuated a new predicament: what if, as now suggested, reason and beneficence would not, after all, triumph in a wicked world?

The sensibility, or sentimentality, cult thus painted a more sombre scene than that recently envisaged by the sanguine *Spectator*: the embattled individual could not count on a happy ending. Yet such trials had their compensations: distress, disappointment and defeat confirmed moral superiority and heightened the piquancy of personal integrity. And in any case, as leery critics always insinuated, through the frisson of such fictions, did not such a cult provide an open invitation to vicarious thrills and illicit passions, the pleasures of imagined Oedipal rebellion or virtual adultery between the sheets?

The novelty of the novel should not, however, be scanted. It was *via* such fictions and their spin-offs, like digests and magazine short stories taking over from the Bible as the age's master narratives – with *Pamela* supposedly being read out by clergymen from the pulpit

– that the enlightened voyage into the self, its yearnings and ambiguities, was pursued and popularized. The novel, to adapt Bolingbroke, was new philosophy teaching by examples, and dubious ones at that. The upstart genre also marks a decisive embourgeoisement and feminization of culture. With the likes of Charlotte Smith, Maria Edgeworth, Amelia Opie and Mary Brunton proving the bestsellers around 1800, this was the first time ever that women had made a prime contribution, via the printed word, to the shaping of public manners and morals.[45]

Popular bewilderment and reactionary venom were levelled at the novel, saturated as it was with 'modern' values – which compares with some reactions to pop culture today:

> 'Tis NOVEL most beguils the female heart.
> Miss reads – she melts – she sighs –
> Love steals upon her –
> And then – Alas, poor girl! – good night, poor Honour![46]

Countless warnings like that of dramatist George Colman, above, exposed the imputed giddy fantasy life of culture consumers, high on solitary reading. It was widely alleged that their readership comprised 'raw prentices, and green girls', or, in Johnson's phrase, 'the young, the ignorant, and the idle', sucked into the maelstrom of print.[47] The giddy psychological confusion fed by novels supposedly led to such physical consequences as autoerotic cravings which might, in turn, precipitate nervous maladies or even wasting diseases. 'She ran over those most delightful substitutes for bodily dissipation, novels,' reflected Mary Wollstonecraft on her heroine's meretricious mother in *Mary* (1788) – ironically one of her own fictions.[48] The morbid fantasy life novels incited, the novelist was sure, would lead readers astray: 'it frequently happens that women who have fostered a romantic unnatural delicacy of feeling, waste their lives in *imagining* how happy they should have been with a husband who could love them with a fervid increasing affection every day, and all day'.[49] Novels corrupted virtue, charged the critic Richard Berenger, 'cheating' women of marriage. Ladies who would otherwise have made 'good wives and good mothers' were turned from the proper 'affections of social life' by the inflated expectations of 'romantic love' there peddled. He served up a cautionary tale: the only child of a wealthy merchant, 'Clarinda' had abandoned herself to the 'ensnaring practice of reading novels', rejecting a husband because he was no 'imaginary' hero.[50] The educator Vicesimus Knox agreed: novels 'pollute the heart in the recesses of the closet . . . and teach all the malignity of vice in solitude'.[51]

The public disrepute of novels shows in the edginess of their champions. 'Our family,' Jane Austen joshed, 'are great novel readers, and not ashamed of being so'[52] – a defiant remark glossed in *Northanger Abbey* (1818):

there seems almost a general wish of decrying the capacity and undervaluing the labour of the novelist, and of slighting the performances which have only genius, wit, and taste to recommend them. 'I am no novel reader – I seldom look into novels – Do not imagine that I often read novels – It is really very well for a novel'. – Such is the common cant.[53]

But elsewhere the conservative Austen laid bare the novel's dangerous tendency to glamorize private passion over public duty, exposing such follies through Marianne in *Sense and Sensibility* (1811) and the younger Bennet sisters in *Pride and Prejudice* (1813). Above all, the project of modelling one's life on fictional characters was inane and pernicious – witness the caricature comic villain Sir Edward Denham in *Sanditon* (written in 1817), who

had read more sentimental Novels than agreed with him. His fancy had been early caught by all the impassioned, & most exceptionable parts of Richardson; & such Authors as have since appeared to tread in Richardson's steps, so far as Man's determined pursuit of Woman in defiance of every opposition of feeling & convenience is concerned, had since occupied the greater part of his literary hours, & formed his Character.[54]

'Does reading Novels tend more to promote or injure the Cause of Virtue?' debated Edinburgh's Pantheon Society in 1783. Its verdict? – a narrow reprieve, which probably had much to do with the fact that

Hugh Blair, Henry Mackenzie and their Mirror Club had done so much among the Edinburgh literati to promote the genre. In his *Lectures on Rhetoric and Belles Lettres*, also of 1783, Blair rebutted the condemnations, holding that such 'fictional histories' were morally useful 'for conveying instruction, for painting human life and manners, for showing the errors into which we are betrayed by our passions'. Trashing the old 'romances of knight errancy', he praised the modern 'familiar novel' for depicting scenes from everyday life. 'The most moral of all our novel writers,' he added, 'is Richardson the Author of *Clarissa*.' The status of the novel as a genre – instructive? debauching? – was endlessly debated, without resolution, not least within novels themselves, a sure sign that the public preoccupations of the first Enlightenment were yielding to more private fixations.[55]

Novels span 'humanitarian narratives', exploring moral predicaments and social dilemmas. 'Beginning in the eighteenth century,' Thomas Laqueur has proposed, 'a new cluster of narratives came to speak in extraordinarily detailed fashion about the pains and deaths of ordinary people', which engaged readers' sympathies.[56] His question – why the moral franchise should thereby be 'extended at any given time to one group but not another' – is particularly apt in respect of the judgemental, *engagé* novels of the sentimental era. And it is clear that, coupled with the prejudices of their plots (discussed further in chapter 18), their 'realism' gave them a potent middle-class appeal: 'I have heard a party of ladies discuss the conduct of the characters in a new novel,' divulged Robert Southey, 'just as if they were real personages of their acquaintance.'[57] Enlightened psychological writers pondered what made the products of the imagination appear so real. 'The frequent Recurrency of an interesting Event, supposed doubtful, or even fictitious,' reflected David Hartley, attesting the phenomenal power of the imagination, 'does, by degrees, make it appear like a real one, as in Reveries, reading Romances, seeing Plays, &c.' In daydreaming about fictions, brooding on a single episode could eventually make it seem true.[58]

David Hume tellingly called the mind 'a kind of theatre, where several perceptions successively make their appearance; pass, repass, glide away, and mingle in an infinite variety of postures and situations',[59] while the sympathetic projection inherent to fiction-reading chimed with the psychology of Adam Smith's *Theory of Moral Sentiments* (1759).[60] Just as Smithian moral theory envisaged the self performing on a public stage, so novel-reading encouraged fantastic identifications. Readers were led to thrust themselves into the action, while also acting as spectators of themselves. Such a ploy was, of course, far from new, and nor was it exclusive to novel-reading. In the 1760s the young James Boswell recorded himself trying on a whole wardrobe of personae: 'we may be in some degree whatever character we choose'.[61] At times he wanted to model himself on his father, or on his acquaintances (for example, Johnson and the Corsican patriot General Paoli) and he also imagined being Aeneas, MacHeath (from *The Beggar's Opera*) and a 'man of pleasure'; but the part which most drew him in the 'play of my life' was that of Mr Spectator. Boswell confessed to 'strong dispositions to be a Mr Addison', or better still to combine his 'sentiment' with the 'gaiety' of Steele: while a 'small fortune' was not enough to relish London, 'a person of imagination and feeling, such as the Spectator finely describes, can have the most lively enjoyment'. A Wollstonecraftian moralist might have concluded that the tragedy of Boswell's dissolute life lay in his hopeless failure to distinguish fantasies from reality.[62]

Cases like Boswell's help explain the widespread fear that readers at large – especially empty-headed young women – would empathize with the characters and plots of fictions so much that they would confuse them with reality, and hence be led astray. That was, of course, an ancient theme – a topic of Cervantes' *Don Quixote* (1605–15), as is hinted in the title of Charlotte Lennox's popular *The Female Quixote* (1752),[63] which pondered the problem at the heart of all Georgian novels: What is the truth of fiction? Thinking 'romances were real Pictures of Life', Lennox's heroine Arabella drew from such works 'all her Notions and Expectations'. That was, of course, a mistake, but if novels did not, after all, supply 'real pictures', then why should *The Female Quixote* be able to?

Anxieties grew that common readers were being seduced by fiction: were they not biting their nails and wetting their cheeks over the fates of Richardsonian heroines? – Clarissa, noted Sarah Fielding, was 'treated like an intimate Acquaintance by all her Readers'.[64] And the dubious identification of the reader with the fictional, this 'novelization of life', brought a further enigma: the elision of the *author* with his or her characters. This disorientation was heightened by the appearance from 1759 of a startling first-person novel of interiority, Laurence Sterne's *Tristram Shandy*. Its vogue depended in part on its astonishing unconventionality and on its sentimentality, notably in Uncle Toby and Corporal Trim. In large measure, however, it stemmed from the slippage of authorial persona between Tristram himself, the first person singular, and his author, Sterne; as also between Sterne and Parson Yorick, subsequently cast as the hero of *A Sentimental Journey*.[65] Gaily and daringly, Sterne smudged the distinction between character and author, while readers were invited to condone the hero's self-revelatory impulses: 'Ask my pen, – it governs me, – I govern not it.'[66]

Sterne found – or rather, made – himself a celebrity, and his writing seized public attention in a manner unimaginable before the rise of a print culture sustained by a large public. *Two Lyric Epistles* (1760), by the author's friend John Hall-Stevenson, was but the first of an avalanche of imitations and spin-offs praising, defending, attacking, imitating and, above all, publicizing *Tristram Shandy*. Twenty such pieces appeared in just over a year. *The Clockmaker's Outcry against the Author of the Life and Opinions of Tristram Shandy* (1760) deplored the eroticization of clocks brought about by Walter Shandy's domestic routines, while the pseudonymous reference in the novel to the sexual perversions of 'Jeremiah Kunastrokius' led to the publication of 'his' *Explanatory Remarks* in 1760. Fictions begat fictions, life and invention reeled in a masquerade, and media hype was born. Brilliant at self-packaging, the flamboyant Sterne (Tristram/Yorick) turned himself into a star – an English Rousseau – in a manner unmatched before Byron.[67]

Tristram Shandy touched a nerve by exposing those of the hero –

and by implication it served as a work of authorial exhibitionism, drawing back the drapes on Sterne's own febrile imagination. If his parodies of pedantic erudition supplied classic enlightened critiques of learned lumber, what was new were his 'cardiographs of consciousness'.[68] Interiorizing understanding, he drew extensively on fashionable psychologies, notably that of Locke. Sterne's boast – 'I wrote not to be fed but to be famous' – shows that he saw that the reading public might now be mesmerized by makebelieve – and how writers were now assuming the role of directors of public thinking.

Whereas *Tristram Shandy* was comically sentimental, later novels harped on the romantic, the melodramatic and the sexual, notably in the Gothic vogue launched by Horace Walpole's *The Castle of Otranto* (1764). Fascination with the subterranean depths of the emotions engaged writers at the dawn of Romantic self-expression; Coleridge and Wordsworth, whose *Prelude*, begun in 1798, was a meditation on 'the growth of my own mind', both exhaustively analysed their own poetic processes, initially through the lenses of enlightened psychologies, especially those of Locke and Hartley.

The mysteries of consciousness were psychologized and philosophized in autobiographies and diaries as well as in fiction.[69] A striking instance of fiction, philosophy and life folding into each other is offered by *Emma Courtney* (1796), an intensely autobiographical epistolary novel written by the petty bourgeois London Dissenting intellectual Mary Hays.[70] Its heroine, Emma, falls for Augustus Harley, a man whose very name harks back to the hero of Henry Mackenzie's *Man of Feeling*. Her passion unrequited, Emma pursues him monomaniacally, pounding him with love and self-pity, and even proposing sexual surrender ('my friend – I would give myself to you') since her affection 'transcended mere custom' – but to no avail. Tragedy then followed tragedy in a tear-jerking finale.[71]

What is so striking about Hays's book – and what makes it a perfect late Enlightenment cameo – is the manner in which passions and problems were couched in terms lifted from contemporary thought.[72] Hays drew extensively upon the determinism of her friend William Godwin's *Enquiry concerning Political Justice* (1793), as well as

Hartley's associationist psychology. Her heroine was thus driven 'irresistibly' to her passion; what was to blame, insisted Emma in self-vindication, was that faulty sentimental childrearing, especially for girls, which Wollstonecraft had lately condemned: being 'the offspring of sensibility' in a nexus of necessity, her infatuation and its consequences were thus utterly beyond her control.[73] 'Enslaved by passion', she had fallen 'victim' to her own 'mistaken tenderness'. 'Is it virtue then,' she asked, 'to combat, or to yield to, my passions?' The implied answer was obvious.[74]

While Hays's heroine was ostensibly presented 'as a warning' of the mischiefs of 'indulged passion', she was evidently glamorized. Though the stated intention was to bolster the Wollstonecraftian *exposé* of exorbitant female sensibility,[75] Hays combined critique with celebration. Surely aware of this double message, and anticipating charges of immorality, she pitched her appeal to the 'feeling and thinking few', those enlightened readers who soared above 'common rules'.[76]

Hays's *Bildungsroman* was remarkable, but not unique, in its portrait of late Enlightenment selfhood in all its deliciously dangerous ambiguities. Her heroine was the upholder of earnest philosophical principles regarding sincerity, but also a raging emotional inferno; fiercely independent, yet a child of circumstances; strong-willed, while also the product of her environment, driven by forces beyond her control. Above all, the novel was all autobiographical. Emma's fictional miseries precisely embodied Mary Hays's own passion for her first lover, John Eccles, and then for William Frend – a considerable Enlightenment figure in his own right, newly expelled from Cambridge University for his Jacobinism. Emma's correspondence in the novel was almost a carbon copy of Hays's own love letters to Frend and also of her exchanges with Godwin.[77] Thus fact and fiction merged in late Enlightenment subjectivity.

The tale also curiously echoes the life and loves of another William and Mary – Godwin and Wollstonecraft – as written up by the former in his *Memoirs of the Author of the Vindication of the Rights of Woman* (1798) following his wife's death in childbirth. Godwin told the startled world that Mary had flung herself at the married Henry Fuseli; following this she had had a liaison with Gilbert Imlay, by whom she had borne a child out of wedlock; she had then twice attempted suicide before becoming pregnant by Godwin; and finally, she had ignored religion on her deathbed.[78] Nonplussed by such a shameless rigmarole – the life of the feminist scripted as a Minerva Press heroine – Charles Lucas renamed the work 'Godwin's History of the Intrigues of his Own Wife', while 'A Convenient Manual of Speculative Debauchery' was Thomas Mathias's suggested subtitle.[79] Reviewers of such works found it astonishing that authors should expose themselves (and others) so. Such literary exhibitionism, with writers washing their emotional underwear in public, shamelessly exonerating vice and sin, shocked through its subversive conflation of truth and fiction.

It is no accident in this light that in *Mansfield Park* (1814) Jane Austen disapprovingly depicted the morally lax younger members of the Bertram family staging a performance of August von Kotzebue's risqué *Lovers' Vows*, with a view to indulging in unseemly sexual play. She was probably aware of the *Anti-Jacobin Review*'s assault on the modern German drama: *The Rovers*, its burlesque of Kotzebue, advocated 'a discharge of every man (in his own estimation) from every tie which laws, divine or human . . . impose upon him, and to set them [*sic*] about doing what they like, where they like, when they like, and how they like'.[80] Critics thus mocked pernicious late Enlightenment tendencies. By giving free rein to interiority and the imagination, fantasy fictions were being produced which legitimized the revolt of the breast, and challenged standards in the name of the sacred self.

Sensibility and individualism thus fired each other up. The vicarious experience offered by novels released and scripted the outpouring of feelings. Sensibility also catalysed sexual transformation. Supplanting the old Christian order in which sex had been either functional (procreative) or sinful, Eros now became expressive, the supreme secret of the inner, hidden self. In real life, and as mirrored in novels like *Emma Courtney*, the cry of the soul became the libidinous imagination, an erotic demon that would not be denied – be it in the wanton womanizing of Richardson's Lovelace, the yearnings of Clarissa, the sentimental philandering of Parson Yorick, or Emma's passion. Truth was subjectivized, and Eros became the idiom of the modern.[81]

The radicalism of these changes is revealed in the horror they provoked. Pillars of society denounced the epidemic of self-indulgence and predicted moral collapse, catastrophic enfeeblement, hysteria, diseases of civilization and the like – the later anti-Freudian backlash is brought to mind. Male chauvinists balked at the claims of 'new women'.[82]

These developments had ambiguous implications, above all for women. Personal emancipation, however 'authentic', was often achieved at the cost of a restyling which glamorized women into sexual objects, seductively fragile, tearful victims of perilous impulses. The idealization of motherhood encouraged by sensibility likewise fostered the domestic doll's house atmosphere which threatened to smother the Victorian angel in the house.[83] For men the implications were equally complex. Anxieties arose about 'effeminacy', and while sensibility was valued, it fuelled the growing dread of what was later known as homosexuality.[84]

This chapter has traced the late Enlightenment commingling of – indeed confusion between – life and art, reality and fiction. With the print boom, writing became a mirror held up to fashion self-images, as a guidebook for life; enlightened aspirations became privatized. Texts, especially fiction, designed to be read in private, loomed large in such psychological and identity transformations, creating new emotional and imaginative possibilities, further reflections upon selfhood and platforms for socio-ethical criticism. Emotional individualism came to the fore, symbolized by the *Bildungsroman*, and life assumed a new script – what Hazlitt meant by the 'cant of religion' yielding to the 'cant of sentimentality'.[85] It spelt a new and crucial phase in the dynamic enlightened quest for truth and freedom.

13

NATURE

The whole earth . . . is cursed and polluted.

DAVID HUME[1]

Take Nature's path, and mad Opinions leave
All States can reach it, and all heads conceive;

ALEXANDER POPE[2]

Of all the terms that we employ in treating of human affairs, those of *natural* and *unnatural* are the least determinate in their meaning.

ADAM FERGUSON[3]

The key Enlightenment concept was Nature. Deeply enigmatic, it is most easily approached in terms of its opposites. It was an affirmation of an objective and exalted external reality, created by God, repudiating the fallen, decaying cosmos imagined by Calvinism. The natural could also serve as the antithesis of all that was confused and contorted, the deceitful and the meretricious. For early Enlightenment thinkers like Shaftesbury, Nature linked the divine (eternal and transcendental) and the human; it pointed to the purification and perfection of mankind, and extended human sympathies beyond the narrow bounds of artifice. Orderly, objective, rational, grand and majestic, Nature enshrined both norms and ideals. Through such means it was possible to sustain that religion of Nature and natural holiness which climaxed in Romanticism, while reclaiming a domain of creation which previous Christian teachings had vilified.[4] No wonder Pope enjoined 'follow Nature':

> *Unerring Nature*, still divinely bright,
> One *clear*, *unchang'd*, and *Universal* Light,
> Life, Force, and Beauty, must to all impart,
> At once the *Source*, and *End*, and *Test* of *Art*.[5]

Not least, the enlightened deification of Nature involved an affirmation of aesthetic norms rare heretofore in Christian discourse. As stressed in chapter 11, there had been many traditions denying or denigrating the frank gratification of the senses: Platonism, Puritanism, rationalist anti-sensualism, Protestant anti-idolatry and iconoclasm. Having climbed Mont Ventoux, Petrarch did not gaze upon the striking Provençal landscape but opened his copy of St Augustine and rhapsodized over spiritual heights.[6] All that changed with the Enlightenment. It is no accident that the eighteenth century was the first great age of British landscape painting and aesthetic writings.[7]

The Enlightenment did not coin the term 'environment' – that came slightly later, with Thomas Carlyle – but its thinkers were preoccupied with rethinking man's place in Creation. With new readings of God and models of man, perceptions of the place into which God's creature had been put also inevitably changed. This happened in complex ways. Some insight into the ambiguities concerning man's rights and responsibilities towards Nature is offered by an entry in the *Bath Chronicle* for 30 May 1799 concerning the 139th anniversary celebrations of the Restoration of Charles II on the previous day:

It is with much regret that for some years past we have remarked considerable injury to have been suffered by the woods and young timber around this city in consequence of wearing oaken sprigs in the hat, and the decorating of shop-windows and apartments of houses with oaken branches, on the 29 of May. If the practice alluded to be meant as an expression of *Loyalty*, we would just suggest that this is a very improper display of it: since it would never sanction that injury to individuals and loss to the publick, which are produced by these annual depredations on private property.[8]

As hinted, Nature symbolized as public patrimony or even patriotism could easily be at odds with Nature as private property.

Nowadays it is accepted that 'Nature' is a social category. 'Although we are accustomed,' explains Simon Schama, 'to separate nature and human perception into two realms, they are, in fact, indivisible . . . landscape is the work of the mind.'[9] What passes these days in England for Nature – the chequerboard fields, hawthorn hedgerows and coppices which conservationists defend against developers – is largely the product of Enlightenment agri-business, landscape gardening and peasant-cleansing. In declaring 'All Nature is but Art unknown to Thee', Alexander Pope intended to be pious, but he was unwittingly providing the codebreaker to Georgian environmental history.[10]

What framed the mental landscape of the English Enlightenment? Vistas were widening: the Ptolemaic closed world had yielded to the infinite Newtonian universe, while circumnavigators like Captain Cook encouraged poets and philosophers alike to portray the terraqueous globe as an integrated whole, a backdrop to enlightened cosmopolitanism, man as a citizen of the whole world.[11]

Yet horizons on Creation were also shrinking spectacularly. When conceptualizing the universe, a late-eighteenth-century man of science – unlike, say, a founding fellow of the Royal Society – had probably excluded from his range of vision Heaven, Hell and all the Satanic squadrons of demons, spirits and witches omnipresent in Milton.[12] 'The truth,' lamented Carlyle in 1829, 'is men have lost their belief in the Invisible, and believe and hope and work only in the Visible . . . Only the material, the immediate practical, not the divine and spiritual, is important to us.'[13]

But though we catch here anticipations of what Max Weber termed the 'disenchantment of the world', the planet had not yet been reduced to the meaningless mass of congealing magma which paralysed Tennyson and other Victorian honest doubters; with Pope as their guide, the Georgians read Nature as a masterwork of divine artistry – one looked 'thro' Nature, up to Nature's God'. Filing out of church of a Sunday, the devout were meant to gaze up in awe.

In the words of Psalm III, as rhymed and regularized by Joseph Addison:

> The Spacious Firmament on high
> With all the blue Etherial sky
> And spangled Heav'ns, a Shining Frame
> Their great Original proclaim.[14]

In such a confident Latitudinarian world view, there could be no such thing as mere Nature; there was *Creation*, and that remained a sacred auditorium with designated roles, costumes and scripts for all creatures great and small, from herbs and herbivores, up through the Chain of Being to the Psalmist's, or Addison's, great Original:

> See, thro' this air, this ocean, and this earth,
> All matter quick, and bursting into birth.
> Above, how high, progressive life may go!
> Around, how wide! how deep extend below![15]

Perceptions of the terrestrial economy as a drama or, equally, as an estate, matched the daily material realities of the interdependency of man with the natural world.[16] Most people, after all, still lived on the land – in 1700 only one in eight of England's population resided in towns of over 5,000 – and sheep outnumbered people. There was an overwhelming proximity – physical, mental and emotional – between humans, flocks and fields. The sense that everything had its rank and station in Creation squared with popular mentalities whose folk tales mixed up children, wolves, giants and monsters; an élite culture exemplified by Gilbert White's *Natural History and Antiquities of Selborne* (1788/9), where swallows and hedgehogs were humanized into honorary parishioners;[17] and, not least, a creed that was breath-takingly anthropocentric. Unlike certain world religions, Christian theology affirmed that all had been divinely adapted for mankind, because humans alone had immortal souls and so could be saved. Genesis had granted man 'dominion over the fish of the sea, and over the fowl of the air, and over the cattle, and over all the earth and over every creeping thing that creepeth upon the earth'. And even after the Fall and the Flood, had not the Lord reissued His mandate: 'Be fruitful and multiply and replenish the earth and subdue it'?[18]

For enlightened sensibilities, Nature was, in other words, no wilderness occupied by Satan; nor was it intrinsically alive or holy – the Church had always fought pantheistic paganism. Rather Nature was a resource, 'principally designed', asserted the Cambridge divine and Newtonian popularizer Richard Bentley, 'for the being and service and contemplation of man'.[19] 'We can, if need be, ransack the whole globe,' maintained his fellow physico-theologian the Revd William Derham, 'penetrate into the bowels of the earth, descend to the bottom of the deep, travel to the farthest regions of this world, to acquire wealth, to increase our knowledge, or even only to please our eye and fancy.' And so benevolent was Providence that, no matter how acquisitive man might be, 'still the Creation would not be exhausted, still nothing would be wanting for food, nothing for physic, nothing for building and habitation, nothing for cleanliness and refreshment, yea even for recreation and pleasure'.[20] As late as the dawn of the nineteenth century, the Quaker geologist William Phillips could reassure readers that 'everything is intended for the advantage of Man', who is the 'Lord of Creation', a sentiment mirrored in William Paley's *Natural Theology* (1802) and, in the 1830s, in the multi-authored *Bridgewater Treatises*.[21]

Rational religion sustained a sense of a milieu adapted to the daily needs of the rich man in his castle and the poor man at his gate.[22] There were books in brooks, sermons in stones and the writing was on the trees. The trunk was a staff of life, carrying echoes of Calvary; but timber had social morals to point too.

> Hail, old *Patrician* Trees, so great and good!
> Hail, ye *Plebeian* underwood!

sang Abraham Cowley at the Restoration, anticipating Burke's paean to the 'great oaks which shade a country'.[23] As in the body politic, so in Nature everything had its place and purpose, its meanings and morals. Where diseases were endemic, had not God planted natural remedies? The Revd Edmund Stone's discovery in the 1760s of the therapeutic properties of the bark of another tree, the willow – what was to prove the first stage on the road to aspirin – arose in part because he was piously confident that wetlands, as well as causing rheumatism, would yield cures for it – a vindication of an 'all is for the best' optimism of which Dr Pangloss might have been proud.[24] All the environment was thus a stage – in his popular natural history, *An History of the Earth and Animated Nature* (1774), Oliver Goldsmith extolled the 'great theatre of His glory' – and, if God was also the Celestial Artist, Nature was properly to be appreciated through painterly eyes, as a backdrop designed to elicit seemly responses.[25]

This representation of Nature as an ideal habitat arose in part because Addison's generation, basking in the Glorious Revolution, had inherited a profound environmental crisis which it zealously combatted. 'The opinion of the World's Decay is so generally received,' George Hakewill had observed in 1630, 'not onely among the Vulgar, but of the Learned, both Divines and others.'[26] Reformation commentators had affirmed the old classical tropes and biblical prophecies: this vale of tears was a wreck, old and decrepit; the end of the world was nigh.[27] Everywhere, or so chiliastic champions of *mundus senescens* had declared, the climate was deteriorating, the soil growing exhausted and pestilences multiplying. At the Creation, insisted the theologian Thomas Burnet in his *Sacred Theory of the Earth* (1684), the face of the globe had been eggshell smooth; but the very existence of mountains and, furthermore, their perpetual denudation showed that all was cracking up, becoming reduced to 'Ruines and Rubbish'; what modern man inhabited was, by consequence of the Fall, a 'little dirty Planet', a superannuated sphere and punishment for Original Sin.[28]

If Burnet on mutability smacked of Baroque rhetoric, others could point to environmental decay of a directly tangible kind: collapsing cliffs, landslips, earthquakes, volcanic eruptions, silting estuaries and the like. At home John Evelyn deplored smoke pollution and deforestation, while abroad observers on Barbados and other new colonies were alarmed at how rapidly slash-and-burn clearances and plantation monocultures like sugar cane brought on droughts, flash floods and devastating soil erosion, turning once fertile terrain arid.[29] Original Sin and modern greed together explained what many diagnosed as the symptoms of a planet terminally sick.

But such theological eco-pessimism was challenged in enlightened thinking. The Glorious Revolution enthroned a new regime which championed freedom, order, prosperity and progress; and its apologists, notably the Boyle lecturers, provided environmental visions vindicating the new governmental order by naturalizing it. Complementing the political settlement of 1688, and all the more so the Hanoverian succession of 1714, Nature was newly commended for its stability: the 'grand design of Providence', concluded the Newtonian geologist and physician John Woodward in his *An Essay towards a Natural History of the Earth* (1695), was thus the 'Conservation of the Globe' in a 'just aequilibrium'.[30]

In that work, Woodward frankly admitted that events like the Noachian Deluge – which he happily accepted as a literal historical event, confirmed both by the Bible and by physical evidence – *prima facie* suggested 'nothing but tumult and disorder':

yet if we draw somewhat nearer, and take a closer prospect of it . . . we may there trace out a steady hand producing . . . the most consummate order and beauty out of confusion and deformity . . . and directing all the several steps and periods to an end, and that a most noble and excellent one, no less than the happiness of the whole race of mankind.[31]

As with the English monarchy, and also with miracles, the Earth's turbulent revolutionary career was over; all was now equilibrium, the body terrestrial was healthily balanced; and the final global revolution – the Deluge – had been constructive not punitive, a 'Reformation' introducing a new 'constitution' into the 'Government of the Natural World'. Through that revolution the Lord had transformed mankind 'from the most deplorable Misery and Slavery, to a Capacity of being Happy', by rendering the post-diluvial Earth niggardly, forcing man to labour by the sweat of his brow, and thus compelling sober industry.[32]

Enlightened theorists further insisted that the laws of Nature governing the globe were 'immutable' and 'progressive', and familiar phenomena were reinterpreted in the light of presiding divine design.[33] Decomposing mountains had once been taken as dysfunctional, symptoms of a catastrophe (usually Noah's Flood); but now their positive functions were stressed – 'the plains become richer', explained Goldsmith, 'in proportion as the mountains decay'.[34]

No mountains, no rainfall, no fertility – argued a new generation of physical geographers, dismissing the ecological doomsters. In his *Theory of the Earth* (1795), the Scottish physician and geologist James Hutton maintained that the decomposition of mountains produced the detritus which, flowing down rivers to form the seabed, would, millions of years hence, become the basis of new strata, whose ultimate decay would once again form rich soil, and so on, in endless cycles. Likewise with volcanoes and earthquakes, a sore topic after the calamitous Lisbon earthquake of 1755: all such apparently destructive processes were actually integral, it was now claimed, to Nature's benign operations:

When we trace the parts of which this terrestrial system is composed, and when we view the general connection of those several parts, the whole presents a machine of a peculiar construction by which it is adapted to a certain end. We perceive a fabric, erected in wisdom, to obtain a purpose worthy of the power that is apparent in the production of it.[35]

The globe was self-sustaining and self-repairing, Hutton insisted, so as to form an enduring habitat, perfect for man.[36] A reviewer noted the switch from eco-gloom to eco-glory: 'the dreary and dismal view of waste and universal ruin is removed, and the mind is presented with the pleasing prospect of a wise and lasting provision for the economy of nature'.[37]

The Enlightenment's new environmental vision married Newton and Locke. Along with this law-governed Earth machine went a possessive individualism which rationalized God's giving dominion to mankind through a labour theory of property and value: man had the right to appropriate the Earth and its fruits.[38] The biblical mandate to master the Earth and multiply was thereby rationalized. The age of Donne had seen mutability – ''tis all in pieces, all cohaerence gone' – and the Puritans had anticipated apocalyptic fire and floods; but from the 1690s the environment was philosophically stabilized.[39] Both pious Christians like the Boyle lecturers and later Deists like Hutton portrayed a steady-state terrestrial economy,[40] rather as Adam Smith would deem the free market economy self-adjusting and optimal. Illustrating these views, Oliver Goldsmith depicted the Earth as a God-sent 'habitation', a mansion for the Lord's tenant to enjoy – on condition he toiled to improve his estate, for:

while many of his wants are thus kindly furnished, on the one hand, there are numberless inconveniences to excite his industry on the other. This habitation, though provided with all the conveniences of air, pasturage, and water, is but a desert place, without human cultivation.

A world thus furnished with advantages on the one side and incon-veniences on the other, is the proper abode of reason, is the fittest to exercise the industry of a free and a thinking creature.[41]

So, the Earth was not in crisis; it operated by a self-adjusting system governed by universal laws and made for man. Latitudinarian Anglicanism backed such thinking: God was benevolent, the Devil was *de facto* discredited (there might be a *ghost*, but there certainly were no *gremlins*, in the machine). And this philosophy of Nature was further fanfared by pious and edifying nature poetry. Works like Richard Blackmore's *The Creation* (1712) praised the glories of the universe and hymned its Creator.[42] The cleric-poet Edward Young's *The Complaint* – generally referred to by its subtitle, 'Night Thoughts' – was completed by 1746, the same year as James Thomson's *Seasons*, and two years after Mark Akenside's *The Pleasures of Imagination*.[43] Young extolled the natural world, expressive of the vastness of space and the power of God:

> Seas, rivers, mountains, forests, deserts, rocks,
> The promontory's height, the depth profound
> Of subterranean, excavated grots,
> Back-brow'd, and vaulted high, and yawning wide,
> From Nature's structure, or the scoop of Time.[44]

Similar sentiments were expressed in Henry Brooke's *Universal Beauty* (1735):

> For deep, indeed, the Eternal Founder lies,
> And high above his work the Maker flies;
> Yet infinite that work, beyond our soar;
> Beyond what Clarkes can prove, or Newtons can explore![45]

Brooke was not opposed to the new science; he merely wished to make a moral point about pride.

In *The Pleasures of Imagination*, Akenside for his part celebrated Nature, in true Baconian fashion, as God's book:

> some within a finer mould
> She wrought and temper'd with a purer flame.
> To these the fire omnipotent unfolds
> The world's harmonious volume, there to read
> The transcript of himself.[46]

Mid-century blank verse thus raised up hymns to Nature. Environmental philosophy and poetry propped up the enlightened order: God was the architect of natural order, rather as Walpole was the manager of political stability.

And not just stability, *improvement*. As long ago maintained by Weber and Tawney, Protestant theology highlighted the individual's duty of self-realization: cultivating Nature promised spiritual reward no less than daily bread. Enlightened authors had few qualms about man's right – his duty, even – to harness Nature, 'bringing all the headlong tribes of nature into subjection to his will', according to Goldsmith, 'and producing . . . order and uniformity upon earth'.[47] Through natural philosophy, maintained Joseph Glanvill, paraphrasing Bacon, 'nature being known . . . may be mastered, managed, and used in the services of humane life'.[48]

Such views, of course, underwrote what Europeans had been doing anyway for centuries to the environment: clearing forests, embanking, ploughing, planting, mining. Draining and deforestation were praised for freeing the land from dankness and disease, and turning wasteland into wealth.

Radical and feminist historians have recently reproved the aggressive, macho element in post-Baconian thinking for replacing supposedly organic and harmonious notions of Mother Earth with a new vision of Nature exploited, even raped. 'The veneration wherewith men are imbued for what they call nature,' grumbled Robert Boyle in anti-superstitious vein, 'has been a discouraging impediment to the empire of man over the inferior creatures of God: for many have . . . looked upon it, as . . . something impious to attempt.' Fie on such scruples![49] This strain of environmental mastery should be noted, but it must also be kept in perspective. For the key Enlightenment paradigm of man's relation to the environment was not conflictual but cooperative, indeed positively Georgic. 'I have placed thee in a spacious and well-furnished World,' the botanist and Anglican clergyman John Ray imagined God informing mankind:

I have provided thee with Materials whereon to exercise and employ thy Art and Strength . . . I have distinguished the Earth into Hills and Valleys, and Plains, and Meadows, and Woods; all these Parts, capable of Culture and Improvement by thy Industry, I have committed to thee for thy assistance in thy labors of Plowing, and Carrying, and Drawing, and Travel, the laborious Ox, the patient Ass, and the strong and serviceable Horse . . .[50]

Once the Deity had explained to man his place in the divine scheme, Ray reflected upon His assessment of what He saw:

I persuade my self, that the bountiful and gracious Author of Mans Being . . . is well pleased with the Industry of Man, in adorning the Earth with beautiful Cities and Castles, with pleasant Villages and Country-Houses

... and whatever else differenceth a civil and well-cultivated Region from a barren and desolate Wilderness.[51]

The model typically prescribing the relations between man and Nature was thus the farm. According to Ray's contemporary Sir Matthew Hale, God was the great freeholder, the world his estate and man his tenant. 'The end of man's creation,' the Chief Justice explained in legal terminology, 'was to be God's steward, *villicus*, bailiff or farmer of this goodly farm of the lower world.' For this reason was man 'invested with power, authority, right, dominion, trust and care, to correct and abridge the excesses and cruelties of the fiercer animals' – in short, 'to preserve the face of the earth in beauty, usefulness and fruitfulness'.[52] Everyone would have understood Hale's fatherly metaphor of the good steward, be he in the Bible or in Bedfordshire. Nature would yield and yield well, but only if the principles of good husbandry were upheld: matching stock and crops to soils, adopting sound rotations, planning for long-term sustainability – quite literally ploughing back the profits.[53]

Such images of stewardship – paternal not plundering – sanctioned action and ordained environmental ethics and aesthetics. Pioneering in this respect was the work of John Evelyn, whose *Silva, A Discourse of Forest Trees and the Propagation of Timber in His Majesty's Dominions* (1662) condemned wasteful land practices and exposed how, so as to provide charcoal and pasturage, 'prodigious havoc' had been wreaked through the tendency 'to extirpate, demolish, and raze ... all those many goodly woods and forests, which our more prudent ancestors left standing'.[54] Evelyn's belief that sustainable economic growth depended on sound conservation practices set the tone for the new managerial approaches to Nature widely advocated in the eighteenth century.

'Improvement' was a label often applied to the land, serving as a code word for capitalist farming, notably enclosure, while also being applied to landscape gardening. From early works such as John Houghton's periodical, *A Collection for the Improvement of Husbandry and*

Trade (1692–1703), and Timothy Nourse's *Campania Foelix, or a Discourse of the Benefits and Improvements of Husbandry* (1700), agricultural improvement was publicized by a vast new instructional literature. No mere jurist but also an agricultural improver, Henry Home, Lord Kames, brought out *The Gentleman Farmer; Being an Attempt to Improve Agriculture by Subjecting it to the Test of Rational Principles* (1776), which proved so popular that it had run to a fourth edition by 1798.[55]

Meanwhile, agriculture looked also to science. George Fordyce, a pupil of the Edinburgh professor William Cullen, produced *Elements of Agriculture and Vegetation* (1765), promoting the chemical aspects of farming. Dr Alexander Hunter, another who trained for medical practice in Edinburgh, set up the York Agricultural Society and edited *Georgical Essays*, a collection of papers on agriculture published in four volumes between 1770 and 1772.

The King of Brobdingnag memorably stated that 'whoever could make two Ears of Corn, or two Blades of Grass to grow upon a Spot of ground where only one grew before; would deserve better of Mankind, and do more essential Service to his Country, than the whole Race of Politicians put together'.[56] As well as thus serving political economy, agricultural improvement embodied the new relation between man and Nature advocated by enlightened thinking: the exercise of direct control over the soil, thereby making it succumb to man and thus yield greater crops.

The Scot James Hutton, no mere geologist, theorized the underlying philosophy. Having studied medicine at Edinburgh, in 1752 Hutton moved to a Norfolk farm to learn the skills of a practical farmer. During subsequent Continental travels, he observed the methods of foreign husbandry, before returning to his family estate where he made numerous innovations. His latter years were devoted to the ambitious 'Principles of Agriculture', a manuscript (still unpublished) of over one thousand pages which aimed 'to assist the farming community to judge whether they were farming on sound scientific and economic principles; to promote the general good of the country'.[57] The 'Principles' portrayed scientific agriculture as effecting a Promethean transformation of the relationship between man and

Nature: 'agriculture is a scientific operation', wrote Hutton, whereby man becomes 'like a God on earth . . . orders the system of this world, and commands this species of animal to live, and that to die'.[58]

Hutton's friend Erasmus Darwin was another warm advocate of scientific agriculture. In the introduction to his *Phytologia* (1800), he regretted that 'Agriculture and Gardening . . . continue to be only Arts, consisting of numerous detached facts and vague opinions, without a true theory to connect them.'[59] This had to change. The endeavour would progress only when integrated within rational, capitalist enterprise:

pasturage cannot exist without property both in the soil and the herds which it nurtures; and for the invention of arts, and production of tools necessary to agriculture, some must think, and others labour; and as the efforts of some will be crowned with greater success than that of others, an inequality of the ranks of society must succeed.[60]

For its part, the agricultural committee of the Royal Society of Arts (1754) gave prizes for innovations, and enthusiasm for progress found expression in the foundation of agricultural societies such as the Bath and West of England (1777). The Duke of Bedford and other landlords held shows at which go-ahead tenants explained their methods, and prizes were awarded for the best stock. Such enthusiasm led to the establishment in 1793 of the first Board of Agriculture, a private body supported by government funds.

In the business of agricultural improvement, none was more tireless than Arthur Young, farmer, traveller, author, editor of the *Annals of Agriculture* and finally secretary of the new Board of Agriculture.[61] Writing in 1767, he proclaimed, 'Agriculture is beyond all doubt the foundation of every other art, business, or profession' – and he outlined the great Brobdingnagian commandment: 'Make two blades of grass grow where one grew before.' The formula? 'To cultivate That crop, whatever it be, which produces the greatest profit Valued in Money'. The obstacle? The vicious circle of agricultural poverty, with all its dire consequences: put little in and you got little out.[62]

For Young, who regarded it as the 'greatest of manufactures',[63] the new agriculture promised a more efficient environmentalism. The old common fields spelt waste – they were, he argued, a waste of Nature and hence of God's largesse and they were wasteful to individuals and the nation alike. Was it not revealing that the baulks and margins on the open fields were actually known as the 'waste'?[64] So the shift from 'moral economy' to 'political economy', from partial usufruct to complete private ownership, would end the waste of Nature and ensure the gain of all: 'The universal benefit resulting from enclosures, I consider as fully proved.'[65] The capitalist farm and the common fields thereby became parables of industry and idleness respectively. Young traversed the nation, raising anthems to environmental betterment, as here when visiting Norfolk:

All the country from Holkham to Houghton was a wild sheepwalk before the spirit of improvement seized the inhabitants, and this glorious spirit has wrought amazing effects: for instead of boundless wilds and uncultivated wastes inhabited by scarce anything but sheep, the country is all cut into enclosures, cultivated in a most husbandlike manner, richly manured, well peopled, and yielding a hundred times the produce that it did in its former state.[66]

Enclosure did not merely improve the land. Though, according to Young, 'the Goths and Vandals of open fields' still touched 'the civilization of enclosures', enclosing had 'changed the men as much as it has improved the country': 'When I passed from the conversation of the farmers I was recommended to call on, to that of men whom chance threw in my way, I seemed to have lost a century in time, or to have moved 1,000 miles in a day.'[67] In this national improvement drive, the captains of agriculture should rightly be the nobility, although they too must abandon notorious aristocratic waste: 'there is fifty times more lustre in the waving ears of corn, which cover a formerly waste acre, than in the most glittering star that shines at *Almack's*'.[68] Yet the basic message was simplicity itself: 'He, who is the Best Farmer, is with me the Greatest Man': presumably Farmer George (the King was an agricultural enthusiast) was meant to read that.[69]

With over 2,000 enclosure Acts and more than six million acres of land affected, enclosure and progressive agriculture in general presented a model to enlightened minds of proper environmental superintendence, wedding profit to paternalism, yet also incorporating cherished values. Traditional arcadian, pastoral myths – Nature as spontaneous bucolic bounty – could still be accommodated.

> O the Pleasure of the Plains,
> Happy Nymphs and happy Swains,
> Harmless, Merry, Free, and Gay,
> Dance and sport the Hours away.[70]

Thus sang the chorus in Handel's *Acis and Galatea* (1718). A quasi-physiocratic doctrine could also be grafted on – Nature as the root of all value or, in Adam Smith's dictum, 'land constitutes by far the greatest, the most important, and the most durable part of the wealth of every extensive country'.[71] And finally the Protestant ethic would serve as fertilizer: labour consecrated private gain into a public and ecological good. Hence it became the received wisdom that what was good for farming was good for the nation; a friend of England was a friend of the Earth. Robert Andrews, Esquire, and his new bride, Frances, as famously painted by Gainsborough, surely agreed: ownership, affluence and aesthetics clearly coalesced in their politics of landscape. Lords of all they surveyed, no waste ground, no peasants, paupers and poachers, and not even any happy nymphs encroached upon their power and privacy.[72]

Yet this vision of environmental bounty, if primarily Whig and patrician, was not exclusive to the privileged. It could equally serve those who envisaged the economy of Nature as supporting the march of mankind. 'Three-fourths of the habitable globe, are now uncultivated,' commented the scandalized William Godwin, rationalizing the biblical 'go forth and multiply' into political radicalism. Properly managed, Nature would sustain boundless human improvement: 'Myriads of centuries of still increasing population may pass away, and the earth be yet found sufficient for the support of its inhabitants.'[73] Not just that but, for Godwin and many others, the domestication of Nature furthered the civilizing process – for wild environments bred wild people. As Addison and Steele's *Spectator* buffed up the bourgeoisie, agriculture was sowing civility in the shires.[74] This cosy consensus remained in place until Malthus's dismal *Essay on the Principle of Population* (1798). The parson's version of the eco-system as a zero-sum game not only deflated revolutionary utopians; it amounted to an abandonment of shared broad-church assumptions about how environmental management guaranteed human progress.[75]

Enlightened apologists, as has been said, represented the environment as a farm, promoting policies for the responsible management of natural resources for private profit and long-term public benefit. The mastering of the wild was a source of pride.

> I sing Floods muzled, and the Ocean tam'd,
> Luxurious Rivers govern'd, and reclam'd
> Waters with Banks confin'd, as in Gaol,
> Till Kinder Sluces let them go on Bail;
> Streams curb'd with Dammes like Bridles, taught t'obey,
> And run as strait, as if they saw their way . . .[76]

ran a verse celebration of the draining of the Fens, penned by Sir Jonas Moore, Charles II's Surveyor-general of the Ordnance: one need not be a devout Foucauldian to catch the tenor of this fantasy of the great confinement of Nature. Taming the wilderness remained a favourite theme. 'When we behold rich improvements of a wild and uncultivated soil,' enthused the Cumbrian chauvinist John Dalton, 'we are struck with wonder and astonishment, to see the face of Nature totally changed.'[77]

But as the wild was being rendered both profitable and pleasing, another facet of the environment was becoming a problem: the garden, traditionally designed to be a rather formal and often walled appendage to the country seat.[78] Affluence and ambition threatened to change all that: why think small in an age of aristocratic aggrandizement marked by ever statelier homes? 'May not a whole Estate,' suggested Joseph Addison, 'be thrown into a kind of garden by frequent Plantations . . . A man might make a pretty Landskip of his own Possessions' – that is, create the impression that one's property stretched boundlessly throughout Nature – an illusion enhanced by William Kent's invention of the ha-ha.[79] But Addison's modest proposal merely compounded the problem of the garden, since it seemed to destabilize the distinctive elements of the estate.

So long as Nature had worn a wild air, its antonym, the garden, was bound to be orderly – hence the classical formal gardens of the Renaissance, with their chessboard plans, mazes, hedges, alleys and statuary, seemingly echoing model cities and serving as citadels protecting civilization against the horrid wilderness. But as Nature itself became regularized into a farm, and geometrized by the parliamentary surveyors' charts and chains, so artifice inevitably lost its compelling rationale. With Nature tamed, wildness itself could at last become aesthetically prized, rather as, once enlightened élites had divested themselves of a belief in witchcraft and diabolical possession, the supernatural was ripe for repackaging in Gothic novels and ghost stories.

Repudiating what were increasingly denounced as the claustrophobia of the Italian garden and the sterile symmetries of Versailles, the English garden was refashioned to follow Nature, shedding its overt artifice and manicured paraphernalia. The great house abandoned the formal garden, while also tucking the home farm and kitchen garden out of sight. Inspired by 'Capability' Brown, a generation of gardeners fostered a new arcadian escapism by turning the great house into an island lapped by a sea of parkland, whose austere simplicity – mere turf, tree clumps and sheets of water – could pass for Nature, thanks to the art that concealed art.[80]

The cultural psychology underlying this new departure was perfectly understood by that great Victorian gardener John Claudius Loudon:

As the lands devoted to agriculture in England were, sooner than in any other country in Europe, generally enclosed with hedges and hedgerow trees, so the face of the country in England . . . produced an appearance which bore a closer resemblance to country seats laid out in the geometrical style; and, for this reason, an attempt to imitate the irregularity of nature in laying out pleasure grounds was made in England . . . sooner than in any other part of the world.[81]

Taste never stands still; soon Brown was in his turn being mocked as one obsessed with shaving, trimming and cropping, and his successors, notably Humphry Repton and Richard Payne Knight, while upholding his touchstone of artless Nature, took it to its logical conclusion. Paying court to fancy, they unashamedly brought wildness right up to the house itself by waving 'the wand of enchantment' over the estate, as urged by Marmaduke Milestone, the Reptonian landscaper in Peacock's *Headlong Hall*, who promised to impart 'a new outline to the physiognomy of the universe'.[82] Some were predictably intimidated by this new proximity of naked Nature. 'Knight's system appears to me the jacobinism of taste,' muttered Anna Seward, deploring the 'uncurbed and wild luxuriance, which must soon render our landscape-island as rank, weedy, damp and unwholesome as the incultivate savannas of America'.[83]

Yet this new noble savagery in landscaping was hard to resist completely, since it was sanctioned by a sea change in taste. 'The wildness pleases,' Lord Shaftesbury had declared at the beginning of the century: 'We . . . contemplate her with more Delight in these original Wilds than in the artificial Labyrinths and wildernesses of the palace.'[84] And such judgements, with their Whiggish, liberty-loving credentials, wrought great changes in the aesthetics of the environment.

Take mountains. The *mundus senescens* trope had regarded them as pathological, Nature's pimples. Joshua Poole's poet's handbook, *English Parnassus* (1657), commended some sixty epithets for them, many expressing distaste – 'insolent, surly, ambitious, barren, . . . unfrequented, forsaken, melancholy, pathless', and so forth. 'Mountain gloom' lingered long: as late as 1747 the *Gentleman's Magazine* judged Wales 'a dismal region, generally ten months buried in snow and eleven in clouds'.[85]

The aesthetic ennoblement of mountains owed something to the much-mocked but nevertheless influential critic John Dennis, who championed Longinus. While describing the Alps as 'Ruins upon Ruins', he could relish their 'tremendous' and 'dreadful' qualities.[86] Within a generation, responses had turned to awestruck admiration. 'Not a precipice, not a torrent, not a cliff but is pregnant with religion and poetry,' fluttered Thomas Gray as he crossed the Alps in 1739.[87] Such thoughts were possible because mountains could be validated through the eye of art, and perceived more as paintings than as mere natural objects: 'Precipices, mountains, torrents, wolves, rumblings, Salvator Rosa' – so wrote Horace Walpole in 1739.[88] Indeed, the very essence of the Picturesque creed, theorized in the 1780s by William Gilpin, was that the test of a scene lay in how well it actualized the qualities making a fine painting.[89] The true challenge, however, to the aesthetics of civilized order came with Edmund Burke's *A Philosophical Enquiry into the Origin of our Ideas of the Sublime and the Beautiful* (1757), which extolled the stupendous, rugged and bleak and all else productive of 'ideas elevating, awful and of a magnificent kind'. Crags, precipices and torrents, windswept ridges, unploughed uplands – these now became the very acme of taste, precisely because they had not been ruled and refined by the human hand.[90] 'Compared to this what are the cathedrals or palaces built by men!' rhetoricized Sir Joseph Banks on seeing Fingal's Cave; and he supplied the answer to his own question:

mere models or playthings, imitations as diminutive as his works will always be when compared with those of nature. What is now the boast of the architect! regularity the only part in which he fancied himself to exceed his mistress, Nature, is here found in her possession, and here it has been for ages undescribed.[91]

Through such sentiments there emerged what has been called 'natural supernaturalism', the neo-pagan and Romantic notion that Nature is sacred and 'measureless to man', feelings perhaps mirrored in the new respect for living beings evident in, say, the vegetarianism of Shelley's *Vindication of Natural Diet* (1813).[92]

*

The cult of the sublime threatened aesthetic disorientation; and what constituted choice scenery was being called into question at precisely the moment when the countryside itself was experiencing a disturbing intrusion: heavy industry. If caves, crags and chasms could be sublime, and hence tasteful, what about furnaces and factories? Two locations became laboratories for this unplanned aesthetic experiment: Shropshire and Derbyshire. 'Coalbrookdale itself is a very romantic spot,' commented Arthur Young, still on the road, in 1785:

it is a winding glen between two immense hills . . . all thickly covered with wood, forming the most beautiful sheets of hanging wood. Indeed too beautiful to be much in unison with that variety of horrors art has spread at the bottom: the noise of the forges, mills, &c. with all their vast machinery, the flames bursting from the furnaces with the burning of the coal and the smoak of the lime kilns, are altogether sublime.[93]

The agronome's aesthetic bafflement is what we might expect. Anna Seward, being a poet, had more definite ideas. She was no enemy to industry and enthused about Birmingham, where 'Hedges, thickets, trees, upturn'd, disrooted' had been improved into 'mortar'd piles, the streets elongated, and the statelier square' – that is, urbanization and industry created civilization. But the right place for industry was in town, and her tone changed when she turned to once-lovely Shropshire:

> O, violated COLEBROOK! . . .
>   – Now we view
> Their fresh, their fragrant, and their silent reign
> Usurpt by Cyclops; – hear, in mingled tones,
> Shout their throng'd barge, their pondr'ous engines clang
> Through thy coy dales; while red the countless fires,
> With umber'd flames, bicker on all thy hills,
> Dark'ning the Summer's sun with columns large
> Of thick, sulphureous smoke.[94]

John Sell Cotman's 1802 watercolour *Bedlam Furnace, near Madeley* suggests a similarly disapproving judgement on a nearby industrial site. For Cotman, industry clearly ravaged nature – indeed forged Bedlam. The Romantic conviction was gaining ground that industry wrecked the environment, both physically and aesthetically.[95]

Industrial Derbyshire became another focus of aesthetic controversy. Its economy and beauties found many champions – notably Joseph Wright, who painted local worthies like the cotton spinner Richard Arkwright – and also renowned locations: Dovedale, Matlock High Tor and the Derwent valley with its caves, castles, mines, mineral springs and factories. Praising Wright's 'sweet and magic pencil', James Pilkington's *View of the Present State of Derbyshire* (1789) declared: 'Perhaps no country . . . can boast of finer scenes.' Wright's *Arkwright's Mill. View of Cromford, near Matlock* (*c.* 1782–3) shows nature and industry as twin sources of delight, complementing each other. In his sets for *The Wonders of Derbyshire*, staged in 1779 at Drury Lane, the painter and theatre designer Philip James de Loutherberg likewise sought to show how industry and dramatic scenery both partook of the sublime.[96]

Not everyone was convinced. 'Speaking as a tourist,' remarked that crusty traveller John Byng, Viscount Torrington, in 1790, 'these vales have lost their beauty; the rural cot has given way to the lofty red mill . . . the simple peasant . . . is changed to an impudent mechanic . . . the stream perverted from its course by sluices and aqueducts.'[97] His indignation grew when he lighted upon 'a great flaring mill' in the 'pastoral vale' of Aysgarth:

All the vale is disturb'd; treason and levelling systems are the discourse; the rebellion may be near at hand . . . Sir Rd. Arkwright may have introduced much wealth into his family and into the country, but as a tourist I execrate his schemes.[98]

As is evident, for Byng, as for Anna Seward, natural disorder presaged social disorder.

Byng's condemnations were endorsed by aesthetic experts. The landscape theorist Uvedale Price loved the 'striking natural beauties' of the river Derwent, and hence deplored the factories erected on its banks near Matlock: 'nothing can equal them for the purpose of disbeautifying an enchanting piece of scenery'; 'if a prize were given for ugliness', he quipped, those factories would win.[99]

More tellingly still, it even came to be argued that what had long been championed as agricultural improvement actually spelt environmental degradation and aesthetic impoverishment. Capitalist agriculture had always, of course, had its critics. Oliver Goldsmith's *The Deserted Village* (1770) damned the depopulating effects of enclosure; William Cowper censured the rural asset-stripping that enclosure unleashed – 'Estates are landscapes ... gaz'd upon awhile and auctioneer'd away'; and John Clare later took up the charge most forcibly.[100] But what is remarkable is that some erstwhile enthusiasts also grew disgruntled. Even Arthur Young came to question his sacred cow, recognizing how improvement had made conditions worse for rural labourers: 'I had rather that all the commons of England were sunk in the sea, than that the poor should in future be treated on enclosing as they have been hitherto.'[101]

It is a crisis reflected in the career of Humphry Repton, after Brown the leading British landscaper of the Enlightenment. Embittered by difficulties and debts, his last work includes a homily on the irresponsibility of the landed interest. 'I have frequently been asked,' he reflected,

whether the Improvement of the Country in beauty has not kept pace with the increase of its wealth ... I now may speak the truth ... The taste of the country has bowed to the shrine which all worship; and the riches of individuals have changed the face of the country.[102]

Repton illustrated these distasteful changes by executing a delicious parody of his own technique. He had won fame through his 'Red Book', in which he presented clients and the public with 'before' and 'after' scenes which showed the merits of landscaping. But now he contrasted the horrors of a recently 'improved' estate with the original, before it had been sold by its 'ancient proprietor' to one of the *nouveaux riches*.

The unimproved prospect was attractive. In the foreground Repton presented an 'aged beech' shading the road, its branches pointing to a family relaxing on a bench; nearby was a stile and a public footpath leading through a park full of 'venerable trees'; on the right lay a leafy common. The feeling was one of landed benevolence.

All had then been wrecked by the new proprietor, for whom 'money supersedes every other consideration':

> By cutting down the timber and getting an act to enclose the common, [he] had doubled all the rents. The old mossy and ivy-covered pale was replaced by a new and lofty close paling; not to confine the deer, but to exclude mankind . . . the bench was gone, the ladder-stile was changed to a caution about man-traps and spring-guns, and a notice that the footpath was stopped by order of the commissioners.[103]

This *nouveau riche* was perhaps the model for Sir Simon Steeltrap in Thomas Peacock's *Crotchet Castle* (1831), who, as 'a great preserver of game and public morals' had 'enclosed commons and woodlands; abolished cottage-gardens; taken the village cricket-ground into his own park – out of pure regard to the sanctity of Sunday; shut up footpaths and alehouses'.[104] For villagers and onlookers alike, the environment had thus been ruined. Small wonder perhaps that the painter John Constable was to declare that 'a gentleman's park is my aversion. It is not beauty because it is not nature.'[105]

William Blake too hated commercial capitalism, its metaphysical foundations (the three witches: Bacon, Locke and Newton) and its artistic toadies (Reynolds), its callousness and ugliness. The poem popularly known as 'Jerusalem' (actually the prefatory verses to his epic *Milton* (1804–8)) looks back to England's green and pleasant land, contrasting it with the modern 'dark satanic mills'. But if that makes Blake sound like an aesthetic tourist, scouting round Coalbrookdale or Derwentdale, nothing could be further from the truth. Blake was a Londoner through and through, born in Soho, resident in Lambeth; indeed, those dark satanic mills may well have been not Arkwrightian cotton factories but the steam-powered Albion Flour Mills on bankside opposite Blackfriars.[106] And when Blake wrote about the New Jerusalem, where in the green and pleasant land did he imagine it?

The fields from Islington to Marybone,
To Primrose Hill and Saint John's Wood,
Were builded over with pillars of gold;
And there Jerusalem's pillars stood.[107]

Environments, as this Blakean coda shows, are imagined landscapes, and ecology lies in the eye of the beholder. Enlightened culture created environments of the senses and the soil that fantasized the harmony of human production and natural sustainability.[108] At the heart of enlightened attitudes towards Nature, however, lay a nest of paradoxes. Enlightened man, especially in his Picturesque embodiment, wanted to discover Nature unspoilt by man; and yet, when he found it, he could not resist the impulse, if only in the imagination, to 'improve' it, aesthetically or agriculturally.[109] By the close of the eighteenth century, utilitarian Nature – Nature improved – was becoming problematized and Romanticism was making it transcendental, holy and subjective. Under Romanticism, Nature became the new religion.

14

DID THE MIND
HAVE A SEX?

He for God only, she for God in him.

JOHN MILTON[1]

why . . . must a *female* be made Nobody?

FANNY BURNEY[2]

Was not the world a vast prison, and women born slaves?'

MARY WOLLSTONECRAFT[3]

Woman has everything against her.

CATHARINE MACAULAY[4]

I do not think I ever opened a book in my life which had not something to say upon woman's inconstancy . . . But perhaps you will say, these were all written by men.

JANE AUSTEN[5]

I am persuaded if there was a commonwealth of rational horses (as Doctor Swift has supposed) it would be an established maxim amongst them that a mare could not be taught to pace.

LADY MARY WORTLEY MONTAGU[6]

The world the Enlightenment inherited and critiqued was a man's world, patriarchal both in actuality and by *imprimatur* – after all, the key apology for the Stuarts had actually been titled *Patriarcha*.[7] Scripture, the law and other authorities jointly confirmed male superiority and the subordination of women.[8] 'By marriage, the husband and wife are one person in law,' stated the leading jurist William Blackstone; 'that is, the very being or legal existence of the woman is suspended during the marriage, or at least is incorporated and consolidated into that of her husband.'[9] Every wife, bar a queen regnant, glossed *The Laws Respecting Women* (1777), was under her husband's authority, as was her movable property: 'She can't let, set, sell, give away, or alienate any thing without her husband's consent.'[10] An anonymous poet grumbled:

> In youth, a father's stern command
> And jealous eyes control her will,
> A lordly brother watchful stands
> To keep her closer captive still.
>
> The tyrant husband next appears,
> With awful and contracted brow;
> No more a lover's form he wears:
> Her slave's become her sovereign now.[11]

Such mandates were echoed by other males who set themselves up as experts. In his comprehensive *History of Women*, published in 1779, William Alexander listed, not uncritically, the judicial exclusions to which they were subjected. 'We allow a woman to sway our sceptre, but by law and custom we debar her from every other government but that of her own family,' he observed, 'as if there were not a public employment between that of superintending the kingdom, and the affairs of her own kitchen, which could be managed by the genius and capacity of women.'[12] Historically, women had been condemned to an unenviable role, 'for the most part, but improperly, or slightly educated; and at all times kept in a state of dependence, by the restrictions of a severe legislation'.[13] There were grounds for optimism, however, added the Scottish surgeon in a typically enlightened gesture. Women had begun as 'slaves', but society was advancing, and progress always went hand in glove with improvements in the status of women – it was, indeed, a litmus test of the civilizing process.[14]

Sentiments abounded which sound slighting, if not contemptuous or downright misogynistic:

That bold, independent, enterprising spirit, which is so much admired in boys, should not, when it happens to discover itself in the other sex, be encouraged, but suppressed. Girls should be taught to give up their opinions betimes, even if they should know themselves to be in the right.

This pronouncement, surprising though it might seem, came from the pen of a woman, Hannah More.[15] Other writers – and not only men – endorsed the gendered *status quo*, deeming it ordained by God and Nature. 'You must lay it down for a Foundation in general,' dogmatized the Earl of Halifax in his *Advice to a Daughter* (1688), 'that there is Inequality in the Sexes, and that for the better Oeconomy of the World, the Men, who were to be the Lawgivers, had the larger share of Reason bestow'd upon them.'[16] Men were thus not merely on top, but their superiority lay in an unequal divine apportioning of that essential Enlightenment quality, reason. 'Women are only children of a larger growth,' ribbed a fellow peer, Lord Chesterfield: 'they have an entertaining tattle, and sometimes wit, but for solid, reasoning good sense, I never in my life knew one that had it, or who reasoned or acted consequentially for four-and-twenty hours together.'[17] Others, while avoiding such insults, nevertheless colluded in their underlying assumptions. Hannah More again, who penned *Strictures on the Modern System of Female Education* (1779), held that the 'real' aim of the education of girls should be to make them 'good daughters, good wives, good mistresses, good members of society and good Christians'.[18] 'Keep your knowledge of Latin a dead secret,' Sir William Hamilton alerted his niece when launching her into fashionable society: 'a lady's being learned is commonly looked upon as great fault.'[19] Such advice was given by men and women alike, in the conviction that they had a lady's true interests at heart.

Many bridled at such humiliations. 'We Live and Dye,' ventured Margaret Cavendish, Duchess of Newcastle, in 1663, 'as if we were produced from Beasts, rather than from Men.'[20] 'There is no part of the world where our sex is treated with so much contempt as England,' observed Lady Mary Wortley Montagu a couple of generations later; 'we are educated in the grossest ignorance, and no art omitted to stifle our natural reason.'[21] Given the smug rhetoric praising British liberty over oriental despotism, it is richly ironic that, domiciled in Constantinople as the wife of the British ambassador, she concluded that Turkish ladies were freer than their English counterparts. Envying those she befriended at the baths,[22] Lady Mary contrasted the female solidarity she saw there to London's backbiting tea parties. Polygamy notwithstanding, Turkish women enjoyed some freedom on account of the veil, that 'perpetual Masquerade' which 'gives them entire Liberty of following their Inclinations without Danger of Discovery'.[23] Wryly, she saw herself as the captive one, imprisoned as she was in the 'machine' – her stays, within which the local women assumed her Lord had caged her.[24]

Lady Mary's resentment towards the conspiracy of conventions perpetuating female subservience was widely shared. Like Jane Austen later, Judith Drake, author of an *Essay in Defence of the Female Sex* (1696) – which had gone through five editions by 1750 – observed that nothing could truly be learned about women from books, because their authors were typically men, and 'as men are parties against us their evidence may justly be rejected'. Citing nevertheless the authority of 'some learned Men', she countered that 'all Souls are equal, and alike, and that consequently there is no such distinction, as Male and Female Souls'. Thus, 'how falsely we are deem'd, by the Men, [to be] wanting in that Solidity of Sense which they so vainly value themselves upon . . . Our Souls are as perfect as theirs, and the Organs they depend on are generally more refined.'[25]

Both ideologically and practically, women were thus discriminated against in the Georgian century. There was nothing new in that, although, some feminists argue, such prejudices were being intensified by an idealization of feminine virtues and sensibilities, which set them on a pedestal, and by fresh attempts (discussed below) to ground 'separate spheres' in biology. Collective male opinion certainly enjoined ladylikeness, with James Thomson lecturing the 'British Fair' on their duties:

> Well-order'd Home Man's best Delight to make;
> And by submissive Wisdom, modest skill,
> With every gentle Care-eluding Art,
> To raise the Virtues, animate the bliss,
> Even charm the Pains to something more than Joy
> And sweeten all the Toils of human Life:
> This be the female Dignity and Praise.[26]

Too much should not be made of such prescriptions, however, for in many respects Enlightenment culture was quite women-friendly. There is manifest, if uneven, evidence of a general softening of patriarchy, in actuality though not in black-letter law. Expectations among the educated regarding courtship, engagement and marriage and parental behaviour towards children, were all undergoing that sea change which Lawrence Stone has styled the rise of 'affective individualism', the move from patriarchal distance and deference towards greater intimacy and even equality.[27] Despite the obdurate inequality of the law, marriage became idealized in terms of affable companionship, and presented as a mutual exchange. 'Husband and wife are always together and share the same society,' gasped the Prussian visitor von Archenholz: 'it is the rarest thing to meet the one without the other. They pay all their visits together. It would be more ridiculous to do otherwise in England than it would be to go everywhere with your wife in Paris.'[28]

Such developments entailed new norms for male behaviour. Figures like Squire Western (in *Tom Jones*), the rake Lovelace (in *Clarissa*) and Tyrrell (in William Godwin's *Caleb Williams* (1794)) were demonized as the unacceptable, unenlightened face of machismo, abusing male prerogatives and power. The tyrannical father and the injustice of the double standard were condemned. 'Of all things in nature,' commented the early feminist Laetitia Pilkington, 'I most wonder why men should be severe in their censures on our sex, for a failure in point of chastity: is it not monstrous, that our seducers should be our accusers?'[29] Others raised quizzical eyebrows. 'It is the Interest of the Society,' ironized the arch-cynic Bernard de Mandeville, 'to preserve Decency and Politeness, that Women should linger, waste, and die, rather than relieve themselves in an unlawful Manner.'[30] Would-be modernizers of masculinity commended domestic virtues. Richard Steele's publications – the extraordinarily advanced *The Christian Hero* (1701) and his sentimental comedy *The Tender Husband* (1705) – headed the early campaign to polish conjugal conduct;[31] the hero of Richardson's final novel, *Sir Charles Grandison* (1753–4), set new standards for the sympathetic male; while David Hume praised the vogue for mixed company where 'both sexes meet in an easy and social manner; and the tempers of men, as well as their behaviour, refine apace'.[32] Such socializing led not to effeminacy, as was widely feared, but to a superior masculinity: 'The male sex among a polite people, discover their authority in more generous, though not a less evident manner; by civility, by respect, and in a word by gallantry.'[33]

And so, the 'man of feeling' became prized, as the patriarchalist dictum that matrimony was monarchy in microcosm yielded to a new ideal of the household as a sanctuary of emotional warmth and vehicle of socialization.[34] While the 'molly' (homosexual), macaroni and fribble were vilified as sensibility taken to excess, enlightened discourse – the conquest of despotism by politeness – prized males who were neither 'foppish' nor 'licentious', and aimed to reconcile 'manly liberty' with 'the goodly order of the universe'. Shaftesbury's ideal, for instance, conjuring up a model that looked back to Baldassare Castiglione's Renaissance 'Courtyer' and forward to *Sir Charles Grandison*, would possess 'a mind subordinate to reason, a temper humanized and fitted to all natural affections'.[35]

And as shifting cultural values commended a greater domestic mutuality, the public position of women also arguably improved. Women played vital parts in Georgian public life, in politics (both street and salon), in philanthropic and patriotic activities and in leisured culture (as both patrons and performers).[36] Despite current feminist assertions that women were being excluded from urban public spaces through fear of sexual harassment and dread of losing their 'reputation',[37] English women enjoyed a Europe-wide fame – or notoriety – for their remarkable public independence: 'In Great-Britain the ladies are as free as the gentlemen,' John Potter remarked in 1762, 'and we have no diversions, or public amusements, in which the one may not appear, without any offence, as frankly as the other.' He exaggerated, of course, but the historian Joyce Ellis observes that 'urban women walked about freely, unveiled and for the most part unchaperoned', to visit friends, the theatre and even the coffee house.[38] There were a few mixed coffee houses and clubs,[39] and female and mixed debating societies proliferated in London from the 1770s, their topics including questions like that posed on 12 November 1798 at the Westminster Forum: 'Does the clause of Obedience in the Marriage ceremony, bind a Wife to obey her Husband at all times?' If *The Times* moaned predictably that 'the debating ladies would be much better employed at their needle and thread', its protests were to no avail: at least four dozen sets of rooms in the metropolis were hired out to such societies.[40]

Above all, the participation and perhaps also the status of women were improving through the new opportunities provided by print culture, especially once Aphra Behn, Delarivière Manley and Eliza Haywood achieved early literary fame,[41] and other women shone intellectually. Anne Conway's Cartesian *The Principles of the Most Ancient and Modern Philosophy* appeared in Latin in 1690, while Catherine Trotter Cockburn published one of the first vindications of Locke. Across the board, female education improved: 'All our ladies read now,' commented Dr Johnson in 1778.[42] He of course disparaged female pretensions (a woman preacher, famously, was like a dog walking on its hind legs) and no female authors figured in his *Lives of the English Poets* (1779–81), but such exclusions were being eroded as women played an increasing part in print culture.

In 1777 Richard Samuel exhibited at the Royal Academy a group portrait of *The Nine Living Muses of Great Britain*, which was then reproduced in *Johnson's Ladies New and Polite Pocket Memorandum*. It was a modern pantheon adorned in classical drapes: Elizabeth Carter, bluestocking and translator of the Stoic Epictetus; Angelica Kaufmann, one of two female members of the Royal Academy; Anna Laetitia Barbauld, educationalist, poet and essayist; the singer Elizabeth Linley; Catharine Macaulay, educationalist and author of an 8-volume *History of England* (1763–83); Elizabeth Montagu, 'Queen of the Blues [bluestockings]' and head of a renowned literary salon; Elizabeth Griffith, the Irish actress, novelist and playwright; Hannah More, poet, novelist and Evangelical; and the novelist Charlotte Lennox.

Women won their spurs in public culture; they appear in George Ballard's *Memoirs of Several Ladies of Great Britain who have been Celebrated for their Writings or Skill in the Learned Languages, Arts and Sciences* (1752), Theophilus Cibber's *Lives of the Poets* (1753), in the *Catalogue of 500 Celebrated Authors of Great Britain, Now Living* (1788), in the *New Biographical Dictionary* (1796) and in the *Literary Memoirs of Living Authors of Great Britain* (1798), while they form the exclusive subject matter of Mary Hays's 6-volume *Female Biography* (1803).[43] The periodicals boom, to which women themselves contributed, forced writers to appeal to mixed readerships; while items sympathetic to female aspirations regularly cropped up in the press, not least, if oddly, in the *Gentleman's Magazine*.[44]

Indeed, nearly all the bestselling novelists at the turn of the century were women: Maria Edgeworth, Elizabeth Hamilton, Amelia Opie, Mary Brunton, Jane and Anna Maria Porter and Sydney Owenson – only Sir Walter Scott could match them for sales. Joanna Baillie was the top dramatist of the day, and women also figured in poetry – at least 339 women poets published under their own names between 1760 and 1830 and a further eighty-two anonymous ones have been identified. In her *Thoughts on the Condition of Women* (1799), Mary Robinson listed over two dozen eminent female literary critics, essayists, historians, biographers, translators and classicists, maintaining that her sex had written 'the best novels that have been written, since those of Smollett, Richardson, and Fielding'.[45]

With such tensions existing between male ideologies and women's claims to a place in the sun as cultural producers, controversy inevitably flared as to the true nature of the sex. Alongside familiar scriptural, metaphysical and psychological teachings, one truth claim which loomed large – inevitably so, in an age of science – was biology. Physiological and medical studies, many insisted, would finally crack the secret of women's nature, and hence of their proper social position: anatomy was destiny. And, according to many medical experts, such a 'science of women' dictated a gendered order formally compatible with the *status quo*, though one which, far from endorsing Halifaxian female *inferiority*, viewed the sexes as possessing (broadly speaking) *equivalent* but *different* endowments.[46]

According to anatomical and physiological thinking, the female constitution was specially designed by God and Nature for childbearing, while psychologically too they were meant to be soft and nurturing, thereby suiting them to matrimony and that 'chief end of their being', motherhood. The ancient Aristotelian idea that the female body was a botched version of the male, with her organs of reproduction inversions of the male equivalents (the vagina as an outside-in penis) was replaced, it has been argued, by the idea that male and female bodies were radically different. Anatomical structures that had been thought common to men and women, like the skeleton and the nervous system, were now differentiated. Organs such as ovaries and testicles, which had previously shared a name, became distinctively labelled. Some studies of women's brains held that they were smaller than men's, thereby indicating their unfitness for intellectual pursuits.[47]

Such conclusions hinged in particular on a gendered reading of the nervous system: women's nerves were viewed as more sensitive than men's, and their ability to control their impulses by will power was also questioned. Given these biological facts of life, claimed self-styled biomedical experts, the social good demanded that women should devote themselves earnestly to the maternal role for which Nature had fashioned them. They must cease to be mere butterflies, but nor should they emulate men; rather, they must follow Nature and be 'themselves'.[48]

This doctrine was spelt out in extreme form by Jean-Jacques

Rousseau, who hailed the true woman as the incarnation of feeling, all heart – or, in Mary Wollstonecraft's devastating summary, a house slave 'without a mind'.[49] While full-blown Rousseauvian views won little favour in Britain, English writers, male and female alike, approved some aspects of them. A warm admirer of Rousseau's pedagogical treatise *Émile* (1762), Wollstonecraft herself was one among many who endorsed his notion that women's unique endowment lay in childrearing. They could be good mothers and sound educators, however, only by cultivating the rational faculties with which – despite Rousseau's nonsense – they had been blessed. If the male must 'necessarily fulfil the duties of a citizen, or be despised', his wife should be equally intent to 'manage her family, educate her children, and assist her neighbours'. Committed to promoting education and moral training so that future generations would prove worthy daughters, wives and mothers, Wollstonecraft deemed it a tyranny that they had to 'remain immured in their families groping in the dark'. The ideal marriage should be one based on neither sexual attraction nor romantic passion, but on mutual respect, affection and compatibility.[50]

A few males who piqued themselves on being paladins of enlightenment did, however, take up Rousseau's pet project (announced in *Sophie* (1762), the companion to *Émile*) of grooming a female for her privileged role as protectress of the race. Thomas Day of the Lunar Society, a great admirer of Rousseau and his vision of women as softly submissive,[51] put theory into practice by acquiring a living doll to transform, Pygmalion-fashion, into the perfect wife, an angel schooled to despise fashion, live in domestic retirement and devote herself to her husband and offspring. Aided by a friend, Day selected for his experiment a blonde girl of twelve from the Shrewsbury orphanage, whom he named Sabrina Sidney (after the River Severn and his political hero, the Whig martyr Algernon Sidney). He then went to the London Foundling Hospital where he chose her an 11-year-old brunette companion, Lucretia. To avoid scandal, he took his protégées to France, where he endeavoured to fire them with a Rousseauvian contempt for luxury, dress, title and frivolity, deploying an educational plan which followed the Genevan's. They quarrelled, however, irked him and finally caught smallpox – while Lucretia proved 'invincibly stupid'. After a year, Day returned to England, apprenticed the latter to a milliner and set Sabrina up in Lichfield.[52] His experiments in training his intended's temper proved, however, deeply disillusioning. When he dropped melted sealing wax on Sabrina's arm in order to inure her to pain – a good Rousseauvian experiment – she actually flinched; worse, when he fired blanks at her skirts, she shrieked. Concluding that she was a poor subject, he packed her off to boarding school – later he decided she also had a weak mind and abandoned her.[53] Eventually Day found a congenial soulmate in one Esther Milner; thanks to her husband's repeated efforts, she was successfully hardened into a spartan lifestyle, abandoning her harpsichord and accepting that she would be denied servants. In his didactic novel *Sandford and Merton* (1783), Day then went on to paint the portrait of a perfect Rousseauvian lady, who rose before dawn, dedicated herself to housewifery and wholly renounced the fashionable vices which, enlightened feminists believed, trivialized the sex and spoilt them for their natural duties.

While Day was regarded as quixotic even by his cronies, the notion that Nature had endowed woman with a sacred duty to fulfil her biological endowment as guardian of morality appealed to many. In her first book, *Thoughts on the Education of Daughters* (1787), Mary Wollstonecraft gloried in woman as nurse of the rising generation[54] and, on that elevated basis, expressed her profound contempt for simpering, whimpering, flirtatious spoilt coquettes – those who, in making love their vocation, 'always retain the pretty prattle of the nursery, and do not forget to lisp, when they have learnt to languish', thus turning sexuality into the Trojan horse of oppression.[55] The foibles of the senseless sisterhood who pandered to men and to their own vanity merely perpetuated female weakness: 'imbecility in females,' spat Jane Austen, 'is a great enhancement of their personal charms'.[56] Aware how sexuality could destroy the sisterhood, Wollstonecraft particularly deplored that complicity between beauties and beaux which locked the former in subjection: enticed by men to display 'infantile airs', women's 'strength of body and mind are sacrificed to libertine notions of beauty'.[57] For that reason she denounced the false system of education designed to make women 'alluring mistresses' rather than 'affectionate wives and rational mothers'.[58] True strength in a woman demanded self-control and abstention from sentimentality or seductiveness:

Novels, music, poetry, and gallantry, all tend to make women the creatures of sensation, and their character is thus formed in the mould of folly . . . This overstretched sensibility naturally relaxes the other powers of the mind, and prevents intellect from attaining the sovereignty which it ought.[59]

Sense must triumph over sensibility, that *'manie* of the day', claimed Wollstonecraft; praising Locke, she commended mental self-discipline.[60]

Influential, if equivocal, in promoting positive images of women were Addison and Steele, whose writings advanced a civilizing mission for the sex. Mingling raillery with reproach, they urged improved female education: ladies should comport themselves more rationally, so as to be good companions to their husbands and examples to their children. The essayists flattered women by honouring their role, if, in Swift's tart phrase, 'fair sexing it'.[61]

Launched in 1709, Steele's *Tatler* was targeted not just at 'publick spirited men' but also at 'the Fair Sex, in Honour of whom I have invented the title of this Paper'.[62] That barbed compliment belittled women's discourse ('tattle') while its author was not above dabbling in it himself. 'I do not mean it an injury to women,' he wrote, 'when I say there is a sort of sex in souls.' That was a view reiterated by the *Spectator*: 'The soul of a man and that of a woman,' it pronounced, 'are made very unlike, according to the employments for which they are designed.'[63] Confronting Poulain de la Barre's view, endorsed by John Dunton, that *'l'esprit n'a pas de sexe'* ('the mind has no sex'), Addison ventured the counter-possibility that there may be 'a kind of Sex in the very Soul'.[64] Odd though it may now seem, prominent ladies welcomed Addison's view and his attitude towards them.

'The Women have infinite obligation to him,' complimented the bluestocking Mrs Elizabeth Montagu:

before his time, they used *to nickname Gods creatures, & make their ignorance their pride*, as Hamlet says. Mr Addison has shown them, ignorance, false delicacy, affectation & childish fears, are disgraces to a female character, which should be soft not weak, gentle, but not timorous. He does all he can to cure our sex of their feminalities without making them masculine.[65]

Women who considered themselves enlightened – if lacking any aspiration to become like men – might thus believe that inclusion within the Spectatorial rational circle of polite print culture enhanced their status.

Pondering Addison's modest proposal, and wondering 'if there is really a sex in the soul', the character Savillon in Henry Mackenzie's novel *Julia de Roubigné* (1777) concluded that 'custom and education have established one, in our idea'.[66] There, of course, lay the rub: if the soul was indeed gendered, was that the work of Nature or nurture? – a question which Addison, normally such a loyal Lockean, unaccountably failed to address, indeed like Locke himself.

All hinged on the capacity for rationality, that great instrument of humanity and liberation. Did women naturally partake of rationality precisely as men? If so, the existing socio-legal order must surely be oppressive. Likewise, if, as post-1688 ideology insisted, monarchs were no longer kings by Divine Right but by contract, on what grounds could fathers and husbands legitimately claim their ascendancy over women?[67]

> Wife and servant are the same,
> But only differ in the name:[68]

– in a modest couplet Lady Mary Chudleigh thus got to the heart of the gender, if not the servant, problem!

Responses to this conundrum were complex and confused. Locke had stated that all minds, male and female alike, began as blank sheets of paper and hence were equally receptive to training.[69] He did not, however, pursue the logic of this line of thought to the point of questioning women's current legal or professional status.[70] Various female writers built upon Locke's work. Seeing womanhood as 'manly, noble, full of strength and majesty', the Whig educational theorist Catharine Macaulay mocked 'the notion of a sexual difference in the human character' – it would be disproved by 'close observation of Nature' – and advocated unisex education.[71]

The implications of a common rationality were both simple and complex. Bathsua Makin, in her *Essay to Revive the Antient Education of Gentlewomen* (1673), and Judith Cook, in her *Essay in Defence of the Female Sex* (1696), held that education was a fundamental right – and were not well-instructed ladies, in any case, national assets?[72] The most articulate voice of such opinions was Mary Astell, although her positions defy crude feminist pigeon-holing. Newcastle-born, she moved to London in 1687 and became the intellectual companion of John Norris, 'the last Cambridge Platonist', who attacked Locke's sensationalist epistemology for marginalizing God. Unlike later female intellectuals, Astell rejected Locke: in her view his *The Reasonableness of Christianity* (1695) threatened the Christian faith and the Anglican Church, and she rebutted his contractual theory of government in her *The Christian Religion* (1705), which reinstated the ideal of sacred kingship.[73] Denouncing Shaftesbury as 'deistical', she rejected Whiggery in favour of passive obedience,[74] while, in ecclesiastical politics, her *A Fair Way with the Dissenters and Their Patrons* (1704) and *An Impartial Enquiry Into the Causes of Rebellion and Civil War in This Kingdom* (1704) upheld the penalization of Dissenters and endorsed Tory doctrines of non-resistance.[75]

Astell was not so conservative, however, when it came to the status of women. In *Some Reflections upon Marriage* (1700), she repudiated the 'Tame, Submissive and Depending Temper' of 'those Women who find themselves born for Slavery', assailing the doctrine of familial 'absolute Sovereignty': 'if all Men are born free, how is it that all Women are born Slaves'? Yet, while championing the spiritual independence of women and deploring their trivialization as decorative charms, she also warned against those who might blow 'the

Trumpet of Rebellion' and lead wives on 'to Resist, or to Abdicate the Perjur'd Spouse'.[76] Politically a High Church Tory, Mary Astell had no desire to undermine the Christian gendered hierarchy: women were men's spiritual equals but wives must obey husbands.

Astell's prime aspiration lay in better education, so as to ensure and enhance women's development as moral and spiritual agents: cultivation of the mind was a right. Though men were made for the active life and women for the contemplative, for that their souls must be properly nurtured. The solution she advanced to this end was a female 'monastery', which would be 'not only a retreat from the world for those who desire that advantage, but likewise, an institution and previous [i.e., early] discipline to fit us to do the greatest good in it'.[77] Her idea of a female educational enclave found various later echoes, including Sarah Scott's utopian novel *Millenium Hall* (1762), which pictures a woman-only philanthropic community in which a group of ladies create a feminine utopia caring for the elderly, the poor, the sick and the handicapped. The community is mainly made up of women who have suffered abuse from men and it is more sentimental, less intellectual than Astell's proposed college.[78]

Enlightened thinkers insisted that women were endowed with rational souls equivalent to men's; hence, their minds deserved to be educated. As Astell's case may suggest, much rarer, however, was any call – either by women, or by men chivalrously speaking on their behalf – for greater freedom, social, economic or political, or for radically new roles and rights. Likewise, despite – or, perhaps, because of – extensive castigation of the double standard, demands for what would later be called sexual emancipation were uncommon. A rare forthright repudiation of the *status quo* was Wollstonecraft's *A Vindication of the Rights of Woman* (1792), significantly a work of the Revolutionary era.[79]

Though a lifelong Anglican, Wollstonecraft gained her intellectual and political education from Richard Price and the cluster of rational Dissenters in the London suburb of Newington Green, where she ran a school in the 1780s. Politicization came gradually, as she made her way through a turbulent life and became successively an educationalist (*Thoughts on the Education of Daughters*), a novelist (*Mary, a Fiction* (1788)), a children's writer (*Original Stories from Real Life* (1788)) and a reviewer for the *Analytical Review*. *A Vindication of the Rights of Men* (1790), her reply to Burke's *Reflections*, cast Burke as a toady to power and an apologist for oppression.[80]

A Vindication of the Rights of Woman (1792) protested against the failings and misdirection of female education. Incensed that a woman should be trained to consider that her true purpose in life lay in pleasing men, Wollstonecraft inveighed against the encouragement of 'listless inactivity and stupid acquiescence'. Women were 'kept in ignorance under the specious name of innocence', and men sought in them only 'docility, good humour, and flexibility – virtues incompatible with any vigorous exertion of intellect'. 'Kind instructors!' she fumed, 'what were we created for? To remain, it may be said, innocent; they mean in a state of childhood.'[81]

Presenting herself as a 'philosopher' and a 'moralist', Wollstonecraft politicized her rejection of subordination. ''Til society is very differently constituted,' she expostulated, 'parents, I fear, will still insist on being obeyed, because they will be obeyed.' The answer to it all? – a 'Revolution in female manners'. How it would be brought about and exactly what that would entail were hardly clear, however.[82] Nevertheless, her plea found some echoes. The Dissenter Anna Laetitia Barbauld proclaimed in 1795 in *The Rights of Woman*:

> Yes, injured Woman! rise, assert thy right!
> Woman! too long degraded, scorned, oppressed;
> O born to rule in partial Law's despite,
> Resume thy native empire o'er the breast . . .[83]

while in *A Letter to the Women of England, on the Injustice of Mental Subordination* (1799), addressed to her 'unenlightened country-women', Mary Robinson similarly rallied her sex: 'Shake off the trifling, glittering shackles, which debase you . . . Let your daughters be liberally, classically, philosophically and usefully educated.'[84]

However dramatic, all such proclamations were also remarkable for what they omitted. Wollstonecraft urged women to develop their talents, but she had no plans for votes for women or political activism. Nor did male reformers argue the case on their behalf. The democrat Major Cartwright refuted the idea that women were fit for the vote,[85] and, in his *Essay on Government* (1824), the Benthamite James Mill likewise excluded women, advancing hoary clichés about virtual representation (their interest 'is involved either in that of their fathers, or in that of their husbands').[86]

Nevertheless, enlightened women who talked politics had gone out on a limb, and they were widely attacked. Not content to deny that women were men's equals, John Bennett's *Strictures on Female Education* (1787) warned against female 'over-education', for then 'the world would be deprived of its fairest ornaments . . . and man of that gentle bosom, on which he can recline amidst the toils of labour'.[87] Demonizing Wollstonecraft, the Revd Richard Polwhele accused unruly women of overturning God-given order:

> I shudder at the new unpictur'd scene,
> Where unsex'd woman vaunts her imperious mien;
> Where girls, affecting to dismiss the heart,
> Invoke the Proteus of petrific art;
> With equal ease, in body or in mind,
> To Gallic freaks or Gallic faith resign'd.[88]

Appealing to Nature (that 'grand basis of all laws human and divine'), the Cornish cleric ruled that the woman who defied her place would 'soon "walk after the flesh, in the lust of uncleanness, and despise government"', while graciously accepting that 'the crimsoning blush of modesty, will always be more attractive than the sparkle of confident intelligence'.[89]

It was, moreover, a classic case of 'women beware women'. Margaret Cavendish – labouring under the sobriquet 'mad Madge' – was attacked by others of her sex for her outlandish views, as was Aphra Behn for her audacity. 'Wit in women is apt to have bad consequences,' tartly reflected Lady Mary Wortley Montagu, *à propos* the spirited Laetitia Pilkington: 'I am sorry to say the generality of women who have excelled in wit have failed in chastity.'[90] In turn Catharine Macaulay was ostracized by fellow bluestockings for writing in too political a vein – and for marrying a man thirty-six years her junior: both Elizabeth Montagu and Hannah More refused to read her writings.[91] The latter also chided such 'female politicians' as Mary Wollstonecraft,[92] as did Mrs Chapone, for whom the *Rights of Woman* was marred by 'many absurdities, improprieties, and odious indelicacies'.[93] For her part, Laetitia-Matilda Hawkins, in her *Letters on the Female Mind, Its Powers and Pursuits* (1793), scapegoated Helen Maria Williams, a radical living in Paris who was putting out sympathetic accounts of the Revolution. 'Our Maker never designed us for anything but what he created us, *a subordinate* class of beings,' she insisted, endorsing the gendered *status quo* and boasting that she considered 'the regulation of a kingdom's interests as far too complex a subject for me to comprehend. I would dissuade my countrywomen from the study.'[94]

Such responses betray defensive anxieties – as with Caesar's wife, it was essential to be above suspicion. Women knew that they had too much to lose: emulating men in dirty fields like politics, they would cede the moral and spiritual superiority derived from unblemished virtue. They had to stick together as they ran the gauntlet in a man's world. What was endlessly reiterated, moreover, was the demand for mental cultivation, to make women fit to be responsible adults pulling their social and familial weight, and to endow them with some sort of independence and a degree of rational control over their lives as moral agents. This was what counted to the circles gathering round such bluestockings as Elizabeth Carter, the translator of Epictetus, and Elizabeth Montagu – a lady, complimented Dr Johnson, who 'exerts more mind in conversation than any person I ever met with'.[95] In her *Letters on the Improvement of the Mind* (1773), a hugely popular work reprinted at least sixteen times, another bluestocking, Mrs Chapone, demanded that women's minds be treated like men's.[96] The prime call was thus not for socio-sexual reorganization but for the acceptance of mental and spiritual equality and the right to education so as to end 'Perpetual Babyism'.[97] Women must think for themselves: as so often with the British Enlightenment, the envisaged solution lay in emancipating the mind.

The age of reason has been portrayed by postmodernist feminists such as Catherine Belsey as a disaster for women: 'The Enlightenment commitment to truth and reason, we can now recognise, has meant historically a single truth and a single rationality, which have conspired in practice to legitimate the subordination of . . . women.'[98] Other feminists demur, some going so far as to argue that women, far from being disadvantaged by the Enlightenment, were its very vanguard: in the guise of consumers, cultivators and communicators of feeling, women were to the fore in the birth of the Modern. 'The modern individual,' declares the critic Nancy Armstrong, 'was first and foremost a woman.'[99]

15

EDUCATION: A PANACEA?

I consider a human soul without education like marble in the quarry.

JOSEPH ADDISON[1]

He that undertakes the education of a child undertakes the most important duty of society.

THOMAS DAY[2]

We will venture to say, that there is no class of men to whom a nation is so much indebted as to those employed in instructing the young: For if it be education that forms the only distinction between the civilized and the savage, much certainly is due to those who devote themselves to the office of instruction.

ENCYCLOPAEDIA BRITANNICA (1800)[3]

The model enlightened person was the educated adult, presumed affluent, independent – and male: a 'Mr Spectator', a man of sense or feeling. It was also believed that women were, in principle, at least honorary members of this club, rather than associates of some *salon des refusées*. But what of others?

Children were evidently crucial. Special attention was newly fixed on them, for they would be the standardbearers of that brighter morrow so dear to progressive minds.[4] And opinions about children were undergoing radical change. Mainstream Christian doctrine was put in a nutshell by the leading Evangelical educator Hannah More: were not infants 'beings who bring into the world a corrupt nature, and evil disposition, which it should be the great end of education to rectify'?[5] In line with such Original Sin tenets – the biblical spare the rod and spoil the child – brutal, indeed bloody, childrearing practices had been both preached and practised. Often rationalized by a theology of sin, much traditional upbringing – and not only for the poor – was stern, and beatings were the lot of the young, at home, at school and in the workplace, in the belief that minors were, in a broadly Filmerian sense, the property of their parents or those *in loco parentis*. Some historians have further argued that pre-industrial society scarcely even entertained a distinctive concept of children, seeing them simply as Lilliputian adults: what possible reason could there then be to privilege their condition?[6]

But by 1780 Miss More was on the back foot, for the enlightened had challenged hardline views of children as wicked sinners. Deeming human nature improvable and looking to a brighter future, they knew there could be no progress without a fresh model of the child and a generous vision of education's potential. As with so much else, Locke held the key.[7]

'Of all the men we meet with,' maintained Locke in his *Some Thoughts concerning Education* (1693), 'nine parts of ten are what they are, good or evil, useful or not, by their education. It is that which makes the great difference in mankind.'[8] Whereas Protestant rigorists queried whether the young could truly be schooled into virtue – wickedness was too ingrained to be corrigible by mortal means alone – Locke by contrast likened the infant mind to 'white paper, or wax, to be moulded and fashioned as one pleases'[9] – although it was not precisely a matter of 'as one pleases', for parents were not (as they were for Filmer) owners of their offspring, but trustees, required by God to bring up their children to be rational, responsible Christians.[10]

Locke did not idealize infant innocence – sentimentality came later, and child worship began only with Romanticism. He did, however, regard human nature as malleable: as babies were born indeterminate and more or less identical, so their future temper would hinge upon their upbringing in the widest sense. Much followed from this. Education must not be narrowly scholastic: it was not about being learned but about learning for life, a training in character, habit and conduct. The reader might be surprised, he warned, how little he had said about books: but bookishness was not the point.[11] What counted was to discipline the mind in the correct habits of thinking so as to mould a good disposition. Applying the empiricist epistemology of his *Essay concerning Human Understanding*, Locke insisted that instead of pedantic scholasticism on the one hand or silly fairy stories on the other – works 'as should fill his head with perfectly useless trumpery' – children should be trained to use their powers of observation in getting to know the world at hand. Light-headed imagination must yield to solid sense,[12] and Locke particularly warned parents against letting servants scare children with 'Notions of Spirits and Goblins . . . of Raw-Head and Bloody Bones'. Once such 'Bug-bear Thoughts . . . got into the tender Minds of Children', he maintained, they could not be 'got out again', making them 'afraid of their Shadows and Darkness all their Lives after'.[13]

The usual see-saw of whippings and indulgence produced pettish, peevish youngsters who lacked self-control. However, such self-control was paramount. Crucial to this 'art of stifling their desires' were encouragement and example.[14] The tutor must proceed not through threats and force but by appeals to reason and by winning over the will. Addressed to the higher faculties – brains not buttocks – education should proceed psychologically, through praise and blame, esteem and shame, to instil discipline and build character.

As befitted a physician, Locke did not neglect health. 'Most children's constitutions,' he maintained, 'are either spoiled, or at least harmed, by cockering [mollycoddling].'[15] Children should swim a lot, and even in winter their feet should be washed daily in cold water – better still, shoes should 'leak and let in water'.[16] Girls' clothes should be loose: 'Narrow breasts, short and stinking breath, ill lungs and crookedness are the natural and almost constant effects of hard bodices and clothes that pinch.'[17]

Diet should be simple, meals irregular – stomachs should not be pandered to – but excretion regular. Costiveness 'being an indisposition I had a particular reason to inquire into', Locke had found infants could be trained to go to stool directly after breakfast.[18] Pampering was wrong, 'for if the child must have grapes or sugar-plums when he has a mind to them . . . why, if he is grown up, must he not be satisfied too, if his desires carry him to wine or women?'[19] Holding that education's goal was 'virtue' and that that lay in 'the power of denying ourselves the satisfaction of our own desires, when reason does not authorise them', he urged that children should be made to 'go without their longings even from their very cradles'.[20] Hardening was one thing, however; cruelty was another: a 'slavish discipline' would produce a 'slavish temper'.[21] Rewards and punishments ought not to take a physical form, but rather involve 'esteem and disgrace'. If fear and awe gave parents their first hold over children, love and friendship would follow.[22] Locke thus entertained no rose-tinted vision: children gloried in dominion, and parents must distinguish between the 'wants of nature' and the 'wants of fancy' – which should never be gratified.[23]

On the positive side, faculties should be stimulated. Rote learning was useless, curiosity counted. Locke did not completely anticipate Rousseau's faith in finding out by doing and learning through mistakes, but he certainly disapproved of dinning dead matter into young heads: they must remain receptive and eager to learn.[24] While Locke was far from indifferent to breeding and bearing, unlike Lord Chesterfield later, his accent was not on the trappings of civilization but on the development of responsible, rational creatures capable of meeting their Christian duties.[25] Regarding girls as endowed with reason much like boys, he foresaw 'no great difference' in the training of the sexes.[26]

Locke's views proved exceptionally influential – 'Mr Lock's excellent Treatise of Education, is known to every Body,' stated Chambers' *Cyclopaedia* as early as 1728.[27] Three-quarters of a century later, *Some Thoughts concerning Education* had come out in at least 25 English, 16 French, 3 German, 6 Italian, 1 Swedish and 2 Dutch editions. His faithful follower, Isaac Watts, held that his theories on government and education had together 'laid the Foundations of true Liberty, and the Rules of Just Restraint for the younger and elder Years of

Man'.[28] With a nod at Locke, James Talbott urged founders of charity schools to pay particular attention to infants, since their minds resembled 'blank Paper, or smooth Wax . . . capable of any Impression',[29] and John Clarke's *Essay upon the Education of Youth in Grammar-schools* (1720) likewise endorsed his psychological approach: the only book on the subject 'worth the Perusal', he insisted, was 'Mr Locke's'.[30] Such views, such acclaim, were everywhere. Indeed, pedagogics became all the rage: a staggering 200 educational treatises were published in English between 1762 and 1800.[31]

Locke proved amazingly influential over enlightened educationalists. As already noted, the Whig Catharine Macaulay echoed him, arguing for unisex education. She called on parents to reject 'the absurd notion, that the education of females should be of an opposite kind to that of males' – they should give the same education to both. 'Let your children be brought up together; let their sports and studies be the same; let them enjoy, in the constant presence of those who are set over them, all that freedom which innocence renders harmless, and in which Nature rejoices.'[32]

Staunch patriot that she was, she opposed swaddling as a French habit.[33] Children should be fed with fruit, eggs, vegetables and little meat – 'the taste of flesh is not natural to the human palate'. Sugar was bad ('Nature never intended to deprive us of our teeth'); 'warm liquors, warm beds, and warm nightcaps' were out, cold baths and 'hardy habits' in. Mothers should not overdress infants, never put girls in stays, nor let them wear shoes or socks. Baby talk was banned. With heavy irony, breastfeeding was also ruled out: how could 'a fine lady' possibly be expected to give up 'all her amusements' merely to 'nourish her offspring with wholesome food'?[34]

Other educationalists, while singing Locke's praises, put slants of their own on his theories, especially after the appearance of Rousseau's *Émile* in 1762. 'In 1765 . . . I formed a strong desire to educate my son according to the system of Rousseau,' recalled Richard Lovell Edgeworth, the Lunar Society member and inventor.[35] The experiment, however, proved a disaster. Little Dick (predictably) grew unmanageable: 'I found myself entangled in difficulties with regard to my child's mind and temper,' the father had to admit: 'It was difficult to urge him to any thing that did not suit his fancy' – and even the Genevan guru criticized the results when he saw them.[36] Evidence of Rousseau's influence remained, however, in Edgeworth's monumental *Practical Education* (1798), co-written with his daughter Maria,[37] which stressed learning by doing, and promoted technical, scientific and practical instruction – education that was in the widest sense 'experimental'.[38]

Like Locke, the Edgeworths held that the infant should be treated as a rational being, 'lured sympathetically to think for itself, and kindled to delight in the development of its intellectual powers'. Children should be spurred to speak and act freely; games should teach dexterity, toys should be instructive and practical, and attention held by sympathy. Memory should be trained not by cramming but by 'well arranged associations', and the teacher should encourage the child 'to generalise his ideas, and to apply his observations and his principles'.[39] The ideal 'school' would be a household upon an estate, complete with pets and farm animals.

For the Edgeworths, all education worth the name must rest on a true – that is, Lockean – psychology. Sidelining textbook learning, they maintained that what counted was the development of talents and the ripening of judgement, intellectual and moral. Nothing was to be left to chance; the learning environment was to be carefully regulated and contact with servants monitored, lest children catch 'awkward and vulgar tricks'.[40]

Practical Education went beyond Locke in some respects, notably in its accent on science and handiwork. Edgeworth had early 'amused [himself] with mechanics',[41] and all through his life he dabbled with improved carriages and communications – exemplary enlightened projects. Signally silent on ladylike 'accomplishments' – and religion, too[42] – the authors would have a girl learn mechanics and chemistry rather than, as Rousseau favoured, dressing dolls; she should become 'a good oeconomist, a good mistress, as well as a good mother of a family'.[43]

Edgeworth *père et fille* practised what they preached. They studied the growth of Maria's numerous younger siblings and, rather remarkably, they conducted experiments on Peter the 'wild boy'. Caught in the woods outside Hanover, Germany in 1724, Peter – young, dumb and animal-like – had been brought to England and placed under the tutelage of Dr John Arbuthnot, who undertook to educate him and study his development. *Practical Education* describes the psychological experiments the Edgeworths performed upon Peter, who was by then quite an old man, in order to put the nature/nurture controversy to the test. While he had 'all his senses in remarkable perfection', Peter could only articulate 'imperfectly a few words, in particular King George'.[44] Experiments were devised to gauge his idiocy, and attempts made to activate his faculties by disrupting his 'automatic habits'.[45] For instance, in a daily routine, after Peter fetched water, the Edgeworth children would tip it out of the pail and replace it with a shilling – but all he ever did was to repeat the chore.[46] Tests like that were essential to the aim of their father and elder sister to make education an 'experimental science'.[47]

No mere theorist, Richard Edgeworth was warmly committed to education's social mission. Advocating universal schooling for Ireland, he condemned the blinkered attitudes of those who feared that mass literacy would prove a timebomb. Instruction would not only mend the habits of the poor, it would make them more law-abiding: of 3,000 boys educated at the Gloucester Sunday school, he pointed out, only one had turned to crime.[48]

The Edgeworths and others in late Enlightenment circles made a religion of education. Richard's son-in-law, the radical physician Thomas Beddoes, enthused over giving children 'rational toys' – chemicals, wood for carpentry, scientific instruments and simple machines to take to bits. Citing Thomas Day's slightly shocking view that 'the soul of a child . . . essentially resides in his senses',[49] Beddoes endorsed Locke's experientialism. Concepts not derived from the senses (for instance, hellfire) were meaningless, and parrot learning a tool of despotism, a form of brain-washing designed to implant conformity. Proper education was vital for 'humanizing the minds of the people. Upon this the welfare of civil society immediately depends.'[50]

One logical consequence of Beddoes's thinking was universal education, as advocated in his *Extract of a Letter on Early Instruction* (1792). But on the execution of this matter the enlightened were hardly of a mind. Though Nonconformists were ardent educators, they adamantly opposed state-run schooling, lest that buttress the Church of England monopoly. Here, Priestley took on the crusty Revd John Brown.[51] In his *Thoughts on Civil Liberty, Licentiousness and Faction* (1765), Brown had commended uniform Anglican instruction for the nation on the model of the revered Sparta.[52] What Brown desired, Priestley deplored. Doubtless, standardized state education was best for maintaining the *status quo* – but that was precisely what the Dissenter detested! How could society truly profit by standing still? 'Were the best formed state in the world to be fixed in its present condition,' Priestley explained, 'I make no doubt but that in a course of time it would be the worst.'[53] Like John Stuart Mill later, he gloried in difference: 'The various character of the Athenians was certainly preferable to the uniform character of the Spartans.'[54] And diversity demanded educational pluralism.

Moreover, the British educational system had been designed to educate men for the Church. Circumstances had changed, however, and boys now needed to be trained for an 'active and civil life', particularly in commerce, and for this the modern curriculum should be geared to history and 'civil policy'.[55] Education for the lower orders should be strictly functional, however. Sounding oddly like the Sunday school pioneer Hannah More, whose rule was 'no writing for the poor',[56] Priestley entertained limited horizons for labourers' children, looking to schooling to teach them reading, writing and arithmetic while also keeping them docile: 'Those who have the poorest prospects in life can be taught contentment in their station, and a firm belief in the wisdom and goodness of Providence.'[57]

Dissenting academies won Priestley's praise as the ideal form of higher education, especially as their atmosphere grew increasingly liberal. It was said in 1711 of the Gloucester Academy, where the textbooks included Locke's *Essay*, that its tutor, Samuel Jones, allowed his students 'all imaginable liberty of making objections against his opinion'. Teaching at the Kibworth and Hinckley academies from 1715, John Jennings also introduced his students to Locke, and encouraged 'the greatest freedom of inquiry'. In teaching divinity, remarked Philip Doddridge while a Kibworth student, 'Mr Jennings . . . is sometimes a Calvinist, sometimes an Arminian, and sometimes a Baxterian, as truth and evidence determine him'. Doddridge upheld the same liberal tradition in his own Northampton academy,[58] which was continued after his death in 1751 by Caleb Ashworth at Daventry. When Priestley arrived in 1752 he found Ashworth open-minded: 'The general plan of our studies,' he wrote, 'was exceedingly favourable to free inquiry', for the two tutors 'were of different opinions; Dr Ashworth taking the orthodox side of every question, and Mr Clark, the sub-tutor, that of heresy.'[59]

As to the best mode of education, no consensus held. Locke, who loathed his six years at Westminster under the sadistic Dr Busby, favoured personal tutors; some preferred the old endowed public or grammar schools, others the new commercial academies. For the poor there were dame and charity schools and, by the end of the century, Sunday schools.[60] Enlightened thought, however, united in criticizing the ancient English universities, particularly Oxford, which was damned by alumni like Adam Smith, Jeremy Bentham and Edward Gibbon, who jeered at the fellows' 'dull and deep potations'.[61] In 1715, at government request, Humphrey Prideaux submitted a reform scheme. Condemning life fellowships and the majority of tutors – 'I could scarce committ a dog to their charge' – he urged that a 'Drone Hall' be endowed for superannuated dons.[62] Despite the modernization of the curriculum and rationalization of examinations at Cambridge, university reform came to little in England, however, at a time when in Scotland Edinburgh and Glasgow were going from strength to strength. It was sites beyond academe which supported and stimulated enlightenment in England.

*

Alongside the welter of manuals and self-improvement texts,[63] a key development at this time lay in the virtual invention of juvenile literature, meeting the demand of enlightened parents and tutors for books combining instruction, edification and rational amusement. Suggestive perhaps of Ariès's denial of 'childhood' in traditional society, writings or games created specifically for children hardly existed up to the Restoration: much of what, from today's viewpoint, might be mistaken as writing for children – fairy stories or chapbooks, for instance – formed part of popular culture at large.[64] In the eighteenth century, however, child-oriented books became common, bearing the Enlightenment stamp; and some entrepreneurs specialized in tailoring print capitalism for children, notably John Newbery, publisher of *Tom Telescope* (1761) and *Goody Two-Shoes* (1765).[65]

Reflecting the enlightened view that books needed to entertain and edify all at once, *Goody Two-Shoes* was crammed with messages like

> he that will thrive
> must rise by five.

As with Hogarth's idle and industrious apprentices, in the new children's literature the good got on while the bad came to sticky ends.[66] Violence was condemned, especially cruelty to animals;[67] Locke taught children not to be nasty while, in his *Treatise on the Education of Children and Youth* (1679), the devout Isaac Watts insisted that they should not be allowed to 'set up Cocks to be banged with Cudgels': children who tormented animals turned into tyrants.[68]

Indeed, paralleling its reconfiguration of the child, the Enlightenment rethought the status of animals and man's relations to them.[69] Traditional agrarian society had instilled no-nonsense views which were ratified by Christian doctrine. Man was lord of Creation, because he alone was endowed with an immortal soul; God had granted Adam dominion over the animals; man might tame them, harness them, hunt them, kill, cook and eat them.[70]

Things changed during the long eighteenth century. For affluent town-dwellers, contact with the animal world grew more attenuated: they might now never see animals being born, broken in or slaughtered; indeed, they might not even ride horseback any longer but rattle around in carriages. The educated came to relate to animals, not through working with them but through mind and heart. For one thing, the new science taught that it was society's right, duty and pleasure to investigate that Nature from which it was now becoming further and further divorced. Bug-hunting and beetle-collecting became fashionable, and animals were increasingly sacrificed for scientific research, the Revd Stephen Hales, for instance, performing pioneering – and extremely gruesome – experiments upon various species, from frogs to horses.[71] While such pursuits could involve vivisecting or dissecting, any qualms they might arouse were stilled by the thought that it was all in the service of the nobler goal of understanding Nature and Nature's God.

Urban society was not, however, only intellectually curious: it manifested new sensibilities. Along with children, slaves, noble savages, orphans, the blind, deaf and dumb, and fallen women, animals became objects of sympathy, and the philanthropic thrust for sparing their sufferings came, significantly, not from prelates or Parliament, magnates or the masses, but from the educated professional bourgeoisie. Casual violence – 'swinging cats' and other heartless pastimes – was targeted in Hogarth's *Four Stages of Cruelty* print sequence of 1751, and cruel sports like bear-baiting and cock-fighting came under attack.

As workplace ties with animals dwindled, so a radically new claim emerged: humans and animals were basically the same. Forget the soul, both had feelings. 'The question is not,' explained Jeremy Bentham, 'Can they reason? nor, can they talk? but, Can they suffer?'[72] Pets were humanized, Bentham himself keeping a 'beautiful pig' which would 'grunt contentedly as he scratched its back and ears'. And Sterne's Uncle Toby, for his part, could not hurt a fly that had 'buzz'd about his nose'.[73] Enlightened thinking thus led to a distinct softening of attitudes towards the animal world. Versifying Shaftesbury and Hutcheson, James Thomson expressed pity:

But let not on thy Hook the tortur'd worm
Convulsive twist in agonizing Folds;
Which, by rapacious Hunger swallowed deep,
Gives, as you tear it from the bleeding Breast
Of the weak helpless uncomplaining Wretch,
Harsh Pain and Horror to the tender Hand . . .[74]

while Soame Jenyns and others supposed brutes would enjoy an afterlife.[75]

Animal experiments were being 'published every day with ostentation' by doctors bent on extending the 'arts of torture', complained Samuel Johnson in 1758.[76] And they included, he jibed, those whose 'favourite amusement is to nail dogs to tables and open them alive'.[77] Such experimentation became crucial to this science versus sentiment dilemma, notably in the artist Joseph Wright's depiction of *An Experiment on a Bird in the Air Pump* (1768), a painting designed to excite compassion. Sacrificed by an itinerant lecturer to demonstrate the vacuum, a breathless bird, trapped in a belljar, flutters: Will it live or will it die? Some of the audience are held rapt by the demonstration of the gas laws, others shudder in horror. What Wright's composition also symbolized was the new separation of man and Nature. Traditionally the icon of the Holy Ghost, the dove is now isolated, physically and emblematically, from the humans by the experimental apparatus.[78]

Animals thus became both 'good causes' and also marks of the uptake of enlightened ideas. Thomas Day, that omnipurpose enlightened man, championed dumb beasts. Believing that the breaking-in they received was both cruel and unnecessary – treat an animal well and it would need no severity – he tried out his theory on a colt. He had no more success, however, than he did with Rousseau's theories on how to train a wife. The horse bolted, throwing him from the saddle, and the humanitarian died from his injuries, the English Enlightenment's authentic martyr.[79]

Educationalists were insistent that children should adopt new attitudes towards animals – and that animals themselves could even teach lessons. Sarah Trimmer's *Fabulous Histories Designed for the Amusement and Instruction of Young People* (1786) pointed, for example, to 'the exact regularity with which they discharge the offices of cleanliness and economy'. The idle might be admonished by the bee, a false servant by a dog.[80] The bestselling *Tom Telescope,* John Newbery's children's science primer, urged compassion: stealing bird's eggs or tormenting fledglings was barbaric. Nor must kindness be but caprice: Tom told of a neighbour who treated creatures well so long as they amused him, but who also raged 'at poor children who were shivering at his gate, and sent them away empty-handed'.[81]

Enlightened pedagogy taught that rectitude lay not in title, place or birth, but in inner goodness. Classic as an exposure of aristocratic vice was Thomas Day's bestselling *Sandford and Merton* (1783–9), which went through some forty-five English editions, besides being translated into French and German.[82] Tommy Merton was a toff, Harry Sandford a farmer's son. The tale related honest Harry's encounters with Tommy's family, and his revulsion at their values.[83] 'I don't know,' proclaimed the plain-speaking frontispiece, 'that there is upon the face of the earth a more useless, more contemptible, and more miserable animal than a wealthy, luxurious man without business or profession, arts, sciences, or exercises'[84] – an adage the book illustrated with deadly earnestness. As exemplified by the Mertons, the Quality had no qualities: 'As to . . . industry, economy and punctuality in discharging our obligations, or keeping our words,' Harry commented, 'these were qualities which were treated there as fit for nothing but the vulgar . . . the great object of all their knowledge and education is only to waste, to consume, to destroy.'[85]

Nor would *Sandford and Merton* and its ilk have any truck with levity. Appeal to the fancy, enlightened writers fretted, and children would prove reprobate, not responsible.[86] That is one reason why science was widely commended in children's books: it prized truthfulness and was dedicated to developing reasoning powers. *The Newtonian System of Philosophy* by 'Tom Telescope' taught Newtonianism through the prism of enlightened empiricism.[87] 'All our ideas,' explained the little Lockean, 'are obtained either by sensation or reflection, that is to say, by means of our five senses, as seeing, hearing, smelling, tasting, and touching, or by the operations of the mind.' Selling over 25,000 copies between 1760 and 1800, this book reveals how widely Locke and Newton, associated with humanitarianism, were shaping young minds.

Lucy Aikin's *Poetry for Children* (1803) rejected 'the fairy fictions of the last generation', which were fortunately ceasing to be a threat, for 'the wand of reason' had banished 'dragons and fairies, giants and witches'.[88] The Dissenting author also dismissed novels which gave a 'false picture of the real world', yet she defended verse, provided it was wholesome and improving. The children's tracts which William Godwin wrote and sold from his bookshop off Oxford Street were in a similar literal-minded and moralistic mould: 'My ancestors were respectable heads of families,'[89] declaims a priggish character abused by a supercilious aristocrat in his *Dramas for Children* (1808): his parents had 'bequeathed to me, it is true, a condition in which I am called upon to labour; but I inherit also from them a love of independence, and an abhorrence of every mean or dishonest action'.[90] In his didactic tales, little boys – and sometimes even little girls – floor knaves and giants, since reason and justice are on their side (although the matter-of-fact philosopher was careful to give all his fabulous features rational explanations, partly to stave off nightmarish fears of ogres).[91]

The chief figure in this class of progressive juvenile writing was Anna Barbauld, sister of the Dissenting physician John Aikin. In her influential *Evenings at Home: Or the Juvenile Budget Opened* (1794–8), slavery and empire are condemned and science, industry and business commended.[92] Such heavy-handed moralizing made Charles Lamb mad. 'Mrs Barbauld's stuff has banished all the old classics of the nursery,' he raged to Coleridge:

Think what you would have been now, if instead of being fed with tales and old wives' fables in childhood, you had been crammed with geography and natural history! . . . Damn them! I mean the cursed Barbauld crew, those blights and blasts of all that is human in man and child.[93]

The likes of Locke, the Edgeworths and the liberal Dissenting circles surrounding Mrs Barbauld wanted to enlighten the young for their future as rational, responsible adults: childhood thus formed a stage on the great turnpike of improvement. However, Romanticism would soon be fantasizing childhood as the purest expression of the human and seek to protect it from the developers.[94]

The model of the malleable child, awaiting improvement, was readily transferred by enlightened thinkers to classes of people thought not, or not yet, fully responsible, notably 'victims' of self-induced vices nevertheless believed capable of correction and reform. Enlightened environmentalism held that, since such 'unfortunates' had lapsed into error or crime through no real fault of their own, blame should be pinned on circumstances or on the true villains – the libertine who seduced the maid, the heartless society which reduced workers to pauperdom and beggars to thieving (see chapter 9).[95] Deliverance would come not, as the churches had prescribed, through confession, prayer or the blood of the Saviour, but through re-education under suitable philanthropic guidance. (For humane-style societies, also see chapter 9.)

The Enlightenment took up the cause of the individual or minority, oppressed by bigotry or superstition. 'Freaks' and 'monsters' like dwarves and hermaphrodites attracted sympathy and scientific interest – if also voyeurism.[96] In enlightened thinking, erstwhile villains might be transformed into victims. In his *Reasons for Naturalizing the Jews* (1714), the Deist John Toland proposed, for instance, that Jews ought to be accorded equal status in society. Emancipation was attempted through the Jew Bill, passed in 1753, although public clamour led to its revocation in the next year.[97] In her novel *Harrington* (1817), Maria Edgeworth undertook a personal act of reparation for what she came to recognize as her own unthinking anti-Semitism. A previous work, *The Absentee* (1812), had elicited a complaint from a Jewish reader, on account of its crass stereotyping of a Jewish character. *Harrington*, a radical revision of *The Merchant of Venice*, was meant to make amends.[98]

*

When progressives addressed the relations between enlightened (or enlightening) Europeans and the world's other inhabitants, they often construed such people as children of another kind. Speaking of the 'wild boy' of Hanover, Lord Monboddo considered Peter's story 'a brief chronicle or abstract of the history of the progress of human nature, from the mere animal to the first state of civilized life'.[99]

The work of discovery proceeded. James Cook ('I whose ambition leads me not only farther than any other man has been before me, but as far as I think it is possible for man to go') was the first European to see the Antarctic pack ice.[100] Exploration was news. 'Africa is indeed coming into fashion,' Horace Walpole told Sir Horace Mann in 1774, upon James Bruce's return from Abyssinia. Five years later, Mungo Park's account of his *Travels in the Interior Districts of Africa* proved a bestseller, 1,500 copies going within months. And, alongside the real, imaginary voyages cued the enlightened for their encounters with the Other: *Robinson Crusoe, Captain Singleton, Gulliver's Travels, Roderick Random, Rasselas, Vathek* or the *Marvellous Adventures of the Baron Munchausen*. To the moon, to the underworld, to the Pacific or the Indian Oceans – imaginary voyagers ventured everywhere, while a host of literary works featured exotic worlds, like Aphra Behn's immensely popular *Oroonoko or the Royal Slave* (1688), discussed below.[101]

'The great Map of Mankind is unrolled at once,' rejoiced Edmund Burke: 'and there is no state or gradation of barbarism, and no mode of refinement which we have not at the same moment under our view.'[102] Enlightened minds could thus be proud of opening up the globe: would that not promote the diffusion of knowledge, the unification of mankind and the cause of peace so devoutly wished?[103] Such hopes of course fed optimism about the relations between the West and the rest. Progressives believed that navigation and science were demythologizing the Other, debunking such hoary fantasies as the great Southern Continent, while ethnography banished from the maps the 'monstrous races of men' – Cyclops, dogheads, the man-eating Anthropophagi and giants – though new 'savages' ominously appeared, to fill the gaps they had only just vacated.[104]

Exotic lands and peoples posed the question of difference. Were the 'there and now' of Africa and the Indies exactly the same as the 'here and then' of a bygone Europe? Were the tropics living history? And should the ways of strange and faraway peoples challenge the certainties of the 'civilized', as with Man Friday's bewilderment at Crusoe? It was, however, the savagely indignant Swift who put civilization firmly in the dock.[105] 'To say the truth,' Gulliver blurts out, with regard to European discoveries,

I had conceived a few scruples with relation to the distributive justice of princes upon those occasions. For instance, a crew of pirates are driven by a storm they know not whither, at length a boy discovers land from the topmast, they go on shore to rob and plunder, they see an harmless people, are entertained with kindness, they give the country a new name, they take formal possession of it for the king . . . they murder two or three dozen of the natives . . . return home, and get their pardon . . . Ships are sent with the first opportunity, the natives driven out or destroyed, their princes tortured to discover their gold . . . and this execrable crew of butchers employed in so pious an expedition, is a modern colony sent to convert and civilize an idolatrous and barbarous people.

'But this description, I confess,' concludes Swift's hero with evident relief, 'doth by no means affect the British nation.'[106] Indeed, the pretensions of Europeans to be lords of human kind were attacked and mocked, and anti-colonial thinking ran strong. Locke denied any right of conquest, Adam Smith shuddered at its economic and strategic costs, while others adopted the humanitarian stance. 'I do not much wish well to discoveries,' opined Samuel Johnson, 'for I am always afraid they will end in conquest and robbery.' 'Emancipate your Colonies!' was the advice Jeremy Bentham addressed to the French Revolutionaries some years later.[107]

Growing face-to-face awareness of human diversity prompted the construction of enlightened anthropologies.[108] Difference had customarily been explained by the Bible narrative. Just a few thousand years previously, mankind had been created in Eden. In the dispersal of tribes, by consequence of the Noachian Deluge and the Tower of Babel, corruption had set in, resulting in a multiplication of degenerate tongues, faiths, myths and customs while, thanks to the curse of Ham, his seed had sunk into blackness and barbarity. This Christian master narrative, postulating monogenesis (the original unity of the human race) and a descent from civilization into savagery, commanded broad support. It offered a plausible framework for empirical studies – for instance, comparative analyses of religion – and moral directives, too: natives had to be treated with Christian justice, since all were God's children. Such views still informed the inquiries of Britain's most distinguished early nineteenth-century anthropologist, James Cowles Prichard, author of *Researches into the Physical History of Mankind* (1813). By then, however, that Quaker-born Edinburgh-educated pupil of Dugald Stewart was on the defensive, energetically combating new naturalizing theories, which owed something to observation if as much to speculation.[109]

Stadial sociologies of the kind developed by John Millar (surveyed above in chapter 10) shaped enlightened anthropology, purporting as they did to trace not degeneration from Paradise but man's progress from primitivism. The enlightened 'rudeness to refinement' reference frame challenged the biblical account at various points. It questioned regression from an initial Edenic state, and it also suggested that evidence of similar beliefs and customs among populations worldwide was to be read not, as heretofore, as proof of dispersion from a common source, but as indications of parallel psychological responses to those archetypal traumas faced by primitives the world over: fear, wonder, helplessness, ignorance.[110]

Racial differentiation – Why are some people black? was the way the question was posed – also became problematized. Enlightened discourses came up with various solutions. Some held that negritude was a product of living in the tropics, perhaps even a *beneficial* adaptation to a fierce climate – a solution according with malleability models. Challenging such radical environmentalism, opponents countered that if Negroes had been blackened in the course of time by exposure to the equatorial sun, then why did the skin of their descendants not then lighten after living in colder climes? To others, pigmental indelibility indicated polygenism: blacks formed a distinct species altogether, a separate creation. Addressing the 'Diversity of Men and Languages', Lord Kames was one of many who wrestled with the evidence of human variety. He concluded that there must have been special creations,[111] hinting that blacks might be related to orang-utans and similar great apes then being unearthed in the tropics.[112] Various implications might follow: polygenism might mean that blacks were indelibly different, inferior, yet uniquely adapted to living near the Equator – a way slavery could be rationalized. Debate was heated and unresolved, and there was no single Enlightenment party line, especially as non-Europeans were so diverse as to resist homogenization.

China became an object of study and topic for lively debate,[113] as did Hindu India, with the mastering of Sanskrit above all by Sir William Jones, first president of the Asiatic Society.[114] Knowledge of Islam was diffused through translations of histories, scientific works and sacred writings, the Koran being translated into English in 1734 by George Sale, and 'philosophical' travellers wrote popular texts about the Muslim World, notable among them Lady Mary Wortley Montagu's letters on the Ottoman Empire.[115] With information thus increasing, the 'orientalist' debate grew fiercer.[116]

Stereotypes of the East had been deeply entrenched since medieval times: the great Asiatic emperors were fiendish despots; Islam was a cheat, fabricated by an 'imposter'; the Asiatic imagination had produced an exotic, sensual, tawdry art. Enlightened thinking some- what challenged such negative *clichés*. Deists and unbelievers could find in Islam traces of 'natural' religion (a pristine monotheism) surviving better than in Christianity. Mahomet was thus portrayed in Gibbon's *Decline and Fall* as a heroic figure, and Islam as relatively tolerant of other faiths.[117] A favourite device was the 'noble sage' (or brahmin), a parallel to the noble savage, who, doing the reversed Grand Tour in Europe, could hold the mirror up to Christendom. Oliver Goldsmith's *The Citizen of the World* (1762) thus featured the wise Chinaman, a certain Lien Chi Altangi, who anatomized the British scene in a series of letters home.[118] The vogue for chinoiserie (wallhangings, lamps, carved ivories, rugs, ceramics, patterns) popularized Eastern art – witness the pagoda in Kew Gardens and the Prince Regent's pavilion in Brighton (where Chinese and Indian motifs idiosyncratically merge). There was also a cult of oriental tales, such as in William Beckford's *Vathek* (1786).

But if some aspects of the Orient received sympathy, underlying assumptions were hardly shaken. Progress theorists found in Asia the great counter-example: stagnation. Flaunting utilitarian contempt for all that was backward, Bentham's acolyte James Mill deemed Hinduism 'gross and disgusting', Indian law 'impossibly backward' and Indian art 'rude' . The subcontinentals were dirty, dishonest, effete and disgustingly 'sensuous'. 'One shelf of English books,' Lord Macaulay was soon to conclude, 'is worth more than all the libraries of India.'[119]

And what was to be made of the natives of the Americas, Africa and the newly discovered Pacific islands? Christianity had regarded primitives as the heathen sons of Ham or Cain, and such dismissive attitudes were easily secularized and rationalized. The nomadism of the native American Indians placed them at the foot of the Scottish 4-stage civilization pyramid, while Lockeans might hold that their failure to develop agriculture condoned confiscation of the soil they so signally wasted.[120]

Yet enlightened thinkers could also idealize natives as children of Nature – innocent of Old World corruption, they were virtuous and noble – and Deists might fantasize that they displayed an intuitive knowledge of the Supreme Being. It was the conquering white man who was the true barbarian – especially the Spaniards incited by blood-thirsty priests. Such views fuelled the cult of the noble savage.[121]

Herein also lay some of the roots and rationales for the mounting critique of slavery.[122] As of 1700, few publicly questioned the slave trade's propriety: it was integral to the commercial economy which ensured Britain's greatness. The institution might be euphemized, one author writing in 1740 not of 'enslaving' but rather of 'ransoming the Negroes from their national Tyrants' by transplanting them to colonies where 'under the benign Influences of the Law, and Gospel, they are advanced to much greater Degrees of Felicity'. Indeed, idealization had been possible: James Grainger's *The Sugar-Cane* (1764) presented contented black swains enjoying the pastoral idylls of the plantations:

> Well-fed, well-cloath'd, all emulous to gain
> Their master's smile, who treated them like men.[123]

Sentiments, however, changed rapidly and radically. Nobody, surely, was born a slave – did not Locke's refutation of Filmer show that, in the state of Nature, all were free? Servitude must thus be the product of violence and injustice. The conspicuous humanity and cultural achievements of Africans living in England – for instance, the writer Olaudah Equiano or Sterne's friend Ignatius Sancho – proved that they were not the depraved sons of Ham.[124] Moreover, the law was gradually turning. In 1772, Lord Mansfield, in delivering the judgement of the Court of King's Bench in the case of the slave James Somersset, seemingly ruled that slavery was illegal within Britain itself.[125]

Leading Enlightenment figures joined a swelling chorus of castigation.[126] 'Slavery . . . is a crime so monstrous against the human species,' wrote that unfailing barometer Thomas Day, 'that all those who practise it deserve to be extirpated from the earth.'[127] In 1791, his Lunar Society friend Josiah Wedgwood manufactured thousands of cameos of a kneeling slave, manacled hands raised in supplication, bearing the motto: 'Am I not a man and a brother?' Meanwhile, another member of the Society, Erasmus Darwin, decried the trade in verse:

> Hear, oh, BRITANNIA! potent Queen of ideas,
> On whom fair Art, and meek Religion smiles,
> How AFRIC's coasts thy craftier sons invade
> With murder, rapine, theft, – and call it Trade!

– The SLAVE, in chains, on supplicating knee,
Spreads his wide arms, and lifts his eyes to Thee;
With hunger pale, with wounds and toil oppress'd,
'ARE WE NOT BRETHREN?' sorrow choaks the rest; –
– AIR! bear to heaven upon thy azure flood
Their innocent cries! – EARTH! cover not their blood![128]

'Let the colonists reflect upon this,' wrote Bentham, appalled by the savage slave laws, 'if such a code be necessary, the colonies are a disgrace and an outrage upon humanity; if not necessary, these laws are a disgrace to the colonists themselves.'[129] Weighing all in his utilitarian balance, he conceded that sugar and coffee brought happiness, but 'if they are only to be obtained by keeping three hundred thousand men in a state in which they cannot be kept but by the terror of such executions: are there any considerations of luxury or enjoyment that can counterbalance such evils?'[130] Another utilitarian, the Revd William Paley, fiercely denied the old argument from 'necessity':

It is said, that [the land] could not be cultivated with quite the same conveniency and cheapness, as by the labour of slaves; by which means, a pound of sugar, which the planter now sells for sixpence, could not be afforded under sixpence-halfpenny – and this is the necessity![131]

In such campaigns for the mind, rational Dissent was predictably to the fore. Defoe condemned the slave trade and pleaded for better treatment in his *Life of Colonel Jacque* (1722).[132] Ultra-sensitive to abrogations of the 'natural right' to liberty, Joseph Priestley deplored slavery's reduction of men to 'mere brutes', 'so that they are deprived of every advantage of their rational nature'. For his part, the progressive Baptist minister Robert Robinson of Cambridge denounced the trade as an infringement of natural rights: children should be taught about 'the histories of consciences oppressed, property plundered, families divided and flourishing states ruined by exercises of arbitrary power', while the radical Unitarian Thomas Cooper proclaimed opposition to the trade to be the duty of all Englishmen 'who claim

Freedom as our birth-right'.[133] If it was the Evangelical lobby which in the event secured in Parliament the abolition of the trade, the groundswell of criticism owed much to enlightened liberalism.[134]

Noble savages had long been romanticized. In Aphra Behn's *Oroonoko*, the hero, a young and handsome African prince, falls in love with Imoinda, daughter of his noble foster-father. The two are divided first by the intervention of the king, who covets Imoinda for himself, and then by their sale into slavery. Reunited in Guiana (Surinam), the British colony which Behn had visited, Oroonoko and Imoinda lead a doomed slave rebellion, before he is finally driven to his death by the colonists. The moral was plain: the African 'royal slave' was far nobler than the Europeans (but then he was a prince, blessed with a 'Roman' nose!).[135]

In view of the dilemmas raised in such fictions, the question became pressing: what should be done with noble savages? Since they shared a universal human nature, was not civilization their entitlement? Should they not have the opportunity to be educated and westernized? The young Polynesian Omai provided a test case. Brought back to England, he was lionized, elevated to the status of prince by his hosts, fêted at Court and subjected to the public glare, being painted by Joshua Reynolds – in classical draperies![136] Rather like Peter the 'wild boy' and Thomas Day's Sabrina, however, he turned out to be a let-down to wellwishers expecting him to become a paragon of improvement. He proved a slow learner, his English remained poor and, returning home on Cook's third voyage, he distressed his mentors by taking with him not 'useful' assets like agricultural tools but a jack-in-the-box and a suit of armour.[137]

James Cook nevertheless believed he had descried among the Polynesians those features of civilized life which a Smith or a Miller would have deemed essential to progress: law, marriage, property and rank.[138] For this reason, he picked a bone with the sentimentalized picture painted of them by the French commander, Bougainville: it was an insult to the Tahitians to portray them as lacking private property – they were not so primitive. The down-to-earth Yorkshireman, himself a husbandman's son, who prided himself on not being blinded by fancy, noted that almost every tree upon the islands was actually the property of one of the natives. Nor was their much-vaunted free love the result of primitivism. Far from sanctioning promiscuity, Tahitian sexual morality was not all that different from that actually practised in England or France. True, Cook admitted, when his vessel had first landed, it was besieged by loose women eager to trade their favours, but would not Tahitians find the same if they paddled into Portsmouth?

The armchair *philosophe* Diderot was more of a myth-maker than the voyager, but Cook himself thought within enlightened categories of his own. His 'defence' (as he saw it) of Tahitian sexual mores stemmed from the widespread uniformitarian, cosmopolitan conviction that human nature was the same the whole world over. Moreover, he accepted the political economists' tenet, that private property and social differentiation were the *sine qua non* of any flourishing society. Unlike the naked Australian Aborigines, the Tahitians were thriving: evidently, they must possess systems of social rank and private property.

The mere fact that the Polynesians boasted *different* customs and lifestyles from the Europeans did not automatically make them *inferior*, still less did it warrant exploiting or enslaving them. There was certainly no right of conquest: 'to shed the blood of these peoples is a capital crime,' held Lord Morton, writing to Cook, 'for we are dealing with human beings from the hand of the same almighty Creator ... They are the natural, and in a strict sense, the legal owners of the various territories they inhabit.'[139] Cook endorsed the tolerationist maxim that one should not sit in judgement but rather seek to understand other peoples in the light of their circumstances.[140] Towards the European encroachment on their lands he did so much to further he was less than affirmative:

we debauch their morals already too prone to vice, and we introduce among them wants and perhaps disease which they never before knew, and which serve only to disturb that happy tranquillity which they and their forefathers enjoyed. If anyone denies the truth of this assertion let him tell me what the natives of the whole extent of America have gained by the commerce they have had with Europeans.[141]

Such ambiguities towards exotic peoples – rather as with peasants – characterize the noble savage as figured in late Enlightenment sentimental culture. The title of a 1779 poem about the paradise island of Tahiti speaks for itself: *The Injured Islanders*. Oberea, queen of Otaheite, implores its discoverer, Captain Wallis, to restore the islanders to their former peace and happiness. Contrasting the present with the island's previous state ('Ere Lux'ry taught Ambition to be great'), she declares:

> Canst thou forget, how cheerful, how content
> Taheitee's Sons their Days of Pleasure spent![142]

Meanwhile, in his *Humanity* (1788), Courtney Melmoth presented a similar picture of harmless natives, so 'peaceful and blest where rich Bananas grew', before corruption came with the white man.[143]

Modernizers were optimists; they thought in terms not of hopeless depravity but of problems to be settled. They prided themselves upon their benevolence and prized their power to bring improvement: those not yet enlightened were either innocents or victims. None was damned, none beyond rescue – education and philanthropy would allow them to enter the ranks of the civilized. Though postmodernism accuses enlightened thinkers of the 'imperialism' of reason, their strategies repudiated both rigid hierarchical views of differential human worth and Calvinist convictions of universal reprobation and damnation.[144]

Children and animals were simple cases. As we have seen, however, non-Europeans presented more complicated moral and practical dilemmas. And there were tough nuts to crack nearer home.

16

THE VULGAR

Some must think and others labour.

ERASMUS DARWIN[1]

The people were the acid test. Enlightenment liberalism deemed freedom mankind's native condition: no one was lawfully born into slavery. The *tabula rasa* of Lockean epistemology levelled consciousness; the uniformitarian doctrine of human nature ascribed parity of endowments and needs to all; and anti-privilege arguments depicted life as a race, with all starting on the same line. Fraternity of a sort was proclaimed: 'Am I not a Man and a Brother?'[2]

The attitudes of enlightened élites towards the populace at large were, nevertheless, profoundly ambiguous, often implying not unity or equality but two nations, two mentalities, two sorts of men – and the irksome proximity of odorous beings who were less than fully rational, and certainly not fine Addisonian gentlemen. Horace's *odi profanum vulgus et arceo* ('I hate, I scorn, the Vulgar Throng') fell often from classically educated lips, echoing the biblical 'many are called, but few are chosen'.[3] 'The bulk of mankind,' opined Swift, 'is as well qualified for flying as for thinking.'[4] What then informed enlightened attitudes to the poor? And did they prove the Enlightenment's Waterloo?

Progressive élites liked the people, selectively at least, and particular individuals were praised as diligent, deserving and devoted. Hogarth painted his domestics, while Samuel Johnson left his manservant Francis Barber an annuity of £70 in his will and Lord Chesterfield bequeathed two years' wages to his servants, 'my equals by Nature, and my inferiors only by the difference of our fortunes'. Talented people rising from the ranks were welcomed, if condescendingly, into polite society. Thanks to the support of the local clergy, the agricultural labourer Stephen Duck gained Queen Caroline's patronage as the 'Thresher Poet', while Robert Burns won provisional acclaim amongst the Edinburgh literati as the 'Heaven-taught ploughman'.[5]

Baconianism prized the craft skills of the knowing hand over the cloistered academic's waffle, and in some fields village wisdom remained valued. Though the enlightened now pooh-poohed astrology and clairvoyance, physicians might still honour oral medical lore, at least once purged of its magical relics. Lady Mary Wortley Montagu picked up smallpox inoculation from Turkish folk practice, and the Gloucestershire country doctor Edward Jenner got the clue for vaccination from the gossip of dairymaids.[6]

If the triumphal advance of metropolitan print culture weakened traditional oral culture, it also sparked interest in it; popular mentalities became objects of fascination, and there was a drive to pickle and preserve folklore, songs and sayings.[7] Addison, for instance, in 1711 surprised *Spectator* readers by devoting a paper to the old ballad 'Chevy Chase'. Convinced, like his fellow Augustans, that true literature must obey the 'rules', he cast it, however, as 'an heroic poem', likening it to the *Aeneid* and praising its 'majestic simplicity'.[8] The Northamptonshire clergyman Thomas Percy inspired the ballad revival in 1765 with his *Reliques of English Poetry*. A grocer's son who had snobbishly changed his name from 'Pearcy' so as to claim descent from the Earls of Northumberland, he included in these 'reliques' – a conscious archaism – a number of famous lyrics, such as 'Barbara Allen' and 'Sir Patrick Spence', as well as 'Chevy Chase'. Though he did not see ballads as springing from the folk mind – they were rather the compositions of medieval minstrels enjoying Court patronage – the *Reliques* achieved fame, in Britain and Europe alike, as a corpus of folksongs.[9]

In Scotland, interest in the people's muse led to the publication of *Orpheus Caledonius* (1725); Evan Evans edited *Some Specimens of the Poetry of the Antient Welsh Bards* (1764) and Rhys Jones brought out *Gorchestion*

Beirdd Cymru ('Masterpieces of the Welsh Poets') in 1773. This recovery of popular song culminated in the Ossianic poems, the literary fraud of the century.[10] Largely with a view to vindicating Celtic civilization in the post-Culloden years, James Macpherson produced his *Fragments of Ancient Poetry, Collected in the Highlands of Scotland, and Translated from the Galic or Erse Language* (1760), verses which he claimed he had heard crofters recite, supposedly deriving from Ossian, the 'Highland Homer': the conviction that the poetic imagination was strongest in those 'closest to nature' seemed to be borne out. Admirers funded further forays to collect more Gaelic 'fragments', and two epics followed, also by the old bard: *Fingal* (1762) and *Temora* (1763). Despite growing misgivings about their authenticity, by 1800 there were at least ten editions of the works at home and innumerable versions in German, Italian, Spanish, French, Dutch, Danish, Swedish, Polish, and Russian.[11]

Cast as the true mouthpieces of popular inspiration, Celtic bards were pictured plucking harps and chanting a popular idiom of heroism, love and death. Soon Wordsworth was to venerate the common people in the *Lyrical Ballads* (1798), declaring that 'low and rustic life was generally chosen because in that situation the essential passions of the heart find a better soil . . . [they] speak a plainer and more emphatic language'.[12]

Enlightened élites could also express sympathies towards the lower orders at large, towards the new John Bull figure (envisioned in the Georgian century as infinitely put-upon): their labours sustained the land, they bore the heat of the day with scant reward or thanks. The dignity of toil won salon sympathy,[13] while the late Enlightenment wept over cottagers and carters oppressed by rapacious landlords, brutish squires and others who exploited their probity, ignorance or vulnerability. Oliver Goldsmith's *The Deserted Village* (1770) lamented the victims of enclosure: it was a bad day for Britain when its peasantry was wantonly dispossessed in order to gratify greed:

> Ill fares the land, to hastening ills a prey,
> Where wealth accumulates, and men decay.[14]

While rustics could thus be cast as goodness unsullied by Quality Street depravity, educated élites overall were neither so sympathetic nor so sanguine.[15] For Deists, the rabble was credulous, needing ceremonies, creeds and even clergymen to keep them in check. The Newtonian physician George Cheyne brusquely distinguished society's 'Quick Thinkers, Slow Thinkers and No Thinkers',[16] while rusticity was always good for a laugh. 'I remember, as my goods were once carrying into my lecture-room, at a certain town,' recalled the itinerant lecturer Benjamin Martin, appealing to audience snobbery,

the rabble crouded about the door, to know what it was; and one wiser than the rest immediately cries out, *'Tis a ZHOW come to town*; and what do we give to zee't? A GUINEA, replies the other. Z—nds, says the fellow, this is the D—l of a *Zhow*; why *Luck-man-zshure*, none but he *gentlevauke* can see this.[17]

Who, at bottom, were to be admitted through the pearly gates into the enlightened Elysium of reason? The people, of course – but that was always a slippery notion. The 'people', according to the Revd John Brown, writing in 1765, were 'the landed gentry, the beneficed country clergy, many of the more considerable merchants and men in trade, the substantial and industrious freeholders or yeomen' – evidently, some people were far more equal than others.[18] Three years later, one 'Regulus', writing in the *Political Register*, excluded from the ranks of the 'people' the 'illiterate rabble, who have neither capacity for judging of matters of government, nor property to be concerned for'.[19] If habitually assumed, the drawing of such social discriminations required tact. 'All men by nature are equal,' explained Locke, but

I cannot be supposed to understand all sorts of Equality: Age or Virtue may give men a just Precedency; Excellency of Parts and Merit may place others above the Common Level; Birth may subject some, and Alliance or Benefits others, to pay an Observance to those to whom Nature, Gratitude or other Respects may have made it due.[20]

The beauty of Christianity lay in its being a faith adapted for the ignorant, for 'where the hand is used to the plough and the spade, the head is seldom elevated to sublime notions':[21] Locke's condescension – 'the greatest part cannot know and therefore they must believe'[22] – sanctioned the Deist double-truth doctrine: religion for the rational, superstition for the simple.

Some were less forbearing. In *The Seasons* (1730), James Thomson contrasted the 'enlightened few' whose 'godlike minds Philosophy exalts' with the stupidity of the 'sequacious herd', 'to mystic faith/ And blind amazement prone' and terrified by comets passing across the heavens – witness the proverbial swain running 'to catch the falling glory' of the rainbow.[23] The learned Elizabeth Carter, translator of Epictetus, was hardly amused to find she had won a reputation with Hodge not just for forecasting the weather, but even for conjuring – 'I really thought,' she wrote through gritted teeth, 'there had been no such nonsense left even among the lowest of the people.'[24] Popular belief in prodigies, portents and other superstitions riled the élite, if gratifying their sense of superiority: 'The short-sighted vulgar,' reflected Bernard de Mandeville, 'in the Chain of Causes seldom can see further than one Link.'[25] 'Ask any of the vulgar, why he believes in an omnipresent creator of the world,' invited Hume, 'he will never mention the beauty of final causes, of which he is wholly ignorant . . . He will tell you of the sudden and unexpected death of such a one. The fall and bruise of such another: the excessive drought of this season.'[26]

Terms, in short, were tricky. Henry Fielding famously defined 'no body' as 'all the people in Great Britain, except about 1200'.[27] Shaftesbury praised the 'people' to the skies – there could be no 'public', except where the 'people' were 'included'. Yet by that epithet he understood, in classic Polybian mode, the free citizens of a commonwealth, 'such as have seen the World, and inform'd themselves of the Manners and Customs of the several Nations of Europe' – the numerical majority were thereby excluded.[28] Lacking a free spirit, the 'mere Vulgar' could act only out of 'servile Obedience' – and even then, they 'often stand in need of such a rectifying

Object as the Gallows before their Eyes' – indeed 'a devil and a hell may prevail where a gaol and a gallows are thought insufficient'.[29]

Such status distinctions formed the reflexes of enlightened minds. 'A Man of Polite Imagination,' held the *Spectator*, 'is let into a great many Pleasures that the Vulgar are not capable of receiving.'[30] Taste would tell – indeed, it had become, teased James Miller's *The Man of Taste* (1735), the true badge of distinction: 'fine ladies and gentlemen dress with taste . . . the painters paint with taste'.[31] David Hume for his part addressed 'the elegant part of mankind, who are not immersed in mere animal life'.[32] 'Refinement and delicacy', wrote Mary Anne Radcliffe, elevated ladies above the 'poor and abject', oblivious to manners.[33] Blunter still was the poet William Shenstone: 'the Vulgar are generally in the wrong'.[34]

In this parade of discrimination, the prospect of being judged vulgar was insupportable. The Scottish Common Sense philosopher Thomas Reid naturally distinguished the likes of himself from the mob: 'The vulgar are satisfied with knowing the fact . . . But a philosopher is impatient to know how this event is produced, to account for it, or assign its cause.'[35] But imagine his horror when he found himself hoisted by his own petard: rebuked by Hume's criticism, 'to my great humiliation,' he conceded, 'I find myself classed with the vulgar'.[36] It had, of course, long been feared that 'peasantry', like smallpox, was catching, Locke fretting lest domestics pass on silly whimsies about goblins and witches, thereby imprinting false associations of ideas (see chapter 9).[37] Equally worrying, the masses might mimic polite culture and, perhaps by reading novels, 'indulge in dangerous dreams of pre-eminence':[38]

> And if the rustics grew refined,
> Who would the humble duties mind?
> They might, from scribbling odes and letters,
> Proceed to dictate to their betters.[39]

Overall, then, the definition of the 'people' lay in the eye of the beholder, and there was a repertoire of 'peoples' to enact varied ideological roles, be they as paragons or pariahs. If in their benevolent dreams the enlightened liked to imagine a perfected populace, it was strictly on their own terms; and in the short run, the people were portrayed mainly as problems.

The enlightened temper was upbeat, and solutions to the people problem presented themselves to the sanguine. Hopes were vested in prospects of progress: today's vulgar might be tomorrow's polite. In the 1780s Mrs Thrale thus pointed to the improvement in 'female manners' perceptible since the turn of the century. When she read out the *Spectator* to her pre-teen daughters, they burst out laughing at its 'vulgarisms'; most tellingly, 'the maid who was dressing my hair' joined in. If, seventy years on, even a servant might seem more suave than Mr Spectator himself, was that not reassuring indeed? The *Gentleman's Magazine* concurred in noting how vulgarity of speech was quite out – only 'the lowest class' now said 'sweat'. 'We are every day growing more delicate,' ironized its author, 'and, without doubt, at the same time more virtuous; and shall, I am confident, become the most refined and polite people in the world.'[40] If peasantry was catching, why not politeness too?

History hinted that all might be riding the civilization escalator. Looking back in 1801, the Revd Richard Warner bemoaned how 'the sports which sufficiently satisfied our ancestors of the sixteenth and seventeenth centuries' had been 'the pranks of mountebanks, the feats of jugglers, tumblers, and dancers, the jests of itinerant mimes or mummers, and the dangerous amusement of the quintane, diversified occasionally by . . . the elegant pastime of bull-baiting'. In the past, even superior people had dabbled in coarse fun. Fortunately, all had changed: 'as national manners gradually refined, the ideas of elegance were proportionally enlarged, and publick amusements insensibly approximated to the taste and splendour which they at present exhibit'.[41]

If time itself was thus educative, schooling would speed things up. Initiatives for mass schooling largely came from Christian philanthropists – the charity school movement in the early decades of the eighteenth century and Sunday schools towards its close.[42] But, as seen in the previous chapter, enlightened thinking played its part, too – as in the schemes of education devised by Andrew Bell and Joseph Lancaster which trail-blazed that 'steam engine of the moral world', the mechanized monitorial method of teaching. Deployed in a division of labour, student monitors were to funnel instruction down from a single teacher to the pupils. 'Such is the intellectual organ,' wrote Bell in 1797, 'which puts the whole scholastic machine in motion; such . . . the principle on which every schoolroom, factory, workhouse, poorhouse, prison house, the administration of the poor laws, and every public or even private institution of any magnitude should be conducted.'[43] The entrepreneur Robert Owen's new model society at New Lanark hinged upon enlightened faith in popular perfectibility and the malleability of man. That atheist follower of Locke and Helvétius laid on extensive schooling facilities designed to mould his workforce into happy hands.[44]

Time and teaching might thus prove effective. Such processes, however, needed a helping hand. Energies had to be invested in discrediting and suppressing 'brutal' habits, to render the herd more restrained. Dissociating themselves from popular pastimes now deemed 'vulgar', élites set about cleaning up or closing down such violent amusements as bear-baiting, newly declared offensive to reason, morality, sobriety, law and order.[45] Progressive opinion denounced plebeian drunkenness, fornication and waste, and attempted to promote a new self-respect among the labouring classes, to fit them to the new manufacturing economy. In his *Address to the Young Inhabitants of the Pottery* (1783), published after local food riots, the ceramics manufacturer Josiah Wedgwood, a man whose 'eleventh commandment' was 'Thou shalt not be idle', denounced popular dissipations and detailed the tangible improvements industry would offer to the working population, if they cooperated and gave up inebriety, poor timekeeping, fecklessness and the leisure preference.[46] His physician friend Erasmus Darwin campaigned against the evils of drink, as did his fellow radical, physician Thomas Beddoes.[47]

Anti-alcohol propaganda was produced by many 'friends of the people'. James Parkinson, a doctor with impeccably enlightened credentials – he was a leading member of the radical London Corresponding Society – wrote *The Way to Health* (1802) as a handbill intended for display in public places to be read by the labouring poor.[48] He spoke man to man – that is, enlightened expert to hayseed: 'As most of you are men who benefit society by your labours, gaining your livelihood by the sweat of your brows, you will not be surprised that I commence my instructions, with a few remarks on Exercise and Labour.'[49] Manual work was framed within a pastoral vision: honest toil would endow labourers with sound constitutional health.[50] Quoting John Armstrong, the sentimental Scottish medical poet, Parkinson endorsed the view that 'By health the peasant's toil is well repaid', for 'strength is increased by being used, and lost by being too much hoarded'.[51]

Drunks were thus appealed to in print, as were those who had fallen foul of the law. As explained earlier, enlightened models of causality and personality suggested new notions of blame and guilt. Certain groups like witches, who had traditionally been vilified, were now cast as victims. That was true also of whores, increasingly depicted as products of circumstance and hence as objects of sympathy.

Prostitution was widely debated. Pondering the culpability of streetwalkers, the magistrate John Fielding demanded in 1758, 'What must become of the Daughters of working widows, where Poverty and Illiterateness conspire to expose them to every Temptation?' Answer: 'They become Prostitutes from Necessity even before their Passions can have any Share of their Guilt.'[52] What alternative did they have? 'Scant are the means of subsistence allowed to the female sex . . . and those so much engrossed by our sex; so small the profits . . . and so difficult often the power of obtaining employment.' Employers were loath to hire city girls, preferring the exploitable innocence of those up from the country.[53] Punitiveness only made bad worse. As Jonas Hanway wrote in his *Defects of Police* (1775):

Treat a woman, young in age, and not old in sin, as a *felon*, her sense of shame will be extinguished: she will be tempted to look on herself as an *outcast* of human nature: she will continue to sin without control: her heart will grow petrified: she will grow indifferent to all events, caring not how soon, or in what manner, she leaves a world, where she finds so little mercy, and such unrelenting severity against her.[54]

Enlightened thinking thus deflected blame away from the individual harlot. In his *A Modest Defence of the Public Stews* (1724), Bernard de Mandeville maintained that, in utilitarian terms, commercial sex was a lesser evil in view of male sexual drives, and the only way to prevent the molestation of 'virtuous' women.[55] The predominant image, however, was that of whore as victim: neither intrinsically virtuous nor vicious, she was a child of society, typically pictured, as in Hogarth's *A Harlot's Progress* (1730–31), as a guileless girl who had come up to the wicked city only to be exploited by hardened bawds and heartless clients. The enlightened framework was thus one not of personal guilt and atonement but of social problems and engineered solutions.[56]

So what was to be done? Enlightened minds strategically came up with institutional answers: not punishment but rehabilitation, not whippings but reformatories. London's Magdalen Hospital was set up in 1758 for just this purpose, aiming to remove whores from risk, teach them discipline and an honest trade, and then place them in a situation.[57] Just as children could be educated, so problem people could be retrained.

In that reconditioning process, the enlightened physician often cast himself as possessing a brief extending to the diagnosis and treatment of social disorders. In a sick society riddled with idiocies and injustices, it was the upright doctor, according to enlightened figures like Thomas Beddoes, who was best placed to prescribe for the people's good[58] – witness his *The History of Isaac Jenkins, and of the Sickness of Sarah his Wife, and their Three Children* (1792).[59]

In this improving tale pitched at the labouring poor a Shropshire labourer's family is overtaken by illness. Unable to afford the doctor, the Jenkinses buy some medicine from the local quack. When they can no longer pay him, the huckster stops calling – 'your quack doctors', asides the narrator, 'care not a farthing whether they cure or kill, all they want is to fleece those that know no better'.[60]

Luckily, Surgeon Langford rides past one day, *en route* to attend the parson, injured (in a typical enlightened anti-clerical touch!) while out shooting. Langford gets talking to Sarah, hears that the children are sick, treats them for free and listens to her tale of woe. Her husband has taken to drink. This lapse, interpolates the preachy physician, stems not from inherent depravity but from a terrible accident which has befallen the family (some louts caused a horse to bolt and it trampled the Jenkinses' eldest son to death). The grief-stricken Isaac is now drowning his sorrows, and the family suffers. While condemning the 'heinous practice of drunkenness', the narrator judges that Isaac is to be 'pitied' not 'blamed': 'the poor are well disposed, and do wrong oftener for want of knowing better than from wickedness'.[61]

The doctor has a heart-to-heart with Isaac, prescribes some medicines and shames him back to work. A loan from Langford enables the family to pay off the publican. Obeying doctor's orders, Isaac recovers – unlike his nasty master Simcox, who (in another class-oriented barb) comes to a disgustingly wretched end, his debauchery leading to death from dropsy. All ends happily, with Isaac learning the difference between 'plenty with sobriety . . . and beggary with drunkenness and discontent'.[62] An 'epilogue' for the 'refined reader' urges that, in the light of Locke, the poor should be viewed not as scoundrels but as victims of circumstances, capable of coming good, given proper care and attention.[63] The parable thus teaches the rescue of miscreants, not through grace but through enlightened succour, and thanks not to priests but to physicians.[64]

In practice, the bottom line lay in perspectives and programmes aimed at those whose destitution was judged likely to prove a drain on the nation or a flashpoint of disturbance. What was to be done about poverty? Reason looked askance at those aspects of Christ's teachings which saw holiness in the beggar and which took no heed for the morrow. Why reward laziness? Give thoughtlessly, warned

Joseph Priestley in a fundraising sermon for his newly founded local hospital, the Leeds Infirmary, and 'with the best intention in the world, you may be doing nothing better than encouraging idleness, profligacy and imposture'.[65] The natural law rational individualism advanced by Locke held that each had a duty to take care of himself and of his own, and better his condition.[66] Long before Lady Thatcher, Christian economists quoted St Paul: 'if any would not work, neither should he eat',[67] while Mr Spectator's merchant friend Sir Andrew Freeport considered hand-outs to beggars worse than useless, for they would be confirmed in their idleness.[68]

This is not to say that enlightened élites rejected charity – quite the reverse. Giving could be a duty, indeed a 'luxury' to be enjoyed by superior souls.[69] Yet it should never be indiscriminate; it had to be properly targeted and calibrated; and it must produce results, neither impoverishing the donor nor debauching the recipient. Addressing the workings of charity, the enlightened analysed impulse and action, causes and consequences, weighing beneficence alongside value for money. If it sprang purely from the heart, philanthropy could all too easily be counter-productive, demoralizing and a prey to fraud. Yet charity was something that had to be dispensed, rather than dispensed with. It was, after all, the cardinal virtue, the armorial bearings of genteel humanity, a generosity soaring above sordid miserliness and the institutionalized dribblings of the parish Poor Law. Herein the Georgians sought to steer between the Scylla of sentimentality and the Charybdis of calculation, while guiding a generous heart with a heedful head.

On this, as on so many other matters, the enlightened were nothing if not self-congratulatory. The generosity of donors, stated the Leeds Infirmary's Annual Report in 1784, proved that 'the charity of Mankind . . . has been progressive, and reflects peculiar Lustre on the present Period'.[70] In giving freely, Priestley held, we 'reap all the advantages of the real refinements and true polish of the present age';[71] and, in a similar vein, another hospital fundraiser, William Watts, urged fellow citizens to be 'charitable in an age, and nation, and instance, in which Charity abounds'.[72] The East Midlands could lead the world: 'In this, and every other humane, polite, charitable, and Christian, regard, may the very respectable county of Leicester ever, under the divine influence, be an example and praise to this land of Liberty and social Virtue.'[73] Other arguments also carried weight. The infirmary, so Priestley pointed out, was 'the cheapest of all charities, the most great good being done with the least expense'.[74]

There was thus a role for rational philanthropy. But that had to be set in the context of another reality: the parish Poor Laws, calls on which were mounting ominously. Why did poverty persist, worsen even, despite prosperity and that institution? Might these laws perhaps create or exacerbate the very disease they claimed to cure? Should then the Poor Laws be reformed? Enlightened England brought fierce controversy over the running sore of poverty in a flourishing capitalist economy.

Since Elizabethan times, England had been proud of its national statutory Poor Laws – unlike Catholic Europe and Calvinist Scotland, where alms distribution was left in the hands of the Church.[75] As the 1662 Law of Settlement confirmed, responsibility lay with the parish. A destitute person had the right to outdoor relief in his parish and no other. The flipside of the settlement was the entitlement to remove: a parish had no responsibility for those without a settlement there, and the vagrant poor, old and sick were whipped away.

Early in the eighteenth century, overseers of the poor seem to have been fairly generous with doles: so long as labour remained in short supply, it made good sense to husband it. But then numbers and rates soared. In 1700 the annual cost was around £600,000; by 1776 it had shot up to £1,500,000, and then it went through the roof to £4.2 million in 1803.

The search for explanations and solutions got tied in knots because, at every level, public attitudes to the poor were so conflicting. The able-bodied were often blamed for their own fate. 'When wages are good,' Defoe groused of the 'undeserving',

they won't work any more than from hand to mouth; or if they do work they spend it in riot or luxury, so that it turns to no account to them. Again as soon as trade receives a check, what follows? Why then they grow clamorous and noisy, mutinous and saucy another way, and in the meantime they disperse, run away, and leave their families upon the parishes, and wander about in beggary and distress.[76]

In his *An Inquiry into the Causes of the Late Increase of Robbers* (1751), Henry Fielding levelled similar indictments. The principal causes of crime were the 'luxurious' habits of the 'lowest sort of people', along with maladministration of the Poor Laws. Trade booms and the commercialization of leisure had created vicious tastes and expectations among the poor. 'To be born for no other purpose than to consume the fruits of the earth is the privilege . . . of very few,' he grimaced. Gin and gaming were sapping industry, while the Poor Laws, compromised by administrative bungling and misplaced giving, made bad worse.[77] 'The miseries of the labouring poor,' Frederick Morton Eden later pontificated, 'arise, less from the scantiness of their income . . . than from their own improvidence and unthriftiness.'[78] Only certain cadres, in other words, qualified for the new enlightened status of 'victim': for most, reason required responsibility.

To encourage that virtue, many therefore stipulated that wages must be held low. 'The only way to make the poor industrious,' ruled Sir William Temple, 'is to lay them under the necessity of labouring all the time they can spare from rest and sleep.' 'Everyone but an idiot,' echoed Arthur Young, a century on, 'knows that the lower class must be kept poor or they will never be industrious.'[79] The drawback with low-wage solutions, however, as was pointed out, was that they kept labourers at destitution's door: the slightest accident, illness or trade downswing would instantly turn a sturdy family penurious, and hence publicly chargeable.[80]

There was never a shortage of schemers touting solutions. One much-canvassed, though long-term, answer was, as we have seen, to recondition minds, train up the lower classes in habits of industry, piety, thrift and frugality. Improving tracts, charity schools, sermons and the like aimed to build character and teach the laws of labour. But that would take time. Hence a nostrum which increasingly found favour was to attach strings to hand-outs; notably, relief should mean loss of liberty. The *deus ex machina* was to be the workhouse, 'a mill to grind rogues honest, and idle men industrious', in Jeremy Bentham's adage (see chapter 18). There the poor would earn their keep (thus sparing the ratepayers), and be taught discipline and skills – several birds would be killed with one utilitarian stone.

Locke, almost inevitably, was an early advocate. Prepared for the Board of Trade, his *An Essay on the Poor Law* (1697) briskly diagnosed the causes of poverty and unemployment, which were neither 'scarcity of provisions nor want of employment', but 'the relaxation of discipline and the corruption of manners' – Locke the policymaker invariably sounds harsher than Locke the philosopher. Hence the first step towards 'setting the poor on work ought to be a restraint of their debauchery by a strict execution of the laws against it'.[81] Guardians of the poor were to create boot camp working schools and require master craftsmen and farmers to employ ex-pupils as apprentices. 'Begging drones' – the able-bodied idle – should be dragooned into service at sea, and orphaned children placed in workhouses and made to labour up to fourteen hours a day, from the age of three for boys and five for girls, sustained by a 'watery gruel'.[82]

The philanthropic Quakers John Bellers and Thomas Firmin, contemporaries of Locke, held that, along with workhouses, the training-up of children in habits of industry and putting them to work would also solve the indigence problem.[83] In his *Proposals for Raising a College of Industry of All Useful Trades and Husbandry* (1696), Bellers declared, in standard mercantilist fashion, that 'there cannot be too many labourers in a nation', and proposed a colony of some 300 producers, run on a joint stock basis – 'a Community something like the example of primitive Christianity, that lived in common'.[84]

Workhouses were first tried from 1697 in Bristol; hundreds more were set up during the next few decades. From some quarters the institution received the most lavish, if sinister, praise; in *The Fleece* (1757), John Dyer saluted the happy workhouse as a solution for society's flotsam and jetsam:

> Ho, ye poor, who seek,
> Among the dwellings of the diligent,
> For sustenance unearn'd; who stroll abroad
> From house to house, with mischievous intent,
> Feigning misfortune: Ho, ye lame, ye blind;
> Ye languid limbs, with real want oppress'd,
> Who tread the rough highways, and mountains wild,
> Through storms, and rains, and bitterness of heart;
> Ye children of affliction, be compell'd
> To happiness.[85]

When they failed to deliver the promised goods, however, revised schemes had to be advanced for making workhouses more disciplined and cost-effective. Jeremy Bentham recommended the establishing of a compulsory and universal system, the National Charity Company, a private concern licensed by the State with a view to rounding up beggars and paupers and sequestering them in workhouses. The company would possess the authority to sweep the idle off the streets – they would be 'compelled to come in'.[86] In particular it was to target the young, who would be trained in habits of industry: 'not a particle of time,' wrote Bentham, 'shall remain necessarily unemploy'd' (see chapter 18). Administrative minutiae were specified to make the workhouse cost-efficient: waste of money and time would be avoided by 'moral bookkeeping'. Like the Panopticon,[87] the National Charity Company would be operated by a privatized farming-out system – for Bentham was convinced that state jobs bred jobbery, whereas competitive tendering made for efficiency.

Confronted with pauperism, some hardliners concluded that capitalism itself was producing poverty – and that this might be inevitable and even advantageous. 'Poverty,' asserted the utilitarian Scot Patrick Colquhoun, along Mandevillian lines, is 'a most necessary and indispensable ingredient in society'.[88] No poverty, no incentive to labour, no industry. Certainly, attention increasingly focused upon the balance – or, rather, the newly feared disequilibrium – between wealth and the population rate.

Previously, populousness had always been praised. 'The increase of hands and the right employing of them,' wrote Locke, 'is the great art of government';[89] Sir William Petty held that 'people are the chiefest, most fundamental and precious commodity'; while Nicholas Barbon declared people 'the riches and strength of the country'.[90] Mercantilism had welcomed the proliferation of industrious hands. By late in the eighteenth century, however, the perceived danger was overpopulation, as the Revd Joseph Townsend argued in his *A Dissertation on the Poor Laws* (1786), a work which anticipates Malthus.[91] Well-meaning attempts at social improvement must founder, the Anglican rationalist explained, because of man's inordinate procreative drives. Interventions to relieve poverty invariably made bad worse: 'It seems to be a law of nature, that the poor should be to a certain degree improvident, that there may always be some to fulfil the most servile, the most sordid, and the most ignoble offices in the community.' The only recourse was to 'leave one appetite to regulate another' – and stomach the consequences.[92]

Townsend thus endorsed the conviction of late Enlightenment political economists that Nature, or the market, must determine success and failure, wealth and poverty. Such were matters not for state regulation but for individual responsibility.[93] Similar views were fleshed out in Thomas Robert Malthus's *An Essay on the Principle of Populations* (1798).[94] In an age deferring to scientific facts and figures, his forte lay in iron laws of Nature numerically expressed.[95] Food supplies crept up arithmetically: 2, 4, 6, etc.; human population leapt geometrically: 2, 4, 16, and so forth. The implication of this simple arithmetic was, as Mr Micawber would have spotted, misery, that is, the positive checks of famine, war and pestilence – unless, as later editions of the *Essay* stressed, the poor pre-empted Nature by employing the salutary preventive check of moral restraint: abstinence and delayed marriage would mitigate misery.

The Malthusian trap was a smart card to play. No one, the clergyman claimed, could be a truer friend of humanity, none more liberal or eager for improvement; it was hardly his fault if Nature's niggardliness frustrated these goals, and there was not room for all at 'Nature's mighty feast'.[96] There was no arguing with numbers, asserted the enlightened pessimist whom Thomas Love Peacock would label 'Mr Fax'.[97]

One certain way to keep people off the parish, and a putative long-term means therefore of keeping down the numbers of the poor, was to abolish relief entirely. This modest proposal, advocated by Townsend and mulled over by Malthus, held that relief, far from alleviating poverty, stoked it, because it took away motives for prudence. Remove the safety net and people *would* provide for themselves. 'Hunger will tame the fiercest animals,' asserted the realist Townsend: 'it will teach decency and civility, obedience and subjection.' This audacious stroke, however – let natural sanctions apply and all will find its own level – was never tried. Flattering themselves on their humanity, Georgian statesmen shrank from it; anyway, relief was a useful bait: the hand that fed would not be bitten, and the Poor Laws served major social regulatory functions.[98]

Enlightened attitudes towards the masses were profoundly ambiguous, though in general the poor were regarded as more of a nuisance than a threat – despite disturbances and riots, the élite did not seriously believe the third estate was going to rise in arms. However, as will be seen, that fear flared with good reason in the 1790s.[99] Humanitarianism thus continued to parade itself, but when Blake asked

> Is this a holy thing to see
> In a rich and fruitful land
> Babes reduc'd to misery
> Fed with a cold and usurous hand?[100]

no one answered his charge.

The drive to reform popular culture through implanting bourgeois rationality doubtless reveals the limits of élite sympathies and, in a sense, validates 'cultural imperialism' accusations.[101] But to see trumpeted Enlightenment programmes as nothing other than attempts at social control is rather trite. What is historically distinctive is that the Moderns approached and tackled the people problem and problem people through models of improvement. Just as there was a new optimism that children were educable and mental illness curable, so the rogue too might be made honest and the harlot turned into a good housekeeper.[102]

The wider politics of this *Kulturkampf* have been hotly contested. Some historians, notably Robert Muchembled in his analysis of 'acculturation' in France, have argued that Church and State systematically set about curbing popular culture, so as to strengthen central authority. His views have been criticized, however, for exaggerating both the conspiratorial nature of élite cultural cleansing and its efficacy.[103] From a somewhat different tack, others have stressed how the new shibboleth of rationality served the élite more through cultural hegemony: science undermined the magical basis of popular culture, rooted in the soil, while the old 'moral economy' was assailed by a new individualistic, competitive political economy, supposedly grounded on the laws of Nature.[104] In these 'coercive' and 'hegemonic' readings alike, popular culture is portrayed as mastered from above through policing or propaganda. In England, however, it makes sense to stress seduction no less than suppression. Modernizing outlooks triumphed less through imposition than infiltration, *via* supply and demand mechanisms exploiting opportunities in the commercial exchange of print capitalism. Better communications and the spread of newspapers, magazines and instructional books made country folk *au fait* with metropolitan culture and attuned them to its fashions.[105] The hidden persuaders of the market were another plank in the enlightened platform.

17

THE PURSUIT OF WEALTH

[T]he desire of bettering our condition, a desire which . . . comes
with us from the womb, and never leaves us till we go into the
grave.

ADAM SMITH[1]

Britain prospered under the House of Hanover, a consumer society emerged, and enlightened discourse set about fostering
and rationalizing, while also questioning, such controversial developments. Among the earliest and most prolific of the economic boosters
was Daniel Defoe. A Dissenter educated at the Newington Green
Academy – one noted for its 'laboratory' including an 'air pump' –
Defoe was a classic transitional figure, straddling the old world of
distrustful Puritan asceticism and the new one of reason, desire and
abundance.[2] Learned in demonology and the supernatural – witness
his *Political History of the Devil* and *System of Magick* (both published in
1726) – he was responsible for the century's most celebrated ghost
story, *True Relation of the Apparition of One Mrs Veal* (1706) as well as a
History of Apparitions (1727).[3] Yet he tended to have modern political
jobbery in mind when he spoke of the Devil, and he also has the ring
of the true modern: man 'is a *Charte Blanche*', he wrote in Lockean
idiom, 'and the soul is plac'd in him like a piece of clean paper, upon
which the precepts of life are to be written by his instructors'.[4] Works
like *Tour thro' the Whole Island of Great Britain* (1724–7) puffed the
nation's enterprise, commerce and industry.

A perennial moralizer, fretful about waste, greed, vanity and pride,
Defoe dignified wealth accumulation with middle-class values. Trade
was 'certainly the most Noble, most Instructive, and Improving of

any way of Life', he declared, since it encouraged personal prudence and was responsible for 'enlivening the whole Frame' of society.[5] Economic dealings were amenable to scientific inquiry and rational calculation: 'Nothing obeys the Course of Nature more exactly than Trade, Causes and Consequences follow as directly as Day and Night.'[6] For this happy fact, the Lord was to be praised, and Defoe hymned 'the Harmony of the Creation, and the Beauty and Concern of Providence, in preparing the World for Trade'.[7]

In mainstream mercantilist fashion, Defoe believed that the great hope for Britain's future lay in the expansion of foreign commerce, particularly with the colonies, whose potential had barely as yet been exploited. Trade would not just make Britain rich, it would do God's work, 'civilizing the Nations where we and other Europeans are already settled; bringing the naked Savages to Clothe, and instructing barbarous Nations how to live'.[8]

Modern commercial society was endlessly talked up in the early Enlightenment: 'Trade is the Principal . . . Requisite to aggrandize a Nation,' claimed de Mandeville;[9] the *Spectator* waxed lyrical about its benefits;[10] while Henry Fielding marvelled at how commerce had 'indeed given a new Face to the whole Nation . . . and hath almost totally changed the Manners, Customs and Habits of the People'.[11] For almost the first (and last) time, the trading classes got a good press. Merchants, beamed Addison, 'knit Mankind together in a mutual Intercourse of good Offices, distribute the Gifts of Nature, find Work for the Poor, add Wealth to the Rich, and Magnificence to the Great'.[12] But if this market society was to flourish, it evidently needed credible analyses of and apologetics for economic activity.

In endorsing the market, modern opinion brought to a head a remarkable series of transformations in attitudes towards work and wealth. Each in its own way, Greek philosophy and Christian theology had condemned the love of lucre. The churches had deemed gold vulgar, greed evil, profit without labour usurious. Prices and wage rates had been widely regulated, out of a godly distrust of excess and in the belief that there truly existed a just price, inscribed within a divinely ordained system of distributive justice intelligible to scholastics and magistrates. Since profiteering from necessities was particularly unethical, it had been made an object of legislation – above all, the grain trade was regulated so that none should starve, or riot.[13] These beliefs were complemented in the popular mind by the ancient piety that, everyone being the son of Adam, all were entitled to some access to God's soil, at least in the form of common land and grazing rights, an expression of what E. P. Thompson has called 'customs in common'.[14]

The Christian duty to conduct personal economic dealings in an orderly manner had been mirrored in the commonwealth at large. 'Mercantilism' was the economic outlook which dominated the Stuart century and beyond, aptly reaching its apogee in the writings of Sir James Steuart, before being shot down by Adam Smith's *An Inquiry into the Nature and Causes of the Wealth of Nations* (1776).[15] Mercantilism (called by Smith 'the modern system') took good housekeeping as its model, projecting individual prudence on to the nation. Advocates like Sir Thomas Mun, a director of the East India Company and author of *England's Treasure by Forraign Trade* (1664), measured national economic well-being principally in terms of a favourable balance of trade generated by export surpluses. Associating wealth with money or gold and silver, mercantilism's advocates approved the hoarding of reserves. Everything conducive to wealth or bullion accumulation and a favourable trade balance was the proper object of government regulation, notably the promotion of exports, the limitation of imports and the management of key monopolies.

Enlightened thinking was to mount a sustained attack on such policies for being unscientific and hence futile. Hume's essay 'Of the Balance of Trade' (1787), addressed to those who have 'a strong jealousy with regard to the balance of trade, and a fear, that all their gold and silver may be leaving them', argued that a nation never need be apprehensive of losing its money if it preserved its people and its industry, because there existed an automatic economic mechanism which 'must for ever, in all neighbouring countries, preserve money nearly all proportionable to the art and industry of each nation'.[16] The doctrines of mercantilism were thus short-sighted: how they had become established was then explained by Adam Smith.

Overseas expansion, above all the discovery of the New World, according to Smith, had transformed the commercial regions of Europe into 'the manufacturers for the numerous and thriving culti- vators of America, and the carriers, and in some respects the manu- facturers too, for almost all the different nations of Asia, Africa, and America'. These profitable distribution circuits bred the illusion that wealth creation was essentially a matter of controlling currency and trade – in other words, traffic management. The true source of wealth had thereby been masked. 'It cannot be very difficult,' Smith remarked, with his usual deadpan wit, 'to determine who have been the contrivers of this whole mercantile system; not the consumers, we may believe, whose interest has been entirely neglected.'[17] In place of regulation, labour and consumption – that is, at bottom, desire – were to be set at the heart of the new thinking.

Mercantilism's faith in interference, critics increasingly argued, was superficial, opportunistic and often sinister. Failing to fathom the systemic mechanisms of wealth, money, trade and exchange, regulation had made bad worse, especially when that 'insidious and crafty animal, vulgarly called a statesman or politician' was pulling the strings. What was instead needed was a well-informed grasp of the macro-economics of cash transfers, the relations between wealth and bullion, money and commodities, the short and the long term. Economic policy must be grounded in empirical realities not rulers' wish lists, and certainly not the machinations of monopolists.[18]

A profound revaluation was simultaneously under way in the understanding of economic activity itself. The old 'moral economy' was coming under fire from a new 'political economy'[19] which laid claim to a superior rationale, a scientific grasp of wealth creation and the satisfaction of wants – a purported analysis of actualities rather than aspirations, what really happened and not what the likes of Clarendon or Colbert decreed. Flashpoints in these debates included the deregulation of grain markets and the enclosure question – total privatization of property replacing usufruct.[20]

Distancing themselves from pious precepts, privileges and practice, enlightened analysts insisted that, like it or not, economic activity was inexorably governed by fundamental laws of its own. Ideals such as the moral economy, the just price, the proper reward for labour and so forth might all be very admirable, but they were fatally flawed. They did not, for one thing, reflect human nature. Man was, if not nakedly rapacious *à la* Hobbes, at least an accumulative creature – and therein lay the motivation for economic activity, rooted as it was in the constant human desire for self-improvement. Ignoring or expecting to override such omnipresent motives would end in failure.[21]

The moral economy was thus self-defeating, whereas the new political economy prided itself upon being grounded on a proper grasp of ends and means, individual and system, self and social – natural science, in particular Newtonian physics, often being invoked to prove how economic forces 'gravitated' to an equilibrium. 'The Circulation of Commerce,' explained Josiah Tucker, 'may be conceived to proceed from the Impulse of two distinct Principles of Action in Society, analogous to the Centrifugal and centripetal Powers in the Planetary System.'[22] Smith drew on precisely the same model: prices were 'continually gravitating, if one may say so, towards the natural price'.[23]

In the nature of things, economic activity, like water, would thus find its own level, and so regulation was futile, indeed utterly counter-productive. It was a view given algebraic expression in the crucial 1690s by Charles Davenant, who explained how the market price of corn would prevail, regardless of legislative interferences, however well-intentioned:

because if *B* will not give it, the same may be had from *C* & *D* or if from neither of them, it will yield such a price in foreigne Countries; and from hence arises what wee commonly call Intrinsick value . . . Each Commodity will find its Price . . . The supream power can do many things, but it cannot alter the Laws of Nature, of which the most originall is, That every man should preserve himself.[24]

'Trade is in its Nature free, finds its own Channel, and best directeth its own Course,' Davenant dogmatized in impeccably liberal hydrostatic tones: 'Wisdom is most commonly in the Wrong, when it pretends to direct Nature.'[25] Since profit-seeking was only human nature, it was best to leave trade free and let the economic players get on with it. 'The main spur to Trade, or rather to Industry and Ingenuity,' opined his contemporary Dudley North, 'is the exorbitant Appetites of Men, which they will take pains to gratifie, and so be disposed to work, when nothing else will incline them to it; for did Men content themselves with bare Necessaries, we should have a poor World.'[26] Here, as so often, enlightened thinking appealed to Nature against the mildewed wisdom of cloistered scholars and pontificating divines.

Pioneering amongst the liberal theorists of this school was, predictably, Locke. Not only property but exchange and money too were, in his scheme, pre-established in the state of Nature, subject to the laws of Nature and human rationality and industry. Value was created by labour. Hence economic regulation, beyond the legal protection of property, formed no day to day part of the State's remit.[27]

The new political economy thus repudiated religio-moral or statesmanly policing of wealth in favour of a 'scientific' endorsement of 'natural' economic forces. Christian commandments against greed were sidelined, and the pursuit of gain secularized, privatized and valorized. Dr Johnson – a moral rigorist, yet also a hard-nosed realist – was confident that 'there are few ways in which a man can be more innocently employed than in getting money',[28] and when Adam Smith's mentor, Francis Hutcheson, proposed his distinction between the violent and the tranquil passions, he too set 'the calm desire of wealth' among the latter.[29]

It was Adam Smith who systematized the new political economy, grounding it in a science of human appetite, specifically in 'the desire of bettering our condition'.[30] Given the ceaseless urge to 'self-improvement', 'every man', it followed, 'lives by exchanging . . . and the society itself grows to be what is properly a commercial society'.[31] Selfishness, in short, made the world go round: 'It is not from the benevolence of the butcher, the brewer, or the baker, that we expect our dinner, but from their regard to their own interest.'[32] Smith's formula – let the market-place decide – expresses the enlightened inclination to trust in Nature and its resultant play of wants and needs. In so doing, he was forced to confront the old civic humanist prescriptions. Could *enrichissez-vous* prove compatible with socio-political stability? Would not the pursuit of affluence compromise virtue, and 'luxury', as neo-Harringtonians feared, subvert liberty, set class against class and corrupt the commonwealth?

Like Hume, Smith was no narrow 'economist', he was engaged with the study of man at large, notably the philosophy of scientific inquiry, aesthetics, language, ethics and social laws. Drawing attention to the 'great scramble' of commercial society,[33] he had no illusions about 'the bad effects of a political economy, in some degree both partial and oppressive', not least in creating alienation amongst the workforce.[34] *An Inquiry into the Nature and Causes of the Wealth of Nations* must thus be assessed in terms of its wider contribution to enlightened discussions about freedom, justice, subject–state relations and the quality of life in commercial society.

In his early student lectures at Glasgow, Smith proposed 'opulence and freedom' as 'the two greatest blessings men can possess'.[35] That was a coupling perhaps designed to shock. Two contrasting concepts of liberty had been in circulation in Antiquity.[36] In the Stoic view, as expounded, for instance, by Seneca and Epictetus, freedom was a state of tranquillity in which the cravings of the flesh were curbed by the rational will. There was also the 'civic' view, proposed by Cicero and Livy, for whom liberty lay in political activity aimed at realizing the common good. Rejecting both the political passivity of the former and the 'direct action' of the latter, Smith held that the key to enlightened desiderata was commerce, where every man 'becomes

in some measure a merchant'.[37] Classical thinkers would have condemned such a society as rather inglorious, but for Smith it chimed
with that 'general disposition to truck, barter and exchange'[38] which
achieved its full expression only in commercial society, indeed in a
nation of shopkeepers.

Restlessness, stated Smith, was the spur to opulence, 'an augmentation of fortune' being the means by which 'the greater part of men
propose and wish to better their condition'.[39] Commercial society
thus squared with human nature. What was truly 'unnatural', it
followed, was the Stoic ideal of 'tranquillity', teaching as it did a
perfection 'beyond the reach of human nature'.[40] Whereas Stoicism
disparaged economic life, Smith construed 'selfishness' as everyone's
laudable desire to get on.[41] Downplaying the commonwealth tradition, moreover, he held, like Hume, that the proper stage for
human energies was not the public or political arena, neither honour
nor glory, but private, self-regarding pursuits. For Graeco-Roman
thinkers, time spent meeting household needs was beneath the dignity
of the true male citizen – indeed, fit only for inferiors, peasants,
artisans, women and slaves; for Smith, by contrast, it was the natural
business of humanity at large. Indeed, it was a public benefit, for
economic exchange forged supportive social networks: in a 'civilized
and thriving country', even the 'very meanest person' could not be
provided with even the shirt on his back without the 'joint labour
of a great multitude of workmen'.[42] From such interdependency
commercial society's unique strength was derived.

For Smith, dependency was of course corrupting – a view impeccably classical and central to the civic humanist equation of freedom
with independence.[43] According to the neo-Harringtonians, however, the chief source of corruption and threat to independence lay
in the growth of commerce, paper money, the credit nexus and the
public debt (see chapter 8). Smith rejected this thinking. While never
denying that dependency spelt corruption, he counter-insisted that
'commerce is one great preventive' of its occurrence. Economic
activity was thus not pathological but prophylactic, protecting a
sound constitution. For the civic humanists, history had been a

descent into decadence; for Smith, on the contrary, it was more a pageant of progress.

In Smith's variant on the 'four stages' theory, the 'lowest and rudest state of society' was the age of hunters.[44] In that mode of production, 'there is scarce any property', but that absence also ruled out dependency.[45] By contrast, the second age – that of shepherds – brought growing inequality and with it subordination.[46] Thanks to 'the superiority of his fortune', the Tartar chieftain supported a thousand retainers for whom he was 'necessarily both their general and their judge'.[47] Much the same still held for the third age, that of farmers. Just as the nomad warlord was the head shepherd, so in the third age power lay with the greatest landowners.[48]

The fourth, or commercial, age marked a watershed: at long last the natural propensity to 'truck, barter and exchange' was given free rein to establish its beneficial networks of interdependency. Countering Rousseau, who portrayed trade as breeding corruption, Smith thought commercial society brought a wholly new and superior form of freedom, that of liberty under the law, the true hallmark of civilization. Probing the secret of this conjunction of opulence and freedom, luxury and civilization – one, he noted, highlighted earlier by Hume[49] – Smith directed his gaze on the collapse of the feudal lords.

A great feudal landholder would use his wealth rather like the nomad chief, maintaining hordes of retainers and dependants: what other outlet was there to lavish his surplus upon?[50] As opportunities for consumption arose, however, they were naturally seized – 'consumption' was, after all, for Smith 'the sole end and purpose of all production'.[51] What had permitted this break-through into commodity consumption was 'the silent and insensible operation of foreign commerce', whose effects were to prove dramatic indeed: 'for a pair of diamond buckles perhaps, or for something as frivolous and useless,' he explained,

the feudal lords exchanged the maintenance, or what is the same thing, the price of the maintenance of a thousand men for a year, and with it the whole weight and authority which it could give them . . . and thus for the gratification of the most childish, the meanest and the most sordid of all vanities, they gradually bartered their whole power and authority.[52]

The intrusion of such 'trinkets or baubles'[53] – in other words, 'domestic luxury'[54] – into the feudal sphere in the long run emancipated moneyed, commercial society from the thrall of personal dependency. Once tenants attained independence, proprietors were 'no longer capable of interrupting the regular execution of justice'. The law and order typical of a post-feudal society in which every man was an autonomous economic agent became the guarantor of modern liberty.[55]

Freed from dependence on a particular lord and master, individuals in a commercial society came to enjoy an independence unique to the impersonal market and to its contractual social system. This social 'revolution of the greatest importance to the publick happiness' could not be put down to deliberate action, for neither landholders nor merchants had any 'knowledge or foresight of that great revolution' and neither had 'the least intention to serve the publick'.[56] Civic humanist faith in the primacy of political and personal *virtù* notwithstanding, the general good was not brought about by conscious design, by the will of some great man or senate.

The liberty characteristic of commercial society rested in part on the wealth which cost-efficiencies brought. Success came from scale: bigger markets permitted specialization, which in turn spelt productivity. Hence, in Smith's immortal pin manufacture example, ten workers could make 48,000 pins a day thanks to the division of labour, whereas each on his own could not have turned out a score. Market society thereby bred a 'universal opulence which extends itself to the lowest ranks of the people'.[57] By contrast, independence Rousseau-style condemned the multitude to being 'miserably poor', with, in Smith's view, no compensations at all. Impoverished societies were callous: frequently, he noted, they resorted to 'destroying, and sometimes abandoning their infants, their old people, and those afflicted with lingering diseases'. Opulence, by contrast, was a 'blessing'; only in a developed market society was material plenty enjoyed: the 'common day labourer in Britain has more luxury in his way of living than an Indian sovereign', while his abode 'exceeds that of many an African king, the absolute master of the lives and liberties of 10,000 naked savages'. A peasant in a 'civilized and thriving' nation was thus better off than a savage prince.[58]

For all its gross inequalities,[59] commercial society also enshrined the second great human blessing: liberty. Free of feudal ties, individuals were, for example, entitled to change jobs at will – Smith denounced the 'violent' Asian practice of forcing a son to follow in his father's trade.[60] Together with secure inheritance rights, occupational choice made individuals free 'in our present sense of the word'[61] in the system of natural liberty where every man 'is left perfectly free to pursue his own interest his own way'.[62]

Personal liberty carried political implications. It was the 'highest impertinence and presumption' of governments 'to watch over the economy of private people' by such measures as sumptuary laws;[63] economic well-being derived not from royal decree but from the confidence conferred by an impersonal law-governed system of public liberty. The superiority of modern constitutional liberty over Classical republicanism lay in the fact that liberty under the law was liberty for all, whereas – compare Hume's judgement on Sparta – political liberty in Antiquity had been enjoyed only by a few and sustained by a slave system as unproductive as it was unpalatable.[64] Unlike Mandeville, Smith thought wealth was actually increased by the 'liberal reward of labour', for that was an incentive to industriousness.[65] Where wages were high, workmen were more 'active, diligent and expeditious' – in England more than Scotland, in urban rather than rural areas.[66] Since workmen constituted the bulk of the populace, whatever improved their lot made for a flourishing society.[67]

For Smith, modern liberty was tempered by justice.[68] While critical of Hume for reducing justice to questions of utility, he closely followed his old crony. In *The Theory of Moral Sentiments* (1759) Smith maintained what made society work was not generosity (merchants got by without it)[69] but justice – 'the main pillar that upholds the whole edifice'.[70] That virtue was negative in the sense that its prime requirement lay in not injuring others: 'we may often fulfil all the rules of justice by sitting still and doing nothing'.[71] In this respect, Smith's thinking contradicted both Aristotle and Rousseau, since he believed it possible to fulfil public duties passively, simply by obeying the law. In an orderly commercial society, support for the *status quo* was the 'best expedient' of a 'good citizen'.[72] Freedom and the just life were not exclusive to those well born and wealthy enough to pursue an active 'republican' political existence.

It was here that Smith's break with civic humanism most clearly surfaced, for he did not share Adam Ferguson's qualms that legalism would sap society's lifeblood. In his *An Essay on the History of Civil Society* (1767), Ferguson had argued that liberty was at risk when national felicity was measured by the 'mere tranquillity which may attend an equitable administration'[73] – that was 'more akin to despotism than we are apt to imagine'.[74] A government system requiring no personal involvement, he feared, would 'lay the political spirit to rest'. Hence, while modern society doubtless embodied important liberties, he was uneasy that its members would grow 'unworthy of the freedom they possess'.[75] To endure, civil liberty required the 'individual to act in his station for himself and the public'.[76] While conceding that the Spartan model was anachronistic, true 'rights' were sustainable only by individual political action.[77]

Smith pooh-poohed such rhetorical appeals to the civic spirit. The public good did not depend upon a 'general will', it would best be promoted through the interplay of particular wills. This, of course, was the message of the 'Invisible Hand' – each 'intends only his own gain' but in so doing 'frequently promotes that of the society more effectually than when he really intends to promote it'.[78] Indeed, he tartly asided, 'I have never known much good done by those who affected to trade for the publick good.'[79] Politicians were, in fact, positive menaces to the liberty enshrined in the rule of law, for all too often they pursued agendas affecting citizens in ways 'evidently contrary to the justice and equality of treatment which the sovereign owes to the different orders of his subjects'.[80] Government should limit itself to defence, the maintenance of justice through 'exact administration', and 'certain publick works' like education.[81] The complexity and interdependence of commercial society rendered civic humanist heroics obsolete.

To view Smith's 'Invisible Hand' in purely economic terms would thus be myopic and shallow. What is significant in both Hume and Smith is the de-politicization of the hallowed ideal of the 'public good'. For them individual happiness and material well-being had moved centre stage, and identification of the 'good' as some towering political or moral virtue lost its purchase. Social interdependence upstaged any conception of society predicated on acts of individual virtue.

In the light of this dissonance between individual will and social outcomes, Smith held that the consequences of luxury were bene-ficial, even if the cause was footling – all those 'sordid and childish' diamond buckles![82] Though he might occasionally moralize as to how the 'real happiness of human life' was to be found in the beggar's 'peace of mind', by contrast to the specious 'pleasures of wealth and greatness' conjured up by the imagination, such Stoicism hardly dominated his thinking.[83] He never belittled, however, the role of the imagination in firing economic activity.[84] Imagination, as cast from Hobbes onwards, might be 'but a Fiction of the mind'[85] but it was that which made it such a powerful stimulus. It was precisely because 'the pleasures of wealth and greatness . . . strike the imagination as something grand and beautiful and noble' that men would commit themselves to the toil responsible for all 'the sciences and arts which ennoble and embellish human life'.[86] How could this be a matter for regret? Imagination had transformed 'rude forests' into 'agreeable and fertile plains';[87] goods were produced and consumed because they met not fixed needs but rather 'desires'.[88] 'The whole industry of human life,' Smith concluded, 'is employed not in procuring the supply of our three humble necessities, food, cloaths, and lodging, but in procuring the conveniences of it according to the nicety and delicacy of our taste.'[89] Stoics and others bent upon 'real' satisfactions alone were in truth condemning mankind to misery.[90]

This rejection of traditional civic humanism and its Rousseauvian variant in favour of a 'natural system of liberty' squared with Smith's own proclivity to trust the individual, as it also did with Benthamite utilitarianism. Smith and Bentham together provided the intellectual underpinnings for the emergent body of *laissez-faire* political economy.[91] Such views bred optimism, and, as so often, enlightenment proved patriotic.

The Enlightenment piloted a transition from *homo civilis* to *homo economicus*, which involved the rationalization of selfishness and self-interest as enlightened ideology, the privatization of virtue and the de-moralization of luxury, pride, selfishness and avarice. Corporatism yielded to individualism. 'To provide for us in our necessities,' commented Edmund Burke, elsewhere the defender of paternalism, 'is not in the power of Government'; regulation 'against free trade in provisions' was 'senseless, barbarous and, in fact, wicked'. The great danger, he concluded, 'is in Governments intermeddling too much'.[92] That is what enabled Hazlitt to aside that 'the science of Political Economy means the divine right of landlords'.[93] With *laissez-faire* in the saddle, economic activity, divorced from traditional values, assumed a morality of its own – the rectitude of making your own way in the world as *homo faber*, an independent rational actor beholden to none.

Capitalist consumer society was thus legitimized in terms of Nature, desire and individual freedom. Superseding traditional moral disapproval, the new ideology taught how self-enrichment could be personally enhancing and socially cohesive. Political economy fused burgeoning capitalism and social order into a single enlightened discourse. Individualism, however, was not always so readily accommodated.

18

REFORM

Correspondent to *discovery* and *improvement* in the natural world, is *reformation* in the moral.

JEREMY BENTHAM[1]

The Enlightenment which discovered the liberties, also invented the disciplines.

MICHEL FOUCAULT[2]

[A]ll knowledge will be subdivided and extended; and *knowledge*, as Lord Bacon observes, being *power*, the human powers will, in fact, be increased; nature, including both its materials, and its laws, will be more at our command; men will make their situation in this world abundantly more easy and comfortable; they will probably prolong their existence in it, and will grow daily more happy, each in himself, and more able (and, I believe, more disposed) to communicate happiness to others. Thus, *whatever was the beginning of this world, the end will be glorious and paradisiacal, beyond what our imaginations can now conceive.*

JOSEPH PRIESTLEY[3]

T he late Enlightenment continued to chant the old war-cries of law, liberty, free thought, toleration, but increasingly it was elements of the post-1688 order which formed their target. Initially the enlightened vanguard had been made up of landed gentlemen protesting against popes and priests, kings and courtiers; scions of the senatorial ranks, they comprised a highly superior elite, landed, wealthy and cultivated.[4] As time went on, however, and print capitalism did its work, protest was taken up by those hailing from the middling ranks and below, and by further segments of the traditionally excluded such as women and minority groups such as Dissenters,[5] hitting home against all those 'haves' bedded down in the *status quo*, that is, the 'moderate Enlightenment' Whig state as sanctified by the constitution, the Glorious Revolution, Rule Britannia and so forth. Thus, having emphasized that liberal intellectuals flourished 'in the Whig and Erastian political order that dominated eighteenth-century England', Margaret Jacob rightly adds that 'late in the century and only within select circles, the English promoters of scientific improvement turned their zeal against the established social and political order'.[6] The Mancunian Dissenting physician John Aikin hit the nail on the head: 'your natural connections,' he cautioned his son in a public letter of 1790, 'are not with kings and nobles. You belong to the most virtuous, the most enlightened, the most independent part of the community, the middle class.'[7] Aikin's sister, the children's writer Anna Barbauld, equally congratulated her co-religionists for belonging to 'that middle rank of life where industry and virtue most abound': 'we have no favours to blind us, no golden padlock to our tongues';[8] while Mary Wollstonecraft, pleased to have been spared the 'pestiferous purple', likewise held that 'the middle rank contains most virtue and abilities' – there it was that 'talents thrive best'.[9]

'I bless God,' Joseph Priestley assured his Birmingham buddies, 'that I was born a Dissenter, not manacled by the chains of so debasing a system as that of the Church of England, and that I was not educated at Oxford or Cambridge.'[10] As is evident, there was a new pride in being at odds with 'the world' – with all those mighty men, from magistrates and moneybags up to the House of Lords: 'What is a peer of the realm,' demanded Holcroft, 'but man educated in vice, nurtured in prejudice from his earliest childhood, and daily breathing the same infectious air he first respired!'[11] Meanwhile, these rising voices of righteous anger took it upon themselves to speak for life's victims – they might even shed a tear, like Burns, for a wee timorous mouse. Their creed has thus been paraphrased: 'Society –

cultivated society – is always wrong. The individual who has courage to act against it is always right.'[12] Post-1688 Britain had been supported by progressives as just and free, but the spirit of criticism now charged new generations of activists with a fresh rectitude and more radical energies.

Above all, the late Enlightenment mounted an attack on 'Old Corruption', that nexus of aristocratic capitalism, landed and commercial power, title and wealth, backed by the monster oligarchic state which William Cobbett was soon to dub 'the Thing'.[13] Forget official ideology: the constitution was not in truth, critics now claimed, the palladium of freedom. Rather, argued those aiming to apply the knife to the tumours of the State, the apparatus of government and the social hierarchy remained repressive, if often in covert ways. 'The public character of England . . . was gone,' bemoaned the radical anarchist William Godwin, reprising earlier 'civic humanist' rhetoric: 'I perceived that we were grown a commercial and arithmetical nation . . . Contractors, directors, and upstarts, – men fattened on the vitals of their fellow-citizens – have taken the place which was once filled by the Wentworths, the Seldens, and the Pyms.'[14] That such a remark might just as easily have been uttered by the Burke who excoriated 'calculators' shows how late Enlightenment radicals could be no less hostile to commercialism than any paternalist reactionary: if they had little else in common, Burke, Wilberforce and Godwin all detested high-life vice.[15]

In a swelling chorus, those audibly distancing themselves from the Establishment power machine commended independence. In the preface to his *Dictionary*, the Midlander and self-made man Samuel Johnson boasted of completing his *magnum opus* 'without any patronage of the great', dismissing the idea of an academy for English because he could 'never wish to see dependence multiplied'.[16] David Hume's 'Disdain of all Dependence' rings out from his very first surviving letter (to Michael Ramsey, on 4 July 1727): a man who was 'entirely master of his own disposition' was fortunate, indeed.[17] For Adam Smith, too, the desideratum was 'the highest degree of self-command': 'nothing,' he taught his students, 'tends so much to corrupt and enervate and debase the mind as dependency';[18] while his protégé John Millar also prized 'the independence of the inquiring mind'.[19] 'Oh misery of Dependence!' cries a character in Fanny Burney's play *The Witlings* (1779).[20] Rebutting the French Revolution, the erstwhile radical Archdeacon Paley might laud 'the divine spirit of dependence and subordination',[21] but that was a red rag to an enlightened bull: 'The first lesson of enlightened reason', proclaims a character in Mary Hays's radical feminist novel *The Memoirs of Emma Courtney* (1796), 'the principle by which alone man can become what man is capable of being, is independence'.[22]

In the last third of the eighteenth century criticism crescendo'd against the political oppressiveness, social corruption and moral licentiousness of blue blood. In a secularization of the Protestant right of private judgement and priesthood of all believers, middle-class pundits applauded honesty and sincerity.[23] A new moral earnestness urged strict and strenuous self-examination. For some, truth now lay within the breast, a sincere heart being the steadfast sentinel against temptation;[24] for others, it was a clear head and self-control which must serve as the guardians of uprightness. Whichever, the David of integrity would fell the Goliath of pride.

Novels provided prime vehicles for the critique of corruption. With plots centring on family conflict and generational feuds, the angry sentimental fictions of the 1780s and 1790s scorned aristocratic privilege and presumption, melodramatized the heartrending oppression of labourers, servants, daughters and tenants, and, especially in women's writings, assailed the double standard. Virtue was a child of the cottage, while vice festered at Court. Elizabeth Inchbald's *Nature and Art* (1796) told a tale of two cousins: one, spoilt by rich parents, went to the dogs, while the other was providentially cast away upon a tropical island and reared by noble savages. With her motifs of the honest native as a foil to the corrupt grandee, and the homespun country girl seduced by the vicious squire, Inchbald pointed up a popular moral: integrity was the supreme virtue, degeneracy the most heinous vice.[25] Like many, she sentimentalized cosy bourgeois domesticity.

Thomas Holcroft, author of *The Adventures of Hugh Trevor* (1794) and many other biting tales, was another *engagé* novelist in this didactic mould. A shoemaker's son radicalized by successive experiences as a stable boy, shoemaker, stocking-weaver, stroller, teacher, playwright and translator, he had the common touch, and tirelessly popularized the new philosophy in a deluge of plays, novels, essays, reviews, biographies, histories, travels and translations. His detestation of the cruel and the corrupt was tempered by an enlightened environmentalism: 'men are rendered selfish and corrupt by the baneful influence of the system under which they live . . . They are not in love with baseness, it is forced upon them.'[26]

Remembered by his friend William Hutton as 'barely a Christian', Robert Bage, a Midlands paper manufacturer on the margins of the Lunar Society, produced a string of benignly ironic novels bristling with similar late Enlightenment messages. His stock plot involved a moral trial: the hero and heroine must prove themselves worthy of each other, not, as in romantic narratives, by transcendental passion but by more rational tests of probity, selflessness and social merit.[27] In *Hermsprong: Or Man as He is Not* (1796), a young man of German origin, a supporter of the French Revolution and a reader of Paine, fetches up in a Cornish village and saves the life of the daughter of Lord Gronsdale – a stock Bage villain who is a depraved tyrant in his various incarnations as borough-monger, landlord and father. Falling in love with her, Hermsprong nevertheless feels, inspired as he is by impeccable political correctness, dutybound to lecture her on her shortcomings. She for her part plays the dutiful daughter, and he refuses to marry her while she remains enslaved to custom and prejudice.[28] Tested by heart and head alike, the *status quo* was thus found wanting by the taxing standards of late Enlightenment moralism.

A new political radicalism also emerged, triggered by the 'Wilkes and Liberty' agitation in the 1760s against the abuses of executive power,[29] and taken up by the Society of the Supporters of the Bill of Rights (1769), whose leading figures included the London alderman, John Sawbridge (father of Catharine Macaulay), and the Revd John Horne, later known as Horne Tooke.[30] The society put forward an 11-point programme to be imposed upon parliamentary candidates, including anti-bribery laws, 'full and equal representation of the people in parliament', annual elections, redress of grievances before granting supplies, bans on pensions and places, attention to the Irish problem and restoration to America of the 'essential right of taxation' – demands which became the backbone of the radical agenda.[31]

The Declaration of Independence (1776) and the American war proved crucial to British radicalization, for 'enlightened' England became cast in the new and unaccustomed role of old regime oppressor, while enlightened aspirations were realized in the New Republic. America had long had its allure: 'in the beginning all the World was America,' judged Locke,[32] while George Berkeley declared,

> Westward the course of empire takes its way;
>   The first four acts already past,
> A fifth shall close the drama with the day;
>   Time's noblest offspring is the last.[33]

America came to be identified with the future – the French-born author J. Hector St John de Crèvecoeur tellingly dubbed the American the 'new man'.[34] Richard Price's *Observations on the Nature of Civil Liberty* (1776), which sold a stunning 60,000 copies, supported the colonists' right to self-government and portrayed their country as the new nation whose citizens would truly enjoy the personal and civil freedoms only dreamed of in the old. 'With heart-felt satisfaction,' he proclaimed, 'I see the revolution in favour of universal liberty which has taken place in America; – a revolution which opens a new prospect in human affairs, and begins a new aera in the history of mankind.'[35] For his part, Jeremy Bentham came to admire 'that newly created nation, one of the most enlightened, if not the most enlightened, at this day on the globe';[36] while in Blake's epic poem

America: A Prophecy (1793), Orc, the spirit of revolution, arises from the ocean to proclaim an end to empire: 'The King of England looking westward trembles at the vision.'[37]

Meanwhile, the Society for Promoting Constitutional Information had been founded in 1780 to pump out propaganda for political reform, its activists including Rational Dissenters and such prominent reformers as John Jebb, the ubiquitous Thomas Day and Major John Cartwright. Four years earlier, in his *Take Your Choice*, Cartwright had drafted the radical programme of annual parliaments, universal male suffrage, the ballot, equal representation and payment of members; for half a century, in speeches and pamphlets, he then tirelessly campaigned for reform, helping to found the Friends of the People in 1792 and the Hampden Club in 1812. Growing steadily, by 1782 the SPCI endorsed the Radical programme of parliamentary reform favoured by yet another Radical caucus, the Westminster Association, whose members included Sir William Jones and Horne Tooke, both philologists. The radical Whig the Duke of Richmond graced its dinner in 1782, drinking toasts to 'Magna Carta', 'The Majesty of the People' and 'America in our arms, Despotism at our feet'. Too radical to command widespread support, it faltered, however, after the failure of Pitt's Parliamentary Reform Bill in 1785, but the French Revolution revitalized its efforts to enlighten the rising generation.[38]

The archetypal enlightened radical of this era was James Burgh, a Scot who settled in London in the 1740s and began a long career of reformist idealism.[39] Urging a thorough reformation of 'sentiments and manners', he looked in his early writings to a grand national association of upright aristocrats, proceeding to spend the early 1760s instructing the young George III as to how to cleanse the Augean stables of Westminster and unify the people. The 'moralist in Babylon' became politicized, proposing, in the more populist atmosphere of the 1770s, a 'Grand National Association for Restoring the Constitution'. Written 'in the spirit of a true independent Whig', his *Political Disquisitions* (1774–5) resurrected the canonical commonwealth authors in support of public liberty, targeting the peerage, lamenting national degeneracy and urging constitutional checks on tyranny and corruption. His early critiques of the enervating effects of luxury turned into portents of national disaster: 'Ten millions of people are not to sit still and see a villainous junta overthrow their liberties.'[40]

Burgh's rhetoric derived from the Bible.[41] 'Assert thy supreme dominion over those who impiously pretend to be thy vicegerents upon earth,' he charged the Lord of Hosts: 'Arise . . . Let thy lightnings enlighten the world.'[42] His politics, however, increasingly expressed the values and idiom of the new liberalism. Just as Smith damned monopolies and aristocratic prodigality, and Priestley sought 'free scope to abilities', so Burgh began to demand for all 'an equal chance to rise to honours'. Fairness and equal opportunities became the swelling refrain among such circles. 'All men should start from equal situations and with equal advantages, as horses do on the turf,' declared the Dissenting minister David Williams, an admirer of Priestley and Franklin: 'afterwards everything is to depend on ability and merit.'[43] Godwin likewise looked to a meritocratic race of life: 'let us start fair, render all the advantages and honours of social institutions accessible to every man in proportion to his talents and exertions'.[44] Liberalism was a child of the late Enlightenment.

Political reformers made common cause with those pressing for the enlargement of religious liberties. While the trend among Presbyterian Dissenters was towards Socinianism or Unitarianism,[45] Anglican rationalists expressed growing hostility to the tyranny of the Thirty-nine Articles. Their inspiration was Edmund Law, master of Peterhouse and presiding genius of the liberal turn in Cambridge divinity. His pupil Francis Blackburne, rector of Richmond in Yorkshire, allegedly owed his convictions to a 'worthy old lay gentleman' who told him: 'Young man, let the first book thou readest at Cambridge be "Locke upon Government".'[46] A stalwart liberal in politics and religion alike, Blackburne held in *The Confessional* (1766) that since the Bible, and the Bible alone, was the religion of Protestants, no church had the right to demand subscription beyond an avowal of the Scriptures as the word of God. In any case, the Articles were

theologically suspect, and compulsory subscription bred spiritual
dishonesty.

A campaign was mounted for the abolition of subscription and the
modification of the Articles, headed by Socinian-leaning Anglicans
like Theophilus Lindsey, the vicar of Catterick. A meeting at the
Feathers Tavern in London led to the presentation of a petition to
the House of Commons in 1772, embodying Blackburne's proposal
to replace subscription with a profession of belief in the Scriptures.
On its rejection, Lindsey left the Church, followed by his son-in-law,
John Disney. Shortly afterwards, with the support of the Earl of
Shelburne, the Duke of Grafton and other grandees, Lindsey opened
England's first designated Unitarian church, in Essex Street off the
Strand. Blessed with such superior patrons, Unitarianism became a
force in the land; by 1800 nearly 200 chapels had sprung up.[47]

Amongst Lindsey's allies had been John Jebb, another protégé of
Law at Peterhouse, where he lectured in mathematics and the Greek
Testament. Jebb campaigned for the reform of the Cambridge tripos,
proposing annual examinations. Developing Unitarian leanings, he
too participated in the Feathers Tavern Petition, subsequently
resigning his living and taking up medicine.[48] 'It is now well known',
he asserted,

that a majority of the thinking clergy are disposed to embrace the hypothesis
of Arius or Socinus, with regard to the person of Jesus. And that the opinion
of Athanasius, though sanctified by the acts of uniformity, is now exploded
by almost every reader of the Bible.[49]

Wishful thinking, doubtless, but none the less a sign of the times.

Paralleling these liberal tendencies within Anglicanism, but
altogether weightier in its consequences, was the radicalization of
Nonconformity. Under William and Mary, Dissent had achieved
freedom of worship but not civil equality. Subsequent decades
brought for many Nonconformists a shift from theological soul-
searching to a more rational and political stance; and they flexed
their muscles with a growing sense of historical destiny. 'Your very
existence depends on your changing the reason of your dissent which

used to be an opinion of superior orthodoxy and superior purity of faith and worship,' David Williams apprised fellow Nonconformists in 1777,

for another which is the only rational and justifiable reason of dissent – the inalienable and universal right of private judgement, and the necessity of an unrestrained enquiry and freedom of debate and discussion on all subjects of knowledge, morality, and religion. This may be called *Intellectual Liberty*. This should be the general reason of dissent.[50]

Exercising 'Intellectual Liberty' in those 'shaking times', Rational Dissent gravitated towards Unitarianism, the enlightened mode of Protestantism *par excellence* whose high priest was Joseph Priestley.[51]

A polymath born with a perpetual-motion pen – his works fill twenty-six volumes, and he died, almost inevitably, correcting proofs[52] – Priestley championed freedom of inquiry more than any other as the rationale of a rational Christian life of endless progress. 'Train our youth to the new light which is now almost everywhere bursting out in favour of the civil rights of men,' he called upon the Hackney Academy in 1791, and

let every young mind expand itself, catch the rising gale, and partake of the glorious enthusiasm, the great objects of which are the flourishing state of science, arts, manufactures, and commerce, the extinction of wars, with the calamities incident to mankind for them, the abolishing of all useless distinctions, which were an offspring of a barbarous age.[53]

Largely ignored by most historians of the Enlightenment, Priestley is central to the distinctive arc of British developments.

Born in 1733 the son of a poor Yorkshire cloth-dresser, on his mother's early death Priestley was adopted by a well-to-do aunt, a Presbyterian but no bigot, who kept open house for the local Dissenting ministers, even ones 'obnoxious on account of their heresy . . . if she thought them honest and good men'.[54]

As a lad, Priestley felt the full Calvinist horrors: 'Believing that a new birth, produced by the immediate agency of the Spirit of God, was necessary to salvation,' he was to recall, 'and not being able to satisfy myself that I had experienced anything of the kind, I felt occasionally such distress of mind as it is not in my power to describe.'[55] These brushes with Calvinist 'darkness' drove him to 'a peculiar sense of the value of rational principles of religion'[56] – for, after all, the heretics taking tea at his aunt's showed that 'honest and good men' could legitimately think for themselves.[57]

Destined for the Presbyterian ministry, Priestley was educated at grammar school until he was sixteen, later reading his way into Chaldean, Syriac and Arabic, as well as modern languages, mathematics, physics and philosophy. At nineteen he entered the Daventry Academy, a liberal institution he always cherished. 'While your Universities resemble pools of stagnant water,' he told William Pitt in a public letter in 1787, 'ours [i.e., the Nonconformist academies] are like rivers, which, taking their natural course, fertilize a whole country.'[58] Unlike hidebound Oxbridge, their very methods fostered inquiry, claimed Priestley, who rejoiced in free interchange and became a fierce controversialist. 'I do not recollect,' stated one of his pupils, 'that he ever showed the least displeasure at the strongest objections that were made to what he delivered.'[59]

At Daventry, Priestley hit on David Hartley's *Observations on Man* (1749), which account of the workings of the mind by 'the laws of association' quite won him over. The transparent simplicity of Hartley's philosophy gratified Priestley's no-nonsense Lockean bent: no mystifying 'faculties' or 'innate instincts', only ideas and their causes and effects. Moreover, Hartley implied that education was everything, and the prospects of progress boundless. By pointing to perfectibility through learning, associationism justified faith in both education and progress.[60] Not least, the pious Hartley's rejection of free will and mind–body dualism convinced Priestley he could be a determinist, a materialist and a Christian all at once: 'compared with Dr Hartley, I consider Mr Hume as not even a child'.[61] Hume's conservative politics, in any case, were as distasteful to Priestley as his flippant unbelief.[62] Hartley's earnest morality and faith, by contrast, were after his own heart. Anthony Collins's *Philosophical Inquiry concerning Human Liberty and Necessity* (1714) had already sapped his belief in free will, and Hartley now provided him with an alternative. He proved a lifelong disciple: in 1775 he abridged the *Observations* as *Hartley's Theory of the Human Mind on the Principle of the Association of Ideas* (1775), fifteen years later producing a new edition of Collins's *Philosophical Inquiry*.[63]

In 1755, aged twenty-two, Priestley gained his first congregation, at Needham Market, Suffolk. He was not a success – he stammered, and his Arian theological unorthodoxies galled his flock. Moving to Nantwich in Cheshire, he set up a school, buying scientific instruments, including an 'electrical machine' and an airpump, before becoming in 1761 'Tutor of the languages' to the Nonconformist academy at Warrington, soon to become the most illustrious of the Dissenters' universities. There he gave the world his reflections on criticism, grammar, history and law, his *Chart of Biography* (1765) and *New Chart of History* (1769) proving popular teaching texts.[64] The polymath was never daunted: he was the self-taught lawyer whose *A Few Remarks on Blackstone's Commentaries* (1769) bearded England's most erudite jurist, and the stutterer who published a *Course of Lectures on Oratory and Criticism* (1777).[65] Specialization was arcane and suspect.

On visits to London, Priestley made friends with scientists and philosophers, notably Benjamin Franklin and Richard Price, the Nonconformist divine, actuary and statistician.[66] Contacts with the former led to *The History and Present State of Electricity, with Original Experiments* (1767), the work which put the understanding of electricity on a scientific footing.[67] His electrical inquiries, he proudly reported, were the first to show experimentally that 'the attraction of electricity is subject to the same laws as that of gravitation, and is therefore as the square of the distances'.[68] That work also contained his thoughts on scientific method. While at heart a Baconian fact-collector, the free-thinking controversialist did not dismiss theory, only dogmatism. 'A philosopher who has been long attached to a favourite hypothesis . . . will not, sometimes, be convinced of its falsity by the plainest evidence of fact.'[69]

In 1767 Priestley accepted an invitation to address the people of Mill Hill, Leeds, a congregation which found his religious stance congenial. He had long abandoned both orthodox Trinitarianism and the Atonement.[70] Now the enlightened champion of the plain and simple moved from Arianism to Socinianism, denying not only that Christ was 'of the same substance' as God the Father but that he was divine at all. The Messiah was just 'a man like ourselves', 'a man approved by God', neither unerring nor unblemished – 'as much a creature of God as a loaf of bread'. His bold Socinianism rejected Christ worship as 'idolatrous' – theological levelling indeed! – while Trinitarianism, he railed, was just as bad as transubstantiation.[71] Priestley's *Theological Repository*, set up in 1769, was the first magazine avowedly dedicated to free religious inquiry.[72]

Priestley's later theological writings, notably *An History of the Corruptions of Christianity* (1782) and his *History of Early Opinions Concerning Jesus Christ* (1786), were devoted to proving that Socinianism squared with the Gospels.[73] Yet he was doomed, he lamented, to pleasing none: 'The greater part of my philosophical acquaintance ridicule my attachment to Christianity, and yet the generality of Christians will not allow me to belong to them at all.'[74] Indeed: the unbeliever Gibbon told him to stick to 'those sciences in which real and useful improvements *can* be made',[75] while, for their part, Christians were ill disposed to embrace a materialist and a determinist who rejected Original Sin, the Trinity and the Atonement. He was 'one of the most dangerous enemies of Christianity', judged John Wesley; detesting 'enthusiasm', Priestley retaliated in an anonymous *Appeal to the Professors of Christianity* (1770),[76] while the Methodists paraded their Christian love in a hymn:

> Stretch out thy hands, thou Triune God:
> The Unitarian fiend expel
> And chase his doctrine back to Hell.[77]

Attacks left Priestley quite undaunted, however, as he saw the hand of Providence at work everywhere. 'Even the persecutors,' explained *The Doctrine of Philosophical Necessity Illustrated* (1777), 'are only giving the precedence to the persecuted, and advancing them to a much higher degree of perfection.'[78] The ways of God were thus progressive. On his younger son's early death in 1795, he expressed the belief that he 'had the foundation of something in his character, on which a good superstructure may be raised hereafter'.[79] Even the dead were destined to improve.

Priestley's Leeds years were not wholly given over to the demystification of theology, however. In 1772 he published a history of optics,[80] before plunging into chemistry – with a characteristic utilitarian bent, his first chemical publication taught how to substitute artificial soda water for imported spa waters. Addressing the problem of 'different kinds of air', or the composition of the atmosphere, his *Experiments and Observations on Different Kinds of Air* (1774) augmented knowledge of what he called 'dephlogisticated air' – today's oxygen, although he never approved the name or the Lavoisierian theory behind it.[81] Science won Priestley national fame, and in 1771 Joseph Banks proposed him as 'scientific observer' on Cook's second Pacific expedition. But his theological heterodoxy had grown notorious, and the design was scuppered. The next year, however, the Earl of Shelburne made him 'librarian and literary companion', a post he held until 1780, when he moved to Birmingham.

Priestley's first philosophical publication appeared in 1774: *An Examination of Dr Reid's Inquiry into the Human Mind on the Principles of Commonsense, Dr Beattie's Essay on the Nature and Immutability of Truth, and Dr Oswald's Appeal to Common Sense on Behalf of Religion*. Piously aimed as it was at Hume, the thinking of Reid and his fellow Scottish Common Sense philosophers might have won Priestley's imprimatur.[82] But he was a loyal disciple of Hartley and, *via* Hartley, of Locke's 'way of ideas', over which the Scots had qualms, spying therein the root of all Humean evil. Reid's *Inquiry* was but 'an ingenious piece of sophistry', Priestley judged, and, turning to the Presbyterian minister and philosopher James Oswald, he found it 'unaccountable . . . that such a performance should ever have excited any other sentiments than those of contempt, in any person who had been initiated into the elements of this kind of knowledge by Mr Locke'.[83] In replacing Locke's and Hartley's scientific theories of mind with 'such a number of independent, arbitrary, instinctive principles, that the very enumeration of them is really tiresome', Common Sense philosophy was, he deemed, obscurantist.[84] 'Common sense' was in truth but a euphemism for mystification, a roadblock to further inquiry. All their so-called 'instinctive' truths – belief, for example, in an 'external world' – could be derived from experience by means of a single crystal-clear principle: association.

In his edition of Hartley, Priestley proposed that 'the whole man is made up of some uniform composition, and that the property of perception is the result . . . of such an organical structure as that of the brain'.[85] Such materialism predictably created a furore: 'In all the newspapers,' protested Priestley, 'I was represented as an unbeliever in revelation, and no better than an Atheist.'[86] He was resolved, however, to show that that charge was unwarranted, both religiously and philosophically.

Theologically, conceded his *Disquisitions Relating to Matter and Spirit* (1777), materialism had been deemed at odds with immortality. Man was not, however, 'naturally' immortal at all but only so because God had chosen to resurrect him. That was primarily a resurrection of the body – and of the mind only as a result of its being incorporated. Philosophical anti-materialism was based upon discredited conceptions of matter as inert, impenetrable and solid.[87] Hence there was no incompatibility between matter and mental powers, but there were sound reasons for rejecting the traditional doctrine of two opposed substances, mind and matter, for dualism (which he identified with Popery) could never explain how the twain could possibly interact.

In 1777 again, in his *Doctrine of Philosophical Necessity Illustrated*, Priestley drew heavily on Collins and Hartley to clinch his case against free will.[88] It was theologically erroneous, because it precluded Providence; it was metaphysical moonshine, because it made action unintelligible; and it was ethically objectionable, because it left moral choice arbitrary. In such doctrinal tussles, his old comrade Richard Price proved a worthy antagonist, their correspondence (published as *A Free Discussion of the Doctrines of Materialism and Philosophical Necessity* (1778)) being held up as a model of candour. Price argued that

Christianity preached the free will which alone would ground moral responsibility; Priestley rejected it as arbitrary, irrational and counter-Providential: 'we have no more reason . . . to conclude that a man can move himself, that is, that he can will without motives, than that a stone can move itself': God alone had that power.[89] For Priestley, terms like base or blameworthy should be scrapped: rather it should be said that individuals had acted from motives good or ill and that social happiness would be increased or diminished by this or that action. Adroit social manipulation of 'rewards and punishments' would promote morality and law-abidingness.[90]

Such ethical utilitarianism also watermarked Priestley's political thinking. He cared little for high politics, disdaining the 'language of any party'; what concerned him was freedom. But here his experiences as a Dissenter radicalized him, as he became less inclined to accept that liberty could thrive in the prevailing socio-political soil.

Priestley's early *Essay on the First Principles of Government* (1768) distinguished between two sorts of liberty, civil and political.[91] The former consisted in civil liberty, 'that power over their own actions, which the members of the state reserve to themselves, and which their officers must not infringe'; the latter was 'the right to magistracy' – that is, voting and office-holding.[92] Of the two, it was civil liberty which was fundamental (the two great freedoms upon which he insisted being religion and education). Questions of political leadership, by contrast, were pragmatic – who was least corruptible by power? 'The good and happiness of the members, that is, the majority of the members of any state,' he wrote, 'is the great standard by which everything related to that state must finally be determined' (on reading this, Bentham 'cried out, as it were in an inward ecstasy *Eureka*').[93] Government should no longer intervene in many matters customarily taken for its province, and resistance was sanctioned, if the existing order were destructive of the greatest happiness or of civil liberties. On toleration, Priestley far out-Locked Locke, favouring 'unbounded liberty in matters of religion' – 'full toleration' for Roman Catholics and atheists no less than Dissenters.[94]

Up to the 1760s, while defending minorities, however, Priestley was still fairly content with the constitution; and, if disdaining the established Church as an alliance of 'worldly minded men, for their temporal emolument', he had not urged its disestablishment. Over the years, however, his pamphlets in defence of Dissenters grew more strident.[95] In 1785, in his *Reflections on the Present State of Free Inquiry in this Country*, he spoke of Dissenters as 'laying gunpowder, grain by grain, under the old building of error and superstition, which a single spark may hereafter inflame so as to produce an instantaneous explosion' – hence the nickname 'Gunpowder Joe'.[96]

In 1780 Priestley took up residence in Birmingham, joining the Lunar Society. Living in the new industrial heartlands, he grew warmly sympathetic towards the *laissez-faire* attitudes of the Midlands industrialists. He then criticized the Poor Laws, which in his view had 'debased the very nature of man . . . defeated the purposes of Providence with respect to him, and . . . reduced him to a condition below that of any of the brutes'.[97] While he warned against centralizing legislation, on social discipline Priestley proved stern. Capital punishment, solitary confinement and meagre diets could all be effective utilitarian deterrents; and since prevention was the point of punishment, at bottom it was better that the innocent suffer than the guilty escape.

Crucial to his later politics was the French Revolution: as British opinion hardened, Priestley grew more radical. As is clear from his *Letters to Edmund Burke Occasioned by His Reflections on the Revolution in France* (1791) and his anonymous *A Political Dialogue on the General Principles of Government* of the same year,[98] he had ceased to think of the British as the best of constitutions, while the Anglican Church now seemed a 'fungus upon the noble plant of Christianity'.[99] Abandoning the view that sovereignty lay in the balance of king, Commons and Lords, 'our only proper sovereign', he now held, 'is the Parliament'.[100] Hereditary titles and kingship were feudal relics which must fall before the 'prevailing spirit of industry and commerce'.[101] Long 'a Unitarian in religion but a Trinitarian in politics', he now paraded as a Unitarian in both: 'in every state as in every single person there ought to be but one will',[102] and that was the people's: reform the

House of Commons and 'every other reform could be made without any difficulty whatever'.[103] Denouncing in his *Letter to Pitt* (1787) the Prime Minister's failure to relieve the Nonconformists by abolishing the Test Acts, Priestley scorned his kowtowing to the bishops, who were 'recorded in all histories, as the most jealous, the most timorous, and of course the most vindictive of all men'.[104] Such inflammatory statements made enemies aplenty.

On 14 July 1791 a dinner was organized in Birmingham – Priestley was not himself present – by 'Friends of the Revolution' to commemorate the storming of the Bastille. With the connivance of the authorities, a mob chanting 'Damn Priestley' stormed and burned the local Dissenting chapels, before turning on Priestley's own house, destroying his library and laboratory. The French duly honoured him with a seat in the National Assembly, but this hardly enhanced his popularity back home, especially after France's declaration of war in 1793. And so, in 1794, Priestley sailed for America, settling in Northumberland, Pennsylvania. Though he failed to gain a permanent congregation – Unitarianism was also regarded as suspect in America – he did deliver a series of Socinian lectures, published in *Discourses Relating to the Evidence of Revealed Religion* (1794–9).[105] Alarmed by the political intolerance he encountered in the New World as well (and finding good servants hard to come by), Priestley, with his habitual candour, told his hosts that there was 'less virtue as well as less knowledge in the United States than in most European countries'.[106]

Before Priestley went west, he had explicated the 'second coming': 'The Present State of Europe Compared with Antient Prophecies' (1794) expressed his persuasion 'that the calamitous times foretold in the Scriptures are at hand'. Study of the prophecies of the Book of Daniel led him to anticipate Christ's return within twenty years: 'I take it that the ten horns of the great beast in revelations, mean the ten crowned heads of Europe,' he explained, 'and that the execution of the king of France is the falling off of the first of those horns', while Nelson's victories fulfilled Isaiah's prophecies. Normal in the age of Newton, such immersion in the prophetic books was becoming an anachronism.[107]

Bold, energetic and plain-speaking, Priestley embodied the ultimate plain man's Enlightenment: truth was simple, open to all. His commitment to natural rights jibed with his utilitarianism, and both served the overriding goal of improvement. His liberalism, which preached freedom from state tyranny, priests and superstition, went with an endorsement of new institutions – factories, gaols, schools, hospitals – meant to instruct and discipline. In the fight against the mystifications of power, materialism promised a future in which science would deliver happiness to the people.[108] Paramount in all this was mental autonomy: 'should free inquiry lead to the destruction of Christianity itself,' he reflected,

it ought not, on that account, to be discontinued; for we can only wish for the prevalence of Christianity on the supposition of its being true; and if it fall before the influence of free inquiry, it can only do so in consequence of its not being true.[109]

Such statements epitomized the Dissenting politics of candour and impartiality: truth would prevail given fair opportunities, liberty would bring enlightenment, and enlightenment abet mankind.[110] The Providentialist in Priestley was also confident that out of discord unity would ultimately emerge: 'The consequence of free discussion,' he wrote in 1787, 'would in time, produce a rational and permanent uniformity. For truth, we need not doubt, will finally prevail in every contest.'[111]

The call for reform came in many different guises, with different idioms and priorities, though all had much in common. Perhaps the most systematically radical of the late Enlightenment reformers was Jeremy Bentham, whose exceptionally lengthy life was single-mindedly devoted to the reform, first and foremost of the law (where 'all is darkness') but also of the State, according to the criterion of utility.[112]

The son of a Tory lawyer, after attending Westminster school Bentham went up to Oxford as a 12-year-old stripling in 1760. Upon graduating, he enrolled at Lincoln's Inn, briefly returning, however, to his *alma mater* to hear the lectures of the celebrated professor of law William Blackstone. Published anonymously in that *annus mirabilis* 1776, Bentham's first work, the *Fragment on Government*, debunked the jurist's complacent paeans to the British constitution and common law.[113] While attracting only passing interest, the pithy, witty *Fragment* was fundamental to Bentham's project, since it formulated the principle of utility which drove all his later theorizing:

Nature has placed mankind under the governance of two sovereign masters, *pain* and *pleasure*. It is for them alone to point out what we ought to do, as well as to determine what we shall do. On the one hand the standard of right and wrong, on the other the chain of causes and effects, are fastened to their throne. They govern us in all we do, in all we say, in all we think: every effort we can make to throw off our subjection, will serve but to demonstrate and confirm it. In words a man may pretend to abjure their empire: but in reality he will remain subject to it all the while. The *principle of utility* recognizes this subjection, and assumes it for the foundation of that system, the object of which is to rear the fabric of felicity by the hands of reason and of law. Systems which attempt to question it, deal in sounds instead of senses, in caprice instead of reason, in darkness instead of light.[114]

While Bentham elaborated these archetypal enlightened views over the course of the next half century, training his searchlight into the shadowy recesses of power and the law, his basic principles never wavered.

The proper goal of society was the happiness of its members, and it was the legislator's job to aid that end.[115] Well-being consisted in maximizing individual pleasure and minimizing pain. Government should ensure the welfare of all, each person counting equally, be he patrician or pleb. The securing of the happiness of the greatest number was to be achieved through a proper mixture of personal freedom and administrative measures. Fundamental to state policy were security of the person and property. Also important was parity of treatment and of fortunes. Other things being equal, equality maximized public happiness, because all had a comparable capacity to experience pleasure and pain; with inequality, each additional unit of wealth brought diminishing returns. Absolute equality was unnatural, however, on account of differentials in talents, industry, etc. – nor was confiscation the way to maximize utility or pleasure, owing to the pain felt by losers and the alarm spread in the community if property were rendered precarious. Attacks on security were, after all, attacks on expectation, that imaginative chain which bound the present to the future. Security was thus a primary goal, although gross inequalities could be whittled away over time.

Government, which was to serve the people, needed to be transparent and accountable. The glare of publicity would protect subjects against misrule. Government must create a system which harmonized interests, using the law to ensure the coalescence of interest and duty. Laws must engage with motives – hence it was crucial that those 'springs of action' be thoroughly analysed and classified in the creation of a 'logic of the will'.[116] Sanctions – sources of pleasure or pain inducing men to act in certain ways – came in five sorts: physical, political, moral (or popular), religious and sympathetic. Only the political sanction was directly in the sovereign's hands, but the State also had at its disposal indirect means of persuasion, like public opinion.

It was up to government, manipulating the system of sanctions, to provide a framework of laws and punishment which would expedite optimal individual action. But though everyone potentially knew his own interest, the uneducated, like children, seeing no further than their noses, would grab opportunities to steal or squander without regard to the future. Education, discipline and the law were therefore necessary. Primarily an engine of social control, the law must be both knowable and known; all must understand that infractions would be detected and punished.

A true child of the Enlightenment, Bentham believed power had ensconced itself by mystification. Monarchy, the Church, the peerage and the professions – all had cooked up self-serving mythologies: Divine Right, the ancient constitution, theology, ritual, precedent. Especially obnoxious was the lawyer's worship of the tyranny of tradition: 'Ah! when will the yoke of custom – custom, the blind tyrant of which other tyrants make their slave – ah! when will that misery-perpetuating yoke be shaken off? – When will Reason be seated on her Throne?'[117]

Power must be scrutinized, fictions exposed. The pleasure–pain nexus was real, however, because it was grounded in human nature. The greatest happiness of the greatest number was the only scientific measure of right and wrong. All other criteria (convention, contract, honour, divine will, and so forth) either ultimately boiled down to variants on utility or were mendacious blather: even the rights of man were a kind of nonsense.[118] Every social arrangement had to be appraised in terms of its consequences – its happiness-producing tendency. Hence, in drawing up laws, the statesman had to take dispositions and intentions into account.[119]

This is why Bentham believed the analysis of motives so important. At bottom, all sanctions were reducible to the physical, that is, expectations of calculable pleasures and fears of tangible pains. The cash value of a pleasure or a pain would vary according to its intensity, duration, certainty, propinquity, fecundity (its likelihood of being followed by sensations of the *same* kind) and purity (the probability of not being followed by sensations of the *opposite* type).[120] A comprehensive knowledge of what moved men would be the grounding of a science of the law.

Bentham revered all the canonical Enlightenment heroes, notably Bacon: '*fiat lux*,' cried Bentham, 'were the words of the Almighty: – *Fiat experimentum*, were the words of the brightest genius he ever made'.[121] Locke was another of his idols, as was Helvétius: 'A digest of the laws is a work that could not have been executed with advantage before Locke and Helvétius had written', for both had exposed the witchery of words.[122] And his philosophical radicalism patently embodied key enlightened values.

Like others from Locke to Horne Tooke, Bentham abhorred loose language, creating, to rectify this, a new lexicon of law and politics. Ironically, however, his quest for precision involved obscure neologisms and linguistic solipsism, leading Hazlitt to quip that Bentham ought to be translated into English.[123]

He was furthermore an unabashed materialist, denying the superiority of the so-called spiritual over the physical – 'quantities of pleasure being equal, pushpin is as good as poetry' – and betraying none of the Christian humanist aversion to sensory hedonism.[124] A cash value could be put on everything. Bentham's materialism shows in his attitude towards the disposal of his own body – a contentious issue.[125] Early in life Bentham had directed that his corpse should be dissected 'if I should chance to die of any such disease' whose study would advance 'the art of Surgery or science of Physic'. Later, he conducted investigations into embalming techniques, leading to his *Auto-icon; or, Farther Uses of the Dead to the Living* (1831). In the form of the 'auto-icon', the stuffed bodies of great men should be put on show as edification and the process would be cheaper than carving statues.[126]

Bentham was a staunch individualist. Happiness was the individual's aim; everyone knew best where his own happiness lay; and, *ceteris paribus*, government or society should interfere as little as possible. He thus endorsed the *laissez-faire* economics of Adam Smith, trusting to a natural market-place identification of interests. Whilst suspicious of natural rights theories ('nonsense on stilts'), he reach conclusions similar to Priestley as to the paramountcy of individual liberty, and, as already discussed, he sought a liberalization of the laws regulating sexuality.[127]

Loathing privilege, Bentham detested the Christianity of the churches. Organized religion was despotism and theology was bunk. 'A man who after reading the scriptures can bring himself to fancy the doctrines of the Athanasian Creed,' he declared in 1777, was in a 'state of prepared imbecility'.[128] In time-honoured Deist fashion, *Not Paul but Jesus*, published over forty-five years later, proved the apostle an impostor,[129] while, around the same time, Bentham also denounced 'cold, selfish, priest-ridden, lawyer-ridden, lord-ridden, squire-ridden, soldier-ridden England'.[130]

Benthamism was a philosophy of action *par excellence*; alongside the Poor Laws (see chapter 16 above), the chief crusade to which Bentham devoted himself was prison reform, by then a major cause for concern.

As noted in chapter 9, the British penal system was a prime target for criticism: there was little rationality in the statute book, in the sentences of the Bench, or in punishments like the pillory – justice was a whimsical mix of brutality and mercy. The severity of the penal code was counter-productive, especially in view of its arbitrariness, and gaols were 'schools of vice'.[131] Confusion, reformers argued, must be replaced by consistency, and physical punishments reinforced by psychological sanctions.

In response to such critiques, late in the century the modern prison began to be devised, its advocates, like those of workhouses and lunatic asylums, displaying an ardent faith in salvation by bricks and mortar. With the old lock-ups denounced as dens of depravity and disease, new model prisons – efficient, disciplined, accountable, economical – were touted as the solution to the problems of criminality. Long-term prison sentences, reformers taught, would finally deliver authentic punishment, because they took away that sweetest of the rights of man: liberty. For that same reason, they would deter. And most important of all, they would *rehabilitate*. Whereas the traditional menu of corporal and capital punishments was brutalizing, the carefully calibrated regime of the new purpose-built and scientifically administered penitentiary would mould men anew, replacing caprice, cruelty and corruption by the application of 'a just measure of pain'.[132]

Some reformers, notably religious Evangelicals like Jonas Hanway and John Howard, pinned their hopes on the 'separate system', securing prisoners in solitary confinement, enforcing silent segregation. Traditional prisoner subcultures would thereby be crushed, criminality would cease to be contagious and solitude would work a change of heart.

Bentham shared many, but not all, such views, setting out his own *via* the architectural jewel of the Panopticon, 'a new mode of obtaining power of mind over mind, in a quantity hitherto without example'. The basic structure of this building was to be circular or polygonal, with cells around the circumference. At the core would be a central inspection area of galleries and lodge, from which authority could exercise constant surveillance while remaining itself invisible. High-tech building methods would make this possible. The pillars, arches, staircases and galleries were to be made of cast iron, for it was lighter, more flexible, less bulky and perhaps cheaper than stone or brick. Also, it would not harbour putrid infection and was fire-resistant. Glass was to be used extensively, in skylights, and there would be two large windows for each cell. The penitentiary's distinctive design, with its central conning-station (the spider in the web) ensuring the complete visibility of all prisoners, each in his own cell, aimed to achieve absolute control and regularity through total surveillance.[133]

No less important was the programme of management. Convicts would be worked extremely hard – by way of punishment, to meet the costs of their crime, and to instil discipline. An inmate would work fourteen hours a day at sedentary labour and spend one and a half hours eating his two meals a day, half an hour for breakfast and an hour for dinner: no 'particle' of time would be unaccounted for – and convicts would be under constant surveillance. The scheme – a 'mill for grinding rogues honest'[134] – embodied utilitarian simplicity: 'Morals reformed – health preserved – industry invigorated – instruction diffused – public burthens lightened – economy seated as it were upon a rock – the gordian knot of the Poor Laws not cut but untied – all by simple Idea in Architecture!'[135]

Bentham submitted three utilitarian criteria for prison administration: leniency (a convict ought not to suffer bodily in ways prejudicial to health or life); severity (the prisoner's condition ought not to be more eligible than that of paupers); and economy (saving those reservations, economy must prevail).[136] Humanity and efficiency were thus meant to go hand in hand.[137]

Bentham entertained a godlike vision of the power of his new science: 'J. B. the most ambitious of the ambitious,' he mused: 'His empire – the empire he aspires to – extending to, and comprehending, the whole human race, in all places . . . at all future time.'[138] His was a lifelong fantasy of mastery, to serve the cause of maximizing utility. 'If it were possible to find a method of becoming master of everything which might happen to a certain number of men,' he thus pondered:

to dispose of everything around them so as to produce on them the desired impression, to make certain of their actions, of their connections, and of all the circumstances of their lives, so that nothing could escape, nor could oppose the desired effect, it cannot be doubted that a method of this kind would be a very powerful and a very useful instrument which governments might apply to various objects of the utmost importance.[139]

Bentham did not merely dream of playing God, he turned utilitarianism into a secular religion. 'I dreamt t'other night that I was a founder of a sect', he wrote: 'of course a personage of great sanctity and importance: it was called the sect of the Utilitarians.'[140] In this, he was spot-on. Unlike most other figures in the eddying stream of the British Enlightenment, he had dependable and devoted disciples: legal reforms, notably the campaign to reduce capital statutes, were pursued by Samuel Romilly;[141] his secretary (and St Paul), James Mill, a low-born Scot consumed with hatred of aristocratic corruption, developed Benthamite political thinking in a democratic direction;[142] the artisan Francis Place – like Bentham, a violent atheist and a birth-controller – helped usher his master's *Not Paul but Jesus* (1823) through the press.[143]

Utility, however, was no Benthamite monopoly – after all, the idea itself had emerged from various sources, including the Revd John Gay, Francis Hutcheson and Joseph Priestley. Of the theological utilitarians, the high priest was William Paley.[144] His first book, *The Principles of Moral and Political Philosophy* (1785), destined to become a Cambridge set text, reveals the striking theological radicalism of the pre-1789 era. Slavery was 'abominable tyranny'; inequality of property was an evil *per se*; and 'it is a mistake to suppose that the rich man maintains his servants, tradesmen, tenants and labourers: the truth is, they maintain him'. There should be, he argued, a 'complete toleration of all dissenters from the established church', while the Oath of Allegiance 'permits resistance to the king, when his ill behaviour or imbecility is such, as to make resistance beneficial to the community'. Not least he related the parable of the pigeons, which ridiculed the 'paradoxical and unnatural' distribution of property, ninety-nine out of a hundred birds 'gathering all they got into a heap' and keeping it for 'one, and the weakest, perhaps worst pigeon of the flock'.[145] Strong stuff from a Cambridge divine, and small surprise that in 1802 the *Anti-Jacobin Review* 'hesitated not to affirm' that in it 'the most determined Jacobin might find a justification of his principles, and a sanction for his conduct'.[146]

The 'second Enlightenment' decisively underwrote earlier commitments to freedom, toleration and constitutionality. Its thrust, however, lay in stressing the shortcomings rather than the success of the British socio-political order, and it pressed for the completion of commitments half-fulfilled. The aspirations and demands of this 'Enlightenment within the Enlightenment' were well summed up by the Manchester cotton manufacturer, Dissenter and political activist, Thomas Walker:

[We do not seek] an equality of wealth and possessions . . . The equality insisted on by the friends of Reform is AN EQUALITY OF RIGHTS . . . that every person may be equally entitled to the protection and benefit of society; may equally have a voice in the election of those persons who make the laws . . . and may have a fair opportunity of exerting to advantage any talents he may possess. The rule is not 'let all mankind be perpetually equal' – God and nature have forbidden it. But 'let all mankind start fair in the Race of life'.[147]

Commonplace in the 1770s and 1780s, these views found wellwishers across a broad spectrum. By 1794, however, the time Walker was writing, they had become contentious.

19

PROGRESS

Nature revolves, but man advances.

EDWARD YOUNG[1]

All well written books, that discuss the actions of men, are in reality so many histories of the progress of mind.

THOMAS HOLCROFT[2]

[W]e live but to improve.

ANNIE WATT[3]

No Man can pretend to set Bounds to the Progress that may yet be made in Agriculture and Manufacture ... is it not much more natural and reasonable to suppose, that we are rather at the Beginning only, and just got within the Threshold, than that we are arrived at the *ne plus ultra* of useful Discoveries?

JOSIAH TUCKER[4]

[D]rink success to Philosophy and Trade.

ERASMUS DARWIN[5]

History is progressive, proclaimed enlightened activists in an ever-swelling chorus, as they crested the wave in an age of improvement.[6] 'Rousseau exerts himself to prove that all *was* right originally,' commented Mary Wollstonecraft, 'a crowd of authors that all *is* now right: and I, that all will *be* right.'[7] Sights became fixed on the future – though not the Apocalypse of Christian eschatology but one end-on with the here and now. Indeed, the Enlightenment

424

brought the birth of science fiction and the futurological novel –
Samuel Madden's *Memoirs of the Twentieth Century* (1733), for instance,
or the anonymous and none too chronologically inaccurate *The Reign
of George VI, 1900–1925* (1763).[8]

The scent of progress was pervasive. The Anglican Edmund Law
professed his faith in the 'continual Improvement of the World in
general', while the Scot John Millar taught of how 'one of the most
remarkable differences between man and other animals consists in
that wonderful capacity for the improvement of his faculties'.[9] 'Who
even at the beginning of this century,' asked Richard Price, fired by
rational Dissent,

would have thought, that, in a few years, mankind would acquire the power
of subjecting to their wills the dreadful force of lightning, and of flying in
aerostatic machines? . . . Many similar discoveries may remain to be made
. . . and it may not be too extravagant to expect that (should civil governments throw no obstacles in the way) the progress of improvement will not
cease till it has excluded from the earth most of its worst evils, and restored
that Paradisiacal state which, according to the Mosaic History, preceded
the present state.[10]

Even 'Population' Malthus set off his demographic gloom against
intellectual glory, celebrating 'the great and unlooked for discoveries
that have taken place of late years in natural philosophy . . . the
ardent and unshackled spirit of inquiry that prevails'.[11] In all this,
self-improvement became a keynote. In his *Letters from a Father to his
Son* (1796), John Aikin stressed how man was 'an improvable being',
and (glaring daggers at Burke) countered 'Declamations against
improvement' and the 'Sneering manner of opposing' by stressing
how 'Perfection' was 'attainable in civil institutions'.[12]

Late Enlightenment belief in progress was, to be sure, a secular
theodicy – progress was the opium of enlightenment – but as a piece
of religiose myth-making, 'all will be right' was not complacent in
precisely the same way as earlier Leibnizian 'all is for the best'
optimism. The world, as Wollstonecraft explained, was not perfect
yet: rather it was man's duty to perfect it, through criticism, reform,

education, knowledge, science, industry and sheer energy. The stunning information revolution then in train would make all the difference: the temporal 'second cause' of advancement, proclaimed David Hartley, was 'the diffusion of knowledge to all ranks and orders of men, to all nations, kindred, tongues, and peoples', a progress which 'cannot now be stopped, but proceeds ever with an accelerated velocity'.[13] And all this optimism about the future, this dropping of ancestral fears about 'forbidden knowledge', was buoyed up by the conviction, in the thinking of the likes of Hartley, Price and Priestley, that Providence – the 'first cause' – guaranteed such developments,[14] or, as suggested in the model of the Deist Erasmus Darwin, social progress was underwritten by biological evolution at large.

Progress was the universalization of 'improvement', that ultimate Georgian buzzword. The public got hooked on novelty. Landscapes, gardens, manufactures, manners, taste, art and literature – all were constantly talked up as 'improving', while advertisers puffed the 'latest' in sartorial or culinary elegance or the 'modern method' in commerce, and literary classics were modernized for the masses. Not all were sold on it – Swiftian satirists ridiculed novelty for novelty's sake – and for that very reason the public had to be endlessly reassured that change was truly educative, morally edifying and socially advantageous.[15]

Traditional doubts about the past and the present were addressed and allayed by Gibbon, a man constitutionally sceptical of facile credos. Would not, as civic humanists feared, the calamities that had destroyed Rome recur in 'this enlightened age'? No: the great 'source of comfort and hope', soothed the *Decline and Fall*, was the permanency of improvement. From savagery man had 'gradually arisen to command the animals, to fertilize the earth, to traverse the ocean, and to measure the heavens'. Such betterment had no doubt been 'irregular', with 'vicissitudes of light and darkness', yet the 'experience of four thousand years should enlarge our hopes' – since technical skills could never be lost, no people would 'relapse into their original barbarism'. At bottom, therefore, mankind could 'acquiesce in the pleasing conclusion that every age of the world has increased, and still increases, the real wealth, the happiness, the knowledge, and perhaps the virtue, of the human race'. Moreover, progress had no foreseeable limits, for, once made, gains were irreversible. 'Observations on the Fall of the Empire in the West', the long essay which rounded off the first half of Gibbon's history, explained that any new 'Gothic' invaders could succeed only by first assimilating modern achievements, not least military technology: 'before they can conquer they must cease to be barbarians'.[16] In short, by 1800, progress was the big idea, set to turn into the great panacea, or *ignis fatuus*, of Whiggery in Macaulay's 'march of mind' – and as such to be sent up by that enlightened tailender Thomas Love Peacock.[17]

As already highlighted in chapter 6, science and positive knowledge were mighty generators of optimism. Over time, the culture of science spread more widely and rapidly, percolating down through society and rippling out into the provinces.[18] While the Royal Society remained the nation's senior scientific society, further bodies were added in the capital, notably the Linnean Society of London (1788) and the Royal Institution (1799). The Royal Society of Edinburgh was set up in 1783, and its Irish counterpart, the Royal Irish Academy, in 1785. In the English regions science, Dissent and political reformism joined forces in the Lunar Society of Birmingham, and in similar organizations in Manchester, Newcastle and other commercial and industrializing centres. Science was acclaimed as integral not just to utility but to the civilizing process. Launching a literary and philosophical society in Newcastle-upon-Tyne, the Unitarian minister William Turner underscored its cultural no less than its practical value: would not such societies 'increase the pleasures and advantage of social intercourse'?[19] The leading light in Manchester, Thomas Henry, similarly pronounced the pursuit of natural philosophy preferable to 'the tavern, the gaming table, or the brothel'.[20] To realize this vision of science as rational culture, the Literary and Philosophical Society of Manchester had been set up in 1781, including among its early promoters local physicians and manufacturers, and among its honorary members Erasmus Darwin, Joseph Priestley and Josiah Wedgwood.

The most energetic of such gatherings embodying enlightened faith in science was the Lunar Society, which brought together likeminded luminaries from the West Midlands. Though, at the beginning of the eighteenth century, Birmingham was still a small market town, rapid expansion followed; by 1760, it had already grown considerably, to 30,000 inhabitants, and in Matthew Boulton's Soho factory it gained a machine-tool works of international repute. William Hutton, later the author of a patriotic history of the city, found in Birmingham an ethos he had not encountered elsewhere: 'I had been among dreamers, but now I saw men awake.'[21]

From about 1765 a group of friends – leading industrialists, scientists, educators, Dissenting ministers and physicians – began to meet at Boulton's home, once a month at full moon, to discuss innovations in science and technology and the new industrial order they were instrumental in creating. 'The association of Lunar members and their activities,' it has been claimed, 'shows a conscious shaping of their world and a deliberate application to solve the problems of industrializing England that fits ill the picture of classic harmony and Augustan balance which is, somehow, at the same time also regarded as characteristic of eighteenth-century England' – or, more pithily, 'a nation of Newtons and Lockes became a nation of Boultons and Watts'.[22]

'Improvement' was a label also often applied to the use of the land, serving as a codeword for capitalist farming, notably enclosure. The improving spirit in agriculture, discussed in chapter 13, was increasingly associated with science. In the introduction to his 600-page *Phytologia* (1800), Erasmus Darwin, for instance, expressed his regrets that 'Agriculture and Gardening . . . continue to be only Arts, consisting of numerous detached facts and vague opinions, without a true theory to connect them'.[23] This had to change. Those domains would truly progress only when made fully rational and businesslike, thanks to the teachings of political economy. 'Pasturage cannot exist

without property both in the soil and the herds which it nurtures,'
he insisted,

and for the invention of arts, and production of tools necessary to agriculture, some must think, and others labour; and as the efforts of some will be
crowned with greater success than that of others, an inequality of the ranks
of society must succeed.[24]

With capitalist agriculture being thus cast as rational, farming
became managed as a form of manufacturing, with Robert Bakewell's
fat sheep serving, rather like Newton's prism, as icons of enlightenment.[25] The Leicestershire stockrearer explicitly bred sheep, cattle
and pigs as meat-producing engines, selected so as to maximize
expensive cuts and minimize bones and waste: animals were thus
turned into machines.[26]

As this example hints, if agriculture was celebrated – indeed, in
Arthur Young's phrase, as 'the greatest of all manufactures'[27] – it was
another branch of progress which now received the warmest praise:
manufacturing. Progressives had long expressed their fascination
with industry in the traditional meaning of skilled work, promoting
the image of *homo faber*:

> These are thy blessings, Industry, rough power!
> Whom labour still attends, and sweat, and pain;
> Yet the kind source of every gentle art
> And all the soft civility of life:
> Raiser of human kind![28]

sang James Thomson in 1744.

Overcome with despair, Robinson Crusoe surveyed his predicament: 'I was wet, had no clothes to shift me, nor anything either to
eat or drink, to comfort me; neither did I see any prospect before
me, but that of perishing with hunger, or being devoured by wild
beasts.' Salvation came, however, for Defoe's hero in the implements
and weapons he fished out from the shipwreck: knives and forks, a
spade and pickaxe, needles and thread, muskets, gunpowder and
shot. Implements formed the basis of civilization reborn: 'I had never

handled a tool in my life; and yet, in time, by labour, application, and contrivance I found at last that I wanted nothing but I could have made, especially if I had the tools.'[29]

Innovation was advancing on a broad front. Water-wheel technology became a model of experimental efficiency, and the engineer John Smeaton perfected lighthouse design. In 1758 the 'Improved Birmingham Coach' had blazoned on its side 'FRICTION ANNIHILATED', and by 1801 Richard Trevithick had a perfected steam carriage. Above all, textile technology was transformed and the steam engine revolutionized power. Industrialization gathered pace and production grew rapidly: averaging about £9 million a year in 1780, exports had rocketed to £22 million by the century's close. Iron and steel shipments, running at 16,770 tons in 1765–74, had almost doubled by 1800. Over the same period, cottons exports rose from £236,000 to a staggering £5,371,000.[30]

At the dawn of this stunning transformation, John Dalton's *Descriptive Poem* (1755) carried a telling preface. It opened with a paean to agriculture:

When we behold rich improvements of a wild and uncultivated soil, in their state of maturity, without having observed their rise and progress, we are struck with wonder and astonishment, to see the face of Nature totally changed.

But then it significantly changed tack:

But how great and rational soever the pleasure of such a sight may be, it is still surpassed by that arising from the extraordinary increase of a trading Town, and new plantations of Houses and Men. Such was the satisfaction the author felt at the appearance of the town and harbour of Whitehaven, after an absence of somewhat less than thirty years.[31]

Admiringly recording technological progress with pen or paints, writers and artists encultured nascent industrialization. The Derbyshire painter Joseph Wright portrayed local industrial worthies with emblems of their enterprise: the geologist John Whitehurst with a stratigraphical section, the lead-mining squire Francis Hart with a chunk of galena and the factory owner Richard Arkwright with a model spinning frame – while Arkwright's cotton mills at Cromford also caught his eye.[32]

The appeal of manufacturing to enlightened minds was many-sided. Technology became headline news as the cutting edge of novelty. 'The people in London, Manchester and Birmingham are steam mill mad,' Matthew Boulton assured James Watt.[33] Industry also formed a prime instance of disciplined rationality. An experimentalist in his own right, Josiah Wedgwood the potter aimed to 'make such machines of Men as cannot err', introducing clocking-on to ensure punctuality among his workforce.[34] In 1783 he applauded the progress visible across the West Midlands:

Industry and the machine have been the parent of this happy change. A well directed and long continued series of industrious exertions, has so changed, for the better, the face of our country, its buildings, lands, roads and the manners and deportment of its inhabitants, too.[35]

Business, in other words, promoted not just wealth but well-being too.

Manufacturing was producing, boosters claimed, a new breed of heroes, principally the 'captain of industry', retailed as the self-made man, raising capital for factories, forges and foundries, ploughing back profits, organizing productive capacity, recruiting, training and deploying the workforce and calculating market trends and opportunities. Long before Samuel Smiles, the industrialist was vaunted as a national hero. One of the children's tales in Anna Barbauld's improving *Evenings at Home: Or the Juvenile Budget Opened* (1794–8) celebrates Richard Arkwright's rise to fame and fortune. 'This is what manufacturers can do,' Papa explains to his children, in an enlightened idiom approaching profanity: 'here man is a kind of creator, and like the great Creator, he may please himself with his work and say it is good.' Showing his youngsters round a factory, the fictional father insists what fun it all is: there is 'more entertainment to a cultivated mind in seeing a pin made, than in many a fashionable diversion'.[36]

The entrepreneur was hailed as the exemplar of modern energy. 'I shall never forget Mr Boulton's expression to me,' recalled James Boswell of a visit to the Soho works: '"I sell here, Sir, what all the world desires to have, – Power." He had about seven hundred people at work . . . he seemed to be a father to this tribe.'[37] In a motif congenial to minds analysing the transition from feudal to commercial society, industry was commended as the means to beat swords into ploughshares, supplanting war with peaceful rivalry. 'Do you really think we can make a compleat conquest of France?' Josiah Wedgwood inquired in 1771 about market prospects – the very thought made his 'blood move quicker'.[38]

Wedgwood, like Boulton, was one of a remarkable new breed of men conspicuous for pursuing business through enlightened thinking. Though of meagre formal education, he displayed a consummate faith in reason, and a passion for measuring, weighing, observing, recording and experimenting: all problems in ceramics manufacture would, he maintained, 'yield to experiment'.[39] His rational outlook extended beyond business to Unitarianism in religion and radicalism in politics – he was hostile to slavery, and a warm supporter of the American colonists and later of the French Revolution. He thought big: 'I shall Astonish the World All at Once,' he declared to his partner, Thomas Bentley, 'for I hate piddling you know.'[40] Becoming 'vase-maker general to the universe', he died worth half a million.

If the businessman might thus figure as Britain's answer to the enlightened absolutist, Robert Owen was the Sun King among entrepreneurs, a consummate illustration of the application of enlightened ideas to the empire of industry. Born in mid-Wales, Owen got his first employment as an errand boy; then he moved into drapery, rising to take a partnership in a Manchester firm, before, at the turn of the century, becoming partner and manager of the New Lanark Mills on Clydeside. For the next two decades he combined entrepreneurship with social reform. In his *A New View of Society* (1813) – in today's jargon it would be called his 'mission statement' – Owen urged rational social rebuilding on the basis of universal education. Manufacturing would provide the foundation for happiness, but only once divested of the arbitrariness of the market and reorganized according to social utility. Character could be moulded by correct environmental influence. If the labouring classes were currently ignorant, brutalized and criminal, society must shoulder the blame.

Owen trumpeted the changes he saw all around him and which he was helping to bring about. 'Those who were engaged in the trade, manufactures, and commerce of this country thirty or forty years ago formed but a very insignificant portion of the knowledge, wealth, influence or population of the Empire,' he explained:

Prior to that period, Britain was essentially agricultural. But, from that time to the present, the home and foreign trade have increased in a manner so rapid and extraordinary as to have raised commerce to an importance, which it never previously attained in any country possessing so much political power and influence.[41]

Laissez-faire was futile, however, for ensuring long-term prosperity and welfare – market forces would produce 'the most lamentable and permanent evils', unless there were 'legislative interference and direction'.[42] Though industrialization held out the promise of untold human benefit, under the competitive system some grew fabulously rich while others were doomed to poverty. Co-operation was needed to effect industry's potential social advantages. Since people were products of circumstances, education would make all the difference, according to Owen's plan for a 'national, well digested, unexclusive system for the formation of character, and general amelioration of the lower orders':

On the experience of a life devoted to the subject I hesitate not to say, that the members of any community may by degrees be trained to live *without idleness, without poverty, without crime, and without punishment;* for each of these is the effect of error in the various systems prevalent throughout the world. *They are all the necessary consequences of ignorance.*[43]

In his New Lanark factory village, the provision of schooling, along with such amenities as a museum, would programme workers for happiness. Here was a veritable social experiment in action:

The experiment cannot fail to prove the certain means of renovating the moral and religious principles of the world, by showing whence arise the various opinions, manners, vices and virtues of mankind, and how the best or the worst of them may, with mathematical precision, be taught to the rising generation.[44]

An unbeliever, Owen secularized Christian idioms in envisaging 'the foretold millennium . . . when the slave and the prisoner, the bond-man and the bond-woman, and the child and the servant, shall be set free for ever, and oppression of body and mind shall be known no more'.[45] While hardly approving, Robert Southey nevertheless found this pioneer of Heaven on Earth remarkable. 'What ideas individuals may attach to the term Millennium, I know not,' Southey recalled, hearing Owen hold forth,

but I know that society may be formed so as to exist without crime, without poverty, with health greatly improved, with little, if any, misery, and with intelligence and happiness increased an hundred-fold; and no obstacle whatsoever intervenes at this moment, except ignorance, to prevent such a state of society from becoming universal.

To overcome that obstacle, a school, a museum, a music hall and a ballroom had been built, Southey noted, reflecting the entrepreneur's desire to increase the happiness of his work people a hundredfold. Owen was thus a logical *terminus ad quem* of enlightened thought, imagining and realizing comprehensive benevolent control within a scheme of industrialization, and displaying Helvétius-like concern with education and discipline over his 'human machines'.[46]

Uniting science and imagination, poetry and social theory, many penned anthems to improvement, from the Poet Laureate Henry James Pye's *Progress of Refinement* (1783) to Shelley's *The Triumph of Life*, uncompleted at his death in 1822.[47] Modelled on Lucretius's *De rerum natura*, Richard Payne Knight's *The Progress of Civil Society* (1796) was divided into six books whose very titles – 'Of Hunting', 'Of Pasturage', 'Of Agriculture', 'Of Arts, Manufactures, and Commerce', 'Of

Climate and Soil' and 'Of Government and Conquest' – clearly show that he was setting enlightened speculative anthropology to verse, giving a poetic rendition of the lessons of Adam Smith's stages of society:

> Each found the produce of his toil exceed
> His own demands, of luxury or need;
> Whence each the superfluity resign'd,
> More useful objects in return to find:
> Each freely gave what each too much possess'd,
> In equal plenty to enjoy the rest.[48]

The most notable and prominent poetic prophet of progress, however, was Erasmus Darwin. Born near Nottingham in 1731, Darwin was the son of an 'honest and industrious' lawyer with a taste for antiquities.[49] In 1750 the lad went up to St John's College, Cambridge, then crossed the Tweed (like so many others) to complete his medical training in Edinburgh. He then set up in medical practice in Lichfield, which proved his home for twenty-five years.

Though, like Priestley, a stammerer, the energetic and ebullient Darwin was a domineering talker, becoming noted for his wit and raillery directed against conventions and Christianity. From the 1760s he became familiar with the circle which developed into the Lunar Society, with its 'learned insane'. His earliest close friend was Matthew Boulton, at that time still primarily a buckle manufacturer. Darwin was flirting with the idea of building a 'fiery chariot'; though Boulton was not convinced of the practicality of such a steam carriage, Darwin's enthusiasm drew him to steam and thus paved the way for his partnership with James Watt. In the late 1760s Darwin's 'favourite friend' was Dr William Small, who had arrived from America with a letter of recommendation from Benjamin Franklin, but he also grew close to Josiah Wedgwood, whose pottery works had opened in 1760. On promoting the first major English canal, the Trent and Mersey, the energetic Wedgwood found a staunch ally in Darwin, who helped by writing pamphlets and drumming up influential support for the costly investment.

The next addition to Darwin's set was Richard Lovell Edgeworth, who shared with him a desire to design a carriage which would not overturn. Both were also keen educationalists – Darwin's interest being partly stimulated by an acquaintance with Jean-Jacques Rousseau, then living in exile in Derbyshire; Edgeworth's *Practical Education* (1798) (see chapter 15) proved far more substantial than Darwin's no less progressive, *Plan for the Conduct of Female Education* (1797).[50]

The Glasgow-based James Watt had pioneered the separate condenser as an improvement to the steam engine. Coming to England in 1767 with his invention still undeveloped, he visited Darwin, already a steam enthusiast, and disclosed the blueprint of his invention. Darwin and Watt became fast friends, and over the years Watt looked to him for encouragement, ideas and medical counsel. In the same year Darwin's old Edinburgh chum, James Keir, retired from the army to live at West Bromwich, where at his Tipton alkali works he succeeded in making caustic soda from salt on a large scale and thus helped launch industrial chemistry.

From the late 1760s this group of friends – Boulton, Darwin, Small, Wedgwood, Edgeworth, Watt and Keir – with later additions (notably Joseph Priestley, who settled in Birmingham in 1780) would occasionally meet up. The gatherings grew more regular, held monthly at full moon, to help light them home – hence Lunar Society – at the very hub of the modern technological world.

A physician first and foremost, Darwin practised for some forty years, and *Zoonomia* (1794–6) – his 1,400-page *magnum opus* which in its third edition ran to 2,000 pages – was essentially a work of medical theory, heavily influenced by Hartleyan materialist neurophysiology.[51] Despite his busy practice, Darwin poured his boundless energies into many other channels. In 1771 he was dabbling with a speaking machine or mechanical voicebox;[52] in the next year he had long discussions with Wedgwood and the engineer James Brindley about extending the Grand Trunk Canal; with his friend Brooke Boothby he founded the Lichfield Botanic Society, which in time brought out translations of Linnaeus. His botanic interests also blossomed on a site west of Lichfield, where in 1778 he established a botanic garden, the inspiration of his later poem of the same name.[53]

Uniting arts and sciences, medicine, physics and technology, the corpulent Darwin was not only a man of the broadest interests but the very embodiment of enlightened values. 'All those who knew him will allow that sympathy and benevolence were the most striking features,' wrote Keir. 'He despised the monkish abstinences and the hypocritical pretensions which so often impose on the world. The communication of happiness and the relief of misery were by him held as the only standard of moral merit.'[54]

Darwin's was a benevolence independent of – indeed, hostile to – Christian values and motives. From early years, he had rejected Christianity in favour of Deism. 'That there exists a superior Ens Entium, which formed these wonderful creatures, is a mathematical demonstration,' he proclaimed, but reason gave no warrant for believing that that First Cause was a Jehovah: 'That He influences things by a particular providence, is not so evident . . . The light of Nature affords us not a single argument for a future state.'[55] Indeed, he found the Christian Almighty quite repellent: how could a truly loving Father visit terrible diseases upon innocent children?[56] Darwin regarded the notion of a jealous Lord as quite perverse; he loathed the Church's fixation upon punishment, guilt and suffering; and his *Zoonomia* pathologized religious enthusiasm and superstition, diagnosing such religiosity as symptomatic of madness.[57] Like many other enlightened scoffers, Darwin had a taste for the blasphemous: his speaking machine, for example, was meant to recite 'the Lord's prayer, the creed, and ten Commandments in the vulgar tongue'.[58]

Championing Hartley's philosophy, Darwin was a materialist through and through. 'Dr Darwin often used to say,' remembered the pious Quaker Mrs Schimmelpenninck,

Man is an eating animal, a drinking animal, and a sleeping animal, and one placed in a material world, which alone furnishes all the human animal can desire. He is gifted besides with knowing faculties, practically to explore and to apply the resources of this world to his use. These are realities. All else is nothing; conscience and sentiment are mere figments of the imagination.[59]

(One suspects that, in front of his male cronies, Darwin used a phrase other than 'a sleeping animal'.)

Anti-Christian materialism shaped Darwin's humanitarianism: bigots loved blaming, but men of reason would inquire and sympathize. Hearing of an infanticidal mother, he wrote a commiserating letter to his correspondent:

The Women that have committed this most unnatural Crime, are real Objects of our greatest Pity; their education has produced in them so much Modesty, or Sense of Shame, that this artificial Passion overturns the very Instincts of Nature! – what Struggles must there be in their Minds, what agonies! . . .

Hence the Cause of this most horrid Crime is an excess of what is really a Virtue, of the Sense of Shame, or Modesty. Such is the Condition of human Nature![60]

Politically Darwin was a dyed-in-the-wool liberal. His books and letters echo with condemnations of bloodshed ('I hate war'), despotism and slavery.[61] 'I have just heard,' he raged on one occasion to Josiah Wedgwood, 'that there are muzzles or gags made at Birmingham for the slaves in our island. If this be true, and such an instrument could be exhibited by a speaker in the House of Commons, it might have a great effect.'[62] From its outset he supported the French Revolution, and after the 1791 Birmingham riots he wrote to Priestley deploring his victimization by fanatics – while also courteously advising him to quit his theological maunderings and get on with something more useful, namely scientific experiments. 'Almost all great minds in all ages of the world, who have endeavoured to benefit mankind, have been persecuted by them,' he wrote to him, on behalf of the Derby Philosophical Society:

Galileo for his philosophical discoveries was imprisoned by the inquisition; and Socrates found a cup of hemlock his reward for teaching 'there is one

God'. Your enemies, unable to conquer your arguments by reason, have had recourse to violence.[63]

Darwin's politics were, however, never revolutionary. Law, order and property were essential components of the social progress which would be achieved within the framework of free-market capitalism and industrialization.

Articulating his myriad ideas and outlooks, Darwin developed the first comprehensive theory of biological evolution: 'would it be too bold to imagine, that all warm-blooded animals have arisen from one living filament, which The Great First Cause endued with animality?'[64] Though different from the now generally accepted theory of his grandson, Charles, Erasmus Darwin's speculations were well grounded in the science of his day and gave voice to philosophical tenets central to the Enlightenment.[65] Nature, he contended, was everywhere in motion: the butterfly emerged from the caterpillar, and creatures adapted themselves to their environment – 'the hares and partridges of the latitudes which are long buried in snow, become white during the winter months'.[66] Through 'artificial or accidental cultivation', moreover, beings underwent 'great changes' transmitted from generation to generation, as in the breeding of pedigree cats and dogs.[67] Man's capacity to produce artificial breeds via domestication seemed to be transforming the very face of Nature: 'Many of these enormities of shape are propagated, and continued as a variety at least, if not as a new species of animal.'[68]

Nature thus changed and, for Darwin, the starting point for understanding its dynamics lay in the inherent motility possessed by organized matter: 'In every contraction of the fibre there is an expenditure of the sensorial power, or spirit of animation.'[69] Living beings were those entities which did not react solely in a mechanical manner to environmental inputs, but possessed an inherent responsiveness of their own:[70] living bodies, in short, were those with the capacity to interact with their environment.[71]

Fibres had the power to contract, producing 'irritation'; irritation led to 'sensation'; while, in their turn, pleasure and pain generated feelings of desire and aversion, creating the superior plane of bodily operation, volition, which constituted a creature's capacity to act in response to pleasure and pain sensations. Volition should not, however, be confused (he explained, drawing on Hartley and Priestley) with the discredited theological conception of free will, which was no better than an arbitrary act of the mind or understanding.[72]

Probing the functions of the mind, Darwin addressed the links between volition and habit. Frequent repetition of an action built up patterns of behaviour; once habits were established, subsequent performance demanded less conscious play of mind. The tyro at the piano thus had to give all his concentration, whereas the expert pianist could attend to other things as well. Habit did not supersede volition, it merely pitched it on to a higher plane, better adapted to the complex needs of beings simultaneously performing a multiplicity of actions.[73]

The power of the will to advance from isolated acts to behaviour patterns supplied a comprehensive model for the understanding of change. Animals – humans included – were not born inherently endowed with a repertoire of dispositions, capacities, propensities and skills. Schooled in Locke, Darwin rubbished innate ideas and their Scottish Common Sense variant. Rather, he noted, on the repetition of particular actions, habits formed,[74] which, undergoing modification over time, tailored behaviour to environmental pressures, opportunities and niches. The sanctions of the senses – pleasures and pains – enabled organisms to learn and, through learning, to progress. Sense responses translated, *via* habit, into the volition which gave all creatures the capacity to change and be progressive.[75]

What enabled such adaptive behaviour to assume truly complex forms, especially in humans, was a further power of the organism: association.[76] This associative capacity – Darwin had in mind the classic conception of the association of ideas as spelt out by Locke, Hartley and Hume – was like gravitational attraction,[77] and it was the key to the exceptionally subtle interactivity of organic behaviour as a whole. For Darwin, the expression of emotion – anger, fear, laughter – comprised the learnt product of chains of responses, transmitted from parents to offspring, over the generations, by the power of imitation.

Association was crucial to Darwin's concept of progress, and thus to his evolutionism. Through that mechanism, behaviour attained ever more complex expression, generating, for instance, the sense of beauty and feelings of sympathy which created mutual affection among mankind and other sociable animals. Through imagination the brain became the storehouse of experience.[78] And the imagination in turn played a crucial role in reproduction.

Controversy had long raged over the mechanics of generation and heredity. Darwin repudiated the 'preformationist' theory, popular among the early mechanical philosophers, that foetal growth amounted to little more than the mechanistic enlargement of microscopic parts 'given' from the beginning: offspring did not remain carbon copies down the generations, he retorted.[79] Most importantly, he was convinced that the mind had a part to play in hereditary transmission to the offspring. Views of that kind were not uncommon, for folklore and certain medical theorists alike credited to the mother's imagination the power to impress its contents upon the embryo at conception – 'monstrous' births had been explained in that way.[80] That view was rejected by Darwin, but he did propose an analogous (and equally sexist) doctrine, the idea that it was the *male* imagination which impressed itself upon the conceptus.[81] A mechanism was thus provided whereby 'improvements', the products of experience, could be passed on to offspring: as with his contemporary Lamarck, Erasmus Darwin's evolutionary theory built in the idea of the inheritance of acquired characteristics.

Darwin held sexual reproduction optimal for the future of a species: simpler, pre-sexual forms of reproduction – for example, that of plant bulbs – led to deterioration over the generations.[82] In any case, sexual coupling provided the opportunity for 'joy', and it carried a further advantage: by supplying the means whereby the 'ideas' of the mind or imagination could be conveyed to the next generation, sexual breeding could be evolutionarily progressive, the adaptations of one generation being passed down to the next.[83]

Analysis of living beings showed that life contained the capacity for repeated, continued, gradual modifications 'in part produced by their own exertions in consequence of their desires and aversions, of their pleasures and their pains, or of irritations, or of associations; and many of these acquired forms or propensities are transmitted to their posterity'.[84] Hence the argument for evolution was predicated upon, and clinched by, the general animation of life, leading Darwin to hail the evolutionary process as a whole:

would it be too bold to imagine that . . . all warm-blooded animals have arisen from one living filament, which The Great First Cause endued with animality, with the power of acquiring new parts, attended with new propensities, directed by irritations, sensations, volitions, and associations; and thus possessing the faculty of continuing to improve by its own inherent activity, and of delivering down those improvements by generation to its posterity, world without end?[85]

As a radical alternative to Genesis, evolution was first established in largely biomedical terms in Darwin's *Zoonomia*. Its human and social implications were further spelt out in his didactic poem *The Temple of Nature*, posthumously published in 1803. A sublime panorama of change was there unfolded, from the coagulation of nebulae up to modern society, from mushrooms to monarchs. Irritation was the initial trigger of the life forces, unlocking the potentialities of animated powers, leading to the awakening of feelings:

> Next the long nerves unite their silver train,
> And young SENSATION permeates the brain;
> Through each new sense the keen emotions dart,
> Flush the young cheek, and swell the throbbing heart.[86]

Sensation in turn quickened the perceptions of pleasure and pain and triggered volition:

> From pain and pleasure quick VOLITIONS rise,
> Lift the strong arm, or point the inquiring eyes.[87]

These then produced association and the awakening of mind:

> Last in thick swarms ASSOCIATIONS spring,
> Thoughts join to thoughts, to motions motions cling;
> Whence in long trains of catenation flow
> Imagined joy, and voluntary woe.[88]

And with the association of ideas came habit, imitation, imagination and the higher mental powers, which in their turn generated language, the arts and sciences, the love of beauty and the moral and social powers engendered by sympathy. Through such evolutionary processes man had become the lord of creation – his preeminence did not stem from a divine mission or from any innate Cartesian endowments, but because of basic physical facts: highly sensitive hands, for instance, had permitted the development of superior powers of volition and understanding.[89]

'All nature exists in a state of perpetual improvement', and so life possessed the potential for unlimited improvement.[90] The endless mutual competition of burgeoning organic forms within the terraqueous globe also resulted in death, destruction and even extinction:

> From Hunger's arm the shafts of Death are hurl'd,
> And one great Slaughter-house the warring world![91]

Nevertheless, rather as for Adam Smith, in Darwin's view the law of competition brought about net improvement, and the aggregate rise of population spelt not Malthusian misery but an augmentation of happiness on a cosmic felicific calculus:

> Shout round the globe, how Reproduction strives
> With vanquish'd Death – and Happiness survives;
> How Life increasing peoples every clime,
> And young renascent Nature conquers Time.[92]

Darwin's evolutionism provided the British Enlightenment's most sublime theory of boundless improvement.[93]

Contrast the epic of human progress, implicit or explicit in most late Enlightenment opinion and given tangible form by Darwin, to such earlier visions as *Paradise Lost* and the *Essay on Man*. For Milton, what was fundamental was the relationship between God and man – Adam's offence lay in his violation of God's command – and man's destiny was couched in a transcendental revelation. Pope for his part presented a view of the human condition as fixed on a divinely ordained scale:

> Plac'd on this isthmus of a middle state,
> A being darkly wise, and rudely great . . .[94]

With a static 'Chain of Being' in mind,[95] Pope viewed beings as suspended between the divine and the animal, a predicament at once laughable and lamentable,

> Created half to rise, and half to fall;
> Great lord of all things, yet a prey to all.[96]

Darwin, by contrast, painted a wholly optimistic, naturalistic and this-worldly picture, grounded on evolution. Human capacities were the products of biological and physiological development which extended to 'the progress of the Mind'.[97] Not only was there no Miltonic Lucifer and Fall, neither was there any Popean conflict countenanced between mind and body, man and Nature. Viewing humanity from Nature's perspective, not God's, Darwin granted a far more elevated position to mankind: man alone had consciousness of the natural order. Whereas Pope scorned pride as hubristic, for Darwin, as for Hume before him, pride and its triumphs had their legitimate basis in Nature. The mankind Pope satirized, Darwin celebrated.

Darwin's vision of evolution had potent ideological implications. His writings amount to an early and full vindication of industrial society, rationalized through a social biology.[98] In his naturalistic theodicy, struggle, sexual selection and competition were presented as part of the natural order. Yet no less prominent in his vision were love, sympathy and co-operation – his poems and letters give abundant testimony to his enduring hatred of violence, cruelty, war and empire.[99] Nor was his a merely mechanical view of man; indeed, he was concerned to *rescue* man from the aspersion of being nothing other than a machine. He stressed man's inner energies and drives, both the capacity and the need to learn, the inventiveness and adaptiveness of *homo faber*, the man who makes himself. Darwin offered a vision of man for the machine age, but not of man the machine.

Progress proved the ultimate Enlightenment gospel. It kindled optimism and pointed to a programme: the promise of a better future would expose and highlight whatever remained wrong in the present. It was a vision of hope, a doctrine of change. If *Paradise Lost* told mankind's tale in terms of disobedience, sin and punishment – and perhaps redemption – so as to justify the ways of God to man; and if the *Essay on Man* offered an enigmatic view of man as a riddle, even if in principle at least capable of improvement through self-knowledge, Darwin and his peers presented a man-centred view of man making himself – a Promethean vision of infinite possibilities. God had become a distant cause of causes; what counted was man acting in Nature. The theodicy, the master narrative, had become secularized.[100]

20

THE REVOLUTIONARY ERA: 'MODERN PHILOSOPHY'

The Voluntary Actions of Men Originate in their Opinions.

WILLIAM GODWIN[1]

[S]uch is the irresistible nature of truth, that all it asks, and all it wants, is the liberty of appearing. The sun needs no inscription to distinguish him from darkness.

THOMAS PAINE[2]

The English national memory gloried in the Glorious Revolution. Recording centennial junketings in Norwich, the *Norfolk Chronicle* reported on 1 November 1788:

The Revolution is undoubtedly the most illustrious and happy aera in the British annals ... Hence Britain has been ... the grand bulwark of the liberties of Europe and of the Protestant religion. Hence agriculture, manufactures and commerce have risen to a height which has surprisingly increased the wealth of the community. Hence science, polite literature and the arts of social life have been improved in a manner that ... cannot be equalled in any part of universal history.[3]

Over a hundred gentlemen had supped at the city centre tavern the Maid's Head with a Dissenter in the chair. 'The immortal memory of King William' produced three cheers; 'The Bishop of the Diocese' was fêted, as were 'the Lord Lieutenant' and 'the City Members'. There were more radical toasts too: 'the Majesty of the People' and 'freedom to slaves'. Nearer home, the diners had a whipround for the miserable debtors languishing in the city's gaols.[4] The event captures the true flavour of the English Enlightenment, progressive but not incendiary, broad church and confident enough to include toasts to prelates and people alike, to embrace Anglicans and Dissenters, and to extend sympathy to unfortunates. Such relaxed, tolerant optimism did not long survive the outbreak of the French Revolution.

Initially, John Bull applauded the storming of the Bastille. 'How much the greatest event that has ever happened in the world,' proclaimed the Whig leader Charles James Fox; it was 'the dawn of universal liberty', cheered Erasmus Darwin, while his crony Josiah Wedgwood 'rejoiced' in the 'glorious revolution' – a telling phrase.[5] For a while the atmosphere was festive, with much gadding around wearing *bonnets rouges* and salutations as '*citoyen*' (comparable with the reaction in Europe to the destruction of the Berlin Wall two centuries later). Wordsworth's

> I see, I see! glad Liberty succeed
> With every patriot virtue in her train![6]

caught the mood. To share in the exhilaration, young William crossed the Channel in 1790, landing just before the anniversary of 'that great federal day', 14 July. Writing later in the *Prelude* (although by then the salad days radical had changed his tune) he recalled:

> Europe at that time was thrilled with joy,
> France standing on the top of golden hours,
> And human nature seeming born again.[7]

Dancing around the bonfire of the *ancien régime* was easy, but the Revolution also had to be understood within the great pageant of history. This was what was in his mind when, on 4 November 1789, Richard Price rose to deliver an address to commemorate the Glorious Revolution.[8] That had gone down in British political wisdom as a conservative event: James II, insisted constitutionalists, had in reality 'abdicated' and the great chain of legality had never been snapped. Daringly, the reverend doctor, taking it upon himself to link it with current events in France, challenged such a reading of 1688. What Britain had begun, France was completing: now the tocsin had sounded for the rights of the people. Hence his peroration had a truly radical ring. 'Tremble all ye oppressors of the world!' thundered the frail old Dissenter:

What an eventful period is this! I am thankful that I have lived to it; and I could almost say, *Lord, now lettest thou thy servant depart in peace, for mine eyes have seen thy salvation.* I have lived to see a diffusion of knowledge, which has undermined superstition and error – I have lived to see the rights of men better understood than ever; and nations panting for liberty, which seemed to have lost the idea of it. – I have lived to see THIRTY MILLIONS of people, indignant and resolute, spurning at slavery, and demanding liberty with an irresistible voice . . . After sharing in the benefits of one Revolution, I have been spared to be a witness of two other Revolutions, both glorious.[9]

Wagging his finger at the 'oppressors', Price warned:

You cannot now hold the world in darkness. Struggle no longer against increasing light and liberality. Restore to mankind their rights; and consent to the correction of abuses, before they and you are destroyed together.[10]

And he challenged his compatriots: if they supported the real principles of 1688 and were true believers in liberty, they *must* embrace the French Revolution.

It was Edmund Burke who took up the gauntlet. His *Reflections on the Revolution in France* (1790) never doubted its magnitude: 'the most astonishing that has hitherto happened in the world'. But the veteran Whig, who had defended the American rebels back in the 1770s and many another liberal cause besides, damned the revolutionaries ('the ablest architects of ruin') as 'cannibal philosophers' set on destroying an edifice laboriously erected over the centuries: 'The French have . . . completely pulled down to the ground their monarchy, their church, their nobility, their law, their revenue, their army, their navy, their commerce, their arts and their manufactures.' Theirs was a wrecking rage: 'The age of chivalry is gone,' wrote Burke, 'that of sophisters, economists and calculators has succeeded. The glory of Europe is extinguished for ever.' Evidently politics should not be reduced to a science.[11] Burke never scanted reform – 'a state without the means of some change is without the means of its conservation'[12] – but, he insisted, change must come gradually and it must be consensual.

Not even Burke's rhetoric could stem the tide. Political societies sprang up, comprising radical craftsmen and the petty bourgeoisie, headed by journalists, intellectuals and disaffected gentlemen. The clamour was renewed for constitutional reform. 'Frenchmen, you are already free,' declared the London Corresponding Society in 1792, 'but the Britons are preparing to be so.'[13] 'For God's sake, send us the word of enlightenment,' ran one letter the Society received the next year.[14] Demanding parliamentary reform, the Society of Friends of the People, also founded in 1792, deemed Britain not a paradise of liberty but a prison of oligarchy: only one Englishman in eight possessed the franchise, and a numerical majority of MPs were elected by just over 11,000 voters.[15]

Many returned Burke's fire – the *Reflections* drew at least thirty-eight replies, including Mary Wollstonecraft's *Vindication of the Rights of Men* (1790), which reproved his 'mortal antipathy to reason'.[16] But it was above all Tom Paine who pleaded the people's cause against a corrupt Establishment and its hirelings. Attacking a regime first installed by a 'banditti of ruffians', the *Rights of Man* (1791–2) spoke directly to the cobblers, printers, weavers and carpenters who were the soul of urban radicalism and the torchbearers of plebeian enlightenment. Alarmed by Paine – 'our peasantry,' whinged T. J. Mathias, 'now read the *Rights of Man* on mountains, and moors, and by the way side'[17] – in May 1792 Pitt issued a proclamation against 'seditious writings'. Paine prudently fled, but left his inspiration behind. The title of his *The Age of Reason*, which appeared the next year and carried the attack to the churches, became the radical catchphrase. Were they prepared to remain the 'footballs and shuttlecocks of tyrants'? demanded the Nore mutineers of 1797: 'No. The age of reason has at last revolved.'[18]

Some hoped, others feared, that the revolutionary blaze would leap the Channel. Jacobin doctrines were inflammatory enough, and the tinder of discontent everywhere: soaring inflation, agrarian riots (notably over enclosures) and unsettling industrialization. Insurrection was in the air, old paternalism was crumbling, and deference with it. Awarding ancestral vengefulness a new weapon, an anonymous versifier warned the Quality:

> On Swill and Grains you wish the poor to be fed
> And underneath the Gullintine we could wish to see your heads.

while a notice nailed to a church door expressed new sentiments: 'Downe with your Constitucion Arect a republick':[19] no longer 'ours', now the constitution was 'yours'. This new 'them and us' mood was captured by Thomas Walker. The people had grown aware, noted the Manchester manufacturer, 'how the *few* have permanently contrived to live in affluence and luxurious indulgence, while the *many* drag on an existence laborious and miserable, in ignorance and vice, in pain and poverty!'[20]

Yet the old order was not decisively tested. Once France declared war, radicals at home found themselves in a cleft stick. The Terror alienated many erstwhile supporters;[21] the propertied closed ranks, and patriotic support, spontaneous or staged, swelled in 'Church and King' demonstrations against foreign enemies and domestic 'traitors' like Priestley. The proclamation against 'Seditious Writings' (1792) made mention of Tom Paine dangerous, and he was hanged in effigy.[22]

The Scottish trials of 1793–4, with radical leaders sentenced to transportation for attending an alternative parliament, served warning to militants elsewhere. In England, meanwhile, Pitt had set up spy networks, believing, or professing to believe, that the radical societies threatened a 'whole system of insurrection . . . laid in the modern doctrine of the rights of man'.[23] In April 1794 habeas corpus was suspended, and in the next month a high treason prosecution was launched against leading London radicals, including Horne Tooke, John Thelwall and Thomas Hardy.[24] For the government, their acquittal later in the year proved a blessing in disguise, since their martyrdom would have lent credence to the charges that Pitt was bent on tyranny.[25]

The radical surge subsided, and after 1794 it was economic misery that kept opposition alive. When in October 1795 – a year of sky-rocketing wheat prices – stones were thrown at the King's coach, Pitt seized the opportunity to batten down the hatches still further by means of the 'Two Acts'. The Seditious Meetings Act prohibited assemblies of more than fifty people without a JP's permission, while the Treasonable Practices Act extended the sedition laws. Charles James Fox, leader of the opposition Whig rump, retorted that all parliamentary reformers were, technically at least, now liable to transportation, while Samuel Taylor Coleridge, still in his radical phase, prophesied that 'the cadaverous tranquillity of despotism will succeed the generous order . . . of freedom'.[26] Opposition had been muzzled by 1795, and at crisis point public opinion fell into line behind the government, judging that Britain's priority was national salvation. Things were different in Ireland, however, where political discontent came to a boil in the revolutionary nineties, with an alliance between native Irish resistance and Jacobin ideology through the inspiration of Wolfe Tone and the United Irishmen movement – defeated in the end by internal dissensions and ferocious repression.[27]

If, however, the threat of revolution receded, commentators sensed that the old order was disappearing, too. English society was in turmoil, now no longer based on a rural order still to be found throughout most of the Continent. Labourers were leaving the land – or rather being turfed off it by enclosure and the other innovations brought by agrarian capitalism. 'Two causes, and only two, will rouse a peasantry to rebellion,' opined Robert Southey, a radical turned Tory: 'intolerable oppression, or religious zeal.' But that moderately comforting scenario no longer applied: 'A manufacturing poor is more easily instigated to revolt: they have no local attachments . . . they know enough of what is passing in the political world to think themselves politicians.'[28] England's rulers must pay heed: 'If the manufacturing system continues to be extended, I believe that revolution inevitably must come, and in its most fearful shape.'[29]

Friends of enlightenment became friends of the Revolution. The London Corresponding Society set about disseminating political knowledge, so as to effect 'a Revolution in the Minds of [the] Nation . . . An enlightened nation immediately becomes free.'[30] The chief oracle of enlightened philosophy was Thomas Paine.[31]

Born a Quaker, Paine had had a chequered career as a staymaker, schoolmaster and excise officer before migrating to America and vindicating the rebellion in his book *Common Sense* (1776). Returning to Europe after the outbreak of the French Revolution, he fanned insurrectionary flames in Britain. The first part of his *Rights of Man* was published in March 1791 at 3s. – dear enough, the government hoped, to keep it out of the hands of the swinish multitude. Within a few weeks, however, aided by the London Constitutional Society, which distributed it, 50,000 copies had been sold.[32] Upon appeals to Paine to make it available in cheaper format,[33] the second part, appearing a year later, was issued in a 6d. edition, accompanied by a cheap reprint of the first.[34] By 1793, a staggering 200,000 copies were allegedly in circulation – Burke's *Reflections* sold only a seventh of that number.[35]

'When, in countries that are called civilized,' declaimed Paine, painting a sombre picture of oppression, 'we see age going to the workhouse and youth to the gallows, something must be wrong in the system of government.' What was to blame? In Paine's view, privilege: 'the idea of hereditary legislators is as . . . absurd as an hereditary author'.[36] Power came from the people and must ever dwell in them: 'The vanity and presumption of governing beyond the grave, is the most ridiculous and insolent of all tyrannies.'[37]

Paine jeered at the very words prince and peer which, depending as they did upon the nonsense of hereditariness, were insults to reason: 'mankind are not now to be told they shall not think or they shall not read'. Arbitrary power that squandered millions on pensions, patronage and warfare, must end, and be replaced by government by 'election and representation' : the only safeguard against the abuse of power lay in universal manhood suffrage.

Paine was bold in his predictions – monarchy and aristocracy would not 'continue seven years longer in any of the enlightened countries of Europe' – but, true to his Quaker colours, he did not preach bloodshed. Nor did he envisage strict equality. 'The floor of freedom is as level as water', but that 'that property will ever be unequal is certain', on account of differentials in talents and industry.[38]

Paine's quarrel with Burke concerned the stranglehold of history. Burke had contended that the Revolutionary Settlement bound posterity, thus denying the people's right to choose or cashier their own governors. But the parliament of 1688 had actually done precisely that, asserted Paine, and 'every age and generation must be as free to act for itself, *in all cases*, as the ages and generations which preceded it'. 'Governing beyond the grave' was arrant tyranny, and Burke's lament for the 'age of chivalry' quite absurd: he 'pities the plumage, but forgets the dying bird'.[39]

The origin of the rights of man lay in the origin of man himself: the Creation. All histories, and particularly the Mosaic – 'whether taken as divine authority or merely historical' – agreed 'in establishing one point, the unity of man, by which I mean that . . . all men are born equal, and with equal natural rights'.[40] Upon these rights civil rights were grounded, which existed for the same Lockean reason as did civil society, because not all natural rights could be safeguarded by the individual alone. Some, such as freedom of religion, remained untouched in civil society; others, such as the right to judge and act in one's own case, were relinquished in exchange for justice. Legitimate government rested upon popular sovereignty.

Part Two of the *Rights of Man* took as its departure point the American Revolution, since the New World had been 'the only spot in the political world, where the principles of universal reformation could begin'. The diversity of its settlers with their myriad faiths had compelled a spirit of compromise, and tilling the wilderness required cooperation. Whereas the American regime promoted prosperity, Europe was awash with 'hordes of miserable poor', while 'the greedy hand of government' invaded 'every corner and crevice of industry'.[41]

There was a seeming contradiction in Paine's position which arose out of his populism. He embraced liberalism: man was born free, and the State, set up by contract, was 'no farther necessary than to supply the few cases to which society and civilization are not conveniently competent'. In other words, 'government, even in its best state, is but a necessary evil', a 'badge of lost innocence'.[42] Yet in the concluding chapters of Part Two, he painted a picture of an energetic State meeting the needs of the people: relief for a quarter of a million poor families, universal elementary education, family allowances for children under fourteen, old age pensions, maternity benefits, funeral allowances, workshops for youngsters and public works for London's poor. To pay for this Paine looked to military cuts and a graduated income tax. The civilized society was the one which could say: 'my poor are happy'.[43]

The Rights of Man became the radical bible. Its follow-up, *The Age of Reason* (1794–96), was no less an Enlightenment text, translating the élitist Deist critique of theologians and prelates into a populist idiom.[44] Brimming with indignation against the Old Testament's cruel and arbitrary God, it ridiculed the 'riddles' of the Scriptures, and praised natural religion: 'Every religion is good that teaches man to be good.'[45] 'I do not believe,' ran Paine's anti-creed, 'in the creed professed by the Jewish Church, by the Roman Church, by the Greek Church, by the Turkish Church, by the Protestant Church, nor by any church that I know of. My own mind is my own church.'[46] Established religion insulted reason, the Bible was packed with obscenities, bishops were the toadies of tyrants and churches were set up 'to terrify and enslave mankind, and monopolize power and profit'. As soon as the destruction of priestcraft put an end to mystery-mongering, 'the present age will hereafter merit to be called the Age of Reason'.[47] Paine embraced enlightened cosmopolitanism – 'My country,' he insisted, 'is the world' – and he looked forward to when 'the present generation will appear to the future as the Adam of a new world'.[48] Hugely popular as the voice of hope, he was hymned in a profane anthem:

> GOD save great Thomas Paine,
> His 'Rights of Man' explain
>   To every soul.
> He makes the blind to see

> What dupes and slaves they be,
> And points out liberty,
> From pole to pole.[49]

To others, however, Paine was the Devil incarnate; his books were proscribed, and the booksellers who distributed them imprisoned.[50]

Many political theories burst upon the scene at the end of the eighteenth century, embodying this or that strand of enlightened thinking, and often also drawing upon other traditions – Christian, utopian or populist. Philosophically, the most radical of these was Godwin's anarchism.[51]

Born in 1756 the son of a Dissenting minister, William Godwin was schooled at that hotbed of criticism, Hoxton Nonconformist Academy, moving on to become minister to a Dissenting congregation at Ware in Hertfordshire. His Calvinist faith was shaken, first by his reading Rousseau, d'Holbach and Helvétius, and then by Joseph Priestley's teachings. Unlike Gunpowder Joe, he would not stop at Unitarianism; after five years he quit the ministry and soon turned atheist. Moving to London in 1783 at the age of twenty-seven, Godwin remained there for the rest of his long life, eking out a living in Grub Street while getting involved in radical politics – he was, in fact, present at Richard Price's 1789 sermon.

Godwin conceived his great work in May 1791, just after *The Rights of Man* appeared – unlike Paine, however, he would transcend the rhetoric of representation and address the fundamentals. Appearing in February 1793, *An Enquiry concerning the Principles of Political Justice* instantly made Godwin's name:[52] it was 'a book which . . . in effect directed the whole course of my life,' recalled the radical Crabb Robinson, who was 'willing even to become a martyr for it'.[53]

The *Enquiry* blended Lockean empiricism and Hartleyan determinism, sensationalism and utilitarianism in a unique synthesis.[54] Individual differences arose from education and external influences. Denying innate ideas and instincts, Godwin even doubted whether man could truly be said to have a mind as such, using the word only provisionally as a shorthand to signify the lattices of thought which produced the complex of personal identity. Reason prescribed to the individual a duty to work for the greatest happiness through unflinching exercise of intellect and unfettered private judgement. 'Sound reasoning and truth, when adequately communicated, must always be victorious over error,' he insisted: 'truth is omnipotent . . . man is perfectible.'[55] Truth would triumph, because evil was at bottom not wickedness but ignorance.

Misery prevailed, however, and tyranny, high-life debauchery and rampant capitalism were to blame.[56] Unlike Paine and most other radicals, Godwin sought not the reform of government but its abolition. Unnecessary and counterproductive, government created the evils it pretended to eradicate, just as free-market capitalism spawned the servitude of needless wants and the burdens of wasted labour. The answer lay in the euthanasia of government itself.

Wrongs were at bottom the product of faulty education: 'all vice is nothing more than error and mistake reduced into practice, and adopted as the principle of our conduct'.[57] Such false values would disappear once people acquired a rational understanding of their duties. Subjective sentiments like honour, generosity, gratitude, filial affection, promises, gallantry or friendship had no place in a true moral philosophy or a just society. For example, in the case of a lethal fire, one ought to save the life of the great French writer Fénelon (expounded Godwin, in a parable which became notorious) rather than Fénelon's sister or one's mother; for by rescuing the moralist one would be doing right by mankind rather than pandering to subjective feelings.[58]

Also to disappear in this expurgation of the irrational was the entire panoply of the law and punishment.[59] The judicial system did not operate efficiently; punishment, old style and new style alike, was the infliction of pain to no avail, and the gallows were no argument.[60] It made no sense, moreover, given Godwin's strict Priestleyan determinism. A man, like a knife, was set in motion from without – the weapon was moved by 'material impulse', the man by 'inducement and persuasion'. Hence 'the assassin cannot help the murder he

[21]   [22]

Conviviality

Socialbility, the enlightened agreed, made for the healthy, well-balanced individual and the polished, stable state. They went about ensuring conviviality through the colonizing of congenial urban spaces, like Covent Garden (where everything could be found from a fruit and vegetable market to quack doctors and high-class brothels) [21], and fashionable new institutions like free-masonry [22]. Given half a chance, English men would set up a club where they could be at ease smoking, talking or indulging themselves in blissful silence [23].

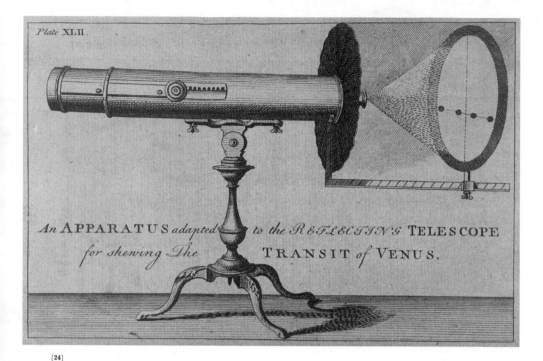

Plate XLII.

An APPARATUS *adapted* to the REFLECTING TELESCOPE
for shewing The TRANSIT *of* VENUS.

[24]

Science

If anything was thought to guarantee the superiority of the Moderns over the Ancients, it was the progress of science. That advance was most tangibly embodied in instruments, widely offered for sale to grace middle-class drawing rooms [24], and in popular scientific lectures, such as those of Adam Walker whose discourses on astronomy and other sciences 'completely captivated' the young Shelley [25]. The efforts of the likes of Walker to draw electricity down from the clouds might seem to others, however, laughable or impious [26].

[25]

[26]

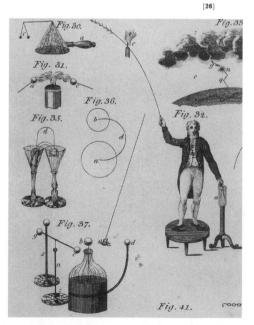

[28]

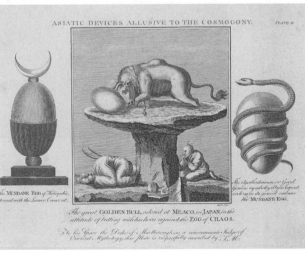

ASIATIC DEVICES ALLUSIVE TO THE COSMOGONY.

The MUNDANE EGG of Heliopolis, adorned with the Lunar Crescent.

The great GOLDEN BULL, adored at MEACO, in JAPAN, in the attitude of butting with his horns against the EGG of CHAOS.

The Agathodæmon, or Good Genius, symbolized by a Serpent, ending in its general contour the MUNDANE EGG.

To his Grace the Duke of Marlborough, as a consummate Judge of Oriental Mythology, this Plate is respectfully inscribed by, L. M.

New Horizons

Discovery was the watchword of enlightened science and exploration, and the progress of geographical and enthnographical knowledge squared perfectly with the imperial and commercial ambitions of the Georgian state. The result was often deeply ambiguous. Hunting walrus may not have gone down well with the new love of animals [**27**], and the slave trade between West Africa and the New World certainly came under increasing fire [**28**]. To Western eyes, the wonders of the East often remained weird, contributing to a growing sense of European superiority over all other civilisations [**29**].

[30]

[31]

[33]

Portraiture

The Enlightenment venerated the famous, and so it is no surprise to find the Scottish philosopher David Hume being portrayed in all his glory by his compatriot Allan Ramsay [30], or the leading female intellectuals and artists being deified as the 'Nine Living Muses of Great Britain' [31]. But, before he became the autocrat of English science, Sir Joseph Banks was evidently prepared to be depicted more glamorously [32];

[34]

[37]

Lancelot Brown retained his 'plain man' stance [33], Erasmus Darwin was all determination [34], James Hutton the geologist was caught lost in thought [35], and his fellow Lunar Society member, Joseph Priestley obviously wanted to go down in history 'warts and all' [36]. In his caricature of Lord Kames, Hugo Arnot and Lord Monboddo, James Kay caught the disputatiousness of the Scottish Enlightenment [37].

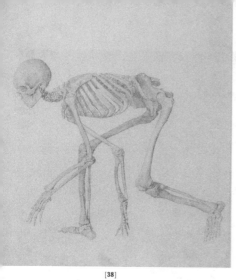

[38]

The Science of Man

The science of man being central to the Enlightenment, artists gave themselves over to studies of the human skeleton [**38**]. The newly founded Royal Academy included a Professor of Anatomy whose task it was to teach art and anatomy to the life class [**39**]. Intense interest in the relations between foetus and mother in the womb helped underpin and reinforce the new conviction of the crucial importance of maternal love and good mothering [**41, 42**]. The doctor was accorded a newly heroic role, witness the involvement of the Quaker physician, John Coakley Lettsom in the activities of the Royal Humane Society, set up to resuscitate victims of drowning [**43**]. Yet if health counted for more, the Enlightenment was haunted by the spectre of the hypochondriac, the person who made himself (or increasingly herself) sick through too much thinking [**40**].

[39]

[40]

THE HYPOCHONDRIAC

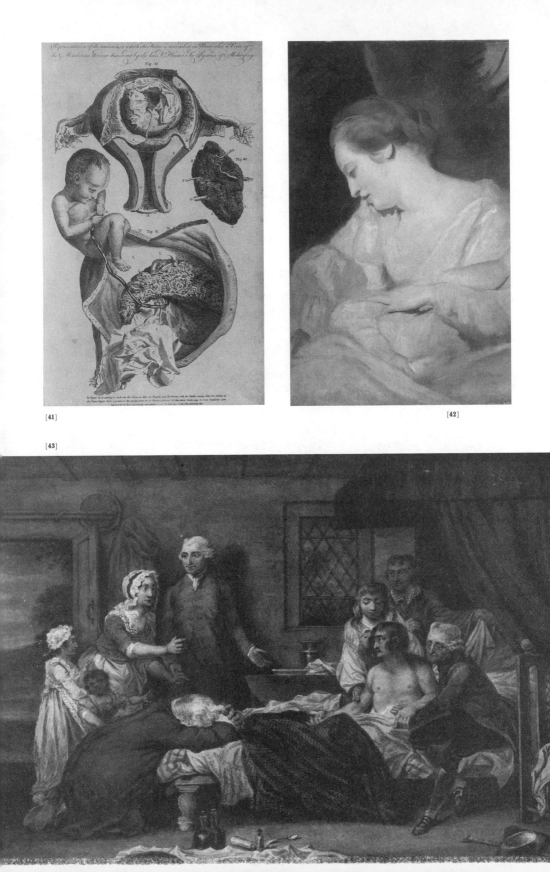

[41]

[42]

[43]

[44]

Industry

As befitted a burgeoning commercial and manufacturing nation, embarking on what proved to be the world's first 'industrial revolution', the links between art, artistry, and artisanship were prized in enlightened England. Quite apart from the famous Joseph Wright of Derby, other provincial artists glorified in manufacturing processes, as here with James Cranke of Warrington's depiction of glassmaking [44], while Zoffany caught a master spectacle-maker at work [45]. The pride of craftsmen shines through in their elaborate tradecards: Richard Siddall 'at the Golden Head in Panton Street near Haymarket makes and sells all manner of chymical and Galenical medicines' [46].

[46]

commits any more than the dagger'.[61] Hating a murderer was thus as irrational as hating his weapon. Disapproval might be in order, indeed, but 'our disapprobation of vice will be of the same kind as our disapprobation of an infectious distemper'. In a necessitarian universe, dominated by a 'chain of events', it was folly (argued this lapsed Calvinist) to hold malefactors responsible for their crimes: society should be so reconstituted and people so re-educated that they had no motive for committing them.

Infringements on individual judgement were 'tyranny' and must be minimized: Godwin thus frowned upon marriage, cohabitation, orchestras, concerts and stage plays because all stifled 'individuality'.[62] Government was 'an evil', and the most that was needed by way of popular control was a parish committee, in the Anglo-Saxon mould.[63] Make private judgement paramount, and one might expect a future in which 'there will be no war, no crimes, no administration of justice, as it is called, and no government'.[64]

Indeed, not only all that, but there would also be 'no disease, no anguish, no melancholy and no resentment. Each man will seek with ineffable ardour, the good of all.'[65] Once people comported themselves truly rationally, ill-health and ageing would disappear and immortality succeed. This would not lead to overpopulation, since sexual appetites, being themselves irrational, would also wither away, and copulation cease. The consequence? 'The whole will be a people of men, and not of children. Generation will not succeed generation, nor truth have . . . to recommence her career every thirty years': a middle-aged bachelor's heaven, indeed.[66]

Citing Franklin's supposition that 'mind will one day become omnipotent over matter', Godwin reflected: 'if the power of intellect can be established over all other matter, are we not inevitably led to ask, why not over the matter of our own bodies?'[67] Duty must supplant desire:

Reasonable men now eat and drink not from the love of pleasure, but because eating and drinking are essential to our healthful existence. Reasonable men will then propagate their species, not because a certain sensible pleasure is annexed to this action, but because it is right the species should be propagated.[68]

Godwin's mission was to grind beliefs and behaviour down to their atoms, for, after all, 'individuality is of the very essence of intellectual excellence'.[69] He extolled the very soul of enlightenment – ceaseless criticism, self-examination and perpetual vigilance – for the unexamined life was not worth living. 'The wise man is satisfied with nothing . . . The wise man is not satisfied with his own attainments, or even with his principles and opinions. He is continually detecting errors in them; he suspects more; there is no end to his revisals and enquiries.'[70] Godwin's faith was also vested in gradualism – 'we shall have many reforms, but no revolutions' – for violence was coercion, and all coercion was useless or worse.[71] Improvement had to come from 'the enlightened and the wise', from within, and from the mind: 'There is no effectual way of improving the institutions of any people but by enlightening their understandings.'[72] 'Reason,' it followed, 'is the only legislator.'[73]

In many respects Godwin was a dogmatic rationalist, but he was certainly not oblivious to complexity. In his novel *Things as They Are, or the Adventures of Caleb Williams* (1794), he continued to expose corruption in precisely the manner commended by the *Enquiry*: England has its Bastilles; the workings of the law betrayed its trumpeted impartiality; between the mighty and the weak justice did not apply; brutal squires suborned the law to tyrannize their inferiors; due legal process did not touch the noble murderer Falkland whereas it hounded innocents like Caleb. But *Caleb Williams* also explores problems arising from the principles of *Political Justice*, though not chewed over there. Apprised of Falkland's fatal secret – he has murdered the brutal Tyrrel – Caleb is beset by threats pressing him to conceal it. In the revised ending to the novel, where the hero's final revelation of the truth leaves Falkland a broken man, Godwin in effect questions the philosophy expounded in the *Enquiry*: that inexorable pursuit of truth and justice which makes no concessions to humanity. The *Enquiry*'s conviction that 'truth is omnipotent' is revealed to be questionable when its quest traps Caleb in the destructive power nexus he has sought to escape. The catastrophe is framed by Falkland's question: 'Will a reasonable man sacrifice to barren truth, when benevolence, humanity and every consideration that is dear to the human heart require that it should be superseded?'[74]

In assailing cant, in cutting the cackle, in envisaging a total transformation of conduct on the basis of private reason, Godwin drove enlightened logic further than any, even Bentham. His very extremism – especially his chillingly Houyhnhnm-like model of a rational, passion-free man – was a gift to the satirists. Godwin clones prate their way through the comic novels of the day – Mr Subtile in Isaac D'Israeli's *Vaurien* (1797), Dr Myope in Elizabeth Hamilton's thematic *Memoirs of Modern Philosophers* (1800).[75] 'His folly in thus eternally making himself a mark for abuse is inconceivable,' guffawed Southey: 'Come kick me – is his eternal language.'[76] Nevertheless, among reforming circles Godwin proved vastly influential, honoured as the man who drove enlightened thinking to its logical conclusions.

Godwin was not alone in advocating the abolition of power in the name of justice. The 1790s produced a crop of utopians, including William Hodgson, whose *The Commonwealth of Reason* (1795) pitted reason against corruption, and came out with ringing vindications of liberty ('the power of doing every thing . . . which does not trench upon the rights of another').[77] Particularly impressive, however, was Thomas Spence.

One of nineteen children of a Newcastle artisan, Spence was brought up as a member of the Sandemanians, a religious sect believing in community of goods among church members: as with Godwin and so many others, his later thinking was a rationalization of early religious views. Following an attempt in the 1770s by the Newcastle Corporation to enclose and appropriate the Town Moor, Spence harangued the local Philosophical Society on the parochial ownership of land. To propagate his radical ideas, in 1792 he moved to London, set up shop 'At the Hive of Liberty' off High Holborn and reissued his land reform proposals as 'The Real Rights of Man' in his *The Meridian Sun of Liberty* (1796).[78] He also issued a penny weekly called *Pig's Meat, or Lessons for the Swinish Multitude* – an 'up yours' to Burke, which contained selections from Harrington, Locke, Voltaire and others from the Enlightenment pantheon.[79]

Land nationalization was Spence's cure-all. Land in 'Spenceonia' would be vested in corporate ownership, and held on parochial leases. A parish council would govern the community, running schools, trades and the militia. Communal ownership was a birthright: 'That property in land and liberty among men in a state of nature ought to be equal, few, one would be fain to hope, would be foolish to deny.'[80]

Spence's politics thus stood Harrington on his head. In *Oceana*, land had secured independence; for Spence, by contrast, landownership was the tool of aristocratic oppression. His *The Restorer of Society to its Natural State* (1807) argued that, far from being divinely ordained by the great Landowner in the Sky, property originated in naked aggression. Land, the people's birthright, had become a field of blood, for anybody with money could cheat the people of their due.[81]

As with land, with language too, Spence was a leveller. His *Grand Repository of the English Language* (1775) proposed a revised alphabet based on the impeccably egalitarian principle of one letter, one sound. Spelling had deviated from the spoken word so drastically that written language had been turned into the 'property of the few', to remedy which Spence created new signs. His book formed part of the enlightened drive to demystify language by exposure of its roots and by simplification.[82]

The prime language reformer in this mould was, however, Horne Tooke, indicted in 1794 for 'compassing and imagining the king's death'. Elaborating in his *The Diversions of Purley* (1786) an etymological theory all his own, the bold political radical revealed how language had become suborned in the power politics of 'metaphysical Imposture'.[83] His 'philosophy of signs' traced individual words back to their Anglo-Saxon roots, presenting a narrative of the English tongue which buttressed the 'Norman Yoke' theory of state power. Defying the orthodoxies of the grammarians, Tooke served up a drastically simplified account of the parts of speech and the meaning of individual words, combating philological élitism ('imposture') of all kinds, be it that of the Tory dictionary-maker Samuel Johnson, the idealist metaphysician Lord Monboddo, or the courtly James Harris, whose *Hermes, or a Philosophical Inquiry concerning Universal Grammar* (1751) had treated hierarchical language structures as the reflections of natural and social hierarchies. Like the Burkean myth of history, Harris's theory was, in Tooke's eyes, an ideological ruse, designed to confer legitimacy upon the present order. Philology must untangle the mystification of power woven by words.[84]

The radical doctor Thomas Beddoes equally pointed to 'the long delusions which words have supported, the deadly animosities, public and private, to which they have given rise'.[85] Likewise Charles Pigott, whose *Political Dictionary, Explaining the True Meaning of Words* (1795) also unmasked official signs as tools of oppression. What, for instance, were bank notes but 'small slips of thin, silky paper, on which are engraved strong and forcible arguments in favour of arbitrary power'? Another likeminded demystifier, William Frend, also exposed paper money as a medium of idolatry, fearing that 'money-craft' would 'become as dangerous as priest-craft'.[86] Locke's radical suspicion of words was alive and well.

Land reform also found expression in the communitarian schemes of the young Samuel Taylor Coleridge and Robert Southey for setting up a 'pantisocracy' in America, that land of radical dreams:[87]

> Where dawns, with hope serene, a brighter day
> Than e'er saw Albion in her happiest times.[88]

Fired by Revolutionary fervour and hounded by creditors, Coleridge had quit Cambridge University in 1793, gravitating to the company of young radicals in Bristol, notably Southey, and throwing himself into poetry, preaching and pamphleteering. The friends projected a utopian community on the banks of the Susquehanna river, Pennsylvania, untainted by the Old World.[89] Twelve men and twelve women, 'familiar with each other's dispositions', were to set sail for America.

Two or three hours' labour a day would suffice, and the ample leisure would be spent in study, discussion and childrearing. 'Could they realize their plan,' wrote Thomas Poole, a friend with his feet upon the ground, 'they would, indeed, realize the age of reason; but however perfectible human nature may be, I fear it is not yet perfect enough to exist long under the regulations of such a system.'[90]

Though their plans, predictably, fell through, young Coleridge, on angelic wings, remained a beacon of enlightenment: his *Watchman* (1796), with its Baconian masthead 'Knowledge is Power', declared, 'A People are Free in Proportion as They Form Their Own Opinions'.[91] Having made 'a diligent, I *may* say, an intense study of Locke, Hartley and others',[92] he had espoused a creed of Unitarianism, determinism, materialism and progress,[93] enthusing to Southey about the 'corporeality of thought'.[94] Radical intellectuals like Godwin, Darwin and Priestley had paved the way;[95] moral improvement would be gradual but inevitable; and society, guided by a 'small but glorious band . . . of thinking and disinterested Patriots', was to reparadise the world.[96] Coleridge's *Religious Musings* (1794) presented 'a Vision' of human destiny, moving to a 'blest future', *viz*: 'The present State of Society. The French Revolution, Millennium. Universal Redemption. Conclusion' – there it was, all history in a nutshell.[97] If English Romanticism was, in large measure, to be the creation of Coleridge's circle, it was thus a child of the Enlightenment, albeit one that repudiated its paternity.

For Coleridge's views changed. 'I have snapped my squeaking baby-trumpet of Sedition,' he announced in 1798, '& the fragments lie scattered in the lumber-room of Penitence.'[98] Tellingly, having named his first son Hartley, Coleridge christened his second Berkeley, to signal his switch from materialism to idealism. He had 'overthrown the doctrine of Association, as taught by Hartley', he wrote to Poole in 1801, 'and with it all the irreligious metaphysics of modern Infidels – especially, the doctrine of Necessity'.[99]

Becoming increasingly, like Southey, a Church and King reactionary, Coleridge abandoned enlightened empiricism for German idealism and transcendentalism. Looking back to earlier religious traditions, and sideways to Kantian metaphysics, he trashed Locke in favour of a theory of mind which forefronted its innate activity; developed a doctrine of the organic 'imagination', over and against what he disparaged as the old passive and mechanical faculty of 'fancy'; and contended that man was naturally religious. Regarding exploded empiricism as a sorry chapter in 'the long and ominous eclipse of philosophy',[100] he would rescue and revive the (neo-) Platonism discarded by the Lockeans.

Coleridge's animus grew ever more blazing. 'Newton was a mere materialist,' he wrote in 1801. 'Mind, in his system, is always passive, – a lazy Looker-on on an external world.'[101] Hence the bitterness of Coleridge's later years, when he surveyed the aftermath of enlightened philosophy:

State of nature, or the Ourang Outang theology of the origin of the human race, substituted for the Book of Genesis, Ch. I–X. Rights of nature for the duties and privileges of citizens. Idea-less facts, misnamed proofs from history, grounds of experience, etc., substituted for principles and the insight derived from them ... Government by journeymen clubs; by reviews, magazines, and above all by newspapers.[102]

No wonder Peacock guyed this oracle: 'there is too much commonplace light in our moral and political literature,' pronounced Mr Flosky in *Nightmare Abbey*, paraphrasing Coleridge's *Lay Sermons* (1817), 'and light is a great enemy to mystery.'[103]

That the Romantic rejection of enlightenment did not automatically spell political conservatism,[104] however, is clear from the career of William Blake. A prophet of liberty, the London artist-poet's roots lay in the seventeenth-century antinomian sects, doused in a later spiritualism.[105] His early *An Island in the Moon* (*c.* 1784–5) lampooned Priestley as 'Inflammable Gass', whose challenge to the other philosophers – 'Your reason – Your reason?' – Blake turned into his name, Urizen, for the idol of abhorred materialism.[106]

For Blake the Behmenist spiritualist, enlightenment's sin lay in its materialism, which denied alike the glory of God and the miracle of man. Materialism stemmed from the vile trinity of Bacon, Locke and

Newton. 'Bacon's Philosophy has Ruin'd England,' he bewailed: 'his first principle is Unbelief';[107] the 'Loom of Locke', with its denial of spiritual genius, was hardly less evil.[108] The monochrome materialism of enlightened philosophy mirrored the sordid realities of capitalist oppression: industrialism, poverty, slavery, prostitution, war.[109] And rationalism itself was, finally, a profanation of divine mystery:

> Mock on, Mock on Voltaire, Rousseau:
> Mock on, Mock on: 'tis all in vain!
> You throw the sand against the wind,
> And the wind blows it back again.[110]

Enlighteners bent on demystification held that the sleep of reason bred monsters. Blake, however, regarded reason itself as the sick man's dream, begetting 'mind forg'd manacles'. He, by contrast, was divinely inspired:[111] 'every honest man is a prophet,' he declared, recuperating the discredited idea of divine madness[112] and remaining ever a 'son of Liberty',[113] all in a rage against an evil Establishment worshipping that diabolical trinity:

> . . . May God us keep
> From Single vision & Newton's sleep![114]

Counter-enlightenment was as old as enlightenment itself: Swift's misanthropic impersonations of gung-ho buttonholing rationalizers, Johnson's sombre realism, those like William Law who held rational religion no religion at all, and perhaps that wing of Scottish Common Sense philosophy which hounded David Hume.[115] The 1790s saw such thinking set upon a more coherent footing, with a reassertion of the frailty or depravity of human nature.

Reaction became philosophized on 1 November 1790, with Burke's *Reflections*. 'We are afraid to put men to live and trade each on his own private stock of reason,' he declared, 'because we suspect that this stock in each man is small . . . Prejudice is of ready application in the emergency . . . Prejudice renders a man's duty his habit.'[116] Mobilizing corporate traditionalism against atomistic individualism,

Burke pulled the rug out from under enlightened faith in permanent progress. 'We know that we have made no discoveries,' he insisted, 'and we think that no discoveries are to be made, in morality; nor many in the great principles of government, nor in the ideas of liberty, which were understood before we were born'.[117]

Moreover, the seasoned Whig bared the dark secret of revolutionary fervour: new enlightenment was but old illumination writ large, the Revolution enthusiasm resurrected – but, this time, enthusiasm without religion. The radical cause was thereby tarred by Burke with the brush of such cranky cults as mesmerism. Prophets like Price who proclaimed the millennium, and rationalist metaphysicians who touted a do-it-yourself State – all provided sitting targets: there was nothing to choose, Burke implied, between sophisters and the mindless mob.[118]

Another who linked British radicalism to the French Revolution, and the *philosophes* to rank illuminism, was the Edinburgh professor John Robison, author of *Proofs of a Conspiracy against All the Religions and Governments of Europe* (1798), who urged the Moderns to abandon the 'bloodstained road': 'Illumination,' he pronounced, 'turns out to be worse than darkness.'[119] Most reactionaries, however, were more homespun. The lawyer John Reeves issued in November 1792 the prospectus of an association 'for protecting Liberty and Property against republicans and levellers'. Believing liberty's fate hung on the defence of property, Reeves dubbed the Radicals 'levellers'.[120] Others too harped on this potent fear, hitherto deployed by enlightened activists against religious enthusiasts. 'The true Christian will never be a leveller,' insisted Arthur Young, 'will never listen to French politics, or to French philosophy.'[121]

The lunacy seemingly pumping up enlightened ideas was meat and drink to the *Anti-Jacobin Review*, which rejoiced in Gillrayan caricatures of *sans culotte* crackpots:

> I am a hearty Jacobin,
> Who owns no God, and dreads no Sin,
> Ready to dash through thick and thin
> For Freedom . . .[122]

and reduced the agenda of enlightenment to *Dunciad*-like twaddle:

> Reason, Philosophy, 'fiddledum, diddledum'
> Peace and Fraternity, higgledy, piggledy
> Higgledy piggledy, 'fiddledy, diddledum'.[123]

A print in the magazine for August 1798 shows the apostles of reason turned devout, worshipping at the altar of 'The New Morality': Godwin, a jackass, braying aloud from *Political Justice*: Paine, a crocodile, in stays; Holcroft, an 'acquitted felon', in leg irons; while from a 'Cornucopia of Ignorance' pour the *Wrongs of Woman* and Godwin's *Memoirs* of Mary Wollstonecraft.[124] Significantly, the *Review* pinpointed the root of all modern evils: 'We have long considered the establishment of newspapers in this country as a misfortune to be regretted.'[125] Yet, by its mere existence, the *Anti-Jacobin* tacitly embraced the same philosophy – print power; indeed, it shared the masthead beloved of the radicals: Magna est Veritas et Praevalebit ('Great is Truth and will Prevail').[126]

In 'The Loves of the Triangles', a skit on Erasmus Darwin's *The Loves of the Plants* (1789), the *Anti-Jacobin* parodied Godwinian perfectibilist pretensions:

We contend, that if, as is demonstrable, we have risen from a level with the *cabbages of the field* to our present comparatively intelligent and dignified state of existence, by the mere exertion of our own *energies*; we should, if these *energies* were not repressed and subdued by the operation of prejudice, and folly, by KING-CRAFT and PRIEST-CRAFT . . . continue to exert and expand ourselves: [raising] Man from his present biped state, to a rank more worthy of his endowments and aspirations; to a rank in which he would be, as it were, *all* MIND . . . and never die, but *by his own consent*.[127]

Other satires chortled at similar rationalist tripe. In her *Letters of a Hindoo Rajah* (1796), Elizabeth Hamilton presented philosophers with names like Mr Vapour and characterized by quirks like vegetarianism, solemnly training young sparrows to swarm bees.[128] Her later *Memoirs of Modern Philosophers* (1800) burlesqued Mary Hays in the guise of Bridgetina Botherim, planning to settle in primal felicity among the Hottentots. Two progressive cults – the noble savage and perfectibilism – were killed with one stone when Mr Glib – Godwin again! – met the dumpy Bridgetina returning from a walk:

'How d'ye do, citizen Miss?' cried he, as soon as he observed her. 'Exerting your energies, I see. That's it! energies do all. Make your legs grow long in a twinkling . . . No short legs in an enlightened society. All the Hottentots tall and straight as maypoles.'[129]

Evangelicalism too repudiated the enlightened. The well-connected Bristol schoolmistress and playwright Hannah More rose to prominence in the 1780s as a religious and political conservative – she was to name her pet cats 'Passive Obedience' and 'Non-Resistance'.[130] Her *Thoughts on the Importance of the Manners of the Great to General Society* (1788) and *An Estimate of the Religion of the Fashionable World* (1791) castigated Addisonian politeness: 'Under the beautiful mask of an enlightened philosophy, all religious restraints are set at nought.' 'Without holiness,' she held, 'no man shall see the Lord.'[131] From early days she assumed a very English stance against the Revolution, telling Horace Walpole in November 1789, 'I can figure to myself no greater mischiefs than despotism and popery, except anarchy and atheism', and later exclaiming: 'From liberty, equality and the rights of man, good Lord deliver *us*.'[132]

The people were being poisoned by print. 'Novels,' Miss More lamented, 'are now become mischievous', for 'they are . . . at once employed to diffuse destructive politics, deplorable profligacy, and impudent infidelity'. While the plebs pored over Paine, the heroines of trashy novels dieted exclusively on tea, 'novels and metaphysicks'.[133] Whatever next? When *The Rights of Man* was promptly followed by Wollstonecraft's *Vindication of the Rights of Woman* (1792), she exploded: 'the next influx of that irradiation, which our enlightenment is pouring in upon us, will illuminate the world with grave descants on the rights of youth – the rights of children – the rights of babies!' (She guessed right: in 1797 Thomas Spence produced his *Rights of Infants*.)[134]

Still, recognizing that print had to be fought with print, in 1795

More devised her 'Cheap Repository Tracts'; priced at around a penny each, their sales were amazing – in the first six weeks, 300,000 copies of the various tracts were sold wholesale, and by March 1796, the total had reached 2,000,000 copies.[135] In order 'to counteract the pernicious doctrines, which, owing to the French Revolution, were then becoming seriously alarming', she had set the ball rolling back in 1793 with *Village Politics* – it has been dubbed 'Burke for Beginners' – addressing it to 'all the Mechanics, Journeymen, and Labourers in Great Britain'. Hammering home the message of obedience to superiors, another of her books, *The Riot; or, Half a Loaf is Better than No Bread* (1795), takes the form of a dialogue between Jack Anvil, an honest blacksmith, and Tom Hod, a mason, who has been seduced by the works of his namesake, Tom Paine, and who wants 'a new constitution, liberty and equality'. 'What book art reading?' Jack asks Tom, 'Why dost look so like a hang dog?'

TOM: (looking on his book.) Cause enough. Why I find here that I'm very unhappy, and very miserable; which I should never have known if I had not had the good luck to meet with this book. O 'tis a precious book!

JACK: A good sign tho'; that you can't find out you're unhappy without looking into a book for it. What is the matter?

TOM: Matter? Why I want liberty.

JACK: Liberty! What has one fetched a warrant for thee? Come man, cheer up, I'll be bound for thee. – Thou art an honest fellow in the main, tho' thou dost tipple and prate a little too much at the Rose and Crown.

TOM: No, no, I want a new constitution.

JACK: Indeed! Why I thought thou hadst been a desperate healthy fellow. Send for the doctor then.

TOM: I'm not sick; I want Liberty and Equality, and the Rights of Man.

JACK: O now I understand thee. What thou art a leveller and a republican I warrant . . .

TOM: I'm a friend to the people. I want a reform . . . I want freedom and happiness, the same as they have got in France.

Patient Jack then has to explain to surly Tom that 'when this levelling comes about, there will be no infirmaries, no hospitals, no charity-schools, no Sunday-schools . . . For who is to pay for them? Equality can't afford it',[136] before going on to cite St Paul on obeying the powers that be, and to reassure his mate that England has the best king, laws and liberty in the world. All ends happily with Tom agreeing to 'mind his own business', and both singing 'The Roast Beef of England'.[137] Along similar lines, Miss More's *History of Mr Fantom the New-fashioned Philosopher and his Man William* (179?) features a rash footman character called William Wilson, who has been debauched by radical philosophy and ends up being hanged: '*New-Fashioned Philosopher*' says it all.[138]

Another who assailed enlightenment from the Evangelical corner was William Wilberforce.[139] 'Rational religion' was, he maintained, mere 'nominal Christianity', rational Christians were well-nigh heathens and faith had to be 'vital', a religion of the True Cross.[140] Back in 1785 Wilberforce, then a young MP for Hull, recorded his 'despair of the republic', precipitated by 'the universal corruption and profligacy of the times'. Convinced it was a matter of 'reform or ruin', he unfolded his mission: 'God Almighty has set before me two great objects,' he solemnly recorded in his diary on 28 October 1787, 'the suppression of the slave trade and the reformation of manners.' His Evangelicalism was grounded on human depravity – man 'is an apostate creature, fallen from his high original, degraded in his nature' – and Christ crucified.[141] It had become the 'commonly received opinion', asserted his *A Practical View of the Prevailing Religious System of Professed Christians in the Higher and Middle Classes in this Country Contrasted with Real Christianity* (1797) – to become the Evangelicals' handbook – 'that provided a man admit in general terms the truth of Christianity . . . we have no great reason to be dissatisfied with him'.[142] Countering not just Latitudinarianism at large but specifically Paley's utilitarianism ('it is a happy world after all'),[143] Wilberforce reasserted a more sombre divinity, stressing man's probationary state, moral trial and redemption:

Christianity appears to me to consider the world as in a state of alienation from God . . . It ought to be the grand object of every moral writer . . . to produce in us that true and just sense of the intensity of the malignity of sin . . . Now, here, Dr Paley appears to me to fail.[144]

Certain of sinfulness, Wilberforce made the Atonement once more central to Christianity. The political consequences must be heeded: it was 'to the decline of religion and morality', he wrote, 'that our national difficulties must both directly and indirectly be chiefly ascribed'.[145]

The most striking instance of the retreat into reaction is Thomas Robert Malthus. His father, Daniel, a personal friend of Rousseau, had been a torchbearer of enlightenment and had had his Bob educated by the most advanced teachers, notably Gilbert Wakefield of the Warrington Academy and William Frend, who tutored him from 1784 at Jesus College, Cambridge (from which he was later expelled for his Jacobinism). Schooled in Locke and Hartley, the son had been groomed to become a philosophical radical – before what might now be called his Oedipal revolt.[146]

The champagne fizz of revolution had naturally created great expectations, but were they rationally justified? asked Malthus in his *Essay on the Principles of Population* (1798). Radicals promised perfectibility, yet was mankind truly about to realize such Promethean dreams?[147] Unlike Burke and Wilberforce, Malthus never denied the attraction of the 'new dawn', but his mood was wary. The programme of boundless progress was intrinsically self-defeating – knowledge would produce growth, growth would increase wealth, wealth would then fuel a population explosion – and that demanded attention to home truths:

population must always be kept down to the level of the means of subsistence; but no writer . . . has inquired particularly into the means by which this level is effected: and it is a view of these means, which forms, to his mind, the strongest obstacle in the way to any very great future improvement of society.[148]

Malthus had thus hit upon the visionaries' blind spot. For mercantilists and utilitarians, the more people the better – underpopulated kingdoms lacked labourers, soldiers and taxpayers. But, countered Malthus, the implications of such an increase had never been thought through by prophets of progress like Godwin and the Marquis de Condorcet, author of the *Esquisse d'un Tableau Historique des Progrès de l'Esprit Humain* (1795). Fantasy had outrun thought: 'I have certainly no right to say that they purposely shut their eyes,' ironized the Anglican clergyman, yet 'we are all of us too prone to err'.[149]

Countering the daydreamers, Malthus posed as the sober realist, scorning rhetoric and 'mere conjectures' in favour of facts.[150] He alone had adopted the scientific approach to those questions of production and reproduction 'explained in part by Hume, and more at large by Dr Adam Smith'.[151] The issue lay in the discrepancies between great expectations and demographic reality. 'Were the rising generation free from the "killing frost" of misery', population 'must rapidly increase', for affluence would induce earlier marriage.[152] Condorcet had glimpsed this overpopulation abyss, but had shrunk from its implications.[153] He was to be honoured for recognizing that rising population was an *obstacle* rather than an *opportunity*, but faulted for then ducking the issue.[154]

Where Condorcet was complacent, Malthus was all concern:[155] surging population was bound to stymie improvement. Radical plans were ravishing – Godwin's philosophy was 'by far the most beautiful and engaging of any that has yet appeared'[156] – but utopian bubbles were pricked by natural facts. Zealots ascribed all evils to the *ancien régime*; abolish the old order and, hey presto, everything was possible. But 'the great error under which Mr Godwin labours throughout his whole work, is, the attributing almost all the vices and misery that are seen in civil society to human institutions'.[157] The real obstacle was not the vices of the politicians but the nature of things.

How then did Nature balance production and reproduction? 'I think,' Malthus proposed, 'I may fairly make two postulata', namely that 'food is necessary to the existence of man' and that 'the passion between the sexes is necessary, and will remain nearly in its present state' ('These two laws ... appear to have been fixed laws of our nature').[158] Population would thus inevitably tend to outrun resources and precipitate crisis: famine, epidemics and war. That was the great problem the radicals had never faced – they had merely come up with frivolous suggestions, notably Godwin's silly surmise 'that the passion between the sexes may in time be extinguished'.[159] Nature herself, in other words, foiled dreams of social equality.[160] Grant these iron laws, and gloom was the only realism: 'that the superior power of population cannot be checked, without producing misery or vice . . . bear too convincing a testimony'.[161]

Malthus thus spelt out a dismal future, with Nature ever poised to avenge herself against hubristic man. Subsequent editions of the *Essay* did at least suggest that catastrophe could be avoided – through 'moral restraint'. Those unable to support families should abstain from marriage or, within marriage, desist from sex. (Parson Malthus abhorred contraception, for that sanctioned vice.)

Malthus was to be rebutted by many opponents, from all moral and political quarters; and in many ways the Malthusian controversy was the crux of the Enlightenment: Are man and Nature good? Thundering on through the nineteenth century, it mainly lies well beyond the scope of this book; however, it would be worthwhile to look briefly at two doctors who early refuted him, since both did so on the basis of enlightened reasoning.

In 1805 the Dissenting physician Charles Hall brought out *The Effects of Civilization on the People in European States*, which later acquired an anti-Malthusian 'Appendix'.[162] Like the parson, the doctor too was haunted by the spectre of poverty; Hall, however, insisted that the root of the problem lay in the iniquitous political system. Society had split into two nations, rich and poor – 'the deaths of the poor are to those of the rich as two to one'. The occupations of the latter were harmful to their health; their moral education was neglected, their minds uncultivated, their lot insupportable. All this was due to an exploitative economic order.[163] Malthus, Hall noted, 'does not consider civilization as chargeable with any thing on this account, because, as he says, the same want and misery must necessarily happen in every system', but that was false! Politics played the major part; rulers created the problem and then blamed Nature. Seeking a solution, Hall, like Spence and others, looked to land redistribution.

A second critic was the Dissenter Thomas Jarrold.[164] Born in 1770, he was educated in medicine at Edinburgh University, going on to practise in Manchester, where he mixed with the manufacturing community, writing *Anthropologia, or Dissertations on the Form and Colour in Man* (1808) and other works on education, character and poverty.[165] In *Dissertations on Man, Philosophical, Physiological and Political; In answer to Mr Malthus's 'Essay on the Principle of Population'* (1806), Jarrold contended that misery was not man's *natural* lot: 'there is no physical cause of war, none of famine, none of pestilence'. Calamity 'arises out of some act of human folly, or is the consequence of ignorance'.[166] Since man was thus the agent of his own destruction, the prevalence of misery did not prove its necessity.[167] The spectre of overpopulation was in any case unfounded. Increase was checked by many forces. Savage tribes were too warlike to expand, while in civilized societies various groups – prostitutes and professors, for instance – produced few offspring. Because 'man is not a mere animal', fertility was not a biological constant but a social variable.[168]

Hall and Jarrold equally refuted Malthus, but from diametrically opposite positions. For Hall, hunger and poverty were the progeny not of Nature but of capitalism; for Jarrold, much as for Erasmus Darwin, modern capitalist society offered the escape from those Malthusian dilemmas. Hall believed, like Godwin, that political action would eradicate poverty; Jarrold, that any overpopulation threat would wither away with growing prosperity. Both accused Malthus of a fatalism that followed from fathering on Nature arrangements which were essentially manmade, historical and political. Against Malthus's degrading vision – man as a slave to sexual appetites – both Hall and Jarrold defended divine design and human dignity. And both looked forward to better things – 'the period is hastening when the condition of mankind will be far better than it now is,' Jarrold concluded; 'already I fancy I have seen the first dawning of this wished-for morning'.[169] Both thus boldly reaffirmed enlightened optimism.

*

Overall, however, the war years which culminated in the battle of Waterloo in 1815 were black times for the enlightened, who found themselves at odds with the political nation and the government, and involved in rearguard actions to defend the century's gains, notably freedom of speech and assembly and the other basic liberties won after 1688. Not only were they opposed by new ideologies of reaction, but erstwhile allies were jumping ship.

Some remained steadfast, however, like young Byron, whose lordly satire expressed a staunchly enlightened hostility to turncoat Romantics, Evangelicals and Tories.[170] Another was William Hazlitt, who at the age of twenty had been mesmerized by the radical Coleridge. The son of a Unitarian minister, while still a child Hazlitt had read the *Tatler, Tom Jones* and all the other modern classics ('buried treasure') in his father's study, and thus bore impeccably enlightened credentials. Failing as an artist, he was to scrape a living as a prolific and pungent lecturer, journalist and essay-writer. Turbulent, inveterate and finally embittered, Hazlitt had a sense of being a loner ('born under Saturn') which owed much to his Nonconformist origins. Reflecting on the dissidence of Dissent, he remarked, 'it was my misfortune (perhaps) to be bred among Dissenters . . . [he was educated at the Hackney Academy] who look with too jaundiced an eye at others, and set too high a value on their own peculiar pretensions. From being proscribed themselves, they learn to proscribe others.'[171]

Hazlitt had hailed the French Revolution: 'a new world,' he wrote, 'was opening to the astonished sight . . . Nothing was too mighty for this new-begotten hope; and the path that led to human happiness seemed as plain as the pictures in the *Pilgrim's Progress* leading to Paradise.'[172] And, proscribed and proscribing, he remained an unwavering Jacobin:[173] 'The love of liberty consists in the hatred of tyrants.'[174] A prose Byron, Hazlitt characterized his times as the age of betrayal: England had betrayed itself, and France the Revolution; the Lake Poets betrayed their Jacobinism; the English politicians betrayed the constitution and the spirit of liberty; Burke betrayed his liberal principles, Bentham betrayed humanity and Malthus and Godwin betrayed experience. The depths of Hazlitt's disillusionment followed from a sense of enlightened hopes dashed. 'I am no politician,' he insisted in 1819 in his *Political Essays*:

and still less can I be said to be a partyman: but I have a hatred of tyranny, and a contempt for its tools . . . I deny that liberty and slavery are convertible terms, that right and wrong, truth and falsehood, plenty and famine, the comforts or wretchedness of a people, are matters of perfect indifference. That is all I know of the matter; but on these points I am likely to remain incorrigible.[175]

The reign of George III thus drew to a close with a mad monarch, with enlightened men like Hazlitt mourning the triumph of unreason, and with Swift's ghost cackling in the background.[176]

21

LASTING LIGHT?

Books have always a secret influence on the understanding.

SAMUEL JOHNSON[1]

He that effects, by his writings or by his actions, a permanent change in the minds of men, deserves to be considered of no less importance in the history of the human species, than a statesman or conqueror who produces a revolution in a kingdom.

THOMAS DAY[2]

The eighteenth century ... has been, of all that are past, the most honourable to human nature. Knowledge and virtue were increased and diffused; arts, sciences, useful to men, ameliorating their condition, were improved more than in any former equal period.

JOHN ADAMS[3]

Postmodernism has one virtue at least – it has reopened inquiries into modernity and its origins.[4] When, why, how did the 'modern' self and 'modern' society come into being? Should we root back as far as the 'self-fashioning' men of the Renaissance, or pitch our inquiries further forward?[5] This book has rated the eighteenth century crucial to the creation of modern mentalities, claiming that British thinkers were prominent, indeed precocious, in such processes. To speak of enlightenment in Britain does not merely make sense; not to do so would be nonsense.

As contemporaries of all political stripes agreed, modern attitudes were inseparable from the explosion of print culture. 'By this art we

seem to be secured against the future perishing of human improvement,' declared William Godwin.

Knowledge is communicated to too many individuals to afford its adversaries a chance of suppressing it. The monopoly of science [that is, know-
ledge] is substantially at an end. By the easy multiplication of copies, and
the cheapness of books, everyone has access to them. The extreme inequality
of information among different members of the same community, which
existed in ancient times, is diminished.[6]

Professing that printing had aided 'the emancipation of mankind',
Godwin credited Cardinal Wolsey's clairvoyance in stating: 'we must
destroy the press; or the press will destroy us'.[7]

The end of censorship spelt a new order. Supporters of the Glorious
Revolution trumpeted press freedom, which subsequent radicals
expected to usher in further transformations – although in the dark
days of the 1790s the pen might seem threatened once again.

> Oh save, oh save, in this eventful hour
> The tree of knowledge from the axe of power . . .[8]

beseeched the fearful Erasmus Darwin in *The Temple of Nature*. What
enlightened activists were heralding was a new order presided over
and masterminded by the writer as fighter. And since, back in the
1740s, David Hume had frankly confessed that 'governors have
nothing to support them but opinion', the logic of the situation
required traditionalists to retaliate in kind: not just for progressives
but for everybody, the word had become the sword.[9]

Integral to these developments was an emergent cadre of cultural
producers and brokers – from Hume down to Blotpage and his ilk –
prefiguring in some ways what Coleridge would shortly dub the
clerisy.[10] 'In opulent or commercial society,' observed Adam Smith,
'to think or reason comes to be, like every other employment, a
particular business, which is carried on by a very few people, who
furnish the public with all the thought and reason possessed by the
vast multitudes that labour.'[11]

The illustrious historian Franco Venturi once wrote of eighteenth-century England that its 'struggles' were 'not those of a nascent intelligentsia'; but he was surely wrong.[12] Thinkers come in many guises, and the Italian avant-garde of the age of the *carbonari*, which is what Venturi perhaps had in mind, along with the French *philosophes*, naturally were not modelled on those of Georgian London, Manchester or Birmingham – or Edinburgh and Dublin, for that matter. But British writers were hardly minor promoters of change, be they the 'true Whigs' meeting at the Grecian coffee house under Queen Anne, mocking hellfire and damning tyrants and papists, the Lunar Society's liberal technocrats, the rosy-cheeked pantisocrats enthused by Coleridge or the authors milling around the bookshop of the radical London publisher Joseph Johnson and eating his suppers. John Aikin, Anna Barbauld, Erasmus Darwin – this is to go through an alphabetical list of just the more celebrated – John Disney, Richard Lovell Edgeworth, Thomas Erskine, George Fordyce, William Frend, Henry Fuseli, William Godwin, Mary Hays, Thomas Henry, Thomas Holcroft, Theophilus Lindsey, John Newton, Thomas Paine, Richard Price, Joseph Priestley, Horne Tooke, George Walker and Mary Wollstonecraft, and, slightly later, Humphry Davy, Maria Edgeworth, William Hazlitt, Thomas Robert Malthus, Henry Crabb Robinson and William Wordsworth: all these intellectual notables were linked with just one single publisher.[13] Such personages hardly resemble a cloak and dagger crew; few styled themselves, like Hazlitt, 'Jacobin', and some were to become downright reactionary. But that merely illustrates the complex and volatile allegiances of the knowledge-mongers in the high-tension French Revolutionary years. By what criterion would such a roll of 'philosophers' – ones who, in the enlightened sense of the term, 'ought to be something greater, and better than another man'[14] – be denied the title of a 'nascent intelligentsia'?

While this ideas élite included ministers of religion, both Anglican and Dissenting, it was rapidly becoming detached from any primary identification with the organized churches; nor was it principally bankrolled by the Court, by grandees or by the ministry. Increasingly, writers and thinkers functioned as autonomous individuals, at bottom beholden to none but themselves, the public who bought their writings or subscribed to their lectures, and such cultural middlemen as publishers. 'From a sociological point of view,' the German sociologist Karl Mannheim once observed, 'the decisive fact of modern times . . . is that this monopoly of the ecclesiastical interpretation of the world, which was held by the priestly caste, is broken, and . . . a free intelligentsia has arisen.' Mannheim's reading illuminates the British scene better than Venturi's.[15]

New personae for the modern thinker were being forged: not the pedant, cooped up in a college, or the 'dull and deep potations' don, but an urban, sociable sort, in the vanguard of humanity, in touch with the people for whom he spoke and wrote, be he an essayist or an itinerant scientific lecturer. A generation or so later, celebrating 'The Hero as Man of Letters', Thomas Carlyle eulogized the achievements of literary men and freelance intellectuals in spreading the word, eclipsing the pulpit and the despatch box: 'literature is our Parliament'.[16] And if, by the mid-Victorian era, John Stuart Mill would accuse public opinion of imposing a conformist straitjacket, its enlightened precursor was, by and large, regarded as a force for criticism and change.[17]

With the rise of *belles lettres*, novels, magazines, newspapers and pulp fiction, Britain found itself awash with print, and elaborate feedback loops emerged, real and virtual, linking authors and auditors. Enlightened men of letters assumed a multiplicity of garbs: as scourges, reformers, hand-wringing Jeremiahs, satirists, gossip columnists, prophets, gurus, watchdogs, publicists and tribunes of the people.[18] Many assumed dramatic poses – self-promoting, self-advertising, even laceratingly self-confessional, as when Godwin or Mary Hays 'told all'. Intellectuals came to exude the air of a narcissistic *bien-pensant* coterie writing about each other,[19] surreptitiously propagating the idea that writers and artists were the people who really counted, the true legislators of the world.

Secular thinkers set themselves up as critics and above all as teachers. They would be the educators of mankind, possessed, like Peacock's Scythrop – a.k.a. Percy Bysshe Shelley – of a passion 'for reforming the world',[20] a mission which meant stealing fire from the gods and bringing it down to earth, or at least countering convention with Promethean aspirations.

This coming intelligentsia prided itself upon being at the cutting edge of thought: it would strike off the shackles of tradition, prejudice, vested interests and oppression, and defend the first principles of freedom: habeas corpus, free speech, a free press, free trade, universal education. Refinement, or, in a later, modified idiom, self-improvement, came to the fore. Everyone was to make himself – with a little help from his guru, be he Mr Spectator or Tom Telescope.

From Bacon's *New Atlantis* to Robert Owen's *New View of Society*, the great buzzword was novelty. New terms were being coined and old ones acquiring new meanings: intellectual, autobiography, rationalism, humanitarian, utilitarian, public opinion, romanticism, ideology, primitive, decade, progressive, modernize, contemporary, antiquated, journalist and many more keywords of modernity. Predictably, neologism was itself a neologism, and 'radical' as a political noun a 1790s minting.[21] Thought wars spawned multiple '-isms' and '-ologies', a development dazzlingly parodied in the satires of that last Enlightenment wit, Thomas Love Peacock. 'Men have been found,' observed his Sir Telegraph Paxarett in *Melincourt* (1817), 'very easily permutable into *ites* and *onians*, *avians* and *arians* . . . Trinitarians, Unitarians, Anythingarians.'[22] There was a new pluralism of the pen in paper wars which some called anarchy, fearing it would lead to what the *British Critic* dubbed 'a state of literary warfare' in which defenders of the established order were dutybound 'to wield the pen, and shed the ink'.[23]

Enlightened minds piqued themselves upon being not just new but *different*. Burke jeered at the 'dissidence of dissent',[24] and, following in his footsteps, J. C. D. Clark is on the right track in concluding that what 'did more than anything to break down the old order' was 'the advance of Dissent'.[25] Clark, however, defines 'Dissent' too narrowly in ecclesiastical terms – better far to have characterized it as an ecumenical expression of the drive to criticize, question and subvert. How telling to be confronted with the reaction of Mary Shelley –

that child (quite literally) of the Enlightenment – when she eventually said goodbye to all that.[26] The deluge of personal tragedies that was her early life, beginning with the death of her mother, Mary Wollstonecraft, brought home the wretched folly of radical over-reaching. Marriage to Shelley had left her with one small son. Told that young Percy should, like his father, be encouraged to think for himself, she recoiled in horror: 'Oh God, teach him to think like other people.' And, to make sure that this happened without a hitch, she sent him to Harrow. He rose without trace to become a Member of Parliament and, reassuringly, a conformist nonentity.[27]

It has not been the claim of this book that Britain was unique, or even necessarily first, in producing a crop of ideas unknown anywhere else.[28] But neither should we be dismissive. Perry Anderson concluded, as we have seen, that Britain produced 'no ferment of ideas', and Robert Palmer judged the phrase English Enlightenment 'jarring and incongruous'. But against such naysayers, I have argued for the importance of Locke and Newton, Addison and Steele, Hume and Smith, Hartley and Bentham, Price and Priestley, and many another, both in changing mentalities in Britain and, to some degree, in influencing developments abroad. In any novelty competition, British authors can certainly hold a candle to their Continental *confrères*. If the Enlightenment had a 'father', Locke's paternity claim is better than any other, and Bentham was the most innovative exponent of a utilitarianism destined to exert a worldwide appeal; there was no freer free-thinker than Anthony Collins, no more ornery liberal individualist than Joseph Priestley while, for his part, William Godwin, the author of anarchism, undertook an astonishing root and branch rational rethink of politico-moral life from first principles. Doubtless the prosy egghead whom Hazlitt called a 'metaphysician grafted upon the Dissenting minister' utterly lacked Diderot's charm and impish wit: but his model of the autonomous new man remains breathtakingly original and challenging.

It has not been my intention to write the history of 'enlightenment in one country', but in two key respects Britain did indeed do it 'my way', and a stress on the 'Englishness of the English Enlightenment' has some validity.[29] Enlightenment came early to the British Isles, and so its champions were exercised not only with having to *create* it but also then to *defend* it once achieved – theirs became a labour not just of criticizing and demolishing but of explaining, vindicating and extending. In Britain enlightenment was thus both an end and also a beginning.[30] The 'mission accomplished' mentality, however, certainly did not preclude ongoing criticism and subversion, the problematizing of the progressive. Not least, the late Enlightenment involved a restless quest for personal self-discovery among newly articulate circles not dissimilar to the 1960s youth revolt against the complacency of Western democracies, confronting the credibility gap between rhetoric and reality.

The other regard in which the British Enlightenment was distinctive from that typical on the Continent was its pervasive individualism. Locke stressed personal rights against the ruler; Hume prized private life over civic virtue; Smith championed the individual actor in the free market – the invisible hand would bring public good out of private; Bentham held all equal and every man the best judge of his own interests, while Godwin formulated a systematic anarchism. The hallmark of British thinking lay in casting progress as a matter of individual improvement or (as with hospitals, schools and charities) as the work of voluntary associations. Kantian categorical imperatives found their English counterparts in a hedonic calculus. At variance with Foucault's stress on discipline, surveillance and control, much enlightened thinking was directed towards dissent and disestablishment, was about dismantling 'the Thing' – or doing your own thing.[31]

Enlightened endeavours blossomed early. The Locke–Addison trinity of liberty, self-interest and polish gained a firm hold in polite society, being devalued and debunked only by dogged self-marginalizers like Swift, Wesley and Blake.[32] Over the longer haul, however, the pursuit of a free, open, yet stable society – combining dynamic individualism with social orderliness – was derailed by late-century social and ideological fractures; to switch metaphors, the chickens of possessive individualism were at last, just as the doomsters had warned, coming home to roost.[33]

Undergoing socio-political growing pains and tensions, liberal ideologies began to shiver into fragments. For some, as we have seen, libertarian rhetoric led to Jacobin radicalism – witness Tom Paine's very titles: *Common Sense*, *The Age of Reason* and *The Rights of Man*. Bourgeois liberalism, as endorsed by the Whiggish *Edinburgh Review* (founded in 1802), for its part put a different face upon enlightened ideology: individualism was there to obey the iron laws of political economy; social harmonization demanded time and work discipline, penology and scientific poor laws; while humanitarian impulses bled into proto-Victorian sentimentality.[34] Meanwhile, Establishment apologists began to draw conclusions of their own from enlightened premises. Malthus in particular put a new gloss on desire, recruiting science to prove how legislative action could not, after all, relieve suffering and starvation.[35] More dramatically, French Revolutionary turmoil led many to change sides.

Yet, in the long run, enlightened ideologies were not discarded: they had bored too deep into the bones. By providing secular legitimation for capitalism, they continued to inform Victorian self-help liberalism and free-market ideology – the road from Smith to Smiles.[36] By touting rational self-help, they promised a meliorist, moralized future which immunized native radicals against Marxist creeds of class war or communitarian socialism. Phrenology, secularism and Fabianism were all, in their own ways, Enlightenment legacies. John Stuart Mill could declare at the beginning of the Victorian age that every Englishmen was by implication 'a Benthamite or a Coleridgian': the former were evidently children of the Enlightenment.[37] The famous Halévy thesis perhaps needs modifying: perhaps it was not Methodism but rather the Enlightenment which inoculated the English against the French, indeed against all subsequent revolutions.[38]

None of these developments was unambiguous or without the most profound tensions. Enlightened activism always involved clashing interests, and its elastic ideological resources could be deployed for radical ends or equally by sections of the propertied, plutocratic and polite against those they sought to discredit, convert or marginalize. Mine has been no tale of 'progress', but rather one of *Kulturkampf*, racked with contradictions, struggles and ironies, and leaving in its wake multiple casualties and victims.

It is this continuing ideological warfare which shows that the Enlightenment's big idea really did take root. 'Should free inquiry lead to the destruction of Christianity itself,' it will be remembered Joseph Priestley once reflected, 'it ought not, on that account, to be discontinued; for we can only wish for the prevalence of Christianity on the supposition of its being true; and if it fall before the influence of free inquiry, it can only do so in consequence of its not being true.'[39] Substitute 'Enlightenment' for 'Christianity' and Priestley's statement becomes a fair gloss on the modern commitment to free inquiry, that liberty tree planted by the Enlightenment, that impious demand to know 'your reason, your reason' and to deny and defy forbidden knowledge.[40] One further substitution shall close this book. Combining hope, humanity and humility, William Hazlitt paid generous tribute to Thomas Holcroft, that most pugnacious of the late enlighteners:

He believed that truth had a natural superiority over error, if it could only be heard; that if once discovered, it must, being left to itself, soon spread and triumph; and that the art of printing would not only accelerate this effect, but would prevent those accidents which had rendered the moral and intellectual progress of mankind hitherto so slow, irregular and uncertain.[41]

Transferred to the British Enlightenment at large, there could be no more accurate summary of its ideals.

NOTES

INTRODUCTION

1 J. G. A. Pocock, 'Clergy and Commerce' (1985), p. 528.

2 J. G. A. Pocock, 'Post-Puritan England and the Problem of the Enlightenment' (1980), p. 91.

3 The Revd Richard Price, *A Discourse on the Love of our Country* (1789), pp. 11–12.

4 For instance, Robert Darnton puts Locke and Toland in a 'pre-Enlightenment': 'George Washington's False Teeth' (27 March 1997). I can see no reason for detaching from the Enlightenment proper its most influential philosopher of empiricism, freedom and toleration and its most challenging Deist. I am likewise dubious about talk of 'anticipations', as, for instance, in A. C. Kors and Paul J. Korshin (eds.), *Anticipations of the Enlightenment in England, France and Germany* (1987).

5 'Eighteenth-century people,' it has been aptly noted, 'were generally quite precise with their gender signifiers, and seldom used terms like "man" to mean anyone other than the males of the species': Margaret R. Hunt, *The Middling Sort* (1996), p. xiii. A contemporary observation nevertheless deserves consideration:

The word Man is used for one of the human species, for a male, for a full grown person, a corpse, a statue, a picture, or a piece of wood upon a chessboard, yet we never mistake the meaning, being directed thereto by what gave occasion for its being employed.

Abraham Tucker, *The Light of Nature Pursued* (1997 [1768]), vol. i, p. 241.

6 Confusion easily sets in: aficionados of typos will relish the following: 'when we speak of the Scottish Englishtenment [sic] . . .': Pocock, 'Post-Puritan England and the Problem of the Enlightenment', p. 92.

7 Norman Davies, *The Isles* (1999); Alexander Grant and Keith Stringer (eds.), *Uniting the Kingdom? The Making of British History* (1995).

8 See, for political theory, J. G. A. Pocock, *The Machiavellian Moment* (1975), and *Virtue, Commerce and History* (1985); for culture, John Brewer, *The Pleasures of the Imagination* (1997); for patriotism, Linda Colley, *Britons* (1992).

9 John Yolton's accounts of Locke and the Lockean tradition are exemplary: *John Locke and the Way of Ideas* (1956), *Locke: An Introduction* (1985), and *Locke and French Materialism* (1991).

10 A further aspect of the 'English-speaking Enlightenment' is here totally omitted: the American experience. Other scholars have already done the American job for me, notably Henry F. May, *The Enlightenment in America* (1976), and Ernest Cassara, *The Enlightenment in America* (1988).

11 For English exceptionalism, see E. P. Thompson, 'The Peculiarities of the English', in his *The Poverty of Theory and Other Essays* (1978), pp. 35–91.

12 For valuable instances of that kind of scholarship, see Fania Oz-Salzberger, *Translating the Enlightenment* (1995); Vincenzo Ferrone, *The Intellectual Roots of the Italian*

Enlightenment (1995); Franco Venturi, 'Scottish Echoes in Eighteenth-Century Italy' (1985), pp. 345–62.

13 Henry Steele Commager, *The Empire of Reason* (1978).

14 J. L. Talmon, *The Rise of Totalitarian Democracy* (1952).

15 For the Frankfurt School's road from Enlightenment to Auschwitz, see M. Horkheimer and T. Adorno, *The Dialectic of Enlightenment* (1990), p. 6. However good as polemic, it is historical baloney; after all, the Nazis loathed the *philosophes*. It should, however, be remembered that in Nazi usage *Aufklärung* (enlightenment) meant 'propaganda'.

16 Michel Foucault, 'What is Enlightenment?' (1984). For discussion, see David R. Hiley, 'Foucault and the Question of Enlightenment' (1985–6); Christopher Norris, ' "What is Enlightenment?" ' (1994); Jürgen Habermas, 'Taking Aim at the Heart of the Present' (1986).

17 On this 'mind-forg'd manacles' world fantasized by historically uninformed postmodernists, see Terry Castle, *The Female Thermometer* (1994), p. 13. See also Jonathan Dollimore, *Death, Desire and Loss in Western Culture* (1998), p. 123, on Jean Baudrillard's crazed postmodernist reading:

> The main claim is that Enlightenment rationality is an instrument not of freedom and democratic empowerment but, on the contrary, of repression and violence. Likewise with the Enlightenment's secular emphasis upon a common humanity; for Baudrillard this resulted in what he calls 'the cancer of the Human' – far from being an inclusive category of emancipation, the idea of a universal humanity made possible the demonizing of difference and the repressive privileging of the normal.

18 The previous lines read: 'one of the few things that stands between us and an accelerated descent into darkness is the set of values inherited from the eighteenth-century Enlightenment. This is not a fashionable view': Eric Hobsbawm, *On History* (1997), p. 254. For similar views, see also Robert Wokler, 'The Enlightenment Project and its Critics' (1997). Dismal structuralist and postmodernist readings of the Enlightenment, which stigmatize reason as an instrument of exclusion, ideological control and disciplinary power, have also been torpedoed by Robert Darnton in 'George Washington's False Teeth'. The politics of Enlightenment in American postmodernism are exhaustively treated in Karlis Racevskis, *Postmodernism and the Search for Enlightenment* (1993).

19 Mark Goldie, 'Priestcraft and the Birth of Whiggism' (1993), p. 210. 'In France,' judged E. P. Thompson, along similar lines:

> the armies of Orthodoxy and Enlightenment faced each other. [But] . . . the Enlightenment proceeded in Britain not like one of those flood-tides massing against a crumbling dyke, but like the tide which seeps into the eroded shores, mudflats and creeks, of an estuary whose declivities are ready to receive it.

'The Peculiarities of the English' in *The Poverty of Theory and Other Essays* (1978), p. 58.

20 Joseph Priestley and Richard Price, *A Free Discussion of the Doctrines of Materialism and Philosophical Necessity* (1994 [1780]).

21 The rallying cry was Robert Darnton's 'In Search of the Enlightenment' (1971). For recent assessments, see Haydn T. Mason (ed.), *The Darnton Debate* (1998); Peter Burke (ed.), *New Perspectives on Historical Writing* (1991), especially Jim Sharpe, 'History from Below', pp. 24–41; John Bender, 'A New History of the Enlightenment?' (1992); and for light and shade, see P. Hulme and L. Jordanova (eds.), *Enlightenment and its Shadows* (1990).

22 'Enlightened' beliefs were not exclusive to enlightened activists. Espousal of this or that 'enlightened' conviction does not automatically turn an individual into a 'spokesman'; nor did the enlightened corner the market in decency or criticism. Jonathan Swift, for instance, ridiculed obfuscatory metaphysics, Roman Catholicism and occultism as intensely as Locke or Hume, but his misanthropic Christianity equally led him to denounce progressives as presumptuous. To ring-fence the Enlightenment in Britain would involve a travesty of the open and pluralist character of the culture.

23 Cited in Yolton, *Locke: An Introduction*, p. 1.

24 See Mark Goldie (ed.), *Locke: Political Essays* (1997), p. xiii.

25 Janet Semple, *Bentham's Prison* (1993), p. 100.

26 R. A. Knox, *Enthusiasm* (1950), p. 388.

27 William Hazlitt, *The New School of Reform* (1901–6 [1862]), p. 188.

28 For wise words on enlightened casuistry regarding ends, means and lesser evils, see Jean Starobinski, *The Remedy in the Disease* (1992).

29 W. J. Bate, J. M. Bullitt, and L. F. Powell (eds.), *Samuel Johnson: The Idler and Adventurer* (1963), p. 457.

30 George Birkbeck Hill, *Boswell's Life of Johnson* (1934–50), vol. ii, p. 170. See also Alvin Kernan, *Printing Technology, Letters and Samuel Johnson* (1987), p. 19.

31 David Hume, *Essays Moral, Political and Literary* (1898 [1741–2]), vol. i, essay vii, p. 54.

32 As will become apparent, I subscribe to the school which views eighteenth-century Britain as a cauldron of change rather than that 'place of rest and refreshment' hailed in George Saintsbury's *The Peace of the Augustans* (1916). I argue my case in 'English Society in the Eighteenth Century Revisited' (1990), and 'The New Eighteenth Century Social History' (1997).

1 A BLIND SPOT?

1 Perry Anderson, 'Origins of the Present Crisis' (1965), p. 17.

2 Immanuel Kant, *Beantwortung der Frage* (1912–22 [1784]), vol. iv, p. 169. For a translation see Isaac Kramnick (ed.), *The Portable Enlightenment Reader* (1995), pp. 1–7. Another eminent contributor was Moses Mendelssohn: James Schmidt, 'The Question of Enlightenment' (1989). On such societies, see Richard van Dülmen, *The Society of the Enlightenment* (1992), pp. 52f.

3 'Our age,' Kant maintained, 'is, in especial degree, the age of criticism, and to criticism everything must submit': see Norman Kemp Smith (ed.), *Emmanuel Kant's Critique of Pure Reason* (1963), p. 9; R. Koselleck, *Critique and Crisis* (1988), p. 121.

4 See Dorinda Outram, *The Enlightenment* (1995), pp. 2f.

5 Kant broadened his outlook by reading, being famously awakened from his 'dogmatical slumbers' by reading Hume's *Inquiry concerning Human Understanding* (1748).

6 Jeremy Black (ed.), *Eighteenth Century Europe 1700–1789* (1990), p. 402; C. B. A. Behrens, *Society, Government and the Enlightenment* (1985).

7 For examples, see chapter 2 below and elsewhere in this book. Prussians like Pastor Moritz and Johann Wilhelm von Archenholz were scared to find so much liberty in England; Kant might possibly have had the same reaction had he ever gone west. My comments do not, of course, impugn Kant's philosophical genius, for which see Ernst Cassirer, *Kant's Life and Thought* (1982); J. B. Schneewind, *The Invention of Autonomy* (1998).

8 For censorship, see Eckhart Hellmuth, 'Enlightenment and the Freedom of the Press' (1998); Black (ed.), *Eighteenth Century Europe 1700–1789*, p. 404. For Phillips, see George S. Marr, *The Periodical Essayists of the Eighteenth Century* (1971), p. 57.

9 Anthony Ashley Cooper, 3rd Earl of Shaftesbury, to Jean Le Clerc (1706), quoted in B. Rand, *The Life, Unpublished Letters and Philosophical Regimen of Anthony, Earl of Shaftesbury* (1900), p. 353. Shaftesbury began his 'Letter Concerning Enthusiasm' by observing that modern Britons were fortunate to live in a culture of criticism: 1688 made all the difference: 'I think Late England since the Revolution, to be better . . . than Old England by many a degree': Anthony Ashley Cooper, 3rd Earl of Shaftesbury, *Characteristicks of Men, Manners, Opinions, Times* (1999 [1711]), vol. i, p. 10.

10 Any naive belief in an 'age of reason' was destroyed by Carl Becker's waspish *The Heavenly City of the Eighteenth Century Philosophers* (1932). For the concept of modernity, see Marshall Berman, *All That is Solid Melts into Air* (1983), and Miles Ogborn, *Spaces of Modernity* (1998), who notes (p. 10) that it has been stated that 'against the backdrop of the Enlightenment, modernity is associated with the release of the individual from the bonds of tradition, with the progressive differentiation of society, with the emergence of civil society, with political equality, with innovation and change. All of these accomplishments are associated with capitalism, industrialism, secularisation, urbanisation and rationalisation.'

11 Peter Gay, *The Enlightenment, An Interpretation*, vol. i: *The Rise of Modern Paganism* (1967), vol. ii: *The Science of Freedom* (1970).

12 Influential in revisionism was Robert Darnton, 'In Search of the Enlightenment' (1971), and 'The High Enlightenment and the Low-Life of Literature in Pre-Revolutionary France' (1982); see also Haydn T. Mason (ed.), *The Darnton Debate* (1998). Outram, *The Enlightenment*, offers a succinct survey of Enlightenment historiography.

13 Ernst Cassirer, *The Philosophy of the Enlightenment* (1951), p. 174. Compare John Stuart Mill's verdict that Bentham 'was not a great philosopher': F. R. Leavis (ed.), *Mill on Bentham and Coleridge* (1962), p. 48.

14 L. M. Marsak (ed.), *The Enlightenment*

(1972); L. G. Crocker (ed.), *The Age of Enlightenment* (1969). Robert Anchor's *The Enlightenment Tradition* (1967), a general survey, discusses only one Briton more than passingly: David Hume (pp. 61–4). Among the nineteen Enlightenment protagonists she biographically spotlights, Dorinda Outram includes just two Britons, Locke and Newton, unaccountably omitting Hume, Bentham and Smith: see *The Enlightenment*, pp. 128–32.

15 James Schmidt (ed.), *What is Enlightenment?* (1996). There is a reason for this: the book focuses on Kant. An honourable exception is Isaac Kramnick (ed.), *The Portable Enlightenment Reader* (1995).

16 J. V. Price, 'Religion and Ideas' (1978); Christopher Hill, *Reformation to Industrial Revolution* (1969), p. 281; A. R. Humphreys, *The Augustan World* (1954); Pat Rogers, *The Augustan Vision* (1974); Kenneth Clark, quoted in R. W. Harris, *Reason and Nature in the Eighteenth Century* (1968), p. 234; for similar judgements, see Douglas Bush, *Science and English Poetry, a Historical Sketch 1590–1950* (1967), ch. 3.

17 Henry Steele Commager, *The Empire of Reason* (1977), p. 4; Robert R. Palmer, 'Turgot: Paragon of the Continental Enlightenment' (1976), p. 608. Some years earlier Alfred Cobban deemed the term Enlightenment 'hardly naturalized in English': *In Search of Humanity* (1960), p. 7.

18 W. O. Chadwick, *The Secularization of the European Mind in the Nineteenth Century* (1975); and see the *Oxford English Dictionary*, 2nd ed. (1989–), under 'Enlightenment'. For 'illuminati' etc., see Richard van Dülmen, *The Society of the Enlightenment* (1992), p. 105.

19 *The Shorter Oxford English Dictionary on Historical Principles* (1973), quoted by Arthur Wilson, 'The Enlightenment Came First to England' (1983), p. 3. Wilson acknowledges the Enlightenment in England, but oddly claims that its contribution was over by *c.*1700 (p. 4).

On philistinism: 'I wish I may be well

enough to listen to these intellectuals,' sighed Lord Byron as early as 1813: quoted in Raymond Williams, *Keywords* (1988), p. 141 – see Williams's wider discussion of the introduction of the largely negative 'intellectual'; see also W. E. Houghton, *The Victorian Frame of Mind 1830–1870* (1957), and, for a knockabout example of British anti-intellectualism, Paul Johnson, *Intellectuals* (1988).

20 John Redwood, *Reason, Ridicule and Religion* (1976). The most heinous charge there levelled against English free-thinkers was that they 'endangered the Church and most severely [sic] led to a seeming decay of manners' (p. 196). Redwood's opinionated book at least recognizes how radically old tenets were attacked – it truly was an age of crisis in a 'divided society'. It must be used with extra caution, since it is riddled with factual errors, mostly uncorrected in the 1996 reprint. Mention should also be made of John Gascoigne, *Joseph Banks and the English Enlightenment* (1994), which recognizes the phenomenon described in this book.

21 J. C. D. Clark, *English Society, 1688–1832* (1985), and *Revolution and Rebellion* (1986). Clark's denial of enlightenment on the grounds that 'no one in the English-speaking world then referred to "the Enlightenment" ' is wilful: *The Language of Liberty* (1994), p. 14: after all, many contemporaries spoke of 'this enlightened age'. For critiques, see Joanna Innes, 'Jonathan Clark, Social History, and England's Ancien Regime' (1987); G. S. Rousseau: 'Revisionist Polemics' (1989); Frank O'Gorman, 'Recent Historiography of the Hanoverian Regime' (1986); Jeremy Black, ' "England's Ancien Regime"?' (1988).

22 Indeed, not only no controversy, but a dearth of syntheses. The last major survey of Georgian thought is, almost unbelievably, Leslie Stephen's *History of English Thought in the Eighteenth Century*, published in 1876! Though himself an agnostic, and hence a child of the Enlightenment, Stephen's tone is schoolmasterly, berating sceptics for being glib rather than honest doubters like himself. Few Victorians sympathized with the age. The Oxford don Mark Pattison bantered that 'the genuine Anglican omits that period from the history of the Church altogether': B. W. Young, 'Knock-Kneed Giants' (1993), p. 87. For debates on the 'scientific revolution', see chapter 6.

23 F. M. Voltaire, *Letters concerning the English Nation* (1926 [1733]), pp. 41–2; Ahmad Gunny, *Voltaire and English Literature* (1979). In 1753 Voltaire congratulated William Lee, an English Grand Tourist, upon coming from 'the only nation where the least shadow of liberty remains in Europe': Jeremy Black, *Convergence or Divergence?* (1994), pp. 144–5; for discussion, see Daniel Roche, *France in the Enlightenment* (1988), p. 11. For other admiring visitors to England, see A. C. Cross, *'By the Banks of the Thames'* (1980).

24 See the introduction in F. M. Voltaire, *Philosophical Dictionary* (1962 [1764]), p. 9.

25 Voltaire, *Letters concerning the English Nation*, pp. 73, 76. Voltaire declared: 'Perhaps no Man ever had a more judicious or more methodical Genius, or was a more acute Logician than Mr Locke.'

26 Denis Diderot, *Oeuvres complètes* (1875–7), vol. ii, p. 80. Voltaire and Montesquieu, 'the true originators' of the Enlightenment, 'were the pupils and followers of England's philosophers and great men': quoted in Gay, *The Enlightenment*, vol. i, p. 12, from *Oeuvres complètes*, vol. iii, p. 416.

27 Quoted in Joseph Texte, *Jean-Jacques Rousseau and the Cosmopolitan Spirit in Literature* (1899), pp. 86–7.

28 Texte, *Jean-Jacques Rousseau and the Cosmopolitan Spirit in Literature*, p. 260.

29 Edward Gibbon, *Memoirs of My Life* (1966 [1796]), p. 125; Joséphine Grieder, *Anglomania in France, 1740–1789* (1985).

30 Franco Venturi, *Utopia and Reform in the Enlightenment* (1971), p. 67.

31 Diderot, *Oeuvres complètes*, vol. iii, p. 416,

quoted in Gay, *The Enlightenment*, vol. i, p. 12.

32 Norman Torrey, *Voltaire and the English Deists* (1930); Ahmad Gunny, *Voltaire and English Literature* (1979); I. O. Wade, *The Structure and Form of the French Enlightenment* (1977), vol. i, ch. 5; M. C. Jacob, 'Newtonianism and the Origins of the Enlightenment' (1977); and Ross Hutchison, *Locke in France (1688–1734)* (1991). Benjamin Franklin acknowledged Wollaston's *The Religion of Nature Delineated* as crucial to his mental development: Douglas Anderson, *The Radical Enlightenment of Benjamin Franklin* (1997), p. 6; Franco Venturi, *Utopia and Reform in the Enlightenment* (1971), p. 60.

33 R. L. Cru, *Diderot as a Disciple of English Thought* (repr. 1966), ch. 3.

34 Jean-Jacques Rousseau, *The Confessions of Jean-Jacques Rousseau* (1954 [1781–8]), p. 110. The *Spectator* was translated into French in 1714, the *Guardian* in 1725, the *Tatler* in 1734.

35 Mary P. Mack, *Jeremy Bentham, An Odyssey of Ideas, 1748–1792* (1962), p. 4.

36 See A. Rupert Hall, 'Newton in France: A New View' (1975). For long, Newton was synonymous with English supremacy. A Greek science journal stated early in the nineteenth century: 'After Bacon, dawned Newton, to the brilliance and eternal glory of England': George N. Vlahakis, 'The Greek Enlightenment in Science' (1999), p. 330.

37 Dorat, 'Idée de la poesie allamande' (1768), p. 43, quoted in Texte, *Jean-Jacques Rousseau and the Cosmopolitan Spirit in Literature*, p. 335.

38 Jean Le Rond d'Alembert, *Preliminary Discourse to the Encyclopedia of Diderot* (1995 [1751]), p. 109.

39 Cru, *Diderot as a Disciple of English Thought*, p. 351. Diderot and Sterne were friends. Shakespeare swept Germany in the early 1770s. Ossian enjoyed a great vogue, James Macpherson's *Fragments of Ancient Poetry Collected in the Highlands* (1760) being translated into German (1768), French (1777), Russian (1792), Dutch (1805), Danish (1807–9) and

Czech (1827), while it also figured in the plot of Goethe's *Werther* (1774): Jeremy Black, *Convergence or Divergence?* (1994), p. 155. Lichtenberg vowed to give up Klopstock's *Messias* 'twice over' for a small part of *Robinson Crusoe*: M. L. Mare and W. H. Quarrell, *Lichtenberg's Visits to England as Described in his Letters and Diaries* (1938), p. xxiii.

40 Quoted in Texte, *Jean-Jacques Rousseau and the Cosmopolitan Spirit in Literature*, p. 335.

41 Geoffrey Hawthorn, *Enlightenment and Despair* (1976), p. 10.

42 Gay, *The Enlightenment*, vol. 1, p. 3. Gay's emphasis on the homogeneity of the Enlightenment was challenged early by Betty Behrens in her review in the *Historical Journal* (1968), pp. 190–95; see also Henry F. May, *The Enlightenment in America* (1976).

43 L. M. Marsak (ed.), *The Enlightenment* (1972), p. 3; Lester G. Crocker, introduction to John W. Yolton (ed.), *The Blackwell Companion to the Enlightenment* (1991), p. 1. For France as the 'hearth' of the Enlightenment, see Darnton, 'George Washington's False Teeth'. Daniel Roche calls Paris the 'capital of the Enlightenment': *France in the Enlightenment* (1998), p. 641.

44 R. R. Palmer, *The Age of the Democratic Revolution* (1959–64).

45 The Enlightenment has also been read through the prism of 'modernization theory': A. M. Wilson, 'The Philosophes in the Light of Present-day Theories of Modernization' (1967); H. B. Applewhite and D. G. Levy, 'The Concept of Modernization and the French Enlightenment' (1971); Joyce Appleby, 'Modernization Theory and the Formation of Modern Social Theories in England and America' (1978).

46 Gay, *The Enlightenment*, vol. i, p. 3.

47 J. H. Plumb, *In the Light of History* (1972), lamented how 'very few' eighteenth-century Englishmen adopted a 'materialist philosophy' and explained this as a revival of 'unreason'. The implied contrast with France is questionable. With such thinkers as

Hartley, Priestley and Erasmus Darwin, England had its fair share, as later chapters will document.

48 See the discussions, for instance, in Roy Porter and Mikuláš Teich (eds.), *The Enlightenment in National Context* (1981).

49 For the French High Enlightenment as 'a pretty mild affair', see Robert Darnton, 'In Search of the Enlightenment', pp. 118–19.

50 A. C. Kors, *D'Holbach's Coterie* (1976), has shown how conventional were the lives even of most of d'Holbach's circle – as one might expect from their titled backgrounds.

51 According to D. Spadafora, *The Idea of Progress in Eighteenth Century Britain* (1990), pp. 10–11: 'to the extent that the French Enlightenment had anything like a British counterpart, it was located not in England but in Scotland.'

52 In any case, certain systematic writings were indeed produced, notably Bentham's gargantuan codification of the law.

53 Joseph Addison and Richard Steele, *The Spectator* (1965), vol. i, no. 10, p. 44 (12 March 1711); Cicero, *Tusculan Disputations* (1927), V.iv.10, pp. 434–5. For pioneering studies of the social production of knowledge and letters, see J. H. Plumb, 'The Public, Literature and the Arts in the Eighteenth Century' (1972), and *The Commercialization of Leisure* 1973); Pat Rogers, *Grub Street* (1972). See chapter 4 below.

54 Thompson, 'The Peculiarities of the English', p. 42; Roy Porter and Mikuláš Teich (eds.), *The Enlightenment in National Context*. See the reflections on Englishness in Nikolaus Pevsner, *The Englishness of English Art* (1976).

55 E. P. Thompson hoped to 'rescue the poor stockinger, the Luddite cropper, the "obsolete" hand-loom weaver, the "utopian" artisan, and even the deluded follower of Joanna Southcott, from the enormous condescension of posterity': *The Making of the English Working Class* (1968), p. 13.

56 Thompson, 'The Peculiarities of the English', p. 58.

57 J. H. Plumb, 'Reason and Unreason in the Eighteenth Century', in *In the Light of History* (1972), pp. 23–4. A fine study which bears out Plumb's remarks is Kathleen Wilson, *The Sense of the People* (1995).

58 For social change, see J. A. Sharpe, *Early Modern England* (1987); Trevor May, *An Economic and Social History of Britain, 1760–1970* (1987); John Rule, *Albion's People* (1992), and *The Vital Century* (1992); Jeremy Black, *An Illustrated History of Eighteenth-Century Britain, 1688–1793* (1996); Roy Porter, *English Society in the Eighteenth Century* (1990).

59 C. Hibbert (ed.), *An American in Regency England* (1968), p. 47.

60 R. Nettel (ed.), *Journeys of a German in England in 1782* (1965), p. 33.

61 A. F. Prévost, *Mémoires et aventures d'un homme de qualité* (1927 [1728–31]), p. 136.

62 R. Brimley Johnson (ed.), *Bluestocking Letters* (1926), p. 90.

63 Tobias Smollett, *Travels through France and Italy* (1766), vol. ii, pp. 197–8. See also C. Maxwell, *The English Traveller in France, 1698–1815* (1932); Brian Dolan, *Exploring European Frontiers* (1999).

64 John Locke, *An Essay concerning Human Understanding* (1975 [1690]), bk I, ch. 1, para. 6, p. 46. See also J. L. Axtell, *The Educational Works of John Locke* (1968); Alexander Pope, *An Essay on Man*, in J. Butt (ed.), *The Poems of Alexander Pope* (1965 [1733–4]), p. 516, l. 2.

65 For example, the development of a political economy (see chapter 17 below). Utilitarianism is the blueprint for a capitalist economy.

66 The phrase is Adam Smith's: *Lectures on Jurisprudence* (1982 [1762–3]), vol. iv, p. 163.

67 [John Gay], 'A Dissertation Concerning the Fundamental Principle and Immediate Criterion of Virtue', in W. King, *An Essay on the Origin of Evil* (1721), pp. xvii–xviii.

68 W. Paley, *The Principles of Moral and Political Philosophy* (1785), p. 61.

69 Joseph Priestley, *Lectures On History* (1793), vol. ii, p. 47.

70 See Joseph Butler, *Fifteen Sermons Preached at the Rolls Chapel* (1726), sermon xi, p. 70, discussed in Donna T. Andrew, *Philanthropy and Police* (1989), p. 39. See also Christopher Cunliffe (ed.), *Joseph Butler's Moral and Religious Thought* (1992).

71 Joseph Priestley, *Lectures on History and General Policy* (1788), vol. ii, p. 231. See also J. A. Passmore, *Priestley's Writings on Philosophy, Science and Politics* (1965), p. 260.

72 Madame du Boccage, *Letters concerning England, Holland and Italy* (1770), vol. i, pp. 28–9.

73 H. C. Robbins-Landon, *Haydn in England 1791–1795* (1976), p. 97. Haydn's concerts and commissions earned him extraordinary fees. Netting £800 from his benefit concert in 1794, he commented, 'this one can only make in England'.

74 E. P. Thompson, 'The Moral Economy of the English Crowd in the Eighteenth Century' (1971).

75 J. Passmore, *The Perfectibility of Man* (1970), pp. 158f.

76 Thus God and Nature link'd the gen'ral frame
And bade self-love and social be the same.

Alexander Pope, *An Essay of Man*, bk III, ll. 317–18, in J. Butt (ed.), *The Poems of Alexander Pope*, p. 535; C. H. Vereker, *Eighteenth-Century Optimism* (1967); A. O. Lovejoy, *The Great Chain of Being* (1936).

77 Anthony Ashley Cooper, 3rd Earl of Shaftesbury, *Characteristicks of Men, Manners, Opinions, Times* (1999 [1711]), vol. i, p. 273.

78 Sir F. M. Eden, *The State of the Poor* (1797), vol. i, p. 468. Eden is here drawing upon Adam Smith.

79 'There is no place in the world, where a man may live more according to his own mind, or even his whims, than in London': Pastor Wendeborn, *A View of England* (1791), vol. i, p. 184.

80 See Lawrence Stone, *The Family, Sex and Marriage in England, 1500–1800* (1977), ch. 9; J. H. Plumb, 'The New World of the Children in Eighteenth-Century England'

(1975); D. Owen, *English Philanthropy, 1660–1960* (1965); B. Rodgers, *Cloak of Charity: Studies in Eighteenth-Century Philanthropy* (1949). The capitalist economy, licensed by Enlightenment political economy, was, of course, creating the very ills which this humanitarianism wished to stamp out.

81 E. P. Thompson, 'Patrician Society, Plebian Culture' (1974), and 'Eighteenth-Century English Society' (1978), p. 139; Ian Gilmour, *Riot, Risings and Revolution* (1992); Nicholas Rogers, *Crowds, Culture and Politics in Georgian Britain* (1998).

82 J. W. von Archenholz, *A Picture of England* (1790), p. 24.

83 Madame du Boccage, *Letters concerning England, Holland and Italy*, p. 44.

84 Quoted in G. May, *Madame Roland and the Age of Revolution* (1970), p. 131 (the whole of ch. 9 is illuminating); Neil McKendrick, John Brewer and J. H. Plumb, *The Birth of a Consumer Society* (1982).

85 'Of the First Principles of Government' (1741), in David Hume, *Selected Essays* (1993), p. 25.

86 See the suggestive remarks in Michel Foucault, *Discipline and Punish* (1977) and Michael Ignatieff, *A Just Measure of Pain* (1978).

87 See Thompson, 'Patrician Society, Plebian Culture', for a gloss on this concept.

88 See J. Woodward, *To Do the Sick No Harm* (1974); M. G. Jones, *The Charity School Movement* (1938).

89 Nettel, *Journeys of a German in England in 1782*, pp. 30, 69; M. Grosley, *A Tour to London, or New Observations on England* (1772), vol. iii, p. 168; C. de Saussure, *A Foreign View of England in 1725–29* (1995), p. 25; Hibbert, *An American in Regency England*, p. 25; Abbé Prévost, *Adventures of a Man of Quality in England* (1930), p. 119.

90 Peter Burke, *Popular Culture in Early Modern Europe* (1978).

91 [Anon.], *A History of Little Goody Two Shoes* (1766), title page.

92 Quoted in Hibbert, *An American in Regency England*, p. 52.

93 Obviously there is a parallel with politics as interpreted in J. H. Plumb's *The Growth of Political Stability in England 1675–1725* (1967). On remoulding human nature, see J. A. Passmore, 'The Malleability of Man in Eighteenth-Century Thought' (1965).

94 Voltaire, *Letters concerning the English Nation*, p. 34. Voltaire was echoing Addison's celebration of the concourse at the Royal Exchange – 'so rich an Assembly of Countrymen and Foreigners consulting together upon the private Business of Mankind, and making this Metropolis *a kind of Emporium for the whole Earth*': Addison and Steele, *The Spectator*, vol. i, no. 69, p. 293 (Saturday, 19 May 1711). The Amsterdam Exchange had been admired for the same reasons.

95 F. A. Pottle (ed.), *Boswell's London Journal* (1950), p. 63; 'learn retenu': F. A. Pottle (ed.), *Boswell in Holland, 1763–1764* (1952), pp. 47, 49, 390.

96 Samuel Johnson, letter to Richard Congreve (25 June 1735), in R. W. Chapman (ed.), *The Letters of Samuel Johnson* (1952), vol. i, p. 6.

97 D. Hartley, *Observations on Man* (1749), vol. ii, p. 255.

98 J. Brewer, 'Commercialization and Politics' (1982).

99 Henry Fielding, 'An Essay on Conversation', in *Miscellanies, by H. F., Esq.* (1743), vol. i, p. 159.

100 Shaftesbury, *Characteristicks of Men, Manners, Opinions, Times*, vol. i, p. 39.

101 For the sociable presentation of self, see R. Sennett, *The Fall of Public Man* (1977); F. L. Lucas, *The Search for Good Sense* (1958), and *The Art of Living* (1959); S. M. Brewer, *Design for a Gentleman* (1963).

102 American academics in particular have seized upon Jürgen Habermas's notion of the creation of a 'public sphere' (a sector made up of private individuals understood to have their roots primarily in the private realm, including the family). Since the importance of public opinion in Georgian England has never been denied, this is to reinvent the wheel. See, however, Jürgen Habermas, *The Structural Transformation of the Public Sphere* (1989), and 'Further Reflections on the Public Sphere' (1992); for helpful expositions, see Craig Calhoun, 'Introduction: Habermas and the Public Sphere', in *Habermas and the Public Sphere* (1992), pp. 1–50; Geoff Eley, 'Nations, Publics and Political Cultures' in Calhoun, *Habermas and the Public Sphere*, pp. 289–339; Robert C. Holub, *Jürgen Habermas: Critic in the Public Sphere* (1991). For hints towards a critique, see Dena Goodman, 'The Public and the Nation' (1995), an introduction to an issue of *Eighteenth Century Studies* devoted to Habermas and history.

103 The play on swords and pens (and by implication, pricks) had long been commonplace: 'thy Pen, is full as harmlesse as thy Sworde', deemed Sir Carr Scrope at the Restoration: Warren Chernaik, *Sexual Freedom in Restoration Literature* (1995), p. 80.

2 THE BIRTH OF AN IDEOLOGY

1 John Dryden, 'Secular Masque' (1700), in *The Poems of John Dryden* (1959), pp. 202–3.

2 Quoted in Joseph Texte, *Jean-Jacques Rousseau and the Cosmopolitan Spirit in Literature* (1899), p. 60.

3 Maurice Cranston, *John Locke: A Biography* (1957), p. 42. For Stuart politics, see Mark Kishlansky, *A Monarchy Transformed* (1996); Derek Hirst, *Authority and Conflict* (1986); Barry Coward, *The Stuart Age* (1980). For interregnum radicalism, see Christopher Hill, *The World Turned Upside Down* (1972), and *God's Englishman* (1970).

4 E. S. De Beer (ed.), *The Diary of John Evelyn* (1955), vol. iii, p. 246.

5 Ronald Hutton, *The Restoration* (1985); J. R. Jones (ed.), *The Restored Monarchy, 1660–1688* (1979). For continuing threats, see Richard Greaves, *Deliver Us From Evil* (1986), *Enemies Under His Feet* (1990), and *Secrets of the Kingdom* (1992); Michael R. Watts, *The Dissenters* (1978), vol. i, p. 222. The 1662 rising was viciously put down.

6 Ursula Henriques, *Religious Toleration in England 1783–1833* (1961), p. 9; Robert S. Bosher, *The Making of the Restoration Settlement* (1951).

7 On Hobbes, see Quentin Skinner, *Reason and Rhetoric in the Philosophy of Hobbes* (1996), and chapter 3 below. For the trappings of Divine Right kingship, see Raymond Henry Payne Crawfurd, *The King's Evil* (1911); Marc Bloch, *The Royal Touch* (1973).

8 On Restoration culture, see Paula R. Backscheider, *Spectacular Politics* (1994); John Brewer, *The Pleasures of the Imagination* (1997), ch. 1; James Anderson Winn, *John Dryden and His World* (1987); Michael Foss, *The Age of Patronage* (1971).

9 Michael Hunter, *Science and Society in Restoration England* (1981), *The Royal Society and its Fellows 1660–1700* (1994), and *Establishing the New Science* (1989).

10 For international politics, see Jeremy Black, *A System of Ambition?* (1991).

11 Watts, *The Dissenters*, vol. i, pp. 221f.

12 See John Kenyon, *The Popish Plot* (1972); Paul Hammond, 'Titus Oates and "Sodomy" ' (1997); John Miller, *Popery and Politics in England 1660–1688* (1973).

13 See W. A. Speck, *Reluctant Revolutionaries* (1988); Robert Beddard (ed.), *The Revolution of 1688* (1991).

14 J. R. Jones (ed.), *Liberty Secured?* (1992); J. G. A. Pocock (ed.), *Three British Revolutions, 1641, 1688, 1776* (1980); Geoffrey Holmes, *The Making of a Great Power* (1993); Lois G. Schwoerer's *The Revolution of 1688–1689* (1992) stresses, against recent revisionism, the radicalism of the Bill of Rights.

15 G. J. Schochet, *Patriarchalism in Political Thought* (1975); for Shaftesbury's rebuttal of Divine Right theory, see Paul Hammond, 'The King's Two Bodies' (1991), p. 33.

16 Though, of course, billed in later English ideology as the revolution to end all revolutions: Christopher Hill, *Some Intellectual Consequences of the English Revolution* (1980), p. 19.

17 For political tensions under William and Mary, see Geoffrey Holmes and W. A. Speck, *The Divided Society* (1967); Geoffrey Holmes (ed.), *Britain after the Glorious Revolution 1689–1714* (1969), and *The Birth of Britain* (1994); J. P. Kenyon, *Revolution Principles* (1977); Clyve Jones (ed.), *Britain in the First Age of Party, 1684–1750* (1987), pp. 195–219; Holmes and Speck, *The Divided Society*. For refugees, see I. Scoutland (ed.), *Huguenots in Britain and their French Background, 1550–1800* (1987).

18 Geoffrey Holmes, *British Politics in the Age of Anne* (1987).

19 John Brewer, *The Sinews of Power* (1989); Geoffrey Holmes, *Augustan England* (1982).

20 For rancour under Anne, see Geoffrey Holmes, *The Trial of Doctor Sacheverell* (1973).

21 Caroline Robbins, *The Eighteenth-century Commonwealthmen* (1968).

22 See Cranston, *John Locke: A Biography*; John Marshall, *John Locke: Resistance, Religion and Responsibility* (1994).

23 Mark Goldie (ed.), *Locke: Political Essays* (1997), pp. xiiif. This contains an excellent introduction.

24 John Dunn, *Locke* (1984), p. 23.

25 Marshall, *John Locke: Resistance, Religion and Responsibility*, p. xvi.

26 Quoted in J. W. Gough, *John Locke's Political Philosophy* (Oxford: Clarendon Press, 1950), p. 134; J. C. D. Clark, *English Society, 1688–1832* (1985), p. 47: Hearne groused that Locke's *Essay* was 'much read and studied at

Cambridge'. On unbelievers, see Michael Hunter, 'The Problem of "Atheism" in Early Modern England' (1985).

27 Margaret C. Jacob, *The Cultural Meaning of the Scientific Revolution* (1988), p. 97; compare also her earlier remark: 'The Enlightenment, in both its moderate and radical forms, began in England,' in *The Radical Enlightenment* (1981), p. 79, and her view (p. 84) that 'the actual roots of the European Enlightenment . . . lay in the English revolutionary experience against Stuart absolutism as well as in the Continental opposition to French absolutism'. For the wider European radicalism of the 1680s, see P. G. M. C. Hazard, *The European Mind, 1680–1715* (1964), and Margaret Jacob, 'The Crisis of the European Mind' (1987).

28 'The Enlightenment, in both its moderate and radical forms, began in England but achieved intellectual maturity in Europe': Jacob, *The Radical Enlightenment*, p. 79, and 'The European Enlightenment begins in 1689' (p. 84).

29 For early Hanoverian politics, see J. H. Plumb, *The Growth of Political Stability in England, 1675–1725* (1967); G. Holmes, 'The Achievement of Stability' (1981); Jeremy Black (ed.), *Britain in the Age of Walpole* (1984), and *The Politics of Britain, 1688–1800* (1993); Hiram Caton, *The Politics of Progress* (1988). For Jacobites, see Paul Kleber Monod, *Jacobitism and the English People, 1688–1788* (1989).

30 Reed Browning, *Political and Constitutional Ideas of the Court Whigs* (1982).

31 For Continental censorship, see Robert Darnton, *The Forbidden Best-Sellers of Pre-Revolutionary France* (1996).

32 J. G. A. Pocock, 'Conservative Enlightenment and Democratic Revolutions' (1989), p. 84.

33 J. G. A. Pocock, 'Post-Puritan England and the Problem of the Enlightenment' (1980), p. 105.

34 J. G. A. Pocock, 'Clergy and Commerce' (1985); compare Jacob, *The Radical Enlightenment*, p. 94.

35 Pocock, 'Clergy and Commerce', p. 528; compare Jacob, *The Radical Enlightenment*, p. 94.

36 J. G. A. Pocock, *The Machiavellian Moment* (1975), p. 477, and *Barbarism and Religion* (1999), vol. i, p. 294. Like Pocock, Jacob sees the English ploughing a *Sonderweg*: Margaret C. Jacob, *The Cultural Meaning of the Scientific Revolution* (1988), p. 139.

37 J. C. D. Clark applies *'ancien régime'* to Hanoverian England in *English Society, 1688–1832* (1985) and in *Revolution and Rebellion* (1986).

38 Jacob, *The Radical Enlightenment*, p. 94.

39 Margaret C. Jacob, *The Newtonians and the English Revolution, 1689–1720* (1976). She has also claimed that there was a more radical movement to the left of Pocock's conservative Enlightenment: *The Radical Enlightenment*.

40 Jacob, *The Cultural Meaning of the Scientific Revolution*, p. 124.

41 The battle for supremacy between 'Old' and 'New' Labour in the 1990s affords some parallel.

42 For Swift, see David Nokes, *Jonathan Swift: A Hypocrite Reversed* (1985), p. 295; see also Isaac Kramnick, *Bolingbroke and His Circle* (1968); Bertrand A. Goldgar, *The Curse of Party* (1961), and *Walpole and the Wits* (1976); J. A. Downie, 'Walpole: The Poet's Foe' (1984).

43 Clark, *English Society, 1688–1832*, and *Revolution and Rebellion*; C. B. Wilde, 'Hutchinsonians, Natural Philosophy and Religious Controversy in Eighteenth-century Britain' (1980). For Whig Cambridge, see chapter 3.

44 Sir William Temple, *Observations upon the United Provinces of the Netherlands* (1972 [1673]); Simon Schama, *The Embarrassment of Riches* (1988).

45 Quoted in Brewer, *The Pleasures of the Imagination*, p. 52.

46 Compare Kevin Sharpe, *Criticism and Compliment* (1987); Kevin Sharpe and Peter Lake (eds), *Culture and Politics in Early Stuart England* (1993); Michael Foss, *The Age of Patronage* (1971).

47 J. M. Beattie, *The English Court in the Reign of George I* (1967); R. O. Bucholz, *The Augustan Court* (1993).

48 On the marvel of the metropolis, see Miles Ogborn, *Spaces of Modernity* (1998); Roy Porter, 'Visiting London' (1994); M. Byrd, *London Transformed* (1978).

49 Samuel Johnson, 'London' (1738), in Patrick Cruttwell (ed.), *Samuel Johnson: Selected Writings* (1986), p. 42.

50 For Londoners' delight in looking at themselves, see Roy Porter, 'Capital Art' (1997).

51 Aytoun Ellis, *The Penny Universities* (1956); Bryant Lillywhite, *London Coffee Houses* (1963).

52 Brewer, *The Pleasures of the Imagination*, p. 44.

53 See Geoffrey Alan Cranfield, *The Press and Society from Caxton to Northcliffe* (1978), p. 89.

54 *The Craftsman* (4 October 1729), quoted in Herbert M. Atherton, *Political Prints in the Age of Hogarth* (1974), p. 61. See also *The Craftsman* (20 March 1727): 'I could wish, Sir, that you would now and then, of an Evening, come incog. to the publick Coffee houses, as some of your Predecessors have done; for then you will be truly informed, of the Opinions and Sentiments of Mankind': Simon Varey (ed.), *Lord Bolingbroke: Contributions to the Craftsman* (1982), p. 8. Jonathan Swift demurred: 'It is the Folly of too many to mistake the Echo of a London Coffee house for the Voice of the Kingdom': *The Conduct of the Allies* (1711), p. 47.

55 C. de Saussure, *A Foreign View of England in 1725–29* (1995 [1902]), p. 111.

56 James L. Clifford (ed.), *Dr Campbell's Diary of a Visit to England in 1775* (1947), p. 58.

57 For clubs, see Peter Clark, *Sociability and Urbanity* (2000); Kathleen Wilson, *The Sense of the People* (1995), p. 67; Marie Mulvey Roberts, 'Pleasures Engendered by Gender' (1996); Howard William Troyer, *Ned Ward of Grub Street* (1968), p. 151. For European comparisons, see Richard van Dülmen, *The Society of the Enlightenment* (1992), pp. 1f., 85.

58 If all Johnson's friends had got together, reflected Boswell, 'we should have a very capital university': R. W. Chapman (ed.), *Samuel Johnson, A Journey to the Western Islands of Scotland and James Boswell, The Journal of a Tour to the Hebrides* (1970), p. 228.

59 D. G. C. Allan, *William Shipley: Founder of the Royal Society of Arts* (1968), p. 8.

60 For enlightened sociability see Brewer, *The Pleasures of the Imagination*, p. 44. For salons, see Dena Goodman, *The Republic of Letters* (1994). Daniel Defoe proposed a London university in *Augusta Triumphans or The Way to Make London the Most Flourishing City in the Universe* (1728).

61 Margaret C. Jacob, *Living the Enlightenment* (1992), p. 32, and *The Radical Enlightenment*, p. 110; for wider European dimensions, see Ulrich Im Hof, *The Enlightenment* (1994), p. 139; van Dülmen, *The Society of the Enlightenment*, pp. 151f. Masons found Newtonian metaphors attractive. In 1779, for example, the Kent vicar and freemason James Smith, preaching before his lodge, praised benevolence: 'Attraction binds the universe as benevolence binds men': Jacob, *Living the Enlightenment*, p. 56.

62 Jacob, *The Radical Enlightenment*, p. 110; John Money, 'Freemasonry and the Fabric of Loyalism in Hanoverian England' (1990); John Brewer, 'English Radicalism in the Age of George III' (1980), p. 359.

63 Wilson, *The Sense of the People*, p. 71.

64 On the politics of the theatre, see Marc Baer, *The Theatre and Disorder in Late Georgian London* (1991).

65 Brewer, *The Pleasures of the Imagination*, p. 60; Iain Pears, *The Discovery of Painting* (1988); David H. Solkin, *Painting for Money* (1993).

66 Richard D. Altick, *The Shows of London* (1978), p. 25.

67 Quoted and discussed in Roy Porter, 'John Hunter: A Showman in Society' (1993–4), pp. 21–2.

68 Altick, *The Shows of London*, pp. 60, 35, 47.

69 The masquerade offered a bold form of freedom, for, as Fielding observed, to 'masque the face' was 't'unmasque the mind': quoted in Terry Castle, *Masquerade and Civilization* (1986), p. 73. Pat Rogers, *Eighteenth Century Encounters* (1985), pp. 11–17, 28; Pears, *The Discovery of Painting*, pp. 77–87; Louise Lippincott, *Selling Art in Georgian London* (1983).

70 Paula R. Backscheider, *Spectacular Politics* (1994), p. 172.

71 Quoted in P. Clark and P. Slack, *English Towns in Transition, 1500–1700* (1976), p. 156.

72 Trevor Fawcett, *The Rise of English Provincial Art* (1974); Peter Borsay, 'The Rise of the Promenade' (1986), and *The English Urban Renaissance* (1989); Phyliss Hembry, *The English Spa 1560–1815* (1990).

73 Paul Langford, *A Polite and Commercial People* (1989); Jonathan Barry and Christopher Brooks (eds), *The Middling Sort of People* (1994).

74 Neil McKendrick, 'Introduction. The Birth of a Consumer Society' (1982); Maxine Berg and Helen Clifford (eds), *Consumers and Luxury* (1999); John Brewer and Roy Porter (eds), *Consumption and the World of Goods* (1993); Lorna Weatherill, *Consumer Behaviour and Material Culture, 1660–1760* (1988); Carole Shammas, *The Pre-Industrial Consumer in England and America* (1990).

75 Addison and Steele, *The Spectator* (1965), vol. i, no. 69, p. 293 (Saturday, 19 May 1711). Other books puffing England included William Camden's *Britannia* (1695), edited and modernized by Bishop Gibson, and Edward Chamberlayne's *Angliae Notitia* (1669).

76 Alexander Catcott, *The Antiquity and Honourableness of the Practice of Marchandize* (sn, 1744), p. 14, quoted in David Dabydeen, 'Eighteenth-century English Literature on Commerce and Slavery' (1985), p. 26.

77 Edward Young, *The Merchant* (1730), vol. ii, p. 1, quoted in Dabydeen, 'Eighteenth-century English Literature on Commerce and Slavery', p. 31.

78 Quoted in Ogborn, *Spaces of Modernity*, p. 202. On roads see Henry Homer, *An Enquiry into the Means of Preserving and Improving the Publick Roads of This Kingdom* (1767), pp. 3, 6, 8. A Warwickshire clergyman, Homer claimed that there had never been a 'more astonishing Revolution accomplished [in transportation] in the internal System of any Country, than has been within the Compass of a few Years in that of England': 'Every Thing wears the Face of Dispatch'.

79 C. Bruyn Andrews (ed.), *The Torrington Diaries* (1934–8), vol. ii, p. 149: 'I wish with all my heart that half the turnpike roads of the kingdom were plough'd up,' he groused: 'I meet milkmaids on the road, with the dress and looks of strand misses.'

80 Ogborn, *Spaces of Modernity*, p. 203; Howard Robinson, *The British Post Office* (1948), pp. 99f.; John Rule, *The Vital Century* (1992), pp. 224–5, 249; Daniel Roche, *France in the Enlightenment* (1998), p. 234.

81 *The Times* (28 February 1794).

82 George Colman in *St James's Chronicle* (6 August 1761).

83 Quoted in Langford, *A Polite and Commercial People*, p. 117.

84 L. Simond, *An American in Regency England* (1968), p. 59.

85 Quoted in Robert DeMaria Jr, *Johnson's Dictionary and the Language of Learning* (1986), pp. 132–3. Compare Oliver Goldsmith's remark that 'Learning is most advanced in populous cities . . . where the members of this large university, if I may so call it, catch manners as they rise, study life not logic, and have the world as correspondents': *Enquiry into the Present State of Polite Learning in Europe* (1759), pp. 183–4.

86 E. P. Thompson, quoted in Linda Colley, 'Radical Patriotism in Eighteenth-century England' (1989), p. 183.

87 Jeremy Black (ed.), *Britain in the Age of Walpole* (1984), p. 1.

88 James Thomson, *The Masque of Alfred* (1740), in Roger Lonsdale (ed.), *The New Oxford Book of Eighteenth-century Verse* (1984), p. 192. Freedom created a flourishing commerce, the consequence of which was:

> The muses, still with freedom found,
>> Shall to thy happy coast repair;
> Blest Isle! with matchless beauty crowned,
>> And manly hearts to guard the fair!
> 'Rule, Britannia, rule the waves,
> Britons never will be slaves.'

89 Oliver Goldsmith, 'The Comparative View of Races and Nations' (1760), p. 286. For the secularization of the Protestant notion of the chosen nation into a kind of manifest destiny, see Christopher Hill, *The World Turned Upside Down* (1972), p. 248.

90 Charles Churchill, *The Duellist* (1984 [1764]), p. 512.

91 Jeremy Black, *The British and the Grand Tour* (1985), p. 174. See also Black's 'Ideology, History, Xenophobia and the World of Print in Eighteenth-century England' (1991). Touring Italy, Gibbon abhorred the oppression, and found the once-famous university of Padua a 'dying taper': Gibbon, *Memoirs of My Life*, p. 135.

92 Black, *The British and the Grand Tour* (1985), p. 180.

93 C. de Saussure, *A Foreign View of England in 1725–29* (1995), p. 111.

94 Madame Van Muyden (ed. and trans.), *A Foreign View of England in the Reigns of George I & George II* (1902), p. 67.

95 Johann Wilhelm von Archenholz, *A Picture of England* (1791), p. 85.

96 Carl Philip Moritz, *Journeys of a German in England* (1982 [1783]), p. 36.

97 Joachim Schlör, *Nights in the Big City* (1998); Porter, 'Visiting London'.

98 In 1752 Dr Lyttelton observed in Cornwall that there were very few cottages without sash windows. Six years later Mrs Montagu, visiting Lumley Castle, complained it had been excessively 'modernized by sash-windows': B. Sprague Allen, *Tides in English Taste (1619–1800)* (1958), vol. ii, p. 73. Note the new use of 'modernized'.

99 Robert E. Schofield, *The Lunar Society of Birmingham* (1963), pp. 196, 347; Wolfgang Schivelbusch, *Disenchanted Night* (1988), p. 11. For further information, see D. King-Hele (ed.), *The Letters of Erasmus Darwin* (1981), p. 146 (Darwin wrote eleven letters to Wedgwood, mainly about oil-lamps); Benjamin Rumford, 'Of the Management of Light in Illumination' (1970 [1812]). Many Lunar Society luminaries were painted by that painter of light, Joseph Wright; see Benedict Nicolson, *Joseph Wright of Derby* (1968); see also Michael Baxandall, *Shadows and Enlightenment* (1995).

100 Quoted in Caroline A. Davidson, *A Woman's Work is Never Done* (1982), p. 33.

101 Isaiah 9:2; Matthew 4:16; John 1:9; I Corinthians 13:12. Compare Rosalie L. Colie, *Light and Enlightenment* (1957). The passage from Isaiah was set in Handel's *Messiah*.

102 Frederick J. Powicke, *The Cambridge Platonists* (1971), pp. 23f. Cambridge Platonists insisted that one light did not extinguish another. For an exclusively Christian view of light see Charles Wesley's 'Morning Hymn' (1740):

> Christ, whose glory fills the skies,
>> Christ, the true, the only light . . .

Anthologized in Lonsdale, *The New Oxford Book of Eighteenth-century Verse*, p. 335.

103 Isaac Newton, *Opticks, or A Treatise of the Reflections, Refractions, Inflections & Colours of Light* (1704); George Berkeley, *An Essay towards a New Theory of Vision*, 2nd edn (1709); G. N. Cantor, 'The History of "Georgian" Optics' (1978); Marjorie Hope Nicolson, *Newton Demands the Muse* (1946).

104 James Thomson, 'Ode to the Memory

of Sir Isaac Newton' (1727), in Lonsdale, *The New Oxford Book of Eighteenth-century Verse*, p. 190.

105 Alexander Pope, 'Epitaph: Intended for Sir Isaac Newton in Westminster Abbey' (1730), in John Butt (ed.), *The Poems of Alexander Pope* (1965), p. 808.

106 Joseph Priestley spoke of the 'change from darkness to light, from superstition to sound knowledge': *Memoirs of Dr Joseph Priestley, Written on Himself* (1904 [1795]), p. 156.

107 Jeremy Black (ed.), *Eighteenth Century Europe 1700–1789* (1990), p. 186.

108 Gilbert Stuart, *The History of the Establishment of the Reformation of Religion in Scotland* (1780), p. 206.

109 Gibbon, *Memoirs of My Life*, p. 186; Thomas Spence, *The Meridian Sun of Liberty* (1796); Mary Wollstonecraft, *A Vindication of the Rights of Men with A Vindication of the Rights of Woman* (1995 [1790 and 1792]), p. 112; Edmund Burke, *Reflections on the Revolution in France* (1790), p. 207. The Burkean sublime, of course, reinstated darkness: Edmund Burke, *Philosophical Enquiry into the Origin of Our Ideas of the Sublime and the Beautiful* (1757).

110 Thomas Paine, 'American Crisis' (1776–83), in *The Complete Writings of Thomas Paine* (1945), vol. i, p. 125.

111 In his *Dictionary of the English Language* (1755), Johnson divided vision into four categories –

1. Sight; the faculty of seeing.
2. The act of seeing.
3. A supernatural appearance; a spectre; a phantom.
4. A dream; something shown in a dream. A dream happens to a sleeping, a vision may happen to a waking man. A dream is supposed natural, a vision miraculous; but they are confounded.

– two related to perception of the visible, two to the invisible. The Lockean tradition dismissed perception of the invisible (spectres, phantoms, supernatural ghosts, miracles, dreams) as the work of a diseased imagination.

112 William Paley, *Natural Theology* (1802), p. 81, quoted in Searby, *A History of the University of Cambridge*, vol. iii, p. 299.

113 See the discussions in Robert A. Ferguson, *The American Enlightenment 1750–1820* (1997), p. 28; Leigh Schmidt, *Hearing Things* (2000), ch. 1; and chapter 3 below. Locke viewed human psychology in terms of 'the Bounds between the enlightened and dark Parts of Things'.

114 Rogers, *Eighteenth Century Encounters*, p. 1. The device is equivocal: the glasses help him see but confirm that his vision is poor.

115 Richard Price, *A Discourse on the Love of Our Country* (1789), pp. 15–16.

116 Thomas Paine, *The Rights of Man* (1984 [1791]), p. 159.

117 Quoted in Theo Barker (ed.), *The Long March of Everyman 1750–1960* (1978), p. 64.

118 George Birkbeck Hill, *Boswell's Life of Johnson* (1934–50), vol. iii, p. 3; see the discussion in D. Spadafora, *The Idea of Progress in Eighteenth-century Britain* (1990), p. 40.

119 Hill, *Boswell's Life of Johnson*, vol. iii, p. 3, and vol. iv, p. 217. 'I do sincerely think,' the biographer opined, 'that this age is better than ancient times': James Boswell, 'On Past & Present', *The Hypochondriack* (January 1782), in M. Bailey (ed.), *Boswell's Column* (1951), no. 52, p. 267.

120 Jeremy Bentham, *A Fragment on Government* (1988 [1776]), p. 3.

121 Clark, *English Society, 1688–1832*, p. 42. My passage is a précis of Clark.

3 CLEARING AWAY THE RUBBISH

1 Isaac Watts, *Logick* (1724), introduction.

2 Basil Willey, *The Eighteenth Century Background* (1962), p. 1: Willey stressed escape achieved ('One meets everywhere a sense of relief'); no less important was escape sought. Throughout the long eighteenth century, the themes of imprisonment and deliverance remained to the fore: John Bender, *Imagining the Penitentiary* (1987).

3 Peter Burke, *The Renaissance Sense of the Past* (1970).

4 For Blake's phrase, see G. Keynes (ed.), *The Complete Writings of William Blake* (1957), p. 170.

5 See W. B. Carnochan, *Confinement and Flight* (1977); for the theme in folklore, see Marina Warner, *From the Beast to the Blonde* (1994). For Christian tellings, see Christopher Hill, *A Turbulent, Seditious and Factious People* (1989), and *The English Bible and the Seventeenth-century Revolution* (1993).

6 John Toland, quoted in Stephen H. Daniel, *John Toland: His Methods, Manners, and Mind* (1984), p. 6; Linda Colley, *Britons* (1992); John Lucas, *England and Englishness* (1990).

7 For an analysis of such prejudices, see Christopher Hill, *Antichrist in Seventeenth-century England* (1971).

8 P. C. Almond's *Heaven and Hell in Enlightenment England* (1994) illuminates the Rational Protestant rejection of the Greek metaphysics colouring Christian theology; see also J. G. A. Pocock, *Virtue, Commerce, and History* (1985), p. 143. For Plato as mystagogue, see Joseph Priestley, *An History of the Corruptions of Christianity* (1871 [1721]), pp. 9, 113, 132, where he was tarred with the brush of 'oriental philosophy'. See chapter 5 below.

9 Henry St John, Viscount Bolingbroke, *Essays on Human Knowledge*, in *The Works of Lord Bolingbroke* (1969 [reprint of 1841 edn]), vol. iii, p. 294.

10 Edward Gibbon, *The History of the Decline and Fall of the Roman Empire* (1994 [1776]), vol. i, pp. 398–9.

11 On 'priestcraft', see below, chapter 5. Catholicism was doubly dangerous since it was so seductive. Not a few Enlightenment figures underwent temporary conversion, including Pierre Bayle, Edward Gibbon and James Boswell: Colin Haydon, *Anti-Catholicism in Eighteenth-century England, c.1714–80* (1993).

12 J. E. Norton (ed.), *The Letters of Edward Gibbon* (1956), vol. ii, p. 245; commented on by Iain McCalman: 'Mad Lord George and Madame La Motte' (1996); Pocock, *Virtue, Commerce, and History*, p. 155.

13 For the trauma of the wars of religion, see Christopher Hill, *Some Intellectual Consequences of the English Revolution* (1980); Michael Heyd, *'Be Sober and Reasonable': The Critique of Enthusiasm in the Seventeenth and Early Eighteenth Centuries* (1995); R. A. Knox, *Enthusiasm* (1950).

14 Samuel Butler, *Hudibras, Part I and II and Selected Other Writings* (1973 [1663]), The First part, canto 1, 'The Argument', p. 7, ll. 193–5.

15 See R. F. Jones, *Ancients and Moderns* (1936); Joseph M. Levine, *The Battle of the Books* (1992).

16 See Elisabeth Labrousse, *Bayle* (1983).

17 Well discussed in Jonathan Brody Kramnick, *Making the English Canon* (1999).

18 Bentham's favourite term: Jeremy Bentham, *The Book of Fallacies* (1824); 'The season of Fiction is now over,' he pronounced in his *A Fragment on Government* (1988 [1776]), p. 53 – Mary P. Mack notes that 'as early as *A Fragment on Government* he denounced "the pestilential breath of Fiction" ': *Jeremy Bentham, An Odyssey of Ideas, 1748–1792* (1962), p. 76.

19 Jones, *Ancients and Moderns*, p. 261. As Thomson's words make evident, rhetorics contrasting old and new, fiction and fact,

were far from exclusive to the
Enlightenment.

20 Quoted in David L. Jacobson and Ronald
Hamowy (eds.), *The English Libertarian Heritage*
(1994), p. 272.

21 G. J. Warnock, *Berkeley* (1969), p. 15. See
also Ian Tipton, *Berkeley: The Philosophy of
Immaterialism* (1995); Peter Walmsley, *The
Rhetoric of Berkeley's Philosophy* (1990).

22 Anthony Ashley Cooper, 3rd Earl of
Shaftesbury, *Characteristicks of Men, Manners,
Opinions, Times* (1999 [1711]), 'Miscellany III',
vol. ii, ch. 1; ''Tis the persecuting Spirit has
rais'd the bantering one': 'Sensus
Communis', section 4.

23 Shaftesbury, 'Miscellany III', in
Characteristicks of Men, Manners, Opinions, Times,
vol. ii, ch. 1, p. 206. Lawrence E. Klein,
Shaftesbury and the Culture of Politeness (1994),
p. 34. He speared Calvinism and Hobbes
with the same argument: their moralities of
fear took the virtue out of virtue; thus they
were both ungenteel. Shaftesbury's preferred
dialogue form shows his leanings towards
intellectual openness: Michael Prince,
Philosophical Dialogue in the British Enlightenment
(1996).

24 Thomas Sprat, *The History of the Royal
Society of London, for the Improving of Natural
Knowledge* (1667), p. 43; P. B. Wood,
'Methodology and Apologetics' (1980); Hans
Aarsleff, *From Locke to Saussure* (1982), pp. 8f;
Robert Markley, *Fallen Languages* (1993).

25 Samuel Johnson, *A Dictionary of the English
Language* (1755), para. 17; he nevertheless
defended words, concluding: 'I wish . . . that
signs might be made permanent, like the
things they denote.' See Robert DeMaria Jr,
Johnson's Dictionary and the Language of Learning
(1986), p. 155.

26 George Berkeley, *Treatise concerning
the Principles of Human Knowledge* (1710),
p. 152.

27 C. H. Hull (ed.), *The Economic Writings of
Sir William Petty* (1899), vol. i, p. 244. See also
Richard Olson, *The Emergence of the Social

Sciences, 1642–1792* (1993); Alessandro
Roncaglia, *Petty: The Origins of Political
Economy* (1985); Richard Stone, *Some British
Empiricists in the Social Sciences, 1650–1900*
(1997), pp. 41f.

28 Alexander Pope, *The Dunciad* (1728), book
IV, ll. 653–6 in John Butt (ed.), *The Poems of
Alexander Pope* (1965), p. 800.

29 Pope was, indeed, in some measure
popularizing Shaftesbury and Bolingbroke,
both of whom derived many of their ideas
from Locke: Brean S. Hammond, *Pope and
Bolingbroke* (1984).

30 See C. G. Caffentzis, *Clipped Coins, Abused
Words, and Civil Government* (1989), p. 46.
Locke, who oversaw the great recoinage of
1695–6, believed the value of legal tender
must be seen to be intrinsic – it should not
depend upon the politicians: John Dunn,
Locke (1984), p. 40. Fears over clipped and
counterfeit coins paralleled anxieties over
false faces, and other forms of false pretences
in an age of image-making: see Roy Porter,
'Making Faces' (1985).

31 Walter J. Ong, *Orality and Literacy* (1982);
Elizabeth L. Eisenstein, *The Printing Press as an
Angent of Change* (1979). For parallel
iconoclasm in art, see Andrew Graham-
Dixon, *A History of British Art* (1996).

32 Of course there is something arbitrary in
picking out three precursors: others were
immensely influential too. Spinoza readily
doubled with Hobbes as the atheist
bogeyman. See R. L. Colie, 'Spinoza and the
Early English Deists' (1959).

33 For discussion, see John Cottingham,
Descartes (1986); Marjorie Hope Nicolson,
'The Early Stage of Cartesianism in
England' (1929); Martin Hollis (ed.), *The Light
of Reason* (1973); William Barrett, *Death of the
Soul* (1987), pp. 14f.; Sylvana Tomaselli, 'The
First Person' (1984); Roger Smith, 'Self-
Reflection and the Self' (1997).

34 Alan Gabbey, 'Cudworth, More and the
Mechanical Analogy' (1992); Rosalie L.
Colie, *Light and Enlightenment* (1957), p. 124;

G. A. J. Rogers, 'Descartes and the English' (1985).

35 There was, for instance, the lover's gland: 'The Pineal Gland . . . smelt very strong of Essence and Orange-Flower Water . . . We observed a large *Antrum* or Cavity in the *Sinciput*, that was filled with Ribbons, Lace and Embroidery': Joseph Addison and Richard Steele, *The Spectator* (1965), vol. ii, no. 275, p. 571 (Tuesday, 15 January 1712). Or the free-thinker's, which Berkeley purported to visit. The understanding he found 'narrower than ordinary, insomuch that there was not any room for a Miracle, Prophesie, or Separate Spirit . . . I discover'd Prejudice in the Figure of a Woman standing in a Corner': *Guardian* (1713), no. 39, p. 155 (Saturday, 25 April 1713). In a narrative purporting to be the biography of Martin Scriblerus, who in vain devoted his life to the pursuit of knowledge, chapter 12 describes his 'Enquiry after the *Seat* of the *Soul*': 'At length he grew fond of the *Glandula Pinealis*, dissecting many Subjects to find out the different Figure of this Gland, from whence he might discover the cause of the different Tempers in mankind': Charles Kerby-Miller, *Memoirs of the Extraordinary Life, Works, and Discoveries of Martinus Scriblerus* (1988 [1742]), p. 286.

36 F. M. Voltaire, *Letters concerning the English Nation* (1926 [1733]), pp. 84f.; see also A. Rupert Hall, 'Newton in France' (1975).

37 See Lisa Jardine, *Francis Bacon: Discovery and the Art of Discourse* (1974); Charles Webster, *The Great Instauration* (1975); Barbara J. Shapiro, *Probability and Certainty in Seventeenth-century England* (1983).

38 See Quentin Skinner, *Reason and Rhetoric in the Philosophy of Hobbes* (1996); Samuel I. Mintz, *The Hunting of Leviathan* (1962).

39 Thomas Hobbes, *Leviathan* (1968 [1651]), pt 1, ch. 4, p. 105.

40 Hobbes, *Leviathan*, pt 1, ch. 4, p. 106.

41 How we came to translate *Spirits*, by the word *Ghosts*, which signifieth nothing, neither in heaven, nor earth, but the Imaginary inhabitants of man's brain, I examine not: but this I say, the word *Spirit* in the text signifieth no such thing; but either properly a real *substance*, or Metaphorically, some extraordinary *ability* or *affection* of the Mind, or of the Body.

Hobbes, *Leviathan*, pt 3, ch. 34, p. 43. See Jeffrey Barnouw, 'Hobbes's Psychology of Thought' (1990).

42 Hobbes, *Leviathan* (1968 [1651]), pt 1, ch. 11, p. 160; Mintz, *The Hunting of Leviathan*, p. 30.

43 Hobbes, *Leviathan*, pt 1, ch. 11, p. 161.

44 Hobbes, *Leviathan*, pt 1, ch. 11, p. 161. For secularized Calvinism, see Christopher Hill, *The World Turned Upside Down* (1972), p. 313.

45 Warren Chernaik, *Sexual Freedom in Restoration Literature* (1995), p. 27; Mintz, *The Hunting of Leviathan*, p. 23: 'In Hobbes's hands,' Mintz observes, 'nominalism and materialism became the instruments of a powerful scepticism about the real or objective existence of absolutes, and in particular about such absolutes as divine providence, good and evil, and an immortal soul.'

46 Hobbes, *Leviathan*, ch. 46.

47 Mintz, *The Hunting of Leviathan*, pp. 50, 61.

48 David Hume, *Essays Moral, Political and Literary* (1898 [1741–2]), vol. ii, p. 135. As needs no saying, Enlightenment rhetoric can sound, albeit playfully, as bigoted and intolerant as any.

49 For the '*Under-Labourer*', see John Locke, *An Essay concerning Human Understanding* (1975 [1690]), 'Epistle to the Reader', p. 10. Although knowledge was far from absolute, Locke believed, 'it yet secures their great Concernments, that they have Light enough to lead them to the Knowledge of their Maker, and the sight of their own Duties.' Locke was deeply interested in the new science and had a large collection of scientific books. See also John C. Biddle, 'Locke's Critique of Innate Principles and Toland's

Deism' (1990), p. 141. For the limits of reason, see Robert Voitle, 'The Reason of the English Enlightenment' (1963).

50 Generally see Maurice Cranston, *John Locke: A Biography* (1957); John W. Yolton, *John Locke and the Way of Ideas* (1956), and *Locke: An Introduction* (1985); Dunn, *Locke*; Peter Schouls, *Reasoned Freedom* (1992) is a good philosophical exposition. On the *Essay*, Katharine M. Morsberger, 'John Locke's *An Essay concerning Human Understanding*' (1996) is helpful.

51 Locke, *An Essay concerning Human Understanding*, bk IV, ch. 3, p. 21; bk I, ch. 3, p. 27.

52 Locke, *An Essay concerning Human Understanding*, bk I, ch. 3, para. 12, p. 73. See discussion in Mark Goldie (ed.), *Locke: Political Essays* (1997), p. xix.

53 Locke, *An Essay concerning Human Understanding*, bk III, ch. 10, para. 34, p. 508. He continued that 'all the Art of Rhetorick' is 'for nothing else but to insinuate wrong Ideas, move the Passions, and thereby mislead the Judgement'. Peter Walmsley, 'Prince Maurice's Rational Parrot' (1995) brings out Locke's distrust of language, as does Markley, *Fallen Languages*. The whole of Locke's book III is relevant.

54 Locke, *An Essay concerning Human Understanding*, bk II, ch. 10, para. 34, p. 508.

55 Locke, *An Essay concerning Human Understanding*, bk III, ch. 10, para. 34, p. 508; see Cranston, *John Locke: A Biography*, pp. 272f. Sterne's hero remarks: 'Well might Locke write a chapter upon the imperfections of words': Laurence Sterne, *Tristram Shandy* (1967 [1759–67]), pp. 354–5.

56 Locke, *An Essay concerning Human Understanding*, bk III, ch. 10, para. 31; bk III, ch. 10, para. 9, p. 495. Locke feared a new Babel: bk III, ch. 6, para. 29, p. 456.

57 Aarsleff, *From Locke to Saussure*, p. 27. The linguistic cleansing here urged was parodied by Swift in a *reductio ad absurdum*, in which he broached the scheme of the Academy of Lagado 'for entirely abolishing all Words whatsoever; And this was urged as a great Advantage in Point of Health as well as Brevity . . . since Words are only Names for Things, it would be more convenient for all Men to carry about them, such Things as were necessary to express the particular Business they are to discourse on': Jonathan Swift, *Gulliver's Travels* (1954 [1726]), bk III, pp. 51–85. (Penguin edn, p. 230.) Swift both shared and satirized enlightened critiques of intellectual nonsense: see J. R. R. Christie, 'Laputa Revisited' (1989); Deborah Baker Wyrick, *Jonathan Swift and the Vested Word* (1988); Christopher Fox, *Locke and the Scriblerians* (1988).

58 Locke, *An Essay concerning Human Understanding*, bk IV, ch. 16, para. 14.

59 Quoted in Alan P. F. Sell, *John Locke and the Eighteenth-century Divines* (1997), p. 9.

60 Locke, *An Essay concerning Human Understanding*, bk IV, ch. 13; bk IV, ch. 18, para. 2.

61 Locke, *An Essay concerning Human Understanding*, bk IV, ch. 18, para. 5: 'Nothing that is contrary to, and inconsistent with the clear and self-evident Dictates of Reason, has a Right to be urged, or assented to, as a matter of Faith, wherein Reason hath nothing to do.' Failure to acknowledge this had resulted in religions being filled with superstition.

62 Locke, *An Essay concerning Human Understanding*, bk IV, ch. 18, para. 2. In the fourth edition, Locke added an attack on enthusiasm: see chapter 5.

63 Locke, *An Essay concerning Human Understanding*, bk IV, ch. 17, para. 2.

64 Locke, *An Essay concerning Human Understanding*, bk IV, ch. 27, para. 6.

65 Locke, *An Essay concerning Human Understanding*, bk IV, ch. 17, para. 15.

66 Locke, *An Essay concerning Human Understanding*, bk I, ch. 1, para. 6, p. 46. For Locke and the new science, see G. A. J. Rogers, 'The Empiricism of Locke and Newton' (1979), 'Locke, Anthropology and

Models of the Mind' (1993), 'Boyle, Locke and Reason' (1990), and 'Locke, Newton and the Cambridge Platonists on Innate Ideas' (1990). For the idea of a tongue scientifically unambiguous and shorn of misleading rhetoric, see W. K. Wimsatt, *Philosophic Words* (1948).

67 Biddle, 'Locke's Critique of Innate Principles and Toland's Deism'; Charles Taylor, *Sources of the Self* (1989), p. 164.

68 Locke, *An Essay concerning Human Understanding*, bk II, ch. 1, para. 2, p. 104.

69 Locke, *An Essay concerning Human Understanding*, bk II, ch. 11, para. 17, pp. 162–3; Taylor, *Sources of the Self*, p. 167. Early in book I of the *Essay concerning Human Understanding*, Locke asks: 'Whence comes it [the mind] by that vast store [of ideas], which the busy and boundless Fancy of Man has painted on it, with an almost endless variety?' (which was the same as asking, 'Whence has it all the materials of Reason and Knowledge?'), and replies: 'To this I answer, in one word, From *Experience*' (bk I, ch. 2, para. 1).

70 Locke, *An Essay concerning Human Understanding*, bk II, ch. 1, para. 5: Locke's statement – 'whatsoever the mind perceives in itself, or is the immediate object of perception, thought, or understanding, that I call *idea*' – was quoted by Samuel Johnson in his *Dictionary sub* 'idea'.

71 As Berkeley among others argued, in a further attack upon the false thought worlds created by the philosophers. See Barrett, *Death of the Soul*, p. 35.

72 Locke, *An Essay concerning Human Understanding*, bk II, ch. 11, para. 2; bk II, ch. 11, para. 1.

73 Locke, *An Essay concerning Human Understanding*, bk II, ch. 11, para. 2; Martin Kallich, *The Association of Ideas and Critical Theory in Eighteenth-century England* (1970); Ernest Lee Tuveson, *The Imagination as a Means of Grace* (1960).

74 Locke, *An Essay concerning Human Understanding*, bk II, ch. 33.

75 Locke, *An Essay concerning Human Understanding*, bk II, ch. 21, para. 73.

76 Locke, *An Essay concerning Human Understanding*, bk II, ch. 23, para. 13.

77 Locke, *An Essay concerning Human Understanding*, bk III, ch. 6, para. 9.

78 Locke, *An Essay concerning Human Understanding*, bk IV, ch. 3, para. 6.

79 'There is a real justice in seeing the European Enlightenment as Locke's legacy': Dunn, *Locke*, p. 21.

80 E. S. De Beer (ed.), *The Correspondence of John Locke* (1976–89), letter 1659, vol. iv, p. 727. As late as 1768, Locke's *Essay* was placed on the Index of Prohibited Books in Portugal.

81 Yolton, *John Locke and the Way of Ideas*, p. 88; Sell, *John Locke and the Eighteenth-century Divines*, p. 29.

82 For Tindal, see his *Rights of the Christian Church Asserted* (sn, 1706); and for Swift, see his *Bickerstaff Papers* (1957 [1708–9]), p. 80, quoted in John Valdimir Price, 'The Reading of Philosophical Literature' (1982), p. 167. Locke's idea of personality also came in for satire: Kerby-Miller (ed.), *Memoirs of the Extraordinary Life, Works, and Discoveries of Martinus Scriblerus*, 1950.

83 For Chambers, see under entry for 'Idea'; William Wollaston, *The Religion of Nature Delineated* (1724), p. 17, in Yolton, *John Locke and the Way of Ideas*, p. 69.

84 William R. Paulson, *Enlightenment, Romanticism and the Blind in France* (1988), pp. 21–38; Marjorie Hope Nicolson, *Newton Demands the Muse* (1946), pp. 82–4; see also Locke, *An Essay concerning Human Understanding*, bk II, ch. 9, para. 8.

85 William Cheselden, 'An Account of Some Observations Made by a Young Gentleman' (1727–8); Richard C. Allen, *David Hartley on Human Nature* (1999), p. 140. See also G. N. Cantor, 'The History of "Georgian" Optics' (1978); Luke Davidson, ' "Identities Ascertained" ' (1996).

86 Alan Bewell, *Wordsworth and the*

Enlightenment (1989), p. 26; Jonathan Rée, *I See a Voice* (1999), pp. 334–7.

87 William Warburton, *Letters from a Late Eminent Prelate to One of His Friends* (1808), p. 207: letter of 3 March 1759. The friend was Richard Hurd.

88 Bolingbroke, *On Human Knowledge*, in *The Works of Lord Bolingbroke* (1969; repr. of 1841 edn [1754–77]), vol. v, p. 166. Reason was to Bolingbroke, as to Locke, a candle to light the traveller on a dark night.

89 Watts, *Logick*; see Arthur Paul Davis, *Isaac Watts: His Life and Works* (1948), p. 86.

90 Isaac Watts, *Philosophical Essays on Various Subjects* (1733), preface. Locke's writings were 'sun-beams': Sell, *John Locke and the Eighteenth-century Divines*, pp. 36, 163.

91 Sell, *John Locke and the Eighteenth-century Divines*, p. 5; J. Yolton, 'Schoolmen, Logic and Philosophy' (1986), p. 570.

92 John Gascoigne, *Cambridge in the Age of the Enlightenment* (1989), pp. 7f.; Peter Searby, *A History of the University of Cambridge* (1997), vol. iii, p. 152.

93 W. S. Howell, *Eighteenth-century British Logic and Rhetoric* (1971), pp. 273–4; Anand C. Chitnis, *The Scottish Enlightenment* (1976), p. 159.

94 Abraham Tucker, *The Light of Nature Pursued* (1997 [1768]), vol. i, p. 44. Tucker thematically contrasted the 'land of philosophy', which was open country, with the 'land of metaphysics', overgrown with thickets (vol. ii, p. 76).

95 Mary P. Mack, *Bentham, An Odyssey of Ideas, 1748–1792*, p. 120. Bentham, however, was not naive about language:

To say that, in discourse, fictitious language ought never, on any occasion, to be employed, would be as much as to say that no discourse in the subject of which the operations, or affections, or other phenomena of the mind are included, ought ever to be held.

Chrestomathia (1816), quoted in Bender, *Imagining the Penitentiary*, p. 138.

96 Addison and Steele, *The Spectator*, 11 papers, vol. III, nos. 411–42, pp. 535–82.

After categorizing the 'primary' sources of the imagination's pleasures, chiefly those objects or prospects distinguished by greatness, uncommonness or beauty, Addison then turned to the 'secondary' pleasures' of the imagination. See the discussion in Malcolm Andrews, *The Search for the Picturesque* (1989), pp. 39–40; Tuveson, *The Imagination as a Means of Grace*. For Locke on abuse of words, see *Spectator*, no. 373; on personal identity, no. 578. Addison succeeded Locke as Commissioner of Appeals in 1704.

97 Addison and Steele, *The Spectator*, vol. III, no. 413, pp. 546–7 (Tuesday, 24 June 1712).

98 Sir Richard Steele, Joseph Addison and others, the *Guardian*, vol. I, no. 24, p. 95 (24 June 1712).

99 Kenneth MacLean, *John Locke and English Literature of the Eighteenth Century* (1936), p. 1; see also Gerd Buchdahl, *The Image of Newton and Locke in the Age of Reason* (1961). For Locke as an educationalist, see chapter 15, and for his influence abroad, see John W. Yolton, *Locke and French Materialism* (1991), and Ross Hutchison, *Locke in France (1688–1734)* (1991). Robert DeMaria Jr calls Locke Johnson's 'principal philosopher': *Johnson's Dictionary and the Language of Learning*, p. 50.

100 *Covent-Garden Journal* no. 30, quoted in MacLean, *John Locke and English Literature of the Eighteenth Century*, p. 2.

101 Laurence Sterne, *The Life and Opinions of Tristram Shandy* (1967 [1759–67]), vol. I, ch. 4, p. 39; Judith Hawley, 'The Anatomy of *Tristram Shandy*' (1993); Sterne perhaps had in mind this passage of Locke's *Some Thoughts concerning Education*: 'Let not any fearful apprehensions be talked into them, nor terrible objects surprise them. This often so shatters and discomposes the spirits, that they never recover it [sic] again.' J. L. Axtell, *The Educational Writings of John Locke* (1968), section 115, p. 221. At a later stage, Tristram felt obliged to come back and explain Locke's *Essay*:

I will tell you in three words what the book is. – It is a history. – A history! of who? what? where? when? Don't hurry yourself – It is a history-book, Sir, (which may possibly recommend it to the world) of what passes in a man's own mind.

Sterne, *Tristram Shandy*, vol. ii, ch. 2, p. 107.

102 Mary Hays, *Memoirs of Emma Courtney* (1996 [1796]), p. 23.

103 Samuel Richardson, *Pamela* (1883–4 [1740]), vol. iii, p. 330, letter 90. Parents, she

recommended, should be careful not to 'indulge their children in bad habits, and give them their head, at a time when, like wax, their tender minds may be moulded into what shape they please'.

104 Charles Strachey (ed.), *The Letters of the Earl of Chesterfield to His Son* (1932), vol. i, p. 292, letter 168.

105 John Passmore, *The Perfectibility of Man* (1970), pp. 171–212.

106 Taylor, *Sources of the Self*, p. 174.

4 PRINT CULTURE

1 Alexander Pope, *The Dunciad* (1728), l. 1, in John Butt (ed.), *The Poems of Alexander Pope* (1965), p. 349.

2 Samuel Johnson, *A Dictionary of the English Language* (1755), preface.

3 W. J. Bate, J. M. Bullitt, and L. F. Powell (eds.), *Samuel Johnson: The Idler and Adventurer* (1963), no. 115, p. 457 (11 December 1753).

4 George Birkbeck Hill, *Boswell's Life of Johnson* (1934), vol. iii, p. 293 (16 April 1778).

5 For censorship on the Continent, see Robert Darnton, *The Forbidden Best-Sellers of Pre-Revolutionary France* (1996), and *The Business of Enlightenment* (1979). For a metahistory of the impact of the book, see Ernest Gellner, *Plough, Sword and Book* (1991).

6 See discussion in Adrian Johns, *The Nature of the Book* (1998), pp. 187f.

7 This was then repeated in the *Salisbury Journal* (18 March 1754): C. Y. Ferdinand, *Benjamin Collins and the Provincial Newspaper Trade in the Eighteenth Century* (1997), p. 155. A degree of theatrical censorship was introduced by the Licensing Act (1737).

8 James Raven, Naomi Tadmore and Helen Small (eds), *The Practice and Representation of Reading in Britain 1500–1900* (1996), pp. 4ff.; John Feather, 'The Power of Print' (1997), and *A History of British Publishing* (1988); Marjorie Plant, *The English Book Trade* (1965).

9 Richard D. Altick, *The English Common Reader* (1957), p. 49.

10 James Sutherland, *Defoe* (1937), p. 68.

11 A. Beljame, *Men of Letters and the English Public in the Eighteenth Century, 1660–1744* (1948), p. 309; A. S. Collins, *Authorship in the Days of Johnson* (1927), p. 21.

12 See John Brewer, *The Pleasures of the Imagination* (1997), p. 428; Clifford Siskin, *The Work of Writing* (1998). A Foucauldian might modify Pope and write of the appearance of the 'author function': Michel Foucault, 'What is an Author?' (1977); see the discussion in Roger Chartier, *The Order of Books* (1994), p. 29.

13 William Worthington, *An Essay on the Scheme and Conduct, Procedure and Extent of Man's Redemption* (sn, 1743), pp. 155–6; Edmund Law, *Considerations on the State of the World, with Regard to the Theory of Religion* (1745), p. 25.

14 George Davie, *The Democratic Intellect* (1961), p. 66; T. C. Smout, *A History of the Scottish People, 1560–1830* (1969), p. 478; R. A. Houston, 'Scottish Education and Literacy, 1600–1800' (1989).

15 According to a parliamentary survey, in 1819 there were 4,167 'endowed' schools in England, including grammar schools, with 165,433 pupils; 14,282 unendowed schools, from 'dame schools' to Dissenting academies, with 478,849 pupils; and for the children of the poor, 5,162 Sunday schools with 452,817 pupils. See John Lawson and Harold Silver, *A Social History of Education in England* (1973), pp. 226–66.

16 E. G. Hundert, *The Enlightenment's Fable* (1994), p. 122; Soame Jenyns, *Free Inquiry into the Nature and Origin of Evil* (1757), pp. 49–50. Johnson put Jenyns in his place:

The privileges of education may sometimes be improperly bestowed, but I shall always fear to withhold them, lest I should be yielding to the suggestions of pride, while I persuade myself that I am following the maxims of policy; and under the appearance of salutary restraints, should be indulging the lust of dominion, and that malevolence which delights in seeing others depressed.

Samuel Johnson, 'A Review of Soame Jenyns' "A Free Inquiry into the Nature and Origin of Evil" ' (1757), in B. Bronson (ed.), *Samuel Johnson, Rasselas, Poems and Selected Prose* 3rd edn (1971), p. 224.

17 Edward Gibbon, *Memoirs of My Life* (1966 [1796]), p. 36.

18 Brewer, *The Pleasures of the Imagination*, p. 187; John Money, 'Teaching in the Market-Place, or "*Caesar Adsum Jam Forte; Pompey Aderat*" ' (1993). Professor Money is engaged on a biography of Cannon.

19 G. D. H. and Margaret Cole (eds.), *The Opinions of William Cobbett* (1944), p. 17; George Spater, *William Cobbett: The Poor Man's Friend* (1982), p. 18; Cobbett went on to Dryden, Pope and Goldsmith, who were his favourites, and also Milton, Marvell, Butler, Cowley, Churchill, Thomson and Cowper, some Byron, Wordsworth and Southey, and the novels of Fielding, Sterne, Le Sage and Cervantes. He studied Blackstone's *Commentaries*, Watts's *Logic*, and Blair's *Lectures on Rhetoric*, and some of Bacon, Evelyn, Gibbon, Addison, Paley, Johnson and William Temple.

20 Samuel Bamford, *The Autobiography of Samuel Bamford* (1848–9; repr. 1967), vol. i, pp. 23, 40; see also Patricia Anderson, *The Printed Image and the Transformation of Popular Culture 1790–1860* (1991), pp. 31, 90: 'My mind was ever desiring more of the silent but exciting conversation with books.'

21 John Clare, 'The Autobiography, 1793–1824', in J. W. and A. Tibble (eds.), *The Prose of John Clare* (1951), p. 14.

22 David Vincent, *Literacy and Popular Culture* (1989), and *Bread, Knowledge and Freedom* (1982).

23 James Lackington, *Memoirs of the First Forty-five Years of the Life of James Lackington*, 7th edn (1794), pp. 254–5.

24 Lackington, *Memoirs of the First Forty-five Years of the Life of James Lackington*, pp. 232, 257; see Altick, *The English Common Reader 1800–1900*, pp. 36ff.; Roy McKeen Wiles, 'The Relish for Reading in Provincial England Two Centuries Ago' (1976), pp. 85–115.

25 See Altick, *The English Common Reader 1800–1900*, p. 57. Apprenticed to a cobbler, Lackington became a Methodist and set about educating himself, going without food to buy books. In 1774 he moved to London, working as a cobbler. On his first London Christmas he went to get Christmas dinner – but bought instead a copy of Edward Young's *Night Thoughts* (1742–5). Becoming a bookseller and selling with small profits, he increased the value of his stock to £25 within six months. In 1779, he published his first catalogue, listing a stock of 12,000 volumes. By the 1790s, when his annual sales were counted in tens of thousands of volumes, he proclaimed: 'I found the whole of what I am possessed of, in Small Profits, bound by Industry, and clasped by Economy': *Memoirs of the First Forty-five Years of the Life of James Lackington*, pp. 210–14, 256–9, 268.

26 Samuel Johnson, 'Milton', in *The Lives of the Most Eminent English Poets* (1939 [1779–81]), vol. i, pp. 103–4, quoted in Altick, *The English Common Reader 1800–1900*, p. 41. A Prussian visitor to London wrote that his landlady, a tailor's widow, 'reads her Milton and tells me that her late husband first fell in love with her, because of the good style in which she read that poet': Carl Philip Moritz, *Journeys of a German in England* (1982 [1783]), p. 30.

27 William Hazlitt, *Life of Thomas Holcroft* (1816), in P. P. Howe (ed.), *The Complete Works of William Hazlitt*, vol. iii, p. 42; see also A. S. Collins, *The Profession of Letters* (1973 [1928]), p. 31.

28 Indeed, it may have actually dipped towards 1800 amid rapid population growth and the disruptions of early industrialization. See R. A. Houston, *Literacy in Early Modern Europe* (1988); David Cressy, 'Literacy in Context' (1993). Between 1650 and 1800 female literacy in England increased from under 15 per cent to about 36 per cent: Margaret R. Hunt, *The Middling Sort* (1996), p. 85.

29 Quoted in Keith Hanley and Raman Selden (eds.), *Revolution and English Romanticism* (1990), p. 2; Dror Wahrman, 'National Society, Communal Culture' (1992).

30 These terms were developed by Rolf Engelsing, who claimed a 'reading revolution'. See his *Der Burger als Lesser* (1974). For discussion, see Dorinda Outram, *The Enlightenment* (1995), p. 19; Robert Darnton, 'History of Reading' (1991); Robert Darnton and Daniel Roche (eds.), *Revolution in Print* (1989); Roger Chartier, *Forms and Meanings* (1995), and *The Order of Books*.

31 Brewer, *The Pleasures of the Imagination*, p. 169. 'Receipts in physic' means medical remedies. For a classic 'intensive' reader, see the portrait of Anthony Liddell offered by Thomas Bewick: *A Memoir of Thomas Bewick, Written by Himself* (1961 [1862]), p. 29: Liddell read the Bible, Josephus and Jeremy Taylor's sermons.

32 Quoted in Brewer, *The Pleasures of the Imagination*, p. 169.

33 John Brown, *An Estimate of the Manners and Principles of the Times* (1757), pp. 25–6.

34 Samuel Johnson thought sermons

essential to any gentleman's library: J. C. D. Clark, *Samuel Johnson: Literature, Religion and English Cultural Politics from the Restoration to Romanticism* (1994), p. 125.

35 David Vaisey (ed.), *The Diary of Thomas Turner of East Hoathley* (1984), p. 347. Turner read Locke on 26 May 1757.

36 In 1758, Samuel Johnson judged that 'almost every large town has its weekly historian': Bate, Bullitt and Powell (eds.), *Samuel Johnson: The Idler and Adventurer* (1958–71), no. 30, p. 22 (11 November 1758). For newspapers, see Roy McKeen Wiles, *Freshest Advices* (1965); Michael Harris, *London Newspapers in the Age of Walpole* (1987); Michael Harris and Alan Lee (eds.), *The Press in English Society from the Seventeenth to the Nineteenth Centuries* (1986); Jeremy Black, *The English Press in the Eighteenth Century* (1986); Geoffrey Alan Cranfield, *The Development of the Provincial Newspaper 1700–1760* (1962), and *The Press and Society from Caxton to Northcliffe* (1978); Hannah Barker, *Newspapers, Politics and Public Opinion in Late Eighteenth-century England* (1998).

37 Samuel Johnson, preface to the *Gentleman's Magazine*, 1740, quoted in Cranfield, *The Development of the Provincial Newspaper 1700–1760*, p. 93.

38 G. Crabbe, *The News-paper* in Norma Dalrymple-Champneys (ed.), *George Crabbe: The Complete Poetical Works* (1988), vol. i, p. 182. On newness, see C. John Sommerville, *The News Revolution in England* (1997).

39 Joseph Addison and Richard Steele, *The Spectator* (1965), vol. iv, pp. 90–94 (Friday, 8 August 1712); see vol. v, no. 625, pp. 134–7 (Friday, 26 November 1714) for the 'pleasure of news'.

40 C. Y. Ferdinand, *Benjamin Collins and the Provincial Newspaper Trade in the Eighteenth Century* (1997), p. 196.

41 James Boswell, *The Life of Samuel Johnson* (1946 [1791]), vol. i, p. 424; Hill, *Boswell's Life of Johnson*, vol. ii, p. 170. Johnson also said that 'books have a secret influence on the understanding': quoted in Brewer, *The Pleasures of the Imagination*, p. 167.

42 C. de Saussure, *A Foreign View of England in 1725–29* (1995 [1902]), p. 102.

43 Collins, *The Profession of Letters*, p. 19.

44 Alexander Catcott, *A Treatise on the Deluge*, 2nd edn (1768), p. vi. For this dyed in the wool reactionary, see Roy Porter and Michael Neve, 'Alexander Catcott: Glory and Geology' (1977).

45 Josiah Tucker, *Four Tracts* (1774), pp. 89–90.

46 In full it runs:

Non fumum ex fulgore, sed ex fumo dare lucem Cogitat, ut speciosa dehinc miracula promat.

Horace, *Ars poetica*, 1. 143.

47 Richmond P. Bond (ed.), *Studies in the Early English Periodical* (1957), p. 17; Erin Mackie, *Market à la Mode* (1997).

48 Bond, *Studies in the Early English Periodical*, p. 19.

49 Samuel Johnson, *The Lives of the Most Eminent English Poets*, vol. ii, pp. 362–4.

50 The *Female Spectator* was preceded by the *Female Tatler* (1709–10), but, while professedly handled by 'Mrs Crackenthorpe', it was actually an all male affair. See Gabrielle M. Firmager (ed.), *The Female Spectator* (1992), p. 5; Cheryl Turner, *Living by the Pen* (1992), p. 149; Kathryn Shevelow, *Women and Print Culture* (1989); Paula McDowell, *The Women of Grub Street* (1998).

51 Margaret Beetham, *A Magazine of Her Own?* (1996). Eliza Haywood (1693–1756) was a friend of Richard Steele. Her *The Female Spectator* (1744–6) was a collection of moral tales and reflections in twenty-four monthly parts. She wrote several popular novels, among them *The History of Miss Betsy Thoughtless* (1751).

52 C. L. Carlson, *The First Magazine* (1938); Terry Belanger, 'Publishers and Writers in Eighteenth-century England' (1982), p. 5. For some of its functions, see Roy Porter, 'Laymen, Doctors and Medical Knowledge in the Eighteenth Century' (1985), and 'Lay Medical Knowledge in the Eighteenth Century' (1985).

53 Bond, *Studies in the Early English Periodical*, p. 27; Benjamin Christie Nangle, *The Monthly Review* (1934–5); Derek Roper, *Reviewing Before the Edinburgh* (1978), p. 21.

54 M. Bailey (ed.), *Boswell's Column* (1951), p. 21.

55 G. McEwen, *The Oracle of the Coffee House* (1972), p. 57; Michael Mascuch, *Origins of the Individualist Self* (1997), p. 148; John Dunton, *The Life and Errors of John Dunton, Citizen of London* (1960 [1818]).

56 McEwen, *The Oracle of the Coffee House*, pp. 23f., 130.

57 A phrase used by John Byrom: H. Talon (ed.), *Selections from the Journals and Papers of John Byrom, Poet – Diarist – Shorthand Writer* (1950), p. 47.

58 Daniel Defoe, 'On Pope's Translation of Homer' (1725), in William Lee, *Daniel Defoe: His Life and Recently Discovered Writings* (1869), vol. ii, p. 410. Talk followed of 'novel manufactories': Collins, *Authorship in the Days of Johnson*, p. 21; Alvin Kernan, *Printing Technology, Letters and Samuel Johnson* (1987), pp. 17f.

59 Henry Fielding, *The Author's Farce* (1966 [1730]), p. 28; Brean S. Hammond, *Professional Imaginative Writing in England, 1670–1740* (1997), p. 28; Philip Pinkus, *Grub St Stripped Bare* (1968), p. 71.

60 John Clive, 'The Social Background of the Scottish Renaissance' (1970), p. 227; Frederick A. Pottle (ed.), *Boswell's London Journal, 1762–1763* (1950), p. 287.

61 Pat Rogers, *Grub Street* (1972). Grub Street ran just outside the city wall in Cripplegate, near Bethlem Hospital. The use of the term to denote the home of shabby hack-writing emerged in the Restoration. Pope extended this idea in *The Dunciad*, that epic of Grub Street, with its hacks, dunces and poetasters as attendants to the Queen of Dulness. See also Johnson's *An Account of the Life of Richard Savage*, 2nd edn (1748).

62 The narrator of the *Memoirs of Martin Scriblerus* thus boasted of getting his education amongst 'the Learned of that Society', and it perhaps provided the germ for the idea of the Grand Academy of Lagado in *Gulliver's Travels*: Rogers, *Grub Street*, p. 182.

63 For 'pimps', see Frank Donoghue, *The Fame Machine* (1996), p. 44.

64 Johnson, *An Account of the Life of Richard Savage*; Richard Holmes, *Dr Johnson and Mr Savage* (1993). It was a label ironically self-affixed by Coleridge amongst others: Earl Leslie Griggs (ed.), *Collected Letters of Samuel Taylor Coleridge* (1956), vol. i, p. 185, letter 105 (22 February 1796).

65 John Dennis, *The Characters and Conduct of Sir John Edgar, Call'd by Himself Sole Monarch of the Stage in Drury-Lane* (1720), in E. N. Hooker (ed.), *The Critical Works of John Dennis* (1943), vol. ii, pp. 191–2; Martha Woodmansee, 'The Genius and the Copyright' (1984), pp. 417–32; Mark Rose, *Authors and Owners* (1993). A conceptual focus is offered by Foucault, 'What is an Author?'; Hammond, *Professional Imaginative Writing in England, 1670–1740*, p. 5.

66 Johns, *The Nature of the Book* (1998), p. 353; Hammond, *Professional Imaginative Writing in England, 1670–1740*, p. 23; John Feather, *Publishing, Piracy and Politics* (1994).

67 Not a bad advance, being a hundred times the annual income of a labourer. See Collins, *Authorship in the Days of Johnson*, pp. 9–10, 25; Kernan, *Printing Technology, Letters and Samuel Johnson*, p. 10.

68 Collins, *Authorship in the Days of Johnson*, p. 47; James Aikman Cochrane, *Dr Johnson's Printer* (1964).

69 James Ralph, *The Case of Authors by Profession or Trade, Stated with Regard to Booksellers, the State and the Public* (1758), p. 22.

70 Gibbon, *Memoirs of My Life*, p. 153.

71 Gibbon, *Memoirs of My Life*, p. 157.

72 Patron was defined by Johnson as 'one who countenances, supports or protects. Commonly a wretch who supports with insolence, and is paid with flattery': see Robert DeMaria Jr, *Johnson's Dictionary and the Language of Learning* (1986), p. 211; Dustin Griffin, *Literary Patronage in England, 1650–1800* (1996).

73 R. W. Chapman (ed.), *Samuel Johnson, A Journey to the Western Islands of Scotland and James Boswell, The Journal of a Tour to the Hebrides* (1970), pp. 196–7.

74 Hill, *Boswell's Life of Johnson*, vol. i, p. 262, from James Boswell (ed.), *The Celebrated Letter from Samuel Johnson, LLD to Philip Dormer Stanhope, Earl of Chesterfield* (1790).

75 Samuel Johnson, *The Vanity of Human Wishes* (1749), ll. 159–60, in Patrick Cruttwell (ed.), *Samuel Johnson: Selected Writings* (1986), p. 143.

76 Oliver Goldsmith, *Selected Essays* (1910), p. 65.

77 Altick, *The English Common Reader* (1957), p. 36.

78 Altick, *The English Common Reader*, p. 56; Roy McKeen Wiles, *Serial Publication in England before 1750* (1957). A letter in the *Grub-Street Journal* complained of 'that strange Madness of publishing Books by piecemeal, at six or twelve Pennyworth a Week': 'The Bible can't escape. I bought the other Day, three Pennyworth of the Gospel, made easy and familiar to Porters, Carmen, and Chimney-Sweepers . . . Well, what an Age of Wit and Learning have I the happiness to live in!': Cranfield, *The Development of the Provincial Newspaper 1700–1760*, p. 52.

79 An alliance of forty London booksellers attempted to steal Bell's thunder by publishing an upmarket collection of British poets, for which Samuel Johnson wrote his famous prefaces: Johnson, *The Lives of the Most Eminent English Poets*.

80 Stanley Morrison, *John Bell (1745–1831)* (1930), p. 88.

81 Hazlitt's father purchased Cooke's 'Select Edition of the British Novels' from 1792, the first being *Tom Jones* – a work 'sweet in the mouth'. The boy soon read *Joseph Andrews*, and in due course the works of Smollett and Sterne: Catherine Macdonald Maclean, *Born Under Saturn* (1943), pp. 49–51; Altick, *The English Common Reader*, p. 54; Olivia Smith, *The Politics of Language 1791–1819* (1984), p. 157.

82 Pat Rogers, *The Augustan Vision* (1974), p. 8; John Feather, *The Provincial Book Trade in Eighteenth-century England* (1985), p. 29; Jack Lindsay, *William Blake: His Life and Work* (1978), p. 3.

83 Brewer, *The Pleasures of the Imagination*, p. 178.

84 'Madam, a circulating library in a town is as an evergreen tree of diabolical knowledge! It blossoms through the year! – and depend upon it, Mrs Malaprop, that they who are so fond of handling the leaves, will long for the fruit at last': Richard Brinsley Sheridan, *The Rivals* (1961 [1775]), act I, scene ii, ll. 33–7. On libraries see Paul Kaufman, *Borrowings from the Bristol Library, 1773–1784* (1960); M. Kay Flavell, 'The Enlightened Reader and the New Industrial Towns' (1985); James Raven, 'From Promotion to Proscription' (1996), p. 175 – Raven proclaims a 'library revolution'. Great houses might even contain servants' libraries: Joanna Martin (ed.), *A Governess in the Age of Jane Austen* (1988), p. 67.

85 W. R. Scott, *Adam Smith as Student and Professor* (1937), pp. 344–5, from the draft for the *Wealth of Nations*, written in 1769 but expunged from the published text: as society progressed, 'philosophy, or speculation . . . naturally becomes, like every other employment, the sole occupation of a particular class of citizens': Adam Smith, 'Early Draft of Part of *The Wealth of Nations*' (1762), in *Lectures on Jurisprudence* (1982), pp. 570–74. See discussion in Outram, *The Enlightenment*, p. 14; see also Adam Smith, *An Inquiry into the Nature and Causes of the Wealth of Nations* (1976 [1776]), bk I, ch. 1, para. 9.

86 Jonathan Swift, 'On Poetry' (1733), ll. 353–6, in *The Complete Poems* (1983), p. 531. Swift wrote a 'Digression Concerning Criticks',

where 'a *True Critick*' is presented as 'a sort of Mechanick, set up with a Stock and Tools for his Trade, at as little Expence as a *Taylor*': Jonathan Swift, *A Tale of a Tub* (1975 [1704]), p. 62; see also Paul Fussell, *The Rhetorical World of Augustan Humanism* (1965), p. 85.

87 Cole (eds), *The Opinions of William Cobbett*, p. 42. Characteristically Cobbett qualified: 'The only critics that I look to are the public.'

88 For Steele: 'In a Nation of Liberty, there is hardly a Person in the whole Mass of the People more absolutely necessary than a Censor': Donald F. Bond (ed.), *The Tatler* (1987), vol. ii, no. 144, p. 318 (Saturday, 11 March 1710). Terry Eagleton, *The Function of Criticism* (1984), pp. 31, 4: for Eagleton, the irony of Enlightenment criticism lay in the fact that 'while its appeal to standards of universal reason signifies a resistance to absolutism, the critical gesture itself is typically conservative and corrective, revising and adjusting particular phenomena to its implacable model of discourse'.

89 Samuel Johnson, *The Rambler* (1969 [1750–52]), vol. i, p. xxviii.

90 Donoghue, *The Fame Machine*.

91 Edward A. Bloom and Lilian D. Bloom, *Joseph Addison's Sociable Animal* (1971).

92 Addison and Steele, *The Spectator*, vol. i, no. 10, p. 54.

93 Anthony Ashley Cooper, 3rd Earl of Shaftesbury, *Characteristicks of Men, Manners, Opinions, Times* (1999 [1711]); Lawrence E. Klein, *Shaftesbury and the Culture of Politeness* (1994); Robert Voitle, *The Third Earl of Shaftesbury: 1671–1713* (1984).

94 Shaftesbury, *Characteristicks of Men, Manners, Opinions, Times*, vol. ii, p. 207.

95 David Hume, 'Of Essay Writing' (1741), in *Selected Essays* (1993), p. 2.

96 David Hume, *A Treatise of Human Nature*, 2nd edn (1978 [1739–40]), p. 269; Ernest Campbell Mossner, *The Life of David Hume* (1954), ch. 6.

97 David Hume, *A Treatise of Human Nature* (1969 [1739–40]), p. 21.

98 David Hume, *The Life of David Hume, Esq.* (1741–2), in David Hume, *The Philosophical Works of David Hume* (1874–5; repr. 1987), vol. 3, p. 2.

99 Hume, *The Life of David Hume, Esq.*, in David Hume, *Essays Moral, Political and Literary* (1898), vol. 4, p. 5. Unlike Hume, Hugh Blair complimented Locke's style: his 'celebrated Treatise on Human Understanding' was a model of 'the greatest clearness and distinctness of Philosophical Style, with very little approach to ornament': Hugh Blair, *Lectures on Rhetoric and Belles Lettres* (1783), vol. iii, lecture 37, p. 81.

100 See the discussion in Stephen Copley, 'Commerce, Conversation and Politeness in the Early Eighteenth-century Periodical' (1995); Jerome Christensen, *Practising Enlightenment* (1987).

101 Blair, *Lectures on Rhetoric and Belles Lettres*, vol. iii, pp. 78, 79, 80.

102 Smith, *An Inquiry into the Nature and Causes of the Wealth of Nations*, vol. i, bk I, ch. i, p. 21, para. 9.

103 Smith, *An Inquiry into the Nature and Causes of the Wealth of Nations*, vol. i, bk I, ch. 1, p. 21, para. 9.

104 For Smith's universal observer, see John Barrell, *English Literature in History, 1730–80* (1983).

105 Compare Jean Le Rond D'Alembert, *Preliminary Discourse to the Encyclopedia of Diderot* (1995).

106 For instructional and educational books, see Isabel Rivers (ed.), *Books and Their Readers in Eighteenth-century England* (1982); John Ashton, *Chap-books of the Eighteenth Century* (1882); Victor Neuberg, *Popular Literature* (1977), pp. 113f.

107 See S. F. Pickering Jr, *John Locke and Children's Books in Eighteenth-century England* (1981), and chapter 15, below.

108 Herbert M. Atherton, *Political Prints in the Age of Hogarth* (1974); Barbara Maria Stafford, *Artful Science* (1994); Anderson, *The Printed Image and the Transformation of Popular Culture*

1790–1860, pp. 17f.; Marcus Wood, *Radical Satire and Print Culture 1790–1822* (1994); Michael Duffy (ed.), *The English Satirical Print, 1600–1832* (1986); Ronald Paulson, *Representations of Revolution (1789–1820)* (1983); Brian Maidment, *Popular Prints, 1790–1870* (1995).

109 DeMaria, *Johnson's Dictionary and the Language of Learning*; J. Harris, *Lexicon Technicum* (1736): it had 1,200 subscribers. For encyclopaedias, see Frank A. Kafker (ed.), *Notable Encyclopedias of the Seventeenth and Eighteenth Centuries* (1981), p. 108; Robert Collison, *Encyclopaedias* (1964), p. 99; Richard Yeo, *Encyclopaedic Visions* (forthcoming). Theology received little attention in the *Lexicon Technicum*.

110 Ephraim Chambers, *Cyclopaedia, Or an Universal Dictionary of Arts and Sciences* (1728).

111 Abraham Rees, *The Cyclopaedia* (1819).

112 *Encyclopaedia Britannica* (1771). See Collison, *Encyclopaedias*, pp. 138f.

113 Thus, Laurence Sterne drew heavily upon Chambers for the learned humour in *Tristram Shandy*: see Judith Hawley, 'The Anatomy of *Tristram Shandy*' (1993).

114 Brewer, *The Pleasures of the Imagination*, p. 463; Jonathan Brody Kramnick, *Making the English Canon* (1999).

115 Quoted in B. Sprague Allen, *Tides in English Taste (1619–1800)* (1858), p. 85.

116 Michael Dobson, *The Making of the National Poet* (1992); Jonathan Bate, *Shakespearean Constitutions* (1989); Robert W. Babcock, *The Genesis of Shakespeare Idolatry, 1766–1799* (1931).

117 F. M. Voltaire, *Letters concerning the English Nation* (1926 [1733]), p. 165; Brewer, *The Pleasures of the Imagination*, p. 473.

118 Jonathan Swift, letter to Dean Sterne (26 September 1710), quoted in Michael Foss, *Man of Wit to Man of Business* (1988), p. 163.

119 Thomas Beddoes, *Hygëia* (1802–3), vol. iii, ch. 9, p. 163. In the persona of his hero, Sterne facetiously asks the reader: 'is this good for your worship's eyes?': Sterne, *The Life and Opinions of Tristram Shandy*, p. 268. For the pathology of reading, see Roy Porter, 'Reading: A Health Warning' (1999).

120 Brown, *An Estimate of the Manners and Principles of the Times*, vol. i, pp. 42–3.

121 Hill, *Boswell's Life of Johnson*, vol. iii, p. 332.

122 Henry Mackenzie, *The Mirror* (1779–80).

123 The phrase is Goldsmith's: Thomas Schlereth, *The Cosmopolitan Ideal in Enlightenment Thought* (1977), p. 3; see Kramnick, *Making the English Canon*; Anne Goldgar, *Impolite Learning* (1995); Benedict Anderson, *Imagined Communities* (1983); Lorraine Daston, 'The Ideal and Reality of the Republic of Letters in the Enlightenment' (1991).

124 Anthony Pasquin [pseud.], *Memoirs of the Royal Academicians* (1796), p. 148. Many would arraign the public:

> There still remains to mortify a Wit,
> The many-headed Monster of the Pit:
> A sense-less, worth-less, and unhonour'd
>   crowd;
> Who to disturb their betters mighty proud,

Alexander Pope, 'The First Epistle of the Second Book of Horace' (1733), ll. 304–7, in Butt, *The Poems of Alexander Pope*, p. 646.

125 Gibbon, *Memoirs of My Life*, pp. 162–3.

126 Samuel Johnson, *Life of Gray* (1915), p. 14.

5 RATIONALIZING RELIGION

1 Thomas Sprat, *The History of the Royal Society of London* (1667), p. 374.

2 Edward Moore on Sunday observance, in the *World* magazine, no. 21, quoted in George S. Marr, *The Periodical Essayists of the Eighteenth Century* (1971), p. 144.

3 For historiography, see Sheridan Gilley, 'Christianity and the Enlightenment' (1981). For background, see Gerald R. Cragg, *From Puritanism to the Age of Reason* (1950), *The Church and the Age of Reason* (1960), and *Reason and Authority in the Eighteenth Century* (1964); David Hempton, *Religion and Political Culture in Britain and Ireland* (1996); Jane Garnett and Colin Matthew (eds.), *Revival and Religion since 1700* (1993); Sheridan Gilley and W. J. Sheils, *A History of Religion in Britain* (1994); James Downey, *The Eighteenth Century Pulpit* (1969).

This chapter is extremely selective, chiefly dealing with the question of religious rationality. It essentially omits the heated discussions taking place on particular doctrines, for instance questions of the soul and of Heaven and Hell and the afterlife; see, however, the account in Roy Porter, 'The Soul and the English Enlightenment' (forthcoming); and P. C. Almond, *Heaven and Hell in Enlightenment England* (1994); B. W. Young, ' "The Soul-sleeping System" ' (1994); Colleen McDannell and Bernhard Lang, *Heaven – A History* (1988).

4 Edward Gibbon, *Memoirs of My Life* (1966 [1796]), p. 139. 'Cassock'd huntsmen' was a coinage of the poet George Crabbe. 'Gay' Quakers were those who abandoned seventeenth-century costume and accepted some worldly pleasures.

5 Joseph Addison and Richard Steele, *The Spectator* (1965), vol. 1, no. 112, p. 459 (9 July 1711); John Beresford (ed.), *The Diary of a Country Parson* (1978–81).

6 John Walsh, Colin Haydon and Stephen Taylor (eds), *The Church of England c.1689–c.1833* (1993), p. 19.

7 Quoted in Hiram Caton, *The Politics of Progress* (1988), p. 207; Roland N. Stromberg, *Religious Liberalism in Eighteenth-century England* (1954), p. 2. For High Church men see George Every, *The High Church Party 1699–1718* (1956). Many historians treat such 'atheists' as mere bogeymen, but David Berman counter-argues that they were actually numerous but forced to resort to subterfuge: *A History of Atheism in Britain from Hobbes to Russell* (1988), p. 43. In his *Answer to Priestley's Letters to a Philosophical Unbeliever* (sn, 1782), William Hammon wrote (p. xvii):

as to the question whether there is such an existent Being as an atheist, to put that out of all manner of doubt, I do declare upon my honour that I am one. Be it therefore for the future remembered, that in London in the kingdom of England, in the year of our Lord one thousand seven hundred and eighty-one, a man publicly declared himself to be an atheist.

8 Joseph Texte, *Jean-Jacques Rousseau and the Cosmopolitan Spirit in Literature* (1899), p. 59; C. John Sommerville, *The Secularization of Early Modern England* (1992), p. 185. In London in 1766, Alessandro Verri wrote: 'Nobody even talks about religion here': quoted in Nicholas Davidson, 'Toleration in Enlightenment Italy' (2000), p. 230.

9 For the age of Watts, the Wesleys and Cowper, see Horton Davies, *Worship and Theology in England from Watts and Wesley to Martineau, 1690–1900* (1996). Isaac Watts's *The Psalms of David Imitated in the Language of the New Testament* (1719) contained such well-known hymns as 'O God, our help in ages past'.

10 William Law, *The Absolute Unlawfulness of the Stage Entertainment Fully Demonstrated* (1726), p. 11. For Law, see A. Whyte, *Characters and Characteristics of William Law* (1898); for the quotation see John Brewer, *The Pleasures of the Imagination* (1997), p. 333. Law discerned a Trojan horse: 'the infidelity which is now openly declared for pretends to support itself upon the sufficiency, excellency and absolute perfections of reason or Natural Religion': William Law, *A Serious Call to a Devout and Holy Life* (1729), introduction. Gibbon wrote of him: 'his last compositions are darkly tinctured with the incomprehensible visions of Jacob Behmen': Gibbon, *Memoirs of My Life*, p. 22.

11 See M. Quinlan, *Samuel Johnson: A Layman's Religion* (1964); C. F. Chapin, *The Religious Thought of Samuel Johnson* (1968). For 'the quiver of Omnipotence' see W. J. Bate, J. M. Bullitt, and L. F. Powell (eds), *Samuel Johnson: The Idler and Adventurer* (1963), no. 120, p. 468.

12 Jonas Hanway, *A Journal of Eight Days' Journey*, 2 vols., 2nd edn (1757), vol. i, p. 35.

13 In the middle of the century John Leland found the attacks of Deists still threatening: *A View of the Principal Deistical Writers That Have Appeared in England in the Last and Present Century* (1754).

14 Edmund Burke, *Reflections on the Revolution in France and on the Proceedings in Certain Societies in London Relative to That Event* (1982 [1790]), p. 186. For Bolingbroke's Deism see Ronald W. Harris, *Reason and Nature in the Eighteenth Century, 1714–1780* (1968), p. 151. Johnson too was rude about Bolingbroke, in his *Dictionary* defining 'Irony' as 'A mode of speech in which the meaning is contrary to the words: as, Bolingbroke was a holy man'. For Bolingbroke, see H. T. Dickinson, *Bolingbroke* (1970).

15 Certainly that was the view of that earnest agnostic, Leslie Stephen: *History of English Thought in the Eighteenth Century* (1962 [1876]).

16 Mary Wollstonecraft, *Thoughts on the Education of Daughters* (1995 [1787]), p. 132. A contemporary who certainly did read the Deists was Hazlitt: Catherine Macdonald Maclean, *Born Under Saturn* (1943), p. 58.

17 Joseph Butler, *The Analogy of Religion to the Constitution and Course of Nature* (n.d.), advertisement.

18 Norman Torrey, *Voltaire and the English Deists* (1930). Like those thinkers, Voltaire, while passionately anti-Catholic, remained for most of his life a Deist, seeing belief in God as the foundation of order.

19 Claude Rawson, *Satire and Sentiment 1660–1830* (1994), p. 200.

20 Joseph Granvill's *Vanity of Dogmatizing* (1661) – significant title! – analysed on

Baconian lines man's proneness to error, and denounced dogmatism. Locke opposed 'untractable Zealots in different and opposite Parties', moved as they were by unreasoning 'enthusiasm': R. D. Stock, *The Holy and the Daemonic from Sir Thomas Browne to William Blake* (1982), p. 85. John Fletcher Clews Harrison, *The Second Coming* (1979).

21 Michael R. Watts, *The Dissenters* (1978), vol. i, p. 263: Sacheverell called Dissenters 'miscreants begat in rebellion, born in sedition, and nursed in faction'. On church courts, see John Addy, *Sin and Society in the Seventeenth Century* (1989).

22 Increasingly it was the laity who led in policing vice through bodies like the Society for the Reformation of Manners and the Proclamation Society; the Evangelical revival was spearheaded by non-ecclesiastics like William Wilberforce: T. C. Curtis and W. A. Speck, 'The Societies for the Reformation of Manners' (1976); Sommerville, *The Secularization of Early Modern England*, charts the shift from 'a religious culture to a religious faith' (p. 1); C. John Sommerville, 'The Secularization Puzzle' (1994); Pieter Spierenburg, *The Broken Spell* (1991). See also the opening of chapter 9.

23 'If the voice of our priests was clamorous and bitter, their hands were disarmed of the powers of persecution': Gibbon, *Memoirs of My Life*, p. 159.

24 C. de Saussure, *A Foreign View of England in 1725–29* (1995 [1902]), p. 132.

25 Jeremy Gregory, 'Christianity and Culture' (1997), p. 113. They thus in some ways anticipated Coleridge's 'clerisy'.

26 Robert Southey, *Letters from England by Don Manuel Alvarez Espriella* (1984 [1807]), p. 111.

27 Maurice Cranston, *John Locke: A Biography* (1957), p. 125.

28 Samuel Butler, *Hudibras, Parts I and II and Selected Other Writings* (1973 [1663–78]), p. 7, ll. 193–5. Butler mocked the 'darkness' of the Puritans' illumination:

'Tis a Dark-Lanthorn of the Spirit,
Which none see by but those that bear it:
A Light that falls down from on high,
For spiritual Trades to cozen by:
An Ignis Fatuus, that bewitches,
And leads Men into Pools and Ditches.

29 Loathing for the 'tyrannical' Christian God was powerfully expressed by William Godwin, *The Enquirer* (1965 [1797]), p. 135.

30 Henry St John, Viscount Bolingbroke, *The Idea of a Patriot King*, in Henry St John, Viscount Bolingbroke, *The Works of Lord Bolingbroke* (1969 [reprint of 841 edn), vol. ii, p. 382.

31 On Locke and religion, see John Marshall, *John Locke; Resistance, Religion and Responsibility* (1994); Ashcraft, 'Anticlericalism and Authority in Lockean Political Thought'. On the debate surrounding his views, see Alan P. F. Sell, *John Locke and the Eighteenth-century Divines* (1997).

32 John Locke, Journal (8 February 1677): R. I. Aaron and J. Gibb (eds), *An Early Draft of Locke's Essay Together with Excerpts from His Journals* (1936), p. ii.

33 John Locke, *The Reasonableness of Christianity* (1695), p. 2.

34 John Locke, *An Essay concerning Human Understanding* (1975 [1690]), bk IV, ch. 19, para. 4, p. 698; Ernest Campbell Mossner, *Bishop Butler and the Age of Reason* (1990), p. 43; see discussion in Basil Willey, *The Eighteenth Century Background* (1962), p. 35.

35 John Locke, *Works* (1714), vol. vi, p. 157.

36 Locke, *The Reasonableness*, in *Works* (1714), vol. vii, p. 113.

37 Locke, *The Reasonableness of Christianity*, in *Works*, vol. vii, p. 125.

38 Locke, *The Reasonableness of Christianity*, in *Works*, vol. vii, p. 133.

39 Locke, *The Reasonableness of Christianity*, in *Works*, vol. vii, p. 135.

40 Locke, *The Reasonableness of Christianity*, in *Works*, vol. vii, p. 139.

41 Acts 17:22–9.

42 Locke, *The Reasonableness of Christianity*, in *Works*, vol. vii, p. 176.

43 Marshall, *John Locke: Resistance, Religion and Responsibility*, p. 454.

44 Quoted in Willey, *The Eighteenth Century Background*, p. 3. Such positions, as will be shown below, were readily exploited by Deists, who drove their logic to the limits. Quoting this passage, Anthony Collins continued: 'And even these he justly observes, are of less moment than any of those parts of religion which in their own nature tend to the Happiness of human Society': *Discourse of Freethinking* (sn, 1713), p. 136.

45 John Tillotson, *The Works of the Most Reverend Dr John Tillotson* (1820), vol. i, p. 475.

46 Tillotson, *The Works of the Most Reverend Dr John Tillotson*, vol. i, p. 468. For analysis, see Norman Sykes, *Church and State in England in the Eighteenth Century* (1934); see also Downey, *The Eighteenth Century Pulpit*, pp. 10, 15. See also John Tillotson, *The Works of the Most Reverend Dr John Tillotson*, vol. i, sermon 6, pp. 152–73.

47 'The Life of Jesus Christ Consider'd as Our Example', Tillotson, *The Works of the Most Reverend Dr John Tillotson*, vol. i, sermon 6, p. 71. Tom Paine later styled Jesus 'a virtuous and an amiable man', a 'virtuous reformer'.

48 David Hume, 'Of Miracles', in David Hume, *Enquiries concerning Human Understanding and concerning the Principles of Morals* (1966 [1751]), pp. 109f.; W. M. Spellman, *The Latitudinarians and the Church of England, 1660–1700* (1993), p. 60; R. M. Burns, *The Great Debate on Miracles* (1981).

49 Quinlan, *Samuel Johnson: A Layman's Religion*, p. 28. The Deist Anthony Collins called him the man 'whom all English freethinkers own as their head': *Discourse of Freethinking*, p. 171.

50 Samuel Clarke, *A Demonstration of the Being and Attributes of God* (1705), quoted in Stephen,

History of English Thought in the Eighteenth Century, vol. i, pp. 100–4; J. P. Ferguson, *An Eighteenth Century Heretic* (1976), pp. 23f.; Peter Gay, *The Enlightenment* (1967), p. 326; Peter Searby, *A History of the University of Cambridge* (1997), vol. iii, p. 281, who brings out Clarke's friendship with the Arian William Whiston.

51 Quoted in David Brown, 'Butler and Deism' (1992), p. 9.

52 Samuel Clarke, *The Scripture-doctrine of the Trinity* (1712); John Redwood, *Reason, Ridicule and Religion* (1976), ch. 7. Compare M. Greig, 'The Reasonableness of Christianity?' (1993). Isaac Watts too sweated over the Trinity for twenty years, until he had to admit that he had only 'learned more of my own ignorance', and he was finally driven to chide his Maker for leaving him in such a quandary: 'Surely I ought to know the God whom I worship, whether he be one pure and simple or whether thou art a threefold deity': Stromberg, *Religious Liberalism in Eighteenth-century England*, p. 36.

53 William Derham, *Physico-Theology* (1713), p. 467.

54 Addison and Steele, *The Spectator*, vol. iv, no. 465, pp. 141–5 (Saturday, 23 August 1712).

55 Quoted in Nigel Smith, 'The Charge of Atheism and the Language of Radical Speculation, 1640–1660' (1992), p. 131.

56 For a conspectus, see O. P. Grell and B. Scribner (eds.), *Tolerance and Intolerance in the European Reformation* (1996); O. P. Grell, J. I. Israel and N. Tyacke (eds.), *From Persecution to Toleration* (1991); W. K. Jordan, *The Development of Religious Toleration in England* (1965 [1932–40]); Elisabeth Labrousse, 'Religious Toleration' (1974); Henry Kamen, *The Rise of Toleration* (1967); John Christian Laursen and Cary J. Nederman (eds.), *Beyond the Persecuting Society* (1998); and O. P. Grell and Roy Porter (eds.), *Toleration in the Enlightenment* (2000).

57 See John Dunn, 'The Claim to Freedom of Conscience' (1991); Henry Kamen, *The*

Rise of Toleration (1967), pp. 231f.; Cranston, *John Locke: A Biography*, p. 100; John W. Yolton, *Locke: An Introduction* (1985), pp. 77f.; John Dunn, *Locke* (1984), p. 26.

58 Kamen, *The Rise of Toleration*, p. 204.

59 Ursula Henriques , *Religious Toleration in England 1783–1833* (1961), pp. 11–12.

60 The Blasphemy Act made it an offence if any person educated in the Christian religion 'shall by writing, printing, teaching, or advised speaking deny any one of the persons in the Holy Trinity to be God, or shall assert or maintain there are more gods than one, or shall deny the Christian religion to be true, or shall deny the Holy Scriptures of the Old and New Testament to be of divine authority'. See Michael Hunter, 'Aikenhead the Atheist' (1992). Executions for religious offences long continued elsewhere: as late as 1782 a maid servant was executed as a witch in the Swiss canton of Glarus.

61 Daniel Defoe, *Robinson Crusoe* (1719), p. 240; Brean S. Hammond, *Professional Imaginative Writing in England, 1670–1740* (1997), p. 273. See J. B. Bury, *A History of Freedom of Thought* (nd), pp. 138–40. William Warburton sallied: 'Orthodoxy is my doxy. Heterodoxy is the other man's doxy': S. C. Carpenter, *Eighteenth Century Church and People* (1959), p. 146.

62 F. M. Voltaire, *Letters concerning the English Nation* (1926 [1733]), p. 34, quoted in Arthur Wilson, 'The Enlightenment Came First to England' (1983), p. 7; F. M. Voltaire, *Philosophical Dictionary* (1979 [1764]), p. 387. Everyone could go to Heaven the way they liked.

63 Southey, *Letters from England by Don Manuel Alvarez Espriella*, p. 159. For the proliferation of sects the world over, see William Hodgson, *The Commonwealth of Reason* (1795), pp. 31–4:

And as religion seems to be a subject on which men may perhaps never be perfectly agreed; since no one can, by any thing like demonstrative evidence, prove that the tenets of the particular sect to which he belongs, is more acceptable to the Supreme Being, than those of another sect, whether he be BAPTIST, JEW, GENTILE, MAHOMETAN, ARMENIAN, CHRISTIAN, ANTICHRISTIAN, ADAMITE, DUNKER, SWEDENBURGIAN, WORSHIPER OF THE SUN, WORSHIPER OF THE MOON, UNIVERSALIST, EUTYCHIAN, ADRAMMELECHIAN, PHILADELPHIAN, QUARTODECIMANIAN, PRE-DESTINARIAN, AGONYCLITE, BONASIAN, BASILIDIAN

– the list goes on and on –

it follows of course, that setting up one species of religion, in preference to others, or nationalizing it, by countenancing, protecting, and supporting in idleness and luxury such drones as MUFTIS, POPES, TA-HO-CHANGS, GREAT LAMAS, PARSONS, ARCHBISHOPS, DEACONESSES, RECTORS, HIGH-PRIESTS, DOCTORS OF DIVINITY, HO-CHANGS, NUNS, RABBIS, MONKS, ABBES, CARMELITES, JESUITS, CARTHUSIANS, DOMINICANS, FRANCISCANS, LADY ABBESSES, MASORITES, LAMAS, CARDINALS, EMIRS, VICARS, PROPHETS, PREBENDS, TALAPOINS, BONZES, BRAMINS, APOSTLES, SEERS, PRIMONTRES, BENEDICTINES, JACOBINES, FEUILLANS, BERNARDINES, FRERES DE L'ORDRE DE LA MERCY, CORDELIERS, CAPUCHINS, RECOLLECTS . . . and other such useless beings, or *as they emphatically style each other* IMPUDENT IMPOSTORS, who being too proud and lazy to work, have availed themselves of man's credulity, and the corruption of the executive power, to get laws enacted, enabling them to steal with impunity from the laborious and industrious citizens; and who not content with thus cheating mankind, have contrived to defraud each other in the division of the spoil, by giving to one, because he wears a cap of a particular form, and of his own invention, TEN OR TWELVE THOUSAND POUNDS A YEAR, whilst the poor devils who read all their tenets to the infatuated multitude are allowed by these *meek, moderate, temperate, sober, honest, chaste, virtuous, modest, dignified*, and *superior* interpreters of what, *as they say of each other*, each impiously chooses to call God's holy word, perhaps FIFTEEN OR TWENTY POUNDS A YEAR; but then their motto is *patience, and perhaps I may be a cardinal, pope, mufti, Ta-ho-chang, Great Lama, or high-priest.*

After listing such a gallimaufry of competing sectarians, Hodgson drew the inevitable enlightened conclusion:

it follows, I say, that these establishments, which produce such caterpillars, who pretend that an all just God has sent them to devour the good things of this world, without contributing to the labour of producing them, can be attended with no other consequence than that unhappy one of exciting the most rancorous animosities and implacable resentments betwixt those whose immediate interest consists in preserving the utmost cordiality, harmony, and fraternity, with each other, because they are at every instant endeavouring to gain superiority the one over the other, by engendering the most vicious hatred in their followers against all who happen to dissent from their particular doctrine; I therefore propose, as religion is a subject merely of opinion, and consequently ought to be free as the circumambient air, This premised, I think it proper and suitable to my subject, to set out with a declaration of rights, founded on the broad and permanent basis of LIBERTY, FRATERNITY AND EQUALITY, as I conceive it is on the imperishable foundation of these rights alone, that those laws and regulations can be built, which shall truly and faithfully have for object, what ought to be considered the most important of all human pursuits – THE HAPPINESS OF THE HUMAN RACE LIVING TOGETHER IN SOCIETY.

Quoted in Gregory Claeys (ed.), *Utopias of the British Enlightenment* (1994), p. 208.
64 [Anon.], *Some Reflections on Prescience* (1731), p. 2.
65 Locke, *An Essay concerning Human Understanding*, vol. ii, ch. 23, para. 15. Locke's raising the possibility of 'thinking matter' was less to advance materialism than to deny that it was not for man to circumscribe divine powers: John W. Yolton, *Thinking Matter* (1983).
66 Locke, *An Essay concerning Human Understanding*, vol. ii, ch. 23, para. 31.

67 John Locke, *A Letter to . . . Edward [Stillingfleet], Ld Bishop of Worcester . . .* (1697), p. 303; Yolton, *Locke: An Introduction*, p. 88; generally, see William Rounseville Alger, *The Destiny of the Soul* (1878).
68 Locke, *A Letter to . . . Edward [Stillingfleet], Ld Bishop of Worcester . . .*, p. 304.
69 See Yolton, *Locke: An Introduction*, p. 88.
70 Quoted in Sell, *John Locke and the Eighteenth-century Divines*, p. 197.
71 On his deathbed, Shaftesbury supposedly talked of the Socinian notions 'imbibed from Mr Locke and his tenth chapter of "Human Understanding" ': H. R. Fox Bourne, *Life of John Locke* (1876), vol. i, p. 469.
72 'It seems likely that Locke's chief impact in eighteenth-century England was not to import contractarianism into politics, but Arianism into religion': J. C. D. Clark, *English Society, 1688–1832* (1985), p. 47. At Cambridge, John Jebb's lectures 'made so much noise' because he 'had been charged with propagating Socinianism and Fatalism ([to] which Mr Locke's chapter on power is thought to look)': quoted in J. C. D. Clark, *The Language of Liberty 1660–1832* (1994), p. 314; see Stromberg, *Religious Liberalism in Eighteenth-century England*, p. 98.
73 [Charles Leslie], *The Charge of Socinianism against Dr Tillotson Considered* (sn, 1695), p. 13.
74 Redwood, *Reason, Ridicule and Religion*, p. 142.
75 John Dryden, *Absolom and Achitophel* (1681), in John Sargeaunt (ed.), *The Poems of John Dryden* (1959), p. 42, ll. 1–2.
76 Stephen H. Daniel, *John Toland: His Methods, Manners, and Mind* (1984), p. 34; Mark Goldie, 'Priestcraft and the Birth of Whiggism' (1993), p. 219.
77 Ashcraft, 'Anticlericalism and Authority in Lockean Political Thought', p. 74. Locke's early writings express his opposition to the political embroilments of the clergy, blaming the Civil War on the 'ambition . . . pride and hypocrisy' of those 'malicious men'. People were 'hoodwinked' by the

clergy, and 'a veil is cast over their eyes' (p. 82).

78 Richard Baron, *The Pillars of Priestcraft and Orthodoxy Shaken* (1768), vol. i, pp. iii, vi; Justin A. I. Champion, *The Pillars of Priestcraft Shaken* (1992); Goldie, 'Priestcraft and the Birth of Whiggism', p. 214.

79 Peter Harrison, *'Religion' and the Religions in the English Enlightenment* (1990), p. 79.

80 Charles F. Bahmueller, *The National Charity Company* (1981), p. 98; James E. Crimmins, *Secular Utilitarianism* (1990). In 1818, Bentham published his *Church of Englandism, and Its Catechism Examined* (1818), in which he outlined the programme of a moral Christianity simplified in the extreme; and it was about the same time that he composed his *Not Paul but Jesus* (sn, 1823), in which he devoted himself to proving that Paul was an impostor and an ambitious man, that his doctrine was on almost all points different from the doctrine of Jesus, and that he was the true Antichrist.

81 Mary Thale (ed.), *The Autobiography of Francis Place (1771–1854)* (1972), p. xvii: 'twaddler' was a favourite expression of his for priest.

82 Journal for Tuesday, 7 September 1824: John Clare, 'The Autobiography, 1793–1824', in J. W. and A. Tibble (eds.), *The Prose of John Clare* (1970 [1951]), p. 103.

83 William Wollaston, *The Religion of Nature Delineated* (1724). Franklin singled out that book as the stimulus which launched his career: Douglas Anderson, *The Radical Enlightenment of Benjamin Franklin* (1997), p. 6.

84 Matthew Tindal, *The Rights of the Christian Church Asserted* (sn, 1706); see Christopher Cunliffe (ed.), *Joseph Butler's Moral and Religious Thought* (1992), pp. 11f.

85 Matthew Tindal, *Christianity as Old as the Creation; Or The Gospel a Republication of the Religion of Nature* (1733), p. 7; Harrison, *'Religion' and the Religions in the English Enlightenment*, p. 167.

86 Tindal, *Christianity as Old as the Creation*, pp. 7, 10.

87 Tindal, *Christianity as Old as the Creation*, p. 10.

88 Tindal, *Christianity as Old as the Creation*, p. 23.

89 For primitive monotheism, see Jan Assmann, *Moses the Egyptian* (1997), p. 80. Compare Pope's:

> Nor think, in NATURE'S STATE they blindly trod;
> The state of nature was the reign of God . . .

Alexander Pope, *An Essay on Man* (1733–4) in John Butt (ed.), *The Poems of Alexander Pope* (1965), p. 530, ll. 247–8.

90 Tindal, *Christianity as Old as the Creation*, p. 92.

91 Bury, *A History of Freedom of Thought*, pp. 144–5.

92 L. S. Sutherland and L. G. Mitchell (eds.), *The History of the University of Oxford* (1986), vol. v, p. 455.

93 Tindal, *Christianity as Old as the Creation* (1733), p. 49; Ernest Mossner, *Bishop Butler and the Age of Reason* (1990), p. 76.

94 Hans W. Frei, *The Eclipse of Biblical Narrative* (1974), pp. 52f.

95 See William H. Trapnell, 'Who Thomas Woolston Was' (1988), 'What Thomas Woolston Wrote' (1991), and *Thomas Woolston: Madman and Deist?* (1994).

96 Thomas Woolston, *Six Discourses on the Miracles of Our Saviour and Defences of His Discourses* (1979 [1727–30]); Stock, *The Holy and the Daemonic from Sir Thomas Browne to William Blake*, p. 99; Trapnell, 'What Thomas Woolston Wrote', p. 17.

97 See, for instance, Thomas Sherlock, *Trial of the Witnesses* (1729). The pamphlet purports to be the report of a trial held at the Inns of Court, with the Apostles charged with giving false evidence in the case of the Resurrection. A 'not guilty' verdict is returned. Samuel Johnson deplored the 'Old Bailey theology', 'in which the apostles are being tried once a week for the capital crime of forgery'.

98 For the following, see T. L. Bushell, *The Sage of Salisbury* (1968), p. 18.

99 Bushell, *The Sage of Salisbury*, p. 51.

100 Thomas Chubb, 'Human Nature Vindicated', in *A Collection of Tracts* (1730), p. 342, quoted in Bushell, *The Sage of Salisbury*, p. 88.

101 For Toland, see Daniel, *John Toland: His Methods, Manners and Mind*; R. E. Sullivan, *John Toland and the Deist Controversy* (1982); Margaret C. Jacob, *The Newtonians and the English Revolution, 1689–1720* (1976), pp. 210–11.

102 John Toland, *Christianity Not Mysterious* (1696), p. 6, quoted in Simon Eliot and Beverley Stern (eds.), *The Age of Enlightenment* (1979), vol. i, p. 31; James O'Higgins, *Anthony Collins: The Man and His Works* (1970), p. 52.

103 Toland, *Christianity Not Mysterious*, preface, p. xxvii.

104 Toland, *Christianity Not Mysterious*, p. 6.

105 John C. Biddle, 'Locke's Critique of Innate Principles and Toland's Deism' (1990), p. 148.

106 John Toland, *Tetradymus* (1720), p. 45.

107 John Toland, *Pantheisticon, Sive Formula Celebrandae Sodalitatis Socraticae* (sn, 1720), quoted in Frank E. Manuel, *The Eighteenth Century Confronts the Gods* (1967), p. 67. For Toland's pantheism, see Margaret C. Jacob, *The Radical Enlightenment* (1981), p. 49.

108 John Toland, *Letters to Serena* (1704).

109 John Toland, *Letters to Serena*, p. 71.

> Natural Religion was easy first and plain,
> Tales made it Mystery, Offrings made it Gain;
> Sacrifices and Shows were at length prepar'd,
> The Priests ate Roast-meat, and the People star'd.

Daniel, *John Toland: His Methods, Manners and Mind*, p. 34.

110 See O'Higgins, *Anthony Collins: The Man and His Works*. David Berman infers that Collins was an atheist: Berman, *A History of Atheism in Britain*. There is, however, no evidence for this view. Gentlemen like Collins professed a Deity who upheld order; such a belief would square with their own interests as land and property owners.

111 Anthony Collins, *A Discourse of the Grounds and Reasons of the Christian Religion* (sn, 1724), p. vi.

112 Sell, *John Locke and the Eighteenth-century Divines*, p. 209; O'Higgins, *Anthony Collins: The Man and His Works*, pp. 6ff.

113 O'Higgins, *Anthony Collins: The Man and His Works*, p. 6. Much was made in Radical circles of Collins' connections with Locke, to insinuate that Locke was more radical than he was. Forged letters of Locke to Collins were published in the *Gentleman's Magazine* in 1753: Margaret C. Jacob, *Living the Enlightenment* (1992), p. 61.

114 O'Higgins, *Anthony Collins: The Man and His Works*, p. 12. The *Discourse* went too far for circumspect Whigs who publicly disowned him (their private feelings are less clear): see O'Higgins, *Anthony Collins: The Man and His Works*, p. 89; Yolton, *Thinking Matter*, p. 42.

115 Quoted in O'Higgins, *Anthony Collins: The Man and His Works*, p. 10.

116 Swift produced a magnificent parody in *Mr Collins' Discourse of Free-thinking* (1713), p. 7. 'The priests tell me,' he ironized, 'I am to believe the Bible, but Free-thinking tells me otherwise in many Particulars. The Bible says the Jews were a nation favoured by God; but I who am a Free-thinker say, that cannot be, because the Jews lived in a corner of the earth, and Free-thinking makes it clear that those who live in Corners cannot be Favourites of God.' 'Free-thinker' was a term used by Locke in 1697 to describe Toland. In 1711 there appeared a periodical named the *Freethinker*.

117 Quoted in O'Higgins, *Anthony Collins: The Man and His Works*, pp. 78, 89f.

118 Collins, *A Discourse of the Grounds and Reasons of the Christian Religion*; Bury, *A History of Freedom of Thought*, p. 140; Frei, *The Eclipse of Biblical Narrative*, pp. 70f.

119 Hobbes professed to be a Christian but emptied Christianity of all its traditional meanings, portraying God simply as the source of irresistible power. Belief in the natural immortality of the soul was a relic of 'Greek demonology': Thomas Hobbes, *Leviathan* (1968 [1651]), p. 405.

120 Charles Blount, *Anima Mundi* (1679); Harrison, *'Religion' and the Religions in the English Enlightenment*, p. 73; Champion, *The Pillars of Priestcraft Shaken*, p. 142.

121 Charles Leslie, *A Short and Easy Method with the Deists* (1698); Searby, *A History of the University of Cambridge*, vol. iii, p. 277.

122 The following depends heavily on Manuel, *The Eighteenth Century Confronts the Gods*, pp. 66f., and Harrison, *'Religion' and the Religions in the English Enlightenment*, pp. 16f.

123 S. I. Tucker, *Enthusiasm* (1972). The fourth edition of Locke's *Essay concerning Human Understanding* contains an additional chapter entitled 'Of Enthusiasm', in which Locke attacks Protestant extremists claiming to have private illuminations from God. These he refuses to dignify with the name of 'revelation', calling them 'the ungrounded fancies of a man's own brain': Cranston, *John Locke: A Biography*, p. 277.

124 John Trenchard, *The Natural History of Superstition* (1709); Manuel, *The Eighteenth Century Confronts the Gods*, p. 74. Trenchard then went on to collaborate with John Gordon on the *Independent Whig* (1720), whose essays on politics and religion proved amazingly successful, seeing many re-editions, making its way across the Atlantic and being translated into French by the atheist d'Holbach.

125 Mandeville too took up this Lucretian idea that religion had originated in fear:

Primitive man saw an invisible enemy behind every Mischief and every Disaster that happens to him, of which the Cause is not very plain and obvious; excessive Heat and Cold; Wet and Drought, that are offensive; Thunder and Lightning, even when they do no visible Hurt; Noises in the dark, Obscurity itself, and every thing that is frightful and unknown . . . finding all his Enquiries upon earth in vain, he would lift up his Eyes to the Sky.

Bernard de Mandeville, *The Fable of the Bees* (1924 [1714]), vol. ii, pp. 208–12. See Redwood, *Reason, Ridicule and Religion*, p. 34.

126 Trenchard, *The Natural History of Superstition*, pp. 10–11; Manuel, *The Eighteenth Century Confronts the Gods*, p. 75.

127 Trenchard, *The Natural History of Superstition*, pp. 12–13.

128 Trenchard, *The Natural History of Superstition*, p. 15. See also John Beaumont, *An Historical, Physiological and Theological Treatise of Spirits, Apparitions, Witchcrafts and Other Magical Practices* (1705).

129 Trenchard, *The Natural History of Superstition*, pp. 14–15; Manuel, *The Eighteenth Century Confronts the Gods*, p. 77.

130 Trenchard, *The Natural History of Superstition*, p. 19; Manuel, *The Eighteenth Century Confronts the Gods*, p. 78. For the psychopathologization of enthusiasm, see Michael Heyd, *'Be Sober and Reasonable'* (1995); Hillel Schwartz, *Knaves, Fools, Madmen, and 'That Subtile Effluvium'* (1978), and *The French Prophets* (1980).

131 Anthony Ashley Cooper, 3rd Earl of Shaftesbury, *Characteristicks of Men, Manners, Opinions, Times* (1999 [1711]), vol. i, p. 86. Thus, 'above all other enslaving Vices, and Restrainers of Reason and just Thought, the most evidently ruinous and fatal to the Understanding is that of Superstition, Bigotry, and vulgar Enthusiasm' (vol. i, p. 153).

132 Shaftesbury, *Characteristicks of Men, Manners, Opinions, Times*, 'Letter concerning Enthusiasm', vol. i, p. i; Manuel, *The Eighteenth Century Confronts the Gods*, p. 79; see also Robert Voitle, *The Third Earl of Shaftesbury: 1671–1713* (1984). Shaftesbury stated: 'Ridicule is the proper antidote to every development of enthusiasm. Instead of breaking the bones of the French charlatans, we had the good sense to make them the subject of a puppet-show at Bartle'my fair': 'Letter concerning Enthusiasm', in Shaftesbury, *Characteristicks of Men, Manners, Opinions, Times*, vol. i, p. 19. Shaftesbury's teacher, Locke, had added a chapter against enthusiasm in the fourth edition of his *Essay*.

Enthusiasm was satirized in Swift's *A Tale of a Tub* (1975 [1704]).

133 Shaftesbury, *Characteristicks of Men, Manners, Opinions, Times*, vol. i, p. 8; Manuel, *The Eighteenth Century Confronts the Gods*, p. 79.

134 Shaftesbury, *Characteristicks of Men, Manners, Opinions, Times* (1999), vol. i, p. 13.

135 Robert Kreiser, *Miracles, Convulsions and Ecclesiastical Politics in Early Eighteenth-century Paris* (1978); Daniel Roche, *France in the Enlightenment* (1998), p. 373; Stanley Tweyman (ed. and intro.), *Hume on Miracles* (1996), p. 31.

136 Conyers Middleton, *Free Enquiry into the Miraculous Powers which are Supposed to Have Subsisted in the Christian Church from the Earliest Ages* (1749). That is why it was upon reading Middleton that the adolescent Gibbon converted to Catholicism.

137 Hume had published his *Enquiry concerning Human Understanding* in 1748 and had high hopes for it, but 'on my return from Italy, I had the Mortification to find all England in a Ferment on account of Dr Middletons Free Enquiry; while my Performance was entirely overlooked and neglected'; discussed in John Valdimir Price, 'The Reading of Philosophical Literature' (1982), p. 171. See Ernest Campbell Mossner, 'The Religion of David Hume' (1990).

138 See David Hume, 'Of Miracles', first published in *Philosophical Essays concerning Human Understanding* (1748), contained in *Enquiries concerning the Human Understanding and concerning the Principles of Morals* (1966), section X, 'Of Miracles', part I, p. 86:

A miracle is a violation of the laws of nature; and as a firm and unalterable experience has established

these laws, the proof against a miracle, from the very nature of the fact, is as entire as any argument from experience can possibly be imagined . . . It is no miracle that a man, seemingly in good health, should die on a sudden: because such a kind of death, though more unusual than any other, has yet been frequently observed to happen. But it is a miracle, that a dead man should come to life; because that has never been observed in any age or country. There must, therefore, be a uniform experience against every miraculous event, otherwise the event would not merit that appellation. And as a uniform experience amounts to a proof, there is here a direct and full *proof*, from the nature of the fact, against the existence of any miracle; nor can such a proof be destroyed, or the miracle rendered credible, but by an opposite proof, which is superior.

See Tweyman (ed. and intro.), *Hume on Miracles*; James E. Force, 'Hume and Johnson on Prophecy and Miracles' (1990); Donald T. Siebert, 'Johnson and Hume on Miracles' (1990).

139 See Hume, 'Of Miracles' (1741–2), in *Enquiries concerning the Human Understanding and concerning the Principles of Morals*, pt 1, p. 86.

140 Hume, *Enquiries concerning the Human Understanding and concerning the Principles of Morals*, p. 130.

141 David Hume, *Essays Moral, Political and Literary* (1898 [1741–2]).

142 David Hume, 'Of Superstition and Enthusiasm' (1741–2), in *Selected Essays* (1993), p. 39.

143 J. G. A. Pocock, *Virtue, Commerce, and History* (1985), p. 153; see also John B. Stewart, *Opinion and Reform in Hume's Political Philosophy* (1992), p. 277.

144 David Hume, 'Natural History of Religion' (1741–2), in *Essays Moral, Political and Literary*, vol. ii, p. 363.

145 David Hume, *Hume's Dialogues concerning Natural Religion* (1947).

146 Gladys Bryson, *Man and Society* (1968), p. 230.

147 See the account of their last meeting in Boswell's journal, 3 March 1777, in Charles M. Weis and Frederick A. Pottle (eds), *Boswell in Extremes, 1776–1778* (1971), pp. 11–15, especially p. 11: 'He then said flatly that the Morality of every Religion was bad, and I really thought, was not jocular when he said that when he heard a man was religious, he concluded he was a rascal, though he had known some instances of very good men being religious'; see A. N. Wilson, *God's Funeral* (1999), p. 22.

148 Hume to Boswell, 7 July 1776. Charles M. Weis and Frederick A. Pottle (eds.), *Boswell in Extremes, 1776–1778* (1971), p. 11.

149 David Hume, *The Philosophical Works of David Hume* (1874–5; repr. 1987), vol. 3, p. 83.

150 Hume, *Essays Moral, Political and Literary*, vol. i, p. 54, essay vii.

151 For Hume, see Berman, *A History of Atheism in Britain from Hobbes to Russell*, p. 101; Don Locke, *A Fantasy of Reason* (1980), p. 340: 'In my forty-fourth year I ceased to regard the name of Atheist with the same complacency I had done for several preceding years.' In 1818 he began an autobiographical essay 'Of Religion', opening with the round declaration 'I am an unbeliever'. See also Percy Bysshe Shelley, *The Necessity of Atheism* (1811), and Wilson, *God's Funeral*. Godwin declared: 'For my part I had rather be damned with Plato and Lord Bacon, than go to Heaven with Paley and Malthus': Harold Orel, *English Romantic Poets and the Enlightenment* (1973), p. 181.

152 Wilson, *God's Funeral*.

153 David Hume, *Letters* (1932), vol. i, p. 62.

See the discussion in Stewart, *Opinion and Reform in Hume's Political Philosophy*, p. 106.

154 Pocock, *Virtue, Commerce, and History*, pp. 153f. Gibbon drew on Hume's discussion of superstition and enthusiasm.

155 For Gibbon's mock surprise at the flap his impieties caused, see Gibbon, *Memoirs of My Life*, p. 159.

156 Sell, *John Locke and the Eighteenth-century Divines*, p. 165. The transition from a religious to a political framework of thought in the Enlightenment is well discussed in Michel de Certeau, 'The Formality of Practices', in *The Writing of History* (1988), pp. 149–51; B. W. Young, *Religion and Enlightenment in Eighteenth-century England* (1998). See also Hans W. Frei: 'If historical periods may be said to have a single chronological and geographical starting point, modern theology began in England at the turn from the seventeenth to the eighteenth century': *The Eclipse of Biblical Narrative*, p. 51. Rational Dissenters looked back with gratitude to Locke, above all for his stand on toleration. See Sell, *John Locke and the Eighteenth-century Divines*, p. 165.

157 Gibbon, *Memoirs of My Life*, p. 80.

158 Richard Polwhele, preface to George Lavington, *Enthusiasm* (1833), p. cxiv: 'The mania of Methodism has seized the West of England, and is now spreading at this instant through its remotest parts.'

159 Jonathan Swift, *An Argument to Prove That the Abolishing of Christianity in England . . .* (1717), p. 9.

160 William Blake, 'Annotations to Dr Thornton's "New Translation of the Lord's Prayer"' (1827) in G. Keynes (ed.), *Blake: Complete Writings* (1969), p. 787.

6 THE CULTURE OF SCIENCE

1 And new Philosophy calls all in doubt,
The Element of fire is quite put out,
The Sun is lost, and th'earth, and no mans wit
Can well direct him where to looke for it.

John Donne, *The First Anniversarie* (1611), quoted in Victor I. Harris, *All Coherence Gone* (1966), pp. 20–21.

2 The concept of a 'scientific revolution'

remains contested, though whether what happened amounted to a 'revolution' does not affect the argument in this chapter: see I. Bernard Cohen, *Revolution in Science* (1985); H. Floris Cohen, *The Scientific Revolution* (1994); John Henry, *The Scientific Revolution and the Origins of Modern Science* (1997); Roy Porter and Mikuláš Teich (eds), *The Scientific Revolution in National Context* (1992); John A. Schuster, 'The Scientific Revolution' (1990). Michael Fores's 'Science and the "Neolithic Paradox"' (1983) attacks the 'myth' of the Scientific Revolution; Steven Shapin's *The Scientific Revolution* (1996) opens provocatively: 'there was no such thing as the Scientific Revolution, and this is a book about it' (p. 1).

3 The Archangel Raphael's warning to man: John Milton, *Paradise Lost* (1667), bk VIII, ll. 167–8. See Marjorie Hope Nicolson, *The Breaking of the Circle* (1960), p. 167, and *Science Demands the Muse* (1966).

4 'The Battle Royal' (1694) by William Pittis, reprinted in *The Original Works of William King* (1776), vol. i, pp. 221–2. The fact that Burnet's cause was taken up by the Deist Charles Blount did not help; Roy Porter, 'Creation and Credence' (1979).

5 Alexander Pope, *The Dunciad* (1728), bk IV, ll. 453–4, in John Butt (ed.), *The Poems of Alexander Pope* (1965), pp. 788–9.

6 Jonathan Swift, *Gulliver's Travels* (1954 [1726]), p. 165; J. R. R. Christie, 'Laputa Revisited' (1989); Douglas Patey, 'Swift's Satire on "Science" and the Structure of *Gulliver's Travels*' (1991); Roslynn D. Haynes, *From Faust to Strangelove* (1994), p. 44. From the viewpoint of this book it is significant that it was sunbeams that Swift's virtuosi hoped to produce: *Gulliver's Travels*, 'A Voyage to Laputa', pt III, section 5.

7 Michael Hunter, *Science and Society in Restoration England* (1981), and *Establishing the New Science* (1989). The June 1999 issue of the *British Journal for the History of Science* is devoted to the eighteenth-century Royal Society.

8 Richard S. Westfall, *Science and Religion in Seventeenth-century England* (1970); John Hedley Brooke, *Science and Religion* (1991).

9 'Natural philosophy' was the contemporary term for what would later be modified into 'science'. The salience of the distinction is stressed in Andrew Cunningham, 'Getting the Game Right' (1988).

10 J. Spedding, R. L. Ellis and D. D. Heath (eds), *The Works of Francis Bacon* (1857–74), vol. iv, p. 57.

11 For Bacon's image and influence, see Charles Webster, *The Great Instauration* (1975); R. F. Jones, *Ancients and Moderns* (1936).

12 P. B. Wood, 'Methodology and Apologetics' (1980); Peter Dear, '*Totius in Verba*' (1985).

13 For biography, see R. S. Westfall, *Never at Rest* (1980); Frank E. Manuel, *A Portrait of Isaac Newton* (1968).

14 Betty Jo Teeter Dobbs, *The Janus Face of Genius* (1991).

15 Frank F. Manuel, *Isaac Newton, Historian* (1963), and *The Religion of Isaac Newton* (1974).

16 Isaac Newton, *Mathematical Principles of Natural Philosophy* (1962 [1687]).

17 Norman Hampson, *The Enlightenment* (1968), p. 34; Manuel, *Isaac Newton, Historian*.

18 A. Rupert Hall, *Philosophers at War* (1980).

19 Betty Jo Teeter Dobbs and Margaret C. Jacob, *Newton and the Culture of Newtonianism* (1995); Simon Schaffer, 'Newtonianism' (1990); Marie Boas Hall, *Promoting Experimental Learning* (1991). For their Cambridge roots, see Peter Searby, *A History of the University of Cambridge* (1977), vol. iii, pp. 150f. For Desaguliers, see Margaret C. Jacob, *The Radical Enlightenment* (1981), p. 124.

20 Steven Shapin, 'The Social Uses of Science' (1980); Gerald Dennis Meyer, *The Scientific Lady in England, 1650–1760* (1955).

21 Searby, *A History of the University of Cambridge*, vol. iii, p. 150; James A. Force, *William Whiston: Honest Newtonian* (1985).

22 Newton surpassed conquerors like Alexander the Great: F. M. Voltaire, *Letters* *concerning the English Nation* (1926 [1733]), p. 65.

23 Henry Guerlac, *Newton on the Continent* (1981); A. Ruper Hall, 'Newton in France' (1975).

24 Henry Guerlac, 'Where the Statue Stood' (1977).

25 James Thomson, 'Summer', ll. 1545–8, in James Thomson, *Works* (1744), vol. i, p. 141; Richard Yeo, 'Genius, Method and Mortality' (1988); Gerd Buchdahl, *The Image of Newton and Locke in the Age of Reason* (1961); Marjorie Hope Nicolson, *Newton Demands the Muse* (1946).

26 William Wordsworth, *The Prelude* (1970 (text of 1805)), p. 35. In his early years Coleridge too was an ardent Newtonian:

> There, Priest of Nature! dost thou shine,
> NEWTON! a King among the Kings divine.

Quoted in Ian Wylie, *Young Coleridge and the Philosophers of Nature* (1989), pp. 32–3.

27 Even Blake could be ambiguous: Donald D. Ault, *Visionary Physics* (1974).

28 C. B. Wilde, 'Hutchinsonians, Natural Philosophy and Religious Controversy in Eighteenth-century Britain' (1980).

29 Schaffer, 'Newtonianism'.

30 Newton, *Mathematical Principles of Natural Philosophy*, 'General Scholium', vol. ii, p. 547.

31 Such images were for public consumption – in person, Newton was an imperious egoist: see Manuel, *A Portrait of Isaac Newton*. Science presented itself as harmonious, but in truth there were endless priority and property disputes: see R. Iliffe, ' "In the Warehouse" ' (1992).

For Newtonian methodology, rhetoric and the language of science, see J. V. Golinski, 'Language, Discourse and Science' (1990); for the rejection of 'metaphysics', see Gary Hatfield, 'Metaphysics and the New Science' (1990); G. A. J. Rogers, 'The Empiricism of Locke and Newton (1979), and 'Locke's *Essay* and Newton's *Principia*' (1990).

32 Westfall, *Never at Rest*, p. 863.

33 'I make great doubt,' insisted Boyle, 'whether there be not some phenomena in nature which the atomists cannot satisfactorily explain by any figuration, motion or connection of material particles whatsoever': Robert Boyle, *Some Considerations Touching the Usefulnesse of Experimental Natural Philosophy* (1663), in Thomas Birch (ed.), *The Works of the Honourable Robert Boyle* (1744), vol. ii, pp. 47f. On Boyle, see Michael Hunter (ed.), *Robert Boyle Reconsidered* (1994).

34 Norman Sykes, *Church and State in England in the Eighteenth Century* (1934), p. 153; John Gascoigne, 'From Bentley to the Victorians' (1988); Margaret C. Jacob, 'Reflections on the Ideological Meaning of Western Science from Boyle and Newton to the Postmodernists' (1995), and *The Newtonians and the English Revolution, 1689–1720* (1976), p. 18, which 'stresses what previous commentators have ignored – [Newtonianism's] usefulness to the intellectual leaders of the Anglican church as an underpinning for their vision of what they liked to call the "world politick" '. Coleridge quipped that for rationalists God was the Sunday name for gravitation: R. W. Harris, *Romanticism and the Social Order* (1969), p. 234.

35 J. T. Desaguliers, *The Newtonian System of the World* (1728), ll. 17–18, quoted in Jacob, *The Radical Enlightenment*, p. 124. There were other ways of putting science to use for the wider purposes of state, notably political arithmetic: see Julian Hoppit, 'Political Arithmetic in Eighteenth-century England' (1996); Andrea Rusnock, 'Biopolitics' (1999); Peter Buck, 'People Who Counted' (1982).

36 Desaguliers, *The Newtonian System of the World*, p. 8.

37 Desaguliers, *The Newtonian System of the World*, p. 8.

38 For the fate of one of Newton's disciples, see Force, *William Whiston: Honest Newtonian*.

39 Dennis R. Dean, *James Hutton and the History of Geology* (1992); Roy Porter, 'Philosophy and Politics of a Geologist' (1978); Toland's pantheistic view of active matter challenged orthodox Newtonianism: Stephen H. Daniel, *John Toland: His Methods, Manners, and Mind* (1984), pp. 12f.

40 William Paley, *Natural Theology* (1802), ch. 1, 'State of Argument'. The watch illustration was commonplace – in Bolingbroke, etc. – long before Paley made it his own. He probably adapted it from Abraham Tucker's *The Light of Nature Pursued* (1768), vol. i, p. 523; vol. ii, p. 83.

41 Paley, *Natural Theology*, ch. 1. For the Pope quotation, see *An Essay on Man* (1733–4), l. 332, in Butt, *The Poems of Alexander Pope*, p. 546.

42 Yes, according to Richard Dawkins's *The Blind Watchmaker* (1986).

43 The following discussion examines changing ideas of the very micro stuff of nature (ontology). Chapter 13 explores new theories of the meaning of natural order in the terraqueous globe.

44 For matter theory, the order of nature and the will of God, see Robert E. Schofield, *Mechanism and Materialism* (1970); Arnold Thackray, *Atoms and Powers* (1977); Simon Schaffer, 'Natural Philosophy' (1980); P. M. Heimann and J. E. McGuire, 'Newtonian Forces and Lockean Powers' (1971); P. M. Heimann, 'Newtonian Natural Philosophy and the Scientific Revolution' (1973), ' "Nature is a Perpetual Worker" ' (1973), and 'Voluntarism and Immanence' (1978); Peter Harman, *Metaphysics and Natural Philosophy* (1982).

45 For materialism on the Continent, see Aram Vartanian, *Diderot and Descartes* (1953); Thomas L. Hankins, *Science and the Enlightenment* (1985); for Erasmus Darwin, see chapter 19 below. See also Theodore Brown, 'From Mechanism to Vitalism in Eighteenth-century English Physiology' (1974).

46 Joseph Priestley, *Disquisitions Relating to Matter and Spirit* (1777), pp. 1–7. Priestley saw himself as completing Newton's empiricism, that is, not feigning fictitious entities: Robert E. Schofield, *The Enlightenment of Joseph Priestley* (1997), and see below, chapter 18; John W. Yolton, *Thinking Matter* (1983), pp. 113f.

47 Robert Greene, *The Principles of the Philosophy of the Expansive and Contractive Forces* (1727); John Rowning, *A Compendious System of Natural Philosophy* (1735–42). For non- and anti-Newtonian theories, see C. B. Wilde, 'Hutchinsonianism, Natural Philosophy and Religious Controversy in Eighteenth-century Britain' (1980), and 'Matter and Spirit as Natural Symbols in Eighteenth-century British Natural Philosophy' (1982).

48 James Hutton, *An Investigation of the Principles of Knowledge, and of the Progress of Reason, from Sense to Science and Philosophy* (1794).

49 James Hutton, *Theory of the Earth* (1795), vol. i, p. 200.

50 Schofield, *Mechanism and Materialism*, p. 263, and see below, chapter 18.

51 Harriet Ritvo, *The Animal Estate* (1987), p. 8.

52 For popularization, see Simon Schaffer, 'Natural Philosophy and Public Spectacle in the Eighteenth Century' (1983); the essays contained in *British Journal for the History of Science*, vol. xxviii (March 1995); and Roger Cooter and Stephen Pumfrey, 'Separate Spheres and Public Places' (1994).

53 Steven Shapin and Simon Schaffer, *Leviathan and the Air-pump* (1985), a book which raises and, *via* a concrete case study, attempts to resolve the crucial question of how the new science established its truth status, a problem to which Shapin has returned in *A Social History of Truth* (1994). In this period *scientific* truth became normative for and definitive of truth in general. See also Larry Stewart, 'Public Lectures and Private Patronage in Newtonian England' (1986), 'The Selling of Newton' (1986), and 'Other Centres of Calculation' (1999).

54 Margaret C. Jacob, *The Cultural Meaning of the Scientific Revolution* (1988), p. 142.

55 Richard D. Altick, *The Shows of London*

(1978), p. 81; Desmond King-Hele, *Erasmus Darwin and the Romantic Poets* (1986).

56 Roy Porter, 'Sex and the Singular Man' (1984); for other medical showmen see Roy Porter, *Health for Sale* (1989).

57 Geoffrey Alan Cranfield, *The Development of the Provincial Newspaper 1700–1760* (1962), p. 216. For Jurin, see Andrea Rusnock, *The Correspondence of James Jurin (1684–1750) Physician and Secretary of the Royal Society* (1996). For itinerant lecturers, see A. E. Musson and Eric Robinson, *Science and Technology in the Industrial Revolution* (1969); Larry Stewart, *The Rise of Public Science* (1992), p. 94.

58 John R. Millburn, *Benjamin Martin: Author, Instrument-maker and Country-showman* (1976).

59 Millburn, *Benjamin Martin: Author, Instrument-maker and Country-showman*, p. 4.

60 Gerard Turner, 'Instruments' (2000); Patricia Fara, *Sympathetic Attractions* (1996); Michael Adas, *Machines as the Measure of Men* (1989). For science and women, see Alice N. Walters, 'Conversation Pieces' (1997).

61 On science for children, see James A. Secord, 'Newton in the Nursery' (1985). Robert Collison, *Encyclopaedias* (1964); Frank A. Kafker (ed.), *Notable Encyclopedias of the Seventeenth and Eighteenth Centuries* (1981). Richard Yeo, *Encyclopaedic Visions* (forthcoming), quotes Charles Lamb's droll confession that he was 'a whole encyclopaedia behind the rest of the world'. See also above, chapter 4.

62 Quoted in D. Spadafora, *The Idea of Progress in Eighteenth-century Britain* (1990), p. 326.

63 Jan Golinski, *Science as Public Culture* (1992); Stewart, *The Rise of Public Science*, p. 22. For such projectors, see Margaret R. Hunt, *The Middling Sort* (1996), pp. 175f.

64 Benjamin Vaughan, *New and Old Principles of Trade Compared* (1788), quoted in Nicholas A. Hans, *New Trends in Education in the Eighteenth Century* (1966), p. 13.

65 [Thomas Bentley], *Letters on the Utility and Policy of Employing Machines to Shorten Labour*

(1780), quoted in Hans, *New Trends in Education in the Eighteenth Century*, p. 14.

66 D. G. C. Allan, *William Shipley: Founder of the Royal Society of Arts* (1968), p. 112.

67 Spadafora, *The Idea of Progress in Eighteenth-century Britain*, pp. 53, 211. In his 'Navigation, or the Triumph of the Thames' (1778), the personified nations, summoned by Mercury, god of commerce, discharge their products into the lap of Father Thames. Barry stressed the superiority of the Moderns: James Barry, *An Account of a Series of Pictures in the Great Room of the Society of Arts . . . at the Adelphi* (1783), in *The Works of James Barry, Esq.* (1809), vol. ii, p. 323.

68 See James Johnston Abraham, *Lettsom, His Life, Times, Friends and Descendants* (1933); Thomas Joseph Pettigrew, *Memoirs of the Life and Writings of the Late John Coakley Lettsom* (1817).

69 Pettigrew, *Memoirs of the Life and Writings of the Late John Coakley Lettsom*, vol. ii, p. 3.

70 Pettigrew, *Memoirs of the Life and Writings of the Late John Coakley Lettsom*, vol. i, p. 21.

71 Pettigrew, *Memoirs of the Life and Writings of the Late John Coakley Lettsom*, vol. i, p. 118.

72 Pettigrew, *Memoirs of the Life and Writings of the Late John Coakley Lettsom*, vol. ii, pp. 129–30.

73 See John Gascoigne, *Joseph Banks and the English Enlightenment* (1994); H. B. Carter, *Joseph Banks 1743–1820* (1988).

74 Robert Hooke, *Micrographia* (1665), p. 5.

75 Hooke, *Micrographia*, preface, p. 7.

76 L. Krüger, L. Daston and M. Heidelberger (eds.), *The Probabilistic Revolution* (1987), pp. 237–60; I. Hacking, *The Emergence of Probability* (1975), and *The Taming of Chance* (1990).

77 Robert Brown, *The Nature of Social Laws, Machiavelli to Mill* (1984), pp. 58f. See also below, chapter 17.

78 Adam Smith, *Essays on Philosophical Subjects* (1980 [1795]), bk II, sect. 12, p. 45. See also Lorraine Daston and Katharine Park, *Wonders and the Order of Nature 1150–1750* (1998), pp. 326f.

79 Smith, *Essays on Philosophical Subjects*, p. 51. 'As ignorance begot superstition,' he wrote, 'science gave birth to the first theism that arose amongst those nations, who were not enlightened by divine Revelation.' See discussion in D. D. Raphael, 'Adam Smith: Philosophy, Science, and Social Science' (1979).

80 For marginalization, see Patrick Curry, *Prophecy and Power* (1989); Gloria Flaherty, 'The Non-Normal Sciences' (1995).

81 Ann Geneva, *Astrology and the Seventeenth-century Mind* (1995).

82 Curry, *Prophecy and Power*.

83 Bernard S. Capp, *Astrology and the Popular Press* (1979), p. 239; Simon Schaffer, 'Newton's Comets and the Transformation of Astrology' (1987).

84 Capp, *Astrology and the Popular Press*, pp. 243–5; Curry, *Prophecy and Power*, p. 90.

85 Capp, *Astrology and the Popular Press*, pp. 167–81.

86 Marc Bloch, *The Royal Touch* (1973).

87 George Birkbeck Hill, *Boswell's Life of Johnson* (1934–50), vol. iii, p. 323.

88 Ephraim Chambers, *Cyclopaedia*, 2nd edn (1738 [1728]), vol. ii, unpaginated, 'Medicine'.

89 Samuel Wood, *Strictures on the Gout* (1775), p. 6.

90 Roy Porter, *Doctor of Society* (1991).

91 Thomas Beddoes (ed.), *Chemical Experiments and Opinions* (1790), p. 60, and *A Letter to Erasmus Darwin* (1793), p. 29.

92 Beddoes, *A Letter to Erasmus Darwin*, p. 58.

93 Beddoes, *A Letter to Erasmus Darwin*, p. 62.

94 Beddoes, *A Letter to Erasmus Darwin*, p. 62.

95 John Aikin, *Letters from a Father to His Son*, 3rd edn (1796 [1792–3]), p. 47.

96 Joseph Priestley, *An Essay on the First Principles of Government* (1768), p. 7.

97 Joseph Priestley, *Experiments and Observations on Different Kinds of Air* (1774–7), p. xiv; Maurice Crosland, 'The Image of Science as a Threat' (1987).

98 See Kevin C. Knox, 'Lunatick Visions' (1999). For the enduring rhetoric of the mad scientist and the irrational rationalist, see Haynes, *From Faust to Strangelove*.

7 ANATOMIZING HUMAN NATURE

1 Alexander Pope, *An Essay on Man* (1733–4), epistle ii, ll. 1–2, in John Butt (ed.), *The Poems of Alexander Pope* (1965), p. 516.

2 J. Y. T. Greig (ed.), *The Letters of David Hume* (1932), vol. i, p. 34.

3 Laurence Sterne, *The Life and Opinions of Tristram Shandy* (1967 [1759–67]), vol. vii, ch. 33, p. 500.

4 David Hume, *A Treatise of Human Nature* (1978 [1739]), p. xv. The potential benefits were inestimable: "Tis impossible to tell what changes and improvements we might make in these sciences were we thoroughly acquainted with the extent and force of human understanding.'

5 John Bunyan, *Pilgrim's Progress* (1678), discussed in Michael R. Watts, *The Dissenters* (1978), p. 263, and Christopher Hill, *A Turbulent, Seditious and Factious People* (1989).

6 Arthur Paul Davis, *Isaac Watts: His Life and Works* (1948), p. 7.

7 Donald F. Bond (ed.), *The Tatler* (1987), vol. ii, no. 87, p. 48 (Saturday, 29 October 1709).

8 William Shakespeare, *Hamlet*, act III, scene i, l. 130.

9 For Johnson's convictions, see Paul K. Alkon, *Samuel Johnson and Moral Discipline* (1967); Maurice Quinlan, *Samuel Johnson: A Layman's Religion* (1964); C. F. Chapin, *The Religious Thought of Samuel Johnson* (1968); R. Voitle, *Samuel Johnson the Moralist* (1961); G. Irwin, *Samuel Johnson: A Personality in Conflict* (1971); more broadly, on humanist morality, see Herschel Baker, *The Dignity of Man* (1947); J. B. Bamborough, *The Little World of Man* (1952).

10 Quoted in Paul Fussell, *The Rhetorical World of Augustan Humanism* (1965), p. 8; see also pp. 110f.

11 W. J. Bate and A. B. Straus (eds), *Samuel Johnson: The Rambler* (1969), vol. iii, no. 196, pp. 257–61 (Saturday, 1 February 1752); Samuel Johnson, *Life of Thomas Browne*, in *The Lives of the Most Eminent English Poets* (1939 [1779–81]); George Birkbeck Hill, *Boswell's Life of Johnson* (1934–50), vol. i, p. 198; Fussell, *The Rhetorical World of Augustan Humanism*, p. 53.

12 Hill, *Boswell's Life of Johnson*, vol. iv, p. 188.

13 Fussell, *The Rhetorical World of Augustan Humanism*, p. 65.

14 Jonathan Swift, *A Tale of a Tub, and Other Satires* (1975 [1704]), p. 133. For Swift's misanthropy, see Jove's address, in the 'Day of Judgment':

> Offending race of human kind,
> By nature, learning, reason blind;

Jonathan Swift, *The Complete Poems* (1983), p. 317.

15 Discussed in Fussell, *The Rhetorical World of Augustan Humanism*, p. 303.

16 Pope, *An Essay on Man*, epistle ii, l. 10, in Butt, *The Poems of Alexander Pope*, p. 516.

17 Pope, *An Essay on Man*, epistle ii, ll. 183–4, in Butt, *The Poems of Alexander Pope*, p. 522. See also Brean S. Hammond, *Pope and Bolingbroke* (1984).

18 Lancelot ('Capability') Brown got his soubriquet because of his legendary ability to see the 'capabilities' in noblemen's grounds. Enlightened moralists felt the same about human nature.

19 John Andrew Bernstein, 'Shaftesbury's Optimism and Eighteenth-century Social Thought' (1987); Robert Voitle, *The Third Earl of Shaftesbury: 1671–1713* (1984).

20 Anthony Ashley Cooper, 3rd Earl of Shaftesbury, *Characteristicks of Men, Manners,*

Opinions, Times (1999 [1711]), vol. ii, p. 67; Robert E. Norton, *The Beautiful Soul* (1995).

21 Shaftesbury, *Characteristicks of Men, Manners, Opinions, Times*, 'The Moralists', vol. ii, pt II, sect. 4, p. 49, discussed in Lawrence E. Klein, *Shaftesbury and the Culture of Politeness* (1994), p. 68; Basil Willey, *The Eighteenth Century Background* (1962), p. 73.

22 Shaftesbury, *Characteristicks of Men, Manners, Opinions, Times*, 'Sensus Communis', vol. i, sect. 1, p. 38. See also Klein, *Shaftesbury and the Culture of Politeness*, p. 168.

23 Klein, *Shaftesbury and the Culture of Politeness*, p. 2.

24 Thomas Hobbes, *Leviathan* (1968 [1651]). Hobbes's epistemology and moral philosophy have been discussed above in chapter 3.

25 Sir Isaac Newton, *Opticks* (1721), Query 31, p. 381; see discussion in Hume, *A Treatise of Human Nature*, introduction.

26 For the science of mind, see Elie Halévy, *The Growth of Philosophic Radicalism* (1792). The project also naturally attracted sceptics and satirists: see Christopher Fox, *Locke and the Scriblerians* (1988).

27 For the European background, see Ulrich Im Hof, *The Enlightenment* (1994), p. 182; Knud Haakonssen, *Natural Law and Moral Philosophy* (1996).

28 David Hume, *Enquiries concerning the Human Understanding and concerning the Principles of Morals* (1966 [1748]), pt I, sect. viii, pp. 83–4. See D. Spadafora, *The Idea of Progress in Eighteenth-century Britain* (1990), p. 269. Statements to this effect were legion. See, for instance, Viscount Bolingbroke's view that 'men of all countries and languages, who cultivate their reason, judge alike': *Of the True Use of Retirement and Study*, in *The Works of Lord Bolingbroke* (1969; repr. of 1841 edn), vol. iv, p. 163. For Mandeville's opinion that 'human Nature is every where the same', see *The Fable of the Bees* (1924 [1714]), vol. i, p. 275.

29 On the state of nature, see Ronald L. Meek, *Social Science and the Ignoble Savage* (1975); Robert Wokler, 'Anthropology and Conjectural History in the Enlightenment' (1995).

30 On Locke's anthropology, see G. A. J. Rogers, 'Locke, Anthropology and Models of the Mind' (1993).

31 See William Knight, *Lord Monboddo and Some of His Contemporaries* (1900); discussion of an 'original' state amounted to a recasting of original sin.

32 Adam Ferguson, *An Essay on the History of Civil Society* (1995 [1767]), p. 14.

33 Francis Hutcheson, *A Short Introduction to Moral Philosophy* (1747), p. 2; *cf.* his *A System of Moral Philosophy* (1755), vol. i, pp. 1–2; Vincent Hope, *Virtue by Consensus* (1989); Gladys Bryson, *Man and Society* (1968), p. 19. The son of an Ulster Dissenting minister, Francis Hutcheson (1694–1746) developed a theology which replaced Calvinism with rationalism. In 1729 he accepted the chair of moral philosophy at the University of Glasgow, remaining there until his death in 1747. In metaphysics he largely followed Locke, but he was most important for his ethical writings.

34 Bryson, *Man and Society*, p. 131. For a human anatomy that would 'undress nature', see also Mandeville, *The Fable of the Bees*, vol. ii, pp. 3, 142. See Roger Smith, *The Fontana History of the Human Sciences* (1997), ch. 3, pp. 215–59.

35 Johnson's sense of mental struggle is well conveyed in Gloria Sybil Gross, *This Invisible Riot of the Mind* (1992).

36 And also, by extension, with independent gentlemen: 'when the free spirit of a nation turns itself this way, judgments are formed: critics arise; the public eye and ear improve; a right taste prevails': quoted in John Barrell, *The Political Theory of Painting from Reynolds to Hazlitt* (1986), p. 34.

37 G. J. Barker-Benfield, *The Culture of Sensibility* (1992), p. 205; Michael Prince, *Philosophical Dialogue in the British Enlightenment* (1996), p. 35.

38 Hutcheson undertook to explain 'the Principles of the late Earl of Shaftesbury' and to show the errors of 'the Author of the *Fable of the Bees*': John B. Stewart, *Opinion and Reform in Hume's Political Philosophy* (1992), p. 76.

39 Francis Hutcheson, *An Inquiry into the Original of Our Ideas concerning Beauty, Order, Harmony, Design* (1973 [1725]), p. 2; John Darling, 'The Moral Teaching of Francis Hutcheson' (1989); J. Mordaunt Crook, 'The Arcadian Vision' (1988), pp. 48–9. 'The Mind . . . is passive, and has not Power directly to prevent the perception of Ideas': Hutcheson, *An Inquiry into the Original of Our Ideas concerning Beauty, Order, Harmony, Design*, p. 2.

40 David Hume, 'Of the Standard of Taste' (1741), in *Selected Essays* (1993), p. 136; David Marshall, 'Arguing by Analogy' (1995).

41 Archibald Alison, *Essays on the Nature and Principles of Taste* (1790), p. 55; Martin Kallich, *The Association of Ideas and Critical Theory in Eighteenth-century England* (1970).

42 For associationism, see John P. Wright, 'Association, Madness, and the Measures of Probability in Locke and Hume' (1987); Hume, *A Treatise of Human Nature*, bk I, pt I, sections 1–4, pp. 1–13.

43 Hobbes, *Leviathan*, p. 6; see the discussion in Edward Hundert, 'Performing the Passions in Commercial Society' (1998), p. 150; Charles Taylor, *Sources of the Self* (1989), pp. 172f.

44 John Locke, *An Essay concerning Human Understanding* (1975 [1690]), bk II, chs. 27–9; H. E. Allison, 'Locke's Theory of Personal Identity' (1977); R. C. Tennant, 'The Anglican Response to Locke's Theory of Personal Identity' (1982); D. P. Behan, 'Locke on Persons and Personal Identity' (1979); Taylor, *Sources of the Self*, p. 172; Sylvana Tomaselli, 'The First Person' (1984); John Marshall, *John Locke; Resistance, Religion and Responsibility* (1994), p. 399.

45 Locke's theory of the person proved unsettling: 'What initially strikes a modern reader of his earliest critics . . . is their honest sense of befuddlement over what Locke is saying about the self': Fox, *Locke and the Scriblerians*, pp. 50f. For satires on Locke, see Roger S. Lund, 'Martinus Scriblerus and the Search for a Soul' (1989).

46 Locke, *An Essay concerning Human Understanding*, bk IV, ch. 9, p. 618, quoted in Patricia Meyer Spacks, *Imagining a Self* (1976), p. 2.

47 Lawrence E. Klein, *Shaftesbury and the Culture of Politeness* (1994), pp. 73, 83–90. Shaftesbury obviously hints at Sterne on the self: see Max Byrd, *Tristram Shandy* (1985).

48 See below, chapters 18 and 20, and the debates on topics such as insanity: chapter 9. The emergent novel obviously provided a forum for exploring the enigmas of the self.

49 J. P. Ferguson, *An Eighteenth-century Heretic* (1976), contains a fine discussion; see also James O'Higgins, *Anthony Collins: The Man and His Works* (1970), p. 72f.; John W. Yolton, *Thinking Matter* (1983). For the meaning of dreams, see Jennifer Ford, *Coleridge on Dreaming* (1998); Fox, *Locke and the Scriblerians*, p. 51.

50 Anthony Collins, *An Answer to Mr Clarke's Third Defence to His Letter to Mr Dodwell* (1708), p. 66; quoted in Fox, *Locke and the Scriblerians*, p. 53. Collins argued, like Locke, that personal identity did not reside in the flesh but 'solely in Consciousness', proceeding to carry Locke's theory to conclusions he never countenanced. Clarke had objected that if personal identity consisted in consciousness and if that were fleeting, the Resurrection of the same person would be impossible. 'To which I answer,' replied Collins, 'if Personal Identity consists in Consciousness, as before explained . . . Consciousness can perish no more at the Dissolution of the Body, than it does every Moment we cease to think, or be conscious': Anthony Collins, *A Philosophical Inquiry concerning Human Liberty* (1790 [1717]),

p. 66. Given the impermanent nature of these distinct acts, Collins argued, 'we are not conscious, that we continue a Moment the same individual numerical Being' (p. 66).

51 Gladys Bryson, *Man and Society* (1968), p. 8; Daniel Carey, 'Reconsidering Rousseau' (1998), p. 27.

52 Hutcheson, *An Inquiry into the Original of Our Ideas of Beauty, Order, Harmony, Design*, sect. iii, fig. 8; Bryson, *Man and Society*, p. 8.

53 Hutcheson, *A Short Introduction to Moral Philosophy in Three Books*, pp. 2f., for the following.

54 Bryson, *Man and Society*, p. 155.

55 Hutcheson, *A Short Introduction to Moral Philosophy in Three Books*, p. 4.

56 Hutcheson, *A Short Introduction to Moral Philosophy in Three Books*, p. 17.

57 Hutcheson, *A Short Introduction to Moral Philosophy in Three Books*, p. 2.

58 For Common Sense philosophy, see Selwyn Alfred Grave, *The Scottish Philosophy of Common Sense* (1960); Keith Lehrer, *Thomas Reid* (1989).

59 The word appears in Nathan Bailey's *Universal Etymological English Dictionary* (1721), which went through thirty editions: Gary Hatfield, 'Remaking the Science of the Mind' (1995); Christopher Fox, 'Introduction: Defining Eighteenth-century Psychology', in *Psychology and Literature in the Eighteenth Century* (1987), p. 3.

Michel Foucault held that in the eighteenth century 'psychology did not exist': *Madness and Civilization* (1967), p. 197. As the above literature makes clear, this claim is wrong.

60 Fernando Vidal, 'Psychology in the Eighteenth Century' (1993); John Christie, 'The Human Sciences' (1993).

61 Fox, *Psychology and Literature in the Eighteenth Century* (1987), and 'Crawford, Willis, and *Anthropologie Abstracted*' (1988).

62 David Hartley, *Observations on Man* (1791 [1749]), vol. i, p. 2.

63 Mandeville, *The Fable of the Bees*, vol. ii, p. 79.

64 Mandeville, *The Fable of the Bees*, vol. i, p. 72. Mandeville was reopening issues raised by Hobbes. For the following, see E. G. Hundert, *The Enlightenment's Fable* (1994); Dario Castiglione, 'Excess, Frugality and the Spirit of Capitalism' (1992); R. I. Cook, *Bernard Mandeville* (1974); M. M. Goldsmith, *Private Vices, Public Benefits* (1985); T. A. Horne, *The Social Thought of Bernard Mandeville* (1978).

65 Bernard de Mandeville, *The Virgin Unmask'd* (1709), pp. 25, 87.

66 Mandeville, *The Fable of the Bees*; Rudolf Dekker, ' "Private Vices, Public Virtues" Revisited' (1992); J. Martin Stafford, *Private Vices, Publick Benefits?* (1997).

67 Mandeville, *The Fable of the Bees*, vol. i, p. 20.

68 Mandeville, *The Fable of the Bees*, vol. i, p. 24.

69 Mandeville, *The Fable of the Bees*, vol. i, p. 26.

70 Mandeville, *The Fable of the Bees*, vol. i, pp. 323–69.

71 Mandeville, *The Fable of the Bees*, vol. i, p. 212.

72 Mandeville, *The Fables of the Bees*, vol. i, p. 10.

73 Mandeville, *The Fable of the Bees*, vol. i, p. 76. For luxury, see John Sekora, *Luxury: The Concept in Western Thought, Eden to Smollett* (1977), p. 80; for pride, see Hundert, *The Enlightenment's Fable*, p. 73.

74 Mandeville, *The Fable of the Bees*, vol. i, p. 76.

75 Mandeville, *The Fable of the Bees*, vol. i, p. 407.

76 Pope, *An Essay on Man*, epistle iii, ll. 317–18, in Butt, *The Poems of Alexander Pope*, p. 535.

77 'The attentive Reader, who peruses the foregoing part of this Book, will soon perceive that two Systems cannot be more opposite than his Lordship's and mine': Mandeville, *The Fable of the Bees*, vol. ii, p. 324.

78 Francis Hutcheson, *Thoughts on Laughter*, and *Observations on the Fable of the Bees* (1989 [1758]), discussed in Hundert, *The Enlightenment's Fable*, p. 37.

79 Hume, *A Treatise of Human Nature*, subtitle. It notoriously fell 'deadborn from the press'. For Hume's life, see above, chapter 4. Generally on Hume, see Philippa Foot, 'Locke, Hume, and Modern Moral Theory' (1991); Peter Jones (ed.), *The 'Science' of Man in the Scottish Enlightenment* (1989); Nicholas Phillipson, *Hume* (1989); John B. Stewart, *The Moral and Political Philosophy of David Hume* (1963).

80 Hume, *A Treatise of Human Nature*, p. 269.

81 Hume, *A Treatise of Human Nature*, p. xvi.

82 Hume, *A Treatise of Human Nature*, p. xvii.

83 Hume, *A Treatise of Human Nature*, bk I, section iv.

84 Hume, *Enquiries concerning the Human Understanding and concerning the Principles of Morals*, sect. viii, pt i, p. 83.

85 Hume, *A Treatise of Human Nature*, bk I, sect. i; bk I, sect. xii, 'Of the Probability of Causes'.

86 Hume, *A Treatise of Human Nature*, bk I, sect. vi. Hume wrote (p. 259):

We now proceed to explain the nature of *personal identity*, which has become so great a question in philosophy, especially of late years in *England*, where all the abstruser sciences are study'd with a peculiar ardour and application. And here 'tis evident, the same method of reasoning must be continu'd, which has so successfully explain'd the identity of plants, and animals, and ships, and houses, and of all the compounded and changeable productions either of art or nature. The identity, which we ascribe to the mind of man, is only a fictitious one.

87 For Hume on pride, see Stewart, *Opinion and Reform in Hume's Political Philosophy*, p. 123. Some moralists, argued Hume, try to quash all pride as 'purely pagan and natural', but this would render us incapable of achieving much: Hume, *A Treatise of Human Nature*, bk III, sect. ii, p. 600.

88 Stewart, *Opinion and Reform in Hume's Political Philosophy*, p. 127.

89 Radical novels of the 1790s were often subtitled 'Man as he is', or some variant. Hume wanted to reconcile society to man as he is.

90 See Mossner's interesting discussion in his introduction to David Hume, *A Treatise of Human Nature* (1969 [1739]), p. 22.

91 Hume, *A Treatise of Human Nature*, bk II, sect. iii, p. 416.

92 Hartley, for instance, dismissed eternal punishment: Richard C. Allen, *David Hartley on Human Nature* (1999), pp. xx, 38.

93 Generally on Hartley, see Barbara Bowen Oberg, 'David Hartley and the Association of Ideas' (1976); C. U. M. Smith, 'David Hartley's Newtonian Neuropsychology' (1987); M. E. Webb, 'A New History of Hartley's *Observations on Man*' (1988), and 'The Early Medical Studies and Practice of Dr David Hartley' (1989); Margaret Leslie, 'Mysticism Misunderstood' (1972); Spadafora, *The Idea of Progress in Eighteenth-century Britain*, p. 153; Allen, *David Hartley on Human Nature*.

94 Locke stated, 'I shall not at present meddle with the physical considerations of the mind' – 'These are speculations which, however curious and entertaining, I shall decline': Locke, *An Essay concerning Human Understanding*, bk I, ch. 1, p. 43.

95 For Gay, see Halévy, *The Growth of Philosophic Radicalism*, pp. 7f.

96 Quoted in R. V. Sampson, *Progress in the Age of Reason* (1956), p. 46; for Hartley's influence, see R. M. Young, 'David Hartley' (1970), and 'Association of Ideas' (1973); Yolton, *Thinking Matter*, p. 158.

97 Hartley, *Observations on Man*, vol. i, p. 83.

98 This argument, developed by the Revd John Gay, was taken over by Abraham Tucker in his *The Light of Nature Pursued* (1768). See the discussion in Allen, *David Hartley on Human Nature*, p. 267.

99 Hartley, *Observations on Man*, vol. i, pp. 473–4.

100 Smith, *The Fontana History of the Human Sciences*, pp. 216–17; Hatfield, 'Remaking the Science of the Mind'.

101 Dugald Stewart, 'Dissertation: Exhibiting the Progress of Metaphysical, Ethical and Political Philosophy since the Revival of Letters in Europe', in Sir William Hamilton (ed.), *The Collected Works of Dugald Stewart* (1854–60), vol. i, p. 479.

8 THE SCIENCE OF POLITICS

1 Edward Gibbon, *Memoirs of My Life* (1966 [1796]), p. 51.

2 David Hume, 'That Politics may be Reduced to a Science' (1741–2), in *Selected Essays* (1993), pp. 13–24; Jonathan Swift, *Gulliver's Travels* (1985 [1726]), bk ii, p. 176: 'Voyage to Brobdingnag', Gulliver speaking:

But I take this Defect among them to have risen from their Ignorance; but not having hitherto reduced *Politicks* into a *Science*, as the more acute Wits of Europe have done . . . He [the king] confined the Knowledge of governing within very narrow bounds; to common Sense and Reason, to Justice and Lenity, to the Speedy Determination of Civil and criminal Causes.

3 J. T. Desaguliers, *The Newtonian System of the World* (1728), preface, p. 32, ll. 175–6:

But boldly let thy *perfect model* be
NEWTON's (the only true) *Philosophy*.

4 E. P. Thompson, *The Making of the English Working Class* (1965), p. 79.

5 Robert Filmer, *Patriarcha, and Other Political Works of Sir Robert Filmer* (1949); Mark

Kishlansky, *A Monarchy Transformed* (1996); Paul Kleber Monod, *Jacobitism and the English People, 1688–1788* (1989).

6 For Locke's politics, see Peter Laslett, 'The English Revolution and Locke's *Two Treatises of Government*' (1956); John Marshall, *John Locke; Resistance, Religion and Responsibility* (1994); Richard Ashcraft, *Revolutionary Politics and Locke's Two Treatises of Government* (1986); John Dunn, *The Political Thought of John Locke* (1969). A useful anthology of political thinking is David Williams (ed.), *The Enlightenment* (1999).

7 John Locke, *Two Treatises of Government* (1988 [1690]), bk i, ch. 1, sect. 1, p. 141. Locke added: 'Slavery is so vile and miserable an Estate of Man, and so directly opposite to the generous Temper and Courage of our Nation; that 'tis hardly to be conceived, that an Englishman, much less a Gentleman, should plead for't': bk i, ch. 1, sect. 1, p. 141. The key to Filmer's philosophy, as Locke saw it, was that 'no Man is Born free': bk i, ch. 1, sect. 1, p. 142.

8 Locke, *Two Treatises of Government*, bk i, ch. 1, sect. 1, p. 141.

9 Locke, *Two Treatises of Government*, treatise 2, ch. 1, sect. 2, p. 268. For the politics of property, see H. T. Dickinson, *Liberty and Property* (1977); John Brewer and Susan Staves (eds), *Early Modern Conceptions of Property* (1995).

10 Locke, *Two Treatises of Government*, treatise 2, ch. 2, sect. 6, p. 271. Locke explained that this was because men were 'all the workmanship of one omnipotent and infinitely wise Maker, all the servants of one sovereign Master, sent into the world by His order, and about His business'. For the key idea of civil society, see Marvin B. Becker, *The Emergence of Civil Society in the Eighteenth Century* (1994).

11 Locke, *Two Treatises of Government*, treatise 2, ch. 9, sect. 124, pp. 350–51.

12 Locke, *Two Treatises of Government*, treatise 2, ch. 9, sect. 135, pp. 357–8.

13 Locke, *Two Treatises of Government*, treatise 2, ch. 13, sect. 149, p. 367.

14 Locke, *Two Treatises of Government*, treatise 2, ch. 14, sect. 168, pp. 379–80: 'people are not so easily got out of their old forms as some are apt to suggest'.

15 Locke, *Two Treatises of Government*, treatise 2, ch. 19, sect. 225, p. 415.

16 Locke, *Two Treatises*, treatise 2, ch. 5, sect. 25, p. 286. For discussion of property, see C. B. Macpherson, *The Political Theory of Possessive Individualism* (1964).

17 Locke, *Two Treatises of Government*, treatise 2, ch. 5, sect. 25, p. 286. *Cf.* Psalms 115, verse 16.

18 Locke, *Two Treatises of Government*, treatise 2, ch. 5, sect. 32, pp. 290–91; Richard Ashcraft, 'Lockean Ideas, Poverty, and the Development of Liberal Political Theory' (1995).

19 Locke, *Two Treatises of Government*, treatise 2, ch. 5, sect. 27, pp. 287–8.

20 Locke, *Two Treatises of Government*, treatise 2, ch. 5, sect. 35, p. 292.

21 Locke, *Two Treatises of Government*, treatise 2, ch. 5, sect. 36, p. 293.

22 Locke, *Two Treatises of Government*, treatise 2, ch. 5, sect. 37, p. 294.

23 Locke, *Two Treatises of Government*, treatise 2, ch. 5, sect. 46, p. 300.

24 Locke, *Two Treatises of Government*, treatise 2, ch. 5, sect. 46, p. 300.

25 Locke, *Two Treatises of Government*, treatise 2, ch. 5, sect. 47, p. 300.

26 Locke, *Two Treatises of Government*, treatise 2, ch. 5, sect. 50, p. 302.

27 Joseph Tucker, *A Treatise concerning Civil Government* (1781), p. 33; W. George Shelton, *Dean Tucker and Eighteenth-century Economic and Political Thought* (1981); J. G. A. Pocock, 'Josiah Tucker on Burke, Locke, and Price' (1985). Similar criticisms were made by Hume, by Blackstone and by Burke. 'The only true and natural foundations of society,' wrote Blackstone, 'are the wants and the fears of individuals': Isaac Kramnick,

Republicanism and Bourgeois Radicalism (1990), pp. 73f.; J. C. D. Clark, *The Language of Liberty 1660–1832* (1994), ch. 3.

28 Laslett, 'The English Revolution and Locke's *Two Treatises of Government*'; Ashcraft, *Revolutionary Politics and Locke's Two Treatises of Government*.

29 J. G. A. Pocock, *Virtue, Commerce and History* (1985), p. 48.

30 J. G. A. Pocock, *The Machiavellian Moment* (1975), pp. 406f., and *Virtue, Commerce and History*, pp. 75f. In his *Commonwealth of Oceana* (1656), James Harrington (1611–77) offered an ideal constitution for England. Property, especially landed property, determined the distribution of power within a state. To prevent executive powers from remaining with the same individuals, he proposed a limited tenure of office. His ideas shaped the development of the 'country' ideology, with its stress on opposition to centralized power and suspicion of corruption.

31 Henry St John, first Viscount Bolingbroke (1678–1751), a Tory politician, was Secretary at War from 1704 to 1708, allying with Robert Harley. Supporting a Stuart restoration, after Queen Anne's death he fled to France, and was briefly the Pretender's secretary of state. Pardoned in 1723 but refused his Lords seat, he unleashed a literary onslaught on Walpole in the *Craftsman*, lambasting the corrupt 'Robinocracy', demanding frequent elections and limits on placemen and standing armies: H. T. Dickinson, *Bolingbroke* (1970); Isaac Kramnick, *Bolingbroke and His Circle* (1968); Simon Varey (ed.), *Lord Bolingbroke: Contributions to the Craftsman* (1982); John B. Stewart, *Opinion and Reform in Hume's Political Philosophy* (1992), p. 63.

32 Caroline Robbins, *The Eighteenth-century Commonwealthmen* (1968); Nicholas Phillipson and Quentin Skinner (eds.), *Political Discourse in Early Modern Britain* (1993); John Robertson, 'The Scottish Enlightenment at the Limits of the Civic Tradition' (1983).

33 J. G. A. Pocock, 'Machiavelli, Harrington and English Political Ideologies' (1972), and 'Civic Humanism and its Role in Anglo-American Thought' (1972).

34 Robbins, *The Eighteenth-century Commonwealthmen*; Shelley Burtt, *Virtue Transformed* (1992); Malcolm Jack, *Corruption and Progress* (1989); Pocock, *The Machiavellian Moment*, p. 467; David L. Jacobson and Ronald Hamowy (eds.), *The English Libertarian Heritage* (1994).

35 The pair then turned out another highly successful weekly in the early 1720s, the *Independent Whig*, promoting anti-clericalism and free-thinking (see chapter 5). It says something about the 'pen for hire' ethos of the day that on Trenchard's death in 1723, Gordon's radicalism came to an end. He became Walpole's press adviser, accepted a position as the First Commissioner of Wine Licenses, and in time became a leading court writer, a pillar of the 'corruption' against which he had railed: Marie P. McMahon, *The Radical Whigs, John Trenchard and Thomas Gordon* (1990).

36 Jacobson (ed.), *The English Libertarian Heritage* (1965), letters 59–68, p. xxxix.

37 Jacobson (ed.), *The English Libertarian Heritage*, letter 62, p. xxxvi.

38 Jacobson (ed.), *The English Libertarian Heritage*, letter 45, p. xxxvii.

39 Jacobson (ed.), *The English Libertarian Heritage*, letter 60, p. xxxviii.

40 Jacobson (ed.), *The English Libertarian Heritage*, letter 60, p. xxxix, p. 47.

41 For the constitution, see J. A. W. Gunn, *Beyond Liberty and Property* (1983); and Ernest Neville Williams, *The Eighteenth Century Constitution, 1688–1815* (1960).

42 James Thomson, *Liberty* (1735), p. 45, ll. 814–16. Thomson and other 'patriots' had a political agenda of their own, using 'patriotism' to support the Prince of Wales against George II.

43 Johann Wilhelm von Archenholz, *A Picture of England* (1791), quoted in Harry

Ballam and Roy Lewis (eds.), *The Visitors' Book* (1950), p. 79; Nicholas Rogers, *Crowds, Culture and Politics in Georgian Britain* (1998), p. 274.

44 Quoted in C. Y. Ferdinand, *Benjamin Collins and the Provincial Newspaper Trade in the Eighteenth Century* (1997), p. 155. For the limits of press freedom on the Continent, see Ulrich Im Hof, *The Enlightenment* (1994), p. 150.

45 Geoffrey Alan Cranfield, *The Development of the Provincial Newspaper 1700–1760* (1962), p. 273; Marilyn Butler (ed.), *Burke, Paine, Godwin, and the Revolution Controversy* (1984), p. 6. On the press as guardian of English liberties, recall Henry Tilney's quizzing of the suspicious Catherine Morland:

What have you been judging from? Remember the country and the age in which we live. Remember that we are English, that we are Christians. Consult your own understanding, your own sense of the probable, your own observation of what is passing around you – Does your education prepare us for such atrocities? Do our laws connive at them? Could they be perpetrated without being known, in a country like this, where social and literary intercourse is on such a footing; where every man is surrounded by a neighbourhood of voluntary spies, and where roads and newspapers lay everything open?

Jane Austen, *Northanger Abbey* (1975 [1818]), p. 172.

46 William Blackstone, *Commentaries on the Laws of England* (1979 [1765–9]), quoted in Butler, *Burke, Paine, Godwin, and the Revolution Controversy*, p. 6; James T. Boulton, *The Language of Politics in the Age of Wilkes and Burke* (1963), p. 19; H. T. Dickinson, *The Politics of the People in Eighteenth-century Britain* (1995), p. 169; Eckhart Hellmuth, ' "The Palladium of All Other English Liberties" ' (1990).

47 Quoted in Butler, *Burke, Paine, Godwin, and the Revolution Controversy*, p. 6.

48 J. Almon, *Memoirs of a Late Eminent Bookseller* (sn, 1790), pp. 148f. The Berlin Wednesday Club was arguing, in 1783, in *favour* of censorship – not surprisingly, as many of its members were civil servants: Eckhart Hellmuth, 'Enlightenment and the Freedom of the Press' (1998).

49 Quoted in Stewart, *Opinion and Reform in Hume's Political Philosophy*, p. 306.

50 Pat Rogers, *Hacks and Dunces* (1980), pp. 8–9.

51 Alan P. F. Sell, *John Locke and the Eighteenth-century Divines* (1997), p. 2. All ideologues looked back to 1688 as securing English law and liberties (Bill of Rights, the Toleration Act, the Act of Settlement, the Union with Scotland, Defoe's *Iure Divino* (1704)).

52 Anthony Ashley Cooper, 3rd Earl of Shaftesbury, *Characteristicks of Men, Manners, Opinions, Times* (1999 [1711]), vol. i, p. 60.

53 Shaftesbury, *Characteristicks of Men, Manners, Opinions, Times*, vol. i, p. 39.

54 Henry St John, Viscount Bolingbroke, 'Idea of the Patriot King' (1738), in *The Works of Lord Bolingbroke* (1969 [1754–98]), vol. iii, p. 123: 'The landed men are the true owners of our political vessel; the moneyed men, as such, are but passengers in it', quoted in Leslie Stephen, *History of English Thought in the Eighteenth Century* (1962 [1876]), vol. ii, p. 178. There was of course endless social satire targeted against the vulgarity of mere money: Colin Nicholson, *Writing and the Rise of Finance* (1994).

55 James Harris, *Hermes* (1751), in *The Works of James Harris, Esq.* (1801), vol. i, ch. 5, p. 438.

56 For the consolidation of the State, see John Brewer, *The Sinews of Power* (1989); P. Corrigan and D. Sayer, *The Great Arch* (1985); John Cannon (ed.), *The Whig Ascendancy* (1981); J. H. Plumb, *The Growth of Political Stability in England 1675–1725* (1967); Jeremy Black, *The Politics of Britain, 1688–1800* (1993).

57 For accusations of a 'sham', see D. Hay, 'Property, Authority and the Criminal Law' (1975); Peter Linebaugh, *The London Hanged* (1991).

58 John Brown, *An Estimate of the Manners and*

Principles of the Times (1757), pp. 29, 35–6: Brown believed Britain was 'gliding down to Ruin', just like 'degenerate and declining *Rome*': he eventually committed suicide. See Jack, *Corruption and Progress*; D. Spadafora, *The Idea of Progress in Eighteenth-century Britain* (1990), p. 214; Howard D. Weinbrot, *Augustus Caesar in 'Augustan' England* (1978).

59 See the discussions above in chapters 1 and 4. For the political thinking of Addison and Steele, see Nicholas Phillipson, 'Politics and Politeness in the Reigns of Anne and the Early Hanoverians' (1993), pp. 211–45.

60 Joseph Addison and Richard Steele, *The Spectactor* (1965), vol. i, no. 124, p. 507 (Monday, 23 July 1711); see the discussion in Erin Mackie, *Market à la Mode* (1977), p. 208.

61 Donald F. Bond (ed.), *The Tatler* (1987), vol. i, p. 8, dedication. Steele said, 'it is no small discouragement to me, to see how slow a progress I make in the reformation of the world': Bond, *The Tatler* (1987), vol. ii, no. 139, pp. 297–301 (Tuesday, 28 February 1710). Note that eighty years later the leading Spanish literary journal, the *Espíritu de los majores diarios*, had but 765 subscribers.

62 John Gay, *The Present State of Wit* (sn, 1711), p. 20.

63 Addison and Steele, *The Spectator* (1965), vol. i, no. 10, p. 44 (Monday, 12 March 1711).

64 Addison and Steele, *The Spectator*, vol. i, no. 10, pp. 44–7 (Monday, 12 March 1711).

65 Addison and Steele, *The Spectator*, vol. ii, no. 219, pp. 351–4 (Saturday, 10 November 1711), and vol. ii, no. 275, pp. 570–73 (Tuesday, 15 January 1712). See Edward A. Bloom, Lilian D. Bloom and Edmund Leites, *Educating the Audience* (1984); Scott Black, 'Social and Literary Form in the *Spectator*' (1999); Peter Burke, *The Art of Conversation* (1993); Stephen Copley, 'Commerce, Conversation and Politeness in the Early Eighteenth-century Periodical' (1995); Michael Ketcham, *Transparent Designs* (1985);

David Castronovo, *The English Gentleman* (1987); George C. Brauer, *The Education of a Gentleman* (1959). For the tag, *Totus mundus agit histrionem*, see Addison and Steele, *The Spectator*, vol. iii, no. 370, p. 393 (Monday, 5 May 1712).

66 Addison and Steele, *The Spectator*, vol. i, no. 125, pp. 509–10 (Tuesday, 24 July 1711).

67 Addison and Steele, *The Spectator*, vol. ii, no. 262, p. 517 (Monday, 31 December 1711). He was as good as his word, although for his pains he then incurred Pope's derisive portrait as 'Atticus' ('Willing to wound, yet afraid to strike/Just hint a fault and hesitate dislike'): Alexander Pope, *An Epistle to Dr Arbuthnot* (1735), in John Butt (ed.), *The Poems of Alexander Pope* (1965), p. 604, ll. 203–4.

68 Addison and Steele, *The Spectator*, vol. ii, no. 262, p. 519 (Monday, 31 December 1711). Compare Swift's professed aim in *A Tale of a Tub*.

69 Addison and Steele, *The Spectator*, vol. i, no. 81, pp. 346–9 (Saturday, 2 June 1711).

70 Addison and Steele, *The Spectator*, vol. ii, no. 169, pp. 164–7 (Thursday, 13 September 1711).

71 Scott Paul Gordon, 'Voyeuristic Dreams' (1995). 'Mr Spectator' went 'masked': Terry Castle, *Masquerade and Civilization* (1986); Lee Davison, Tim Hitchcock, Tim Keirn and Robert B. Shoemaker (eds), *Stilling the Grumbling Hive* (1992).

72 George S. Marr, *The Periodical Essayists of the Eighteenth Century* (1971), p. 57.

73 Ernest Cassara, *The Enlightenment in America* (1988), p. 43. 'Addison,' wrote Macaulay, 'reconciled wit with virtue, after a long and disastrous separation, during which wit had been led astray by profligacy and virtue by fanaticism': quoted in Terry Eagleton, *The Function of Criticism* (1984), p. 4.

74 See the analyses in Christopher J. Berry, *The Idea of Luxury* (1994), pp. 147f.; Jean-Christophe Agnew, *Worlds Apart* (1986); John Sekora, *Luxury* (1977); James Raven, *Judging New Wealth* (1992).

75 Hume, 'Of the Protestant Succession' (1741–2), in *Selected Essays* (1993), p. 297; see also David Hume, *The History of England under the House of Tudor* (1754–62), vol. iii, ch. 23, p. 296, and Spadafora, *The Idea of Progress in Eighteenth-century Britain*, p. 309. Broadly on Hume's politics, see Duncan Forbes, *Hume's Philosophical Politics* (1975), and 'Sceptical Whiggism, Commerce and Liberty' (1975); John B. Stewart, *The Moral and Political Philosophy of David Hume* (1963), and *Opinion and Reform in Hume's Political Philosophy*; Nicholas Phillipson, *Hume* (1989).

76 Hume, 'Of Civil Liberty' (1741–2), in *Selected Essays*, p. 52. For these ideas, see Phillipson, 'Politics and Politeness in the Reigns of Anne and the Early Hanoverians'.

77 Robertson, 'The Scottish Enlightenment at the Limits of the Civic Tradition', pp. 152–3.

78 Hume, 'On the Origin of Government' (1741–2), in *Selected Essays*, pp. 28–32, *A Treatise of Human Nature* (1978 [1740]), bk III, pt 2, ch. 1, and 'Of Justice', in David Hume, *Enquiries concerning the Human Understanding and concerning the Principles of Morals* (1966 [1777]), pp. 183–204; Jonathan Harrison, *Hume's Theory of Justice* (1981); Christopher J. Berry, *Social Theory of the Scottish Enlightenment* (1997), chs. 2–3.

79 Hume, *A Treatise of Human Nature*, bk III, pt 2, sect. 2, pp. 498–500. Such views anticipate Smith's.

80 Robertson, 'The Scottish Enlightenment at the Limits of the Civic Tradition', p. 152.

81 Hume, 'Of Luxury' (1741–2), in *Selected Essays*, pp. 167–77. From 1760 this essay was retitled 'Of Refinement in the Arts'. Gibbon agreed: the fall of Rome had been due not to luxury but to despotism: see Pocock, *Virtue, Commerce, and History*, p. 148. For the Rome debate, see Howard Erskine-Hill, *The Augustan Idea in English Literature* (1983); Philip Ayres, *Classical Culture and the Idea of Rome in Eighteenth-century England* (1997); Sekora, *Luxury*, p. 110.

82 Hume, 'Of the Rise and Progress of the Arts and Sciences' (1741–2), in *Selected Essays*, pp. 56–77.

83 See the discussion in Robertson, 'The Scottish Enlightenment at the Limits of the Civic Tradition', p. 163.

84 Hume, 'Of Civil Liberty', in *Selected Essays*, p. 54. Gibbon too denied that modern monarchies were tyrannies:

The abuses of tyranny are restrained by the mutual influence of fear and shame; republics have acquired order and stability; monarchies have imbibed the principles of freedom, or, at least, of moderation; and some sense of honour and justice is introduced into the most defective constitutions by the general manners of the times.

Edward Gibbon, *The History of the Decline and Fall of the Roman Empire* (1994 [1781]), vol. ii, ch. 38, p. 514.

85 David Hume, *The Philosophical Works of David Hume* (1882 [1741–2]), vol. iii, pp. 301–2, quoted in Hiram Caton, *The Politics of Progress* (1988), p. 329.

86 Hume, 'Of Refinement in the Arts' (1741–2), in *Selected Essays*, p. 168.

87 While a student at the University of Glasgow from 1737 to 1740 Smith attended the lectures of Francis Hutcheson. He lectured on rhetoric, *belles lettres*, and, finally, jurisprudence in Edinburgh from 1748 to 1751, when he was appointed professor of logic at Glasgow, moving soon after to Hutcheson's old chair of moral philosophy, which he held until 1763. At Glasgow, he lectured on literature as well as on law, government and ethics, and in 1759 he published *The Theory of Moral Sentiments*. Nicholas Phillipson, 'Adam Smith as Civic Moralist' (1983). See also T. D. Campbell, *Adam Smith's Science of Morals* (1971); V. Brown, *Adam Smith's Discourse* (1994); Forbes, 'Sceptical Whiggism, Commerce and Liberty'; Donald Winch, *Adam Smith's Politics* (1978).

88 Adam Smith, *The Theory of Moral Sentiments* (1976 [1759]), pt III, ch. 3, para. 20, quoted in Phillipson, 'Adam Smith as Civic Moralist', p. 185.

89 A man might pursue his desires to the full extent of his powers, so long as moral limits were accepted: 'In the race for wealth, and honours, and preferments, he may run as hard as he can, and strain every nerve and every muscle, in order to outstrip all his competitors. But if he should justle, or throw down any of them, the indulgence of the spectators is entirely at an end': Smith, *The Theory of Moral Sentiments*, p. 83.

90 Smith, *The Theory of Moral Sentiments*, p. 113.

91 Smith, *The Theory of Moral Sentiments*, p. 112, quoted in Nicholas Phillipson, 'Adam Smith as Civic Moralist', p. 189.

92 Phillipson, 'Adam Smith as Civic Moralist', pp. 189–92.

93 David Hume: 'But why, in the greater society or confederation of mankind, should not the case be the same as in particular clubs and companies': Hume, *Enquiries concerning Human Understanding and concerning the Principles of Morals*, p. 281.

94 Smith, *The Theory of Moral Sentiments*, p. 112. By the second edition (1761), it has been argued, Smith was withdrawing from an ethics overwhelmingly based upon a moderate and informed public opinion towards a moral code which underlined the pre-eminence of the individual and internal conscience. Smith there made public the concept of a 'tribunal within the breast', 'the abstract man', the 'representative of mankind', which acted as the 'supreme judge' of men's sentiments: John Dwyer, *Virtuous Discourse* (1987), p. 141.

95 Robert Burns, 'To a Louse' (1786), in *The Poetical Works of Burns* (1974), p. 44 – virtually a gloss on Smith.

96 E. G. Hundert, *The Enlightenment's Fable* (1994), p. 173. 'It is the great fallacy of Dr Mandeville's book *The Fable of the Bees* to represent every passion as wholly vicious': Smith, *The Theory of Moral Sentiments*, pt VII, sect. 2, p. 312.

97 Quoted in Michael Ignatieff, 'John Millar and Individualism' (1983), p. 329.

9 SECULARIZING

1 J. G. A. Pocock, *The Machiavellian Moment* (1975), p. 451.

2 Pieter Spierenburg, *The Broken Spell* (1991); Ronald Hutton, *The Rise and Fall of Merry England* (1994). For a balanced adaptation of Weber's Protestant ethic, see Keith Thomas, *Religion and the Decline of Magic* (1971), especially the conclusion. C. John Sommerville's *The Secularization of Early Modern England* (1992) is widely regarded as exaggerating the secularization process. By way of prelude, see the discussion at the beginning of chapter 5.

3 Samuel Pepys, *The Diary of Samuel Pepys* (1970–83), vol. vi, pp. 83, 100, 101; Henri Misson, *Memoirs and Observations in His Travels over England* (1719), pp. 36–7; on time, see

D. S. Landes, *Revolution in Time* (1983); on clock ownership, see Lorna Weatherill, *Consumer Behaviour and Material Culture, 1660–1760* (1988), pp. 25–8; Stuart Sherman, *Telling Time* (1996).

4 M. Grosley, *A Tour to London* (1772), vol. i, p. 107.

5 Robert Southey, *Letters from England by Don Manuel Alvarez Espriella* (1984 [1807]), p. 361.

6 For these quotations and discussion, see E. P. Thompson, 'Time, Work-Discipline and Industrial Capitalism' (1991), pp. 385–6; Neil McKendrick, 'Josiah Wedgwood and Factory Discipline' (1961).

7 Thompson, 'Time, Work-Discipline and Industrial Capitalism'.

8 Charles Strachey (ed.), *The Letters of the Earl*

of Chesterfield to His Son (1924), vol. i, p. 192.

9 On hospitals, see J. Woodward, *To Do the Sick No Harm* (1974); Roy Porter, 'The Gift Relation' (1989). For the Magdalen, see Vivien Jones (ed.), *Women in the Eighteenth Century* (1990), p. 87; Miles Ogborn, *Spaces of Modernity* (1998), pp. 39–74.

10 P. J. Bishop, *A Short History of the Royal Humane Society* (1974); Elizabeth H. Thomson, 'The Role of the Physician in Humane Societies of the Eighteenth Century' (1963). Carolyn Williams has shown that the Humane Society was promoted within a framework of polite values: 'The Genteel Art of Resuscitation' (1982). Inspired by the Society, newspapers began to carry advice for dealing with accident victims. Thus *Jopson's Coventry Mercury* (31 May 1784):

a correspondent has communicated the following directions for the recovery of persons seemingly drowned. – In the first place, strip them of all their wet cloaths; rub them and lay them in hot blankets before the fire: blow with your breath strongly, or with a pair of bellows into the mouth of the person, holding the nostrils at the same time: afterwards introduce the small end of a lighted tobacco-pipe into the fundament, putting a paper pricked full of holes near the bowl of it, through which you must blow into the bowels . . .

For Humane Society insertions in the *Gentleman's Magazine*, see Roy Porter, 'Lay Medical Knowledge in the Eighteenth Century' (1985), pp. 140, 156.

11 Max Weber's concept: *The Protestant Ethic and the Spirit of Capitalism* (1930).

12 Mark Jackson, *New-Born Child Murder* (1996), pp. 46f.

13 Thomas Robert Malthus, *An Essay on the Principle of Population as it Affects the Future Improvement of Society* (1798). See also chapters 17 and 20.

14 Julian Hoppit, 'Political Arithmetic in Eighteenth-century England' (1996).

15 Ulrich Tröhler, 'Quantification in British Medicine and Surgery 1750–1830' [1978];

James C. Riley, *Sickness, Recovery and Death* (1989).

16 G. Miller, *The Adoption of Inoculation for Smallpox in England and France* (1957); Andrea Rusnock, *The Correspondence of James Jurin (1684–1750)* (1996).

17 I. Hacking, *The Taming of Chance* (1990); Lorraine J. Daston, *Classical Probability in the Enlightenment* (1988), and 'The Domestication of Risk' (1987); Tore Frängsmyr, J. L. Heilbron, Robin E. Rider (eds), *The Quantifying Spirit in the Eighteenth Century* (1990); Geoffrey Clark, *Betting on Lives* (1999).

18 Christopher Fox, Roy Porter and Robert Wokler (eds), *Inventing Human Science* (1995); Richard Olson, *Science Deified and Science Defied* (1990), vol. ii, and *The Emergence of the Social Sciences, 1642–1792* (1993).

19 For press support for inoculation, see C. Y. Ferdinand, *Benjamin Collins and the Provincial Newspaper Trade in the Eighteenth Century* (1997), p. 157; see also Simon Schaffer, 'A Social History of Plausibility' (1993).

20 C. Bruyn Andrews (ed.), *The Torrington Diaries* (1954 [1781–94]), vol. ii, p. 120; Clark, *Betting on Lives*. For the roles of knowledge, data and quantification in conceptualizing a more regulated world, see Peter L. Bernstein, *Against the Gods* (1996); Siegfried Giedion, *Mechanization Takes Command* (1948); Roy Porter, 'Accidents in the Eighteenth Century' (1996).

21 Cecil Henry L'Estrange Ewen, *Lotteries and Sweepstakes* (1932). The elimination of lotteries – for defying Providence – was central to the Evangelical platform: Ford K. Brown, *Fathers of the Victorians* (1961), p. 107.

22 James Kelly, *That Damned Thing Called Honour* (1995); V. G. Kiernan, *The Duel in European History* (1989).

23 William Cadogan thus justified his *Essay upon Nursing, and the Management of Children* (1748): 'this business has been too long fatally left to the management of women, who cannot be supposed to have proper knowledge to fit them for such a task' (p. 3).

See the discussion in Adrian Wilson, *The Making of Man-Midwifery* (1995).

24 V. Fildes, *Breasts, Bottles and Babies* (1986), and *Wetnursing* (1988).

25 C. Hardyment, *Dream Babies* (1983).

26 'When I think of dying, it is always without pain or fear': Desmond King-Hele (ed.), *The Letters of Erasmus Darwin* (1981), p. 279, letter 95E, to Richard Lovell Edgeworth (15 March 1795).

27 Hume retained to the end the capacity to madden Boswell. See the account of their final meeting in Boswell's journal (3 March 1777) in Charles M. Weis and Frederick A. Pottle (eds.), *Boswell in Extremes, 1776–1778* (1971), pp. 11–15, especially p. 11: 'He [Hume] then said flatly that the Morality of every Religion was bad, and I really thought, was not jocular when he said that when he heard a man was religious, he concluded he was a rascal.' The pious Christian Boswell was also disappointed when he attended the deathbed of Lord Kames:

'I said the doctrine of eternity of Hell's torments did harm'. 'No', said he. 'Nobody believes it'. I could make nothing of him tonight.

Ian Simpson Ross, *Lord Kames and the Scotland of His Day* (1972), p. 370.

28 Philippe Ariès, *L'homme devant la mort* (1977). Ariès felt repugnance towards Enlightenment rituals of dying; for alternative views, see Nigel Llewellyn, *The Art of Death* (1991); John McManners, *Death and the Enlightenment* (1981); Roy Porter, 'Death and the Doctors in Georgian England' (1989).

29 See Warren Chernaik, *Sexual Freedom in Restoration Literature* (1995), p. 8.

30 See Gibbon's comment:

In old age, the consolation of hope is reserved for the tenderness of parents, who commence a new life in their children; the faith of enthusiasts who sing Hallelujahs above the clouds, and the vanity of authors who presume the immortality of their name and writings.

Edward Gibbon, *Memoirs of My Life* (1966 [1796]), p. 188.

31 See Alan Bewell, *Wordsworth and the Enlightenment* (1989), p. 215. Compare Locke's demystification of darkness.

32 Ralph A. Houlbrooke, *Death, Religion and the Family in England, 1480–1750* (1998), pp. 329–30.

33 C. J. Lawrence, 'William Buchan: Medicine Laid Open' (1975); Roy Porter, 'Spreading Medical Enlightenment' (1992).

34 W. Buchan, *Observations concerning the Prevention and Cure of the Venereal Disease* (1796), p. xxii.

35 Buchan, *Observations concerning the Prevention and Cure of the Venereal Disease*, p. xxvi, quoting Benjamin Rush, *An Account of the Bilious Remitting Yellow Fever* (1794).

36 Buchan, *Domestic Medicine* (1769), p. 730. People might look dead but be recoverable: see pp. 730–58.

37 Buchan, *Domestic Medicine*.

38 Roy Porter, *Doctor of Society* (1991), throughout.

39 Thomas Beddoes, *Hygëia* (1802–3), vol. ii, essay vi, p. 46.

40 Roy Porter, 'Civilization and Disease' (1991).

41 Charles F. Bahmueller, *The National Charity Company* (1981), p. 7; see discussion in David Lieberman, *The Province of Legislation Determined* (1989), p. 211.

42 A key theme of V. A. C. Gatrell, *The Hanging Tree* (1994).

43 Bahmueller, *The National Charity Company*, p. 6. See below chapters 16 and 18.

44 Robert Poole, ' "Give Us Our Eleven Days!" ' (1995).

45 Paul Langford, *A Polite and Commercial People* (1989), p. 300.

46 S. I. Tucker, *Protean Shape* (1967), esp. pp. 33–48.

47 *Gentleman's Magazine* no. 58 (1788), p. 947, discussed in Penelope J. Corfield (ed.), *Language, History and Class* (1991), p. 102. The suggestion was originally Addison's.

48 Robert DeMaria Jr, *Johnson's Dictionary and the Language of Learning* (1986), p. 6; John Barrell, *English Literature in History, 1730–80* (1983), pp. 149–50; Carey McIntosh, *The Evolution of English Prose, 1700–1800* (1999), discusses the gentrification, standardization and codification of the language. Radical language reform schemes are mentioned in chapter 20; theories of language are discussed in chapter 10.

In the preface to his *Dictionary*, Johnson opposed the formation of an English academy for the improvement of the language because he could 'never wish to see dependence multiplied' (para. 90), being proud that he completed his book 'without any patronage of the great' (para. 94). See the discussion in Barrell, *English Literature in History, 1730–80*, ch. 9. Defoe favoured an English academy partly to encourage learning, partly to stabilize the language – see James T. Boulton (ed.), *Selected Writings of Daniel Defoe* (1975), p. 29.

49 Jeremy Black, introduction to Jeremy Black and Jeremy Gregory (eds), *Culture, Politics and Society in Britain, 1660–1800* (1991), pp. 5–6.

50 Thomas Sheridan, *British Education* (sn, 1756), pp. 241–2, quoted in John Brewer, *The Pleasures of the Imagination* (1997), p. 475.

51 William Hogarth, *The Analysis of Beauty* (1753), title page; see the discussion in Ronald Paulson, *Hogarth, The 'Modern Moral Subject'* (1992–3), vol. iii, pp. 56–151.

52 D. V. Glass, *Numbering the People* (1973).

53 N. Robinson, *A New System of the Spleen* (1729), p. 174; see Akihito Suzuki, 'An Anti-Lockean Enlightenment?' (1994), and 'Mind and Its Disease in Enlightenment British Medicine' [1992]; and more broadly, Roy Porter, *Mind Forg'd Manacles* (1987).

54 Jonathan Andrews, Asa Briggs, Roy Porter, Penny Tucker and Keir Waddington, *The History of Bethlem* (1997); Michel Foucault, *La Folie et la Déraison* (1961); Andrew Scull, *The Most Solitary of Afflictions* (1993).

55 Alexander Crichton, *An Inquiry into the Nature and Origin of Mental Derangement* (1798), quoted in Richard Hunter and Ida Macalpine, *Three Hundred Years of Psychiatry* (1963), p. 559; thus, to refer back to the discussion in chapter 7, in the emerging field of psychiatry too, Christian pneumatology was being elbowed aside by a naturalistic 'psychology'.

56 William Battie, *A Treatise on Madness* (1758), and John Monro, *Remarks on Dr Battie's Treatise on Madness* (1962 [1758]), pp. 61–2. Battie drew on Locke's psychology, not least his distinction between idiots and the insane:

In fine, the defect in *naturals* seems to proceed from want of quickness, activity, and motion in the intellectual Faculties, whereby they are deprived of Reason: whereas *mad Men*, on the other side seem to suffer by the other Extreme. For they do not appear to me to have lost the Faculty of Reasoning: but having joined together some *Ideas* very wrongly, they mistake them for Truths; and they err as men do, that argue right from wrong Principles.

John Locke, *An Essay concerning Human Understanding* (1975 [1690]), bk II, ch. 11, pp. 160–61.

57 Thomas Arnold, *Observations on the Nature, Kinds, Causes and Prevention of Insanity* (1782–6), vol. ii, p. 432.

58 Erasmus Darwin, *Zoonomia* (1794–6), bk IV, pp. 83–4.

59 C. Hibbert (ed.), *An American in Regency England* (1968), p. 109; Samuel Tuke, *Description of the Retreat* (1813).

60 For what follows, see Michael MacDonald, 'The Secularization of Suicide in England, 1600–1800' (1986); Michael MacDonald and Terence R. Murphy, *Sleepless Souls* (1990); S. E. Sprott, *The English Debate on Suicide from Donne to Hume* (1961); R. Bartel, 'Suicide in Eighteenth-century England' (1959); and, for the *longue durée*, Georges Minois, *History of Suicide* (1999).

61 MacDonald and Murphy, *Sleepless Souls*, pp. 180–81.

62 David Hume, *On Suicide* (1741–2), in *Selected Essays* (1993), p. 315.

63 I thought of Chatterton, the marvellous Boy,
   The sleepless Soul that perished in its pride.

William Wordsworth, 'Resolution and Independence' (1802), quoted in MacDonald and Murphy, *Sleepless Souls*, p. 192. Chatterton's suicide was widely interpreted as consequent upon an excess of sensibility: Janet Todd, *Sensibility: An Introduction* (1986), p. 53.

64 Thomas, *Religion and the Decline of Magic*.

65 MacDonald and Murphy, *Sleepless Souls*, p. 323.

66 Alexander Pope, 'Elegy to the Memory of an Unfortunate Lady' (1817), ll. 6–10, in John Butt (ed.), *The Poems of Alexander Pope* (1965), p. 262.

67 Thomas Laqueur, 'Bodies, Details, and Humanitarian Narrative' (1989). For discussion, see above, chapter 12.

68 See generally Thomas, *Religion and the Decline of Magic*.

69 For Priestley on ghosts, see John Towill Rutt (ed.), *The Theological and Miscellaneous Works of Joseph Priestley* (1817–32), vol. iii, p. 50 and vol. iv, pt 1, 'Remarks concerning the Penetrability of Matter'; Simon Schaffer, 'States of Mind' (1990), pp. 241f.

70 For Bentham on ghosts, see John Bowring (ed.), *The Works of Jeremy Bentham* (1995 [1843]), vol. x, pp. 11–21.

71 Porter, *Mind Forg'd Manacles*, pp. 63f.; Stuart Clark, *Thinking with Demons* (1997).

72 Of course it changed elsewhere, too. For France, see Robert Mandrou, *Magistrats et sorciers en France au XVIIe siècle* (1968).

73 Thomas Hobbes, *Leviathan* (1968 [1651]), p. 92. Hobbes was the bogeyman who confirmed the old dictum that denial of witchcraft was the Devil's work.

74 Joseph Addison and Richard Steele, *The Spectator* (1965), vol. i, no. 117, pp. 480–82 (14 July 1711). The following section draws heavily on James Sharpe, *Instruments of Darkness* (1996) and Ian Bostridge, *Witchcraft and Its Transformation, c.1650–c.1750* (1997).

75 Addison and Steele, *The Spectator*, vol. i, no. 117, pp. 480–82 (14 July 1711).

76 Francis Hutchinson, *An Historical Essay concerning Witchcraft* (1718), p. vi. Hutchinson, subsequently bishop of Down and Connor, also wrote a *Short View of the Pretended Spirit of Prophecy* (1708).

77 Hutchinson, *An Historical Essay concerning Witchcraft*, p. viii.

78 See Sharpe, *Instruments of Darkness*, pp. 284–5; R. D. Stock, *The Holy and the Daemonic from Sir Thomas Browne to William Blake* (1982), p. 81.

79 Hutchinson, *An Historical Essay concerning Witchcraft*, pp. 229, 230.

80 Hutchinson, *An Historical Essay concerning Witchcraft*, p. 69.

81 Hutchinson, *An Historical Essay concerning Witchcraft*, p. 63. Note the villain/victim reversal.

82 See Thomas Gordon, *The Humorist*, 3rd edn (1724), pp. 74–7; R. D. Stock, *The Holy and the Daemonic from Sir Thomas Browne to William Blake* (1982), p. 82. For Gordon's politics, see chapter 8 above.

83 Joseph Juxon, *A Sermon upon Witchcraft* (1736), p. 24; Sharpe, *Instruments of Darkness*, pp. 372–4.

84 [Anon.], *A System of Magick* (1727). Like Shaftesbury, the author recommended laughing at such pretenders.

85 [Anon.], *A Discourse on Witchcraft* (1736), ch. 3, p. 6. Magic and witchcraft originated in 'Heathen Fables'.

86 *Reading Mercury and Oxford Gazette* (15 March 1773). After a ducking, the poor woman was 'happily' saved from a second by a magistrate.

87 *Lloyd's Evening Post* (2 January 1761). Similar newspaper items abound.

88 Hutchinson, *An Historical Essay concerning Witchcraft*, pp. 130–31.

89 Christopher Smart, *The Genuine History of the Good Devil of Woodstock* (1802).

90 K. M. Briggs, *Pale Hecate's Team* (1962); Diane Purkiss, *The Witch in History* (1996), pp. 179–249.

91 Jonathan Keates, *Purcell: A Biography* (1995), pp. 107, 180; Sharpe, *Instruments of Darkness*, p. 291; Stock, *The Holy and the Daemonic from Sir Thomas Browne to William Blake*, pp. 83–4.

92 Ronald Paulson, *Hogarth: His Life, Art and Times* (1974), pp. 404f. See also Maximillian Rudwin, *The Devil in Legend and Literature* (1959); Sharpe, *Instruments of Darkness*, pp. 257–8, 291–2. For Wesley's defence of witchcraft and satanic interventions, see Owen Davies, 'Methodism, the Clergy, and the Popular Belief in Witchcraft and Magic' (1997).

93 W. K. Wimsatt, *Samuel Johnson on Shakespeare* (1960), p. 128.

94 For this new bogeyman/anti-hero, see B. Easlea, *Witch-hunting, Magic and the New Philosophy* (1980), pp. 249–50; Bram Dijkstra, *Idols of Perversity* (1986); David Dabydeen, *Hogarth's Blacks* (1985); Hugh Honour, *The Image of the Black in Western Art* (1989), vol. iv; Luther Link, *The Devil: A Mask without a Face* (1995).

95 For the supernatural in children's literature, see Bruno Bettelheim, *The Uses of Enchantment* (1977); Bette P. Goldstone, *Lessons to be Learned* (1984); Ruth B. Bottigheimer, 'Fairy Tales and Folk-tales' (1996).

96 In Lamb's pseudo-Jacobean drama, *John Woodvil* (1802), one passage, later cancelled, runs:

> I can remember when a child the maids
> Would place me on their lap, as they undrest me,
> As silly women use, and tell me stories
> Of Witches – Make me read 'Glanvil on Witchcraft' . . .

Charles Lamb, 'Witches, and Other Night Fears', *London Magazine* (October 1821), p. 384; Geoffrey Summerfield, *Fantasy and Reason* (1984), pp. 254–62. Lamb's

assumption that children absorb witch beliefs from nurses of course echoes John Locke, who had written 'the Ideas of Goblines and Sprights have really no more to do with Darkness than Light, yet let but a foolish Maid inculcate these often on the Mind of a Child, and . . . he shall never be able to separate them again so long as he lives, but Darkness shall ever afterwards bring with it those frightful Ideas': Locke, *An Essay concerning Human Understanding*, bk II, ch. 33, para. 10, pp. 397–8.

97 Edmund Burke, *Philosophical Enquiry into the Origin of Our Ideas of the Sublime and the Beautiful* (1757). Burke argued that the two strongest instincts known to man were self-preservation and the social impulse. All that directly threatened self-preservation caused terror; and terrifying experiences were the source of the sublime. Our experience of the sublime was far greater in intensity than our experience of beauty. The thrill of the sublime, this 'agreeable horror', depended on one's being able to enjoy danger at a safe distance: see Eagleton, *The Ideology of the Aesthetic*; Hipple, *The Beautiful, the Sublime, and the Picturesque in Eighteenth-century Aesthetic Theory*; Monk, *The Sublime: A Study of Critical Theories in Eighteenth Century England*; Andrew Ashfield and Peter de Bolla (eds), *The Sublime: A Reader in British Eighteenth-century Aesthetic Theory* (1996), pp. 131–43; Tom Furniss, *Edmund Burke's Aesthetic Ideology* (1993); Terry Castle, *The Female Thermometer* (1994). For the sublime, see also chapter 13.

98 Marjorie Hope Nicolson, *Mountain Gloom and Mountain Glory* (1959); M. H. Abrams, *Natural Supernaturalism* (1971), p. 102.

99 Robert Lowth, *Lectures on the Sacred Poetry of the Hebrews* (1787), p. 50.

100 A. Blackwall, *The Sacred Classics Defended and Illustrated* (1725), pp. 250–54; Stock, *The Holy and the Daemonic from Sir Thomas Browne to William Blake*, p. 107.

101 Compare the apocalyptic set pieces in James Thomson's *The Seasons* (1726–30) or

Edward Young's *Night Thoughts* (1742–5): for the biblical narrative aestheticized, see Abrams, *Natural Supernaturalism*, p. 38.

102 Blackwall, *The Sacred Classics Defended and Illustrated*, pp. 277–8. Pandaemonium was staged in West End theatres – what had been religion in Milton had turned into spectacle: R. D. Altick, *The Shows of London* (1978), p. 123; Humphrey Jennings, *Pandaemonium 1660–1886* (1985).

103 James Usher, *Clio*, 2nd edn (1769), pp. 101, 103, 107–9, 116, 237–40; Stock, *The Holy and the Daemonic from Sir Thomas Browne to William Blake*, pp. 107–8.

104 Castle, *The Female Thermometer*, p. 120; see also E. J. Clery, *The Rise of Supernatural Fiction* (1995), esp. pp. 172f.; Chris Baldick, *In Frankenstein's Shadow* (1987); Stephen Bann (ed.), *Frankenstein, Creation and Monstrosity* (1994); David Punter, *The Literature of Terror* (1980); Christopher Frayling, *Nightmare, The Birth of Horror* (1996).

105 N. Powell, *Fuseli's 'The Nightmare'* (1956).

106 T. E. Hulme, 'Romanticism and Classicism' (1936 [1923]), p. 118. For Blake as visionary, see David V. Erdman, *Blake, Prophet against Empire* (1954).

107 Christopher Hill, *The English Bible and the Seventeenth-century Revolution* (1993), illuminates the demotion of the Bible after the Restoration, along with Antichrist and millennialism. See also his *Antichrist in Seventeenth-century England* (1971); for the persistence of such themes, see John Fletcher Clews Harrison, *The Second Coming* (1979).

108 David Nokes, *Jonathan Swift: A Hypocrite Reversed* (1985). This, of course, brings to mind Carl Becker's celebrated critique: *The Heavenly City of the Eighteenth-century Philosophers* (1932).

109 Quoted in Schaffer, 'States of Mind', p. 247; Mary P. Mack, *Jeremy Bentham, An Odyssey of Ideas, 1748–1792* (1962), p. 337.

110 Mack, *Jeremy Bentham, An Odyssey of Ideas, 1748–1792*, p. 370.

111 John Neville Figgis, *The Divine Right of Kings* (1965); Raymond Henry Payne Crawfurd, *The King's Evil* (1977 [1911]); Marc Bloch, *The Royal Touch* (1973).

112 Lorraine Daston and Katharine Park, *Wonders and the Order of Nature 1150–1750* (1988); Roger Shattuck, *Forbidden Knowledge* (1996).

113 Daniel Defoe, *A System of Magic* (1727).

114 Discussed in Langford, *A Polite and Commercial People*, p. 285.

115 For continuing absorption in the supernatural, see Schaffer, 'A Social History of Plausibility'; and for fascination with freaks, see Dennis Todd, *Imagining Monsters* (1995).

116 Daston and Park, *Wonders and the Order of Nature 1150–1750*.

117 Katherine C. Balderston (ed.), *Thraliana: The Diary of Mrs Hester Lynch Thrale 1776–1809* (1942), vol. ii, p. 786; see also, for the marginalization of occult beliefs, Simon Schaffer, 'Newton's Comets and the Transformation of Astrology' (1987); Kevin C. Knox, 'Lunatick Visions' (1999).

10 MODERNIZING

1 George Birkbeck Hill, *Boswell's Life of Johnson* (1934–50), vol. ii, p. 365.

2 Sidney Pollard, *The Idea of Progress* (1968); Robert Nisbet, *History of the Idea of Progress* (1980); D. Spadafora, *The Idea of Progress in Eighteenth-century Britain* (1990).

3 David Hume, 'Of the Study of History' (1741), in *Essays Moral, Political and Literary* (1898 [1741–2]), vol. ii, p. 389. For a discussion of David Hume as historian, see J. G. A. Pocock, *Barbarism and Religion* (1999), vol. ii, sect. 3.

4 Christopher Hill, *The English Bible and the 17th-Century Revolution* (1993), p. 427.

5 Pocock, *Barbarism and Religion*, vol. ii, p. 210.

6 Edward Gibbon, *The History of the Decline and Fall of the Roman Empire* (1994 [1776]), vol. i, ch. 15, p. 446:

The theologian may indulge the pleasing task of describing Religion as she descended from heaven, arrayed in her native purity. A more melancholy duty is imposed on the historian. He must discover the inevitable mixture of error and corruption which she contracted in a long residence upon earth, among a weak and degenerate race of beings.

See Pocock, *Barbarism and Religion*.

7 For Pope, Thomas Hearne the Oxford antiquarian was the prototype dunce:

But who is he, in closet close y-pent,
Of sober face, with learned dust besprent?
Right well mine eyes arede the myster wight,
On parchment scraps y-fed, and Wormius hight.

Alexander Pope, *The Dunciad* (1728), bk III, ll. 185–9, in John Butt (ed.), *The Poems of Alexander Pope* (1965), p. 758. In true enlightened fashion, Hearne was pictured shut off from the world, neglecting life in indiscriminate fascination with bits of paper.

8 Edwin Jones, *The English Nation* (1998), pp. 70f.

9 Quoted in Jones, *The English Nation*, p. 154; see also Spadafora, *The Idea of Progress in Eighteenth-century Britain*, p. 223.

10 Hume, 'Of the Study of History', in *Essays Moral, Political and Literary*, vol. ii, p. 389.

11 Hume, 'Of the Study of History', in *Essays Moral, Political and Literary*, vol. ii, p. 389. According to Lord Monboddo, 'The history of manners is the most valuable. I never set a high value on any other history': reported by James Boswell, in R. W. Chapman (ed.), *Samuel Johnson, A Journey to the Western Islands of Scotland and James Boswell, The Journal of a Tour to the Hebrides* (1970), p. 209.

12 Hume, 'Of the Study of History' in *Essays Moral, Political and Literary*, vol. ii, p. 389. Gilbert Burnet called the Middle Ages 'the Darkness' and referred to its writers as 'that Rubbish'; for Gibbon's similar usage, see Edward Gibbon, *Memoirs of My Life* (1966 [1796]), p. 49.

13 Samuel Johnson was sceptical about 'real authentick history':

JOHNSON: That certain Kings reigned, and certain battles were fought, we can depend upon as true; but all the colouring, all the philosophy of history is conjecture.

BOSWELL: Then, Sir, you would reduce all history to no better than an almanack, a mere chronological series of remarkable events.

Hill, *Boswell's Life of Johnson*, vol. ii, pp. 365–6.

14 See James William Johnson, *The Formation of English Neo-classical Thought* (1967), p. 33.

15 Henry St John, Viscount Bolingbroke, *The Works of Lord Bolingbroke* (1969 [reprint of 1841 edn]), vol. ii, letter 2, p. 183. See J. B. Black, *The Art of History* (1965), pp. 30–31.

16 Karen O'Brien, *Narratives of Enlightenment* (1997), p. 14; Laird Okie, *Augustan Historical Writing* (1992), p. 48. For the theme of escape, see above, chapter 3.

17 Generally, for what follows, see Burton Feldman and Robert D. Richardson, *The Rise of Modern Mythology* (1973).

18 Samuel Shuckford, *The Sacred and Profane History of the World Connected* (1728); Peter Harrison, *'Religion' and the Religions in the English Enlightenment* (1990), p. 143.

19 See, for discussion, Hans W. Frei, *The Eclipse of Biblical Narrative* (1974); Harrison, *'Religion' and the Religions in the English Enlightenment*, p. 148.

20 William Warburton, *The Divine Legation of Moses Demonstrated* (1738–41); Frei, *The Eclipse of Biblical Narrative*, p. 151.

21 John Toland, *Letters to Serena* (1704), letter 3, p. 71; Feldman and Richardson, *The Rise of Modern Mythology*, p. 27; Stephen H. Daniel, *John Toland: His Methods, Manners, and Mind*

(1984), p. 32. Toland also did a translation of Aesop.

22 Quoted in Daniel, *John Toland: His Methods, Manners and Mind*, p. 32.

23 Daniel, *John Toland: His Methods, Manners, and Mind*, pp. 33–4.

24 Frank E. Manuel, *The Eighteenth Century Confronts the Gods* (1967), p. 15; Feldman and Richardson, *The Rise of Modern Mythology* (1973), pp. 28, 34. Hume's views have already been discussed in chapter 5.

25 Adam Ferguson, *An Essay on the History of Civil Society* (1995 [1767]), pp. 76–7.

26 Ferguson, *An Essay on the History of Civil Society*, p. 77.

27 Ferguson, *An Essay on the History of Civil Society*, p. 77.

28 W. K. Wimsatt, *Samuel Johnson on Shakespeare* (1960), p. 128.

29 Speaking animals were always a challenge. Locke discussed parrots: Peter Walmsley, 'Prince Maurice's Rational Parrot' (1995). From the Greeks onwards, man has been prized as the rational animal, *homo sapiens*, and the clinching proof of that rationality has been articulate speech. The rest of Creation may jabber and bay, bark or bray, howl or mew, or even sing the dawn chorus, but man alone has words, makes sentences, constructs arguments: Allan Ingram, *The Madhouse of Language* (1991).

30 Christopher J. Berry, 'James Dunbar and the Enlightenment Debate on Language' (1987); Stephen K. Land, 'Adam Smith's "Considerations concerning the First Formation of Languages" ' (1977), and *The Philosophy of Language in Britain* (1986).

31 See Hans Aarsleff, *The Study of Language in England, 1780–1860* (1983), and *From Locke to Saussure* (1982).

32 Spadafora, *The Idea of Progress in Eighteenth Century Britain*, p. 360.

33 E. G. Hundert, *The Enlightenment's Fable* (1994), p. 90. John Locke, *The Philosophical Works of John Locke* (1905), vol. ii, p. 8.

34 William Warburton, *The Divine Legation of*

Moses Demonstrated, Part I, bk IV, section 4, in *Works* (1788), vol. ii, p. 83. Part I of the *Divine Legation* was published in 1737, part II in 1741.

35 Warburton, *The Divine Legation of Moses Demonstrated*, part 1, bk IV, section 4, in *Works*, vol. ii, p. 83; see also William Godwin, *An Enquiry concerning Political Justice* (1985 [1793]), p. 158. For the history of such ideas, see Jonathan Rée, *I See a Voice* (1999), pp. 128f.

36 James Burnett, Lord Monboddo, *Of the Origin and Progress of Language* (1773–92; repr. 1970), vol. i, pp. 214–15.

37 Monboddo, *Of the Origin and Progress of Language*, vol. i, p. 574; Berry, 'James Dunbar and the Enlightenment Debate on Language'.

38 E. L. Cloyd, *James Burnett, Lord Monboddo* (1972), pp. 64–89.

39 Such views had their own prehistory, for in 1699 Edward Tyson had published an anatomical comparison of a human being and a great ape which he named *Homo sylvestris*, thus including it within the human genus. As a result, the orang-utan was sometimes called, in English translation, 'wild man of the woods': Robert Wokler, 'From *l'homme physique* to *l'homme moral* and Back' (1993), 'Anthropology and Conjectural History in the Enlightenment' (1995), and 'Apes and Races in the Scottish Enlightenment' (1988).

40 Monboddo, *Of the Origin and Progress of Language*, vol. i, pp. 187–8. Monboddo noted that he had his information from Buffon.

41 Monboddo, *Of the Origin and Progress of Language*, vol. i, p. 257.

42 Monboddo's views were delightfully reworked by Peacock in *Melincourt* (1817), which starred Sir Oran Haut-Ton, Bart, a great ape who successfully passed as a (silent) backbench MP: David Garnett (ed.), *The Novels of Thomas Love Peacock* (1948), pp. 120f.

43 Roy Porter, *The Making of the Science of*

Geology (1977); and for race, see below, chapter 15.

44 Porter, *The Making of the Science of Geology*; P. Rossi, *The Dark Abyss of Time* (1984).

45 T. Goddard Bergin and Max H. Fisch (trans.), *The New Science of Giambattista Vico* (1948 [3rd edn, 1744]).

46 'It is tempting to observe that the Enlightenment was born and organized in those places where the contact between a backward world and a modern one, was chronologically more abrupt, and geographically closer': Franco Venturi, *Utopia and Reform in the Enlightenment* (1971), p. 133. For discussion, see Dorinda Outram, *The Enlightenment* (1995), p. 6.

47 Thomas Schlereth, *The Cosmopolitan Ideal in Enlightenment Thought* (1977).

48 Linda Colley, 'Britishness and Otherness' (1992); Gerald Newman, *The Rise of English Nationalism* (1987) – a work strong on the covert history of English nationalism. There is no room to explore here the complex interactions between England, Scotland, Wales and Ireland in the eighteenth century: see Hugh Kearney, *The British Isles* (1989); Jeremy Black, *The Politics of Britain, 1688–1800* (1993); Norman Davies, *The Isles* (1999).

49 A good instance lies in Adam Smith's review in the first *Edinburgh Review* (1755): see the discussion below.

50 Hill, *Boswell's Life of Johnson*, vol. ii, p. 50.

51 David Nokes, *Jonathan Swift: A Hypocrite Reversed* (1985), p. 111; Joseph McMinn, *Jonathan's Travels* (1994).

52 On Wales, see Gwyn Williams, 'Romanticism In Wales' (1988); Peter D. G. Thomas, *Politics in Eighteenth-century Wales* (1998); Geraint H. Jenkins, *The Foundations of Modern Wales: 1642–1780* (1987); D. Moore (ed.), *Wales in the Eighteenth Century* (1976); Philip Jenkins, *The Making of a Ruling Class* (1983). Peacock wrote:

Harry Headlong, Esquire, was, like all other Welsh squires, fond of shooting, hunting, racing, drinking, and other such innocent amusements . . . But, unlike other Welsh squires, he had actually suffered certain phenomena, called books, to find their way into his house.

Headlong Hall (1816), in Garnett, *The Novels of Thomas Love Peacock*, p. 10. The *Gentleman's Magazine* said in 1747 that Wales was acknowledged 'a dismal region, generally ten months buried in snow and eleven in clouds': quoted in David Pepper, *The Roots of Modern Environmentalism* (1984), p. 80. Insofar as the English thought about Wales at this time, it was largely for the mountains. See Malcolm Andrews, *The Search for the Picturesque* (1989), ch. 6.

53 See Whitney R. D. Jones, *David Williams: The Hammer and the Anvil* (1986).

54 Gwyn Williams, *Madoc: The Making of a Myth* (1979). Welsh Jacobinism was, in the event, small beer. The French who landed in Pembrokeshire were surprised to find themselves met not by enthusiasts but by hostile peasants armed with billhooks, and they surrendered without a shot being fired.

55 Eric Hobsbawm and Terence Ranger (eds), *The Invention of Tradition* (1983). On Druids, see pp. 62–6.

56 For Ireland, see W. E. H. Lecky, *A History of Ireland in the Eighteenth Century* (1972); Constantia Maxwell, *Dublin under the Georges, 1714–1830* (1946); Roy Foster (ed.), *The Oxford Illustrated History of Ireland* (1991); David Dickson, *New Foundations* (1987); Mary Pollard, *Dublin's Trade in Books 1550–1800* (1990); Norman Vance, *Irish Literature: A Social History* (1990).

57 Theobald Wolfe Tone, *An Argument on Behalf of the Catholics of Ireland* (sn, 1791); see Stella Tillyard, *Citizen Lord* (1997); Foster, *The Oxford Illustrated History of Ireland*, pp. 180–84. See below, chapter 20.

58 For general developments, see T. C. Smout, *A History of the Scottish People, 1560–1830* (1969); Charles Camic, *Experience And*

Enlightenment (1983); R. A. Houston, *Social Change in the Age of Enlightenment* (1994); T. M. Devine, *The Scottish Nation, 1700–2000* (1999), pp. 64f.

59 On the universities, see George Davie, *The Democratic Intellect* (1961); Margaret Forbes, *Beattie and His Friends* (1904); Richard Sher, *Church and University in the Scottish Enlightenment* (1985); Roger L. Emerson, *Professors, Patronage and Politics* (1992); Paul B. Wood, *The Aberdeen Enlightenment* (1993). For the literary tradition, see David Craig, *Scottish Literature and the Scottish People 1680–1830* (1961).

60 For the important new idea of 'civil society', see Marvin B. Becker, *The Emergence of Civil Society in the Eighteenth Century* (1994); John Dwyer, *Virtuous Discourse* (1987).

61 There is a balanced discussion in David Allan, *Virtue, Learning and the Scottish Enlightenment* (1993), p. 18. For the Scottish Enlightenment in general, see Anand C. Chitnis, *The Scottish Enlightenment: A Social History* (1976), and *The Scottish Enlightenment and Early Victorian Society* (1986); Alexander Broadie (ed.), *The Scottish Enlightenment: An Anthology* (1997); Christopher J. Berry, *Social Theory of the Scottish Enlightenment* (1997); David Daiches, *The Scottish Enlightenment* (1986); Nicholas Phillipson, 'The Scottish Enlightenment' (1981), 'Towards a Definition of the Scottish Enlightenment' (1973), and 'Culture and Society in the Eighteenth Century Province' (1974); Nicholas Phillipson and Rosalind Mitchison (eds.), *Scotland in the Age of Improvement* (1970); R. H. Campbell and Andrew S. Skinner (eds.), *The Origins and Nature of the Scottish Enlightenment* (1982); Jane Rendall, *The Origins of the Scottish Enlightenment* (1978).

62 A. Allardyce (ed.), *Scotland and Scotsmen in the Eighteenth Century, from the MSS of John Ramsay* (1888), vol. i, pp. 6–7, quoted in Allan, *Virtue, Learning and the Scottish Enlightenment*, p. 18. 'It is well known that between 1723 and 1740 . . . [the] writings of

Locke and Clarke, of Butler and Berkeley, presented a wide and interesting field of inquiry': John Ramsay of Ochtertyre, quoted in Ian Simpson Ross, *Lord Kames and the Scotland of His Day* (1972), p. 60.

63 Quoted by Hugh Trevor-Roper, 'The Scottish Enlightenment' (1967), p. 1649, from Dugald Stewart, *The Collected Works of Dugald Stewart* (1854–60), vol. i, p. 551. Trevor-Roper himself subscribes to the Victorian view that the Scottish Enlightenment should largely be seen as a massive rejection of traditional Calvinism.

64 Janet Adam Smith, 'Some Eighteenth-century Ideas of Scotland' (1970), p. 108.

65 John B. Stewart, *Opinion and Reform in Hume's Political Philosophy* (1992), p. 234.

66 J. Y. T. Greig (ed.), *The Letters of David Hume* (1932), vol. ii, p. 310.

67 Angus Calder, *Revolutionary Empire* (1981), p. 534; Smith, 'Some Eighteenth-century Ideas of Scotland', p. 108.

68 Quoted in Chitnis, *The Scottish Enlightenment: A Social History*, p. 12. Hume, of course, did not think it was one bit strange, exclaiming: 'This is the historical age and we are the historical people': see the discussion in David Daiches, *Robert Burns* (1952), p. 2.

69 Forbes, *Beattie and His Friends*; Selwyn Alfred Grave, *The Scottish Philosophy of Common Sense* (1960).

70 John Robertson (ed.), *A Union for Empire* (1995).

71 See, for instance, Devine, *The Scottish Nation, 1700–2000*, pp. 105–23.

72 Chapman, *Samuel Johnson, A Journey to the Western Islands of Scotland and James Boswell, The Journal of a Tour to the Hebrides*, p. 51; see Claire Lamont, 'Dr Johnson, the Scottish Highlander, and the Scottish Enlightenment' (1989).

73 Michael Hunter, 'Aikenhead The Atheist' (1992).

74 Kames denied the reality of free will while claiming God had given man the illusion of it: Henry Home, Lord Kames, *Essays on the Principles of Morality and Natural Religion* (1751), p. 147. He later abandoned the doctrine of the fallacious sense of liberty and became a frank necessitarian. See Ross, *Lord Kames and the Scotland of His Day*, p. 152; Stewart, *Opinion and Reform in Hume's Political Philosophy*, p. 13; Gladys Bryson, *Man and Society* (1968), p. 54.

75 On the Moderates, see Sher, *Church and University in the Scottish Enlightenment*; Ian D. L. Clark, 'From Protest to Reaction' (1970).

76 Brian Hepworth, *The Rise of Romanticism* (1978), p. 233; Dwyer, *Virtuous Discourse*, p. 20.

77 For Robertson as historian, see Pocock, *Barbarism and Religion*, vol. ii, section 4.

78 Dwyer, *Virtuous Discourse*, p. 12. Approximately the same circulation as an English provincial newspaper.

79 David Dunbar McElroy, *Scotland's Age of Improvement* (1969); Dwyer, *Virtuous Discourse*, p. 26; Ross, *Lord Kames and the Scotland of his Day*, p. 67.

80 'Of Luxury' (1741–2), later retitled 'Of Refinement in the Arts', in David Hume, *Selected Essays* (1993), p. 169: see Christopher J. Berry, *The Idea of Luxury* (1994), p. 143.

81 John Clive, 'The Social Background of the Scottish Renaissance' (1970), p. 227; Houston, *Social Change in the Age of Enlightenment*.

82 Peter Jones, 'The Scottish Professoriate and the Polite Academy' (1983).

83 Adam Smith in the *Edinburgh Review*, quoted in Ross, *Lord Kames and the Scotland of His Day*, p. 177. The *Review* spoke of Scotland as being 'in a state of early youth, guided and supported by the more mature strength of her kindred country': see the discussion in Daiches, *Robert Burns*, p. 28.

84 Craig, *Scottish Literature and the Scottish People 1680–1830*, p. 52.

85 Ferguson, *An Essay on the History of Civil Society*, p. 97; David Kettler, *The Social and Political Thought of Adam Ferguson* (1965); William C. Lehmann, *Adam Ferguson and the Beginnings of Modern Sociology* (1930). See also

Pocock, *Barbarism and Religion*, vol. ii, section 6. Ferguson is discussed further in chapter 17.

86 Berry, *Social Theory of the Scottish Enlightenment*, ch. 3.

87 See Istvan Hont and Michael Ignatieff (eds), *Wealth and Virtue* (1983); Knud Haakonssen, *Natural Law and Moral Philosophy* (1996). For Smith's *Wealth of Nations*, see chapter 17.

88 A key figure in the neo-Harringtonian lineage, Fletcher had argued in the immediate pre-Union years the cause of a Scottish form of civic virtue, to be preserved by safeguarding an autonomous parliament and militia: Robertson (ed.), *A Union for Empire*, and *Andrew Fletcher: Political Works* (1997).

89 For a general discussion of Hume and politics, see above, chapter 8. For the proverbial Sparta, see Elizabeth Rawson, *The Spartan Tradition in European Thought* (1969); Berry, *The Idea of Luxury*. For Hume's undermining of traditional Scottish patriotic history, see Colin Kidd, *Subverting Scotland's Past* (1993), ch. 9.

90 David Hume, *A Treatise of Human Nature* (1978 [1739–40]), p. 273; Peter Jones (ed.), *The 'Science' of Man in the Scottish Enlightenment* (1989), and (ed.), *Philosophy and Science in the Scottish Enlightenment* (1988). The discussion following takes elements of the broad account of Hume's case for modernization, already set out in chapter 8, and applies them specifically to the Scottish debate.

91 Hume, 'Of Refinement in the Arts', in *Selected Essays*, p. 169.

92 Hume, 'Of Commerce' (1741–2), in *Selected Essays*, p. 157.

93 Hume, 'Of Commerce', in *Selected Essays*, p. 161.

94 Hume, 'Of Refinement in the Arts', in *Selected Essays*, p. 170; cf. Berry, *The Idea of Luxury*, pp. 144–5.

95 Hume, 'Of Commerce', in *Selected Essays*, p. 163.

96 Hume, 'Of Refinement in the Arts', in *Selected Essays*, p. 175.

97 Hume, 'Of Refinement in the Arts', in *Selected Essays*, p. 176.

98 Hume, 'Of the Standard of Taste' (1741–2), in *Selected Essays*, pp. 133–54.

99 Hume, 'Of Refinement in the Arts', in *Selected Essays*, p. 169.

100 Hume, 'Of Refinement in the Arts', in *Selected Essays*, p. 170.

101 Albert O. Hirschman, *The Passions and the Interests* (1977), p. 60; Pocock, *Barbarism and Religion*, p. 331; see Montesquieu, *The Spirit of Laws* (1750 [1748]), bk XX, ch. 1.

102 Hume, 'Of Refinement in the Arts', in *Selected Essays*, p. 172.

103 Hume, 'Of Commerce', in *Selected Essays*, pp. 157f.

104 Hume, 'Of the Populousness of Ancient Nations' (1741–2), in *Selected Essays*, pp. 223–274, and 'Of Commerce' in *Selected Essays*, p. 157.

105 Hume, 'Of Commerce', in *Selected Essays*, p. 159.

106 Hume, 'Of Commerce', in *Selected Essays*, p. 162.

107 Hume, *A Treatise of Human Nature*, pp. 487–8.

108 Hume, 'Of Commerce', in *Selected Essays*, p. 160.

109 Hume, 'Of Civil Liberty' (1758 [1741]), in *Selected Essays*, p. 56.

110 Hume, 'Of Interest' (1741–2), in *Selected Essays*, p. 180.

111 Hume, 'Of the Rise and Progress of Arts and Sciences' (1741–2), in *Selected Essays*, p. 67.

112 Hume, *A Treatise of Human Nature*, pp. xx–xxi.

113 Hume, 'Of Commerce', in *Selected Essays*, p. 157.

114 Hume, 'Of Refinement in the Arts', in *Selected Essays*, p. 174.

115 Hume, *A Treatise of Human Nature*, pp. 417, 437.

116 Hume, 'Of Commerce', in *Selected Essays*, pp. 154–67.

117 Hume, 'Of Commerce', in *Selected Essays*, p. 160.

118 For Kames, see Henry Home, Lord Kames, *Sketches of the History of Man* (1774); Ross, *Lord Kames and the Scotland of His Day*; William C. Lehmann, *Henry Home, Lord Kames, and the Scottish Enlightenment* (1971); for the law, see David Lieberman, 'The Legal Needs of a Commercial Society' (1983), and *The Province of Legislation Determined* (1989); Alan Bewell, *Wordsworth and the Enlightenment* (1989), p. 15.

Another subscriber to similar stadial notions was the historian William Robertson. As he put it in his *The History of America* (1777), 'In every inquiry concerning the operations of men when united together in society, the first object of attention should be their mode of subsistence. Accordingly as that varies, their laws and policy must be different': Ronald L. Meek, *Social Science and the Ignoble Savage* (1975), p. 2; see also Karen O'Brien, 'Between Enlightenment and Stadial Theory' (1994); Ronald L. Meek, 'Smith, Turgot and the Four Stages Theory' (1971); Berry, *Social Theory of the Scottish Enlightenment*, ch. 5.

119 Chitnis, *The Scottish Enlightenment: A Social History*, p. 101. Kames's enlightened optimism about human nature was attacked by Samuel Johnson. Of the *Sketches of the History of Man* (1774), Johnson observed:

> in this book it is maintained that virtue is natural to man, and that if we would but consult our own hearts we should be virtuous. Now after consulting our own hearts all we can, and with all the helps we have, we find how few of us are virtuous. This is saying a thing which all mankind know not to be true.

Hill, *Boswell's Life of Johnson*, vol. iii, p. 353.

120 Quoted in Lieberman, *The Province of Legislation Determined*, p. 149.

121 Henry Home, Lord Kames, *Historical*

Law Tracts, 3rd edn (1776), vol. i, pp. 30–31; Chitnis, *The Scottish Enlightenment: A Social History*, p. 101; Meek, *Social Science and the Ignoble Savage*, p. 102.

122 Ross, *Lord Kames and the Scotland of His Day*, p. 208.

123 Kames, *Historical Law Tracts*, vol. i, p. 77.

124 Kames, *Historical Law Tracts*, vol. i, p. 78.

125 Allan, *Virtue, Learning and the Scottish Enlightenment*, p. 163.

126 Pocock, *Barbarism and Religion*, vol. ii, p. 320.

127 Adam Smith, *Lectures on Justice, Police Revenue and Arms*, ed. Edwin Cannan (Oxford: Clarendon Press, 1896), pp. 107–8, quoted in Chitnis, *The Scottish Enlightenment: A Social History*, p. 104. Wordsworth was later to grumble: 'A Scotch Professor cannot write three minutes together upon the Nature of Man, but he must be dabbling with his savage state, with his agricultural state, his Hunter state &c &c': Bewell, *Wordsworth and the Enlightenment*, p. 30.

Stadial theories were also satirized by Peacock. In *Crotchet Castle* (1831), Mr MacQuedy is the great exponent:

MR MACQUEDY: Nothing is so easy as to lay down the outlines of perfect society . . . (*Producing a large scroll.*) 'In the infancy of society – '

THE REV. DR FOLLIOTT: Pray, Mr MacQuedy, how is it that all gentlemen of your nation begin every thing they write with the 'infancy of society'?

MR MACQUEDY: Eh, sir, it is the simplest way to begin at the beginning. 'In the infancy of society, when government was invented to save a percentage; say two and a half per cent – '

Garnett, *The Novels of Thomas Love Peacock*, p. 686.

128 Smith, *An Inquiry into the Nature and Causes of the Wealth of Nations*, vol. ii, bk V, ch. 1, p. 715, quoted in Chitnis, *The Scottish Enlightenment: A Social History*, p. 104. Smith's views are analysed more fully below in chapter 17.

129 William C. Lehmann, *John Millar of*

Glasgow, 1735–1801 (1960), p. 326. For Millar, see the discussion in Michael Ignatieff, 'John Millar and Individualism' (1983), and in general Lehmann, *John Millar of Glasgow, 1735–1801*.

130 Lehmann, *John Millar of Glasgow, 1735–1801*, p. 125.

131 Quoted in Chitnis, *The Scottish Enlightenment: A Social History*, pp. 100–101. See also Lehmann, *John Millar of Glasgow, 1735–1801*, p. 125.

132 John Millar, *Observations concerning the Distinction of Ranks in Society* (1771), p. 4.

133 Millar, *Observations concerning the Distinction of Ranks in Society*, p. 3. Scotland did not have a monopoly on stadial theories; they were for instance deployed by Gibbon: see discussion in J. G. A. Pocock, 'Clergy and Commerce' (1985). There was less urgency, however, in the task of applying such theories to explain English history (which was less of an enigma).

134 Stewart, *The Collected Works of Dugald Stewart*, vol. x, pp. 32–4, 37; Bryson, *Man and Society*, p. 87; H. M. Höpfl, 'From Savage to Scotsman' (1978); Wokler, 'Anthropology and Conjectural History in the Enlightenment' (1995). For another aspect of Stewart, see S. Rashid, 'Dugald Stewart, Baconian Methodology and Political Economy' (1985); Stewart, *The Collected Works of Dugald Stewart*, vol. x, pp. 32–4, 37. Stewart was himself a great luminary, as witness Lord John Russell's tribute (1812):

> To nearer worlds the source of life and light,
> To further orbs a guide amid the night
> Each sun, effulgent, fills its radiant throne,
> Gilds other systems, and preserves his own;
> Thus we mark Stewart on his fame reclined,
> Enlighten all the Universe of Mind.

Quoted in Chitnis, *The Scottish Enlightenment and Early Victorian Society*, p. 21.

135 Millar, *Observations concerning the Distinction of Ranks in Society*, pp. 94–5. Women, judged Hume and Millar, were a 'school of

manners'. Compare the views of William Alexander on women and society discussed in chapter 14. See also Berry, *Social Theory of the Scottish Enlightenment*, p. 109.
136 John S. Gibson, 'How Did the Enlightenment Seem to the Edinburgh Enlightened?' (1978); Istvan Hont, 'The "Rich Country–Poor Country" Debate in Scottish Classical Political Economy' (1985).
137 Bryson, *Man and Society*, p. 31; Adam Ferguson, *Institutes of Moral Philosophy, for the Use of Students in the College of Edinburgh*, 2nd edn (1773); Bewell, *Wordsworth and the Enlightenment*, pp. 14–15.

11 HAPPINESS

1 Quoted in Iain Pears, *The Discovery of Painting* (1988), p. 21.
2 Alexander Pope, *An Essay on Man* (1733–4), epistle IV, ll. 1–2, in John Butt (ed.), *The Poems of Alexander Pope* (1965), p. 536.
3 Cited in Mary P. Mack, *Jeremy Bentham, An Odyssey of Ideas, 1748–1792* (1962), pp. 204.
4 H. Digby Beste, *Personal and Literary Memorials* (1829), p. 209. I owe this quotation to Michael Neve.
5 For the Greeks, see A. W. H. Adkins, *From the Many to the One* (1970); H. North, *Sophrosyne* (1966); Peter Quennell, *The Pursuit of Happiness* (1988), pp. 167–9.
6 For Renaissance attitudes, see Herschel Baker, *The Dignity of Man* (1947); J. B. Bamborough, *The Little World of Man* (1952); W. Kaiser, *Praisers of Folly* (1963); M. M. Bakhtin, *Rabelais and His World* (1968).
7 Raymond Williams, *The Country and the City* (1973), pp. 35–45; Kevin Sharpe, *Criticism and Compliment* (1987).
8 See Alasdair MacIntyre, *A Short History of Ethics* (1966); Peter Brown, *The World of Late Antiquity* (1971). Even Christian theology, Bentham later noted, did not fundamentally decry happiness; that was to be attained, however, only upon the heavenly reunion of the soul with its Maker.
9 For Christianity, see Morton W. Bloomfield, *The Seven Deadly Sins* (1952); Jean Delumeau, *Sin and Fear* (1990); Piero Camporesi, *The Fear of Hell* (1990). For death, see Nigel Llewellyn, *The Art of Death* (1991); Philippe Ariès, *Western Attitudes towards Death* (1976); and John McManners, *Death and the Enlightenment* (1981).

10 Edward Gibbon, *Memoirs of My Life* (1966 [1796]), p. 23. By contrast he thanked fate for his own good fortune:

When I contemplate the common lot of mortality, I must acknowledge that I have drawn a high prize in the lottery of life. The far greater part of the globe is overspread with barbarism or slavery: in the civilized world the most numerous class is condemned to ignorance and poverty; and the double fortune of my birth in a free and enlightened country in an honourable and wealthy family is the lucky chance of an unit against millions. [p. 186.]

11 Samuel Johnson, *The Rambler* (1969), vol. i, no. 32, p. 175 (7 July 1750). For *Rasselas*, see B. Bronson, *Samuel Johnson, Rasselas, Poems and Selected Prose*, 3rd edn (1971).
12 John Tillotson, *The Works of the Most Reverend Dr John Tillotson* (1820), vol. ii, p. 205.
13 George Savile, marquis of Halifax, *The Character of a Trimmer*, 2nd edn (1689), p. 17. Compare Byron's remark: 'I am almost most religious upon a sunshiny day': L. A. Marchand (ed.), *Byron's Letters and Journals* (1973–82), vol. ix, p. 46. For Addison commending 'Chearfulness in Religion', see Joseph Addison and Richard Steele, *The Spectator* (1965), vol. iv, no. 494, pp. 251–4 (26 September 1712).
14 Conflict between the self-interested rational individual and the hierarchical

society forms the premise of James L. Clifford (ed.), *Man versus Society in Eighteenth-century Britain* (1968).

15 John Hedley Brooke, *Science And Religion* (1991); A. O. Lovejoy, *The Great Chain of Being* (1936); Margaret C. Jacob, *The Newtonians and the English Revolution, 1689–1720* (1976).

16 On such environmental views, see C. Glacken, *Traces on the Rhodian Shore* (1967).

17 Richard B. Schwartz, *Samuel Johnson and the Problem of Evil* (1975).

18 William Paley, *Natural Theology* (1802), p. 490; M. L. Clark, *Paley: Evidences for the Man* (1974).

19 Abraham Tucker, *The Light of Nature Pursued* (1768), vol. ii, pt III, ch. 28, pp. 373, 375.

20 Lawrence E. Klein, *Shaftesbury and the Culture of Politeness* (1994). Shaftesbury was echoed by Sterne: Parson Yorick, Tristram tells us, 'had an invincible dislike and opposition in his nature to gravity', being 'mercurial and sublimated': Laurence Sterne, *The Life and Opinions of Tristram Shandy* (1967 [1759–67]), vol. i, ch. 11, p. 55. Sterne himself wrote:

'I have not managed my miseries like a wise man – and if God, for my consolation under them, had not poured forth the spirit of Shandeism into me, which will not suffer me to think two moments upon any grave subject, I would else, just now, lay down and die – die –'

Letter to John Hall-Stevenson (1761), in Lewis P. Curtis (ed.), *Letters of Laurence Sterne* (1935), p. 139.

21 John Darling, 'The Moral Teaching of Francis Hutcheson' (1989).

22 On benevolence, see G. J. Barker-Benfield, *The Culture of Sensibility* (1992).

23 C. B. Macpherson, *The Political Theory of Possessive Individualism* (1962).

24 Roy Porter, 'Medical Science and Human Science in the Enlightenment' (1995).

25

The Wants of the Mind are infinite, Man naturally Aspires and as his Mind is elevated, his Senses grow more refined, and more capable of Delight; his Desires are inlarged, and his Wants increase with his Wishes, which is for every thing that is rare, can gratifie his Senses, adorn his Body and promote the Ease, Pleasure and Pomp of Life.

Nicholas Barbon, *A Discourse of Trade* (1905 [1690]), p. 14, quoted in Christopher J. Berry, *The Idea of Luxury* (1994), p. 112.

For the psychological individualism entailed in such views, see J. O. Lyons, *The Invention of the Self* (1978); Patrick Meyer Spacks, *Imagining a Self* (1976); Charles Taylor, *Sources of the Self* (1989); G. S. Rousseau, 'Psychology' (1980).

26 Adam Smith, *An Inquiry into the Nature and Causes of the Wealth of Nations* (1976 [1776]), bk II, ch. 3, para. 28, p. 341. For further discussion, see below, chapter 17.

27 Quoted in Stephen Copley (ed.), *Literature and the Social Order in Eighteenth-century England* (1984), pp. 121, 115.

28 Gary Hatfield, 'Remaking the Science of the Mind' (1995); David Carrithers, 'The Enlightenment Science of Society' (1995).

29 Locke, *An Essay concerning Human Understanding*, bk I, ch. 2, p. 55, para. 15; J. A. Passmore, 'The Malleability of Man in Eighteenth-century Thought' (1965); G. A. J. Rogers, 'Locke, Anthropology and Models of the Mind' (1993).

30 For Locke's theory of mind and its influence, see John W. Yolton, *John Locke and the Way of Ideas* (1956), and *Thinking Matter* (1983); Kenneth MacLean, *John Locke and English Literature of the Eighteenth Century* (1936).

31 Maurice Cranston, *John Locke: A Biography* (1957), p. 124. See also a Locke manuscript, quoted on p. 123:

It is a man's proper business to seek happiness and avoid misery. Happiness consists in what delights and contents the mind, misery is what disturbs, discomposes or torments it. I will therefore make it my business to seek satisfaction and delight and avoid uneasiness and disquiet and to have as much of the one and as little of the other as may be.

32 For Hartley, see M. E. Webb, 'A New History of Hartley's *Observations on Man*' (1988).
33 Philippa Foot, 'Locke, Hume, and Modern Moral Theory' (1991). Eighteenth-century thinking emphasized the pleasurability of moral acts, as in philanthropy: Betsy Rodgers, *Cloak of Charity* (1949).
34 Charles Strachey (ed.), *The Letters of the Earl of Chesterfield to His Son* (1924), vol. ii, p. 68 (19 July 1750); F. L. Lucas, *The Search for Good Sense* (1958) has a sensible essay on Chesterfield. See also his *The Art of Living* (1959); S. M. Brewer, *Design for a Gentleman* (1963).
35 Henry Fielding, 'An Essay on Conversation' (1972 [1743]), pp. 199, 204.
36 Soame Jenyns, *Free Inquiry into the Nature and Origin of Evil* (1757), p. 46; P. Rompkey, *Soame Jenyns* (1984).
37 See Albert O. Hirschman, *The Passions and the Interests* (1977); J. Viner, *The Role of Providence in the Social Order* (1972); Istvan Hont and Michael Ignatieff (eds), *Wealth and Virtue* (1983); Joyce Oldham Appleby, 'Consumption in Early Modern Social Thought' (1993).
38 For counter-currents reasserting traditional, conservative, Christian thinking, see J. H. Plumb, 'Reason and Unreason in the Eighteenth Century', in *In the Light of History* (1972), pp. 3–24; Maurice J. Quinlan, *Victorian Prelude* (1941); for international comparisons and contrasts, see Robert Mauzi, *L'Idée du bonheur dans la littérature et la pensée française au XVIII siècle* (1960), and, largely for Italy, Piero Camporesi, *Exotic Brew* (1992).
39 In the eighteenth century, Jeremy Bentham of course attempted to do just that – to create a calibration of pleasure. For his felicific calculus, see chapter 18.

40 For Britain as a commercial society generating a 'consumer revolution', see Neil McKendrick, John Brewer and J. H. Plumb, *The Birth of a Consumer Society* (1982). Because the Dutch had created modern pleasures before Britain, they had first to come to terms with their moral dilemmas: see Simon Schama, *The Embarrassment of Riches* (1988).
41 For material culture, see Chandra Mukerji, *From Graven Images* (1983); Alan Macfarlane, *The Culture of Capitalism* (1987).
42 'By this invention,' wrote the first British aeronaut James Tytler, respecting ballooning, in the *Encyclopaedia Britannica*, 'the schemes of transporting people through the atmosphere, formerly though chimerical, are realized; and it is impossible to say how far the art of navigation may be improved, or with what advantages it may be attended.' See C. Gillispie, *The Montgolfier Brothers and the Invention of Aviation 1783–1784* (1983).
43 On aristocratic lifestyles, see David Cannadine, *The Decline and Fall of the British Aristocracy* (1990); J. V. Beckett, *The Aristocracy in England, 1660–1914* (1986); G. E. Mingay, *English Landed Society in the Eighteenth Century* (1963); Lawrence Stone and Jeanne C. Fawtier Stone, *An Open Elite?* (1984). For a collective biography of a pleasure-loving aristocratic family, see Stella Tillyard, *Aristocrats* (1994).
44 Classic is Thorstein Veblen, *The Theory of the Leisure Class* (1912).
45 The pioneer work came from J. H. Plumb, *The Commercialization of Leisure in Eighteenth-century England* (1973); see also J. H. Plumb, *Georgian Delights* (1980).
46 Ronald Hutton, *The Rise and Fall of Merry England* (1994); Nicholas Rogers, *Crowds, Culture and Politics in Georgian Britain* (1998), pp. 24ff.; David Cressy, *Bonfires and Bells* (1989).
47 Mark Girouard, *Life in the English Country House* (1978); Jeremy Black, *The British and the Grand Tour* (1985); Lawrence Stone, 'The Residential Development of the West End of

London in the Seventeenth Century' (1980).

48 R. W. Malcolmson, *Popular Recreations in English Society 1700–1850* (1973); Barry Reay (ed.), *Popular Culture in Seventeenth-century England* (1985), p. 6; Peter Burke, *Popular Culture in Early Modern Europe* (1978); Ronald Hutton, *The Stations of the Sun* (1996), pp. 23f.

49 For cultural performers, see Emmett L. Avery (ed.), *The London Stage 1600–1800* (1968); Paula R. Backscheider, *Spectacular Politics* (1994); and on the commercialization of the visual arts, see Pears, *The Discovery of Painting*; Louise Lippincott, *Selling Art in Georgian London* (1983).

50 Maxine Berg, *The Age of Manufactures, 1700–1820* (1994); Maxine Berg and Helen Clifford (eds), *Consumers and Luxury* (1999); Neil McKendrick, introduction to McKendrick, Brewer and Plumb, *The Birth of a Consumer Society*, pp. 1–8.

51 For the spread of objects of pleasure, see Carole Shammas, *The Pre-industrial Consumer in England and America* (1990); Lorna Weatherill, *Consumer Behaviour and Material Culture, 1660–1760* (1988), and 'The Meaning of Consumer Behaviour in Late Seventeenth- and Early Eighteenth-century England' (1993); T. H. Breen, ' "Baubles of Britain" ' (1988), and 'The Meanings of Things' (1993); B. Fine and E. Leopold, 'Consumerism and the Industrial Revolution' (1990).

52 Peter Borsay (ed.), *The Eighteenth-century Town* (1990); Peter Borsay and Angus McInnes, 'The Emergence of a Leisure Town' (1990).

53 'Fashion is infinitely superior to merit in many respects': Josiah Wedgwood in a 1779 letter to his partner Bentley, in Ann Finer and George Savage (eds), *The Selected Letters of Josiah Wedgwood* (1965), p. 235.

54 Alison Adburgham, *Shopping in Style* (1979); David Alexander, *Retailing in England during the Industrial Revolution* (1970); Hoh-cheung Mui and Lorna H. Mui, *Shops and Shopkeeping in Eighteenth-century England* (1989). London's

pavements – unknown in Paris – aided window-shoppers.

55 Clare Williams (ed. and trans.), *Sophie in London* (1933), p. 87.

56 Williams, *Sophie in London*, p. 237; Robert Southey noted the splendour of English shops: *Letters from England by Don Manuel Alvarez Espriella* (1984 [1807]), p. 361.

57 For resorts, see William Biggs Boulton, *The Amusements of Old London* (1969).

58 For Vauxhall, see Miles Ogborn, *Spaces of Modernity* (1998), p. 119. Paralleling the pleasure garden was the masquerade: Terry Castle, *Masquerade and Civilization* (1986).

59 For the theatre, see Marc Baer, *The Theatre and Disorder in Late Georgian London* (1991); Kristina Straub, *Sexual Suspects* (1991).

60 Cressy, *Bonfires and Bells*, p. 19.

61 On sport, see Hugh Cunningham, *Leisure in the Industrial Revolution, c.1780–c.1880* (1980); R. Longrigg, *The English Squire and His Sport* (1977); John K. Walton and James Walvin (eds), *Leisure in Britain 1780–1939* (1983); Dennis Brailsford, *Sport, Time and Society* (1990), *British Sport* (1992), and *Bareknuckles* (1988); John Ford, *Prizefighting* (1971); W. Vamplew, *The Turf* (1974).

62 John Ashton, *The History of Gambling in England* (1898); Cecil Henry L'Estrange Ewen, *Lotteries and Sweepstakes* (1932).

63 H. C. Robbins-Landon, *Handel and His World* (1984); Eric David Mackerness, *A Social History of English Music* (1964).

64 Richard D. Altick, *The Shows of London* (1978), pp. 121–33, 303–16; Ricky Jay, *Learned Pigs and Fireproof Women* (1986), pp. 277–8.

65 Admirably discussed in Plumb, *The Commercialization of Leisure in Eighteenth-century England*, and *Georgian Delights*.

66 Kenneth Hudson, *A Social History of Museums* (1975); Edward Miller, *That Noble Cabinet* (1973).

67 Roger Elbourne, *Music and Tradition in Early Industrial Lancashire 1780–1840* (1980).

68 Peter Clark, *The English Alehouse* (1983).

The 1730s and 1740s saw the gin craze: Peter Clark, 'The "Mother Gin" Controversy in the Early Eighteenth Century' (1988); Roy Porter, 'The Drinking Man's Disease' (1985). Compare Jordan Goodman, *Tobacco in History* (1993).

69 For general introductions, see Lawrence Stone, *The Family, Sex and Marriage in England, 1500–1800* (1977); P.-G. Boucé (ed.), *Sexuality in Eighteenth-century Britain* (1982); Tim Hitchcock, *English Sexualities, 1700–1800* (1997); Jean H. Hagstrum, *Sex and Sensibility* (1980).

70 Frederick A. Pottle (ed.), *Boswell's London Journal, 1762–1763* (1950); V. Bullough, 'Prostitution and Reform in Eighteenth-century England' (1987); A. R. Henderson, 'Female Prostitution in London, 1730–1830' [1992]; Randolph Trumbach, *Sex and the Gender Revolution* (1998), vol. i; Peter Martin, *A Life of James Boswell* (1999).

71 William Wimsatt Jr and Frederick A. Pottle, *Boswell for the Defence 1769–1774* (1960), p. 108 (10 April 1772); Susan Manning, 'Boswell's Pleasures, the Pleasures of Boswell' (1997); Bruce Redford, 'Boswell's "Libertine" Correspondences' (1984); David M. Weed, 'Sexual Positions' (1997–8).

72 Pottle, *Boswell's London Journal*, p. 84 (14 December 1762).

73 Boswell's sex life and sexual attitudes have been analysed in Stone, *The Family, Sex and Marriage in England, 1500–1800*, pp. 572–99.

74 Peter Wagner, *Eros Revived* (1986); Lynn Hunt (ed.), *The Invention of Pornography, 1500–1800* (1993); David Foxon, *Libertine Literature in England, 1660–1745* (1965); Patrick J. Kearney, *The Private Case* (1981), and *A History of Erotic Literature* (1982); A. D. Harvey, *Sex in Georgian England* (1994); Karen Louise Harvey, 'Representations of Bodies and Sexual Difference in Eighteenth-century English Erotica' [1999]. Women too contributed to the genre: see Ros Ballaster, *Seductive Forms* (1992).

75 John Cleland, *Memoirs of a Woman of Pleasure* (1985 [1748–9]), p. 144.

76 Cleland, *Memoirs of a Woman of Pleasure*; Leo Braudy, '*Fanny Hill* and Materialism' (1970–71); see Randolph Trumbach, 'Modern Prostitution and Gender in Fanny Hill' (1987).

77 The fullest discussion is Roy Porter and Lesley Hall, *The Facts of Life* (1994).

78 Desmond King-Hele, *Doctor of Revolution* (1977), p. 240.

79 The prick and the pen were merged: Warren Chernaik, *Sexual Freedom in Restoration Literature* (1995), pp. 10–11; G. J. Barker-Benfield, *The Culture of Sensibility* (1992), p. 41; Gilbert Burnet, *Some Passages of the Life and Death of the Right Honourable John, Earl of Rochester* (1680), pp. 57, 72.

80 In *A Modest Defence of Publick Stews* (1724), Mandeville made the case for legalized and publicly regulated prostitution as a means of protecting other women from seduction and rape. Men must, one way or another, have sexual relief, and 'our Business is to contrive a Method how they may be gratify'd, with as little Expence of Female Virtue as possible' (p. 44). Prostitution was a private vice with clear public benefits, and should be made more safe and convenient for clients and customers.

81 John Wilkes, *An Essay on Woman* (1972 [1763]), p. 213. See also George Rudé, *Wilkes and Liberty* (1962); Adrian Hamilton, *The Infamous Essay on Woman* (1972); Peter D. G. Thomas, *John Wilkes: A Friend to Liberty* (1996), p. 4. For Wilkes's rakish activities, see Donald McCormick, *The Hell-Fire Club* (1958); Kathleen Wilson, *The Sense of the People* (1995), p. 219.

82 Strachey (ed.), *The Letters of the Earl of Chesterfield to His Son*, vol. ii, p. 133 (25 March 1751).

83 Erasmus Darwin, *The Botanic Garden* (1789–91), vol. i, ll. 57–64. Genista is broom. Darwin compared plant promiscuity with the newly discovered information about free love in Polynesia. For more on Darwin, see below, chapter 19.

84 Janet Browne, 'Botany for Gentlemen' (1989); Darwin, *The Botanic Garden*, vol. i, ll. 57–64.

85 Discussed in Marilyn Butler, *Romantics, Rebels and Reactionaries* (1981), pp. 129f.

86 Brian Fothergill (ed.), *Sir William Hamilton: Envoy Extraordinary* (1969); Giancarlo Carabelli, *In the Image of Priapus* (1996); Butler, *Romantics, Rebels and Reactionaries*, p. 130ff. William Blake too became preoccupied with sexual freedom and erotic energy ('the lineaments of gratified desire'), or perhaps with the perils of phallic sexuality and the evils of thwarted sexuality. He produced erotic engravings: see Peter Ackroyd, *Blake* (1995), p. 281.

87 See Michael Clarke and Nicholas Penny (eds), *The Arrogant Connoisseur* (1982), pp. 14, 59; Marilyn Butler, *Peacock Displayed* (1979), p. 32. Christianity, according to Payne Knight, had transformed 'the Creator and Generator Bacchus' into a 'jealous and irascible God'; Frank E. Manuel, *The Eighteenth Century Confronts the Gods* (1967), p. 259.

88 Butler, *Peacock Displayed*, p. 30.

89 Charles F. Bahmueller, *The National Charity Company* (1981), pp. 98f.; Jeremy Bentham, 'Offenses against One's Self: Paederasty' (1978 and 1979 [originally written *c.* 1785 but not published]). On Enlightenment attitudes towards homosexuality, see G. S. Rousseau, 'The Pursuit of Homosexuality in the Eighteenth Century' (1987); and Trumbach, *Sex and the Gender Revolution*, vol. i.

90 Discussed in Anand C. Chitnis, *The Scottish Enlightenment: A Social History* (1976), pp. 47f.

91 Chitnis, *The Scottish Enlightenment: A Social History*, p. 47.

92 Chitnis, *The Scottish Enlightenment: A Social History*, p. 48.

93 Chitnis, *The Scottish Enlightenment: A Social History*, p. 48.

94 Derek Jarrett, *The Ingenious Mr Hogarth* (1976); Michael Duffy (ed.), *The English Satirical Print, 1600–1832* (1986). For the pleasures of the bourgeoisie, see Peter Earle, *The World of Defoe* (1976), and *The Making of the English Middle Class* (1989).

95 For a reassessment of the Victorian 'anti-sensual' reaction, see Michael Mason, *The Making of Victorian Sexual Attitudes* (1994).

12 FROM GOOD SENSE TO SENSIBILITY

1 M. Bentham-Edwards (ed.) *The Autobiography of Arthur Young* (1898), p. 421.

2 W. A. Speck, 'Politicians, Peers, and Publication by Subscription 1700–50' (1982), p. 65, and the valuable discussion in Pat Rogers (ed.), *The Context of English Literature* (1978), introduction, p. 13.

3 See Stephen Mennell, *Norbert Elias: Civilization and the Human Self-image* (1989); Alain Boureau, *et al.* (eds), *A History of Private Life* (1989), vol. iii; Michelle Perrot (ed.), *A History of Private Life* (1990), vol. iv; Dena Goodman, 'Public Sphere and Private Life' (1992).

4 See George Birkbeck Hill, *Boswell's Life of Johnson* (1934–50), vol. i, p. 266; for attacks on aristocratic corruption, see below, chapter 18.

5 On the middling ranks, and their participation in public life, see Geoffrey Holmes, *Augustan England* (1982); Penelope Corfield, *Power and the Professions in Britain 1700–1850* (1995); Peter Earle, *The Making of the English Middle Class* (1989); Margaret R. Hunt, *The Middling Sort* (1996).

6 Coined by William Taylor in 1797. For selfhood, see S. D. Cox, *'The Stranger within Thee'* (1980); J. O. Lyons, *The Invention of the*

Self (1978); Charles Taylor, *Sources of the Self* (1989); Quentin Skinner, 'Who Are "We"?' (1991); Michael Mascuch, *Origins of the Individualist Self* (1997).

7 Gordon Rattray Taylor, *The Angel Makers* (1958).

8 Jean-Jacques Rousseau, *The Confessions of Jean-Jacques Rousseau* (1965 [1781–8]), p. 17. Translating Rousseau's *Discours sur les sciences et les arts* in 1751, William Howyer dismissed Rousseau's ideas, insisting he gave them currency only because of their great 'singularity'. For Rousseau's radical critique, see Mark Hulliung, *The Autocritique of Enlightenment* (1994); for his influence, see Edward Duffy, *Rousseau in England* (1979), pp. 14f.; and for his importance in transforming ideas of the self, see Richard Sennett, *The Fall of Public Man* (1977). Rousseau is echoed by Walter Shandy's comment on his child Tristram: thanks to the accidents of his birth, Tristram should 'neither think, nor act like any other man's child': Laurence Sterne, *The Life and Opinions of Tristram Shandy* (1967 [1759–67]), p. 572.

9 H. Whitbread (ed.), *I Know My Own Heart* (1987). Rousseau was endlessly quoted: see, for instance, Mary Hays, *Memoirs of Emma Courtney* (1996 [1796]), p. 8. For an exemplary study of how reality came to mirror the fictional imagination, see John Bender, *Imagining the Penitentiary* (1987).

10 Hill, *Boswell's Life of Johnson*, vol. ii, p. 437, n.2. See Penelope Murray (ed.), *Genius: The History of an Idea* (1989); G. Tonelli, 'Genius: From the Renaissance to 1770' (1973).

11 Charles Strachey (ed.), *The Letters of the Earl of Chesterfield to his Son* (1924), vol. ii, p. 136. For Chesterfield on women, see chapter 14.

12 Adam Smith, *An Inquiry into the Nature and Causes of the Wealth of Nations* (1976 [1776]), bk I, ch. 2, para. 4, pp. 28–9; Simon Schaffer, 'Genius in Romantic Natural Philosophy' (1990).

13 Joseph Priestley, *Memoirs of Dr Joseph*

Priestley, Written on Himself (1904 [1795]), p. 70; William Godwin, *The Enquirer* (1965 [1797]), p. 17.

14 Alexander Pope, *Essay on Criticism* (1711), in John Butt (ed.), *The Poems of Alexander Pope* (1965), p. 153, ll. 297–300.

15 Paul Fussell, *The Rhetorical World of Augustan Humanism* (1965), p. 104; John Barrell, *The Political Theory of Painting from Reynolds to Hazlitt* (1986), pp. 124, 151f.

16 Mark Akenside, *The Pleasures of Imagination* (1744). On fear of imagination, see M. V. De Porte, *Nightmares and Hobbyhorses* (1974); Donald F. Bond, ' "Distrust" of Imagination in English Neoclassicism' (1937), and 'The Neo-Classical Psychology of the Imagination' (1937); S. Cunningham, 'Bedlam and Parnassus' (1971). For Johnson's phrase, see Roy Porter, 'The Hunger of Imagination' (1985).

17 For proto-Romantic ideas of genius, see J. Engell, *The Creative Imagination* (1981); Schaffer, 'Genius in Romantic Natural Philosophy'.

18 Edward Young, *Conjectures on Original Composition* (1759), p. 42; R. W. Harris, *Romanticism and the Social Order* (1969), p. 238; Howard Mumford Jones, *Revolution and Romanticism* (1974), p. 270.

19 Young, *Conjectures on Original Composition*, p. 42.

20 Young, *Conjectures on Original Composition*, pp. 52, 53–54.

21 William Sharpe, *A Dissertation upon Genius* (1755); Alexander Gerard, *An Essay upon Genius* (1774).

22 Quoted in G. Becker, *The Mad Genius Controversy* (1978), p. 26; Roy Porter, 'Bedlam and Parnassus' (1987).

23 Joseph Warton's *The Enthusiast* (1744) contrasted England and France, preferring 'Gothick battlements' to the artificialities of continental and classical taste:

> What are the lays of artful Addison,
> Coldly correct, to Shakespear's warblings
> wild?

Quoted in Ronald W. Harris, *Reason and Nature in the Eighteenth Century* (1968), p. 16. See C. Thacker, *The Wildness Pleases: The Origins of Romanticism* (1983).

24 On the refiguring of enthusiasm, see R. A. Knox, *Enthusiasm* (1950); M. Abrams, *The Mirror and the Lamp* (1953). For (pre-) Romanticism, see David Aers, Jonathan Cook and David Punter, *Romanticism and Ideology* (1981).

25 Michael Ferber, *The Social Vision of William Blake* (1985), p. 29.

26 See Janet Todd, *Sensibility: An Introduction* (1986); G. J. Barker-Benfield, *The Culture of Sensibility* (1992); Adela Pinch, *Strange Fits of Passion* (1996); Michael Prince, *Philosophical Dialogue in the British Enlightenment* (1996); Bruce Redford, *The Converse of the Pen* (1986).

27 C. Campbell, *The Romantic Ethic and the Spirit of Modern Consumerism* (1989), p. 90.

28 Especially when targeted at women: Margaret Beetham, *A Magazine of Her Own?* (1996); Kathryn Shevelow, *Women and Print Culture* (1989).

29 Roy Porter, 'Madness and the Family before Freud' (1998).

30 John Mullan, *Sentiment And Sociability* (1988); G. S. Rousseau, 'Towards a Semiotics of the Nerve' (1991), and 'Nerves, Spirits and Fibres' (1991).

31 See the introduction by Roy Porter to George Cheyne, *The English Malady* (1990 [1733]).

32 G. S. Rousseau, 'Nerves, Spirits and Fibres'.

33 Thomas Trotter, *A View of the Nervous Temperament* (1807); Roy Porter, 'Addicted to Modernity' (1992).

34 Roy Porter, 'Consumption: Disease of the Consumer Society?' (1991).

35 Roy Porter, 'Civilization and Disease' (1991), *Doctor of Society* (1991), and ' "Expressing Yourself Ill" ' (1991).

36 As ever, there were counter-currents. Gibbon was proud that 'my nerves are not tremblingly alive': Edward Gibbon, *Memoirs of My Life* (1966 [1796]), p. 188. Many deplored sensibility as an affectation.

37 Barker-Benfield, *The Culture of Sensibility*, p. 133.

38 Generally on the novel, see Ian Watt, *The Rise of the Novel* (1957); John J. Richetti, *Popular Fiction before Richardson* (1992 [1969]); Michael McKeon, *The Origins of the English Novel, 1600–1740* (1987); R. F. Brissenden, *Virtue in Distress* (1974). On the sense of self-identification, see Alan Richardson, *Literature, Education, and Romanticism* (1994).

39 Marilyn Butler, *Jane Austen and the War of Ideas* (1975), p. 9.

40 See Todd, *Sensibility: An Introduction*, p. 90.

41 Todd, *Sensibility: An Introduction*, pp. 65–128; Barker-Benfield, *The Culture of Sensibility*, pp. 71f.; Taylor, *The Angel Makers*, p. 265.

42 Robert D. Mayo, *The English Novels in the Magazines, 1740–1815* (1962), p. 223.

43 Edward Copeland, *Women Writing about Money* (1995), p. 49; Katharine M. Rogers, *Feminism in Eighteenth-century England* (1982), pp. 152f.

44 Mary Hays has one of her characters exclaim: ' "I have no home;" said I, in a voice choked with sobs – "I am an alien in the world – and alone in the universe" ': *Memoirs of Emma Courtney*, p. 161.

45 Janet Todd, *The Sign of Angellica* (1989). Among men, only Sir Walter Scott achieved comparable popularity. See below, chapter 14.

46 George Colman, prologue to *Polly Honeycombe* (1760); Jacqueline Pearson, *Women's Reading in Britain, 1750–1835* (1999).

47 *Critical Review*, no. 2 (November 1756), p. 379. Writing in 1750, Johnson portrayed fiction as dangerous:

These books are written chiefly to the young, the ignorant, and the idle, to whom they serve as lectures of conduct, and introductions into life. They are the entertainments of minds unfurnished with ideas, and therefore easily susceptible of impressions; not fixed by principles, and therefore easily following the current of fancy; not informed by experience, and consequently open to every false suggestion and partial account.

Samuel Johnson, *The Rambler* (1969), vol. i, no. 4, p. 21 (Saturday, 31 March 1750).
48 Mary Wollstonecraft, *Mary: A Fiction* (1788), pp. 1–2. That book showed women disoriented by light reading: the mother 'was chaste, according to the vulgar acceptation of the word, that is, she did not make any actual *faux pas*; she feared the world, and was indolent; but then, to make amends for this seeming self-denial, she read all the sentimental novels, dwelt on the love-scenes, and, had she thought while she read, her mind would have been contaminated'. The pleasures such novels imparted were 'bodily' or 'animal': Barker-Benfield, *The Culture of Sensibility*, p. 328.

On masturbation and the novel, see Thomas W. Laqueur, *'Amor Veneris, vel Dulcedo Appelatur'* (1989); Eve Kosofsky Sedgwick, 'Jane Austen and the Masturbating Girl' (1995). For the paradoxes of advice literature warning against the perils of reading, see Roy Porter, 'Forbidden Pleasures' (1995).
49 Sylvana Tomaselli (ed.), *Mary Wollstonecraft: A Vindication of the Rights of Men with A Vindication of the Rights of Woman* (1995), p. 102.
50 Peter H. Pawlowicz, 'Reading Women' (1995), p. 45.
51 Vicesimus Knox, *Liberal Education* (1789), vol. i, p. 301.
52 A. S. Collins, *The Profession of Letters* (1973 [1928]), p. 95; R. W. Chapman (ed.), *Jane Austen's Letters to Her Sister Cassandra & Others* (1952), p. 38: letter to Cassandra (18 December 1798).
53 Jane Austen, *Northanger Abbey* (1975 [1818]), p. 58.
54 Jane Austen, *Lady Susan, The Watsons, Sanditon*, ed. Margaret Drabble (1974 [written 1817]), p. 191; for Austen's conservative moralism, see Butler, *Jane Austen and the War of Ideas*, pp. 287–8.

55 John Dwyer, *Virtuous Discourse* (1987), pp. 26, 141.
56 Thomas Laqueur, 'Bodies, Details, and Humanitarian Narrative' (1989), pp. 176–7; Gary Kelly, *The English Jacobin Novel, 1780–1805* (1976).
57 Robert Southey, *Letters from England by Don Manuel Alvarez Espriella* (1984 [1807]), p. 348.
58 David Hartley, *Observations on Man, His Frame, His Duty, and His Expectations* (1749), vol. i, p. 377.
59 David Hume, *A Treatise of Human Nature* (1978 [1739–40]), bk I, sect. 6, p. 253.
60 As discussed in Dwyer, *Virtuous Discourse*, pp. 170–71. And see above, chapter 8.
61 Patricia Meyer Spacks, *Imagining a Self* (1976), p. 16; Boswell loved to reflect upon his own self: 'And as a lady adjusts her dress before a mirror, a man adjusts his character by looking at his journal': quoted in Spacks, *Imagining a Self*, p. 228.
62 Frederick A. Pottle (ed.), *Boswell's London Journal, 1762–1763* (1950), p. 62. See the discussion in John Brewer, *The Pleasures of the Imagination* (1997), p. 32; Spacks, *Imagining a Self*, p. 231. Boswell, of course, wrote a magazine column under the penname of 'The Hypochondriack': M. Bailey (ed.), *Boswell's Column* (1951).
63 Charlotte Lennox, *The Female Quixote* (1989 [1752]).
64 Lennox, *The Female Quixote*, p. 15; Mullan, *Sentiment And Sociability*, pp. 57–113; Pawlowicz, 'Reading Women', p. 45.
65 It was perceived from the beginning as a 'fashionable' novel – hence Samuel Johnson's assurance to Boswell that 'nothing odd will do long, *Tristram Shandy* did not last': Hill, *Boswell's Life of Johnson*, vol. i, p. 449. Sterne said of his book: ''Tis . . . a picture of myself' and signed letters 'Tristram' or 'Yorick': Max Byrd, *Tristram Shandy* (1985), p. 8.
66 Sterne, *The Life and Opinions of Tristram Shandy*, quoted in Spacks, *Imagining a Self*, p. 134.

67 Frank Donoghue, *The Fame Machine* (1996), pp. 74, 85f.; Arthur Cash, *Laurence Sterne: The Later Years* (1986), ch. 2.

68 Peter Conrad, *Shandyism* (1978), p. 31.

69 For Gothic, see E. J. Clery, *The Rise of Supernatural Fiction* (1995); David Punter, *The Literature of Terror* (1980); M. H. Abrams, *Natural Supernaturalism* (1971), p. 74; Alan Bewell, *Wordsworth and the Enlightenment* (1989).

70 Born to a family of Rational Dissenters who encouraged her literary leanings, Mary Hays (1760–1843) moved in the circles of Thomas Holcroft, Anna Laetitia Barbauld, William Godwin and Mary Wollstonecraft. Like the *Memoirs of Emma Courtney*, her second novel, *The Victim of Prejudice* (1799), was also violently criticized. She produced a feminist tract, *Appeal to the Men of Great Britain in Behalf of Women* (1798), and *Female Biography* (1803).

71 Hays, *Memoirs of Emma Courtney*, p. 4.

72 See the introduction by Eleanor Ty to Hays, *Memoirs of Emma Courtney*; Marilyn L. Brooks, 'Mary Hays: Finding a "Voice" in Dissent' (1995); Kelly, *The English Jacobin Novel, 1780–1805*, pp. 12, 85. Hays directly quotes from Rousseau, Wollstonecraft, Helvétius, Abraham Tucker, Godwin, Sterne, Holcroft, Hartley ('indissoluble chains of association and habit') and Richardson, and alludes to many others, including Locke.

73 Hays, *Memoirs of Emma Courtney*, p. 4.

74 Barker-Benfield, *The Culture of Sensibility*, p. 365.

75 Hays, *Memoirs of Emma Courtney*, pp. 3–5. She was a 'woman to whom education has given a sexual character': p. 117.

76 Hays, *Memoirs of Emma Courtney*, p. 119.

77 A fellow of Jesus College, Cambridge, William Frend converted to Unitarianism, and supported the campaign to abolish subscription to the Thirty-nine Articles. He was excluded from the college as a consequence of his involvement with the French Revolution. He became a freelance writer and teacher in London until 1806, when he became actuary to the Rock Life Assurance Company. Frida Knight, *University Rebel* (1971); Peter Searby, *A History of the University of Cambridge* (1997), vol. iii, p. 410.

78 Barker-Benfield, *The Culture of Sensibility*, p. 369.

79 Don Locke, *A Fantasy of Reason* (1980), p. 135.

80 *The Anti-Jacobin*, no. 30 (4 June 1798); Butler, *Jane Austen and the War of Ideas*, pp. 92, 235; Edward Copeland, 'Money Talks' (1989), p. 156. Kotzebue's *Lovers' Vows* (1798) attacked marrying for money and exalted relations based on feeling.

81 Taylor, *The Angel Makers*; Hagstrum, *Sex And Sensibility*. See also the discussion of sex in chapter 11.

82 Philip Carter, 'An "Effeminate" or "Efficient" Nation?' (1997), and 'Mollies, Fops and Men of Feeling' [1995].

83 Leonore Davidoff and Catherine Hall, *Family Fortunes* (1987).

84 Rictor Norton, *Mother Clap's Molly House* (1992); Randolph Trumbach, *Sex and the Gender Revolution* (1998), vol. i.

85 William Hazlitt, *Selected Writings* (1970), p. 447.

13 NATURE

1 David Hume, *Dialogues concerning Natural Religion* (1947 [1779]), pt X, p. 194: 'Demea', the spokesman for orthodox Christianity, is speaking.

2 Alexander Pope, *An Essay on Man* (1733–4),

epistle IV, ll. 29–30, in John Butt (ed.), *The Poems of Alexander Pope* (1965), p. 537; compare:

Nor think, in NATURE'S STATE they blindly trod;

The state of nature was the reign of God . . .

Pope, *An Essay on Man*, epistle III, ll. 147–8, p. 530.

3 Adam Ferguson, *An Essay on the History of Civil Society* (1995 [1767]), p. 15.

4 A wonderful discussion of these topics is A. O. Lovejoy's ' "Nature" as Aesthetic Norm' (1955).

5 Alexander Pope, *Essay on Criticism* (1711), ll. 70–73, in Butt, *The Poems of Alexander Pope*, p. 146.

6 'I was abashed . . . I closed the book, angry with myself that I should still be admiring earthly things': quoted in R. W. Harris, *Reason and Nature in the Eighteenth Century* (1968), p. 22.

7 Andrew Graham-Dixon, *A History of British Art* (1996). The history of aesthetics is beyond the scope of this book, but see chapter 7 above and Malcolm Andrews, *The Search for the Picturesque* (1989); Stephen Copley (ed.), *The Politics of the Picturesque* (1994); Walter John Hipple, *The Beautiful, the Sublime, and the Picturesque in Eighteenth-century Aesthetic Theory* (1957); Walter Jackson Bate, *From Classic to Romantic* (1946); Andrew Ashfield and Peter de Bolla (eds.), *The Sublime: A Reader in British Eighteenth-century Aesthetic Theory* (1996).

8 Trevor Fawcett (ed.), *Voices of Eighteenth-century Bath* (1995), p. 191.

9 Simon Schama, *Landscape and Memory* (1995), pp. 6–7.

10 Pope, *An Essay on Man*, epistle I, l. 289, in Butt, *The Poems of Alexander Pope*, p. 515. For 'thinking the environment', see Denis Cosgrove and Stephen Daniels (eds.), *The Iconography of Landscape* (1988); Yi-fu Tuan, *Topophilia* (1974); Derek Wall, *A Reader in Environmental Literature, Philosophy and Politics* (1994); Clive Ponting, *A Green History of the World* (1991); Donald Worster, *The Wealth of Nature* (1993), and *Nature's Economy* (1985).

11 Roy Porter, 'The Terraqueous Globe' (1980); B. Smith, *European Vision and the South Pacific, 1768–1850* (1960); Barbara Maria Stafford, *Voyage Into Substance* (1984); Neil Rennie, *Far-fetched Facts* (1995).

12 Marijke Gijswijt-Hofstra, Brian P. Levack and Roy Porter, *Witchcraft and Magic in Europe* (1999), vol. v.

13 [Thomas Carlyle], 'Signs of the Times, An Addiction to Prophecy, Not a favourable Indication, Either of Nations or Individuals' (1829).

14 Pope, *An Essay on Man*, epistle IV, ll. 332, in Butt, *The Poems of Alexander Pope*, p. 546; for Addison, see Basil Willey, *The Eighteenth Century Background* (1962), p. 51. Addison remarked: 'we find the Works of Nature still more pleasant, the more they resemble those of Art': quoted in Andrews, *The Search for the Picturesque*, p. vii. For another popular instance of cosmic poetry, see Richard Blackmore, *Creation* (1712).

15 Pope, *An Essay on Man*, epistle I, ll. 233–46, in Butt, *The Poems of Alexander Pope*, p. 513. For Pope on the Chain of Being, see *An Essay on Man*, epistle I, ll. 233–36; see also A. O. Lovejoy, *The Great Chain of Being* (1936).

16 Keith Thomas, *Man and the Natural World* (1983).

17 Marina Warner, *From the Beast to the Blonde* (1994); Gilbert White, *The Natural History and Antiquities of Selborne* (1977 [1789]).

18 Genesis, 1: 26, 28. See C. Glacken, *Traces on the Rhodian Shore* (1967); J. A. Passmore, *The Perfectibility of Man* (1972), and *Man's Responsibility for Nature* (1980), pp. 6f.

19 Richard Bentley, 'Eight Sermons Preached at the Hon. Robert Boyle's Lecture in the Year MDCXCII', in A. Dyce (ed.) *The Works of Richard Bentley* (1838 [1693]), vol. iii, p. 175. See discussion in Thomas, *Man and the Natural World*, p. 18.

20 William Derham, *Physico-Theology* (1713), pp. 54–5, 112. Derham was ordained in 1682, and from 1689 was vicar at Upminster, Essex, where he conducted amateur studies into meteorology, astronomy, natural history and mechanics. The work reached twelve editions.

21 William Phillips, *An Outline of Mineralogy and Geology* (1815), pp. 193, 191; William Paley,

Natural Theology (1802). The *Bridgewater Treatises* formed a series of natural theological works produced during the 1830s, in accordance with the will of the Earl of Bridgewater, the aim being to illustrate the argument from Divine Design. They are discussed in Charles C. Gillispie, *Genesis and Geology* (1951).

22 See John Hedley Brooke, *Science and Religion* (1991).

23 Abraham Cowley, 'Of Solitude' (1668), in John Sparrow (ed.), *The Mistress with Other Select Poems of Abraham Cowley* (1926), p. 178; Edmund Burke, *Reflections on the Revolution in France* (1790), p. 76.

24 Miles Weatherall, *In Search of a Cure* (1990), p. 10.

25 Oliver Goldsmith, *An History of the Earth and Animated Nature* (1774), vol. i, p. 401.

26 George Hakewill, *An Apologie*, 2nd ed. (1630), preface; Yi-fu Tuan, *The Hydrologic Cycle and the Wisdom of God* (1968), p. 65.

27 Gordon Davies, *The Earth in Decay* (1969).

28 Thomas Burnet, *The Sacred Theory of the Earth* (1965 [1684–90; Latin original, 1681]), quoted in Glacken, *Traces on the Rhodian Shore*, p. 411.

29 John Evelyn, *Silva* (1776 [1662]); see also Richard Grove, *Green Imperialism* (1995).

30 John Woodward, *An Essay towards a Natural History of the Earth* (1695), pp. 30, 32. See the discussion in Margaret C. Jacob, *The Newtonians and the English Revolution, 1689–1720* (1976); Tuan, *The Hydrologic Cycle and the Wisdom of God*, p. 76.

31 Woodward, *An Essay towards a Natural History of the Earth*, p. 35.

32 Woodward, *An Essay towards a Natural History of the Earth*, pp. 61, 94.

33 Roy Porter, 'Creation and Credence' (1979).

34 Goldsmith, *An History of the Earth and Animated Nature*, vol. i, p. 163.

35 James Hutton, *Theory of the Earth* (1795), vol. i, p. 3; Dennis R. Dean, *James Hutton and the History of Geology* (1992).

36 See Hutton, *Theory of the Earth*; T. D. Kendrick, *The Lisbon Earthquake* (1956).

37 Jean Jones, 'James Hutton's Agricultural Research and His Life as a Farmer' (1985).

38 C. B. Macpherson, *The Political Theory of Possessive Individualism* (1964); Anthony Pagden, *Lords of All the World* (1995).

39 G. Williamson, 'Mutability, Decay and Seventeenth-century Melancholy' (1961); Victor I. Harris, *All Coherence Gone* (1966).

40 Hutton held that 'a proper system of the earth should lead us to see that wise construction, by which this earth is made to answer the purpose of its intention, and to preserve itself from every accident by which the design of this living world might be frustrated': Hutton, *Theory of the Earth*, vol. i, p. 275.

41 Goldsmith, *An History of the Earth and Animated Nature*, vol. i, p. 400. Writers commonly celebrated the fusion of the beautiful with the useful:

> What pleasing scenes the landscape wide
>   displays!
> The 'enchanting prospect bids for ever gaze . . .
> To social towns, see! wealthy Commerce brings
> Rejoicing Affluence on his silver wings,
> On verdant hills, see! flocks innumerous feed,
> Or thoughtful listen to the lively reed.
> See! golden harvests sweep the bending plains;
> 'And Peace and Plenty own a Brunswick
>   reigns'.

John Langhorne, 'Studley Park' (nd), ll. 83–4, 91–6, quoted in John Barrell, *The Idea of Landscape and the Sense of Place 1730–1840* (1972), p. 74. The well-cultivated landscape is the beautiful one.

42 Richard Blackmore's *Creation* (1712), p. xx, opposed 'Bigots in Atheism', who celebrated the universe while slighting its creator:

> I would th'Eternal from his Works assert,
> And sing the Wonders of Creating Art. [p. 4.]

R. D. Stock, *The Holy and the Daemonic from Sir Thomas Browne to William Blake* (1982), p. 120.

43 For Thomson, see Robert Inglesfield, 'Shaftesbury's Influence on Thomson's "Seasons" ' (1986); for Young, see Stock, *The Holy and the Daemonic from Sir Thomas Browne to William Blake*, p. 188. Akenside addressed superior souls:

> To these the Sire Omnipotent unfolds
> The world's harmonious volume, there to read
> The transcript of Himself. On every part
> They trace the bright impressions of his hand:
> In earth or air, the meadow's purple stores,
> The moon's mild radiance, or the virgin's form
> Blooming with rosy smiles, they see portray'd
> That uncreated beauty, which delights
> The mind supreme.

Mark Akenside, *The Pleasures of Imagination* (1744), in *The Poetical Works of Mark Akenside* (1866), bk I, ll. 99–107.

44 Edward Young, *Night Thoughts on Life, Death and Immortality* (1780).

45 Henry Brooke, *Universal Beauty* (1735).

46 Akenside, *The Pleasures of Imagination*, in *The Poetical Works of Mark Akenside*, bk I, ll. 97–107.

47 Goldsmith, *An History of the Earth and Animated Nature*, vol. i, p. 401; Max Weber, *The Protestant Ethic and the Spirit of Capitalism* (1930); Richard Tawney, *Religion and the Rise of Capitalism* (1926).

48 Francis Bacon, 'Of Heresies' (1597), in J. Spedding, R. L. Ellis and D. D. Heath (eds.), *The Works of Francis Bacon* (1857–74), vol. vii, p. 253, and *New Atlantis* (1627), in *The Works of Francis Bacon*, vol. iii, p. 156; Joseph Glanvill, *Plus Ultra, Or the Progress and Advancement of Knowledge Since the Days of Aristotle* (1668). See the discussion in Carolyn Merchant, *The Death of Nature* (1980), p. 188.

49 René Descartes, *Le Monde* (1664), quoted in Brian Easlea, *Science and Sexual Oppression* (1981), p. 72: Robert Boyle, 'A Free Inquiry into the Vulgarly Received Notion of Nature Made in an Essay Addressed to a Friend, To Which is Pre-Fixed the Life of the Author by Thomas Birch', in *The Works of the Honourable Robert Boyle* (1744), vol. iv, p. 363; Passmore, *Man's Responsibility for Nature*, p. 11; for the critique, see, for instance, Merchant, *The Death of Nature*.

50 John Ray, *The Wisdom Of God Manifested in the Works of the Creation* (1691), pp. 113–14. Civilization was better than Arcadia:

If a Country thus planted and adorned, thus polished and civilized, thus improved to the height . . . be not preferred before a Barbarous and Inhospitable *Scythia* . . . or a rude and unpolished *America* peopled with slothful and naked *Indians*, instead of well-built Houses, living in pitiful Huts and Cabans, made of Poles set end-ways; then surely the brute Beasts Condition, and manner of Living . . . is to be esteem'd better than Man's, and Wit and Reason was in vain bestowed on him. [p. 118.]

51 Ray, *The Wisdom Of God Manifested in the Works of the Creation*, ll. 117–18.

52 Matthew Hale, *The Primitive Origination of Mankind* (1677), sect. 4, ch. 8, p. 370.

53 G. E. Mingay, *A Social History of the English Countryside* (1990).

54 Evelyn, *Silva*, p. 1.

55 Ian Simpson Ross, *Lord Kames and the Scotland of His Day* (1972), p. 351.

56 Jonathan Swift, *Gulliver's Travels* (1954 [1726]), pt II, ch. 7, p. 143.

57 Jones, 'James Hutton's Agricultural Research and His Life as a Farmer', p. 579.

58 James Hutton, 'Principles of Agriculture', quoted in Maureen McNeil, *Under the Banner of Science* (1987), pp. 172–3; Jones, 'James Hutton's Agricultural Research and His Life as a Farmer'.

59 Erasmus Darwin, *Phytologia* (1800), p. vii: *Phytologia* is in three parts: 1) 'physiology of vegetation', with detailed accounts of plant structure and functioning (pp. 1–139); 2) 'economy of vegetation', covering seed growth, photosynthesis, nutrition, manures, drainage, aeration and diseases (pp. 141–372); 3) 'agriculture and horticulture', with the accent on productivity, of fruits, seeds, root crops and flowers (pp. 373–578).

60

This inequality of mankind in the present state of the world is too great for the purposes of producing the greatest quantity of human nourishment, and the greatest sum of human happiness; there should be no slavery at one end of the chain of society, and no despotism at the other.

Darwin, *Phytologia*, pt II, pp. 415, 416.

61 J. G. Gazley, *The Life of Arthur Young* (1973), pp. 20f.; G. E. Mingay (ed.), *Arthur Young and His Times* (1975). See also Merchant, *The Death of Nature*, p. 236.

62 Arthur Young, *The Farmer's Letters to the People of England* (1767), p. 84, letter 3.

63 McNeil, *Under the Banner of Science*, p. 7.

64 J. M. Neeson, *Commoners* (1993).

65 Young, *The Farmer's Letters to the People of England*, p. 91. For 'moral economy', see E. P. Thompson, *Customs in Common* (1991). For enclosure, see M. Turner, *English Parliamentary Enclosure* (1980), and *Enclosures in Britain, 1750–1830* (1984).

66 Arthur Young, *A Six Weeks' Tour through the Southern Counties of England and Wales* (1768), p. 21.

67 Arthur Young, *View of the Agriculture of Oxfordshire* (1809), p. 36. The preceding sentences run:

The Oxfordshire farmers . . . are now in the period of a great change in their ideas, knowledge, practice, and other circumstances. Enclosing to a greater proportional amount than in almost any other county in the kingdom has changed the men as much as it has improved the country; they are now in the ebullition of this change; a vast amelioration has been wrought, and is working; and a great deal of ignorance and barbarity remains. The Goths and Vandals of open fields touch the civilization of enclosures. Men have been taught to think, and till that moment arrives nothing can be done effectively.

68 Young, *The Farmer's Letters to the People of England*, p. 306. For the involvement of the nobility in progressive agriculture, see G. E. Mingay, *English Landed Society in the Eighteenth Century* (1963).

69 Arthur Young, *A Six Months' Tour through the North of England*, 2nd edn (1771), vol. i, p. xiv, quoted in Gazley, *The Life of Arthur Young*, p. 45.

70 For the bucolic, see Raymond Williams, *The Country and the City* (1973); for pastoral painting, see Ann Bermingham, *Landscape and Ideology* (1986); Christiana Payne, *Toil and Plenty* (1993); Nigel Everett, *The Tory View of Landscape* (1994).

71 Adam Smith, *An Inquiry into the Nature and Causes of the Wealth of Nations* (1976 [1776]), vol. i, bk 1, ch. 11.n, p. 258.

72 For Gainsborough's painting of the couple, see Cosgrove and Daniels, *The Iconography of Landscape*; John Berger *et al.*, *Ways of Seeing* (1972), pp. 106–8; Graham-Dixon, *A History of British Art*, p. 110.

73 William Godwin, *An Enquiry concerning Political Justice* (1985 [1793]), p. 769.

74 Roy Porter, 'Medical Science and Human Science in the Enlightenment' (1995); James Dunbar, *Essays on the History of Mankind in Rude and Cultivated Ages* (1780).

75 Thomas Robert Malthus, *An Essay on the Principle of Population* (1798); M. Turner (ed.), *Malthus and His Times* (1986).

76 Jonas Moore, *The History or Narrative of the Great Level of the Fenns, Called Bedford Level* (1685), p. 72.

77 John Dalton, *A Descriptive Poem Addressed to Two Ladies at Their Return from Viewing the Mines at Whitehaven* (1755), p. iii. This Dalton was not the atomic chemist.

78 On English gardening and landscaping, see Christopher Hussey, *English Gardens and Landscapes, 1700–1750* (1967); C. Thacker, *The Wildness Pleases* (1983); Tom Williamson, *Polite Landscapes* (1996).

79 Joseph Addison and Richard Steele, *The Spectator* (1965), vol. iii, no. 414, pp. 551–2 (Wednesday 25 June 1712); see also no. 111, in which Addison protests against the excessive formality of the Continental garden. For the ha-ha, see Thacker, *The Wildness Pleases*, pp. 32–3.

80 Dorothy Stroud, *Capability Brown* (1975); Williamson, *Polite Landscapes*, pp. 77–99.

81 J. C. Loudon, *The Suburban Gardener and Villa Companion* (1838), p. 162.

82 For Payne Knight, see Marilyn Butler, *Peacock Displayed* (1979), pp. 6, 30f.; Richard Payne Knight, *The Progress of Civil Society* (1796); Thomas Peacock, *Headlong Hall* (1816), in David Garnett (ed.), *The Novels of Thomas Love Peacock* (1948), p. 22.

83 A. Constable (ed.), *The Letters of Anna Seward, 1784–1807* (1811), vol. iv, p. 10.

84 Anthony Ashley Cooper, 3rd Earl of Shaftesbury, *The Moralists* (1709), quoted in Thacker, *The Wildness Pleases*, p. 12; Shaftesbury there expressed his preference for 'Things of a natural kind: where neither Art, nor the Conceit or Caprice of Man has spoil'd their genuine order'. He continued:

O glorious *Nature*! supremely Fair, and sovereignly Good! All-loving and All-lovely, All-divine! Whose Looks are so becoming, and of such infinite Grace; whose Study brings such Wisdom, and whose Contemplation such Delight; whose every single Work affords an ampler Scene, and is a nobler Spectacle than all which every Art presented! – O mighty *Nature*! Wise Substitute of *Providence*! impower'd *Creatress*! O Thou impowering *Deity*, Supreme Creator! Thee I invoke, and Thee alone adore.

Shaftesbury, *The Moralists*, sect. 1, in *Characteristicks of Men, Manners, Opinions, Times* (1711), p. 158, quoted in Brian Hepworth, *The Rise of Romanticism* (1978), p. 81; Willey, *The Eighteenth Century Background*, p. 62.

85 See Joshua Poole, *English Parnassus* (1657), pp. 137–8; *The Gentleman's Magazine* (1747), quoted in David Pepper, *The Roots of Modern Environmentalism* (1984), p. 80; Marjorie Hope Nicolson, *Mountain Gloom and Mountain Glory* (1959).

86 John Dennis, cited in Christopher Hussey, *The Picturesque* (1967), p. 87.

87 Paget Toynbee and L. Whibley (eds), *The Correspondence of Thomas Gray* (1935), vol. i, p. 128.

88 Horace Walpole, letter to Richard West (28 September 1739), in W. S. Lewis (ed.), *The Yale Edition of Horace Walpole's Correspondence* (1937–83), vol. xiii, p. 181.

89 For William Gilpin, see Andrews, *The Search for the Picturesque*. The idea goes back to classical aesthetics: 'We find the Works of Nature still more pleasant, the more they resemble those of Art,' wrote Joseph Addison in the *Spectator* in 1712: Addison and Steele, *The Spectator*, no. 414, p. 549 (Wednesday, 25 June 1712).

90 Edmund Burke, *Philosophical Enquiry into the Origin of Our Ideas of the Sublime and the Beautiful* (1757), p. 52. See above, chapter 9, for a fuller discussion.

91 Joseph Banks in T. Pennant, *A Tour in Scotland, and Voyages to the Hebrides* (1774–6), vol. ii, p. 262. For Banks, see John Gascoigne, *Joseph Banks and the English Enlightenment* (1994).

92 Percy Bysshe Shelley, *Vindication of Natural Diet* (1813).

93 For Young, see his *Annals of Agriculture and Other Useful Arts* (1784–1815), vol. iv (1785), pp. 166–8; Barry Trinder, *The Industrial Revolution in Shropshire* (1973); Francis D. Klingender, *Art and the Industrial Revolution* (1975 [1947]); Bermingham, *Landscape and Ideology*, p. 79.

94 Sir Walter Scott (ed.), *The Poetical Works of Anna Seward* (1810), vol. ii, pp. 314–15.

95 Bermingham, *Landscape and Ideology*, p. 80; see also Stephen Daniels, *Fields of Vision* (1993).

96 James Pilkington, *View of the Present State of Derbyshire* (1789), p. 49. For key discussions of the above, see Daniels, *Fields of Vision*, pp. 60f; Charlotte Klonk, *Science and the Perception of Nature* (1996).

97 C. Bruyn Andrews (ed.), *The Torrington Diaries* (1934–8), vol. ii, p. 194.

98 Andrews, *The Torrington Diaries*, vol. iii, p. 81.

99 Uvedale Price, *Essays on the Picturesque, as Compared with the Sublime and the Beautiful* (1810), vol. i, p. 198.

100 Oliver Goldsmith, *The Deserted Village* (1770); William Cowper, *The Task* (1785), bk III, ll. 755–6, in James Sambrook (ed.), *W. Cowper, The Task and Selected Other Poems* (1994), p. 136; Roger Sales, *English Literature in History, 1780–1830* (1983); Barrell, *The Idea of Landscape and the Sense of Place, 1730–1840*, and *The Dark Side of the Landscape* (1980).

101 Young, *Annals of Agriculture and Other Useful Arts*, vol. xxvi, p. 214.

102 Humphry Repton, *Fragments on the Theory and Practice of Landscape Gardening* (1816), p. 191. There is a delightful spoof on Repton in Tom Stoppard's *Arcadia*, in which the landscaper Noakes insists that 'irregularity' is 'one of the chiefest principles of the Picturesque style': *Arcadia* (1993), p. 11; Stephen Daniels, *Humphry Repton: Landscape Gardening and the Geography of Georgian England* (1999).

103 Repton, *Fragments on the Theory and Practice of Landscape Gardening*, p. 193.

104 Thomas Peacock, *Crotchet Castle* (1831), in Garnett, *The Novels of Thomas Love Peacock*, p. 85.

105 C. R. Leslie, *Memoirs of the Life of John Constable* (1949), p. 111.

106 Peter Ackroyd, *Blake* (1995), p. 130.

107 William Blake, 'Jerusalem' (1804–20), in G. Keynes (ed.), *Blake: Complete Writings* (1969), p. 649.

108 Jon Mee, *Dangerous Enthusiasm* (1992); Blake, 'Jerusalem', in Keynes, *Blake: Complete Writings*, pp. 480–81, 649.

14 DID THE MIND HAVE A SEX?

1 John Milton, *Paradise Lost* (1667), bk IV, l. 299.

2 Fanny Burney, diary (1768), quoted in Patricia Meyer Spacks, *The Adolescent Idea* (1981), p. 23. She addressed her diary to 'Dear Nobody': see B. G. Shrank and D. J. Supino (eds.), *The Famous Miss Burney* (1976), p. 5.

3 Mary Wollstonecraft, *Maria or The Wrongs of Woman* (1994 [1798]), p. 11. She used the 'vast prison' phrase elsewhere, autobiographically: see *Letters, Written During a Short Residence in Sweden, Norway, and Denmark* (1976 [1796]), p. 102.

4 Catharine Macaulay, *Letters On Education* (1790), p. 212.

5 Jane Austen, *Persuasion* (1965 [1818]), p. 237. The passage continues: 'Men have had every advantage of us in telling their own story. Education has been theirs in so much higher a degree; the pen has been in their hands.' Such comments were common: compare Mary Astell, *The Christian Religion, as Profess'd by a Daughter of the Church of England* (1705), p. 293:

the Men being the Historians, they seldom condescend to record the great and the good Actions of Women; and when they take notice of them, 'tis with this wise Remark, That such Women *acted above their Sex*. By which one must suppose they wou'd have their Readers understand, That they were not Women who did those Great Actions, but that they were Men in Petticoats.

6 Isobel Grundy, *Lady Mary Wortley Montagu. Comet of the Enlightenment* (1999), p. 526.

7 Robert Filmer, *Patriarcha* (1949 [1680]); G. J. Schochet, *Patriarchalism in Political Thought* (1975).

8 For gender relations, see Anthony Fletcher, *Gender, Sex and Subordination in England, 1500–1800* (1995); Mary Abbott, *Family Ties* (1993); Ralph A. Houlbrooke, *The English Family,*

1450–1700 (1984); Susan D. Amussen, *An Ordered Society* (1988).

For women and the Enlightenment, see Bridget Hill, *Eighteenth-century Women: An Anthology* (1984), and *Women, Work and Sexual Politics in Eighteenth-century England* (1994); Margaret Hunt, Margaret Jacob, Phyllis Mack and Ruth Perry, *Women and the Enlightenment* (1984); Anne Laurence, *Women in England 1500–1760* (1994); Alice Browne, *The Eighteenth-century Feminist Mind* (1987); Laura Brown, *Ends of Empire* (1993); Barbara Caine, *English Feminism 1780–1980* (1997); Natalie Zemon Davis and Arlette Farge (eds.), *A History of Women in the West* (1993), vol. iii, and Phyllis Mack, 'Women and the Enlightenment: Introduction', (1984).

9 William Blackstone, *Commentaries on the Laws of England* (1979 [1765–9]), vol. i, p. 430. Mary Wollstonecraft called marriage 'legal prostitution': Claire Tomalin, *The Life and Death of Mary Wollstonecraft* (1974), p. 106.

10 Quoted in Linda Colley, *Britons: Forging the Nation 1707–1837* (1992), p. 238.

11 Anon., quoted in Roger Lonsdale (ed.), *Eighteenth-century Women Poets* (1989), p. 136.

12 William Alexander, *The History of Women* (1779), vol. ii, p. 336, quoted by Colley, *Britons: Forging the Nation 1707–1837*, p. 238. Modern politeness had raised respect for women; refinement and women were mutually reinforcing and advanced together.

13 Alexander, *The History of Women*, vol. i, p. 210.

14 Only with commercial society did women cease to be the slaves or idols of the other sex, and become their 'friends and companions'; only in Europe were women neither 'abject slaves' nor 'perpetual prisoners', but 'intelligent beings': Alexander, *The History of Women*, vol. i, p. 300.

15 Hannah More, quoted in Spacks, *The Adolescent Idea*, p. 120. More was aiming to make young women compliant to spare them future grief, but the sentiments also squared with her evangelical Christianity and social

conservatism. For more on More see below and chapter 20.

16 George Savile, marquis of Halifax, *The Lady's New Year's Gift* (1688), introduction; see discussion in Vivien Jones (ed.), *Women in the Eighteenth Century* (1990), p. 18.

17 Charles Strachey (ed.), *The Letters of the Earl of Chesterfield to His Son* (1932), vol. i, p. 261; *cf.* Felicity A. Nussbaum, *The Brink of All We Hate* (1984). Such views were often predicated upon gendered notions of duty. According to Lord Kames, 'To make a good husband, is but one branch of a man's duty; but it is the chief duty of a woman, to make a good wife': see Spacks, *The Adolescent Idea*, p. 121.

18 Hannah More, *Essays on Various Subjects* (1778), p. 133. This passage was copied out by the governess Agnes Porter: Joanna Martin (ed.), *A Governess in the Age of Jane Austen* (1988), p. 58.

19 M. G. Jones, *Hannah More* (1952), p. 50; Sylvia Harcstark Myers, *The Bluestocking Circle* (1990), p. 4. In the first volume of the *Athenian Mercury*, John Dunton provided space for questions from women. In May 1691 it was asked 'Whether it be proper for Women to be Learned?': G. McEwen, *The Oracle of the Coffee House* (1972), p. 103. He later set up the *Ladies Mercury* (1693).

20 Margaret Cavendish, duchess of Newcastle, *Orations of Divers Sorts* (sn, 1663), p. 225, quoted in Hilda Smith, *Reason's Disciples* (1982), p. 82. Note the deep cultural anxieties: Andrew Hiscock, 'Here's No Design, No Plot, Nor Any Ground' (1997).

21 Letter (10 October 1753), in Lady Mary Wortley Montagu, *Letters and Works*, 3rd edn (1861), vol. ii, p. 242. For Montagu on female education, see Grundy, *Lady Mary Wortley Montagu. Comet of the Enlightenment*, pp. 503ff. Anne Finch deemed women 'Education's more than Nature's fools': Sara Mendelson and Patricia Crawford, *Women in Early Modern England* (1998), p. 252.

22 Montagu, *Letters and Works*, vol. i, p. 314;

Grundy, *Lady Mary Wortley Montagu. Comet of the Enlightenment*, pp. 152f.

23 Montagu, *Letters and Works*, vol. i, p. 328.

24 Felicity A. Nussbaum, 'Polygamy, *Pamela*, and the Prerogative of Empire' (1995); Katharine M. Rogers, *Feminism in Eighteenth-century England* (1982), p. 54, a letter of 1 April 1717, to Lady —; Katharine M. Rogers, *Before Their Time* (1979), p. 54.

25 Judith Drake, *Essay in Defence of the Female Sex* (1696), pp. 11–12, 23, 143, quoted and valuably discussed in Estelle Cohen, ' "What the Women at All Times Would Laugh At" ' (1997), p. 134.

26 James Thomson, 'Autumn', in *The Seasons* (1744), pp. 157–8, ll. 610–16; discussed in Gordon Rattray Taylor, *The Angel Makers* (1958), p. 19. For the domestic woman constructed 'in and by print', see Kathryn Shevelow, *Women and Print Culture* (1989), p. 5.

27 On the new conjugality and egalitarian family, and companionate marriage, see R. Trumbach, *The Rise of the Egalitarian Family* (1978); Lawrence Stone, *The Family, Sex and Marriage in England, 1500–1800* (1977); L. A. Curtis, 'A Case Study of Defoe's Domestic Conduct Manuals Suggested by *The Family, Sex and Marriage in England 1500–1800*' (1981).

28 Harry Ballam and Roy Lewis (eds.), *The Visitors' Book* (1950), p. 89.

29 Browne, *The Eighteenth-century Feminist Mind*, p. 148. On the double standard, see Rogers, *Feminism in Eighteenth-century England*, p. 10.

30 Bernard de Mandeville, *The Fable of the Bees* (1924 [1714]), vol. i, p. 151.

31 For a fine example of this in practice, see Stella Tillyard, *Aristocrats* (1994). On Steele, see Jean H. Hagstrum, *Sex and Sensibility* (1980), p. 166; Brean S. Hammond, *Professional Imaginative Writing in England, 1670–1740* (1997), p. 178.

32 Quoted in Philip Carter, 'An "Effeminate" or "Efficient" Nation?' (1997), p. 438. Lady Mary Wortley Montagu praised 'the frequency of the mixed Assemblies' that her granddaughters enjoyed in the 'enlightened' 1760s, which provided 'a kind of Public Education, which I have always considered as necessary for girls as for boys': quoted in Jones, *Hannah More*, p. 7; on the new masculinity, see Michèle Cohen, *Fashioning Masculinity* (1996).

33 Carter, 'An "Effeminate" or "Efficient" Nation?', p. 438; see also David Castronovo, *The English Gentleman* (1987).

34 On the 'man of feeling', see G. J. Barker-Benfield, *The Culture of Sensibility* (1992).

35 Anthony, 3rd Earl of Shaftesbury, *Characteristicks* (1723), vol. i, p. 48; vol. ii, pp. 12, 24, 148; Jones, *Women in the Eighteenth Century*, p. 11. Philip John Carter, 'Mollies, Fops and Men of Feeling' [1995]; Rictor Norton, *Mother Clap's Molly House* (1992); Susan Staves, 'A Few Kind Words for the Fop' (1982).

36 Colley, *Britons: Forging the Nation 1707–1837*, ch. 6; the involvement of women in out of doors political activity, especially canvassing, is documented in Nicholas Rogers, *Crowds, Culture and Politics in Georgian Britain* (1998), ch. 7, pp. 215–47.

37 Anna Clark, *Women's Silence, Men's Violence* (1987), and *The Struggle for the Breeches* (1995).

38 John Potter, *Observations on the Present State of Music and Musicians* (1762), p. 106; Joyce Ellis, ' "On The Town" ' (1995), p. 22. Assumptions about the restrictiveness of separate spheres are also questioned in Lawrence E. Klein, 'Gender and the Public/Private Distinction in the Eighteenth Century' (1995); Amanda Vickery, *The Gentleman's Daughter* (1998).

39 Helen Berry, ' "Nice and Curious Questions" ' (1997).

40 Vickery, *The Gentleman's Daughter*, p. 257; Almack's Club was mixed and there was a female coffee house in Bath: Mary Thale, 'Women in London Debating Societies in 1780' (1995).

41 Cheryl Turner, *Living by the Pen* (1992), p. 46.

42 George Birkbeck Hill, *Boswell's Life of Johnson* (1934–50), vol. iii, p. 333. Predictably, Johnson also went on to warn against novels. See also Jacqueline Pearson, *Women's Reading in Britain, 1750–1835* (1999).

43 Kate Davies, 'Living Muses' [1995]; John Brewer, *The Pleasures of the Imagination* (1997), p. 78. For such achievers, see Dale Spender, *Mothers of the Novel* (1986); Myers, *The Bluestocking Circle*, p. 276; Jane Spencer, *The Rise of the Woman Novelist, from Aphra Behn to Jane Austen* (1986); on women's cultural underachievement, see Germaine Greer, *The Obstacle Race* (1979), and *Slip-Shod Sibyls* (1995). For women's involvement in science, see Gerald Dennis Meyer, *The Scientific Lady in England, 1650–1760* (1955); Myra Reynolds, *The Learned Lady in England 1650–1760* (1920); Patricia Phillips, *The Scientific Lady* (1990).

44 Kathryn Shevelow sees the domestic woman as being constructed 'in and by print': Shevelow, *Women and Print Culture*, p. 5; Jean E. Hunter, 'The Eighteenth-century Englishwoman' (1976); only one quarter of the articles in the *Gentleman's Magazine* supported the traditional idea of women as the weaker sex to be kept from study and public activities. Most relevant articles were sympathetic to women, being concerned with lack of educational opportunities, lack of career opportunities, the injustice of marriage and the need for equality between the sexes. In 'The Female Sex Not the Weakest' (pp. 588–9 (October 1735)), 'Climene' argues that 'women were inferior to men in nothing but brute strength'; women were deprived of learning because of the jealousy of men.

45 Mary Robinson, *Thoughts on the Condition of Women, and on the Injustice of Mental Subordination* (1799), p. 95; see the discussion in Anne K. Mellor, 'British Romanticism, Gender, and Three Women Artists' (1995), p. 121; and Cohen, ' "What the Women at All Times Would Laugh At" ', p. 138.

46 'Sometime in the eighteenth century, sex as we know it was invented': Thomas W. Laqueur, *Making Sex* (1990), p. 149. Laqueur argues that traditional 'one-sex hierarchical' models yielded in the eighteenth century to the idea that the male and the female were radically different in anatomy and hence in temperament and function. While this hypothesis has weaknesses, both empirical and conceptual, Laqueur is right to perceive that *difference* between the sexes became a burning issue and strongly accentuated in certain schools of thought. For enlightened attempts to create the 'science of women', see Londa Schiebinger, *The Mind Has No Sex?* (1989); Lynn Salkin Sbiroli, 'Generation and Regeneration' (1993); Ludmilla Jordanova, 'Natural Facts' (1980); Sylvana Tomaselli, 'Reflections on the History of the Science of Woman' (1991).

47 Laqueur, *Making Sex*, p. 148 and throughout.

48 Ornella Moscucci, *The Science of Woman* (1990).

49 Mary Wollstonecraft, *A Vindication of the Rights of Women*, in *A Vindication of the Rights of Men with A Vindication of the Rights of Woman* (1995), p. 171; on Rousseau and women, see Sylvana Tomaselli, 'The Enlightenment Debate on Women' (1985).

50 Wollstonecraft, *A Vindication of the Rights of Men with A Vindication of the Rights of Woman*, pp. 151, 236, and *Thoughts on the Education of Daughters* (1995 [1787]); E. Yeo (ed.), *Mary Wollstonecraft and 200 Years of Feminism* (1997); Ludmilla Jordanova, *Nature Depicted* (1999).

51 The youthful Day's Rousseau worship knew no bounds: 'Were all the books in the world to be destroyed . . . the second book I should wish to save, after the Bible, would be Rousseau's *Emilius*. . . . Every page is big with important truth'. See Marilyn Butler, *Jane Austen and the War of Ideas* (1975), p. 127.

52 Richard Lovell Edgeworth, *Memoirs* (1820), vol. i, pp. 220–22.

53 Edgeworth, *Memoirs*, vol. i, p. 334; Desmond Clarke, *The Ingenious Mr Edgeworth* (1965), p. 86.

54 See Tomaselli, 'The Enlightenment Debate on Women'.

55 Wollstonecraft, *A Vindication of the Rights of Men*, in *A Vindication of the Rights of Men with A Vindication of the Rights of Woman* (1995), p. 8; Patricia Meyer Spacks, *Imagining a Self*, p. 69.

56 Jane Austen, *Northanger Abbey* (1995 [1818]), p. 99.

57 Wollstonecraft, *A Vindication of the Rights of Women*, in *A Vindication of the Rights of Men with A Vindication of the Rights of Woman*, p. 77; see also Barker-Benfield, *The Culture of Sensibility*, p. 347.

58 For the critique of coquettishness, see Wollstonecraft, *A Vindication of the Rights of Men with A Vindication of the Rights of Woman*, pp. 6, 74, 137; Gary Kelly, '(Female) Philosophy in the Bedroom' (1997).

59 Wollstonecraft, *A Vindication of the Rights of Woman*, in *A Vindication of the Rights of Men with A Vindication of the Rights of Woman*, p. 137.

60 Wollstonecraft, *A Vindication of the Rights of Woman*, in *A Vindication of the Rights of Men with A Vindication of the Rights of Woman*, pp. 6, 214; Felicity A. Nussbaum, *The Autobiographical Subject* (1989); Syndy McMillen Conger, *Mary Wollstonecraft and the Language of Sensibility* (1994). Locke was much admired. Lady Mary Wortley Montagu told her daughter that 'Mr Locke . . . has made a more exact dissection of the Human mind than any Man before him': John Valdimir Price, 'The Reading of Philosophical Literature' (1982), p. 166. Debate rages among feminist scholars: for Locke cast as an anti-feminist, see Carole Pateman, *The Sexual Contract* (1988).

61 Claude Rawson, *Satire and Sentiment 1660–1830* (1994), p. 209. Swift was hardly one to talk, given his condescending relationships with, and attitudes towards, his own female friends.

62 Donald F. Bond (ed.), *The Tatler* (1987); Shevelow, *Women and Print Culture*, pp. 17, 93;

M. Mahl and H. Koon (eds.), *The Female Spectator* (1977).

63 Bond, *The Tatler*, vol. ii, no. 172, p. 444 (Tuesday, 16 May 1710).

64 Joseph Addison and Richard Steele, *The Spectator* (1965), vol. ii, no. 128, pp. 8–11 (Friday, 27 July 1711); Poulain de la Barre, *De l'égalité des deux sexes* (1673), for whom, see Cohen, ' "What the Women at All Times Would Laugh At" ', p. 125; and Browne, *The Eighteenth-century Feminist Mind*, p. 122; see the discussion in Erin Mackie, *Market à la Mode* (1977), p. 165. For the *Spectator* on companionate marriage, see nos. 105–8.

65 Quoted in Myers, *The Bluestocking Circle*, p. 123.

66 Henry Mackenzie, *Julia de Roubigné* (1777), vol. ii, letter 30, pp. 73–4; Janet Todd, *Sensibility: An Introduction* (1986), p. 100.

67 For these issues, see Janet Todd, *The Sign of Angellica* (1989). For a denunciation of the 'divine right' of husbands, see Wollstonecraft, *A Vindication of the Rights of Woman*, in *A Vindication of the Rights of Men with A Vindication of the Rights of Woman*, pp. 112–13: 'The divine right of husbands, like the divine right of kings, may, it is hoped, in this enlightened age, be contested without danger.'

68 Lady Mary Chudleigh, 'To the Ladies' (1705), in Lonsdale, *Eighteenth-century Women Poets*, p. 36.

69 James L. Axtell, *The Educational Works of John Locke* (1968). Locke's views are further explored in chapter 15.

70 Nowhere does Locke ever indicate, for instance, that women merit rights of political participation. It is noteworthy, however, that Locke treated marriage as a purely civil convention rather than a natural arrangement, and his anthropological observations in the *Essay concerning Human Understanding* included, without overt criticism, societies which sanctioned divorce or polygamy.

71 Jones, *Women in the Eighteenth Century*, p. 101; Myers, *The Bluestocking Circle*, p. 104;

Bridget Hill, *The Republican Virago* (1992), p. 158 – 'Republican virago' was Burke's slur. See also Macaulay, *Letters On Education* (1790).

72 Ian H. Bell, *Literature and Crime in Augustan England* (1991), p. 103. Similar arguments may be found in Lady Mary Chudleigh's *The Ladies' Defence* (1701) and *Woman Not Inferior to Man* (1739), by 'Sophia'. Many such works were anonymous. Mary Astell also published anonymously, knowing 'that when a women appears in Print, she must certainly run the gauntlet'. In her 1702 defence of Locke, Catherine Cockburn explained her anonymity in terms of the belief 'that the name of a woman would be a prejudice against a work of that nature': Catharine Cockburn, *A Defence of the Essay of Human Understanding Written by Mr Lock* (1702). Many writings by males, of course, also appeared anonymously.

73 Warren Chernaik, *Sexual Freedom in Restoration Literature* (1995), pp. 125–6; Bridget Hill, *The First English Feminist* (1986), pp. 50f.; Rogers, *Before Their Time*, pp. 28f. Astell published *A Serious Proposal to the Ladies for the Advancement of Their True and Greatest Interest* (1694), *Letters concerning the Love of God* (1695), *A Serious Proposal to the Ladies: Part II* (1697), *Some Reflections Upon Marriage* (1700), *Moderation Truly Stated* (1704), *A Fair Way with the Dissenters and Their Patrons* (1704), *An Impartial Enquiry into the Causes of Rebellion and Civil War in This Kingdom* (1704), *The Christian Religion, as Profess'd by a Daughter of the Church of England* (1705), and *Bart'lemy Fair or an Enquiry after Wit* (1709).

74 Ruth Perry, *The Celebrated Mary Astell* (1986).

75 Barker-Benfield, *The Culture of Sensibility*, pp. 73, 194, 221–8; Ruth Perry has rather implausibly praised Astell for seeing through capitalist modernism: 'Mary Astell and the Feminist Critique of Possessive Individualism' (1990).

76 Astell, *Some Reflections upon Marriage*, preface, quoted in Warren Chernaik, *Sexual Freedom in Restoration Literature* (1995), pp. 125–

63; Astell, of course, raised the perpetual issue of the congruency between domestic and political relations. As Lady Brute (in Vanbrugh's *The Provok'd Wife* (1697)) asked: 'The argument's good between king and people, why not between husband and wife?'

77 Astell, *A Serious Proposal to the Ladies for the Advancement of Their True and Greatest Interest*; Hill, *The First English Feminist*, p. 49; Rogers, *Feminism in Eighteenth-century England*, p. 29.

78 Sarah Scott, *A Description of Millennium Hall and the Country Adjacent* (1996 [1762]); Gregory Claeys (ed.), *Utopias of the British Enlightenment* (1994), p. xv. Compare the female community in Clara Reeve's *The School for Widows* (1791).

79 Tomalin, *The Life and Death of Mary Wollstonecraft*.

80 Gary Kelly, *Revolutionary Feminism* (1992).

81 Spacks, *Imagining a Self*, p. 183; Wollstonecraft, *A Vindication of the Rights of Woman*, in *A Vindication of the Rights of Men with A Vindication of the Rights of Woman*, p. 137.

82 Wollstonecraft, *A Vindication of the Rights of Men with A Vindication of the Rights of Woman*, pp. 250, 292.

83 Roger Lonsdale (ed.), *The New Oxford Book of Eighteenth Century Verse* (1984), p. 816:

> YES, injured Woman! rise, assert thy right!
> Woman! too long degraded, scorned, oppressed;
> O born to rule in partial Law's despite,
> Resume thy native empire o'er the breast!

Note that, while admiring Wollstonecraft's writings, Mrs Barbauld was 'too correct in conduct to visit her': Rogers, *Feminism in Eighteenth-century England*, p. 218. She had a reputation for starchiness. According to Coleridge, she disapproved of his *Ancient Mariner* on the grounds that it was implausible and had no moral.

84 Quoted in Cohen, ' "What the Women at All Times Would Laugh At" ', p. 138.

85 H. R. Dickinson, *The Politics of the People in Eighteenth-century Britain* (1995), p. 184. See chapter 18 below.

86 James Mill, *Essay On Government* (1824), p. 22.

87 John Bennett, *Strictures on Female Education Chiefly as it Relates to the Culture of the Heart, in Four Essays* (1787), p. 124.

88 [Richard Polwhele], *The Unsex'd Females* (1798), p. 7.

89 [Polwhele], *The Unsex'd Females*, pp. 6, 16. Wollstonecraft's death was divine retribution (pp. 29–30):

I cannot but think, that the Hand of Providence is visible, in her life, her death, and the Memoirs themselves. As she was given up to her 'heart's lusts', and let 'to follow her own imaginations', that the fallacy of her doctrines, and the effects of an irreligious conduct, might be manifested to the world; and as she died a death that strongly marked the distinction of the sexes, by pointing out the destiny of women, and the diseases to which they are liable; so her husband was permitted, in writing her Memoirs, to labour under a temporary infatuation, that every incident might be seen without a gloss – every fact exposed without an apology.

Cited in Todd, *The Sign of Angellica*, p. 215.

90 Todd, *The Sign of Angellica*, p. 131. Wit, unless rigorously controlled, 'is the most dangerous Companion that can lurk in a Female Bosom', insisted Wetenhall Wilkes in 1744: Spacks, *The Adolescent Idea*, p. 23.

91 Hill, *The First English Feminist*, p. 145; Myers, *The Bluestocking Circle*, p. 44. The same fate awaited Hester Thrale when she married Giuseppi Piozzi – Elizabeth Montagu became hysterical over the marriage, which 'has taken such horrible possession of my mind I cannot advert to any other subject': Rogers, *Feminism in Eighteenth-century England*, p. 216: Mrs Thrale had become 'a disgrace upon her sex'.

92 Todd, *The Sign of Angellica*, p. 131;

Tomalin, *The Life and Death of Mary Wollstonecraft*, p. 244.

93 Myers, *The Bluestocking Circle*, pp. 238, 257; Mrs Chapone also disapproved of Macaulay, for her politics and erotic adventurism alike.

94 Laetitia-Matilda Hawkins, *Letters on the Female Mind, Its Powers and Pursuits* (1793), vol. i, p. 142:

It cannot, I think, be truly asserted, that the intellectual powers know no difference of sex. Nature certainly intended a distinction . . . the feminine intellect has less strength and more acuteness. Consequently in our exercise of it, we show less perseverance and more vivacity.

95 Rogers, *Feminism in Eighteenth-century England*, p. 32. Elizabeth Carter (1717–1806) was the eldest daughter of a clergyman who taught her Latin, Greek and Hebrew; she learned French and taught herself Italian, Spanish and German, with some Portuguese and Arabic. She also studied mathematics, geography, history and astronomy, and wrote music. In 1758, she earned £1,000 for her translation of Epictetus, which Samuel Richardson published by subscription.

96 Myers, *The Bluestocking Circle*, p. 231. Hester Chapone's *Letters on the Improvement of the Mind* (1773) was reprinted at least sixteen times in the eighteenth century.

97 Mary Hays, *Appeal to the Men of Great Britain in Behalf of Women* (1798), p. 97, discussed in Browne, *The Eighteenth-century Feminist Mind*, p. 117.

98 Catherine Belsey, 'Afterword: A Future for Materialist-Feminist Criticism?' (1991), p. 262. The Enlightenment was also a disaster for 'black people' and 'the non-Western world'.

99 Nancy Armstrong, *Desire and Domestic Fiction* (1987), p. 8; see the focused discussion in Miles Ogborn, *Spaces of Modernity* (1998), p. 42.

15 EDUCATION: A PANACEA?

1 Joseph Addison and Richard Steele, *The Spectator* (1965), vol. ii, no. 215, p. 338.

2 James Keir (ed.), *An Account of the Life and Writings of Thomas Day* (1791), p. 104, quoted in B. Simon, *The Two Nations and the Educational Structure 1780–1870* (1974 [1960]), p. 25.

3 'Teachers', in *Encyclopedia Britannica*, 4th edn (1800), vol. xx, p. 230.

4 On children, broadly, see J. H. Plumb, 'The New World of the Children in Eighteenth-century England' (1975); Ivy Pinchbeck and Margaret Hewitt, *Children in English Society* (1969–73); Hugh Cunningham, *The Children of the Poor* (1991), and *Children and Childhood in Western Society Since 1500* (1995). Lawrence Stone has questioned parental affection towards children before the eighteenth century, Linda Pollock has reasserted it: Lawrence Stone, *The Family, Sex and Marriage in England, 1500–1800* (1977); Linda Pollock, *Forgotten Children* (1983), and *A Lasting Relationship: Parents and Children over Three Centuries (1987)*.

5 M. G. Jones, *Hannah More* (1952), p. 117.

6 Philippe Ariès, *Centuries of Childhood* (1973); Stone, *The Family, Sex and Marriage in England, 1500–1800*. See also Ilana Krausman Ben-Amos, *Adolescence and Youth in Early Modern English History* (1994) and Patricia Meyer Spacks, *The Adolescent Idea* (1981) for the earlier absence of modern ideas of adolescence.

7 J. A. Passmore, *The Perfectibility of Man* (1970), pp. 159f.

8 John Locke, *Some Thoughts concerning Education* (1693), in James L. Axtell, *The Educational Writings of John Locke* (1968), p. 114. On child-rearing, see D. Beekman, *The Mechanical Baby* (1979); C. Hardyment, *Dream Babies* (1983). It would be wrong to exaggerate Locke's originality as a pedagogue: he is part of a great chain of Renaissance educators. His influence, however, is undeniable.

9 Maurice Cranston, *John Locke: A Biography* (1957), pp. 239ff. Axtell, *The Educational Writings of John Locke*, p. 325; see the discussion in D. Spadafora, *The Idea of Progress in Eighteenth-century Britain* (1990), p. 167.

10 'A slavish bondage to parents cramps every faculty of the mind,' Mary Wollstonecraft pointed out: 'and Mr Locke very judiciously observes, that if the mind be curbed and humbled too much in children; if their spirits be abased and broken much by too strict an hand over them; they lose all their vigour and industry.' Mary Wollstonecraft, *A Vindication of the Rights of Woman*, in *A Vindication of the Rights of Men with A Vindication of the Rights of Woman* (1995 [1790 and 1792]), p. 247. Her reference is to Locke, *Some Thoughts concerning Education*, para. 46, in Axtell, *The Educational Works of John Locke*, p. 148, paras. 2 and 46.

11 Axtell, *The Educational Writings of John Locke*, p. 253.

12 Isaac Kramnick, 'Children's Literature and Bourgeois Ideology' (1983), pp. 21–2. Kramnick paraphrases and quotes Locke's *Some Thoughts concerning Education* (1899 [1693]), pp. 149 and 156.

13 Axtell, *The Educational Writings of John Locke*, pp. 242–3: 'If Children were let alone, they would be no more afraid in the Dark, than in broad Sun-shine'; S. F. Pickering Jr, *John Locke and Children's Books in Eighteenth-century England* (1981), pp. 43, 60.

14 Axtell, *The Educational Writings of John Locke*, p. 19.

15 Axtell, *The Educational Writings of John Locke*, p. 116.

16 Axtell, *The Educational Writings of John Locke*, p. 117.

17 Axtell, *The Educational Writings of John Locke*, pp. 116, 123. See also Maurice

Cranston, *John Locke: A Biography* (1957), p. 240.

18 Axtell, *The Educational Writings of John Locke*, p. 134: 'if a Man, after his first Eating in the Morning, would presently sollicite Nature, and try, whether he could strain himself so as to obtain a Stool, he might in time, by a constant Application, bring it to be Habitual'.

19 Axtell, *The Educational Writings of John Locke*, p. 140.

20 Axtell, *The Educational Writings of John Locke*, pp. 118, 143.

21 Axtell, *The Educational Writings of John Locke*, pp. 118, 150.

22 Axtell, *The Educational Writings of John Locke*, p. 146.

23 Axtell, *The Educational Writings of John Locke*, pp. 208–9.

24 Axtell, *The Educational Writings of John Locke*, p. 212.

25 Axtell, *The Educational Writings of John Locke*, p. 152.

26 Axtell, *The Educational Writings of John Locke*, p. 117: Locke says that children 'love to be treated as Rational creatures sooner than is imagined' (p. 181). On breeding, see George C. Brauer, *The Education of a Gentleman* (1959).

27 Ephraim Chambers, *Cyclopaedia, Or an Universal Dictionary of Arts and Sciences* (1728), vol. i, p. 279. 'Everybody' means 'everybody who counts': Pickering, *John Locke and Children's Books in Eighteenth-century England*, p. 10.

28 Isaac Watts, *Philosophical Essays on Various Subjects* (1733), p. viii; M. J. M. Ezell, 'John Locke's Images of Childhood' (1983/4).

29 James Talbot, *The Christian Schoolmaster* (1707), p. 24.

30 Pickering, *John Locke and Children's Books in Eighteenth-century England*, p. 10. Among later admirers of Locke's educational views was the utilitarian law reformer Samuel Romilly. See his *Memoirs of the Life of Sir Samuel Romilly* (1971 [1840]), vol. i, p. 279.

31 Lawson and Silver, *A Social History of Education in England* (1973).

32 Quoted in Bridget Hill, *The Republican Virago* (1992), p. 146.

33 Catharine Macaulay, *Letters On Education* (1790), p. 27, discussed in Hill, *The Republican Virago*, p. 158.

34 Hill, *The Republican Virago*, p. 159.

35 Richard Lovell Edgeworth, *Memoirs* (1820), vol. i, p. 173, cited in Desmond Clarke, *The Ingenious Mr Edgeworth* (1965), p. 166; Robert E. Schofield, *The Lunar Society of Birmingham* (1963), p. 55.

36 Edgeworth, *Memoirs*, vol. i, pp. 253–4, 268–9. Dick migrated to Carolina and led a dissipated life.

37 Clarke, *The Ingenious Mr Edgeworth*, p. 164; Mitzi Myers, 'Shot From Canons' (1995). Marilyn Butler, *Maria Edgeworth: A Literary Biography* (1972).

38 Clarke, *The Ingenious Mr Edgeworth*, p. 163. *Practical Education* was, actually, a team effort, with contributions from family and friends, and Maria delegated to put it down on paper – the beginning of a literary partnership, she wrote, 'which for so many years was the joy and pride of my life'.

39 Clarke, *The Ingenious Mr Edgeworth*, p. 40.

40 Clarke, *The Ingenious Mr Edgeworth*, p. 40.

41 Clarke, *The Ingenious Mr Edgeworth*, p. 50.

42 Marilyn Butler, *Romantics, Rebels and Reactionaries* (1981), p. 94. A century and a half earlier, John Milton in his *Of Education* (1644), p. 2, had thought religion the very point of education: 'The end then of learning is to repair the ruins of our first parents by regaining to know God aright.'

43 Edgeworth, *Memoirs*, vol. ii, pp. 527, 549.

44 Michael Newton, 'The Child of Nature' (1996).

45 R. L. Edgeworth and M. Edgeworth, *Practical Education* (1798), vol. i, p. 63. This was one of many experiments integral to the authors' goal of making education an 'experimental science' (vol. i, pp. v–vi). For children as objects of (thought) experiments, see Larry Wolff, 'When I Imagine a Child (1998).

46 Edgeworth and Edgeworth, *Practical Education*, vol. i, p. 64.

47 Edgeworth and Edgeworth, *Practical Education*, vol. i, p. xii.

48 Clarke, *The Ingenious Mr Edgeworth*, p. 202.

49 Thomas Beddoes, appendix to J. E. Stock, *Life of Thomas Beddoes MD* (1811); Dorothy A. Stansfield, 'Thomas Beddoes and Education' (Spring 1979), and *Thomas Beddoes MD 1760–1808, Chemist, Physician, Democrat* (1984), p. 83.

50 Roy Porter, *Doctor of Society* (1991), pp. 39f., 79f.

51 For Priestley on education, see J. A. Passmore, *Priestley's Writings on Philosophy, Science and Politics* (1965), pp. 285–313; H. McLachlan, *Warrington Academy, Its History and Influence* (1943); Joseph Priestley, *An Essay on a Course of Liberal Education for Civil and Active Life* (1765).

52 John Brown, *Thoughts on Civil Liberty, Licentiousness and Faction* (1765).

53 Joseph Priestley, *An Essay on the First Principles of Government* (1771), in John Towill Rutt (ed.), *The Theological and Miscellaneous Works of Joseph Priestley* (1817–32), vol. xxii, p. 119. See Peter N. Miller (ed.), *Joseph Priestley: Political Writings* (1993), p. xix.

54 Priestley, *An Essay on the First Principles of Government*, in Rutt, *The Theological and Miscellaneous Works of Joseph Priestley*, vol. xxii, p. 46.

55 Enlightened men advocated practical education for commerce. Wedgwood thought it 'a very idle waste of time for any boys intended for trade to learn Latin, as they seldom learnt it to any tolerable degree of perfection, or retained what they learnt. Besides they did not want it, and the time would be much better bestowed in making themselves perfect in French and accounts': Ann Finer and George Savage (eds), *The Selected Letters of Josiah Wedgwood* (1965), p. 244.

56 W. Roberts (ed.), *Memoirs of the Life and Correspondence of Mrs Hannah More* (1834), vol. iii, p. 133.

57 Joseph Priestley, *Miscellaneous Observations Relating to Education* (1778), p. 129.

58 Michael R. Watts, *The Dissenters* (1978), vol. i, p. 371.

59 Watts, *The Dissenters*, vol. i, p. 467.

60 See, for instance, John Lawson and Harold Silver, *A Social History of Education in England* (1973); H. McLachlan, *English Education under the Test Acts* (1931); Nicholas A. Hans, *New Trends in Education in the Eighteenth Century* (1966).

61 Edward Gibbon, *Memoirs of My Life* (1966 [1796]), p. 53.

62 V. H. H. Green, 'Reformers and Reform in the University' (1986), p. 607.

63 For instances, see Victor Neuberg, *The Penny Histories*, in *Milestones in Children's Literature*, and *Popular Education in Eighteenth-century England* (1971).

64 Ariès, *Centuries of Childhood*; see the pioneering discussion in Plumb, 'The New World of the Children in Eighteenth-century England'.

65 See [Anon.], *A History of Little Goody Two Shoes* (1766); James A. Secord, 'Newton in the Nursery' (1985). Newbery was a commercial innovator who virtually invented the children's publishing trade. Goody Two-Shoes had gone through sixty-six British editions by 1850: Margaret R. Hunt, *The Middling Sort* (1996), p. 78.

66 *Little Goody Two-Shoes* was thoroughly uplifting, combining the themes of female agency in the face of adversity with the pursuit of literacy and virtue and successful social mobility. The orphaned Margery Meanwell and her younger brother Tommy are cast penniless upon the world. Ignored by their relatives, they are helped by a local clergyman who buys them clothes and sends Tommy off to sea. Meanwhile, little Margery teaches herself to read and becomes so adept that she begins teaching other children. She also becomes precociously wise, advising a testy gentleman to rise early and eat sparingly, combating superstitious beliefs and preventing a robbery at the house of her father's old enemy and former landlord, Sir Timothy – thus demonstrating her capacity to return good for evil. In time, her reputation earns her the position of schoolmistress of the local school, where she continues to teach children to read using her alphabet blocks, combining this with preaching obedience to authority and the value of early rising and hard work. She inveighs against cock-throwing, torturing insects and whipping horses and dogs, and she continues to dispense wise advice to villagers and to spread rational problem-solving wherever she goes. In the fullness of time a gentleman falls in love with her and marries her, at which point her brother Tommy serendipitously reappears, having made his fortune in Africa, and endows her with a rich settlement.

67 Richardson's villain, Lovelace, comments how cruelty to women often begins in cruelty to animals: Samuel Richardson, *Clarissa* (1748), vol. iii, letter 75, pp. 347–50.

68 Axtell, *The Educational Works of John Locke*, p. 225.

69 James Turner, *Reckoning with the Beast* (1980), p. 7; Pickering, *John Locke and Children's Books in Eighteenth-century England*, p. 19.

70 Keith Thomas, *Man and the Natural World* (1983); Christianity had maintained (witness Peacock's clergyman, the Revd Dr Gaster) that 'all animals were created solely and exclusively for the use of man' – lacking a soul, they were not ends in themselves, and Cartesianism had denied them consciousness: Thomas Peacock, *Headlong Hall* (1816), in David Garnett (ed.), *The Novels of Thomas Love Peacock* (1948), p. 15. See the discussion in chapter 13.

71 David Elliston Allen, *The Naturalist in Britain* (1976); Nicolaas A. Rupke (ed.), *Vivisection in Historical Context* (1987);

Macdonald Daly, 'Vivisection in Eighteenth-century Britain' (1989).

72 K. Tester, *Animals and Society* (1991), p. 96.

73 Turner, *Reckoning with the Beast*, p. 13; Laurence Sterne, *The Life and Opinions of Tristram Shandy* (1967 [1759–67]), p. 131.

74 James Thomson, 'Spring', in *The Seasons* (1744), p. 19, ll. 386–91.

75 Turner, *Reckoning with the Beast*, p. 49.

76 John Wiltshire, *Samuel Johnson in the Medical World* (1991), p. 129.

77 Wiltshire, *Samuel Johnson in the Medical World*, p. 125.

78 'An Experiment on a Bird in the Air Pump', in Benedict Nicolson, *Joseph Wright of Derby: Painter of Light* (1968), pp. 43–5, 112–13.

79 Schofield, *The Lunar Society of Birmingham*, p. 215.

80 Kramnick, 'Children's Literature and Bourgeois Ideology', p. 26. Isaac Watts wrote *Against Idleness and Mischief* (1715):

> How doth the little busy bee
> > Improve each shining hour,
> And gather honey all the day
> > From every opening flower!

Anthologized in Roger Lonsdale (ed.), *The New Oxford Book of Eighteenth-century Verse* (1984), p. 74.

81 J. H. Plumb, 'The New World of the Children in Eighteenth-Century England' (1975), p. 303.

82 Thomas Day, *The History of Sandford and Merton* (1783–9). See F. J. H. Darton, *Children's Books in England*, 3rd edn (1982), pp. 145–7.

83 Kramnick, 'Children's Literature and Bourgeois Ideology'.

84 Kramnick, 'Children's Literature and Bourgeois Ideology', p. 37. Kramnick is quoting Day.

85 Kramnick, 'Children's Literature and Bourgeois Ideology'.

86 [Tom Telescope], *The Newtonian System of Philosophy* (1761); Geoffrey Summerfield, *Fantasy and Reason* (1984); Pickering, *John Locke*

and Children's Books in Eighteenth-century England;
Bette P. Goldstein, *Lessons to be Learned* (1984);
Susan Pedersen, 'Hannah More Meets
Simple Simon' (1986); Joyce Whalley,
Cobwebs to Catch Flies (1975).

87 [Tom Telescope], *The Newtonian System of
Philosophy* purported to be 'the substance of
six lectures read to the Lilliputian Society':
Plumb, 'The New World of the Children in
Eighteenth-century England', p. 302; Secord,
'Newton in the Nursery'. It was not the first
popular science book for children: as early as
1710 there appeared [Anon.], *A Short and Easie
Method to Give Children an Idea or True Notion of
Celestial and Terrestrial Beings* (1710).

88 Pickering, *John Locke and Children's Books in
Eighteenth-century England*, p. 41.

89 Kramnick, 'Children's Literature and
Bourgeois Ideology', p. 227; Marina Warner,
No Go the Bogeyman (1998), p. 318.

90 Kramnick, 'Children's Literature and
Bourgeois Ideology, pp. 227–8.

91 Warner, *No Go the Bogeyman*, p. 318.

92 Kramnick, 'Children's Literature and
Bourgeois Ideology', pp. 228–9; Pickering,
*John Locke and Children's Books in
Eighteenth-century England*, p. 146. For the role
of women in the anti-slavery movement, see
Moira Ferguson, *Subject To Others* (1992),
which explores how women spoke for blacks
and slaves.

93 'Think,' Lamb told Coleridge, 'what you
would have been now, if you had been
crammed with geography and natural
history': Pickering, *John Locke and Children's
Books in Eighteenth-century England*, p. 61.

94 Peter Coveney, *The Image of Childhood*
(1968).

95 See Ian H. Bell, *Literature and Crime in
Augustan England* (1991).

96 Dennis Todd, *Imagining Monsters* (1995);
Alice Domurat Dreger, *Hermaphrodites and the
Medical Invention of Sex* (1998).

97 John Toland, *Reasons for Naturalising the
Jews in Great Britain and Ireland* (1714). On
Jews, see Frank Felsenstein, *A Paradigm of

Otherness* (1995); Todd M. Endelman, *The
Jews of Georgian England 1714–1830* (1979); and
the wider discussion in Ulrich Im Hof, *The
Enlightenment* (1994), p. 245, and Hiram
Caton, *The Politics of Progress* (1988), p. 246.

98 Warner, *No Go the Bogeyman*, p. 163.

99 The parallel was drawn long before
Victorian social commentators began talking
of 'darkest England', partly because of the
discovery of so-called 'wild boys' and 'wild
girls' (people displaying the characteristics
and problem features associated with
'savages'): Newton, 'The Child of Nature';
Alan Bewell, *Wordsworth and the Enlightenment*,
p. 62.

100 James Cook, *Journals* (1955–68), vol. ii,
p. 322.

101 Felicity A. Nussbaum, 'Polygamy,
Pamela, and the Prerogative of Empire'
(1995), p. 217; Henry Steele Commager, *The
Empire of Reason* (1978), p. 52; Gregory Claeys
(ed.), *Utopias of the British Enlightenment* (1994),
p. xi. The functions of imaginary voyages are
well discussed in Charles Kerby-Miller,
*Memoirs of the Extraordinary Life, Works, and
Discoveries of Martinus Scriblerus* (1988), p. 316.
For travels within Europe, see Brian Dolan,
Exploring European Frontiers (1999).

102 Edmund Burke, in a letter to W.
Robertson, in W. Robertson, *Works* (1840),
quoted in Ronald L. Meek, *Social Science and
the Ignoble Savage* (1975), p. 173; see also Peter
Marshall and Gwyndyr Williams, *The Great
Map of Mankind* (1982).

103 Meek, *Social Science and the Ignoble Savage*,
p. 173.

104 Jonathan Lamb, *Preserving the Self in the
South Seas* (forthcoming).

105 Daniel Defoe, *Robinson Crusoe* (1985
[1719]). For a classic interpretation of
Robinson Crusoe as representative of the age,
see Ian Watt, *The Rise of the Novel* (1957),
pp. 60–90.

106 Jonathan Swift, *Gulliver's Travels* (1985
[1726]), p. 243, discussed in Laura Brown,
Ends of Empire (1993), p. 170; Dennis

Todd, 'The Hairy Maid at the Harpsichord' (1992).

107 George Birkbeck Hill, *Boswell's Life of Johnson* (1934–50), vol. i, p. 308. Jeremy Bentham, *Emancipate Your Colonies!*, in John Bowring (ed.), *The Works of Jeremy Bentham* (1995 [1843]), vol. iv, p. 407.

108 On eighteenth-century anthropology, see H. F. Augstein (ed.), *Race: The Origins of an Idea, 1760–1850* (1996); J. S. Slotkin, *Readings in Early Anthropology* (1965).

109 See M. T. Hodgen, *Early Anthropology in the Sixteenth and Seventeenth Centuries* (1964); H. F. Augstein, *James Cowles Prichard's Anthropology* (1999).

110 Hugh West, 'The Limits of Enlightenment Anthropology (1989); Robert Wokler, 'From *l'homme physique* to *l'homme moral* and Back' (1993), and 'Anthropology and Conjectural History in the Enlightenment' (1995).

111 Ian Simpson Ross, *Lord Kames and the Scotland of His Day* (1972), p. 337; Ivan Hannaford, *Race. The History of an Idea in the West* (1996).

112 Henry Home, Lord Kames, *Sketches of the History of Man* (1774); Robert Wokler, 'Apes and Races in the Scottish Enlightenment' (1988); Martin Bernal, *Black Athena* (1987), vol. i; Christopher J. Berry, ' "Climate" in the Eighteenth Century' (1974).

113 H. Honour, *Chinoiserie* (1961); J. J. Clarke, *Oriental Enlightenment* (1997); William W. Appleton, *A Cycle of Cathay* (1951).

114 Peter Marshall (ed.), *The British Discovery of Hinduism in the Eighteenth Century* (1970); Hans Aarsleff, *The Study of Language in England, 1780–1860* (1983), ch. 4.

115 See Isobel Grundy, *Lady Mary Wortley Montagu. Comet of the Enlightenment* (1999), pp. 152f. For the Koran, see Rana Kabbani, *Europe's Myths of Orient* (1986), p. 31; Sarah Searight, *The British in the Middle East* (1979), p. 82; Ahmad Gunny, *Images of Islam in Eighteenth-century Writing* (1996).

116 Edward Said, *Orientalism* (1978).

117 Roy Porter, *Gibbon* (1988), p. 131; Gunny, *Images of Islam in Eighteenth-century Writing*.

118 See Oliver Goldsmith, *Citizen of the World* (1762); Appleton, *A Cycle of Cathay*, p. 122; V. G. Kiernan, *The Lords of Human Kind* (1972), p. 22. Deists like Matthew Tindal held up Confucians as sages who recognized that the essence of religion was morality.

119 Quoted in Michael Adas, *Machines as the Measure of Men* (1989), p. 169; and see the discussion of James Mill in J. W. Burrow, *Evolution and Society* (1966, 1970), pp. 42–62. For the growing Western defamation of Eastern knowledge as childish, see Roberta Bivins, 'Expectations and Expertise' (1999).

120 Anthony Pagden, *Lords of All the World* (1995), p. 77. Lockeans denied the legitimacy of the argument from conquest.

121 Lois Whitney, *Primitivism and the Idea of Progress* (1934). The phrase 'noble savage' is Dryden's. The fiction was satirized in Edmund Burke, *A Vindication of Natural Society* (1982 [1756]).

122 See David Brion Davis, *The Problem of Slavery in Western Culture* (1966); Angus Calder, *Revolutionary Empire* (1981); Hugh Honour, *The Image of the Black in Western Art* (1989), vol. iv; Roxann Wheeler, 'The Complexion of Desire' (1999); Markman Ellis, *The Politics of Sensibility* (1996).

123 James Grainger, *The Sugar-Cane* (1764), bk I, ll. 611–12. See Lonsdale, *The New Oxford Book of Eighteenth-century Verse*, p. 520; David Dabydeen (ed.), *The Black Presence in English Literature* (1985), and *Hogarth's Blacks* (1985). Johnson was hostile: he stunned 'some very grave men at Oxford', Boswell reports, by proposing the toast: 'Here's to the next insurrection of the negroes in the West Indies': Hill, *Boswell's Life of Johnson*, vol. iii, p. 200.

124 Vincent Carretta (ed.), *Unchained Voices* (1996), and (ed.), *Olaudah Equiano: The Interesting Narrative and Other Writings* (1995).

125 See Folarin Shyllon, *Black People in Britain*

1555–1833 (1977), p. ix. The first edition of William Blackstone's *Commentaries on the Laws of England* (1979 [1765–9]), declared 'that a slave or negro, the instant he lands in England, becomes a freeman': Carretta, *Unchained Voices*, p. 5.

126 See Ferguson, *Subject to Others*, for protests by women.

127 Quoted in Carretta, *Unchained Voices*, p. 6. Day wrote an anti-slavery poem called *The Dying Negro* (1773).

128 Erasmus Darwin, *The Botanic Garden* (1789–91), pt II, pp. 421–30. For Wedgwood's anti-slavery sentiments, see Finer and Savage (eds.), *The Selected Letters of Josiah Wedgwood*, p. 310. See also David Turley, *The Culture of English Antislavery, 1780–1860* (1991); Shyllon, *Black People in Britain 1555–1833*, p. 9.

129 F. J. Klingberg, *The Anti-Slavery Movement in England* (1926), p. 51.

130 Klingberg, *The Anti-Slavery Movement in England*, p. 51.

131 William Paley, *The Complete Works of William Paley* (1824), vol. iii, pp. 146f.; Klingberg, *The Anti-Slavery Movement in England*, p. 51.

132 Daniel Defoe, *The History and Remarkable Life of Colonel Jacque, Commonly Call'd* (1722).

133 David Turley, *The Culture of English Antislavery, 1780–1860* (1991), pp. 25f.

134 For abolitionism, see J. Walvin, *Slavery and British Society, 1776–1848* (1982), and *Black and White* (1973); J. Walvin and D. Eltis (eds.), *Abolition of the Atlantic Slave Trade* (1981); J. Walvin, M. Craton and D. Wright (eds.), *Slavery, Abolition and Emancipation* (1976). Black voices to some extent spoke in the enlightened idiom, but they were primarily Christian: Carretta, *Unchained Voices*.

135 Aphra Behn, *Oroonoko or the Royal Slave* (1688), p. 30.

136 Paul Langford, *A Polite and Commercial People* (1989), p. 514.

137 T. B. Clark, *Omai: The First Polynesian Ambassador to England* (1941), pp. 76–89.

138 For Polynesia, see Bernard Smith, *Imagining the Pacific* (1992); Barbara Maria Stafford, *Voyage Into Substance* (1984); Neil Rennie, *Far-fetched Facts* (1995).

139 James Cook, quoted in Hof, *The Enlightenment*, p. 227.

140 Roy Porter, 'The Exotic as Erotic' (1989).

141 Cook, *Journals*, vol. ii, p. 175.

142 Whitney, *Primitivism and the Idea of Progress*, p. 58.

143 Whitney, *Primitivism and the Idea of Progress*, p. 64; R. D. Altick, *The Shows of London* (1978), p. 47.

144 Kiernan, *The Lords of Human Kind*; Simon Schaffer, 'Visions of Empire: Afterword' (1996); Karlis Racevskis, *Postmodernism and the Search for Enlightenment* (1993).

16 THE VULGAR

1 Erasmus Darwin, quoted in Maureen McNeil, *Under the Banner of Science* (1987), p. 111.

2 Josiah Wedgwood, 'An Address to Young Inhabitants of the Pottery' (1783), p. 22. See above, chapter 15.

3 Joseph Trapp, *Lectures On Poetry* (1742), quoted in Brian Hepworth, *The Rise of Romanticism* (1978), p. 58. See Henry Fielding's *The Covent-Garden Journal*, no. 33 (Saturday, 23 April 1752), which carried the tag: '*Odi profanum vulgus.* – Hor. I hate profane rascals', and which banteringly spoke of 'this very learned and enlightened age'. For 'many are called', see David Hartley, *Observations on Man, His Frame, His Duty, and His Expectations* (1791), vol. ii, p. 405.

4 Quoted in Leslie Stephen, *History of English Thought in the Eighteenth Century* (1962), vol. i, p. 197. Some luminaries assumed a nastier tone. 'The Church, like the Ark of Noah, is worth saving,' spat Bishop Warburton to his friend Richard Hurd, 'not for the sake of the unclean beasts and vermin that almost filled it, but for the little corner of rationality that was as much disturbed by the stink within as by the tempest without': William Warburton, *Letters from a Late Eminent Prelate to One of His Friends* (1808), letter 47, quoted in S. C. Carpenter, *Eighteenth-century Church and People* (1959), p. 148.

5 See Jenny Uglow, *Hogarth: A Life and a World* (1997); Colin Franklin, *Lord Chesterfield, His Character and Characters* (1993), p. 35; David Craig, *Scottish Literature and the Scottish People 1680–1830* (1961), p. 59. For images of the vulgar, see John Brewer, *The Common People and Politics, 1750–1800* (1986).

6 Roy Porter, 'The People's Health in Georgian England' (1995); G. Miller, *The Adoption of Inoculation for Smallpox in England and France* (1957).

7 'The histories of mankind that we possess are histories only of the higher classes,' noted Thomas Robert Malthus: *An Essay on the Principle of Population* (1798), p. 32; John Brand (ed.), *Observations on Popular Antiquities* (1777).

8 Peter Burke, *Popular Culture in Early Modern Europe* (1978), p. 285.

9 Thomas Percy, *Reliques of Ancient English Poetry* (1765); Burke, *Popular Culture in Early Modern Europe*, p. 5; Bob Bushaway, *By Rite* (1982); Richard M. Dorson (ed.), *Peasant Customs and Savage Myths* (1968).

10 Jeremy Black, *An Illustrated History of Eighteenth-century Britain, 1688–1793* (1996), p. 158; Paul Baines, *The House of Forgery in Eighteenth-century Britain* (1999), pp. 103–24.

11 *Fragments of Ancient Poetry Collected in the Highlands of Scotland* (1760), *Fingal* (1762), and *Temora* (1763) purported to be translations of ancient Gaelic poetry, but were mainly his own invention. Hugh Blair vindicated the poems, in terms of the 'enthusiasm' of primitives in the 'infancy of societies', in his *A Critical Dissertation on the Poems of Ossian* (1765):

the poet was then the prophet. For the growing European interest in cultures and a past that were neither Christian nor classical, see Kirsti Simonsuuri, *Homer's Original Genius* (1979); Craig, *Scottish Literature and the Scottish People 1680–1830*, p. 107.

12 William Wordsworth, preface to the *Lyrical Ballads* (1798), in *The Prose Works of William Wordsworth* (1974), vol. i, p. 124.

13 See Keith Thomas (ed.), *The Oxford Book of Work* (1999), pp. 16, 80f.

14 Oliver Goldsmith, *The Deserted Village* (1770), p. 4. There is sentimentality about peasants too in Thomas Gray's *Elegy Written in a Country Church-yard* (1751):

> Let not Ambition mock their useful toil,
> Their homely joys and destiny obscure;
> Nor Grandeur hear, with a disdainful smile,
> The short and simple annals of the poor.

Thomas Gray, *Selected Poems* (1997), p. 23. Raymond Williams, *The Country and the City* (1973).

15 On negative attitudes to the poor, see Daniel A. Baugh, *Poverty, Protestantism and Political Economy* (1977–8); A. L. Beier, ' "Utter Strangers to Industry, Morality and Religion" ' (1988).

16 Roy Porter, 'Civilization and Disease' (1991). As ever, one must be alert to equivocations: in a somewhat Rousseauvian manner, Cheyne thought clodhoppers were healthier.

17 Quoted in John R. Millburn, *Benjamin Martin: Author, Instrument-Maker and Country-Showman* (1976), p. 41.

18 John Brown, *Thoughts on Civil Liberty, Licentiousness and Faction* (1765); for Brown, see James L. Clifford (ed.), *Man versus Society in Eighteenth-century Britain* (1968), p. 29. In mid-seventeenth-century debates, spokesmen like Henry Ireton commonly said that by the 'people' they did not mean the 'poor'; C. B. Macpherson, *The Political Theory of Possessive Individualism* (1964), pp. 227f.

19 Carl B. Cone, *The English Jacobins* (1968),

pp. 11–12. In 1752, in the *Covent Garden Journal*, Henry Fielding published his 'Modern Glossary', which caustically defined 'no body' as 'all the people in Great Britain, except about 1200': Gerald Newman, *The Rise of English Nationalism* (1987), p. 70. Compare David Hume in his essay 'Of Commerce' (1741–2): 'The greater part of mankind may be divided into two classes; that of shallow thinkers, who fall short of the truth; and that of abstruse thinkers, who go beyond it': David Hume, *Selected Essays* (1993), p. 154. 'Rabble' was a favourite word of Hume's.

20 Quoted in John Marshall, *John Locke; Resistance, Religion and Responsibility* (1994), p. 298. Compare C. B. Macpherson, *Democratic Theory* (1973).

21 John Locke, *The Reasonableness of Christianity* (1695), p. 302, quoted in Cone, *The English Jacobins*, p. 12.

22 Locke, *The Reasonableness of Christianity*, p. 279. Locke disposed of claims to priesthood by lower-class believers: 'day-labourer and tradesmen, the spinster and dairymaids' must be told what to believe. 'The greatest part cannot know and therefore they must believe.'

23 James Thomson, 'Summer', in *The Seasons*, in *Works* (1744), l. 1710, quoted by Marjorie Hope Nicolson, *Science Demands the Muse* (1966), p. 32. In one of the first flights ever undertaken by a large balloon, staged in 1787, just outside Paris, frightened peasants mistook it for the moon falling when it came to rest, attacking and badly damaging it: Margaret C. Jacob, *Scientific Culture and the Making of the Industrial West* (1997), p. 132.

24 Paul Langford, *A Polite and Commercial People* (1989), p. 282.

25 Bernard de Mandeville, *The Fable of the Bees* (1924 [1714]), vol. i, p. 91.

26 David Hume, *Hume's Dialogues concerning Natural Religion* (1947 [1779]), section 6, p. 185.

27 Quoted in Newman, *The Rise of English Nationalism*, p. 70.

28 Anthony Ashley Cooper, 3rd Earl of Shaftesbury, *Characteristicks of Men, Manners, Opinions, Times*, 4th edn (1727), Second Characters, pp. 22–3, quoted in John Barrell, *The Political Theory of Painting from Reynolds to Hazlitt* (1986), p. 34.

29 Shaftesbury, *Characteristicks of Men, Manners, Opinions, Times* (1999 [1723]), vol. i, p. 70.

30 Joseph Addison and Richard Steele, *The Spectator* (1965), vol. iii, no. 411, p. 539. 'Some men,' opined Lord Bolingbroke, 'are . . . designed to take care of that government on which the common happiness depends': Lord Bolingbroke, *A Letter on the Spirit of Patriotism* (1738), in Henry St John, Viscount Bolingbroke, *The Works of Lord Bolingbroke* (1969 [reprint of 1841 ed.] [1754–98]), vol. ii, p. 353.

31 James Miller, *The Man of Taste* (1735), p. 27.

32 David Hume, 'Of Essay Writing' (1742), in *Essays Moral, Political and Literary* (1898 [1741–2]), vol. ii, pp. 367–70, quoted in Stephen Copley, 'Commerce, Conversation and Politeness in the Early Eighteenth-century Periodical' (1995). Hume contrasted the 'rabble without doors'. Other key writings which built a social distinction into taste include Alexander Gerard's *Essay On Taste* (1759) and Lord Kames's *Elements of Criticism* (1762).

33 G. J. Barker-Benfield, *The Culture of Sensibility* (1992), p. 291.

34 Iain Pears, *The Discovery of Painting* (1988), p. 48.

35 Thomas Reid, 'Of the Powers We Have by Means of Our External Senses', in *Essays on the Intellectual Powers of Man* (sn, 1785), p. 128, discussed in John W. Yolton, *Perceptual Acquaintance from Descartes to Reid* (1984), p. 3.

36 Thomas Reid, *The Works of Thomas Reid* (1846–63), p. 302.

37 Mary Wollstonecraft dismissed servants as 'ignorant and cunning': Mary Wollstonecraft, *Thoughts on the Education of*

Daughters (1995 [1787]), p. 118. Her husband, William Godwin, warned against the vile character of servants, but explained that it was not their fault: their servile situation made them hateful: William Godwin, *The Inquirer* (1965 [1797]), essay IV: 'Of Servants', p. 201.

38 Chudleigh is quoted in Moira Ferguson (ed.), *First Feminists* (1985), p. 217.

39 Jane West, 'To the Hon Mrs C[ockayn]e' (1791), quoted in Clifford Siskin, *The Work of Writing* (1998), p. 130.

40 Katherine Balderston (ed.), *Thraliana: The Diary of Mrs Hester Lynch Thrale* (1942 [1776–1809]), vol. ii, p. 547, quoted in Alice Browne, *The Eighteenth-century Feminist Mind* (1987), p. 125; the *Gentleman's Magazine* (1791), quoted in Maurice J. Quinlan, *Victorian Prelude* (1965), pp. 66–7.

41 Richard Warner, *The History of Bath* (1801), p. 349; see John Rule, *Albion's People* (1992), p. 158.

42 M. G. Jones, *The Charity School Movement* (1938), and *Hannah More* (1952), pp. 92–5.

43 Joyce Taylor, *Joseph Lancaster: The Poor Child's Friend* (1996); John Lawson and Harold Silver, *A Social History of Education in England* (1973), pp. 241–6.

44 For Owen, see chapter 19. Education and enlightened ideas of children have been discussed in chapter 15.

45 Burke, *Popular Culture in Early Modern Europe*; Lee Davison, Tim Hitchcock, Tim Keirn and Robert B. Shoemaker (eds), *Stilling the Grumbling Hive* (1992); R. W. Malcolmson, *Popular Recreations in English Society, 1700–1850* (1973). For contestation over magic and the occult arts, see chapter 9.

46 Neil McKendrick, 'Josiah Wedgwood and Factory Discipline' (1961), pp. 52–3; E. P. Thompson, 'Time, Work-Discipline and Industrial Capitalism' (1991); Ann Finer and George Savage (eds), *The Selected Letters of Josiah Wedgwood* (1965), p. 310.

47 Desmond King-Hele, *Erasmus Darwin: A Life of Unequalled Achievement* (1999), pp. 199–200.

48 James Parkinson, *The Way to Health, Extracted from the Villager's Friend and Physician* (1802). For Parkinson, see Arthur D. Morris, *James Parkinson, His Life and Times* (1989).

49 James Parkinson, *The Villager's Friend and Physician*, 2nd edn (1804), p. 66.

50 For background to such pastoral assumptions, see John Barrell, *The Dark Side of the Landscape* (1980).

51 Parkinson, *The Villager's Friend and Physician*, p. 9.

52 John Fielding, *A Plan for a Preservatory and Reformatory for the Benefit of Deserted Girls and Penitent Prostitutes* (1758), p. 7; see also John Bender, *Imagining the Penitentiary* (1987); Ian H. Bell, *Literature and Crime in Augustan England* (1991); Donna T. Andrew, *Philanthropy and Police* (1989), p. 116; W. A. Speck, 'The Harlot's Progress in Eighteenth-century England' (1980). The image of the prostitute as the victim of seduction runs through Georgian literature.

53 Donna T. Andrew, *Philanthropy and Police* (1989), p. 124. Similar views – that thieves turned to crime out of necessity – were earlier aired by Daniel Defoe, for instance in *The History and Remarkable Life of Colonel Jacque, Commonly Call'd* (1722).

54 Jonas Hanway, *Defects of Police* (1775), p. 54.

55 Bernard de Mandeville, *A Modest Defence of the Public Stews* (1724).

56 See V. Bullough, 'Prostitution and Reform in Eighteenth-century England' (1987); D. A. Coward, 'Eighteenth-century Attitudes to Prostitution' (1980); A. R. Henderson, 'Female Prostitution in London, 1730–1830' [1992]; Stanley D. Nash, 'Social Attitudes towards Prostitution in London from 1752 to 1829' [1980]; John B. Radner, 'The Youthful Harlot's Curse' (1976).

57 Saunders Welch, *A Proposal to . . . Remove the Nuisance of Common Prostitutes from the Streets* (sn, 1758); R. Dingley, *Proposals for Establishing a Place of Reception for Penitent Prostitutes* (1758); Sherrill Cohen, *The Evolution of Women's*

Asylums since 1500 (1992), p. 130; Sarah Lloyd, ' "Pleasure's Golden Bait" ' (1996); S. Nash, 'Prostitution and Charity' (1984); Miles Ogborn, *Spaces of Modernity* (1998), pp. 34–79.

58 The importance for Beddoes of science as the basis of medical authority is stressed in Roy Porter, *Doctor of Society* (1991).

59 Thomas Beddoes, *The History of Isaac Jenkins* (sn, 1792) (the following quotations are from the 1796 edition). Sold cheaply or given away, this work went through numerous editions. In 1796 Beddoes claimed that an astonishing 40,000 copies of the tract been sold or distributed.

60 Beddoes, *The History of Isaac Jenkins*, p. 5.

61 Beddoes, *The History of Isaac Jenkins*, p. 37.

62 Beddoes, *The History of Isaac Jenkins*, p. 40.

63 Beddoes, *The History of Isaac Jenkins*, p. 43.

64 For Beddoes on education, see Porter, *Doctor of Society*, pp. 39f.

65 Joseph Priestley, *A Sermon on Behalf of the Leeds Infirmary Preached at Mill Hill Chapel* (sn, 1768), p. 18. See the discussion in Roy Porter, 'The Gift Relation' (1989), p. 164.

66 For attitudes to charity, see Andrew, *Philanthropy and Police*; Gertrude Himmelfarb, *The Idea of Poverty* (1984). 'Homo economicus' is discussed further in chapter 17.

67 See Andrew, *Philanthropy and Police*, pp. 17, 19.

68 Addison and Steele, *The Spectator*, vol. ii, no. 232, pp. 401–5 (Monday, 26 November 1711). Addison continued: 'Am I against all acts of charity? God forbid! I know of no virtue in the gospel that is in more pathetic expressions recommended to our practice . . . Our blessed Saviour treats the exercise and neglect of charity towards a poor man, as the performance or breach of this duty towards himself.'

69 Betsy Rodgers, *Cloak of Charity* (1949), pp. 163f; D. Owen, *English Philanthropy, 1660–1960* (1965), pp. 69f.

70 J. T. Anning, *The General Infirmary at Leeds* (1963), vol. i, p. i.

71 Priestley, *A Sermon on Behalf of the Leeds Infirmary Preached at Mill Hill Chapel*, p. 10.

72 E. R. Frizelle and J. D. Martin, *Leicester Royal Infirmary, 1771–1971* (1971), p. 24, quoted in Porter, 'The Gift Relation', p. 163.

73 William Watts, in Frizelle and Martin, *Leicester Royal Infirmary, 1771–1971*, p. 24, quoted in Porter, 'The Gift Relation', p. 176.

74 Priestley, *A Sermon on Behalf of the Leeds Infirmary Preached at Mill Hill Chapel*, p. 10, quoted in Porter, 'The Gift Relation', p. 163.

75 Paul Slack, *The English Poor Law, 1531–1782* (1995); George R. Boyer, *An Economic History of the English Poor Law, 1750–1850* (1990); Brian Inglis, *Poverty and the Industrial Revolution* (1971); J. R. Poynter, *Society and Pauperism* (1969); G. W. Oxley, *Poor Relief in England and Wales: 1601–1834* (1974); M. E. Rose, *The English Poor Law 1760–1830* (1971).

76 Daniel Defoe, quoted in Oxley, *Poor Relief in England and Wales: 1601–1834*, p. 35.

77 Henry Fielding, 'An Enquiry into the Causes of the Late Increase of Robbers' (1751) in *An Enquiry into the Causes of the Late Increase of Robbers and Related Writings* (1988), quoted in Nicholas Rogers, 'Confronting the Crime Wave' (1992), p. 84. 'The sufferings of the poor are indeed less observed than their misdeeds,' noted Fielding. 'They starve and freeze and rot among themselves, but they beg and steal and rob among their betters.'

78 Sir F. M. Eden, *The State of the Poor* (1797), various locations.

79 Sir William Temple, *The Works of Sir William Temple, Bart*, 2 vols. (London: Churchill, 1720). Temple makes similar comments throughout; Arthur Young, *The Farmer's Tour through the East of England* (1771), vol. 4, p. 361. Young, however, recognized that incentives counted, for 'the great engine wherewith the poor may be governed and provided for the most easily and the most cheaply is property'.

80 It was in part for such reasons that Adam Smith advocated the liberal reward of labour: see chapter 17.

81 See discussions in Mark Goldie (ed.),

Locke: Political Essays (1997), p. xiii; Marshall, *John Locke; Resistance, Religion and Responsibility*, p. 331; Rule, *Albion's People*, p. 124; Beier, ' "Utter Strangers to Industry, Morality and Religion" '.

82 Marshall, *John Locke; Resistance, Religion and Responsibility*, p. 324; Maurice Cranston, *John Locke: A Biography* (1957), p. 424; Richard Ashcraft, 'Lockean Ideas, Poverty, and the Development of Liberal Political Theory' (1995), p. 48.

83 George Clarke (ed.), *John Bellers: His Life, Times and Writings* (1993 [1987]); Michael Ignatieff, *A Just Measure of Pain* (1978), p. 13; W. H. G. Armytage, *Heavens Below* (1961), pp. 29–30. For Firmin, see Mitchell Dean, *The Constitution of Poverty* (1991), p. 41.

84 Clarke, *John Bellers: His Life, Times and Writings*; Armytage, *Heavens Below*, p. 29.

85 John Dyer, *The Fleece* (1757), bk II, ll. 239–48, anthologized in Roger Lonsdale (ed.), *The New Oxford Book of Eighteenth-century Verse* (1984), p. 172.

86 Charles F. Bahmueller, *The National Charity Company* (1981), pp. 152, 193. The ecclesiastical echo of *compellare intrare* is obvious.

87 Bahmueller, *The National Charity Company*, pp. 92, 142.

88 Patrick Colquhoun, *The State of Indigence* (1799), p. 18.

89 John Locke, *Two Treatises of Government* (1988 [1690]), vol. ii, p. 42; Goldie, *Locke: Political Essays*, p. xxv.

90 Dean, *The Constitution of Poverty*, pp. 27–8: William Petty argued that 'Fewness of people is real poverty': William Petty, *Treatise of Taxes and Contributions* (1662), p. 34.

91 Sylvana Tomaselli, 'Moral Philosophy and Population Questions in Eighteenth-century Europe' (1989); Frederick G. Whelan, 'Population and Ideology in the Enlightenment' (1991).

92 J. Townsend, *A Dissertation on the Poor Laws* (1786), p. 34. For discussion, see Kenneth Smith, *The Malthusian Controversy* (1951), pp. 28–9.

93 Dean, *The Constitution of Poverty*, p. 69.

94 Malthus, *An Essay on the Principle of Population*. For Malthus's ideas, see James R. Bonar, *Malthus and His Work* (1966); Donald Winch, *Malthus* (1987); Smith, *The Malthusian Controversy*; Andrew Pyle (ed.), *Population: Contemporary Responses to Thomas Malthus* (1994), p. 129. For a definitive biography, see Patricia James, *Population Malthus: His Life and Times* (1979). Malthus is briefly discussed here in terms of population and poverty; for a wider account of his politics, see chapter 20.

95 Mary Poovey, *A History of the Modern Fact* (1998).

96 Malthus, *An Essay on the Principle of Population*, 2nd edn (1803), p. 531. Malthus argued that:

> A man . . . if he cannot get subsistence from his parents on whom he has a just demand, and if the society do not want his labour, has no claim of *right* to the smallest portion of food, and, in fact, has no business to be where he is. At nature's mighty feast there is no vacant cover for him.

97 Thomas Peacock, *Melincourt* (1817), in David Garnett (ed.), *The Novels of Thomas Love Peacock* (1948), pp. 103f.

98 Townsend, *A Dissertation on the Poor Laws*, p. 20.

99 Ian Gilmour, *Riot, Risings and Revolution* (1992); J. Stevenson, *Popular Disturbances in England, 1700–1870* (1979).

100 William Blake, 'Holy Thursday' (1793), in G. Keynes (ed.), *Blake: Complete Writings* (1969), p. 211, ll. 1–4.

101 Karlis Racevskis, *Postmodernism and the Search for Enlightenment* (1993); Robert Darnton, 'George Washington's False Teeth' *The New York Review* (27 March 1997). For the reform of popular culture, see Burke, *Popular Culture in Early Modern Europe*, p. 208.

102 M. Foucault, *Discipline and Punish* (1979). Underpinning this was the notion of a native virtue, corrupted by society: see Lois Whitney, *Primitivism and the Idea of Progress* (1934).

This limitation to populism was not an aberration unique to Britain. In France the *philosophes* wished to reform, not to revolutionize, society, and the outlook of Voltaire and others to the common people was generally severe. *Philosophes* sought not to heed but to help the peasantry, whose lot was to be alleviated to make them more useful and society stronger: H. C. Payne, *The Philosophes and the People* (1976).

103 R. Muchembled, *Popular Culture and Elite Culture in France, 1400–1750* (1985).

104 Larry Stewart, 'The Selling of Newton' (1986); Margaret C. Jacob, *The Cultural Meaning of the Scientific Revolution* (1988), pp. 116f.

105 Neil McKendrick, John Brewer and J. H. Plumb, *The Birth of a Consumer Society* (1982); Dror Wahrman, 'National Society, Communal Culture' (1992).

17 THE PURSUIT OF WEALTH

1 Adam Smith, *An Inquiry into the Nature and Causes of the Wealth of Nations* (1976 [1776]), vol. i, bk II, ch. 3, p. 341.

2 Paula Backscheider, *Daniel Defoe: His Life* (1989). A butcher's son, Daniel Defoe (1660–1731) for a time he made his living as a merchant, but was bankrupted. He wrote extensively about trade, notably *The Complete English Tradesman* (1969 [1726]). He pioneered adventurous novels with exotic plots, including *Robinson Crusoe* (1719), *Moll Flanders* (1722), *Roxana* (1724) and *The History and Remarkable Life of Colonel Jacque, Commonly Call'd* (1722). He was responsible for the *Review* (1704–13), in which he was sponsored by Robert Harley, though he later wrote for the Whigs. In *A Tour Through the Whole Island of Great Britain* (1724–6) he offered an account of the country that stressed improvement and the value of commerce.

3 For Defoe on demons, see Peter Earle, *The World of Daniel Defoe* (1976), p. 43f.

4 Daniel Defoe, *The Compleat English Gentleman* (1729), in James T. Boulton, *Selected Writings of Daniel Defoe* (1975), p. 247.

5 Daniel Defoe, *The Review* (3 January 1706), quoted in Denis Donoghue, *England, Their England* (1988), p. 65. For his praise of the commercial classes, see *The Complete English Tradesman*, vol. i, pp. 368–87. For his economic views, see T. K. Meier, *Defoe and the Defense of Commerce* (1987); Simon Schaffer,

'Defoe's Natural Philosophy and the Worlds of Credit' (1989), and 'A Social History of Plausibility' (1993).

6 Daniel Defoe, *Review* (1706), vol. ii, p. 26, quoted in Donoghue, *England, Their England*, p. 65.

7 Defoe, *Review*, (Thursday, 5 February 1713), vol. ix, p. 109, quoted in Donoghue, *England, Their England*, p. 65.

8 Daniel Defoe, preface to *A Plan of the English Commerce* (1728), p. x.

9 Bernard de Mandeville, *The Fable of the Bees* (1924 [1714]), vol. i, p. 116.

10 Edward A. Bloom and Lillian D. Bloom, *Joseph Addison's Sociable Animal* (1971), pp. 11–83.

11 Henry Fielding, *An Enquiry into the Causes of the Late Increase of Robbers* (1751), p. xi; Nancy F. Koehn, *The Power of Commerce* (1994), p. 25.

12 Joseph Addison and Richard Steele, *The Spectator* (1965), vol. i, no. 69, p. 296 (Saturday, 19 May 1711).

13 For traditional Christian economics, see Richard Tawney, *Religion and the Rise of Capitalism* (1926).

14 E. P. Thompson, *Customs in Common* (1991); Robert W. Gordon, 'Paradoxical Property' (1995); and the discussion in John Rule, *The Vital Century* (1992), p. 79.

15 On mercantilism, see D. C. Coleman, *The Economy of England 1450–1750* (1977); Michel

Foucault, *The Order of Things* (1970), pp. 174–80.

16 David Hume, 'Of the Balance of Trade' (1741–2), in *Selected Essays* (1993), p. 191. See the discussion in Ronald L. Meek (ed.), *Precursors of Adam Smith* (1973), pp. 61f.

17 Smith, *An Inquiry into the Nature and Causes of the Wealth of Nations*, vol. ii, bk IV, ch. 8, p. 661.

18 W. L. Letwin, *The Origins of Scientific Economics* (1963), pp. 41–5; Erich Roll, *A History of Economic Thought* (1938); J. A. Schumpeter, *History of Economic Analysis* (1954), pp. 186–7; Louis Dumont, *From Mandeville to Marx* (1977), pp. 34–6.

19 The title of book IV of Smith, *An Inquiry into the Nature and Causes of the Wealth of Nations*.

20 Joyce Oldham Appleby, *Economic Thought and Ideology in Seventeenth-century England* (1978), and 'Ideology and Theory' (1976); for the old norms, see E. P. Thompson, 'The Moral Economy of the English Crowd in the Eighteenth Century' (1971); Keith Snell, *Annals of the Labouring Poor* (1985); J. M. Neeson, *Commoners* (1993). Analysed by Thompson, Snell and Neeson, the agrarian debate will not be covered further here.

21 For human nature and economics, see Albert O. Hirschman, *The Passions and the Interests* (1977); James Thompson, *Models of Value* (1996); Sylvana Tomaselli, 'Political Economy' (1995).

22 Koehn, *The Power of Commerce*, pp. 74f; W. George Shelton, *Dean Tucker and Eighteenth-century Economic and Political Thought* (1981); Robert Brown, *The Nature of Social Laws, Machiavelli to Mill* (1984), p. 58; J. G. A. Pocock, 'Josiah Tucker on Burke, Locke, and Price' (1985); Jacob Viner, *The Role of Providence in the Social Order* (1972), p. 92. Warburton is said to have remarked that Tucker, dean of Gloucester, made trade his religion.

23 Smith, *An Inquiry into the Nature and Causes of the Wealth of Nations*, vol. i, bk I, ch. 7, pp. 74–5. Prices should thus be natural: 'When the quantity brought to market is just sufficient to supply the effectual demand, and no more, the market price naturally comes to be either exactly, or as nearly as can be judged of, the same with the natural price' (bk VII). To Smith, the laws of supply and demand should operate as naturally as the laws of gravitation.

24 Charles Davenant, 'A Memorial concerning the Coyn of England' (1695), in Abbot Payson Usher (ed.), *Two Manuscripts by Charles Davenant* (1942), pp. 20–21.

25 Charles Davenant, *An Essay on the East-India-Trade* (sn, 1696), pp. 25, 34.

26 See Dudley North, *Discourses Upon Trade* (1691), quoted in Appleby, *Economic Thought and Ideology in Seventeenth-century England*, p. 169; Terence Hutchison, *Before Adam Smith* (1988); compare Alessandro Roncaglia, *Petty: The Origins of Political Economy* (1985).

27 Joyce Oldham Appleby, 'Locke, Liberalism and the Natural Law of Money' (1976); C. G. Caffentzis, *Clipped Coins, Abused Words, and Civil Government* (1989). For Locke, see Patrick Hyde Kelly (ed.) *Locke on Money* (1991).

28 Hirschman, *The Passions and the Interests*, p. 58.

29 Hirschman, *The Passions and the Interests*, p. 65. See above, chapter 7.

30 Smith, *An Inquiry into the Nature and Causes of the Wealth of Nations*, vol. i, bk II, ch. 3, p. 341. For discussions of Smith which transcend the limited and often anachronistic concerns of modern economists, see Donald Winch, *Adam Smith's Politics* (1978), and *Riches and Poverty* (1996). Stephen Copley and Kathryn Sutherland (eds.), *Adam Smith's Wealth of Nations* (1995); V. Brown, *Adam Smith's Discourse* (1994).

31 Smith, *An Inquiry into the Nature and Causes of the Wealth of Nations*, vol. i, bk I, ch. IV, p. 37.

32 Smith, *An Inquiry into the Nature and Causes of the Wealth of Nations*, vol. i, bk I, ch. 2, pp. 26–7. For Sir James Steuart, it was 'the combination of every private interest which forms the public good'; 'publick happiness', therefore, as Smith explained, was often the unintended result of all the members of a society acting 'merely from a view to their own interest', and in pursuit of the principle 'of turning a penny wherever a penny was to be got': quoted in John Barrell, *The Political Theory of Painting from Reynolds to Hazlitt* (1986), p. 49.

33 Adam Smith, *Lectures on Jurisprudence* (1982 [lectures given 1762–3]), vol. iv, p. 163. The following depends heavily upon Christopher J. Berry, *The Idea of Luxury* (1994), pp. 152–73.

34 Smith, *An Inquiry into the Nature and Causes of the Wealth of Nations*, vol. II, bk IV, ch. 9, p. 674. Smith was not oblivious to the drawbacks of the manufacturing system:

The man whose whole life is spent in performing a few simple operations, of which the effects too are, perhaps, always the same, or very nearly the same, has no occasion to exert his understanding, or to exercise his invention in finding out expedients for removing difficulties which never occur. He naturally loses, therefore, the habit of such exertion, and generally becomes as stupid and ignorant as it is possible for a human creature to become.

(Smith, *An Inquiry into the Nature and Causes of the Wealth of Nations*, vol. ii, bk V, ch. 1, p. 782.)

35 Smith, *Lectures on Jurisprudence*, p. 185.

36 Berry, *The Idea of Luxury*, p. 153.

37 Smith, *An Inquiry into the Nature and Causes of the Wealth of Nations*, vol. i, bk I, ch. 4, p. 37.

38 Smith, *An Inquiry into the Nature and Causes of the Wealth of Nations*, vol. i, bk I, ch. 2, p. 30; the phrase is often repeated.

39 Smith, *An Inquiry into the Nature and Causes of the Wealth of Nations*, vol. i, bk II, ch. 3, p. 341.

40 Adam Smith, *The Theory of Moral Sentiments* (1976 [1759]), pp. 60, 292. Smith departed from the physiocrats regarding the source of value: Daniel Roche, *France in the Enlightenment* (1998), p. 122.

41 'Digression on the Corn Trade' in Smith, *An Inquiry into the Nature and Causes of the Wealth of Nations*, vol. i, bk IV, ch. 5, p. 540:

The natural effort of every individual to better his own condition, when suffered to exert itself with freedom and security, is so powerful a principle, that it is alone, and without any assistance, not only capable of carrying on the society to wealth and prosperity, but of surmounting a hundred impertinent obstructions with which the folly of human laws too often encumbers its operations.

42 Smith, *An Inquiry into the Nature and Causes of the Wealth of Nations*, vol. i, bk I, ch. 1, pp. 22–3.

43 Smith, *Lectures on Jurisprudence*, p. 333.

44 Smith, *An Inquiry into the Nature and Causes of the Wealth of Nations*, vol. ii, bk V, ch. 1, p. 689. For Hume, see Eugene Rotwein, *David Hume: Writings on Economics* (1970).

45 Smith, *An Inquiry into the Nature and Causes of the Wealth of Nations*, vol. ii, bk V, ch. 1, p. 709.

46 Smith, *Lectures on Jurisprudence*, p. 14; Smith, *An Inquiry into the Nature and Causes of the Wealth of Nations*, vol. ii, bk V, ch. 1, p. 714.

47 Smith, *An Inquiry into the Nature and Causes of the Wealth of Nations*, vol. ii, bk V, ch. 1, p. 712.

48 Smith, *An Inquiry into the Nature and Causes of the Wealth of Nations*, vol. ii, bk V, ch. 1, p. 717.

49 David Hume, *The History of England* (1894 [1754–62]), vol. iii, p. 99; *cf.* vol. ii, p. 602. For Hume's economics, see Rotwein, *David Hume: Writings on Economics*; Meek, *Precursors of Adam Smith*, p. 43. For Smith's tributes to Hume, see Smith, *An Inquiry into the Nature and Causes of the Wealth of Nations*, vol. i, bk III, ch. 4, p. 412.

50 Smith, *An Inquiry into the Nature and Causes of the Wealth of Nations*, vol. i, bk III, ch. 4, p. 413.

51 Smith, *An Inquiry into the Nature and Causes of the Wealth of Nations*, vol. ii, bk IV, ch. 3, p. 660.

52 Smith, *An Inquiry into the Nature and Causes of the Wealth of Nations*, vol. i, bk III, ch. 4, p. 419.

53 Smith, *An Inquiry into the Nature and Causes of the Wealth of Nations*, vol. ii, bk V, ch. 1, p. 712. Hume spoke of 'worthless toys and gewgaws': John B. Stewart, *Opinion and Reform in Hume's Political Philosophy* (1992), p. 193.

54 Smith, *Lectures on Jurisprudence*, pp. 227, 416, 420.

55 Smith, *An Inquiry into the Nature and Causes of the Wealth of Nations*, vol. i, bk III, ch. 4, p. 421.

56 Smith, *An Inquiry into the Nature and Causes of the Wealth of Nations*, vol. i, bk III, ch. 4, p. 422; on 'unintended consequences', see Christopher J. Berry, *Social Theory of the Scottish Enlightenment* (1997), pp. 39–47.

57 Smith, *An Inquiry into the Nature and Causes of the Wealth of Nations*, vol. i, bk I, ch. 1, p. 22.

58 Smith, *An Inquiry into the Nature and Causes of the Wealth of Nations*, vol. i, bk I, ch. 1, p. 24.

59 As Smith frankly put it, 'civil government, so far as it is instituted for the security of property, is in reality instituted for the defence of the rich against the poor, or of those who have some property against those who have none at all'. Smith, *An Inquiry into the Nature and Causes of the Wealth of Nations*, vol. ii, bk V, ch. 1, p. 715.

60 Smith, *An Inquiry into the Nature and Causes of the Wealth of Nations*, vol. i, bk I, ch. 7, p. 80. He also believed the Law of Settlement under the Poor Law was an unacceptable infringement on freedom: Smith, *An Inquiry into the Nature and Causes of the Wealth of Nations*, vol. ii, bk V, ch. 1, p. 715.

61 Smith, *An Inquiry into the Nature and Causes of the Wealth of Nations*, vol. i, bk III, ch. 3, p. 400.

62 Smith, *An Inquiry into the Nature and Causes of the Wealth of Nations*, vol. ii, bk IV, ch. 9, p. 687.

63 Smith, *An Inquiry into the Nature and Causes of the Wealth of Nations*, vol. i, bk II, ch. 3, p. 346.

64 Smith, *Lectures on Jurisprudence*, p. 226.

65 Smith, *An Inquiry into the Nature and Causes of the Wealth of Nations*, vol. i, bk I, ch. 8, p. 99.

The liberal reward of labour, as it encourages the propagation, so it increases the industry of the common people. The wages of labour are the encouragement of industry, which like every other human quality, improves in proportion to the encouragement it receives. A plentiful subsistence increases the bodily strength of the labourer, and the comfortable hope of bettering his condition . . . Where wages are high, accordingly, we shall always find the workmen more active, diligent, and expeditious than where they are low.

See A. W. Coats, 'Changing Attitudes to Labour in the Mid-Eighteenth Century' (1958). Smith saw labour as creating wealth; in this respect he owed something to the French physiocrats: Ian Ross, 'The Physiocrats and Adam Smith' (1984).

66 Smith, *An Inquiry into the Nature and Causes of the Wealth of Nations*, vol. i, bk I, ch. 8, p. 99.

67 Smith, *An Inquiry into the Nature and Causes of the Wealth of Nations*, vol. i, bk I, ch. 8, p. 99.

68 For this theme, see Istvan Hont and Michael Ignatieff, 'Needs and Justice in the *Wealth of Nations*: An Introductory Essay', in Istvan Hont and Michael Ignatieff (eds), *Wealth And Virtue* (1983), pp. 1–44. The authors' claim that 'the *Wealth of Nations* was centrally concerned with the issue of justice' seems overstated (p. 2).

69 Smith, *The Theory of Moral Sentiments*, p. 86.

70 Smith, *The Theory of Moral Sentiments*, p. 86; cf. David Hume, *A Treatise of Human Nature* (1978 [1739–40]), p. 497.

71 Smith, *The Theory of Moral Sentiments*, p. 82.

72 Smith, *The Theory of Moral Sentiments*, p. 231.

73 Adam Ferguson, *An Essay on the History of Civil Society* (1995 [1767]), p. 255. The context of the *Essay* has been discussed in chapter 10.

74 Ferguson, *An Essay on the History of Civil Society*, p. 255.

75 Ferguson, *An Essay on the History of Civil Society*, p. 210.

76 Ferguson, *An Essay on the History of Civil Society*, p. 152.

77 Ferguson, *An Essay on the History of Civil Society*, p. 155.

78 Smith used the phrase three times, in the *Wealth of Nations*, the *Moral Sentiments*, and the *History of Astronomy* (1795): Berry, *Social Theory of the Scottish Enlightenment*, p. 44. See also Smith, *An Inquiry into the Nature and Causes of the Wealth of Nations*, vol. i, bk IV, ch. 2, p. 456.

79 Smith, *An Inquiry into the Nature and Causes of the Wealth of Nations*, vol. i, bk 4, ch. 2, p. 456. For discussion of the 'invisible hand', see Ronald Hamowy, *The Scottish Enlightenment and the Theory of Spontaneous Order* (1987), pp. 13–22 (for Smith); pp. 22–5 (for Ferguson).

80 Smith, *An Inquiry into the Nature and Causes of the Wealth of Nations*, vol. ii, bk IV, ch. 8, p. 654.

81 See the discussion in Smith, *An Inquiry into the Nature and Causes of the Wealth of Nations*, vol. ii, bk V, ch. 1, pp. 707–23.

82 This dissonance is obviously reminiscent of 'Mandeville's paradox'.

83 Smith, *The Theory of Moral Sentiments*, pp. 183–5.

84 Smith, *The Theory of Moral Sentiments*, p. 51.

85 Thomas Hobbes, *Leviathan* (1968 [1651]), vol. ii, p. 16.

86 Smith, *The Theory of Moral Sentiments*, p. 183.

87 Smith, *The Theory of Moral Sentiments*, p. 229.

88 Smith, *The Theory of Moral Sentiments*, p. 50. Barbon had earlier written of such 'wants of the mind'. See the discussion in chapter 15.

89 Smith, *Lectures On Jurisprudence*, p. 488.

90 Smith, *The Theory of Moral Sentiments*, p. 223. This is of course also Mandeville's sentiment.

91 This is one of the main themes of Elie Halévy, *The Growth of Philosophic Radicalism* (1972).

92 Edmund Burke, *The Works and Correspondence of the Right Honourable Edmund Burke* (1852), vol. ii, p. 398, letter from Burke to Arthur Young (23 May 1797).

93 Catherine Macdonald Maclean, *Born Under Saturn* (1943), p. 549.

18 REFORM

1 Jeremy Bentham, *A Fragment on Government* (1988 [1776]), p. 3.

2 Michel Foucault, *Discipline and Punish* (1979), p. 222.

3 Joseph Priestley, *An Essay on the First Principles of Government* (1768), pp. 7–9.

4 For this Anglo-Latin educational and cultural tradition, see J. C. D. Clark, *Samuel Johnson: Literature, Religion and English Cultural Politics from the Restoration to Romanticism* (1994), p. 2.

5 On that 'two cultures' divide, the *Norwich Gazette* once announced that 'a Latin Epigram . . . was some Time since published in this Paper; but, as the greater Part of our Readers are unacquainted with that Language, the Author has been prevailed upon to put the same Sentiments into English': Geoffrey Alan Cranfield, *The Development of the Provincial Newspaper 1700– 1760* (1962), p. 105. A new audience had come into being: Peter Burke, '*Heu Domine, Adsunt Turcae*' (1991).

6 Margaret C. Jacob, *The Cultural Meaning of the Scientific Revolution* (1988), p. 139.

7 John Aikin, *An Address to the Dissenters of England on Their Late Defeat* (1790), p. 18; see Isaac Kramnick, *Republicanism and Bourgeois*

Radicalism (1990), p. 60; Penelope Corfield, *Power and the Professions in Britain 1700–1850* (1995).

8 Anna Barbauld, *Address to Opposers of the Repeal of the Corporation and Test Acts* (1790), pp. 18, 25.

9 Mary Wollstonecraft, *A Vindication of the Rights of Woman* (1792), in *A Vindication of the Rights of Men with A Vindication of the Rights of Woman* (1995), p. 132. 'Thank heaven I am not a Lady of Quality,' Wollstonecraft once remarked: Claire Tomalin, *The Life and Death of Mary Wollstonecraft* (1974), p. 59.

10 Joseph Priestley, *A View of the Principles and Conduct of the Protestant Dissenters with Respect to the Civil and Ecclesiastical Constitution of England* (1769), p. 5, and *Familiar Letters Addressed to the Inhabitants of the Town of Birmingham in Refutation of Several Charges Advanced Against the Dissenters and Unitarians, by the Revd Mr Madan* (1790–92), letter 4, p. 6; Richard Price, *The Evidence for a Future Period of Improvement in the State of Mankind, with the Means and Duty of Promoting It* (1787), pp. 41–4.

11 Thomas Holcroft, *The Adventures of Hugh Trevor* (1973 [1794]), pp. 9, 158.

12 Crane Brinton, *The Political Ideas of the English Romanticists* (1926), p. 39. In Mary Hays, *Memoirs of Emma Courtney* (1996 [1796]), p. 49, a character exclaims the anti-Pope philosophy of 'whatever is, is wrong': 'we may trace most of the faults, and the miseries of mankind, to the vices and errors of political institutions'.

13 Philip Harling, *The Waning of 'Old Corruption'* (1996), p. 1.

14 Quoted in Jeremy Black, *An Illustrated History of Eighteenth-century Britain, 1688–1793* (1996), p. 51.

15 See the discerning discussion in Marilyn Butler, *Romantics, Rebels and Reactionaries* (1981).

16 Samuel Johnson, preface to *A Dictionary of the English Language* (1755).

17 Ernest Mossner, *The Life of David Hume* (1970 [1954]), pp. 10, 365; Charles Camic,

Experience and Enlightenment (1983), p. 56. For other relevant remarks from Hume's correspondence, see J. Y. T. Greig (ed.), *The Letters of David Hume* (1932), vol. i, pp. 86, 161, 170, 193, 355, 392, 451, 504; John B. Stewart, *The Moral and Political Philosophy of David Hume* (1963), p. 187.

18 Adam Smith, *The Theory of Moral Sentiments* (1976 [1759]), pp. 245, 254.

19 William C. Lehmann, *John Millar of Glasgow, 1735–1801: His Life and Thought and His Contributions to Sociological Analysis* (1960), p. 35.

20 Edward Copeland, *Women Writing about Money* (1995), p. 167.

21 William Paley, *Reasons for Contentment Addressed to the Labouring Part of the British Public* (1793), p. 12. Hazlitt dubbed Paley a 'shuffling Divine': Catherine Macdonald Maclean, *Born Under Saturn* (1943), p. 194. For his earlier radicalism, see later in this chapter.

22 Hays, *Memoirs of Emma Courtney*, p. 140. She says: 'The small pittance bequeathed to me was insufficient to preserve me from dependence. – *Dependence!* – I repeated to myself, and I felt my heart die within me' (p. 31).

23 'Sincerity,' wrote William Godwin, 'once introduced into the manners of mankind, would necessarily bring every other virtue in its train': William Godwin, *Enquiry concerning Political Justice* (1985 [1793]), p. 26.

24 Wordsworth was soon to call true poetry the 'spontaneous overflow of powerful feelings': Alan Bewell, *Wordsworth and the Enlightenment* (1989), pp. 30f.

25 Mrs Inchbald, *Nature And Art* (1796).

26 William Hazlitt, *Life of Thomas Holcroft* (1816), in *The Complete Works of William Hazlitt* (1932), vol. iii, p. 140; Holcroft, *The Adventures of Hugh Trevor*; Gary Kelly, *The English Jacobin Novel, 1780–1805* (1986), p. 114. Holcroft was a passionate supporter of the French Revolution: 'Hey for the new Jerusalem! The millennium! And peace and eternal beatitude be with the soul of Thomas Paine': quoted in Marilyn Butler, *Jane Austen and the War of Ideas* (1975), p. 49. Sincerity must replace secrecy, benevolence self-love, and truth ignorance.

27 Butler, *Jane Austen and the War of Ideas*, p. 42. In Robert Bage's *Man as He is* (1792), the impoverished Quaker heroine refuses to marry the rich baronet until he proves himself a valuable member of society.

28 Robert Bage, *Hermsprong, or Man as He is Not* (1951 [1796]), ch. 76, p. 233.

29 John Cannon, *Parliamentary Reform 1640–1832* (1972), p. 66; Peter D. G. Thomas, *John Wilkes: A Friend to Liberty* (1996); James T. Boulton, *The Language of Politics in the Age of Wilkes and Burke* (1963); George Rudé, *Wilkes and Liberty* (1962).

30 On post-1760 politics, see H. T. Dickinson, *The Politics of the People in Eighteenth-century Britain* (1995), pp. 236f.; J. G. A. Pocock (ed.), *The Varieties of British Political Thought, 1500–1800* (1993); John Brewer, 'English Radicalism in the Age of George III' (1980), pp. 323–67; Kramnick, *Republicanism and Bourgeois Radicalism*.

31 Carl B. Cone, *The English Jacobins* (1968), p. 50.

32 John Locke, *Two Treatises of Government* (1988 [1690]), p. 301; discussed in John Dunn, *Locke* (1984), p. 39.

33 George Berkeley, 'On the Prospect of Planting Arts and Learning in America' (1752), in Roger Lonsdale (ed.), *The New Oxford Book of Eighteenth-century Verse* (1984), p. 175; W. H. G. Armytage, *Yesterday's Tomorrows* (1968), p. 26.

34 J. Hector St John de Crèvecoeur, *Letters from an American Farmer and Sketches of Eighteenth-century America* (1997 [1782]), p. 64.

35 Richard Price, *Observations on the Importance of the American Revolution* (1784), pp. 1–2, 5; D. O. Thomas, *The Honest Mind* (1977), p. 264.

36 Mary P. Mack, *Jeremy Bentham, An Odyssey of Ideas, 1748–1792* (1962), p. 410.

37 William Blake, *America: A Prophecy* (1793),

pt 4, l. 12, in G. Keynes (ed.), *Blake: Complete Writings* (1969), p. 197; David V. Erdman, *Blake, Prophet against Empire* 3rd edn (1954). Bentham admired America: though deploring the natural rights metaphysics of the Declaration of Independence and the Constitution, he hailed 'that newly created nation, one of the most enlightened, if not the most enlightened, at this day on the globe': Mack, *Jeremy Bentham, An Odyssey of Ideas, 1748–1792*, p. 410.

38 Kramnick, *Republicanism and Bourgeois Radicalism*, pp 183f.; Dickinson, *The Politics of the People in Eighteenth-century Britain*, pp. 237f.; Peter Searby, *A History of the University of Cambridge* (1997), vol. iii, p. 297.

39 Kramnick, *Republicanism and Bourgeois Radicalism*, pp. 175ff.; Carla Hay, *James Burgh, Spokesman for Reform in Hanoverian England* (1979); Gerald Newman, *The Rise of English Nationalism* (1987), p. 197.

40 James Burgh, *Political Disquisitions* (1775), discussed in Newman, *The Rise of English Nationalism*, p. 197.

41 J. C. D. Clark, *The Language of Liberty 1660–1832* (1994), p. 33.

42 Burgh, *Political Disquisitions*, vol. iii, pp. 458–60.

43 [David Williams], *Incidents in My Own Life Which Have Been Thought of Some Importance* (1980 [1802?]). In a newly inaugurated chapel in Margaret Street, London, 'where all matters of faith should be omitted and pure morality taught', Williams was the first person in Europe to conduct a form of public worship based on simple deism. He was passionately in favour of freedom of expression. 'I do not see why thieves should not be allowed to preach the principles of theft; seducers of seduction; adulterers of adultery, and traitors of treason': quoted by Martin Fitzpatrick, 'Toleration and the Enlightenment Movement' (2000), p. 44. See also J. Dybikowski, *On Burning Ground* (1993).

44 Joseph Priestley, *Lectures on History and General Policy*, 4th edn (1826 [1788], lecture 18,

p. 337; James Burgh, *Crito* (1767), vol. ii, p. 68; David Williams, *Lectures On Education* (1789), pp. 4, 64; Godwin, *An Enquiry concerning Political Justice*, pp. 42, 472; Isaac Kramnick, 'Eighteenth-century Science and Radical Social Theory' (1986).

45 Michael R. Watts, *The Dissenters* (1978), p. 380.

46 Leslie Stephen, *History of English Thought in the Eighteenth Century* (1962 [1876]), vol. i, p. 358.

47 Martin Fitzpatrick, 'Heretical Religion and Radical Political Ideas in Late Eighteenth-century England' (1990), pp. 350–52; Searby, *A History of the University of Cambridge*, vol. iii, pp. 407f.; A. M. C. Waterman, 'A Cambridge "Via Media" in Late Georgian Anglicanism' (1991).

48 Searby, *A History of the University of Cambridge*, vol. iii, p. 405; Anthony Page, 'Enlightenment and a "Second Reformation" ' (1998), which stresses Jebb's praise of Locke and Newton. William Cole, the antiquarian and diehard Tory, denounced Lindsey as one of 'a restless generation who will never be contented till they have overturned the Constitution in Church and State'.

49 Anthony Hadley Lincoln, *Some Political and Social Ideas of English Dissent, 1763–1800* (1938), p. 320.

50 Quoted in Dickinson, *The Politics of the People in Eighteenth-century Britain*, p. 168.

51 Joseph Barber, tutor at the Evangelical Independent Academy at Hoxton from 1778 to 1791: see Alan P. F. Sell, *John Locke and the Eighteenth-century Divines* (1997), p. 14. Unitarianism was defined in 1792 by the *Monthly Review* as denying the Trinity, the pre-existence and atonement of Christ, and the existence of a spiritual principle in man distinct from the body; and maintaining the absolute unity of God, the proper humanity of Christ, the necessity and efficacy of good works, and the sufficiency of repentance without a vicarious sacrifice, to obtain pardon from a placable Deity: see G. M.

Ditchfield, 'Anti-trinitarianism and Toleration in Late Eighteenth-century British Politics' (1991), p. 48. For Socinianism, see Roland N. Stromberg, *Religious Liberalism in Eighteenth-century England* (1954); Knud Haakonssen (ed.), *Enlightenment and Religion* (1997); Lincoln, *Some Political and Social Ideas of English Dissent, 1763–1800*; Fitzpatrick, 'Heretical Religion and Radical Political Ideas in Late Eighteenth-century England'; Ursula Henriques, *Religious Toleration in England 1783–1833* (1961); H. McLachlan, *The Unitarian Movement in the Religious Life of England* (1931).

52 It will be remembered that Hume, on his deathbed, imagined pleading with Charon for more time so that he could finish correcting a work for the press. Of the dead Priestley, it was written:

> Here lies at rest,
>   In oaken chest,
> Together packed most nicely,
>   The bones and brains,
> Flesh, blood, and veins,
>   And soul of Dr Priestley.

Quoted in Horton Davies, *Worship and Theology in England from Watts and Wesley to Martineau, 1690–1900* (1996), p. 91. For biographies of Priestley, see Ann Holt, *A Life of Joseph Priestley* (1931); Robert E. Schofield, *The Enlightenment of Joseph Priestley* (1997).

53 Joseph Priestley, *Proper Objects of Education in the Present State of the World* (1791), pp. 22, 39. On the liberal atmosphere of the Academy, see Maclean, *Born Under Saturn*, p. 65.

54 Joseph Priestley, *Memoirs of Dr Joseph Priestley, Written on Himself* (1904 [1795]), p. 4, para. 10. For what follows see J. A. Passmore, *Priestley's Writings on Philosophy, Science and Politics* (1965); Schofield, *The Enlightenment of Joseph Priestley*.

55 Priestley, *Memoirs of Dr Joseph Priestley, Written on Himself*, p. 5, para. 13.

56 Priestley, *Memoirs of Dr Joseph Priestley, Written on Himself*, p. 6, para. 14.

57 Revulsion grew among Nonconformists against strict Calvinism. Late in life Lucy Aikin recollected how, around 1750, Dissenters had broken free from 'the chains and darkness of Calvinism, and their manners softened with their system': Cone, *The English Jacobins*, p. 13.

58 Joseph Priestley, *Letter to the Right Honourable William Pitt* (1787), in John Towill Rutt (ed.), *The Theological and Miscellaneous Works of Joseph Priestley* (1817–32), vol. xix, p. 128; for the liberalism of Nonconformist academies, see Watts, *The Dissenters*, pp. 370, 466. When Joseph Priestley joined the staff at Warrington in 1761 he found that all three of its tutors were Arians.

59 Rutt, *The Theological and Miscellaneous Works of Joseph Priestley*, vol. i, p. 50n.

60 See especially Joseph Priestley, *An Examination of Dr Reid's Inquiry into the Human Mind on the Principles of Commonsense . . .* (1774), p. xxxvii; Joseph Priestley, *Disquisitions Relation to Matter and Spirit* (1777), p. 120. Priestley was more 'indebted' to Hartley's *Observations* than to any other book except the Bible: *An Examination of Dr Reid's Inquiry into the Human Mind on the Principles of Commonsense . . .*, p. 2.

61 Joseph Priestley, *Letters to a Philosophical Unbeliever*, letter IV, 'An Examination of Mr Hume's Dialogues on Natural Religion', vol. iv, p. 368.

62 Joseph Priestley, *Additional Letters to a Philosophical Unbeliever, in Answer to Mr William Hammon [i.e. Matthew Turner]* (1782).

63 Joseph Priestley, *Hartley's Theory of the Human Mind on the Principle of the Association of Ideas* (1775), and his introduction to Anthony Collins, *A Philosophical Inquiry concerning Human Liberty* (1790).

64 Joseph Priestley, *The Rudiments of English Grammar* (1969 [1761]), *A Chart of Biography* (1765), and *New Chart of History* (1769).

65 Joseph Priestley, *Course of Lectures on Oratory and Criticism* (1777), and *Remarks on Some Paragraphs in the Fourth Volume of Dr Blackstone's Commentaries on the Laws of England, Relating to the Dissenters* (1769).

66 Carl B. Cone, *Torchbearer of Freedom* (1952); Jack Fruchtman, Jr, *The Apocalyptic Politics of Richard Price and Joseph Priestley* (1983); William D. Hudson, *Reason and Right* (1970).

67 Joseph Priestley, *The History and Present State of Electricity, with Original Experiments* (1767).

68 Priestley, *The History and Present State of Electricity, with Original Experiments*, p. 711.

69 Priestley, *The History and Present State of Electricity, with Original Experiments*, p. 420.

70 Joseph Priestley, *The Scripture Doctrine of Remission* (1761).

71 Watts, *The Dissenters*, p. 477.

72 H. McLachlan, *English Education under the Test Acts* (1931), p. 168; Fitzpatrick, 'Heretical Religion and Radical Political Ideas in Late Eighteenth-century England', p. 352.

73 Joseph Priestley, *An History of the Corruptions of Christianity* (1871 [1782]), *An History of Early Opinions concerning Jesus Christ* (1786), and Priestley wrote of 'dreadful corruptions' (p. x), and attacked the 'atonement' and 'original sin' as being unbiblical (pp. 93, 107). He praised the clergy in England for being 'enlightened'; condemned 'idolatry' (p. 108) and the deification of Jesus (p. 108) – all such was Platonizing (p. 113), and 'oriental philosophy' (p. 132); for Priestley the 'Universal Parent of mankind commissioned Jesus Christ to invite men to the practice of virtue, by the assurance of his mercy to the penitent' (p. 301).

74 Joseph Priestley, preface to *Letters to the Revd Edward Burn*, in Rutt, *The Theological and Miscellaneous Works of Joseph Priestley*, vol. xix, p. 310.

75 Letter from Gibbon (28 January 1783), in J. E. Norton (ed.), *The Letters of Edward Gibbon* (1956), vol. ii, p. 321.

76 [Joseph Priestley], *An Appeal to the Serious and Candid Professors of Christianity . . . by a Lover of the Gospel* (1775).

77 Passmore, *Priestley's Writings on Philosophy, Science and Politics*, p. 17.

78 Joseph Priestley, *The Doctrine of Philosophical Necessity Illustrated* (1777), in Rutt, *The Theological and Miscellaneous Works of Joseph Priestley*, vol. iv, p. 450. Priestley called himself a 'Necessarian'.

79 Passmore, *Priestley's Writings on Philosophy, Science and Politics*, p. 18.

80 Joseph Priestley, *The History of the Present State of the Discoveries Relating to Vision, Light, and Colours* (1772).

81 Joseph Priestley, *Experiments and Observations on Different Kinds of Air* (1774–7); R. G. W. Anderson and Christopher Lawrence (eds.), *Science, Medicine and Dissent* (1987); William H. Brock, *The Fontana History of Chemistry* (1992), pp. 99–101.

82 Priestley, *An Examination of Dr Reid's Inquiry into the Human Mind on the Principles of Commonsense*; Michael Barfoot, 'Priestley, Reid's Circle and the Third Organon of Human Reasoning' (1987). Reid resisted Locke's way of ideas, Berkeley's idealism and Hume's scepticism: all undermined the belief in a divinely created reality which common sense provided. In his *An Inquiry into the Human Mind on the Principles of Common Sense* (1764), he questioned the notion that reality consisted simply of 'ideas', arguing that belief in an external reality was intuitive, and not mediated by sensory perceptions. Keith Lehrer, *Thomas Reid* (1989), p. 5.

83 Priestley, 'An Examination of Dr Reid's Inquiry into the Human Mind on the Principles of Common Sense', in Rutt, *The Theological and Miscellaneous Works of Joseph Priestley*, vol. iii, pp. 4–5.

84 Priestley, introduction to 'Remarks on Dr Reid's Inquiry into the Principles of the Human Mind', in Rutt, *The Theological and Miscellaneous Works of Joseph Priestley*, vol. iii, p. 27.

85 Priestley, *Hartley's Theory of the Human Mind on the Principle of the Association of Ideas* (1775), in Rutt, *The Theological and Miscellaneous Works of Joseph Priestley*, vol. iii, p. 182.

86 Priestley, *Memoirs of Dr Joseph Priestley, Written on Himself*, p. 52, para. 124.

87 Priestley, *Disquisitions Relating to Matter and Spirit*. See also the contextualized discussion in chapter 6.

88 Priestley, *The Doctrine of Philosophical Necessity Illustrated*.

89 Joseph Priestley and Richard Price, *A Free Discussion of the Doctrines of Materialism and Philosophical Necessity* (1778) in Rutt, *The Theological and Miscellaneous Works of Joseph Priestley*, vol. iv, p. 72. These ideas obviously prefigure Godwin's: see chapter 20.

90 Priestley and Price, *A Free Discussion of the Doctrines of Materialism and Philosophical Necessity*, in Rutt, *The Theological and Miscellaneous Works of Joseph Priestley*, vol. iv, p. 74.

91 Priestley, *An Essay on the First Principles of Government* (1768): see Elie Halévy, *The Growth of Philosophic Radicalism* (1972), p. 22; Joseph Priestley, *Political Writings* (1993).

92 Priestley, *An Essay on the First Principles of Government*, in Rutt, *The Theological and Miscellaneous Works of Joseph Priestley*, vol. xxii, p. 11.

If I be asked what I mean by *liberty*, I should chose, for the sake of greater clearness, to divide it into two kinds, *political* and *civil*; and the importance of having clear ideas on this subject will be my apology for the innovation. POLITICAL LIBERTY, I would say, *consists in the power, which the members of the state reserve to themselves, of arriving at the public offices, or, at least, of having votes in the nomination of those who fill them*: and I would choose to call CIVIL LIBERTY *that power over their own actions, which the members of the state reserve to themselves, and which their officers must not infringe.*

Priestley, *Political Writings*, p. 12.

93 Priestley, *An Essay on the First Principles on Government*, in Rutt, *The Theological and Miscellaneous Works of Joseph Priestley*, vol. xxii,

p. 13; Mack, *Jeremy Bentham, An Odyssey of Ideas, 1748–1792*, p. 103.

94 [Joseph Priestley], *A Free Address to Those Who Have Petitioned for the Repeal of the Late Act of Parliament in Favour of the Roman Catholics* (1780); see Halévy, *The Growth of Philosophic Radicalism*, pp. 133f.

95 Priestley, *An Essay on the First Principles of Government*, in Rutt (ed.), *The Theological and Miscellaneous Works of Joseph Priestley*, vol. xxii, p. 57, and *A Free Address to Those Who Have Petitioned for the Repeal of the Late Act of Parliament in Favour of the Roman Catholics*; Halévy, *The Growth of Philosophic Radicalism*, p. 22.

96 Joseph Priestley, *Reflections on the Present State of Free Inquiry in This Country* (1785), in Rutt, *The Theological and Miscellaneous Works of Joseph Priestley*, vol. xviii, p. 544; Maurice Crosland, 'The Image of Science as a Threat' (1987). This explains Dr Johnson's response: 'Ah Priestley, an evil man, Sir. His work unsettles everything': quoted in Boswell Taylor, *Joseph Priestley: The Man of Science* (1954), p. 11.

97 Joseph Priestley, 'Some Considerations on the State of the Poor in General' (1787), in Rutt, *The Theological and Miscellaneous Works of Joseph Priestley*, vol. xxv, p. 314; Kramnick, *Republicanism and Bourgeois Radicalism*, p. 54.

98 Joseph Priestley, *Letters to Edmund Burke Occasioned by His Reflections on the Revolution in France, &c.* (1791), and his anonymous *A Political Dialogue on the General Principles of Government* (1791).

99 Priestley, *Letters to the Right Hon. Edmund Burke*, in Rutt, *The Theological and Miscellaneous Works of Joseph Priestley*, vol. xxii, p. 203.

100 Priestley, *The Doctrine of Philosophical Necessity Illustrated* (1777), in Rutt, *The Theological and Miscellaneous Works of Joseph Priestley*, vol. xxii, p. 168.

101 Priestley, *A Political Dialogue on the General Principles of Government*, in Rutt, *The Theological and Miscellaneous Works of Joseph Priestley*, vol. xxv, p. 92.

102 Priestley, *A Political Dialogue on the General Principles of Government*, in Rutt, *The Theological and Miscellaneous Works of Joseph Priestley*, vol. xxv, p. 96.

103 Priestley, *A Political Dialogue on the General Principles of Government*, in Rutt, *The Theological and Miscellaneous Works of Joseph Priestley*, vol. xxv, p. 107.

104 Joseph Priestley, *Letter to the Right Hon. William Pitt* (1787), in Rutt, *The Theological and Miscellaneous Works of Joseph Priestley*, vol. xix, p. 118.

105 Joseph Priestley, *Discourses Relating to the Evidence of Revealed Religion* (1794–9); Kramnick, *Republicanism and Bourgeois Radicalism*, p. 75; Watts, *The Dissenters*, p. 486.

106 Joseph Priestley, *Letters to the Inhabitants of Northumberland* (1801), in Rutt, *The Theological and Miscellaneous Works of Joseph Priestley*, vol. xxv, p. 18.

107 Joseph Priestley, in Rutt, *The Theological and Miscellaneous Works of Joseph Priestley*, vol. ii, p. 404; Ian Wylie, *Young Coleridge and the Philosophers of Nature* (1989), p. 63. Nelson's victories were to fulfil the predictions contained in Isaiah 19, and Napoleon was the deliverer promised to Egypt.

108 Priestley, *Disquisitions Relating to Matter and Spirit*; Kramnick, *Republicanism and Bourgeois Radicalism*, p. 97; John W. Yolton, *Thinking Matter* (1983), p. 113.

109 Joseph Priestley, *The Importance and Extent of Free Inquiry in Matters of Religion* (1785), in Rutt, *The Theological and Miscellaneous Works of Joseph Priestley*, vol. xv, p. 78; Priestley, *Political Writings*, p. xxiv. Compare Godwin's teachings about truth and 'free inquiry'.

110 See Joseph Priestley, *Letter to the Right Honourable William Pitt* (1787).

111 Priestley, *Letter to the Right Honourable William Pitt* in Rutt, *The Theological and Miscellaneous Works of Joseph Priestley*, vol. xix, p. 125.

112 Generally on Bentham, see Mack, *Jeremy Bentham, An Odyssey of Ideas, 1748–1792*; J. Dinwiddy, *Bentham* (1989); Ross Harrison,

Bentham (1983); Bentham, *A Fragment on Government*, p. 29.

113 Bentham, *A Fragment on Government*. Bentham thought it 'the very first publication by which men at large were invited to break loose from the trammels of authority and ancestor-worship on the field of law' (p. vi). On the law and law reform see David Lieberman, *The Province of Legislation Determined* (1989). It can hardly be an accident that both Bentham and Gibbon came from Jacobite Tory families.

114 Bentham, *A Fragment on Government*, p. 3.

115 For the following exposition, see Harrison, *Bentham*.

116 James E. Crimmins, *Secular Utilitarianism* (1990), p. 88.

117 D. J. Manning, *The Mind of Jeremy Bentham* (1968), pp. 37, 59, citing Bentham's *Plan of Parliamentary Reform* (1817), p. cxcviii.

118 For expositions, see Dinwiddy, *Bentham*; Harrison, *Bentham*; Mack, *Jeremy Bentham, An Odyssey of Ideas, 1748–1792*. 'I am sorry,' he wrote to Brissot, 'that you have undertaken to publish a Declaration of Rights. It is a metaphysical work – the *ne plus ultra* of metaphysics. It may have been a necessary evil, – but it is nevertheless an evil': Halévy, *The Growth of Philosophic Radicalism*, p. 174.

119 Bentham, *A Fragment of Government and An Introduction to the Principles of Morals and Legislation*; Charles F. Bahmueller, *The National Charity Company* (1981), p. 203.

120 Bentham, *A Fragment on Government and An Introduction to the Principles of Morals and Legislation*; Halévy, *The Growth of Philosophic Radicalism*, p. 30.

121 Mack, *Jeremy Bentham, An Odyssey of Ideas, 1748–1792*, p. 129.

122 Mack, *Jeremy Bentham, An Odyssey of Ideas, 1748–1792*, pp. 120, 129. Bentham substituted the method of 'paraphrasis': to define a word was to resolve the idea it represents into simpler ones based on sense impressions, that is, on pleasures and pains: Mack, *Jeremy Bentham, An Odyssey of Ideas, 1748–1792*, p. 155.

123 William Hazlitt, *The Spirit of the Age* (1971 [1825]), p. 25.

124 Pushpin was a tavern game. Bentham's views on sex have been discussed above in chapter 11.

125 Simon Schaffer, 'States of Mind' (1990), p. 288; Ruth Richardson, *Death, Dissection and the Destitute* (1987); Tim Marshall, *Murdering to Dissect* (1995).

126 For Bentham's will (24 August 1769) see A. Taylor Milne (ed.), *The Correspondence of Jeremy Bentham* (1981), vol. i, p. 136. Bentham's auto-icon sits in state in University College, London.

127 John Bowring, *The Works of Jeremy Bentham* (1995 [1843]), vol. ii, p. 501.

128 Schaffer, 'States of Mind', p. 274; Crimmins, *Secular Utilitarianism*.

129 Halévy, *The Growth of Philosophic Radicalism*, p. 291.

130 Bowring, *The Works of Jeremy Bentham*, vol. x, p. 595.

131 For Bentham, see Janet Semple, *Bentham's Prison* (1993), p. 28; see also Jonas Hanway, *Solitude in Imprisonment* (1776), p. 210 – Hanway rather than Bentham was the architect of the solitary system, the latter fearing that excessive solitude would drive prisoners mad. Margaret Delacy, *Prison Reform in Lancashire, 1700–1850* (1986); R. Evans, *The Fabrication of Virtue* (1982); Foucault, *Discipline And Punish*; Michael Ignatieff, *A Just Measure of Pain* (1978); V. A. C. Gatrell, *The Hanging Tree* (1994); John Bender, *Imagining the Penitentiary* (1987); Norval Morris and David J. Rothman (eds.), *The Oxford History of the Prison* (1995). More generally on the rise of disciplinary society, see Mitchell Dean, *The Constitution of Poverty* (1991).

132 Ignatieff, *A Just Measure of Pain*.

133 Semple, *Bentham's Prison*, p. 116.

134 Milne, *The Correspondence of Jeremy Bentham*, vol. iv, p. 342.

135 Semple, *Bentham's Prison*, pp. 100, 288, and 'Foucault and Bentham: A Defence of

Panopticism' (1992); Jeremy Bentham, *The 'Panopticon' Writings* (1995), p. 100; Jeremy Bentham, *Panopticon* (1791).

136 Halévy, *The Growth of Philosophic Radicalism*, p. 84; see discussion in Semple, *Bentham's Prison*, p. 112.

137 Foucault, *Discipline And Punish*; Ignatieff, *A Just Measure of Pain*; Duncan Forbes, *Hume's Philosophical Politics* (1975). For Bentham, moreover, the beauty of the panopticon – that 'magnificent instrument with which I then dreamed of revolutionizing the world' – was that it could be adapted to serve all manner of social purposes as a model of efficient control: it could even be accommodated to battery-farming.

138 Semple, *Bentham's Prison*, p. 301.

139 Bentham, *Panopticon*. Bentham knew he was playing God. The scheme, he wrote, would combine 'the apparent omnipresence of the inspector (if divines will allow me the expression)' with 'the extreme facility of his real presence'.

140 Mack, *Jeremy Bentham, An Odyssey of Ideas, 1748–1792*, p. 337. Bentham recognized his own 'madness'. 'I do not like to look among Panopticon papers. It is like opening a drawer where devils are locked up – it is breaking into a haunted house': quoted in Gertrude Himmelfarb, *Victorian Minds* (1968), p. 32.

141 Samuel Romilly, *Memoirs of the Life of Sir Samuel Romilly* (1971 [1840]).

142 B. Mazlish, *James and John Stuart Mill: Father and Son in the Nineteenth Century* (1975); Halévy, *The Growth of Philosophic Radicalism*, p. 249. 'If I had time to write a book,' James Mill claimed in 1817, 'I would make the human mind as plain as the road from Charing Cross to St Paul's': Schaffer, 'States of Mind', p. 289.

143 Dudley Miles, *Francis Place 1771–1854: The Life of a Remarkable Radical* (1988), pp. 139f.; Mary Thale (ed.), *The Autobiography of Francis Place (1771–1854)* (1972); Bahmueller, *The National Charity Company*, p. 94. For other

sexual radicals, see M. L. Bush (ed.), *What Is Love?* (1998); Place commented on the christening of Queen Victoria's daughter: 'Surely the time will come when these Barbaric Ceremonies will cease': Thale, *The Autobiography of Francis Place*, pp. xii, xxiii.

144 Waterman, 'A Cambridge "Via Media" in Late Georgian Anglicanism', p. 423; M. L. Clark, *Paley: Evidences for the Man* (1974). While fairly radical, Paley supposedly declined to support Jebb's anti-subscription campaign, on the grounds that he could not afford to keep a conscience. For theological utilitarians before Paley, see Jacob Viner, *The Role of Providence in the Social Order* (1972), p. 71.

145

If you should see a flock of pigeons in a field of corn: and if, instead of each picking what and where it liked, you should see ninety-nine of them gathering all they had got into a heap, reserving nothing for themselves but the chaff and refuse, keeping this heap for one – and that the weakest, perhaps, and the worst pigeon of the flock: sitting round and looking on all winter whilst this one was devouring, throwing about and wasting it: and, if a pigeon more hardy or hungry than the rest touched a grain of the hoard, all the others instantly flying upon it, and tearing it to pieces – If you should see this, you would see nothing more than what is today practised and established among men.

William Paley, *The Principles of Moral and Political Philosophy* (1785), p. 93. See Searby, *A History of the University of Cambridge*, vol. iii, p. 307; Waterman, 'A Cambridge "Via Media" in Late Georgian Anglicanism', p. 423.

146 Searby, *A History of the University of Cambridge*, vol. iii, p. 307; Paley, *The Principles of Moral and Political Philosophy*, and *Reasons for Contentment Addressed to the Labouring Poor of the British Public* (1793).

147 Thomas Walker, *A Review of Some of the Political Events Which Have Occurred in Manchester During the Last Five Years, etc.* (1794),

p. 46, quoted in Kramnick, *Republicanism and Bourgeois Radicalism*, p. 57. See also Frida

Knight, *The Strange Case of Thomas Walker* (1957).

19 PROGRESS

1 Edward Young, *Night Thoughts on Life, Death and Immortality* (1780), bk vi, l. 691.

2 Thomas Holcroft, preface to *The Adventures of Hugh Trevor* (1973 [1794]), pp. vi–vii.

3 Annie Watt to her son Gregory, quoted in Margaret C. Jacob, *Scientific Culture and the Making of the Industrial West* (1997), p. 124.

4 Josiah Tucker, *Four Tracts* (1774), p. 23.

5 Desmond King-Hele (ed.), *The Letters of Erasmus Darwin* (1981), p. 16, letter 63a, to Matthew Boulton (1 July 1763).

6 For historical visions, see Stephen Bann, *The Clothing of Clio* (1984); Laird Okie, *Augustan Historical Writing* (1992); Karen O'Brien, *Narratives of Enlightenment* (1997).

7 Mary Wollstonecraft, *A Vindication of the Rights of Woman* (1792), in *A Vindication of the Rights of Men with A Vindication of the Rights of Woman* (1995), p. 82. For discussions, see Jerome Hamilton Buckley, *The Triumph of Time* (1967); Robert Nisbet, *History of the Idea of Progress* (1980); Sidney Pollard, *The Idea of Progress* (1968); R. V. Sampson, *Progress in the Age of Reason* (1956); D. Spadafora, *The Idea of Progress in Eighteenth-century Britain* (1990); Ernest Lee Tuveson, *Millennium and Utopia* (1964).

8 See Paul K. Alkon, *Origins of Futuristic Fiction* (1987); I. F. Clarke, *The Pattern of Expectation 1644–2001* (1979), p. 16.

9 Quoted in William C. Lehmann, *John Millar of Glasgow, 1735–1801: His Life and Thought and His Contributions to Sociological Analysis* (1960), p. 218.

10 Richard Price, *Observations on the Nature of Civil Liberty, the Principles of Government, and the Justice and Policy of the War with America* (1776), p. 5, and *The Evidence for a Future Period of Improvement in the State of Mankind* (1787), p. 12; Spadafora, *The Idea of Progress in*

Eighteenth-century Britain, p. 237; for Law, see R. S. Crane, *The Idea of the Humanities and Other Essays Historical and Critical* (1967), vol. i, pp. 216–18.

11 Thomas Robert Malthus, *An Essay on the Principle of Population* (1798), pp. 1–2.

12 John Aikin, *Letters from a Father to His Son*, 3rd edn (1796 [1792–3]), contents list.

13 David Hartley, *Observations on Man, His Frame, His Duty and His Expectations* (1749), p. 376; quoted in Martin Fitzpatrick, 'Heretical Religion and Radical Political Ideas in Late Eighteenth-century England' (1990), p. 343.

14 The 'state of the world at present,' Joseph Priestley told his students in the 1760s, 'is vastly preferable to what it was in any former period.' There was the 'greatest certainty' that posterity 'will be wiser, and therefore the fairest presumption that they will be better than we are'. 'Thus whatever was the beginning of this world, the end will be glorious and paradisiacal, beyond what our imaginations can now conceive': *Lectures On History* (1793), lectures 38 and 56, in John Towill Rutt (ed.), *The Theological and Miscellaneous Works of Joseph Priestley* (1817–32), vol. xxiv, pp. 225, 425.

15 J. H. Plumb, 'The Acceptance of Modernity' (1982), p. 332; Stephen Daniels, *Fields of Vision* (1993), pp. 80f.; Miles Ogborn, *Spaces of Modernity* (1998), p. 23.

16 Edward Gibbon, *The History of the Decline and Fall of the Roman Empire* (1994 [1781]), vol. ii, ch. 38, p. 516; see the discussion in Joseph M. Levine, *The Battle of the Books* (1992), pp. 178f.; Nisbet, *History of the Idea of Progress*, p. 187; Spadafora, *The Idea of Progress in Eighteenth-century Britain*; and J. G. A. Pocock, *Barbarism and Religion* (1999), vol. ii.

17 Buckley, *The Triumph of Time*. Compare Peacock's Mr Foster in *Headlong Hall* (1816) who 'held forth with great energy on the subject of roads and railways, canals and tunnels, manufactures and machinery'. 'In short,' said he, 'every thing we look on attests the progress of mankind in all the arts of life, and demonstrates their gradual advancement towards a state of unlimited perfection': David Garnett (ed.), *The Novels of Thomas Love Peacock* (1948), p. 11.

18 John Money, 'Public Opinion in the West Midlands, 1760–1793' [1967], 'Taverns, Coffee Houses and Clubs' (1971), *Experience and Identity* (1977), and 'Birmingham and the West Midlands 1760–1793 (1990); Jacob, *Scientific Culture and the Making of the Industrial West*; Kathleen Wilson, *The Sense of the People* (1995).

19 William Turner, *Speculations on the Propriety of Attempting the Establishing a Literary Society in Newcastle upon Tyne* (np, 1793), p. 3.

20 Thomas Henry, 'On the Advantages of Literature and Philosophy in General, and Especially on the Consistency of Literary and Philosophical with Commercial Pursuits' (1785), pp. 7 and 9. Erasmus Darwin sought 'gentlemanlike facts' for the Derby Philosophical Society: see A. E. Musson and Eric Robinson, *Science and Technology in the Industrial Revolution* (1969), p. 192.

21 William Hutton, *An History of Birmingham*, 3rd edn (1795), pp. 88–91.

22 Robert E. Schofield, *The Lunar Society of Birmingham* (1963), p. 440; Paul Langford, *Englishness Identified* (2000), p. 76. Darwin further helped found a similar society in Derby: Eric H. Robinson, 'The Derby Philosophical Society' (1953). The Society, and especially Erasmus Darwin's role in it, is discussed below. Musson and Robinson, *Science and Technology in the Industrial Revolution*.

23 Erasmus Darwin, *Phytologia* (1800), p. vii.

24 Inequality was progressive provided it stopped short of the extremes of despotism and slavery. The 'inequality of mankind in the present state of the world' Darwin judged 'too great for the purposes of producing the greatest quantity of human nourishment, and the greatest sum of human happiness': Darwin, *Phytologia*, pt ii, pp. 415, 416. 'Some must think' is *Zoonomia*, 3rd edn (1801 [1794–6]), pt ii, p. 416.

25 G. E. Mingay (ed.), *Arthur Young and His Times* (1975); Harriet Ritvo, 'Possessing Mother Nature' (1995).

26 Ritvo, 'Possessing Mother Nature'. Compare Josiah Wedgwood's aims with his workers: see below.

27 Quoted in Maureen McNeil, *Under the Banner of Science* (1987), p. 168.

28 James Thomson, 'The Development of Civilization' from 'Autumn', *The Seasons* (1744), ll. 1826–30.

29 Daniel Defoe, *Robinson Crusoe* (1985 [1719]), p. 85.

30 Pat Hudson, *The Industrial Revolution* (1989).

31 Francis D. Klingender, *Art and the Industrial Revolution* (1975), p. 25; Maxine Berg, *The Age of Manufactures, 1700–1820* (1994); for historiography, see David Cannadine, 'The Present and the Past in the English Industrial Revolution, 1880–1980' (1984); Julian Hoppit, 'Understanding the Industrial Revolution' (1987).

32 Klingender, *Art and the Industrial Revolution*; Charlotte Klonk, *Science and the Perception of Nature* (1996); Daniels, *Fields of Vision* (1993), p. 57.

33 H. M. Dickinson, *Matthew Boulton* (1937), p. 113.

34 Neil McKendrick, 'Josiah Wedgwood and Factory Discipline' (1961).

35 Josiah Wedgwood, *An Address to the Young Inhabitants of the Pottery* (1783), p. 22.

36 Isaac Kramnick, 'Children's Literature and Bourgeois Ideology' (1983).

37 George Birkbeck Hill, *Boswell's Life of Johnson* (1934–50), Friday 22 March, vol. 2, p. 459.

38 Daniels, *Fields of Vision*, p. 49.

39 Quoted in J. H. Plumb, *Men and Places*

(1966), p. 134. Erasmus Darwin bantered that a fool is 'a man who never tried an experiment in his life'.

40 Quoted in Stephen Daniels, 'The Political Iconography of Woodland in Later Georgian England' (1988), p. 44.

41 Robert Owen, *Observations on the Effect of the Manufacturing System* (1815), pp. 1–2. Owen's co-operative villages were denounced by Cobbett as 'parallelograms of pauperism'.

42 Owen, *Observations on the Effect of the Manufacturing System*, pp. 3–9.

43 Owen, *Report to the County of Lanark* (1969 [1813]), p. 129.

44 Robert Owen, *A New View of Society* (1813), pp. 28–9. Owen, *Report to the County of Lanark*; W. H. G. Armytage, *Heavens Below* (1961), p. 77. His grand scheme for new men in a new society was:

a national, well digested, unexclusive system for the formation of character, and general amelioration of the lower orders. On the experience of a life devoted to the subject I hesitate not to say, that the members of any community may by degrees be trained to live *without idleness, without poverty, without crime, and without punishment*; for each of these is the effect of error in the various systems prevalent throughout the world. *They are all the necessary consequences of ignorance.*

Owen, *Report to the County of Lanark*, p. 129. This has a very Godwinian ring.

45 Robert Owen, *The Book of the New Moral World* (1836), vol. i, p. 3.

46 Quoted in Armytage, *Heavens Below*, p. 77.

47 Bewell, *Wordsworth and the Enlightenment*, pp. 6–7; Edward Duffy, *Rousseau in England* (1979), pp. 2f., Percy Bysshe Shelley, *The Triumph of Life* (1965 [1824]).

48 Richard Payne Knight, *The Progress of Civil Society* (1796), pp. 77–8; Bewell, *Wordsworth and the Enlightenment*, p. 6. See McNeil, *Under the Banner of Science*; Michael Clarke and Nicholas Penny (eds.), *The Arrogant Connoisseur* (1982), pp. 10f.; Ronald L. Meek, *Social Science and the Ignoble Savage* (1975), p. 211.

49 See McNeil, *Under the Banner of Science*; Desmond King-Hele, *Erasmus Darwin: A Life of Unequalled Achievement* (1999), *The Letters of Erasmus Darwin* (1981), and *Erasmus Darwin and the Romantic Poets* (1986).

50 R. L. Edgeworth and M. Edgeworth, *Practical Education* (1798); Erasmus Darwin, *Plan for the Conduct of Female Education* (1797).

51 Darwin's chief works are *The Botanic Garden* (1789–91), *Zoonomia* (1794–6), *Phytologia* (1800), and *The Temple of Nature* (1803). For 'theory' in *Zoonomia*, see vol. i, p. viii.

52 Schofield, *The Lunar Society of Birmingham*, pp. 75, 108, 154.

53 Darwin, *The Botanic Garden*; Janet Browne, 'Botany for Gentlemen' (1989).

54 Cited in Charles Darwin, *Life of Erasmus Darwin* (1887), pp. 35–6.

55 King-Hele, *The Letters of Erasmus Darwin*, p. 8, letter no. 54A, to Thomas Oakes (23[?] November 1754). Coleridge was impressed by Darwin when he visited Derby in 1796 – but found him no Christian:

Derby is full of curiosities, the cotton, the silk mills, Wright, the painter, and Dr Darwin, the everything, except the Christian! Dr Darwin possesses, perhaps, a greater range of knowledge than any other man in Europe, and is the most inventive of philosophical men. He thinks in a *new* train on all subjects except religion. He bantered me on the subject of religion . . . He deems that there is a certain *self-evidence* in infidelity, and becomes an atheist by intuition. Well did St Paul say: 'Ye have an evil *heart* of unbelief'.

Earl Leslie Griggs (ed.), *Collected Letters of Samuel Taylor Coleridge* (1956–68), vol. i, pp. 177, 178, 216.

56 King-Hele, *The Letters of Erasmus Darwin*, p. 104, letter no. 81A, to James Watt (6 January 1781).

57 King-Hele, *Doctor of Revolution* (1977), p. 75.

58 King-Hele, *Erasmus Darwin: A Life of Unequalled Achievement*, p. 102.

59 C. C. Hankin (ed.), *Life of Mary Anne*

Schimmelpenninck (1858), vol. i, pp. 151–3, 242.

60 King-Hele, *The Letters of Erasmus Darwin*, p. 42, letter no. 67A, to unknown man (7 February 1767). Mark Jackson, *New-Born Child Murder* (1996).

61 Darwin, *Zoonomia*, vol. ii, pp. 526–7: 'In the present insane state of human society . . . war and its preparations employ the ingenuity and labour of almost all nations; and mankind destroy or enslave each other with as little mercy as they destroy and enslave the bestial world.'

62 King-Hele, *The Letters of Erasmus Darwin*, p. 189, letter no. 89D, to Josiah Wedgwood (13 April 1789). For slave collars, see Folarin Shyllon, *Black People in Britain 1555–1833* (1977), p. 9.

63 Thus requested, however, to 'leave the unfruitful fields of polemical theology', Priestley objected: 'Excuse me, however, if I still join theological to philosophical studies, and if I consider the former as greatly superior in importance to mankind to the latter': King-Hele, *Erasmus Darwin: A Life of Unequalled Achievement*, p. 257.

64 Darwin, *Zoonomia*, 3rd edn, vol. ii, p. 505, as quoted in McNeil, *Under the Banner of Science*, pp. 100f.

65 MacNeil, *Under the Banner of Science*; King-Hele, *Doctor of Revolution*; Roy Porter, 'Erasmus Darwin: Doctor of Evolution?' (1989); P. J. Bowler, *Evolution: The History of an Idea* (1984).

66 Darwin, *Zoonomia*, vol. i, p. 514.

67 Darwin, *Zoonomia*.

68 Darwin, *Zoonomia*, vol. i, p. 505.

69 Darwin, *Zoonomia*, vol. i, p. 92. See also Karl Figlio, 'Theories of Perception and the Physiology of Mind in the Late Eighteenth Century' (1975).

70 Darwin, *Zoonomia*, vol. i, p. 148.

71 Darwin, *Zoonomia*, vol. i, p. 96.

72 Darwin, *Zoonomia*, vol. i, p. 72:

All our emotions and passions seem to arise out of the exertions of these two faculties of the animal sensorium. Pride, hope, joy, are the names of particular pleasures; shame, despair, sorrow, are the names of peculiar pains; and love, ambition, avarice, of particular desires: hatred, disgust, fear, anxiety, of particular aversions.

73 Darwin, *Zoonomia*, vol. i, p. 376.

74 The education of the mind through imitation and habit is a key theme of Darwin's *Plan for the Conduct of Female Education*. Darwin's views on imitation are spelt out most graphically in *The Temple of Nature* (1803), p. 107, canto 3, ll. 285–8.

75 See Darwin, *Zoonomia*, vol. i, p. 376:

Man is termed by Aristotle an imitative animal; this propensity to imitation not only appears in the actions of children, but in all the customs and fashions of the world.

76 Darwin, *Zoonomia*, vol. i, pp. 38, 61, 76.

77 Darwin, *Zoonomia*, vol. i, p. 13.

Association is an exertion or change of some extreme part of the sensorium residing in the muscles or organs of sense, in consequence of some antecedent or attendant fibrous contractions.

78 Darwin, *Zoonomia*, vol. ii, p. 255.

79 Darwin, *Zoonomia*, vol. ii, p. 263; McNeil, *Under the Banner of Science*, pp. 98f.

80 Darwin, *Zoonomia*, vol. ii, pp. 264, 270; see James Blondel, *The Strength of Imagination in Pregnant Women Examin'd* (1727); Dennis Todd, *Imagining Monsters* (1995).

81 Darwin, *Zoonomia*, vol. ii, p. 270.

82 Darwin, *Phytologia*, pt 3, p. 557.

83 Darwin, *Zoonomia*, vol. ii, pp. 13–14. Darwin thus celebrated the joyous eroticism of Tahiti: 'about 100 males and 100 females, who form one promiscuous marriage':

Thus where pleased VENUS, in the southern main,

Sheds all her smiles on Otaheite's plain,

Wide o'er the isle her silken net she draws,

And the Loves laugh at all but Nature's laws.

The Botanic Garden, p. 200, canto 4. See the discussion in chapter 11 above.

84 Darwin, *Zoonomia*, vol. ii, p. 235.

85 Darwin, *Zoonomia*, vol. ii, p. 240.

86 Darwin, *The Temple of Nature*, p. 24, canto 1, ll. 269–72.

87 Darwin, *The Temple of Nature*, p. 25, canto 1, ll. 273–4.

88 Darwin, *The Temple of Nature*, p. 25, canto 1, ll. 277–80; compare p. 107, canto 3, ll. 279–86:

> Hence when the inquiring hands with contact fine
>
> Trace on hard forms the circumscribing line;
>
> Which then the language of the rolling eyes
>
> From distant scenes of earth and heaven supplies;
>
> Those clear idea of the touch and sight
>
> Rouse the quick sense to anguish or delight;
>
> Whence the fine power of *IMITATION* springs,
>
> And the outlines of external things.

89 Darwin, *The Temple of Nature*, p. 86, canto 3, ll. 41–6.

90 Darwin, *Zoonomia*, vol. ii, p. 318.

91 Darwin, *The Temple of Nature*, p. 134, canto 4, ll. 65–6.

92 Darwin, *The Temple of Nature*, p. 166, canto 4, ll. 451–4.

93 In the counter-revolutionary age, it met a frosty reception: Norton Garfinkle, 'Science and Religion in England, 1790–1800' (1955).

94 Alexander Pope, *An Essay on Man* (1733–4), epistle 2, l. 10, in John Butt (ed.), *The Poems of Alexander Pope* (1965), p. 516.

95 See A. O. Lovejoy, *The Great Chain of Being* (1936).

96 Pope, *An Essay on Man*, epistle ii, ll. 15–16, in Butt, *The Poems of Alexander Pope*, p. 516.

97 Darwin, *The Temple of Nature*, p. 86, canto 3, ll. 43–6.

98 McNeil, *Under the Banner of Science*.

99 Darwin, *The Temple of Nature*, pp. 139–40, canto 4, ll. 369–82:

> So human progenies, if unrestrain'd,
>
> By climate friended, and by food sustain'd,
>
> O'er seas and soils, prolific hordes! would spread
>
> Erelong, and deluge their terraqueous bed;
>
> But war, and pestilence, disease, and dearth
>
> Sweep the superfluous myriads from the earth . . .
>
> The births and deaths contend with equal strife,
>
> And every pore of Nature teems with Life;
>
> Which buds or breathes from Indus to the Poles,
>
> And Earth's vast surface kindles as it rolls!

100 This is one of the themes of M. H. Abrams, *Natural Supernaturalism* (1971).

20 THE REVOLUTIONARY ERA: 'MODERN PHILOSOPHY'

1 William Godwin, *An Enquiry concerning Political Justice* (1985 [1793]), title of bk I, ch. 5.

2 Thomas Paine, *The Complete Writings of Thomas Paine* (1945), vol. i, p. 354.

3 C. B. Jewson, *Jacobin City* (1975), pp. 12–13.

4 For the air of self-congratulation, see Nicholas Rogers, *Crowds, Culture and Politics in Georgian Britain* (1998), p. 180: 'The jubilee was an opportunity to glory in British achievements, not dwell on past and present failures'.

For late eighteenth-century politics, see I. R. Christie, *Wars and Revolutions* (1982), and *Stress and Stability in Late Eighteenth-Century Britain* (1984); James T. Boulton, *The Language of Politics in the Age of Wilkes and Burke* (1963); Philip Anthony Brown, *The French Revolution in English History* (1965); E. P. Thompson, *The Making of the English Working Class* (1968); Gregory Claeys, 'The French Revolution Debate and British Political Thought' (1990); Carl B. Cone, *The English Jacobins* (1968);

Clive Emsley, *British Society and the French Wars 1793–1815* (1979); Keith Hanley and Raman Selden (eds.), *Revolution and English Romanticism* (1990).

5 Desmond King-Hele (ed.), *The Letters of Erasmus Darwin* (1981), p. 200, letter no. 90A, to James Watt (19 January 1790): 'I feel myself becoming all French both in chemistry and politics': see Ann Finer and George Savage (eds.), *The Selected Letters of Josiah Wedgwood* (1965), p. 319.

6 William Wordsworth, *The Prelude* (1850 version), bk VI, l. 339, in J. Wordsworth, M. H. Abrams and S. Gill (eds.), *William Wordsworth, the Prelude 1799, 1805, 1850* (1979), p. 205. The fact that Wordsworth's words were written later does not, of course, invalidate their recreation of the aura of '89.

7 Wordsworth, *The Prelude* (1850 version), bk IX, l. 161, in Wordsworth, Abrams and Gill, *William Wordsworth, the Prelude 1799, 1805, 1850*, p. 320.

8 As the doyen of Dissenting ministers, Price was originally meant to give the commemorative sermon at the Presbyterian chapel in London's Old Jewry the previous year, the one-hundredth anniversary of the Glorious Revolution. Price did not wish to abolish the monarchy, and he preferred the existing 'mixed' form of government to a democracy.

9 Richard Price, *A Discourse on the Love of our Country* (1789), pp. 49, 50.

10 Price, *Discourse on the Love of Our Country*, pp. 50–51.

11 Edmund Burke, *Reflections on the Revolution in France* (1790), p. 113.

12 Burke, *Reflections on the Revolution in France*, in L. G. Mitchell (ed.), *The Writings and Speeches of Edmund Burke* (1989), vol. viii, p. 207. See also Peter Stanlis, *Edmund Burke: The Enlightenment and Revolution* (1991).

13 Clive Emsley, *British Society and the French Wars 1793–1815* (1979), p. 14.

14 Theo Barker (ed.), *The Long March of Everyman 1750–1960* (1978), p. 62. This comes from papers confiscated during the Treason Trials of 1794.

15 John Cannon, *Parliamentary Reform 1640–1832* (1972).

16 Mary Wollstonecraft, *A Vindication of the Rights of Men*, in *A Vindication of the Rights of Men with A Vindication of the Rights of Woman* (1995), p. 8; Gary Kelly, *Revolutionary Feminism* (1992).

17 T. J. Mathias, *The Pursuits of Literature, Or What You Will* (1794), advertisement to pt IV, p. 238.

18 Philip Anthony Brown, *The French Revolution in English History* (1965), p. 157.

19 For this and the preceding quotations, see Emsley, *British Society and the French Wars 1793–1815*, pp. 86–7.

20 Thomas Walker, *A Review of Some of the Political Events Which Have Occurred in Manchester during the Last Five Years* (1794), pp. 1–2.

21 'The French are plunging into a degree of barbarism,' declared the liberal Samuel Romilly, 'which, for such a nation, and in so short a period, surpasses all imagination. All religion is already abolished . . . We may soon expect to see all books exterminated': Samuel Romilly, *Memoirs of the Life of Sir Samuel Romilly* (1971 [1840]), vol. ii, p. 37.

22 Paine became a bogey. 'At Redruth in Cornwall, a miner,' noted the *Gentleman's Magazine* obituary column in 1795, 'he was drinking at the Three Compasses in that town, and, in a fit of inebriety, blasphemed the Evangelists, wished perdition to all the kings of the earth, and drank Tom Paine's health; when, on a sudden, his jaw became locked, and he died on the spot in the most excruciating torments': *Gentleman's Magazine*, no. 65 (1795), p. 495.

23 Quoted in Emsley, *British Society and the French Wars 1793–1815*, p. 161.

24 Gregory Claeys (ed.), *The Politics of English Jacobinism* (1995), which has a fine introduction; Christina Bewley and David Bewley, *Gentleman Radical* (1998).

25 Clive Emsley, *Policing and Its Context, 1750–1870* (1983), p. 25; H. R. Dickinson, *The Politics of the People in Eighteenth-century Britain* (1995), p. 237.

26 For this, including the quotations, see Emsley, *British Society and the French Wars 1793–1815*, p. 56; on early Coleridge, see Ian Wylie, *Young Coleridge and the Philosophers of Nature* (1989), p. 51.

27 See Maurice Colgan, 'Prophecy Against Reason' (1985); Roy Foster (ed.), *The Oxford Illustrated History of Ireland* (1991), pp. 134ff. The United Irishmen failed, partly because they were too dependent on French support: Marianne Elliott, *Partners in Revolution* (1982).

28 Robert Southey, *Letters from England by Don Manuel Alvarez Espriella* (1984 [1807]), p. 375. For a contemporary assessment of Southey, see William Hazlitt, *The Spirit of the Age* (1971 [1825]), pp. 365–84.

29 Southey, *Letters from England by Don Manuel Alvarez Espriella*, p. 375.

30 John Dinwiddy, 'Conceptions of Revolution in the English Radicalism of the 1790s' (1990), p. 547.

31 Marilyn Butler (ed.), *Burke, Paine, Godwin, and the Revolution Controversy* (1984); Mark Philp, *Paine* (1989); G. Claeys, *Thomas Paine. Social and Political Thought* (1989); Jack Fruchtman Jr, *Thomas Paine: Apostle of Freedom* (1994); John Keane, *Tom Paine: A Political Life* (1995).

32 Thomas Paine, *The Complete Writings of Thomas Paine* (1945), vol. i, p. xxviii. Jack Fruchtman Jr, *Thomas Paine and the Religion of Nature* (1993).

33 Paine, *The Complete Writings of Thomas Paine*, vol. ii, p. 486.

34 Paine, *The Complete Writings of Thomas Paine*, vol. ii, p. 481.

35 Richard D. Altick, *The English Common Reader 1800–1900* (1957), p. 69.

36 Paine, *The Complete Writings of Thomas Paine*, vol. i, p. 198. 'A Friend to the People', who pseudonymously produced *A Review of the Constitution of Great Britain* (1791), dismissed the Lords as 'political monsters' and 'mere creatures' of the Crown. The British people, he insisted, were in worse plight than the subjects of the Sultan: 'In Turkey, the tyger Despotism springs upon his single victim, and gluts himself with carnage; but in England, the monster, Aristocracy, extending over the devoted million her ten thousand fangs, sucks from every pore of the people, a never ceasing stream of blood'. Quoted in Cannon, *Parliamentary Reform 1640–1832*, p. 163.

37 Paine, *The Complete Writings of Thomas Paine*, vol. i, p. 251; see the discussion in Gregory Claeys (ed.), *Political Writings of the 1790s* (1995), vol. i, p. 64.

38 Paine, *The Complete Writings of Thomas Paine*, ed. Philip S. Foner, 2 vols (New York: Citadel Press, 1945), vol. i, p. 447.

39 Paine, *The Complete Writing of Thomas Paine*, vol. i, p. 260.

40 Paine, *The Complete Writings of Thomas Paine*, vol. i, p. 274.

41 Gregory Claeys, 'The French Revolution Debate and British Political Thought' (1990).

42 Paine, *The Complete Writings of Thomas Paine*, vol. i, pp. 357–8.

no man is capable, without the aid of society, of supplying his own wants; and those wants acting upon every individual, impel the whole of them into society, as naturally as gravitation acts to a centre. But she [nature] has gone further. She has not only forced man into society, by a diversity of wants, which the reciprocal aid of each other can supply, but she has implanted in him a system of social affections, which, though not necessary to his existence, are essential to his happiness. There is no period of life when this love of society ceases to act. (vol. I, p. 357.)

43 Paine, *The Complete Writings of Thomas Paine*, vol. i, p. 431.

44 Paine, *The Complete Writings of Thomas Paine*, vol. i, pp. 459–604; Fruchtman, *Thomas Paine and the Religion of Nature*.

Fruchtman approaches Paine as a secular preacher.

45 Paine, *The Complete Writings of Thomas Paine*, vol. i, p. 451. Religious toleration was not enough because it was a form of intolerance:

Toleration is not the opposite of Intolerance, but is the *counterfeit* of it. Both are despotisms. The one assumes to itself the right of witholding Liberty of Conscience, and the other of granting it.

vol. i, p. 291.

46 Paine, *The Complete Writings of Thomas Paine*, vol. i, p. 464.

47 Quoted in Wylie, *Young Coleridge and the Philosophers of Nature*, p. 1.

48 Paine, *The Complete Writings of Thomas Paine*, vol. i, p. 274.

49 Joseph Mather, 'God Save Great Thomas Paine' (1792?), in Roger Lonsdale (ed.), *The New Oxford Book of Eighteenth-century Verse* (1984), p. 790.

50 Paine, *The Complete Writings of Thomas Paine*, vol. i, p. xxxi.

51 Godwin, *An Enquiry concerning Political Justice*, p. 665.

52 Don Locke, *A Fantasy of Reason* (1980); Mark Philp, *Godwin's Political Justice* (1986). The Cabinet did discuss prosecution, on 25 May 1793, but, at £1 16s. they thought it too expensive to be dangerous.

53 Godwin, *An Enquiry concerning Political Justice*, p. 13.

54 Locke, *A Fantasy of Reason*; Peter H. Marshall, *William Godwin* (1984).

55 Godwin, *An Enquiry concerning Political Justice*, p. 140. See ch. 4, pp. 96–115: 'The Characters of Men Originate in Their External Circumstances'.

56 Godwin, *An Enquiry concerning Political Justice*, p. 32.

57 Godwin, *An Enquiry concerning Political Justice*, p. 104.

58 Such play was made of this that in the third edition Fénelon's valet was consigned to the flames instead: Godwin, *An Enquiry concerning Political Justice*, p. 169; Locke, *A Fantasy of Reason*, p. 168.

59 It was impossible to punish people into virtue:

Let us consider the effect that coercion produces upon the mind of him against whom it is employed. It cannot begin with convincing; it is no argument; it begins with producing the sensation of pain, and the sentiment of distaste. It begins with violently alienating the mind from the truth with which we wish it to be impressed.

Godwin, *An Enquiry concerning Political Justice*, pp. 22–3.

60 Like Paley and Bentham, Godwin did not see punishment as a rational retaliation. Punishment should not be inflicted

because there is apprehended to be a certain fitness and propriety in the nature of things, that render suffering, abstractedly from the benefit to result, the suitable concomitant of vice . . . Punishment ought to be inflicted because public interest demands it.

Godwin, *An Enquiry concerning Political Justice*, p. 648.

61 Godwin, *An Enquiry concerning Political Justice*, p. 633.

62 Godwin wondered: 'shall we have concerts of music? . . . Shall we have theatrical exhibitions? This seems to include an absurd and vicious cooperation': Godwin, *An Enquiry concerning Political Justice*, p. 759. Godwin disapproved of cohabitation because it led to 'thwarting, bickering and unhappiness', and marriage was 'a monopoly, and the worst of monopolies' (p. 762); he stressed: 'individuality is of the very essence of intellectual excellence' (p. 775).

63 Godwin, *An Enquiry concerning Political Justice*, pp 19, 556.

64 Godwin, *An Enquiry concerning Political Justice*, p. 776.

65 Godwin, *An Enquiry concerning Political Justice*, p. 777, quoted in Locke, *A Fantasy of Reason*, p. 8.

66 Godwin, *An Enquiry concerning Political Justice*, p. 776.

67 Godwin, *An Enquiry concerning Political Justice*, p. 730.

68 Godwin, *An Enquiry concerning Political Justice*, p. 769.

69 Godwin, *An Enquiry concerning Political Justice*, p. 529: 'Individuals are everthing, and society, abstracted from the individuals of which it is composed, nothing.'

70 Godwin, *An Enquiry concerning Political Justice*, p. 268.

71 Godwin, *An Enquiry concerning Political Justice*, pp. 34, 251: 'we shall have many reforms, but no revolutions', for 'Revolutions are the produce of passion, not of sober and tranquil reason'; truth must be advanced by 'sober and tranquil reason', by 'communication and discussion': Locke, *A Fantasy of Reason*, p. 102. Once there was enlightenment, 'the chains fall off themselves' (Godwin, *An Enquiry concerning Political Justice*, p. 33). Hence Godwin's claim: 'My creed is a short one'; 'I am in principle a Republican, but in practice a Whig' (see Locke, *A Fantasy of Reason*, p. 104).

72 Godwin, *An Enquiry concerning Political Justice*, pp. 184–5, quoted in Locke, *A Fantasy of Reason*, p. 3.

73 Godwin, *An Enquiry concerning Political Justice*, p. 221, quoted in Locke, *A Fantasy of Reason*, p. 4.

74 Quoted in Hanley and Selden (eds.), *Revolution and English Romanticism*, p. 151.

75 There were lots of snarling or ironic variations on 'modern philosophy', one being Wordsworth's 'philosophism': see Edward Duffy, *Rousseau in England* (1979), p. 55; for 'modern philosophy', see Lois Whitney, *Primitivism and the Idea of Progress* (1934), p. 320. Godwin's commitment to reason led Hazlitt to speak of his 'Arctic Circle'.

76 Butler, *Burke, Paine, Godwin, and the Revolution Controversy*, p. 76.

77 William Hodgson, *The Commonwealth of Reason* (1795), p. 46. Like other liberals, Hodgson proposed that marriage should be but a civil contract.

78 'That property in land and liberty among men in a state of nature ought to be equal, few, one would be fain to hope, would be foolish to deny': Thomas Spence, *The Real Rights of Man* (1793), a lecture delivered at Newcastle-upon-Tyne on 8 November 1775 and published in 1796 as *The Meridian Sun of Liberty* and reprinted in M. Beer (ed.), *The Pioneers of Land Reform* (1920), pp. 5–16. Spence was imprisoned for a few months in 1794 and again in 1801.

79 Armytage, *Heavens Below*, p. 70; Butler, *Burke, Paine, Godwin, and the Revolution Controversy*, p. 189; Olivia Smith, *The Politics of Language 1791–1819* (1984), p. 80.

80 Spence, *The Meridian Sun of Liberty*, quoted in Armytage, *Heavens Below*, p. 70; Gregory Claeys (ed.), *Utopias of the British Enlightenment* (1994), p. xviii.

81 Spence, *The Meridian Sun of Liberty*. For Spence as Harrington reversed, see Roger Sales, *English Literature in History: 1780–1830, Pastoral and Politics* (1983), p. 26. Like Godwin, Spence saw society as a federation of parishes.

82 Armytage, *Heavens Below*, p. 72; Smith, *The Politics of Language 1791–1819*, p. 112.

Spence's dedicatory poem to *A Supplement to the History of Robinson Crusoe* (1782) used his specialized alphabet, which he termed the Kruzonian Manner:

> And dho mi bwk's in kwer Lingo
> I wil it send tw St. Domingo
> Tw dhe Republik ov dhe 'Inkaz
> For an egzampl how tw fram Looz
> For hw kan tel but dhe Mileneum
> Ma tak its riz from mi pwr Kraneum

Quoted in Marcus Wood, *Radical Satire and Print Culture 1790–1822* (1994), p. 86.

83 Horne Tooke, *The Diversions of Purley* (1786), vol. ii, p. 51b; D. Rosenberg, ' "A New Sort of Logick and Critick" ' (1991); Bewley and Bewley, *Gentleman Radical*.

84 For Tooke, see Hans Aarsleff, *The Study of Languge in England, 1780–1860* (1983), p. 71; Butler, *Burke, Paine, Godwin, and the Revolution Controversy*, p. 19. For Harris, see Smith, *The Politics of Language 1791–1819*, p. 20.

According to Hazlitt, Tooke examined, 'with jealous watchfulness, the meaning of words to prevent being entrapped by them': William Hazlitt, 'The Late Mr Horne Tooke' (1825), in *The Complete Works of William Hazlitt* (1930–34), vol. xi, p. 54.

85 Thomas Beddoes, *Observations on the Nature of Demonstrative Evidence* (1793), p. 151.

86 See Kevin C. Knox, 'Lunatick Visions' (1999). Frend has been discussed in chapter 14 above.

87 Armytage, *Heavens Below*, p. 63. For America's reputation post-1776 as a land of freedom, see above, chapter 18. Young Southey had been expelled from Westminster for editing a magazine, the *Flagellant*, against flogging and other undemocratic practices. He carried around a copy of Goethe's *Werther*.

88 'On the Prospect of Establishing a Pantisocracy in America' (1826), in Samuel Taylor Coleridge, *The Complete Poems* (1997), p. 58.

89 Coleridge's later account stated; 'I was a sharer in the general vortex, though my little world described the path of its revolution in an orbit of its own': Barbara E. Rooke (ed.), *The Collected Works of Samuel Taylor Coleridge: The Friend I* (1969), vol. iv, p. 223. He explained: 'The leading Idea of Pantisocracy is to make men *necessarily* virtuous by removing all Motives to Evil – all possible Temptations': Earl Leslie Griggs (ed.), *Collected Letters of Samuel Taylor Coleridge* (1956–68), vol. i, p. 114, letter 65, to Robert Southey (21 October 1794).

90 Richard Holmes, *Coleridge: Early Visions* (1989), p. 72; Armytage, *Heavens Below*, p. 64.

91 See the discussion of his early activities in Samuel Taylor Coleridge, *Biographia Literaria*

(1817), pp. 81f.; Wylie, *Young Coleridge and the Philosophers of Nature*, p. 66.

92 Holmes, *Coleridge: Early Visions*, p. 79.

93 Defending his unorthodox opinions to Southey, Coleridge affirmed his attachment not only to Hartley, but implicitly to Priestley and his 'materialism': 'I am a compleat Necessitarian – and understand the subject as well almost as Hartley himself – but I go farther than Hartley and believe the corporeality of thought – namely, that it is motion': 'Lecture 1795 on Politics and Religion' (1795), in Lewis Patton and Peter Mann (eds.), *The Collected Works of Samuel Taylor Coleridge* (1971), p. lviii.

94 Wylie, *Young Coleridge and the Philosophers of Nature*, p. 44.

95
> Nor will I not thy holy guidance bless,
> And hymn thee, Godwin! with an ardent lay;

'To William Godwin' (1795), in Coleridge, *The Complete Poems*, p. 74.

96 Wylie, *Young Coleridge and the Philosophers of Nature*, p. 109.

97 M. H. Abrams, *Natural Supernaturalism* (1971), p. 338.

98 Griggs, *Collected Letters of Samuel Taylor Coleridge*, vol. i, p. 397, letter 238, to George Coleridge (*c.* 10 March 1798). On Coleridge and Wordsworth, see Alan Bewell, *Wordsworth and the Enlightenment* (1989); Richard Holmes, *Coleridge* (1982); Butler, *Romantics, Rebels and Reactionaries*, and 'Romanticism in England' (1988); R. J. White, *The Political Thought of Samuel Taylor Coleridge* (1938).

99 Griggs, *Collected Letters of Samuel Taylor Coleridge*, vol. ii, p. 706, letter 387, to Thomas Poole (Monday, 16 March 1801).

100 Samuel Taylor Coleridge, *A Lay Sermon Addressed to the Higher and Middle Classes on the Existing Distresses and Discontents* (1817), in R. J. White (ed.), *Political Tracts of Wordsworth, Coleridge and Shelley* (1953), p. 83.

101 Griggs, *Collected Letters of Samuel Taylor*

Coleridge, vol. ii, p. 709, letter 388, to Thomas Poole (23 March, 1801).

102 Samuel Taylor Coleridge, *On the Constitution of the Church and State* (1830), in John Colmer (ed.), *The Collected Works of Samuel Taylor Coleridge* (1976), vol. x, pp. 66, 68. For Coleridge's philosophy, see Holmes, *Coleridge*; Harold Orel, *English Romantic Poets and the Enlightenment* (1973); Wylie, *Young Coleridge and the Philosophers of Nature*.

103 Thomas Peacock, *Nightmare Abbey* (1818), in David Garnett (ed.), *The Novels of Thomas Love Peacock* (1948), pp. 115, 359–60. Flosky asks: 'How can we be cheerful when we are surrounded by a reading public, that is growing too wise for its betters?'

104 Southey, Hazlitt remarked, 'had missed his way in Utopia and found it at Old Sarum': David Garnett, introduction to Thomas Peacock, *Melincourt* (1817), in *The Novels of Thomas Love Peacock*, p. 98.

105 Michael Ferber, *The Social Vision of William Blake* (1985), p. 125.

106 Peter Ackroyd, *Blake* (1995); Jacob Bronowski, *William Blake and the Age of Revolution* (1972); Ferber, *The Social Vision of William Blake*; David V. Erdman, *Blake, Prophet against Empire*, 3rd edn (1954); Morton D. Paley, *Energy and the Imagination* (1970).

107 William Blake, 'Annotations to Sir Joshua Reynolds' Discourses' (*c.* 1808), in G. Keynes (ed.), *Blake: Complete Writings* (1969), p. 985, discussed in Marjorie Hope Nicolson, *Newton Demands the Muse* (1946), p. 170; Jack Lindsay, *William Blake: His Life and Work* (1978), p. 60.

108 William Blake, 'Jerusalem: The Emanation of the Giant Albion' (written and etched 1804–20), ll. 15–16, in Keynes, *The Complete Works of William Blake* (1956), p. 636. See discussion in Orel, *English Romantic Poets and the Enlightenment*, p. 49.

109 Romantic criticism of 'mechanism' became ubiquitous. 'Were we required,' wrote Thomas Carlyle, 'to characterise this age of course by any single epithet, we should be temped to call it, not an Heroical, Devotional, Philosophical, or Moral age, but above all others, the Mechanical Age': [T. Carlyle], 'Signs of the Times', *Edinburgh Review* (1829), p. 453.

110 William Blake, *Poems and Fragments from the Note-book* (c. 1800–1803) in *Blake: Complete Writings* (1966), p. 418. Note how Blake's language is about 'vision' not 'light' in the enlightenment sense. Enlightenment sensationalism limited vision.

111 'I am not ashamed, afraid, or averse to tell you,' he informed his London patron Thomas Butts, 'that I am under the direction of Messengers from Heaven, Daily & Nightly': Lindsay, *William Blake: His Life and Work*, p. 147; Bronowski, *William Blake and the Age of Revolution*, p. 28; for his visions of angels, see Ackroyd, *Blake*, p. 195.

112 William Blake, 'Annotations to Richard Watson's "An Apology to the Bible"' (1798). It is of course significant that Blake found himself battling against the spokesmen not for atheism but for rational Christianity. See Iain McCalman, 'New Jerusalems' (1997).

113 Ackroyd, *Blake*, pp. 72–3.

114 William Blake, *Letter to Thomas Butts* (22 November 1802), in *Blake: Complete Writings*, p. 818.

115 For such anti-enlightenment traditions, see Bernard M. Schilling, *Conservative England and the Case against Voltaire* (1950); D. W. Bebbington, *Evangelicalism in Modern Britain* (1988); Clement Hawes, *Christopher Smart and the Enlightenment* (1999); Margaret Forbes, *Beattie and His Friends* (1904); Edward J. Bristow, *Vice and Vigilance* (1977); Grayson Ditchfield, *The Evangelical Revival* (1997). For Bowdlerism, see N. Perrin, *Dr Bowdler's Legacy* (1970). Beattie called Hume's *Treatise* a 'vile effusion': David Hume, *A Treatise of Human Nature* (1969 [1739–40]), p. 19.

116 Edmund Burke, *Reflections on the Revolution in France* (1790), pp. 129–30.

117 Edmund Burke, *Reflections on the Revolution in France* (1790), in *Works* (1826), vol. v, p. 185.

Burke's 'apostasy' is well discussed in John Cannon, *Parliamentary Reform 1640–1832* (1972), p. 168.

Burke's intellectual conservatism was mocked by the Dissenter John Aikin, who warned his son that he would nowadays hear many saying: 'Thank heaven! I am no philosopher; I pretend not to be wiser than those who have gone before me. I do not boast of the discovery of new principles': John Aikin, *Letters from a Father to His Son*, 3rd edn (1796), p. 45.

118 Simon Schaffer, 'Genius in Romantic Natural Philosophy' (1990), p. 86 and, 'States of Mind' (1990), p. 244.

119 Quoted in Schaffer, 'Genius in Romantic Natural Philosophy', p. 88, from John Robison, *Proofs of a Conspiracy against All the Religions and Governments of Europe* (1798); see also R. B. Clark, *William Gifford: Tory Satirist, Critic, and Editor* (1980); Amos Hofman, 'Opinion, Illusion and the Illusion of Opinion' (1993).

120 Emily Lorraine de Montluzin, *The Anti-Jacobins 1798–1800* (1988), p. 16.

121 Arthur Young, *An Enquiry into the State of the Public Mind* (1798), p. 25; Harry T. Dickinson, 'Popular Loyalism in Britain in the 1790s' (1990); Montluzin, *The Anti-Jacobins 1798–1800*, p. 7.

122 The poem appeared in 1798: Charles Edmonds (ed.), *Poetry of the Anti-Jacobin* (1854), p. 115; Marcus Wood, *Radical Satire and Print Culture 1790–1822* (1994); Montluzin, *The Anti-Jacobins 1798–1800*, p. 14.

123 G. Canning, 'The Soldier's Friend' (nd), in L. Sanders (ed.), *Selections from the Anti-Jacobin* (1904), p. 29; Edmonds, *Poetry of the Anti-Jacobin*, pp. 29–30.

124 Locke, *A Fantasy of Reason*, p. 160.

125 Quoted in A. Aspinall, *Politics and the Press c. 1780–1850* (1949), p. 9.

126 *Anti-Jacobin Review*, no. 1 (July 1798), p. 2; Montluzin, *The Anti-Jacobins 1798–1800*, p. 28.

127 Edmonds, *Poetry of the Anti-Jacobin*, p. 110;

this was a direct hit at Godwin's notion of self-willed immortality: Maureen McNeil, *Under the Banner of Science* (1987), p. 86; Wylie, *Young Coleridge and the Philosophers of Nature*, p. 70.

128 Mrs Elizabeth Hamilton, *Letters of a Hindoo Rajah* (1999 [1796]), p. 257.

129 Mrs Elizabeth Hamilton, *Memoirs of Modern Philosophers* (1800), vol. ii, p. 9; Marilyn Butler, *Jane Austen and the War of Ideas* (1975), p. 108; Locke, *A Fantasy of Reason*, p. 116. For mockery of 'modern philosophy', see Whitney, *Primitivism and the Idea of Progress*, p. 306. Bridgetina had first met the divine words of Godwin's *Political Justice* on some proof sheets that had been used as wrapping paper for snuff. 'I read and sneezed, and sneezed and read,' she tells us, 'till the germ of philosophy began to fructify my soul. From that moment I became a philosopher, and need not to inform you of the important consequences.'

130 M. G. Jones, *Hannah More* (1952), p. 104; Ford K. Brown, *Fathers of the Victorians* (1961), p. 126; Muriel Jaeger, *Before Victoria* (1967); Boyd Hilton, *The Age of Atonement* (1988); Ian Bradley, *The Call to Seriousness* (1976).

131 Hannah More, *An Estimate of the Religion of the Fashionable World* (1791), pp. 31–2; Jones, *Hannah More*, p. 109; R. W. Harris, *Romanticism and the Social Order* (1969), p. 134.

132 W. S. Lewis (ed.), *The Correspondence of Horace Walpole* (1961), vol. xxxi, p. 329; W. Roberts (ed.), *Memoirs of the Life and Correspondence of Mrs Hannah More* (1834), vol. ii, p. 357.

133 Whitney, *Primitivism and the Idea of Progress*, p. 239.

134 She guessed right. In 1797 Thomas Spence produced *The Rights of Infants* (1797). Roberts, *Memoirs of the Life and Correspondence of Mrs Hannah More*, vol. iii, p. 100. As shown in chapter 15, More believed it was 'a fundamental error to consider children as innocent beings': Jones, *Hannah More*, p. 117.

See Jon Klancher, *The Making of English Reading Audiences, 1790–1832* (1987), p. 12.

135 Altick, *The English Common Reader 1800–1900*, p. 75; Butler, *Burke, Paine, Godwin, and the Revolution Controversy*, p. 180.

136 Hannah More, *Village Politics* (1793), and *The Riot* (1795), pp. 3–4. Quoted in Butler, *Burke, Paine, Godwin, and the Revolution Controversy*, p. 180.

137 More, *Village Politics* (1793).

138 *The History of Mr Fantom the New-Fashioned Philosopher* (1805) was the story of a prosperous business man with little true education, who longed to cut a figure. He alighted upon a copy of Paine and became carried away by the new philosophy. Trueman explained to Fantom that philosophers did not understand the true cause of human misery: sin.

139 Ian Bradley, *The Call to Seriousness* (1976), p. 19.

140 Brown, *Fathers of the Victorians* (1961), p. 1; Jaeger, *Before Victoria*, p. 14. Religion had been reduced, thought Wilberforce, to a *comme il faut*: Roland N. Stromberg, *Religious Liberalism in Eighteenth-century England* (1954), p. 119.

141 Robert Isaac Wilberforce and Samuel Wilberforce, *The Life of William Wilberforce* (1838), vol. i, p. 84; Bradley, *The Call to Seriousness*, p. 94; William Wilberforce, *A Practical View of the Prevailing Religious System of Professed Christians in the Higher and Middle Classes in This Country Contrasted with Real Christianity* (1797), p. 12; Hilton, *The Age of Atonement*.

142 Wilberforce, *A Practical View of the Prevailing Religious System of Professed Christians in the Higher and Middle Classes in This Country Contrasted with Real Christianity*, p. 12.

143 William Paley, *Natural Theology* (1802), p. 490.

144 William Wilberforce, letter to Ralph Creyke (8 January 1803), in *The Correspondence of William Wilberforce* (1840), vol. i, pp. 247–53; see discussion in Hilton, *The Age of Atonement*, p. 4.

145 Wilberforce, *A Practical View of the Prevailing Religious System of Professed Christians in the Higher and Middle Classes of This Country Contrasted with Real Christianity*, p. 489. Sydney Smith mocked the 'patent Christianity which has been for some time manufacturing at Clapham': quoted in Harris, *Romanticism and the Social Order*, p. 54.

146 Patricia James, *Population Malthus: His Life and Times* (1979), p. 25. For Rousseau's influence, see Duffy, *Rousseau in England*; for Daniel Malthus, see Elie Halévy, *The Growth of Philosophic Radicalism* (1972), p. 235.

147 Thomas Robert Malthus, *An Essay on the Principle of Population* (1966 [1798]), pp. 2–3; M. Turner (ed.), *Malthus and His Times* (1986).

148 Malthus, *An Essay on the Principle of Population*, preface, p. iii.

149 Malthus, *An Essay on the Principle of Population*, pp. 8–9.

150 Malthus, *An Essay on the Principle of Population*, p. 10.

151 Malthus, *An Essay on the Principle of Population*, p. 8.

152 Malthus, *An Essay on the Principle of Population*, pp. 150–52.

153 Malthus, *An Essay on the Principle of Population*, p. 152.

154 Malthus, *An Essay on the Principle of Population*, p. 153.

155 Malthus, *An Essay on the Principle of Population*, p. 174.

156 Malthus, *An Essay on the Principle of Population*, pp. 174–5.

157 Malthus, *An Essay on the Principle of Population*, p. 176.

158 Malthus, *An Essay on the Principle of Population*, pp. 11–12.

159 Malthus, *An Essay on the Principle of Population*, pp. 12–13.

160 Malthus, *An Essay on the Principle of Population*, pp. 16–17.

161 Malthus, *An Essay on the Principle of Population*, pp. 37–8.

162 Charles Hall, *The Effects of Civilization on the People in European States* (1805). On Hall, see

Kenneth Smith, *The Malthusian Controversy* (1951), pp. 50f.; Roy Porter, 'The Malthusian Moment' (2000).

163 Hall, *The Effects of Civilization on the People in European States*, p. 10, quoted in Smith, *The Malthusian Controversy*, p. 51.

164 For Thomas Jarrold, see Smith, *The Malthusian Controversy*, pp. 56f.

165 Thomas Jarrold, *Anthropologia* (1808).

166 Thomas Jarrold, *Dissertations on Man, Philosophical, Physiological and Political* (1806), p. 69.

167 Jarrold, *Dissertations on Man, Philosophical, Physiological and Political*, p. 73.

168 Jarrold, *Dissertations on Man, Philosophical, Physiological and Political*, p. 267.

169 Jarrold, *Dissertations on Man, Philosophical,*

Physiological and Political, p. 366; Porter, 'The Malthusian Moment'.

170 See Frederick Raphael, *Byron* (1982).

171 Catherine Macdonald Maclean, *Born Under Saturn* (1943), pp. 85, 385.

172 Brown, *The French Revolution in English History*, p. 49.

173 Maclean, *Born Under Saturn*, pp. 23, 334.

174 William Hazlitt, *Political Essays* (1819), in *The Collected Works of William Hazlitt* (1901–6), vol. iii, p. 175; Seamus Deane, *The French Revolution and Enlightenment in England 1789–1832* (1988), p. 142; Maclean, *Born Under Saturn*, p. 332.

175 Hazlitt, *Political Essays* in *The Collected Works of William Hazlitt*, preface, vol. vii, p. 31.

176 Knox, 'Lunatick Visions'.

21 LASTING LIGHT?

1 W. J. Bate, J. M. Bullitt, and L. F. Powell (eds.), *Samuel Johnson: The Idler and Adventurer* (1963), no. 137, p. 491.

2 James Keir (ed.), *An Account of the Life and Writings of Thomas Day* (1791), p. 104.

3 Letter from John Adams to Thomas Jefferson (13 November 1815), in Charles Francis Adams (ed.), *The Works of John Adams* (1850–56), vol. x, p. 174.

4 Perry Anderson, *The Origins of Postmodernity* (1988); Karlis Racevskis, *Postmodernism and the Search for Enlightenment* (1993); Marshal Berman, *All That is Solid Melts into Air* (1983), pp. 34f.

5 Stephen Greenblatt, *Renaissance Self-Fashioning* (1980); Miles Ogborn, *Spaces of Modernity* (1998), pp. 7ff.

6 William Godwin, *An Enquiry concerning Political Justice* (1985 [1793]), p. 281.

7 Godwin, *An Enquiry concerning Political Justice*, p. 529. For a parody of the voice of Reaction against printing, see Daniel Eaton [pseud. 'Antitype'], *The Pernicious Effects of the Art of Printing upon Society, Exposed* (1794).

8 Erasmus Darwin, *The Temple of Nature* (1803), canto IV, p. 152, ll. 283–6.

9 David Hume, 'Of the First Principles of Government' (1741–2), in *Selected Essays* (1993), p. 24.

10 Coleridge imagined a 'clerisy' comprising a mixture of different sorts of writers, intellectuals and opinion-makers, balancing the clashing forces of permanency and progression. It would 'secure and improve that civilisation, without which the nation could be neither permanent nor progressive'. For Coleridge it would perform a conservative function, however, whereas the enlightened intelligentsia was reforming and progressive: *On the Constitution of Church and State* (1830); Richard Holmes, *Coleridge* (1982), pp. 64f.; R. W. Harris, *Romanticism and the Social Order* (1969), p. 229.

11 W. R. Scott, *Adam Smith as Student and Professor* (1937), pp. 344–5, from the draft for the *Wealth of Nations* composed in 1769, and excised from the published text of 1776.

12 Franco Venturi, *Utopia and Reform in the Enlightenment* (1971), p. 132. For dissent, see

E. P. Thompson, 'The Peculiarities of the English' (1978), p. 58; J. G. A. Pocock, *Barbarism and Religion* (1999), vol. i, pp. 53ff.

13 Gerald Tyson, *Joseph Johnson: A Liberal Publisher* (1979), p. 121.

14 Joseph Priestley, *The History and Present State of Electricity, with Original Experiments* (1767), p. xx.

15 Karl Mannheim, *Ideology and Utopia* (1936), pp. 11–12.

16 Quoted in Terry Eagleton, *The Function of Criticism* (1984), p. 46. Hazlitt famously dubbed Cobbett 'a kind of fourth estate': see Harris, *Romanticism and the Social Order*, p. 60.

17 See John Stuart Mill, *On Liberty* (1859).

18 Marilyn Butler, *Romantics, Rebels and Reactionaries* (1981), p. 69.

19 Classic is William Hazlitt's *The Spirit of the Age* (1971 [1825]), which deified and demonized the great thinkers he knew. This was the age of the great vogue for literary anecdotes: see John Nichols, *Literary Anecdotes of the Eighteenth Century* (1967 [1812]).

20 Thomas Peacock, *Nightmare Abbey* (1918), in David Garnett (ed.), *The Novels of Thomas Love Peacock* (1948), p. 363:

He now became troubled with the passion for reforming the world. He built many castles in the air, and peopled them with secret tribunals, and bands of illuminati . .

'Action', thus he soliloquised, 'is the result of opinion, and to new-model opinion would be to new-model society. Knowledge is power; it is in the hands of a few, who employ it to mislead the many, for their own selfish purposes of aggrandizement and appropriation. What if it were in the hands of a few who should employ it to lead the many? What if it were universal, and the multitude were enlightened?

The libertarian Shelley deemed poets the unacknowledged legislators of the world: see Butler, *Romantics, Rebels and Reactionaries*, p. 147.

21 Raymond Williams, *Keywords* (1988); Penelope J. Corfield (ed.), *Language, History and Class* (1991), p. 102. Battles were fought over words: Johnson would not admit 'civilization' into his *Dictionary*.

22 Thomas Peacock, *Melincourt* (1817), in Garnett, *The Novels of Thomas Love Peacock*, p. 124.

23 *British Critic*, no. 18 (July–December 1801), p. i, quoted in Emily Lorraine de Montluzin, *The Anti-Jacobins 1798–1800* (1988), p. 2. It was the high noon of reviewing: see John Clive, *Scotch Reviewers* (1957).

24 Quoted in J. G. A. Pocock (ed.), *The Varieties of British Political Thought, 1500–1800* (1993), p. 278.

25 J. C. D. Clark, *English Society, 1688–1832* (1985), pp. 69, 89.

26 Frankenstein captures key aspects of the Romantic critique of enlightened values: Chris Baldick, *In Frankenstein's Shadow* (1987); Stephen Bann (ed.), *Frankenstein, Creation and Monstrosity* (1994).

27 Claire Tomalin, *The Life and Death of Mary Wollstonecraft* (1974), p. 255. Perhaps he resembled the simian Sir Oran Haut-Ton in Peacock's *Melincourt*: Garnett, *The Novels of Thomas Love Peacock*, pp. 97f. Presumably she yearned at all costs that her son should not turn into a Dr Frankenstein.

28 For the ferments across Europe, see Roy Porter and Mikuláš Teich (eds.), *The Enlightenment in National Context* (1981). Britain, of course, had various 'firsts', from freemasonry to the steam engine.

29 The English *Sonderweg* thesis receives support from Koselleck's view that the split between *raison d'état* and the dreams of intellectuals, in his view so pathogenic on the Continent, was absent from Britain: R. Koselleck, *Critique and Crisis* (1988), pp. 2f.

30 Here I concur, as stated earlier, with J. G. A. Pocock, 'Post-Puritan England and the Problem of the Enlightenment' (1980), ideas elaborated in Pocock's *Barbarism and Religion*, vols. i and ii.

31 France was the nation of *L'état, c'est moi*. In England the monarch ceased to be seen in that way, and few wanted an enlightenment led by enlightened absolutism. Contrast Daniel Roche, *France in the Enlightenment* (1998), pp. 32f.

32 'The enquiry in England is not whether a Man has Talents & Genius, But whether he is Passive & Polite & a Virtuous Ass & obedient to Noblemen's Opinions': G. Keynes (ed.), *Blake: Complete Writings* (1969), pp. 452–3.

33 For which, see E. P. Thompson, *The Making of the English Working Class* (1965); H. Perkin, *The Origins of Modern English Society* (1969).

34 For example, Maurice Quinlan, *Victorian Prelude* (1941); Muriel Jaeger, *Before Victoria* (1956); Boyd Hilton, *The Age of Atonement* (1988).

35 See J. R. Poynter, *Society and Pauperism* (1969).

36 Louis Dumont, *From Mandeville to Marx* (1977); Sir Isaiah Berlin, *Four Essays on Liberty* (1969); John Gray, *Enlightenment's Wake* (1995).

37 F. R. Leavis (ed.), *Mill on Bentham and Coleridge* (1962).

38 Elie Halévy, *A History of the English People in the Nineteenth Century*, 2nd edn (1961), vol. i.

39 Joseph Priestley, *The Importance and Extent of Free Inquiry in Matters of Religion* (sn, 1785), in John Towill Rutt (ed.), *The Theological and Miscellaneous Works of Joseph Priestley* (1817–32), vol. xv, p. 78.

40 Roger Shattuck, *Forbidden Knowledge* (1996).

41 William Hazlitt, *Life of Thomas Holcroft* (1816), in *The Complete Works of William Hazlitt* (1932), vol. iii, pp. 132–3.

BIBLIOGRAPHY

R. I. Aaron and J. Gibb (eds.), *An Early Draft of Locke's Essay Together with Excerpts from His Journals* (Oxford: Clarendon Press, 1936)

Hans Aarsleff, *From Locke to Saussure: Essays on the Study of Language and Intellectual History* (Minneapolis: University of Minnesota Press, 1982)

——, *The Study of Language in England, 1780–1860* (Minneapolis: University of Minnesota Press, 1983)

Mary Abbot, *Family Ties: English Families 1540–1920* (London: Routledge, 1993)

James Johnston Abraham, *Lettsom, His Life, Times, Friends and Descendants* (London: William Heinemann, 1933)

M. H. Abrams, *The Mirror and the Lamp* (London: Oxford University Press, 1953)

——, *Natural Supernaturalism; Tradition and Revolution in Romantic Literature* (London and New York: Oxford University Press, 1971)

Peter Ackroyd, *Blake* (London: Sinclair-Stevenson, 1995)

Charles Francis Adam (ed.), *The Works of John Adams*, 10 vols. (Boston: Little, Brown, 1850–56)

Michael Adas, *Machines as the Measure of Men: Science, Technology, and Ideologies of Western Dominance* (Ithaca, NY: Cornell University Press, 1989)

Alison Adburgham, *Shopping in Style: London from the Restoration to Edwardian Elegance* (London: Thames & Hudson, 1979)

Joseph Addison and Richard Steele, *The Spectator*, Donald Bond (ed.), 5 vols. (Oxford: Clarendon Press, 1965)

John Addy, *Sin and Society in the Seventeenth Century* (London and New York: Routledge, 1989)

A. W. H. Adkins, *From the Many to the One: A Study of Personality and Views of Human Nature in the Context of Ancient Greek Society, Values and Beliefs* (London: Constable, 1970)

David Aers, Jonathan Cook and David Punter, *Romanticism and Ideology: Studies in English Writing, 1765–1830* (London: Routledge & Kegan Paul, 1981)

Jean-Christophe Agnew, *Worlds Apart: The Market and the Theater in Anglo-American Thought, 1550–1750* (Cambridge: Cambridge University Press, 1986)

John Aikin, *An Address to the Dissenters of England on Their Late Defeat* (London: Johnson, 1790)

——, *Letters from a Father to His Son, on Various Topics Relative to Literature and the Conduct of Life*, 3rd edn (London: J. Johnson, 1796 [1792–3])

Lucy Aikin, *Poetry for Children* (London: Phillips, 1803)

Mark Akenside, *The Pleasures of Imagination* (London: Dodsley, 1744)

——, *The Poetical Works of Mark Akenside* (London: Bell and Daldy, 1866)

Jean Le Rond D'Alembert, *Preliminary Discourse to the Encyclopedia of Diderot*, Richard N. Schwab (trans. and ed.) (Chicago: University of Chicago Press, 1995)

David Alexander, *Retailing in England during the Industrial Revolution* (London: Athlone Press, 1970)

William Alexander, *The History of Women, from the Earliest Antiquity to the Present Time, Giving Some Account of Almost Every Interesting Particular concerning that Sex among All Nations*, 2 vols. (London: W. Strahan and T. Cadell, 1779)

William Rounseville Alger, *The Destiny of the Soul. A Critical History of the Doctrine of a Future Life and a Complete Bibliography of the Subject*, 10th edn (New York: W. J. Widdleton, 1878)

Archibald Alison, *Essays on the Nature and Principles of Taste* (Edinburgh: Bell and Bradfute, 1790)

Paul K. Alkon, *Samuel Johnson and Moral Discipline* (Evanston, Ill.: Northwestern University Press, 1967)

——, *Origins of Futuristic Fition* (Athens, GA, and London: University of Georgia Press, 1987)

David Allan, *Virtue, Learning and the Scottish Enlightenment: Ideas of Scholarship in Early Modern History* (Edinburgh: Edinburgh University Press, 1993)

D. G. C. Allan, *William Shipley: Founder of the Royal Society of Arts. A Biography with Documents* (London: Hutchinson, 1968)

A. Allardyce (ed.), *Scotland and Scotsmen in the Eighteenth Century, from the MSS of John Ramsay*, 2 vols. (Edinburgh: Blackwood, 1888)

B. Sprague Allen, *Tides in English Taste (1619–1800): A Background for the Study of Literature*, 2 vols. (New York: Pageant Books, 1958)

David Elliston Allen, *The Naturalist in Britain: A Social History* (London: Allen Lane, 1976)

Richard C. Allen, *David Hartley on Human Nature* (New York: State University of New York Press, 1999)

H. E. Allison, 'Locke's Theory of Personal Identity: A Re-Examination', in I. C. Tipton (ed.), *Locke on Human Understanding: Selected Essays* (Oxford: Oxford University Press, 1977), 105–22

J. Almon, *Memoirs of a Late Eminent Bookseller* (London: sn, 1790)

P. C. Almond, *Heaven and Hell in Enlightenment England* (Cambridge: Cambridge University Press, 1994)

Richard D. Altick, *The English Common Reader: A Social History of the Mass Reading Public 1800–1900* (Chicago: Chicago University Press, 1957)

——, *The Shows of London: A Panoramic History of Exhibitions, 1600–1862* (Cambridge, Mass.: Belknap Press, 1978)

Susan D. Amussen, *An Ordered Society: Gender and Class in Early Modern England* (Oxford: Basil Blackwell, 1988)

Robert Anchor, *The Enlightenment Tradition* (New York: Harper & Row, 1967)

Benedict Anderson, *Imagined Communities: Reflections on the Origin and Spread of Nationalism* (London: Verso Editions and New Left Books, 1983)

Douglas Anderson, *The Radical Enlightenment of Benjamin Franklin* (Baltimore: Johns Hopkins University Press, 1997)

Patricia Anderson, *The Printed Image and the Transformation of Popular Culture 1790–1860* (Oxford: Clarendon Press, 1991)

Perry Anderson, *The Origins of Postmodernity* (London: Verso, 1998)

Perry Anderson and Robin Blackburn (eds.), *Towards Socialism* (London: Fontana, 1965)

R. G. W. Anderson and Christopher Lawrence, *Science, Medicine and Dissent: Joseph Priestley (1733–1804)* (London: Wellcome Trust/Science Museum, 1987)

Donna T. Andrew, *Philanthropy and Police: London Charity in the Eighteenth Century*

(Princeton, NJ: Princeton University Press, 1989)

C. Bruyn Andrews (ed.), *The Torrington Diaries: Containing the Tours through England and Wales of the Hon. John Byng (Later Fifth Viscount Torrington) between the Years 1781 and 1794*, 4 vols. (London: Eyre and Spottiswoode, 1934–8; 1954)

Jonathan Andrews, Asa Briggs, Roy Porter, Penny Tucker and Keir Waddington, *The History of Bethlem* (London: Routledge, 1997)

Malcolm Andrews, *The Search for the Picturesque: Landscape Aesthetics and Tourism in Britain, 1760–1800* (Aldershot: Scolar Press, 1989)

J. T. Anning, *The General Infirmary at Leeds*, vol. i: *The First Hundred Years* (Edinburgh: E. & S. Livingstone, 1963)

[Anon.], *A Short and Easie Method to Give Children an Idea or True Notion of Celestial and Terrestrial Beings* (sn: sl, 1710)

——, *A System of Magick; Or, a History of the Black Art. Being an Historical Account of Mankind's Most Early Dealing with the Devil; and How the Acquaintance on Both Sides First Began . . .* (London: J. Roberts, 1727)

——, *Some Reflecting on Prescience: In Which the Nature of Divinity is Enquired Into* (London: Roberts, 1731)

——, *A History of Little Goody Two Shoes* (London: J. Newbery, 1766)

——, *A Discourse on Witchcraft. Occasioned by a Bill Now Depending in Parliament, to Repeal the Statute Made in the First Year of the Reign of King James I, Intituled An Act against Conjuration, Witchcraft, and Dealing with Evil and Wicked Spirits* (London: J. Read, 1736)

Joyce Oldham Appleby, 'Locke, Liberalism and the Natural Law of Money', *Past and Present*, lxxi (1976), 43–69

——, 'Ideology and Theory: The Tension between Political and Economic Liberalism in Seventeenth-century England', *American Historical Review*, lxxxi (1976), 499–515

——, *Economic Thought and Ideology in Seventeenth-century England* (Princeton: Princeton University Press, 1978)

——, 'Consumption in Early Modern Social Thought', in John Brewer and Roy Porter (eds.), *Consumption and the World of Goods* (London: Routledge, 1993), 162–75

William W. Appleton, *A Cycle of Cathay: The Chinese Vogue in England During the Seventeenth and Eighteenth Centuries* (New York: Columbia University Press, 1951)

Johann Wilhelm Von Archenholz, *A Picture of England: Containing a Description of the Laws, Customs and Manners of England* (Dublin: P. Byrne, 1791)

Philippe Ariès, *Centuries of Childhood: A Social History of the Family* (Harmondsworth: Penguin Books, 1973)

——, *Western Attitudes towards Death: From the Middle Ages to the Present* (London: Marion Boyars, 1976)

——, *L'homme devant la mort* (Paris: Seuil, 1977), trans. by Helen Weaver as *The Hour of Our Death* (London: Allen Lane, 1981)

Nancy Armstrong, *Desire and Domestic Fiction: A Political History of the Novel* (New York: Oxford University Press, 1987)

W. H. G. Armytage, *Heavens Below: Utopian Experiments in England 1560–1960* (London: Routledge & Kegan Paul, 1961)

——, *Yesterday's Tomorrows: A Historical Survey of Future Societies* (London: Routledge & Kegan Paul, 1968)

Thomas Arnold, *Observations on the Nature, Kinds, Causes and Prevention of Insanity*, 2 vols. (Leicester: Robinson and Cadell, 1782–6)

Richard Ashcraft, *Revolutionary Politics and Locke's Two Treatises of Government* (Princeton, NJ: Princeton University Press, 1986)

——, 'Anticlericalism and Authority in Lockean Political Thought', in Roger D. Lund (ed.), *The Margins of Orthodoxy: Heterodox Writing and Cultural Response, 1660–1750* (Cambridge: Cambridge University Press, 1995), 73–96

——, 'Lockean Ideas, Poverty, and the

Development of Liberal Political Theory', in John Brewer and Susan Staves (eds.), *Early Modern Conceptions of Property* (London and New York: Routledge, 1995), 43–61

Andrew Ashfield and Peter de Bolla (eds.), *The Sublime: A Reader in British Eighteenth-century Aesthetic Theory* (Cambridge: Cambridge University Press, 1996)

John Ashton, *Chap-books of the Eighteenth Century* (London: Chatto & Windus, 1882)

——, *The History of Gambling in England* (London: Duckworth & Co., 1898)

A. Aspinall, *Politis and the Press c. 1780–1850* (London: Home and Van Thal, 1949)

Jan Assmann, *Moses the Egyptian: The Memory of Egypt in Western Monotheism* (Cambridge, Mass.: Harvard University Press, 1997)

Mary Astell, *A Serious Proposal to the Ladies for the Advancement of Their True and Greatest Interest* (London: Wilkin, 1694)

——, *Letters Concerning the Love of God* (London: Wilkin, 1695)

——, *A Serious Proposal to the Ladies: Part II* (London: Wilkin, 1697)

——, *Some Reflections upon Marriage, Occasioned by the Duke and Duchess of Mazarine's Case* (London: Nutt, 1700)

——, *A Fair Way with the Dissenters and Their Patrons* (London: Wilkin, 1704)

——, *An Impartial Enquiry into the Causes of Rebellion and Civil War in This Kingdom* (London: Wilkin, 1704)

——, *Moderation Truly Stated* (London: Wilkin, 1704)

——, *The Christian Religion, as Profess'd by a Daughter of the Church of England* (London: R. Wilkin, 1705)

——, *Bart'lemy Fair or an Enquiry after Wit* (London: Wilkin, 1709)

Herbert M. Atherton, *Political Prints in the Age of Hogarth: A Study of the Ideographic Representation of Politics* (Oxford: Clarendon Press, 1974)

H. F. Augstein (ed.), *Race: The Origins of an Idea, 1760–1850* (Bristol: Thoemmes Press, 1996)

——, *James Cowles Prichard's Anthropology: Remaking the Science of Man in Early Nineteenth-century Britain* (Amsterdam: Rodopi, 1999)

Donald D. Ault, *Visionary Physics: Blake's Response to Newton* (Chicago: Chicago University Press, 1974)

Jane Austen, *Northanger Abbey* (Harmondsworth: Penguin, 1975 [1818])

——, *Persuasion* (Harmondsworth: Penguin, 1965 [1818])

——, *Lady Susan, The Watsons, Sanditon,* Margaret Drabble (ed.) (Harmondsworth: Penguin, 1974)

Emmett L. Avery (ed.), *The London Stage. Part 2: 1700–1729,* 11 vols. (Carbondale, Ill.: Southern Illinois University Press, 1968)

James L. Axtell, *The Educational Writings of John Locke: A Critical Edition with Introduction and Notes* (Cambridge: Cambridge University Press, 1968)

Philip Ayres, *Classical Culture and the Idea of Rome in Eighteenth-century England* (Cambridge: Cambridge University Press, 1997)

Robert W. Babcock, *The Genesis of Shakespeare Idolatry, 1766–1799: A Study in English Criticism of the Late Eighteenth Century* (Chapel Hill: University of North Carolina Press, 1931)

Paula R. Backscheider, *Daniel Defoe: His Life* (Baltimore: Johns Hopkins University Press, 1989)

——, *Spectacular Politics: Theatrical Power and Mass Culture in Early Modern England* (Baltimore: Johns Hopkins University Press, 1994)

Marc Baer, *The Theatre and Disorder in Late Georgian London* (Oxford: Clarendon Press, 1991)

Robert Bage, *Man as He is,* 4 vols. (London: Lane, 1792)

——, *Hermsprong, or Man as He is Not,* V. Wilkins (ed.) (London: Turnstile Press, 1951 [London: Lane, 1796])

Charles F. Bahmueller, *The National Charity*

Company: Jeremy Bentham's Silent Revolution (Berkeley: University of California Press, 1981)

M. Bailey (ed.), *Boswell's Column* (London: William Kimber, 1951)

Nathan Bailey, *Universal Etymological English Dictionary* (London: Bell, 1721)

Paul Baines, *The House of Forgery in Eighteenth-century Britain* (Aldershot: Ashgate, 1999)

Herschel Baker, *The Dignity of Man: Studies in the Persistence of an Idea* (Cambridge, Mass.: Harvard University Press, 1947)

M. M. Bakhtin, *Rabelais and His World*, trans. by H. Iswoldsky (Cambridge, Mass.: MIT Press, 1968)

Katherine Balderston (ed.), *Thraliana: The Diary of Mrs Hester Lynch Thrale, Later Mrs Piozzi, 1776–1809*, 2 vols. (Oxford: Clarendon Press, 1942)

Chris Baldick, *In Frankenstein's Shadow: Myth, Monstrosity, and Nineteenth-century Writing* (Oxford: Clarendon Press, 1987)

Harry Ballam and Roy Lewis (eds.), *The Visitors' Book: England and the English as Others Have Seen Them* (London: Max Parrish, 1950)

Ros Ballaster, *Seductive Forms: Women's Amatory Fiction, 1684–1740* (Oxford: Clarendon Press, 1992)

J. B. Bamborough, *The Little World of Man: An Account of Renaissance Psychological Theory* (London: Longmans, Green, 1952)

Samuel Bamford, *The Autobiography of Samuel Bamford*, vol. i: *Early Days* (London: Simpkin, Marshall & Co., 1848–9; repr., London: Frank Cass, 1967)

Stephen Bann, *The Clothing of Clio: A Study of the Representation of History in Nineteenth-century Britain and France* (Cambridge: Cambridge University Press, 1984)

—— (ed.), *Frankenstein, Creation and Monstrosity* (London: Reaktion Books, 1994)

Anna Barbauld, *Address to Opposers of the Repeal of the Corporation and Test Acts* (London: Johnson, 1790)

N. Barbon, *A Discourse of Trade* (London:

Thomas Milbourn, 1690; repr. J. Hollander (ed.), Baltimore: Johns Hopkins University Press, 1905)

Michael Barfoot, 'Priestley, Reid's Circle and the Third Organon of Human Reasoning', in R. G. W. Anderson and Christopher Lawrence (eds.), *Science, Medicine and Dissent: Joseph Priestley (1733–1804)* (London: Wellcome Trust/Science Museum, 1987), 81–9

Hannah Barker, *Newspapers, Politics and Public Opinion in Late Eighteenth-century England* (Oxford: Clarendon Press, 1998)

Theo Barker (ed.), *The Long March of Everyman 1750–1960* (Harmondsworth: Penguin, 1978)

G. J. Barker-Benfield, *The Culture of Sensibility: Sex and Society in Eighteenth-century Britain* (Chicago: University of Chicago Press, 1992)

Jeffrey Barnouw, 'Hobbes's Psychology of Thought: Endeavours, Purpose and Curiosity', *History of European Ideas*, x (1990), 519–45

Richard Baron, *The Pillars of Priestcraft and Orthodoxy Shaken*, 2nd edn, 4 vols. (London: Cadell, 1768)

Poulain de la Barre, *De l'égalité des deux sexes* (Paris: du Puis, 1673)

John Barrell, *The Idea of Landscape and the Sense of Place 1730–1840: An Approach to the Poetry of John Clare* (London: Cambridge University Press, 1972)

——, *The Dark Side of the Landscape: The Rural Poor in English Painting, 1730–1840* (Cambridge: Cambridge University Press, 1980)

——, *English Literature in History, 1730–80: An Equal, Wide Survey* (London: Hutchinson, 1983)

——, *The Political Theory of Painting from Reynolds to Hazlitt: The Body of the Public* (New Haven, Conn.: Yale University Press, 1986)

William Barrett, *Death of the Soul. Philosophical Thought from Descartes to the Computer*

(Oxford: Oxford University Press, 1987)

James Barry, *The Works of James Barry, Esq., Historical Painter*, 2 vols. (London: Cadell and Davies, 1809)

Jonathan Barry and Christopher Brooks (eds.), *The Middling Sort of People: Culture, Society and Politics in England, 1550–1800* (Basingstoke: Macmillan, 1994)

R. Bartel, 'Suicide in Eighteenth-century England: The Myth of a Reputation', *Huntingdon Library Quarterly*, xxiii (1959), 145–55

Jonathan Bate, *Shakespearean Constitutions: Politics, Theatre, Criticism 1730–1830* (Oxford: Clarendon Press, 1989)

Walter Jackson Bate, *From Classic to Romantic: Premises of Taste in Eighteenth-century England* (Cambridge, Mass.: Harvard University Press, 1946)

W. J. Bate, J. M. Bullitt, and L. F. Powell (eds.), *Samuel Johnson: The Idler and Adventurer* (New Haven, Conn.: The Yale Edition of the Works of Samuel Johnson, Yale University Press, 1963)

W. J. Bate and A. B. Straus (eds.), *Samuel Johnson: The Rambler*, 3 vols. (New Haven, Conn.: The Yale Edition of the Works of Samuel Johnson, Yale University Press, 1969)

William Battie, *A Treatise on Madness* (London: Whiston & White, 1758)

Daniel A. Baugh, *Poverty, Protestantism and Political Economy: English Attitudes towards the Poor 1660–1800* (Clark Library, Los Angeles: University of California, Los Angeles, 1977–8)

Michael Baxandall, *Shadows and Enlightenment* (London and New Haven: Yale University Press, 1995)

J. M. Beattie, *The English Court in the Reign of George I* (Cambridge: Cambridge University Press, 1967)

John Beaumont, *An Historical, Physiological and Theological Treatise of Spirits, Apparitions, Witchcrafts and Other Magical Practises . . . With a Refutation of Dr Bekker's World*

Bewitch'd; and Other Authors that Have Opposed the Belief of Them (London: Brown, 1705)

D. W. Bebbington, *Evangelicalism in Modern Britain: A History from the 1730s to the 1980s* (London: Routledge, 1988)

Carl Becker: *The Heavenly City of the Eighteenth-century Philosophers* (New Haven: Yale University Press, 1932)

G. Becker, *The Mad Genius Controversy* (London & Beverly Hills: Sage, 1978)

Marvin B. Becker, *The Emergence of Civil Society in the Eighteenth Century* (Indiana: Indiana University Press, 1994)

J. V. Beckett, *The Aristocracy in England, 1660–1914* (Oxford: Basil Blackwell, 1986)

Robert Beddard (ed.), *The Revolutions of 1688* (Oxford: Clarendon Press, 1991)

Thomas Beddoes (ed.), *Chemical Experiments and Opinions; Extracted From a Work Published in the Last Century* (Oxford: Clarendon Press, 1790)

——, *The History of Isaac Jenkins, and of the Sickness of Sarah His Wife, and Their Three Children* (Madeley: sn, 1792)

——, *Observations on the Nature of Demonstrative Evidence; with an Explanation of Certain Difficulties in the Elements of Geometry, and Reflections on Language* (London: Johnson, 1793)

——, *A Letter to Erasmus Darwin . . . on a New Method of Treating Pulmonary Consumption, and Some Other Diseases Hitherto Found Incurable* (Bristol: Bulgin & Rosser, 1793)

——, *Hygëia: or Essays Moral and Medical, on the Causes Affecting the Personal State of Our Middling and Affluent Classes*, 3 vols. (Bristol: Phillips, 1802–3)

D. Beekman, *The Mechanical Baby: A Popular History of the Theory and Practice of Child-raising* (London: Dennis Dobson, 1979)

E. S. De Beer (ed.), *The Diary of John Evelyn*, 6 vols. (Oxford: Oxford University Press, 1955)

—— (ed.), *The Correspondence of John Locke*, 8 vols. (Oxford: Clarendon Press, 1976–89)

Margaret Beetham, *A Magazine of Her Own?*

Domesticity and Desire in the Woman's Magazine 1800–1914 (London and New York: Routledge, 1996)

D. P. Behan, 'Locke on Persons and Personal Identity', *Canadian Journal of Philosophy*, ix (1979), 53–75

Aphra Behn, *Oroonoko or the Royal Slave* (London: Canning, 1688)

A. L. Beier, ' "Utter Strangers to Industry, Morality and Religion": John Locke on the Poor', *Eighteenth-century Life*, xii (1988), 28–41

Terry Belanger, 'Publishers and Writers in Eighteenth-century England', in Isabel Rivers (ed.), *Books and Their Readers in Eighteenth-century England* (Leicester: Leicester University Press, 1982), 5–25

A. Beljame, *Men of Letters and the English Public in the Eighteenth Century, 1660–1744* (London: Kegan Paul, Trench, Trubner, 1948)

Ian H. Bell, *Literature and Crime in Augustan England* (London: Routledge, 1991)

John Bellers, *Proposals for Raising a College of Industry of All Useful Trades and Husbandry* (London: Sowle, 1696)

Catherine Belsey, 'Afterword: A Future for Materialist-Feminist Criticism?' in Valerie Wayne (ed.), *The Matter of Difference: Materialist-Feminist Criticism of Shakespeare* (Ithaca: Cornell University Press, 1991)

Ilana Krausman Ben-Amos, *Adolescence and Youth in Early Modern England* (New Haven and London: Yale University Press, 1994)

John Bender, *Imagining the Penitentiary. Fiction and the Architecture of Mind in Eighteenth-century England* (Chicago: University of Chicago Press, 1987)

——, 'A New History of the Enlightenment?', *Eighteenth-century Life*, xvi (1992), 1–20

John Bennett, *Strictures on Female Education Chiefly as It Relates to the Culture of the Heart, in Four Essays* (London: T. Cadell, 1787)

Jeremy Bentham, *An Introduction to the Principles of Morals and Legislation* (London: Payne, 1789)

——, *Panopticon; or, The Inspection-House*, 3 vols. (London: Payne, 1791)

——, *Plan of Parliamentary Reform* (London: Wooler, 1817)

——, *Church of Englandism, and Its Catechism Examined* (London: Wilson, 1818)

——, *Not Paul but Jesus* (London: sn, 1823)

——, *The Book of Fallacies* (London: Hunt, 1824)

——, *A Fragment of Government and An Introduction to the Principles of Morals and Legislation*, W. Harrison (ed.) (Oxford: Basil Blackwell, 1948 [1776 and 1789])

——, 'Offenses against One's Self: Paederasty', *Journal of Homosexuality*, iii (1978), 389–405; iv (1979), 91–109

——, *A Fragment on Government*, Ross Harrison (intro.), J. H. Burns and H. L. A. Hart (eds.), (Cambridge: Cambridge University Press, 1988 [1776])

——, *The 'Panopticon' Writings*, Miran Bozovic (ed.) (London: Verso, 1995)

M. Bentham-Edwards (ed.), *The Autobiography of Arthur Young* (London: Smith, Elder, 1898)

[Thomas Bentley], *Letters on the Utility and Policy of Employing Machines to Shorten Labour* (London: Becket, 1780)

John Beresford (ed.), *The Diary of a Country Parson: The Rev. James Woodforde, 1758–1802*, 5 vols. (Oxford: Oxford University Press, 1978–81)

Maxine Berg, *The Age of Manufactures, 1700–1820: Industry, Innovation and Work in Britain* (London: Routledge, 1994)

Maxine Berg and Helen Clifford (eds.), *Consumers and Luxury: Consumer Culture in Europe 1650–1850* (Manchester: Manchester University Press, 1999)

T. Goddard Bergin and Max H. Fish (trans.), *The New Science of Giambattista Vico* (Ithaca, NY: Cornell University Press, 1948 [trans. of 3rd edn, 1744])

George Berkeley, *An Essay towards a New Theory of Vision*, 2nd edn (Dublin: Aaron Rhames, 1709)

——, *Treatise concerning the Principles of Human Knowledge* (Dublin: Pepyat, 1710)

Isaiah Berlin, *Four Essays on Liberty* (London: Oxford University Press, 1969)

David Berman, *A History of Atheism in Britain from Hobbes to Russell* (London: Croom Helm, 1988)

Marshall Berman, *All That is Solid Melts into Air: The Experience of Modernity* (London: Verso, 1983)

Ann Bermingham, *Landscape and Ideology: The English Rustic Tradition 1740–1860* (Berkeley: University of California Press, 1986)

Martin Bernal, *Black Athena: The Afroasiatic Roots of Classical Civilization*, vol. i: *The Fabrication of Ancient Greece, 1785–1985* (London: Free Association Books, 1987)

John Andrew Bernstein, 'Shaftesbury's Optimism and Eighteenth-century Social Thought', in A. C. Kors and Paul J. Korshin (eds.), *Anticipations of the Enlightenment in England, France and Germany* (Philadelphia: University of Pennsylvania Press, 1987), 86–101

Peter L. Bernstein, *Against the Gods: The Remarkable Story of Risk* (New York: John Wiley, 1996)

Christopher J. Berry, ' "Climate" in the Eighteenth Century: James Dunbar and the Scottish Case', *Texas Studies in Literature and Language*, xvi (1974), 281–92

——, 'James Dunbar and the Enlightenment Debate on Language', in Jennifer J. Carter and Joan H. Pittock (eds.), *Aberdeen and the Enlightenment. Proceedings of a Conference Held at the University of Aberdeen* (Aberdeen University Press, 1987), 241–50

——, *The Idea of Luxury: A Conceptual and Historical Investigation* (Cambridge: Cambridge University Press, 1994)

——, *Social Theory of the Scottish Enlightenment* (Edinburgh: Edinburgh University Press, 1997)

Helen Berry, ' "Nice and Curious Questions": Coffee Houses and the Representations of Women in John Dunton's *Athenian Mercury*', *Seventeenth Century*, xii (1997), 257–76

H. Digby Beste, *Personal and Literary Memorials* (London: Henry Colburn, 1829)

Bruno Bettelheim, *The Uses of Enchantment: The Meaning and Importance of Fairy Tales* (New York: Vintage, 1977)

Alan Bewell, *Wordsworth and the Enlightenment: Nature, Man, and Society in the Experimental Poetry* (New Haven and London: Yale University Press, 1989)

Thomas Bewick: *A Memoir of Thomas Bewick, Written by Himself* (London: The Cresset Press, 1961 [1862])

Christina Bewley and David Bewley, *Gentleman Radical: A Life of John Horne Tooke, 1736–1812* (London: Tauris, 1998)

John C. Biddle, 'Locke's Critique of Innate Principles and Toland's Deism', in John W. Yolton (ed.), *Philosophy, Religion and Science in the Seventeenth and Eighteenth Centuries* (Rochester: University of Rochester Press, 1990), 140–51

Thomas Birch (ed.), *The Works of the Honourable Robert Boyle*, 5 vols. (London: Millar, 1744)

P. J. Bishop, *A Short History of the Royal Humane Society* (London: The Society, 1974)

Roberta Bivins, 'Expectations and Expertise: Early British Responses to Chinese Medicine', *History of Science*, xxxvii (1999), 459–89

Jeremy Black (ed.), *Britain in the Age of Walpole* (London: Macmillan, 1984)

——, *The British and the Grand Tour* (London: Croom Helm, 1985)

——, *The English Press in the Eighteenth Century* (London: Croom Helm, 1986)

—— (ed.), *Eighteenth-century Europe 1700–1789* (London: Macmillan, 1990)

——, 'Ideology, History, Xenophobia and the World of Print in Eighteenth-century England', in Jeremy Black and Jeremy Gregory (eds.), *Culture, Politics and Society in*

Britain, 1660–1800 (Manchester: Manchester University Press, 1991), 184–216

——, *A System of Ambition? British Foreign Policy 1660–1793* (London: Longman, 1991)

——, *The Politics of Britain, 1688–1800* (Manchester and New York: Manchester University Press, 1993)

——, *An Illustrated History of Eighteenth-century Britain, 1688–1793* (Manchester: Manchester University Press, 1996)

Jeremy Black and Jeremy Gregory (eds.), *Culture, Politics and Society in Britain, 1660–1800* (Manchester: Manchester University Press, 1991)

J. B. Black, *The Art of History* (New York: Russell & Russell, 1965)

Scott Black, 'Social and Literary Form in the *Spectator*', *Eighteenth Century Studies*, xxxiii (1999), 21–42

Richard Blackmore, *Creation: A Philosophical Poem, in Seven Books* (London: Buckley, Tonson, 1712)

William Blackstone, *Commentaries on the Laws of England*, 4 vols. (Oxford: Clarendon Press, 1765–9; facsimile, Chicago: University of Chicago Press, 1979)

A. Blackwall, *The Sacred Classics Defended and Illustrated* (London: J. Bettenham, 1725)

Hugh Blair, *A Critical Dissertation on the Poems of Ossian* (London: Becket and de Hondt, 1765)

——, *Lectures on Rhetoric and Belles Lettres*, 3 vols. (Dublin: Whitestone, Colles, etc., 1783)

Marc Bloch, *The Royal Touch: Sacred Monarchy and Scrofula in England and France*, J. E. Anderson (trans.) (London: Routledge & Kegan Paul, 1973)

James Blondel, *The Strength of Imagination in Pregnant Women Examin'd* (London: Peele, 1727)

Edward A. Bloom and Lillian D. Bloom, *Joseph Addison's Sociable Animal: In the Market Place, on the Hustings, in the Pulpit* (Providence: Brown University Press, 1971)

Edward A. Bloom, Lillian D. Bloom and Edmund Leites, *Educating the Audience: Addison, Steele, and Eighteenth-century Culture* (Los Angeles: William Andrews Clark Memorial Library, 1984)

Morton W. Bloomfield, *The Seven Deadly Sins: An Introduction to the History of a Religious Concept, with Special Reference to Medieval Literature* (East Lansing: Michigan State University Press, 1952)

Charles Blount, *Anima Mundi* (London: W. Cademan, 1679)

Madame du Boccage, *Letters concerning England, Holland and Italy*, 2 vols. (London: E. and C. Dilly, 1770)

Henry St John, Viscount Bolingbroke, *The Works of Lord Bolingbroke*, 7 vols. (London: David Mallett, 1754–98; Farnborough: Gregg International, 1969 [repr. of 1841 edn])

James R. Bonar, *Malthus and His Work* (London: Macmillan, 1885; repr. Frank Cass, 1966)

Donald F. Bond, ' "Distrust" of Imagination in English Neoclassicism', *Philological Quarterly*, xiv (1937), 54–69

——, 'The Neo-Classical Psychology of the Imagination', *ELH*, iv (1937), 245–64

—— (ed.), *The Tatler*, 3 vols. (Oxford and New York: Clarendon Press, 1987)

Richmond P. Bond (ed.), *Studies in the Early English Periodical* (Chapel Hill: University of North Carolina Press, 1957)

Peter Borsay, 'The Rise of the Promenade: The Social and Cultural Use of Space in the English Provincial Town, *c.* 1660–1800', *British Journal for Eighteenth-century Studies*, ix (1986), 125–40

——, *The English Urban Renaissance: Culture and Society in the Provincial Town 1660–1770* (Oxford: Clarendon Press, 1989)

—— (ed.), *The Eighteenth-century Town: A Reader in English Urban History 1688–1820* (London: Longman, 1990)

Peter Borsay and Angus McInnes, 'The Emergence of a Leisure Town: Or an Urban Renaissance?', *Past and Present*, cxxvi (1990), 189–202

Robert S. Bosher, *The Making of the Restoration Settlement* (London: Dacre Press, 1951)

Ian Bostridge, *Witchcraft and its Transformation, c. 1650–c. 1750* (Oxford: Clarendon Press, 1997)

James Boswell (ed.), *The Celebrated Letter from Samuel Johnson, LLD to Philip Dormer Stanhope, Earl of Chesterfield* (London: Dilly, 1790)

——, *The Life of Samuel Johnson*, 2 vols. (London: J. M. Dent, 1946 [1790])

Ruth B. Bottigheimer, 'Fairy Tales and Folktales', in Peter Hunt (ed.), *International Companion Encyclopaedia of Children's Literature* (London and New York: Routledge, 1996), 162–65

P.-G. Boucé (ed.), *Sexuality in Eighteenth-century Britain* (Manchester: Manchester University Press, 1982)

James T. Boulton, *The Language of Politics in the Age of Wilkes and Burke* (London: Routledge and Kegan Paul, 1963)

—— (ed.), *Selected Writings of Daniel Defoe* (Cambridge: Cambridge University Press, 1975)

William Biggs Boulton, *The Amusements of Old London: being a Survey of the Sports and Pastimes, Tea Gardens and Parks, Playhouses and Other Diversions of the People of London from the Seventeenth to the Beginning of the Nineteenth Century* (New York and London: Benjamin Blom, 1969)

Alain Boureau, *et al.* (eds.), *A History of Private Life*, vol. iii: *Passions of the Renaissance*, Arthur Goldhammer (trans.) (Cambridge, Mass.: Harvard University Press, 1989)

H. R. Fox Bourne, *The Life of John Locke*, 2 vols. (London: H. S. King, 1876)

P. J. Bowler, *Evolution: The History of an Idea* (Berkeley: University of California Press, 1984)

John Bowring, *The Works of Jeremy Bentham*, 11 vols. (Edinburgh: William Tait, 1843; John Hill Burton (intr.), Bristol: Thoemmes Press, 1995)

George R. Boyer, *An Economic History of the English Poor Law, 1750–1850* (Cambridge and New York: Cambridge University Press, 1990)

Robert Boyle, *Some Considerations Touching the Usefulnesse of Experimental Natural Philosophy* (Oxford: Davis, 1663)

——, *The Works of the Honourable Robert Boyle*, T. Birch (ed.), 5 vols. (London: A. Millar, 1744)

Ian Bradley, *The Call to Seriousness: The Evangelical Impact on the Victorians* (London: Jonathan Cape, 1976)

Leo Brady, 'Fanny Hill and Materialism', *Eighteenth-century Studies*, iv (1970–71), 21–40

Dennis Brailsford, *Bareknuckles: A Social History of Prize-fighting* (Cambridge: Lutterworth, 1988)

——, *Sport, Time and Society* (London: Routledge, 1990)

——, *British Sport: A Social History* (London: Lutterworth Press, 1992)

John Brand (ed.), *Observations on Popular Antiquities: Chiefly Illustrating the Origin of Our Vulgar Customs, Ceremonies and Superstitions* (London: Johnson, 1777; London: Chatto & Windus, 1913)

George C. Brauer, *The Education of a Gentleman: Theories of Gentlemanly Education in England 1660–1775* (New York: Bookman Associates, 1959)

T. H. Breen, ' "Baubles of Britain": The American and Consumer Revolutions of the Eighteenth Century', *Past and Present*, cxix (1988), 73–104

——, 'The Meanings of Things: Interpreting the Consumer Economy in the Eighteenth Century', in John Brewer and Roy Porter (eds.), *Consumption and the World of Goods* (London and New York: Routledge, 1993), 249–60

John Brewer, 'English Radicalism in the Age

of George III', in J. G. A. Pocock (ed.), *Three British Revolutions: 1641, 1688, 1776* (Princeton: Princeton University Press, 1980), 323–67

——, *The Common People and Politics, 1750–1800: Popular Political Participation in Cartoon and Caricature* (Cambridge: Chadwyck Healey, 1986)

——, *The Sinews of Power. War, Money and the English State 1688–1783* (London: Unwin Hyman, 1989)

——, *The Pleasures of the Imagination: English Culture in the Eighteenth Century* (London: HarperCollins, 1997)

John Brewer and Roy Porter (eds.), *Consumption and the World of Goods* (London: Routledge, 1993)

S. M. Brewer, *Design for a Gentleman: The Education of Philip Stanhope* (London: Chapman and Hall, 1963)

K. M. Briggs, *Pale Hecate's Team* (New York: The Humanities Press, 1962)

Crane Brinton, *The Political Ideas of the English Romanticists* (London: Oxford University Press, 1926)

R. F. Brissenden, *Virtue in Distress: Studies in the Novel of Sentiment from Richardson to Sade* (London: Macmillan, 1974)

Edward J. Bristow, *Vice and Vigilance: Purity Movements in Britain since 1700* (Dublin: Gill and Macmillan, 1977)

Alexander Broadie (ed.), *The Scottish Enlightenment: An Anthology* (Edinburgh: Canongate, 1997)

William H. Brock, *The Fontana History of Chemistry* (London: Fontana, 1992)

Jacob Bronowski, *William Blake and the Age of Revolution* (London: Routledge & Kegan Paul, 1972)

B. Bronson (ed.), *Samuel Johnson, Rasselas, Poems and Selected Prose*, 3rd edn (San Francisco: Rinehart, 1971)

Henry Brooke, *Universal Beauty* (London: J. Wilcox, 1735)

John Hedley Brooke, *Science and Religion: Some Historical Perspectives* (Cambridge: Cambridge University Press, 1991)

Marilyn L. Brooks, 'Mary Hays: Finding a "Voice" in Dissent', *Enlightenment and Dissent*, xiv (1995), 3–24

David Brown, 'Butler and Deism', in Christopher Cunliffe (ed.), *Joseph Butler's Moral and Religious Thought* (Oxford: Clarendon Press, 1992), 7–28

Ford K. Brown, *Fathers of the Victorians: The Age of Wilberforce* (Cambridge: Cambridge University Press, 1961)

John Brown, *An Estimate of the Manners and Principles of the Times*, 2 vols. (London: L. Davis & C. Reymers, 1757)

——, *Thoughts on Civil Liberty, Licentiousness and Faction* (Newcastle-upon-Tyne: Davis and Reymers, 1765)

Laura Brown, *Ends of Empire: Women and Ideology in Early Eighteenth-century English Literature* (Ithaca and London: Cornell University Press, 1993)

Peter Brown, *The World of Late Antiquity: From Marcus Aurelius to Muhammad* (London: Thames & Hudson, 1971)

Philip Anthony Brown, *The French Revolution in English History* (London: Frank Cass, 1965)

Robert Brown, *The Nature of Social Laws, Machiavelli to Mill* (Cambridge: Cambridge University Press, 1984)

Sanborn C. Brown (ed.), *Collected Works of Count Rumford*, vol. iv: *Light and Armament* (Cambridge, Massachusetts: Belknap Press, 1970)

Theodore Brown, 'From Mechanism to Vitalism in Eighteenth-century English Physiology', *Journal of the History of Biology*, vii (1974), 179–216

V. Brown, *Adam Smith's Discourse: Canonicity, Commerce and Conscience* (London: Routledge, 1994)

Alice Browne, *The Eighteenth-century Feminist Mind* (Brighton: Harvester Press, 1987)

Janet Browne, 'Botany for Gentlemen: Erasmus Darwin and *The Loves of the Plants*', *Isis*, lxxx (1989), 593–612

Reed Browning, *Political and Constitutional Ideas of the Court Whigs* (Baton Rouge: Louisiana State University Press, 1982)

Gladys Bryson, *Man and Society: The Scottish Inquiry of the Eighteenth Century* (New York: Kelley, 1968)

W. Buchan, *Domestic Medicine, or a Treatise on the Prevention and Cure of Diseases by Regimen and Simple Medicines* (Edinburgh: Balfour, Auld & Smellie, 1769)

——, *Observations concerning the Prevention and Cure of the Venereal Disease* (London: Chapman, 1796)

Gerd Buchdahl, *The Image of Newton and Locke in the Age of Reason* (London and New York: Sheed and Ward, 1961)

R. O. Bucholz, *The Augustan Court: Queen Anne and the Decline of Court Culture* (Stanford, CA: Stanford University Press, 1993)

Peter Buck, 'People Who Counted: Political Arithmetic in the Eighteenth Century', *Isis*, lxxiii (1982), 28–45

Jerome Hamilton Buckley, *The Triumph of Time: A Study of the Victorian Concepts of Time, History, Progress, and Decadence* (Cambridge, Mass.: Belknap Press, 1967)

V. Bullough, 'Prostitution and Reform in Eighteenth-century England', in R. P. Maccubbin (ed.), *'Tis Nature's Fault: Unauthorized Sexuality during the Enlightenment* (Cambridge: Cambridge University Press, 1987), 61–74

John Bunyan, *Pilgrim's Progress* (London: Nathaniel Ponder, 1678)

James Burgh, *Crito; or, Essays on Various Subjects*, 2 vols. (London: J. Dodsley, 1766, 1767)

——, *Political Disquisitions; or, An Enquiry into Public Errors, Defects, and Abuses*, 3 vols. (Philadelphia: Robert Bell, 1775)

Edmund Burke, *Philosophical Enquiry into the Origin of Our Ideas of the Sublime and the Beautiful* (London: R. and J. Dodsley, 1757)

——, *Reflections on the Revolution in France and on the Proceedings in Certain Societies in London Relative to that Event. In a Letter Intended to have been Sent to a Gentleman in Paris* (London: J. Dodsley, 1790; Conor Cruise O'Brien (ed.), Harmondsworth: Penguin, 1982)

——, *The Works and Correspondence of the Right Honourable Edmund Burke*, 8 vols. (London: Francis and John Rivington, 1852)

——, *A Vindication of Natural Society*, Frank N. Pagano (ed.) (London: Cooper, 1756; North Shadeland, Indianapolis: Liberty Classics, 1982)

Peter Burke, *The Renaissance Sense of the Past* (New York: St Martin's Press, 1970)

——, *Popular Culture in Early Modern Europe* (London: Temple Smith, 1978)

——, 'Heu Domine, Adsunt Turcae: A Sketch for the Social History of Post-Medieval Latin', in Peter Burke and Roy Porter (eds.), *Language, Self and Society: A Social History of Language* (Cambridge: Polity Press, 1991), 23–50

—— (ed.), *New Perspectives on Historical Writing* (Cambridge: Polity Press, 1991)

——, *The Art of Conversation* (Cambridge: Polity Press, 1993)

Gilbert Burnet, *Some Passages of the Life and Death of the Right Honourable John, Earl of Rochester* (London: Chiswel, 1680)

Thomas Burnet, *The Sacred Theory of the Earth*, translated from the 1681 Latin original (London: Centaur Press, 1956 [1684–90])

R. M. Burns, *The Great Debate on Miracles, from Joseph Glanvill to David Hume* (Lewisburg, PA: Bucknell University Press, 1981)

Robert Burns, *The Poetical Works of Burns* (Boston: Houghton Mifflin, 1974)

J. W. Burrow, *Evolution and Society: A Study in Victorian Social Theory* (Cambridge: Cambridge University Press, 1966, 1970)

Shelley Burtt, *Virtue Transformed: Political Argument in England, 1688–1740* (Cambridge: Cambridge University Press, 1992)

J. B. Bury, *A History of Freedom of Thought* (London: Williams and Norgate, nd)

M. L. Bush (ed.), *What is Love? Richard Carlile's Philosophy of Sex* (London: Verso, 1998)

Bob Bushaway, *By Rite: Custom, Ceremony and Community in England, 1700–1880* (London: Junction Books, 1982)

T. L. Bushell, *The Sage of Salisbury: Thomas Chubb 1679–1747* (London: Vision Press, 1968)

Joseph Butler, *Fifteen Sermons Preached at the Rolls Chapel* (London: Knapton, 1726)

——, *The Analogy of Religion to the Constitution and Course of Nature* (London: Religion Tract Society, n.d.)

Marilyn Butler, *Maria Edgeworth: A Literary Biography* (Oxford: Clarendon Press, 1972)

——, *Jane Austen and the War of Ideas* (Oxford: Clarendon Press, 1975)

——, *Peacock Displayed: A Satirist in His Context* (London: Routledge and Kegan Paul, 1979)

——, *Romantics, Rebels and Reactionaries: English Literature and Its Background 1760–1830* (Oxford and New York: Oxford University Press, 1981)

—— (ed.), *Burke, Paine, Godwin, and the Revolution Controversy* (Cambridge: Cambridge University Press, 1984)

——, 'Romanticism in England', in Roy Porter and Mikuláš Teich (eds.), *Romanticism in National Context* (Cambridge: Cambridge University Press, 1988)

Samuel Butler, *Hudibras, Parts I and II and Selected Other Writings*, John Wilders and Hugh de Quehen (eds.) (Oxford: Clarendon Press, 1973 [1663])

John Butt (ed.), *The Poems of Alexander Pope* (London: Methuen, 1965)

M. Byrd, *London Transformed: Images of the City in the Eighteenth Century* (New Haven and London: Yale University Press, 1978)

Max Byrd, *Tristram Shandy* (London: Allen & Unwin, 1985)

James Byrne, *Glory, Jest and Riddle: Religious Thought in the Enlightenment* (London: SCM Press Ltd, 1996)

William Cadogan, *Essay upon Nursing, and the Management of Children* (London: J. Roberts, 1748)

C. G. Caffentzis, *Clipped Coins, Abused Words, and Civil Government. John Locke's Philosophy of Money* (New York: Autonomedia, 1989)

Barbara Caine, *English Feminism, 1780–1980* (Oxford: Oxford University Press, 1997)

Angus Calder, *Revolutionary Empire: The Rise of the English-speaking Empires from the Fifteenth Century to the 1780s* (London: Jonathan Cape, 1981)

Craig Calhoun (ed.), *Habermas and the Public Sphere* (Cambridge, Mass. and London: MIT Press, 1992)

William Camden, *Britannia* (London: Churchill, 1695)

Charles Camic, *Experience and Enlightenment: Socialization for Cultural Change in Eighteenth-century Scotland* (Edinburgh: Edinburgh University Press, 1983)

C. Campbell, *The Romantic Ethic and the Spirit of Modern Consumerism* (Oxford: Basil Blackwell, 1989)

R. H. Campbell and Andrew S. Skinner (eds.), *The Origins and Nature of the Scottish Enlightenment* (Edinburgh and New York: Edinburgh University Press, 1982)

T. D. Campbell, *Adam Smith's Science of Morals* (London: Allen & Unwin, 1971)

Piero Camporesi, *The Fear of Hell: Images of Damnation and Salvation in Early Modern Europe*, Lucinda Byatt (trans.) (Oxford: Basil Blackwell, 1990)

——, *Exotic Brew: Hedonism and Exoticism in the Eighteenth Century* (Cambridge: Polity Press, 1992)

David Cannadine, 'The Present and the Past in the English Industrial Revolution, 1880–1980', *Past and Present*, ciii (1984), 131–72

——, *The Decline and Fall of the British Aristocracy* (New Haven, Conn.: Yale University Press, 1990)

John Cannon, *Parliamentary Reform 1640–1832* (London: Cambridge University Press, 1972)

—— (ed.), *The Whig Ascendancy: Colloquies on Hanoverian England* (London: Edward Arnold, 1981)

G. N. Cantor, 'The History of "Georgian" Optics', *History of Science*, xvi (1978), 1–21

Bernard S. Capp, *Astrology and the Popular Press: English Almanacs, 1500–1800* (London: Faber & Faber, 1979)

Giancarlo Carabelli, *In the Image of Priapus* (London: Duckworth, 1996)

Daniel Carey, 'Reconsidering Rousseau: Sociability, Moral Sense and the American Indian from Hutcheson to Bartram', *British Journal for Eighteenth-century Studies*, xxi (1998), 25–38

C. L. Carlson, *The First Magazine. A History of the Gentleman's Magazine* (Providence, R. I.: Brown University Studies 5, 1938)

[T. Carlyle], 'Signs of the Times, An Addiction to Prophecy, Not a Favourable Indication, Either of Nations or Individuals', *Edinburgh Review*, xlix (1829), 439–59

W. B. Carnochan, *Confinement and Flight. An Essay on English Literature of the Eighteenth Century* (Berkeley, CA: University of California Press, 1977)

S. C. Carpenter, *Eighteenth-century Church and People* (London: Murray, 1959)

Vincent Carretta (ed.), *Olaudah Equiano: The Interesting Narrative and Other Writings* (New York: Penguin Books, 1995)

—— (ed.), *Unchained Voices: An Anthology of Black Authors in the English-speaking World of the Eighteenth Century* (Lexington, KY: The University Press of Kentucky, 1996)

David Carrithers, 'The Enlightenment Science of Society', in Christopher Fox, Roy S. Porter and Robert Wokler (eds.), *Inventing Human Science: Eighteenth-century Domains* (Berkeley, CA: University of California Press, 1995), 232–70

H. B. Carter, *Joseph Banks 1743–1820* (London: British Museum (Natural History), 1988)

Philip John Carter, 'Mollies, Fops and Men of Feeling: Aspects of Male Effeminacy and Masculinity in Britain c. 1700–1780' [University of Oxford, D.Phil., 1995]

Philip Carter, 'An "Effeminate" or "Efficient" Nation? Masculinity and Eighteenth-century Social Documentary', *Textual Practice*, xi (1997), 429–43

Arthur Cash, *Laurence Sterne: The Later Years* (London: Methuen, 1986)

Ernest Cassara, *The Enlightenment in America* (Lanham: University Press of America, 1988)

Ernst Cassirer, *The Philosophy of the Enlightenment*, Fritz C. A. Koelln and James P. Pettegrove (trans.) (Princeton, NJ: Princeton University Press, 1951)

——, *Kant's Life and Thought* (New Haven: Yale University Press, 1981)

Dario Castiglione, 'Excess, Frugality and the Spirit of Capitalism: Readings of Mandeville on Commercial Society', in Joseph Melling and Jonathan Barry (eds.), *Culture in History: Production, Consumption and Values in Historical Perspective* (Exeter: University of Exeter Press, 1992), 155–79

Terry Castle, *Masquerade and Civilization: The Carnivalesque in Eighteenth-century English Culture and Fiction* (London: Methuen, 1986)

——, *The Female Thermometer: Eighteenth-century Culture and the Invention of the Uncanny* (Oxford: Oxford University Press, 1994)

David Castronovo, *The English Gentleman: Images and Ideals in Literature and Society* (New York: Ungar, 1987)

Alexander Catcott, *The Antiquity and Honourableness of the Practice of Marchandize. A Sermon* (Bristol: sn, 1744)

——, *A Treatise on the Deluge*, 2nd edn (Bristol: E. Allen, 1768)

Hiram Caton, *The Politics of Progress: The Origins and Development of the Commercial Republic, 1600–1835* (Gainesville: University of Florida Press, 1988)

Margaret Cavendish, duchess of Newcastle, *Orations of Divers Sorts* (London: sn, 1663)

Michael de Certeau, *The Writing of History*, Tom Conley (trans.) (New York: Colombia University Press, 1988)

Ephraim Chambers, *Cyclopaedia, Or an Universal Dictionary of Arts and Sciences: Containing the Definitions of the Terms, and Accounts of the Things Signify'd Thereby, in the Several Arts, Both Liberal and Mechanical, and the Several Sciences*, 2 vols. (London: Printed for James & John Knapton *et al.*, 1728; 2nd edn, 2 vols., London: Midwinter, 1738)

Justin A. I. Champion, *The Pillars of Priestcraft Shaken: The Church of England and its Enemies, 1660–1730* (Cambridge: Cambridge University Press, 1992)

C. F. Chapin, *The Religious Thought of Samuel Johnson* (Ann Arbor, Mich.: University of Michigan Press, 1968)

R. W. Chapman (ed.), *Jane Austen's Letters to Her Sister Cassandra & Others* (London: Oxford University Press, 1952)

—— (ed.), *Samuel Johnson, A Journey to the Western Islands of Scotland and James Boswell, The Journal of a Tour to the Hebrides* (Oxford: Oxford University Press, 1970 [1775 and 1785])

Hester Chapone, *Letters on the Improvement of the Mind: Addressed to a Young Lady*, 2 vols. (London: J. Walter, 1773)

Roger Chartier, *The Order of Books: Readers, Authors and Libraries in Europe between the Fourteenth and Eighteenth Centuries*, Lydia Cochrane (trans.) (Cambridge: Polity Press, 1994)

——, *Forms and Meanings: Texts, Performances, and Audiences from Codex to Computer* (Philadelphia: University of Pennsylvania Press, 1995)

Warren Chernaik, *Sexual Freedom in Restoration Literature* (Cambridge: Cambridge University Press, 1995)

William Cheselden, 'An Account of Some Observations Made by a Young Gentleman, Who was Born Blind, or Lost His Sight So Early, That He Had No Remembrance of Ever Having Seen, and was Couch'd Between 13 and 14 Years', *Philosophical Transactions*, xxxv (1727–8), 447–50

Anand C. Chitnis, *The Scottish Enlightenment: A Social History* (London: Croom Helm, 1976)

——, *The Scottish Enlightenment and Early Victorian Society* (London: Croom Helm, 1986)

Jerome Christensen, *Practising Enlightenment: Hume and the Formation of a Literary Career* (Madison: University of Wisconsin Press, 1987)

I. R. Christie, *Wars and Revolutions: England 1760–1815* (London: Edward Arnold, 1982)

——, *Stress and Stability in Late Eighteenth-century Britain: Reflections on the British Avoidance of Revolution* (Oxford: Oxford University Press, 1984)

J. R. R. Christie, 'Laputa Revisited', in J. J. R. Christie and S. Shuttleworth (eds.), *Nature Transfigured* (Manchester: Manchester University Press, 1989), 45–60

John Christie, 'The Human Sciences: Origins and Histories', *History of the Human Sciences*, vi (1993), 1–12

Thomas Chubb, *A Collection of Tracts* (London: for the author, 1730)

Lady Mary Chudleigh, *The Ladies' Defence* (London: Deeve, 1701)

[Lady Mary Chudleigh], *Women Not Inferior to Men or A Short and Modest Vindication of the Natural Right of the Fair Sex to a Perfect Equality of Power, Dignity, and Esteem with the Men* (London: sn, 1739)

Charles Churchill, *The Duellist* (London: Kearsly, 1764), in Roger Lonsdale (ed.), *The New Oxford Book of Eighteenth Century Verse*, p. 512.

Gregory Claeys, *Thomas Paine. Social and Political Thought* (Winchester, Mass.: Unwin Hyman, 1989)

——, 'The French Revolution Debate and

British Political Thought', *History of Political Thought*, i (1990), 59–80

—— (ed.), *Utopias of the British Enlightenment* (Cambridge: Cambridge University Press, 1994)

—— (ed.), *Political Writings of the 1790s*, 8 vols. (London: Pickering and Chatto, 1995)

—— (ed.), *The Politics of English Jacobinism: Writings of John Thelwall* (Pennsylvania: Pennsylvania State University Press, 1995)

Anna Clark, *Women's Silence, Men's Violence: Sexual Assault in England, 1770–1845* (New York: Pandora, 1987)

——, *The Struggle for the Breeches: Gender and the Making of the British Working Class* (Berkeley, CA: University of California Press, 1995)

Geoffrey Clark, *Betting on Lives: The Culture of Life Insurance in England, 1695–1775* (Manchester: Manchester University Press, 1999)

Ian D. L. Clark, 'From Protest to Reaction: The Moderate Regime in the Church of Scotland, 1752–1805', in N. T. Phillipson and Rosalind Mitchison (eds.), *Scotland in the Age of Improvement: Essays in Scottish History in the Eighteenth Century* (Edinburgh: Edinburgh University Press, 1970), 200–224

J. C. D. Clark, *English Society, 1688–1832: Ideology, Social Structure and Political Practice During the Ancien Régime* (Cambridge: Cambridge University Press, 1985) 2nd edn: *English Society, 1660–1832: Religion, Ideology and Politics During the Ancien Régime* (Cambridge: Cambridge University Press, 2000)

——, *Revolution and Rebellion: State and Society in England in the Seventeenth and Eighteenth Centuries* (Cambridge: Cambridge University Press, 1986)

——, *The Language of Liberty 1660–1832: Political Discourse and Social Dynamics in the Anglo-American World* (Cambridge: Cambridge University Press, 1994)

——, *Samuel Johnson: Literature, Religion and English Cultural Politics from the Restoration to Romanticism* (Cambridge: Cambridge University Press, 1994)

M. L. Clark, *Paley: Evidences for the Man* (London: SPCK, 1974)

Peter Clark, *The English Alehouse: A Social History, 1200–1830* (London: Longman, 1983)

——, 'The "Mother Gin" Controversy in the Early Eighteenth Century', *Transactions of the Royal Historical Society*, xxxviii (1988), 63–84

——, *Sociability and Urbanity: Clubs and Societies in the Eighteenth Century* (Leicester: Leicester University Press, 2000)

P. Clark and P. Slack, *English Towns in Transition, 1500–1700* (London: Oxford University Press, 1976)

R. B. Clark, *William Gifford: Tory Satirist, Critic, and Editor* (New York: Russell and Russell, 1980)

Stuart Clark, *Thinking with Demons: The Idea of Witchcraft in Early Modern Europe* (Oxford: Clarendon Press, 1997)

T. B. Clark, *Omai: The First Polynesian Ambassador to England* (San Francisco: Colt Press, 1941)

Desmond Clarke, *The Ingenious Mr Edgeworth* (London: Oldbourne, 1965)

George Clarke (ed.), *John Bellers: His Life, Times and Writings* (London: Routledge and Kegan Paul, 1987; York: Sessions, 1993)

I. F. Clarke, *The Pattern of Expectation 1644–2001* (London: Jonathan Cape, 1979)

J. J. Clarke, *Oriental Enlightenment: The Encounter between Asian and Western Thought* (London: Routledge, 1997)

Michael Clarke and Nicholas Penny (eds.), *The Arrogant Connoisseur: Richard Payne Knight 1751–1824* (Manchester: Manchester University Press, 1982)

Samuel Clarke, *The Scripture-doctrine of the Trinity* (London: Strahan, 1712)

——, *A Demonstration of the Being and Attributes of God* (London: James Knapton, 1705)

John Cleland, *Memoirs of a Woman of Pleasure*,

Peter Sabor (ed.) (Oxford: Oxford University Press, 1985 [1784–9])

E. J. Clery, *The Rise of Supernatural Fiction* (Cambridge: Cambridge University Press, 1995)

James L. Clifford (ed.), *Dr Campbell's Diary of a Visit to England in 1775* (Cambridge: Cambridge University Press, 1947)

—— (ed.), *Man Versus Society in Eighteenth-century Britain: Six Points of View* (Cambridge: Cambridge University Press, 1968)

John Clive, *Scotch Reviewers: The 'Edinburgh Review' 1802–1815* (London: Faber & Faber, 1957)

——, 'The Social Background of the Scottish Renaissance', in Nicholas Phillipson and Rosalind Mitchison (eds.), *Scotland in the Age of Improvement: Essays in Scottish History in the Eighteenth Century* (Edinburgh: Edinburgh University Press, 1970), 225–44

E. L. Cloyd, *James Burnett, Lord Monboddo* (Oxford: Clarendon Press, 1972)

A. W. Coats, 'Changing Attitudes to Labour in the Mid-Eighteenth Century', *Economic History Review*, xi (1958), 35–51

James Aikman Cochrane, *Dr Johnson's Printer: The Life of William Strahan* (London: Routledge and Kegan Paul, 1964)

Catharine Cockburn, *A Defence of the Essay of Human Understanding Written by Mr Lock* (London: W. Turner, 1702)

Estelle Cohen, ' "What the Women at All Times Would Laugh At": Redefining Equality and Difference, circa 1660–1760', *Osiris*, xii (1997), 121–42

I. Bernard Cohen, *Revolution in Science* (Cambridge, Mass.: Belknap Press, 1985)

H. Floris Cohen, *The Scientific Revolution: A Historiographical Inquiry* (Chicago: University of Chicago Press, 1994)

Michèle Cohen, *Fashioning Masculinity: National Identity and Language in the Eighteenth Century* (London and New York: Routledge, 1996)

Sherrill Cohen, *The Evolution of Women's Asylums since 1500: From Refugees for Ex-Prostitutes to Shelters for Battered Women* (New York: Oxford University Press, 1992)

G. D. H. and Margaret Cole (eds.), *The Opinions of William Cobbett* (London: The Cobbett Publishing Co. Ltd, 1944)

D. C. Coleman, *The Economy of England 1450–1750* (London: Oxford University Press, 1977)

Samuel Taylor Coleridge, *Biographia Literaria: or Biographical Sketches of My Literary Life and Opinions* (London: Rest Fenner, 1817)

——, *On the Constitution of the Church and State: According to the Idea of Each: With Aids Towards a Right Judgment on the Late Catholic Bill* (London: Hurst, Chance, 1830)

——, *The Complete Poems*, William Keach (ed.) (Harmondsworth: Penguin, 1997)

Maurice Colgan, 'Prophecy Against Reason: Ireland and the Apocalypse', *British Journal for Eighteenth-century Studies*, viii (1985), 209–16

Rosalie L. Colie, *Light and Enlightenment: A Study of the Cambridge Platonists and the Dutch Arminians* (Cambridge: Cambridge University Press, 1957)

R. L. Colie, 'Spinoza and the Early English Deists', *Journal of the History of Ideas*, xx (1959), 23–46

Linda Colley, 'Radical Patriotism in Eighteenth-century England', in Raphael Samuel (ed.), *Patriotism: The Making and Unmaking of British National Identity*, vol. i: *History and Politics* (London and New York: Routledge, 1989), 169–87

——, 'Britishness and Otherness: An Argument', *Journal of British Studies*, xxxi (1992), 309–22

——, *Britons: Forging the Nation 1707–1837* (New Haven and London: Yale University Press, 1992)

A. S. Collins, *Authorship in the Days of Johnson: Being a Study of the Relation Between Author, Patron, Publisher and Public, 1726–1780* (London: Robert Holden & Co. Ltd, 1927)

——, *The Profession of Letters: A Study of the Relation of Author to Patron, Publisher and*

Public, 1780–1832 (London: George
Routledge & Sons Ltd, 1928; repr.,
Clifton, NJ: Augustus M. Kelley,
1973)

Anthony Collins, *Discourse of Free-thinking*
(London: sn, 1713)

——, *A Discourse of the Grounds and Reasons of the
Christian Religion* (London: sn, 1724)

——, *An Answer to Mr Clarke's Third Defence to
His Letter to Mr Dodwell* (London: Baldwin,
1708)

——, *A Philosophical Inquiry concerning Human
Liberty* (London: Robinson, 1717;
republished with a preface by Joseph
Priestley, London: Johnson, 1790)

Robert Collison, *Encyclopaedias: Their History
throughout the Ages* (New York: Hafner,
1964)

George Colman, *Polly Honeycombe, A Dramatick
Novel of One Act* (London: T. Becket, 1760)

John Colmer (ed.), *The Collected Works of
Samuel Taylor Coleridge* (Princeton:
Princeton University Press, 1976)

Patrick Colquhoun, *The State of Indigence, and
the Situation of the Casual Poor in the Metropolis
Explained* (London: Baldwin, 1799)

Henry Steele Commager, *The Empire of
Reason: How Europe Imagined and America
Realized the Enlightenment* (London:
Weidenfeld & Nicolson, 1978)

Carl B. Cone, *Torchbearer of Freedom: The
Influence of Richard Price on Eighteenth-century
Thought* (Lexington, Ky: University of
Kentucky Press, 1952)

——, *The English Jacobins: Reformers in Late
Eighteenth-century England* (New York:
Charles Scribner's Sons, 1968)

Syndy McMillen Conger, *Mary Wollstonecraft
and the Language of Sensibility* (London and
Toronto: Associated University Press,
1994)

Peter Conrad, *Shandyism* (Oxford: Blackwell,
1978)

A. Constable (ed.), *The Letters of Anna Seward,
1784–1807*, 6 vols. (Edinburgh: A.
Constable & Co., 1811)

James Cook, *Journals*, J. C. Beaglehole (ed.), 3
vols. (Cambridge: Cambridge University
press, 1955–68)

R. I. Cook, *Bernard Mandeville* (New York:
Twayne Publishers, 1974)

Roger Cooter and Stephen Pumfrey,
'Separate Spheres and Public Places:
Reflections on the History of Science
Popularization and Science in Popular
Culture', *History of Science*, xxxii (1994),
237–67

Edward Copeland, 'Money Talks: Jane
Austen and the *Lady's Magazine*', in J.
David Grey (ed.), *Jane Austen's Beginnings:
The Juvenilia and 'Lady Susan'* (Ann Arbor
and London: U.M.I. Research Press,
1989), 153–71

——, *Women Writing about Money: Women's
Fiction in England, 1790–1820* (Cambridge
and New York: Cambridge University
Press, 1995)

Stephen Copley (ed.), *Literature and the Social
Order in Eighteenth-century England* (London:
Croom Helm, 1984)

—— (ed.), *The Politics of the Picturesque:
Literature, Landscape and Aesthetics since 1770*
(Cambridge: Cambridge University Press,
1994)

——, 'Commerce, Conversation and
Politeness in the Early Eighteenth-century
Periodical', *British Journal for
Eighteenth-century Studies*, xviii (1995),
63–77

Stephen Copley and Kathryn Sutherland
(eds.), *Adam Smith's Wealth of Nations: New
Interdisciplinary Essays* (Manchester:
Manchester University Press, 1995)

Penelope J. Corfield (ed.), *Language, History and
Class* (Oxford: Basil Blackwell, 1991)

——, *Power and the Professions in Britain 1700–
1850* (London: Routledge, 1995)

P. Corrigan and D. Sayer, *The Great Arch:
English State Formation as Cultural Revolution*
(Oxford: Basil Blackwell, 1985)

Denis Cosgrove and Stephen Daniels (eds.),
The Iconography of Landscape: Essays on the

Symbolic Representation, Design and Use of Past Environments (Cambridge: Cambridge University Press, 1988)

John Cottingham, *Descartes* (Oxford: Basil Blackwell, 1986)

Peter Coveney, *The Image of Childhood* (Harmondsworth: Penguin, 1968)

Barry Coward, *The Stuart Age: A History of England 1603–1714* (New York: Longman Press, 1980)

D. A. Coward, 'Eighteenth-century Attitudes to Prostitution', *Studies on Voltaire and the Eighteenth Century*, clxxxix (1980), 363–99

William Cowper, *The Task* (London: J. Johnson, 1785)

S. D. Cox, *'The Stranger within Thee': The Concept of the Self in Late Eighteenth-century Literature* (Pittsburgh: Pittsburgh University Press, 1980)

Gerald R. Cragg, *The Church and the Age of Reason* (Harmondsworth: Penguin, 1960)

——, *Reason and Authority in the Eighteenth Century* (Cambridge: Cambridge University Press, 1964)

David Craig, *Scottish Literature and the Scottish People 1680–1830* (London: Chatto & Windus, 1961)

R. S. Crane, *The Idea of the Humanities and Other Essays Historical and Critical*, 2 vols. (Chicago: University of Chicago Press, 1967)

Geoffrey Alan Cranfield, *The Development of the Provincial Newspaper 1700–1760* (Oxford: Clarendon Press, 1962)

——, *The Press and Society from Caxton to Northcliffe* (London: Longman, 1978)

Maurice Cranston, *John Locke: A Biography* (London: Longmans, Green & Co., 1957)

Raymond Henry Payne Crawfurd, *The King's Evil* (Oxford: Clarendon Press, 1911; New York, AMS Press, 1977)

David Cressy, *Bonfires and Bells* (London: Weidenfeld & Nicolson, 1989)

——, 'Literacy in Context: Meaning and Measurement in Early Modern England', in John Brewer and Roy Porter (eds.),

Consumption and the World of Goods (London and New York: Routledge, 1993), 305–19

J. Hector St John de Crèvecoeur, *Letters from an American Farmer and Sketches of Eighteenth-century America* (Oxford: Oxford University Press, 1997 [1782])

Alexander Crichton, *An Inquiry into the Nature and Origin of Mental Derangement*, 2 vols. (London: T. Cadell & Davis, 1798)

James E. Crimmins, *Secular Utilitarianism: Social Science and the Critique of Religion in the Thought of Jeremy Bentham* (Oxford: Clarendon Press, 1980)

J. Mordaunt Crook, 'The Arcadian Vision: Neo-Classicism and the Picturesque', in G. W. Clarke (ed.), *Rediscovering Hellenism* (Cambridge: Cambridge University Press, 1988), 43–59

Maurice Crosland, 'The Image of Science as a Threat: Burke versus Priestley and the "Philosophical Revolution"', *British Journal for the History of Science*, xx (1987), 277–307

Patrick Cruttwell (ed.), *Samuel Johnson: Selected Writings* (Harmondsworth: Penguin, 1986)

Christopher Cunliffe (ed.), *Joseph Butler's Moral and Religious Thought* (Oxford: Clarendon Press, 1992)

Andrew Cunningham, 'Getting the Game Right: Some Plain Words on the Identity and Invention of Science', *Studies in the History and Philosophy of Science*, xix (1988), 365–89

Hugh Cunningham, *Leisure in the Industrial Revolution*, c. *1780*–c. *1880* (London: Croom Helm, 1980)

——, *The Children of the Poor: Representations of Childhood Since the Seventeenth Century* (Oxford: Basil Blackwell, 1991)

——, *Children and Childhood in Western Society Since 1500* (London: Longman, 1995)

S. Cunningham, 'Bedlam and Parnassus: Eighteenth-century Reflections', *Eighteenth Century Studies*, xxiv (1971), 36–55

Andrew Curran, Robert P. Maccubbin and David F. Morrill (eds.), 'Faces of

Monstrosity in Eighteenth-century Thought', *Eighteenth-century Life*, xxi (1997)

Patrick Curry, *Prophecy and Power: Astrology in Early Modern England* (Cambridge: Polity Press, 1989)

L. A. Curtis, 'A Case Study of Defoe's Domestic Conduct Manuals Suggested by *The Family, Sex and Marriage in England 1500–1800*', *Studies in Eighteenth Century Culture*, x (1981), 409–28

Lewis P. Curtis (ed.), *Letters of Laurence Sterne* (Oxford: Clarendon Press, 1935)

T. C. Curtis and W. A. Speck, 'The Societies for the Reformation of Manners: A Case Study in the Theory and Practice of Moral Reform', *Literature and History*, iii (1976), 45–64

David Dabydeen, *Hogarth's Blacks: Images of Blacks in Eighteenth-century English Art* (Kingston, Surrey: Dangeroo Press, 1985)

—— (ed.), *The Black Presence in English Literature* (Manchester: Manchester University Press, 1985)

——, 'Eighteenth-century English Literature on Commerce and Slavery', in David Dabydeen (ed.), *The Black Presence in English Literature* (Manchester: Manchester University Press, 1985), 26–49

David Daiches, *Robert Burns* (London: G. Bell & Sons, 1952)

——, *The Scottish Enlightenment* (Edinburgh: Saltire Society, 1986)

Norma Dalrymple-Champneys, *George Crabbe: The Complete Poetical Works*, 3 vols. (Oxford: Clarendon Press, 1988)

John Dalton, *A Descriptive Poem Addressed to Two Ladies at Their Return from Viewing the Mines at Whitehaven* (London: J. and J. Rivington, 1755)

Macdonald Daly, 'Vivisection in Eighteenth-century Britain', *British Journal for Eighteenth-century Studies*, xii (1989), 57–68

Stephen H. Daniel, *John Toland: His Methods, Manners and Mind* (Kingston and Montreal: McGill-Queen's University Press, 1984)

Stephen Daniels, 'The Political Iconography of Woodland in Later Georgian England', in Denis Cosgrove and Stephen Daniels (eds.), *The Iconography of Landscape: Essays on the Symbolic Representation, Design and Use of Past Environments* (Cambridge: Cambridge University Press, 1988)

——, *Fields of Vision: Landscape Imagery and National Identity in England and the United States* (Cambridge: Polity Press, 1993)

——, *Humphry Repton: Landscape Gardening and the Geography of Georgian England* (New Haven: Yale University Press, 1999)

John Darling, 'The Moral Teaching of Francis Hutcheson', *British Journal for Eighteenth-century Studies*, xii (1989), 165–74

Robert Darnton, 'In Search of the Enlightenment: Recent Attempts to Create a Social History of Ideas', *Journal of Modern History*, xliii (1971), 113–32

——, *The Business of Enlightenment: A Publishing History of the Encyclopédie, 1775–1800* (Cambridge, Mass.: Harvard University Press, 1979)

——, 'History of Reading', in Peter Burke (ed.), *New Perspectives on Historical Writing* (Cambridge: Polity Press, 1991)

——, *The Forbidden Best-Sellers of Pre-Revolutionary France* (London: HarperCollins, 1996)

——, 'George Washington's False Teeth', *New York Review* (27 March 1997)

Robert Darnton and Daniel Roche (eds.), *Revolution in Print: The Press in France 1775–1800* (Berkeley: University of California Press, 1989)

F. J. H. Darton, *Children's Books in England*, 3rd edn (Cambridge: Cambridge University Press, 1982)

Charles Darwin, *Life of Erasmus Darwin* (London: John Murray, 1887)

Erasmus Darwin, *Zoonomia; or, The Laws of Organic Life*, 2 vols. (London: Johnson, 1794–6)

——, *Plan for the Conduct of Female Education* (Derby: Drewry, 1797)

——, *Phytologia: or, The Philosophy of Agriculture and Gardening* (London: T. Bensley, 1800)

——, *Zoonomia; or the Laws of Organic Life*, 2 vols., 3rd edn (London: Johnson, 1801 [1794–6])

——, *The Temple of Nature; or, The Origin of Society: A Poem with Philosophical Notes* (London: Johnson, 1803)

——, *The Botanic Garden, A Poem in Two Parts. Part I. Containing the Economy of Vegetation. Part II. The Loves of the Plants. With Philosophical Notes*, 2 vols. (London: Johnson, 1789–91)

Lorraine J. Daston, 'The Domestication of Risk: Mathematical Probability and Insurance 1650–1830', in L. Krüger, L. Daston and M. Heidelberger (eds.), *The Probabilistic Revolution* (Ann Arbor, MI: University of Michigan Press, 1987), 237–60

——, *Classical Probability in the Enlightenment* (Princeton, NJ: Princeton University Press, 1988)

——, 'The Ideal and Reality of the Republic of Letters in the Enlightenment', *Science in Context*, iv (1991), 367–86

Lorraine Daston and Katharine Park, *Wonders and the Order of Nature 1150–1750* (New York: Zone Books, 1998)

Charles Davenant, *An Essay on the East-India-trade* (London: sn, 1696)

Leonore Davidoff and Catherine Hall, *Family Fortunes: Men and Women of the English Middle Class, 1780–1850* (London: Hutchinson, 1987)

Caroline A. Davidson, *A Woman's Work is Never Done: A History of Housework in the British Isles, 1650–1950* (London: Chatto & Windus, 1982)

Luke Davidson, ' "Identities Ascertained": British Ophthalmology in the First Half of the Nineteenth Century', *Social History of Medicine*, ix (1996), 313–33

Nicholas Davidson, 'Toleration in Enlightenment Italy', in O. P. Grell and Roy Porter (eds.), *Toleration in the Enlightenment* (Cambridge: Cambridge University Press, 2000), 230–49

George Davie, *The Democratic Intellect. Scotland and Her Universities in the Nineteenth Century* (Edinburgh: Edinburgh University Press, 1961)

Gordon Davies, *The Earth in Decay* (London: MacDonald, 1969)

Horton Davies, *Worship and Theology in England from Watts and Wesley to Martineau, 1690–1900* (Grand Rapids, Mich.: William B. Eerdmans Publishing Company, 1996)

Kate Davies, 'Living Muses: The Politics of Embodiment 1750–1780' [MA Dissertation, University of York, 1995]

Norman Davies, *The Isles* (London: Macmillan, 1999)

Owen Davies, 'Methodism, the Clergy, and the Popular Belief in Witchcraft and Magic', *History*, lxxxii (1997), 252–65

Arthur Paul Davis, *Isaac Watts: His Life and Works* (London: Independent Press Ltd, 1948)

David Brion Davis, *The Problem of Slavery in Western Culture* (Ithaca, NY: Cornell University Press, 1966)

Natalie Zemon Davis and Arlette Farge (eds.), *A History of Women in the West*, vol. iii: *Renaissance and Enlightenment Paradoxes* (Cambridge, Mass.: Harvard University Press, 1993)

Lee Davison, Tim Hitchcock, Tim Keirn and Robert B. Shoemaker (eds.), *Stilling the Grumbling Hive: The Response to Social and Economic Problems in England, 1689–1750* (Stroud: Alan Sutton, 1992)

Richard Dawkins, *The Blind Watchmaker* (London: Longmans, 1986)

Thomas Day, *The History of Sandford and Merton*, 3 vols. (London: J. Stockdale, 1783–9)

Dennis R. Dean, *James Hutton and the History of Geology* (Ithaca, NY: Cornell University Press, 1992)

Mitchell Dean, *The Constitution of Poverty*.

Towards a Genealogy of Liberal Governance (London: Routledge, 1991)

Peter Dear, '*Totius in Verba*: Rhetoric and Authority in the Early Royal Society', *Isis*, lxxvi (1985), 145–61

Daniel Defoe, *Robinson Crusoe* (Harmondsworth: Penguin, 1985 [London: J. Roberts, 1719])

——, *The History and Remarkable Life of Colonel Jacque, Commonly Call'd* (London: J. Brotherton, 1722)

——, *Moll Flanders* (London: Chetwood and Edling, 1722)

——, *Roxana* (London: Warner, 1724)

——, *A Tour Thro' the Whole Island of Great Britain* (London: Strahan, 1724–6)

——, *A System of Magick* (London: J. Roberts, 1727)

——, *The Complete English Tradesman in Familiar Letters, Directing him in all the Several Parts and Progressions of Trade*, 2nd edn, 2 vols. (London: Charles Rivington, 1727, repr. New York: Augustus M. Kelley, 1969)

——, *Augusta Triumphans or The Way to Make London the Most Flourishing City in the Universe* (London: J. Roberts, 1728)

——, *A Plan of the English Commerce* (London: Rivington, 1728)

——, *The Compleat English Gentleman*, Karl Bulbring (ed.) (London: David Nutt, 1890 [1729])

——, *Review*, A. W. Secord (ed.), 22 vols. (New York: Columbia University Press, 1938)

——, *A Tour Thro' the Whole Island of Great Britain*, Pat Rogers (abridged and ed.) (Harmondsworth: Penguin, 1971 [1724–6])

Rudolf Dekker, ' "Private Vices, Public Virtues" Revisited: The Dutch Background of Bernard Mandeville', *History of European Ideas*, xiv (1992), 481–98

Margaret Delacy, *Prison Reform in Lancashire, 1700–1850* (Manchester: Chetham Society, 1986)

Jean Delumeau, *Sin and Fear: The Emergence of a Western Guilt Culture, Thirteenth–Eighteenth Centuries* (New York: St Martin's Press, 1990)

Robert DeMaria Jr, *Johnson's Dictionary and the Language of Learning* (Oxford: Clarendon Press, 1986)

William Derham, *Physico-Theology: or a Demonstration of the Being and Attributes of God, from His Works of Creation* (London: Innys, 1713)

J. T. Desaguliers, *The Newtonian System of the World: The Best Model of Government, an Allegorical Poem* (Westminster: J. Roberts, 1728)

T. M. Devine, *The Scottish Nation, 1700–2000* (Harmondsworth: Allen Lane, 1999)

H. M. Dickinson, *Matthew Boulton* (Cambridge: Cambridge University Press, 1937)

H. T. Dickinson, *Bolingbroke* (London: Constable, 1970)

——, 'Popular Loyalism in Britain in the 1790s', in Eckhart Hellmuth (ed.), *The Transformation of Political Culture: England and Germany in the Late Eighteenth Century* (London: Oxford University Press, 1990)

——, *The Politics of the People in Eighteenth-century Britain* (New York: St Martin's Press, 1995)

David Dickson, *New Foundations: Ireland, 1660–1800* (Dublin: Helicon, 1987)

Bram Dijkstra, *Idols of Perversity. Fantasies of Feminine Evil in Fin de Siècle Culture* (Oxford: Oxford University Press, 1986)

R. Dingley, *Proposals for Establishing a Place of Reception for Penitent Prostitutes* (London: W. Faden, 1758)

John Dinwiddy, 'Conceptions of Revolution in the English Radicalism of the 1790s', in Eckhart Hellmuth (ed.), *The Transformation of Political Culture: England and Germany in the Late Eighteenth Century* (London: Oxford University Press, 1990)

——, *Bentham* (Oxford: Oxford University Press, 1989)

G. M. Ditchfield, 'Anti-Trinitarianism and Toleration in Late Eighteenth-century

British Politics: The Unitarian Petition of 1792', *Journal of Ecclesiastical History*, xlii (1991), 39–67

Grayson Ditchfield, *The Evangelical Revival* (London: UCL Press, 1997)

Betty Jo Teeter Dobbs, *The Janus Face of Genius. The Role of Alchemy in Newton's Thought* (Cambridge: Cambridge University Press, 1991)

Betty Jo Teeter Dobbs and Margaret C. Jacob, *Newton and the Culture of Newtonianism* (Atlantic Highlands, NJ: Humanities Press, 1995)

Michael Dobson, *The Making of the National Poet: Shakespeare, Adaptation and Authorship, 1660–1769* (New York: Oxford University Press, 1992)

Brian Dolan, *Exploring European Frontiers: British Travellers in the Age of Enlightenment* (Basingstoke: Macmillan, 1999)

Jonathan Dollimore, *Death, Desire and Loss in Western Culture* (London: Allen Lane, 1998)

Denis Donoghue, *England, Their England: Commentaries on English Language and Literature* (New York: Alfred A. Knopf, 1988)

Frank Donoghue, *The Fame Machine: Book Reviewing and Eighteenth-century Literary Careers* (Stanford: Stanford University Press, 1996)

Richard M. Dorson (ed.), *Peasant Customs and Savage Myths: Selections from the British Folklorists*, 2 vols. (London: Routledge & Kegan Paul, 1968)

Judith Drake, *Essay in Defence of the Female Sex* (London: Roper and Wilkinson, 1696)

Alice Domurat Dreger, *Hermaphrodites and the Medical Invention of Sex* (Cambridge, Mass.: Harvard University Press, 1998)

John Dryden, *The Poems of John Dryden*, John Sargeaunt (ed.) (London: Oxford University Press, 1959)

James Downey, *The Eighteenth Century Pulpit* (Oxford: Clarendon Press, 1969)

J. A. Downie, 'Walpole: The Poet's Foe', in

Jeremy Black (ed.), *Britain in the Age of Walpole* (London: Macmillan, 1984), 171–88

Edward Duffy, *Rousseau in England: The Context for Shelley's Critique of the Enlightenment* (Berkeley: University of California Press, 1979)

Michael Duffy (ed.), *The English Satirical Print, 1600–1832*, 7 vols. (Cambridge: Chadwyck-Healey, 1986)

Richard van Dülmen, *The Society of the Enlightenment: The Rise of the Middle Class and Enlightenment Culture in Germany*, Anthony Williams (trans.) (Cambridge: Polity Press, 1992)

Louis Dumont, *From Mandeville to Marx: The Genesis and Triumph of Economic Ideology* (Chicago: University of Chicago Press, 1977)

James Dunbar, *Essays on the History of Mankind in Rude and Cultivated Ages* (London: R. Strahan, 1780)

John Dunn, *The Political Thought of John Locke* (Cambridge: Cambridge University Press, 1969)

——, *Locke* (Oxford: Oxford University Press, 1984)

——, 'The Claim to Freedom of Conscience: Freedom of Speech, Freedom of Thought, Freedom of Worship?' in O. P. Grell, J. I. Israel and N. Tyacke (eds.), *From Persecution to Toleration: The Glorious Revolution and Religion in England* (Oxford: Oxford University Press, 1991)

John Dunton, *The Life and Errors of John Dunton, Citizen of London*, 2 vols. (London: J. Nichols & Bentley, 1818); repr. as *The Life and Errors of John Dunton, Citizen of London: With the Lives and Characters of More than a Thousand Contemporary Divines and Other Persons of Literary Eminence, to Which are Added Dunton's Conversation in Ireland, Selections from His Other Genuine Works and a Faithful Portrait of the Author* (New York: Burt Franklin, 1960)

John Dwyer, *Virtuous Discourse: Sensibility and*

Community in Late Eighteenth-century Scotland (Edinburgh: John Donald, 1987)

J. Dybikowski, *On Burning Ground: An Examination of the Ideas, Projects and Life of David Williams* (Studies on Voltaire and the Eighteenth Century, Oxford: the Voltaire Foundation, 1993)

A. Dyce (ed.), *The Works of Richard Bentley*, 3 vols. (London: Francis Macpherson, 1838)

John Dyer, *The Fleece* (London: Dodsley, 1757)

Terry Eagleton, *The Function of Criticism: From 'The Spectator' to Post-Structuralism* (London: Verso Editions and NLB, 1984)

——, *The Ideology of the Aesthetic* (Oxford: Basil Blackwell, 1990)

Peter Earle, *The World of Defoe* (London: Weidenfeld & Nicolson, 1976)

——, *The Making of the English Middle Class: Business, Society and Family Life in London, 1660–1730* (London: Methuen, 1989)

B. Easlea, *Witch-hunting, Magic and the New Philosophy: An Introduction to Debates of the Scientific Revolution 1450–1750* (Sussex: Harvester, 1980)

——, *Science and Sexual Oppression: Patriarchy's Confrontation with Woman and Nature* (London: Weidenfeld & Nicolson, 1981)

Daniel Eaton [pseud. 'Antitype'], *The Pernicious Effects of the Art of Printing upon Society, Exposed* (London: Eaton, 1794)

Richard Lovell Edgeworth, *Memoirs*, 2 vols. (London: R. Hunter, 1820)

R. L. Edgeworth and M. Edgeworth, *Practical Education*, 2 vols. (London: J. Johnson, 1798)

Sir F. M. Eden, *The State of the Poor: A History of the Labouring Classes in England, with Parochial Reports*, 3 vols. (London: J. Davis, 1797)

Charles Edmonds (ed.), *Poetry of the Anti-Jacobin* (London: Willis, 1854)

Elizabeth L. Eisenstein, *The Printing Press as an Agent of Change*, 2 vols. (Cambridge: Cambridge University Press, 1979)

Roger Elbourne, *Music and Tradition in Early Industrial Lancashire 1780–1840* (Woodbridge, Suffolk: The Folklore Society, 1980)

Simon Eliot and Beverley Stern (eds.), *The Age of Enlightenment*, 2 vols (London: Ward Lock, 1979)

Marianne Elliott, *Partners in Revolution: The United Irishmen and France* (New Haven: Yale University Press, 1982)

Aytoun Ellis, *The Penny Universities: A History of the Coffee Houses* (London: Secker & Warburg, 1956)

Joyce Ellis, ' "On The Town": Women in Augustan England', *History Today*, xlv (1995), 20–27

Markman Ellis, *The Politics of Sensibility: Race, Gender and Commerce in the Sentimental Novel* (New York: Cambridge University Press, 1996)

Roger L. Emerson, *Professors, Patronage and Politics: The Aberdeen Universities in the Eighteenth Century* (Aberdeen: Aberdeen University Press, 1992)

Clive Emsley, *British Society and the French Wars 1793–1815* (London: Macmillan, 1979)

——, *Policing and Its Context, 1750–1870* (London: Macmillan, 1983)

Encyclopaedia Britannica: or, A Dictionary of Arts and Sciences, Complied upon a New Plan. In Which the Different Sciences and Arts are Digested into Distinct Treaties or Systems; and the Various Technical Terms, &c. are Explained as They Occur in the Order of the Alphabet (Edinburgh: A. Bell and C. Macfarquhar, 1771); 4th edn (1800)

Todd M. Endelman, *The Jews of Georgian England 1714–1830: Tradition and Change in a Liberal Society* (Philadelphia: Jewish Publication Society of America, 1979)

J. Engell, *The Creative Imagination* (Cambridge, Mass.: Harvard University Press, 1981)

Rolf Engelsing, *Der Burger als Lesser* (Stuttgart: Metzler, 1974)

David V. Erdman, *Blake, Prophet against Empire: A Poet's Interpretation of the History of His Own Times*, 3rd edn (Princeton, NJ: Princeton University Press, 1954)

Howard Erskine-Hill, *The Augustan Idea in English Literature* (London: Edward-Arnold, 1983)

John Evelyn, *Silva, or a Discourse of Forest Trees* (York: J. Dodsley, 1776 [1662])

Nigel Everett, *The Tory View of Landscape* (New Haven, Conn.: Yale University Press, 1994)

George Every, *The High Church Party 1688–1718* (London: The Church Historical Society, 1956)

Cecil Henry L'Estrange Ewen, *Lotteries and Sweepstakes: An Historical, Legal and Ethical Survey of Their Introduction, Suppression and Re-Establishment in the British Isles* (London: Heath Cranton, 1932)

M. J. M. Ezell, 'John Locke's Images of Childhood: Early Eighteenth-century Responses to *Some Thoughts Concerning Education*', *Eighteenth Century Studies*, xvii (1983/4), 139–55

Patricia Fara, *Sympathetic Attractions. Magnetic Practices, Beliefs, and Symbolism in Eighteenth-century England* (Princeton, NJ: Princeton University Press, 1996)

Trevor Fawcett, *The Rise of English Provincial Art: Artists, Patrons and Institutions Outside London, 1800–1830* (Oxford: Oxford University Press, 1974)

—— (ed.), *Voices of Eighteenth-century Bath. An Anthology of Contemporary Texts Illustrating Events, Daily Life and Attitudes at Britain's Leading Georgian Spa* (Bath: Ruton, 1995)

John Feather, *The Provincial Book Trade in Eighteenth-century England* (Cambridge: Cambridge University Press, 1985)

——, *A History of British Publishing* (London: Croom Helm, 1988)

——, *Publishing, Piracy and Politics. An Historical Study of Copyright in Britain* (London: Mansell, 1994)

——, 'The Power of Print: Word and Image in Eighteenth-century England', in Jeremy Black (ed.), *Culture and Society in Britain 1660–1800* (Manchester: Manchester University Press, 1997), 51–68

Burton Feldman and Robert D. Richardson, *The Rise of Modern Mythology* (Bloomington: Indiana University Press, 1973)

Frank Felsenstein, *A Paradigm of Otherness: Anti-Semitic Stereotypes in English Popular Culture, 1660–1830* (Baltimore: Johns Hopkins University Press, 1995)

Michael Ferber, *The Social Vision of William Blake* (Princeton: Princeton University Press, 1985)

C. Y. Ferdinand, *Benjamin Collins and the Provincial Newspaper Trade in the Eighteenth Century* (Oxford; Clarendon Press, 1997)

Adam Ferguson, *An Essay on the History of Civil Society* (Edinburgh: Miller and Cadell, 1767)

——, *Institutes of Moral Philosophy, for the Use of Students in the College of Edinburgh*, 2nd edn (Edinburgh: A. Kincaid, W. Creech, and J. Bell, 1773)

——, *An Essay on the History of Civil Society*, Fania Oz-Salzberger (ed.) (Cambridge: Cambridge University Press, 1995 [1767])

J. P. Ferguson, *An Eighteenth-century Heretic: Dr Samuel Clarke* (Kineton: The Roundwood Press, 1976)

Moira Ferguson (ed.), *First Feminists: British Women Writers, 1578–1799* (Bloomington: Indiana University Press, 1985)

——, *Subject to Others: British Women Writers and Colonial Slavery, 1700–1843* (London: Routledge, 1992)

Robert A. Ferguson, *The American Enlightenment 1750–1820* (Cambridge, Mass.: Harvard University Press, 1997)

Vincenzo Ferrone, *The Intellectual Roots of the Italian Enlightenment: Newtonian Science, Religion, and Politics in the Early Eighteenth Century*, Sue Brotherton (trans.) (Atlantic Highlands, NJ: Humanities Press, 1995)

Henry Fielding, 'An Essay on Conversation', in *Miscellanies, by H. F., Esq.*, 3 vols. (London: Millar, 1743) and H. K. Miller (ed.), *Miscellanies by Henry Fielding Esq.* (Oxford: Oxford University Press, 1972)

——, *The Author's Farce* (London: J. Roberts,

1730); C. B. Woods (ed.) (Lincoln: University of Nebraska Press, 1966)

——, *An Inquiry into the Causes of the Late Increase of Robbers, with Some Proposals for Remedying This Growing Evil* (London: A. Millar, 1751)

——, *An Enquiry into the Causes of the Late Increase of Robbers and Related Writings*, Malvin R. Zirker (ed.) (Middletown, CT: Wesleyan University Press, 1988)

John Fielding, *A Plan for a Preservatory and Reformatory for the Benefit of Deserted Girls and Penitent Prostitutes* (London: B. Francklin, 1758)

John Neville Figgis, *The Divine Right of Kings* (New York: Harper, 1965)

Karl M. Figlio, 'Theories of Perception and the Physiology of the Mind in the Late Eighteenth Century', *History of Science*, xiii (1975), 177–212

V. Fildes, *Breasts, Bottles and Babies. A History of Infant Feeding* (Edinburgh: Edinburgh University Press, 1986)

——, *Wetnursing* (Oxford: Basil Blackwell, 1988)

Robert Filmer, *Patriarcha, and Other Political Works of Sir Robert Filmer*, Peter Laslett (ed.) (Oxford: Basil Blackwell, 1949 [1680])

B. Fine and E. Leopold, 'Consumerism and the Industrial Revolution', *Social History*, xv (1990), 151–79

Ann Finer and George Savage (eds.), *The Selected Letters of Josiah Wedgwood* (London: Cory, Adams & Mackay, 1965)

Gabrielle M. Firmager (ed.), *The Female Spectator: Being Selections from Mrs Eliza Haywood's Periodical, First Published in Monthly Parts (1774–6)* (Bristol: Bristol Classical Press, 1992)

Martin Fitzpatrick, 'Heretical Religion and Radical Political Ideas in Late Eighteenth-century England', in Eckhart Hellmuth (ed.), *The Transformation of Political Culture: England and Germany in the Late Eighteenth Century* (London: Oxford University Press, 1990), 339–72

——, 'Toleration and the Enlightenment Movement', in O. P. Grell and Roy Porter (eds.), *Toleration in Enlightenment Europe* (Cambridge: Cambridge University Press, 2000), 23–68

Gloria Flaherty, 'The Non-Normal Sciences: Survivals of Renaissance Thought in the Eighteenth Century', in Christopher Fox, Roy S. Porter and Robert Wokler (eds.), *Inventing Human Science: Eighteenth-century Domains* (Berkeley, CA: University of California Press, 1995), 271–91

M. Kay Flavell, 'The Enlightened Reader and the New Industrial Towns: A Study of the Liverpool Library 1758–1790', *British Journal for Eighteenth Century Studies*, viii (1985), 17–36

Anthony Fletcher, *Gender, Sex and Subordination in England 1500–1800* (New Haven and London: Yale University Press, 1995)

Philippa Foot, 'Locke, Hume, and Modern Moral Theory: A Legacy of Seventeenth- and Eighteenth-century Philosophies of Mind', in G. S. Rousseau (ed.), *The Languages of Psyche: Mind and Body in Enlightenment Thought* (Berkeley/Los Angeles/Oxford: University of California Press, 1991), 81–106

Duncan Forbes, *Hume's Philosophical Politics* (Cambridge: Cambridge University Press, 1975)

——, 'Sceptical Whiggism, Commerce and Liberty', in A. S. Skinner and T. Wilson (eds.), *Essays on Adam Smith* (Oxford: Clarendon Press, 1975), 179–201

Margaret Forbes, *Beattie and His Friends* (London: Constable, 1904)

James A. Force, *William Whiston: Honest Newtonian* (Cambridge: Cambridge University Press, 1985)

James E. Force, 'Hume and Johnson on Prophecy and Miracles: Historical Context', in John W. Yolton (ed.), *Philosophy, Religion and Science in the Seventeenth and Eighteenth Centuries* (Rochester, NY: University of Rochester Press, 1990), 127–39

Jennifer Ford, *Coleridge on Dreaming: Romanticism, Dreams and the Medical Imagination* (Cambridge: Cambridge University Press, 1998)

John Ford, *Prizefighting. The Age of Regency Boximania* (Newton Abbot: David and Charles, 1971)

Michael Fores, 'Science and the "Neolithic Paradox" ', *History of Science*, xxi (1983), 141–63

Michael Foss, *The Age of Patronage: The Arts in England 1660–1750* (London: Hamish Hamilton, 1971)

——, *Man of Wit to Man of Business: The Arts and Changing Patronage 1660–1750* (Bristol: Bristol Classical Press, 1988)

Roy Foster (ed.), *The Oxford Illustrated History of Ireland* (New York: Oxford University Press, 1991)

Brian Fothergill (ed.), *Sir William Hamilton: Envoy Extraordinary* (London: Faber and Faber, 1969)

Michel Foucault, *La Folie et la Déraison: Histoire de la Folie à l'Age Classique* (Paris: Librairie Plon, 1961); trans. and abridged by Richard Howard as *Madness and Civilization: A History of Insanity in the Age of Reason* (London: Tavistock Publications, 1967)

——, *The Order of Things: An Archeology of the Human Sciences* (London: Tavistock, 1970; London: Routledge, 1989)

——, 'What is an Author?', in *Language, Counter-Memory, Practice: Selected Essays and Interviews*, Donald F. Bouchard (ed.), Donald F. Bouchard and Sherry Simon (trans.) (Ithaca, NY: Cornell University Press, 1977), 113–38

——, *Discipline And Punish: The Birth of the Prison* (Harmondsworth: Penguin, 1979)

——, 'What is Enlightenment?' in Paul Rabinow (ed.), *The Foucault Reader* (New York: Pantheon Books, 1984), pp. 32–50

Christopher Fox (ed.), *Psychology and Literature in the Eighteenth Century* (New York: AMS Press, 1987)

——, 'Crawford, Willis, and *Anthropologie Abstracted*: Some Early-English Uses of Psychology', *Journal of the History of the Behavioral Sciences*, xxiv (1988), 378–80

——, *Locke and the Scriblerians: Identity and Consciousness in Early Eighteenth-century Britain* (Berkeley, CA: University of California Press, 1988)

Christopher Fox, Roy Porter and Robert Wokler (eds.), *Inventing Human Science: Eighteenth-century Domains* (Berkeley, CA: University of California Press, 1995)

David Foxon, *Libertine Literature in England, 1660–1745* (New Hyde Park, New York: University Books, 1965)

Tore Frängsmyr, J. L. Heilbron, Robin E. Rider (eds.), *The Quantifying Spirit in the Eighteenth Century* (Berkeley, CA: University of California Press, 1990)

Colin Franklin, *Lord Chesterfield, His Character and Characters* (Aldershot: Scolar Press, 1993)

Christopher Frayling, *Nightmare, The Birth of Horror* (London: BBC Books, 1996)

Hans W. Frei, *The Eclipse of Biblical Narrative: A Study in Eighteenth- and Nineteenth-century Hermeneutics* (New Haven and London, Yale University Press, 1974)

['A Friend to the People'], *A Review of the Constitution of Great Britain* (London: Ridgeway, 1791)

E. R. Frizelle and J. D. Martin, *Leicester Royal Infirmary, 1771–1971* (Leicester: Leicester No. 1 Hospital Management Committee, 1971)

Jack Fruchtman, Jr, *The Apocalyptic Politics of Richard Price and Joseph Priestley: A Study in Late Eighteenth-century English Republican Millennialism* (Philadelphia: American Philosophical Society, 1983)

——, *Thomas Paine and the Religion of Nature* (Baltimore: Johns Hopkins University Press, 1993)

——, *Thomas Paine: Apostle of Freedom* (New York and London: Four Walls Eight Windows, 1994)

Tom Furniss, *Edmund Burke's Aesthetic Ideology: Language, Gender and Political Economy in Revolution* (Cambridge: Cambridge University Press, 1993)

Paul Fussell, *The Rhetorical World of Augustan Humanism. Ethics and Imagery from Swift to Burke* (Oxford: Clarendon Press, 1965)

Alan Gabbey, 'Cudworth, More and the Mechanical Analogy', in Richard Kroll, Richard Ashcraft, Perez Zagorin (eds.), *Philosophy, Science and Religion in England 1640–1700* (Cambridge: Cambridge University Press, 1992), 109–48

Norton Garfinkle, 'Science and Religion in England, 1790–1800: The Critical Response to the Work of Erasmus Darwin', *Journal of the History of Ideas*, xvi (1955), 376–88

David Garnett (ed.), *The Novels of Thomas Love Peacock* (London: Rupert Hart-Davis, 1948)

Jane Garnett and Colin Matthew (eds.), *Revival and Religion since 1700: Essays for John Walsh* (London: The Hambledon Press, 1993)

John Gascoigne, 'From Bentley to the Victorians: The Rise and Fall of Newtonian Natural Theology', *Science in Context*, ii (1988), 219–56

——, *Cambridge in the Age of the Enlightenment: Science, Religion and Politics from the Restoration to the French Revolution* (Cambridge: Cambridge University Press, 1989)

——, *Joseph Banks and the English Enlightenment: Useful Knowledge and Polite Culture* (Cambridge and New York: Cambridge University Press, 1994)

V. A. C. Gatrell, *The Hanging Tree: Execution and the English People 1770–1868* (Oxford: Oxford University Press, 1994)

John Gay, *The Present State of Wit* (London: sn, 1711)

Peter Gay, *The Enlightenment, An Interpretation*, vol. i: *The Rise of Modern Paganism* (London: Weidenfeld & Nicolson, 1967); vol. ii: *The Science of Freedom* (London: Weidenfeld & Nicolson, 1970)

J. G. Gazley, *The Life of Arthur Young* (Philadelphia: American Philosophical Society, 1973)

Ernest Gellner, *Plough, Sword and Book: The Structure of Human History* (London: Paladin Grafton Books, 1991)

Ann Geneva, *Astrology and the Seventeenth-century Mind: William Lilly and the Language of the Stars* (Manchester: Manchester University Press, 1995)

Alexander Gerard, *Essay on Taste* (London: A. Millar, 1759)

——, *An Essay on Genius* (London: Strahan, 1774)

Edward Gibbon, *The History of the Decline and Fall of the Roman Empire*, David Womersley (ed.), 3 vols. (London: Allen Lane, 1994 [1776–88])

——, *Memoirs of My Life*, G. A. Bonnard (ed.) (London: Nelson, 1966 [1796])

Edmund Gibson and Edward Chamberlayne, *Angliae Notitia* (London: Martyn, 1669)

John S. Gibson, 'How Did the Enlightenment Seem to the Edinburgh Enlightened?', *British Journal for Eighteenth-century Studies*, i (1978), 46–50

Siegfried Giedion, *Mechanization Takes Command: A Contribution to Anonymous History* (New York: Oxford University Press, 1948)

Marijke Gijswijt-Hofstra, Brian P. Levack and Roy Porter, *Witchcraft and Magic in Europe*, vol. 5: *The Eighteenth and Nineteenth Centuries* (London: Athlone, 1999)

Sheridan Gilley, 'Christianity and the Enlightenment: An Historical Survey', *History of European Ideas*, i (1981), 103–21

Sheridan Gilley and W. J. Sheils, *A History of Religion in Britain: Practice and Belief from Pre-Roman Times to the Present* (Oxford: Blackwell, 1994)

Charles C. Gillispie, *Genesis and Geology: A Study in the Relations of Scientific Thought, Natural Theology, and Social Opinion in Great*

Britain, 1790–1850 (Cambridge, Mass.: Harvard University Press, 1951)

——, *The Montgolfier Brothers and the Invention of Aviation 1783–1784* (Princeton: Princeton University Press, 1983)

Ian Gilmour, *Riot, Risings and Revolution. Governance and Violence in Eighteenth-century England* (London: Hutchinson, 1992)

Mark Girouard, *Life in the English Country House* (New Haven and London: Yale University Press, 1978)

C. Glacken, *Traces on the Rhodian Shore: Nature and Culture in Western Thought from Ancient Times to the End of the Eighteenth Century* (Berkeley, CA: University of California Press, 1967)

Joseph Glanvill, *Plus Ultra, Or the Progress and Advancement of Knowledge Since the Days of Aristotle* (London: James Collins, 1668)

D. V. Glass, *Numbering the People: The Eighteenth-century Population Controversy and the Development of Census and Vital Statistics in Britain* (Farnborough, Hants: Saxon House, 1973)

William Godwin, *The Enquirer. Reflections on Education, Manners and Literature* (New York: Augustus M. Kelley, 1965 [1797])

——, *An Enquiry concerning Political Justice and Its Influence on Modern Morals and Happiness*, Isaac Kramnick (eds.) (Harmondsworth: Penguin, 1985 [London: G. G. J. and J. Robinson, 1793])

——, *Caleb Williams*, Maurice Hindle (ed.) (Harmondsworth: Penguin, 1988 [1794])

Anne Goldgar, *Impolite Learning. Conduct and Community in the Republic of Letters 1680–1750* (New Haven and London: Yale University Press, 1995)

Bertrand A. Goldgar, *The Curse of Party. Swift's Relations with Addison and Steele* (Lincoln: University of Nebraska Press, 1961)

——, *Walpole and the Wits: The Relation of Politics to Literature, 1722–1742* (Lincoln: University of Nebraska Press, 1976)

Mark Goldie, 'Priestcraft and the Birth of Whiggism', in Nicholas Phillipson and Quentin Skinner (eds.), *Political Discourse in Early Modern Britain* (Cambridge: Cambridge University Press, 1993), 209–31

—— (ed.), *Locke: Political Essays* (Cambridge: Cambridge University Press, 1997)

M. M. Goldsmith, *Private Vices, Public Benefits: Bernard Mandeville's Social and Political Thought* (Cambridge: Cambridge University Press, 1985)

Oliver Goldsmith, 'The Comparative View of Races and Nations', in *The Royal Magazine or Gentleman's Monthly Companion* (London: J. Coote, 1760)

——, *The Deserted Village* (London: W. Griffin, 1770)

——, *An History of the Earth and Animated Nature*, 8 vols. (London: J. Nourse, 1774)

——, *Enquiry into the Present State of Polite Learning in Europe* (London: Dodsley, 1759)

——, *Citizen of the World* (London: the author, 1762)

——, *Selected Essays*, J. H. Lobban (ed.) (Cambridge: Cambridge University Press, 1910)

Bette P. Goldstone, *Lessons to be Learned: A Study of Eighteenth-century English Didactic Children's Literature* (New York, Berne, and Frankfurt-am-Main: Peter Lang, 1984)

J. V. Golinski, 'Language, Discourse and Science', in R. C. Olby, G. N. Cantor, J. R. R. Christie, and M. J. S. Hodge (eds.), *Companion to the History of Modern Science* (London: Routledge, 1990), 110–26

Jan Golinski, *Science as Public Culture: Chemistry and Enlightenment in Britain, 1760–1820* (Cambridge and New York: Cambridge University Press, 1992)

Dena Goodman, 'Public Sphere and Private Life: Towards a Synthesis of Current Historiographical Approaches to the Old Regime', *History and Theory*, xxxi (1992), 1–20

——, *The Republic of Letters: A Cultural History of the French Enlightenment* (Ithaca, NY and

London: Cornell University Press, 1994)

Jordan Goodman, *Tobacco in History: The Cultures of Dependence* (London: Routledge, 1993)

Robert W. Gordon, 'Paradoxical Property', in John Brewer and Susan Staves (eds.), *Early Modern Conceptions of Property* (London and New York: Routledge, 1995), 95–110

Scott Paul Gordon, 'Voyeuristic Dreams: Mr Spectator and the Power of Spectacle', *The Scriblerian and the Kit-Cats*, xxxvi (1995), 3–23

Thomas Gordon, *The Humourist*, 3rd edn (London: T. Woodward, 1724)

J. W. Gough, *John Locke's Political Philosophy* (Oxford: Clarendon Press, 1950)

Andrews Graham-Dixon, *A History of British Art* (London: BBC, 1996)

James Grainger, *The Sugar-Cane: A Poem in Four Books, with Notes* (London: Dodsley, 1764)

Alexander Grant and Keith Stringer (eds.), *Uniting the Kingdom? The Making of British History* (London: Routledge, 1995)

Joseph Granvill, *Vanity of Dogmatizing* (London: H. Eversden, 1661)

Selwyn Alfred Grave, *The Scottish Philosophy of Common Sense* (Oxford: Clarendon Press, 1960)

Thomas Gray, *Selected Poems* (London: Bloomsbury Classics, 1997)

Richard Greaves, *Deliver Us from Evil: The Radical Underground in Britain, 1660–1663* (New York: Oxford University Press, 1986)

——, *Enemies under His Feet: Radicals and Nonconformists in Britain, 1664–1677* (Stanford: Stanford University Press, 1990)

——, *Secrets of the Kingdom: British Radicals from the Popish Plot to the Revolution of 1688–89* (Stanford: Stanford University Press, 1992)

V. H. H. Green, 'Reformers and Reform in the University', in L. S. Sutherland and L. G. Mitchell (eds.), *The History of the University of Oxford*, vol. v: *The Eighteenth Century* (Oxford: Clarendon Press, 1986), 607–37

Stephen Greenblatt, *Renaissance Self-Fashioning: From More to Shakespeare* (Chicago: University of Chicago Press, 1980)

Robert Greene, *The Principles of the Philosophy of the Expansive and Contractive Forces* (Cambridge: Cambridge University Press, 1727)

Germaine Greer, *The Obstacle Race* (London: Secker & Warburg, 1979)

——, *Slip-Shod Sibyls. Recognition, Rejection and the Woman Poet* (London: Viking, 1995)

Jeremy Gregory, 'Christianity and Culture: Religion, the Arts and the Sciences in England, 1660–1800', in Jeremy Black (ed.), *Culture and Society in Britain* (Manchester: Manchester University Press, 1997), 102–3

J. Y. T. Greig (ed.), *The Letters of David Hume*, 2 vols. (Oxford: Clarendon Press, 1932)

M. Greig, 'The Reasonableness of Christianity?: Gilbert Burnet and the Trinitarian Controversy of the 1690s', *Journal of Ecclesiastical History*, xliv (1993), 631–51

O. P. Grell, J. I. Israel and N. Tyacke (eds.), *From Persecution to Toleration: The Glorious Revolution and Religion in England* (Oxford: Oxford University Press, 1991)

O. P. Grell and B. Scribner (eds.), *Tolerance and Intolerance in the European Reformation* (Cambridge: Cambridge University Press, 1996)

Dustin Griffin, *Literary Patronage in England, 1650–1800* (Cambridge: Cambridge University Press, 1996)

Earl Leslie Griggs (ed.), *Collected Letters of Samuel Taylor Coleridge*, 6 vols. (Oxford: Clarendon Press, 1956–1968)

M. Grosley, *A Tour to London, or New Observations on England*, 3 vols. (Dublin: J. Ekshaw, 1772)

Gloria Sybil Gross, *This Invisible Riot of the Mind: Samuel Johnson's Psychological Theory*

(Baltimore: Johns Hopkins University Press, 1992)

Richard Grove, *Green Imperialism. Colonial Expansion, Tropical Island Edens and the Origins of Environmentalism 1600–1800* (Cambridge: Cambridge University Press, 1995)

Isobel Grundy, *Lady Mary Wortley Montagu. Comet of the Enlightenment* (Oxford: Oxford University Press, 1999)

Henry Guerlac, 'Where the Statue Stood: Divergent Loyalties to Newton in the Eighteenth Century', in *Essays and Papers in the History of Modern Science* (Baltimore: Johns Hopkins University Press, 1977), 131–45

——, *Newton on the Continent* (Ithaca: Cornell University Press, 1981)

J. A. W. Gunn, *Beyond Liberty and Property: The Process of Self-recognition in Eighteenth-century Political Thought* (Kingston: McGill-Queen's University Press, 1983)

Ahmad Gunny, *Images of Islam in Eighteenth-century Writing* (London: Grey Seal, 1996)

Knud Haakonssen, *Natural Law and Moral Philosophy: From Grotius to the Scottish Enlightenment* (Cambridge: Cambridge University Press, 1996)

—— (ed.), *Enlightenment and Religion: Rational Dissent in Eighteenth-century Britain* (Cambridge: Cambridge University Press, 1997)

Jürgen Habermas, *The Structural Transformation of the Public Sphere: An Inquiry into a Category of Bourgeois Society*, Thomas Burger (trans.) (Cambridge: Polity, 1989); originally published as *Strukturwandel der Öffentlicheit* (Berlin: Luchterhand, 1962)

——, 'Taking Aim at the Heart of the Present', in D. C. Hoy (ed.), *Foucault: A Critical Reader* (Oxford: Basil Blackwell, 1986), 103–19

——, 'Further Reflections on the Public Sphere', in Craig Calhoun (ed.), *Habermas and the Public Sphere* (Cambridge, Mass. and London, 1992), 421–61

I. Hacking, *The Emergence of Probability* (Cambridge: Cambridge University Press, 1975)

——, *The Taming of Chance* (Cambridge: Cambridge University Press, 1990)

Jean H. Hagstrum, *Sex and Sensibility. Ideal and Erotic Love from Milton to Mozart* (Chicago and London: The University of Chicago Press, 1980)

George Hakewill, *An Apologie*, 2nd edn (Oxford: William Turner, 1630; first published 1627)

Matthew Hale, *The Primitive Origination of Mankind* (London: William Godbid, 1677)

Elie Halévy, *The Growth of Philosophic Radicalism* (London: Faber & Faber, 1972)

——, *A History of the English People in the Nineteenth Century*, vol. 1, *England in 1815*, 2nd edn, E. I. Watkin and D. A. Barker (trans.) (London: Benn, 1961)

George Savile, Marquis of Halifax, *The Lady's New Year's Gift, Or Advice to a Daughter* (London: Randal Taylor, 1688)

——, *The Character of a Trimmer*, 2nd edn (London: Baldwin, 1689)

A. Rupert Hall, 'Newton in France: A New View', *History of Science*, xiii (1975), 233–50

——, *Philosophers at War: The Quarrel between Newton and Leibniz* (Cambridge: Cambridge University Press, 1980)

Charles Hall, *The Effects of Civilization on the People in European States: Observations on the Principal Conclusion in Mr Malthus's Essay on Population* (London: the author, 1805)

Marie Boas Hall, *Promoting Experimental Learning: Experiment and the Royal Society 1660–1727* (Cambridge: Cambridge University Press, 1991)

Adrian Hamilton, *The Infamous Essay on Woman: Or John Wilkes Seated Between Vice and Virtue* (London: André Deutsch, 1972)

Elizabeth Hamilton, *Memoirs of Modern Philosophers* (Bath: R. Cruttwell, 1800)

——, *Letters of a Hindoo Rajah* (London: G. G. and J. Robinson, 1796; London: Broadview, 1999)

Sir William Hamilton (ed.), *The Collected Works of Dugald Stewart*, 11 vols. (Edinburgh: Constable, 1854–60)

William Hammond, *Answer to Priestley's Letters to a Philosophical Unbeliever* (London: sn, 1782)

Brean S. Hammond, *Pope and Bolingbroke: A Study of Friendship and Influence* (Columbia: University of Missouri Press, 1984)

——, *Professional Imaginative Writing in England, 1670–1740: 'Hackney for Bread'* (Oxford: Clarendon Press, 1997)

Paul Hammond, 'The King's Two Bodies: Representations of Charles II', in J. Black and J. Gregory (ed.), *Culture, Politics and Society in Britain 1660–1800* (Manchester: Manchester University Press, 1991), 13–48

——, 'Titus Oates and "Sodomy" ', in Jeremy Black (ed.), *Culture and Society in Britain* (Manchester: Manchester University Press, 1997), 85–101

Ronald Hamowy, *The Scottish Enlightenment and the Theory of Spontaneous Order* (Carbondale: South Illinois University Press, 1987)

Norman Hampson, *The Enlightenment* (Harmondsworth: Penguin Books, 1968)

C. C. Hankin (ed.), *Life of Mary Anne Schimmelpenninck*, 2 vols. (London: Longmans, 1858)

Thomas L. Hankins, *Science and the Enlightenment* (Cambridge and New York: Cambridge University Press, 1985)

Keith Hanley and Raman Selden (eds.), *Revolution and English Romanticism: Politics and Rhetoric* (Hemel Hempstead: Harvester Wheatsheaf, 1990)

Ivan Hannaford, *Race. The History of an Idea in the West* (Baltimore: Johns Hopkins University Press, 1996)

Nicholas A. Hans, *New Trends in Education in the Eighteenth Century* (London: Routledge and Kegan Paul, 1966)

Jonas Hanway, *A Journal of Eight Days' Journey*, 2nd edn (London: H. Woodfall, 1757)

——, *Solitude In Imprisonment* (London: Bew, 1776)

——, *Defects Of Police* (London: J. Dodsley, 1775)

C. Hardyment, *Dream Babies: Child Care from Locke to Spock* (London: Jonathan Cape, 1983)

Philip Harling, *The Waning of 'Old Corruption': The Politics of Economical Reform in Britain, 1779–1846* (Oxford: Oxford University Press, 1996)

Peter Harman, *Metaphysics and Natural Philosophy* (Brighton: Harvester Press, 1982)

James Harrington, *Commonwealth of Oceana* (London: J. Streater, 1656)

James Harris, *Lexicon Technicum: or, An Universal English Dictionary of Arts and Sciences: Explaining Not Only the Terms of Art, But the Arts Themselves*, 5th edn (London: J. Walthoe, 1736)

——, *Hermes, Or a Philosophical Inquiry, concerning Universal Grammar* (1751), in *The Works of James Harris, Esq.*, 2 vols. (London: F. Wingrave, 1801)

Michael Harris and Alan Lee (eds.), *The Press in English Society from the Seventeenth to the Nineteenth Centuries* (London and Toronto: Associated University Presses, 1986)

R. W. Harris, *Reason and Nature in the Eighteenth century, 1714–1780* (London: Blandford Press, 1968)

——, *Romanticism and the Social Order* (London: Blandford Press: London, 1969)

Victor I. Harris, *All Coherence Gone* (London: Frank Cass & Co., 1966)

John Fletcher Clews Harrison, *The Second Coming: Popular Millenarianism, 1780–1850* (London: Routledge & Kegan Paul, 1979)

Jonathan Harrison, *Hume's Theory of Justice* (Oxford: Oxford University Press, 1981)

Peter Harrison, *'Religion' and the Religions in the English Enlightenment* (Cambridge: Cambridge University Press, 1990)

Ross Harrison, *Bentham* (London: Routledge & Kegan Paul, 1983)

David Hartley, *Observations on Man, His Frame, His Duty, and His Expectations*, 2 vols.

(London: Richardson, 1749; 3 vols. London: Johnson, 1791)

A. D. Harvey, *Sex in Georgian England. Attitudes and Prejudices from the 1720s to the 1820s* (London: Duckworth, 1994)

Karen Louise Harvey, 'Representations of Bodies and Sexual Difference in Eighteenth-century English Erotica' [PhD thesis, University of London, 1999]

Gary Hatfield, 'Metaphysics and the New Science,' in David C. Lindberg and Robert S. Westman (eds.), *Reappraisals of the Scientific Revolution* (Cambridge, New York, Port Chester, Melbourne, Sydney: Cambridge University Press, 1990), 93–166

——, 'Remaking the Science of the Mind: Psychology as Natural Science', in Christopher Fox, Roy S. Porter and Robert Wokler (eds.), *Inventing Human Science: Eighteenth-century Domains* (Berkeley, CA: University of California Press, 1995), 184–231

Clement Hawes, *Christopher Smart and the Enlightenment* (New York: St Martin's Press, 1999)

Laetitia-Matilda Hawkins, *Letters on the Female Mind, Its Powers and Pursuits; Addressed to Miss H. M. Williams, with Particular Reference to Her Letters from France* (London: Hookham and Carpender, 1793)

Judith Hawley, 'The Anatomy of *Tristram Shandy*', in Marie Mulvey Roberts and Roy Porter (eds.), *Literature and Medicine During the Eighteenth Century* (London and New York: Routledge, 1993), 84–100

Carla Hay, *James Burgh, Spokesman for Reform in Hanoverian England* (Washington, DC: University Press of America, 1979)

D. Hay, 'Property, Authority and the Criminal Law' in D. Hay *et al.* (eds.), *Albion's Fatal Tree* (London: Allen Lane, 1975), 17–64

Colin Haydon, *Anti-Catholicism in Eighteenth-century England, c. 1714–80: A Political and Social Study* (Manchester: Manchester University Press, 1993)

Mary Hays, *Appeal to the Men of Great Britain in Behalf of Women* (London: Johnson and Bell, 1798)

——, *The Victim of Prejudice* (London: Johnson, 1799)

——, *Female Biography* (London: R. Phillips, 1803)

——, *Memoirs of Emma Courtney*, Eleanor Ty (ed.) (Oxford: Oxford University Press, 1996 [1796])

Roslynn D. Haynes, *From Faust to Strangelove: Representations of the Scientist in Western Literature* (Baltimore and London: Johns Hopkins University Press, 1994)

Eliza Haywood, *The History of Miss Betsy Thoughtless*, 4 vols. (London: Gardner, 1751)

P. G. M. C. Hazard, *The European Mind, 1680–1715*, J. L. May (trans.) (Harmondsworth: Penguin, 1964)

William Hazlitt, *Political Essays* (London: W. Hone, 1819)

——, *The Collected Works of William Hazlitt*, A. R. Waller and A. Glover (eds.), 13 vols. (London: Dent, 1901–6)

——, *The Complete Works of William Hazlitt*, P. P. Howe (ed.), 21 vols. (London: J. M. Dent, 1930–34)

——, *The New School of Reform* in *The Collected Works of William Hazlitt*, A. R. Waller and A. Glover (eds.), 13 vols. (London: Dent, 1901–6), vol. 7, essay xvii

——, *Selected Writings*, Ronald Blythe (ed.) (Harmondsworth: Penguin, 1970)

——, *The Spirit of the Age* (Menston, Yorks: Scolar Press, 1971 [1825])

P. M. Heimann, 'Newtonian Natural Philosophy and the Scientific Revolution', *History of Science*, xi (1973), 1–7

——, ' "Nature is a Perpetual Worker": Newton's Aether and Eighteenth-century Natural Philosophy', *Ambix*, xx (1973), 1–25

——, 'Voluntarism and Immanence:

Conceptions of Nature in Eighteenth-century Thought', *Journal of the History of Ideas*, xxxix (1978), 271–83

P. M. Heimann and J. E. McGuire, 'Newtonian Forces and Lockean Powers: Concepts of Matter in Eighteenth-century Thought', *Historical Studies in the Physical Sciences*, iii (1971), 233–306

Eckhart Hellmuth, ' "The Palladium of All Other English Liberties". Reflections on the Liberty of the Press in England During the 1760s and 1770s', in Eckhart Hellmuth (ed.), *The Transformation of Political Culture: England and Germany in the Late Eighteenth Century* (London: Oxford University Press, 1990), 467–501

——, 'Enlightenment and the Freedom of the Press: The Debate in the Berlin Mittwochsgesellschaft 1783–84', *History*, lxxxiii (1998), 420–44

Phyllis Hembry, *The English Spa 1560–1815: A Social History* (London: Athlone, 1990)

David Hempton, *Religion and Political Culture in Britain and Ireland: From the Glorious Revolution to the Decline of Empire* (Cambridge: Cambridge University Press, 1996)

A. R. Henderson, 'Female Prostitution in London, 1730–1830' [PhD dissertation, University of London, 1992]

E. Henderson, *Life of James Ferguson F. R. S., in a Brief Autobiographical Account* (Edinburgh: Fullerton, 1867)

Ursula Henriques, *Religious Toleration in England 1783–1833* (London: Routledge, 1961)

John Henry, *The Scientific Revolution and the Origins of Modern Science* (London: Macmillan, 1997)

Thomas Henry, 'On the Advantages of Literature and Philosophy in General, and Especially on the Consistency of Literary and Philosophical with Commercial Pursuits', in *Memoirs of the Manchester Literary and Philosophical Society*, i (1785), 7–29

Brian Hepworth, *The Rise of Romanticism: Essential Texts* (Manchester: Carcanet, 1978)

Michael Heyd, *'Be Sober and Reasonable': The Critique of Enthusiasm in the Seventeenth and Early Eighteenth Centuries* (Leiden; New York; Koln: E. J. Brill, 1995)

C. Hibbert (ed.), *An American in Regency England* (London: Maxwell, 1968); orig. pub. as [L. Simond], *Journal of a Tour and Residence in Great Britain during the Years 1810 and 1811, by a French Traveller* (Edinburgh: A. Constable, 1815)

David R. Hiley, 'Foucault and the Question of Enlightenment', *Philosophy and Social Criticism*, xi (1985–6), 63–83

Bridget Hill, *Eighteenth-century Women: An Anthology* (London: Allen and Unwin, 1984)

——, *The First English Feminist: Reflections upon Marriage and Other Writings by Mary Astell* (Aldershot: Gower, 1986)

——, *The Republican Virago: The Life and Times of Catharine Macaulay* (Oxford: Clarendon Press, 1992)

——, *Women, Work and Sexual Politics in Eighteenth-century England* (London: UCL Press, 1994)

Christopher Hill, *God's Englishman: Oliver Cromwell and the English Revolution* (Harmondsworth: Penguin, 1970)

——, *Antichrist in Seventeenth-century England* (London: Oxford University Press, 1971)

——, *The World Turned Upside Down: Radical Ideas during the English Revolution* (Harmondsworth: Penguin, 1972; repr. 1978)

——, *Some Intellectual Consequences of the English Revolution* (London: Weidenfeld and Nicolson, 1980)

——, *A Turbulent, Seditious and Factious People: John Bunyan and His Church 1628–1688* (Oxford: Oxford University Press, 1989)

——, *The English Bible and the Seventeenth-century Revolution* (London: Allen Lane, 1993)

George Birkbeck Hill, *Boswell's Life of Johnson*, L. F. Powell (ed., rev. and enl.), 6 vols. (Oxford: Clarendon Press, 1934–50)

Boyd Hilton, *The Age of Atonement: The Influence of Evangelicalism on Social and Economic Thought, 1795–1865* (Oxford: Clarendon Press, 1988)

Gertrude Himmelfarb, *Victorian Minds* (London: Weidenfeld & Nicolson, 1968)

——, *The Idea of Poverty: England in the Early Industrial Age* (London: Faber & Faber; New York: Knopf, 1984)

Walter John Hipple, *The Beautiful, the Sublime, and the Picturesque in Eighteenth-century Aesthetic Theory* (Carbondale: Southern Illinois University Press, 1957)

Albert O. Hirschman, *The Passions and the Interests: Political Arguments for Capitalism Before Its Triumph* (Princeton, NJ: Princeton University Press, 1977)

Derek Hirst, *Authority and Conflict: England 1603–1658* (London: Edward Arnold, 1986)

Andrew Hiscock, ' "Here's No Design, No Plot, Nor Any Ground": The Drama of Margaret Cavendish and the Disorderly Woman', *Women's Writing*, iv (1997), 401–20

Tim Hitchcock, *English Sexualities, 1700–1800* (Basingstoke: Macmillan, 1997)

Thomas Hobbes, *Leviathan: or, the Matter, Forme and Power of a Commonwealth Ecclesiasticall and Civil*, C. B. Macpherson (ed.) (Harmondsworth: Penguin, 1968 [1651])

Eric Hobsbawm, *On History* (London: Weidenfeld & Nicolson, 1997)

Eric Hobsbawm and Terence Ranger (eds.), *The Invention of Tradition* (Cambridge: Cambridge University Press, 1983)

M. T. Hodgen, *Early Anthropology in the Sixteenth and Seventeenth Centuries* (Philadelphia: University of Pennsylvania Press, 1964)

William Hodgson, *The Commonwealth of Reason by William Hodgson, Now Confined in the Prison of Newgate, London, For Sedition* (London: the author, 1795)

Ulrich Im Hof, *The Enlightenment*, William E. Yuill (trans.) (Oxford: Blackwell, 1994)

Amos Hofman, 'Opinion, Illusion and the Illusion of Opinion: Barruel's Theory of Conspiracy', *Eighteenth Century Studies*, xxvii (1993), 27–60

William Hogarth, *The Analysis of Beauty* (London: the author, 1753)

Thomas Holcroft, *The Adventures of Hugh Trevor*, Seamus Deane (ed.) (Oxford: Oxford University Press, 1973 [1794])

Martin Hollis (ed.), *The Light of Reason: Rationalist Philosophers of the Seventeenth Century* (London: Collins Fontana, 1973)

Geoffrey Holmes, 'The Achievement of Stability: The Social Context of Politics from the 1680s to the Age of Walpole', in J. Cannon (ed.), *The Whig Ascendancy: Colloquies on Hanoverian England* (London: Edward Arnold, 1981), 1–22

—— (ed.), *Britain after the Glorious Revolution 1689–1714* (London: Macmillan, 1969)

——, *The Trial of Doctor Sacheverell* (London: Eyre Methuen, 1973)

——, *Augustan England: Professions, State and Society 1680–1730* (London: Allen and Unwin, 1982).

——, *British Politics in the Age of Anne* (London: Hambledon, 1987)

——, *The Making of a Great Power: Late Stuart and Early Georgian Britain 1660–1722* (London: Longmans, 1993)

——, *The Birth of Britain: A New Nation 1700–1710* (Oxford: Blackwell, 1994)

Geoffrey Holmes and W. A. Speck, *The Divided Society: Parties and Politics in England, 1694–1716* (London: Edward Arnold, 1967)

Richard Holmes, *Coleridge* (Oxford: Oxford University Press, 1982)

——, *Coleridge: Early Visions* (London: Hodder & Stoughton, 1989)

——, *Dr Johnson and Mr Savage: A Biographical Mystery* (London: Hodder & Stoughton, 1993)

Ann Holt, *A Life of Joseph Priestley* (London: Oxford University Press, 1931)

Henry Homer, *An Enquiry into the Means of Preserving and Improving the Publick Roads of This Kingdom* (Oxford: S. Parker, 1767)

Hugh Honour, *Chinoiserie: The Vision of Cathay* (London: John Murray, 1961)

——, *The Image of the Black in Western Art*, vol. iv: *From the American Revolution to World War I* (Cambridge, Mass.: Harvard University Press, 1989)

Istvan Hont, 'The "Rich Country–Poor Country" Debate in Scottish Classical Political Economy', in Istvan Hont and Michael Ignatieff (eds.), *Wealth and Virtue: The Shaping of Political Economy in the Scottish Enlightenment* (Cambridge: Cambridge University Press, 1983), 271–315

Istvan Hont and Michael Ignatieff (eds.), *Wealth and Virtue: The Shaping of Political Economy in the Scottish Enlightenment* (Cambridge: Cambridge University Press, 1983)

Robert Hooke, *Micrographia* (London: J. Martyn and J. Allestry, 1665)

E. N. Hooker (ed.), *The Critical Works of John Dennis*, 2 vols. (Baltimore: Johns Hopkins University Press, 1943)

Vincent Hope, *Virtue by Consensus: The Moral Philosophy of Hutcheson, Hume, and Adam Smith* (Oxford: Clarendon Press, 1989)

H. M. Höpfl, 'From Savage to Scotsman: Conjectural History in the Scottish Enlightenment', *Journal of British Studies* (1978), 19–40

Julian Hoppit, 'Political Arithmetic in Eighteenth-century England', *Economic History Review*, xlix (1996), 516–40

——, 'Understanding the Industrial Revolution', *Historical Journal*, xxx (1987), 211–24

M. Horkheimer and T. Adorno, *The Dialectic of Enlightenment*, J. Cumming (trans.) (New York: Continuum, 1990)

T. A. Horne, *The Social Thought of Bernard Mandeville: Virtue and Commerce in Early Eighteenth-century England* (London: Macmillan, 1978)

Ralph A. Houlbrooke, *The English Family, 1450–1700* (London and New York: Longman, 1984)

——, *Death, Religion and the Family in England, 1480–1750* (Oxford: Clarendon Press, 1998)

R. A. Houston, *Literacy in Early Modern Europe: Culture and Education, 1500–1800* (London: Longman, 1988)

——, 'Scottish Education and Literacy, 1600–1800: An International Perspective', in T. M. Devine (ed.), *Improvement and Enlightenment* (Edinburgh: John Donald, 1989), 43–61

——, *Social Change in the Age of Enlightenment: Edinburgh, 1660–1760* (Oxford: Clarendon Press, 1994)

W. S. Howell, *Eighteenth-century British Logic and Rhetoric* (Princeton, NJ: Princeton University Press, 1994)

Kenneth Hudson, *A Social History of Museums* (London: Macmillan, 1975)

Pat Hudson, *Britain's Industrial Revolution* (London: Arnold, 1989)

William D. Hudson, *Reason and Right: A Critical Examination of Richard Price's Moral Philosophy* (London: Macmillan, 1970)

C. H. Hull (ed.), *The Economic Writings of Sir William Petty*, 2 vols. (Cambridge: Cambridge University Press, 1899)

Mark Hulliung, *The Autocritique of Enlightenment: Rousseau and the Philosophes* (Cambridge, Mass.: Harvard University Press, 1994)

P. Hulme and L. Jordanova (eds.), *Enlightenment and Its Shadows* (London and New York: Routledge, 1990)

T. E. Hulme, 'Romanticism and Classicism' (1923), in Herbert Read (ed.), *Speculations* (London: Kegan Paul, Trench, Trubner, 1936)

David Hume, *A Treatise of Human Nature*, Ernest C. Mossner (ed.) (Harmondsworth: Penguin, 1969 [1739–40])

——, *A Treatise of Human Nature*, L. A. Selby-Bigge (ed.), 2nd edn revised by Peter H. Nidditch (Oxford: Clarendon Press, 1978 [1739–40])

——, *Philosophical Essays Concerning Human Understanding* (London: A. Millar, 1748)

——, *Essays Moral, Political and Literacy*, T. H. Green and T. H. Grose (eds.), 2 vols. (London: Longman's, Green & Co., 1898 [1741–2])

——, *The Philosophical Works of David Hume*, T. H. Green and T. H. Grose (eds.), 4 vols. (London: Longman's, Green & Co., 1882 [1741–2])

——, *Enquiries concerning Human Understanding and concerning the Principles of Morals*, L. A. Selby-Bigge (ed.) (Oxford: Clarendon Press, 1966 [1748 and 1751])

——, *The History of England Under the House of Tudor*, 6 vols. (London: A. Millar, 1754–62; George Routledge, 1894)

——, *Dialogues concerning Natural Religion*, Norman Kemp Smith (ed.) (Edinburgh: Thomas Nelson, 1947 [1779])

——, *Hume's Dialogues concerning Natural Religion*, Norman Kemp Smith (ed.) (Edinburgh: Thomas Nelson, 1947 [1779])

——, *Selected Essays*, Stephen Copley and Andrew Edgar (eds.) (Oxford: Oxford University Press, 1993)

E. G. Hundert, *The Enlightenment's Fable: Bernard Mandeville and the Discovery of Society* (Cambridge: Cambridge University Press, 1994)

——, 'Performing the Passions in Commercial Society: Bernard Mandeville and the Theatricality of Eighteenth-century Thought', in Kevin Sharpe and Steven N. Zwicker (eds.), *Refiguring Revolutions: Aesthetics and Politics from the English Revolution to the Romantic Revolution* (Berkeley, CA: University of California Press, 1998), 141–72

Lynn Hunt (ed.), *The Invention of Pornography, 1500–1800* (New York: Zone Books, 1993)

Margaret Hunt, Margaret Jacob, Phyllis Mack, and Ruth Perry, *Women and the Enlightenment* (New York: Institute for Research in History, 1984)

Margaret R. Hunt, *The Middling Sort: Commerce, Gender, and the Family in England, 1680–1780* (Berkeley, CA and London: University of California Press, 1996)

Jean E. Hunter, 'The Eighteenth-century Englishwoman: According to the *Gentleman's Magazine*', in Paul Fritz and Richard Morton (eds.), *Women in the Eighteenth Century and Other Essays* (Toronto: Samuel Stevens, Hakkert, 1976), 73–88

Michael Hunter, *Science and Society in Restoration England* (Cambridge: Cambridge University Press, 1981)

——, 'The Problem of "Atheism" in Early Modern England', *Transactions of the Royal Historical Society*, xxxv (1985), 135–57

——, *Establishing the New Science: The Experience of the Early Royal Society* (Woodbridge: Boydell and Brewer, 1989)

——, 'Aikenhead the Atheist: The Context and Consequences of Articulate Irreligion in the Late Seventeenth Century', in Michael Hunter and David Wootton (eds.), *Atheism from the Reformation to the Enlightenment* (Oxford: Clarendon Press, 1992), 221–54

—— (ed.), *Robert Boyle Reconsidered* (Cambridge: Cambridge University Press, 1994)

——, *The Royal Society and Its Fellows 1660–1700: The Morphology of an Early Scientific Institution* (Oxford: Alden Press, 1994)

Richard Hunter and Ida Macalpine, *Three Hundred Years of Psychiatry: 1535–1860* (London: Oxford University Press, 1963)

Christopher Hussey, *English Gardens and Landscapes, 1700–1750* (London: Country Life, 1967)

——, *The Picturesque* (London: F. Cass and Co., 1967)

Francis Hutcheson, *Short View of the Pretended Spirit of Prophecy* (London: Morphew, 1708)

——, *An Inquiry into the Original of Our Ideas of Beauty, Order, Harmony, Design* (London: Darby, 1725; The Hague: Martinus Nijhoff, 1973)

——, *A Short Introduction to Moral Philosophy, in Three Books, Containing the Elements of Ethicks and the Law of Nature* (Glasgow: R. Foulis, 1747)

——, *A System of Moral Philosophy*, 2 vols., ed. by his son (London: R. Foulis, 1755)

——, *Thoughts on Laughter, and Observations on the Fable of the Bees* (Bristol: Thoemmes Reprint, 1989 [1758])

——, *Short View of the Pretended Spirit of Prophecy* (London: Morphew, 1708)

——, *An Historical Essay concerning Witchcraft. With Observations upon Matters of Fact; Tending to Clear the Texts of the Sacred Scriptures, and Confute the Vulgar Errors about That Point, and Also Two Sermons. One in Proof of the Christian Religion; the Other concerning the Good and Evil Angels* (London: R. Knaplock & D. Midwinter, 1718)

Ross Hutchison, *Locke in France (1688–1734)* (Oxford: The Voltaire Foundation, 1991)

Terence Hutchison, *Before Adam Smith: The Emergence of Political Economy, 1662–1776* (Oxford and New York: Blackwell, 1988)

James Hutton, *An Investigation of the Principles of Knowledge, and of the Progress of Reason, from Sense to Science and Philosophy*, 3 vols. (Edinburgh: Strahan and T. Cadell, 1794)

——, *Theory of the Earth*, 2 vols. (Edinburgh: Cadell, Davies and Creech, 1795)

Ronald Hutton, *The Restoration: A Political and Religious History of England and Wales, 1658–1667* (Oxford: Oxford University Press, 1985)

——, *The Rise and Fall of Merry England* (Oxford: Oxford University Press, 1994)

——, *The Stations of the Sun. A History of the Ritual Year in Britain* (Oxford: Oxford University Press, 1996)

William Hutton, *An History of Birmingham*, 3rd edn (Birmingham: Pearson, 1795)

Michael Ignatieff, *A Just Measure of Pain: The Penitentiary in the Industrial Revolution, 1750–1850* (London: Macmillan, 1978)

——, 'John Millar and Individualism', in Istvan Hont and Michael Ignatieff (eds.), *Wealth and Virtue: The Shaping of Political Economy in the Scottish Enlightenment* (Cambridge: Cambridge University Press, 1983), 317–44

R. Iliffe, ' "In the Warehouse": Privacy, Property and Priority in the Early Royal Society', *History of Science*, xxx (1992), 29–62

Mrs Inchbald, *Nature and Art* (London: Robinson, 1796)

Robert Inglesfield, 'Shaftesbury's Influence on Thomson's "Seasons" ', *British Journal for Eighteenth-century Studies*, ix (1986), 141–56

Brian Inglis, *Poverty and the Industrial Revolution* (London: Hodder & Stoughton, 1971)

Allan Ingram, *The Madhouse of Language: Writing and Reading Madness in the Eighteenth Century* (London and New York: Routledge, 1991)

G. Irwin, *Samuel Johnson: A Personality in Conflict* (Auckland: Auckland University Press, 1971)

Malcolm Jack, *Corruption and Progress: The Eighteenth Century Debate* (New York: AMS Press, 1989)

Mark Jackson, *New-Born Child Murder: Women, Illegitimacy and the Courts in Eighteenth-century England* (Manchester and New York: Manchester University Press, 1996)

Margaret C. Jacob, *The Newtonians and the English Revolution, 1689–1720* (Hassocks: Harvester Press, 1976)

——, *The Radical Enlightenment: Pantheists, Freemasons and Republicans* (London: Allen & Unwin, 1981)

——, 'The Crisis of the European Mind: Hazard Revisited', in Phyllis Mack and Margaret Jacob (eds.), *Politics and Culture in Early Modern Europe* (Cambridge: Cambridge University Press, 1987), 251–71

——, *The Cultural Meaning of the Scientific Revolution* (New York: Alfred A. Knopf, 1988)

——, *Living the Enlightenment: Freemasonry and Politics in Eighteenth-century Europe* (New York: Oxford University Press, 1992)

——, 'Reflections on the Ideological Meaning of Western Science from Boyle and Newton to the Postmodernists', *History of Science*, xxxiii (1995), 333–57

——, *Scientific Culture and the Making of the Industrial West* (Oxford: Oxford University Press, 1997)

David L. Jacobson (ed.), *The English Libertarian Heritage: From the Writings of John Trenchard and Thomas Gordon in* The Independent Whig *and* Carto's Letters (Indianapolis, New York, Kansas City: Bobbs-Merrill, 1965).

David L. Jacobson and Ronald Hamowy (eds.), *The English Libertarian Heritage* (San Francisco: Fox and Wilkes, 1994)

Muriel Jaeger, *Before Victoria, Changing Standards and Behaviour 1787–1837* (Harmondsworth: Penguin, 1967)

Patricia James, *Population Malthus: His Life and Times* (London: Routledge and Kegan Paul, 1979)

Lisa Jardine, *Francis Bacon: Discovery and the Art of Discourse* (Cambridge: Cambridge University Press, 1974)

Derek Jarrett, *The Ingenious Mr Hogarth* (London: Joseph, 1976)

Thomas Jarrold, *Dissertations on Man, Philosophical, Physiological and Political; in Answer to Mr Malthus's 'Essay on the Principle of Population'* (London: Cadell and Davis, 1806)

——, *Anthropologia, or Dissertations on the Form and Colour in Man* (London: Cadell and Davis, 1808)

Ricky Jay, *Learned Pigs and Fireproof Women* (New York: Warner Books, 1986)

Geraint H. Jenkins, *The Foundations of Modern Wales: 1642–1780* (Oxford: Clarendon Press; Cardiff: University of Wales Press, 1987)

Philip Jenkins, *The Making of a Ruling Class: The Glamorganshire Gentry 1640–1790* (Cambridge: Cambridge University Press, 1983)

Humphrey Jennings, *Pandaemonium 1660–1886: The Coming of the Machine as Seen by Contemporary Observers*, Mary-Lou Jennings and Charles Madge (eds.) (London: André Deutsch, 1985)

Soame Jenyns, *Free Inquiry into the Nature and Origin of Evil. In Six Letters* (London: R. and J. Dodsley, 1757)

C. B. Jewson, *Jacobin City: A Portrait of Norwich in Its Reaction to the French Revolution 1788–1902* (Glasgow: Blackie, 1975)

Adrian Johns, *The Nature of the Book: Print and Knowledge in the Making* (Chicago: Chicago University Press, 1998)

James William Johnson, *The Formation of English Neo-classical Thought* (Princeton, NJ: Princeton University Press, 1967)

Samuel Johnson, *An Account of the Life of Richard Savage*, 2nd edn (London: Cave, 1748)

——, *A Dictionary of the English Language* (London: Strahan, 1755)

——, *Life Of Gray* (Oxford: Clarendon Press, 1915)

——, *The Lives of the Most Eminent English Poets*, 4 vols., C. H. Firth (ed.) (Oxford: Clarendon Press, 1939 [London: Bathurst, 1781])

——, *The Rambler*, W. J. Bate and Albrecht B. Straus (eds.), 3 vols. (New Haven, Conn.: Yale University Press, 1969 [1750–52])

Clyve Jones (ed.), *Britain in the First Age of Party, 1684–1750* (London: Hambledon, 1987)

Edwin Jones, *The English Nation: The Great Myth* (Stroud: Sutton, 1998)

Howard Mumford Jones, *Revolution and Romanticism* (Cambridge, Mass.: Harvard University Press, 1974)

J. R. Jones (ed.), *The Restored Monarchy, 1660–*

1688 (Totowa, NJ: Rowman & Littlefield, 1979)

—— (ed.), *Liberty Secured? Britain Before and After 1688* (Stanford: Stanford University Press, 1992)

Jean Jones, 'James Hutton's Agricultural Research and His Life as a Farmer', *Annals of Science*, xlii (1985), 573–601

M. G. Jones, *The Charity School Movement* (Cambridge: Cambridge University Press, 1938)

——, *Hannah More* (Cambridge: Cambridge University Press, 1952)

Peter Jones, 'The Scottish Professoriate and the Polite Academy', in Istvan Hont and Michael Ignatieff (eds.), *Wealth and Virtue: The Shaping of Political Economy in the Scottish Enlightenment* (Cambridge: Cambridge University Press, 1983), 89–118

—— (ed.), *Philosophy and Science in the Scottish Enlightenment* (Edinburgh: John Donald Publishers, 1988)

—— (ed.), *The 'Science' of Man in the Scottish Enlightenment: Hume, Reid, and Their Contemporaries* (Edinburgh: Edinburgh University Press, 1989)

R. F. Jones, *Ancients and Moderns: A Study of the Background of the Battle of the Books* (St Louis: Washington University Press, 1936)

Vivien Jones (ed.), *Women in the Eighteenth Century: Constructions of Femininity* (London: Routledge, 1990)

Whitney R. D. Jones, *David Williams: The Hammer and the Anvil* (Cardiff: University of Wales Press, 1986)

W. K. Jordan, *The Development of Religious Toleration in England*, 4 vols. (Cambridge, Mass.: Harvard University Press, 1932–1940; repr. Gloucester, Mass.: Peter Smith, 1965)

Ludmilla Jordanova, 'Natural Facts: A Historical Perspective on Science and Sexuality', in C. MacCormack and M. Strathern (eds.), *Nature, Culture and Gender* (Cambridge: Cambridge University Press, 1980), 42–69

Ludmilla Jordanova, *Nature Depicted* (Harlow: Longman, 1999)

Joseph Juxon, *A Sermon upon Witchcraft: Occasion'd by a Late Illegal Attempt to Discover Witches by Swimming. Preached at Twyford in the County of Leicester, July 11, 1736* (London: H. Woodfall, 1736)

Rana Kabbani, *Europe's Myths of Orient* (Bloomington: Indiana University Press, 1986)

Frank A. Kafker (ed.), *Notable Encyclopedias of the Seventeenth and Eighteenth Centuries: Nine Predecessors of the Encyclopédie* (Oxford: The Voltaire Foundation at The Taylor Institution, 1981)

W. Kaiser, *Praisers Of Folly* (Cambridge, Mass.: Harvard University Press, 1963)

Martin Kallich, *The Association of Ideas and Critical Theory in Eighteenth-century England: A History of a Psychological Method in English Criticism* (The Hague: Mouton, 1970)

Henry Kamen, *The Rise of Toleration* (London: Weidenfeld & Nicolson, 1967)

Henry Home, Lord Kames, *Essays on the Principles of Morality and Natural Religion* (Edinburgh: Felming, 1751)

——, *Elements of Criticism* (Edinburgh: Millar, 1762)

——, *Sketches of the History of Man*, 2 vols. (Edinburgh: W. Creech, 1774)

——, *Historical Law Tracts*, 2 vols., 3rd edn (Edinburgh: Miller, Kincaid and Bell, 1776)

Paul Kaufman, *Borrowings from the Bristol Library, 1773–1784: A Unique Record of Reading Vogues* (Charlottesville, Va: Bibliographical Society of the University of Virginia, 1960)

John Keane, *Tom Paine: A Political Life* (London: Bloomsbury, 1995)

Hugh Kearney, *The British Isles: A History of Four Nations* (Cambridge: Cambridge University Press, 1989)

Patrick J. Kearney, *The Private Case: An Annotated Bibliography of the Private Case Erotica Collection in the British (Museum)*

Library (London: Jay Landesman, 1981)

——, *A History of Erotic Literature* (London: Macmillan, 1982)

Jonathan Keates, *Purcell: A Biography* (London: Chatto & Windus, 1995)

James Keir (ed.), *An Account of the Life and Writings of Thomas Day* (London: Stockdale, 1791)

Gary Kelly, *The English Jacobin Novel, 1780–1805* (Oxford: Clarendon Press, 1976)

——, *Revolutionary Feminism: The Mind and Career of Mary Wollstonecraft* (New York: St Martin's Press, 1992)

——, '(Female) Philosophy in the Bedroom: Mary Wollstonecraft and Female Sexuality', *Women's Writing*, iv (1997), 143–54

James Kelly, *That Damned Thing Called Honour: Duelling in Ireland 1570–1860* (Cork: Cork University Press, 1995)

Patrick Hyde Kelly (ed.), *Locke On Money*, 2 vols. (Oxford: Clarendon Press, 1991)

T. D. Kendrick, *The Lisbon Earthquake* (London: Methuen, 1956)

J. P. Kenyon, *Revolution Principles: The Politics of Party 1689–1720* (Cambridge: Cambridge University Press, 1977)

John Kenyon, *The Popish Plot* (London: Heinemann, 1972)

Charles Kerby-Miller (ed.), *Memoirs of the Extraordinary Life, Works, and Discoveries of Martinus Scriblerus* (Oxford: Oxford University Press, 1988 [1742])

Alvin Kernan, *Printing Technology, Letters and Samuel Johnson* (Princeton, NJ: Princeton University Press, 1987)

Michael Ketcham, *Transparent Designs: Reading, Performance and Form in the Spectator Papers* (Athens, Ga: University of Georgia Press, 1985)

David Kettler, *The Social and Political Thought of Adam Ferguson* (Columbus: Ohio State University Press, 1965)

Geoffrey Keynes (ed.), *The Letters of William Blake* (London: Hart Davis, 1956)

—— (ed.), *Blake: Complete Writings* (London: Oxford University Press, 1969)

V. G. Kiernan, *The Lords of Human Kind* (Harmondsworth: Penguin, 1972)

——, *The Duel in European History: Honour and the Reign of Aristocracy* (Oxford: Oxford University Press, 1989)

Desmond King-Hele, *Doctor of Revolution: The Life and Genius of Erasmus Darwin* (London: Faber & Faber, 1977)

—— (ed.), *The Letters of Erasmus Darwin* (Cambridge: Cambridge University Press, 1981)

——, *Erasmus Darwin and the Romantic Poets* (London: Macmillan, 1986)

——, *Erasmus Darwin: A Life of Unequalled Achievement* (London: DLM, 1999)

Mark Kishlansky, *A Monarchy Transformed: Britain 1603–1714* (Harmondsworth: Penguin, 1996)

Jon Klancher, *The Making of English Reading Audiences, 1790–1832* (Madison: University of Wisconsin Press, 1987)

Lawrence E. Klein, *Shaftesbury and the Culture of Politeness: Moral Discourse and Cultural Politics in Early Eighteenth-century England* (Cambridge: Cambridge University Press, 1994)

——, 'Gender and the Public/Private Distinction in the Eighteenth Century: Some Questions about Evidence and Analytic Procedure', *Eighteenth Century Studies*, xxix (1995), 97–110

F. J. Klingberg, *The Anti-Slavery Movement in England: A Study in English Humanitarianism* (New Haven: Yale University Press, 1926)

Francis D. Klingender, *Art and the Industrial Revolution*, A. Elton (ed.) (London: Evelyn, Adams and Mackay, 1968)

Charlotte Klonk, *Science and the Perception of Nature. British Landscape Art in the Late Eighteenth and Early Nineteenth Centuries* (New Haven and London: Yale University Press, 1996)

Frida Knight, *The Strange Case of Thomas Walker:*

Ten Years in the Life of a Manchester Radical (London: Lawrence and Wishart, 1957)

——, *University Rebel: The Life of William Frend (1756–1841)* (London: Victor Gollancz, 1971)

Richard Payne Knight, *The Progress of Civil Society: A Didactic Poem in Six Books* (London: W. Bulmer and G. Nicol, 1796)

William Knight, *Lord Monboddo and Some of His Contemporaries* (London: John Murray, 1900)

Kevin C. Knox, 'Lunatick Visions: Prophecy, Scientific Public and the Signs of the Times in 1790s London', *History of Science*, xxxvii (1999), 427–58

R. A. Knox, *Enthusiasm: A Chapter in the History of Religion* (London: Clarendon Press, 1950)

Vicesimus Knox, *Liberal Education: or a Practical Treatise on the Methods of Acquiring Useful and Polite Learning*, 10th edn (London: Dilly, 1789 [1781])

Nancy F. Koehn, *The Power of Commerce: Economy and Governance in the First British Empire* (Ithaca, NY: Cornell University Press, 1994)

A. Kors, *D'Holbach's Coterie: An Enlightenment in Paris* (Princeton, NJ: Princeton University Press, 1976)

R. Koselleck, *Critique and Crisis: Enlightenment and the Pathogenesis of Modern Society* (Oxford: Berg, 1988)

August Friedrich Kotzebue, *Lovers' Vows* (London: G. G. Robinson and J. Robinson, 1798)

Isaac Kramnick, *Bolingbroke and His Circle: The Politics of Nostalgia in the Age of Walpole* (Cambridge, Mass.: Harvard University Press, 1968)

——, 'Children's Literature and Bourgeois Ideology: Observations on Culture and Industrial Capitalism in the Later Eighteenth Century', *Studies in Eighteenth-century Culture*, xii (1983), 11–44

——, 'Eighteenth-century Science and Radical Social Theory: The Case of

Joseph Priestley's Scientific Liberalism', *Journal of British Studies*, xxv (1986), 1–30

——, *Republicanism and Bourgeois Radicalism: Political Ideology in Late Eighteenth-century England and America* (Ithaca, NY: Cornell University Press, 1990)

Jonathan Brody Kramnick, *Making the English Canon: Print Capitalism and the Cultural Past, 1700–1770* (Cambridge: Cambridge University Press, 1999)

Robert Kreiser, *Miracles, Convulsions and Ecclesiastical Politics in Early Eighteenth-century Paris* (Princeton, NJ: Princeton University Press, 1978)

L. Krüger, L. Daston and M. Heidelberger (eds.), *The Probabilistic Revolution* (Ann Arbor, MI: University of Michigan Press, 1987)

Elisabeth Labrousse, 'Religious Toleration', in P. P. Wiener (ed.), *Dictionary of the History of Ideas*, 5 vols. (New York: Scribner's, 1974), vol. iv, 112–21

——, *Bayle* (Oxford: Oxford University Press, 1983)

James Lackington, *Memoirs of the First Forty-five Years of the Life of James Lackington*, 7th edn (London: for the author, 1794)

Charles Lamb, 'Witches, and Other Night Fears', *London Magazine* (October 1821), 384

Jonathan Lamb, *Preserving the Self in the South Seas* (Cambridge: Cambridge University press, forthcoming)

Claire Lamont, 'Dr Johnson, the Scottish Highlander, and the Scottish Enlightenment', *British Journal for Eighteenth-century Studies*, xii (1989), 47–56

Stephen K. Land, 'Adam Smith's "Considerations concerning the First Formation of Languages"', *Journal of the History of Ideas*, xxxviii (1977), 677–90

——, *The Philosophy of Language in Britain: Major Theories from Hobbes to Thomas Reid* (New York: ASM Press, 1986)

D. S. Landes, *Revolution in Time: Clocks and the Making of the Modern World* (Cambridge,

Mass.: Harvard University Press, 1983)

Paul Langford, *A Polite and Commercial People: England 1727–1783* (Oxford: Oxford University Press, 1989)

——, *Englishness Identified: Manners and Character 1650–1850* (Oxford: Oxford University Press, 2000)

Thomas Laqueur, 'Bodies, Details, and Humanitarian Narrative', in Lynn Hunt (ed.), *The New Cultural History* (Berkeley, CA: University of California Press, 1989), 176–204

——, '*Amor Veneris, Vel Dulcedo Appelatur*', in M. Feher (ed.), *Fragments for a History of the Human Body*, iii (New York: Zone, 1989), 91–131

——, *Making Sex. Gender and the Body from Aristotle to Freud* (Cambridge, Mass.: Harvard University Press, 1990)

Peter Laslett, 'The English Revolution and Locke's *Two Treatises of Government*', *Cambridge Historical Journal*, xii (1956), 40–55

Anne Laurence, *Women in England 1500–1760: A Social History* (London: Weidenfeld & Nicolson, 1994)

John Christian Laursen and Cary J. Nederman (eds.), *Beyond the Persecuting Society* (Philadelphia, PA: University of Pennsylvania Press, 1998)

Edmund Law, *Considerations on the State of the World, with Regard to the Theory of Religion* (Cambridge: Bentham, 1745)

William Law, *The Absolute Unlawfulness of the Stage Entertainment Fully Demonstrated* (London: William Innys, 1726)

——, *A Serious Call to a Devout and Holy Life* (London: William Innys, 1729)

C. J. Lawrence, 'William Buchan: Medicine Laid Open', *Medical History*, xix (1975), 20–35

John Lawson and Harold Silver, *A Social History of Education in England* (London: Methuen, 1973)

F. R. Leavis (ed.), *Mill on Bentham and Coleridge* (London: Chatto & Windus, 1962)

W. E. H. Lecky, *A History of Ireland in the Eighteenth Century*, L. P. Curtis, Jr (abridge. and intro.) (Chicago: University of Chicago Press, 1972)

William Lee, *Daniel Defoe: His Life and Recently Discovered Writings*, 3 vols. (London: John Camden Hotten, 1869)

William C. Lehmann, *Adam Ferguson and the Beginnings of Modern Sociology* (New York: Columbia University Press, 1930)

——, *John Millar of Glasgow, 1735–1801: His Life and Thought and His Contributions to Sociological Analysis* (Cambridge: Cambridge University Press, 1960)

——, *Henry Home, Lord Kames, and the Scottish Enlightenment: A Study in National Character and the History of Ideas* (The Hague: Nijhoff, 1971)

Keith Lehrer, *Thomas Reid* (London: Routledge, 1989)

John Leland, *A View of the Principal Deistical Writers that Have Appeared in England in the Last and Present Century* (London: Dodsley, 1754)

Charlotte Lennox, *The Female Quixote, or the Adventures of Arabella*, 2 vols. (London: A. Millar, 1752; Oxford: Oxford University Press, 1989)

[Charles Leslie], *The Charge of Socinianism against Dr Tillotson Considered, By a True Son of the Church* (Edinburgh: sn, 1695)

Charles Leslie, *A Short and Easy Method with the Deists* (London: Onley, 1698)

C. R. Leslie, *Memoirs of the Life of John Constable* (London: John Lehmann, 1949)

Margaret Leslie, 'Mysticism Misunderstood: David Hartley and the Idea of Progress', *Journal of the History of Ideas*, xxxiii (1972), 625–32

W. L. Letwin, *The Origins of Scientific Economics* (London: Methuen, 1963)

Joseph M. Levine, *The Battle of the Books: History and Literature in the Augustan Age* (Ithaca, NY: Cornell University Press, 1992)

W. S. Lewis (ed.), *The Correspondence of Horace*

Walpole, 48 vols. (New Haven, Conn.: Yale University Press, 1961)

——— (ed.), *The Yale Edition of Horace Walpole's Correspondence*, 48 vols. (London: Oxford University Press, 1937–83)

David Lieberman, 'The Legal Needs of a Commercial Society: The Jurisprudence of Lord Kames', in Istvan Hont and Michael Ignatieff (eds.), *Wealth and Virtue: The Shaping of Political Economy in the Scottish Enlightenment* (Cambridge: Cambridge University Press, 1983), 203–34

———, *The Province of Legislation Determined: Legal Theory in Eighteenth-century Britain* (Cambridge: Cambridge University Press, 1989)

Bryant Lillywhite, *London Coffee Houses: A Reference Book of Coffee Houses of the Seventeenth, Eighteenth and Nineteenth Centuries* (London: Allen & Unwin, 1963)

Anthony Hadley Lincoln, *Some Political and Social Ideas of English Dissent, 1763–1800* (Cambridge: Cambridge University Press, 1938)

Jack Lindsay, *William Blake: His Life and Work* (London: Constable, 1978)

Peter Linebaugh, *The London Hanged: Crime and Civil Society in the Eighteenth Century* (London: Allen Lane, 1991)

Luther Link, *The Devil: A Mask without a Face* (London: Reaktion Books, 1995)

Louise Lippincott, *Selling Art in Georgian London: The Rise of Arthur Pond* (New Haven, Conn.: Yale University Press, 1983)

Nigel Llewellyn, *The Art of Death: Visual Culture In the English Death Ritual* c. *1500–c. 1800* (London: Victoria and Albert Museum, 1991)

Sarah Lloyd, ' "Pleasure's Golden Bait": Prostitution, Poverty and the Magdalen Hospital', *History Workshop Journal*, xli (1996), 51–72

Don Locke, *A Fantasy of Reason: The Life and Thought of William Godwin* (London: Routledge & Kegan Paul, 1980)

John Locke, *An Essay concerning Human Understanding*, Peter H. Nidditch (ed.) (Oxford: Clarendon Press, 1975 [1690])

———, *Two Treatises of Government*, Peter Laslett (ed.) (Cambridge: Cambridge University Press, 1988 [1690])

———, *Some Thoughts Concerning Education*, R. H. Quick (ed.) (London: sn, 1899 [1693])

———, *The Reasonableness of Christianity* (London: Awnsham and John Churchill, 1695)

———, *A Letter to . . . Edward [Stillingfleet], Ld Bishop of Worcester . . .* (London: Churchill, 1697)

———, *The Philosophical Works of John Locke*, J. A. St John (ed.), 2 vols. (London: George Bell & Sons, 1905)

R. Longrigg, *The English Squire and His Sport* (London: Michael Joseph, 1977)

Roger Lonsdale (ed.), *The New Oxford Book of Eighteenth-century Verse* (Oxford: Oxford University Press, 1984)

——— (ed.), *Eighteenth-century Women Poets* (Oxford: Oxford University Press, 1989)

J. C. Loudon, *The Suburban Gardener and Villa Companion* (London: for the author, 1838)

A. O. Lovejoy, *The Great Chain of Being* (Cambridge, Mass.: Harvard University Press, 1936)

Robert Lowth, *Lectures on the Sacred Poetry of the Hebrews* (London: Johnson, 1787)

F. L. Lucas, *The Search for Good Sense* (London: Cassell, 1958)

———, *The Art of Living* (London: Cassell, 1959)

John Lucas, *England and Englishness: Ideas of Nationhood in English Poetry 1688–1900* (London: The Hogarth Press, 1990)

Roger D. Lund, 'Martinus Scriblerus and the Search for a Soul', *Papers in Literature and Language*, xxv (1989), 135–90

J. O. Lyons, *The Invention of the Self* (Carbondale, Ill.: Southern Illinois University Press, 1978)

Catharine Macauly, *Letters on Education* (London: C. Dilly, 1790)

Iain McCalman: 'Mad Lord George and Madame La Motte: Riot and Sexuality in the Genesis of Burke's *Reflections on the Revolution in France*', *Journal of British Studies*, xxxv (1996), 343–67

——, 'New Jerusalems: Prophecy, Dissent, and Radical Culture in England, 1786–1830', in Knud Haakonssen (ed.), *Enlightenment and Religion: Rational Dissent in Eighteenth-century Britain* (Cambridge: Cambridge University Press, 1997), 312–35

Donald McCormick, *The Hell-Fire Club: The Story of the Amorous Knights of Wycombe* (Norwich: Jarrold, 1958)

Colleen McDannell and Bernhard Lang, *Heaven – A History* (New Haven and London: Yale University Press, 1988)

Michael MacDonald, 'The Secularization of Suicide in England, 1600–1800', *Past and Present*, cxi (1986), 50–100

Michael MacDonald and Terence R. Murphy, *Sleepless Souls: Suicide in Early Modern England* (Oxford: Clarendon Press, 1990)

Paula McDowell, *The Women of Grub Street: Press, Politics and Gender in the London Literary Marketplace, 1678–1730* (Oxford: Clarendon Press, 1998)

David Dunbar McElroy, *Scotland's Age of Improvement: A Survey of Eighteenth-century Literary Clubs and Societies* (Washington: Washington State University Press, 1969)

G. McEwen, *The Oracle of the Coffee House: John Dunton's Athenian Mercury* (San Marino, CA: The Huntingdon Library, 1972)

Alan Macfarlane, *The Culture of Capitalism* (Oxford: Basil Blackwell, 1987)

A. McInnes, 'The Emergence of a Leisure Town: Shrewsbury, 1660–1760', *Past and Present*, cxx (1968), 53–87

Carey McIntosh, *The Evolution of English Prose, 1700–1800: Style, Politeness and Print Culture* (Cambridge: Cambridge University Press, 1999)

Alasdair MacIntyre, *A Short History of Ethics* (London: Routledge and Kegan Paul, 1967)

Mary P. Mack, *Jeremy Bentham, An Odyssey of Ideas, 1748–1792* (London: Heinemann, 1962)

Phyllis Mack, 'Women and the Enlightenment: Introduction', *Women & History*, xiv (1984), 1–11

Neil McKendrick, 'Josiah Wedgwood and Factory Discipline', *The Historical Journal*, iv (1961), 30–55

——, 'Introduction. The Birth of a Consumer Society: The Commercialization of Eighteenth-century England', in Neil McKendrick, John Brewer and J. H. Plumb, *The Birth of a Consumer Society: The Commercialization of Eighteenth-century England* (London: Europa, 1982), 1–8

Neil McKendrick, John Brewer and J. H. Plumb, *The Birth of a Consumer Society: The Commercialization of Eighteenth-century England* (London: Europa, 1982)

Henry Mackenzie, *Julia de Roubigné* (London: W. Strahan and T. Cadell, 1777)

——, *The Mirror*, 3 vols. (Edinburgh: William Creech, 1779–80)

Michael McKeon, *The Origins of the English Novel, 1600–1740* (Baltimore: Johns Hopkins University Press, 1987)

Eric David Mackerness, *A Social History of English Music* (London: Routledge & Kegan Paul, 1964)

Erin Mackie, *Market à la Mode: Fashion, Commodity, and Gender in The Tatler and The Spectator* (Baltimore: Johns Hopkins University Press, 1997)

H. McLachlan, *English Education under the Test Acts: Being the History of Non-Conformist Academies 1662–1820* (Manchester: Manchester University Press, 1931)

——, *The Unitarian Movement in the Religious Life of England* (London: George Allen and Unwin, 1931)

——, *Warrington Academy, Its History and Influence* (Manchester: Chetham Society, 1943)

Catherine Macdonald Maclean, *Born under*

Saturn: A Biography of William Hazlitt (London: Collins, 1943)

Kenneth MacLean, *John Locke and English Literature of the Eighteenth Century* (New Haven, Conn.: Yale University Press, 1936)

Marie P. McMahon, *The Radical Whigs, John Trenchard and Thomas Gordon* (Lanham, Md.: University Press of America, 1990)

John McManners, *Death and the Enlightenment* (Oxford: Clarendon Press, 1981)

Joseph McMinn, *Jonathan's Travels: Swift and Ireland* (Belfast: Appletree Press, 1994)

Maureen McNeil, *Under the Banner of Science: Erasmus Darwin and His Age* (Manchester: Manchester University Press, 1987)

C. B. Macpherson, *The Political Theory of Possessive Individualism: Hobbes to Locke* (Oxford: Clarendon Press, 1964)

——, *Democratic Theory: Essays in Retrieval* (Oxford: Oxford University Press, 1973)

James Macpherson, *Fragments of Ancient Poetry Collected in the Highlands of Scotland* (Edinburgh: Hamilton and Balfour, 1760)

——, *Fingal* (London: Becket and De Hondt, 1762)

——, *Temora* (London: Becket and De Hondt, 1763)

Samuel Madden, *Memoirs of the Twentieth Century* (London: Osborn and Longman, 1733)

M. Mahl and H. Koon (eds.), *The Female Spectator: English Women Writers Before 1800* (Bloomington, Ind.: University of Indiana Press, 1977)

Brian Maidment, *Popular Prints, 1790–1870: Reading Popular Graphic Images* (Manchester: Manchester University Press, 1995)

R. W. Malcolmson, *Popular Recreations in English Society, 1700–1850* (Cambridge: Cambridge University Press, 1973)

Thomas Robert Malthus, *An Essay on the Principle of Population as It Affects the Future Improvement of Society, With Remarks on the Speculations of Mr Godwin, M. Condorcet, And Other Writers* (London: J. Johnson, 1798; facsimile repr., London: Macmillan, 1966)

——, *An Essay on the Principle of Population*, 2nd edn (London: J. Johnson, 1803)

Bernard de Mandeville, *The Virgin Unmask'd* (London: Morphew, 1709)

——, *A Modest Defence of the Public Stews; or An Essay Upon Whoring* (London: A. Moore, 1724)

——, *The Fable of the Bees: Or, Private Vices, Publick Benefits*, with a Commentary Critical, Historical, and Explanatory by F. B. Kaye, 2 vols. (Oxford: Clarendon Press, 1924 [London: J. Roberts, 1714])

Robert Mandrou, *Magistrats et sorciers en France au XVIIe siècle: une analyse de psychologie historique* (Paris: Plon, 1968)

Karl Mannheim, *Ideology and Utopia* (New York: Harcourt Brace, 1936)

D. J. Manning, *The Mind of Jeremy Bentham* (London: Longman, 1968)

Susan Manning, 'Boswell's Pleasures, the Pleasures of Boswell', *British Journal for Eighteenth Century Studies*, xx (1997), 17–31

Frank E. Manuel, *The Eighteenth Century Confronts the Gods* (New York: Athenaeum, 1967)

——, *Isaac Newton, Historian* (Cambridge, Mass.: Harvard University Press, 1963)

——, *The Religion of Isaac Newton* (Oxford: Clarendon Press, 1974)

——, *A Portrait of Isaac Newton* (Cambridge, Mass.: Harvard University Press, 1968)

L. A. Marchand (ed.), *Byron's Letters and Journals*, 12 vols. (London: John Murray, 1973–82)

Robert Markley, *Fallen Languages: Crises of Representation in Newtonian England, 1660–1740* (Ithaca, NY: Cornell University Press, 1993)

George S. Marr, *The Periodical Essayists of the Eighteenth Century* (New York: Augustus M. Kelley, 1971)

David Marshall, 'Arguing by Analogy: Hume's Standard of Taste', *Eighteenth-century Studies*, xxviii (1995), 323–43

John Marshall, *John Locke; Resistance, Religion*

and Responsibility (Cambridge: Cambridge University Press, 1994)

Peter Marshall (ed.), *The British Discovery of Hinduism in the Eighteenth Century* (Cambridge: Cambridge University Press, 1970)

Peter Marshall and Glyndyr Williams, *The Great Map of Mankind: British Perceptions of the World in the Age of Enlightenment* (London: Dent, 1982)

Peter H. Marshall, *William Godwin* (New Haven, Conn.: Yale University Press, 1984)

Tim Marshall, *Murdering to Dissect: Grave-robbing, Frankenstein and the Anatomy of Literature* (Manchester: Manchester University Press, 1995)

Joanna Martin (ed.), *A Governess in the Age of Jane Austen* (London: Hambledon Press, 1988)

Peter Martin, *A Life of James Boswell* (London: Weidenfeld & Nicolson, 1999)

Michael Mascuch, *Origins of the Individualist Self. Autobiography and Self-identity in England 1591–1791* (Cambridge: Polity Press, 1997)

Haydn T. Mason (ed.), *The Darnton Debate: Books and Revolution in the Eighteenth Century* (Oxford: Voltaire Foundation, 1998)

Michael Mason, *The Making of Victorian Sexual Attitudes* (Oxford: Oxford University Press, 1994)

T. J. Mathias, *The Pursuits of Literature, Or What You Will: A Satirical Poem*, 4 parts (London: J. Owen, 1794)

Robert Mauzi, *L'Idée du bonheur dans la littérature et la pensée française au XVIII siècle* (Paris: Colin, 1960)

Constantia Maxwell, *Dublin under the Georges, 1714–1830* (London: George G. Harrap, 1946)

Henry F. May, *The Enlightenment in America* (New York: Oxford University Press, 1976)

Robert D. Mayo, *The English Novels in the Magazines, 1740–1815* (Evanston, Ill.: Northwestern University Press, 1962)

B. Mazlish, *James and John Stuart Mill: Father and Son in the Nineteenth Century* (London: Hutchinson, 1975)

Jon Mee, *Dangerous Enthusiasm: William Blake and the Culture of Radicalism in the 1790s* (Oxford: Clarendon Press, 1992)

Ronald L. Meek, 'Smith, Turgot and the Four Stages Theory', *History of Political Economy*, iii (1971), 9–27

—— (ed.), *Precursors of Adam Smith* (London: Dent, 1973)

——, *Social Science and the Ignoble Savage* (Cambridge: Cambridge University Press, 1975)

T. K. Meier, *Defoe and the Defense of Commerce* (Victoria, BC: English Literary Studies, University of Victoria, 1987)

Anne K. Mellor, 'British Romanticism, Gender, and Three Women Artists', in Ann Bermingham and John Brewer (eds.), *The Consumption of Culture, 1600–1800: Image, Object, Text in the 17th and 18th Centuries* (London: Routledge, 1995), 121–42

Sara Mendelson and Patricia Crawford, *Women in Early Modern England* (Oxford: Clarendon Press, 1998)

Stephen Mennell, *Norbert Elias: Civilization and the Human Self-image* (Oxford: Basil Blackwell, 1989)

Carolyn Merchant, *The Death of Nature: Women, Ecology and the Scientific Revolution* (San Francisco: Harper and Row, 1980)

Gerald Dennis Meyer, *The Scientific Lady in England, 1650–1760: An Account of Her Rise, with Emphasis on the Major Roles of the Telescope and Microscope* (Berkeley, CA: University of California Press, 1955)

Conyers Middleton, *Letter from Rome* (London: W. Innys, 1729)

——, *Free Enquiry into the Miraculous Powers Which are Supposed to Have Subsisted in the Christian Church from the Earliest Ages* (London: Manby and Cox, 1749)

Dudley Miles, *Francis Place 1771–1854: The Life of a Remarkable Radical* (Brighton: Harvester, 1988)

James Mill, *Essay on Government* (London: Innes, 1824)

John Stuart Mill, *On Liberty* (London: Parker, 1859)

John Millar, *Observations concerning the Distinction of Ranks in Society* (London: Richardson, 1771)

John R. Millburn, *Benjamin Martin: Author, Instrument-maker and Country-showman* (Noordhoff: Leyden, 1976)

Edward Miller, *That Noble Cabinet: A History of the British Museum* (London: André Deutsch, 1973)

G. Miller, *The Adoption of Inoculation for Smallpox in England and France* (London: Oxford University Press, 1957)

James Miller, *The Man of Taste* (Dublin: Hoey, 1735)

John Miller, *Popery and Politics in England 1660–1688* (Cambridge: Cambridge University Press, 1973)

Peter N. Miller (ed.), *Joseph Priestley: Political Writings* (Cambridge: Cambridge University Press, 1993)

A. Taylor Milne (ed.), *The Correspondence of Jeremy Bentham* (London: Athlone, 1981)

John Milton, *Paradise Lost* (London: Parker, 1667)

——, *Of Education* (London: Underhill, 1644)

G. E. Mingay, *English Landed Society in the Eighteenth Century* (London: Routledge & Kegan Paul, 1963)

—— (ed.), *Arthur Young and His Times* (London: Macmillan, 1975)

——, *A Social History of the English Countryside* (London: Routledge, 1990)

George Minois, *History of Suicide: Voluntary Death in Western Culture* (Baltimore: Johns Hopkins University Press, 1999)

Samuel I. Mintz, *The Hunting of Leviathan* (Cambridge: Cambridge University Press, 1962)

Henri Misson, *Memoirs and Observations in His Travels over England* (London: Browne, 1719)

L. G. Mitchell (ed.), *The Writings and Speeches of Edmund Burke*, viii (Oxford: Clarendon Press, 1989)

James Burnett, Lord Monboddo, *Of the Origin and Progress of Language*, 6 vols. (Edinburgh: Kincaid; London: T. Cadell, 1773–92; repr. New York: Garland, 1970)

John Money, 'Public Opinion in the West Midlands, 1760–1793' (PhD thesis, Cambridge University, 1967)

——, 'Taverns, Coffee Houses and Clubs: Local Politics and Popular Articulacy in the Birmingham Area in the Age of the American Revolution', *The Historical Journal*, xiv (1971), 15–47

——, *Experience and Identity: Birmingham and the West Midlands, 1760–1800* (Manchester: Manchester University Press, 1977)

——, 'Birmingham and the West Midlands 1760–1793: Politics and Regional Identity in the English Provinces in the Later Eighteenth Century', in Peter Borsay (ed.), *The Eighteenth-century Town: A Reader in English Urban History 1688–1820* (London: Longman, 1990), 292–314

——, 'Freemasonry and the Fabric of Loyalism in Hanoverian England', in Eckhart Hellmuth (ed.), *The Transformation of Political Culture* (London: Oxford University Press, 1990), 235–74

——, 'Teaching in the Market-Place, or "Caesar adsum jam forte; Pompey aderat": The Retailing of Knowledge on Provincial England during the Eighteenth Century', in John Brewer and Roy Porter (eds.), *Consumption and the World of Goods in the Seventeenth and Eighteenth Centuries* (London: Routledge, 1993), 335–79

Samuel H. Monk, *The Sublime: A Study of Critical Theories in Eighteenth Century England* (Ann Arbor, MI: University of Michigan Press, 1960)

Paul Kleber Monod, *Jacobitism and the English*

People, 1688–1788 (Cambridge: Cambridge University Press, 1989)

John Monro, *Remarks on Dr Battie's Treatise on Madness*, intro. by R. Hunter and I. Macalpine (London: Dawsons, 1962 [1758])

Lady Mary Wortley Montagu, *Letters and Works*, 3rd edn (London: Henry Bohn, 1861)

Montesquieu, *De l'Esprit des lois* (1748; published as *The Spirit of Laws*, T. Nugent (trans.), 2 vols. (London: J. Nourse and P. Vallant, 1750)

Emily Lorraine de Montluzin, *The Anti-Jacobins 1798–1800: The Early Contributors to the Anti-Jacobin Review* (New York: St Martin's Press, 1988)

D. Moore (ed.), *Wales in the Eighteenth Century* (Swansea: C. Davies, 1976)

Jonas Moore, *The History or Narrative of the Great Level of the Fenns, Called Bedford Level* (London: Moses Pitt, 1685)

Hannah More, *Essays on Various Subjects, Principally Designed for Young Ladies* (London: J. Wilkie and T. Cadell, 1778)

——, *An Estimate of the Religion of the Fashionable World*, 3rd edn (Dublin: Wogan, 1791)

——, *Village Politics. Addressed to all the Mechanics, Journeymen, and Day Labourers, in Great Britain. By Will Chip, a Country Carpenter* (London: Rivington, 1793)

——, *The Riot; or Half a Loaf is Better than No Bread* (London: J. Marshall, 1795)

——, *Strictures on the Modern System of Female Education*, 2 vols. (London: Cadell and Davies, 1799; repr. with intro. by Gina Luria, New York: Garland, 1974)

——, *History of Mr Fantom the New-Fashioned Philosopher* (London: J. Binns, 1805)

Carl Philip Moritz, *Journeys of a German in England: A Walking-tour of England in 1782*, Reginald Nettel (trans. and intro.) (London: Eland Books, 1982 [1783])

Arthur D. Morris, *James Parkinson, His Life and Times* (Boston: Birkhauser, 1989)

Stanley Morrison, *John Bell (1745–1831)*

(Cambridge: Cambridge University Press, 1930)

Katharine M. Morsberger, 'John Locke's *An Essay Concerning Human Understanding*: The "Bible" of the Enlightenment', *Studies in Eighteenth Century Culture*, xxv (1996), 1–19

Ornella Moscucci, *The Science of Woman: Gynaecology and Gender in England, 1800–1929* (Cambridge and New York: Cambridge University Press, 1990)

Ernest Campbell Mossner, *The Life of David Hume* (Oxford: Clarendon Press, 1954)

——, 'The Religion of David Hume', in John W. Yolton (ed.), *Philosophy, Religion and Science in the Seventeenth and Eighteenth Centuries* (Rochester, NY: University of Rochester Press, 1990), 111–21

——, *Bishop Butler and the Age of Reason* (Bristol: Thoemmes, 1990)

R. Muchembled, *Popular Culture and Elite Culture in France, 1400–1750*, L. Cochrane (trans.) (Baton Rouge, La: Louisiana State University Press, 1978; 1985)

Chandra Mukerji, *From Graven Images: Patterns of Modern Materialism* (New York: Columbia University Press, 1983)

Hoh-cheung Mui and Lorna H. Mui, *Shops and Shopkeeping in Eighteenth-century England* (London: Methuen, 1989)

John Mullan, *Sentiment and Sociability: The Language of Feeling in the Eighteenth Century* (Oxford: Clarendon Press, 1988)

Penelope Murray (ed.), *Genius: The History of an Idea* (Oxford: Basil Blackwell, 1989)

A. E. Musson and Eric Robinson, *Science and Technology in the Industrial Revolution* (Manchester: Manchester University Press, 1969)

Mitzi Myers, 'Shot from Canons; or, Maria Edgeworth and the Cultural Production and Consumption of the Eighteenth-century Woman Writer', in Ann Bermingham and John Brewer (eds.), *The Consumption of Culture, 1600–1800: Image, Object, Text* (London: Routledge, 1995), 193–216

Sylvia Harcstark Myers, *The Bluestocking Circle: Women, Friendship, and the Life of the Mind in Eighteenth-century England* (Oxford: Clarendon Press, 1990)

Benjamin Christie Nangle, *The Monthly Review: First Series, 1749–1789 (Second Series, 1790–1815); Indexes of Contributors and Articles*, 2 vols. (Oxford: Clarendon Press, 1934–5)

Stanley D. Nash, 'Social Attitudes towards Prostitution in London, from 1752 to 1829' (PhD thesis, New York University, 1980)

S. Nash, 'Prostitution and Charity: The Magdalen Hospital, a Case Study', *Journal of Social History*, xvii (1984), 617–28

J. M. Neeson, *Commoners: Common Right, Enclosure and Social Change in England, 1700–1820* (Cambridge: Cambridge University Press, 1993)

Victor Neuberg, *The Penny Histories: A Study of Chapbooks for Young Readers over Two Centuries* (London: Oxford University Press, 1968)

——, *Popular Education in Eighteenth-century England* (London: Welbourn Press, 1971)

——, *Popular Literature: A History and Guide from the Beginning of Printing to the Year 1897* (Harmondsworth: Penguin, 1977)

Gerald Newman, *The Rise of English Nationalism: A Cultural History, 1740–1830* (New York: St Martin's Press, 1987)

Isaac Newton, *Opticks, or A Treatise of the Reflexions, Refractions, Inflections & Colours of Light* (London: Smith and Walford, 1704; London: William and John Innys, 1721)

——, *Mathematical Principles of Natural Philosophy*, 2 vols., Florian Cajori (trans.) (Berkeley, CA: University of California Press, 1962 [1687])

Michael Newton, 'The Child of Nature: The Feral Child and the State of Nature' (PhD thesis, University College London, 1996)

John Nichols, *Literary Anecdotes of the Eighteenth Century* (London, for the author, 1812; Colin Clair Fontwell (ed.), Sussex: Centaur Press, 1967)

Colin Nicholson, *Writing and the Rise of Finance: Capital Satires of the Early Eighteenth Century* (Cambridge: Cambridge University Press, 1994)

Benedict Nicolson, *Joseph Wright of Derby: Painter of Light*, 2 vols. (London: Paul Mellon Foundation for British Art, 1968)

Marjorie Hope Nicolson, 'The Early Stage of Cartesianism in England', *Studies in Philology*, xxvi (1929), 356–75

——, *Newton Demands the Muse: Newton's Opticks and the Eighteenth-century Poets* (Princeton, NJ: Princeton University Press, 1946)

——, *Mountain Gloom and Mountain Glory: The Development of the Aesthetics of the Infinite* (Ithaca, NY: Cornell University Press, 1959)

——, *The Breaking of the Circle: Studies in the Effect of the 'New Science' upon Seventeenth-century Poetry* (New York: Columbia University Press, 1960)

Robert Nisbet, *History of the Idea of Progress* (New York: Basic Books, 1980)

David Nokes, *Jonathan Swift: A Hypocrite Reversed: A Critical Biography* (Oxford: Oxford University Press, 1985)

Christopher Norris, ' "What is Enlightenment?": Kant and Foucault', in Gary Gutting (ed.), *The Cambridge Companion to Foucault* (Cambridge: Cambridge University Press, 1994), 159–96

Dudley North, *Discourses Upon Trade* (London: Bassett, 1691); repr. in J. R. McCulloch (ed.), *Early English Tracts on Commerce* (Cambridge: Economic History Society Reprint, 1952)

H. North, *Sophrosyne: Self-knowledge and Self-restraint in Greek Literature* (Ithaca, NY: Cornell University Press, 1966)

J. E. Norton (ed.), *The Letters of Edward Gibbon*, 3 vols. (London: Cassell, 1956)

Rictor Norton, *Mother Clap's Molly House: The Gay Subculture in England 1700–1830* (London: Gay Men's Press, 1992)

Robert E. Norton, *The Beautiful Soul: Aesthetic Morality in the Eighteenth Century* (Ithaca, NY: Cornell University Press, 1995)

Felicity A. Nussbaum, *The Brink of All We Hate: English Satires on Women 1660–1750* (Lexington, Ken.: University Press of Kentucky, 1984)

——, *The Autobiographical Subject: Gender and Ideology in Eighteenth-century England* (Baltimore: Johns Hopkins University Press, 1989)

——, 'Polygamy, *Pamela*, and the Prerogative of Empire', in Ann Bermingham and John Brewer (eds.), *The Consumption of Culture, 1600–1800: Image, Object, Text* (London: Routledge, 1995), 217–36

Barbara Bowen Oberg, 'David Hartley and the Association of Ideas', *Journal of the History of Ideas*, xxxvii (1976), 441–54

Karen O'Brien, 'Between Enlightenment and Stadial Theory: William Robertson on the History of Europe', *British Journal for Eighteenth Century Studies*, xvi (1994), 53–63

——, *Narratives of Enlightenment: Cosmopolitan History from Voltaire to Gibbon* (Cambridge: Cambridge University Press, 1997)

Miles Ogborn, *Spaces of Modernity: London's Geographies, 1680–1780* (New York: The Guilford Press, 1998)

James O'Higgins, *Anthony Collins: The Man and His Works* (The Hague: Nijjoff, 1970)

Laird Okie, *Augustan Historical Writing. Histories of England in the English Enlightenment* (Lanham, Md: University Press of America, 1992)

Richard Olson, *The Emergence of the Social Sciences, 1642–1792* (New York: Twayne, 1993)

——, *Science Deified and Science Defied. The Historical Significance of Science in Western Culture*, vol. ii: *From the Early Modern Age Through the Early Romantic Era ca. 1640 to ca. 1820* (Berkeley, CA: University of California Press, 1990)

Walter J. Ong, *Orality and Literacy: The Technologizing of the Word* (London: Methuen, 1982)

Harold Orel, *English Romantic Poets and the Enlightenment* (Banbury: The Voltaire Foundation, 1973)

Dorinda Outram, *The Enlightenment* (Cambridge: Cambridge University Press, 1995)

D. Owen, *English Philanthropy, 1660–1960* (Cambridge, Mass.: Harvard University Press, 1965)

Robert Owen, *The Book of the New Moral World* (London: Wilson, 1836)

——, *A New View of Society* (London: Cadell and Davies, 1813)

——, *Observations on the Effect of the Manufacturing System* (London: R. Taylor, 1815)

——, *Report to the County of Lanark; A New View of Society*, V. A. C. Gatrell (ed.) (Harmondsworth: Penguin, 1969)

G. W. Oxley, *Poor Relief in England and Wales 1601–1834* (Newton Abbot: David & Charles, 1974)

Fania Oz-Salzberger, *Translating the Enlightenment: Scottish Civic Discourse in Eighteenth Century Germany* (Oxford: Clarendon Press, 1995)

Anthony Pagden, *Lords of All the World: Ideologies of Empire in Spain, Britain and France c. 1500–c. 1800* (New Haven, Conn.: Yale University Press, 1995)

Anthony Page, 'Enlightenment and a "Second Reformation": The Religion and Philosophy of John Jebb (1736–86)', *Enlightenment and Dissent*, xvii (1998), 48–82

Thomas Paine, *Agrarian Justice* (London: Adlard, 1797)

——, *The Complete Writings of Thomas Paine*, Philip S. Foner (ed.), 2 vols. (New York: Citadel Press, 1945)

——, *The Rights of Man*, Henry Collins (ed.) (Harmondsworth: Penguin, 1969 [1791])

Morton D. Paley, *Energy and the Imagination: The Development of Blake's Thought* (Oxford: Clarendon Press, 1970)

William Paley, *The Principles of Moral and Political Philosophy* (London: Faulder, 1785)

——, *Reasons for Contentment Addressed to the Labouring Part of the British Public* (London: Faulder, 1802)

——, *The Complete Works of William Paley* (London: Dove, 1824)

James Parkinson, *The Way to Health, Extracted from the Villager's Friend and Physician* (Broadside, 1802)

——, *The Villager's Friend and Physician, or a Familiar Address on the Preservation of Health and the Removal of Disease on its First Appearance, Supposed to be Delivered by a Village Apothecary, with Cursory Observations on the Treatment of Children, on Sobriety, Industry, etc., intended for the Promotion of Domestic Happiness*, 2nd edn (London: C. Whittingham, 1804)

W. Ll. Parry-Jones, *The Trade in Lunacy: A Study of Private Mad-houses in England in the Eighteenth and Nineteenth Centuries* (London: Routledge and Kegan Paul, 1972)

Anthony Pasquin [pseud.], *Memoirs of the Royal Academicians* (London: Symonds, 1796)

J. A. Passmore, *Priestley's Writings on Philosophy, Science and Politics* (London: Collier Macmillan, 1965)

——, 'The Malleability of Man in Eighteenth-century Thought', in E. R. Wasserman (ed.), *Aspects of the Eighteenth Century* (Baltimore: Johns Hopkins University Press, 1965), 21–46

——, *The Perfectibility of Man* (London: Duckworth, 1970)

——, *Man's Responsibility for Nature* (London: Duckworth, 1980)

Carole Pateman, *The Sexual Contract* (Cambridge: Polity Press, 1988)

Douglas Patey, 'Swift's Satire on ' "Science" ' and the Structure of *Gulliver's Travels*', *English Literary History*, lviii (1991), 809–33

Lewis Patton and Peter Mann (eds.), *The Collected Works of Samuel Taylor Coleridge* (London: Routledge and Kegan Paul, 1971)

Ronald Paulson, *Hogarth: His Life, Art and Times* (New Haven, Conn.: Yale University Press, 1974)

——, *Representations of Revolution (1789–1820)* (New Haven, Conn.: Yale University Press, 1983)

——, *Hogarth, The 'Modern Moral Subject'*: vol. iii: *Art and Politics, 1750–64* (Cambridge: Lutterworth Press, 1992–3)

William R. Paulson, *Enlightenment, Romanticism and the Blind in France* (Princeton, NJ: Princeton University Press, 1988)

Peter H. Pawlowicz, 'Reading Women. Text and Image in Eighteenth-century England', in Ann Bermingham and John Brewer (eds.), *The Consumption of Culture, 1600–1800: Image, Object, Text* (London: Routledge, 1995), 42–53

Christiana Payne, *Toil and Plenty. Images of the Agricultural Landscape in England 1780–1890* (London: Yale, 1993)

H. C. Payne, *The Philosophes and the People* (New Haven, Conn.: Yale University Press, 1976)

Iain Pears, *The Discovery of Painting: The Growth of Interest in the Arts in England 1680–1768* (New Haven, Conn.: Yale University Press, 1988)

Jacqueline Pearson, *Women's Reading in Britain, 1750–1835: A Dangerous Recreation* (Cambridge: Cambridge University Press, 1999)

T. Pennant, *A Tour in Scotland, and Voyages to the Hebrides*, 2 vols. (vol. i, Chester: J. Monk, 1774; vol. ii, London: B. White, 1774–6)

David Pepper, *The Roots of Modern Environmentalism* (London: Croom Helm, 1984)

Samuel Pepys, *The Diary of Samuel Pepys*, 11 vols., R. Latham and W. Matthews (eds.) (London: Bell and Hyman, 1970–83)

Thomas Percy, *Reliques of Ancient English Poetry* (London: J. Dodsley, 1765)

H. Perkin, *The Origins of Modern English Society* (London: Routledge and Kegan Paul, 1969)

N. Perrin, *Dr Bowdler's Legacy – A History of Expurgated Books in England and America* (London: Macmillan, 1970)

Michelle Perrot (ed.), *A History of Private Life*, vol. iv: *From the Fires of Revolution to the Great War*, Arthur Goldhammer (trans.) (Cambridge, Mass.: Belknap Press, 1990)

Ruth Perry, *The Celebrated Mary Astell: An Early English Feminist* (Chicago: University of Chicago Press, 1986)

——, 'Mary Astell and the Feminist Critique of Possessive Individualism', *Eighteenth-century Studies*, xxiii (1990), 444–57

Thomas Joseph Pettigrew, *Memoirs of the Life and Writings of the Late John Coakley Lettsom, With a Selection from his Correspondence* (London: Longman, Hurst, Rees, Orme, and Brown, 1817)

William Petty, *Treatise of Taxes and Contributions* (London: Brooke, 1662)

Nikolaus Pevsner, *The Englishness of English Art* (London: Architectural Press, 1956; Harmondsworth: Penguin, 1976)

Patricia Phillips, *The Scientific Lady: A Social History of Woman's Scientific Interests 1520–1918* (London: Weidenfeld & Nicolson, 1990)

William Phillips, *An Outline of Mineralogy and Geology* (London: William Phillips, 1815)

Nicholas Phillipson, 'Towards a Definition of the Scottish Enlightenment', in Paul Fritz and David Williams (eds.), *City and Society in the Eighteenth Century* (Toronto: Hakkert, 1973), 125–47

——, 'Culture and Society in the Eighteenth Century Province: The Case of Edinburgh and the Scottish Enlightenment', in Lawrence Stone (ed.), *The University of Society*, 2 vols. (Princeton, NJ: Princeton University Press, 1974), ii, 407–48

——, 'The Scottish Enlightenment', in Roy Porter and Mikuláš Teich (eds.), *The Enlightenment in National Context* (Cambridge: Cambridge University Press, 1981), 19–40

——, 'Adam Smith as Civic Moralist', in Istvan Hont and Michael Ignatieff (eds.), *Wealth and Virtue: The Shaping of Political Economy in the Scottish Enlightenment* (Cambridge and New York: Cambridge University Press, 1983), 179–202

——, *Hume* (London: Weidenfeld & Nicolson, 1989)

——, 'Politics and Politeness in the Reigns of Anne and the Early Hanoverians', in J. G. A. Pocock (ed.), *The Varieties of British Political Thought, 1500–1800* (Cambridge: Cambridge University Press, 1993), 211–45

Nicholas Phillipson and Quentin Skinner (eds.), *Political Discourse in Early Modern Britain* (Cambridge: Cambridge University Press, 1993)

Nicholas Phillipson and Rosalind Mitchison (eds.), *Scotland in the Age of Improvement: Essays in Scottish History in the Eighteenth Century* (Edinburgh: Edinburgh University Press, 1970)

Mark Philp, *Godwin's Political Justice* (London: Duckworth, 1986)

——, *Paine* (Oxford: Oxford University Press, 1989)

S. F. Pickering Jr, *John Locke and Children's Books in Eighteenth-century England* (Knoxville, Tenn.: The University of Tennessee Press, 1981)

James Pilkington, *View of the Present State of Derbyshire* (Derby: J. Drewry, 1789)

Adela Pinch, *Strange Fits of Passion: Epistemologies of Emotion, Hume to Austen* (Stanford: Stanford University Press, 1996)

Ivy Pinchbeck and Margaret Hewitt, *Children in English Society*, 2 vols. (London: Routledge and Kegan Paul, 1969–73)

Philip Pinkus, *Grub St Stripped Bare: The Scandalous Lives and Pornographic Works of the Original Grub St. Writers, Together With the*

Battle Songs Which Led Them to Prison, & the Continual Pandering to Public Taste Which Put Them Among the First Almost to Earn a Fitful Living From Their Writing Alone (Hamden, Conn.: Archon Books, 1968)

William Pittis (ed.), *The Original Works of William King*, 3 vols. (London: for the editor, 1776)

Marjorie Plant, *The English Book Trade: An Economic History of the Making and Sale of Books* (London: Allen & Unwin, 1965)

J. H. Plumb, *Men And Places* (Harmondsworth: Pelican, 1966)

——, *The Growth of Political Stability in England 1675–1725* (London: Macmillan, 1967)

——, *In the Light of History* (London: Allen Lane, 1972)

——, *The Commercialization of Leisure in Eighteenth-century England* (Reading: University of Reading, 1973)

——, 'The New World of the Children in Eighteenth-century England', *Past and Present*, lxvii (1975), 64–95

——, *Georgian Delights* (London: Weidenfeld & Nicolson, 1980)

——, 'The New World of the Children in Eighteenth-century England', in Neil McKendrick, John Brewer and J. H. Plumb (eds.), *The Birth of a Consumer Society: The Commercialization of Eighteenth-Century England* (London: Europa, 1982), 286–315

——, 'The Acceptance of Modernity', in Neil McKendrick, John Brewer and J.H. Plumb (eds.), *The Birth of a Consumer Society: The Commercialization of Eighteenth-century England* (London: Europa, 1982), 316–34

J. G. A. Pocock, 'Civic Humanism and Its Role in Anglo-American Thought', in *Politics, Language and Time: Essays on Political Thought and History* (London: Methuen, 1972), pp. 80–103

——, 'Machiavelli, Harrington and English Political Ideologies', in *Politics, Language and Time: Essays on Political Thought and History* (London: Methuen, 1972), 104–47

——, *The Machiavellian Moment. Florentine*

Political Thought and the Atlantic Republican Tradition (Princeton, NJ: Princeton University Press, 1975)

——, 'Post-Puritan England and the Problem of the Enlightenment', in P. Zagorin (ed.), *Culture and Politics from Puritanism to the Enlightenment* (Berkeley, CA: University of California Press, 1980), 91–111

——, 'Clergy and Commerce: The Conservative Enlightenment in England', in L. G. Crocker *et al.* (eds.), *L'Età dei Lumi: studi storici sul settecento europeo in onore di Franco Venturi*, vol. ii (Naples: Jovene, 1985), 523–68

——, *Virtue, Commerce and History: Essays on Political Thought and History, Chiefly in the Eighteenth Century* (Cambridge: Cambridge University Press, 1985)

——, 'Josiah Tucker on Burke, Locke, and Price: A Study in the Varieties of Eighteenth-century Conservatism', in *Virtue, Commerce and History: Essays on Political Thought and History, Chiefly in the Eighteenth Century* (Cambridge: Cambridge University Press, 1985), 157–91

——, 'Conservative Enlightenment and Democratic Revolutions: The American and French Cases in British Perspective', *Government and Opposition*, xxiv (1989), 81–105

—— (ed.), *The Varieties of British Political Thought, 1500–1800* (Cambridge: Cambridge University Press, 1993)

——, *Barbarism and Religion*, 2 vols.: vol. i: *The Enlightenments of Edward Gibbon, 1737–1764*; vol. ii: *Narratives of Civil Government* (Cambridge: Cambridge University Press, 1999)

Mary Pollard, *Dublin's Trade in Books 1550–1800* (Oxford: Clarendon Press, 1990)

Sidney Pollard, *The Idea of Progress: History and Society* (London: Watts & Co., 1968)

Linda Pollock, *Forgotten Children: Parent–Child Relations from 1500–1900* (Cambridge: Cambridge University Press, 1983)

——, *A Lasting Relationship: Parents and Children*

over *Three Centuries* (London: Fourth Estate, 1987)

[Richard Polwhele], *The Unsex'd Females: A Poem, Addressed to the Author of 'The Pursuits of Literature'* (London: Cadell and Davies, 1798)

Richard Polwhele, preface to George Lavington, *The Enthusiasm of Methodists and Papists Considered* (London: Whittaker, 1833)

Clive Ponting, *A Green History of the World* (London: Sinclair-Stevenson, 1991)

Joshua Poole, *English Parnassus* (London: Thomas Johnson, 1657)

Robert Poole, ' "Give Us Our Eleven Days!": Calendar Reform in Eighteenth-century England', *Past and Present*, cxlix (1995) 95–139

Mary Poovey, *A History of the Modern Fact: Problems of Knowledge in the Sciences of Wealth and Society* (Chicago: University of Chicago Press, 1998)

K. Popper, *The Open Society and Its Enemies*, 2 vols. (London: Routledge and Kegan Paul, 1945)

M. V. De Porte, *Nightmares and Hobbyhorses* (San Marino, CA: Huntington Library, 1974)

Roy Porter, *The Making of the Science of Geology* (Cambridge: Cambridge University Press, 1977)

——, 'Philosophy and Politics of a Geologist: George H. Toulmin (1754–1817)', *Journal of the History of Ideas*, xxxix (1978), 435–50

——, 'Creation and Credence: The Career of Theories of the Earth in Britain, 1660–1820', in B. Barnes and S. Shapin (eds.), *Natural Order* (Beverly Hills, CA: Sage Publications, 1979), 97–123

——, 'The Terraqueous Globe', in G. S. Rousseau and R. S. Porter (eds.), *The Ferment of Knowledge: Studies in the Historiography of Eighteenth-century Science* (Cambridge: Cambridge University Press, 1980), 285–324

——, 'Sex and the Singular Man: The Seminal Ideas of James Graham', *Studies on Voltaire & the Eighteenth Century*, ccxxviii (1984), 3–24

——, 'The Drinking Man's Disease: The "Pre-History" of Alcoholism in Georgian Britain', *British Journal of Addiction*, lxxx (1985), 385–96

——, 'Lay Medical Knowledge in the Eighteenth Century: The Case of the *Gentleman's Magazine*', *Medical History*, xxix (1985), 138–68

——, 'Laymen, Doctors and Medical Knowledge in the Eighteenth Century: The Evidence of the *Gentleman's Magazine*', in Roy Porter (ed.), *Patients and Practitioners: Lay Perceptions of Medicine in Pre-Industrial Society* (Cambridge: Cambridge University Press, 1985), 283–314

——, 'Making Faces: Physiognomy and Fashion in Eighteenth-century England', *Etudes Anglaises*, xxxviii (1985), 385–96

——, 'The Hunger of Imagination: Approaching Samuel Johnson's Melancholy', in W. F. Bynum, Roy Porter and M. Shepherd (eds.), *The Anatomy of Madness*, 2 vols. (London: Tavistock, 1985), i, 63–88

——, 'Bedlam and Parnassus: Mad People's Writing in Georgian England', in George Levine (ed.), *One Culture: Essays in Science and Literature* (Madison, Wisconsin: University of Wisconsin Press, 1987), 258–84

——, *Gibbon* (London: Weidenfeld & Nicolson, 1988)

——, *Health for Sale: Quackery in England 1650–1850* (Manchester: Manchester University Press, 1989)

——, 'Erasmus Darwin: Doctor of Evolution?', in James R. Moore (ed.), *History, Humanity and Evolution* (Cambridge: Cambridge University Press, 1989), 39–69

——, 'The Exotic as Erotic: Captain Cook at Tahiti', in G. S. Rousseau and Roy Porter (eds.), *Exoticism in the Enlightenment*

(Manchester: Manchester University
Press, 1989), 117–44

——, 'The Gift Relation: Philanthropy and
Provincial Hospitals in Eighteenth-
century England', in L. Granshaw and R.
Porter (eds.), *The Hospital in History*
(London: Routledge, 1989), 149–78

——, 'Death and the Doctors in Georgian
England', in R. Houlbrooke (ed.), *Death,
Ritual and Bereavement* (London: Routledge,
1989), 77–94

——, *Mind Forg'd Manacles: Madness and
Psychiatry in England from Restoration to
Regency* (London, Athlone Press, 1987;
repr. Harmondsworth, Penguin, 1990)

——, 'English Society in the Eighteenth
Century Revisited', in Jeremy Black (ed.),
*British Politics and Society from Walpole to Pitt:
1742–1789* (London: Macmillan, 1990),
29–52

——, *Doctor of Society: Thomas Beddoes and the
Sick Trade in Late Enlightenment England*
(London: Routledge, 1991)

——, 'Civilization and Disease: Medical
Ideology in the Enlightenment', in J.
Black and J. Gregory (eds.), *Culture, Politics
and Society in Britain 1660–1800*
(Manchester: Manchester University
Press, 1991), 154–83

——, 'Consumption: Disease of the
Consumer Society?', in John Brewer and
Roy Porter (eds.), *Consumption and the World
of Goods* (London: Routledge, 1991), 58–84

——, ' "Expressing Yourself Ill": The
Language of Sickness in Georgian
England', in P. Burke and R. Porter (eds.),
*Language, Self and Society: The Social History of
Language* (Cambridge: Polity Press, 1991),
276–99

——, 'Spreading Medical Enlightenment:
The Popularization of Medicine in
Georgian England, and its Paradoxes', in
Roy Porter (ed.), *The Popularization of
Medicine, 1650–1850* (London: Routledge,
1992), 215–31

——, 'John Hunter: A Showman in Society',

The Transactions of the Hunterian Society
(1993–4), 19–24

——, 'Visiting London', in M. S. Moretti
(ed.), *Il Senso del Nonsenso: Scritti in Memoria
di Lynn Salkin Sbiroli* (Napoli: Edizioni
Scientifiche Italiane, 1994), 93–108

——, 'Medical Science and Human Science
in the Enlightenment', in C. Fox, R.
Porter and R. Wokler (eds.), *Inventing
Human Science: Eighteenth Century Domains*
(Berkeley, CA: University of California
Press, 1995), 53–87

——, 'The People's Health in Georgian
England', in Tim Harris (ed.), *Popular
Culture in England c. 1500–1850* (London:
Macmillan, 1995), 124–42

——, 'Forbidden Pleasures: Enlightenment
Literature of Sexual Advice', in Paula
Bennett and Vernon A. Rosario II (eds.),
*Solitary Pleasures: The Historical, Literary and
Artistic Discourses of Autoeroticism* (New York
and London: Routledge, 1995), 75–100

——, 'Accidents in the Eighteenth Century',
in Roger Cooter and Bill Luckin (eds.),
*Accidents in History: Injuries, Fatalities and
Social Relations* (Amsterdam: Rodopi,
1996), 90–106

——, 'Capital Art: Hogarth's London', in F.
Ogée (ed.), *The Dumb Show. Image and
Society in the Works of William Hogarth*
(Oxford: Voltaire Foundation: *Studies on
Voltaire and the Eighteenth Century*, 1997), 47–
64

——, 'The New Eighteenth-century Social
History', in Jeremy Black (ed.), *Culture and
Society in Britain 1660–1800* (Manchester:
Manchester University Press, 1997), 29–50

——, 'Madness and the Family before Freud:
The Views of the Mad Doctors', *Journal of
Family History*, xxiii (1998), 159–72

——, 'Reading: A Health Warning', in
Robin Myers and Michael Harris (eds.),
Medicine, Mortality and the Booktrade
(Winchester: St Paul's Bibliographies,
1999), 131–52

——, 'The Malthusian Moment', in Brian

Dolan (ed.), *Malthus, Medicine and Morality: 'Malthusianism' After 1798* (Amsterdam: Rodopi, 2000), 57–72

——, 'The Soul and the English Enlightenment', in Duncan Salkeld (ed.), *The History of the Soul* (forthcoming)

Roy Porter and Lesley Hall, *The Facts of Life: The History of Sexuality and Knowledge from the Seventeenth Century* (New Haven, Conn.: Yale University Press, 1994)

Roy Porter and Michael Neve, 'Alexander Catcott: Glory and Geology', *The British Journal for the History of Science*, x (1977), 37–60

Roy Porter and Mikuláš Teich (eds.), *The Enlightenment in National Context* (Cambridge: Cambridge University Press, 1981)

—— (eds.), *The Scientific Revolution in National Context* (Cambridge: Cambridge University Press, 1992)

John Potter, *Observations on the Present State of Music and Musicians* (London: Henderson, 1762)

Frederick A. Pottle (ed.), *Boswell's London Journal, 1762–1763* (London: Heinemann, 1950)

N. Powell, *Fuseli's 'The Nightmare'* (London: Routledge and Kegan Paul, 1956)

Frederick J. Powicke, *The Cambridge Platonists: A Study* (New York: Archon Books, 1971)

J. R. Poynter, *Society and Pauperism* (London: Routledge and Kegan Paul, 1969)

Samuel Jackson Pratt, *Humanity, or, the Rights of Nature: A Poem; in Two Books/by the Author of Sympathy* (London: printed for T. Cadell, 1788)

John Valdimir Price, 'The Reading of Philosophical Literature', in Isabel Rivers (ed.), *Books and Their Readers in Eighteenth-century England* (Leicester: Leicester University Press, 1982), 165–96

Richard Price, *Observations on the Nature of Civil Liberty, the Principles of Government, and the Justice and Policy of the War with America* (London: T. Cadell, 1776)

——, *Observations on the Importance of the American American Revolution, and the Means of Making It a Benefit to the World* (London: Powars and Willis, 1784)

——, *The Evidence for a Future Period of Improvement in the State of Mankind, with the Means and Duty of Promoting It* (London: Goldney, 1787)

——, *A Discourse on the Love of Our Country* (London: T. Cadell, 1789)

Uvedale Price, *Essays on the Picturesque, as Compared with the Sublime and the Beautiful; and, on the Use of Studying Pictures, for the Purpose of Improving Real Landscape*, 3 vols. (London: J. Mawman, 1810)

Joseph Priestley, *The Rudiments of English Grammar* (London: Griffiths, 1761; Menston: Scolar, 1969)

——, *The Scripture Doctrine of Remission* (London: P. F. C. Henderson, 1761)

——, *A Chart of Biography* (London: J. Johnson, 1765)

——, *An Essay on a Course of Liberal Education for Civil and Active Life; . . . To Which are Added Remarks on a Code of Education, Proposed by Dr Brown, in a Late Treatise, Intitled, Thoughts on Civil Liberty, &c.* (London: C. Henderson, 1765)

——, *The History and Present State of Electricity, with Original Experiments* (London: J. Dodsley, 1767)

——, *An Essay on the First Principles of Government; and on the Nature of Political, Civil, and Religious Liberty* (London: J. Dodsley; T. Cadell; J. Johnson, 1768)

——, *A Sermon on Behalf of the Leeds Informary Preached at Mill Hill Chapel* (Leek: sn, 1768)

——, *New Chart of History* (London: J. Johnson, 1769)

——, *A View of the Principles and Conduct of the Protestant Dissenters with Respect to the Civil and Ecclesiastical Constitution of England* (London: J. Johnson, 1769)

——, *Remarks on Some Paragraphs in the Fourth Volume of Dr Blackstone's Commentaries on the Laws of England, Relating to the Dissenters*

(London: J. Johnson and J. Payne, 1769)

——, *An Essay on the First Principles of Government* (1771), in John Towill Rutt (ed.), *The Theological and Miscellaneous Works of Joseph Priestley*, 25 vols. in 26 (London: Smallfield, 1817–32), vol. xxii

——, *The History of the Present State of the Discoveries Relating to Vision, Light, and Colours* (London: J. Johnson, 1772)

——, *An Examination of Dr Reid's Inquiry into the Human Mind on the Principles of Commonsense, Dr Beattie's Essay on the Nature and Immutability of Truth, and Dr Oswald's Appeal to Common Sense on Behalf of Religion* (London: J. Johnson, 1774)

——, *Experiments and Observations on Different Kinds of Air* (London: J. Johnson, 1774–7)

[——], *An Appeal to the Serious and Candid Professors of Christianity . . . by a Lover of the Gospel* (London: J. Johnson, 1775)

——, *Hartley's Theory of the Human Mind on the Principle of the Association of Ideas; With Essays Relating to the Subject of It* (London: J. Johnson, 1775)

——, *Course of Lectures on Oratory and Criticism* (London: J. Johnson, 1777)

——, *The Doctrine of Philosophical Necessity Illustrated: Being an Appendix to the Disquisitions Relating to Matter and Spirit; To Which is Added an Answer to the Letters on Materialism, and on Hartley's Theory of the Mind* (London: J. Johnson, 1777)

——, *Disquisitions Relating to Matter and Spirit*, 2 vols. (London: J. Johnson, 1777)

——, *Miscellaneous Observations Relating to Education: More Especially, as It Respects the Conduct of the Mind. To Which is Added, an Essay on a Course of Liberal Education for Civil and Active Life* (London: J. Johnson, 1778)

——, *A Free Address to Those Who Have Petitioned for the Repeal of the Late Act of Parliament in Favour of the Roman Catholics* (London: J. Johnson, 1780)

——, *Additional Letters to a Philosophical Unbeliever, in Answer to Mr William Hammon [i.e. Matthew Turner]* (Birmingham: Pearson and Rollason, 1782)

——, *The Importance and Extent of Free Inquiry in Matters of Religion: A Sermon* (Birmingham: sn, 1785)

——, *An History of Early Opinions Concerning Jesus Christ, Compiled from Original Writers; Proving that the Christian Church was at First Unitarian* (Birmingham: Pearson and Rollason, 1786)

——, *Letter to the Right Honourable William Pitt* (London: Johnson, 1787)

——, *Lectures on History and General Policy: To Which is Prefixed, An Essay on a Course of Liberal Education for Civil and Active Life* (Birmingham: Pearson and Rollason, 1788)

——, *Letters to Edmund Burke Occasioned by His Reflections on the Revolution in France, &c.* (Birmingham: Thomas Pearson, 1791)

——, *Proper Objects of Education in the Present State of the World: Represented in a Discourse, Delivered on Wednesday, the 27th of April, 1791, at the Meeting-House in the Old-Jewry, London to the Supporters of New College at Hackney by Joseph Priestley. To Which is Subjoined, a Prayer . . . by Thomas Belsham* (London: J. Johnson, 1791)

[——], *A Political Dialogue on the General Principles of Government* (London: Johnson, 1791)

——, *Familiar Letters Addressed to the Inhabitants of the Town of Birmingham in Refutation of Several Charges Advanced against the Dissenters and Unitarians, by the Revd Mr Madan: Also, Letters to the Revd Edward Burn . . . and Considerations of the Differences of Opinion among Christians, Which Originally Accompanied the Reply to the Revd Mr Venn* (Birmingham: J. Thompson, 1790–92)

——, *Lectures on History*, 2 vols. (London: Printed for J. Johnson, 1793)

Joseph Priestley, *The Doctrines of Heathen Religion Compared with Those of Revelation* (Northumberland: John Binns, 1804)

——, *An History of the Corruptions of Christianity*

(London: The British and Foreign Unitarian Association, 1871 [1782])

——, *Lecture on History and General Policy To Which is Prefixed, An Essay on a Course of Liberal Education for Civil and Active Life*, 4th edn (London: T. Tegg, 1826 [1788])

——, *Discourses Relating to the Evidences of Revealed Religion*, 3 vols. (London: Johnson, 1794–9)

——, *Letters to the Inhabitants of Northumberland* (Northumberland: for the author, 1801)

——, *Memoirs of Dr Joseph Priestley, Written on Himself* (London: Allenson, 1904 [1795])

——, *Political Writings*, Peter N. Miller (ed.) (Cambridge: Cambridge University Press, 1993)

Joseph Priestley and Richard Price, *A Free Discussion of the Doctrines of Materialism and Philosophical Necessity* (Bristol: Thoemmes Press, 1994 [1778])

Michael Prince, *Philosophical Dialogue in the British Enlightenment: Theology, Aesthetics, and the Novel* (Cambridge: Cambridge University Press, 1996)

David Punter, *The Literature of Terror: A History of Gothic Fictions from 1785 to the Present Day* (London: Longman, 1980)

Diane Purkiss, *The Witch in History: Early Modern and Twentieth Century Representations* (London: Routledge, 1996)

Andrew Pyle (ed.), *Population: Contemporary Responses to Thomas Malthus* (Bristol: Thoemmes Press, 1994)

Peter Quennell, *The Pursuit of Happiness* (London: Constable, 1988)

Maurice J. Quinlan, *Victorian Prelude: A History of English Manners, 1700–1830* (London: Cass, 1941)

——, *Samuel Johnson: A Layman's Religion* (Madison, Wis.: University of Wisconsin Press, 1964)

Karlis Racevskis, *Postmodernism and the Search for Enlightenment* (Charlottesville, VA: University Press of Virginia, 1993)

John B. Radner, 'The Youthful Harlot's Curse: The Prostitute as Symbol of the City in Eighteenth-century English Literature', *Eighteenth-Century Life*, ii (1976), 59–64

James Ralph, *The Case of Authors by Profession or Trade, Stated with Regard to Booksellers, the Stage and the Public* (London: R. Griffiths, 1758)

D. D. Raphael, 'Adam Smith: Philosophy, Science, and Social Science', in S. C. Brown (ed.), *Philosophers of the Enlightenment* (Brighton: Harvester Press, 1979), 77–93

Frederick Raphael, *Byron* (London: Thames and Hudson, 1982)

S. Rashid, 'Dugald Stewart, Baconian Methodology and Political Economy', *Journal of the History of Ideas*, xlvi (1985), 245–7

James Raven, *Judging New Wealth: Popular Publishing and Responses to Commerce in England 1750–1800* (Oxford: Clarendon Press, 1992)

——, 'From Promotion to Proscription: Arrangements for Reading and Eighteenth-century Libraries', in James Raven, Helen Small and Naomi Tadmor (eds.), *The Practice and Representation of Reading in England* (Cambridge: Cambridge University Press, 1996), 175–201

James Raven, Helen Small and Naomi Tadmore (eds.), *The Practice and Representation of Reading in England* (Cambridge: Cambridge University Press, 1996)

Claude Rawson, *Satire and Sentiment 1660–1830* (Cambridge: Cambridge University Press, 1994)

Elizabeth Rawson, *The Spartan Tradition in European Thought* (Oxford: Clarendon Press, 1969)

John Ray, *The Wisdom of God Manifested in the Works of the Creation* (London: Samuel Smith, 1691)

Barry Reay (ed.), *Popular Culture in Seventeenth-century England* (London: Croom Helm, 1985)

Bruce Redford, 'Boswell's "Libertine"

Correspondences', *Philological Quarterly*, lxiii (1984), 55–73

——, *The Converse of the Pen: Acts of Intimacy in the Eighteenth-century Familiar Letter* (Chicago, Ill.: University of Chicago Press, 1986)

John Redwood, *Reason, Ridicule and Religion: The Age of Enlightenment in England, 1660–1750* (London: Thames & Hudson, 1976; repr. 1996)

Jonathan Rée, *I See a Voice: Language, Deafness and the Senses: A Philosophical History* (London: HarperCollins, 1999)

Abraham Rees, *The Cyclopaedia; or, Universal Dictionary of Arts and Sciences . . . Biography, Geography and History*, 39 vols. (London: Longman, Hurst, Rees, Orme, and Brown, 1819)

Clara Reeve, *The School for Widows: A Novel* (London: Hookham, 1791)

Thomas Reid, *An Inquiry into the Human Mind on the Principles of Common Sense* (Dublin: Ewing, 1764)

——, *The Works of Thomas Reid*, Sir William Hamilton (ed.), 2 vols. with continuous pagination (Edinburgh: Maclachlan and Stewart, 1846–63; Bristol: Thoemmes Press, 1995)

——, *Essays on the Intellectual Powers of Man* (Edinburgh: sn, 1785)

Jane Rendall, *The Origins of the Scottish Enlightenment* (London: Macmillan, 1978)

Neil Rennie, *Far-fetched Facts: The Literature of Travel and the Idea of the South Seas* (Oxford: Clarendon Press, 1995)

Humphry Repton, *Fragments on the Theory and Practice of Landscape Gardening* (London: T. Bensley and Sons, 1816)

Myra Reynolds, *The Learned Lady in England 1650–1760* (Boston, Mass.: Houghton Mifflin, 1920)

Alan Richardson, *Literature, Education, and Romanticism: Reading as Social Practice, 1780–1832* (Cambridge: Cambridge University Press, 1994)

Ruth Richardson, *Death, Dissection and the Destitute: A Political History of the Human Corpse* (London: Routledge & Kegan Paul, 1987)

Samuel Richardson, *Clarissa* (London: Richardson, 1748)

——, *Pamela*, in *Works*, Leslie Stephen (ed.), 12 vols. (London: Southeran, 1883–4 [1740–41])

——, *Pamela*, Peter Sabor (ed.) (Harmondsworth: Penguin, 1980 [1740–41])

John J. Richetti, *Popular Fiction Before Richardson: Narrative Patterns, 1700–1789* (Oxford: Clarendon Press, 1969; repr. 1992)

Harriet Ritvo, *The Animal Estate* (Cambridge, Mass.: Harvard University Press, 1987)

——, 'Possessing Mother Nature. Genetic Capital', in John Brewer and Susan Staves (eds.), *Early Modern Conceptions of Property* (London: Routledge, 1995), 414–26

Isabel Rivers (ed.), *Books and Their Readers in Eighteenth-century England* (Leicester: Leicester University Press, 1982)

Caroline Robbins, *The Eighteenth-century Commonwealthmen: Studies in the Transmission, Development and Circumstances of English Liberal Thought from the Restoration of Charles II until the War with the Thirteen Colonies* (New York: Atheneum, 1968)

H. C. Robbins-Landon, *Handel and His World* (London: Weidenfeld & Nicolson, 1984)

Marie Mulvey Roberts, 'Pleasures Engendered by Gender: Homosociality and the Club', in Roy Porter and Marie Mulvey Roberts (eds.), *Pleasure in the Eighteenth Century* (London: Macmillan, 1996), 48–76

W. Roberts (ed.), *Memoirs of the Life and Correspondence of Mrs Hannah More*, 4 vols. (London: R. B. Seeley and W. Burnside, 1834)

John Robertson, 'The Scottish Enlightenment at the Limits of the Civic Tradition', in Istvan Hont and Michael Ignatieff (eds.),

Wealth and Virtue: The Shaping of Political Economy in the Scottish Enlightenment (Cambridge: Cambridge University Press, 1983), 137–78

—— (ed.), *A Union for Empire: Political Thought and the British Union of 1707* (Cambridge: Cambridge University Press, 1995)

—— (ed.), *Andrew Fletcher: Political Works* (Cambridge: Cambridge University Press, 1997)

William Robertson, *Works*, 8 vols. (Edinburgh: T. Cadell, 1840)

Howard Robinson, *The British Post Office: A History* (Princeton, NJ: Princeton University Press, 1948)

Eric H. Robinson, 'The Derby Philosophical Society', *Annals of Science*, ix (1953), 359–67

Mary Robinson, *Thoughts on the Condition of Women, and on the Injustice of Mental Subordination* (London: Longman and Rees, 1799)

N. Robinson, *A New System of the Spleen* (London: A. Bettesworth, 1729)

John Robison, *Proofs of a Conspiracy against All the Governments and Religions of Europe, Carried on in Secret Meetings of Free Masons, Illuminati, and Reading Societies* (Edinburgh: William Creech, T. Cadell Jr, W. Davies, 1798)

Daniel Roche, *France in the Enlightenment* (Cambridge, Mass.: Harvard University Press, 1998)

Betsy Rodgers, *Cloak of Charity: Studies in Eighteenth-century Philanthropy* (London: Methuen, 1949)

G. A. J. Rogers, 'The Empiricism of Locke and Newton', in S. C. Brown (ed.), *Philosophers of the Enlightenment* (Brighton: Harvester Press, 1979), 1–30

——, 'Descartes and the English', in J. D. North and J. J. Roche (eds.), *The Light and Nature: Essays in the History and Philosophy of Science Presented to A. C. Crombie* (Dordrecht: Martinus Nijhoff, 1985), 281–302

——, 'Boyle, Locke and Reason', in John W. Yolton (ed.), *Philosophy, Religion and Science in the Seventeenth and Eighteenth Centuries*

(Rochester, NY: University of Rochester Press, 1990), 339–50

——, 'Locke, Newton and the Cambridge Platonists on Innate Ideas', in John W. Yolton (ed.), *Philosophy, Religion and Science in the Seventeenth and Eighteenth Centuries* (Rochester, NY: University of Rochester Press, 1990), 351–65

——, 'Locke's *Essay* and Newton's *Principia*', in John W. Yolton (ed.), *Philosophy, Religion and Science in the Seventeenth and Eighteenth Centuries* (Rochester, NY: University of Rochester Press, 1990), 366–84

——, 'Locke, Anthropology and Models of the Mind', *History of the Human Sciences*, vi (1993), 73–87

Katharine M. Rogers, *Before Their Time: Six Women Writers of the Eighteenth Century* (New York: Frederick Ungar Publishing Co., 1979)

——, *Feminism in Eighteenth-century England* (Brighton: Harvester Press, 1982)

Nicholas Rogers, 'Confronting the Crime Wave: The Debate over Social Reform and Regulation, 1749–1753', in Lee Davison, Tim Hitchcock, Tim Keirn and Robert B. Shoemaker (eds.), *Stilling the Grumbling Hive: The Response to Social and Economic Problems in England, 1689–1750* (Stroud: Alan Sutton, 1992), 77–98

——, *Crowds, Culture and Politics in Georgian Britain* (Oxford: Clarendon Press, 1998)

Pat Rogers, *Grub Street: Studies in a Subculture* (London: Methuen, 1972)

——, *The Augustan Vision* (London: Weidenfeld & Nicolson, 1974)

—— (ed.), *The Context of English Literature: The Eighteenth Century* (London: Methuen, 1978)

——, *Hacks and Dunces: Pope, Swift and Grub Street* (London: Methuen, 1980)

——, *Eighteenth Century Encounters* (Brighton: Harvester Press, 1985)

Eirch Roll, *A History of Economic Thought* (London: Faber, 1938)

Samuel Romilly, *Memoirs of the Life of Sir Samuel Romilly: With a Selection from His*

Correspondence Edited by His Sons, 3 vols. (Shannon: Irish University Press, 1971 [1840])

R. Rompkey, *Soame Jenyns* (Boston, Mass.: Twayne Publishers, 1984)

Alessandro Roncaglia, *Petty: The Origins of Political Economy* (Armonk, NY: M. E. Sharpe, 1985)

Barbara E. Rooke (ed.), *The Collected Works of Samuel Taylor Coleridge: The Friend I* (Princeton, NJ (Bollingen Series LXXV): Princeton University Press, 1969)

Derek Roper, *Reviewing Before the Edinburgh: 1788–1802* (London: Methuen, 1978)

Mark Rose, *Authors and Owners: the Invention of Copyright* (Cambridge, Mass.: Harvard University Press, 1993)

M. E. Rose, *The English Poor Law 1760–1830* (Newton Abbot: David & Charles, 1971)

D. Rosenberg, ' "A New Sort of Logick and Critick": Etymological Interpretation in Horne Tooke's *The Diversions of Purley*', in Peter Burke and Roy Porter (eds.), *Language, Self and Society* (Cambridge: Polity Press, 1991), 300–329

Ian Simpson Ross, *Lord Kames and the Scotland of His Day* (Oxford: Clarendon Press, 1972)

——, 'The Physiocrats and Adam Smith', *British Journal for Eighteenth-century Studies*, vii (1984), 177–90

P. Rossi, *The Dark Abyss of Time: The History of the Earth and the History of Nations from Hooke to Vico* (Chicago: University of Chicago Press, 1984)

Eugene Rotwein, *David Hume: Writings on Economics* (Madison, Wisc.: University of Wisconsin Press, 1970)

G. S. Rousseau, 'Psychology', in G. S. Rousseau and Roy Porter (eds.), *The Ferment of Knowledge: Studies in the Historiography of Eighteenth-Century Science* (Cambridge: Cambridge University Press, 1980), 143–210

——, 'The Pursuit of Homosexuality in the Eighteenth Century: "Utterly Confused Category" and/or Rich Repository?', in

R. P. Maccubbin (ed.), *'Tis Nature's Fault: Unauthorized Sexuality during the Enlightenment* (Cambridge: Cambridge University Press, 1987), 132–68

——, 'Towards a Semiotics of the Nerve: The Social History of Language in a New Key', in Peter Burke and Roy Porter (eds.), *Language, Self and Society: A Social History of Language* (Cambridge: Polity Press, 1991), 213–75

——, 'Nerves, Spirits and Fibres: Towards an Anthropology of Sensibility', in *Enlightenment Crossings: Pre- and Post-Modern Discourses* (Manchester: Manchester University Press, 1991), 122–41

Jean-Jacques Rousseau, *The Confessions of Jean-Jacques Rousseau*, J. M. Cohen (trans.) (Harmondsworth: Penguin, 1954 [1781–8])

John Rowning, *A Compendious System of Natural Philosophy* (London: Harding, 1735–42)

George Rudé, *Wilkes and Liberty: A Social Study of 1763–1774* (Oxford, Clarendon Press, 1962)

Maximillian Rudwin, *The Devil in Legend and Literature* (La Salle, Ill.: The Open Court Publishing Company, 1959)

John Rule, *Albion's People: English Society, 1714–1815* (London: Longman, 1992)

——, *The Vital Century: England's Developing Economy 1714–1815* (London: Longman, 1992)

Benjamin Rumford, 'Of the Management of Light in Illumination' (1812), in Sanborn C. Brown (ed.), *Collected Works of Count Rumford*, vol. iv: *Light and Armament* (Cambridge, Mass: Belknap Press, 1970), 97–8

Nicolaas A. Rupke (ed.), *Vivisection in Historical Context* (London: Croom Helm, 1987)

Gordon Rupp, *Religion in England 1688–1791* (Oxford: Clarendon Press, 1986)

Benjamin Rush, *An Account of the Bilious Remitting Yellow Fever* (Philadelphia: Thomas Dobson, 1794)

Andrea Rusnock, *The Correspondence of James*

Jurin (1684–1750), Physician and Secretary of the Royal Society (Amsterdam: Rodopi Press, 1996)

——,: 'Biopolitics: Political Arithmetic in the Enlightenment', in William Clark, Jan Golinski and Simon Schaffer (eds.), *The Sciences in Enlightened Europe* (Chicago: University of Chicago Press, 1999), 49–68

John Towill Rutt (ed.), *The Theological and Miscellaneous Works of Joseph Priestley*, 25 vols. in 26 (London: Smallfield, 1817–32)

Edward Said, *Orientalism* (Harmondsworth: Penguin, 1978)

Roger Sales, *English Literature in History, 1780–1830: Pastoral and Politics* (London: Hutchinson, 1983)

James Sambrook (ed.), *William Cowper, The Task and Selected Other Poems* (London: Longman, 1994)

R. V. Sampson, *Progress in the Age of Reason: The Seventeenth Century to the Present Day* (London: Heinemann, 1956)

L. Sanders (ed.), *Selections from the Anti-Jacobin* (London: Methuen, 1904)

John Sargeaunt (ed.), *The Poems of John Dryden* (London: Oxford University Press, 1959)

J. W. Saunders, *The Profession of English Letters* (London: Routledge and Kegan Paul, 1964)

C. de Saussure, *A Foreign View of England in 1725–29* (London: John Murray, 1902; London: Caliban Books, 1995)

Lynn Salkin Sbiroli, 'Generation and Regeneration: Reflections on the Biological and Ideological Role of Women in France (1786–96)', in Marie Mulvey Roberts and Roy Porter (eds.), *Literature and Medicine During the Eighteenth Century* (London and New York: Routledge, 1993), 266–85

Simon Schaffer, 'Natural Philosophy', in G. S. Rousseau and R. Porter (eds.), *The Ferment of Knowledge: Studies in the Historiography of Eighteenth-century Science* (Cambridge: Cambridge University Press, 1980), 55–91

——, 'Natural Philosophy and Public Spectacle in the Eighteenth Century', *History of Science*, xxi (1983), 1–43

——, 'Newton's Comets and the Transformation of Astrology', in Patrick Curry (ed.), *Astrology, Science and Society* (Woodbridge, Suffolk: The Boydell Press, 1987), 219–43

——, 'Defoe's Natural Philosophy and the Worlds of Credit', in J. H. R. Christie and S. Shuttleworth (eds.), *Nature Transfigured: Science and Literature, 1700–1989* (Manchester: Manchester University Press, 1989), 13–44

——, 'Newtonianism', in R. C. Olby, G. N. Cantor, J. R. R. Christie, and M. J. S. Hodge (eds.), *Companion to the History of Modern Science* (London: Routledge, 1990), 610–26

——, 'States of Mind; Enlightenment and Natural Philosophy', in G. S. Rousseau (ed.), *The Languages of Psyche: Mind and Body in Enlightenment Thought* (Berkeley, CA: University of California Press, 1990), 233–90

——, 'Genius in Romantic Natural Philosophy', in A. Cunningham and N. Jardine (eds.), *Romanticism and the Sciences* (Cambridge: Cambridge University Press, 1990), 82–98

——, 'The Consuming Flame: Electrical Showmen and Tory Mystics in the World of Goods', in John Brewer and Roy Porter (eds.), *Consumption and the World of Goods in the Seventeenth and Eighteenth Centuries* (London and New York: Routledge, 1993), 489–526

——, 'A Social History of Plausibility: County, City and Calculation in Augustan Britain', in Adrian Wilson (ed.), *Rethinking Social History: English Society 1570–1920 and Its Interpretation* (Manchester and New York: Manchester University Press, 1993), 128–57

——, 'Visions of Empire: Afterword', in David Philip Miller and Peter Hanns Reill (eds.), *Visions of Empire: Voyages, Botany, and Representations of Nature* (Cambridge: Cambridge University Press, 1996), 335–52

Simon Schama, *The Embarrassment of Riches: An Interpretation of Dutch Culture in the Golden Age* (London: Fontana, 1988)

——, *Landscape and Memory* (London: HarperCollins, 1995)

Londa Schiebinger, *The Mind Has No Sex? Women in the Origins of Modern Science* (Cambridge, Mass.: Harvard University Press, 1989)

Bernard M. Schilling, *Conservative England and the Case against Voltaire* (New York: Columbia University Press, 1950)

Wolfgang Schivelbusch, *Disenchanted Night: The Industrialisation of Light in the Nineteenth Century*, Angela Davies (trans.) (Oxford, New York and Hamburg: Berg, 1988)

Thomas Schlereth, *The Cosmopolitan Ideal in Enlightenment Thought: Its Form and Function in the Ideas of Franklin, Hume and Voltaire* (Notre Dame, Ind.: University of Notre Dame Press, 1977)

Joachim Schlör, *Nights in the Big City* (London: Reaktion, 1998)

Leigh Schmidt, *Hearing Things: Religion, Illusion and the American Enlightenment* (Cambridge, Mass.: Harvard University Press, 2000)

G. J. Schochet, *Patriarchalism in Political Thought: The Authoritarian Family and Political Speculation and Attitudes Especially in Seventeenth-century England* (Oxford: Blackwell, 1975)

Robert E. Schofield, *The Lunar Society of Birmingham: A Social History of Provincial Science and Industry in Eighteenth-century England* (Oxford: Clarendon Press, 1963)

——, *Mechanism and Materialism: British Natural Philosophy in an Age of Reason* (Princeton, NJ: Princeton University Press, 1970)

——, *The Enlightenment of Joseph Priestley: A Study of His Life and Work from 1733 to 1773* (Philadelphia, PA: Pennsylvania State University Press, 1997)

Peter Schouls, *Reasoned Freedom: John Locke and Enlightenment* (Ithaca, NY: Cornell University Press, 1992)

J. A. Schumpeter, *History of Economic Analysis* (London: Allen and Unwin, 1954)

John A. Schuster, 'The Scientific Revolution', in R. C. Olby, G. N. Cantor, J. R. R. Christie, and M. J. S. Hodge (eds.), *Companion to the History of Modern Science* (London: Routledge, 1990), 217–43

Hillel Schwartz, *Knaves, Fools, Madmen, and 'That Subtile Effluvium': A Study of the Opposition to the French Prophets in England, 1706–1710* (Gainesville, Fla: University Presses of Florida, 1978)

——, *The French Prophets: The History of a Millenarian Group in Eighteenth-century England* (Berkeley and Los Angeles, CA: University of California Press, 1980)

Richard B. Schwartz, *Samuel Johnson and the Problem of Evil* (Madison, Wisc.: University of Wisconsin Press, 1975)

Lois G. Schwoerer, *The Revolution of 1688–1689. Changing Perspectives* (Cambridge: Cambridge University Press, 1992)

Sarah Scott, *A Description of Millenium Hall and the Country Adjacent: Together with the Characters of the Inhabitants and Such Historical Anecdotes and Reflections as May Excite in the Reader Proper Sentiments of Humanity and Lead the Mind to the Love of Virtue; by 'A Gentleman on His Travels'* (London: Newbery, 1762; repr., Peterborough: Broadview Press, 1996)

W. R. Scott, *Adam Smith as Student and Professor* (Glasgow: Jackson, 1937)

Sir Walter Scott (ed.), *The Poetical Works of Anna Seward* (Edinburgh: J. Ballantyne, 1810)

I. Scoutland (ed.), *Huguenots in Britain and Their French Background, 1550–1800* (Basingstoke: Macmillan, 1987)

Andrew Scull, *The Most Solitary of Afflictions: Madness and Society in Britain, 1700–1900* (New Haven, Conn.: Yale University Press, 1993)

Peter Searby, *A History of the University of Cambridge*, vol. iii: *1750–1870* (Cambridge: Cambridge University Press, 1997)

Sarah Searight, *The British in the Middle East* (London and The Hague: East–West Publications, 1979)

James A. Secord, 'Newton in the Nursery: Tom Telescope and the Philosophy of Tops and Balls, 1761–1838', *History of Science*, xxiii (1985), 127–51

Eve Kosofsky Sedgwick, 'Jane Austen and the Masturbating Girl', in Paula Bennett and Vernon A. Rosario II (eds.), *Solitary Pleasures. The Historical, Literary, and Artistic Discourses of Autoeroticism* (New York and London: Routledge, 1995), 133–54

John Sekora, *Luxury: The Concept in Western Thought, Eden to Smollett* (Baltimore: Johns Hopkins University Press, 1977)

Alan P. F. Sell, *John Locke and the Eighteenth-century Divines* (Cardiff: University of Wales Press, 1997)

Janet Semple, 'Foucault and Bentham: A Defence of Panopticism', *Utilitas*, iv (1992), 105–20

——, *Bentham's Prison: A Study of the Panopticon Penitentiary* (Oxford: Clarendon Press, 1993)

Richard Sennett, *The Fall of Public Man* (Cambridge: Cambridge University Press, 1977)

Anthony Ashley Cooper, 3rd Earl of Shaftesbury, *The Moralists* (London: Wyat, 1709)

——, *Characteristicks of Men, Manners, Opinions, Times* (London: Wyat, 1711)

——, *Characteristicks of Men, Manners, Opinions, Times*, 4th edn, 3 vols. (London: J. Darby, 1727)

——, *Characteristicks of Men, Manners, Opinions, Times*, 2 vols., Philip Ayres (ed.) (Oxford: Clarendon Press, 1999 [1711])

Carole Shammas, *The Pre-industrial Consumer in England and America* (Oxford: Clarendon Press, 1990)

Steven Shapin, 'The Social Uses of Science', in G. S. Rousseau and Roy Porter (eds.), *The Ferment of Knowledge: Studies in the Historiography of Eighteenth-century Science* (Cambridge: Cambridge University Press, 1980), 93–142

——, *A Social History of Truth: Civility and Science in Seventeenth-century England* (Chicago: University of Chicago Press, 1994)

——, *The Scientific Revolution* (Chicago and London: University of Chicago Press, 1996)

Steven Shapin and Simon Schaffer, *Leviathan and the Air-pump: Hobbes, Boyle, and the Experimental Life* (Princeton, NJ: Princeton University Press, 1985)

Barbara J. Shapiro, *Probability and Certainty in Seventeenth-century England: A Study of the Relationships between Natural Science, Religion, History, Law and Literature* (Princeton, NJ: Princeton University Press, 1983)

James Sharpe, *Instruments of Darkness: Witchcraft in England, 1550–1750* (London: Hamish Hamilton, 1996)

Jim Sharpe, 'History From Below', in Peter Burke (ed.), *New Perspectives on Historical Writing* (Cambridge: Polity Press, 1991), 24–41

Kevin Sharpe, *Criticism and Compliment: The Politics of Literature in the England of Charles I* (Cambridge: Cambridge University Press, 1987)

Kevin Sharpe and Peter Lake (eds.), *Culture and Politics in Early Stuart England* (Stanford, CA: Stanford University Press, 1993)

William Sharpe, *A Dissertation upon Genius* (London: Bathurst, 1755)

Roger Shattuck, *Forbidden Knowledge. From Prometheus to Pornography* (New York: St Martin's, 1996)

Percy Bysshe Shelley, *The Necessity of Atheism* (Worthing: C. and W. Phillips, 1811)

——, *The Triumph of Life*, D. H. Reiman (ed.) (Urbana, Ill.: University of Illinois Press, 1965 [1824])

W. George Shelton, *Dean Tucker and Eighteenth-century Economic and Political Thought* (New York: St Martin's, 1981)

Richard Sher, *Church and University in the Scottish Enlightenment: The Moderate Literati of Edinburgh* (Princeton, NJ: Princeton University Press, 1985)

Richard Sher and Jeffrey Smitten, *Scotland and America in the Age of the Enlightenment* (Edinburgh: Edinburgh University Press, 1990)

Richard Brinsley Sheridan, *The Rivals* (London: Arnold, 1961 [1775])

Thomas Sheridan, *British Education: or the Source of the Disorders of Great Britain* (London: sn, 1756)

Thomas Sherlock, *Trial of the Witnesses* (Edinburgh: Robertson, 1729)

Stuart Sherman, *Telling Time: Clocks, Diaries and English Diurnal Form, 1660–1785* (Chicago: University of Chicago Press, 1996)

Kathryn Shevelow, *Women and Print Culture: The Construction of Femininity in the Early Periodical* (London: Routledge, 1989)

B. G. Shrank and D. J. Supino (eds.), *The Famous Miss Burney. The Diaries and Letters of Fanny Burney* (New York: John Day, 1976)

Samuel Shuckford, *The Sacred and Profane History of the World Connected*, 2 vols. (London: Knaplock, 1728)

Folarin Shyllon, *Black People in Britain 1555–1833* (London: Oxford University Press, 1977)

B. Simon, *The Two Nations and the Educational Structure 1780–1870* (London: Lawrence and Wishart, 1974 [1960])

L. Simond, *An American in Regency England: The Journal of a Tour in 1810–1811*, C. Hibbert (ed.) (London: Robert Maxwell, 1968)

Kirsti Simonsuuri, *Homer's Original Genius: Eighteenth-century Notions of the Early Greek Epic, 1688–1798* (Cambridge: Cambridge University Press, 1979)

Clifford Siskin, *The Work of Writing: Literature and Social Change in Britain 1700–1830* (Baltimore: Johns Hopkins University Press, 1998)

Quentin Skinner, *Reason and Rhetoric in the Philosophy of Hobbes* (Cambridge: Cambridge University Press, 1996)

——, 'Who are "We"? Ambiguities of the Modern Self', *Inquiry*, xxxiv (1991), 133–53

——, *Reason and Rhetoric in the Philosophy of Hobbes* (Cambridge: Cambridge University Press, 1996)

Paul Slack, *The English Poor Law, 1531–1782* (Cambridge: Cambridge University Press, 1995)

J. S. Slotkin, *Readings in Early Anthropology* (London: Methuen & Co Ltd, 1965)

Christopher Smart, *The Genuine History of the Good Devil of Woodstock. The Story of Jane Gilbert, a Supposed Witch* (London: J. Roach, 1802)

Adam Smith, *An Inquiry into the Nature and Causes of the Wealth of Nations* (London: W. Strahan and T. Cadell, 1776)

——, *An Inquiry into the Nature and Causes of the Wealth of Nations*, 2 vols., R. H. Campbell, A. S. Skinner and W. B. Todd (eds.) (Oxford: Clarendon Press, 1976)

——, *The Theory of Moral Sentiments*, D. D. Raphael and A. L. Macfie (eds.) (Oxford: Clarendon Press, 1976 [1759])

——, *Lectures on Justice, Police, Revenue and Arms*, Edwin Cannan (ed.) (Oxford: Clarendon Press, 1896)

——, *Essays on Philosophical Subjects*, W. P. D. Wightman, J. C. Bryce, and I. S. Ross (eds.) (Oxford: Clarendon Press, 1980)

——, *Lectures On Jurisprudence*, R. Meek, D. Raphael and P. Stein (eds.) (Oxford: Clarendon Press, 1982)

Bernard Smith, *European Vision and the South Pacific, 1768–1850: A Study in the History of Art and Ideas* (Oxford: Clarendon Press, 1960)

——, *Imagining the Pacific: In the Wake of the Cook Voyages* (New Haven, Conn.: Yale University Press, 1992)

C. U. M. Smith, 'David Hartley's Newtonian

Neuropsychology', *Journal of the History of the Behavioral Sciences*, xxiii (1987), 123–36

Hilda Smith, *Reason's Disciples: Seventeenth-century English Feminists* (Urbana, Ill.: University of Illinois Press, 1982)

Janet Adam Smith, 'Some Eighteenth-century Ideas of Scotland', in N. T. Phillipson and Rosalind Mitchison (eds.), *Scotland in the Age of Improvement: Essays in Scottish History in the Eighteenth Century* (Edinburgh: Edinburgh University Press, 1970), 107–24

Kenneth Smith, *The Malthusian Controversy* (London: Routledge and Kegan Paul, 1951)

Nigel Smith, 'The Charge of Atheism and the Language of Radical Speculation, 1640–1660', in Michael Hunter and David Wootton (eds.), *Atheism from the Reformation to the Enlightenment* (Oxford: Clarendon Press, 1992), 131–58

Olivia Smith, *The Politics of Language 1791–1819* (Oxford: Clarendon Press, 1984)

Roger Smith, *The Fontana History of the Human Sciences* (London: Fontana Press, 1997)

Roger Smith, 'Self-Reflection and the Self', in Roy Porter (ed.), *Rewriting the Self: Histories from the Reinaissance to the Present* (London and New York: Routledge, 1997), 49–57

T. C. Smout, *A History of the Scottish People, 1560–1830* (London: Collins, 1969)

Keith Snell, *Annals of the Labouring Poor: Social Change in Agrarian England, 1660–1900* (Cambridge: Cambridge University Press, 1985)

David H. Solkin, *Painting for Money: The Visual Arts and the Public Sphere in Eighteenth-century England* (New Haven, Conn.: Yale University Press, 1993)

C. John Sommerville, *The Secularization of Early Modern England: From Religious Culture to Religious Faith* (New York: Oxford University Press, 1992)

——, 'The Secularization Puzzle', *History Today*, xliv (1994), 14–19

——, *The News Revolution in England* (Oxford: Clarendon Press, 1997)

Robert Southey, *Letters from England by Don Manuel Alvarez Espriella*, Jack Simmons (ed.) (Gloucester: Allan Sutton, 1984 [1807])

Patricia Meyer Spacks, *Imagining a Self: Autobiography and Novel in Eighteenth-century England* (Cambridge, Mass.: Harvard University Press, 1976)

——, *The Adolescent Idea: Myths of Youth and the Adult Imagination* (London: Faber & Faber, 1981)

D. Spadafora, *The Idea of Progress in Eighteenth-century Britain* (New Haven, Conn.: Yale University Press, 1990)

John Sparrow (ed.), *The Mistress With Other Select Poems of Abraham Cowley* (London: The Nonesuch Press, 1926)

George Spater, *William Cobbett: The Poor Man's Friend* (Cambridge: Cambridge University Press, 1982)

W. A. Speck, *The Divided Society: Parties and Politics in England, 1694–1716* (London: Edward Arnold, 1967)

——, 'Politicians, Peers, and Publication by Subscription 1700–50', in Isabel Rivers (ed.), *Books and Their Readers in Eighteenth-century England* (Leicester: Leicester University Press, 1982), 47–68

——, *Reluctant Revolutionaries: Englishmen and the Revolution of 1688* (Oxford: Oxford University Press, 1988)

J. Spedding, R. L. Ellis and D. D. Heath (eds.), *The Works of Francis Bacon*, 14 vols. (London: Longman, 1857–74)

W. M. Spellman, *The Latitudinarians and the Church of England, 1660–1700* (Athens, GA: University of Georgia Press, 1993)

Thomas Spence, *A Supplement to the History of Robinson Crusoe* (Newcastle: T. Saint, 1782)

——, *The Real Rights of Man* (1793), re-issued as *The Meridian Sun of Liberty, or the Whole Rights of Man Displayed and Most Accurately Defined* (London: Spence, 1796), reprinted in *The Pioneers of Land Reform*, M. Beer (ed.) (London: Bell, 1920), 5–16

——, *The Rights of Infants* (London: Spence, 1797)

Jane Spencer, *The Rise of the Woman Novelist, from Aphra Behn to Jane Austen* (Oxford: Blackwell, 1986)

Dale Spender, *Mothers of the Novel: 100 Good Women Writers Before Jane Austen* (London: Pandora, 1986)

Pieter Spierenburg, *The Broken Spell: A Cultural and Anthropological History of Preindustrial Europe* (London: Macmillan, 1991)

Thomas Sprat, *The History of the Royal Society of London, for the Improving of Natural Knowledge* (London: Martyn, 1667)

S. E. Sprott, *The English Debate on Suicide from Donne to Hume* (London: Open Court Publishing Co., 1961)

Barbara Maria Stafford, *Voyage into Substance: Art, Science, Nature, and the Illustrated Travel Account 1760–1840* (Cambridge, Mass.: MIT Press, 1984)

——, *Artful Science: Enlightenment Entertainment and the Eclipse of Visual Education* (Cambridge, Mass.: MIT Press, 1994)

J. Martin Stafford, *Private Vices, Publick Benefits? The Contemporary Reception of Bernard Mandeville* (Solihull: Ismeron, 1997)

Peter Stanlis, *Edmund Burke: The Enlightenment and Revolution* (New Brunswick, NJ: Transaction Pub., 1991)

Dorothy A. Stansfield, 'Thomas Beddoes and Education', *History of Education Society Bulletin*, xxiii (Spring 1979), 7–14

——, *Thomas Beddoes MD 1760–1808, Chemist, Physician, Democrat* (Dordrecht: Reidel, 1984)

Susan Staves, 'A Few Kind Words for the Fop', *Studies in English Literature*, xxii (1982), 413–28

Leslie Stephen, *History of English Thought in the Eighteenth Century*, 2 vols. (London: Smith, Elder, 1876; Harbinger, 1962)

Laurence Sterne, *The Life and Opinions of Tristram Shandy*, Graham Petrie (ed.)

(Harmondsworth: Penguin, 1967 [1759–67])

J. Stevenson, *Popular Disturbances in England, 1700–1870* (London: Longman, 1979)

Dugald Stewart, *The Collected Works of Dugald Stewart*, Sir William Hamilton (ed.), 11 vols. (Edinburgh: T. Constable & Co., 1854–60)

John B. Stewart, *The Moral and Political Philosophy of David Hume* (New York: Columbia University Press, 1963)

——, *Opinion and Reform in Hume's Political Philosophy* (Princeton, NJ: Princeton University Press, 1992)

Larry Stewart, 'Public Lectures and Private Patronage in Newtonian England', *Isis*, lxxvii (1986), 47–58

——, 'The Selling of Newton: Science and Technology in Early Eighteenth-century England', *Journal of British Studies*, xxv (1986), 179–92

——, *The Rise of Public Science: Rhetoric, Technology, and Natural Philosophy in Newtonian Britain, 1660–1750* (Cambridge: Cambridge University Press, 1992)

——, 'Other Centres of Calculation: Or, Where the Royal Society Didn't Count: Commerce, Coffee-Houses and Natural Philosophy in Early Modern London', *British Journal for the History of Science*, xxxii (1999), 133–53

J. E. Stock, *Memoirs of the Life of Thomas Beddoes MD* (London: Murray, 1811)

R. D. Stock, *The Holy and the Daemonic from Sir Thomas Browne to William Blake* (Princeton, NJ: Princeton University Press, 1982)

Lawrence Stone, *The Family, Sex and Marriage in England, 1500–1800* (London: Weidenfeld & Nicolson, 1977)

——, 'The Residential Development of the West End of London in the Seventeenth Century', in Barbara C. Malament (ed.), *After the Reformation: Essays in Honor of J. H. Hexter* (Philadelphia: University of Philadelphia Press, 1980), 167–212

Lawrence Stone and Jeanne C. Fawtier

Stone, *An Open Elite? England 1540–1880* (Oxford: Clarendon Press, 1984)

Richard Stone, *Some British Empiricists in the Social Sciences, 1650–1900* (Cambridge: Cambridge University Press, 1997)

Tom Stoppard, *Arcadia* (London: Samuel French, 1993)

Charles Strachey (ed.), *The Letters of the Earl of Chesterfield to His Son*, 2 vols. (London: Methuen, 1924, 1932)

Roland N. Stromberg, *Religious Liberalism in Eighteenth-century England* (London: Oxford University Press, 1954)

Dorothy Stroud, *Capability Brown* (London: Faber, 1975)

Gilbert Stuart, *The History of the Establishment of the Reformation of Religion in Scotland* (London: Murray, 1780)

R. E. Sullivan, *John Toland and the Deist Controversy: A Study in Adaptations* (Cambridge, Mass.: Harvard University Press, 1982)

Geoffrey Summerfield, *Fantasy and Reason: Children's Literature in the Eighteenth Century* (London: Methuen, 1984)

James Sutherland, *Defoe* (London: Methuen, 1937)

L. S. Sutherland and L. G. Mitchell (eds.), *The History of the University of Oxford*, vol. v: *The Eighteenth Century* (Oxford: Clarendon Press, 1986)

Akihito Suzuki, 'Mind and its Disease in Enlightenment British Medicine' (PhD thesis, University of London, 1992)

——, 'An Anti-Lockean Enlightenment?: Mind and Body in Early Eighteenth-century English Medicine', in Roy Porter (ed.), *Medicine and the Enlightenment* (Amsterdam: Rodopi, 1994), 226–59

——, *Gulliver's Travels* (London: Dent, 1954 [1726])

——, *The Complete Poems*, Pat Rogers (ed.) (New Haven, Conn.: Yale University Press, 1983)

——, *A Tale of a Tub. Written for the Universal Improvement of Mankind . . . To Which is Added, an Account of a Battel between the Ancient and Modern Books in St James' Library (A Discourse Concerning the Mechanical Operation of the Spirit. In a Letter to a Friend)* (London: Nutt, 1704; K. Williams (ed.), London: Dent, 1975)

——, *Mr Collins' Discourse of Free-thinking, Put into Plain English, by Way of Abstract, for the Use of the Poor* (London: Morphew, 1713)

——, *Argument to Prove That the Abolishing of Christianity in England, May, as Things Now Stand, be Attended with Some Inconveniences* (London: Atkins, 1717)

Jonathan Swift, *The Conduct of the Allies* (Edinburgh: Freebairn, 1711)

——, *Bickerstaff Papers*, H. Davis (ed.) (Oxford: Basil Blackwell, 1957 [1708–9])

——, *Gulliver's Travels* (Harmondsworth: Penguin Books, 1985 [1726])

Norman Sykes, *Church and State in England in the Eighteenth Century* (Cambridge: Cambridge University Press, 1934)

James Talbot, *The Christian Schoolmaster* (London: sn, 1707)

J. L. Talmon, *The Rise of Totalitarian Democracy* (Boston, Mass.: Beacon Press, 1952)

H. Talon (ed.), *Selections from the Journals and Papers of John Byrom, Poet – Diarist – Shorthand Writer* (London: Rockliff, 1950)

Richard Tawney, *Religion and the Rise of Capitalism* (New York: Harcourt, Brace and Co., 1926)

Boswell Taylor, *Joseph Priestley: The Man of Science* (London: Macmillan, 1954)

Charles Taylor, *Sources of the Self: The Making of the Modern Identity* (Cambridge: Cambridge University Press, 1989)

Gordon Rattray Taylor, *The Angel Makers: A Study in the Psychological Origins of Historical Change 1750–1850* (London: Secker & Warburg, 1958)

Joyce Taylor, *Joseph Lancaster: The Poor Child's Friend* (West Wickham: The Campanile Press, 1996)

[Tom Telescope], *The Newtonian System of*

Philosophy (London: John Newbery, 1761)

Sir William Temple, *The Works of Sir William Temple, Bart*, 2 vols. (London: Churchill, 1720)

——, *Observations upon the United Provinces of the Netherlands*, G. N. Clark (ed.) (Oxford: Oxford University Press, 1972 [1673])

R. C. Tennant, 'The Anglican Response to Locke's Theory of Personal Identity' *Journal of the History of Ideas*, xliii (1982), 73–90

K. Tester, *Animals and Society. The Humanity of Animal Rights* (London: Routledge, 1991)

Joseph Texte, *Jean-Jacques Rousseau and the Cosmopolitan Spirit in Literature: A Study of the Literary Relations between France and England during the Eighteenth Century* (London: Duckworth, 1899)

C. Thacker, *The Wildness Pleases: The Origins of Romanticism* (London: Croom Helm, 1983)

Arnold Thackray, *Atoms and Powers: An Essay on Newtonian Matter Theory and the Development of Chemistry* (Cambridge, Mass.: Harvard University Press, 1977)

Mary Thale (ed.), *The Autobiography of Francis Place (1771–1854)* (Cambridge: Cambridge University Press, 1972)

——, 'Women in London Debating Societies in 1780', *Gender and History*, xii (1995), 5–24

D. O. Thomas, *The Honest Mind: The Thought and Work of Richard Price* (Oxford: Clarendon, 1977)

Keith Thomas, *Religion and the Decline of Magic: Studies in Popular Beliefs in Sixteenth- and Seventeenth-century England* (London: Weidenfeld & Nicolson, 1971)

——, *Man and the Natural World: Changing Attitudes in England, 1500–1800* (Harmondsworth: Penguin, 1983)

—— (ed.), *The Oxford Book of Work* (Oxford: Oxford University Press, 1999)

Peter D. G. Thomas, *John Wilkes: A Friend to Liberty* (Oxford: Clarendon Press, 1996)

——, *Politics in Eighteenth-century Wales* (Cardiff: University of Wales Press, 1998)

E. P. Thompson, *The Making of the English Working Class* (London: Gollancz, 1965; Harmondsworth: Penguin, 1968)

——, 'The Moral Economy of the English Crowd in the Eighteenth Century', *Past and Present*, 1 (1971), 76–136

——, *The Poverty of Theory and Other Essays* (London: Merlin Press, 1978)

——, 'The Peculiarities of the English', in *idem, The Poverty of Theory and Other Essays* (London: Merlin Press, 1978), 35–91

——, *Customs in Common* (London: Merlin Press, 1991)

——, 'Time, Work-Discipline and Industrial Capitalism', in *Customs in Common* (London: Merlin Press, 1991), 352–403

Elizabeth H. Thomson, 'The Role of the Physician in Humane Societies of the Eighteenth Century', *Bulletin of the History of Medicine*, xxxvii (1963), 43–51

James Thomson, *Liberty* (London: A. Millar, 1735)

——, *The Seasons* (London: A. Millar, 1744)

——, *The Masque of Alfred* in Roger Lonsdale (ed.), *The New Oxford Book of Eighteenth Century Verse* (Oxford: Oxford University Press, 1984), 192

J. W. and A. Tibble (eds.), *The Prose of John Clare* (London: Routledge & Kegan Paul, 1951)

John Tillotson, *The Works of the Most Reverend Dr John Tillotson, Late Lord Archbishop of Canterbury: Containing Two Hundred Sermons and Discourses, on Several Occasions*, T. Birch (ed.), 10 vols. (London: Dove, 1820)

Stella Tillyard, *Aristocrats: Caroline, Emily, Louisa and Sarah Lennox* (London: Chatto & Windus, 1994)

——, *Citizen Lord: Edward Fitzgerald 1763–1798* (London: Chatto & Windus, 1997)

Matthew Tindal, *The Rights of the Christian Church Asserted against the Romish and All Other Priests Who Claim an Independent Power over It* (London: sn, 1706)

——, *Christianity as Old as the Creation; Or the Gospel a Republication of the Religion of Nature* (London: Wilford, 1733)

Ian Tipton, *Berkeley: The Philosophy of Immaterialism* (Bristol: Thoemmes Press, 1995)

Dennis Todd, 'The Hairy Maid at the Harpsichord: Some Speculations on the Meaning of Gulliver's Travels', *Texas Studies in Literature and Language*, xxxiv (1992), 239–83

——, *Imagining Monsters: Miscreations of the Self in Eighteenth-century England* (Chicago: University of Chicago Press, 1995)

Janet Todd, *Sensibility: An Introduction* (London: Methuen, 1986)

——, *The Sign of Angellica: Women, Writing and Fiction, 1660–1800* (London: Virago, 1989)

John Toland, *Christianity Not Mysterious: Or, A Treatise Showing, That There is Nothing in the Gospel Contrary to Reason, Nor Above It, and That No Christian Doctrine can be Properly Call'd a Mystery*, 2nd edn (London: Buckley, 1696)

——, *Letters To Serena* (London: Lintot, 1704)

——, *Reasons for Naturalising the Jews in Great Britain and Ireland* (London: Roberts, 1714)

——, *Pantheisticon, Sive Formula Celebrandae Sodalitatis Socraticae* (London: sn, 1720)

——, *Tetradymus* (London: Brotherton and Meadows, 1720)

Claire Tomalin, *The Life and Death of Mary Wollstonecraft* (London: Weidenfeld & Nicolson, 1974)

Sylvana Tomaselli, 'The First Person: Descartes, Locke and Mind–Body Dualism', *History of Science*, xxii (1984), 185–205

——, 'The Enlightenment Debate on Women', *History Workshop Journal*, xx (1985), 101–24

——, 'Moral Philosophy and Population Questions in Eighteenth-century Europe', in M. S. Teitelbaum and J. M. Winter (eds.), *Population, Resources and Environment* (Cambridge: Cambridge University Press, 1989), 7–29

——, 'Reflections on the History of the Science of Woman', *History of Science*, xxix (1991), 185–205

——, 'Political Economy: The Desire and Needs of Present and Future Generations', in Christopher Fox, Roy S. Porter and Robert Wokler (eds.), *Inventing Human Science: Eighteenth-century Domains* (Berkeley, CA: University of California Press, 1995), 292–322

—— (ed.), *Mary Wollstonecraft: A Vindication of the Rights of Men with A Vindication of the Rights of Woman* (Cambridge: Cambridge University Press, 1995)

Theobald Wolfe Tone, *An Argument on Behalf of the Catholics of Ireland* (Belfast, sn, 1791)

G. Tonelli, 'Genius: From the Renaissance to 1770', in P. P. Wiener (ed.), *Dictionary of the History of Ideas*, vol. ii (New York: C. Scribner's & Sons, 1973), 293–7

Horne Tooke, *The Diversions of Purley* (London: Johnson, 1786)

Norman Torrey, *Voltaire and the English Deists* (New Haven: Yale University Press, 1930)

J. Townsend, *A Dissertation on the Poor Laws by a Well-wisher to Mankind* (London: Dilly, 1786)

Paget Toynbee and L. Whibley (eds.), *Correspondence of Thomas Gray*, 3 vols. (Oxford: Clarendon Press, 1935)

William H. Trapnell, 'Who Thomas Woolston Was', *British Journal for Eighteenth Century Studies*, xi (1988), 143–58

——, 'What Thomas Woolston Wrote', *British Journal for Eighteenth-century Studies*, xiv (1991), 13–30

——, *Thomas Woolston: Madman and Deist?* (Bristol: Thoemmes Press, 1994)

Joseph Trapp, *Lectures on Poetry* (London: Hitch and Davis, 1742)

John Trenchard, *The Natural History of Superstition* (London: Baldwin, 1709)

Hugh Trevor-Roper, 'The Scottish Enlightenment', in Theodore Besterman (ed.), *Studies on Voltaire and the Eighteenth Century*, lviii (1967), 1635–58

Barry Trinder, *The Industrial Revolution in*

Shropshire (Chichester: Phillimore, 1973)

Ulrich Tröhler, 'Quantification in British Medicine and Surgery 1750–1830; with Special Reference to its Introduction into Therapeutics' (PhD Thesis, University of London, 1978)

Thomas Trotter, *A View of the Nervous Temperament* (London: Longman, Hurst, Rees & Owen, 1807)

Howard William Troyer, *New Ward of Grub Street: A Study of Sub-Literary London in the Eighteenth Century* (London: Frank Cass & Co. Ltd, 1968)

Randolph Trumbach, *The Rise of the Egalitarian Family: Aristocratic Kinship and Domestic Relations in Eighteenth-century England* (New York: Academic Press, 1978)

——, 'Modern Prostitution and Gender in Fanny Hill: Libertine and Domesticated Fantasy', in G. S. Rousseau and Roy Porter (eds.), *Sexual Underworlds of the Enlightenment* (Manchester: Manchester University Press, 1987), 69–85

——, *Sex and the Gender Revolution*, vol. i: *Heterosexuality and the Third Gender in Enlightenment London* (Chicago: Chicago University Press, 1998)

Yi-fu Tuan, *The Hydrologic Cycle and the Wisdom of God: A Theme in Geoteleology* (Toronto: University of Toronto Press, 1968)

——, *Topophilia: A Study of Environmental Perception, Attitudes and Values* (Englewood Cliffs, NJ: Prentice-Hall, 1974)

Abraham Tucker, *The Light of Nature Pursued*, 2 vols. in 3 (London: Payne, 1768)

——, *Light of Nature Pursued*, 7 vols. (New York & London: Garland Publishing, 1997 [1768])

Josiah Tucker, *Four Tracts* (Gloucester: Raikes, 1774)

——, *A Treatise concerning Civil Government* (London: Cadell, 1781)

S. I. Tucker, *Protean Shape: A Study in Eighteenth-century Vocabulary and Usage* (London: Athlone Press, 1967)

——, *Enthusiasm: A Study in Semantic Change*

(Cambridge: Cambridge University Press, 1972)

Samuel Tuke, *Description of the Retreat, an Institution near York for Insane Persons of the Society of Friends containing an Account of Its Origin and Progress, the Modes of Treatment, and a Statement of Cases* (York: W. Alexander, 1813)

David Turley, *The Culture of English Antislavery, 1780–1860* (London & New York: Routledge, 1991)

Cheryl Turner, *Living by the Pen: Women Writers in the Eighteenth Century* (London: Routledge, 1992)

G. L'E. Turner, 'Eighteenth-century Scientific Instruments and Their Makers', in Roy Porter (ed.), *The Cambridge History of Science*, vol. iv: *The Eighteenth Century* (Cambridge: Cambridge University Press, 2001), 583–607

James Turner, *Reckoning with the Beast: Animals, Pain, and Humanity in the Victorian Mind* (Baltimore & London: Johns Hopkins University Press, 1980)

M. Turner, *English Parliamentary Enclosure: Its Historical Geography and Economic History* (Folkestone: Dawson, 1980)

——, *Enclosures in Britain, 1750–1830* (London: Macmillan, 1984)

—— (ed.), *Malthus and His Times* (Basingstoke: Macmillan, 1986)

William Turner, *Speculations on the Propriety of Attempting the Establishing a Literary Society in Newcastle upon Tyne* (Newcastle: np, 1793)

Ernest Lee Tuveson, *The Imagination as a Means of Grace: Locke and the Aesthetics of Romanticism* (Berkeley, CA: University of California Press, 1960)

——, *Millennium and Utopia: A Study in the Background of the Idea of Progress* (New York: Harper & Row, 1964)

Stanley Tweyman (ed.), *Human on Miracles* (Bristol: Thoemmes Press, 1996)

Gerald Tyson, *Joseph Johnson: A Liberal Publisher* (Iowa City: University of Iowa Press, 1979)

Jenny Uglow, *Hogarth: A Life and a World* (London: Faber & Faber, 1997)

James Usher, *Clio: or, a Discourse on Taste*, 2nd edn (London: T. Davies, 1769)

Abbot Payson Usher (ed.), *Two Manuscripts by Charles Davenant* (Baltimore: Johns Hopkins University Press, 1942)

David Vaisey (ed.), *The Diary of Thomas Turner of East Hoathley* (Oxford: Oxford University Press, 1984)

W. Vamplew, *The Turf: A Social and Economic History of Horse Racing* (London: Allen Lane, 1974)

Norman Vance, *Irish Literature: A Social History: Tradition, Identity and Difference* (Oxford: Basil Blackwell, 1990)

Simon Varey (ed.), *Lord Bolingbroke: Contributions to the Craftsman* (Oxford: Clarendon Press, 1982)

Aram Vartanian, *Diderot and Descartes. A Study of Scientific Naturalism in the Enlightenment* (Princeton, NJ: Princeton University Press, 1953)

Benjamin Vaughan, *New and Old Principles of Trade Compared* (London: Johnson and Debrett, 1788)

Thorstein Veblen, *The Theory of the Leisure Class* (New York: Macmillan, 1912)

Franco Venturi, *Utopia and Reform in the Enlightenment* (Cambridge: Cambridge University Press, 1971)

——, 'Scottish Echoes in Eighteenth-Century Italy', in Istvan Hont and Michael Ignatieff (eds.), *Wealth and Virtue: The Shaping of Political Economy in the Scottish Enlightenment* (Cambridge: Cambridge University Press, 1983), 345–62

Amanda Vickery, *The Gentleman's Daughter: Women's Lives in Georgian England* (New Haven, Conn.: Yale University Press, 1998)

Fernando Vidal, 'Psychology in the Eighteenth Century: A View from Encyclopaedias', *History of the Human Sciences*, vi (1993), 89–120

David Vincent, *Bread, Knowledge and Freedom: A Study of Nineteenth-century Working Class Autobiography* (London: Routledge, 1982)

——, *Literacy and Popular Culture. England 1750–1914* (Cambridge: Cambridge University Press, 1989)

Jacob Viner, *The Role of Providence in the Social Order: An Essay in Intellectual History* (Philadelphia: American Philsophical Society 1972)

Robert Voitle, *Samuel Johnson the Moralist* (Cambridge, Mass.: Harvard University Press, 1961)

——, 'The Reason of the English Enlightenment', *Studies on Voltaire and the Eighteenth Century*, xxvii (1963), 1735–74

——, *The Third Earl of Shaftesbury: 1671–1713* (Baton Rouge: Louisiana State University Press, 1984)

F. M. Voltaire, *Letters concerning the English Nation* (London: printed for C. Davis and A. Lyon, 1733; Charles Whibley (ed.), London: Peter Davies, 1926)

——, *Philosophical Dictionary*, Theodore Besterman (trans.) (Harmondsworth: Penguin, 1979 [1764])

Peter Wagner, *Eros Revived: Erotica in the Age of Enlightenment* (London: Secker & Warburg, 1986)

Dror Wahrman, 'National Society, Communal Culture: An Argument about the Recent Historiography of Eighteenth-century Britain', *Social History*, xvii (1992), 43–72

Thomas Walker, *A Review of Some of the Political Events Which Have Occurred in Manchester during the Last Five Years: Being a Sequel to the Trial of Thomas Walker, and Others, for a Conspiracy to Overthrow the Constitution and Government of This Country, and to Aid and Assist the French, Being the King's Enemies* (London: J. Johnson, 1794)

Derek Wall, *A Reader in Environmental Literature, Philosophy and Politics* (London: Routledge, 1994)

Peter Walmsley, *The Rhetoric of Berkeley's*

Philosophy (Cambridge: Cambridge University Press, 1990)

——, 'Prince Maurice's Rational Parrot: Civil Discourse in Locke's *Essay*', *Eighteenth-Century Studies*, xxviii (1995), 413–25

John Walsh, Colin Haydon and Stephen Taylor (eds.), *The Church of England c. 1689–c. 1833* (Cambridge: Cambridge University Press, 1993)

Alice N. Walters, 'Conversation Pieces: Science and Politeness in Eighteenth-century England', *History of Science*, cviii (1997), 121–54

John K. Walters and James Walvin (eds.), *Slavery, Abolition and Emancipation: Black Slaves and the British Empire* (London: Longman, 1976)

J. Walvin and D. Eltis (eds.), *Abolition of the Atlantic Slave Trade* (Madison, Wisc.: University of Wisconsin Press, 1981)

William Warburton, *The Divine Legation of Moses Demonstrated*, 2 vols. (London: Gyles, 1738–41)

——, *Works*, 7 vols. (London, sn, 1788)

——, *Letters from a Late Eminent Prelate to One of His Friends* (London: Cadell and Davies, 1808)

Marina Warner, *From the Beast to the Blonde: On Fairy Tales and Their Tellers* (London: Chatto & Windus, 1994)

——, *No Go the Bogeyman: Scaring, Lulling and Making Mock* (London: Chatto & Windus, 1998)

Richard Warner, *The History of Bath* (Bath: Cruttwell, 1801)

G. J. Warnock, *Berkeley* (Harmondsworth: Peregrine, 1969)

Joseph Warton, *The Enthusiast: or Lover of Nature: A Poem* (London: Dodsley, 1744)

A. M. C. Waterman, 'A Cambridge "Via Media" in Late Georgian Anglicanism', *Journal of Ecclesiastical History*, xlii (1991), 419–36

Ian Watt, *The Rise of the Novel: Studies in Defoe,* *Richardson and Fielding* (London: Chatto & Windus, 1957)

Isaac Watts, *Philosophical Essays on Various Subjects* (London: Ford, Hett, 1733)

——, *The Psalms of David Imitated in the Language of the New Testament* (London: Clark, 1719)

——, *Logick: Or, The Right Use of Reason in the Enquiry after Truth. With a Variety of Rules to Guard against Error, in the Affairs of Religion and Human Life, as well as in the Sciences* (London, 1724; 20th edn, Glasgow: William Smith, 1779)

Michael R. Watts, *The Dissenters: From the Reformation to the French Revolution* (Oxford: Clarendon Press, 1978)

Lorna Weatherill, *Consumer Behaviour and Material Culture, 1660–1760* (London: Routledge, 1988)

——, 'The Meaning of Consumer Behaviour in Late Seventeenth- and Early Eighteenth-century England', in John Brewer and Roy Porter (eds.), *Consumption and the World of Goods* (London and New York: Routledge, 1993), 206–27

Miles Weatherall, *In Search of a Cure: A History of the Pharmaceutical Industry* (Oxford: Oxford University Press, 1990)

M. E. Webb, 'A New History of Hartley's *Observations on Man*', *Journal of the History of the Behavioral Sciences*, xxiv (1988), 202–11

——, 'The Early Medical Studies and Practice of Dr David Hartley', *Bulletin of the History of Medicine*, lxiii (1989), 618–36

Max Weber, *The Protestant Ethic and the Spirit of Capitalism* (London: Allen and Unwin, 1930)

Charles Webster, *The Great Instauration. Science, Medicine and Reform 1626–1660* (London: Duckworth, 1975)

Josiah Wedgwood, *An Address to the Young Inhabitants of the Pottery* (Newcastle: Smith, 1783)

David M. Weed, 'Sexual Positions: Men of Pleasure, Economy, and Dignity in Boswell's London Journal', *Eighteenth-century Studies*, xxxi (1997–8), 215–34

Howard D. Weinbrot, *Augustus Caesar in 'Augustan' England: The Decline of a Classical Norm* (Princeton, NJ: Princeton University Press, 1978)

Charles M. Weis and Frederick A. Pottle (eds.), *Boswell in Extremes, 1776–1778* (London: Heinemann, 1971)

Saunders Welch, *A Proposal to Render Effectual a Plan to Remove the Nuisance of Common Prostitutes from the Streets* (London: sn, 1758)

Hugh West, 'The Limits of Enlightenment Anthropology: Georg Forster and the Tahitians', *History of European Ideas*, xx (1989), 147–60

Richard S. Westfall, *Science and Religion in Seventeenth-century England* (Garden City, New York: Doubleday Anchor, 1970)

——, *Never at Rest: A Biography of Isaac Newton* (Cambridge: Cambridge University Press, 1980)

Roxann Wheeler, 'The Complexion of Desire: Racial Ideology and Mid-Eighteenth-century British novels', *Eighteenth-century Studies*, xxxii (1999), 309–32

Frederick G. Whelan, 'Population and Ideology in the Enlightenment', *History of Political Thought*, vii (1991), 35–72

H. Whitbread (ed.), *I Know My Own Heart: The Diaries of Anne Lister (1740–1840)* (London: Virago, 1987)

Gilbert White, *The Natural History and Antiquities of Selborne*, Richard Mabey (ed.) (Harmondsworth: Penguin, 1977 [1789])

R. J. White, *Political Thought of Samuel Taylor Coleridge* (London: Jonathan Cape, 1938)

—— (ed.), *Political Tracts of Wordsworth, Coleridge and Shelley* (Cambridge: Cambridge University Press, 1953)

Lois Whitney, *Primitivism and the Idea of Progress, English Popular Literature in the Eighteenth Century* (Baltimore: Johns Hopkins University Press, 1934)

A. Whyte, *Characters and Characteristics of William Law: Nonjuror and Mystic* (London: Hodder and Stoughton, 1898)

Robert Isaac Wilberforce and Samuel Wilberforce, *The Life of William Wilberforce*, 5 vols. (London: Murray, 1838)

William Wilberforce, *A Practical View of the Prevailing Religious System of Professed Christians in the Higher and Middle Classes in This Country Contrasted with Real Christianity* (London: Cadell and Davies, 1797)

——, *The Correspondence of William Wilberforce*, R. I. and S. Wilberforce (eds.), 2 vols. (London: Murray, 1840)

C. B. Wilde, 'Hutchinsonians, Natural Philosophy and Religious Controversy in Eighteenth-century Britain', *History of Science*, xviii (1980), 1–24

——, 'Matter and Spirit as Natural Symbols in Eighteenth-century British Natural Philosophy', *British Journal for the History of Science*, xv (1982), 99–131

R. McKeen Wiles, *Freshest Advices: Early Provincial Newspapers in England* (Columbus: Ohio State University Press, 1965)

——, 'The Relish for Reading in Provincial England Two Centuries Ago', in Paul J. Korshin (ed.), *The Widening Circle: Essays on the Circulation of Literature in Eighteenth-century Europe* (Philadelphia: University of Pennsylvania Press, 1976), 85–115

——, *Serial Publication in England before 1750* (Cambridge: Cambridge University Press, 1957)

John Wilkes, *An Essay on Woman* (London: André Deutsch, 1972 [1763])

Basil Willey, *The Eighteenth Century Background: Studies on the Idea of Nature in the Thought of the Period* (Harmondsworth: Penguin, 1962)

Carolyn Williams, 'The Genteel Art of Resuscitation', *Transactions of the International Congress of Enlightenment*, viii (1982), 1887–90

Clare Williams (ed. and trans.), *Sophie in London, 1786, Being the Diary of Sophie v. La Roche* (London: Jonathan Cape, 1933)

David Williams, *Lectures On Education* (London: Bell, 1789)

[——], *Incidents in My Own Life Which Have*

been Thought of Some Importance, Peter France (ed.) (Brighton: University of Sussex Library, 1980 [1802])

David Williams (ed.), *The Enlightenment* (Cambridge: Cambridge University Press, 1999)

Ernest Neville Williams, *The Eighteenth Century Constitution, 1688–1815* (Cambridge: Cambridge University Press, 1960)

Gwyn Williams, *Madoc: The Making of a Myth* (London: Eyre Methuen, 1979)

——, 'Romanticism In Wales', in Roy Porter and Mikuláš Teich (eds.), *Romanticism in National Context* (Cambridge: Cambridge University Press, 1988), 1–8

Raymond Williams, *The Country and the City* (London: Chatto & Windus, 1973)

——, *Keywords: A Vocabulary of Culture and Society* (London: Fontana Press, 1988)

G. Williamson, 'Mutability, Decay and Seventeenth-century Melancholy', in *Seventeenth-century Contexts* (London: Faber & Faber, 1961), 73–101

Tom Williamson, *Polite Landscapes: Gardens and Society in Eighteenth-century England* (Stroud: Sutton Publishing, 1996)

Adrian Wilson, The Making of Man-Midwifery (London: University College Press, 1995)

Arthur M. Wilson, 'The Enlightenment Came First to England', in Stephen B. Baxter (ed.), *England's Rise to Greatness, 1660–1763* (Berkeley and Los Angeles, CA: University of California Press, 1983), 1–28

A. N. Wilson, *God's Funeral* (London: John Murray, 1999)

Kathleen Wilson, *The Sense of the People: Politics, Culture and Imperialism in England, 1715–1785* (Cambridge: Cambridge University Press, 1995)

John Wiltshire, *Samuel Johnson in the Medical World: The Doctor and the Patient* (Cambridge: Cambridge University Press, 1991)

W. K. Wimsatt, *Philosophic Words: A Study of Style and Meaning in the Rambler and Dictionary of Samuel Johnson* (New Haven, Conn.: Yale University Press, 1948)

——, *Samuel Johnson on Shakespeare* (Harmondsworth: Penguin, 1960)

William Wimsatt Jr and Frederick A. Pottle, *Boswell for the Defence 1769–1774* (London: Heinemann, 1960)

Donald Winch, *Adam Smith's Politics: An Essay in Historiographic Revision* (Cambridge: Cambridge University Press, 1978)

——, *Malthus* (Oxford: Oxford University Press, 1987)

——, *Riches and Poverty: An Intellectual History of Political Economy in Britain, 1750–1834* (Cambridge: Cambridge University Press, 1996)

James Anderson Winn, *John Dryden and his World* (New Haven, Conn.: Yale University Press, 1987)

Robert Wokler, 'Apes and Races in the Scottish Enlightenment: Monboddo and Kames on the Nature of Man', in Peter Jones (ed.), *Philosophy and Science in the Scottish Enlightenment* (Edinburgh: John Donald, 1988), 152–56

——, 'From *l'homme physique* to *l'homme moral* and Back: Towards a History of Enlightenment Anthropology', *History of the Human Sciences*, vi (1993), 121–38

——, 'Anthropology and Conjectural History in the Enlightenment', in Christopher Fox, Roy S. Porter and Robert Wokler (eds.), *Inventing Human Science: Eighteenth-century Domains* (Berkeley, CA: University of California Press, 1995), 31–52

——, 'The Enlightenment Project and its Critics', in S. E. Liedman (ed.), *The Postmodernist Critique of the Project of Enlightenment, Poznan Studies in the Philosophy of the Sciences and the Humanities*, lviii (1997), 13–30

Larry Wolff, 'When I Imagine a Child: The Idea of Childhood and the Philosophy of Memory in the Enlightenment', *Eighteenth Century Studies*, xxxi (1998), 377–401

William Wollaston, *The Religion of Nature Delineated* (London: Palmer, 1724)

Mary Wollstonecraft, *Thoughts on the Education of Daughters*, Janet Todd (ed.) (Bristol: Thoemmes, 1995 [London: sn, 1787])

——, *Mary: A Fiction* (London: Johnson, 1788)

——, *Letters, Written During a Short Residence in Sweden, Norway and Denmark*, Carol H. Poston (ed.) (Lincoln, Nebraska: University of Nebraska Press, 1976 [1796])

——, *Maria or The Wrongs of Woman*, Anne Mellor (ed.) (New York: Norton, 1994 [1798])

——, *A Vindication of the Rights of Men with A Vindication of the Rights of Woman*, Sylvana Tomaselli (ed.) (Cambridge: Cambridge University Press, 1995 [1790 and 1792])

Marcus Wood, *Radical Satire and Print Culture 1790–1822* (Oxford: Clarendon Press, 1994)

Paul B. Wood, *The Aberdeen Enlightenment: The Arts Curriculum in the Eighteenth Century* (Aberdeen: Aberdeen University Press, 1993)

——, 'Methodology and Apologetics: Thomas Sprat's History of the Royal Society', *British Journal for the History of Science*, xiii (1980), 1–26

——, 'The Natural History of Man in the Scottish Enlightenment', *History of Science*, xxviii (1990), 89–123

Samuel Wood, *Strictures on the Gout* (London: J. Bell and J. Sewel, 1775)

Martha Woodmansee, 'The Genius and the Copyright: Economic and Legal Conditions of the Emergence of the "Author" ', *Eighteenth Century Studies*, xvii (1984), 417–32

J. Woodward, *To Do the Sick No Harm: A Study of the British Voluntary Hospital System to 1875* (London: Routledge and Kegan Paul, 1974)

John Woodward, *An Essay towards a Natural History of the Earth* (London: R. Wilkin, 1695)

Thomas Woolston, *Six Discourses on the Miracles of Our Saviour and Defences of His Discourses* (New York: Garland, 1979 [1727–30])

J. Wordsworth, M. H. Abrams and S. Gill (eds.), *William Wordsworth, the Prelude 1799, 1805, 1850* (London: W. W. Norton, 1979)

William Wordsworth, *The Prelude. Or, Growth of a Poet's Mind (Text of 1805)*, Ernest de Selincourt and Stephen Gill (eds.) (Oxford: Oxford University Press, 1970)

——, *The Prose Works of William Wordsworth*, W. J. B. Owen and Jane Worthington Smyser (eds.), 3 vols. (Oxford: Clarendon Press, 1974)

Donald Worster, *Nature's Economy: A History of Ecological Ideas* (Cambridge: Cambridge University Press, 1985)

——, *The Wealth of Nature. Environmental History and the Ecological Imagination* (New York: Oxford University Press, 1993)

William Worthington, *An Essay on the Scheme and Conduct, Procedure and Extent of Man's Redemption* (London, sn, 1743)

John P. Wright, 'Association, Madness, and the Measures of Probability in Locke and Hume', in Christopher Fox (ed.), *Psychology and Literature in the Eighteenth Century* (New York: AMS Press, 1987), 103–27

Ian Wylie, *Young Coleridge and the Philosophers of Nature* (Oxford: Clarendon Press, 1989)

Deborah Baker Wyrick, *Jonathan Swift and the Vested Word* (Chapel Hill, NC: University of North Carolina Press, 1988)

E. Yeo (ed.), *Mary Wollstonecraft and 200 Years of Feminism* (London: Rivers Oram Press, 1997)

Richard Yeo, 'Genius, Method and Mortality: Images of Newton in Britain, 1760–1860', *Science in Context*, ii (1988), 257–84

——, *Encyclopaedic Visions: Scientific Dictionaries and Enlightenment Culture* (Cambridge: Cambridge University Press, forthcoming)

John W. Yolton, *John Locke and the Way of Ideas* (Oxford: Oxford University Press, 1956)

——, *Thinking Matter: Materialism in Eighteenth-*

692

century Britain (Minneapolis, Minn.: University of Minnesota Press, 1983)

——, *Perceptual Acquaintance from Descartes to Reid* (Minneapolis, Minn.: University of Minnesota Press, 1984)

——, *Locke: An Introduction* (Oxford: Basil Blackwell, 1985)

——, 'Schoolmen, Logic and Philosophy', in L. S. Sutherland and L. G. Mitchell (eds.), *The History of the University of Oxford*, vol. v: *The Eighteenth Century* (Oxford: Clarendon Press, 1986), 565–91

——, *Locke and French Materialism* (Oxford: Clarendon Press, 1991)

Arthur Young, *The Farmer's Letters to the People of England* (London: W. Nicoll, 1767)

——, *A Six Weeks' Tour through the Southern Counties of England and Wales* (London: W. Nicoll, 1768)

——, *A Six Months' Tour Through the North of England*, 4 vols., 2nd edn (London: W. Strahan, 1771)

——, *The Farmer's Tour through the East of England*, 3 vols. (London: Strahan and Nicoll, 1771)

——, *An Enquiry into the State of the Public Mind* (London: Richardson, 1798)

——, *Annals of Agriculture and Other Useful Arts*, 46 vols. (London: Arthur Young, 1784–1815)

——, *View of the Agriculture of Oxfordshire* (London: R. Phillips, 1809)

B. W. Young, ' "The Soul-sleeping System": Politics and Heresy in Eighteenth-century England', *Journal of Ecclesiastical History*, xlv (1994), 64–81

——, *Religion and Enlightenment in Eighteenth-century England: Theological Debate from Locke to Burke* (Oxford: Clarendon Press, 1998)

Edward Young, *Conjectures on Original Composition* (London: Millar and Dodsley, 1759)

——, *Night Thoughts on Life, Death and Immortality* (London: Toplis and Bunney, 1780)

——, *The Merchant* (Dublin: Risk, 1730)

R. M. Young, 'David Hartley', in *Dictionary of Scientific Biography*, vi (New York: Charles Scribner's Sons, 1972), 138–40

R. M. Young, 'Association of Ideas', in P. P. Wiener (ed.), *Dictionary of the History of Ideas* (New York: Charles Scribner's Sons, 1973), 111–18

WORKS OF REFERENCE

Jeremy Black and Roy Porter (eds.), *The Basil Blackwell Dictionary of World Eighteenth-century History* (Oxford: Basil Blackwell, 1994)

Philip P. Wiener (ed.), *Dictionary of the History of Ideas* (New York: Charles Scribner's Sons, 1973)

John W. Yolton (ed.), *The Blackwell Companion to the Enlightenment* (Oxford: Blackwell, 1991)

John Yolton, John Valdimir Price and John Stephens (eds.), *The Dictionary of Eighteenth-century Philosophers*, 2 vols. (Bristol: Thoemmes Press, 1999)

INDEX

Aberdeen 242
  see also Scotland
Académie Royale des Sciences (Paris) 135
accountability 167, 219
  see also morality/morals
Act of Settlement (1701) xvi
Act of Toleration (1689) 31–2, 107
Act of Toleration (1813) 107
Act of Uniformity (1662) 25
Act of Union (1707) xvi–xvii, 34, 242, 243
Act of Union (1801) xvi–xvii
actuarial statistics 207, 208
Adam, Robert 243
Addison, Joseph 4, 8, 35, 36, 40, 69, 79, 93,
  105, 277, 298, 311
  on ballads 365
  on gardens 311–12
  on the imagination 279
  influence/importance 88, 201, 203–4,
    265, 482
  on morals/morality 194–7, 198
  as MP 276
  'Pleasures of the Imagination' 69
  on trade 384
  on witchcraft 220–21, 222
  on women's rights 331–2
  see also The Spectator; Steele, Richard
adult education 353–8, 361, 363
the aesthetic 163–5, 194–7, 215, 226–7,
  261–2, 279, 281, 283, 313–14
  chinoiserie, vogue for 358
  industrialization as threat to 316–18
  possessors of 369
  see also human nature
Africa 148, 354, 359
African Society 148
agricultural improvement 306–9, 317–18,
  428–9, 430, 451
agricultural societies 307, 308
agriculture 147, 148, 267, 297, 301, 306–11
  enclosure 306, 309–10, 317, 318, 366,
    386–7, 451, 459

science and 307–8
  as stewardship 306, 317–18
  see also rural life
Aikenhead, Thomas 244
Aikin, John 154–5, 352, 398
  Letters from a Father . . . 425
Aikin, Lucy:
  Poetry for Children 352
Akenside, Mark 279
  The Pleasures of Imagination 303, 304
alcohol *see* drunkenness
d'Alembert, Jean le Rond 8, 10, 57
  Encyclopédie 57, 92, 246
Alexander, William:
  History of Women 321
Algarotti, Francesco 134
  *Newtonianismo . . . (Sir Isaac Newton's
    Philosophy . . .)* 134
Alison, Sir Archibald 164–5
almanacs 151
  see also printing/books
Almon, John 192
America xviii, 1
  attitudes to 402–3
  Declaration of Independence (1776) 402
  discovery of 52, 240
  emigration to 240
  Fundamental Constitutions of Carolina
    xx–xxi
  Thirteen Colonies 239, 240
  trade with 386
American Revolution 9, 148, 188, 240, 402,
  432, 448, 458
Analytical Review 81, 335
anarchism 455–9
Anderson, Perry 12, 481
Andrews, Robert *and* Frances 310
Anglican Church 5, 25, 99, 185, 404–5
  see also religion
animals 348–51
Anne, Queen of Gt Britain and Ireland 28,
  152